Book 7 of Caesar's Bellum Gallicum:
With Introduction, Text, Vocabulary and Notes

Drew Arlen Mannetter, PhD.

BrownWalker Press
Boca Raton • 2004

Book 7 of Caesar's Bellum Gallicum:
With Introduction, Text, Vocabulary and Notes

BrownWalker Press
Boca Raton , Florida
USA • 2004

ISBN: 1-58112-427-9

BrownWalker.com

Permissions obtained from Oxford University Press.

Front and back cover images from
F.W. Kelsey, Caesar's Gallic War. Published by Allyn and Bacon, 1898.

Library of Congress Cataloging-in-Publication Data

Caesar, Julius.
  [De bello Gallico. Liber 7]
  Book 7 of Caesar's Bellum gallicum / with introduction, text, vocabulary and notes [by] Drew
Arlen Mannetter.
      p. cm.
  Text in Latin and English.
  Includes bibliographical references.
  ISBN 1-58112-427-9 (pbk. : alk. paper)
  1. Gaul--History--Gallic Wars, 58-51 B.C. 2. Caesar, Julius. De bello gallico. Liber 7. I.
Mannetter, Drew Arlen, 1962- II. Title.

PA6237.A7M36 2004
936.4'02--dc22

2004015230

TABLE OF CONTENTS

INTRODUCTION

> "If Caesar instead of Vercingetorix had suffered complete defeat, little doubt that Gaul would long have remained unconquered, and that the course of European history would have been changed. The siege of Alesia may well rank among the decisive military operations of the world's history." (Kelsey,[1] 433)

Book 7 of Caesar's *Gallic Wars* is a narrative like few others in the history of the world. It is a first hand account of the final titanic struggle between two nations, one fighting for hegemony, the other for independent survival. It is hard to overstate the importance for western history of Caesar's Gallic campaigns which culminated in his dramatic victory over the united might of Gaul under the leadership of Vercingetorix at Alesia as described in Book 7. During the first six years of Caesar's Gallic war, 58-53 B.C., (*BG* Books 1-6), he had waged yearly campaigns against select Gallic tribes, the Britons, and the Germans. These campaigns were mainly conducted in a piecemeal fashion, directed against one or two tribes at a time or small coalitions. Although many alliances were made between tribes and many individual leaders temporally emerged, there was no systematic attempted to initiate a pan-Gallic coalition and the Gauls were still too disunited and mutually suspicious of traditionally rival tribes to overcome the unified and disciplined Roman presence. It is in the next year, 52 B.C., (*BG* Book 7), that the Gauls finally find a commander who is capable of uniting nearly all Gaul and challenging Caesar for military and political supremacy. Vercingetorix raises an army from the Gallic states for the final battle at Alesia that numbered 80,000 men inside the city and a relief army of 259,000, for a combined force of 339,000 men, a staggering number. Pitted against them is a Roman army of only 40,000 men, and, of course, the intrepid general Julius Caesar.

I.A: THE LIFE OF GAIUS JULIUS CAESAR

When Caesar was born on July 12, 100 B.C., Rome was still a Republic and had not yet adopted the quasi-monarchial form of government known as the Empire. The ideal of the Roman aristocrat in the Republican period was service to the state, both as politician and general. As a politician, he would serve in the Senate and oversee the smooth operation of the state. As a general, he would subdue foreign enemies and then return to Rome after laying down his command to reassume his position in the Senate (one thinks of the paradigm Cincinnatus). This system, which united the success of Rome to the success of the aristocracy as a whole, functioned remarkably well until the erosion of this ideal began with the first civil war between Sulla and Marius (88-82 B.C.). Both Marius and Sulla broke with established tradition and used their armies, which were loyal to them personally and not Rome, to march on Rome in order to impose their will. While the Republican form of government ultimately survived this ordeal, it was shaken and its basic weaknesses were exposed. The ambition of individual men for power would now supercede the good of the Republic and a mainly ineffective Senate was helpless in presenting a counterbalance to the overwhelming force of personal armies. When Caesar entered the political arena, aristocrats were still nominally committed to the welfare of the state and the ideals of the Republic, but it was very apparent to the ambitious man how the basis of power had shifted from the Senate to the individual leader with a personal army. (Those interested in Rome's transformation from Republic to Empire, and Caesar's role in this transformation, should familiarize themselves with "Part IV: The Fall of the Republic" in Cary and Scullard's *A History of Rome*.[2] These ten chapters examine Roman history from Tiberius and Gaius Gracchus (133) to Actium (31). For those interested in a basic introduction to the history of the Republic to the time of Caesar with special emphasis on the political lessons which Caesar derived see Fuller,[3] 15-48. For information on the development of the Roman army in this period and Roman soldiers in general see Adcock[4] and Watson.[5])

Caesar's early life and career reflected the traditional pattern and conforms exactly to what one would expect from an ambitious member of the Roman nobility. He exercised the customary offices and social prerogatives as he rose up through the *cursus honorum*: Priest of Jupiter (87), marries a daughter of Cinna, Cornelia (84), military service in Asia, won the 'civic crown' (80), prosecutes Dolabella (78), study abroad, captured by pirates (76), military service in the east against Mithradates (74), Quaestor (69), marries Pompey's cousin, Pompeia (67), Curule Aedile (65), Pontifex Maximus (63), Praetor (62), Propraetor in Further Spain (61), the 'first triumvirate' with Pompey and Crassus (60), marries Calpurnia, Consul (59), Proconsul of Gallia Cisalpina, Gallia Narbonensis (Provincia), and Illyricum, for five years (1 March 59 to 28 February 54) (58). (For those interested in the early career of Caesar see Fuller,[6] 49-73 and Taylor.[7] For a discussion of Caesar's physical characteristics and their relationship to coins and busts see Toynbee.[8])

It is at Caesar's assumption of the Proconsulship of Gaul that his personal greatness begins to emerge and his career can be designated extraordinary. Caesar spent eight years in Gaul building a reputation as an exceptional leader and brilliant campaigner by subduing Gaul, twice sailing to Britain, and twice crossing the Rhine into Germany (58-51). In 58 (*BG* Book 1), the Helvetians began a migration across Gaul that Caesar used as a pretext to become embroiled in Gallic affairs. The Gauls were defeated at a battle near Bibracte and forced to return home. Immediately after, Caesar, at the request of Diviciacus the Aeduan, expelled Ariovistus the German from Gaul. In 57 (*BG* Book 2), he campaigned in the north of Gaul against the Belgae. In the pivotal battle of the Sambre River against the Nervii, it was by his personal intervention in the battle (and the reinforcements led by Labienus) that victory was ensured. In 56 (*BG* Book 3), the main campaign against the Veneti, a coastal people, was a combination of maritime and land battles. In 55 (*BG* Book 4), Caesar campaigned both across the Rhine river in Germany and the English Channel in Britain, yet neither campaign was conclusive. In 54 (*BG* Book 5), there was a second expedition to Britain in which Caesar crossed the Thames River. He then returned to Gaul and again needed to subdue the northern Belgic tribes. In 53 (BG Book 6), Caesar crossed the Rhine River a second time, supplied ethnographic information on the Gauls and Germans, and finished the campaign season with several battles in the northeast of Gaul. (For those interested in the full narrative of these battles see *Caesar: The Gallic War*,[9] Books 1-6. For those interested in a secondary analysis of these campaigns see Fuller,[10] 97-126. For a critique of Caesar as a general see Fuller,[11] 315-324. For the relationship between Caesar and his army see Cuff.[12] For Caesar's intentions in governing Gaul see Sherwin-White.[13])

In the longest and most complex book of the *BG*, Book 7 (52), Caesar described the conflict between himself and

Vercingetorix, the Arvernian, who was successful at finally uniting nearly all Gaul against the occupation. The book can be conveniently broken down into four distinct sections. Part 1 (Chapters 1-13) describes how the rebellion begins in central Gaul, with the Carnutes taking the active lead, and subsequently spreads, especially gaining momentum when Vercingetorix is chosen as leader. Once Caesar returns to Gaul and gathers his legions, he storms three Gallic cities in rapid succession: Vellaunodunum, Cenabum, and Noviodunum. In part 2 (Chapters 14-33), the Gauls adopt a scorched-earth policy, although Avaricum, the main city of the Bituriges, they excepted and defended. After a long siege and spirited defense, the city is taken, plundered, and the population put to the sword. In part 3 (Chapters 34-52), it is the Roman army that suffers defeat at Gergovia, a city of the Arverni. In a battle before the city, military discipline breaks down and the Roman soldiers extend themselves too far, only to be overwhelmed by superior numbers of Gauls. In part 4 (Chapters 53-90), the Gauls retreat to Alesia, a city of the Mandubii in central Gaul. Here, Caesar hems in Vercingetorix with eleven miles of fortifications and is forced to build an additional fourteen miles of fortifications facing outward before the relief army arrived. There were three battle before the relief army finally retreats and the interior army surrenders. Although there are further operations in the next two years (*BG* Book 8), the resistance was effectively broken at this battle and the supremacy of the Romans is never again in doubt. (For those interested in the full narrative of these battles see *Caesar: The Gallic War*,[14] Book 7. For those interested in a secondary analysis of this campaign see Fuller,[15] 127-165. For the final two years of the Gallic war see *Caesar: The Gallic War*,[16] Book 8. For a secondary analysis of the final two years of the campaign see Fuller,[17] 158-65.)

Caesar's career did not end with the conquest of Gaul but he now had many political enemies who feared his ambition, abilities, and the loyalty of his army. When the Senate attempted to force him to lay down his command, an act which would make him susceptible to prosecution by his enemies, he initiated civil war by crossing the Rubicon on January 10, 49. He then fought the civil war against the Senate and their chosen leader, Pompey (49-45), winning the final battle over him at Phrasalus in Thessaly (48). Many opponents survived and Caesar campaigned in Egypt (47), North Africa (46), and Spain (45) before the civil war was finally over. During this time, he became Dictator for eleven days to ensure the elections of 48 (49), Consul a second time (48), Dictator a second time (47), Consul a third time and Dictator for ten years (46), Consul a fourth time and Dictator for life (45), Consul a fifth time (44). Although he refused a crown at the festival Lupercalia on February 15, 44, his supreme position eventually led to his assassination on March 15, 44. (For those interested in the full narrative of the civil war see Caesar's *Civil War*,[18] Books 1-3. For a secondary analysis of the civil war see Fuller,[19] 166-307. For Caesar's campaigns in Spain, Egypt, and Africa to end the civil war see the pseudo-Caesar texts *Alexandrian, African, and Spanish Wars*.[20] For a secondary analysis of these campaigns see Fuller,[21] 240-307. For a general discussion of the end of Caesar's political career and life see Fuller,[22] 283-307. For an analysis of Caesar's intention with regard to monarchy see Carson.[23] For the identity and motivations of his assassins see Smith.[24] For Caesar's effect on later political developments see Chilver.[25] For Caesar's clementia in the civil war see Coulter.[26])

The best sources for the biography of Caesar are, of course, those of primary literature. First, the entire *Bellum Gallicum*[27] and *Bellum Civile*[28] by Caesar and the pseudo-Caesar texts *Bellum Alexandrinum, Bellum Africae*, and *Bellum Hispaniense*[29] ought to be read. Then, the ancient biographies of Caesar should also be read prior to turning to secondary sources, those of Suetonius[30] and Plutarch[31] being the best. For anyone interested in all the major sources, Book II of Appian's *The Civil Wars*[32] and Books 37-44 of Dio's *Roman History*[33] are instructive. Once the reader is familiar with primary sources, I consider J. F. C. Fuller's *Caesar: Man, Soldier and Tyrant*[34] the best secondary resource for the historical background, life, and political and military career of Caesar. Fuller maintains a healthy balance between respect for the great man and skepticism of the political opportunist. (For additional biographies see also Gelzer[35] and Yavetz.[36])

I.B THE *COMMENTARII* AS LITERATURE

As a piece of literature, the entire *Bellum Gallicum*, but especially the climax of the war in Book 7, is a masterpiece. The narrative sweeps the reader along as Caesar contacts foreign peoples, customs, cultures, and geographies. The deceptively simple style of Caesar has been noted since his contemporary Cicero who claimed that the *Commentaries* "are like nude figures, straight and beautiful; stripped of all ornament of style as if they had laid aside a garment. His aim was to furnish others with material for writing history, and in perhaps he has succeeded in gratifying the inept, who may wish to apply their curling irons to the material; but men of sound judgment he has deterred from writing, since in history there is nothing more pleasing than brevity clear and correct." (*Brutus*,[37] 262). Current scholarship is beginning to agree with Cicero. H. C. Gotoff claims that "it may be that Caesar had succeeded all too well in disguising his art; that centuries of readers, praising him, predictably, for precisely those virtues assigned to him, have failed to notice his diversity, his deceptiveness, and his power." (Gotoff,[38] 6) and it is the aim of M. F. Williams to treat Caesar "as an artist rather than a self-serving political hack." (Williams,[39] 217). (The best introductory work on Caesar as an author is Adcock's *Caesar as a Man of Letters*.[40] The focus of the book is not Caesar's political or military career, but instead his literary career and it serves as a good introduction to the traditional issues involving Caesar as an author. But, although it covers all the major questions, it does not go into any great depth. For a survey of the traditional topics associated with *Caesarstudien* see Conte,[41] 225-33.)

Much has been written about the genre-busting nature of the *Commentaries*; how they are purported to be *hypomnemata*, the "raw stuff" for historians, but instead transcend and supercede that genre (see Adcock,[42] 6-18). To see that the *Commentaries* transcend *hypomnemata* one must look no further than the underlying dramatic structure of Book 7. A. D. Kahn has analyzed Book 7 and argues that the plot is Aristotelian and that the structure "is constructed on a pattern approximating that in the Senecean plays." (Kahn,[43] 250) He breaks down the book into 5 acts: Prologue (Act 1), chapters 1-13; Act 2, chapters 14-18; Act 3, chapters 29-62; Act 4, chapters 63-74; and Act 5, chapters 75-90. He further suggests that the five council meetings at 1.6, 14.1, 63.4, 75.1, and 89.1 function as the choral odes and set off each major turning point. (Kahn, 251) This underlying structure is daring and innovative; it is a clear indication that Caesar has gone beyond *hypomnemata* and is experimenting with a completely new form. Kahn then delves into characterization (Vercingetorix, Caesar, the Romans, and the Gauls), thought, dramatic and stylistic devices, and diction, all of which combine to elevate the narrative." (Kahn, 251-254) (For dramatic structure in the *Bellum Civile* see Rowe.[44])

The use of speeches is analyzed by C. T. Murphy[45] who argues that indirect discourse is not a sign of immature style, but it is instead a conscious choice by Caesar to use indirect discourse instead of direct. Murphy classifies speeches into four types (deliberations, or debates, hortations of generals to their soldiers, epideictic or ceremonial speeches, forensic or judicial speeches) and categorizes the major 29 rhetorical passages in the *Bellum Gallicum* into three types (epideictic is missing). From this analysis, Murphy concludes that the speeches are organically integrated into the narrative and that "Caesar's concern for decent oratorical niceties is found in both his careful arrangement of the parts of the various speeches, and in his use of rhetorical topics, or 'loci communes'." (Murphy, 123) Murphy maintains that, since all the organization and rhetorical devices present in direct discourse are present in the indirect discourse, just the form, necessitated by the genre, is different. He further points out that in the two main speeches completely in direct discourse in Book 7, those at 7.38 and 7.77, "he is, in fact, doing what later historians are to do with his material: i.e., he takes the substance of what was said and puts it into good rhetorical form." (Murphy, 122) As with dramatic structure, Caesar's use of speeches again supercedes the genre of *hypomnemata*. (For a good review of the secondary literature on speeches and unique, original insights see Nordling.[46] For the two seminal works on speeches (written in German) see Deichgräber[47] and Rasmussen.[48])

A cursory examination of rhetorical devices contained in the *BG*, provided by C. W. Siedler,[49] again demonstrates the high quality of the narrative. Siedler rereads the work aloud and, despite Caesar's noted adherence to the plain style, isolates "three kinds of figures, expressions of idea in a fanciful manner with artistic effect to charm the ears and the minds of his audience for the sake of diversity, impressiveness, vividness, strength, and distinction: Figures of Rhetoric, of Syntax, and of speech." (Siedler, 29) Figures of Rhetoric include alliteration, anaphora, antithesis, assonance, chiasmus, climax, anti-climax, litotes, repetition, rhetorical questions, rhythm, and symmetry. Figures of Syntax include asyndeton, polysyndeton, ellipsis, and syncope. Figures of Speech include simile, metonymy, metaphor, and hyperbole. Unfortunately, Siedler's discussion of each is brief with sparing examples, sometimes even none. In the addenda there is a useful count of instances for these categories.

P. R. Murphy[50] examines word frequency and isolates specific themes in each book of the *Gallic War*. Book 1: *persuasio, timor*; Book 2: *furor*; Book 3: *difficultas Romana*; Book 4: *perfidia, perturbatio Romana*; Book 5: *fuga Britannorum, mors decora Romana, virtus, consilium*; Book 6: *celeritas, consilium, Fortuna*; Book 7: *libertas* balanced by *barbaria, continentia*. This thematic construction demonstrates a high degree of literary accomplishment.

Caesar's use of general reflections is cataloged and arranged into groups by J.D. Craig.[51] Craig makes no attempt to analyze further the general reflections, but merely groups them into three categories. 1) Military hints in generalized form: *BG* 5.33; *BC* 1.44; 3.51, 92.2. 2) General rules which are military but have a wider application: *BG* 3.26; 5.33; 6.35; *BC* 1.21, 72; 3.68.3. 3) Generalizations whose application is as wide as human nature: *BG* 1.14; 3.18; 7.26; *BC* 2.8, 27, 39; 3.1, 32, 104. He then compares 2 instances from *BG* Book 8 and 2 from *Bellum Alexandrinum*. There are no instances in *Bellum Africae* and *Bellum Hispaniense*.

Caesar's style has also been the focus of much study. H.C. Gotoff[52] rejects the prevailing view that Caesar wrote "essentially simple sentences, perhaps achieving some temporal or causal subordination by use of a discrete ablative absolute. He ended his sentence with the verb. Adjectives and genitives would be expected adjacent to their governing nouns, and object phrases precede the prepositional phrases and other adverbial elements that adhere more closely to the verb" and instead believes that "Caesar's style is more complex than the *communis opinio* suggests." (Gotoff, 5 and 15) Gotoff examines elements of this complexity and rejects the developmental argument for Caesar's style since the complexity of the narrative begins with the first book and runs throughout the narrative. He supplies examples of hyperbaton, the unusual position of words and concludes that it is clear that Caesar did not limit himself to the simple sentence, verb last, with which he is associated. (Gotoff, 6-10) He also notes that the subordinating use of ablative absolutes and participial phrases is not "Tulliocentric" but is instead a construction that is closer to Livy than Cicero. (Gotoff, 9-12) Finally, he examines the use of parallelism in constructing periodic sentences and notes that "not only does a practical criticism of Caesar's composition demonstrate a variety of sentence typologies, but it makes clear that Caesar composed beyond the limit of a single sentence, no matter how complex." (Gotoff, 14-15)

J.J. Schlicher[53] sees a pattern of development in Caesar's style. First, he discusses the development of sentence construction in Caesar's narrative and notices the following patterns: "After *BG* i, which, with its over precise and argumentative manner and its rather old-fashion mode of expression, has not yet adapted itself fully to the narrative technique, the first phase (*BG* ii-iv) represents an intensification of the periodical narrative sentence by overloading it with preliminary detail. Relief from this extreme was found in various ways, from *BG* v onward - first, by distributing some of the load carried by a single main verb among several verbs of the sentence; second, by increasing the use of such elements in the sentence as afford an easy transition - namely, the ablative absolute and the participial phrase - and diminishing the number of the more stubborn and specific subordinate clauses; third, by placing some of these, especially the participial constructions, after the dominate verb instead of before it; fourth, by increasing the use of noncommittal words of easy transition, both at the beginning of the sentence and within it. Some of these changes progressed quite steadily from the beginning to the end, while others appeared more spasmodically, and still others did not manifest themselves decisively before the Civil War." (Schlicher, 222) Schlicher also sees three other developmental elements beginning with Book IV. The first is speeches in direct discourse. The second is the notice taken of heroism and daring on the part of individual men of low rank in the army. And finally, he notes the extended descriptive passages, customs, peoples, and dramatic situations. (For more on style see Eden,[54] Radista,[55] and Williams.[56])

In his book *The Face of Battle*,[57] John Keegan includes a critique of Caesar's historical skills and concludes that, when compared to Greek historians, especially Thucydides, Caesar is a second-rate author. As a test-case, he compares Caesar's account of the battle at the River Sambre to Thucydides' account of the battle of Mantinea and concludes that Caesar's description is flawed in four areas: 1) disjunctive movement; 2) uniformity of behavior; 3) simplified characterization; 4) simplified motivation. In each of these areas Keegan sees Thucydides as Caesar's superior. Although Keegan does not use examples from *BG* Book 7, his critique can be applied equally to the major battle-narratives of Avaricum, Gergovia, and Alesia. Upon close examination, Keegan's critiques of Caesar's battle-narratives can not be sustained for any of these major battles (I elsewhere contend that his critiques are not true for the battle at the River Sambre, either). They are not simple, mechanical events which are Caesar-centric, but contain a full range of movement, behavior, characterization, and motivation. Even in battle-narratives Caesar's *Commentaries* are rich and diverse. (For a full critique of Keegan's argument, see Mannetter,[58] 176-196. For battle-narrative see also Pelling.[59])

I.C THE PROBLEM OF CAESAR'S SELF-PRESENTATION AND VERACITY (*TENDENZ*)

No discussion of Caesar's *Commentaries* is complete without addressing the problem of Caesar's self-presentation and veracity (*Tendenz*). The problem of Caesar's self-presentation and veracity has been well documented and the range of the spectrum covers nearly all possible opinions. The literary critique of Asinius Pollio, as cited in Suetonius' *The Deified Julius*,[60] 56, contained four major criticisms of Caesar's work: "Asinius Pollio thinks that they were put together somewhat carelessly and without strict regard for the truth; since in many cases Caesar was too ready to believe the accounts which others gave of their actions, and gave a perverted account of his own, either designedly or perhaps from forgetfulness; and he thinks that he intended to rewrite and revise them." G. B. Conte notes that "whether [his judgments] are malicious or clear-sighted is hard to say." (Conte,[61] 260) Nevertheless, this assessment of Caesar's veracity has served as a wellspring of criticism. (A book which must be read by anyone wishing to come to grips with the problem of veracity in Caesar is Hayden White's *Tropics of Discourse: Essays in Cultural Criticism*. The John Hopkins University Press, 1978. Although the work is not specifically about Caesar, this book on historical theory will clear up many of the alleged "problems" with Caesar's narrative.)

A negative view of Caesar's veracity is presented by S. E. Stevens[62] who examines two episodes to show that "on two important occasions in the Gallic war Caesar did not have the initiative. On one his plan went completely astray and he has not told us." (This is the invasion of Britain) "On the other his moves conformed to those of his adversary and he has written as far as possible to show that his adversary's moves conformed to his." (This is Gergovia and Alesia) (Stevens, 8-16 and 16-18) The remainder of the article deals with the first book of the *Commentaries* which he negatively characterizes as "a tangled web that he had already woven." (Stevens, 165) His final assessment of Caesar is that he is guilty of propaganda of the worst type: "When I made propaganda for the British government during the last war, there were two types of it, the White, in which our aim was to slant the truth but rigorously tell it, and the Black in which we permitted ourselves to swerve deliberately from it in the pursuit of the objective. In both White and Black, Caesar has shown himself, as I have tried to demonstrate, supreme." (Stevens, 179) (For the most negative critique of Caesar see Rambaud.[63] Balsdon has noted of Rambaud's work that "it is more ingenious than convincing." (Balsdon,[64] 28)

A much more moderate view is taken by J. P. V. D. Balsdon[65] who begins with Asinius Pollio's criticism of Caesar's veracity and adds that "Asinius Pollio unfortunately gave no examples of the sort of thing that he criticized. We, however, can easily supply a few." (Balsdon, 20) He discusses the major allegedly whitewashed scenes of Caesar's confrontation of Pompey before Brundisium, the mutiny of the IX legion, and the genocide of the Usipetes and Tencteri. Balsdon dismisses the seriousness of these episodes and simply admits that Caesar did not write "the truth, the whole truth, and nothing but the truth." (Balsdon, 22) Balsdon finally turns to a discussion of minor shadings of the truth and suggests that the dates of composition and publication have much to do with one's assessment of Caesar. He examines the campaign against Ariovistus and concludes that the episode is open to interpretation depending upon "what ... was the Roman estimate of the danger which threatened the northern provinces, and perhaps Italy itself? Was Caesar the only one who thought and spoke in terms of a second invasion of the Cimbri and Teutones?" (Balsdon, 27) His final estimation of Caesar's veracity is that "the truth no doubt lies somewhere between the view of those who reject nearly every word that Caesar wrote and those who believe that every statement of Caesar is true." (Balsdon, 27)

J. F. Gardner[66] also takes the middle road and sees Caesar shading rather than outright lying. She notes of the Gauls that "only occasionally had these presented any real and immediate threat to the security of the Italian peninsula. Nevertheless, they were present in Roman consciousness as a kind of bogeyman. ... Caesar represented the danger to Rome from the Gauls as arising in part from the nature of the Gauls themselves and in part from the pressure they were experiencing from the Germanic people." (Gardner, 181 and 182) Caesar used his *Commen*taries "to bring his successes before the Roman people in the best possible light and - no less important - to justify in advance those actions of his which might serve as a basis for prosecution by his political enemies." (Gardner, 188) He found the Gallic menace a convenient excuse for those actions, and "the emphasis laid on the danger created, both for Caesar and his army and, by implication or sometimes expressly, for the security of Rome and Italy, by the nature of the Gallic peoples themselves is part of the same technique." (Gardner, 189) Thus, while Caesar is not strictly lying, he is using a *topos* which would resonate in the Roman consciousness for his own advancement and Gardner sees this as propaganda. (For more on the historical Gauls and how they fit into the Roman literary tradition see Dauge[67] and Harmond.[68])

On the other end of the spectrum from Stevens is J. C. Collins[69] who advances the view that Caesar's works can scarcely be described as propaganda in the modern sense. While he admits that "here and there he stretched the truth" (Collins, 963), he argues that "the most powerful propaganda is the truth, and the greatest asset of the propagandist is a reputation for truth-telling. We underestimate Caesar if we suppose he was ignorant of this, or if we regard him as a clumsy or habitual fabricator. He felt far too strong a sense of dignitas and personal self-assurance to resort to such methods. The essence of good propaganda is the presentation of true facts in a selected light and with selected emphasis, and this, not lying, is Caesar's main reliance." (Collins, 946-47) Collins separates the *BG* and *BC* as two different works with two different motives and aims. He looks at what Caesar is justifying and how. The *BG* is a positive self-display, not a negative self-defense, which functions as a statement of fact designed to show Caesar as a victorious Roman commander. The *BC* is a self-defense, but one which does not contain gross falsifications. It presents Caesar as right and "on the psychological front intended to remove the grounds of internal opposition in reasonable men and to destroy the credit of the irreconcilables." (Collins, 942) "In the Bellum Civile, on the other hand, he was concerned throughout to show not that he was successful, but that he was in the right, that his adversaries were stupid, un-Roman, and criminal, and that his victory was the victory of the better cause." The Pompeians were depicted as "cruel and vindictive in success, cowardly in battle, abject in defeat. They are boastful and vain, incompetent and stupid, greedy and luxurious, petty-minded and ignoble, time-serving and treacherous, morally repulsive. Their downfall was the inevitable consequence of their folly, ὕβρις, and *inpotentia*." (Collins, 946) Of all the works dedicated to propaganda and veracity, I find Collins to be the most well reasoned and beneficial to an understanding of Caesar.

D. F. Conley[70] also sees a lack of excessive distortion and has advanced an argument against excessive aggrandizement in self-presentation. Conley claims that other factors for victory are emphasized by Caesar and that "the majority of scholars ever since

Mommsen have believed that the *BG* is tendentious - heavily so, most have implied - and in the more recent studies it has generally been asserted that the principal aim or theme of the *Tendenz* is the glorification of Caesar's prowess as Commander-in-Chief. If this were true, we should expect that in those episodes which culminate in a Roman victory (as most do), the contributions of Caesar the commander would consistently loom large in the structure of causes leading to victory, to a point that would arouse suspicion of partiality. The purpose of this article is to demonstrate that this is not the case." (Conley, 173) He then analyzes scenes that are often cited as excessive and argues that, when they are examined in the larger context of the surrounding narrative and all the factors are taken into account, the actual self-aggrandizement is minimal.

I.D THE AIM OF THIS WORK

The aim of this work is to be a useful tool for anyone who desires to read Latin prose and has had at least basic Latin grammar/morphology. For the beginning student, a complete vocabulary is provided so that valuable time is not wasted paging through the dictionary and the notes are abundant so that help is available for any aspect they find difficult. For the more advanced student, the notes are placed last so that the vocabulary can be used alone with the text in order to facilitate speed in reading. The book is designed to be self-sufficient with its own text, vocabulary, and notes, but at the same time is referenced to other works which a student may consult for further information. The text is that found in the Oxford Latin text,[71] broken down into small sense units that are more approachable than large chunks of Latin. The definitions in the basic vocabulary lists are mainly taken from Lewis' *An Elementary Latin Dictionary*,[72] supplemented periodically by definitions found in Kelsey's[73] vocabulary list. Some specialized word uses are taken from the *Oxford Latin Dictionary*[74] (abbreviated *OLD*). In the notes, each grammar and syntax point is referenced to Allan and Greenaugh's *New Latin Grammar*[75] (abbreviated A.G.). A small explanation is provided but the reader is encouraged to look there for further explanation and examples. There are two older commentaries, those of Kelsey[76] and Walker,[77] which were published near the turn of the last century and summarize much archeological and historical scholarship. I cite these two works where I feel that it is useful for understanding the text. The descriptions of tribes and individuals in Appendix A are based upon those found in Kelsey but augmented from other sources and are included as proper names are not normally included in dictionaries and this can be a source of frustration for readers. For those interested in word occurrences, C. M. Birch's *Concordantia et Index Caesaris*[78] is indispensable. Finally, a complete listing of secondary literature can be found in Jürgen von Kroymann's bibliography Caesar und das Corpus Caesarianum in der Neueren Forschung: Gesamtbibliographie 1945-1970.[79]

I. E ACKNOWLEDGEMENTS

I would like to thank all of my teachers, collogues, and students for making this book possible. Thank you to Oxford University Press for the use of the base text. The cover art is reproduced from Kelsey's commentary and was too wonderful to pass by. The map is also from Kelsey, originally produced at the turn of the last century by Bradley and Poates, Engineers, New York. Special thanks to John Craig and Michael Bradsell for technical assistance. My greatest debt of gratitude goes to my wife, Sara, and children, August and Veda, who understood that much time was needed to conclude this project. Thank you one and all.

I.F SELECTED CHRONOLOGY

102 (B.C.) Marius defeats the Teutoni

101	Marius defeats the Cimbri
100	July 12, Caesar born
88-82	The first civil war between Sulla and Marius
87	Caesar elected Flamen Dialis
84	Caesar marries Cornelia, daughter of Cinna
80	Caesar serves in Asia (80-78), wins the "civic crown"
78	Prosecutes Dolabella for extortion
76	Caesar sails to Rhodes to study under Molo, captured by pirates, elected *Tribunus Militum*
74	Raised a company of volunteers at Rhodes, held Caria against Mithradates
69	Caesar Quaestor in Further Spain, Cornelia dies
67	Caesar marries Pompeia
65	Caesar Curule Aedile
63	Caesar Pontifix Maximus
62	Caesar Praetor
61	Governor, as Propraetor, of Further Spain
60	Formed The First Triumvirate with Pompey and Crassus
59	Caesar Consul (1), marries Calpurnia, Pompey marries Caesar's daughter Julia
58-51	Caesar campaigns in Gaul, Britain, and Germany as Proconsul
58	Caesar made Proconsul March 1, 59 - February 28, 54, *BG* 1, campaign against the Helvetii and Ariovistus
57	*BG* 2, campaign against the Belgae
56	*BG* 3, Campaign against the Veneti; conference of Triumvirs at Luca, Caesar's command extended five years, to February, 49
55	*BG* 4, Caesar campaigns in Germany and Britain
54	*BG* 5, Second campaign in Britain, campaign against the northern Belgic tribes; Julia dies
53	*BG* 6, Second campaign in Germany, campaign in north-east Gaul; Crassus killed at Carrahae
52	*BG* 7, Pan-Gallic revolt under Vercingotrix subdued; unrest in Rome, Clodius killed
51-50	*BG* 8 Revolt of the Carnutes and Bellovaci, siege and fall of Uxellodunum; disputes at Rome about Caesar's command and second consulship
49	Senate decrees that Caesar must disband his army, Caesar crosses the Rubicon on January 10, beginning the civil war, Pompey leads the opposition, Caesar dictator (1)
48	Caesar Consul (2), defeat of Pompey at Pharsalus, death of Pompey in Egypt, Caesar in Egypt with Cleopatra
47	Caesar Dictator (2), combats Pompeian remnants, defeats Pharnaces at Zela (*Veni, Vidi, Vici*)
46	Caesar Consul (3), Dictator for ten years (3), defeats Pompeians at Thaspus
45	Caesar Dictator (4) for life, Consul (4), defeats Pompeians at Munda
44	Caesar Consul (5), refuses crown at Lupercalia February 15, assassinated on Ides of March (15TH)

1.A CHAPTERS 1-3: THE GAULS PLAN REBELLION IN SECRET; THE CARNUTES TAKE THE LEAD; THEY SACK CENABUM AND KILL ROMAN CITIZENS

(1.1) **QUIETA Gallia, Caesar, ut constituerat, in Italiam ad conventus agendos proficiscitur.**

ad, *in order to, for the purpose of.*
Caesar, -aris, m., *Caesar.*

conventus, -us, m., *court, assize.*
in, *to, towards.*
proficiscor, -ficisci, -fectus, *set out, depart, proceed.*
ut, *as, just as.*

ago, agere, egi, actus, *manage, conduct, transact, hold.*
constituo, -stituere, -stitui, -stitutus, *resolve upon, determine.*
Gallia, -ae, f., *Gaul.*
Italia, -ae, f., *Italy.*
quietus, a, um, *peaceful, at peace.*

QUIETA Gallia: Ablative absolute with an adjective (**QUIETA**) taking the place of a participle (there is no participle for "being") (see Allen and Greenough's *New Latin Grammar*, henceforth abbreviated A.G., 419.a-20). The ablative absolute is a common construction in Book 7 and it is important to translate it into good idiomatic English. The translation of an ablative absolute varies but should either be translated as a subordinate clause beginning with "when, while, after, since, although, if, seeing as, in, by, etc.", or at times as a coordinate clause, as the context demands. When the passive participle is utilized in Latin, it should be rendered in the active with a personal subject whenever possible, as **coacto exercitu**, "After he had collected the army", not "with the army having been collected" (A.G. 419-20). The year is 52 B.C. and in the previous campaign season Caesar had suppressed a revolt led by the relatives of the deceased Indutiomarus of the Treveri, Acco of the Senones, and Ambiorix of the Eburones; see *BG* 6.1-8, 29-44 (all references will be to the *Bellum Gallicum* unless otherwise noted). Caesar had previously thought that Gaul was subdued, at 2.35.1: **omni Gallia pacata**, 3.7.1: **cum omnibus de causis Caesar pacatam Galliam existimaret**, and 3.28.1: **omni Gallia pacata**; then he described the situation a little less positively as **quietiorem Galliam** at 5.58. Here, the weaker adjective **Quieta** (peaceful, but not subdued) seems to suggest that experience has taught him that Gaul is only quiet on the surface. **QUIETA**: The adjective is used in Book 7 only here and at 6.4 (**quieti**). **Gallia**: See Appendix A. "Between the home territory of the Roman people in the Italian peninsula and the tribes of Gaul and Germany lay two provinces - Cisalpine Gaul, most of whose population were actually already Roman citizens or in possession of Latin rights, and Transalpine Gaul, a province since only 121 B.C., but already in Caesar's time displaying a developed urban civilization based on the Greek model, under the influence of Massilia. By the end of the first century B.C. well-to-do Romans considered the schools of Massilia an acceptable alternative to those of Athens for their son's higher studies (Strabo 4.1.5). On the fringes of the province, however, and beyond in Gaul proper were the long-haired Gauls (hence *Gallia comata*) and beyond them the German tribes." (Gardner, 181; the references for all citations can be found in the Introduction.) Compare the prominent position of **Gallia** in the opening of *BG* Book 1: **GALLIA est omnis divisa** ...; Book 2: **CUM esset Caesar in citeriore Gallia** ...; Book 6: **MULTIS de causis Caesar maiorem Galliae motum exspectans** ... .
Caesar: Nominative subject (A.G. 339). See Appendix A. In Book 7 of the *BG*, Caesar refers to himself only in the third person, either in the singular or occasionally in the plural. Compare the three instances in the *BG* where he refers to himself in the first person: **dixeram** at 2.24.1, **demonstraveram** at 4.27.2, and **scio** at 5.55.5. F. E. Adcock claims that through the use of the third person "it is thus possible that the constant use of his name in the *Commentaries* is not only a convention or a mask of objectiveness, but includes, as it were, the natural, almost automatic, expression of his conscious preeminence." (Adcock, 76) For a full discussion see Adcock, 74-76; C. W. Siedler, 29. J.H. Collins notes of Caesar's presence in the entire *BG* that: "from his dramatic entrance in the sentences I have already quoted from *BG* I.7.1, to the graphic description of the fall of Alesia, *BG* VII, 88, Caesar stands in the center of the action, the efficient, resourceful, alert commander, prepared in mind and body for all eventualities, *acer et indomitus*, as Lucan (I, 146) calls him. He stands forth also as the very embodiment of the Roman *imperium*, ready to beat down Rome's enemies and spread the terror of her name to the Rhine, the ocean, and beyond." (Collins, 941) Compare the prominent position of the noun **Caesar** in the opening of *BG* Book 2: **CUM esset Caesar** ...; Book 3: **CUM in Italiam proficisceretur Caesar** ...; Book 5: **L. Domitio App. Claudio consulibus, discedens ab hibernis Caesar** ...; Book 6: **MULTIS de causis Caesar** ... . In Book 1, **Caesar** (in the dative, **Caesari**) first occurs at 7.1 and in Book 4 **Caesar** first occurs at 5.1.
ut constituerat: The relative adverb **ut** ("as") with the indicative introduces a parenthetical remark (*OLD* **ut** 12). For the reference see *BG* 6.44.3. **constituerat**: The main verb of the subordinate clause (A.G. 278.b). The pronoun **is**, with **Caesar** as the antecedent, is understood as the subject (A.G. 271.a). The pluperfect tense of the verb denotes an action completed in past time (A.G. 477).
in Italiam: Accusative of *place to which* with the preposition **in** (A.G. 426.2). **Italiam**: See Appendix A.
ad conventus agendos: The preposition **ad** with accusative noun and gerundive denotes purpose (A.G. 506). **conventus agendos**: The phrase is an idiom that means "to hold court, the assizes". "The governor of a province from time to time visited the principal cities to administer justice. Caesar's chief object in going up into Cisalpine Gaul, however, was doubtless to get as near Rome as the law allowed, in order to watch the course of events there." (Kelsey, 291) For other instances of Caesar holding the assizes see *BG* 1.54.3, 5.1.5, 5.2.1, and 6.44.3. **agendos**: Plural, masculine, accusative gerundive used as an adjective modifying **conventus** denoting necessity, obligation or propriety (A.G. 500.1).
proficiscitur: The main verb of the main clause (A.G. 278.b). The historical present, giving vividness to the narrative, is present in Chapter 1 (A.G. 469). This usage, common in all languages, comes from imagining past events as going on before our eyes (*repraesentatio*) (A.G. 469 Note). The historical present is used "to lend speed, vividness, excitement, the ancient equivalent of our TV (I like to call it the Television Tense), which brings the past to life before our eyes with a *You Are There* effect." (Siedler, 29) Siedler counts 352 uses of the historical present in Book 7 (Siedler, 46).

(1.1) **Ibi cognoscit de Clodi caede, *de* senatusque consulto certior factus, ut omnes iuniores Italiae coniurarent, dilectum tota provincia habere instituit.**

caedes, -is, f., *killing, slaughter, murder, massacre.*
Claudius, -i, m. *Claudius.*

certus, -a, -um, comp. **-ior**, *certain, positive.*
cognosco, -gnoscere, -gnovi, cognitus, *learn, learn of.*

coniuro, -are, -avi, -atus, *take an oath together.*
de, *about, concerning.*
fio, fieri, factus, *become,* (with certior) *be informed.*
ibi, *in that place, there.*

Italia, -ae, f., *Italy.*
omnis, -e, *every, all.*
-que, *and.*
totus, -a, -um, *the whole, all, all the, entire.*

consultum, -i, n., *resolution, decree.*
dilectus, -us, m., *levy, draft, enlistment.*
habeo, habere, habui, habitus, *have, hold, conduct.*
instituo, -stituere, -stitui, -stitutus, *decide, determine, resolve upon.*
iuniores, -um, m., pl., *younger men.*
provincia, -ae, f., *the province.*
senatus, -us, m., *senate.*
ut, *namely that, to the effect that.*

ibi: Adverb (A.G. 215.5 and 320-21).

cognoscit: Main verb of the coordinate clause ibi ... caede (A.G. 278.a). The pronoun is, with Caesar as the antecedent, is understood as the subject (A.G. 271.a).

de Clodi caede: Prepositional phrase, de with the ablative here means "about, concerning" (*OLD* de 12). Clodi: Possessive genitive with caede (A.G. 343). The singular genitive of nouns in -ius ended, until the Augustan Age, in a single -i (A.G. 49.b). "By Milo, 52 BC." (Edwards, 381) See Appendix A.

de senatusque consulto: Prepositional phrase, de with the ablative here means "about, concerning" (*OLD* de 12). senatus: Possessive genitive with consulto (A.G. 343). -que: The enclitic conjunction connects the two main verbs cognoscit ... instituit (A.G. 324.a). The enclitic is seldom joined to an unemphasized monosyllabic preposition (*de*) and so is connected to senatus (*OLD* -que).

certior factus: Nominative subject of instituit (A.G. 339). The phrase certiorem fieri is an idiom that means "to be informed" (*OLD* facere 12.b). certior: Singular, masculine, nominative comparative adjective modifying factus (A.G. 124). factus: Nominative, perfect, passive participle used as a predicate, where in English a phrase or a subordinate clause would be more natural (A.G. 496). The pronoun is, with Caesar as the antecedent, is understood. In this predicate use, the participle is normally equivalent to a subordinate clause which expresses time, cause, occasion, concession, etc. and can be translated into good idiomatic English with the words "while, when, after, because, although, if, etc." (A.G. 496). The present participle represents the action as in progress at the time indicated by the main verb, the perfect as completed (A.G. 489).

ut ... coniurarent: The conjunction ut ("namely that, to the effect that") with the subjunctive forms an epexegetical clause in apposition to the prepositional phrase *de senatusque consulto* (*OLD* ut 39). coniurarent: The main verb of the subordinate clause (A.G. 278.b). Imperfect subjunctive; the tense of the subjunctive is in secondary sequence and follows the rules for the sequence of tense after the historical present instituit (A.G. 482-85, esp. 485.e). For the purposes of sequence of tense, the historical present is equivalent to the historical perfect tense and is normally followed by the secondary sequence (there will be exceptions) (A.G. 469 and 485.e). "In times of danger, when the levies were made in haste, the soldiers did not take the military oath one by one but in a body, responding to the general." (Kelsey, 400)

omnes iuniores: Nominative subject (A.G. 339). iuniores: Nominative, plural, masculine comparative adjective used substantively ("substantively" simply means "as a noun") (A.G.288). The noun means "the younger men, especially those of military age" (between 17 and 46 years of age) (*OLD* iuniores).

Italiae: Locative case of Italia, ae, f. (A.G. 43.c). See Appendix A.

dilectum: Accusative direct object of the infinitive habere (A.G. 387 and 451.3). "Although recruitment to the Roman army was theoretically based upon conscription, there seems to have been little difficulty in normal times in maintaining the establishment by means of voluntary enlistment, especially in the western provinces. The infrequency with which resort was made to the dilectus is remarkable." (Watson, 31)

tota provincia: Ablative of *place where* without a preposition (A.G. 429.2). "Cisalpine Gaul is meant, as shown by the next sentence." (Kelsey, 400) provincia: See Appendix A.

habere: Complementary infinitive after instituit (A.G. 456 and 563.d). The infinitive is equivalent to a substantive clause of purpose (A.G. 563.d).

instituit: The main verb of the coordinate clause de ... instituit (A.G. 278.a).

(1.2) **Eae res in Galliam Transalpinam celeriter perferuntur.**

celeriter, *quickly, speedily, at once, immediately.*
in, *into, to.*
perfero, -ferre, -tuli, -latus, *convey, bring, report.*
Transalpinus, -a, -um, *beyond the Alps, Transalpine.*

Gallia, -ae, f., *Gaul.*
is, ea, id, *he, she, it; that, this.*
res, rei, f., *matter, affair, circumstance, fact.*

Eae res: Nominative subject (A.G. 339). Eae: Plural, feminine, nominative demonstrative pronoun used as an adjective modifying res (A.G. 296.1 and a). Walker notes on the translation of the pronoun is, ea, id, that "when it is used substantively it is translated by a personal pronoun; when used as an adjective by *this* or *that*; when used as the antecedent of a relative it is translated in various ways, - *the man, a man, such a man, that,* etc." (Walker, 488)

in Galliam Transalpinam: Accusative of *place to which* with the preposition in (A.G. 426.2). Galliam Transalpinam: See Appendix A.

celeriter: Adverb (A.G. 214.b and 320-21).

perferuntur: The main verb of the simple sentence (A.G. 278.1).

(1.2-3) Addunt ipsi et adfingunt rumoribus Galli quod res poscere videbatur, retineri urbano motu Caesarem neque in tantis (3) dissensionibus ad exercitum venire posse.

ad, *to*.
adfingo, -fingere, -finxi, -fictus, *embellish, invent beside*.
dissensio, -onis, f., *difference of opinion, disagreement*.
exercitus, -us, m., *army*.
in, *in, amid*.
motus, -us, m., *tumult, commotion*.
posco, poscere, poposci, *require, make necessary*.
qui, quae, quod, *who, what, which*.
retineo, -tinere, -tinui, -tentus, *detain, keep back*.
tantus, -a, -um, *such, so important*.
venio, venire, veni, ventus, *come*.

addo, -dere, -didi, -ditus, *add, join*.
Caesar, -aris, m., *Caesar*.
et, *and*.
Galli, -orum, m., *the Gauls*.
ipse, -a, -um, *for their own part, themselves*.
neque, *and ... not*.
possum, posse, potui, -----, *be able*.
res, rei, f., *matter, affair, circumstance*.
rumor, -oris, m., *report, rumor*.
urbanus, -a, -um, *of the city* (usually Rome).
videor, videri, visus sum, *seem, appear*.

Addunt: The main verb of the coordinate clause **Addunt ipsi** (A.G. 278.a). The verb comes in the first position when the idea in it is emphatic (A.G. 598.d).
ipsi ... Galli: Nominative subject of **Addunt ... adfingunt** (A.G. 339). **ipsi**: Plural, masculine, nominative demonstrative pronoun used as an adjective modifying **Galli** (A.G. 296.1 and a). The pronoun marks a transition and means "for their own part" (*OLD* ipse 3).
Galli: Notice how vague the term is here; Caesar supplies no specific names of either states or people. Technically, the term Galli only refers to the inhabitants of central Gaul. At *BG* 1.1-2 Caesar differentiates between the three major groups in Gaul (the Belgae in the north, the Aquitani in the south, and the Galli in central Gaul): **Gallia est omnis divisa in partis tris, quarum unam incolunt Belgae, aliam Aquitani, tertiam qui ipsorum lingua Celtae, nostra Galli appellantur.** Caesar uses the term **Galli** (which should refer only to those inhabitants of central Gaul) to refer to the entire coalition of Gauls as a generic term in Book 7 and does not make rigorous distinctions as he does elsewhere in the *BG*. Gardner notes of the Gauls that "only occasionally had these presented any real and immediate threat to the security of the Italian peninsula. Nevertheless, they were present in Roman consciousness as a kind of bogeyman. ... Caesar represented the danger to Rome from the Gauls as arising in part from the nature of the Gauls themselves and in part from the pressure they were experiencing from the Germanic people." (Gardner, 181 and 182) For the nature of the Gauls see **quaeruntur** at 1.4 and **deserantur** at 2.3. For an example of pressure from the Germans, see the encounter with Ariovistus at *BG* 1.30-54. See Appendix A.
et: The conjunction connects the two main verbs **addunt ... adfingunt** (A.G. 324.a).
adfingunt: The main verb of the coordinate clause **adfingunt ... posse** (A.G. 278.a).
rumoribus: Dative indirect object of the transitive verbs **addunt ... adfingunt** (A.G. 362). (**id**, the supplied antecedent of **quod**, is the direct object.)
quod ... videbatur: Relative clause (A.G. 303). **quod**: Singular, neuter, accusative relative pronoun used substantively (A.G. 305). The antecedent is omitted, supply **id** (A.G. 307.c). Accusative direct object of the infinitive **poscere** (A.G. 387 and 451.3). **videbatur**: The main verb of the subordinate clause (A.G. 278.b).
res: Nominative subject (A.G. 339).
poscere: Complementary infinitive after **videbatur** (A.G. 456).
retineri ... Caesarem: Accusative/infinitive construction in indirect discourse (A.G. 577 ff.). The verb of saying is not expressed, but implied in the general drift of the sentence (A.G. 580.a). Siedler notes that the effect of indirect discourse in the *Commentaries* is that "Caesar disarms his audience by his apparent telling of the Truth, as would any experienced reporter who does not feel justified in quoting the exact words ... ." (Siedler, 29) Siedler counts 131 instances of indirect speech in Book 7 (Siedler, 46). **retineri**: Present infinitive; the tense of the infinitive in indirect discourse is relative to that of the verb of saying (A.G. 584). **Caesarem**: See Appendix A.
urbano motu: Ablative of cause without a preposition (A.G. 404).
neque: The conjunction here joins a negative clause to a preceding positive one and means "and ... not" (*OLD* neque 3).
in tantis dissensionibus: Prepositional phrase, **in** with the ablative here means "in, amid" (certain circumstances) (*OLD* in 40).
ad exercitum: Accusative of *place to which* with the preposition **ad** (A.G. 426.2). "6 legions were at Agedincum, 2 among the Lingones, 2 on the borders of the Treveri - 10 in all." (Kelsey, 401)
venire: Complementary infinitive after **posse** (A.G. 456).
(eum) posse: Accusative/infinitive construction in indirect discourse (A.G. 577 ff.). The verb of saying is not expressed, but implied in the general drift of the sentence (A.G. 580.a). The pronoun **eum**, with **Caesarem** as the antecedent, is understood as the accusative subject. **posse**: Present infinitive; the tense of the infinitive in indirect discourse is relative to that of the verb of saying (A.G. 584). The present infinitive **posse** often has a future sense in indirect discourse (A.G 584.b).

(1.3-4) Hac impulsi occasione qui iam ante se populi Romani imperio subiectos dolerent liberius atque audacius de bello consilia inire (4) incipiunt.

ante, *before*.
audacter, comp., **audacius**, *boldly, courageously, fearlessly*.
consilium, -i, n., *plan, plot*.
doleo, dolere, dolui, doliturus, *lament, deplore, take offense*.
iam, *already*.

atque, *and in fact, and even*.
bellum, -i, n., *war, warfare*.
de, *about, concerning*.
hic, haec, hoc, *this; he, she, it*.
impello, -pellere, -puli, -pulsus, *urge on, drive on*,

4

imperium, -i, n., *control, dominion, military authority.*

ineo, -ire, -ivi, or -ii, -itus, *begin, form.*
occasio, -onis, f., *opportunity, favorable moment.*
qui, quae, quod, *who, what, which.*
sui, sibi, se, or sese, nom. wanting, *they*, with or without *themselves.*

incite, impel.
incipio, -cipere, -cepi, -ceptus, *begin, commence, undertake.*
libere, comp. -ius, *freely, openly, boldly.*
populus, -i, m., *people* (as a political whole), *nation.*
Romanus, -a, -um, *Roman.*
subicio, -icere, -ieci, -iectus, *make subject.*

Hac ... occasione: Ablative of cause without a preposition after **impulsi**; the motive which influences the mind of the person acting is expressed by the ablative of cause (A.G. 404). **Hac**: Singular, feminine, ablative demonstrative pronoun used as an adjective modifying **occasione** (A.G. 296.1 and a).

impulsi: Nominative, perfect, passive participle used as a predicate, where in English a phrase or a subordinate clause would be more natural (A.G. 496). The pronoun **ei**, with **Galli** as the antecedent, is understood. Nominative subject of **incipiunt** (A.G. 339).

qui ... dolerent: A relative clause of characteristic; the relative pronoun with the subjunctive is often used to indicate a characteristic of the antecedent, especially where the antecedent is otherwise undefined (A.G. 535). Here the relative expresses cause ("since they") (A.G. 535.e). **qui**: Plural, masculine, nominative relative pronoun used substantively (A.G. 305). The antecedent is **impulsi** (A.G. 307). Nominative subject (A.G. 339). **dolerent**: The main verb of the subordinate clause (A.G. 278.b). Imperfect subjunctive; the tense of the subjunctive is in secondary sequence and follows the rules for the sequence of tense after the historical present **incipiunt** (A.G. 482-85, esp. 485.e).

iam: Adverb (A.G. 215.6, 217.b and 320-21).

ante: Adverb (A.G. 320-21 and 433.1).

se ... subiectos (esse): Accusative/infinitive construction in indirect discourse after **dolerent** (A.G. 577 ff.). **se**: Plural, masculine, accusative direct relative pronoun (A.G. 300.1). The antecedent is **qui**, the subject of **dolerent** (A.G. 299). **subiectos (esse)**: Supply **esse** to form the perfect, passive, infinitive (A.G. 188). Siedler claims that this common ellipsis in Caesar creates speed (Siedler, 31). The tense of the infinitive in indirect discourse is relative to that of the verb of saying (A.G. 584).

populi Romani: Possessive genitive with **imperio** (A.G. 343). This expression has an invariable word order (A.G. 598.k).

imperio: Dative indirect object of the passive infinitive **subiectos (esse)**; verbs which in the active voice take the accusative and dative retain the dative when used in the passive (A.G. 370).

liberius: Comparative adverb (A.G. 218 and 320-21). Liberty for the Gauls is a theme in Book 7. In the first chapter alone it is repeated three times: **liberius, in libertatem**, and **libertatem** (1.3, 1.6, and 1.8). For the noun **libertas** in Book 7 see 1.5, 1.8, 4.4, 37.4, 64.3, 66.4, 71.3, 76.2, 77.13, 77.14, 89.1. See especially the juxtaposition of liberty and slavery in Critignatus' speech at 7.77. Paul Murphy maintains that while liberty is the main theme of the book, Caesar matches almost every mention of it with an instance of Gallic **barbaria** (Paul Murphy, 241). After their concern for liberty in Chapter 1, they massacre Roman merchants at 3.1 and "Vercingetorix *habet dilectum egentium et perditorum* (4.3). Thus the Roman reader felt no sympathy at learning that *hortatur ut communis libertatis causa arma capiant* (4.4). Even less was the (sic) so stirred at learning how Vercingetorix enforced discipline - through death by torture and by burning, through lopping off ears and gouging out eyes (4.10)." (P. Murphy, 241-42) According to Murphy, the only case where **libertas** is not conjoined to **barbaria** is at 89.1-2. (P. Murphy, 242)

atque: The conjunction connects a word (**audacius**) which strengthens or corrects the first term (**liberius**) and means "and in fact, and even" (*OLD* atque 4).

audacius: Comparative adverb (A.G. 218 and 320-21).

de bello: Prepositional phrase, **de** with the ablative here means "about, concerning" (*OLD* de 12).

consilia: Accusative direct object of the infinitive **inire** (A.G. 387 and 451.3). The phrase **consilium inire** is an idiom that means "to form a plan or plot" (*OLD* ineo 7.b). Notice that the noun is here plural, implying numerous plots.

inire: Complementary infinitive after **incipiunt** (A.G. 456).

incipiunt: The main verb of the main clause (A.G. 278.b).

(1.4-5) Indictis inter se principes Galliae conciliis silvestribus ac remotis locis queruntur de Acconis morte; (5) posse hunc casum ad ipsos recidere demonstrant; miserantur communem Galliae fortunam;

ac, *and.*
ad, *on to, to, against.*
communis, -e, *common, in common, public, general.*
de, *about, concerning.*

fortuna, -ae, f., *condition, state, fate, misfortune, circumstance.*
hic, haec, hoc, *this; he, she, it.*
inter, *with, to, among.*

loca, -orum, n., pl., *places.*
mors, mortis, f., *death.*
princeps, -ipis, m., *head man, leader, chief, prince.*
recido, -cidere, -cidi, -casurus, *come upon, fall to the lot of.*
silvestris, -e, *covered with woods, wooded, woody.*

Acco, -onis, m., *Acco.*
casus, -us, m., *misfortune, evil plight.*
concilium, -i, n., *meeting, assembly, council.*
demonstro, -are, -avi, -atus, *point out, show, say, mention, explain.*
Gallia, -ae, f., *Gaul.*
indico, -dicere, -dixi, -dictus, *convoke, call, appoint.*
ipse, -a, -um, *he, they*, with or without *himself, themselves.*
miseror, -ari, -atus, *lament, deplore.*
possum, posse, potui, -----, *be able.*
queror, queri, questus, *complain of, make complaint of.*
remotus, -a, -um, *far off, remote.*
sui, sibi, se, or sese, nom. wanting, *each other, themselves.*

Indictis ... conciliis: Ablative absolute (A.G. 419-20). **Indictis**: The perfect tense of the participle represents the action as completed at the time indicated by the tense of the main verb (A.G. 489). **conciliis**: Notice that the plural noun indicates the widespread nature of the newest revolt. Kahn claims that the council scene functions as a substitute for choral odes between major episodes (Kahn, 251). See also 14.1, 29.1, 63.5-6, 75.1, and 89.1.

inter se: Prepositional phrase, **inter** with the accusative reflexive pronoun here means "with or to each other" (*OLD* **inter**1 15). **se**: Plural, masculine, accusative direct reflexive pronoun (A.G. 300.1). The antecedent is **principes**, the subject of **queruntur** (A.G. 299).

principes: Nominative subject of **queruntur** (A.G. 339).

Galliae: Partitive genitive with **principes** (A.G. 346.a.1).

silvestribus ac remotis locis: Ablative of *place where* without a preposition (A.G. 429.1). **ac**: The conjunction connects the two adjectives modifying **locis** and means "and" (*OLD* **atque** 12). Two adjectives belonging to the same noun are regularly connected by a conjunction (A.G. 323.d). **locis**: The noun **locus** is heterogeneous in Caesar, meaning that the singular is masculine and the plural is neuter (A.G. 106.a). "At 7.1 the Gauls begin their revolt by complaining about the death of Acco in remote forest spots, casting a suspicious light on the conspiracy." (Mannetter, 34)

quaeruntur ... recuperare: C. Murphy classifies this speech as deliberative and analyzes it thus:

I) *Exordium*: **quaeruntur ... fortunam**.

II) *Propositio*: **Omnibus ... vindicent**.

111) *Confirmatio*: **In ... possit**.

IV) *Peroratio*: **Postremo ... recuperare**.

He notes that "Caesar reports a number of speeches in which the Gauls encouraged each other to revolt; here too he uses these speeches to show the motives and beliefs which led the Gauls to rebel. The Gallic leaders invariably represent the Roman rule as intolerable slavery." (C. Murphy, 122-23, 125-126) Kahn notes that "since a strong dramatic conflict requires well-matched antagonists, Caesar characterizes the Gauls objectively, attributing to them nobility of motivation. They are represented as ready to die to regain their freedom, courageous in battle, ingenious in tactics and skilled in engineering. But they exhibit a tragic flaw, instability of character." (Kahn, 253) For their tragic flaw, see **deserantur** at 2.3. In this first speech, in the very opening of Book 7, Caesar sets out the Gauls as a worthy opponent, the noble character type. For a discussion of the Gallic character as 'noble savage' see Mannetter, 28-38. For other instances of the noble character type in Book 7 see Chapter 2, the actions of the Carnutes; 4, Vercingetorix's desire for liberty; 14-15, adopting the scorched earth policy; 22, adapting to, and adopting, Roman techniques; 25, Gauls steadfast in the face of death; 28-29, Vercingetorix checks emotion and retains his composure; 37, Convictolitavis is dedicated to the cause of liberty; 62, the Gauls do not flee in defeat; 76, the Gauls are dedicated to obtaining liberty; 77, Critognatus is unwilling to surrender; 89, Vercingetorix surrenders for the common good.

queruntur: The main verb of the main clause (A.G. 278.b).

de Acconis morte: Prepositional phrase, here **de** with the ablative means "about, concerning" (*OLD* **de** 12). **Acconis**: Possessive genitive with **morte** (A.G. 343). "By flogging him to death (*fustuarium*)." (Edwards, 377) For the reference see *BG* 6.44.2-3. "Caesar's ferocious campaigns had no more than stunned the Gallic tribes, and the hideous fate of Acco like a Domaclean sword hung over the head of every chieftain. Thus it came about that his systematic devastations and slaughterings, instead of compelling coercion, awakened desperation, and they were lead to the one thing he feared most - a coalescence of the tribes in a war of liberation." (Fuller, 132) See Appendix A.

hunc casum posse: Accusative /infinitive construction in indirect discourse after **demonstrant** (A.G. 577 ff.). **hunc**: Singular, masculine, accusative demonstrative pronoun used as an adjective modifying **casum** (A.G. 296.1 and a). **posse**: Present infinitive; the tense of the infinitive in indirect discourse is relative to that of the verb of saying (A.G. 584).

ad ipsos: Prepositional phrase, **ad** with the accusative here means "on to, to, against" (*OLD* **ad** 2). **ipsos**: Plural, masculine, accusative demonstrative pronoun used substantively (296.2 and 298.d). The antecedent is **principes**, the subject of **demonstrant** (A.G. 298). Here, the demonstrative pronoun is used for emphasis instead of the indirect reflexive **se** (A.G. 298.e and 300.b).

recidere: Complementary infinitive after **posse** (A.G. 456).

demonstrant: The main verb of the main clause (A.G. 278.b). The pronoun **ei**, with **principes** as the antecedent, is understood as the subject (A.G. 271.a).

miserantur: The main verb of the simple sentence (A.G. 278.1). The verb comes in the first position when the idea in it is emphatic (A.G. 598.d). The pronoun **ei**, with **principes** as the antecedent, is understood as the subject (A.G. 271.a).

communem ... fortunam: Accusative direct object of **miserantur** (A.G. 387).

Galliae: Possessive genitive with **fortunam** (A.G. 343). See Appendix A.

(1.5-6) **omnibus pollicitationibus ac praemiis deposcunt qui belli initia faciant et sui capitis (6) periculo Galliam in libertatem vindicent.**

ac, *and*.
caput, -itis, n., *head*; by metonymy, *life, safety*.
et, *and*.
Gallia, -ae, f., *Gaul*.
initia, -orum, n., pl., *the initial phase, first part*.
omnis, -e, *all, of every kind, all sorts of*.
pollicitatio, -onis, f., *offer, promise*.
qui, quae, quod, *who, what, which*.
vindico, -are, -avi, -atus, *restore, set free, liberate, deliver*.

bellum, -i, n., *war, warfare*.
deposco, -poscere, -poposci, *request, earnestly call for*.
facio, facere, feci, factus, *cause, occasion, bring about*.
in, *into*.
libertas, -atis, f., *freedom, liberty, independence*.
periculum, -i, n., *risk, danger, hazard*.
praemium, -i, n., *reward, recompense*.
suus, -a, -um, *their*, with or without *own*.

omnibus pollicitationibus ac praemiis: Two ablatives of means (A.G. 409). **ac**: The conjunction connects the two ablative nouns and means "and" (*OLD* **atque** 12).

deposcunt: The main verb of the main clause (A.G. 278.b). The pronoun **ei**, with **principes** as the antecedent, is understood as the subject (A.G. 271.a).

qui ... faciant ... vindicent: A relative clause of characteristic; the relative pronoun with the subjunctive is often used to indicate a characteristic of the antecedent, especially where the antecedent is otherwise undefined (A.G. 535). **qui**: Plural, masculine, nominative relative pronoun used substantively (A.G. 305). The antecedent is omitted, supply **eos** (A.G. 307.c). Nominative subject (A.G. 339). **faciant ... vindicent**: The main verbs of the subordinate clause (A.G. 278.b). Present subjunctives; the tense of the subjunctives is normally in secondary sequence after the historical present **deposcunt** (A.G. 482-85). Here it is in primary sequence through *repraesentatio* (A.G. 485.e and 585.b Note).

belli: Possessive genitive with **initia** (A.G. 343).

initia: Accusative direct object of **faciant** (A.G. 387). The noun **initium** in the plural means "the initial phase, first part" (*OLD* **initium** 3).

et: The conjunction connects the two main verbs in the relative clause **faciant ... vindicent** (A.G. 324.a).

sui capitis: Objective genitive with **periculo** (A.G. 348). **sui**: Singular, neuter, genitive possessive pronoun used as an adjective modifying **capitis** (A.G. 302). **capitis**: Here, the noun **caput** means "the life of a person, especially when endangered" by metonymy ("the use of the name of one thing to indicate some kindred thing") (A.G. 641) (*OLD* **caput** 4).

periculo: Ablative of specification (A.G. 418.a). "As the Romans had no such categories as we make, it is impossible to classify all uses of the ablative. The ablative of *specification* (originally *instrumental*) is closely akin to that of *manner*, and shows some resemblance to *means* and *cause*." (A.G. 418.a Note)

Galliam in libertatem vindicent: The phrase **in libertatem vindicare** is an idiom that means "to free a country (**Galliam**) from oppressive rule, liberate" (*OLD* **vindico** 3.b).

Galliam: Accusative direct object of **vindicent** (A.G. 387). See Appendix A.

in libertatem: Prepositional phrase, **in** with the accusative here means "into" (a state or condition) (*OLD* **in** 2). **libertatem**: For the theme of liberty in Book 7, see **liberius** at 1.3.

(1.6-7) **In primis rationem esse habendam dicunt, prius quam eorum clandestina (7) consilia efferantur, ut Caesar ab exercitu intercludatur.**

ab, *from.*
clandestinus, -a, -um, *secret, hidden.*
dico, dicere, dixi, dictus, *say.*
exercitus, -us, m., *army.*

in primis, *first.*
is, ea, id, *he, she, it; that, this.*
ratio, -onis, f., *plan.*

Caesar, -aris, m., *Caesar.*
consilium, -i, n., *deliberation, plan, design, policy.*
effero, -ferre, extuli, elatus, *spread abroad, publish.*
habeo, habere, habui, habitus, *consider, reckon, devise.*
intercludo, -cludere, -clusi, -clusus, *shut off, cut off.*
prius quam, *before.*
ut, *how, in what way, in what manner.*

In primis: Adverbial phrase, originally a prepositional phrase, **in** with the ablative plural of the adjective **primus** means "first" (*OLD* **imprimis**). This is balanced by **postremo** at 1.8.

rationem esse habendam: Accusative/infinitive construction in indirect discourse after **dicunt** (A.G. 577 ff.). **rationem habendam**: The phrase **rationem habere** is an idiom that means "to take into consideration" (*OLD* **habeo** 19.d). **esse habendam**: The infinitive **esse** with the gerundive forms the second periphrastic (passive) present infinitive implying necessity (A.G. 194.b and 196). The tense of the infinitive in indirect discourse is relative to that of the verb of saying (A.G. 584).

dicunt: The main verb of the main clause (A.G. 278.b). The pronoun **ei**, with **principes** as the antecedent, is understood as the subject (A.G. 271.a).

prius quam ... efferantur: Temporal clause; the conjunction **prius quam** ("before") is common with the imperfect subjunctive when the action that it denotes did not take place. After an historical present (**dicunt**) the present subjunctive is used instead of the imperfect (A.G. 551.b and Note 2). **prius quam**: The conjunction is written as two words (*OLD* **priusquam**). **efferantur**: The main verb of the subordinate clause (A.G. 278.b).

eorum: Plural, masculine, genitive demonstrative pronoun used substantively (A.G. 296.2). The antecedent is **ei** (**principes**), the supplied subject of **dicunt** (A.G. 297.e). Possessive genitive with **consilia** (A.G. 343). The more normal form here would be the indirect reflexive possessive adjective **sua** (as the subordinate clause reflects the thought of the subject of the main clause), but the demonstrative pronoun **eorum** is an allowable (although rare) alternative (A.G. 300.b).

clandestina consilia: Nominative subject (A.G. 339).

ut ... intercludatur: The interrogative adverb **ut** ("how") with the subjunctive forms an indirect question in apposition to **rationem** (A.G. 531.1). **intercludatur**: The main verb of the subordinate clause (A.G. 278.b). Present subjunctive; the tense of the subjunctive is normally in secondary sequence after the historical present **dicunt** (A.G. 575). Here it is in primary sequence through *repraesentatio* (A.G. 485.e and 585.b Note).

Caesar: Nominative subject (A.G. 339). See Appendix A.

ab exercitu: Ablative of separation with the preposition **ab** after **intercludatur** (A.G. 401).

(1.7-8) **Id esse facile, quod neque legiones audeant absente imperatore ex hibernis egredi neque imperator sine praesidio (8) ad** legiones pervenire possit.

absens (part. of absum), -entis, *absent*.
audeo, audere, ausus sum, *venture, dare, risk*.
ex, *from, out of*.
hiberna, -orum, n., pl., (supply castra), *winter-quarters*.

is, ea, id, *he, she, it; that, this*.
neque ... neque, *neither ... nor*.

possum, posse, potui, -----, *be able*.
quod, *because, since, for, as*.
sum, esse, fui, futurus, *be*.

ad, *to*.
egredior, -gredi, -gressus, *go out* or *forth, leave*.
facilis, -e, *easy, not difficult, not hard*.
imperator, -oris, m., *commander-in-chief, commander, general*.
legio, -onis, f., *legion*.
pervenio, -venire, -veni, -ventus, *come to, arrive at, reach*.
praesidium, -i, n., *guard, protection, escort*.
sine, *without*.

Id esse facile: Accusative/infinitive construction in indirect discourse after **dicunt** (A.G. 577 ff.). **Id**: Singular, neuter, accusative demonstrative pronoun used substantively (A.G. 296.2). The antecedent is the idea of separating Caesar from his army contained in the previous indirect question (**ut ... intercludantur**) (A.G. 297.e). **esse**: Present infinitive; the tense of the infinitive in indirect discourse is relative to that of the verb of saying (A.G. 584). **facile**: Singular, neuter, accusative predicate adjective modifying **id** after **esse** (A.G. 283-84).

quod ... audeant ... possit: Causal clause; the conjunction **quod** ("because") normally takes the indicative when the reason is given on the authority of the writer or speaker (A.G. 540.1). Here **quod** takes the subjunctive as a subordinate clause in indirect discourse after **dicunt** (A.G. 580). **audeant ... possit**: The main verbs of the subordinate clause (A.G. 278.b). Present subjunctives; the tense of the subjunctives is normally in secondary sequence after the historical present **dicunt** (A.G. 482-85). Here it is in primary sequence through *repraesentatio* (A.G. 485.e and 585.b Note). Notice the change in subject from the plural **legiones** to the singular **imperator**.

neque ... neque: The repeated conjunction connects the two main verbs in the causal clause and means "neither ... nor" (*OLD* **neque** 7).

legiones: Nominative subject (A.G. 339). "In theory a legion consisted of 6000 men; but battles, accidents, and disease so reduced this number that Caesar's legions probably averaged about 4000 men, or even less. The following table gives the divisions of a legion and their theoretical strength:

century [**centum**, hundred]	= 100 men	
2 centuries	= 1 maniple	= 200 men
3 maniples	= 1 cohort	= 600 men
10 cohorts	= 1 legion	= 6000 men." (Walker, 23)

absente imperatore: Ablative absolute (A.G. 419-20). **absente**: Present participle of **absum** (A.G. 170.b). The participle ends in -e rather than -i in the ablative singular when used in an ablative absolute (A.G. 121.2). The present participle represents the action as in progress at the time indicated by the tense of the main verb (A.G. 489). **imperatore**: I.e., Caesar. "The general was technically called leader (*dux*) until he had won a victory; after the first victory he had a right to the title *imperator*, commander. Caesar used this title from the time he defeated the Helvetii (B.C. 58) until his death." (Kelsey, 25)

ex hibernis: Ablative of *place from which* with the preposition **ex** (426.1). **hibernis**: Plural, neuter, ablative, adjective used substantively (A.G. 288). The noun **castris** is understood from constant association (A.G. 288.c). "The winter-quarters (*hibernia*, or *castra hibernia*) were made more comfortable than the ordinary encampments, by the substitution of straw-thatched huts (*casae*) for tents. Many Roman camps became the nucleus of permanent settlements, which still exist to-day. ... all names of English towns ending in -*chester* point to Roman encampments." (Kelsey, 35)

egredi: Complementary infinitive after **audeant** (A.G. 456).

imperator: Nominative subject (A.G. 339). I.e., Caesar.

sine praesidio: Prepositional phrase, **sine** with the ablative means "without the accompaniment of" (*OLD* **sine** 1).

ad legiones: Accusative of *place to which* with the preposition **ad** (A.G.426.2)

pervenire: Complementary infinitive after **possit** (A.G. 456).

(1.8) Postremo in acie praestare interfici quam non veterem belli gloriam libertatemque quam a maioribus acceperint reciperare.

a(b), *from*.
acies, -ei, f., *line of battle, battle*.
gloria, -ae, f., *fame, renown*.
interficio, -ficere, -feci, -fectus, *slay, kill*.
maiores, -um, m., pl., *forefathers, ancestors, forebears*.
postremo, *at last, finally*.

quam, (*rather*) *than*.
qui, quae, quod, *who, what, which*.
vetus, -eris, *old, former, ancient, long-standing*.

accipio, -cipere, -cepi, -ceptus, *receive*.
bellum, -i, n., *war, warfare*.
in, *in*.
libertas, -atis, f., *freedom, liberty, independence*.
non, *not*.
praesto, -stare, -stiti, -stitus, (imper.) *it is preferable, it is better*.
-que, *and*.
recipero, -are, -avi, -atus, *recover, regain, get back*.

Postremo: Adverb (A.G. 217.b and 320-21).

in acies ... interfici: The infinitive phrase functions as the subject of the impersonal infinitive **praestare** (A.G. 454). **in acie**: Ablative of *place where* with the preposition **in** (locative ablative) (A.G. 426.3).

praestare: Impersonal infinitive construction in indirect discourse after **dicunt** (A.G. 577 ff.). Impersonal use of the verb meaning "it is preferable, it is better" (A.G. 208.c) (*OLD* **praesto** 4). The following infinitive phrase functions as the subject (A.G. 454). Present infinitive; the tense of the infinitive in indirect discourse is relative to that of the verb of saying (A.G. 584).

quam ... reciperare: Relative clause in indirect discourse after **dicunt** (A.G. 279.a). **quam**: Relative adverb meaning "(rather) than" after the comparison implied in **praestare** (*OLD* **quam** 9.b). Here the comparison is being made between the two infinitives **interfici ... reciperare**. **reciperare**: The infinitive construction is regularly continued after a comparative with **quam** in indirect discourse rather than switching to the subjunctive in the dependent clause (A.G. 583.c).

non: Adverb; when **non** is especially emphatic it begins the clause (A.G. 217.e, 320-21, and 599.a).

veterem ... gloriam libertatemque: Two accusative direct objects of the infinitive **reciperare** (A.G. 387 and 451.3). **veterem**: The adjective should be construed with both nouns **gloriam ... libertatem** but agrees in number with only the nearest noun (A.G. 286.a). **libertatem**: For the theme of liberty in Book 7, see **liberius** at 1.3. **-que**: The enclitic conjunction connects the two accusative nouns **gloriam ... libertatem** (A.G. 324.a).

belli: Objective genitive with **gloriam** (A.G. 348).

quam ... acceperint: Relative clause; a subordinate clause in indirect discourse takes the subjunctive (A.G. 303 and 580). **quam**: Singular, feminine, accusative relative pronoun used substantively (A.G. 305). The antecedent is both **gloriam** and **libertatem**, agreeing with the nearest noun (A.G. 305.a). Accusative direct object of **acceperint** (A.G. 387). **acceperint**: Perfect subjunctive; the tense of the subjunctive is normally in secondary sequence after the historical present **dicunt** (A.G. 482-85). Here it is in primary sequence through *repraesentatio* (A.G. 485.e and 585.b Note). The pronoun **ei**, with **principes** as the antecedent, is understood as the subject (A.G. 271.a).

a maioribus: Ablative of source with the preposition **a(b)** (A.G. 403.1). **a**: The preposition **ab** may (but not necessarily, see for example **ab reliquis** at 2.3) lose the consonant 'b' and legthen the quantity of 'ă' to 'ā' before a consonant (*OLD* **ab**). **maioribus**: Irregular comparative adjective used substantively meaning "ancestors, forebears" (A.G. 129 and 291.c Note 3) (*OLD* **maior** 3.b).

(2.1-2) His rebus agitatis, profitentur Carnutes se nullum periculum communis salutis causa recusare, principesque ex (2) omnibus bellum facturos pollicentur;

agito, -are, -avi, -atus, *consider, discuss, debate, deliberate on.*
Carnutes, -um, m., pl., *the Carnutes.*

communis, -e, *common, in common, public, general.*
facio, facere, feci, factus, *bring about, make, carry on.*
nullus, -a, -um, *no, not any.*
periculum, -i, n., *risk, danger, hazard.*
princeps, -cipis, *first in order, foremost.*
-que, *and.*
res, rei, f., *matter, affair, matter of business.*
sui, sibi, se, or **sese**, nom. wanting, *they*, with or without *themselves.*

bellum, -i, n., *war, warfare.*
causa, -ae, f., abl. with the gen., *for the sake of, on account of.*
ex, *from the number of, from among, of.*
hic, haec, hoc, *this; he, she, it.*
omnes, -ium, m., pl., *all men, all.*
polliceor, -licere, -lictus, *promise, offer.*
profiteor, -fiteri, -fessus, *declare openly, avow.*
recuso, -are, -avi, -atus, *refuse, make refusal, decline.*
salus, -utis, f., *prosperity, safety, preservation.*

His rebus agitatis: Ablative absolute (A.G. 419-20). **His**: Plural, feminine, ablative demonstrative pronoun used as an adjective modifying **rebus** (A.G. 296.1 and a). **agitatis**: The perfect tense of the participle represents the action as completed at the time indicated by the tense of the main verb (A.G. 489). An iterative form of **ago** (A.G. 263.2).

profitentur: The main verb of the coordinate clause **His ... recusare** (A.G. 278.a). The historical present, giving vividness to the narrative, is present in Chapter 2 (A.G. 469). This usage, common in all languages, comes from imagining past events as going on before our eyes (*repraesentatio*) (A.G. 469 Note).

Carnutes: Nominative subject (A.G. 339). This tribe had surrendered to Caesar with only the threat conflict the year before, see *BG* 6.2-4 and 6.44. This is the first tribe specifically named in the conspiracy. See Appendix A.

se ... recusare: Accusative/infinitive construction in indirect discourse after **profitentur** (A.G. 577 ff.). **se**: Plural, masculine, accusative direct reflexive pronoun (A.G. 300.1). The antecedent is **Carnutes**, the subject of **profitentur** (A.G. 299). **recusare**: Present infinitive; the tense of the infinitive in indirect discourse is relative to that of the verb of saying (A.G. 584).

nullum periculum: Accusative direct object of the infinitive **recusare** (A.G.387 and 451.3).

communis salutis causa: A preceding genitive with the ablative of **causa** means "for the sake of" (A.G. 359.b and 404.c).

principesque: Plural, masculine, accusative predicate adjective modifying **se**, the supplied subject of **facturos (esse)** (A.G. 283). **-que**: The enclitic conjunction connects the two main verbs **profitentur ... pollicentur** (A.G. 324.a).

ex omnibus: Prepositional phrase, **ex** with the ablative instead of the partitive genitive means "from the number of, from among, of" (A.G. 346.c) (*OLD* **ex** 17). **omnibus**: Plural, masculine, ablative, adjective used substantively (A.G. 288).

bellum: Accusative direct object of the infinitive **facturos (esse)** (A.G. 387 and 451.3).

(se) facturos (esse): Accusative/infinitive in indirect discourse after **pollicentur** (A.G. 577 ff., esp. 580.c). Carry down the pronoun **se** from above as the accusative subject. **facturos (esse)**: Supply **esse** to form the future active infinitive (A.G. 188). The tense of the infinitive in indirect discourse is relative to that of the verb of saying (A.G. 584).

pollicentur: The main verb of the coordinate clause **principesque ... pollicentur** (A.G. 278.a). The pronoun **ei**, with **Carnutes** as the antecedent, is understood as the subject (A.G. 271.a).

(2.2-3) **et, quoniam in praesentia obsidibus cavere inter se non possint ne res efferatur, ut iure iurando ac fide sanciatur petunt collatis militaribus signis, quo more eorum gravissima caerimonia continetur, (3) ne facto initio belli ab reliquis deserantur.**

ab, *by.*

bellum, -i, n., *war, warfare.*

caveo, cavere, cavi, cautus, *to give surety, provide guarantees.*

contineo, -tinere, -tinui, -tentus, *consist of.*

effero, -ferre, extuli, elatus, *spread abroad, publish.*

facio, facere, feci, factus, *bring about, make.*

gravis, -e, sup. **-issimus,** *serious, solemn, important.*

initium, -i, n., *beginning, commencement.*

is, ea, id, *he, she, it; that, this.*

ius iurandum, iuris iurandi, n. (**ius** + gerundive of **iuro**), *oath.*

mos, moris, f., *custom, pratice.*

non, *not.*

peto, petere, petivi, and **petii, petitus,** *ask, request.*

qui, quae, quod, *who, what, which.*

reliqui, -orum, m., pl., *the rest.*

sancio, sancire, sanxi, sanctus, *render sacred, bind, confirm.*

sui, sibi, se, or **sese,** nom. wanting, *each other, themselves.*

ac, *and.*

caerimonia, -ae, f., *religious ceremony, sacred rite, ritual.*

confero, -ferre, -tuli, collatus, *bring together, gather, collect.*

desero, -serere, -serui, -sertus, *leave, abandon, desert.*

et, *but at the same time, and yet.*

fides, ei, f., *pledge of good faith, promise.*

in praesentia (supply **tempora**), *for the moment, for the present, temporarily.*

inter, *with, to, among.*

iuro, see **ius iurandum.**

militaris, -e, *military.*

ne, *lest, so that ... not.*

obses, -idis, m. and f., *hostage.*

possum, posse, potui, -----, *be able.*

quoniam, *since, seeing that, because.*

res, rei, f., *matter, affair, circumstance.*

signum, -i, n., *standard.*

ut, *so that.*

et: The conjunction here has a slight adversative force and means "but at the same time, and yet" *OLD* **et** 14).

quoniam ... petunt: The order of the clauses can be rewritten as: **petunt ut ... sanciatur quoniam ... possint ne ... efferatur.**

quoniam ... possint: Causal clause; the conjunction **quoniam** ("since") introduces a reason given on the authority of the writer or speaker and normally takes the indicative (A.G. 540.a). Here **quoniam** takes the subjunctive as it is dependent upon the purpose clause which follows (**ut ... sanciatur**) and is regarded as an integral part of that clause (attraction) (A.G. 593). For the same construction see also 7.72.2 (do not confuse this with **quoniam** taking the subjunctive in indirect discourse as at 7.64.2 and 89.2). **possint**: The main verb of the subordinate clause (A.G. 278.b). Present subjunctive; the tense of the subjunctive is normally in secondary sequence after the historical present **petunt** (A.G. 482-85). Here it is in primary sequence through *repraesentatio* (A.G. 485.e and 585.b Note). The pronoun **ipsi**, with the participants of the council as the antecedent, is understood as the subject (A.G. 271.a).

in praesentia: Adverbial phrase, originally a prepositional phrase, **in** with the plural, neuter, accusative of **praesens** means "for the moment, for the present, temporarily" (*OLD* **praesens** 16.b).

obsidibus: Ablative of means (A.G. 409).

cavere: Complementary infinitive after **possint** (A.G. 456). Here, the infinitive **cavere** means "to give surety, provide guarantees" F(*OLD* **caveo** 8).

inter se: Prepositional phrase, **inter** with the plural, masculine, accusative reflexive pronoun **se**, "among themselves", is regularly used to express reciprocal action (A.G. 301.f). **se**: Plural, masculine, accusative direct reflexive pronoun (A.G. 300.1). The antecedent is **ipsi**, the supplied subject of **possint** (A.G. 299).

non: Adverb, the adverb generally precedes the verb if it belongs to no one word in particular (A.G. 217.e, 320-21, and 599.a).

(veriti) ne ... efferatur: The conjunction **ne** ("lest") with the subjunctive forms a substantive clause of fearing. Here the verb of fearing, **veriti** (**vereor, vereri, veritus sum,** *fear, dread, be afraid of*) must be supplied in the form of a participle agreeing with **ipsi**, the supplied subject of **possint** (A.G. 564). **efferatur**: The main verb of the subordinate clause (A.G. 278.b). Present subjunctive; the tense of the subjunctive is normally in secondary sequence after the historical present **petunt** (A.G. 482-85). Here it is in primary sequence through *repraesentatio* (A.G. 485.e and 585.b Note).

res: Nominative subject (A.G. 339).

ut ... sanciatur: The conjunction **ut** ("so that") with the subjunctive forms a substantive clause of purpose which is used as the object of the verb **petunt** denoting an action directed toward the future (A.G. 563). **sanciatur**: The main verb of the subordinate clause (A.G. 278.b). Present subjunctive; the tense of the subjunctive is normally in secondary sequence after the historical present **petunt** (A.G. 482-85). Here it is in primary sequence through *repraesentatio* (A.G. 485.e and 585.b Note). The following negative substantive clause of purpose **ne ... deserantur** functions as the subject of the passive verb (A.G. 566).

iure iurando ac fide: Two ablatives of means (A.G. 409). **iure iurando**: The phrase **ius iurandum** is an idiom that means "a binding formula to be sworn to, an oath" (whether or not in legal contexts) (*OLD* **ius2** 5). **iurando**: Singular, neuter, ablative gerundive used as an adjective modifying **iure** denoting necessity, obligation or propriety (A.G. 500.1). **ac**: The conjunction connects the two ablative nouns and means "and" (*OLD* **atque** 12).

petunt: The main verb of the main clause (A.G. 278.b). The pronoun **ei**, with **Carnutes** as the antecedent, is understood as the subject (A.G. 271.a).

collatis militaribus signis: Ablative absolute (A.G. 419-20). **collatis**: The perfect tense of the participle represents the action as completed at the time indicated by the tense of the main verb (A.G. 489). Passive participle of **confero**.

quo ... continetur: Relative clause; a clause dependent on a subjunctive clause (**ut ... sanciatur**) normally takes the subjunctive (attraction) (A.G. 303 and 593). However, when a dependent clause is not regarded as a necessary logical part of the clause, the indicative is used. The indicative serves to emphasize the fact, as true independently of the statement contained in the subjunctive clause (A.G. 593.a Note 1). **quo**: See below. **continetur**: The main verb of the subordinate clause (A.G. 278.b). The present tense is not the historical present but denotes a state as now existing in present time (A.G. 465.1).

quo more: Ablative of specification (A.G. 418). I.e., the custom of swearing before the standards. **quo**: singular, masculine, ablative relative pronoun (A.G. 305). The antecedent is **more** in its own clause (adjectival use) (A.G. 307.b).

eorum: Plural, masculine, genitive demonstrative pronoun used substantively (A.G. 296.2). The antecedent is **ipsi** (the members of the council), the supplied subject of **possint** (A.G. 297.e). Possessive genitive with **caerimonia** (A.G. 343).

gravissima caerimonia: Nominative subject (A.G. 339). **gravissima**: Superlative adjective (A.G. 124).

ne ... deserantur: The conjunction **ne** ("so that ... not") with the subjunctive forms a negative substantive clause of purpose (A.G. 563). The clause functions as the subject of the impersonal verb **sanciatur**; a substantive clause used as the object of a verb becomes the subject when the verb is put into the passive (A.G. 566). **deserantur**: The main verb of the subordinate clause (A.G. 278.b). Present subjunctive; the tense of the subjunctive is normally in secondary sequence after the historical present **petunt** (A.G. 482-85). Here it is in primary sequence through *repraesentatio* (A.G. 485.e and 585.b Note). The pronoun **ei**, with **Carnutes** as the antecedent, is understood as the subject (A.G. 271.a). Kahn notes that although the Gauls are presented with a nobility of character, "they exhibit a tragic flaw, instability of character. They lack perseverance, are fickle, impetuous, susceptible to rumor and prone to swift turnabouts in crisis. In distress they are treacherous. They do not readily submit to authority." (Kahn, 252) Gardner notes that the Gauls are characterized as "impulsive, emotional, easily-swayed, fickle, loving change, credulous, prone to panic, scatter-brained." (Gardner, 185) Caesar subtly inserts this fear of the Carnutes to introduce the second characterization of the Gallic character, the 'barbarian type'. For a discussion of the barbarian character type as opposed to the noble character type in the *BG*, see Mannetter, 9-23. For other instances of the barbarian type in Book 7 see Chapter 3, the unprovoked attack of the Romans; 4, Vercingetorix tortures and maims; 5 the treachery of the Bituriges; 6, Caesar fears Gallic treachery; 8, the Gauls are panic-stricken; 12, the Gauls are fickle; 13, the Gauls are panic-stricken; 17, the Gauls are indolent; 19, the Gauls are full of bravado; 20, Vercingetorix deceives his own people; 21, the Gauls are fickle; 26, the Gauls are terror-stricken; 28, the Gauls are panic-stricken; 32, the Aedui nearly engage in civil war; 37, Convictolitavis betrays Caesar; 38, Litaviccus deceives his own people and slaughters innocent Romans; 40, the Aedui are fickle; 42, the Aedui are treacherous and slaughter innocent Romans; 43, the Aedui are fickle and treacherous as they secretly plot rebellion; 53, the Gauls are full of bravado; 63, the Aedui are fickle; 66, the Gauls are rash and too easily swear an oath; 70, the Gauls are panic-stricken; 76, the Gauls are full of confidence; 77, Critognatus proposed cannibalism. Notice that in some instances the Gauls can exhibit both character types, as at Chapters 4, 37, and 77.

facto initio belli: Ablative absolute (A.G. 419-20). **facto**: The perfect tense of the participle represents the action as completed at the time indicated by the tense of the main verb (A.G. 489). **belli**: Possessive genitive with **initio** (A.G. 343).

ab reliquis: Ablative of agent with the preposition **ab** with the passive verb **deserantur** (A.G. 405). **reliquis**: Plural, masculine, ablative adjective used substantively (A.G. 288). The noun **Gallis** is understood (A.G. 288.b).

(2.3) Tum, collaudatis Carnutibus, dato iure iurando ab omnibus qui aderant, tempore eius rei constituto ab concilio disceditur.

ab, *by, from.*	**adsum, -esse, affui, -----,** *be at hand, be present.*
Carnutes, -um, m., pl., *the Carnutes.*	**collaudo, -are, -avi, -atus,** *praise highly, extol, commend.*
concilium, -i, n., *meeting, assembly, council.*	**constituo, -stituere, -stitui, -stitutus,** *resolve upon, determine.*
discedo, -cedere, -cessi, -cessurus, *go away, depart, leave.*	**do, dare, dedi, datus,** *give.*
is, ea, id, *he, she, it, that, this.*	**iuro,** see **ius iurandum**.
ius iurandum, iuris iurandi, n. (**ius** + gerundive of **iuro**), *oath.*	**omnes, -ium,** m., pl., *all men, all.*
qui, quae, quod, *who, what, which.*	**res, rei,** f., *business, event, matter, affair.*
tempus, -oris, n., *time.*	**tum,** *then, thereupon.*

Tum: Adverb (A.G. 271.b and 320-21).

collaudatis ... dato ... constituto: Notice the asyndeton between the three ablative absolutes (A.G. 323.b). Asyndeton here gives an impression of rapidity to the events. Siedler counts 71 examples of asyndeton in Book 7 (Siedler, 46). See also Siedler, 31.

collaudatis Carnutibus: Ablative absolute (A.G. 419-20). **collaudatis**: The perfect tense of the participle represents the action as completed at the time indicated by the tense of the main verb (A.G. 489). Caesar has previously noted the effect of strong leadership among the Gauls at 5.54.4: **Tantum apud homines barbaros valuit esse aliquos repertos principes inferendi belli tantamque omnibus voluntatum commutationem attulit ... Carnutibus**: See Appendix A.

dato ... aderant: Ablative absolute with a dependent clause (see Gotoff, 9-12).

dato iure iurando: Ablative absolute (A.G. 419-20). **dato**: The perfect tense of the participle represents the action as completed at the time indicated by the tense of the main verb (A.G. 489). **iure iurando**: The phrase **ius iurandum** is an idiom that means "a binding formula to be sworn to, an oath" (whether or not in legal contexts) (*OLD* **ius2** 5). **iurando**: Singular, neuter, ablative gerundive used as an adjective modifying **iure** denoting necessity, obligation or propriety (A.G. 500.1).

ab omnibus: Ablative of agent with the preposition **ab** with the passive participle **dato** (A.G. 405). **omnibus**: Plural, masculine, ablative, adjective used substantively (A.G. 288).

qui aderant: Relative clause (A.G. 303). **qui**: Plural, masculine, nominative relative pronoun used substantively (A.G.305). The antecedent is **omnibus** (A.G. 307). Nominative subject (A.G. 339). **aderant**: The main verb of the subordinate clause (A.G. 278.b).

tempore eius rei constituto: Ablative absolute (A.G. 419-20). **eius rei**: Objective genitive with **tempore** (A.G. 348). **eius**: Singular, feminine, genitive demonstrative pronoun used as an adjective modifying **rei** (A.G. 296.1 and a). **constituto**: The perfect tense of the

participle represents the action as completed at the time indicated by the tense of the main verb (A.G. 489).
ab concilio: Ablative of *place from which* with the preposition **ab** (A.G. 426.1).
(id) disceditur: The main verb of the main clause (A.G. 278.b). Impersonal use of the intransitive passive verb (A.G. 208.d). Supply **id** as the subject (A.G. 318.c).

(3.1-2) Ubi ea dies venit, Carnutes, Cotuato et Conconnetodumno ducibus, desperatis hominibus, Cenabum signo dato concurrunt civisque Romanos qui negotiandi causa ibi constiterant, in his C. Fufium Citam, honestum equitem Romanum, qui rei frumentariae iussu Caesaris praeerat, (2) interficiunt bonaque eorum diripiunt.

bona, -orum, n., pl., *possessions, property, goods.*
Caesar, -aris, m., *Caesar.*
causa, -ae, f., abl. with the gen., *for the sake of, on account of.*
civis, -is, m., *citizen.*
concurro, -currere, -cucurri or **-curri, -cursus**, *run together, run up, rush.*
Cotuatus, -i, m., *Cotuatus.*
dies, -ei, m. and f., *day.*
do, dare, dedi, datus, *give.*
eques, -itis, m., *knight, one of the equestrian order.*
frumentarius, -a, -um, *having to do with grain* or *supplies.*
homo, hominis, m., *man, person.*

ibi, *in that place, there.*
interficio, -ficere, -feci, -fectus, *slay, kill.*
iussus, -us, m., *order, bidding, command.*
praesum, -esse, -fui, -----, *preside over, have command of, have charge of.*
qui, quae, quod, *who, what, which.*
Romanus, -a, -um, *Roman.*
ubi, *when.*

C. Fufius Cita, -i, -ae, m., *Gaius Fufius Cita.*
Carnutes, -um, m., pl., *the Carnutes.*
Cenabum, -i, n., *Cenabum.*
Conconnetodumnus, -i, m., *Conconnetodumnus.*
constituo, -stituere, -stitui, -stitutus, *settle.*
desperatus, -a, -um, *without hope, desperate.*
diripio, -ripere, -ripui, -reptus, *plunder, pillage.*
dux, ducis, m., *leader, general, commander.*
et, *and.*
hic, haec, hoc, *this; he, she, it.*
honestus, -a, -um, *worthy of honor, honorable, upright, noble.*
in, *among.*
is, ea, id, *he, she, it; that, this.*
negotior, -ari, -atus, *transact business, trade.*
-que, *and.*
res, rei, f., (with **frumentaria**) *supply of grain, supplies.*
signum, -i, n., *signal.*
venio, venire, veni, ventus, *come, arrive.*

Ubi ... venit: Temporal clause; the relative adverb **ubi** ("when") with the indicative introduces a subordinate clause (A.G. 543). **venit**: The main verb of the subordinate clause (A.G. 278.b).
ea dies: Nominative subject (A.G. 339). **ea**: Singular, feminine, nominative demonstrative pronoun used as an adjective modifying **res** (A.G. 296.1 and a). **dies**: The noun **dies** is sometimes feminine in the singular, especially in phrases indicating a fixed time (A.G. 97.a).
Carnutes: Nominative subject of **concurrunt ... interficiunt ... diripiunt** (A.G. 339). See Appendix A.
Cotuato et Conconnetodumno ducibus: Ablative absolute with a noun (**ducibus**) taking the place of the participle (there is no participle for "being") (A.G. 419.a-20). **Cotuato**: See Appendix A. **et**: The conjunction connects the two ablative nouns (A.G. 324.a). **Conconnetodumno**: See Appendix A. **ducibus**: A plural predicate noun referring to two singular nouns (A.G. 284.a).
desperatis hominibus: Ablative phrase in apposition to **ducibus** (A.G. 282).
Cenabum: Accusative of *place to which* without a preposition (as the name of a town) (A.G. 427.2). See Appendix A.
signo dato: Ablative absolute (A.G. 419-20). **dato**: The perfect tense of the participle represents the action as completed at the time indicated by the tense of the main verb (A.G. 489).
concurrunt: The main verb of the coordinate clause **Ubi ... concurrunt** (A.G. 278.a). The historical present, giving vividness to the narrative, is present in Chapter 3 (A.G. 469). This usage, common in all languages, comes from imagining past events as going on before our eyes (*repraesentatio*) (A.G. 469 Note).
civisque Romanos: Accusative direct object of **interficiunt** (A.G. 387). **civis**: Accusative plural noun; **-is** for **-es** is the regular form in i-stem nouns (A.G. 65-7 and 74.c). **-que**: The enclitic conjunction connects the two main verbs **concurrunt ... interficiunt** (A.G. 324.a).
qui ... constiterant: Relative clause (A.G. 303). **qui**: Plural, masculine, nominative relative pronoun used substantively (A.G. 305). The antecedent is **civis** (A.G. 307). Nominative subject (A.G. 339). **constiterant**: The main verb of the subordinate clause (A.G. 278.b). The pluperfect tense of the verb denotes an action completed in past time (A.G. 477).
negotiandi causa: The genitive of the gerund with the ablative of **causa** expresses purpose (A.G. 504.b). "The Romans in Gallic cities were chiefly engaged in loaning money, in buying grain and other commodities, and in farming revenues." (Kelsey, 401) **negotiandi**: Singular, neuter, genitive gerund (A.G. 501-02).
ibi: Adverb (A.G. 215.5 and 320-21).
in his: Prepositional phrase, **in** with the ablative here means "among" (*OLD* in 29.b). **his**: Plural, masculine, ablative demonstrative pronoun used substantively (A.G. 296.2). The antecedent is **civis** (A.G. 297.e).
C. Fufium Citam: An accusative phrase in apposition to **his** (A.G. 282). See Appendix A. **C.**: Abbreviated form of the praenomen **Gaius** (A.G. 108.c).
honestum equitem Romanum: An accusative phrase in apposition to the proper noun **C. Fufium Citam** (A.G. 282).
qui ... praeerat: Relative clause (A.G. 303). **qui**: Singular, masculine, nominative relative pronoun used substantively (A.G. 305). The antecedent is **C. Fufium Citam** (A.G. 307). Nominative subject (A.G. 339). **praeerat**: The main verb of the subordinate clause (A.G. 278.b).
rei frumentariae: Dative indirect object of the intransitive compound verb **praeerat** (A.G. 370). The phrase, often translated as 'corn

supply', is actually wheat or grain supply as corn is a new world product. "The soldier's staple food was wheat, issued in the grain, ground by him in a portable hand mill ... and made into a rough kind of bread, probably resembling a chupatty baked on hot stones or embers. He seldom ate meat, was allowed no wine, and drank vinegar when obtainable. His corn ration and clothing were charged against his pay, which Caesar increased from 120 denarii a year to 225; he also allowed his men corn, when it was in plenty, without any restrictions. That the Roman soldier could march and fight as he did on so meager a ration certainly redounds to his astonishing physical endurance." (Fuller, 85)

iussu: Ablative of specification (A.G. 418).

Caesaris: Possessive genitive with **iussu** (A.G. 343). See Appendix A.

interficiunt: The main verb of the coordinate clause **civisque ... interficiunt** (A.G. 278.a). The pronoun **ei**, with **Carnutes** as the antecedent, is understood as the subject (A.G. 271.a). Collins provides this assessment of the Carnutes' actions: "the *negotiatores* on whom the Carnutes fell probably got about what they deserved, and I suspect that C. Fufius Cita had little to learn from those profiteers that Tacitus (Agric. 19) has so severely described. "*Krieg, Handel, und Piraterie: dreieinig sind sie, nicht zu trennen*", and the process of economic penetration and exploitation so cogently described by Cicero for the province: *nummus in Galia nullus sine civium Romanorum tabulis commovetur* (Pro Font. 11) was rapidly extended to *Gallia Comata* by the greedy adventurers who followed Caesar's victories. They were men who knew all the ways of money-getting, omnis vias pecuniae norunt (QF I, 1, 15) and they made the most of their opportunities." (Collins, 938)

bonaque: Accusative direct object of **diripiunt** (A.G. 387). **bona**: Plural, neuter, accusative adjective used substantively meaning "possessions, property" (A.G. 107 and 288) (*OLD* **bonum** 8). **-que**: The enclitic conjunction connects the two main verbs **interficiunt ... diripiunt** (A.G. 324.a).

eorum: Plural, masculine, genitive demonstrative pronoun used substantively (A.G. 296.2). The antecedent is **civis** (A.G. 297.e). Possessive genitive with **bona** (A.G. 343).

diripiunt: The main verb of the coordinate clause **bonaque ... diripiunt** (A.G. 278.a). The pronoun **ei**, with **Carnutes** as the antecedent, is understood as the subject (A.G. 271.a).

(3.2) Celeriter ad omnis Galliae civitates fama perfertur.

ad, *to*.
civitas, -tatis, f., *state, nation*.
Gallia, -ae, f., *Gaul*.
perfero, -ferre, -tuli, -latus, *convey, bring, report*.

celeriter, *quickly, speedily, at once, immediately*.
fama, -ae, f., *report, rumor*.
omnis, -e, *all*.

Celeriter: Adverb (A.G. 214.b and 320-21).

ad omnis Galliae civitates: Accusative of *place to which* with the preposition **ad** (A.G. 426.2). **omnis**: Accusative plural adjective; **-is** for **-es** is the regular form in i-stem adjectives (A.G. 114.a and 116). **Galliae**: Locative case of **Gallia, -ae**, f. (A.G. 43.c). See Appendix A.

fama: Nominative subject (A.G. 339).

perfertur: The main verb of the simple sentence (A.G. 278.1).

(3.2-3) Nam, ubique maior atque inlustrior incidit res, clamore per agros regionesque significant; hanc alii deinceps excipiunt et proximis tradunt, ut (3) tum accidit.

accido, -cidere, -cidi, -----, (imper.), *it happens*.

alii, -orum, m., *other persons, others*.
clamor, -oris, m., *loud call, shout*.
et, *and*.
hic, haec, hoc, *this*; *he, she, it*.
inlustris, -e, comp. **-ior**, *remarkable, noteworthy*.
nam, *for*.
proximi, -orum, m., pl., *the nearest men, next men*.
regio, -onis, f., *region, territory*.
significo, -are, -avi, -atus, *transmit news*.

tum, *then*.
ut, *as*.

ager, -ri, m., *land* (under cultivation), *field, territory, domain*.
atque, *and*.
deinceps, *one after the other, in succession, in turn*.
excipio, -cipere, -cepi, -ceptus, *take up*.
incido, -cidere, -cidi, ------, *occur, happen*.
maior, -or, -us, *very important, weighty, momentous*.
per, *all over, throughout, through*.
-que, *and*.
res, rei, f., *matter, affair, event*.
trado, -dere, -didi, -ditus, *transmit, pass on, deliver, relate*.
ubique, *in whatever place, wherever, anywhere*.

Nam: Conjunction, here explanatory meaning "for" (*OLD* **nam** 2).

ubique ... res: Subordinate clause (A.G. 278.b). **ubique**: Conjunction ("in whatever place, wherever") (*OLD* **ubique**). **res**: See below.

maior atque inlustior ... res: Nominative subject (A.G. 339). **maior**: Irregular comparative adjective (A.G. 129). **atque**: The conjunction connects the two adjectives modifying **res** and means "and" (*OLD* **atque** 12). Two adjectives belonging to the same noun are regularly connected by a conjunction (A.G. 323.d). **inlustior**: Comparative adjective (A.G. 124). **res**: The subject is in the last position (A.G. 597.b).

incidit: The main verb of the subordinate clause (A.G. 278.b). The present tense is not the historical present but denotes a state as now existing in present time (A.G. 465.1).

clamore: Ablative of means (A.G. 409). "On this occasion probably men were posted all along the route, ready to receive and at once transmit news. The Mexicans, whose civilization previous to the coming of Europeans was in some respect analogous to that of the Gauls, carried messages 300 miles in one day by relays of couriers, stationed six miles apart." (Kelsey, 401)

per agros regionesque: Prepositional phrase, **per** with the accusative here means "all over, throughout" (*OLD* **per** 4). **-que**: The enclitic conjunction connects the two accusative nouns in the prepositional phrase (A.G. 324.a).

significant: The main verb of the main clause (A.G. 278.b). The noun **Galli** is understood as the subject (A.G. 271.a). The present tense is not the historical present but denotes a state as now existing in present time (A.G. 465.1).

hanc: Singular, feminine, accusative demonstrative pronoun used substantively (A.G. 296.2). The antecedent is **res** (A.G. 297.e). Accusative direct object of both **excipiunt ... tradunt** (A.G. 387).

alii: Plural, masculine, nominative pronoun used substantively meaning "other persons, others" (*OLD* **alius2** 1). Nominative subject of **excipiunt ... tradunt** (A.G. 339).

deinceps: Adverb (A.G. 217.b and 320-21).

excipiunt: The main verb of the coordinate clause **hanc ... excipiunt** (A.G. 278.a). The present tense is not the historical present but denotes a state as now existing in present time (A.G. 465.1).

et: The conjunction connects the two main verbs in the sentence **excipiunt ... tradunt** (A.G. 324.a).

proximis: Plural, masculine, dative adjective used substantively (A.G. 288). The noun **Gallis** is understood (A.G. 288.b). Dative indirect object of the transitive verb **tradunt** (A.G. 362). Defective superlative adjective (A.G. 130.a).

tradunt: The main verb of the coordinate clause **proximis tradunt** (A.G. 278.a). The present tense is not the historical present but denotes a state as now existing in present time (A.G. 465.1).

ut ... accidit: The relative adverb **ut** ("as") with the indicative introduces a parenthetical remark (*OLD* **ut** 12). **accidit**: The main verb of the subordinate clause (A.G. 278.b). Impersonal use of the verb, supply **id** as the subject (A.G. 207). The tense of the verb is perfect (A.G. 473).

tum: Adverb (A.G. 217.b and 320-21).

(3.3) **Nam quae Cenabi oriente sole gesta essent ante primam confectam vigiliam in finibus Arvernorum audita sunt, quod spatium est milium passuum circiter centum LX.**

ante, *before.*
audio, -ire, -ivi or **-ii, -itus**, *learn* (by hearing), *hear of.*
centum, indeclinable numerical adjective, *hundred.*
conficio, -ficere, -feci, -fectus, *complete, finish.*

gero, gerere, gessi, gestus, *do, carry on, carry out, perform.*
L, in expression of number, *50.*
nam, *for.*
passus, -us, m., *step, pace*, = 4 feet, 10 ¼ inches.
primus, -a, -um, *first.*
quis, -----, quid, *who? what?*
spatium, -i, n., *space, distance.*
vigilia, -ae, f., *watch.*

Arverni, -orum, m., pl., *the Arverni.*
Cenabum, -i, n., *Cenabum.*
ciricter, *about.*
fines, -ium, m., pl., *borders*, hence *territory, country, land.*
in, *in.*
mille, milia, *thousand, thousands.*
orior, oriri, ortus, *rise.*
perfero, -ferre, -tuli, -latus, *convey, bring, report.*
qui, quae, quod, *who, what, which.*
sol, -is, m., *the sun.*
sum, esse, fui, futurus, *be.*
X, in expression of number, = *10.*

Nam: The particle is put before an interrogative pronoun (**quae**) in lively or impatient questions (*OLD* **nam** 7).

quae ... gesta essent: Indirect question with the subjunctive; the phrase is the subject of **audita sunt** (A.G. 573-75). **quae**: Plural, neuter, nominative interrogative pronoun used substantively meaning "what things" (A.G. 148). Nominative subject (A.G. 339). **gesta essent**: The main verb of the subordinate clause (A.G. 278.b). Pluperfect subjunctive; the tense of the subjunctive is in secondary sequence and follows the rules for the sequence of tense for indirect questions after **audita sunt** (A.G. 575).

Cenabi: Locative case of the city name **Cenabum, -i**, n. (A.G. 49.a). See Appendix A.

oriente sole: Ablative of *time when* (A.G. 423.1).

ante primam confectam vigiliam: Prepositional phrase, **ante** with the accusative is here temporal and means "before" (an event) (*OLD* **ante2** 6). "Before 9 P.M.." (Kelsey, 401) **primam**: Ordinal numeral used as an adjective modifying **vigiliam** (A.G. 132-35).

confectam: Accusative, perfect, passive participle modifying **vigiliam** used as a predicate, where in English a phrase or a subordinate clause would be more natural (A.G. 496). **vigiliam**: "The night, from sunset to sunrise, was divided into four watches (*vigiliae*), numbered *prima*, ending at 9 o'clock; *secunda*, ending at midnight; *tertia*, from midnight to 3 A.M.; and *quarta*, from 3 o'clock to sunrise." (Kelsey, 35)

in finibus Arvernorum: Ablative of *place where* with the preposition **in** (locative ablative) (A.G. 426.3). **finibus**: In the plural the noun means "bounds, territories" (A.G. 107). **Arvernorum**: Possessive genitive of the tribe name **Arverni** with **finibus** (A.G. 343). "the Arverni were mentioned as important at 1.31, but this is their first involvement in the action." (Hammond, 237) See Appendix A.

audita sunt: The main verb of the main clause (A.G. 278.b).

quod ... XL: Relative clause (A.G. 303). **quod**: See below. **XL**: See below.

quod spatium: Nominative subject (A.G. 339). **quod**: Singular, neuter nominative relative pronoun (A.G. 305). The antecedent is **spatium** in its own clause (adjectival use) (A.G. 307.b).

est: The main verb of the subordinate clause (A.G. 278.b). The present tense is not the historical present but denotes a state as now existing in present time (A.G. 465.1).

milium passuum circiter centum LX: Possessive genitive (predicate genitive); the possessive genitive often stands in the predicate, connected to its noun (**spatium**) by a verb (**est**) (A.G. 343.b). **milium passuum**: Predicate genitive (A.G. 343.b). "A Roman mile" (4851 feet or about 95 yards less than an English mile) (*OLD* **passus** 2.b). **milium**: Genitive plural; **milia** is here an adjective modifying **passuum** (*OLD* **mille**). **passuum**: "'a pace', the distance from where the foot leaves the ground to where the same foot strikes it again, a measurement of 4 feet, 10 ¼ inches (five Roman feet)." (Walker, 56) **circiter**: Adverb (A.G. 320-21). **centum**: Indeclinable cardinal number used as an adjective modifying **milium** (A.G. 132-35). **LX**: Roman numeral used as an adjective modifying **milium** (A.G. 133).

1.B CHAPTERS 4-5: VERCINGETORIX BECOMES **REX** OF THE ARVERNI AND BUILDS A COALITION OF TRIBES; THE BITURIGES JOIN THE REVOLT
(4.1-2) Simili ratione ibi Vercingetorix, Celtilli filius, Arvernus, summae potentiae adulescens, cuius pater principatum Galliae totius obtinuerat et ob eam causam, quod regnum appetebat, ab civitate erat interfectus, convocatis suis clien(2)tibus facile incendit.

ab, *by.*
appeto, -petere, -petivi or **-petii, -petitus**, *strive after, desire, seek.*
causa, -ae, f., *reason, cause.*
civitas, -tatis, f., *body of citizens, state.*
convoco, -are, -avi, -atus, *call together, summon, assemble.*
facile, *easily, readily, with no trouble.*
Gallia, -ae, f., *Gaul.*
incendo, -cendere, -cendi, -census, *fire, rouse, excite.*
is, ea, id, *he, she, it; that, this.*
obtineo, -tinere, -tinui, -tentus, *gain, acquire, obtain.*
potentia, -ae, f., *might, power, influence.*

qui, quae, quod, *who, what, which.*
regnum, -i, n., *kingship, absolute authority.*
similis, -e, *like, similar.*
suus, -a, -um, *his*, with or without *own.*
Vercingetorix, -igis, m., *Vercingetorix.*

adulescens, -entis, m., *young man, youth.*
Arvernus, -i, m., *an Arvernian.*
Celtillus, -i, m., *Celtillus.*
cliens, -entis, m., *retainer, dependant, client, supporter.*
et, *and.*
filius, -i, m., *son.*
ibi, *in that place, there.*
interficio, -ficere, -feci, -fectus, *slay, kill.*
ob, *on account of, because of, for.*
pater, -tris, m., *father.*
principatus, -us, m., *chief authority, headship, leadership.*
quod, *because, since, for, as.*
ratio, -onis, f., *method, system, way.*
summus, -a, -um, *highest, greatest.*
totus, -a, -um, *the whole of, all.*

Simili ratione: Ablative of manner with a limiting adjective (A.G. 412). This phrase is to be taken with the ablative absolute **convocatis suis clientibus**; i.e. they are called together in the same way that news is spread at 3.2-3.
ibi: Adverb (A.G. 215.5 and 320-21). Vercingetorix's home town is Gergovia.
Vercingetorix: Nominative subject of **incendit** (A.G. 339). This is the first mention of Vercingetorix, the young Arvernian, who will be the supreme leader of the revolt. Kahn claims that "as a dramatic hero, Vercingetorix undergoes a consistent, subtle, and complex development ... ." (Kahn, 252) "A true dramatic character, he grows as he confronts problems. He begins as a mere adventurer who rejects the advice of his elders, hotheaded, power-hungry, self-willed and vicious toward those who would thwart him. Insecure in his command, he is forced to yield to the demand that Avaricum be spared from the scorched earth policy (15), yet he demonstrates his skill in harassing Caesar (16) and his cunning in tricking his own troops into renewed obedience (20) and in hiding from them the pitiful survivors of captured Avaricum (28). He begins to emerge as a truly national leader (29) and an experienced general. He conducts daily strategy meetings and tests and trains his troops in limited skirmishes. As the campaign progresses, he learns to exploit the capacities of his troops and to avoid exposing their weaknesses and develops a strategy appropriate to the Gauls of guerrilla attacks and uncompromising scorched earth. He rallies new allies and husbands his supplies when under siege, all with businesslike administration. But he is no Caesar: he hesitates and misses the decisive moment in an attack on Alesia (82). Finally, after defeat, he displays the dignity of a heroic fighter for freedom, offering to kill himself or to surrender himself to Caesar for the sake of Gaul." (Kahn, 252) Adcock notes that "Vercingetorix is the most Caesarian of all Caesar's antagonists." (Adcock, 54) For the characterization of Vercingetorix, see Adcock, 54-56. Finally, Hammond notes that Vercingetorix is "Caesar's greatest Gallic adversary, and in later times a symbol of Gallic resistance to the threat of invasion. For the Gallic historian Camille Jullian he had the stature of a Hannibal or Mithridates; he became a romantic national icon to the French in the twentieth century, symbolizing the struggle of the Resistance against Hitler, the imperialist aggressor. Montaigne was not the last to question his wisdom in seeking refuge in Alesia (*Essais* 2.24). Following his defeat at Alesia, he surrendered and was put to death in 46 BC after being paraded in Caesar's unprecedented quadruple triumph (see Cassius Dio, 43.19.4)." (Hammond, 237) See Appendix A.
Celtilli: Possessive genitive with **filius** (A.G. 343). See Appendix A.
filius: A nominative noun in apposition to the proper noun **Vercingetorix** (A.G. 282).
Arvernus: A nominative noun in apposition to the proper noun **Vercingetorix** (A.G. 282).
summae potentiae: Genitive of quality (descriptive genitive) modifying **adulescens** (A.G. 345). **summae**: Irregular superlative adjective (A.G. 130.b).
adulescens: A nominative noun in apposition to the proper noun **Vercingetorix** (A.G. 282).
cuius ... obtinuerat ... erat interfectus: Relative clause (A.G. 303). This clause both justifies and explains Vercingetorix's imperial ambitions and forebodes his ultimate failure. **cuius**: Singular, masculine, genitive relative pronoun used substantively (A.G. 305). The antecedent is **Vercingetorix** (A.G. 307). Possessive genitive with **pater** (A.G. 343). **obtinuerat ... erat interfectus**: The main verbs of the subordinate clause (A.G. 278.b). The pluperfect tense of the verbs denotes an action completed in past time (A.G. 477).

pater: Nominative subject of **obtinuerat ... erat interfectus** (A.G. 339). **pater** = Celtilius.

principatum: Accusative direct object of **obtinuerat** (A.G. 387).

Galliae totius: Objective genitive with **principatum** (A.G. 348). **Galliae**: See Appendix A. **totius**: -ius is the regular genitive, singular ending for the adjective **totus** (A.G. 113).

et: The conjunction connects the two main verbs in the relative clause **obtinuerat ... erat interfectus** (A.G. 324.a).

ob eam causam: Prepositional phrase, **ob** with the accusative means "on account of, because of" (*OLD* ob 3.b) (A.G. 221.15.b). **eam**: Singular, feminine, accusative demonstrative pronoun used as an adjective modifying **causam** (A.G. 296.1 and a). "*Ob eam causam* may refer either to the chieftainship or to the attempt at kingship. Celtillus evidently desired to advance from *principatus* to *regnum*." (Edwards, 385)

quod ... appetebat: Causal clause; the conjunction **quod** ("because") takes the indicative when the reason is given on the authority of the writer or speaker (A.G. 540.1). **appetebat**: The main verb of the subordinate clause (A.G. 278.b). The pronoun **is**, with **pater** as the antecedent, is understood as the subject (A.G. 271.a).

regnum: Accusative direct object of **appetebat** (A.G. 387). **principatum ... regnum**: The two nouns mean "leadership .... kingship". The exact meaning of this passage is difficult to interpret since Caesar applies Roman terminology to Gallic political institutions. It seems as though Celtillus was a leader of the Arverni and held an unofficial leadership position over the other Gallic chieftains (**principatum**) which he wanted to solidify into complete hegemony (**regnum**). Exactly why this compelled the Arverni to kill him is left vague. Compare this to the political maneuverings and eventual fate of Orgetorix at *BG* 1.2-4.

ab civitate: Ablative of agent with the preposition **ab** with the passive verb **erat interfectus** (A.G. 405). Presumably the Arverni.

convocatis suis clientibus: Ablative absolute (A.G. 419-20). **convocatis**: The perfect tense of the participle represents the action as completed at the time indicated by the tense of the main verb (A.G. 489). **suis**: Plural, masculine, ablative possessive pronoun used as an adjective modifying **clientibus** (A.G. 302).

facile: Adverb formed from the neuter accusative adjective (A.G. 214.d and 320-21).

incendit: The main verb of the main clause (A.G. 278.b). The historical present, giving vividness to the narrative, is present in Chapter 4 (A.G. 469). This usage, common in all languages, comes from imagining past events as going on before our eyes (*repraesentatio*) (A.G. 469 Note). The pronoun **eos**, with **clientibus** as the antecedent, is understood as the accusative direct object of the transitive verb.

(4.2) Cognito eius consilio ad arma concurritur.

ad, *to*.

cognosco, -gnoscere, -gnovi, cognitus, *learn of, recognize, perceive*.

consilium, -i, n., *plan, plot, design*.

arma, -orum, n., pl., *arms, weapons*.

concurro, -currere, -cucurri or **-curri, -cursus**, *rush*.

is, ea, id, *he, she, it*; *that, this*.

Cognito eius consilio: Ablative absolute (A.G. 419-20). **Cognito**: The perfect tense of the participle represents the action as completed at the time indicated by the tense of the main verb (A.G. 489). **eius**: Singular, masculine, genitive demonstrative pronoun used substantively (A.G. 296.2). The antecedent is **Vercingetorix** (A.G. 296.e). Possessive genitive with **consilio** (A.G. 343).

consilio: Caesar does not specify what his exact intentions are at this stage, whether to lead the Arverni in a rebellion against Rome or more grandly, following his father's ill-fated ambition, to lead all Gaul in a rebellion against Rome. Whatever his initial intention may have been, he quickly passed from one to the other.

ad arma: Prepositional phrase, **ad** with the accusative here means "to" (an act or policy) (*OLD* ad 6).

(id) concurritur: The main verb of the main clause (A.G. 278.b). Impersonal use of the intransitive passive verb (A.G. 208.d). Supply **id** as the subject (A.G. 318.c).

(4.2-3) Prohibetur ab Gobannitione, patruo suo, reliquisque principibus, qui hanc temptandam fortunam non existi(3)mabant; expellitur ex oppido Gergovia;

ab, *by*.

existimo, -are, -avi, -atus, *think, consider, judge*.

fortuna, -ae, f., *fate, chance, fortune*.

Gobannitio, -onis, m., *Gobannitio*.

non, *not*.

patruus, -i, m., *father's brother, uncle*.

prohibeo, -hibere, -hibui, -hibitus, *prevent, hinder*.

qui, quae, quod, *who, what, which*.

suus, -a, -um, *his*, with or without *own*.

ex, *from*.

expello, -pellere, -puli, -pulsus, *drive out, drive away, expel*.

Gergovia, -ae, f., *Gergovia*.

hic, haec, hoc, *this*; *he, she, it*.

oppidum, -i, n., *fortified town, city*.

princeps, -ipis, m., *head man, leader, chief*.

-que, *and*.

reliquus, -a, -um, *remaining, the rest*.

tempto, -are, -avi, -atus, *try, attempt*.

Prohibetur: The main verb of the main clause (A.G. 278.b). The verb comes in the first position when the idea in it is emphatic (A.G. 598.d). The pronoun **is**, with **Vercingetorix** as the antecedent, is understood as the subject (A.G. 271.a).

ab Gobannitione patruo suo reliquisque principibus: Ablative of agent with the preposition **ab** after the passive verb **prohibetur** (A.G. 405). **Gobannitione**: See Appendix A. **patruo**: An ablative noun in apposition to the proper noun **Gobannitione** (A.G. 282). **suo**: Singular, masculine, ablative possessive pronoun used as an adjective modifying **patruo** (A.G. 302). **-que**: The enclitic conjunction connects the two ablative nouns **Gobannitione ... principibus** in the prepositional phrase (A.G. 324.a).

qui ... existimabant: Relative clause (A.G. 303). **qui**: Plural, masculine, nominative relative pronoun used substantively (A.G. 305).

The antecedent is **Gobannitione ... reliquisque principibus** (A.G. 307). Nominative subject (A.G. 339). **existimabant**: The main verb of the subordinate clause (A.G. 278.b).

hanc temptandam (esse) fortunam: Accusative/infinitive construction in indirect discourse after **existimabant** (A.G. 577 ff.). **hanc**: Singular, feminine, accusative demonstrative pronoun used as an adjective modifying **fortunam** (A.G. 296.1 and a). **temptandam (esse)**: Supply **esse** with the gerundive to form the second periphrastic (passive) present infinitive implying necessity (A.G. 194.b and 196). The tense of the infinitive in indirect discourse is relative to that of the verb of saying (A.G. 584).

non: Adverb, the adverb generally precedes the verb if it belongs to no one word in particular (A.G. 217.e, 320-21, and 599.a).

expellitur: The main verb of the simple sentence (A.G. 278.1). The pronoun **is**, with **Vercingetorix** as the antecedent, is understood as the subject (A.G. 271.a).

ex oppido Gergovia: Ablative of *place from which* with the preposition **ex** (A.G. 426.1). **Gergovia**: An ablative proper noun in apposition to the noun **oppido** (A.G. 282). This is the chief city of the Arverni where a major engagement will take place, see Chapters 34-52. See Appendix A.

(4.3) **non destitit tamen, atque in agris habet dilectum egentium ac perditorum.**

ac, *and.*
ager, -ri, m., *land* (under cultivation), *field.*
dilectus, -us, m., *levy, draft, enlistment.*
habeo, habere, habui, habitus, *have, hold, conduct.*
non, *not.*
tamen, *yet, still, for all that, nevertheless, however.*

atque, *and in fact, and even.*
desisto, -sistere, -stiti, -stitus, *leave off, stop, give up.*
egentes, -ium, m., pl., *the needy, the destitute.*
in, *in.*
perditi, -orum, m., pl., *desperate men, the desperate.*

non: Adverb; when **non** is especially emphatic it begins the clause (A.G. 217.e, 320-21, and 599.a).

destitit: The main verb of the coordinate clause **non ... tamen** (A.G. 278.a). The pronoun **is**, with **Vercingetorix** as the antecedent, is understood as the subject (A.G. 271.a).

tamen: Adverb, postpositive (A.G. 320-21 and 324.j).

atque: The conjunction connects a second phrase which strengthens the first phrase (**non ... tamen**) and means "and in fact, and even" (*OLD* **atque** 4).

in agris: Ablative of *place where* with the preposition **in** (locative ablative) (A.G. 426.3).

habet: The main verb of the coordinate clause **in ... perditorum** (A.G. 278.a). The pronoun **is**, with **Vercingetorix** as the antecedent, is understood as the subject (A.G. 271.a).

dilectum egentium ac perditorum: Caesar characterizes the common people this way at *BG* 6.13.1-3: **Nam plebes paene servorum habetur loco, quae nihil audet per se, nullo adhibetur consilio. Plerique, cum aut aerealieno aut magnitudine tributorum aut iniuria potentiorum premuntur, sese in servitutem dicant nobilibus,** *quibus* **in hos eadem omnia sunt iura quae dominis in servos.**

dilectum: Accusative direct object of **habet** (A.G. 387).

egentium ac perditorum: Two objective genitives with **dilectum** (A.G. 348). **egentium**: Plural, masculine, genitive adjective used substantively (A.G. 288). The noun **virorum** is understood (A.G. 288.b). **ac**: The conjunction connects the two substantive adjectives and means "and" (*OLD* **atque** 12). **perditorum**: Plural, masculine, genitive adjective used substantively (A.G. 288). The noun **virorum** is understood (A.G. 288.b). Not a very propitious start for the young commander, raising an army in the countryside from the dregs of society after being rejected by his own relatives. This beginning makes his meteoric rise all the more astonishing.

(4.3-5) **Hac coacta manu, quoscumque adit ex civitate ad suam senten(4)tiam perducit; hortatur ut communis libertatis causa arma capiant, magnisque coactis copiis advisarios suos a quibus (5) paulo ante erat eiectus expellit ex civitate.**

a(b), *by.*
adeo, -ire, -ivi, or **-ii, -itus**, *go to, approach, visit.*
ante, *before.*
capio, capere, cepi, captus, *take, take up, seize.*
civitas, -tatis, f., *body of citizens; state, nation.*
communis, -e, *common, in common, public, general.*
eicio, -icere, -ieci, -iectus, *throw out, cast out, thrust out, expel.*
expello, -pellere, -puli, -pulsus, *drive out, drive away, remove, expel.*
hortor, -ari, -atus, *urge, encourage, exhort, incite, press.*
magnus, -a, -um, *great, large, powerful.*
paulo, *by a little, just a little.*
-que, *and.*
quiscumque, quaecumque, quodcumque, *whoever, whatever, whichever.*
suus, -a, -um, *his, with or without own.*

ad, *to.*
advisarius, -i, m., *opponent, enemy, adversary.*
arma, -orum, n., pl., *arms, weapons.*
causa, -ae, f., abl. with the gen., *for the sake of, on account of.*
cogo, cogere, coegi, coactus, *bring together, collect, gather, assemble.*
copiae, -arum, f., pl., *forces, troops.*
ex, *from the number of, from among, of, from.*
hic, haec, hoc, *this; he, she, it.*
libertas, -atis, f., *freedom, liberty, independence.*
manus, -us, f., *band, force.*
perduco, -ducere, -duxi, -ductus, *bring over, gain over.*
qui, quae, quod, *who, what, which.*
sententia, -ae, f., *way of thinking, view, purpose.*
ut, *so that.*

Hac coacta manu: Ablative absolute (A.G. 419-20). **Hac**: Singular, feminine, ablative demonstrative pronoun used as an adjective modifying **manu** (A.G. 296.1 and a). **coacta**: The perfect tense of the participle represents the action as completed at the time indicated by the tense of the main verb (A.G. 489).

quoscumque ... civitate: Relative clause (A.G. 303). **quoscumque**: Plural, masculine, accusative indefinite relative pronoun (A.G. 151.a). Accusative direct object of **adit** (A.G. 387). **civitate**: See below.

adit: The main verb of the subordinate clause (A.G. 278.b). The pronoun **is**, with **Vercingetorix** as the antecedent, is understood as the subject (A.G. 271.a).

ex civitate: Prepositional phrase with **quoscumque**, **ex** with the ablative instead of the partitive genitive means "from the number of, from among, of" (A.G. 346.c) (*OLD* **ex** 17). **civitate**: The noun here means "the persons living in an organized community, the citizens of a state" (*OLD* **civitas** 2).

ad suam sententiam: Prepositional phrase, **ad** with the accusative here means "to" (an act or policy) (*OLD* **ad** 6). **suam**: Singular, feminine, accusative possessive pronoun used as an adjective modifying **sententiam** (A.G. 302).

perducit: The main verb of the main clause (A.G. 278.b). The pronoun **is**, with **Vercingetorix** as the antecedent, is understood as the subject (A.G. 271.a).

hortatur: The main verb of the coordinate clause **hortatur ... capiant** (A.G. 278.a). The pronoun **is**, with **Vercingetorix** as the antecedent, is understood as the subject (A.G. 271.a).

ut ... capiant: The conjunction **ut** ("so that") with the subjunctive forms a substantive clause of purpose which is used as the object of the verb **hortatur** denoting an action directed toward the future (A.G. 563). **capiant**: The main verb of the subordinate clause (A.G. 278.b). Present subjunctive; the tense of the subjunctive is normally in secondary sequence after the historical present **hortatur** (A.G. 482-85). Here it is in primary sequence through *repraesentatio* (A.G. 485.e and 585.b Note). The pronoun **ei**, with **quoscumque** as the antecedent, is understood as the subject (A.G. 271.a).

communis libertatis causa: A preceding genitive with the ablative of **causa** means "for the sake of" (A.G. 359.b and 404.c).

libertatis: For the theme of liberty in Book 7, see **liberius** at 1.3.

arma: Accusative direct object of **capiant** (A.G. 387).

magnisque coactis copiis: Ablative absolute (A.G. 419-20). **-que**: The enclitic conjunction connects the two main verbs **hortatur ... expellit** (A.G. 324.a). **coactis**: The perfect tense of the participle represents the action as completed at the time indicated by the tense of the main verb (A.G. 489). **copiis**: The plural of the noun is used to mean "troops" (A.G. 107).

advisarios suos: Accusative direct object of **expellit** (A.G. 387). **suos**: Plural, masculine, accusative possessive pronoun used as an adjective modifying **advisarios** (A.G. 302).

a quibus ... erat eiectus: Relative clause (A.G. 303). **a quibus**: Ablative of agent with the preposition **a(b)** after passive verb **erat eiectus** (A.G. 405). **quibus**: Plural, masculine, ablative relative pronoun used substantively (A.G. 305). The antecedent is **advisarios** (A.G. 307). **erat eiectus**: The main verb of the subordinate clause (A.G. 278.b). The pronoun **is**, with **Vercingetorix** as the antecedent, is understood as the subject (A.G. 271.a). The pluperfect tense of the verb denotes an action completed in past time (A.G. 477).

paulo: Adverb (A.G. 320-21).

ante: Adverb (A.G. 320-21 and 433.1).

expellit: The main verb of the coordinate clause **magnisque ... civitate** (A.G. 278.a). The pronoun **is**, with **Vercingetorix** as the antecedent, is understood as the subject (A.G. 271.a).

ex civitate: Ablative of *place from which* with the preposition **ex** (A.G. 426.1). Notice how much more ruthless Vercingetorix is than his enemies, they banish him **ex oppido**, he banishes them **ex civitate**.

(4.5) Rex ab suis appellatur. Dimittit quoque versus legationes, obtestatur (6) ut in fide maneant.

ab, *by.*
dimitto, -mittere, -misi, -missus, *send in different directions, send about.*
in, *in.*
maneo, manere, mansi, mansus, *stay, remain, continue.*
quoque versus, *in every direction.*
sui, -orum, m., pl., *his men, with or without own.*

appello, -are, -avi, -atus, *name.*
fides, -ei, f., *good faith, loyalty, alliance.*
legatio, -onis, f., *deputation, embassy, envoys.*
obtestor, -ari, -atus, *implore, adjure.*
rex, regis, m., *king, ruler, chieftain.*
ut, *so that.*

Rex: Nominative predicate noun with the passive verb **appellatur** (A.G. 283). Notice the prominent position of the noun. "The word **rex** is applied to the following persons in the *BG*: **Ariovistus** (1.31); **Carvilius** (5.22); **Catuvolcus** (6.31); **Cavarinus** (5.54); **Cingetorix** (5.22); **Commius** (4.21); **Diviciacus** (2.4); **Galba** (2.4); **Segovax** (5.22); **Taximagulus** (5.22); **Teutomatus** (7.31); **Vercingetorix** (7.4); **Voccio** (1.53); it belongs also by implication to **Ambiorix** (6.31, 5.24)." (Kelsey, 100) See Appendix A.

ab suis: Ablative of agent with the preposition **ab** with the passive verb **appellatur** (A.G. 405). **suis**: Plural, masculine, ablative possessive pronoun used substantively to denote a special class (A.G. 302.d).

appellatur: The main verb of the simple sentence (A.G. 278.1). The pronoun **is**, with **Vercingetorix** as the antecedent, is understood as the subject (A.G. 271.a).

Dimittit: The main verb of the coordinate clause **Dimittit ... legationes** (A.G. 278.a). The pronoun **is**, with **Vercingetorix** as the antecedent, is understood as the subject (A.G. 271.a). The verb comes in the first position when the idea in it is emphatic (A.G. 598.d).

appellatur ... Dimittit: Notice the impression that the juxtaposition of the two main verb makes: immediately upon being named **rex** Vercingetorix decisively acts in that capacity.

quoque versus: Adverb, sometimes written as two words (A.G. 320-21) (*OLD* **quoqueversus**).

legationes: Accusative direct object of **Dimittit** (A.G. 387).

obtestatur: The main verb of the coordinate clause **obtestatur ... maneant** (A.G. 278.a). The pronoun **is**, with **Vercingetorix** as the antecedent, is understood as the subject (A.G. 271.a). Notice the asyndeton between the two main verbs **Dimittit ... obtestatur** which creates an impression of rapidity (A.G. 323.b).

ut ... maneant: The conjunction **ut** ("so that") with the subjunctive forms a substantive clause of purpose which is used as the object of the verb **obtestatur** denoting an action directed toward the future (A.G. 563). **maneant**: The main verb of the subordinate clause (A.G. 278.b). Present subjunctive; the tense of the subjunctive is normally in secondary sequence after the historical present **obtestatur** (A.G. 482-85). Here it is in primary sequence through *repraesentatio* (A.G. 485.e and 585.b Note). The noun **civitates** is understood as the subject (A.G. 271.a).

in fide maneant: The phrase **in fide manere** is an idiom that means "to remain loyal" (*OLD* **fides1** 8).

in fide: Prepositional phrase, **in** with the ablative here means "in" (expressing an abstract location) (*OLD* **in** 26).

(4.6-7) Celeriter sibi Senones, Parisios, Pictones, Cadurcos, Turonos, Aulercos, Lemovices, Andos, reliquosque omnis qui Oceanum attingunt adiungit: omnium (7) consensu ad eum defertur imperium.

ad, *to, into the hands of.*
advisarius, -i, m., *opponent, enemy, adversary.*
attingo, -tingere, -tigi, -tactus, *border on, extend to, adjoin.*
Cadurci, -orum, m., pl., *the Cadurci.*
consensus, -us, m., *united opinion, agreement, assent.*
imperium, -i, n., *command, military authority.*
Lemovices, -um, m., pl., *the Lemovices.*
omnes, -ium, m., pl., *all men, all.*
Parisii, -orum, m., pl., *the Parisii.*
-que, *and.*
reliqui, -orum, m., pl., *the rest.*
sui, sibi, se, or **sese**, nom. wanting, *him*, with or without *-self.*

adiungo, -iungere, -iunxi, -iunctus, *add, unite.*
Andi, -orum, m., pl., *the Andi.*
Aulerci, -orum, m., pl., *the Aulerci.*
celeriter, *quickly, speedily, at once, immediately.*
defero, -ferre, -tuli, -latus, *confer upon, bestow.*
is, ea, id, *he, she, it; that, this.*
Oceanus, -i, m., *Ocean, the sea.*
omnis, -e, *all.*
Pictones, -um, m., pl., *the Pictones.*
qui, quae, quod, *who, what, which.*
Senones, -um, m., pl., *the Senones.*
Turoni, -orum, m., pl., *the Turoni.*

Celeriter: Adverb (A.G. 214.b and 320-21). Notice the use of the same adverb at 4.8 and 5.1. Mark Williams does not believe that word repetitions in Caesar are due to inability or carelessness, but that he has had a reason for writing as he did (Williams, 217-219). Here he is emphasizing the speed of the building momentum of the rebellion.

sibi: Singular, masculine, dative direct reflexive pronoun (A.G. 300.1). The antecedent is **Vercingetorix**, the subject of **adiungit** (A.G. 299). Indirect object of the transitive verb **adiungit** (A.G. 362).

Senones, Parisios, Pictones, Cadurcos, Turonos, Aulercos, Lemovices, Andos, reliquosque omnis: Nine accusative direct objects of **adiungit** (A.G. 387). Note the asyndeton construction in the catalog (A.G. 323.b). See Appendix A for each of the eight tribes.

reliquos: Plural, masculine, accusative adjective used substantively (A.G. 288). The noun **tribos** is understood (A.G. 288.b). **-que**: The enclitic conjunction is used to connect the last member of a series (A.G. 323.c.3). **omnis**: Accusative plural adjective modifying **reliquos**; **-is** for **-es** is the regular form in i-stem adjectives (A.G. 114.a and 116).

qui ... attingunt: Relative clause (A.G. 303). **qui**: Plural, masculine, nominative relative pronoun used substantively (A.G. 305). The antecedent is **reliquos** (A.G. 307). Nominative subject (A.G. 339). **attingunt**: The main verb of the subordinate clause (A.G. 278.b). The present tense is not the historical present but denotes a state as now existing in present time (A.G. 465.1).

Oceanum: Accusative direct object of **attingunt** (A.G. 387). The noun means "the ocean" (envisaged by the ancients as a sea flowing around the land mass of the known world); especially with reference to the Atlantic (*OLD* **Oceanus** 2). See Appendix A.

adiungit: The main verb of the main clause (A.G. 278.b). The pronoun **is**, with **Vercingetorix** as the antecedent, is understood as the subject (A.G. 271.a).

consensu: Ablative of specification (A.G. 418).

omnium: Plural, masculine, genitive adjective used substantively (A.G. 288). Possessive genitive with **consensu** (A.G. 343).

ad eum: Prepositional phrase, **ad** with the accusative here means "to, into the hands of" (*OLD* **ad** 24). **eum**: Singular, masculine, accusative demonstrative pronoun used substantively (A.G. 296.2). The antecedent is **Vercingetorix** (A.G. 297.e).

defertur: The main verb of the simple sentence (A.G. 278.1).

imperium: Nominative subject (A.G. 339). The subject is in the last position (A.G. 597.b). "= the position of commander-in-chief." (Kelsey, 401) Notice that it is only the Arverni who call Vercingetorix **rex**; the other tribes only confer the imperium on him.

(4.7-8) Qua oblata potestate omnibus his civitatibus obsides imperat, certum numerum (8) militum ad se celeriter adduci iubet;

ad, *to.*

celeriter, *quickly, speedily, at once, immediately.*
civitas, -tatis, f., *state, nation.*
impero, -are, -avi, -atus, *order to furnish, demand.*

miles, -itis, m., *soldier, foot-solider.*
obses, -idis, m. and f., *hostage.*
omnis, -e, *all.*
qui, quae, quod, *who, which, what.*

adduco, -ducere, -duxi, -ductus, *lead* or *bring to, bring up, lead.*
certus, -a, -um, *fixed, definite.*
hic, haec, hoc, *this; he, she, it.*
iubeo, iubere, iussi, iussus, *order, give orders, bid, command.*
numerus, -i, m., *number, amount.*
offero, -ferre, obtuli, oblatus, *offer, present.*
potestas, -atis, f., *power, lordship, authority.*
sui, sibi, se, or **sese**, nom. wanting, *him*, with or without *-self.*

Qua oblata potestate: Ablative absolute (A.G. 419-20). **Qua**: Singular, feminine, ablative relative pronoun (A.G. 305). The antecedent is **potestate** in its own clause (adjectival use) (A.G. 307.b). The relative does not introduce a relative clause but is a connecting relative; at the beginning of a clause the pronoun is often best rendered by a personal or demonstrative pronoun, with or without *and* (A.G. 308.f). **oblata**: The perfect tense of the participle represents the action as completed at the time indicated by the tense of the main verb (A.G. 489).

omnibus his civitatibus: Dative indirect object of the normally intransitve verb **imperat** (A.G. 369). **his**: Plural, feminine, dative demonstrative pronoun used as an adjective modifying **civitatibus** (A.G. 296.2 and a).

obsides: Accusative direct object of the normally intransitive verb **imperat** (A.G. 369 and 387).

imperat ... iubet: Vercingetorix wastes no time wielding the imperium he has been given; see also 64.1-2. In this regard he is swift and decisive, making him much like Caesar himself.

imperat: The main verb of the coordinate clause **Qua ... imperat** (A.G. 278.a). The pronoun **is**, with **Vercingetorix** as the antecedent, is understood as the subject (A.G. 271.a).

certum numerum ... adduci: Subject accusative with the infinitive after **iubet**. The construction is equivalent to a substantive clause of purpose (A.G. 563.a).

militum: Partitive genitive with **numerum** (A.G. 346.a.1).

ad se: Prepositional phrase, **ad** with the accusative here means "to" (*OLD* **ad** 1). **se**: Singular, masculine, accusative indirect reflexive pronoun (A.G. 300.2). The antecedent is **is** (**Vercingetorix**), the supplied subject of **iubet** (A.G. 299).

celeriter: Adverb (A.G. 214.b and 320-21). Notice the use of the same adverb at 4.6 and 5.1.

iubet: The main verb of the coordinate clause **certum ... iubet** (A.G. 278.a). The pronoun **is**, with **Vercingetorix** as the antecedent, is understood as the subject (A.G. 271.a). Notice the asyndeton between the two main verbs **imperat ... iubet** (A.G. 323.b).

(4.8-9) armorum quantum quaeque civitas domi quodque ante tempus efficiat con(9)stituit; in primis equitatui studet.

ante, *before*.	**arma, -orum**, n., pl., *implements of war, arms, armor, weapons*.
civitas, -tatis, f., *state, nation*.	**constituo, -stituere, -stitui, -stitutus**, *establish, determine, fix*.
domus, -us, f., *house, home*.	**efficio, -ficere, -feci, -fectus**, *produce, make, construct*.
equitatus, -us, m., *cavalry*.	**in primis**, *especially, above all*.
quantus, -a, -um, *how great, how much, how large*.	**-que**, *and*.
quisque, -----, quidque, *each, every*.	**quis, -----, quid**, *who? what?* (as adj., **qui, quae, quod**).
studeo, -ere, -ui, -----, *be eager for, eagerly desire*.	**tempus, -oris**, n., *time*.

armorum: Partitive genitive with **quantum** (346.3. Note 1).

quantum ... quod... efficiat: A double indirect question with the subjunctive; the phrase is the object of **constituit** (A.G. 573-75).

quantum: Singular, neuter, accusative interrogative pronoun used substantively (*OLD* **quantum1** 1). Accusative direct object of **efficiat** (A.G. 387). **quod**: See below. **efficiat**: The main verb of the subordinate clause (A.G. 278.b). Present subjunctive; the tense of the subjunctive is normally in secondary sequence after the historical present **constituit** (A.G. 575). Here it is in primary sequence through *repraesentatio* (A.G. 485.e and 585.b Note).

quaeque civitas: Nominative subject of **efficiat** (A.G. 339). **quaeque**: Singular, feminine, nominative indefinite pronoun used as an adjective modifying **civitas** (A.G. 151.g).

domi: Locative case of the noun **domus, -us**, f. (A.G. 427.1).

quodque ante tempus: Prepositional phrase, **ante** with the accusative is here temporal and means "before" (*OLD* **ante2** 6). **quod**: Singular, neuter, accusative interrogative pronoun used as an adjective modifying **tempus** (A.G. 148.b). **-que**: The enclitic conjunction connects the two interrogative pronouns **quantum ... quod** (A.G. 324.a). **ante**: A monosyllabic preposition is often placed between a noun and its adjective (A.G. 599.d.2).

constituit: The main verb of the main clause (A.G. 278.b). The pronoun **is**, with **Vercingetorix** as the antecedent, is understood as the subject (A.G. 271.a).

in primis: Adverbial phrase, originally a prepositional phrase, **in** with the ablative plural of **primus** means "especially, above all" (*OLD* **imprimis**).

equitatui: Dative indirect object of the intransitive verb **studet** (A.G. 368.3). Vercingetorix must know that Caesar is poorly equipped with cavalry and that the cavalry he does have is Gallic and not very trustworthy. In Chapter 65 Caesar will send for German cavalry to make up for the deficit.

studet: The main verb of the simple sentence (A.G. 278.1). The pronoun **is**, with **Vercingetorix** as the antecedent, is understood as the subject (A.G. 271.a).

(4.9-10) Summae diligentiae summam imperi severitatem addit; magnitudine supplici (10) dubitantis cogit.

addo, -dere, -didi, -ditus, *add, join*.	**cogo, cogere, coegi, coactus**, *compel, force, oblige*.
diligentia, -ae, f., *care, diligence*.	**dubito, -are, -avi, -atus**, *waver, be irresolute, hesitate, delay*.
imperium, -i, n., *command, control, military authority*.	**magnitudo, -inis**, f., *greatness, extent*.
severitas, -tatis, f., *sternness, rigor, severity*.	**summus, -a, -um**, *highest, greatest*.
supplicium, -i, n., *punishment*.	

Summae diligentiae: Dative indirect object of the transitive verb **addit** (A.G. 362). **Summae**: Irregular superlative adjective (A.G. 130.b).

summam ... severitatem: Accusative direct object of **addit** (A.G. 387). **summam**: Irregular superlative adjective modifying **severitatem** (A.G. 130.b). Notice the emphasis that the repetition of the superlative adjective (**Summae ... summam**) creates.

imperi: Partitive genitive with **severitatem** (A.G. 346.a.1). The singular genitive of nouns in **-ium** ended, until the Augustan Age, in a single **-i** (A.G. 49.b).

addit: The main verb of the simple sentence (A.G. 278.1). The pronoun **is**, with **Vercingetorix** as the antecedent, is understood as the subject (A.G. 271.a).

magnitudine: Ablative of means (A.G. 409).

supplici: Possessive genitive with **magnitudine** (A.G. 343). The singular genitive of nouns in **-ium** ended, until the Augustan Age, in a single **-i** (A.G. 49.b).

dubitantis: Plural, masculine, accusative present participle used substantively (A.G. 494.a). Accusative direct object of **cogit** (A.G. 387). Accusative plural; **-is** for **-es** is the regular form of the present participle (A.G. 117-18).

cogit: The main verb of the simple sentence (A.G. 278.1). The pronoun **is**, with **Vercingetorix** as the antecedent, is understood as the subject (A.G. 271.a).

(4.10) **Nam maiore commisso delicto igne atque omnibus tormentis necat, leviore de causa auribus desectis aut singulis effossis oculis domum remittit, ut sint reliquis documento et magnitudine poenae perterreant alios.**

alii, -orum, m., *other persons, others.*	**atque**, *and.*
auris, is, f., *ear.*	**aut**, *or.*
causa, -ae, f., *reason, cause.*	**committo, -mittere, -misi, -missus**, *commit, do, perpetrate.*
de, *with regard to, in the matter of.*	**delictum, -i**, n., *offense, fault, crime.*
deseco, -care, -cui, -ctus, *cut off.*	**documentum, -i**, n., *evidence, proof, warning.*
domus, -us, f., *house, home.*	**effodio, -fodere, -fodi, -fossus**, *dig out, tear out.*
et, *and.*	**ignis, -is**, m., *fire.*
levis, -e, comp. **-ior**, *less serious.*	**magnitudo, -inis**, f., *greatness, extent.*
maior, -or, -us, *greater, larger.*	**nam**, *for instance.*
neco, -are, -avi, -atus, *put to death, kill, destroy.*	**oculus, -i**, m., *eye.*
omnis, -e, *all, of every kind, all sorts of.*	**perterreo, -terrere, -----, -territus**, *greatly alarm, frighten, terrify, dismay.*
poena, -ae, f., *punishment, penalty.*	**reliqui, -orum**, m., pl., *the rest.*
remitto, -mittere, -misi, -missus, *send back.*	**singuli, -ae, -a**, *one apiece, single.*
sum, esse, fui, futurus, *be.*	**tormentum, -i**, n., *torture, torment, suffering.*
ut, *so that.*	

Nam: Causal conjunction introducing an example or illustration meaning "for instance" (*OLD* **nam** 3.c).

maiore commisso delicto ... necat: A disguised conditional statement (A.G. 521).

maiore commisso delicto: An ablative absolute standing as the protasis of the conditional statement and equivalent to **si qui delictum maius commiserunt** (A.G. 419-20, 420.4 and 521.a). **maiore**: Irregular comparative adjective (A.G. 129). **delicto**: The perfect tense of the participle represents the action as completed at the time indicated by the tense of the main verb (A.G. 489).

igne: Ablative of instrument (A.G. 409).

atque: The conjunction connects the two ablative nouns **igne ... tormentis** and means "and" (*OLD* **atque** 12).

omnibus tormentis: Ablatives of means (A.G. 409).

necat: The main verb of the apodosis of the conditional statement (A.G. 512). The main verb of the coordinate clause **Nam ... necat** (A.G. 278.a). The pronoun **is**, with **Vercingetorix** as the antecedent, is understood as the subject (A.G. 271.a). The pronoun **eos**, with the men committing the crime as the antecedent, is understood as the direct object.

leviore de causa ... remittit: A disguised conditional statement (A.G. 521).

leviore de causa: Prepositional phrase standing as the protasis of the conditional statement and equivalent to **si qui levius peccaverunt** (A.G. 521.a and Kelsey, 401). Prepositional phrase, **de** with the ablative here means "with regard to, in the matter of " (*OLD* **de** 13). **leviore**: Comparative adjective (A.G.124). **de**: A monosyllabic preposition is often placed between a noun and its adjective (A.G. 599.d.2).

auribus desectis: Ablative absolute (A.G. 419-20). **desectis**: The perfect tense of the participle represents the action as completed at the time indicated by the tense of the main verb (A.G. 489).

aut: The conjunction connects the two ablative absolutes and excludes the alternative (A.G. 324.e).

singulis effossis oculis: Ablative absolute (A.G. 419-20). **singulis**: Distributive numeral used as an adjective modifying **oculis** (A.G. 136-37). **effossis**: The perfect tense of the participle represents the action as completed at the time indicated by the tense of the main verb (A.G. 489).

domum: Accusative of *place to which* without a preposition (A.G. 427.2).

remittit: The main verb of the apodosis of the conditional statement (A.G. 512). The main verb of the coordinate clause **leviore ... alios** (A.G. 278.a). The pronoun **is**, with **Vercingetorix** as the antecedent, is understood as the subject (A.G. 271.a). The pronoun **eos**, with the maimed men as the antecedent, is understood as the direct object.

ut sint ... perterreant: The conjunction **ut** ("so that") with the subjunctive forms a final (purpose) clause (A.G. 531-532). **sint ... perterreant**: The main verbs of the subordinate clause (A.G. 278.b). Present subjunctives; the tense of the subjunctive is normally in secondary sequence after the historical present **remittit** (A.G. 482-85). Here it is in primary sequence through *repraesentatio* (A.G. 485.e and 585.b Note). The pronoun **ei**, with the punished men as the antecedent, is understood as the subject of both verbs (A.G. 271.a).

reliquis documento: Dative of the purpose or end (double dative). The dative of an abstract noun (**documento**) is used to show that for which a thing serves or which it accomplishes, often with another dative of the person or thing affected (**reliquis**). The verb is usually a form of **sum (sint)** (A.G. 382.1). **reliquis**: Plural, masculine, dative adjective used substantively (A.G. 288). The noun **Gallis** is understood (A.G. 288.b).

et: The conjunction connects the two verbs in the final clause (A.G. 324.a).

magnitudine: Ablative of means (A.G. 409).

poenae: Possessive genitive with **magnitudine** (A.G. 343).

alios: Plural, masculine, accusative pronoun used substantively meaning "other persons, others" (*OLD* **alius2** 1). Accusative direct object of **perterreant** (A.G. 387).

(5.1-2) His suppliciis celeriter coacto exercitu, Lucterium Cadurcum, summae hominem audaciae, cum parte copiarum in (2) Rutenos mittit; ipse in Bituriges proficiscitur.

audacia, -ae, f., *boldness, daring, insolence, impudence.*
Cadurcus, -i, m., *a Cadurcan.*
cogo, cogere, coegi, coactus, *bring together, collect, gather, assemble.*
cum, *with.*
hic, haec, hoc, *this; he, she, it.*
in, *into the country of, against.*

Lucterius, -i, m., *Lucterius.*
pars, partis, f., *part, portion.*
Ruteni, -orum, m., pl., *the Ruteni.*
supplicium, -i, n., *punishment.*

Bituriges, -um, m., pl., *the Bituriges.*
celeriter, *quickly, speedily, at once, immediately.*
copiae, -arum, f., pl., *forces, troops.*
exercitus, -us, m., *army.*
homo, hominis, m., *man, person.*
ipse, -a, -um, *he, they, with or without himself, themselves.*
mitto, mittere, misi, missus, *send, despatch.*
proficiscor, -ficisci, -fectus, *set out, depart, proceed.*
summus, -a, -um, *highest, greatest.*

His suppliciis celeriter coacto exercitu: Ablative absolute (A.G. 419-20). **His suppliciis**: Ablative of means (A.G. 409). **His**: Plural, neuter, ablative demonstrative pronoun used as an adjective modifying **suppliciis** (A.G. 296.1 and a). **celeriter**: Adverb (A.G. 214.b and 320-21). Notice the use of the same adverb at 4.6 and 4.8. **coacto exercitu**: The noun, participle element of the ablative absolute (A.G. 419-20). **coacto**: The perfect tense of the participle represents the action as completed at the time indicated by the tense of the main verb (A.G. 489).

Lucterium: Accusative direct object of **mittit** (A.G. 387). See Appendix A.

Cadurcum: An accusative noun in apposition to the proper noun **Lucterium** (A.G. 282).

summae ... audaciae: Genitive of quality (descriptive genitive) modifying **hominem** (A.G. 345). **summae**: Irregular superlative adjective (A.G. 130.b).

hominem: An accusative noun in apposition to the proper noun **Luterium** (A.G.282).

cum parte copiarum: Ablative of accompaniment with the preposition **cum** (A.G. 413). **copiarum**: Partitive genitive with **parte** (A.G 346.a.1).

in Rutenos: Accusative of *place to which* with the preposition **in** meaning "into the country of" (A.G. 426.2). **Rutenos**: See Appendix A. The Rutini do join with the Arverni, see 7.1-2.

mittit: The main verb of the main clause (A.G. 278.b). The historical present, giving vividness to the narrative, is present in Chapter 5 (A.G. 469). This usage, common in all languages, comes from imagining past events as going on before our eyes (*repraesentatio*) (A.G. 469 Note). The pronoun **is**, with **Vercingetorix** as the antecedent, is understood as the subject (A.G. 271.a).

ipse: Singular, masculine, nominative demonstrative pronoun used substantively (296.2 and 298.d). The antecedent is **Vercingetorix** at 4.1 (A.G. 298). The pronoun distinguishes the principle person (**Vercingetorix**) from a subordinate person (**Lucterium**) (A.G. 298.3). Nominative subject (A.G. 339).

in Bituriges: Accusative of *place to which* with the preposition **in** meaning "into the country of" (A.G. 426.2). **Bituriges**: See Appendix A. The Bituriges do join with the Arverni, see 5.7

proficiscitur: The main verb of the simple sentence (A.G. 278.1).

(5.2-3) Eius adventu Bituriges ad Aeduos, quorum erant in fide, legatos mittunt, subsidium rogatum, quo facilius hostium copias sustinere (3) possint.

ad, *to.*
Aedui, -orum, m., pl., *the Aedui.*
copiae, -arum, f., pl., *forces, troops.*
fides, -ei, f., *protection, alliance.*
in, *in.*
legatus, -i, m., *envoy, ambassador.*
possum, posse, potui, -----, *be able.*

adventus, -us, m., *coming, approach, arrival.*
Bituriges, -um, m., pl., *the Bituriges.*
facile, comp. -ius, *easily, readily, with no trouble.*
hostis, -is, m., *enemy, foe;* pl., *the enemy.*
is, ea, id, *he, she, it; that, this.*
mitto, mittere, misi, missus, *send, despatch.*
qui, quae, quod, *who, which, what.*

22

quo, *so that* (by that degree), *in order that, that, that thereby.*
subsidium, -i, n., *support, relief, reinforcement, help, aid.*
sustino, -tinere, -tinui, -tentus, *hold out against, withstand.*

rogo, -are, -avi, -atus, *ask, request.*
sum, esse, fui, futurus, *be.*

Eius: Singular, masculine, genitive demonstrative pronoun used substantively (A.G. 296.2). The antecedent is **ipse** (**Vercingetorix**) (A.G. 297.e). Possessive genitive with **adventu** (A.G. 343).
adventu: Either an ablative of cause without a preposition; the motive which influences the mind of the person acting is expressed by the ablative of cause (A.G. 404) or an ablative of *time when* (A.G. 423.1).
Bituriges: Nominative subject of **mittunt** (A.G. 339). See Appendix A.
ad Aeduos: Prepositional phrase, **ad** with the accusative here means "to" (*OLD* **ad** 1). **Aeduos**: See Appendix A.
quorum ... fide: Relative clause (A.G. 303). **quorum**: Plural, masculine, genitive relative pronoun used substantively (A.G. 305). The antecedent is **Aeduos** (A.G. 307). Possessive genitive with **fide** (A.G. 343).
erant: The main verb of the subordinate clause (A.G. 278.b). Supply **ei**, with **Bituriges** as the antecedent, as the subject (A.G. 271.a).
in fide: Prepositional phrase, **in** with the ablative here means "in" (*OLD* **in** 37). The prepositional phrase is in the predicate position after **erant** (A.G. 272).
legatos: Accusative direct object of **mittunt** (A.G. 387).
mittunt: The main verb of the main clause (A.G. 278.b).
subsidium: Accusative direct object of the supine **rogatum** (A.G. 387 and 509).
rogatum: The supine in **-um** is used after a verb of motion (**mittunt**) to express purpose (A.G. 509).
quo facilius ... possint: Final clause; the ablative **quo** (= **ut eo**) is used as a conjunction in a final (purpose) clause with the subjunctive (A.G. 531.a). **quo**: In a final clause with a comparative, the conjunction means "so that by that degree" (*OLD* **quo2** 3.b). **facilius**: Comparative adverb (A.G. 218 and 320-21). **possint**: The main verb of the subordinate clause (A.G. 278.b). Present subjunctive; the tense of the subjunctive is normally in secondary sequence after the historical present **mittunt** (A.G. 482-85). Here it is in primary sequence through *repraesentatio* (A.G. 485.e and 585.b Note). The pronoun **ei**, with **Bituriges** as the antecedent, is understood as the subject (A.G. 271.a).
hostium: Partitive genitive with **copias** (A.G. 346.a.1). The enemy is Vercingetorix and his army.
copias: Accusative direct object of the infinitive **sustinere** (A.G. 387 and 451.3).
sustinere: Complementary infinitive after **possint** (A.G. 456).

(5.3-4) Aedui de consilio legatorum, quos Caesar ad exercitum reliquerat, copias equitatus peditatusque subsidio (4) Biturigibus mittunt.

ad, *with.*
Bituriges, -um, m., pl., *the Bituriges.*
consilium, -i, n., *instruction, instigation.*
de, *on, at.*
exercitus, -us, m., *army.*
mitto, mittere, misi, missus, *send, despatch.*
perfidia, -ae, f., *faithlessness, bad faith, treachery.*
qui, quae, quod, *who, which, what.*
subsidium, -i, n., *support, relief, reinforcement, help, aid.*

Aedui, -orum, m., pl., *the Aedui.*
Caesar, -aris, m., *Caesar.*
copiae, -arum, f., pl., *forces, troops.*
equitatus, -us, m., *cavalry.*
legatus, -i, m., *deputy, legate.*
peditatus, -us, m., *infantry.*
-que, *and.*
relinquo, -linquere, -liqui, -lictus, *leave, leave behind.*

Aedui: Nominative subject of **mittunt** (A.G. 339). See Appendix A.
de consilio legatorum: Prepositional phrase, **de** with the ablative of **consilium** means "on someone's instructions, at someone's instigation" (*OLD* **consilium** 2.c). **legatorum**: Possessive genitive with **consilio** (A.G. 343). "All governors of provinces were given several **legati**, deputies or assistants. These legates were not strictly military officers, but were to be employed by the governors in any way they saw fit. Caesar introduced the innovation of putting a legate in command of each legion just before a battle. When one or more legions were detached from the main army for special service, Caesar put a legate in command; the legates were left in command of the winter-quarters during Caesar's absence. But no one legate was in permanent command of any one legion." (Walker, 25)
quos ... reliquerat: Relative clause (A.G. 303). The Aedui were old and steadfast allies of the Romans and had assisted Caesar in various ways from the opening of *BG* Book 1; see especially *BG* 2.14-15, 5.54. **quos**: Plural, masculine, accusative relative pronoun used substantively (A.G. 305). The antecedent is **legatorum** (A.G. 307). Accusative direct object of **reliquerat** (A.G. 387).
reliquerat: The main verb of the subordinate clause (A.G. 278.b). The pluperfect tense of the verb denotes an action completed in past time (A.G. 477).
Caesar: Nominative subject (A.G. 339). See Appendix A.
ad exercitum: Prepositional phrase, **ad** with the accusative here means "with" (*OLD* **ad** 16.a).
copias: Accusative direct object of **mittunt** (A.G. 387).
equitatus peditatusque: Two partitive genitives with **copias** (A.G. 346.a.1). **-que**: The enclitic conjunction connects the two genitive nouns (A.G. 324.a).
subsidio Biturigibus: Dative of the purpose or end (double dative). The dative of an abstract noun (**subsidio**) is used to show that for which a thing serves or which it accomplishes, often with another dative of the person or thing affected (**Biturigibus**) (A.G. 382.1).
Biturigibus: See Appendix A.
mittunt: The main verb of the main clause (A.G. 278.b).

(5.4-6) **Qui cum ad flumen Ligerim venissent, quod Bituriges ab Aeduis dividit, paucos dies ibi morati (5) neque flumen transire ausi domum revertuntur legatisque nostris renuntiant se Biturigum perfidiam veritos revertisse, quibus id consili fuisse cognoverint ut, si flumen transissent, (6) una ex parte ipsi, altera Arverni se circumsisterent.**

ab, *from.*
Aedui, -orum, m., pl., *the Aedui.*
Arverni, -orum, m., pl., *the Arverni.*
Bituriges, -um, m., pl., *the Bituriges.*
cognosco, -gnoscere, -gnovi, cognitus, *learn, ascertain, recognize.*
cum, *after, when.*
divido, -videre, -visi, -visus, *separate, divide.*
ex, *on.*
ibi, *in that place, there.*

is, ea, id, *he, she, it; that, this.*
Liger, -eris, m., *the Loire River.*
neque, *and ... not.*
pars, partis, f., *side.*
perfidia, -ae, f., *faithlessness, bad faith, treachery.*
qui, quae, quod, *who, which, what.*

reverto, -ere, reverti, *return, come back, go back.*
sui, sibi, se, or sese, nom. wanting, *they*, with or without *themselves*; *them*, with or without *-selves.*
sum, esse, fui, futurus, *be.*

unus, -a, -um, *one.*
venio, venire, veni, ventus, *come.*

ad, *to.*
alter, -era, -erum, *the other, second.*
audeo, audere, ausus sum, *venture, dare, risk.*
**circumsisto, -sistere, -steti, or -stiti, -----, *surround.*
consilium, -i, n., *plan, design, scheme.*
dies, -ei, m., and f., *day.*
domus, -us, f., *house, home.*
flumen, -inis, n., *stream, river.*
ipse, -a, -um, *he, they*, with or without *himself, themselves.*
legatus, -i, m., *deputy, legate.*
moror, -ari, -atus, *delay, wait, stay.*
noster, -tra, -trum, *our, our own.*
paucus, -a, um, *few.*
-que, *and.*
renuntio, -are, -avi, -atus, *bring back word, report, announce.*
si, *if.*

transeo, -ire, -ivi, or -ii, -itus, *go over, go across, cross over.*
ut, *namely that, to the effect that.*
vereor, -eri, -itus, *fear, be afraid of.*

Qui ... morati ... ausi: Nominative subject of **revertuntur ... renuntiant** (A.G. 339). **Qui:** Plural, masculine, nominative relative pronoun used substantively (A.G. 305). The antecedent is **equitatus peditatusque** (i.e. the Aedui) (A.G. 307). The relative does not introduce a relative clause but is a connecting relative; at the beginning of a clause the pronoun is often best rendered by a personal or demonstrative pronoun, with or without *and* (A.G. 308.f). **morati:** Nominative, perfect, deponent participle used as a predicate, where in English a phrase or a subordinate clause would be more natural (A.G. 496). **ausi:** Nominative, perfect, semi-deponent participle used as a predicate, where in English a phrase or a subordinate clause would be more natural (A.G. 192 and 496).

cum ... venissent: Temporal clause; **cum** ("after, when") with the pluperfect subjunctive describes the circumstances that preceded the action of the main verb (A.G. 546). **venissent:** The main verb of the subordinate clause (A.G. 278.b). The pronoun **ei**, with **Qui** (the Aedui) as the antecedent, is understood as the subject (A.G. 271.a).

ad flumen Ligerim: Accusative of *place to which* with the preposition **ad** (A.G. 426.2). **flumen:** Caesar never uses the synonym **fluvius** or **amnis**. (See Adcock, 16) **Ligerim:** An accusative proper noun in apposition to **flumen** (A.G. 282). The accusative singular of the third declension masculine i-stem noun **Liger** ends in **-im**, not **-em** (A.G. 73-75, esp. 74.d and 75.a.1). See Appendix A.

quod... dividit: Relative clause (A.G. 303). **quod:** Singular, neuter, nominative relative pronoun used substantively (A.G. 305). The antecedent is **flumen** (A.G. 307). Nominative subject (A.G. 339). **dividit:** The main verb of the subordinate clause (A.G. 278.b). The present tense is not the historical present but denotes a state as now existing in present time (A.G. 465.1).

Bituriges: Accusative direct object of **dividit** (A.G. 387). See Appendix A.

ab Aeduis: Ablative of separation with the preposition **ab** after **dividit** (A.G. 401). **Aeduis:** See Appendix A.

paucos dies: Accusative of *time how long* (A.G. 423.2). **dies:** The noun **dies** is normally masculine gender (A.G. 97.a).

ibi: Adverb (A.G. 215.5 and 320-21).

neque: The conjunction here joins a negative clause (**ausi**) to a preceding positive one (**morati**) and means "and ... not" (*OLD* **neque** 3).

flumen: Accusative direct object of the infinitive **transire** (A.G. 387 and 451.3).

transire: Complementary infinitive after the participle **ausi** (A.G. 456 and 488).

domum: Accusative of *place to which* without a preposition (A.G. 427.2).

revertuntur: The main verb of the coordinate clause **Qui ... revertuntur** (A.G. 278.a).

legatisque nostris: Dative indirect object of the transitive verb **renuntiant** (the infinitive clause **se ... revertisse** functions as the direct object (A.G. 560-62)) (A.G. 362). **-que:** The enclitic conjunction connects the two main verbs **revertuntur ... renuntiant** (A.G. 324.a). **nostris:** Plural, masculine, dative possessive pronoun used as an adjective modifying **legatis** (A.G. 302).

renuntiant: The main verb of the coordinate clause **legatisque ... circumsisterent** (A.G. 278.a).

se ... veritos revertisse: Accusative/infinitive construction in indirect discourse after **rennuntiant** (A.G. 577 ff.). **se:** Plural, masculine, accusative direct reflexive pronoun (A.G. 300.1). The antecedent is **Qui** (the Aedui), the subject of **renuntiant** (A.G. 299). **veritos:** Accusative, perfect, deponent participle used as a predicate modifying **se**, where in English a phrase or a subordinate clause would be more normal (A.G. 496). **revertisse:** Perfect infinitive; the tense of the infinitive in indirect discourse is relative to that of the verb of saying (A.G. 584).

perfidiam: Accusative direct object of the participle **veritos** (A.G. 387 and 488).

Biturigum: Possessive genitive of the tribe name **Bituriges** with **perfidiam** (A.G. 343). See Appendix A.

quibus ... cognoverint: Relative clause; a subordinate clause in indirect discourse takes the subjunctive (A.G. 303 and 580). **quibus**: Plural, masculine, dative relative pronoun used substantively (A.G. 305). The antecedent is **Biturigum** (A.G. 307). Dative of possession with **fuisse** (A.G. 373). **cognoverint**: The main verb of the subordinate clause (A.G. 278.b). Perfect subjunctive; the tense of the subjunctive is normally in secondary sequence after the historical present **renuntiant** (A.G. 482-85). Here it is in primary sequence through *repraesentatio* (A.G. 485.e and 585.b Note). The pronoun **ei**, with **Qui** (the Aedui) as the antecedent, is understood as the subject (A.G. 271.a).

id ... fuisse: Accusative/infinitive construction in indirect discourse after **cognoverint** (A.G. 577 ff.). **id**: Singular, neuter, accusative demonstrative pronoun used substantively (A.G. 296.2). The pronoun is explained by the following **ut** clause (**ut ... circumsisterent**) (A.G. 297.e). **fuisse**: Perfect infinitive; the tense of the infinitive in indirect discourse is relative to that of the verb of saying (A.G. 584).

consili: Partitive genitive with **id** (A.G. 346.a.3). The singular genitive of nouns in -**ium** ended, until the Augustan Age, in a single -**i** (A.G. 49.b).

ut si ... transissent ... circumsisterent: A subordinate conditional statement in indirect statement after **renuntiant** (A.G. 512.c). The apodosis, as an epexegetical **ut** clause, takes the subjunctive rather than the infinitive and the protasis, as a clause subordinate to a subjunctive clause, also takes the subjunctive (A.G. 512.c and 589).

ut ... circumsisterent: The apodosis of the conditional statement (A.G. 512.c and 589). The conjunction **ut** ("namely that, to the effect that") with the subjunctive forms an epexegetical clause in apposition to the neuter pronoun **id** (*OLD* **ut** 39). **circumsisterent**: The main verb of the subordinate clause (A.G. 278.b). Imperfect subjunctive; the tense of the subjunctive is in secondary sequence after the historical present **renuntiant** (A.G. 482-85, esp. 485.e).

si ... transissent: The conjunction **si** ("if") with the subjunctive forms the protasis of the conditional statement (A.G. 589). A clause dependent on a subjunctive clause (**ut ... circumsisterent**) takes the subjunctive when regarded as an integral part of that clause (attraction) (A.G. 593). **transissent**: The main verb of the subordinate clause (A.G. 278.b). Pluperfect subjunctive; the tense of the subjunctive is in secondary sequence after the historical present **renuntiant** (A.G. 482-85, esp. 485.e). Contracted form of **transivissent** (A.G. 181.b). According to Siedler, syncope is "another indication of Speed, almost poetic, of stripping forms of words, especially verbs, down to their bare bones." (Siedler, 31). The pronoun **ei**, with **Qui** (the Aedui) as the antecedent, is understood as the subject (A.G. 271.a).

flumen: Accusative direct object of **transissent** (A.G. 387).

una ex parte ... altera: Ablative of *position* with the preposition **ex** meaning "on the one side ... on the other side" (A.G. 429.b). **una**: Declinable cardinal number used as an adjective modifying **parte** (A.G. 132-35). **ex**: A monosyllabic preposition is often placed between a noun and its adjective (A.G. 599.d.2). **altera**: Singular, feminine, ablative adjective used substantively (A.G. 288). This is an ellipsis of **altera ex parte** (A.G. 323.b).

ipsi: Plural, masculine, nominative demonstrative pronoun used substantively (A.G. 296.2). The antecedent is **Biturigum** (A.G. 298). First nominative subject of **circumsisterent** (A.G. 339). The pronoun is here emphatic (A.G. 298.d.1).

Arverni: Second nominative subject of **circumsisterent** (A.G. 339). That is, Vercingetorix and his army. See Appendix A.

se: Plural, masculine, accusative indirect reflexive pronoun (A.G. 300.2). The antecedent is **Qui** (the Aedui), the subject of **renuntiant** (A.G. 299). Accusative direct object of **circumsisterent** (A.G. 387).

(5.6-7) Id eane de causa, quam legatis pronuntiarunt, an perfidia adducti fecerint, quod nihil nobis constat, non videtur pro (7) certo esse proponendum.

adduco, -ducere, -duxi, -ductus, *induce, prevail upon, influence.*
certus, -a, -um, *certain, positive.*

de, *from, on account of.*
is, ea, id, *he, she, it; that, this.*
-ne ... an, *whether ... or.*
non, *not.*
perfidia, -ae, f., *faithlessness, bad faith, treachery.*
pronuntio, -are, -avi, -atus, *tell openly, declare.*

qui, quae, quod, *who, which, what.*
videor, videri, visus sum, *seem good, right,* or *proper.*

causa, -ae, f., *reason, cause.*
consto, -stare, -stiti, -staturus, *be certain, ascertained, known.*
facio, facere, feci, factus, *do, act.*
legatus, -i, m., *deputy, legate.*
nihil, n., *nothing.*
nos, nostrum, *we, us.*
pro, *for.*
propono, -ponere, -posui, -positus, *put forward, present, declare.*
quod, *because, since, for, as.*

Id ... fecerint: This phrase could be written in full as: **Id eane de causa quam legatis pronuntiarunt fecerint an id perfidia adducti fecerint ...**

Id: Accusative direct object of **fecerint** (A.G.387). Singular, neuter, accusative demonstrative pronoun used substantively (A.G. 296.2). The antecedent is the idea of returning contained in the previous sentence (A.G 297.e).

eane de causa: Prepositional phrase; **de** with the ablative here means "from, on account of" (*OLD* **de** 14). **-ne**: See below. **ea**: Singular, feminine, ablative demonstrative pronoun use as an adjective modifying **causa** (296.1 and a).

-ne ... an ... fecerint: A double indirect question with the subjunctive; the phrase is the object of the infinitive **esse proponendum** (A.G. 573-75). **-ne ... an**: The two interrogative particles mean "whether ... or" (A.G. 335). **fecerint**: The main verb of the subordinate clause (A.G. 278.b). Perfect subjunctive; the tense of the subjunctive is normally in secondary sequence after the historical present **videtur** (A.G. 575). Here it is in primary sequence through *repraesentatio* (A.G. 485.e and 585.b Note). The pronoun **ei**, with

Qui (the Aedui) at 5.4 as the antecedent, is understood as the subject (A.G. 271.a).

quam ... pronuntiarunt: Relative clause; a clause dependent on a subjunctive clause (**-ne ... fecerint**) normally takes the subjunctive (attraction) (A.G. 303 and 593). However, when a dependent clause is not regarded as a necessary logical part of the clause, the indicative is used. The indicative serves to emphasize the fact, as true independently of the statement contained in the subjunctive clause (A.G. 593.a Note 1). **quam**: Singular, feminine, accusative relative pronoun used substantively (A.G. 305). The antecedent is **causa** (A.G. 307). Accusative direct object of **pronuntiarunt** (A.G. 387). **pronuntiarunt**: The main verb of the subordinate clause (A.G. 278.b). The pronoun **ei**, with **Qui** (the Aedui) at 5.4 as the antecedent, is understood as the subject (A.G. 271.a). Contracted form of **pronuntiaverunt** (A.G. 181.b).

legatis: Dative indirect object of the transitive verb **pronuntiarunt** (A.G. 362).

perfidia: Ablative of cause without a preposition after **adducti**; the motive which influences the mind of the person acting is expressed by the ablative of cause (A.G. 404).

adducti: Nominative, perfect, passive participle used substantively as a predicate where in English a phrase or a subordinate clause would be more natural (A.G. 496). The pronoun **ei**, with **Qui** (the Aedui) at 5.4 as the antecedent, is understood. Nominative subject (A.G. 339).

quod ... constat: Causal clause; the conjunction **quod** ("because") takes the indicative when the reason is given on the authority of the writer or speaker (A.G. 540.1). **constat**: The main verb of the subordinate clause (A.G. 278.b).

nihil: Nominative subject (A.G. 339). Indeclinable noun, used only as nominative and accusative singular (A.G. 103.a).

nobis: Plural, masculine, dative personal pronoun used substantively (A.G. 143 and 295). Dative indirect object of the intransitive verb **constat** (A.G. 366).

non ... proponendum: Caesar allows their action to speak louder than words, as we are immediately told (and this is meant to be ironically humorous) that **Bituriges eorum discessu statim cum Arvernis iunguntur**. Kahn notes that "in effect his characters are what they do and not what he says about them." (Kahn, 251)

non: Adverb, the adverb generally precedes the verb if it belongs to no one word in particular (A.G. 217.e, 320-21, and 599.a).

videtur: The main verb of the main clause (A.G. 278.b). Impersonal use of the verb (A.G. 208.c). The impersonal passive verb means "to seem good, right, or proper" (*OLD* **video** 24). The following infinitive phrase functions as the subject (A.G. 208.c and 454).

pro certo esse proponendum: The infinitive phrase functions as the subject of the impersonal verb **videtur** (A.G. 454). **pro certo**: Prepositional phrase, **pro** with the neuter ablative of the adjective **certus** means "as or for certainty" (*OLD* **certus** 3.b). **esse proponendum**: Second periphrastic (passive) present infinitive, **esse** with the gerundive denotes necessity (A.G. 194.b and 196, 500.2). The infinitive functions as the subject of the impersonal verb **videtur** (A.G. 454).

(5.7) **Bituriges eorum discessu statim cum Arvernis iunguntur.**

Arverni, -orum, m., pl., *the Arverni.*
cum, *with.*
is, ea, id, *he, she, it; that, this.*
statim, *immediately, straightaway, at once.*

Bituriges, -um, m., pl., *the Bituriges.*
discessus, -us, m., *departure, going away.*
iungo, iungere, iunxi, iunctus, *join together, join, unite.*

Note the dry irony in the sentence.

Bituriges: Nominative subject (A.G. 339). See Appendix A.

eorum: Plural, masculine genitive demonstrative pronoun used substantively (A.G. 296.2). The antecedent is **Qui** (the Aedui) at 5.4 (297.e). Possessive genitive with **discessu** A.G. 343.

discessu: Ablative of *time when* (A.G. 423.1).

statim: Adverb (A.G. 215.2 and 320-21).

cum Arvernis: Ablative of accompaniment with the preposition **cum** (A.G. 413). **Arvernis**: See Appendix A.

iunguntur: The main verb of the simple sentence (A.G. 278.1).

1.C CHAPTERS 6-10: CAESAR RETURNS FROM ITALY AND ASSEMBLES HIS LEGIONS; VERCINGETORIX ATTACKS GORGOBINA OF THE BOII; CAESAR SETS OUT TO AID THEM

(6.1-2) **His rebus in Italiam Caesari nuntiatis, cum iam ille urbanas res virtute Cn. Pompei commodiorem in statum pervenisse intellegeret, in Transalpinam Galliam profectus (2) est.**

Caesar, -aris, m., *Caesar.*

commodus, -a, -um, comp **-ior**, *advantageous, favorable, suitable.*
Gallia, -ae, f., *Gaul.*
iam, *already.*
in, *into; to, into; to, towards.*

is, ea, id, *he, she, it; that, this.*
nuntio, -are, -avi, -atus, *announce, report.*
proficiscor, -ficisci, -fectus, *set out, depart, proceed.*
status, -us, m., *position, situation, condition.*
urbanus, -a, -um, *of the city* (usually referring to Rome).

Cn. Pompeus, -i, m., *Gnaeus Pompeius Magnus, Pompey.*
cum, *since, seeing that.*
hic, haec, hoc, *this; he, she, it.*
ille, illae, illud, *that; he, she, it.*
intellego, -legere, -lexi, -lectus, *understand, perceive, ascertain.*
Italia, -ae, f., *Italy.*
pervenio, -venire, -veni, -ventus, *come, come to.*
res, rei, f., *matter, affair, event.*
Transalpinus, -a, um, *beyond the Alps, Transalpine.*
virtus, -utis, f., *vigor, energy, effort.*

His rebus in Italiam Caesari nuntiatis: Ablative absolute (A.G. 419-20). **His**: Plural, feminine, ablative demonstrative pronoun used as an adjective modifying **rebus** (A.G. 296.1 and a). **in Italiam**: Accusative of *place to which* with the preposition **in** (A.G. 426.2). **Italiam**: See Appendix A. **Caesari**: Dative indirect object of the passive participle **nuntiatis**; verbs which in the active voice take the accusative and dative retain the dative when used in the passive (A.G. 365). See Appendix A. **nuntiatis**: The perfect tense of the participle represents the action as completed at the time indicated by the tense of the main verb (A.G. 489).

cum ... intellegeret: Causal clause; the relative adverb **cum** ("since") with the subjunctive forms a clause expressing cause (A.G. 549). **intellegeret**: The main verb of the subordinate clause (A.G. 278.b). Imperfect subjunctive; the tense of the subjunctive is in secondary sequence and follows the rules for the sequence of tense after **profectus est** (A.G. 482-85).

iam: Adverb (A.G. 215.6, 217.b and 320-21).

ille: Singular, masculine, nominative demonstrative pronoun used substantively (A.G. 296.2). The antecedent is **Caesari** (A.G. 297.e). Nominative subject (A.G. 339).

urbanas res ... pervenisse: Accusative/infinitive construction in indirect discourse after **intellegeret** (A.G. 577 ff.). **pervenisse**: Perfect infinitive; the tense of the infinitive in indirect discourse is relative to that of the verb of saying (A.G. 584).

virtute: Ablative of means (A.G. 409). "'energetic action'. Pompey was made sole consul for a time with great authority." (Kelsey, 402) "A deliberate irony, with Caesar, writing in late 50, maintaining the fiction of reliance on Pompey's friendship. Rioting after the death of Clodius on 18 January led directly to Pompey's selection as *consul sine collega*, and to calls that he be made dictator: so both were now locked in a struggle for security and supremacy." (Hammond, 237)

Cn. Pompei: Possessive genitive with **virtute** (A.G. 343). See Appendix A. **Cn.**: Abbreviated form of the praenomen **Gnaeus** (A.G. 108.c). Pompey was still nominally Caesar's ally as a member of the Triumvirate. However, relations by this time were exceedingly strained (see Fuller, 172-75).

commodiorem in statum: Prepositional phrase, **in** with the accusative here means "into, to" (a state or condition) (*OLD* **in** 2).

commodiorem: Comparative adjective modifying **statum** (A.G. 124). **in**: A monosyllabic preposition is often placed between a noun and adjective (A.G. 599.d.2).

in Transalpinam Galliam: Accusative of *place to which* with the preposition **in** (A.G. 426.2). **Transalpinam Galliam**: See Appendix A.

profectus est: The main verb of the main clause (A.G. 278.b). The pronoun **is**, with **ille** (**Caesar**) as the antecedent, is understood as the subject (A.G. 271.a).

(6.2-3) Eo cum venisset, magna difficultate adficiebatur, qua (3) ratione ad exercitum pervenire posset.

ad, *to*.

cum, *after, when*.
eo, *thither, there*.
magnus, -a, -um, *great, large*.
possum, posse, potui, -----, *be able*.
ratio, -onis, f., *plan, course, method*.

adficio, -ficere, -feci, -fectus, *to be involved in, annoy, afflict*.
difficultas, -tatis, f., *difficulty, trouble, embarrassment*.
exercitus, -us, m., *army*.
pervenio, -venire, -veni, -ventus, *come to, reach*.
quis, -----, quid, *who? what?* (as adj., **qui, quae, quod**).
venio, venire, veni, ventus, *come*.

Eo: Adverb (A.G. 217.a and 320-21). The adverb is standing outside the temporal clause.

cum venisset: Temporal clause; the relative adverb **cum** ("after, when") with the pluperfect subjunctive describes the circumstances that preceded the action of the main verb (A.G. 546). **venisset**: The main verb of the subordinate clause (A.G. 278.b). The pronoun **is**, with **ille** (**Caesar**) as the antecedent, is understood as the subject (A.G. 271.a).

magna difficultate: Ablative of manner with a limiting adjective (A.G. 412).

adficiebatur: The main verb of the main clause (A.G. 278.b). The pronoun **is**, with **ille** (**Caesar**) as the antecedent, is understood as the subject (A.G. 271.a).

qua ... posset: Indirect question with the subjunctive; the phrase depends on the expression of uncertainty in the phrase **magna difficultate adficiebatur** (A.G. 573-75). **qua**: See below. **posset**: The main verb of the subordinate clause (A.G. 278.b). Imperfect subjunctive; the tense of the subjunctive is in secondary sequence and follows the rules for the sequence of tense for indirect questions after **adficiebatur** (A.G. 575). The pronoun **is**, with **ille** (**Caesar**) as the antecedent, is understood as the subject (A.G. 271.a).

qua ratione: Ablative of manner with a limiting adjective (A.G. 412). **qua**: Singular, feminine, ablative interrogative pronoun used as an adjective modifying **ratione** (A.G. 148).

ad exercitum: Prepositional phrase, **ad** with the accusative here means "to" (*OLD* **ad** 1).

pervenire: Complementary infinitive after **posset** (A.G. 456).

(6.3-4) Nam, si legiones in provciam arcesseret, se absente in itinere proelio dimi(4)caturas intellegebat;

absens (part. of **absum**), **-entis**, *absent*
dimico, -are, -avi, -atus, *fight, contend, struggle*.
intellego, -legere, -lexi, -lectus, *understand, perceive, ascertain*.
legio, -onis, f., *legion*.
proelium, -i, n., *battle, combat, engagement*.
si, *if*.

arcesso, -sere, -sivi, -situs, *send for, summon*.
in, *to, towards; on, during*.
iter, itineris, n., *line of march, march, road, route*.
nam, *for*.
provcia, ae, f., *the province*.
sui, sibi, se, or **sese**, nom. wanting, *he, with or without himself*.

Nam: Conjunction, here explanatory meaning "for" (*OLD* **nam** 2).

si ... arcesseret ... (esse) dimicaturas: Conditional statement in indirect discourse after **intellegebat** (A.G. 589). The protasis, as a dependent clause, is in the subjunctive and the apodosis, as the principal clause, is in the infinitive (A.G. 589.1-2).

si ... arcesseret: The conjunction **si** ("if") with the subjunctive forms the protasis of the conditional statement (A.G. 589.1).

arcesseret: The main verb of the subordinate clause (A.G. 278.b). Imperfect subjunctive; the tense of the subjunctive is in secondary sequence and follows the rules for the sequence of tense after **intellegebat** (A.G. 585). Third conjugation iterative verbs end in **-esso** (A.G. 263.2.b). The pronoun **is**, with **ille** (**Caesar**) as the antecedent, is understood as the subject (A.G. 271.a).

legiones: Accusative direct object of **arcesseret** (A.G. 387).

in proviciam: Accusative of *place to which* with the preposition **in** (A.G. 426.2). **proviciam**: See Appendix A.

se absente: Ablative absolute (A.G. 419-20). **se**: Singular, masculine, ablative indirect reflexive pronoun (A.G. 300.2). The antecedent is **is** (**Caesar**), the supplied subject of **intellegebat** (A.G. 299). **absente**: Present participle of **absum** (A.G. 170.b). The participle ends in **-e** rather than **-i** in the ablative singular when used in an ablative absolute (A.G. 121.2). The present participle represents the action as in progress at the time indicated by the tense of the main verb (A.G. 489).

in itinere: Prepositional phrase, **in** with the ablative of **iter** means "en route, (while) traveling or marching" (*OLD* **iter** 3). "The length of a day's march of course varied greatly, according to the nature of the country and the need for haste. As the soldier had to carry from forty-five to sixty pounds of arms and baggage, and as the army had to halt early in the afternoon to give time for making camp, the rate of march of the army could be nothing like that of an unencumbered individual. Probably when there was no need of haste the average march was no more than twelve to fifteen miles, and a day of rest was given about every fifth day." (Walker, 31)

proelio: Ablative of *place where* without a preposition (A.G. 429.3).

(eas) dimicaturas (esse): The apodosis of the conditional statement (A.G. 589.2). Accusative/infinitive construction in indirect discourse after **intellegebat** (A.G. 577 ff. and 589). Supply the pronoun **eas**, with **legiones** as the antecedent, as the accusative subject. **dimicaturas (esse)**: Supply **esse** to form the future active infinitive (A.G. 184). The tense of the infinitive in indirect discourse is relative to that of the verb of saying (A.G. 584).

intellegebat: The main verb of the main clause (A.G. 278.b). The pronoun **is**, with **ille** (**Caesar**) as the antecedent, is understood as the subject (A.G. 271.a).

(6.4) **si ipse ad exercitum contenderet, ne eis quidem eo tempore qui quieti viderentur, suam salutem recte committi videbat.**

ad, *to*.
contendo, -tendere, -tendi, -tentus, *hasten, make haste, push forward*.
ipse, -a, -um, *he, they*, with or without *himself, themselves*.
ne ... quidem, *not even*.
quietus, a, um, *peaceful, at peace*.
salus, -utis, f., *health, welfare, safety*.
suus, -a, -um, *his*, with or without *own*.
video, videre, visi, visus, *perceive, observe, understand*.

committo, -mittere, -misi, -missus, *intrust, commit*.
exercitus, -us, m., *army*.
is, ea, id, *he, she, it; that, this*.
qui, quae, quod, *who, which, what*.
recte, *safely*.
si, *if*.
tempus, -oris, n., *time*.
videor, videri, visus sum, *seem, appear*.

si ... contenderet ... committi: Conditional statement in indirect discourse after **videbat** (A.G. 589). The protasis, as a dependent clause, is in the subjunctive and the apodosis, as the principal clause, is in the infinitive (589.1-2).

si ... contenderet: The conjunction **si** ("if") with the subjunctive forms the protasis of the conditional statement (A.G. 589.1).

contenderet: The main verb of the subordinate clause (A.G. 278.b). Imperfect subjunctive; the tense of the subjunctive is in secondary sequence and follows the rules for the sequence of tense after **videbat** (A.G. 585).

ipse: Singular, masculine, nominative demonstrative pronoun used substantively (A.G. 296.2 and 298.d). The antecedent is **ille** (**Caesar**) (A.G. 298). Nominative subject (A.G. 339). The pronoun is here emphatic (A.G. 298.d.1).

ad exercitum: Accusative of *place to which* with the preposition **ad** (A.G. 426.2).

ne ... quidem: The negative adverb with the particle means "not even" (*OLD* **ne1** 6). The emphatic word must stand between **ne** and **quidem** (A.G. 322.f).

eis: Plural, masculine, dative demonstrative pronoun used substantively (296.2). The pronoun is correlative to the relative clause **qui ... viderentur** (A.G. 297.d). Dative indirect object of the passive infinitive **committi**; verbs which in the active voice take the accusative and dative retain the dative when used in the passive (A.G. 365).

eo tempore: Ablative of *time when* (A.G. 423.1). **eo**: Singular, neuter, ablative demonstrative pronoun used as an adjective modifying **tempore** (296.1 and a).

qui ... viderentur: Relative clause; a subordinate clause in indirect discourse takes the subjunctive (A.G. 303 and 580). **qui**: Plural, masculine, nominative relative pronoun used substantively (A.G. 305). The antecedent is **eis** (A.G. 307). Nominative subject (A.G. 339). **viderentur**: The main verb of the subordinate clause (A.G. 278.b). Imperfect subjunctive; the tense of the subjunctive is in secondary sequence and follows the rules for the sequence of tense after **videbat** (A.G. 585).

quieti (esse): Plural, masculine, nominative predicate adjective modifying **qui** after **viderentur** (A.G. 283). A predicate adjective after a complementary infinitive takes the case of the subject of the main verb (A.G. 283-84 and 458). Supply **esse** as the complementary infinitive after **viderentur**.

suam salutem ... committti: The apodosis of the conditional statement (A.G. 589.2). Accusative/infinitive construction in indirect discourse after **videbat** (A.G. 577 ff. and 589). **suam**: Singular, feminine, accusative possessive pronoun used as an adjective modifying **salutem** (A.G. 302). **committti**: Present infinitive; the tense of the infinitive in indirect discourse is relative to that of the verb of saying (A.G. 584).

recte: Adverb (A.G. 214.a and 320-21).
videbat: The main verb of the main clause (A.G. 278.b). The pronoun is, with ipse (Caesar) as the antecedent, is understood as the subject (A.G. 271.a).

(7.1-2) Interim Lucterius Cadurcus in Rutenos missus eam (2) civitatem Arvernis conciliat.

Arverni, -orum, m., pl., *the Arverni.*
civitas, -tatis, f., *state, nation.*

in, *into the country of, against.*
is, ea, id, *he, she, it; that, this.*
mitto, mittere, misi, missus, *send.*

Cadurcus, -i, m., *a Cadurcian.*
concilio, -are, -avi, -atus, *win over, make friendly, reconcile.*
interim, *in the meantime, meanwhile.*
Lucterius, i, m., *Lucterius.*
Ruteni, -orum, m., pl., *the Ruteni.*

Interim: Adverb (A.G. 320-21).
Lucterius ... missus: Nominative subject (A.G. 339). Lucterius: See Appendix A. missus: Nominative, perfect, passive, participle used as a predicate, where in English a phrase or a subordinate clause would be more normal (A.G. 496). See 5.1-2 for the reference.
Cadurcus: A nominative noun in apposition to the proper noun Lucterius (A.G. 288).
in Rutenos: Accusative of *place to which* with the preposition in meaning "into the country of" (A.G. 426.2). Rutenos: See Appendix A.
eam civitatem: Accusative direct object of conciliat (A.G. 387). eam: Singular, feminine, accusative demonstrative pronoun used as an adjective modifying civitatem (A.G. 296.1 and a).
Arvernis: Dative indirect object of the transitive verb conciliat (A.G. 362). See Appendix A.
conciliat: The main verb of the simple sentence (A.G. 278.1). The historical present, giving vividness to the narrative, is present in Chapter 7 (A.G. 469). This usage, common in all languages, comes from imagining past events as going on before our eyes (*repraesentatio*) (A.G. 469 Note).

(7.2-3) Progressus in Nitiobriges et Gabalos ab utrisque obsides accipit et magna coacta manu in provinciam Narbonem versus eruptionem facere con (3)tendit.

ab, *from.*

cogo, cogere, coegi, coactus, *bring together, collect, assemble.*

eruptio, -onis, f., *a bursting forth, sally, sortie.*
facio, facere, feci, factus, *make, do.*
in, *into the country of, against; to, into.*
manus, -us, f., *band, force.*
Nitiobriges, -um, m., pl., *the Nitiobriges.*
progredior, -gredi, -gressus, *advance, go forward, proceed.*
utrique, utrourmque, m., pl., *both peoples.*

accipio, -cipere, -cepi, -ceptus, *take to one's self, receive, accept.*
contendo, -tendere, -tendi, -tentus, *hasten, make effort, strive.*
et, *and.*
Gabali, -orum, m., pl., *the Gabali.*
magnus, -a, -um, *great, large.*
Narbo, -onis, m., *Narbo.*
obses, -idis, m. and f., *hostage.*
provincia, -ae, f., *the province.*
versus, *in the direction of, towards.*

Progressus: Nominative, perfect, passive, participle used as a predicate, where in English a phrase or a subordinate clause would be more normal (A.G. 496). The pronoun is, with Lucterius as the antecedent, is understood. Nominative subject of accipit ... contendit (A.G. 339).
in Nitiobriges et Gabalos: Accusative of *place to which* with the preposition in meaning "into the country of" (A.G. 426.2).
Nitiobriges: See Appendix A. et: The conjunction connects the two nouns in the prepositional phrase (A.G. 324.a). Gabalos: See Appendix A.
ab utrisque: Ablative of source with the preposition ab (A.G. 403.1). utrisque: Plural, masculine, ablative pronoun used substantively (*OLD* uterque 3). The antecedent is Nitiobriges et Gabalos (A.G. 313).
obsides: Accusative direct object of accipit (A.G. 387).
accipit: The main verb of the coordinate clause Progressus ... accipit (A.G. 278.a).
et: The conjunction connects the two main verbs accipit ... contendit (A.G. 324.a).
magna coacta manu: Ablative absolute (A.G. 419-20). coacta: The perfect tense of the participle represents the action as completed at the time indicated by the tense of the main verb (A.G. 489).
in provinciam: Accusative of *place to which* with the preposition in (A.G. 426.2). provinciam: See Appendix A.
Narbonem versus: Prepositional phrase, versus is an adverb having prepositional force with the accusative and meaning "in the direction of, towards" (*OLD* versus2 2.a). Narbonem: The city Narbo was the capital of the province. See Appendix A. versus: The adverb regularly follows its noun (A.G. 435).
eruptionem: Accusative direct object of the infinitive facere (A.G. 387 and 451.3).
facere: Complementary infinitive after contendit (A.G. 456).
contendit: The main verb of the coordinate clause magna ... contendit (A.G. 278.a).

(7.3-4) Qua re nuntiata Caesar omnibus consiliis ante(4)vertendum existimavit, ut Nar(5)bonem proficisceretur.

anteverto, -teri, -ti, -----, *prefer, take precedence.*
consilium, -i, n., *plan, design, scheme.*
Narbo, -onis, m., *Narbo.*
omnis, -e, *all, every.*
qui, quae, quod, *who, which, what.*
ut, *namely that, to the effect that.*

Caesar, -aris, m., *Caesar.*
existimo, -are, -avi, -atus, *think, consider, judge.*
nuntio, -are, -avi, -atus, *announce, report.*
proficiscor, -ficisci, -fectus, *set out, depart, proceed.*
res, rei, f., *matter, affair, event.*

Qua re nuntiata: Ablative absolute (A.G. 419-20). **qua**: Singular, feminine, ablative relative pronoun (A.G. 305). The antecedent is **re** in its own clause (adjectival use) (A.G. 307.b). The relative does not introduce a relative clause but is a connecting relative; at the beginning of a clause the pronoun is often best rendered by a personal or demonstrative pronoun, with or without *and* (A.G. 308.f). **nuntiata**: The perfect tense of the participle represents the action as completed at the time indicated by the tense of the main verb (A.G. 489).

Caesar: Nominative subject (A.G. 339). See Appendix A.

omnibus consiliis: Dative indirect object of the intransitive infinitive **antevertendum (esse)** (A.G. 451.3). When intransitive verbs that govern the dative are used impersonally in the passive the dative is retained (A.G. 372).

(id) antevertendum (esse): Accusative/infinitive construction in indirect discourse after **existimavit** (A.G. 577 ff). **antevertendum (esse)**: Supply **esse** to form the second periphrastic (passive) present infinitive with the gerundive implying necessity (A.G. 194.b and 196). The tense of the infinitive in indirect discourse is relative to that of the verb of saying (A.G. 584). Impersonal use of the verb (A.G. 207.d). Supply **id** as the accusative subject (A.G. 318.c).

existimavit: The main verb of the main clause (A.G. 278.b).

ut ... proficisceretur: The conjunction **ut** ("namely that, to the effect that") introduces an epexegetical clause with the subjunctive in apposition to the supplied neuter pronoun **id** (*OLD* **ut** 39). **proficisceretur**: The main verb of the subordinate clause (A.G. 278.b). Imperfect subjunctive; the tense of the subjunctive is in secondary sequence and follows the rules for the sequence of tense after **existimavit** (A.G. 585). The pronoun **is**, with **Caesar** as the antecedent, is understood as the subject (A.G. 271.a).

Narbonem: Accusative of *place to which* without a preposition (being the name of a town) (A.G. 427.2). See Appendix A.

(7.4-5) Eo cum venisset timentis confirmat, praesidia in Rutenis provincialibus, Volcis Arecomicis, Tolosatibus circumque Narbonem, quae loca hostibus erant finitima, constituit;

circum, *in the vicinity of, somewhere near* or *in.*
constituo, -stituere, -stitui, -stitutus, *station, place, establish.*
eo, *thither, there.*

hostis, -is, m., *enemy, foe*; pl., *the enemy.*
loca, -orum, n., pl., *places, positions.*
praesidium, -i, n., *guard, garrison, fortress, redoubt.*
-que, *and.*
Ruteni, -orum, m., pl., *the Ruteni.*
timeo, -ere, -ui, -----, *have fear, be afraid, be apprehensive.*
venio, venire, veni, ventus, *come.*

confirmo, -are, -avi, -atus, *reassure, encourage.*
cum, *after, when.*
finitimus, -a, -um, *bordering on, neighboring, adjoining.*
in, *in, among.*
Narbo, -onis, m., *Narbo.*
provincialis, -e, *of the province.*
qui, quae, quod, *who, which, what.*
sum, esse, fui, futurus, *be.*
Tolosates, -ium, m., pl., *the inhabitants of Tolosa.*
Volcae Arecomici, -arum -orum, m., pl., *the Volci Arecomici.*

Eo: Adverb (A.G. 217.a and 320-21). The adverb is standing outside the temporal clause.

cum venisset: Temporal clause; the relative adverb **cum** ("after, when") with the pluperfect subjunctive describes the circumstances that preceded the action of the main verb (A.G. 546). **venisset**: The main verb of the subordinate clause (A.G. 278.b). The pronoun **is**, with **Caesar** as the antecedent, is understood as the subject (A.G. 271.a).

timentis: Plural, masculine, accusative present participle used substantively (A.G. 494.a). The noun **milites** is understood (A.G. 288.b). Accusative direct object of **confirmat** (A.G. 387). Accusative plural; **-is** for **-es** is the regular form in the present participle (A.G. 117-18).

confirmat: The main verb of the coordinate clause **Eo ... confirmat** (A.G. 278.a). The pronoun **is**, with **Caesar** as the antecedent, is understood as the subject (A.G. 271.a).

praesidia: Accusative direct object of **constituit** (A.G. 387).

in Rutenis provincialibus, Volcis Arecomicis, Tolosatibus: Ablative of *place where* with the preposition **in** (locative ablative) (A.G. 426.3). Note the asyndeton construction (A.G. 323.b). See Appendix A for each tribe. **provincialibus**: "Only a part of the Rutini were in the province." (Kelsey, 402)

circumque Narbonem: Prepositional phrase, **circum** with the accusative here means "in the vicinity of, somewhere near or in" (*OLD* **circum** 5). **-que**: The enclitic conjunction is used to connect the last member of a series (A.G. 323.c.3). **Narbonem**: See Appendix A.

quae ... finitima: Relative clause (A.G. 303). **quae**: See below. **finitima**: Plural, neuter, nominative predicate adjective modifying **loca** after **erant** (A.G. 283-84).

quae loca: Nominative subject (A.G. 339). **quae**: Plural, neuter, nominative relative pronoun (A.G 305). The antecedent is **loca** in its own clause (adjectival use) (A.G. 307.b).

hostibus: Dative after the adjective **finitima** (A.G. 383-84).

erant: The main verb of the subordinate clause (A.G. 278.b).

constituit: The main verb of the coordinate clause **praesidia ... constituit** (A.G. 278.a). The pronoun **is**, with **Caesar** as the antecedent, is understood as the subject (A.G. 271.a). Notice the asyndeton between the two main verbs **confirmat ... constituit** (A.G. 323.b).

(7.5) partem copiarum ex provincia supplementumque quod ex Italia adduxerat in Helvios, qui finis Arvernorum contingunt, convenire iubet.

adduco, -ducere, -duxi, -ductus, *bring up, lead.*
contingo, -tingere, -tigi, -tactus, *touch, extend to, reach.*

copiae, -arum, f., pl., *forces, troops.*
fines, -ium, m., pl., *borders,* hence *territory, country, land.*
in, *into the country of, against.*
iubeo, iubere, iussi, iussus, *order, give orders, bid, command.*
provincia, -ae, f., *the province.*
qui, quae, quod, *who, which, what.*

Arverni, -orum, m., pl., *the Arverni.*
convenio, -venire, -veni, -ventus, *come together, assemble.*
ex, *from, out of.*
Helvii, -orum, m., pl., *the Helvii.*
Italia, -ae, f., *Italy.*
pars, partis, f., *part, portion.*
-que, *and.*
supplementum, -i, n., *reinforcement, reinforcements.*

partem ... supplementumque ... convenire: Two subject accusatives with the infinitive after **iubet**. The construction is equivalent to a substantive clause of purpose (A.G. 563.a). **supplementum**: "The troops lately levied in Cisalpine Gaul (7.1.1); they were seemingly not enrolled with the legions already in the field, nor made separate legions by themselves." (Kelsey, 402) **-que**: The enclitic conjunction connects the two accusative nouns (A.G. 324.a).
copiarum: Partitive genitive with **partem** (A.G. 346.a.1).
ex provincia: Ablative of *place from which* with the preposition **ex** (426.1). **provincia**: See Appendix A.
quod ... adduxerat: Relative clause (A.G. 303). **quod**: Singular, neuter, accusative relative pronoun used substantively (A.G. 305). The antecedent is **supplementum** (A.G. 307). Accusative direct object of **adduxerat** (A.G. 387). **adduxerat**: The main verb of the subordinate clause (A.G. 278.b). The pronoun **is**, with **Caesar** as the antecedent, is understood as the subject (A.G. 271.a). The pluperfect tense of the verb denotes an action completed in past time (A.G. 477).
ex Italia: Ablative of *place from which* with the preposition **ex** (426.1). **Italia**: See Appendix A.
in Helvios: Accusative of *place to which* with the preposition **in** meaning "into the country of" (A.G. 426.2). **Helvios**: See Appendix A.
qui ... contingunt: Relative clause (A.G. 303). **qui**: Plural, masculine, nominative relative pronoun used substantively (A.G. 305). The antecedent is **Helvios** (A.G. 307). Nominative subject (A.G. 339). **contingunt**: The main verb of the subordinate clause (A.G. 278.b). The present tense is not the historical present but denotes a state as now existing in present time (A.G. 465.1).
finis: Accusative direct object of **contingunt** (A.G. 387). Accusative plural noun; **-is** for **-es** is the regular form in i-stem nouns (A.G. 65-7 and 74.c).
Arvernorum: Possessive genitive with **finis** (A.G. 343). See Appendix A.
iubet: The main verb of the main clause (A.G. 278.b). The pronoun **is**, with **Caesar** as the antecedent, is understood as the subject (A.G. 271.a).

(8.1-2) His rebus comparatis, represso iam Lucterio et remoto, quod intrare intra praesidia periculosum putabat, in Helvios (2) proficiscitur.

comparo, -are, -avi, -atus, *prepare, make ready, get together.*
Helvii, -orum, m., pl., *the Helvii.*
iam, *already, by this time.*
intra, *within, inside of.*
Lucterius, -i, m., *Lucterius.*
praesidium, -i, n., *garrison, fortress, redoubt.*
puto, -are, -avi, -atus, *think, consider, believe, judge.*
removeo, -movere, -movi, -motus, *move back, remove.*
res, rei, f., *preparation, affair.*

et, *and.*
hic, haec, hoc, *this; he, she, it.*
in, *into the country of.*
intro, -are, -avi, -atus, *enter, go in.*
periculosus, -a, -um, *full of danger, dangerous.*
proficiscor, -ficisci, -fectus, *set out, depart, proceed.*
quod, *because, since, for, as.*
reprimo, -primere, -pressi, -pressus, *restrain, check.*

His rebus comparatis: Ablative absolute (A.G. 419-20). **His**: Plural, feminine, ablative demonstrative pronoun used as an adjective modifying **rebus** (A.G. 296.1 and a). **comparatis**: The perfect tense of the participle represents the action as completed at the time indicated by the tense of the main verb (A.G. 489).
represso ... putabat: Ablative absolute with a dependent clause.
represso iam Lucterio et remoto: Ablative absolute (A.G. 419-20). Notice the asyndeton between the two ablative absolutes (A.G. 323.b). **represso ... remoto**: The perfect tense of the participles represents the action as completed at the time indicated by the tense of the main verb (A.G. 489). **iam**: Adverb (A.G. 215.6, 217.b and 320-21). **Lucterio**: See Appendix A. **et**: The conjunction connects the two participles modifying **Lucterio** (A.G. 324.a). Two adjectives belonging to the same noun are regularly connected by a conjunction (A.G. 323.d).
quod ... putabat: Causal clause; the conjunction **quod** ("because") takes the indicative when the reason is given on the authority of the writer or speaker (A.G. 540.1). **putabat**: The main verb of the subordinate clause (A.G. 278.b). The pronoun **is**, with **Lucterio** as the antecedent, is understood as the subject (A.G. 271.a).

intrare intra praesidia: The infinitive phrase functions as the subject of the impersonal verb **periculosum (esse)** (A.G. 454). **intra praesidia**: Prepositional phrase, **intra** with the accusative here means "within, inside" (*OLD* intra 1).

periculosum (esse): Impersonal infinitive construction in indirect discourse after **putabat** (A.G. 577 ff). Supply **esse** to form the impersonal verb (A.G. 208.c). **periculosum**: Singular, neuter, accusative predicate adjective after the supplied **esse** (A.G. 283-84). Adjectives meaning *full of, prone to,* are formed from noun-stems with the suffix -osus (A.G. 245).

in Helvios: Accusative of *place to which* with the preposition **in** meaning "into the country of" (A.G. 426.2). **Helvios**: See Appendix A.

proficiscitur: The main verb of the main clause (A.G. 278.b). The historical present, giving vividness to the narrative, is present in Chapter 8 (A.G. 469). This usage, common in all languages, comes from imagining past events as going on before our eyes (*repraesentatio*) (A.G. 469 Note). The pronoun **is**, with **Caesar** as the antecedent, is understood as the subject (A.G. 271.a).

(8.2-3) Etsi mons Cevenna, qui Arvernos ab Helviis discludit, durissimo tempore anni, altissima nive iter impediebat, tamen discussa nive sex in altitudinem pedum atque ita viis patefactis summo militum sudore ad finis (3) Arvernorum pervenit.

ab, *from*.	**ad**, *to*.
altitudo, -onis, f., *depth*.	**altus, -a, um**, sup. -issimus, *high, deep*.
annus, -i, m., *year*.	**Arverni, -orum**, m., pl., *the Arverni*.
atque, *and*.	**Cevenna, -ae**, f., *the Cevennes*.
discludo, -cludere, -clusi, -clusus, *separate*.	**discutio, -cutere, -cussi, -cussus**, *remove, clear away*.
durus, -a, -um, sup. -issimus, *inclement*.	**etsi**, *although, though*.
fines, -ium, m., pl., *borders*, hence *territory, country, land*.	**Helvii, -orum**, m., pl., *the Helvii*.
impedio, -pedire, -pedivi, -peditus, *hinder, obstruct*.	**in**, *to*.
ita, *in this way, so, thus*.	**iter, itineris**, n., *line of march, march, road, route*.
miles, -itis, m., *soldier, foot-solider*.	**mons, montis**, m., *mountain, mountain-range*.
nix, nivis, f., *snow*.	**patefacio, -facere, -feci, -factus**, *lay open, open, clear*.
pervenio, -venire, -veni, -ventus, *come, reach*.	**pes, pedis**, m., *foot*, = .9708 of the English foot.
qui, quae, quod, *who, which, what*.	**sex**, *six*.
sudor, -oris, m., *sweat, toil, effort*.	**summus, -a, -um**, *utmost, greatest*.
tamen, *yet, still, for all that, nevertheless, however*.	**tempus, -oris**, n., *time*.
via, -ae, f., *way, road*.	

Etsi ... impediebat: Concessive clause; the conjunction **etsi** ("although") with the indicative forms a dependent clause which is made clearer by the adversative particle **tamen** ("nevertheless") in the main clause (A.G. 526 and 527.c). **impediebat**: The main verb of the subordinate clause (A.G. 278.b).

mons: Nominative subject (A.G. 339).

Cevenna: A nominative proper noun in apposition to **mons** (A.G. 282). See Appendix A.

qui ... discludit: Relative clause (A.G. 303). **qui**: Singular, masculine, nominative relative pronoun used substantively (A.G. 305). The antecedent is **mons** (A.G. 307). Nominative subject (A.G. 339). **discludit**: The main verb of the subordinate clause (A.G. 278.b). The present tense is not the historical present but denotes a state as now existing in present time (A.G. 465.1).

Arvernos: Accusative direct object of **discludit** (A.G. 387). See Appendix A.

ab Helviis: Ablative of separation with the preposition **ab** after **discludit** (A.G. 401). **Helviis**: See Appendix A.

durissimo tempore: Ablative of *time when* (A.G. 423.1). **durissimo**: Superlative adjective modifying **tempore** (A.G. 124). Note the three superlative adjectives in this sentence (**durissimo, altissima, summo**) which serve to emphasize the magnitude of the undertaking. **tempore**: "It was probably the latter part of February according to the Calendar, but mid-winter in reality." (Kelsey, 402)

anni: Partitive genitive with **tempore** (A.G. 346.a.1).

altissima nive: Ablative means or instrument (A.G. 409). **altissima**: Superlative adjective (A.G. 124).

iter: Accusative direct object of **impediebat** (A.G. 387).

tamen: Adverb, correlative to **etsi** meaning "nevertheless" (A.G. 527.c) (*OLD* tamen 3). The adverb is normally postpositive but not here (A.G. 324.j).

discussa nive sex in altitudinem pedum: Ablative absolute (A.G. 419-20). **discussa**: The perfect tense of the participle represents the action as completed at the time indicated by the tense of the main verb (A.G. 489). **sex ... pedum**: Genitive of quality (measure) with **altitudinem** (A.G. 345.b). **sex**: Indeclinable cardinal number used as an adjective (A.G. 132-35). **in altitudinem**: Prepositional phrase, **in** with the accusative here means "to" (*OLD* in 14).

atque: The conjunction connects the two ablative absolutes and means "and" (*OLD* atque 12).

ita viis patefactis summo militum sudore: Ablative absolute (A.G. 419-20). **ita**: Adverb (A.G. 217.c and 320-21). **viis patefactis**: The noun, participle element of the ablative absolute (A.G. 419-20). **patefactis**: The perfect tense of the participle represents the action as completed at the time indicated by the tense of the main verb (A.G. 489). **summo ... sudore**: Ablative of manner with a limiting adjective (A.G. 412). **summo**: Irregular superlative adjective (A.G. 130.b). **sudore**: The noun here means "sweat," used as a symbol of toil or exertion (*OLD* sudor 2). **militum**: Possessive genitive with **sudore** (A.G. 343). Fuller provides this description of the typical Roman soldier: "It is generally held that his soldiers were close cropped and clean shaven; that they wore long, sleeveless woollen shirts, and in cold we"Ther wollen drawers, puttees, and a blanket-like cloak, which was fashioned together on their right shoulder. Except for metal helmet, large rectangular shield, and possibly a greave on the right leg, which was unprotected by the shield, nothing further is definitely known of their defensive weapons. ... Their offensive weapons were a Spanish sword, a dagger, and a pilum." (Fuller, 84) Kahn assesses the character of the Roman soldiers this way: "Disciplined and courageous, persevering under the harshest trials, they have an intense espirit de corps and reject retreat as a disgrace. Because of their magnificent discipline, Caesar can effect complicated maneuvers in rapid succession, relying upon each man to carry out his responsibility. The key to their morale is their dedication to Rome and their loyalty to their commander. But they have failings. Occasionally, forgetful of their Roman discipline, they rampage, pressing an attack beyond orders and panicking when they are overextended." (Kahn, 252) For disciplined and hardy soldiers in Book 7 see Chapter 17, they withstand hunger at Avaricum; 19, they beg to fight; 24, they overcome obstacles; 41, some hold out against a superior force while others march incredible distances; 50, Lucius Fabius gives his life for his men; 56, they cross the Lorie River without a bridge; 72-74, they build massive siege-works; 79-88, they withstand three assaults from a vastly superior force. For examples of where they overextend in Book 7 see Chapter 28, the fearful slaughter at Avaricum; 47-51, they do not obey the military tribunes and legates; Lucius Fabius (47) is exhibited as the paradigm.

ad finis Arvernorum: Accusative of *place to which* with the preposition **ad** (A.G 296.2). **finis**: Accusative plural noun; **-is** for **-es** is the regular form in i-stem nouns (A.G. 65-7 and 74.c). **Arvernorum**: Possessive genitive with **finis** (A.G. 343). See Appendix A.
pervenit: The main verb of the main clause (A.G. 278.b). The pronoun **is**, with **Caesar** as the antecedent, is understood as the subject (A.G. 271.a).

(8.3-4) Quibus oppressis inopinantibus, quod se Cevenna ut muro munitos existimabant, ac ne singulari quidem umquam homini eo tempore anni semitae patuerant, equitibus imperat ut quam latissime possint vagentur et (4) quam maximum hostibus terrorem inferant.

ac, *and.*
Cevenna, -ae, f., *the Cevennes.*
et, *and.*
homo, hominis, m., *man, person.*
impero, -are, -avi, -atus, *command, order.*
inopinans, -antis, *not expecting, unaware, off one's guard.*
late, sup. -latissime, *far, broad.*
munio, -ire, -ivi, -itus, *fortify, protect, secure.*
ne ... quidem, *not even.*

pateo, patere, patui, -----, *be open, lie open, stand open.*
quam, with sup. -- *as ---- as possible.*
quod, *because, since, for, as.*
singularis, -e, *one by one, solitary, one at a time.*

tempus, -oris, n., *time.*
umquam, *at any time, ever.*
vagor, -ari, -atus, *wander, wander about, roam about, rove.*

annus, -i, m., *year.*
eques, -itis, m., *rider, horseman, cavalryman, trooper.*
existimo, -are, -avi, -atus, *think, consider, judge.*
hostis, -is, m., *enemy, foe;* pl., *the enemy.*
infero, -ferre, intuli, illatus, *inflict, infuse.*
is, ea, id, *he, she, it; that, this.*
maximus, -a, -um, *much.*
murus, -i, m., *wall, rampart.*
opprimo, -primere, -pressi, -pressus, *take by surprise, surprise, fall upon.*
possum, posse, potui, -----, *be able.*
qui, quae, quod, *who, which, what.*
semita, -ae, f., *path, by-way, a narrow path.*
sui, sibi, se, or sese, nom. wanting, *they,* with or without *themselves.*
terror, -oris, m., *fear, dread, alarm, terror.*
ut, *just as, like; so that.*

Quibus ... patuerant: Ablative absolute with a dependent clause.
Quibus oppressis inopinantibus: Ablative absolute (A.G. 419-20). **quibus**: Plural, masculine, ablative relative pronoun used substantively (A.G. 305). The antecedent is **Arvernorum** (A.G. 307). The relative does not introduce a relative clause but is a connecting relative; at the beginning of a clause the pronoun is often best rendered by a personal or demonstrative pronoun, with or without *and* (A.G. 308.f). **oppressis**: The perfect tense of the participle represents the action as completed at the time indicated by the tense of the main verb (A.G. 489). **inopinantibus**: A predicate adjective modifying **Quibus** (A.G. 285.2).
quod ... existimabant ... patuerant: Causal clause depending on **inopinantibus**; the conjunction **quod** ("because) takes the indicative when the reason is given on the authority of the writer or speaker (A.G. 540.1). **existimabant ... patuerant**: The main verbs of the subordinate clause (A.G. 278.b). **existimabant**: The pronoun **ei**, with **Quibus (Arverni)** as the antecedent, is understood as the subject (A.G. 271.a). **patuerant**: The pluperfect denotes an action in indefinite time, but prior to some past time referred to (A.G. 477).
se ... munitos (esse): Accusative infinitive construction in indirect discourse after **existimabant** (A.G. 577 ff.). **se**: Plural, masculine, accusative direct reflexive pronoun (A.G. 300.1). The antecedent is **ei (Arverni)**, the supplied subject of **existimabant** A.G. 299). **munitos (esse)**: Supply **esse** to form the perfect, passive infinitive (A.G. 187). The tense of the infinitive in indirect discourse is relative to that of the verb of saying (A.G. 584).
Cevenna: Ablative of means (A.G. 409). See Appendix A.
ut muro: The relative adverb **ut** ("just as, like") with the noun here introduces a simile (*OLD* ut 7). **muro**: Ablative of means (A.G. 409).
ac: The conjunction connects the two main verbs in the causal clause **existimabant ... patuerant** and means "and" (*OLD* atque 12).
ne ... quidem: The negative adverb with the particle means "not even" (*OLD* ne1 6). The emphatic word must stand between **ne** and **quidem** (A.G. 322.f).
singulari ... homini: Dative indirect object of the intransitive verb **patuerant** (A.G. 366). "Much less a body of troops." (Edwards, 391)
umquam: Adverb (A.G. 217.b and 320-21).
eo tempore: Ablative of *time when* (A.G. 423.1). **eo**: Singular, neuter, ablative demonstrative pronoun used as an adjective modifying **tempore** (A.G. 296.1 and a).

anni: Partitive genitive with **tempore** (A.G. 346.a.1).

semitae: Nominative subject (A.G. 339).

equitibus: Dative indirect object of the normally intransitive verb **imperat** (A.G. 369).

imperat: The main verb of the main clause (A.G. 278.b). The pronoun **is**, with **Caesar** as the antecedent, is understood as the subject (A.G. 271.a).

ut ... vagentur ... inferant: The conjunction **ut** ("so that") with the subjunctive forms a substantive clause of purpose which is used as the object of the verb **imperat** denoting an action directed toward the future (A.G. 563). **vagentur ... inferant**: The main verbs of the subordinate clause (A.G. 278.b). Present subjunctives; the tense of the subjunctives is normally in secondary sequence after the historical present **imperat** (A.G. 482-85). Here it is in primary sequence through *repraesentatio* (A.G. 485.e and 585.b Note). The pronoun **ei**, with **equitibus** as the antecedent, is understood as the subject of both verbs (A.G. 271.a).

quam latissime possint: Relative clause (A.G. 279.a). A clause dependent on a subjunctive clause (**ut ... vagentur**) will itself take the subjunctive if regarded as an integral part of that clause (attraction) (A.G. 593). **quam**: The relative adverb with the superlative denotes the highest possible degree "as broadly as possible" (A.G. 291.c) (*OLD* **quam** 7). **latissime**: Superlative adverb (A.G. 218 and 320-21). **possint**: The main verb of the subordinate clause (A.G. 278.b). Present subjunctive; the tense of the subjunctive is normally in secondary sequence after the historical present **imperat** (A.G. 482-85). Here it is in primary sequence through *repraesentatio* (A.G. 485.e and 585.b Note). The pronoun **ei**, with **equitibus** as the antecedent, is understood as the subject (A.G. 271.a).

et: The conjunction connects the two main verbs in the purpose clause **vagentur ... inferant** (A.G. 324.a).

quam maximum: Relative clause (A.G. 279.a). Here there is an ellipsis of the verb **posse** (*OLD* **quam** 7.b). **quam**: The relative adverb **quam** with the superlative denotes the highest possible degree "as much (fear) as possible" (A.G. 291.c) (*OLD* **quam** 7).

maximum: An irregular superlative adjective modifying **terrorem** (A.G. 129).

terrorem: Accusative direct object of **inferant** (A.G. 387).

hostibus: Dative indirect object of the transitive verb **inferant** (A.G. 362).

(8.4-5) **Celeriter haec fama ac nuntii ad Vercingetorigem perferuntur; quem perterriti omnes Arverni circumsistunt atque obsecrant ut suis fortunis consulat, ne[ve] ab hostibus diripiantur, praesertim (5) cum videat omne ad se bellum translatum.**

ab, *by.*

ad, *to; to, into the hands of.*

atque, *and then.*

celeriter, *quickly, speedily, at once, immediately.*

consulo, -sulere, -sului, -sultus, *have regard for, look out for.*

diripio, -ripere, -ripui, -reptus, *ravage, plunder, pillage.*

fortunae, -arum, f., pl., *possessions, property, fortune.*

hostis, -is, m., *enemy, foe;* pl., *the enemy.*

nuntius, -i, m., *message, tidings.*

omnis, -e, *all, the whole.*

perterreo -terrere, -----, -territus, *greatly alarm, frighten, terrify, dismay.*

qui, quae, quod, *who, which, what.*

suus, -a, -um, *their*, with or without *own.*

ut, *so that.*

video, videre, visi, visus, *perceive, observe, understand.*

ac, *and.*

Arverni, -orum, m., pl., *the Arverni.*

bellum, -i, n., *war, warfare.*

circumsisto, -sistere, -steti, or **-stiti, -----**, *stand around, surround, take a position around.*

cum, *since, seeing that, because, in that.*

fama, -ae, f., *report, rumor.*

hic, haec, hoc, *this; he, she, it.*

ne[ve], *and not, and that not, nor.*

obsecro, -are, -avi, -atus, *beseech, implore, beg.*

perfero, -ferre, -tuli, -latus, *convey, bring, report.*

praesertim, *especially, particularly.*

sui, sibi, se, or **sese**, nom. wanting, *them*, with or without *-selves.*

transfero, -ferre, -tuli, -latus, *transfer, direct, turn.*

Vercingetorix, -igis, m., *Vercingetorix.*

Celeriter: Adverb (A.G. 214.b and 320-21).

haec fama ac nuntii: Two nominative subjects (A.G. 339). **haec**: Singular, feminine, nominative demonstrative pronoun used as an adjective modifying **fama** (A.G. 296.1 and a). **ac**: The conjunction connects the two nominative nouns and means "and" (*OLD* **atque** 12).

ad Vercingetorigem: Prepositional phrase, **ad** with the accusative here means "to" (*OLD* **ad** 1). **Vercingetorigem**: See Appendix A.

perferuntur: The main verb of the simple sentence (A.G. 278.1).

quem: Singular, masculine, accusative relative pronoun used substantively (A.G. 305). The antecedent is **Vercingetorigem** (A.G. 307). Accusative direct object of **circumsistunt** and **obsecrant** (A.G. 387). The relative does not introduce a relative clause but is a connecting relative; at the beginning of a clause the pronoun is often best rendered by a personal or demonstrative pronoun, with or without *and* (A.G. 308.f).

perterriti omnes Arverni: Nominative subject of **circumsistunt ... obsecrant** (A.G. 339). **perterriti**: Nominative, perfect, passive, participle used as a predicate, where in English a phrase or a subordinate clause would be more normal (A.G. 496). **Arverni**: See Appendix A.

circumsistunt: The main verb of the coordinate clause **quem ... circumsistunt** (A.G. 278.a).

atque: The conjunction connects the two main verbs **circumsistunt ... obsecrant** and means "and then" (*OLD* **atque** 7).

obsecrant: The main verb of the coordinate clause **obsecrant ... translatum** (A.G. 278.a).

ut ... consulat: The conjunction **ut** ("so that") with the subjunctive forms a substantive clause of purpose which is used as the object of the verb **obsecrant** denoting an action directed toward the future (A.G. 563). **consulat**: The main verb of the subordinate clause (A.G. 278.b). Present subjunctive; the tense of the subjunctive is normally in secondary sequence after the historical present **obsecrant** (A.G.

482-85). Here it is in primary sequence through *repraesentatio* (A.G. 485.e and 585.b Note). The pronoun **is**, with **quem** (**Vercingetorix**) as the antecedent, is understood as the subject (A.G. 271.a).

suis fortunis: Dative indirect object of the intransitive use of the verb **consulat** (A.G. 366). **suis**: Plural, feminine, dative possessive pronoun used as an adjective modifying **fortunis** (A.G. 302).

ne[ve] ... diripiantur: The conjunction **ne[ve]** with the subjunctive forms a negative substantive clause of purpose which is used as the object of the verb **obsecrant** denoting an action directed toward the future (A.G. 563). **ne[ve]**: The conjunction after **ut** adds a negative purpose clause to a positive one and means "and that ... not" (*OLD* **neve** 2). **[ve]**: Deleted by Dittenberger, resulting in a clause of fearing. **diripiantur**: The main verb of the subordinate clause (A.G. 278.b). Present subjunctive; the tense of the subjunctive is normally in secondary sequence after the historical present **obsecrant** (A.G. 482-85). Here it is in primary sequence through *repraesentatio* (A.G. 485.e and 585.b Note). The pronoun **ei**, with **Arverni** as the antecedent, is understood as the subject (A.G. 271.a).

ab hostibus: Ablative of agent with the preposition **ab** after the passive verb **diripiantur** (A.G. 405).

praesertim: Adverb modifying **cum** (A.G. 320-21).

cum videat: Causal clause; the relative adverb **cum** ("since") with the subjunctive forms a clause expressing cause (A.G. 549). **videat**: The main verb of the subordinate clause (A.G. 278.b). Present subjunctive; the tense of the subjunctive is normally in secondary sequence after the historical present **obsecrant** (A.G. 482-85). Here it is in primary sequence through *repraesentatio* (A.G. 485.e and 585.b Note). The pronoun **is**, with **quem** (**Vercingetorix**) as the antecedent, is understood as the subject (A.G. 271.a).

omne ... bellum translatum (esse): Accusative/infinitive construction in indirect discourse after **videat** (A.G. 577 ff.). **translatum (esse)**: Supply **esse** to form the perfect, passive infinitive (A.G. 200). The tense of the infinitive in indirect discourse is relative to that of the verb of saying (A.G. 584).

ad se: Prepositional phrase, **ad** with the accusative here means "to, into the hands of" (*OLD* **ad** 24). **se**: Plural, masculine, accusative indirect reflexive pronoun (A.G. 300.2). The antecedent is **Arverni**, the subject of **obsecrant** (A.G. 299).

(8.5) Quorum ille precibus permotus castra ex Biturigibus movet in Arvernos versus.

Arverni, -orum, m., pl., *the Arverni.*
castra, -orum, n., pl., *camp, encampment.*
ille, illae, illud, *that; he, she, it.*

moveo, movere, movi, motus, *move.*

prex, precis, f., *prayer, entreaty, supplication.*

Bituriges, -um, m., pl., *the Bituriges.*
ex, *from the country of, from.*
in ... versus, *into the country of, towards, in the direction of.*
permoveo, -movere, -movi, -motus, *deeply move, influence, induce.*
qui, quae, quod, *who, which, what.*

Quorum: Plural, masculine genitive relative pronoun used substantively (A.G. 305). The antecedent is **Arverni** (A.G. 307). Possessive genitive with **precibus** (A.G. 343). The relative does not introduce a relative clause but is a connecting relative; at the beginning of a clause the pronoun is often best rendered by a personal or demonstrative pronoun, with or without *and* (A.G. 308.f).

ille ... permotus: Nominative subject (A.G. 339). **ille**: Singular, masculine, nominative demonstrative pronoun used substantively (A.G. 296.2). The antecedent is **quem** (**Vercingetorix**) (A.G. 297.e). **permotus**: Nominative, perfect, passive participle used as a predicate where in English a phrase or a subordinate clause would be more natural (A.G. 496).

precibus: Ablative of cause without a preposition (A.G. 404).

castra: Accusative direct object of **movet** (A.G. 387). In the plural the noun means "camp" (A.G. 107).

ex Biturigibus: Ablative of *place from which* with the preposition **ex** ("from the country of") (A.G. 426.1). **Biturigibus**: See Appendix A.

movet: The main verb of the simple sentence (A.G. 278.1).

in Arvernos versus: Accusative of *place to which* with the preposition **in ... versus** meaning "into the country of" (A.G. 426.2). **Arvernos**: See Appendix A. **versus**: Adverb, placed after the prepositional phrase **in** with the accusative (pleonastic) (*OLD* **versus2** 1.b).

(9.1-2) At Caesar biduum in his locis moratus, quod haec de Vercingetorige usu ventura opinione praeceperat, per causam supplementi equitatusque cogendi ab exercitu dis(2)cedit;

ab, *from.*
biduum, -i, n., *space of two days, two days.*
causa, -ae, f., *pretext, feigned cause, pretense.*

de, *from, by, on the part of.*

equitatus, -us, m., *cavalry.*
hic, haec, hoc, *this; he, she, it.*
loca, -orum, n., pl., *places, positions.*
opinio, -onis, f., *supposition, conjecture, expectation.*
praecipio, -cipere, -cepi, -ceptus, *anticipate, suspect.*
quod, *because, since, for, as.*
usus, -us, m., (with **venio**), *course of events.*

at, *but, but on the other hand.*
Caesar, -aris, m., *Caesar.*
cogo, cogere, coegi, coactus, *bring together, collect, assemble.*
discedo, -cedere, -cessi, -cessurus, *go away, depart, leave.*
exercitus, -us, m., *army.*
in, *in.*
moror, -ari, -atus, *delay, wait, stay.*
per, *on.*
-que, *and.*
supplementum, -i, n., *reinforcement, reinforcements.*
venio, venire, veni, ventus, *occur.*

Vercingetorix, -igis, m., *Vercingetorix.*

At: Conjunction, introduces a change of subject (A.G. 324.d) (*OLD* **at** 2).

Caesar ... moratus: Nominative subject of **discedit** (A.G. 339). **Caesar**: See Appendix A. **moratus**: Nominative, perfect, deponent participle used as a predicate where in English a phrase or a subordinate clause would be more natural (A.G. 496).

biduum: Accusative of *time how long* (A.G. 423.2).

in his locis: Ablative of *place where* with the preposition **in** (locative ablative) (A.G. 426.3). **his**: Plural, neuter, ablative demonstrative pronoun used as an adjective modifying **locis** (A.G. 296.1 and a).

quod ... praeceperat: Causal clause; the conjunction **quod** ("because") takes the indicative when the reason is given on the authority of the writer or speaker (A.G. 540.1). **praeceperat**: The main verb of the subordinate clause (A.G. 278.b). The pronoun **is**, with **Caesar** as the antecedent, is understood as the subject (A.G. 271.a). The pluperfect tense of the verb denotes an action completed in past time (A.G. 477).

haec ... usu ventura (esse): Accusative/infinitive construction in indirect discourse after **praeceperat** (A.G. 577 ff.). **haec**: Plural, neuter, accusative demonstrative pronoun used substantively (A.G. 296.2). The antecedent is the idea of the movement of Vercingetorix's troops at 8.5 (A.G. 297.e). **usu**: Ablative of specification (A.G. 418). **ventura (esse)**: Supply **esse** to form the future active infinitive (A.G. 187). The tense of the infinitive in indirect discourse is relative to that of the verb of saying (A.G. 584). The phrase **usu venire** is an idiom that means "to occur in the course of events" (*OLD* **venio** 15.c).

de Vercingetorige: Prepositional phrase, **de** with the ablative here means "from, by" (*OLD* **de** 14). **Vercingetorige**: See Appendix A.

opinione: Ablative of means after **praeceperat** (A.G. 409).

per causam supplementi equitatusque cogendi: Prepositional phrase, **per** with the accusative of **causa** with the genitive means "on the pretext of" (*OLD* **causa** 5). **per causam**: "Used of a fictitious or assumed reason through pretended anxiety about the new force, etc. In reality Caesar had no intention of going back to the Province to look after his recruits stationed there, but pushed on to Agedincum and joined his legiones before even his own men suspected that this was his destination. Great caution was necessary to keep information of his proposed movements from the Gauls." (Kelsey, 402) **supplementi equitatusque cogendi**: Two objective genitives after **causam** (A.G. 348). **equitatus**: "Caesar had no Roman cavalry. During his first six years in Gaul he had none but Gallic cavalry, but in the seventh year he secured some Germans and found them much more effective. They were useless against a line of infantry, but met the enemy's cavalry. Caesar employed them especially as scouts and raiders, or in pursuit of a routed enemy." (Walker, 28) **cogendi**: Singular, masculine, genitive gerundive used as an adjective modifying both nouns **supplementi equitatusque**, but agrees in gender and number with only the nearest noun (A.G. 286.a and 500.1).

ab exercitu: Ablative of separation with the preposition **ab** after **discedit** (A.G. 401).

discedit: The main verb of the main clause (A.G. 278.b). The historical present, giving vividness to the narrative, is present in Chapter 9 (A.G. 469). This usage, common in all languages, comes from imagining past events as going on before our eyes (*repraesentatio*) (A.G. 469 Note).

(9.2-3) Brutum adulescentem his copiis praeficit; hunc monet ut in omnis partis equites quam latissime pervagentur: daturum se operam ne longius triduo ab castris (3) absit.

ab, *from.*

adulescens, -entis, m., *the junior.*

castra, -orum, n., pl., *camp, encampment.*

do, dare, dedi, datus, (with **operam**) *devote one's attention, apply oneself, take pains.*

hic, haec, hoc, *this; he, she, it.*

late, sup. **-issime**, (with **quam**) *as far as possible.*

moneo, -ere, -ui, -itus, *advise, instruct.*

omnis, -e, *all.*

pars, partis, f., *part, region, district, direction.*

praeficio, -ficere, -feci, -fectus, *place over, appoint to command.*

sui, sibi, se, or **sese**, nom. wanting, *he*, with or without *himself.*

ut, *so that.*

absum, -esse, afui, -futurus, *be distant, be absent* or *away from.*

Brutus, -i, m., *Brutus.*

copiae, -arum, f., pl., *forces, troops.*

eques, -itis, m., *rider, horseman, cavalryman, trooper.*

in, *into.*

longius, *longer.*

ne, *so that ... not.*

opera, -ae, f., *effort, work, pains.*

pervagor, -ari, -atus, *roam about.*

quam, (with sup.), *as ---- as possible.*

triduum, -i, n., *space of three days, three days.*

Brutum: Accusative direct object of **praeficit** (A.G. 387). See Appendix A.

adulescentem: An accusative noun in apposition to the proper noun **Brutum** (A.G. 282).

his copiis: Dative indirect object of the transitive verb **praeficit** (A.G. 362). **his**: Plural, feminine, ablative demonstrative pronoun used as an adjective modifying **copiis** (A.G. 296.1 and a).

praeficit: The main verb of the simple sentence (A.G. 278.1). The pronoun **is**, with **Caesar** as the antecedent, is understood as the subject (A.G. 271.a).

hunc: Singular, masculine, accusative demonstrative pronoun used substantively (A.G. 296.2). The antecedent is **Brutum** (A.G. 297.e). Accusative direct object of **monet** (A.G. 387).

monet: The main verb of the main clause (A.G. 278.b). The pronoun **is**, with **Caesar** as the antecedent, is understood as the subject (A.G. 271.a).

ut ... pervagentur: The conjunction **ut** ("so that") with the subjunctive forms a substantive clause of purpose which is used as the object of the verb **monet** denoting an action directed toward the future (A.G. 563). **pervagentur**: The main verb of the subordinate clause (A.G. 278.b). Present subjunctive; the tense of the subjunctive is normally in secondary sequence after the historical present **praeficit** (A.G. 482-85). Here it is in primary sequence through *repraesentatio* (A.G. 485.e and 585.b Note).

in omnis partis: Accusative of *place to which* with the preposition **in** A.G. 426.2). **omnis**: Accusative plural adjective; **-is** for **-es** is the regular form in i-stem adjectives (A.G. 114.a and 116). **partis**: Accusative plural noun; **-is** and **-es** are both accusative forms in mixed i-stem nouns (A.G. 71).

equites: Nominative subject (A.G. 339).

quam latissime: Relative clause (A.G. 279.a). Here there is an ellipsis of the verb **posse** (*OLD* **quam** 7.b). **quam**: The relative adverb with the superlative denotes the highest possible degree "as broadly as possible" (A.G. 291.c) (*OLD* **quam** 7). **latissime**: Superlative adverb (A.G. 218).

daturum (esse) se operam: Accusative/infinitive construction in indirect discourse (A.G. 577 ff.). The verb of saying is not expressed, but implied in the general drift of the sentence (A.G. 580.a). **daturum (esse)**: Supply **esse** to form the future active infinitive (A.G. 202). The tense of the infinitive in indirect discourse is relative to that of the verb of saying (A.G. 584). **daturum ... operam**: The phrase **operam dare** is an idiom that means "to devote one's attention, to apply oneself" (to an activity or task) (*OLD* **opera** 2). **se**: Singular, masculine, accusative direct reflexive pronoun (A.G. 300.1). The antecedent is **Caesar**, the subject of the unexpressed verb of saying (A.G. 299). Accusative subject of the infinitive (A.G. 397.e). **operam**: Accusative direct object of the infinitive **daturum (esse)** (A.G. 387 and 451.3).

ne ... absit: The conjunction **ne** ("so that ... not") with the subjunctive forms a negative (final) purpose clause after **daturum ... operam** (A.G. 531). **absit**: The main verb of the subordinate clause (A.G. 278.b). Present subjunctive; the tense of the subjunctive is normally in secondary sequence after an unexpressed verb of saying (A.G. 482-84). Here it is in primary sequence through *repraesentatio* (A.G. 585.b Note). The pronoun **is**, with **Caesar** as the antecedent, is understood as the subject (A.G. 271.a).

longius triduo: Ablative of comparison; the comparative degree is often followed by the ablative signifying "than" (A.G. 406). **longius**: Comparative adverb (A.G. 218 and 320-21).

ab castris: Ablative of separation with the preposition **ab** after the compound verb **absit** (A.G. 402). **castris**: "A Roman army never halted even for one night without fortifying its camp (**castra**) with a wall and trench. This must have cost two or three hours of hard work; but it made the army safe from attack, and so allowed the general to choose his own time and place for battle; and in case of defeat the camp was a place of refuge." (Walker, 28)

(9.3-4) His constitutis rebus, suis inopinantibus quam (4) maximis potest itineribus Viennam pervenit.

constituo, -stituere, -stitui, -stitutus, *establish, resolve upon, determine.*	**hic, haec, hoc**, *this; he, she, it.*
inopinans, -antis, *not expecting, unaware, off one's guard.*	**iter, itineris**, n., *march.*
maximus, -a, -um, *long*, (with **iter**), *forced.*	**pervenio, -venire, -veni, -ventus**, *come, reach.*
possum, posse, potui, -----, *be able.*	**quam**, (with sup.), *as ---- as possible.*
res, rei, f., *matter, affair.*	**sui, -orum**, m., pl., *his men*, with or without *own.*
Vienna, -ae, f., *Vienna.*	

His constitutis rebus: Ablative absolute (A.G. 419-20). **His**: Plural, feminine, ablative demonstrative pronoun used as an adjective modifying **rebus** (A.G. 296.1 and a). **constitutis**: The perfect tense of the participle represents the action as completed at the time indicated by the tense of the main verb (A.G. 489).

suis inopinantibus: Dative indirect object of the intransitive verb **pervenit** (A.G. 366). "The march to Vienne may have been expected, but not so soon, or it may have been quite unexpected." (Edwards, 392) **suis**: Plural, masculine, dative possessive pronoun used substantively to denote a special class (A.G. 302.d).

quam maximis potest: Relative clause (A.G. 279.a). **quam**: The relative adverb **quam** with the superlative denotes the highest possible degree " (by marches) as long as possible" (A.G. 291.c) (*OLD* **quam** 7). **maximis**: Irregular superlative adjective modifying **itineribus** (A.G. 129). The superlative denotes a very high degree without implying a distinct comparison (A.G. 291.b). **potest**: The main verb of the subordinate clause (A.G. 278.b). The pronoun **is**, with **Caesar** as the antecedent, is understood as the subject (A.G. 271.a).

(maximis) ... itineribus: Ablative of manner with a limiting adjective (A.G. 412). "When we speak of forced marches (**magna itinera, maxima itinera**), we are to think of marches of from eighteen to twenty-five miles a day, or even more. On one occasion he marched four legions, without baggage, fifty Roman miles in less than thirty hours, including all stops." (Walker, 31)

Viennam: Accusative of *place to which* without a preposition (being the name of a town) (A.G. 427.2). See Appendix A.

pervenit: The main verb of the main clause (A.G. 278.b). The pronoun **is**, with **Caesar** as the antecedent, is understood as the subject (A.G. 271.a).

(9.4-5) Ibi nactus recentem equitatum, quem multis ante diebus eo praemiserat, neque diurno neque nocturno itinere intermisso per finis Aeduorum in Lingones, contendit, ubi duae legiones hiemabant, ut, si quid etiam de sua salute ab Aeduis iniretur (5) consili, celeritate praecurreret.

ab, *by.*	**Aedui, -orum**, m., pl., *the Aedui.*
ante, *before, previously.*	**celeritas, -tatis**, f., *speed, quickness, swiftness, rapidity.*
consilium, -i, n., *plan, design, scheme.*	**contendo, -tendere, -tendi, -tentus**, *hasten, push forward, march.*
de, *about, concerning.*	**dies, -ei**, m.,and f., *day.*

diurnus, -a, -um, *of the day, by day.*
eo, *there, thither.*
etiam, *even.*

hiemo, -are, -avi, -atus, *pass the winter, winter.*
in, *into the country of.*
intermitto, -mittere, -misi, -missus, *leave off, discontinue, interrupt*
legio, -onis, f., *legion.*
multus, -a, -um, *many.*

neque ... neque, *neither ... nor.*
per, *through.*

praemitto, -mittere, -misi, -missus, *send forward, before,* or *in advance.*
quis, -----, quid, *any one, anything.*
salus, -utis, f., *welfare, safety.*
suus, -a, -um, *his,* with or without *own.*
ut, *so that.*

duo, -ae, -o, *two.*
equitatus, -us, m., *cavalry.*
fines, -ium, m., pl., *borders,* hence *territory, country, land.*
ibi, *in that place, there.*
ineo, -ire, -ivi, or -ii, -itus, *enter upon, begin, form.*
iter, itineris, n., *journey, march, route.*
Lingones, -um, m., pl., *the Lingones.*
nanciscor, -cisci, nactus or nanctus, *come upon, find, obtain, get, secure.*
nocturnus, -a, -um, *by night, of night.*
praecurro, -currere, -cucurri or -curri, -----, *anticipate, precede.*
qui, quae, quod, *who, which, what.*
recens, -entis, *fresh, unwearied.*
si, *if.*
ubi, *where.*

ibi: Adverb (A.G. 215.5 and 320-21).

nactus: Nominative, perfect, deponent participle used as a predicate where in English a phrase or a subordinate clause would be more natural (A.G. 496). The pronoun is, with Caesar from 9.1 as the antecedent, is understood. Nominative subject of contendit (A.G. 339).

recentem equitatum: Accusative direct object of the participle nactus (A.G. 387 and 488).

quem ... praemiserat: Relative clause (A.G. 303). quem: Singular, masculine, accusative relative pronoun used substantively (A.G. 305). The antecedent is equitatum (A.G. 307). Accusative direct object of praemiserat (A.G. 387). praemiserat: The main verb of the subordinate clause (A.G. 278.b). The pronoun is, with nactus (Caesar) as the antecedent, is understood as the subject (A.G. 271.a). The pluperfect tense of the verb denotes an action completed in past time (A.G. 477).

multis ante diebus: The ablative with the adverb here expresses *distance of time before* ("before, by many days") (A.G. 424.f). ante: Adverb (A.G. 320-21 and 433.1). diebus: The noun dies is normally masculine gender (A.G. 97.a).

eo: Adverb (A.G. 217.a and 320-21).

neque diurno neque nocturno itinere intermisso: Ablative absolute (A.G. 419-20). neque ... neque: The repeated conjunction means "neither ... nor", connecting the two adjectives modifying itinere (*OLD* neque 7). Two adjectives belonging to the same noun are regularly connected by a conjunction (A.G. 323.d). intermisso: The perfect tense of the participle represents the action as completed at the time indicated by the tense of the main verb (A.G. 489).

per finis Aeduorum: Prepositional phrase, per with the accusative here means "through" (*OLD* per 1.c). finis: Accusative plural noun; -is for -es is the regular form in i-stem nouns (A.G. 65-7 and 74.c). Aeduorum: Possessive genitive of the tribe name Aedui with finis (A.G. 343). See Appendix A.

in Lingones: Accusative of *place to which* with the preposition in meaning "into the country of" (A.G. 426.2). Lingones: See Appendix A.

contendit: The main verb of the main clause (A.G. 278.b).

ubi ... hiemabant: Relative clause (A.G. 279.a) The relative adverb ubi ("where") with the indicative forms a subordinate clause (A.G. 278.b). hiemabant: The main verb of the subordinate clause (A.G. 278.b).

duae legiones: Nominative subject (A.G. 339). duae: Declinable cardinal number used as an adjective (A.G. 132-35).

ut si ... iniretur ... praecurreret: A subordinate conditional statement (A.G. 512.c). The apodosis, as a purpose clause dependent on contendit, takes the subjunctive and the protasis, as a clause subordinate to a subjunctive clause, also takes the subjunctive (attraction) (A.G. 512.c and 593).

ut ... praecurreret: The apodosis of the conditional statement (A.G. 512.c). The conjunction ut ("so that") with the subjunctive forms a final (purpose) clause dependent upon contendit (A.G. 531.1). praecurreret: The main verb of the subordinate clause (A.G. 278.b). Imperfect subjunctive; the tense of the subjunctive is in secondary sequence after the historical present tense of contendit (A.G. 482-85, esp. 485.e). The pronoun is, with nactus (Caesar) as the antecedent, is understood as the subject (A.G. 271.a).

si ... iniretur: The conjunction si ("if") with the subjunctive forms the protasis of the conditional statement (A.G. 512). A clause dependent on a subjunctive clause (ut ... praecurreret) takes the subjunctive when regarded as an integral part of that clause (attraction) (A.G. 593). iniretur: The main verb of the subordinate clause (A.G. 278.b). Imperfect subjunctive; the tense of the subjunctive is in secondary sequence after the historical present tense of contendit (A.G. 482-85, esp. 485.e).

quid: Singular, neuter, nominative indefinite pronoun used substantively (A.G. 149). The indefinite quis, -----, quid is used after si (A.G. 310.a). Nominative subject (A.G. 339).

etiam: Adverb (A.G. 322.a and 320-21). The adverb normally proceeds the emphatic word (A.G. 322.a).

de sua salute: Prepositional phrase, de with the ablative here means "about, concerning" (*OLD* de 12). sua: Singular, feminine, ablative possessive pronoun used as an adjective modifying salute (A.G. 302).

ab Aeduis: Ablative of agent with the preposition ab after the passive verb iniretur (A.G. 405). Aeduis: See Appendix A.

consili: Partitive genitive with quid (A.G. 346.a.3). The singular genitive of nouns in -ium ended, until the Augustan Age, in a single -i (A.G. 49.b). The phrase consilium inire is an idiom that means "to hold a consultation, deliberate, take counsel" (*OLD* consilium 1).

celeritate: Ablative of means (A.G. 409). Caesar's speed may be legendary (see also for example 7.12.3, 40.2), but Fuller notes that it has a negative aspect: "the truth is, Caesar was not an organizer; careful preparations - adequate supplies, sufficient fighting forces, and many other requirements needed to assure the success of a campaign - were either distasteful to him, or lost to sight by reliance on his genius to solve all difficulties, as well as his eagerness to respond immediately to every challenge whatever at the moment his means might be." (Fuller, 316) For a full discussion see Fuller, 321-24.

(9.5-6) Eo cum pervenisset, ad reliquas legiones mittit priusque omnis in unum locum (6) cogit quam de eius adventu Arvernis nuntiari posset.

ad, *to.*
Arverni, -orum, m., pl., *the Arverni.*

cum, *after, when.*
eo, *thither, there.*
is, ea, id, *he, she, it; that, this.*
locus, -i, m., *place, location.*
nuntio, -are, -avi, -atus, *announce, report.*
pervenio, -venire, -veni, -ventus, *come to, reach.*

prius ... quam, *before, sooner than.*
reliquus, -a, -um, *remaining, the rest.*

adventus, -us, m., *coming, approach, arrival.*
cogo, cogere, coegi, coactus, *bring together, collect, gather, assemble.*
de, *about, concerning.*
in, *into, to.*
legio, -onis, f., *legion.*
mitto, mittere, misi, missus, *send.*
omnis, -e, *all.*
possum, posse, potui, -----, *it can be done or happen, it is possible.*
-que, *and.*
unus, -a, -um, *one.*

Eo: Adverb (A.G. 217.a and 320-21). The adverb is standing outside the temporal clause.
cum pervenisset: Temporal clause; **cum** ("after, when") with the pluperfect subjunctive describes the circumstances that preceded the action of the main verb (A.G. 546). **pervenisset**: The main verb of the subordinate clause (A.G. 278.b). The pronoun **is**, with **nactus** (**Caesar**) as the antecedent, is understood as the subject (A.G. 271.a).
ad reliquas legiones: Accusative of *place to which* with the preposition **ad** (A.G. 426.2). "as well as these two, there were six quartered at Agedincum and two on the Treveri's borders." (Hammond, 237)
mittit: The main verb of the coordinate clause **Eo ... mittit** (A.G. 278.a). The pronoun **is**, with **nactus (Caesar)** as the antecedent, is understood as the subject (A.G. 271.a).
priusque: Construe **prius** with **quam** below. **-que**: The enclitic conjunction connects the two main verbs **mittit ... cogit** (A.G. 324.a).
omnis: Plural, feminine, accusative adjective used substantively (A.G. 288). The noun **legiones** is understood (A.G. 288.b). Accusative plural adjective; **-is** for **-es** is the regular form in i-stem adjectives (A.G. 114.a and 116). Accusative direct object of **cogit** (A.G. 387).
in unum locum: Accusative of *place to which* with the preposition **in** (A.G. 426.2). **unum**: Declinable cardinal number used as an adjective modifying **locum** (A.G. 132-35).
cogit: The main verb of the coordinate clause **priusque ... posset** (A.G. 278.a). The pronoun **is**, with **nactus (Caesar)** as the antecedent, is understood as the subject (A.G. 271.a).
priusque ... quam ... (id) posset: Temporal clause; **priusquam** ("before") with the imperfect subjunctive is common when the subordinate clause implies purpose or expectancy in the past (A.G. 551.b). **priusque ... quam**: The conjunction is here split (tmesis) (A.G. 640). **posset**: The main verb of the subordinate clause (A.G. 278.b). Impersonal use of the verb, supply **id** as the subject (A.G. 271.a). When used impersonally with the passive infinitive (**nuntiari**), **posse** means "it can be done or happen, it is possible" (*OLD* **possum** 6.b).
de eius adventu: Prepositional phrase, **de** with the ablative here means "about, concerning" (*OLD* **de** 12). **eius**: Singular, masculine, genitive demonstrative pronoun used substantively (A.G. 296.2). The antecedent is **is (Caesar)**, the supplied subject of **cogit** (A.G. 297.e). Possessive genitive with **adventu** (A.G. 343). Here the indirect reflexive possessive adjective **suo** is not used as the subordinate clause does not express the words or thoughts of the main subject (A.G. 300.a).
Arvernis: Dative indirect object of the passive infinitive **nuntiari**, verbs which in the active voice take the accusative and dative retain the dative when used in the passive (A.G. 365). "an oblique rebuttal of the hopes expressed by the Gallic leaders at 7.1. The sequence of events in 7.7-9 is complicated: Vercingetorix had planned, through Lucterius, to rouse the peoples bordering the Province so as to expose it to an invasion force. Caesar prevents this, first by forcing him back on to the defensive, then by concealing his own departure and by gathering his army together safely." (Hammond, 238) See Appendix A.
nuntiari: Complementary infinitive after **posset** (A.G. 456).

(9.6) Hac re cognita, Vercingetorix rursus in Bituriges exercitum reducit atque inde profectus Gorgobinam, Boiorum oppidum, quos ibi Helvetico proelio victos Caesar collocaverat Aeduisque attribuerat, oppugnare instituit.

Aedui, -orum, m., pl., *the Aedui.*
attribuo, -uere, -ui, -utus, *assign, allot, turn over to.*
Boii, -orum, m., pl., *the Boii.*
cognosco, -gnoscere, -gnovi, cognitus, *learn of, know.*
exercitus, -us, m., *army.*
Helveticus, -a, -um, *Helvetian*, (with **proelium**), *the battle with the Helvetii.*
ibi, *in that place, there.*

atque, *and.*
Bituriges, -um, m., pl., *the Bituriges.*
Caesar, -aris, m., *Caesar.*
colloco, -are, -avi, -atus, *place, set, post, station.*
Gorgobina, -ae, f., *Gorgobina.*
hic, haec, hoc, *this; he, she, it.*
in, *into the country of, against.*

inde, *from that place, thence.*

oppidum, -i, n., *fortified town, city.*
proelium, -i, n., *battle, combat, engagement.*
-que, *and.*
reduco, -ducere, -duxi, -ductus, *lead back, conduct back.*
rursus, *again, anew.*
vinco, vincere, vici, victus, *conquer, overcome, defeat, subdue.*

instituo, -stituere, -stitui, -stitutus, *undertake, commence, begin.*
oppugno, -are, -avi, -atus, *attack, storm, besiege.*
proficiscor, -ficisci, -fectus, *set out, depart, proceed.*
qui, quae, quod, *who, which, what.*
res, rei, f., *matter, affair, event, circumstance.*
Vercingetorix, -igis, m., *Vercingetorix.*

Hac re cognita: Ablative absolute (A.G. 419-20). Hac: Singular, feminine, ablative demonstrative pronoun used as an adjective modifying re (A.G. 296.1 and a). cognita: The perfect tense of the participle represents the action as completed at the time indicated by the tense of the main verb (A.G. 489).
Vercingetorix: Nominative subject of reducit (A.G. 339). See Appendix A.
rursus: Adverb (A.G. 216 and 320-21).
in Bituriges: Accusative of *place to which* with the preposition in meaning "into the country of" (A.G. 426.2). Bituriges: See Appendix A.
exercitum: Accusative direct object of reducit (A.G. 387).
reducit: The main verb of the coordinate clause Hac ... reducit (A.G. 278.a).
atque: The conjunction connects the two main verbs reducit ... instituit and means "and" (*OLD* atque 12).
inde: Adverb (A.G. 217.a and 320-21).
profectus: Nominative, perfect, deponent participle used as a predicate where in English a phrase or a subordinate clause would be more natural (A.G. 496). The pronoun is, with Vercingetorix as the antecedent, is understood. Nominative subject of instituit (A.G. 339).
Gorgobinam: Accusative direct object of the infinitive oppugnare (A.G. 387 and 451.3). See Appendix A.
Boiorum: Possessive genitive of the tribe name Boii modifying oppidum (A.G. 343). See Appendix A.
oppidum: An accusative noun in apposition to the proper noun Gorgobinam (A.G. 282).
quos ... victos ... collocaverat ... attribuerat: Relative clause (A.G. 303). For the reference see *BG* 1.28.5. quos ... victos: Accusative direct object of both collocaverat and attribuerat (A.G. 387). quos: Plural, masculine, accusative relative pronoun used substantively (A.G. 305). The antecedent is Boiorum (A.G. 307). victos: Accusative, perfect, passive, participle used as a predicate, where in English a phrase or a subordinate clause would be more normal (A.G. 496). collocaverat ... attribuerat: The main verbs of the subordinate clause (A.G. 278.b). The pluperfect tense of the verbs denotes an action completed in past time (A.G. 477).
ibi: Adverb with collocaverat (A.G. 215.5 and 320-21).
Helvetico proelio: Ablative of *time when* with victos (A.G. 424.d). For the Helvetian campaign see *BG* 1.1-29.
Caesar: Nominative subject (A.G. 339). See Appendix A.
Aeduisque: Dative indirect object of the transitive verb attribuerat (A.G. 362). Aeduis: See Appendix A. -que: The enclitic conjunction connects the two main verbs in the relative clause collocaverat ... attribuerat (A.G. 324.a).
oppugnare: Complementary infinitive after instituit (A.G. 456). Caesar gives a description of Gallic siege tactics at *BG* 2.6.2-3: Gallorum eadem atque Belgarum oppugnatio est haec. Ubi circumiecta multitudine hominum totis moenibus undique in murum lapides iaci coepti sunt murusque defensoribus nudatus est, testudine facta, portas succendunt murumque subruunt. By the fifth year of the war, at *BG* 5.42, the Gauls are being instructed in Roman techniques by Roman prisoners but still lack the technology to be proficient (5.42.3-4): sed nulla ferramentorum copia quae esset ad hunc usum idonea, gladiis caespites circumcidere, manibus sagulisque terram exhaurire videbantur. Under Vercingetorix, the Gauls eventually adopted both Roman methods and technological sophistication (see 84.1-2).
instituit: The main verb of the coordinate clause inde ... instituit (A.G. 278.a).

(10.1-2) Magnam haec res Caesari difficultatem ad consilium capiendum adferebat, si reliquam partem hiemis uno loco legiones contineret, ne stipendiariis Aeduorm expugnatis cuncta Gallia deficeret, quod nullum amicis in eo praesidium videret positum esse; si maturius ex hibernis educeret, ne (2) ab re frumentaria duris subvectionibus laboraret.

ab, *because of.*
adfero, -ferre, attuli, allatus, *produce, cause, occasion.*
amicus, -i, m., *friend, ally.*
capio, capere, cepi, captus, *form.*
contineo, -tinere, -tinui, -tentus, *hold back, keep, retain, detain, shut in.*
deficio, -ficere, -feci, -fectus, *fall away, revolt, rebel.*
durus, -a, -um, *hard, severe, difficult.*
ex, *from, out of.*

frumentarius, -a, -um, *having to do with grain* or *supplies.*
hiberna, -orum, n., pl., (supply castra), *winter-quarters.*
hiems, hiemis, f., *winter.*
is, ea, id, *he, she, it; that, this.*

legio, -onis, f., *legion.*

ad, *for, in order to, for the purpose of, in.*
Aedui, -orum, m., pl., *the Aedui.*
Caesar, -aris, m., *Caesar.*
consilium, -i, n., *plan, council, strategy, policy.*
cunctus, -a, -um, *all together, all.*
difficultas, -tatis, f., *difficulty, trouble.*
educo, ducere, -duxi, -ductus, *lead out, lead forth.*
expugno, -are, -avi, -atus, *storm, take by assault, capture.*
Gallia, -ae, f., *Gaul.*
hic, haec, hoc, *this; he, she, it.*
in, *in the power or capacity of.*
laboro, -are, -avi, -atus, *be hard pressed, in distress, in danger.*
locus, -i, m., *place, location.*

magnus, -a, -um, *great.*
ne, *lest, that.*
pars, partis, f., *part, portion.*
praesidium, -i, n., *protection.*
reliquus, -a, -um, *the remaining.*

si, *if.*
subvectio, -onis, f., *transportation, conveyance.*
video, videre, visi, visus, *perceive, observe, understand.*

mature, comp. -ius, *early.*
nullus, -a, -um, *no, not any.*
pono, ponere, posui, positus, *place, put.*
quod, *because, since, for, as.*
res, rei, f., *matter, circumstance, event;* (with frumentaria) *supply of grain, supplies.*
stipendiarii, -orum, m., pl., *tributaries, dependencies.*
unus, -a, -um, *one.*

Magnam ... difficultatem: Accusative direct object of the transitive verb **adferebat** (A.G. 387).
haec res: Nominative subject (A.G. 339). **haec**: Singular, feminine, nominative demonstrative pronoun used as an adjective modifying **res** (A.G. 296.1 and a).
Caesari: Dative indirect object of the transitive verb **adferebat** (A.G. 362). See Appendix A.
ad consilium capiendum: The preposition **ad** with an accusative noun and gerundive expresses purpose (A.G. 506). **capiendum**: Singular, neuter, accusative gerundive used as an adjective modifying **consilium** denoting necessity, obligation or propriety (A.G. 500.1).
adferebat: The main verb of the main clause (A.G. 278.b).
si ... contineret (vereretur) ne: Supply the imperfect subjunctive verb **vereretur** with **ne** to form a present contrary to fact conditional statement (imperfect subjunctive in both protasis and apodosis) (A.G. 514.C.1).
si ... contineret: The conjunction **si** ("if") with the imperfect subjunctive forms the protasis of the contrary to fact conditional statement (A.G. 517). **contineret**: The main verb of the subordinate clause (A.G. 278.b). The pronoun **is**, with **Caesari** as the antecedent, is understood as the subject (A.G. 271.a).
reliquam partem: Accusative of *how long* (A.G. 423.2).
hiemis: Partitive genitive with **partem** (A.G. 346.1.a).
uno loco: Ablative of *place where* without a preposition (A.G. 429.1-2). **uno**: Declinable cardinal number used as an adjective (A.G. 132-35).
legiones: Accusative direct object of **contineret** (A.G. 387).
(vereretur) ne: Supply the imperfect subjunctive **vereretur** (vereor, vereri, veritus sum, *fear, dread, be afraid of*) with **ne** as the main verb in the apodosis of the conditional statement (A.G. 517). **vereretur**: The pronoun **is**, with **Caesari** as the antecedent, is understood as the subject (A.G. 271.a).
ne ... deficeret: The conjunction **ne** ("lest") with the subjunctive forms a substantive clause of fearing depending on the supplied verb **vereretur** (A.G. 564). **deficeret**: The main verb of the subordinate clause (A.G. 278.b). Imperfect subjunctive; the tense of the subjunctive is in secondary sequence and follows the rules for the sequence of tense after the supplied verb **vereretur**; the imperfect subjunctive in present conditions contrary to fact is regularly followed by the secondary sequence (A.G. 482-85, esp. 485.h).
stipendiariis Aeduorum expugnatis: Ablative absolute (A.G. 419-20). **Aeduorum**: Possessive genitive of the tribe name **Aedui** with **stipendiariis** (A.G. 343). See Appendix A. **expugnatis**: The perfect tense of the participle represents the action as completed at the time indicated by the tense of the main verb (A.G. 489).
cuncta Gallia: Nominative subject of **deficeret** (A.G. 339). **Gallia**: See Appendix A.
quod ... videret: Causal clause; the conjunction **quod** ("because") normally takes the indicative when the reason is given on the authority of the writer or speaker (A.G. 540.1). Here **quod** takes the subjunctive as it is dependent upon a subjunctive clause (**ne ... deficeret**) and is regarded as an integral part of that clause (attraction) (A.G. 593). **videret**: The main verb of the subordinate clause (A.G. 278.b). Imperfect subjunctive; the tense of the subjunctive is in secondary sequence and follows the rules for the sequence of tense after the supplied verb **vereretur**; the imperfect subjunctive in present conditions contrary to fact is regularly followed by the secondary sequence (A.G. 482-85, esp. 485.h). The pronoun **ea**, with **cuncta Gallia** as the antecedent, is understood as the subject (A.G. 271.a).
nullum ... praesidium ... positum esse: Accusative/infinitive construction in indirect discourse after **videret** (A.G. 577 ff.). **positum esse**: Perfect infinitive; the tense of the infinitive in indirect discourse is relative to that of the verb of saying (A.G. 584).
amicis: Dative of reference; the dative in this construction is often called the dative of advantage as denoting the person for whose benefit the action is performed (A.G. 376).
in eo: Prepositional phrase, **in** with the ablative here means "in the power or capacity of" (*OLD* in 26.b). **eo**: singular, masculine, ablative demonstrative pronoun used substantively (A.G. 296.2). The antecedent is **Caesari** (A.G. 297.e).
si ... educeret (vereretur) ne: Supply the imperfect subjunctive verb **vereretur** with **ne** to form a present contrary to fact conditional statement (imperfect subjunctive in both protasis and apodosis) (A.G. 514.c.1).
si ... educeret: The conjunction **si** ("if") with the imperfect subjunctive forms the protasis of the contrary to fact conditional statement (A.G. 517). **educeret**: The main verb of the subordinate clause (A.G. 278.b). The pronoun **is**, with **Caesari** as the antecedent, is understood as the subject (A.G. 271.a). The pronoun **eas**, with **legiones** as the antecedent, is understood as the subject (A.G. 271.a).
maturius: Comparative adverb (A.G. 218). The comparative degree here denotes a considerable or excessive degree of the quality meaning "too" (A.G. 291.a).
ex hibernis: Ablative of *place from which* with the preposition **ex** (A.G. 426.1). **hibernis**: Plural, neuter, ablative adjective used substantively (A.G. 288). The noun **castris** is understood from constant association (A.G. 288.c).
(vereretur) ne: Supply the imperfect subjunctive **vereretur** (vereor, vereri, veritus sum, *fear, dread, be afraid of*) with **ne** as the main verb in the apodosis of the conditional statement (A.G. 517). **vereretur**: The pronoun **is**, with **Caesari** as the antecedent, is understood as the subject (A.G. 271.a).

ne ... laboraret: The conjunction **ne** ("lest") with the subjunctive forms a substantive clause of fearing (A.G. 564). **laboraret**: The main verb of the subordinate clause (A.G. 278.b). Imperfect subjunctive; the tense of the subjunctive is in secondary sequence and follows the rules for the sequence of tense after the supplied verb **vereretur**; the imperfect subjunctive in present conditions contrary to fact is regularly followed by the secondary sequence (A.G. 482-85, esp. 485.h). The pronoun **is**, with **Caesari** as the antecedent, is understood as the subject (A.G. 271.a).

ab re frumentaria: Prepositional phrase, here **ab** with the ablative is causal meaning "because of" (*OLD* **ab** 15).

duris subvectionibus: Ablative of cause without a preposition after **laboraret** (A.G. 404.a).

(10.2) **Praestare visum est tamen omnis difficultates perpeti quam tanta contumelia accepta omnium suorum voluntates alienare.**

accipio, -cipere, -cepi, -ceptus, *receive.*

contumelia, -ae, f., *insult, abuse, indignity.*

omnes, -ium, m., pl., *all men, all.*

perpetior, -peti, -pessus, *bear patiently, endure.*

quam, (*rather*) *than.*

tamen, *yet, still, for all that, nevertheless, however.*

videor, videri, visus sum, *seem proper, seem good, seem best.*

alieno, -are, -avi, -atus, *make strange, alienate, estrange.*

difficultas, -tatis, f., *difficulty, trouble.*

omnis, -e, *all.*

praesto, -stare, -stiti, -stitus, (imper.), *it is preferable, it is better.*

sui, -orum, m., pl., *his men,* with or without *own.*

tantus, -a, -um, *so great, so large, such.*

voluntas, atis, f., *good-will, affection.*

Praestare: Impersonal infinitive in indirect discourse after **visum est** (A.G. 577 ff.). Impersonal use of the verb (A.G. 208.c). The following infinitive phrase functions as the subject (A.G. 454). Present infinitive; the tense of the infinitive in indirect discourse is relative to that of the verb of saying (A.G. 584).

(id) visum est: Impersonal use of the intransitive passive verb (A.G. 208.d). Supply **id** as the subject (A.G. 318.c).

tamen: Adverb, postpositive (A.G. 320-21 and 324.j).

omnis difficultates perpeti: The infinitive phrase functions as the subject of the impersonal verb **Praestare** (A.G. 454). **omnis difficultates**: Accusative direct object of the infinitive **perpeti** (A.G. 387 and 451.3). **omnis**: Accusative plural adjective; **-is** for **-es** is the regular form in i-stem adjectives (A.G. 114.a and 116).

quam ... alienare: Relative clause (A.G. 279.a). **quam**: Relative adverb meaning "(rather) than" after the comparison implied in **Praestare** (*OLD* **quam** 9.b). Here the comparison is being made between the two infinitives **perpeti ... alienare**. **alienare**: The infinitive construction is regularly continued after a comparative with **quam** in indirect discourse rather than switching to the subjunctive in the dependent clause (A.G. 583.c).

tanta contumelia accepta: Ablative absolute (A.G. 419-20). **accepta**: The perfect tense of the participle represents the action as completed at the time indicated by the tense of the main verb (A.G. 489).

omnium suorum: Possessive genitive with **voluntates** (A.G. 343). **suorum**: Plural, masculine, genitive possessive pronoun used substantively to denote a special class (A.G. 302.d).

voluntates: Accusative direct object of the infinitive **alienare** (A.G. 387 and 451.3).

(10.3-4) **(3) Itaque cohortatus Aeduos de supportando commeatu, praemittit ad Boios qui de suo adventu doceant hortenturque ut in fide maneant atque hostium impetum magno (4) animo sustineant.**

ad, *to, towards.*

Aedui, -orum, m., pl., *the Aedui.*

atque, *and.*

cohortor, -ari, -atus, *encourage, urge, exhort, address.*

de, *about, concerning.*

fides, -ei, f., *fidelity, loyalty, alliance.*

hostis, -is, m., *enemy, foe*; pl., *the enemy.*

in, *in.*

magnus, -a, -um, *great.*

praemitto, -mittere, -misi, -missus, *send on before, send in advance.*

qui, quae, quod, *who, which, what.*

sustineo, -tinere, -tinui, -tentus, *bear, endure, withstand.*

ut, *so that.*

adventus, -us, m., *coming, approach, arrival.*

qanimus, -i, m., *courage, spirit, temper, resolution.*

Boii, -orum, m., pl., *the Boii.*

commeatus, -us, m., *supplies, provisions.*

doceo, docere, docui, doctus, *inform, point out, state.*

hortor, -ari, -atus, *urge, encourage, exhort, incite, press.*

impetus, -us, m., *attack, assault, onset, charge.*

itaque, *and so, in consequence, accordingly, therefore.*

maneo, manere, mansi, mansus, *continue, remain.*

-que, *and.*

supporto, -are, -avi, -----, *carry up, bring up, convey.*

suus, -a, -um, *his,* with or without *own.*

Itaque: An adverb expressing the result of the previous ideas meaning "and so, in consequence" (*OLD* **itaque** 1). The adverb stands in the first position (A.G. 599.b).

cohortatus: Nominative, perfect, deponent, participle used as a predicate, where in English a phrase or a subordinate clause would be more normal (A.G. 496). The pronoun **is**, with **Caesari** as the antecedent, is understood. Nominative subject of **praemittit** (A.G. 339).

Aeduos: Accusative direct object of the participle **cohortatus** (A.G. 387 and 488). See Appendix A.

de supportando commeatu: Prepositional phrase, **de** with the ablative here means "about, concerning" (*OLD* **de** 12). **supportando**:

Singular, masculine, ablative of the gerundive modifying **commeatu** used after the preposition **de** (A.G. 507.3).

praemittit: The main verb of the main clause (A.G. 278.b). The historical present, giving vividness to the narrative, is present in Chapter 10 (A.G. 469). This usage, common in all languages, comes from imagining past events as going on before our eyes (*repraesentatio*) (A.G. 469 Note). Here, Caesar switches to the historical present after setting up the background information. Supply **legatos** as the direct object.

ad Boios: Accusative of *place to which* with the preposition **ad** (A.G. 426.2). **Boios**: See Appendix A.

qui ... doceant ... hortenturque: A relative clause of purpose is introduced by a relative pronoun and takes the subjunctive (A.G. 531.2). **qui**: Plural, masculine, nominative relative pronoun used substantively (A.G. 305). The antecedent is omitted, supply **legatos** (A.G. 307.c). Nominative subject (A.G. 339). The relative is here equivalent to **ut ei** (A.G. 531.2 Note). **doceant ... hortentur**: The main verbs of the subordinate clause (A.G. 278.b). Present subjunctives; the tense of the subjunctives is normally in secondary sequence after the historical present **praemittit** (A.G. 482-85). Here it is in primary sequence through *repraesentatio* (A.G. 485.e and 585.b Note). **-que**: The enclitic conjunction connects the two verbs in the relative clause (A.G. 323.a).

de suo adventu: Prepositional phrase, **de** with the ablative here means "about, concerning" (*OLD* de 12). **suo**: Singular, masculine, ablative possessive pronoun used as an adjective modifying **adventu** (A.G. 302).

ut ... maneant ... sustineant: The conjunction **ut** ("so that") with the subjunctive forms a substantive clause of purpose which is used as the object of the verb **hortentur** denoting an action directed toward the future (A.G. 563). **maneant ... sustineant**: The main verbs of the subordinate clause (A.G. 278.b). Present subjunctive; the tense of the subjunctive is normally in secondary sequence after the historical present **praemittit** (A.G. 482-85). Here it is in primary sequence through *repraesentatio* (A.G. 485.e and 585.b Note). The pronoun **ei**, with **Boios** as the antecedent, is understood as the subject of both verbs (A.G. 271.a).

in fide maneant: The phrase **in fide manere** is an idiom that means "to remain loyal" (*OLD* fides1 8).

in fide: Prepositional phrase, **in** with the ablative here means "in" (expressing an abstract location) (*OLD* in 26).

atque: The conjunction connects the two verbs in the purpose clause **maneant ... sustineant** and means "and" (*OLD* atque 12).

hostium: Possessive genitive with **impetum** (A.G. 343). Here the enemy is Vercingetorix who is besieging Gorgobina (9.6).

impetum: Accusative direct object of **sustineant** (A.G. 387).

magno animo: Ablative of manner with a limiting adjective (A.G. 412).

(10.4) Duabus Agedinci legionibus atque impedimentis totius exercitus relictis, ad Boios proficiscitur.

ad, *to, towards*.	**Agedincum, -i**, n., *Agedincum*.
atque, *and*.	**Boii, -orum**, m., pl., *the Boii*.
duo, -ae, -o, *two*.	**exercitus, -us**, m., *army*.
impedimenta, -orum, n., pl., *heavy baggage, baggage*.	**legio, -onis**, f., *legion*.
proficiscor, -ficisci, -fectus, *set out, depart, proceed*.	**relinquo, -linquere, -liqui, -lictus**, *leave, leave behind*.
totus, -a, -um, *the whole of, all*.	

Duabus Agedinci legionibus atque impedimentis totius exercitus relictis: Ablative absolute (A.G. 419-20). **Duabus**: Declinable cardinal number used as an adjective modifying **legionibus** (A.G. 132-35). **Agedinci**: Locative of the city name **Agedincum, -i**, n. (A.G. 49.a). See Appendix A. **atque**: The conjunction connects the two ablative nouns in the ablative absolute **legionibus ... impedimentis** and means "and" (*OLD* atque 12). **impedimentis**: In the plural the noun means "baggage" (A.G. 107). "The heavy baggage (*impedimenta*) consisted of tents, provisions, hand-mills for grinding grain, engines of war, etc., and was carried on pack horses or mules (*iumenta*). These were driven or led by the drivers (*muliones*) and camp servants (*calones*), who were probably slaves." (Walker, 27) **totius exercitus**: Possessive genitive with **impedimentis** (A.G. 343). **totius**: -ius is the regular genitive singular ending for the adjective **totus** (A.G. 113). **relictis**: The perfect tense of the participle represents the action as completed at the time indicated by the tense of the main verb (A.G. 489).

ad Boios: Accusative of *place to which* with the preposition **ad** (A.G. 426.2). **Boios**: See Appendix A.

proficiscitur: The main verb of the main clause (A.G. 278.b). The pronoun **is**, with **cohortatus (Caesar)** as the antecedent, is understood as the subject (A.G. 271.a).

1.D CHAPTERS 11-13: CAESAR CAPTURES VELLAUNODUNUM, CENABUM, AND NOVIODUNUM

Chapter 11: Notice how the tense structure for the main verbs functions in Chapter 11. The action is set up with the perfect tense: **altero die ... instituit ... biduo circumvallavit**. Then the narrative portion is in the historical present: **tertio die ... iubet ... relinquit ... proficiscitur**. Then, the action is again set up with the perfect tense: **pervenit**. Then the historical present is again used for the narrative portion: **differt ... imperat ... iubet ... coeperunt ... intromittit ... potitur ... diripit ... incendit ... donat ... traducit ... pervenit**. (A.G. 469 and 473).

(11.1-2) Altero die cum ad oppidum Senonum Vellaunodunum venisset, ne quem post se hostem relinqueret, quo expeditiore re frumentaria uteretur, oppugnare instituit idque (2) biduo circumvallavit;

ad, *to, towards*.	**alter, -era, -erum**, *the next*.
biduum, -i, n., *space of two days, two days*.	**circumvallo, -are, -avi, -atus**, *surround with a rampart, blockade, invest*.
cum, *after, when*.	**dies, -ei**, m., and f., *day*.
expeditus, -a, -um, comp. **-ior**, *ready, easy, convenient*.	**frumentarius, -a, -um**, *having to do with grain or supplies*.

hostis, -is, m., *enemy, foe.*

is, ea, id, *he, she, it; that, this.*
oppidum, -i, n., *fortified town, city.*

post, *behind.*
quis, -----, quid, *any;* (as adj., qui, quae, or qua, quod).

relinquo, -linquere, -liqui, -lictus, *leave, leave behind.*
Senones, -um, m., pl., *the Senones.*

utor, uti, usus, *avail one's self of, have, enjoy.*
venio, venire, veni, ventus, *come.*

instituo, -stituere, -stitui, -stitutus, *undertake, commence, begin.*
ne, *so that ... not.*
oppugno, -are, -avi, -atus, *attack, assault, storm, besiege.*
-que, *and.*
quo, *so that* (by that degree), *in order that, that, that thereby.*
res, rei, f., (with frumentaria) *supply of grain, supplies.*
sui, sibi, se, or sese, nom. wanting, *him,* with or without *-self.*
Vellaunodunum, -i, n., *Vellaunodunum.*

Altero die: Ablative of *time when* (A.G. 423.1). **die**: The noun **dies** is normally masculine gender (A.G. 97.a).
cum ... venisset: Temporal clause; **cum** ("after, when") with the pluperfect subjunctive describes the circumstances that preceded the action of the main verb (A.G. 546). **venisset**: The main verb of the subordinate clause (A.G. 278.b). The pronoun **is**, with **cohortatus** (**Caesar**) as the antecedent, is understood as the subject (A.G. 271.a).
ad oppidum Senonum: Accusative of *place to which* with the preposition **ad** (A.G. 426.2). **Senonum**: Possessive genitive of the tribe name **Senones** with **oppidum** (A.G. 343). See Appendix A.
Vellaunodunum: An accusative proper noun in apposition to **oppidum** (A.G. 282). See Appendix A.
ne ... reliqueret: The conjunction **ne** ("so that ... not") with the subjunctive forms a negative (final) purpose clause after **oppugnare instituit** (A.G. 531). **reliqueret**: The main verb of the subordinate clause (A.G. 278.b). Imperfect subjunctive; the tense of the subjunctive is in secondary sequence and follows the rules for the sequence of tense after the perfect tense **instituit** (A.G. 482-85). The pronoun **is**, with **cohortatus** (**Caesar**) as the antecedent, is understood as the subject (A.G. 271.a).
quem ... hostem: Accusative direct object of **relinqueret** (A.G. 387). **quem**: Singular, masculine, accusative indefinite pronoun used as an adjective modifying **hostem** (A.G. 148-49). The indefinite pronoun **quis**, -----, **quid** (**qui, quae,** or **qua, quod** when used adjectively) is used after **ne** (A.G. 310.a).
post se: Prepositional phrase, **post** with the accusative here means "behind" (*OLD* post2 1). **se**: Singular, masculine, accusative direct reflexive pronoun (A.G. 300.1). The antecedent is **is** (**Caesar**), the supplied subject of **relinqueret** (A.G. 299). Notice that iconically Caesar (**se**) is surrounded by his enemy (**quem ... hostem**), the very thing he wishes to avoid.
quo expeditiore ... uteretur: Final clause; the ablative **quo** (= **ut eo**) is used as a conjunction in a final (purpose) clause with the subjunctive (A.G. 531.a). **quo**: In a final clause with a comparative, the conjunction means "so that by that degree" (*OLD* quo2 3.b).
expeditiore: Comparative adjective modifying **re frumentaria** (A.G. 124). **uteretur**: The main verb of the subordinate clause (A.G. 278.b). Imperfect subjunctive; the tense of the subjunctive is in secondary sequence and follows the rules for the sequence of tense after the perfect tense **instituit** (A.G. 482-85). The pronoun **is**, with **cohortatus** (**Caesar**) as the antecedent, is understood as the subject (A.G. 271.a).
expeditiore re frumentaria: Ablative direct object of the deponent verb **uteretur** (A.G. 410). "Caesar's base of operations was now at Agedincum. The transportation of supplies to the front as he kept marching south would be endangered if he left towns behind him in possession of the enemy." (Kelsey, 403)
(id) oppugnare: Complementary infinitive after **instituit** (A.G. 456). The pronoun **id**, with **oppidum** as the antecedent, is understood as the accusative direct object of the infinitive.
instituit: The main verb of the coordinate clause **Altero ... instituit** (A.G. 278.a). The pronoun **is**, with **cohortatus** (**Caesar**) as the antecedent, is understood as the subject (A.G. 271.a).
idque: Singular, neuter, accusative demonstrative pronoun used substantively (A.G. 296.2). The antecedent is **oppidum** (A.G. 297.e). Accusative direct object of **circumvallavit** (A.G. 387). **-que**: The enclitic conjunction connects the two main verbs **instituit ... circumvallavit** (A.G. 324.a).
biduo: Ablative of *time within which* (A.G. 423.1).
circumvallavit: The main verb of the coordinate clause **idque ... circumvallavit** (A.G. 278.a). The pronoun **is**, with **cohortatus** (**Caesar**) as the antecedent, is understood as the subject (A.G. 271.a).

(11.2) **tertio die missis ex oppido legatis de deditione, arma conferri, iumenta produci, sescentos obsides dari iubet.**

arma, -orum, n., pl., *arms, armor, weapons.*

de, *about, concerning.*
dies, -ei, m. and f., *day.*
ex, *from.*

iumentum, -i, n., *yoke-animal, beast of burden, draught-animal.*
mitto, mittere, misi, missus, *send.*
oppidum, -i, n., *fortified town, city.*
sescenti, -ae, -a, *six hundred.*

conferro, -ferre, -tuli, collatus, *bring together, gather, collect, convey.*
deditio, -onis, f., *surrender.*
do, dare, dedi, datus, *give.*
iubeo, iubere, iussi, iussus, *order, give orders, bid, command.*
legatus, -i, m., *envoy, ambassador.*
obses, -idis, m. and f., *hostage.*
produco, -ducere, -duxi, -ductus, *bring out, lead forth.*
tertius, -a, -um, *third.*

tertio die: Ablative of *time when* (A.G. 423.1). **tertio**: Ordinal number used as an adjective (A.G. 132-35). **die**: The noun **dies** is normally masculine gender (A.G. 97.a).

missis ex oppido legatis de deditione: Ablative absolute (A.G. 419-20). **missis**: The perfect tense of the participle represents the action as completed at the time indicated by the tense of the main verb (A.G. 489). **ex oppido**: Ablative of *place from which* with the preposition **ex** (A.G. 426.1). **de deditione**: Prepositional phrase, **de** with the ablative here means "about, concerning" (*OLD* **de** 12). **arma conferri, iumenta produci, sescentos obsides dari**: Three subject accusatives with three respective infinitives after **iubet**. The construction is equivalent to a substantive clause of purpose (A.G. 563.a). **iumentum**: Horses, mules, and asses. **sescentos**: Declinable cardinal number used as an adjective modifying **obsides** (A.G. 132-35). Notice the asyndeton construction (A.G. 323.b). Notice the euphony created by the three -i endings of the passive infinitives (A.G. 641). Notice the use of the passive voice with subdued enemies. Compare the use of the active and passive voice at 12.4, 12.5, 62.3-5 and 89.3-5.

iubet: The main verb of the main clause (A.G. 278.b). The historical present, giving vividness to the narrative, is present in Chapter 11 (A.G. 469). This usage, common in all languages, comes from imagining past events as going on before our eyes (*repraesentatio*) (A.G. 469 Note). The pronoun **is**, with **cohortatus (Caesar)** as the antecedent, is understood as the subject (A.G. 271.a).

(11.2-3) **Ea qui conficeret C. Trebonium legatum re(3)linquit.**

C. Trebonius, -i, m., *Gaius Trebonius.*	**conficio, -ficere, -feci, -fectus**, *complete, finish, accomplish, do.*
is, ea, id, *he, she, it; that, this.*	**legatus, -i**, m., *lieutenant, lieutenant-general.*
qui, quae, quod, *who, which, what.*	**relinquo, -linquere, -liqui, -lictus**, *leave, leave behind.*

Ea: Plural, neuter, accusative demonstrative pronoun used substantively meaning "these things" (A.G. 296.2). The antecedent is the actions described in the clause **arma ... dari** (A.G. 297.e). Accusative direct object of **conficeret** (A.G. 387).

qui ... conficeret: A relative clause of purpose is introduced by a relative pronoun and takes the subjunctive (A.G. 531.2). **qui**: Singular, masculine, nominative relative pronoun used substantively (A.G. 305). The antecedent is the following noun **Trebonium** (A.G. 307). Nominative subject (A.G. 339). The relative is here equivalent to **ut is** (A.G. 531.2 Note). **conficeret**: The main verb of the subordinate clause (A.G. 278.b). Imperfect subjunctive; the tense of the subjunctive is in secondary sequence follows the rules for the sequence of tense after the historical present tense of **relinquit** (A.G. 482-85, esp. 485.e).

C. Trebonium: Accusative direct object of **relinquit** (A.G. 387). See Appendix A. **C.**: Abbreviated form of the praenomen **Gaius** (A.G. 108.c).

legatum: An accusative noun in apposition to the proper noun **Trebonium** (A.G. 282).

relinquit: The main verb of the main clause (A.G. 278.b). The pronoun **is**, with **cohortatus (Caesar)** as the antecedent, is understood as the subject (A.G. 271.a).

(11.3-5) **Ipse, ut quam primum iter faceret, Cenabum Car(4)nutum proficiscitur; qui tum primum allato nuntio de oppugnatione Vellaunoduni, cum longius eam rem ductum iri existimarent, praesidium Cenabi tuendi causa quod eo (5) mitterent comparabant.**

adfero, -ferre, attuli, allatus, *bring, convey, deliver.*	**Carnutes, -um**, m., pl., *the Carnutes.*
causa, -ae, f., abl. with the gen., *for the sake of, on account of.*	**Cenabum, -i**, n., *Cenabum.*
comparo, -are, -avi, -atus, *prepare, make ready, get together.*	**cum**, *since, seeing that.*
de, *about, concerning.*	**duco, ducere, duxi, ductus**, *protract, prolong.*
eo, *there, thither.*	**existimo, -are, -avi, -atus**, *think, consider, judge.*
facio, facere, feci, factus, *make, accomplish.*	**ipse, -a, -um**, *he, they*, with or without *himself, themselves.*
is, ea, id, *he, she, it; that, this.*	**.iter, itineris**, n., *journey, march.*
longius, *further, longer.*	**mitto, mittere, misi, missus**, *send.*
nuntius, -i, m., *message, tidings.*	**oppugnatio, -onis**, f., *storming, assault, attack, besieging.*
praesidium, -i, n., *garrison.*	**primum**, (with **quam**), as *soon as possible; first.*
proficiscor, -ficisci, -fectus, *set out, depart, proceed.*	**quam**, as ---- *as possible.*
qui, quae, quod, *who, which, what.*	**res, rei**, f., *matter, affair, event.*
tueor, tueri, -----, *see to, support, guard, protect, defend.*	**tum**, *then, at that time.*
ut, *so that.*	**Vellaunodunum, -i**, n., *Vellaunodunum.*

Ipse: Singular, masculine, nominative demonstrative pronoun used substantively (A.G. 296.2 and 298.d). The antecedent is **Caesari** at 10.1 (A.G. 298). The pronoun **ipse** distinguishes the principle person (**Caesari**) from a subordinate person (**Trebonium**) (A.G. 298.3). Nominative subject of **proficiscitur** (A.G. 339).

ut ... faceret: The conjunction **ut** ("so that") with the subjunctive forms a final (purpose) clause dependent upon **proficiscitur** (A.G. 531.1). **faceret**: The main verb of the subordinate clause (A.G. 278.b). Imperfect subjunctive; the tense of the subjunctive is in secondary sequence after the historical present tense of **proficiscitur** (A.G. 482-85, esp. 485.e). The pronoun **is**, with **Ipse (Caesar)** as the antecedent, is understood as the subject (A.G. 271.a).

quam primum: The relative adverb **quam** with the adverb **primum** means "as soon as possible" (*OLD* **primum2** 4.b). **primum**: Adverb (A.G. 217.b and 320-21).

iter: Accusative direct object of **faceret** (A.G. 387). The phrase **iter facere** is an idiom that means "to march or travel" (*OLD* **iter** 1.b).

Cenabum: Accusative of *place to which* without a preposition (being the name of a town) (A.G. 427.2). "*Cenabum ... as quickly as possible*: problematic, because Cenabum is not on a direct route to Gorgobina from the probable site of Vellaunodunum. Perhaps Caesar takes the need to punish Cenabum for granted, as an unavoidable part of his march." (Hammond, 238) See Appendix A.

Carnutum: Possessive genitive of the tribe name **Carnutes** with **Cenabum** (A.G. 343). See Appendix A.

proficiscitur: The main verb of the main clause (A.G. 278.b).

qui: Plural, masculine, nominative relative pronoun used substantively (A.G. 305). The antecedent is **Carnutum** (A.G. 307). Nominative subject of **comparabant** (A.G. 339). The relative does not introduce a relative clause but is a connecting relative; at the beginning of a clause the pronoun is often best rendered by a personal or demonstrative pronoun, with or without *and* (A.G. 308.f).

tum: Adverb (A.G. 271.b and 320-21).

primum: Adverb (A.G. 214.d, 320-21, and 322.d).

allato nuntio de oppugnatione Vellaunoduni: Ablative absolute (A.G. 419-20). **allato**: The perfect tense of the participle represents the action as completed at the time indicated by the tense of the main verb (A.G. 489). **de oppugnatione**: Prepositional phrase, **de** with the ablative here means "about, concerning" (*OLD* **de** 12). **Vellaunoduni**: Locative of the city name **Vellaunodunum, -i**, n. (A.G. 49.a). See Appendix A.

cum ... existimarent: Causal clause; the relative adverb **cum** ("since") with the subjunctive forms a clause expressing cause (A.G. 549). **existimarent**: The main verb of the subordinate clause (A.G. 278.b). Imperfect subjunctive; the tense of the subjunctive is in secondary sequence and follows the rule for sequence of tense after **comparabant** (A.G. 482-85). The pronoun ei, with **qui** (Carnutes) as the antecedent, is understood as the subject (A.G. 271.a).

longius: Comparative adverb (A.G. 218 and 320-21).

eam rem ductum iri: Accusative/infinitive construction in indirect discourse after **existimarent** (A.G. 577 ff.). **eam**: Singular, feminine, accusative demonstrative pronoun used as an adjective modifying **rem** (A.G. 296.1 and a). **ductum iri**: The future passive infinitive is formed from the passive infinitive of **eo (iri)** and the supine in **-um (ductum)** (A.G. 193 Note and 203.a). The supine does not decline and so remains **ductum**, not **ductam**, which would agree with the accusative subject **rem** (A.G. 159.b). The tense of the infinitive in indirect discourse is relative to that of the verb of saying (A.G. 584).

praesidium: Accusative direct object of **comparabant** (A.G. 387).

Cenabi tuendi causa: The genitive of the noun and gerundive with the ablative **causa** expresses purpose (A.G. 504.b). **Cenabi**: See Appendix A. **tuendi**: Singular, neuter, genitive gerundive used as an adjective modifying **Cenabi** denoting necessity, obligation or propriety (A.G. 500.1).

quod ... mitterent: A relative clause of purpose is introduced by a relative pronoun and takes the subjunctive (A.G. 531.2). **quod**: Singular, neuter, accusative relative pronoun used substantively (A.G. 305). The antecedent is **praesidium** (A.G. 307). Accusative direct object of **mitterent** (A.G. 387). The relative is here equivalent to **ut id** (A.G. 531.2 Note). **mitterent**: The main verb of the subordinate clause (A.G. 278.b). Imperfect subjunctive; the tense of the subjunctive is in secondary sequence and follows the rule for sequence of tense after **comparabant** (A.G. 482-85). The pronoun ei, with **qui** (**Carnutes**) as the antecedent, is understood as the subject (A.G. 271.a).

eo: Adverb (A.G. 217.a and 320-21).

comparabant: The main verb of the main clause (A.G. 278.b).

(11.5-7) **Huc biduo pervenit. Castris ante oppidum positis, diei tempore exclusus in posterum oppugnationem differt, quaeque ad eam rem usui sint milititus (6) imperat et, quod oppidum Cenabum pons fluminis Ligeris contingebat, veritus ne noctu ex oppido profugerent duas (7) legiones in armis excubare iubet.**

ad, *for the purpose of, for.*
arma, -orum, n., pl., *arms.*
castra, -orum, n., pl., *camp, encampment.*
contingo, -tingere, -tigi, -tactus, *touch, extend to, reach.*
differo, differre, distuli, dilatus, *put off, delay.*
et, *and.*
excludo, -cludere, -clusi, -clusus, *hinder, prevent.*

flumen, -inis, n., *stream, river.*
impero, -are, -avi, -atus, *give orders* or *make requisition for, demand.*
is, ea, id, *he, she, it, that, this.*

legio, -onis, f., *legion.*
miles, -itis, m., *soldier, foot-solider.*
noctu, *by night, at night, in the night.*
oppugnatio, -onis, f., *storming, assault, attack, besieging.*
pono, ponere, posui, positus, *place, put.*
posterus, -a, -um, *following, the next.*
-que, *and.*
quod, *because, since, for, as.*
sum, esse, fui, futurus, *be.*

ante, *out in front of, before.*
biduum, -i, n., *space of two days, two days.*
Cenabum, -i, n., *Cenabum*
dies, -ei, m. and f., *day.*
duo, -ae, -o, *two.*
ex, *from, out of.*
excubo, -are, -avi, -atus, *lie out of doors, keep watch* or *guard.*
huc, *hither, here, to this place.*
in, *to; bearing, under.*
iubeo, iubere, iussi, iussus, *order, give orders, bid, command.*
Liger, -eris, *m., the Loire River.*
ne, *lest, that.*
oppidum, -i, n., *fortified town, city.*
pervenio, -venire, -veni, -ventus, *come to, reach.*
pons, pontis, m., *bridge.*
profugio, -fugere, -fugi, -----, *flee, escape.*
qui, quae, quod, *who, which, what.*
res, rei, f., *project, business, operation.*
tempus, -oris, n., *time.*

usus, -us, m., *advantage, profit, benefit.*

vereor, -eri, -itus, *fear, be afraid of.*

Huc: Adverb (A.G. 217.a and 320-21).

biduo: Ablative of *time within which* (A.G. 423.1).

pervenit: The main verb of the simple sentence (A.G. 278.1). The verb is in the perfect tense and indicates that the action is now completed (A.G. 473). The tense will next change to the historical present for the remainder of the chapter. The pronoun **is**, with **Ipse (Caesar)** as the antecedent, is understood as the subject (A.G. 271.a).

Castris ante oppidum positis: Ablative absolute (A.G. 419-20). **ante oppidum**: Prepositional phrase, **ante** with the accusative here means "out in front of" (*OLD* **ante2** 3). **positis**: The perfect tense of the participle represents the action as completed at the time indicated by the tense of the main verb (A.G. 489).

tempore: Ablative of cause without a preposition after **exclusus** (A.G. 404). "I.e., by the lateness of the hour, Caesar reached Cenabum late in the afternoon." (Kelsey, 403)

diei: Partitive genitive with **tempore** (A.G. 346.a.1).

exclusus: Nominative, perfect, passive participle used as a predicate where in English a phrase or a subordinate clause would be more natural (A.G. 496). The pronoun **is**, with **Ipse (Caesar)** as the antecedent, is understood Nominative subject of **differt** (A.G. 339).

in posterum: Prepositional phrase, **in** with the accusative of the adjective **posterus** means "to a point in the future, for the future" (*OLD* **posterus** 1.b). **posterum**: Singular, masculine, accusative adjective used substantively (A.G. 288). The noun **diem** is understood (A.G. 288.b).

oppugnationem: Accusative direct object of **differt** (A.G. 387).

differt: The main verb of the coordinate clause **Castris ... differt** (A.G. 278.a).

quaeque ... sint: A relative clause of characteristic; the relative pronoun with the subjunctive is often used to indicate a characteristic of the antecedent, especially where the antecedent is otherwise undefined (A.G. 535). **quae**: Plural, neuter, nominative relative pronoun used substantively meaning "such things as" (A.G. 148). The antecedent is omitted, supply **ea** (A.G. 307.c). Nominative subject (A.G. 339). **-que**: The enclitic conjunction connects the two main verbs **differt ... imperat** (A.G. 324.a). **sint**: The main verb of the subordinate clause (A.G. 278.b). Present subjunctive; the tense of the subjunctive is normally in secondary sequence after the historical present **imperat** (A.G. 482-85). However, when the historical present is equivalent to the perfect, the primary sequence is allowable when the present time is clearly in the writer's mind (A.G. 482-85, esp. 485.a).

ad eam rem: Prepositional phrase, **ad** with the accusative here means "for the purpose of" (*OLD* **ad** 44). **eam**: Singular, feminine, accusative demonstrative pronoun used as an adjective modifying **rem** (A.G. 296.1 and a).

usui ... militibus: Dative of the purpose or end (double dative). The dative of an abstract noun (**usui**) is used to show that for which a thing serves or which it accomplishes, often with another dative of the person or thing affected (**militibus**). The verb is usually a form of **sum (sint)** (A.G. 382.1).

imperat: The main verb of the coordinate clause **quaeque ... imperat** (A.G. 278.a). The pronoun **is**, with **Ipse (Caesar)** as the antecedent, is understood as the subject (A.G. 271.a).

et: The conjunction connects the main verbs **imperat ... iubet** (A.G. 324.a).

quod ... contingebat: Causal clause; the conjunction **quod** ("because") takes the indicative when the reason is given on the authority of the writer or speaker (A.G. 540.1). **contingebat**: The main verb of the subordinate clause (A.G. 278.b).

oppidum: Accusative direct object of **contingebat** (A.G. 387).

Cenabum: An accusative proper noun in apposition to **oppidum** (A.G. 282). See Appendix A.

pons: Nominative subject (A.G. 339).

fluminis: Partitive genitive with **pons** (A.G. 346.a.1).

Ligeris: A genitive proper noun in apposition to **fluminis** (A.G. 282). See Appendix A.

veritus ne ... profugerent: The conjunction **ne** ("lest") with the subjunctive after the participle **veritus** forms a substantive clause of fearing (A.G. 564). **veritus**: Nominative, perfect, deponent participle used as a predicate where in English a phrase or a subordinate clause would be more natural (A.G. 496). The pronoun **is**, with **Ipse (Caesar)** as the antecedent, is understood. Nominative subject of **iubet** (A.G. 339). **profugerent**: The main verb of the subordinate clause (A.G. 278.b). Imperfect subjunctive; the tense of the subjunctive is in secondary sequence and follows the rules for the sequence of tense after the historical present **iubet** (A.G. 482-85, esp. 485.e). The noun **Cenabenes** ("the inhabitants of Cenabum") is understood as the subject (A.G. 271.a).

noctu: Adverb (ablative or locative of *****noctus**, fourth-declension variant of **nox**) (*OLD* **noctu**) (A.G. 320-21).

ex oppido: Ablative of *place from which* with the preposition **ex** (A.G. 1/1/00426.1).

duas legiones ... excubare: Subject accusative/infinitive construction after **iubet**. The construction is equivalent to a substantive clause of purpose (A.G. 563.a). **duas**: Declinable cardinal number used as an adjective modifying **legiones** (A.G. 132-35).

in armis: Prepositional phrase, **in** with the ablative here means "bearing" (*OLD* **in** 36.b).

iubet: The main verb of the coordinate clause **quod ... iubet** (A.G. 278.a).

(11.7-8) Cenabenes paulo ante mediam noctem silentio ex oppido egressi flumen transire (8) coeperunt.

ante, *before, prior.*

coepi, -isse, coeptus, *begin, start, commence.*

ex, *from, out of.*

medius, -a, -um, *in the middle, midst, middle, mid-.*

oppidum, -i, n., *fortified town, city.*

silentium, -i, m., *silence, stillness.*

Cenabenes, -ium, m., pl., *the inhabitants of Cenabum.*

egredior, -gredi, -gressus, *go out, go forth, come forth, leave.*

flumen, -inis, n., *stream, river.*

nox, noctis, f., *night.*

paulo, *by a little, just a little.*

transeo, -ire, -ivi, or -ii, -itus, *go over, go across, pass* *over, cross over.*

Cenabenses ... egressi: Nominative subject (A.G. 339). **egressi**: Nominative, perfect, deponent participle used as a predicate where in English a phrase or a subordinate clause would be more natural (A.G. 496).
paulo: Adverb (320-21).
ante mediam noctem: Prepositional phrase, **ante** with the accusative here means "before" (a stated time) (*OLD* **ante2** 5). **mediam**: The adjective designates not what object, but what part of it is meant (A.G. 293).
silentio: Ablative of manner without the preposition **cum** (A.G. 412.b).
ex oppido: Ablative of *place from which* with the preposition **ex** (426.1).
flumen: Accusative direct object of the infinitive **transire** (A.G. 387 and 451.3).
transire: Complementary infinitive after **coeperunt** (A.G. 456).
coeperunt: The main verb of the simple sentence (A.G. 278.1). The verb **coepi** has no present tense and so the perfect has present force (A.G. 205).

(11.8-9) Qua re per exploratores nuntiata, Caesar legiones quas expeditas esse iusserat portis incensis intromittit atque oppido potitur, perpaucis ex hostium numero desideratis quin cuncti caperentur, quod pontis atque itinerum (9) angustiae multitudinis fugam intercluserant.

angustiae, -arum, f., pl., *narrowness, difficulties.*	**atque**, *and then; and.*
Caesar, -aris, m., *Caesar.*	**capio, capere, cepi, captus**, *take, seize, capture.*
cuncti, -orum, m., pl., *all in a body.*	**desidero, -are, -avi, -atus**, *lack, lose.*
ex, *from the number of, from among, of.*	**expeditus, -a, -um**, *light-armed, without baggage, ready.*
explorator, -oris, m., *spy, scout.*	**fuga, -ae**, f., *flight.*
hostis, -is, m., *enemy, foe*; pl., *the enemy.*	**incendo, -cendere, -cendi, -census**, *set on fire, burn.*
intercludo, -cludere, -clusi, -clusus, *shut off, cut off, block up.*	**intromitto, -mittere, -misi, -missus**, *send into, send in, let in.*
iter, itineris, n., *road.*	**iubeo, iubere, iussi, iussus**, *order, give orders, bid, command.*
legio, -onis, f., *legion.*	**multitudo, -inis**, f., *great number, large body, multitude, crowd.*
numerus, -i, m., *number.*	**nuntio, -are, -avi, -atus**, *announce, report.*
oppidum, -i, n., *fortified town, city.*	**per**, *by* (means of), *through.*
perpauci, -orum, m., pl., *a very few men.*	**pons, pontis**, m., *bridge.*
porta -ae, f., *city gate*; of a camp, *gate, entrance, passage.*	**potior, potiri, potitus**, *obtain possession of, acquire, obtain.*
qui, quae, quod, *who, which, what.*	**quin**, *so that ... not, that, but that.*
quod, *because, since, for, as.*	**res, rei**, f., *matter, affair, event.*
sum, esse, fui, futurus, *be.*	

Qua re per exploratores nuntiata: Ablative absolute (A.G. 419-20). **Qua**: Singular, feminine, ablative relative pronoun (A.G. 305). The antecedent is **re** in its own clause (adjectival use) (A.G. 307.b). The relative does not introduce a relative clause but is a connecting relative; at the beginning of a clause the pronoun is often best rendered by a personal or demonstrative pronoun, with or without *and* (A.G. 308.f). **per exploratores**: Prepositional phrase, the personal agent, when considered as instrument or means, is often expressed by **per** with the accusative meaning "by" (means of) (A.G. 405.b). **nuntiata**: The perfect tense of the participle represents the action as completed at the time indicated by the tense of the main verb (A.G. 489).
Caesar: Nominative subject of **intromittit ... potitur** (A.G. 339). See Appendix A.
legiones: Accusative direct object of **intromittit** (A.G. 387).
quas ... iusserat: Relative clause (A.G. 303). **iusserat**: The main verb of the subordinate clause (A.G. 278.b). The pronoun **is**, with **Caesar** as the antecedent, is understood as the subject (A.G. 271.a). The pluperfect tense of the verb denotes an action completed in past time (A.G. 477).
quas expeditas esse: Subject accusative/infinitive construction after **iusserat**. The construction is equivalent to a substantive clause of purpose (A.G. 563.a). **quas**: Plural, feminine, accusative relative pronoun used substantively (A.G. 305). The antecedent is **legiones** (A.G. 307). **expeditas**: Plural, feminine, accusative predicate adjective modifying **quas** after **esse** (A.G. 283-84).
portis incensis: Ablative absolute (A.G. 419-20). **incensis**: The perfect tense of the participle represents the action as completed at the time indicated by the tense of the main verb (A.G. 489).
intromittit: The main verb of the coordinate clause **Qua ... intromittit** (A.G. 278.a).
atque: The conjunction connects the two main verbs **intromittit ... potitur** and means "and then" (*OLD* **atque** 7).
oppido: Ablative direct object of the deponent verb **potitur** (A.G. 410).
potitur: The main verb of the coordinate clause **oppido ... intercluserant** (A.G. 278.a).
perpaucis ... intercluserant: Ablative absolute with dependent clauses.
perpaucis ex hostium numero desideratis: Ablative absolute (A.G. 419-20). **perpaucis**: Plural, masculine, ablative adjective used substantively (A.G. 288). The noun **hostibus** is understood (A.G. 288.b). The adverbial prefix **per-**, modifying an adjective, means "very" (A.G. 267.d.1). **ex hostium numero**: Prepositional phrase, **ex** with the ablative in a partitive sense means "from the number of,

from among, of" (*OLD* **ex** 17). **hostium**: Partitive genitive with **numero** (A.G. 346.a.1). **desideratis**: The perfect tense of the participle represents the action as completed at the time indicated by the tense of the main verb (A.G. 489).

quin ... caperentur: Subordinate clause; the conjunction **quin** ("so that ... not") with the subjunctive is used after a verb of lacking (**desideratis**) when it is negatived (here by implication) (A.G. 278.b and 558) (*OLD* **quin** 4). **caperentur**: The main verb of the subordinate clause (A.G. 278.b). Imperfect subjunctive; the tense of the subjunctive is in secondary sequence and follows the rules for the sequence of tense after the historical present **potitur** (A.G. 482-85, esp. 485.e).

cuncti: Plural, masculine, nominative adjective used substantively (A.G. 288). The noun **Cenabenes** is understood (A.G. 288.b). Nominative subject (A.G. 339).

quod ... intercluserant: Causal clause; the conjunction **quod** ("because") normally takes the indicative when the reason is given on the authority of the writer or speaker (A.G. 540.1). Here, the clause is dependent on a subjunctive clause (**quin ... caperentur**) and so should take the subjunctive (attraction) (A.G. 593). But a dependent clause may be closely connected grammatically with a subjunctive clause and still take the indicative if it is not regarded as a necessary logical part of that clause. The use of the indicative emphasizes the fact, as true independently of the statement contained in the subjunctive clause (A.G. 593.a). **intercluserant**: The main verb of the subordinate clause (A.G. 278.b). The pluperfect tense of the verb denotes an action completed in past time (A.G. 477).

pontis atque itinerum: Two possessive genitives with **angustiae** (A.G. 343). **atque**: The conjunction connects the two genitive nouns and means "and" (*OLD* **atque** 12).

angustiae: Nominative subject (A.G. 339). The noun is always plural (A.G. 101).

multitudinis: Possessive genitive with **fugam** (A.G. 343).

fugam: Accusative direct object of **intercluserant** (A.G. 387).

(11.9) **Oppidum diripit atque incendit, praedam militibus donat, exercitum Ligerim traducit atque in Biturigum finis pervenit.**

atque, *and then.*	**Bituriges, -um**, m., pl., *the Bituriges.*
diripio, -ripere, -ripui, -reptus, *ravage, plunder, pillage.*	**dono, -are, -avi, -atus**, *give, present, confer.*
exercitus, -us, m., *army.*	**fines, -ium**, m., pl., *borders*, hence *territory, country, land.*
in, *into.*	**incendo, -cendere, -cendi, -census**, *set on fire, burn.*
Liger, -eris, m., *the Loire River.*	**miles, -itis**, m., *soldier, foot-solider.*
oppidum, -i, n., *fortified town, city.*	**pervenio, -venire, -veni, -ventus**, *come to, reach.*
praeda, -ae, f., *booty, spoil, plunder.*	**traduco, -ducere, -duxi, -ductus**, *lead across, bring over, bring across.*

Notice how the use of five main verbs in one sentence creates a sense of vividness and moves the action along. The piling up of main verbs is not a common feature of Caesar's narrative style; normally there would be one (or two) main verb and the others would be subordinated, i.e. an ablative absolute, **cum** causal clause, participle, etc.. This is a noteworthy sentence.

Oppidum: Accusative direct object of both **diripit** (A.G. 387).

diripit ... incendit ... donat ... traducit ... pervenit: The pronoun **is**, with **Caesar** as the antecedent, is understood as the subject of all five verbs (A.G. 271.a).

diripit: The main verb of the coordinate clause **oppidum ... diripit** (A.G. 278.a).

atque: The conjunction connects the two main verbs **diripit ... incendit** and means "and then" (*OLD* **atque** 7).

incendit: The main verb of the coordinate clause **incendit** (A.G. 278.a). The pronoun **id**, with **oppidium** as the antecedent, is understood as the accusative direct object.

praedam: Accusative direct object of the transitive verb **donat** (A.G. 387). "Including probably the inhabitants of the town as well as their possessions. Caesar thus rewarded his men for the pluck and endurance they had shown during the few weeks preceding." (Kelsey, 403)

militibus: Dative indirect object of **donat** (A.G. 366).

donat: The main verb of the coordinate clause **praedam ... donat** (A.G. 278.a). Notice the asyndeton between the two main verbs **incendit ... donat** (A.G. 323.b).

exercitum Ligerim traducit: Secondary object construction. Transitive verbs compounded with a preposition (**tra(ns)-ducit**) can take a secondary object (**Ligerem**), originally governed by the preposition, in addition to the direct object (**exercitum**) (A.G. 395).

exercitum: Accusative direct object of **traducit** (A.G. 387).

Ligerim: Accusative of the secondary object of **traducit** (A.G. 394-95). The accusative singular of the third declension masculine i-stem noun **Liger** ends in **-im**, not **-em** (A.G. 73-75, esp. 74.d and 75.a.1). See Appendix A.

traducit: The main verb of the coordinate clause **Ligerim ... traducit** (A.G. 278.a).

atque: The conjunction connects the two main verbs **traducit ... pervenit** and means "and then" (*OLD* **atque** 7).

in Biturigum finis: Accusative of *place to which* with the preposition **in** (A.G. 426.2). **Biturigum**: Possessive genitive of the tribe name **Bituriges** with finis (A.G. 343). See Appendix A. **finis**: Accusative plural noun; **-is** for **-es** is the regular form in i-stem nouns (A.G. 65-7 and 74.c).

pervenit: The main verb of the coordinate clause **in ... pervenit** (A.G. 278.a).

(12.1-2) **Vercingetorix, ubi de Caesaris adventu cognovit, oppug(2)natione destitit atque obviam Caesari proficiscitur. Ille oppidum Biturigum positum in via Noviodunum oppugnare instituerat.**

adventus, -us, m., *coming, approach, arrival.*
Bituriges, -um, m., pl., *the Bituriges.*
cognosco, -gnoscere, -gnovi, cognitus, *learn, ascertain, recognize.*
desisto, -sistere, -stiti, -stitus, *leave off, stop, give up.*
in, *on.*

Noviodunum, -i, n., *Noviodunum.*
oppidum, -i, n., *fortified town, city.*

oppugno, -are, -avi, -atus, *attack, assault, storm, besiege.*
proficiscor, -ficisci, -fectus, *set out, depart, proceed.*
Vercingetorix, -igis, m., *Vercingetorix.*

atque, *and then.*
Caesar, -aris, m., *Caesar.*
de, *about, concerning.*
ille, illae, illud, *that; he, she, it.*
instituo, -stituere, -stitui, -stitutus, *undertake, commence, begin.*
obviam, *to meet, against.*
oppugnatio, -onis, f., *storming, assault, attack, besieging.*
pono, ponere, posui, positus, pass., often *be situated.*
ubi, *when.*
via, -ae, f., *way, road.*

Vercingetorix: Nominative subject of **destitit ... proficiscitur** (A.G. 339). See Appendix A.
ubi ... cognovit: Temporal clause; the relative adverb **ubi** ("when") with the indicative introduces a subordinate clause (A.G. 543).
cognovit: The main verb of the subordinate clause (A.G. 278.b). The pronoun **is**, with **Vercingetorix** as the antecedent, is understood as the subject (A.G. 271.a).
de Caesaris adventu: Prepositional phrase, **de** with the ablative here means "about, concerning" (*OLD* de 12). **Caesaris**: Possessive genitive with **adventu** (A.G. 343). See Appendix A.
oppugnatione: Ablative of separation without a preposition after the compound verb **destitit** (A.G. 402).
destitit: The main verb of the coordinate clause **Vercingetorix ... destitit** (A.G. 278.a). The historical present, giving vividness to the narrative, is present in Chapter 12 (A.G. 469). This usage, common in all languages, comes from imagining past events as going on before our eyes (*repraesentatio*) (A.G. 469 Note).
atque: The conjunction connects the two main verbs **destitit ... proficiscitur** and means "and then" (*OLD* atque 7).
obviam: Adverb (A.G. 216, 320-321.d).
Caesari: Dative after the adverb **obviam** (A.G. 370.c). See Appendix A.
proficiscitur: The main verb of the coordinate clause **obviam ... proficiscitur** (A.G. 278.a).
Ille: Singular, masculine, nominative demonstrative pronoun used substantively (A.G. 296.2 and 298.d). The antecedent is **Caesari** (A.G. 298). Nominative subject (A.G. 339). The pronoun marks a change in subject to one previously mentioned (**Caesari**) (A.G. 601.d).
oppidum ... positum: Accusative direct object of the infinitive **oppugnare** (A.G. 387 and 451.3). **positum**: Accusative, perfect, passive participle used as an adjective modifying **oppidum** (A.G. 494.a).
Biturigum: Possessive genitive of the tribe name **Bituriges** with **oppidum** (A.G. 343). See Appendix A.
in via: Prepositional phrase, **in** with the ablative here means "on" (*OLD* in 33).
Noviodunum: An accusative proper noun in apposition to **oppidum** (A.G. 282). Notice that there are two cities by this name. This one (of the Bituriges) is also mentioned at 7.14. The other (of the Aedui) is mentioned at 7.55. "this cannot refer to Noviodunum of the Aedui (Nevers), which is not on his route. It must be some other settlement, between Cenabum and Avaricum." (Hammond, 238) See Appendix A.
oppugnare: Complementary infinitive after **instituerat** (A.G. 456)
instituerat: The main verb of the simple sentence (A.G. 278.1). The pluperfect tense is normally used in a subordinate clause and its use as a main verb is rare (A.G. 477). Here it implies that Caesar had already begun the siege prior to Vercingetorix's decision to come and meet him.

(12.2-4) Quo ex oppido cum legati ad eum venissent oratum ut sibi ignosceret suaeque vitae consuleret, ut celeritate reliquas res conficeret, qua pleraque erat consecutus, (4) arma conferri, equos produci, obsides dari iubet.

ad, *to.*
celeritas, -tatis, f., *speed, quickness, swiftness, rapidity.*

conficio, -ficere, -feci, -fectus, *do thoroughly, complete, finish.*
consulo, -sulere, -sului, -sultus, *have regard for, look out for.*
do, dare, dedi, datus, *give.*
ex, *from, out of.*

is, ea, id, *he, she, it; that, this.*

legatus, -i, m., *envoy, ambassador.*
oppidum, -i, n., *fortified town, city.*
pleraque, -orumque, n., pl., *most things, very many things.*
-que, *and.*
reliquus, -a, -um, *remaining, the rest.*
sui, sibi, se, or sese, nom. wanting, *them*
venio, venire, veni, ventus, *come.*

arma, -orum, n., pl., *arms, armor, weapons.*
confero, -ferre, -tuli, collatus, *bring together, collect, convey.*
consequor, -sequi, -secutus, *obtain, secure, gain.*
cum, *after, when.*
equus, -i, m., *horse.*
ignosco, -gnoscere, -gnovi, -gnotus, *pardon, forgive, excuse.*
iubeo, iubere, iussi, iussus, *order, give orders, bid, command.*
obses, -idis, m. and f., *hostage.*
oro, -are, -avi, -atus, *plead, beg, entreat.*
produco, -ducere, -duxi, -ductus, *bring out, lead forth.*
qui, quae, quod, *who, which, what.*
res, rei, f., *project, business, operation.*
suus, -a, -um, *their,* with or without *own.*
ut, *so that.*

vita, -ae, f., *life*.

Quo ex oppido: Ablative of *place from which* with the preposition **ex** (A.G. 426.1). **Quo**: Singular, neuter, ablative relative pronoun (A.G. 305). The antecedent is **oppido** in its own clause (adjectival use) (A.G. 307.b). The relative does not introduce a relative clause but is a connecting relative; at the beginning of a clause the pronoun is often best rendered by a personal or demonstrative pronoun, with or without *and* (A.G. 308.f). **ex**: A monosyllabic preposition is often placed between a noun and its adjective (A.G. 599.d.2).
cum ... venissent ... consuleret: Temporal clause; **cum** ("after, when") with the pluperfect subjunctive describes the circumstances that preceded the action of the main verb (A.G. 546). **venissent**: The main verb of the subordinate clause (A.G. 278.b). **consuleret**: See below.
legati: Nominative subject (A.G. 339).
ad eum: Prepositional phrase, **ad** with the accusative here means "to" (*OLD* ad 1). **eum**: Singular, masculine, accusative demonstrative pronoun used substantively (A.G. 296.2). The antecedent is **ille (Caesar)** (A.G. 297.e). Here the indirect reflexive pronoun **se** is not used as the subordinate clause does not express the words or thoughts of the main subject (A.G. 300.a).
oratum: The supine in **-um** is used after a verb of motion (**venissent**) to express purpose (A.G. 509).
ut ... ignosceret ... consuleret: The conjunction **ut** ("so that") with the subjunctive forms a substantive clause of purpose which is used as the object of the supine **oratum** denoting an action directed toward the future (A.G. 563). **ignosceret ... consuleret**: The main verbs of the subordinate clause (A.G. 278.b). Imperfect subjunctive; the tense of the subjunctives is in secondary sequence and follows the rules for the sequence of tense after **venisset** (A.G. 482-85). The pronoun **is**, with **Ille (Caesar)** as the antecedent, is understood as the subject of both verbs (A.G. 271.a).
sibi: Plural, masculine, dative indirect reflexive pronoun (A.G. 300.2). The antecedent is **legati**, the subject of **venissent** (A.G. 299). Dative indirect object of the intransitive use of **ignosceret** (A.G. 367).
suaeque vitae: Dative indirect object of the intransitive use of **consuleret** (A.G. 367.c). **suae**: Singular, feminine, dative possessive pronoun used as an adjective modifying **vitae** (A.G. 302). **-que**: The enclitic conjunction connects the two main verbs in the purpose clause **ignosceret ... consuleret** (A.G. 324.a).
ut ... conficeret: The conjunction **ut** ("so that") with the subjunctive forms a final (purpose) clause (A.G. 531.1). This is not a part of the preceding clause **cum ... consuleret** but is dependent on **iubet**. **conficeret**: The main verb of the subordinate clause (A.G. 278.b). Imperfect subjunctive; the tense of the subjunctive is in secondary sequence after the historical present **iubet** (A.G. 482-85, esp. 485.e). The pronoun **is**, with **Ille (Caesar)** as the antecedent, is understood as the subject (A.G. 271.a).
celeritate: Ablative of means (A.G. 409).
reliquas res: Accusative direct object of **conficeret** (A.G. 387).
qua ... erat consecutus: Relative clause; a clause dependent on a subjunctive clause (**ut ... conficeret**) normally takes the subjunctive (attraction) (A.G. 303 and 593). However, when a dependent clause is not regarded as a necessary logical part of the clause, the indicative is used. The indicative serves to emphasize the fact, as true independently of the statement contained in the subjunctive clause (A.G. 593.a Note 1). **qua**: Singular, feminine, ablative relative pronoun used substantively (A.G. 305). The antecedent is **celeritate** (A.G. 307). Ablative of means (A.G. 409). **erat consecutus**: The main verb of the subordinate clause (A.G. 278.b). The pronoun **is**, with **Ille (Caesar)** as the antecedent, is understood as the subject (A.G. 271.a). The pluperfect denotes an action in indefinite time, but prior to some past time referred to (A.G. 477).
pleraque: Plural, neuter, accusative adjective used substantively meaning "most things" (A.G. 288). Accusative direct object of **erat consecutus** (A.G. 387 and 488).
arma conferri, equos produci, obsides dari: Three subject accusatives with three respective infinitives after **iubet**. The construction is equivalent to a substantive clause of purpose (A.G. 563.a). Notice the asyndeton construction (A.G. 323.b). Notice the euphony created by the three **-i** endings of the passive infinitives (A.G. 641). Notice the use of the passive voice with subdued enemies. Compare the use of the active and passive voice at 11.2, 12.5, 62.3-5 and 89.3-5.
iubet: The main verb of the main clause (A.G. 278.b). The pronoun **is**, with **Ille (Caesar)** as the antecedent, is understood as the subject (A.G. 271.a).

(12.4-5) Parte iam obsidum tradita, cum reliqua administrarentur, centurionibus et paucis militibus intromissis qui arma iumentaque conquirerent, equitatus hostium procul visus est, qui agmen (5) Vercingetorigis antecesserat.

administro, -are, -avi, -atus, *administer, arrange for, get ready*.

antecedo, -cedere, -cessi, -----, *go in advance, precede*.
centurio, -onis, m., *centurion*.

cum, *while, when*.
et, *and*.
iam, *already, by this time*.

iumentum, -i, n., *yoke-animal, beast of burden, draught-animal*.
obses, -idis, m. and f., *hostage*.
paucus, -a, -um, *few*.
-que, *and*.
reliqua, -orum, n., pl., *the remaining things*.

agmen, -minis, n., *army on the march, marching column, army*.
arma, -orum, n., pl., *arms, armor, weapons*.
conquiro, -quire, -quisivi, -quisitus, *seek out, hunt up, bring together*.
equitatus, -us, m., *cavalry*.
hostis, -is, m., *enemy, foe*; pl., *the enemy*.
intromitto, -mittere, -misi, -missus, *send into, send in, let in*.
miles, -itis, m., *soldier, foot-solider*.
pars ,partis, f., *part, portion*.
procul, *at a distance, from afar, far off*.
qui, quae, quod, *who, which, what*.
trado, -dere, -didi, -ditus, *hand over, give up, deliver, surrender*.

Vercingetorix, -igis, m., *Vercingetorix.*   video, videre, visi, visus, *perceive, observe, see.*

Parte iam obsidum tradita: Ablative absolute (A.G. 419-20). **iam**: Adverb (A.G. 215.6, 217.b and 320-21). **obsidum**: Partitive genitive with **Parte** (A.G. 346.a.1). **tradita**: The perfect tense of the participle represents the action as completed at the time indicated by the tense of the main verb (A.G. 489).
tradita ... administrarentur ... intromissis: Notice the asyndeton between the three dependent clauses (A.G. 323.b).
cum ... administrarentur: Temporal clause; **cum** (Awhile, when) with the imperfect subjunctive describes the circumstances that accompanied the action of the main verb (A.G. 546). **administrarentur**: The main verb of the subordinate clause (A.G. 278.b).
reliqua: Plural, neuter, nominative adjective used substantively meaning "the remaining things" (A.G. 288). Nominative subject (A.G. 387). **centurionibus ... conquirerent**: Ablative absolute with a dependent clause.
centurionibus et paucis militibus intromissis: Ablative absolute (A.G. 419-20). **centurionibus**: "The centurions commanded centuries, and there were therefore sixty in each legion. On them fell the immediate management of the men in battle. They fought in the ranks like the men and they were expected to set the men an example of conspicuous bravery. They were therefore promoted from the ranks on the basis of their strength and size as well as their skill and gallantry. They could hope for no promotion above the rank of centurion; but there were grades of centurions from one to the other of which they rose." (Walker, 26) For the exploits of unnamed centurions in the *BG* see 1.39, 41; 2.17, 25; 3.3.5, 14; 5.28, 37, 43, 52; 6.12, 39, 40; 7.17, 51. The named centurions are all used to exemplify the virtues or vices of Roman soldiers. See Publius Sextius Baculus 2.25; 3.5; 6.48. Titus Pullo and Lucius Vorenus 5.44. Lucius Fabius 7.47. Marcus Petronius 7.50. **et**: The conjunction connects the two ablative nouns **centurionibus ... militibus** (A.G. 324.a). **intromissis**: The perfect tense of the participle represents the action as completed at the time indicated by the tense of the main verb (A.G. 489).
qui ... conquirerent: A relative clause of purpose is introduced by a relative pronoun and takes the subjunctive (A.G. 531.2). **qui**: Plural, masculine, nominative relative pronoun used substantively (A.G. 305). The antecedent is **centurionibus ... militibus** (A.G. 307). Nominative subject (A.G. 339). The relative is here equivalent to **ut ei** (A.G. 531.2 Note). **conquirerent**: The main verb of the subordinate clause (A.G. 278.b). Imperfect subjunctive; the tense of the subjunctive is in secondary sequence and follows the rules for the sequence of tense after **visus est** (A.G. 482-85).
arma iumentaque: Two accusative direct objects of **conquirerent** (A.G. 387). **-que**: The enclitic conjunction connects the two accusative nouns (A.G. 324.a). **iumenta**: Horses, mules, and asses.
equitatus: Nominative subject (A.G. 339).
hostium: Partitive genitive with **equitatus** (A.G. 346.a.1).
procul: Adverb (A.G. 320-21).
visus est: The main verb of the main clause (A.G. 278.b).
qui ... antecesserat: Relative clause (A.G. 303). **qui**: Singular, masculine, nominative relative pronoun used substantively (A.G. 305). The antecedent is **equitatus** (A.G. 307). Nominative subject (A.G. 339). **antecesserat**: The main verb of the subordinate clause (A.G. 278.b). The pluperfect tense of the verb denotes an action completed in past time (A.G. 477).
agmen: Accusative direct object of **antecesserat** (A.G. 387).
Vercingetorigis: Possessive genitive with **agmen** (A.G. 343). See Appendix A.

(12.5-6) Quem simul atque oppidani conspexerunt atque in spem auxili venerunt, clamore sublato arma capere, portas claudere, murum complere coepe(6)runt.

arma, -orum, n., *arms, weapons.*
auxilium, -i, n., *help, aid, assistance, relief.*
clamor, -oris, m., *outcry, loud call, shout, din.*
coepi, -isse, coeptus, *begin, start, commence.*
conspicio, -spicere, -spexi, -spectus, *observe, see, perceive.*
murus, -i, m., *wall, rampart.*

porta -ae, f., *city gate.*
simul atque, *as soon as.*
tollo, tollere, sustuli, sublatus, *raise.*

atque, see simul; *and.*
capio, capere, cepi, captus, *take, get, seize, take up.*
claudo, claudere, clausi, clausus, *shut, close.*
compleo, -plere, -plevi, -pletus, *fully occupy, fill full.*
in, *into.*
oppidani, -orum, m., pl., *townspeople, inhabitants of a town.*
qui, quae, quod, *who, which, what.*
spes, -ei, f., *hope, expectation.*
venio, venire, veni, ventus, *come.*

Quem: Singular, neuter, accusative relative pronoun used substantively (A.G. 305). The antecedent is **equitatus** (A.G. 307). Accusative direct object of **conspexerunt** (A.G. 387). The relative does not introduce a relative clause but is a connecting relative; at the beginning of a clause the pronoun is often best rendered by a personal or demonstrative pronoun, with or without *and* (A.G. 308.f).
simul atque ... venerunt: Temporal clause; the clause is introduced by the adverb **simul** and the conjunction **atque** ("as soon as") and takes the indicative (A.G. 543). **conspexerunt ... venerunt**: The main verbs of the subordinate clause (A.G. 278.b).
oppidani: Nominative subject of **conspexerunt ... venerunt** (A.G. 339).
atque: The conjunction connects the two verbs in the temporal clause **conspexerunt ... venerunt** and means "and" (*OLD* atque 12).
in spem auxili: Prepositional phrase, **in** with the accusative here means "into" (a state or condition) (*OLD* **in** 2). **auxili**: Objective genitive with **spem** (A.G. 348). The singular genitive of nouns in **-ium** ended, until the Augustan Age, in a single **-i** (A.G. 49.b).
clamore sublato: Ablative absolute (A.G. 419-20). **sublato**: The perfect tense of the participle represents the action as completed at the time indicated by the tense of the main verb (A.G. 489).
capere ... claudere ... complere: Three complementary infinitives after **coeperunt** (A.G. 456). Notice the alliteration of the letter 'c' and the euphony created by the three **-ere** endings of the active infinitives (A.G. 641). Notice that the active voice returns when the

Gauls are again hopeful. Compare the use of the active and passive voice at 11.2, 12.4, 62.3-5 and 89.3-5.

arma ... portas ... murum: Three accusative directs objects of each respective infinitive (A.G. 387 and 451.3).

coeperunt: The main verb of the main clause (A.G. 278.b). The pronoun **ei**, with **oppidani** as the antecedent, is understood as the subject (A.G. 271.a).

(12.6) Centuriones in oppido, cum ex significatione Gallorum novi aliquid ab eis iniri consili intellexissent, gladiis destrictis portas occupaverunt suosque omnis incolumis receperunt.

ab, *by.*

centurio, -onis, m., *centurion.*
cum, *after, when.*

ex, *as a result of, in consequence of.*
gladius, -i, m., *sword.*
incolumis, -e, *safe, unharmed, uninjured, unhurt.*
intellego, -legere, -lexi, -lectus, *understand, perceive, ascertain.*
novus, -a, -um, *new, fresh, strange.*

omnis, -e, *all.*
porta -ae, f., *city gate.*
recipio, -cipere, -cepi, -ceptus, *take back, get back, recover.*
sui, -orum, m., pl., *their men*, with or without *own.*

aliquis, aliqua, aliquid, *some one, any one, anybody, something, anything.*
consilium, -i, n., *plan, scheme, plot.*
destringo, -stringere, -strinxi, -strictus, *unsheathe, draw.*
Galli, -orum, m., *the Gauls.*
in, *in, inside.*
ineo, -ire, -ivi or **-ii, -itus**, *enter upon, begin, form.*
is, ea, id, *he, she, it; that, this.*
occupo, -are, -avi, -atus, *seize upon, seize, take possession of.*
oppidum, -i, n., *fortified town, city.*
-que, *and.*
significatio, -onis, f., *demeanor, behavior.*

Centuriones: Nominative subject of **occupaverunt ... receperunt** (A.G. 339).

in oppido: Ablative of *place where* with the preposition **in** (locative ablative) (A.G. 426.3).

cum ... intellexissent: Temporal clause; **cum** ("after, when") with the pluperfect subjunctive describes the circumstances that preceded the action of the main verb (A.G. 546). **intellexissent**: The main verb of the subordinate clause (A.G. 278.b). The pronoun **ei**, with **Centuriones** as the antecedent, is understood as the subject (A.G. 271.a).

ex significatione Gallorum: Prepositional phrase, **ex** with the ablative here indicates cause and means "as a result of, in consequence of" (*OLD* ex 18). **Gallorum**: Possessive genitive with **significatione** (A.G. 343). See Appendix A.

novi ... consili: Partitive genitive with **aliquid** (A.G. 346.a.3). **consili**: The singular genitive of nouns in **-ium** ended, until the Augustan Age, in a single **-i** (A.G. 49.b).

aliquid ... iniri: Accusative/infinitive construction in indirect discourse after **intellexissent** (A.G. 577 ff.). **aliquid**: Singular, neuter, accusative indefinite pronoun used substantively (A.G. 151.e). **iniri consili**: The phrase **consilium inire** is an idiom that means "to form a plan or plot" (*OLD* ineo 7.b). **iniri**: Present infinitive; the tense of the infinitive in indirect discourse is relative to that of the verb of saying (A.G. 584).

ab eis: Ablative of agent with the preposition **ab** with the passive infinitive **iniri** (A.G. 405). **eis**: Plural, masculine, ablative demonstrative pronoun used substantively (A.G. 296.2). The antecedent is **Gallorum** (A.G. 297.e).

gladiis destrictis: Ablative absolute (A.G. 419-20). **gladiis**: "A straight, heavy, two-edged sword (**gladius**), about two feet long, adapted for either cutting or thrusting. Its scabbard (**vagina**) hung from a belt (**balteus**) which passed over the left shoulder. The sword was thus on the right side, out of the way of the shield. But the higher officers, who carried no shield, wore the sword on the left side." (Walker, 24-25) **destrictis**: The perfect tense of the participle represents the action as completed at the time indicated by the tense of the main verb (A.G. 489).

portas: Accusative direct object of **occupaverunt** (A.G. 38).

occupaverunt: The main verb of the coordinate clause **Centuriones ... occupaverunt** (A.G. 278.a).

suosque omnis incolumis: Accusative direct object of **receperunt** (A.G. 387). **suos**: Plural, masculine, accusative possessive pronoun used substantively to denote a special class (A.G. 302.d). **-que**: The enclitic conjunction connects the two main verbs **occupaverunt ... receperunt** (A.G. 324.a). **omnis**: An accusative, plural, attributive adjective modifying **suos** (A.G. 285.1). **-is** for **-es** is the regular form in i-stem adjectives (A.G. 114.a and 116). **incolumis**: Plural, masculine, accusative adjective modifying **suos** but used to qualify the action of the verb, and so has the force of an adverb (A.G. 290). **-is** for **-es** is the regular form in i-stem adjectives (A.G. 114.a and 116).

receperunt: The main verb of the coordinate clause **suosque ... receperunt** (A.G. 278.a).

(13.1) Caesar ex castris equitatum educi iubet, proelium equestre committit: laborantibus iam suis Germanos equites circiter CCCC summittit, quos ab initio habere secum instituerat.

ab, *from, since.*
Caesar, -aris, m., *Caesar.*
circiter, *about.*
-cum, *with.*
equester, -tris, -tre, *of cavalry, cavalry-.*
equitatus, -us, m., *cavalry.*
Germanus, -a, -um, *of* or *from Germany, German.*

C, in expression of number, = *100.*
castra, -orum, n., pl., *camp, encampment.*
committo, -mittere, -misi, -missus, *join* (battle), *begin.*
educo, -ducere, -duxi, -ductus, *lead out, lead forth.*
eques, -itis, m., *rider, horseman, cavalryman, trooper.*
ex, *from, out of.*
habeo, habere, habui, habitus, *have.*

instituo, -stituere, -stitui, -stitutus, *be accustomed, make a practice.*
initium, -i, n., *beginning, commencement.*

laboro, -are, -avi, -atus, *be hard pressed, be in distress, be in danger.*
qui, quae, quod, *who, which, what.*

summitto, -mittere, -misi, -missus, *send as reinforcement, send as support.*

iam, *already, presently.*
iubeo, iubere, iussi, iussus, *order, give orders, bid, command.*
proelium, -i, n., *battle, combat, engagement.*
sui, sibi, se, or sese, nom. wanting, *him*, with or without *-self.*
sui, -orum, m., pl., *his men*, with or without *own.*

Caesar: Nominative subject (A.G. 339). See Appendix A.
ex castris: Ablative of *place from which* with the preposition **ex** (426.1).
equitatum educi: Subject accusative with the infinitive after **iubet**. The construction is equivalent to a substantive clause of purpose (A.G. 563.a).
iubet: The main verb of the coordinate clause **Caesar ... iubet** (A.G. 278.a). The historical present, giving vividness to the narrative, is present in Chapter 13 (A.G. 469). This usage, common in all languages, comes from imagining past events as going on before our eyes (*repraesentatio*) (A.G. 469 Note).
proelium equestre: Accusative direct object of **committit** (A.G. 387).
committit: The main verb of the coordinate clause **proelium ... committit** (A.G. 278.a). The pronoun **is**, with **Caesar** as the antecedent, is understood as the subject (A.G. 271.a). Notice the asyndeton between the two main verbs **iubet ... committit** (A.G. 323.b).
laborantibus ... suis: Dative indirect object of the transitive verb **summittit** (A.G. 362). **laborantibus**: Present participle used as an adjective modifying **suis** (A.G. 494). **suis**: Plural, masculine, dative possessive pronoun used substantively to denote a special class (A.G. 302.d).
iam: Adverb modifying **laborantibus** (A.G. 215.6, 217.b and 320-21).
Germanos equites circiter CCCC: Accusative direct object of the transitive verb **summittit** (A.G. 387). **circiter**: Adverb (A.G. 433.2). **CCCC**: Roman numeral used as an adjective modifying **equites** (A.G. 133).
summittit: The main verb of the main clause (A.G. 278.b). The pronoun **is**, with **Caesar** as the antecedent, is understood as the subject (A.G. 271.a).
quos ... instituerat: Relative clause (A.G. 303). **quos**: Plural, masculine, accusative relative pronoun used substantively (A.G. 305). The antecedent is **equites** (A.G. 307). Accusative direct object of the infinitive **habere** (A.G. 387 and 451.3). **instituerat**: The main verb of the subordinate clause (A.G. 278.b). The pronoun **is**, with **Caesar** as the antecedent, is understood as the subject (A.G. 271.a). The pluperfect tense of the verb denotes an action completed in past time (A.G. 477).
ab initio: Prepositional phrase, **in** with the ablative of the noun **initium** means "from the beginning" (*OLD* **initium** 1.c). This is a curious locution. Although Kelsey here notes that it means "'from the beginning' of the Gallic War" (Kelsey, 404), there is no evidence for this. Indeed, the case seems to be the opposite in the *BG*; Caesar never mentions auxiliary German cavalry and is always supported instead by Gallic cavalry. In Book 1, he even mounts soldiers of the tenth legion on the horses of Gallic mounted troops to provide a personal escort (1.42). Perhaps he had a small bodyguard from the beginning which played such a small role that it was not worth mentioning. This, however, seems highly unlikely. Although Hammond suggests that it means "presumably of the seventh campaign." (Hammond, 238), there is no evidence for this interpretation either. Nevertheless, Caesar will specifically send for German cavalry in Chapter 65 and that body will play a pivotal role in his eventual success.
habere: Complementary infinitive after **instituerat** (A.G. 456).
secum: Ablative of accompaniment with the preposition **cum** (A.G. 413). **se**: Singular, masculine, ablative direct reflexive pronoun (A.G. 300.1). The antecedent is **is** (**Caesar**), the supplied subject of **instituerat** (A.G. 299). **-cum**: The preposition **cum** ("with") is joined enclitically with the ablative (A.G. 143.f).

(13.2) **(2) Eorum impetum Galli sustinere non potuerunt atque in fugam coiecti multis amissis se ad agmen receperunt.**

ad, *to, towards.*

amitto, -mittere, -misi, -missus, *lose.*
coicio, -icere, -ieci, -iectus, *put, drive, throw.*
Galli, -orum, m., *the Gauls.*
in, *into.*
multi, -orum, m., pl., *many men.*
possum, posse, potui, -----, *be able.*
sui, sibi, se, or sese, nom. wanting, *themselves.*

agmen, -minis, n., *army on the march, marching column, line of march.*
atque, *and.*
fuga, -ae, f., *flight.*
impetus, -us, m., *attack, assault, onset, charge.*
is, ea, id, *he, she, it; that, this.*
non, *not.*
recipio, -cipere, -cepi, -ceptus, (with se), *retreat.*
sustineo, -tinere, -tinui, -tentus, *bear, endure, withstand.*

Eorum: Plural, masculine, genitive demonstrative pronoun used substantively (A.G. 296.2). The antecedent is **Germanos equites** (A.G. 297.e). Possessive genitive with **impetum** (A.G. 343).
impetum: Accusative direct object of the infinitive **sustinere** (A.G. 387 and 451.3).
Galli: Nominative subject (A.G. 339). See Appendix A.
sustinere: Complementary infinitive with **potuerunt** (A.G. 456).
non: Adverb, the adverb generally precedes the verb if it belongs to no one word in particular (A.G. 217.e, 320-21, and 599.a).
potuerunt: The main verb of the coordinate clause **Eorum ... potuerunt** (A.G. 278.a).

atque: The conjunction connects the two main verbs **potuerunt ... receperunt** and means "and" (*OLD* **atque** 12).

in fugam: Prepositional phrase, **in** with the accusative here means "into" (*OLD* **in** 2).

coiecti: Nominative, perfect, passive participle used as a predicate where in English a phrase or a subordinate clause would be more natural (A.G. 496). The pronoun **ei**, with **Galli** as the antecedent, is understood. Nominative subject (A.G. 339).

multis amissis: Ablative absolute (A.G. 419-20). **amissis**: The perfect tense of the participle represents the action as completed at the time indicated by the tense of the main verb (A.G. 489). **multis**: Plural, masculine, ablative adjective used substantively meaning "many men" (A.G. 288).

se: Plural, masculine, accusative direct reflexive pronoun (A.G. 300.1). The antecedent is **coiecti** (**Galli**), the subject of **receperunt** (A.G. 299). Accusative direct object of **receperunt** (A.G. 387).

ad agmen: Accusative of *place to which* with the preposition **ad** (A.G. 426.2).

receperunt: The main verb of the coordinate clause **in ... receperunt** (A.G. 278.a). The reflexive use of **se recipere** in a military context means "to retreat" (*OLD* **recipio** 12).

(13.2-3) Quibus profligatis, rursus oppidani perterriti comprehensos eos quorum opera plebem concitatem existimabant ad (3) Caesarem perduxerunt seseque ei dediderunt.

ad, *to*.

comprehendo, -hendere, -hendi, -hensus, *lay hold of, arrest, capture*.

deddo, -dere, -didi, -ditus, *give up, surrender*.

is, ea, id, *he, she, it; that, this*.

oppidani, -orum, m., pl., *townspeople, inhabitants of the town*.

perterreo, -terrere, -----, -territus, *greatly alarm, frighten, terrify, dismay*.

profligo, -are, -avi, -atus, *put to flight, rout*.

qui, quae, quod, *who, which, what*.

sui, sibi, se, or **sese**, nom. wanting, *themselves*.

Caesar, -aris, m., *Caesar*.

concito, -are, -avi, -atus, *rouse, stir up, excite, provoke*.

existimo, -are, -avi, -atus, *think, consider, judge*.

opera, -ae, f., *effort, work, pains*.

perduco, -ducere, -duxi, -ductus, *bring, conduct, convey*.

plebs, plebis, f., *the common folk, the common people*.

-que, *and*.

rursus, *again, anew*.

Quibus profligatis: Ablative absolute (A.G. 419-20). **quibus**: Plural, masculine, ablative relative pronoun used substantively (A.G. 305). The antecedent is **Galli** (A.G. 307). The relative does not introduce a relative clause but is a connecting relative; at the beginning of a clause the pronoun is often best rendered by a personal or demonstrative pronoun, with or without *and* (A.G. 308.f). **profligatis**: The perfect tense of the participle represents the action as completed at the time indicated by the tense of the main verb (A.G. 489).

rursus: Adverb (A.G. 216 and 320-21).

oppidani perterriti: Nominative subject of **perduxerunt ... dediderunt** (A.G. 339). **perterriti**: Nominative, perfect, passive, participle used as a predicate, where in English a phrase or a subordinate clause would be more normal (A.G. 496).

comprehensos eos: Accusative direct object of **perduxerunt** (A.G. 387). **comprehensos**: Accusative, perfect, passive participle used as a predicate where in English a phrase or a subordinate clause would be more natural (A.G. 496). **eos**: Plural, masculine, accusative demonstrative pronoun used substantively (A.G. 296.2). The pronoun is correlative to the following relative clause **quorum ... existimabant** (A.G. 297.d).

quorum ... existimabant: Relative clause (A.G. 303). **quorum**: Plural, masculine, genitive relative pronoun used substantively (A.G. 305). The antecedent is **eos** (A.G. 307). Possessive genitive with **opera** (A.G. 343). **existimabant**: The main verb of the subordinate clause (A.G. 278.b). The pronoun **ei**, with **oppidani** as the antecedent, is understood as the subject (A.G. 271.a).

opera: Ablative of means (A.G. 409).

plebem concitatem (esse): Accusative/infinitive construction in indirect discourse after **existimabant** (A.G. 577 ff.). **concitatem (esse)**: Supply **esse** to form the perfect, passive infinitive (A.G. 184). The tense of the infinitive in indirect discourse is relative to that of the verb of saying (A.G. 584).

ad Caesarem: Prepositional phrase, **ad** with the accusative here means "to" (*OLD* **ad** 1). **Caesarem**: See Appendix A.

perduxerunt: The main verb of the coordinate clause **Quibus ... perduxerunt** (A.G. 278.a).

seseque: Plural, masculine, accusative direct reflexive pronoun (A.G. 300.1). The antecedent is **ei** (**oppidani**), the supplied subject of **dediderunt** (A.G. 299). Accusative direct object of the transitive verb **dediderunt** (A.G. 387). Reduplicated form of **se** (A.G. 144.b Note 1). **-que**: The enclitic conjunction connects the two main verbs **perduxerunt ... dediderunt** (A.G. 324.a).

ei: Singular, masculine, dative demonstrative used substantively (A.G. 296.2). The antecedent is **Caesarem** (A.G. 297.e). Dative indirect object of the transitive verb **dediderunt** (A.G. 362).

dediderunt: The main verb of the coordinate clause **sese ... dediderunt** (A.G. 278.a).

(13.3) Quibus rebus confectis, Caesar ad oppidum Avaricum, quod erat maximum munitissimumque in finibus Biturigum atque agri fertilissima regione, profectus est, quod eo oppido recepto civitatem Biturigum se in potestatem redacturum confidebat.

ad, *to, towards*.

atque, *and*.

Bituriges, -um, m., pl., *the Bituriges*.

civitas, -tatis, f., *state, nation*.

ager, -ri, m., *land* (under cultivation), *field*.

Avaricum, -i, n., *Avaricum*.

Caesar, -aris, m., *Caesar*.

conficio, -ficere, -feci, -fectus, *complete, finish, accomplish, do*.

confido, -fidere, -fisus sum, *believe, be confident.*
fines, -ium, m., pl., *borders,* hence *territory, country, land.*
is, ea, id, *he, she, it; that, this.*

munitus, -a, -um, sup. -issimus, *fortified, protected secure.*
potestas, -atis, f., *power, control, sway.*
-que, *and.*
quod, *because, since, for, as.*

redigo, -igere, -egi, -actus, *bring or force back, subdue.*
res, rei, f., *project, business, operation.*

sum, esse, fui, futurus, *be.*

fertilis, -e, sup. -issimus, *fertile, fruitful, productive.*
in, *in; into, under.*
maximus, -a, -um, *greatest, very great, largest, very large.*
oppidum, -i, n., *fortified town, city.*
proficiscor, -ficisci, -fectus, *set out, depart, proceed.*
qui, quae, quod, *who, which, what.*
recipio, -cipere, -cepi, -ceptus, *take back, get back, recover.*
regio, -onis, f., *region, territory.*
sui, sibi, se, or sese, nom. wanting, *he,* with or without *himself.*

Quibus rebus confectis: Ablative absolute (A.G. 419-20). **Quibus**: Plural, feminine, ablative relative pronoun (A.G. 305). The antecedent is **rebus** in its own clause (adjectival use) (A.G. 307.b). The relative does not introduce a relative clause but is a connecting relative; at the beginning of a clause the pronoun is often best rendered by a personal or demonstrative pronoun, with or without *and* (A.G. 308.f). **confectis**: The perfect tense of the participle represents the action as completed at the time indicated by the tense of the main verb (A.G. 489).
Caesar: Nominative subject of **profectus est** (A.G. 339). See Appendix A.
ad oppidum: Accusative of *place to which* with the preposition **ad** (A.G. 426.2).
Avaricum: An accusative proper noun in apposition to **oppidum** (A.G. 282). This city will be the focus of the narrative until 7.31. See Appendix A.
quod ... regione: Relative clause (A.G. 303). **quod**: Singular, neuter, nominative relative pronoun used substantively (A.G. 305). The antecedent is **Avaricum** (A.G. 307). Nominative subject (A.G. 339). **regione**: See below.
erat: The main verb of the subordinate clause (A.G. 278.b). Notice that Caesar does not here use the present tense (to denoting a state as now existing in present time) to describe the city as he normally does in city descriptions (see 55.4, 57.1, 58.3, and 68.1) The imperfect tense here foreshadows the complete annihilation of the city.
maximum munitissimumque: Notice the alliteration of the letter 'm' (A.G. 641).
maximum: Singular, neuter, nominative predicate adjective modifying **quod** after **erat** (A.G. 283-84). Irregular superlative adjective (A.G. 129).
munitissimumque: Singular, neuter, nominative predicate adjective modifying **quod** after **erat** (A.G. 283-84). Superlative adjective (A.G. 124). **-que**: The enclitic conjunction connects the two superlative adjectives **maximum muntissimum** (A.G. 324.a). Two adjectives belonging to the same noun are regularly connected by a conjunction (A.G. 323.d).
in finibus Biturigum atque agri fertilissima regione: Ablative of *place where* with the preposition **in** (locative ablative) (A.G. 426.3). **Biturigum**: Possessive genitive of the tribe name **Bituriges** with **finibus** (A.G. 343). See Appendix A. **atque**: The conjunction connects the two ablative nouns in the prepositional phrase **finibus ... regione** and means "and" (*OLD* **atque** 12). **agri**: Genitive of specification with the superlative adjective **fertilissima** (A.G. 349.d). **fertilissima**: Superlative adjective modifying **regione** (A.G. 124).
profectus est: The main verb of the main clause (A.G. 278.b).
quod ... confidebat: Causal clause; the conjunction **quod** ("because") takes the indicative when the reason is given on the authority of the writer or speaker (A.G. 540.1). **confidebat**: The main verb of the subordinate clause (A.G. 278.b). The pronoun **is**, with **Caesar** as the antecedent, is understood as the subject (A.G. 271.a).
eo oppido recepto: Ablative absolute (A.G. 419-20). **eo**: Singular, neuter, ablative demonstrative pronoun used as an adjective modifying **oppido** (A.G. 296.1 and a). **recepto**: The perfect tense of the participle represents the action as completed at the time indicated by the tense of the main verb (A.G. 489).
civitatem: Accusative direct object of the infinitive **redacturum (esse)** (A.G. 387 and 451.3).
Biturigum: Possessive genitive of the tribe name **Bituriges** with **civitatem** (A.G. 343). See Appendix A.
se ... redacturum (esse): Accusative/infinitive construction in indirect discourse after **confidebat** (A.G. 577 ff.). **se**: Singular, masculine, accusative direct reflexive pronoun (A.G. 300.1). The antecedent is **is** (Caesar), the supplied subject of **confidebat** (A.G. 299). **redacturum (esse)**: Supply **esse** to form the future active infinitive (A.G. 186). The tense of the infinitive in indirect discourse is relative to that of the verb of saying (A.G. 584).
in potestatem redacturum: The phrase **in potestatem redigere** is an idiom that means "to bring under the power or control (of)" (*OLD* **redigo** 10.a).
in potestatem: Prepositional phrase, **in** with the accusative here means "into" (a state or condition) (*OLD* **in** 2).

PART 2: THE SIEGE AND SACK OF AVARICUM BY THE ROMANS (7.14-33)
2.A CHAPTERS 14-15: AT VERCINGETORIX'S INSISTENCE A SCORCHED EARTH POLICY IS ADOPTED; DESPITE VERCINGETORIX'S PROTESTATIONS, AVARICUM IS EXCEPTED AND DEFENDED
(14.1) **Vercingetorix, tot continuis incommodis Vellaunoduni, Cenabi, Novioduni acceptis, suos ad concilium convocat.**

accipio, -cipere, -cepi, -ceptus, *suffer, bear.*
Cenabum, -i, n., *Cenabum.*
continuus, -a, -um, *successive, in unbroken succession, continuous.*

ad, *to.*
concilium, -i, n., *meeting, assembly, council.*
convoco, -are, -avi, -atus, *call together, summon,*

56

incommodum, -i, n., *misfortune, disaster, injury, defeat.*
sui, -orum, m., pl., *his men,* with or without *own.*
Vellaunodunum, -i, n., *Vellaunodunum.*

assemble.
Noviodunum, -i, n., *Noviodunum.*
tot, *so many.*
Vercingetorix, -igis, m., *Vercingetorix.*

Vercingetorix ... ad concilium convocat: Kahn claims that the council scene functions as a substitute for choral odes between major episodes. (Kahn, 251) See also 1.4, 29.1, 63.5-6, 75.1, and 89.1
Vercingetorix: Nominative subject of **convocat** (A.G. 339). See Appendix A.
tot continuis incommodis Vellaunoduni, Cenabi, Novioduni acceptis: Ablative absolute (A.G. 419-20). See Chapters 11-13 for the loss of these three cities. **tot:** Indeclinable adjective modifying **incommodis** (A.G. 122.b). **Vellaunoduni, Cenabi, Novioduni:** Notice the asyndeton between the three nouns (A.G. 323.b). **Vellaunoduni:** Locative of the city name **Vellaunodunum, -i, n.** (A.G. 49.a). See 11.1-3. **Cenabi:** Locative of the city name **Cenabum, -i, n.** (A.G. 49.a). See 11.3-9. **Noviodunum:** Locative of the city name **Noviodunum, -i, n.** (A.G. 49.a). See 12 and 13.1-3. Notice that there are two cities by this name. This one (of the Bituriges) is also mentioned at 7.12. The other (of the Aedui) is mentioned at 7.55. See Appendix A for the three cities. **acceptis:** The perfect tense of the participle represents the action as completed at the time indicated by the tense of the main verb (A.G. 489).
suos: Plural, masculine, accusative possessive pronoun used substantively to denote a special class (A.G. 302.d). Accusative direct object of **convocat** (A.G. 387).
ad concilium: Accusative of *place to which* with the preposition **ad** (A.G. 426.2).
convocat: The main verb of the main clause (A.G. 278.b). The historical present, giving vividness to the narrative, is present in Chapter 14 (A.G. 469). This usage, common in all languages, comes from imagining past events as going on before our eyes (*repraesentatio*) (A.G. 469 Note).

Docet ... victis (14.2-10): This speech is classified by C. Murphy as a military address and claims that it performs "the function of preparing the reader for the coming strategy and tactics of the Gauls." (C. Murphy, 122-123). "This policy of avoiding a decisive battle, cutting off the enemy's supplies and harassing at every turn, was the best that, under the circumstances, the Gauls could pursue. The proposal of it reveals in Vercingetorix generalship of a high order. Similar tactics have been employed by many generals - among others, Fabius Maximus, who wore out Hannibal, and our own Washington." (Kelsey, 404)

(14.2) **(2) Docet longe alia ratione esse bellum gerendum atque antea gestum sit.**

alius, -a, -ud, *another, some other, other.*
antea, *previously, before, formerly.*
doceo, docere, docui, doctus, *inform, point out, state.*
longe, *far, by far.*

atque, (other) *than.*
bellum, -i, n., *war, warfare.*
gero, gerere, gessi, gestus, *manage, carry on, wage.*
ratio, -onis, f., *manner, method, fashion.*

Docet: The main verb of the main clause (A.G. 278.b). The verb comes in the first position when the idea in it is emphatic (A.G. 598.d). The pronoun **is,** with **Vercingetorix** as the antecedent, is understood as the subject (A.G. 271.a). The historical present verb introduces indirect speech through the remainder of Chapter 14.
longe: Adverb (A.G. 214.a and 320-21).
alia ratione: Ablative of manner with a limiting adjective (A.G. 412).
esse bellum gerendum: Accusative/infinitive construction in indirect discourse after **Docet** (A.G. 577 ff.). **esse ... gerendum:** A second periphrastic (passive) present infinitive is formed by a combination of the gerundive with the present infinitive of **sum** and denotes obligation, necessity, or propriety (A.G. 194.b and 196). The tense of the infinitive in indirect discourse is relative to that of the verb of saying (A.G. 584). The infinitive is here split (tmesis) (A.G. 640).
(alia) ... atque ... gestum sit: Subordinate clause; a subordinate clause in indirect discourse takes the subjunctive (A.G. 278.b and 580). **atque:** When the conjunction follows the adjective **alius** it means A (other) than (A.G. 407.d). **gestum sit:** The main verb of the subordinate clause (A.G. 278.b). Perfect subjunctive; the tense of the subjunctive is normally in secondary sequence after the historical present **Docet** (A.G. 482-85). Here it is in primary sequence through *repraesentatio* (A.G. 485.e and 585.b Note). The pronoun **id,** with **bellum** as the antecedent, is understood as the subject (A.G. 271.a).
antea: Adverb (A.G. 216 Note and 320-21).

(14.2-3) **Omnibus modis huic rei studendum ut pabu(3)latione et commeatu Romani prohibeantur.**

commeatus, -us, m., *supplies, provisions.*
hic, haec, hoc, *this; he, she, it.*
omnis, -e, *all.*
prohibeo, -hibere, -hibui, -hibitus, *prevent, hinder.*
Romani, -orum, m., pl., *the Romans.*
ut, *namely that, to the effect that.*

et, *and.*
modus, -i, m., *means, way.*
pabulatio, -onis, f., *foraging, getting fodder.*
res, rei, f., *object, outcome.*
studeo, -ere, -ui, -----, *give attention to, concentrate on.*

Omnibus modis: Ablative of manner (A.G. 412).
huic rei: Dative indirect object of the intransitive infinitive **studendum (esse)** (A.G. 368.3). When intransitive verbs that govern the dative are used impersonally in the passive the dative is retained (A.G. 372). **huic:** Singular, feminine, dative demonstrative pronoun used as an adjective modifying **rei** (A.G. 296.1 and a).

(id) **studendum** (**esse**): Accusative/infinitive construction in indirect discourse after **Docet** (A.G. 577 ff.). **studendum** (**esse**): Supply **esse** to form the second periphrastic (passive) present infinitive (A.G. 196). The second periphrastic present infinitive is formed by a combination of the gerundive with the present infinitive of **sum** and denotes obligation, necessity, or propriety (A.G. 194.b). The tense of the infinitive in indirect discourse is relative to that of the verb of saying (A.G. 584). Impersonal use of the intransitive passive infinitive (A.G. 208.d). Supply **id** as the subject (A.G. 318.c).

ut ... prohibeantur: The conjunction **ut** ("namely that, to the effect that") with the subjunctive forms an epexegetical clause in apposition to **huic rei** (*OLD* **ut** 39). **prohibeantur**: The main verb of the subordinate clause (A.G. 278.b). Present subjunctive; the tense of the subjunctive is normally in secondary sequence after the historical present **Docet** (A.G. 482-85). Here it is in primary sequence through *repraesentatio* (A.G. 485.e and 585.b Note).

pabulatione et commeatu: Two ablatives of separation without a preposition after **prohibeantur** (A.G. 401). **et**: The conjunction connects the two ablative nouns (A.G. 324.a).

Romani: Nominative subject (A.G. 339).

(14.3-4) **Id esse facile, quod equitatu ipsi abundent et quod anni tempore suble(4)ventur.**

abundo, -are, -avi, -----, *abound in, be well provided with.*	**annus, -i,** m., *year.*
equitatus, -us, m., *cavalry.*	**et,** *and.*
facilis, -e, *easy, convenient, not difficult, not hard.*	**ipse, -a, -um,** *he, they,* with or without *himself, themselves.*
is, ea, id, *he, she, it; that, this.*	**quod,** *because, since, for, as.*
sublevo, -are, -avi, -atus, *assist, aid.*	**sum, esse, fui, futurus,** *be.*
tempus, -oris, n., *time.*	

Id esse facile: Accusative/infinitive construction in indirect discourse after **Docet** (A.G. 577 ff.). **Id**: Singular, neuter, accusative demonstrative pronoun used substantively (A.G. 296.2). The antecedent is the idea of depriving the Romans of supplies contained in the previous clause (A.G. 297.e). **esse**: Present infinitive; the tense of the infinitive in indirect discourse is relative to that of the verb of saying (A.G. 584). The present tense, where one might expect the future, makes the verb more vivid. **facile**: Singular, neuter, accusative predicate adjective modifying **Id** after **esse** (A.G. 283-84).

quod ... quod: The repetition of words at the beginning of successive clauses is anaphora (A.G. 641).

quod ... abundent: Causal clause; the conjunction **quod** ("because") would normally take the indicative when the reason is given on the authority of the writer or speaker (A.G. 540.1). Here **quod** takes the subjunctive as a subordinate clause in indirect discourse after **Docet** (A.G. 580). **abundent**: The main verb of the subordinate clause (A.G. 278.b). Present subjunctive; the tense of the subjunctive is normally in secondary sequence after the historical present **Docet** (A.G. 482-85). Here it is in primary sequence through *repraesentatio* (A.G. 485.e and 585.b Note).

equitatu: Ablative of means after the verb **abundent** (A.G. 409.a).

ipsi: Plural, masculine, nominative demonstrative pronoun used substantively (A.G. 296.2 and 298.d). The antecedent is **suos** (those being addressed at the council) (A.G. 298). Nominative subject of **abundent ... subleventur** (A.G. 339). The pronoun is here emphatic (A.G. 298.d.1).

et: The conjunction connects the two causal clauses (A.G. 324.a).

quod ... subleventur: Causal clause; the conjunction **quod** ("because") would normally take the indicative when the reason is given on the authority of the writer or speaker (A.G. 540.1). Here **quod** takes the subjunctive as a subordinate clause in indirect discourse after **Docet** (A.G. 580). **subleventur**: The main verb of the subordinate clause (A.G. 278.b). Present subjunctive; the tense of the subjunctive is normally in secondary sequence after the historical present **Docet** (A.G. 482-85). Here it is in primary sequence through *repraesentatio* (A.G. 485.e and 585.b Note).

tempore: Ablative of means (A.G. 409). "it was March, and there would be no forage in the fields until June." (Hammond, 238)

anni: Partitive genitive with **tempore** (A.G. 346.a.1).

(14.4-5) **Pabulum secari non posse; necessario dispersos hostis ex aedificiis petere: hos omnis cotidie ab equitibus (5) deligi posse.**

ab, *by.*	**aedificium, -i,** n., *building.*
cotidie, *daily, every day.*	**deligo, -ligere, -legi, -lectus,** *separate, single out, pick out.*
dispergo, -spergere, -spersi, -spersus, *scatter, scatter about, disperse.*	**eques, -itis,** m., *rider, horseman, cavalryman, trooper.*
ex, *from, out of.*	**hic, haec, hoc,** *this; he, she, it.*
hostis, -is, m., *enemy, foe*; pl., *the enemy.*	**necessario,** *of necessity, unavoidably.*
non, *not.*	**omnis, -e,** *all.*
pabulum, -i, n., *fodder.*	**peto, petere, petivi,** and **petii, petitus,** *seek, get, secure.*
possum, posse, potui, -----, *be able.*	**seco, -are, -avi, -atus,** *cut, reap.*

Pabulum ... posse: Accusative/infinitive construction in indirect discourse after **Docet** (A.G. 577 ff.). **posse**: Present infinitive; the tense of the infinitive in indirect discourse is relative to that of the verb of saying (A.G. 584).

secari: Complementary infinitive after **posse** (A.G. 456).

non: Adverb, the adverb generally precedes the verb if it belongs to no one word in particular (A.G. 217.e, 320-21, and 599.a).

necessario: Adverb (A.G. 320-21).

dispersos hostis ... petere: Accusative/infinitive construction in indirect discourse after **Docet** (A.G. 577 ff.). **dispersos**: Accusative, perfect, passive participle used as a predicate where in English a phrase or a subordinate clause would be more natural (A.G. 496). **hostis**: Accusative plural noun; **-is** for **-es** is the regular form in i-stem nouns (A.G. 65-7 and 74.c). **petere**: Present infinitive; the tense of the infinitive in indirect discourse is relative to that of the verb of saying (A.G. 584). Supply the pronoun **id**, with **pabulum** as the antecedent, as the direct object (A.G. 387 and 451.3).

ex aedificiis: Ablative of source with the preposition **ex** (A.G. 403.1). **aedificiis**: "The granaries and barns where grain and fodder were stored." (Kelsey, 404)

hos omnis ... posse: Accusative/infinitive construction in indirect discourse after **Docet** (A.G. 577 ff.). **hos**: Plural, masculine, accusative demonstrative pronoun used substantively (A.G. 296.2). The antecedent is **hostis** (A.G. 297.e). **omnis**: Accusative plural adjective; **-is** for **-es** is the regular form in i-stem adjectives (A.G. 114.a and 116). **posse**: Present infinitive; the tense of the infinitive in indirect discourse is relative to that of the verb of saying (A.G. 584).

cotidie: Adverb (A.G. 217.b and 320-21).

ab equitibus: Ablative of agent with the preposition **ab** after the passive infinitive **deligi** (A.G. 405).

deligi: Complementary infinitive after **posse** (A.G. 456).

(14.5-6) Praeterea, salutis causa rei familiaris commoda neglegenda: vicos atque aedificia incendi oportere hoc spatio ab via quoqueversus quo pabulandi causa adire (6) posse videantur.

ab, *from.*
aedificium, -i, n., *building.*
causa, -ae, f., abl. with the gen., *for the sake of, on account of, for the purpose of.*
commodum, -i, n., , *advantage, profit, gain, interest.*
hic, haec, hoc, *this; he, she, it.*
neglego, -legere, -lexi, -lectus, *disregard, leave out of consideration.*

pabulor, -ari, -atus, *forage, get fodder.*
praeterea, *besides, further.*
quoqueversus, *in every direction.*
salus, -utis, f., *welfare, safety, preservation.*
via, -ae, f., *way, road.*
vicus, -i, m., *village, hamlet.*

adeo, -ire, -ivi, or **-ii, -itus**, *go to, approach, draw near.*
atque, *and.*

familiaris, -e, *private, estate, household, domestic*
incendo, -cendere, -cendi, -census, *set on fire, burn.*
oportet, oportere, oportuit, (imper.), *it is necessary, it is needful.*
possum, posse, potui, -----, *be able.*
quo, *where.*
res, rei, f., *property.*
spatium, -i, n., *space, distance.*
videor, videri, visus sum, *seem, appear.*

Praeterea: Adverb (A.G. 216 and 320-21).

salutis causa: A preceding genitive with the ablative of **causa** means "for the sake of" A (A.G. 359.b and 404.c).

rei familiaris: Possessive genitive with **commoda** (A.G. 343). The phrase **res familiaris** means "one's private property, estate, patrimony" (*OLD* **familiaris** 1.c).

commoda neglegenda (esse): Accusative/infinitive construction in indirect discourse after **Docet** (A.G. 577 ff.). **neglegenda (esse)**: Supply **esse** to form the second periphrastic (passive) present infinitive (A.G. 196). The second periphrastic present infinitive is formed by a combination of the gerundive with the present infinitive of **sum** and denotes obligation, necessity, or propriety (A.G. 194.b). The tense of the infinitive in indirect discourse is relative to that of the verb of saying (A.G. 584). "Such an appeal to the sentiment of patriotism, in the face of invaders, might well bring response." (Kelsey, 404)

vicos atque aedificia incendi: The infinitive phrase functions as the subject of the impersonal infinitive **oportere** (A.G. 454). **vicos atque aedificia**: Two accusative subjects of the infinitive (A.G. 397.e and 455.2). **atque**: The conjunction connects the two accusative nouns and means "and" (*OLD* **atque** 12).

oportere: Impersonal infinitive construction in indirect discourse after **Docet** (A.G. 577 ff.). Impersonal use of the verb (A.G. 208.c). The previous infinitive phrase functions as the subject (A.G. 454). Present infinitive; the tense of the infinitive in indirect discourse is relative to that of the verb of saying (A.G. 584). Compare this with **oppida incendi oportere** at 14.9. Notice how Vercingetorix begins with a more palatable suggestion - that villages and buildings (**vicos atque aedificia**) be burnt - before suggesting the more radical position of burning entire towns (**oppida**).

hoc spatio: Ablative of degree of difference (A.G. 414 and 425.b). **hoc**: Singular, neuter, ablative demonstrative pronoun used as an adjective modifying **spatio** (A.G. 296.1 and a).

ab via: Ablative of *place from which* with the preposition **ab** (A.G. 426.1).

quoqueversus: Adverb (A.G. 216 and 320-21).

quo ... videantur: Relative clause; a subordinate clause in indirect discourse takes the subjunctive (A.G. 279.a and 580). **quo**: Relative adverb (*OLD* **quo1** 3). **videantur**: The main verb of the subordinate clause (A.G. 278.b). Present subjunctive; the tense of the subjunctive is normally in secondary sequence after the historical present **Docet** (A.G. 482-85). Here it is in primary sequence through *repraesentatio* (A.G. 485.e and 585.b Note). The pronoun **ei**, with **hostis** as the antecedent, is understood as the subject (A.G. 271.a).

pabulandi causa: The genitive of the gerund with the ablative of **causa** expresses purpose (A.G. 504.b). **pabulandi**: Singular, neuter, genitive gerund (A.G. 501-02).

adire: Complementary infinitive after **posse** (A.G. 456).

posse: Complementary infinitive after **videantur** (A.G. 456).

(14.6-7) Harum ipsis rerum copiam suppetere, quod quorum in finibus bellum geratur eorum opibus sub(7)leventur:

bellum, -i, n., *war, warfare.*
fines, -ium, m., pl., *borders*, hence *territory, country, land.*
hic, haec, hoc, *this; he, she, it.*
ipse, -a, -um, *he, they*, with or without *himself, themselves.*
opes, -um, f., pl., *resources, wealth, means, property.*
quod, *because, since, for, as.*
sublevo, -are, -avi, -atus, *relieve, assist, aid, support.*

copia, -ae, f., *quantity, abundance, supply, plenty.*
gero, gerere, gessi, gestus, *carry on, wage.*
in, *in.*
is, ea, id, *he, she, it; that, this.*
qui, quae, quod, *who, which, what.*
res, rei, f., *goods, possessions.*
suppeto, -petere, -petivi, -petitus, *be at hand, available,* or *present.*

Harum ... rerum: Partitive genitive with **copiam** (A.G. 346.a.1). **Harum**: Plural, feminine, genitive demonstrative pronoun used as an adjective with **rerum** (A.G. 296.1.and a).
ipsis: Plural, masculine, dative demonstrative pronoun used substantively (A.G. 296.2 and 298.d). The antecedent is **ipsi** (those being addressed at the council)) (A.G. 298). Dative indirect object of the intransitive verb **suppetere** (A.G. 366). The pronoun is here emphatic (A.G. 298.d.1).
copiam suppetere: Accusative/infinitive construction in indirect discourse after **Docet** (A.G. 577 ff.). **suppetere**: Present infinitive; the tense of the infinitive in indirect discourse is relative to that of the verb of saying (A.G. 584).
quod ... subleventur: The word order here is nearly reverse of the English. The phrase could be rewritten as **quod (ei) subleventur opibus eorum in quorum finibus bellum geratur**.
quod ... subleventur: Causal clause; the conjunction **quod** ("because") would normally take the indicative when the reason is given on the authority of the writer or speaker (A.G. 540.1). Here **quod** takes the subjunctive as a subordinate clause in indirect discourse after **Docet** (A.G. 580). **subleventur**: The main verb of the subordinate clause (A.G. 278.b). Present subjunctive; the tense of the subjunctive is normally in secondary sequence after the historical present **Docet** (A.G. 482-85). Here it is in primary sequence through *repraesentatio* (A.G. 485.e and 585.b Note). The pronoun **ei**, with **ipsis** as the antecedent, is understood as the subject (A.G. 271.a).
quorum ... geratur: Relative clause; a subordinate clause in indirect discourse takes the subjunctive (A.G. 303 and 580). **quorum**: Plural, masculine, genitive relative pronoun used substantively (A.G. 305). The antecedent is the following demonstrative pronoun **eorum** (A.G. 307 Note). Possessive genitive with **finibus** (A.G. 343). **geratur**: The main verb of the subordinate clause (A.G. 278.b). Present subjunctive; the tense of the subjunctive is normally in secondary sequence after the historical present **Docet** (A.G. 482-85). Here it is in primary sequence through *repraesentatio* (A.G. 485.e and 585.b Note).
in finibus: Ablative of *place where* with the preposition **in** (locative ablative) (A.G. 426.3).
bellum: Nominative subject of **geratur** (A.G. 339).
eorum: Plural, masculine, genitive demonstrative pronoun used substantively (A.G. 296.2). The pronoun is correlative to the relative clause **quorum ... geratur** (A.G. 297.d). Possessive genitive with **opibus** (A.G. 343).
opibus: Ablative of means (A.G. 409). In the plural the noun means "resources, wealth" (A.G. 107).

(14.7-9) Romanos aut inopiam non laturos aut magno (8) periculo longius ab castris processuros; neque interesse ipsosne interficiant impedimentisne exuant, quibus amissis (9) bellum geri non possit.

ab, *from.*
aut ... aut, *either ... or.*
castra, -orum, n., pl., *camp, encampment.*
fero, ferre, tuli, latus, *bear, endure, suffer, hold out against.*
impedimenta, -orum, n., pl., *heavy baggage, baggage.*
interficio, -ficere, -feci, -fectus, *slay, kill.*

ipse, -a, -um, *he, they.*
magnus, -a, -um, *great, considerable.*
neque, *and ... not.*
periculum, -i, n., *risk, danger, hazard.*
procedo, -cedere, -cessi, -----, *advance, go forward.*
Romani, -orum, m., pl., *the Romans.*

amitto, -mittere, -misi, -missus, *lose.*
bellum, -i, n., *war, warfare.*
exuo, -uere, -ui, -utus, *strip, strip off, despoil, deprive.*
gero, gerere, gessi, gestus, *carry on, wage.*
inopia, -ae, f., *want, lack, need, scarcity.*
intersum, -esse, -fui, -----, (imper.), *make a difference, is important.*
longius, *further, longer.*
-ne ... -ne, *whether ... or.*
non, *not.*
possum, posse, potui, -----, *be able.*
qui, quae, quod, *who, which, what.*

Romanos ... laturos (esse): Accusative/infinitive construction in indirect discourse after **Docet** (A.G. 577 ff.). **laturos (esse)**: Supply **esse** to form the future active infinitive (A.G. 200). The tense of the infinitive in indirect discourse is relative to that of the verb of saying (A.G. 584).
aut ... aut: The double conjunction introduces each of the practical alternatives in a given situation and means "either ... or", connecting the two infinitives **laturos (esse) ... processuros (esse)** (*OLD* aut 2).
inopiam: Accusative direct object of the infinitive **laturos (esse)** (A.G. 387 and 451.3).
non: Adverb, the adverb generally precedes the verb if it belongs to no one word in particular (A.G. 217.e, 320-21, and 599.a).
magno periculo: Ablative of manner with a limiting adjective (A.G. 412).
longius: Comparative adverb (A.G. 218 and 320-21).
ab castris: Ablative of *place from which* with the preposition **ab** (A.G. 426.1).

(**Romanos**) ... **processuros** (**esse**): Accusative/infinitive construction in indirect discourse after **Docet** (A.G. 577 ff.). Carry down **Romanos** as the accusative subject. **processuros** (**esse**): Supply **esse** to form the future active infinitive (A.G. 186). The tense of the infinitive in indirect discourse is relative to that of the verb of saying (A.G. 584).

neque: The conjunction here joins a negative clause to a preceding positive one and means "and ... not" (*OLD* **neque** 3).

interesse: Impersonal infinitive construction in indirect discourse after **Docet** (A.G. 577 ff.). The following indirect question (**ipsosne** ... **exuant**) functions as the accusative subject of the impersonal infinitive (A.G. 208.c).

-ne ... **interficiant** ... **-ne** ... **exuant**: A double indirect question with the subjunctive after the enclitic question word **-ne** in indirect discourse (A.G. 332, 335 and 573-75). These two substantive clauses function as the accusative subject of the impersonal infinitive **interesse** (A.G. 560-61 and 573). **-ne** ... **-ne**: Interrogative particles introducing a double indirect question meaning "whether ... or" (*OLD* **-ne** 5). **interficiant**: The main verb of the subordinate clause (A.G. 278.b). Present subjunctive; the tense of the subjunctive is normally in secondary sequence after the historical present **Docet** (A.G. 575). Here it is in primary sequence through *repraesentatio* (A.G. 485.e and 585.b Note). The pronoun **ei**, with **ipsis** as the antecedent, is understood as the subject (A.G. 271.a). **exuant**: The main verb of the subordinate clause (A.G. 278.b). Present subjunctive; the tense of the subjunctive is normally in secondary sequence after the historical present **Docet** (A.G. 575). Here it is in primary sequence through *repraesentatio* (A.G. 485.e and 585.b Note). The pronoun **ei**, with **ipsis** as the antecedent, is understood as the subject (A.G. 271.a).

ipsos: Plural, masculine, accusative demonstrative pronoun used substantively (A.G. 296.2). The antecedent is **Romanos** (A.G. 298.1). Accusative direct object of **interficiant** (A.G. 387). The pronoun is here emphatic (A.G. 298.d.1).

impedimentis: Ablative of separation without a preposition after **exuant** (A.G. 401).

quibus ... **possit**: Relative clause; a subordinate clause in indirect discourse takes the subjunctive (A.G. 303 and 580). **quibus**: See below. **possit**: The main verb of the subordinate clause (A.G. 278.b). Present subjunctive; the tense of the subjunctive is normally in secondary sequence after the historical present **Docet** (A.G. 482-85). Here it is in primary sequence through *repraesentatio* (A.G. 485.e and 585.b Note).

quibus amissis: Ablative absolute (A.G. 419-20). **quibus**: Plural, neuter, ablative relative pronoun used substantively (A.G. 305). The antecedent is **impedimentis** (A.G. 307). **amissis**: The perfect tense of the participle represents the action as completed at the time indicated by the tense of the main verb (A.G. 489).

bellum: Nominative subject (A.G. 339).

geri: Complementary infinitive after **possit** (A.G. 456).

non: Adverb, the adverb generally precedes the verb if it belongs to no one word in particular (A.G. 217.e, 320-21, and 599.a).

(**14.9-10**) **Praeterea oppida incendi oportere, quae non munitione et loci natura ab omni sint periculo tuta, neu suis sint ad detrectandam militiam receptacula neu Romanis proposita ad copiam commeatus praedamque tol(10)lendam.**

ab, *from*.

commeatus, -us, m., *supplies, provisions*.

detrecto, -are, -avi, -atus, *decline, refuse, escape*.

incendo, -cendere, -cendi, -census, *set on fire, burn*.

militia, -ae, f., *military service*.

natura, -ae, f., *natural features, situation*.

non, *not*.

oportet, oportere, oportuit, (imper.), *it is necessary, needful*.

periculum, -i, n., *risk, danger, hazard*.

praeterea, *besides, further*.

-que, *and*.

receptaculum, -i, n., *place of shelter, retreat*.

sum, esse, fui, futurus, *be*.

tollo, tollere, sustuli, sublatus, *take away, remove*.

ad, *for, in order to, for the purpose of, in*.

copia, -ae, f., *quantity, abundance, supply, plenty*.

et, *and*.

locus, -i, m., *place, location*.

munitio, -onis, f., *fortification, works of fortifications, defenses*.

neu ... neu, *that neither ... nor*.

omnis, -e, *all, every*.

oppidum, -i, n., *fortified town, city*.

praeda, -ae, f., *booty, spoil, plunder*.

propositus, -a, -um, *exposed, open*.

qui, quae, quod, *who, which, what*.

Romani, -orum, m., pl., *the Romans*.

sui, -orum, m., pl., *his men*, with or without *own*.

tutus, -a, -um, *safe, out of danger, secure*.

Praeterea: Adverb (A.G. 216 and 320-21).

oppida ... **incendi**: The infinitive phrase functions as the subject of the impersonal infinitive **oportere** (A.G. 454). **oppida**: Accusative subject of the infinitive (A.G. 397.e and 455.2). See note on **vicos** above at 14.5.

oportere: Impersonal infinitive construction in indirect discourse after **Docet** (A.G. 577 ff.). Impersonal use of the verb (A.G. 208.c). The previous infinitive phrase functions as the subject (A.G. 454). Present infinitive; the tense of the infinitive in indirect discourse is relative to that of the verb of saying (A.G. 584).

quae ... **sint** ... **tuta**: Relative clause; a subordinate clause in indirect discourse takes the subjunctive (A.G. 303 and 580). In direct discourse the subjunctive would also be utilized as a clause of characteristic (A.G. 534-35). **quae**: Plural, neuter, nominative relative pronoun used substantively (A.G. 305). The antecedent is **oppida** (A.G. 37). Nominative subject (A.G. 339). **sint**: The main verb of the subordinate clause (A.G. 278.b). Present subjunctive; the tense of the subjunctive is normally in secondary sequence after the historical present **Docet** (A.G. 482-85). Here it is in primary sequence through *repraesentatio* (A.G. 485.e and 585.b Note). **tuta**: Plural, neuter, nominative predicate adjective modifying **quae** after **sint** (A.G. 285.2).

non: Adverb; when **non** is especially emphatic it begins the clause (A.G. 217.e, 320-21, and 599.a).

munitione ... **natura**: Two ablatives of means (A.G. 409).

et: The conjunction connects the two ablative nouns (A.G. 324.a).

loci: Possessive genitive with **natura** (A.G. 343).

ab omni ... periculo: Ablative of separation with the preposition ab after the adjective tuta (A.G. 402.a).

neu ... sint ... neu (ea sint): The conjunctions neu ... neu ("that neither ... nor") with the subjunctive introduce a double final (purpose) clause (A.G. 531) (*OLD* neve 3.b). sint: The main verb of the subordinate clause (A.G. 278.b). Present subjunctive; the tense of the subjunctive is normally in secondary sequence after the historical present Docet (A.G. 482-85). Here it is in primary sequence through *repraesentatio* (A.G. 485.e and 585.b Note). Supply the pronoun ea, with oppida as the antecedent, as the subject (A.G. 271.a). neu (sint): Supply sint as the main verb after the second conjunction. Supply ea, with oppida as the antecedent, as the subject (A.G. 271.a).

suis: Plural, masculine, dative possessive pronoun used substantively to denote a special class (A.G. 302.d). Dative of reference; the dative in this construction is often called the dative of advantage as denoting the person for whose benefit the action is performed (A.G. 376).

ad detrectandam militiam: The preposition ad with the accusative gerundive and noun denotes purpose (A.G. 506). detrectandam: Singular, neuter, accusative gerundive used as an adjective modifying militiam denoting necessity, obligation or propriety (A.G. 500.1).

receptacula: Plural, neuter, nominative predicate noun after sint (A.G. 283-84).

Romanis: Dative of reference; the dative in this construction is often called the dative of advantage as denoting the person for whose benefit the action is performed (A.G. 376).

proposita: Plural, neuter, nominative predicate adjective modifying the supplied pronoun ea after the supplied verb sint (A.G. 283-84).

ad copiam commeatus praedamque tollendam: The preposition ad with the two accusative nouns and gerundive denotes purpose (A.G. 506). commeatus: Partitive genitive with copiam (A.G. 346.a.1). -que: The enclitic conjunction connects the two accusative nouns (A.G. 324.a). tollendam: Singular, feminine, accusative gerundive used as an adjective modifying both copiam and praedam denoting necessity, obligation or propriety (A.G. 500.1). The gerundive is understood with each accusative noun copiam ... praedam but agrees in number with only the nearest noun (A.G. 286.a).

(14.10) **Haec si gravia aut acerba videantur, multo illa gravius aestimare, liberos, coniuges in servitutem abstrahi, ipsos interfici; quae sit necesse accidere victis.**

abstraho, -trahere, -traxi, -tractus, *drag away* or *off, take away by force.*

accido, -cidere, -cidi, -----, *fall to, befall, fall to the lot of.*

acerbus, -a, -um, *bitter, harsh.*

aestimo, -are, -avi, -atus, *reckon, regard, consider.*

aut, *or.*

coniunx, coniugis, f., *wife, spouse.*

gravis, -e, *severe, hard, serious, troublesome.*

graviter, comp. -ius, *severely, bitterly, with great displeasure.*

hic, haec, hoc, *this; he, she, it, the former.*

ille, illae, illud, *that; he, she, it, the following.*

in, *into.*

interficio, -ficere, -feci, -fectus, *slay, kill.*

ipse, -a, -um, *he, they,* with or without *himself, themselves.*

liberi, -orum, m., pl., *children.*

multo, *much, by far, greatly.*

necesse, n., *necessary, unavoidable, inevitable.*

qui, quae, quod, *who, which, what.*

servitus, -tutis, f., *slavery, bondage, subjection.*

si, *if.*

sum, esse, fui, futurus, *be.*

videor, videri, visus sum, *be seen, seem, appear.*

vinco, vincere, vici, victus, *conquer, overcome, defeat, subdue.*

Haec ... illa: The combination of neuter pronouns means "the former things ... the following things" (A.G. 297.a-b).

Haec: Plural, neuter, nominative demonstrative pronoun used substantively (A.G. 296.2). The antecedent is the idea of the burning of cities (A.G. 297.a and e). Nominative subject (A.G. 339).

si ... videantur ... aestimare: Conditional statement in indirect discourse after Docet (A.G. 589). The protasis, as a dependent clause, is in the subjunctive and the apodosis, as the principal clause, is in the infinitive (A.G. 589).

si ... videantur: The conjunction si ("if") with the subjunctive forms the protasis of a conditional statement in indirect discourse (A.G. 589.1). videantur: The main verb of the subordinate clause (A.G. 278.b). Present subjunctive; the tense of the subjunctive is normally in secondary sequence after the historical present Docet (A.G. 482-85). Here it is in primary sequence through *repraesentatio* (A.G. 485.e and 585.b Note).

gravia aut acerba (esse): Two plural, neuter, nominative predicate adjectives modifying Haec after videantur (A.G. 283). A predicate adjective after a complementary infinitive takes the case of the subject of the main verb (A.G. 283-84 and 458). Supply esse as the complementary infinitive after videantur. aut: The conjunction connects the two adjectives. Normally, the conjunction excludes the alternative but this distinction is not always observed (A.G. 324.e).

multo: Adverb with the comparative adverb gravius (A.G. 218.a and 320-21).

illa: Plural, neuter, accusative demonstrative pronoun used substantively (A.G. 296.2). The pronoun points ahead to the two infinitive phrases abstrahi ... interfici (A.G. 297.b and e). Accusative direct object of the infinitive aestimare (A.G. 387 and 451.3).

gravius: Comparative adverb (A.G. 218 and 320-21).

(ipsos) aestimare: The apodosis of the conditional statement (A.G. 589.2). Accusative/infinitive construction in indirect discourse after Docet (A.G. 577 ff. and 589). Supply the pronoun ipsos (those being addressed at the council)) as the accusative subject of the infinitive. aestimare: Present infinitive; the tense of the infinitive in indirect discourse is relative to that of the verb of saying (A.G. 584).

liberos, coniuges in servitutem abstrahi: The infinitive clause is in apposition to the pronoun illa (A.G. 452 Note 1). liberos,

coniuges: Two accusative subjects of the infinitive (A.G. 397.e). Notice the asyndeton between the two nouns (A.G. 323.b). **in servitutem**: Prepositional phrase, **in** with the accusative here means "into" (a state or condition) (*OLD* **in** 2).

ipsos interfici: The infinitive clause is in apposition to the pronoun **illa** (A.G. 452 Note 1). **ipsos**: Plural, masculine, accusative demonstrative pronoun used substantively (A.G. 296.2). The antecedent is **ipsi** (those being addressed at the council)) at 14.3 (A.G. 297.d.1). Accusative subject of the infinitive (A.G. 397.e). The pronoun is here emphatic (A.G. 298.d.1). Notice the asyndeton between the two infinitive clauses **abstrahi ... interfici** (A.G. 323.b).

quae ... victis: Relative clause; a subordinate clause in indirect discourse takes the subjunctive (A.G. 303 and 580). **quae**: See below. **victis**: See below.

quae ... accidere victis: The infinitive phrase functions as the subject of the impersonal infinitive **sit necesse** (A.G. 454). **quae**: Plural, neuter, accusative relative pronoun used substantively meaning "which things" (A.G. 305). Accusative subject of the infinitive (A.G. 397.e). **victis**: Dative, perfect, passive participle used as a predicate where in English a phrase or a subordinate clause would be more natural (A.G. 496). The noun **hominibus** is understood (A.G. 288.b). Dative indirect object of the intransitive infinitive **accidere** (A.G. 366 and 451.3).

sit necesse: Impersonal verb, the previous infinitive phrase forms the subject (A.G. 208.c). **sit**: The main verb of the subordinate clause (A.G. 278.b). Present subjunctive; the tense of the subjunctive is normally in secondary sequence after the historical present **Docet** (A.G. 482-85). Here it is in primary sequence through *repraesentatio* (A.G. 485.e and 585.b Note). **necesse**: Singular, neuter, nominative adjective used in the predicate position after **sit** as an indeclinable noun (A.G. 103.a Note 1 and 283-84).

(15.1-2) Omnium consensu hac sententia probata, uno die amplius (2) XX urbes Biturigum incenduntur.

amplius, *more, further*.	**Bituriges, -um**, m., pl., *the Bituriges*.
consensus, -us, m., *united opinion, agreement, consent*.	**dies, -ei**, m. and f., *day*.
hic, haec, hoc, *this*; *he, she, it*.	**incendo, -cendere, -cendi, -census**, *set on fire, burn*.
omnes, -ium, m., pl., *all men, all*.	**probo, -are, -avi, -atus**, *approve, commend*.
sententia, -ae, f., *decision, view, notion, determination*.	**unus, -a, -um**, *one*.
urbs, urbis, f., *city*.	**X**, in expression of number, = *10*.

omnium consensu hac sententia probata: Ablative absolute (A.G. 419-20). **omnium**: Plural, masculine, genitive adjective used substantively (A.G. 288). Possessive genitive with **consensu** (A.G. 343). **consensu**: Ablative of specification (A.G. 418). **hac**: Singular, feminine, ablative demonstrative pronoun used as an adjective modifying **sententia** (A.G. 296.1 and a). **probata**: The perfect tense of the participle represents the action as completed at the time indicated by the tense of the main verb (A.G. 489).

uno die: Ablative of *time within which* (A.G. 423.1). **uno**: Declinable cardinal number used as an adjective (A.G. 132-35). **die**: The noun **dies** is normally masculine gender (A.G. 97.a).

amplius XX urbes: Nominative subject (A.G. 339). **amplius**: Comparative adverb (A.G. 218). **XX urbes**: Nominative subject (A.G. 339). After the comparative **amplius**, without **quam**, a word of number is used with no change in its case. Therefore, **XX urbes** is nominative, and not ablative, after the comparative (A.G. 407.c). **XX**: Roman numeral used as an adjective modifying **urbes** (A.G. 133).

Biturigum: Possessive genitive of the tribe name **Bituriges** with **urbes** (A.G. 343). See Appendix A.

incenduntur: The main verb of the main clause (A.G. 278.b). The historical present, giving vividness to the narrative, is present in Chapter 15 (A.G. 469). This usage, common in all languages, comes from imagining past events as going on before our eyes (*repraesentatio*) (A.G. 469 Note). "This voluntary burning of cities, especially at such a season, evinces a heroic spirit." (Kelsey, 404)

(15.2-3) Hoc idem fit in reliquis civitatibus: in omnibus partibus incendia conspiciuntur; quae etsi magno cum dolore omnes ferebant, tamen hoc sibi solaci proponebant, quod se prope explorata victoria cele(3)riter amissa reciperaturos confidebant.

amitto, -mittere, -misi, -missus, *lose*.	**celeriter**, *quickly, speedily, at once, immediately*.
civitas, -tatis, f., *state, nation*.	**confido, -fidere, -fisus sum**, *believe, be confident*.
conspicio, -spicere, -spexi, -spectus, *observe, see, perceive*.	**cum**, *with*.
dolor, -oris, m., *grief, distress, vexation*.	**etsi**, *although, though*.
exploratus, -a, -um, *established, certain, settled, sure*.	**fero, ferre, tuli, latus**, *bear, endure, suffer*.
fio, fieri, factus, *take place, happen, come about, come to pass*.	**hic, haec, hoc**, *this*; *he, she, it*.
idem, eadem, idem, *the same*.	**in**, *in*.
incendium, -i, n., *fire, conflagration*.	**magnus, -a, -um**, *great, considerable*.
omnis, -e, *all*.	**omnes, -ium**, m., pl., *all men, all*.
pars, partis, f., *part, region, district, direction*.	**prope**, *near, nearly, almost*.
propono, -ponere, -posui, -positus, *put forward, present*.	**qui, quae, quod**, *who, which, what*.
quod, *that, the fact that*.	**recipero, -are, -avi, -atus**, *recover, regain, get back*.
reliquus, -a, -um, *remaining, the rest*.	**solacium, -i**, n., *consolation, comfort*.
sui, sibi, se, or **sese**, nom. wanting, *themselves*; *they*, with or without themselves.	**tamen**, *yet, still, for all that, nevertheless, however*.
victoria, -ae, f., *victory*.	

Hoc idem: Nominative subject (A.G. 339). **Hoc**: Singular, neuter, nominative demonstrative pronoun used substantively meaning "this thing" (A.G. 296.2). The antecedent is the idea above of the burning of the cities (**Omnium ... incenduntur.**) (A.G. 297.e).

idem: Singular, neuter, nominative demonstrative pronoun used as an adjective modifying **hoc** (A.G. 296.1 and a and 298.a).
fit: The main verb of the simple sentence (A.G. 278.1).
in reliquis civitatibus: Ablative of *place where* with the preposition **in** (locative ablative) (A.G. 426.3).
in omnibus partibus: Ablative of *place where* with the preposition **in** (locative ablative) (A.G. 426.3).
incendia: Nominative subject (A.G. 339).
conspiciuntur: The main verb of the simple sentence (A.G. 278.1).
quae: Plural, neuter, accusative relative pronoun used substantively (A.G. 305). The antecedent is **incendia** (A.G. 307). Accusative direct object of **ferebant** (A.G. 387). The relative does not introduce a relative clause but is a connecting relative; at the beginning of a clause the pronoun is often best rendered by a personal or demonstrative pronoun, with or without *and* (A.G. 308.f).
etsi ... ferebant ... (tamen): Concessive clause; the conjunction **etsi** ("although") with the indicative forms a dependent clause which is made clearer by the adversative particle **tamen** ("nevertheless") in the main clause (A.G. 526 and 527.c). **ferebant**: The main verb of the subordinate clause (A.G. 278.b).
magno cum dolore: Ablative of manner with the preposition **cum** (A.G. 412). **cum**: A monosyllabic preposition is often placed between a noun and its adjective (A.G. 599.d.2).
omnes: Plural, masculine, nominative adjective used substantively (A.G. 288). Nominative subject (A.G. 339).
tamen: Adverb, correlative to **etsi**, meaning "nevertheless" (A.G. 527.c) (*OLD* **tamen** 3). The adverb is often postpositive, but not here (A.G. 324.j).
hoc: Singular, neuter, accusative demonstrative pronoun used substantively (A.G. 296.2). The pronoun points ahead to the following clause **quod ... confidebant** (A.G. 297.e). Accusative direct object of **proponebant** (A.G. 387).
sibi: Plural, masculine, dative direct reflexive pronoun (A.G. 300.1). The antecedent is **omnes**, the subject of **proponebant** (A.G. 299). Dative of reference; the dative in this construction is often called the dative of advantage as denoting the person for whose benefit the action is performed (A.G. 376).
solaci: Partitive genitive with **hoc** (A.G. 346.a.3). The singular genitive of nouns in **-ium** ended, until the Augustan Age, in a single **-i** (A.G. 49.b).
proponebant: The main verb of the main clause (A.G. 278.b). The pronoun **ei**, with **omnes** as the antecedent, is understood as the subject (A.G. 271.a).
quod ... confidebant: The conjunction **quod** ("that, the fact that") with the indicative forms a substantive clause in apposition to the previous accusative pronoun **hoc** (A.G. 572 and Note). The indicative is used with **quod** when the statement is regarded as a fact (A.G. 572). **confidebant**: The main verb of the subordinate clause (A.G. 278.b). The pronoun **ei**, with **omnes** as the antecedent, is understood as the subject (A.G. 271.a).
se ... reciperaturos (esse): Accusative/infinitive construction in indirect discourse after **confidebant** (A.G. 577 ff.). **se**: Plural, masculine, accusative direct reflexive pronoun (A.G. 300.1). The antecedent is **ei (omnes)**, the supplied subject of **confidebant** (A.G. 299). **reciperaturos (esse)**: Supply **esse** to form the future, active infinitive (A.G. 187). The tense of the infinitive in indirect discourse is relative to that of the verb of saying (A.G. 584).
prope explorata victoria: Ablative absolute with an adjective (**explorata**) taking the place of a participle (there is no participle for "being") (A.G. 419.a-20). **prope**: Adverb (A.G. 320-21).
celeriter: Adverb modifying **reciperaturos** (A.G. 214.b and 320-21).
amissa: Plural, accusative, neuter perfect passive participle used substantively meaning "losses" (A.G. 494.a). The neuter plural form may refer back to **oppida** at 14.9, but it is more probably meant to denote the broader category of things lost in general (A.G. 288). Accusative direct object of the infinitive **reciperaturos (esse)** (A.G. 387 and 451.3).

(15.3) +Deliberatur+ de Avarico in communi concilio, incendi placeret an defendi.

an, *or, or rather, or indeed.*
communis, -e, *common, in common, public, general.*
de, *about, concerning.*

delibero, -are, -avi, -atus, *deliberate, consult, discuss.*
incendo, -cendere, -cendi, -census, *set on fire, burn.*

Avaricum, -i, n., *Avaricum.*
concilium, -i, n., *meeting, assembly, council.*
defendo, -fendere, -fensi, -fensus, *defend, guard, protect.*
in, *in.*
placeo, placere, placui, placitus, (imper.), *it seems good.*

+Deliberatur+: The main verb of the main clause (A.G. 278.b). Impersonal use of the verb (A.G. 208.c). The following indirect question **incendi ... defendi**) functions as the subject (A.G. 573). The verb comes in the first position when the idea in it is emphatic (A.G. 598.d).
de Avarico: Prepositional phrase, **de** with the ablative here means "about, concerning" (*OLD* **de** 12). **Avarico**: See Appendix A.
in communi concilio: Ablative of *place where* with the preposition **in** (locative ablative) (A.G. 426.3).
incendi ... defendi: The two infinitives function as the subject of the impersonal verb **placeret** (A.G. 208.c and 454). Notice how the infinitives are iconically split as the parties advocating each position would no doubt be physically split in the council.
placeret an: The interrogative word **an** with the subjunctive forms an indirect question which functions as the subject of the impersonal verb **deliberatur** (A.G. 573-75). **placeret**: The main verb of the subordinate clause (A.G. 278.b). Imperfect subjunctive; the tense of the subjunctive is in secondary sequence after the historical present tense of **Deliberatur** (A.G. 485.e and 575). Impersonal use of the verb (A.G. 208.c). The two infinitives function as the subject (A.G. 454). **an**: The particle **utrum** is omitted with the first member (**incendi**) but the question is picked up by the particle **an** with the second member (**defendi**) (A.G. 335 and a).

(15.4-6) **(4) Procumbunt omnibus Gallis ad pedes Bituriges, ne pulcherrimam prope totius Galliae urbem, quae praesidio et ornamento sit civitati, suis manibus succendere cogerentur:**

ad, *to, before.*
civitas, -tatis, f., *state, nation.*
et, *and.*
Galli, -orum, m., *the Gauls.*
ne, *so that ... not.*
ornamentum, -i, n., *distinction, honor.*
praesidium, -i, n., *guard, protection.*
prope, *near, nearly, almost.*
qui, quae, quod, *who, which, what.*

sum, esse, fui, futurus, *be.*
totus, -a, -um, *the whole of, all.*

Bituriges, -um, m., pl., *the Bituriges.*
cogo, cogere, coegi, coactus, *compel, force, oblige.*
Gallia, -ae, f., *Gaul.*
manus, -us, f., *hand.*
omnis, -e, *all.*
pes, pedis, m., *foot.*
procumbo, -cumbere, -cubui, -cubitus, *fall prostrate.*
pulcher, -chra, -chrum, sup. **-pulcherrimus**, *beautiful.*
succendo, -cendere, -censi, -census, *set on fire, set fire to.*
suus, -a, -um, *their*, with or without *own.*
urbs, urbis, f., *city.*

Procumbunt ... Bituriges: The reversal of the normal word order (subject first, verb last) is called hyperbaton (A.G. 596) (Gotoff, 6-10).
Procumbunt: The main verb of the main clause (A.G. 278.b). The verb comes in the first position when the idea in it is emphatic (A.G. 598.d).
omnibus Gallis: Dative of reference; the dative of reference is often used to qualify a whole idea, instead of the possessive genitive modifying a single word (here **pedes**) (A.G. 377). **Gallis**: See Appendix A.
ad pedes: Accusative of *place to which* with the preposition **ad** (A.G 426.2).
Bituriges: Nominative subject (A.G. 339). The subject is in the last position in the clause (A.G. 597.b). See Appendix A.
ne ... cogerentur: The conjunction **ne** ("so that ... not") with the subjunctive forms a negative final (purpose) clause, here dependent on the drift of the main clause rather than any one verb (A.G. 529-532). **cogerentur**: The main verb of the subordinate clause (A.G. 278.b). Imperfect subjunctive; the tense of the subjunctive is in secondary sequence after the historical present tense of **Procumbunt** (A.G. 482-85, esp. 485.e). The pronoun **ei**, with **Bituriges** as the antecedent, is understood as the subject (A.G. 271.a).
pulcherrimam ... urbem: Accusative direct object of the infinitive **succendere** (A.G. 387 and 451.3). "Avaricum occupied a beautiful site, and had many fine open squares." (Kelsey, 404) **pulcherrimam**: Superlative adjective (A.G. 124).
prope: Adverb (A.G. 320-21).
totius Galliae: Partitive genitive with **urbem** (A.G. 346.a.1). **totius**: **-ius** is the regular genitive singular ending for the adjective **totus** (A.G. 113). **Galliae**: See Appendix A.
quae ... sit: Relative clause; a clause depending upon a subjunctive clause (**ne ... cogerentur**) will itself take the subjunctive if regarded as an integral part of that clause (attraction) (A.G. 303 and 593). **quae**: Singular, feminine, nominative relative pronoun used substantively (A.G. 305). The antecedent is **urbem** (A.G. 307). Nominative subject (A.G. 339). **sit**: The main verb of the subordinate clause (A.G. 278.b). Present subjunctive; the tense of the subjunctive is normally in secondary sequence after the historical present **Procumbunt** (A.G. 482-85). Here it is in primary sequence through *repraesentatio* (A.G. 485.e and 585.b Note).
praesidio et ornamento ... civitati: Dative of the purpose or end (double dative). The dative of an abstract noun (**praesidio et ornamento**) is used to show that for which a thing serves or which it accomplishes, often with another dative of the person or thing affected (**civitati**). The verb is usually a form of **sum** (**sit**) (A.G. 382.1). **et**: The conjunction connects the two dative nouns (A.G. 324.a).
suis manibus: Ablative of instrument (A.G. 409). **suis**: Plural, feminine, ablative possessive pronoun used as an adjective modifying **manibus** (A.G. 302).
succendere: Complementary infinitive after **cogerentur** (A.G. 456 and 566.c).

(15.5-6) **(5) facile se loci natura defensuros dicunt, quod prope ex omnibus partibus flumine et palude circumdata unum habeat et (6) perangustum aditum.**

aditus, -us, m., *approach, access, way of approach*

defendo, -fendere, -fensi, -fensus, *defend, guard, protect.*
et, *and.*
facile, *easily, readily, with no trouble.*
habeo, habere, habui, habitus, *have.*
natura, -ae, f., *natural features, situation.*
palus, -udis, f., *marsh, swamp, bog, morass.*
perangustus, -a, -um, *very narrow.*
quod, *because, since, for, as.*

unus, -a, -um, *one.*

circumdo, -dare, -dedi, -datus, *encompass, surround, encircle.*
dico, dicere, dixi, dictus, *say.*
ex, *on.*
flumen, -inis, n., *stream, river.*
locus, -i, m., *place, location.*
omnis, -e, *all.*
pars, partis, f., *side.*
prope, *near, nearly, almost.*
sui, sibi, se, or **sese**, nom. wanting, *they*, with or without *themselves.*

facile: Adverb formed from the neuter accusative adjective (A.G. 214.d and 320-21).
se ... (eam) defensuros (esse): Accusative/infinitive construction in indirect discourse after **dicunt** (A.G. 577 ff.). **se**: Plural.

masculine, accusative direct reflexive pronoun (A.G. 300.2). The antecedent is **ei** (**Bituriges**), the supplied subject of **dicunt** (A.G. 299). **defensuros** (**esse**): Supply **esse** to form the future active infinitive (A.G. 186). The tense of the infinitive in indirect discourse is relative to that of the verb of saying (A.G. 584). Supply the pronoun **eam**, with **urbem** as the antecedent, as the accusative direct object.

loci: Possessive genitive with **natura** (A.G. 343).

natura: Ablative of means (A.G. 409).

dicunt: The main verb of the main clause (A.G. 278.b). The pronoun **ei**, with **Bituriges** as the antecedent, is understood as the subject (A.G. 271.a).

quod ... habeat: Causal clause; the conjunction **quod** ("because") would normally take the indicative when the reason is given on the authority of the writer or speaker (A.G. 540.1). Here **quod** takes the subjunctive as a subordinate clause in indirect discourse after **dicunt** (A.G. 580). **habeat**: The main verb of the subordinate clause (A.G. 278.b). Present subjunctive; the tense of the subjunctive is normally in secondary sequence after the historical present **dicunt** (A.G. 482-85). Here it is in primary sequence through *repraesentatio* (A.G. 485.e and 585.b Note).

prope: Adverb (A.G. 320-21).

ex omnibus partibus: Ablative of *position* with the preposition **ex** (A.G. 429.b).

flumine et palude: Two ablatives of means with the passive participle **circumdata** (A.G. 409). **et**: The conjunction connects the two ablative nouns (A.G. 324.a).

circumdata: Nominative, perfect, passive participle used as a predicate where in English a phrase or a subordinate clause would be more natural (A.G. 496). The pronoun **ea**, with **urbem** as the antecedent, is understood. Nominative subject (A.G. 339).

unum ... et perangustum aditum: Accusative direct object of **habeat** (A.G. 387). **unum**: Declinable cardinal number used as an adjective (A.G. 132-35). **et**: The conjunction connects the two accusative adjectives modifying **aditum** (A.G. 324.a). Two adjectives belonging to the same noun are regularly connected by a conjunction (A.G. 323.d). **perangustum**: The adverbial prefix **per-**, modifying an adjective, means "very" (A.G. 267.d.1).

(15.6) **Datur petentibus venia, dissuadente primo Vercingetorige, post concedente et precibus ipsorum et misericordia vulgi. Defensores oppido idonei deliguntur.**

concedo, -cedere, -cessi, -cessurus, *yield, give way, succumb.*
deligo, -ligere, -legi, -lectus, *choose, select, pick out.*
do, dare, dedi, datus, *give, grant.*
idoneus, -a, -um, *suitable, convenient, fit, capable.*
misericordia, -ae, f., *pity, compassion, mercy.*
peto, petere, petivi, and **petii, petitus,** *seek, ask, request.*
prex, precis, f., *prayer, entreaty, supplication.*
venia, -ae, f., *permission, forbearance.*
vulgus, -i., m., *common people, mass, multitude, crowd.*

defensor, -oris, m., *defender, protector.*
dissuadeo, -suadere, -suasi, -suasus, *object, oppose.*
et ... et, *both ... and.*
ipse, -a, -um, *he, they.*
oppidum, -i, n., *fortified town, city.*
post, *after, afterwards.*
primo, *at first, in the first place.*
Vercingetorix, -igis, m., *Vercingetorix.*

Datur ... venia: The reversal of the normal word order (subject first, verb last) is called hyperbaton (A.G. 596) (Gotoff, 6-10).

Datur: The main verb of the main clause (A.G. 278.b). The verb comes in the first position when the idea in it is emphatic (A.G. 598.d). Here it marks the end of the indirect discourse (A.G. 589.d).

petentibus: Plural, masculine, dative present participle used substantively (494.a). The noun **Biturigibus** is understood (A.G. 288.b). Dative indirect object of the passive verb **Datur**, verbs which in the active voice take the accusative and dative retain the dative when used in the passive (A.G. 365).

venia: Nominative subject (A.G. 339). The subject is in the last position in the clause (A.G. 597.b).

dissuadente primo Vercingetorige: Ablative absolute (A.G. 419-20). **dissuadente**: The participle ends in -e rather than -i in the ablative singular when used in an ablative absolute (A.G. 121.2). The present participle represents the action as in progress at the time indicated by the tense of the main verb (A.G. 489). **primo ... (post)**: Two adverbs (A.G. 320-21). **primo** means "at first", as opposed to **post** "afterwards", giving prominence to the difference in time (A.G. 322.d). **Vercingetorige**: See Appendix A.

(**Vercingetorige**) **post concedente et precibus ipsorum et misericordia vulgi**: Ablative absolute (A.G. 419-20). Carry down **Vercingetorige** as the noun. **post**: Adverb (A.G. 320-21). **concedente**: The participle ends in -e rather than -i in the ablative singular when used in an ablative absolute (A.G. 121.2). The present participle represents the action as in progress at the time indicated by the tense of the main verb (A.G. 489). **et ... et**: The repeated conjunction means "both ... and", connecting the two ablative nouns (A.G. 323.e). **precibus ... misericordia**: Two ablatives of cause after the participle **concedente**; the motive which influences the mind of the person acting is expressed by the ablative of cause (A.G. 404). **ipsorum**: Plural, masculine, genitive demonstrative pronoun used substantively (A.G. 296.2 and 298.d). The antecedent is **petentibus** (A.G. 297.e). Possessive genitive with **precibus** (A.G. 343). The pronoun is here emphatic (A.G. 298.d.1). **misericordia vulgi**: "Because they would lose their homes in winter." (Hammond, 238) **vulgi**: Objective genitive with **misericordia** (A.G. 348). "The exemption of Avaricum from the general destruction of cities was the first great mistake of the Gauls in this campaign, the outcome of which was to be for them so disastrous." (Kelsey, 405)

Defensores ... idonei: Nominative subject (A.G. 339).

oppido: Either a dative indirect object of the passive verb **deliguntur**, verbs which in the active voice take the accusative and dative retain the dative when used in the passive (A.G. 365) or a dative object of the adjective **idonei** (A.G. 384).

deliguntur: The main verb of the simple sentence (A.G. 278.1).

2.B CHAPTERS 16-19: THE SIEGE OF AVARICUM BEGINS; OUTSIDE THE CITY VERCINGETORIX HARASSES THE

ROMANS; THE ROMAN SOLDIERS ENDURE THE HARDSHIP OF FAMINE; CAESAR AVERTS BATTLE IN AN UNFAVORABLE POSITION DESPITE THE PLEAS OF HIS SOLDIERS

(16.1-2) Vercingetorix minoribus Caesarem itineribus subsequitur et locum castris deligit paludibus silvisque munitum ab Avarico longe milia passuum XVI.

ab, *from, away from.*
Caesar, -aris, m., *Caesar.*
deligo, -ligere, -legi, -lectus, *choose, select, pick out.*
I, in expression of number, *1.*
locus, -i, m., *place, location, site.*
milia, -um, n., pl., *thousand, thousands.*
munitus, -a, -um, *fortified, protected, secure.*
passus, -us, m., *step, pace,* = 4 feet, 10 ¼ inches.
silvae, -arum, f., pl., *wooded parts* or *region.*

V, in expression of number, = *5.*
X, in expression of number, = *10.*

Avaricum, -i, n., *Avaricum.*
castra, -orum, n., pl., *camp, encampment.*
et, *and.*
iter, itineris, n., *march, stage.*
longe, *at a distance, far.*
minor, *smaller, less, shorter, briefer.*
palus, -udis, f., *marsh, swamp, bog, morass.*
-que, *and.*
subsequor, -sequi, -secutus, *follow closely upon, follow after. follow up.*
Vercingetorix, -igis, m., *Vercingetorix.*

Vercingetorix: Nominative subject of **subsequitur ... deligit** (A.G. 339). See Appendix A.
minoribus ... itineribus: Ablative of manner with a limiting adjective (A.G. 412). **minoribus**: Irregular comparative adjective (A.G. 129).
Caesarem: Accusative direct object of **subsequitur** (A.G. 387). See Appendix A.
subsequitur: The main verb of the coordinate clause **Vercingetorix ... subsequitur** (A.G. 278.a). The historical present, giving vividness to the narrative, is present in Chapter 16 (A.G. 469). This usage, common in all languages, comes from imagining past events as going on before our eyes (*repraesentatio*) (A.G. 469 Note).
et: The conjunction connects the two main verbs **subsequitur ... deligit** (A.G. 324.a).
locum ... munitum: Accusative direct object of **deligit** (A.G. 387).
castris: Dative of purpose (A.G. 382.2).
deligit: The main verb of the coordinate clause **locum ... XVI** (A.G. 278.a).
paludibus silvisque: Two ablatives of means with **munitum** (A.G. 409). **silvis**: The plural of the noun means "wooded parts or regions" (*OLD* silva 1). **-que**: The enclitic conjunction connects the two ablative nouns (A.G. 324.a).
ab Avarico: Ablative of *place from which* with the preposition **ab** (A.G. 426.1). **Avarico**: See Appendix A.
longe: Adverb (A.G. 214.a and 320-21).
milia passuum XVI: Accusative of *extent of space* (A.G. 425 and 134.d). **milia**: Accusative plural; in the plural **mille** declines as a neuter noun (A.G. 134.d). **passuum**: Partitive genitive with **milia** (A.G. 346.a.2). **XVI**: Roman numeral used as an adjective modifying **milia** (A.G. 133).

(16.2-3) Ibi per certos exploratores in singula diei tempora quae ad Avericum agerentur (3) cognoscebat et quid fieri vellet imperabat.

ad, *at, near.*
Avaricum, -i, n., *Avaricum.*
cognosco, -gnoscere, -gnovi, cognitus, *learn, learn of.*
et, *and.*
fio, fieri, factus, *take place, happen, come about, come to pass.*
impero, -are, -avi, -atus, *command, order, bid, give an order.*
per, *by* (means of), *through.*
singuli, -ae, -a, *several, individual, successive.*
volo, velle, volui, *wish, desire, mean, intend.*

ago, agere, egi, actus, *do, transact, perform.*
certus, -a, um, *fixed, specified.*
dies, -ei, m. and f., *day.*
explorator, -oris, m., *spy, scout.*
ibi, *in that place, there.*
in, *for.*
quis, -----, quid, *who? what?*
tempus, -oris, n., *time.*

Ibi: Adverb (A.G. 215.5 and 320-21).
per certos exploratores: Prepositional phrase, the personal agent, when considered as instrument or means, is often expressed by **per** with the accusative "by" (means of) (A.G. 405.b).
in singula diei tempora: Prepositional phrase dependent on **certos**; **in** with the accusative here means "for" (*OLD* in 23). **singula**: Distributive numeral used as an adjective modifying **tempora** (A.G. 136-37). **diei**: Partitive genitive with **tempora** (A.G. 346.a.1).
quae ... agerentur: Indirect question with the subjunctive; the phrase is the object of **cognoscebat** (A.G. 573-75). **quae**: Plural, neuter, nominative interrogative pronoun used substantively meaning "what things" (A.G. 148). Nominative subject (A.G. 339).
agerentur: The main verb of the subordinate clause (A.G. 278.b). Imperfect subjunctive; the tense of the subjunctive is in secondary sequence and follows the rules for the sequence of tense for indirect questions after **cognoscebat** (A.G. 575).
ad Avericum: Prepositional phrase, with all names of places *at*, meaning *near* (not *in*), is expressed by **ad** with the accusative (A.G. 428.d). **Avericum**: See Appendix A.
cognoscebat: The main verb of the coordinate clause **Ibi ... cognoscebat** (A.G. 278.a). The pronoun **is**, with **Vercingetorix** as the antecedent, is understood as the subject (A.G. 271.a).
et: The conjunction connects the two main verbs **cognoscebat ... imperabat** (A.G. 324.a).

quid ... vellet: Indirect question with the subjunctive; the phrase is the object of **imperabat** (A.G. 573-75). **quid**: See below. **vellet**: The main verb of the subordinate clause (A.G. 278.b). Imperfect subjunctive; the tense of the subjunctive is in secondary sequence and follows the rules for the sequence of tense for indirect questions after **imperabat** (A.G. 575). The pronoun **is**, with **Vercingetorix** as the antecedent, is understood as the subject (A.G. 271.a).

quid fieri: Subject accusative with the infinitive after **vellet**. The construction is equivalent to a substantive clause of purpose (A.G. 563.b.2). **quid**: Singular, neuter, accusative interrogative pronoun used substantively meaning "what" (A.G. 148 and b).

imperabat: The main verb of the coordinate clause **quid ... imperabat** (A.G. 278.a). The pronoun **is**, with **Vercingetorix** as the antecedent, is understood as the subject (A.G. 271.a).

(16.3) **Omnis nostras pabulationes frumentationesque observabat dispersosque, cum longius necessario procederent, adoriebatur magnoque incommodo adficiebat, etsi quantum ratione provideri poterat ab nostris occurrebatur, ut incertis temporibus diversisque itineribus iretur.**

ab, *by*.

adorior, -oriri, -ortus, *fall upon, attack, assail.*

dispergo, -spergere. -spersi, -spersus, *scatter, scatter abroad, disperse.*
eo, ire, ivi, or **ii, iturus**, *move, march, advance.*
frumentatio, -onis, f., *the collecting of grain* or *provisions, foraging.*
incommodum, -i, n., *misfortune, disaster, injury, defeat.*
longius, *further, longer.*
necessario, *of necessity, unavoidably.*
nostri, -orum, m., pl., *our men, our side.*
occurro, -currere, -curri or **-cucurri, -cursurus**, *resist.*
pabulatio, -onis, f., *the act of collecting fodder.*

procedo, -cedere, -cessi, -----, *advance, go forward.*

quantum, *to what degree* or *extent to which.*
ratio, -onis, f., *plan of action.*
ut, *so that.*

adficio, -ficere, -feci, -fectus, *afflict, trouble, weaken, impair.*
cum, *when, whenever, on every occasion that, as often as.*
diversus -a, -um, *in different directions, different.*
etsi, *although, though, even if.*
incertus, -a, -um, *indefinite, not fixed, undetermined.*
iter, itineris, n., *road, route.*
magnus, -a, -um, *great.*
noster, -tra, -trum, *our, our own.*
observo, -are, -avi, -atus, *watch, observe.*
omnis, -e, *all.*
possum, posse, potui, -----, *it can be done or happen, it is possible.*
provideo, -videre, -vidi, -visus, *provide for, look out for.*
-que, *and.*
tempus, -oris, n., *time.*

Omnis nostras pabulationes frumentationesque: Two accusative direct objects of **observabat** (A.G. 387). **Omnis**: Accusative plural predicate adjective modifying both **pabulationes** and **frumentationes** (A.G. 286.a). **-is** for **-es** is the regular form in i-stem adjectives (A.G. 114.a and 116). **nostras**: Plural, feminine accusative possessive pronoun used as an adjective modifying both **pabulationes** and **frumentationes** (A.G. 302). **pabulationes frumentationesque**: Note that the nouns refer to the actions being performed, not the persons performing the actions. **pabulationes**: Fodder for the animals. **frumentationes**: Grain for the humans. **-que**: The enclitic conjunction connects the two accusative nouns **pabulationes frumentationesque** (A.G. 324.a).

observabat: The main verb of the coordinate clause **Omnis ... observabat** (A.G. 278.a). The pronoun **is**, with **Vercingetorix** as the antecedent, is understood as the subject (A.G. 271.a).

dispersosque: Accusative, perfect, passive participle used as a predicate where in English a phrase or a subordinate clause would be more natural (A.G. 496). The nouns **pabulatores** (foragers of fodder) and **frumentatores** (foragers of grain) are understood (A.G. 288.b). The change in the gender from the feminine nouns **pabulationes frumentationesque** to the masculine participle indicates a change from the nouns of action (**pabulationes frumentationesque**) to those doing the action (**pabulatores** and **frumentatores**). Accusative direct object of **adoriebatur** (A.G. 387). **-que**: The enclitic conjunction connects the two main verbs **observabat ... adoriebatur** (A.G. 324.a).

cum ... procederent: Conditional relative clause; the particle **cum** ("when, whenever") may be used as an indefinite relative and has the construction of protasis. Here the imperfect subjunctive is from a present time, contrary to fact condition (A.G. 543). Vercingetorix's plan at 14.4-5 is coming to fruition. **procederent**: The main verb of the subordinate clause (A.G. 278.b). The pronoun **ei**, with **dispersos** as the antecedent, is understood as the subject (A.G. 271.a).

longius: Comparative adverb (A.G. 218 and 320-21).

necessario: Adverb (A.G. 320-21).

adoriebatur: The main verb of the coordinate clause **dispersosque ... adoriebatur** (A.G. 278.a). The pronoun **is**, with **Vercingetorix** as the antecedent, is understood as the subject (A.G. 271.a).

magnoque incommodo: Ablative of manner with a limiting adjective (A.G. 412). **-que**: The enclitic conjunction connects the two main verbs **adoriebatur ... adficiebat** (A.G. 324.a).

adficiebat: The main verb of the coordinate clause **magnoque ... iretur** (A.G. 278.a). The pronoun **is**, with **Vercingetorix** as the antecedent, is understood as the subject (A.G. 271.a). The pronoun **eos**, with **dispersos** as the antecedent, is understood as the direct object.

etsi ... occurrebatur: Concessive clause; the conjunction **etsi** ("although") with the indicative forms a subordinate clause (A.G. 527).

occurrebatur: The main verb of the subordinate clause (A.G. 278.b). The pronoun **is**, with **Vercingetorix** as the antecedent, is understood as the subject (A.G. 271.a).

quantum ratione provideri poterat: A literal translation of this clause is: "to what degree (**quantum**) it was possible (**poterat**) to be provided for (**provideri**) by means of a plan of action (**ratione**)". This, of course, must be rendered into acceptable English.

quantum ... (id) poterat: Relative clause (A.G. 279.a). **quantum**: Relative adverb (*OLD* **quantum2** B). **poterat**: The main verb of the subordinate clause (A.G. 278.b). Impersonal use of the verb, supply **id** as the subject (A.G. 271.a). When used impersonally with the passive infinitive (**provideri**), **posse** means "it can be done or happen, it is possible" (*OLD* **possum** 6.b).

provideri: Complementary infinitive after **poterat** (A.G. 456).

ratione: Ablative of means (A.G. 409).

ab nostris: Ablative of agent with the preposition **ab** after the passive verb **occurrebatur** (A.G. 405). **nostris**: Plural, masculine, ablative possessive pronoun used substantively to denote a special class (A.G. 302.d).

ut ... (id) iretur: The conjunction **ut** ("so that") with the subjunctive forms a clause of result dependent on **occurrebatur** (A.G. 537.1). **iretur**: The main verb of the subordinate clause (A.G. 278.b). Imperfect subjunctive; the tense of the subjunctive is in secondary sequence and follows the rules for the sequence of tense after **occurrebatur** (A.G. 482-85). Impersonal use of the intransitive passive verb (A.G. 208.d). Supply **id** as the subject (A.G. 318.c).

incertis temporibus: Ablative of *time when* (A.G. 423.1).

diversisque itineribus: Ablative of manner with a limiting adjective (A.G. 412). **-que**: The enclitic conjunction connects the two ablative phrases (A.G. 324.a).

Chapters 17-18: Kahn notes that Caesar "juxtaposes in Book 7 the actions of the Romans and the Gauls implicitly to expose the differences between the antagonists. Thus in 17-18 he contrasts the mutual trust existing between the Roman soldiers and their commander with the rowdy insubordination of the Gallic troops and the Gallic leader's trickery in reestablishing discipline." (Kahn, 253)

(17.1-2) **Castris ad eam partem oppidi positis Caesar, quae intermissa a flumine et a paludibus aditum, ut supra diximus, angustum habebat, aggerem apparare, vineas agere, turris duas constituere coepit: nam circumvallare loci natura pro(2)hibebat.**

a(b), *from.*
aditus, -us, m., *approach, access, way of approach.*
ago, agere, egi, actus, *set in motion, move forward.*
apparo, -are, -avi, -atus, *prepare, make ready, get ready.*
castra, -orum, n., pl., *camp, encampment.*

coepi, -isse, coeptus, *begin, start, commence.*

dico, dicere, dixi, dictus, *say.*
et, *and.*
habeo, habere, habui, habitus, *have.*
is, ea, id, *he, she, it; that, this.*
nam, *for, seeing that, inasmuch as.*
natura, -ae, f., *natural features, situation.*
pars, partis, f., *part, portion, side.*
prohibeo, -hibere, -hibui, -hibitus, *prevent, hinder.*
supra, *before, previously.*
ut, *as.*

ad, *at.*
agger, -eris, m., *rampart, mole, mound, dike.*
angustus, -a, -um, *contracted, narrow, close.*
Caesar, -aris, m., *Caesar.*
circumvallo, -are, -avi, -atus, *surround with a rampart, blockade, invest.*
constituo, -stituere, -stitui, -stitutus, *station, place, establish.*
duo, -ae, -o, *two.*
flumen, -inis, n., *flowing water, current, stream, river.*
intermitto, -mittere, -misi, -missus, *leave an interval.*
locus, -i, m., *place, location.*
oppidum, -i, n., *fortified town, city.*
palus, -udis, f., *marsh, swamp, bog, morass.*
pono, ponere, posui, positus, *place, put.*
qui, quae, quod, *who, which, what.*
turris, -is, f., *tower.*
vinea, -ae, f., *arbor-shed, vinea.*

Castris ad eam partem oppidi positis: Ablative absolute (A.G. 419-20). **ad eam partem oppidi**: Prepositional phrase, **ad** with the accusative here means "at" (*OLD* **ad** 13). **eam**: Singular, feminine, accusative demonstrative pronoun used as an adjective modifying **partem** (A.G. 296.1 and a). **oppidi**: Partitive genitive with **partem** (A.G. 346.a.1). **positis**: The perfect tense of the participle represents the action as completed at the time indicated by the tense of the main verb (A.G. 489).

Caesar: Nominative subject of **coepit** (A.G. 339). See Appendix A.

quae ... habebat: Relative clause (A.G. 303). **quae**: See below. **habebat**: The main verb of the subordinate clause (A.G. 278.b).

quae intermissa: Nominative subject (A.G. 339). **quae**: Singular, feminine, nominative relative pronoun used substantively (A.G. 305). The antecedent is **partem** (A.G. 307). **intermissa**: Nominative, perfect, passive participle used as a predicate where in English a phrase or a subordinate clause would be more natural (A.G. 496).

a flumine et a paludibus: Two ablatives of separation with the preposition **a(b)** after **intermissa** (A.G. 402.a). **et**: The conjunction connects the two prepositional phrases (A.G. 324.a).

aditum ... angustum: Accusative direct object of **habebat** (A.G. 387).

ut ... diximus: The relative adverb **ut** ("as") with the indicative introduces a parenthetical remark (*OLD* **ut** 12). For the reference see above at 15.4-6. **diximus**: The main verb of the subordinate clause (A.G. 278.b). The personal pronoun **nos** is understood as the subject but is not expressed except for distinction or emphasis (A.G. 295.a). In Book 7, Caesar refers to himself only in the third person, either in the singular or occasionally in the plural (see **Caesar** at 1.1). Siedler counts 11 uses of the first person plural in Book 7 (Siedler, 46). These uses are at 17.1, 23.2, 25.1, 37.1, 48.1, 58.4, 70.1, 76.1, 79.2, 83.8, and 85.4.

supra: Adverb (A.G. 320-21).

apparare ... agere ... constituere: Three complementary infinitives after **coepit** (A.G. 456).

aggerem ... vineas ... turris duas: Three accusative direct objects of their respective infinitives (A.G. 387 and 451.3). **aggerem**:

"Another means of gaining command of a wall was to raise against it a mound of earth (agger) - more correctly a ramp - which sloped toward the summit of the wall. The men engaged on it approached it under cover of one or more chains of penthouses, and when at work were protected by mantlets. It was an extremely laborious operation, and frequently thousands of tons of earth had to be carried forward in baskets. When completed, one or more moveable towers were at times hauled up the mound so that increased command might be gained." (Fuller, 93) **vineas**: "The penthouse (*vinea*) was a shed, or hut, with open ends. Normally its two sides were of hurdlework and its roof of timber, both protected against fire by a covering of raw hides. It was moved forward by the men inside it, and was used either singly or in chains - that is, end to end - so as to form a continuous covered way. When so used, they were equivalent to modern siege saps." (Fuller, 92) **turris**: Accusative plural noun; **-is** for **-es** is the regular form in i-stem nouns (A.G. 65-7 and 74.c). "The moveable tower was generally built of scaffolding and hurdlework; it was divided into storeys, and protected from fire by raw hides, sometimes by plates of metal. ... The tower was provided with wheels, and was hauled forward by means of cables, pulleys, and capstans along a prepared causeway by hundreds of men, and sometimes it would appear by thousands. When in position, from its upper storeys and summit archers and catapults fired on the defenders of the wall, while on its ground floor a battering-ram pounded the lower part of the wall. When a tower could be brought close up to the wall, under cover of its archers and catapults, a boarding-bridge was let down from it on to the top of the wall to enable a storming party to gain a footing on its battlements." (Fuller, 92-93) **duas**: Declinable cardinal number used as an adjective modifying **turris** (A.G. 132-35). Note the asyndeton between the infinitive phrases (A.G. 323.b).
coepit: The main verb of the main clause (A.G. 278.b).
nam: Conjunction, here explanatory meaning "for" (*OLD* **nam** 2).
(eum) circumvallere: Subject accusative with the infinitive after **prohibebat** (A.G. 558.b Note). The pronoun **eum**, with **Caesar** as the antecedent, is understood as the accusative subject.
loci: Possessive genitive with **natura** (A.G. 343).
natura: Nominative subject (A.G. 339).
prohibebat: The main verb of the simple sentence (A.G. 278.1).

(17.2-3) **De re frumentaria Boios atque Aeduos adhortari non destitit;**

adhortor, -ari, -atus, *encourage, rally, exhort, rouse, urge.*
atque, *and.*
de, *about, concerning.*
frumentarius, -a, -um, *having to do with grain* or *supplies.*
res, rei, f., *supply, supplies.*

Aedui, -orum, m., pl., *the Aedui.*
Boii, -orum, m., pl., *the Boii.*
desisto, -sistere, -stiti, -stitus, *leave off, stop, give up.*
non, *not.*

De re frumentaria: Prepositional phrase, **de** with the ablative here means "about, concerning" (*OLD* **de** 12).
Boios atque Aeduos: Two accusative direct objects of the infinitive **adhortari** (A.G. 387 and 451.3). **Boios**: See Appendix A.
atque: The conjunction connects the two accusative nouns and means "and" (*OLD* **atque** 12). **Aeduos**: See Appendix A.
adhortari: Complementary infinitive after **destitit** (A.G. 456).
non: Adverb, the adverb generally precedes the verb if it belongs to no one word in particular (A.G. 217.e, 320-21, and 599.a).
destitit: The main verb of the simple sentence (A.G. 278.1). The pronoun **is**, with **Caesar** as the antecedent, is understood as the subject (A.G. 271.a).

(17.2-3) **quorum alteri, quod nullo studio agebant, non multum adiuvabant, alteri non magnis facultatibus, quod civitas erat exigua et infirma, celeriter quod habuerunt (3) consumpserunt.**

adiuvo, -iuvare, -iuvi, -iutus, *help, aid, assist, support.*
alter ... alter, -i, m., *the former ... the latter.*
civitas, -tatis, f., *state, nation.*

et, *and.*
facultas, -atis, f., (in the plural), *resources.*
infirmus, -a, -um, *not strong, weak.*
multum, *much, greatly.*
nullus, -a, -um, *no.*
quod, *because, since, for, as.*
sum, esse, fui, futurus, *be.*

ago, agere, egi, actus, *act, deliver.*
celeriter, *quickly, speedily, at once, immediately.*
consumo, -sumere, -sumpsi, -sumptus, *use up, eat up, consume.*
exiguus, -a, -um, *small, scanty, little.*
habeo, habere, habui, habitus, *have.*
magnus, -a, -um, *great.*
non, *not.*
qui, quae, quod, *who, which, what.*
studium, -i, n., *zeal, eagerness, energy, enthusiasm.*

quorum: Plural, masculine, genitive relative pronoun used substantively (A.G. 305). The antecedent is **Boios ... Aeduos** (A.G. 307). Partitive genitive with **alteri** (A.G. 346.a.2). The relative does not introduce a relative clause but is a connecting relative; at the beginning of a clause the pronoun is often best rendered by a personal or demonstrative pronoun, with or without *and* (A.G. 308.f).
alteri ... alteri: Two pronouns meaning "the former ... the latter" (*OLD* **alter2** 5).
alteri: Plural, masculine, nominative pronoun used substantively (A.G. 296.2). The antecedent is **Aeduos** (A.G. 315). Nominative subject of **adiuvabant** (A.G. 339).
quod ... agebant: Causal clause; the conjunction **quod** ("because") takes the indicative when the reason is given on the authority of the writer or speaker (A.G. 540.1). **agebant**: The main verb of the subordinate clause (A.G. 278.b). The pronoun **ei**, with **alteri** as the antecedent, is understood as the subject (A.G. 271.a).

nullo studio: Ablative of manner with a limiting adjective (A.G. 412). "The Aedui had doubtless found the Roman yoke galling, and would gladly have thrown it off if they had dared. Once before they had given Caesar serious trouble by not bringing promised supplies at 1.16." (Kelsey, 405) Indeed, they will soon join with the rest of Gaul and attempt to throw off that galling yoke.

non: Adverb modifying **multum**; the negative precedes the word it especially effects (A.G. 217.e, 320-21, and 599.a).

multum: Adverb, the neuter accusative of an adjective used as an adverb (A.G. 214.d and 320-21).

adiuvabant: The main verb of the coordinate clause **Quorum ... adiuvabant** (A.G. 278.a).

alteri: Plural, masculine, nominative pronoun used substantively (A.G. 296.2). The antecedent is **Boios** (A.G. 315). Nominative subject of **consumpserunt** (A.G. 339).

non ... infirma: Ablative absolute with a dependent clause.

non magnis facultatibus: Ablative absolute with an adjective (**magnis**) taking the place of a participle (there is no participle for "being") (A.G. 419.a-20). The ablative absolute replaces a causal clause ("since") (A.G. 420.2). **non**: Adverb modifying **magnis**; the negative precedes the word it especially effects (A.G. 217.e, 320-21, and 599.a).

quod ... infirma: Causal clause; the conjunction **quod** ("because") takes the indicative when the reason is given on the authority of the writer or speaker (A.G. 540.1). **infirma**: See below.

civitas: Nominative subject (A.G. 339).

erat: The main verb of the subordinate clause (A.G. 278.b).

exigua et infirma: Two singular, feminine, nominative predicate adjectives modifying **civitas** after **erat** (A.G. 283-84). **et**: The conjunction connects the two adjectives (A.G. 324.a). Two adjectives belonging to the same noun are regularly connected by a conjunction (A.G. 323.d).

celeriter: Adverb (A.G. 214.b and 320-21).

quod ... habuerunt: Relative clause (A.G. 303). **quod**: Singular, neuter, accusative relative pronoun used substantively (A.G. 305). The antecedent is omitted, supply **frumentum** (A.G. 307.c). Accusative direct object of **habuerunt** (A.G. 387). **habuerunt**: The main verb of the subordinate clause (A.G. 278.b). The pronoun **ei**, with **alteri** as the antecedent, is understood as the subject (A.G. 271.a).

consumpserunt: The main verb of the coordinate clause **alteri ... consumpserunt** (A.G. 278.a).

(17.3-4) Summa difficultate rei frumentariae adfecto exercitu tenuitate Boiorum, indiligentia Aeduorum, incendiis aedificiorum, usque eo ut compluris dies frumento milites caruerint et pecore ex longinquioribus vicis adacto extremam famem sustentarent, nulla tamen vox est ab eis audita populi Romani maiestate et superioribus victoriis (4) indigna.

ab, *from.*

adigo, -igere, -egi, -actus, *drive in.*
Aedui, -orum, m., pl., *the Aedui.*
Boii, -orum, m., pl., *the Boii.*
complures, -a and **-ia**, *several, a number of, many.*
difficultas, -tatis, f., *difficulty, trouble.*
ex, *from.*
extremus, -a, -um, *utmost, extreme, highest, greatest.*
frumentarius, -a, -um, *having to do with grain* or *supplies.*
incendium, -i, n., *fire, conflagration, a burning.*
indiligentia, -ae, f., *carelessness, negligence.*
longinquus, -a, -um, comp. **-ior**, *far removed, remote, distant.*
miles, -itis, m., *soldier, foot-solider.*
pecus, -oris, n., *cattle.*
res, rei, f., *supply, supplies.*
superior, -or, -us, *former, earlier, previous.*
sustineo, -tinere, -tinui, -tentus, *hold out, bear, endure, withstand.*
tenuitas, -atis, f., *smallness of resources, poverty.*
ut, *so that.*
vicus, -i, m., *village, hamlet.*

adficio, -ficere, -feci, -fectus, *afflict, trouble, weaken, impair.*
aedificium, -i, n., *building.*
audio, -ire, -ivi or **-ii, -itus**, *hear.*
careo, -ere, -ui, -iturus, *be without, lack, want.*
dies, -ei, m. and f., *day.*
et, *and.*
exercitus, -us, m., *army.*
fames, -is, f., *hunger, starvation.*
frumentum, -i, n., *grain.*
indignus, -a, -um, *unworthy, undeserving.*
is, ea, id, *he, she, it; that, this.*
maiestas, -atis, f., *greatness, dignity.*
nullus, -a, -um, *no.*
populus, -i, m., *people* (as a political whole), *nation.*
Romanus, -a, -um, *Roman.*
summus, -a, -um, *utmost, greatest.*
tamen, *yet, still, for all that, nevertheless, however.*
usque eo, *to such an extent, to so great an extent.*
victoria, -ae, f., *victory.*
vox, vocis, f., *utterance, cry, sound, word.*

Summa ... sustentarent: Ablative absolute with a dependent clause.

Summa difficultate rei frumentariae adfecto exercitu tenuitate Boiorum, indiligentia Aeduorum, incendiis aedificiorum: Ablative absolute (A.G. 419-20). **Summa difficultate**: Ablative of manner with a limiting adjective (A.G. 412). **summa**: Defective superlative adjective (A.G. 130.b). **rei frumentariae**: Objective genitive with **difficultate** (A.G. 348). **adfecto exercitu ... (tamen)**: The noun, participle element of the ablative absolute (A.G. 419-20). The ablative absolute here takes the place of a concessive clause ("although") which is made clearer by the adversative particle **tamen** ("nevertheless") in the main clause (A.G. 420.3). **adfecto**: The perfect tense of the participle represents the action as completed at the time indicated by the tense of the main verb (A.G. 489).

tenuitate ... indiligentia ... incendiis: Three ablatives of cause without prepositions (A.G. 404). Notice the asyndeton construction (A.G. 323.b). **Boiorum**: Possessive genitive of the tribe name **Boii** with **tenuitate** (A.G. 343). See Appendix A. **Aeduorum**: Possessive genitive of the tribe name **Aedui** with **indiligentia** (A.G. 343). See Appendix A. **aedificiorum**: Objective genitive with **incendiis** (A.G. 348).

usque eo ut ... caruerint ... sustentarent: The conjunction **ut** ("so that") with the subjunctive forms a clause of result (A.G. 537.1).

usque eo: Two adverbs introducing the result clause meaning "to such an extent" (*OLD* usque 8). **caruerint ... sustentarent**: The main verbs of the subordinate clause (A.G. 278.b). Notice the switch in tenses "from **caruerint**, stating a historical fact, to **sustentarent** ('were bearing up against'), giving the resulting condition and implying that the hunger continued so long as the grain was scarce." (Kelsey, 405) **caruerint**: Perfect subjunctive; although the perfect tense of the subjunctive is normally not allowed after a secondary main verb (**est ... audita**), it is regularly used in result clauses. This construction emphasizes the result (A.G. 484 and 485.c and Note 1). **sustentarent**: Imperfect subjunctive; the tense of the subjunctive is in secondary sequence and follows the rules for the sequence of tense after **est ... audita** (A.G. 482-85).

compluris dies: Accusative of time *how long* (A.G. 423.2). **compluris**: Plural, masculine, accusative comparative adjective, a compound of **plus** (A.G. 120). **-is** for **-es** is an allowable accusative ending for comparative adjectives (A.G. 120-21.c). **dies**: The noun **dies** is normally masculine gender (A.G. 97.a).

frumento: Ablative of separation without a preposition after the verb **caruerint** (A.G. 401).

milites: Nominative subject of **caruerint ... sustentarent** (A.G. 339).

et: The conjunction connects the two main verbs in the result clause (A.G. 323.a).

pecore ex longinquioribus vicis adacto: Ablative absolute (A.G. 419-20). **ex longinquioribus vicis**: Ablative of *place from which* with the preposition **ex** (A.G. 426.1). **longinquioribus**: Comparative adjective (A.G. 124). **adacto**: The perfect tense of the participle represents the action as completed at the time indicated by the tense of the main verb (A.G. 489).

extremam famem: Accusative direct object of **sustentarent** (A.G. 387). **extremam**: Defective superlative adjective (A.G. 130.b).

nulla ... vox: Nominative subject (A.G. 339).

tamen: Adverb, postpositive (A.G. 324.j and 320-21).

est ... audita: The main verb of the main clause (A.G. 278.b). The perfect passive verb is here split (tmesis) (A.G. 640).

ab eis: Ablative of source with the preposition **ab** (A.G. 403.1). **eis**: Plural, masculine, ablative demonstrative pronoun used substantively (A.G. 296.2). The antecedent is **milites** (A.G. 297.e).

populi Romani: Possessive genitive with **maiestate** (A.G. 343). This expression has an invariable word order (A.G. 598.k).

maiestate et superioribus victoriis: Two ablatives of specification after **indigna** (A.G. 418.b). **et**: The conjunction connects the two ablative nouns **maiestate ... victoriis** (A.G. 324.a). **superioribus**: Defective comparative adjective modifying **victoriis** (A.G. 130.b).

indigna: Singular, feminine, nominative predicate adjective modifying **vox** after **est ... audita** (A.G. 283).

(17.4-8) Quin etiam Caesar cum in opere singulas legiones appellaret et, si acerbius inopiam ferrent, se dimissurum oppugnationem diceret, universi ab eo ne id faceret pete(5)bant:

ab, *from.*
appello, -are, -avi, -atus, *address.*
cum, *while, when.*
dimitto, -mittere, -misi, -missus, *give up.*
facio, facere, feci, factus, *do.*

in, *engaged or occupied in.*
is, ea, id, *he, she, it; that, this.*
ne, *so that ... not.*
opus, operis, n., *work, labor.*

quin etiam, *and furthermore, moreover.*
singuli, -ae, -a, *one at a time, several, individual.*

acerbe, comp. **-ius**, *bitterly, severely.*
Caesar, -aris, m., *Caesar.*
dico, dicere, dixi, dictus, *say.*
et, *and.*
fero, ferre, tuli, latus, *bear, endure, suffer, hold out against.*
inopia, -ae, f., *want, lack, need, scarcity.*
legio, -onis, f., *legion.*
oppugnatio, -onis, f., *assault, sieging.*
peto, petere, petivi, and petii, petitus, *seek, ask, request.*
si, *if.*
sui, sibi, se, or sese, nom. wanting, *he*, with or without *himself.*

universi, -orum, m., pl., *all the men together, the whole body, all together.*

Quin etiam: The two adverbs **quin** and **etiam** introduce a statement that corroborates and amplifies what precedes and means "and furthermore" (*OLD* quin 2-3).

Caesar: Nominative subject (A.G. 339). The noun stands outside the **cum** clause but is the subject of the verbs **appellaret ... diceret**. See Appendix A.

cum ... appellaret ... diceret: Temporal clause; the relative adverb **cum** (A while, when) with the imperfect subjunctive describes the circumstances that accompanied the action of the main verb (A.G. 546). **appellaret ... diceret**: The main verbs of the subordinate clause (A.G. 278.b).

in opere: Prepositional phrase, **in** with the ablative here means "engaged or occupied in" (*OLD* in 39).

singulas legiones: Accusative direct object of **appellaret** (A.G 387). **singulas**: Distributive numeral used as an adjective (A.G. 136-37).

et: The conjunction connects the two verbs in the temporal clause **appellaret ... diceret** (A.G. 324.a).

si ... ferrent ... dimissurum (esse): Conditional statement in indirect discourse after **diceret** (A.G. 589). The protasis, as a dependent clause, is in the subjunctive and the apodosis, as the principal clause, is in the infinitive (A.G. 589).

si ... ferrent: The conjunction **si** ("if") with the subjunctive forms the protasis of a conditional statement in indirect discourse (A.G. 589.1). **ferrent**: The main verb of the subordinate clause (A.G. 278.b). Imperfect subjunctive; the tense of the subjunctive is in secondary sequence and follows the rules for the sequence of tense after **diceret** (A.G. 482-85 and 585). The pronoun **eae**, with **legiones** as the antecedent, is understood as the subject (A.G. 271.a).

acerbius: Comparative adverb (A.G. 218, 320-21). The comparative degree here denotes a considerable or excessive degree of the quality meaning "too" (A.G. 291.a).

inopiam: Accusative direct object of **ferrent** (A.G. 387).

se ... dimissurum (esse): The apodosis of the conditional statement (A.G. 589.2). Accusative/infinitive construction in indirect discourse after **diceret** (A.G. 577 ff. and 589). **se**: Singular, masculine, accusative direct reflexive pronoun (A.G. 300.1). The antecedent is **Caesar**, the subject of **diceret** (A.G. 299). **dimissurum (esse)**: Supply **esse** to form the future active infinitive (186). The tense of the infinitive in indirect discourse is relative to that of the verb of saying (A.G. 584).

oppugnationem: Accusative direct object of the infinitive **dimissurum (esse)** (A.G. 387 and 451.3).

universi: Plural, masculine, nominative adjective used substantively (A.G. 288). The noun **milites** is understood (A.G. 288.b). Nominative subject of **petebant** (A.G. 339).

ab eo: Ablative of source with the preposition **ab** (A.G. 403.1). **eo**: Singular, masculine, ablative demonstrative pronoun used substantively (A.G. 296.2). The antecedent is **Caesar** (A.G. 297.e).

ne ... faceret: The conjunction **ne** ("so that ... not") with the subjunctive forms a negative substantive clause of purpose which is used as the object of the verb **petebant** denoting an action directed toward the future (A.G. 563). **faceret**: The main verb of the subordinate clause (A.G. 278.b). Imperfect subjunctive; the tense of the subjunctive is in secondary sequence and follows the rules for the sequence of tense after **petebant** (A.G. 482-85). The pronoun **is**, with **Caesar** as the antecedent, is understood as the subject (A.G. 271.a).

id: Singular, neuter, accusative demonstrative pronoun used substantively (A.G. 296.2). The antecedent is the idea of giving up the siege (A.G. 297.e). Accusative direct object of **faceret** (A.G. 387).

petebant: The main verb of the main clause (A.G. 278.b).

(17.5-8) **sic se compluris annos illo imperante meruisse ut nullam ignominiam acciperent, nusquam incepta re disce(6)derent: hoc se ignominiae laturos loco, si inceptam oppug(7)nationem reliquissent: praestare omnis perferre acerbitates quam non civibus Romanis qui Cenabi perfidia Gallorum (8) interissent parentarent.**

accipio, -cipere, -cepi, -ceptus, *receive, accept, suffer, bear.*
annus, -i, m., *year.*
civis, -is, m., *citizen, fellow-citizen.*
discedo, -cedere, -cessi, -cessurus, *go away, depart, leave.*
Galli, -orum, m., *the Gauls.*
ignominia, -ae, f., *disgrace, dishonor.*
impero, -are, -avi, -atus, *command, order, exercise authority.*
intereo, -ire, -ii, -iturus, *perish, be destroyed, die.*
mereo, -ere, -ui, -itus, *serve as a soldier.*
nullus, -a, -um, *no.*
omnis, -e, *all.*
parento, -are, -----, -atus, *take vengeance, avenge.*
perfidia, -ae, f., *faithlessness, bad faith, treachery.*
quam, (*rather*) *than.*
relinquo, -linquere, -liqui, -lictus, *leave off, give up.*
Romanus, -a, -um, *Roman.*
sic, *so, in this way, thus.*
ut, *so that.*

acerbitas, -tatis, f., *suffering, grief, sorrow, affliction.*
Cenabum, -i, n., *Cenabum.*
complures, -a and -ia, *a number of, many.*
fero, ferre, tuli, latus, *bear, regard, hold.*
hic, haec, hoc, *this; he, she, it.*
ille, illae, illud, *that; he, she, it.*
incipio, -cipere, -cepi, -ceptus, *begin, commence, undertake.*
locus, -i, m., *in the capacity of, by way of, as.*
non, *not.*
nusquam, *nowhere, in no place.*
oppugnatio, -onis, f., *attack, sieging.*
perfero, -ferre, -tuli, -latus, *endure, suffer, bear, submit to.*
praesto, -stare, -stiti, -stitus, (imper.), *it is preferable, it is better.*
qui, quae, quod, *who, which, what.*
res, rei, f., *project, business, operation.*
si, *if.*
sui, sibi, se, or **sese**, nom. wanting, *they*, with or without *themselves.*

sic: The adverb anticipates a following accusative/infinitive construction (*OLD* **sic** 4.b). The verb of saying is unexpressed, but implied in the adverb (A.G. 580.a).

se ... meruisse: Accusative/infinitive construction in indirect discourse (A.G. 577 ff.). The verb of saying is not expressed, but implied in the general drift of the sentence (A.G. 580.a). **se**: Plural, masculine, accusative direct reflexive pronoun (A.G. 300.1). The antecedent is **universi**, the subject of the unexpressed verb of saying (A.G. 299). **meruisse**: Perfect infinitive; the tense of the infinitive in indirect discourse is relative to that of the verb of saying (A.G. 584).

compluris annos: Accusative of time *how long* (A.G. 423.2). **compluris**: Plural, masculine, accusative comparative adjective, a compound of **plus** (A.G. 120). **-is** for **-es** is an allowable accusative ending for comparative adjectives (A.G. 120-21.c).

illo imperante: Ablative absolute (A.G. 419-20). **illo**: Singular, masculine, ablative singular demonstrative pronoun used substantively (A.G. 296.2). The antecedent is **Caesar** (A.G. 297.e). **imperante**: The participle ends in **-e** rather than **-i** in the ablative singular when used in an ablative absolute (A.G. 121.2). Here the present participle denotes an action continued in the present but begun in the past (A.G. 490.1).

ut ... acciperent ... discederent: The conjunction **ut** ("so that") with the subjunctive forms a clause of result dependent on the infinitive **meruisse** (A.G. 537.1). **acciperent ... discederent**: The main verbs of the subordinate clause (A.G. 278.b). Imperfect subjunctives; the tense of the subjunctives is in secondary sequence after the unexpressed verb of saying (A.G. 585). The use of the imperfect tense, rather than pluperfect, is here demanded as the present siege is still an incomplete action (A.G. 484). Notice the asyndeton between the two main verbs (A.G. 323.b). The pronoun **ipsi**, with **universi** as the antecedent, is understood as the subject of both verbs (A.G. 271.a).

nullam ... ignominiam: Accusative direct object of **acciperent** (A.G. 387).

nusquam: Adverb (A.G. 320-21).

incepta re: Ablative absolute A.G. 419-20). **incepta**: The perfect tense of the participle represents the action as completed at the time indicated by the tense of the main verb (A.G. 489).

hoc: Singular, neuter, accusative demonstrative pronoun used substantively (A.G. 296.2). The pronoun points forward to the phrase **si inceptam oppugnationem reliquissent** (A.G. 297.e). Accusative direct object of the infinitive **laturos (esse)** (A.G. 387 and 451.3).

se ... laturos (esse) ... si ... reliquissent: Conditional statement in indirect discourse after the unexpressed verb of saying (A.G. 589). The protasis, as a dependent clause, is in the subjunctive and the apodosis, as the principal clause, is in the infinitive (A.G. 589).

se ... laturos (esse): The apodosis of the conditional statement (A.G. 589.2). Accusative/infinitive construction after the unexpressed verb of saying (A.G. 577 ff. and 589). **se**: Plural, masculine, accusative direct reflexive pronoun (A.G. 300.1). The antecedent is **universi**, the subject of the unexpressed verb of saying (A.G. 299). **laturos (esse)**: Supply **esse** to form the future active infinitive (A.G. 200). The tense of the infinitive in indirect discourse is relative to that of the verb of saying (A.G. 584).

ignominiae ... loco: Ablative of quality (descriptive ablative) with a genitive modifier describing **hoc** (A.G. 415). **ignominiae**: Objective genitive (A.G. 348). **loco**: The noun **locus** with a genitive means "in the capacity of, by way of, as" (*OLD* **locus** 18.c).

si ... reliquissent: The conjunction **si** ("if") with the subjunctive forms the protasis of the conditional statement in indirect discourse (A.G. 589.1). **reliquissent**: The main verb of the subordinate clause (A.G. 278.b). Pluperfect subjunctive; the tense of the subjunctive is in secondary sequence after the unexpressed verb of saying (A.G. 482-85 and 585). The pluperfect tense of the subjunctive is here standing for a future perfect in direct discourse. The future perfect tense denotes action completed (at the time referred to), and hence is represented in the subjunctive by the pluperfect tense in secondary sequence (A.G. 484.c). The pronoun **ipsi**, with **universi** as the antecedent, is understood as the subject (A.G. 271.a).

inceptam oppugnationem: Accusative direct object of **reliquissent** (A.G. 387). **inceptam**: Accusative, perfect, passive participle used as a predicate where in English a phrase or a subordinate clause would be more natural (A.G. 496).

praestare: Impersonal infinitive in indirect discourse after the unexpressed verb of saying (A.G. 577 ff.). Impersonal use of the verb (A.G. 208.c). The following infinitive phrase functions as the subject (A.G. 454). Present infinitive; the tense of the infinitive in indirect discourse is relative to that of the verb of saying (A.G. 584).

omnis perferre acerbitates: The infinitive phrase functions as the subject of the impersonal **praestare** (A.G. 454). **omnis ... acerbitates** The accusative direct object of the infinitive **perferre** (A.G. 387 and 451.3). **omnis**: Accusative plural adjective; **-is** for **-es** is the regular form in i-stem adjectives (A.G. 114.a and 116).

quam ... parentarent: Relative clause; a dependent clause in indirect discourse takes the subjunctive (A.G. 279.a and 580). **quam**: Relative adverb meaning "(rather) than" after the comparison implied in **praestare** (*OLD* **quam** 9.b). The infinitive construction is regularly continued in indirect discourse after **quam**, but not here (A.G. 583.c). **parentarent**: The main verb of the subordinate clause (A.G. 278.b). Imperfect subjunctive; the tense of the subjunctive is in secondary sequence after the unexpressed verb of saying (A.G. 482-85 and 585). The pronoun **ipsi**, with **universi** as the antecedent, is understood as the subject (A.G. 271.a).

non: Adverb; when **non** is especially emphatic it begins the clause (A.G. 217.e, 320-21, and 599.a).

civibus Romanis: Dative indirect object of the intransitive verb **parentarent** (A.G. 366).

qui ... interissent: Relative clause; a subordinate clause in indirect discourse takes the subjunctive (A.G. 303 and 580). **qui**: Plural, masculine, nominative relative pronoun used substantively (A.G. 305). The antecedent is **civibus** (A.G. 307). Nominative subject (A.G. 339). **interissent**: The main verb of the subordinate clause (A.G. 278.b). Pluperfect subjunctive; the tense of the subjunctive is in secondary sequence after the unexpressed verb of saying (A.G. 482-85 and 585).

Cenabi: Locative case of the city name **Cenabum, -i**, n. (A.G. 49.a). See Appendix A.

perfidia: Ablative of cause without a preposition (A.G. 404).

Gallorum: Possessive genitive with **perfidia** (A.G. 343). See Appendix A.

(17.8) **Haec eadem centurionibus tribunisque militum mandabant, ut per eos ad Caesarem deferrentur.**

ad, *to*.
centurio, -onis, m., *centurion*.

hic, haec, hoc, *this*; *he, she, it*.
is, ea, id, *he, she, it*; *that, this*.
miles, -itis, m., *soldier, foot-solider*.
-que, *and*.
ut, *so that*.

Caesar, -aris, m., *Caesar*.
defero, -ferre, -tuli, -latus, *bring to, carry to, report, announce*.
idem, eadem, idem, *the same*.
mando, -are, -avi, -atus, *commit, entrust, commission*.
per, *by* (means of), *through*.
tribunus, -i, m., *tribune*.

Haec eadem: Accusative direct object of the transitive verb **mandabant** (A.G. 387). **Haec**: Plural, neuter, accusative demonstrative pronoun used substantively meaning "these things" (A.G. 296.2). The antecedent is the aggregate of ideas previously expressed by the soldiers at 17.5-8 (sic ... **parentarent**) (A.G. 297.e). **eadem**: Plural, neuter, accusative demonstrative pronoun used as an adjective modifying **Haec** (A.G. 296.1 and a).

centurionibus tribunisque: Two dative indirect objects of the transitive verb **mandabant** (A.G. 362). **-que**: The enclitic conjunction connects the two dative nouns (A.G. 324.a). **tribunisque militum**: "The military tribunes (*tribuni militum*) numbered six to a legion. In earlier times these officers commanded the legion in turn. In Caesar's army they appear to have received appointment for personal rather than military reasons; as the command of the legions had been given over to the lieutenants, the military tribunes were intrusted with subordinate services, such as the leading of troops on the march, the command of detachments smaller than a legion, the securing of supplies, and the oversight of the watches." (Kelsey, 25)

militum: Possessive genitive with **tribunis** (A.G. 343).

mandabant: The main verb of the main clause (A.G. 278.b). The pronoun **ei**, with **universi** as the antecedent, is understood as the subject (A.G. 271.a).

ut ... deferrentur: The conjunction **ut** ("so that") with the subjunctive forms a final (purpose) clause dependent upon **mandabant** (A.G. 531.1). **deferrentur**: The main verb of the subordinate clause (A.G. 278.b). Imperfect subjunctive; the tense of the subjunctive is in secondary sequence and follows the rule for sequence of tense after **mandabant** (A.G. 482-85). The pronoun **ea**, with **haec eadem** as the antecedent, is understood as the subject (A.G. 271.a).

per eos: Prepositional phrase, the personal agent, when considered as instrument or means, is often expressed by **per** with the accusative meaning "by" (means of) (A.G. 405.b). **eos**: Plural, masculine, accusative demonstrative pronoun used substantively (A.G. 296.2). The antecedent is **centurionibus tribunisque militum** (A.G. 297.d).

ad Caesarem: Prepositional phrase, **ad** with the accusative here means "to" (*OLD* ad 1). **Caesarem**: See Appendix A.

(18.1-2) **Cum iam muro turres appropinquassent, ex captivis Caesar cognovit Vercingetorigem consumpto pabulo castra movisse propius Avaricum, atque ipsum cum equitatu expeditisque qui inter equites proeliari consuessent insidiarum causa eo profectum quo nostros postero die pabulatum (2) venturos arbitraretur.**

appropinquo, -are, -avi, -atus, *approach, come near, draw near.*
atque, *and.*
Caesar, -aris, m., *Caesar.*
castra, -orum, n., pl., *camp, encampment.*

cognosco, -gnoscere, -gnovi, cognitus, *learn, ascertain, recognize.*
consumo, -sumere, -sumpsi, -sumptus, *use* or *eat up, devour, consume.*
dies, -ei, m. and f., *day.*
eques, -itis, m., *rider, horseman, cavalryman, trooper.*
ex, *from.*
iam, *already, by this time, presently.*
inter, *among.*

moveo, movere, movi, motus, *move.*
nostri, -orum, m., pl., *our men, our side.*
pabulum, -i, n., *fodder.*
proelior, -ari, -atus, *fight, join battle, engage in battle.*
prope, comp. **-ius**, *near.*
qui, quae, quod, *who, which, what.*
turris, -is, f., *tower.*
Vercingetorix, -igis, m., *Vercingetorix.*

arbitror, -ari, -atus, *think, suppose, consider, believe.*
Avaricum, -i, n., *Avaricum.*
captivus, -i, m., *captive, prisoner.*
causa, -ae, f., abl. with the gen., *for the sake of, on account of.*
consuesco, -suescere, -suevi, -suetus, *be accustomed.*
cum, *after, when; with.*
eo, *to that place.*
equitatus, -us, m., *cavalry.*
expeditus, -i, m., *a light-armed soldier.*
insidiae, -arum, f., pl., *ambush, ambuscade, trap.*
ipse, -a, -um, *he, they*, with or without *himself, themselves.*
murus, -i, m., *wall, rampart.*
posterus, -a, -um, *following, the next.*
proficiscor, -ficisci, -fectus, *set out, depart, proceed.*
-que, *and.*
quo, *where, whither.*
venio, venire, veni, ventus, *come.*

Cum ... appropinquassent: Temporal clause; the relative adverb **cum** ("after, when") with the pluperfect subjunctive describes the circumstances that preceded the action of the main verb (A.G. 546). **appropinquassent**: The main verb of the subordinate clause (A.G. 278.b). Contracted form of **appropinquavissent** (A.G. 181.b).

iam: Adverb (A.G. 215.6, 217.b and 320-21).

muro: Dative indirect object of the intransitive verb **appropinquassent** (A.G. 366).

turres: Nominative subject (A.G. 339).

ex captivis: Ablative of source with the preposition **ex** (A.G. 403.1).

Caesar: Nominative subject (A.G. 339). See Appendix A.

cognovit: The main verb of the main clause (A.G. 278.b).

Vercingetorigem ... movisse: Accusative/infinitive construction in indirect discourse after **cognovit** (A.G. 577 ff.).

Vercingetorigem: See Appendix A. **movisse**: Perfect infinitive; the tense of the infinitive in indirect discourse is relative to that of the verb of saying (A.G. 584).

consumpto pabulo: Ablative absolute (A.G. 419-20). **consumpto**: The perfect tense of the participle represents the action as completed at the time indicated by the tense of the main verb (A.G. 489).

castra: Accusative direct object of the infinitive **movisse** (A.G. 387 and 451.3).

propius Avaricum: The comparative adverb **propius** is here used as a preposition with the accusative and means "nearer" (A.G. 432.a). **Avaricum**: See Appendix A.

atque: The conjunction connects the two accusative/infinitive constructions after **cognovit** and means "and" (*OLD* atque 12).

ipsum ... profectum (esse): Accusative/infinitive construction in indirect discourse after **cognovit** (A.G. 577 ff.). **ipsum**: Singular, masculine, accusative demonstrative pronoun used substantively (A.G. 296.2). The antecedent is **Vercingetorigem** (A.G. 297.e). The pronoun is here emphatic (A.G. 298.d.1). **profectum (esse)**: Supply **esse** to form the perfect deponent infinitive (A.G. 190). The tense of the infinitive in indirect discourse is relative to that of the verb of saying (A.G. 584).

cum equitatu expeditisque: Ablative of accompaniment with the preposition **cum** (A.G. 413). **expeditis**: Plural, masculine, ablative adjective used substantively (A.G. 288). The noun **militibus** is understood (A.G. 288.b). "The light-armed foot-soldiers fought among the cavalry ... Vercingetorix had adopted the German tactics, the superiority of which over their own the Gauls had learned to their cost." (Kelsey, 405-06) **-que**: The enclitic conjunction connects the two ablative nouns in the prepositional phrase (A.G. 324.a).

qui ... consuessent: Relative clause; a subordinate clause in indirect discourse takes the subjunctive (A.G. 303 and 580). **qui**: Plural, masculine, nominative relative pronoun used substantively (A.G. 305). The antecedent is **expeditis** (A.G. 307). Nominative subject (A.G. 339). **consuessent**: The main verb of the subordinate clause (A.G. 278.b). Pluperfect subjunctive; the tense of the subjunctive is in secondary sequence and follows the rule for sequence of tense after **cognovit** (A.G. 482-85). Contracted form of **consuevissent** (A.G. 181.b).

inter equites proeliari: This passage demonstrates Vercingetorix's adaptability. Just as he adopts Roman siege tactics and camp fortifications, he here adopts German cavalry tactics. Caesar describes these tactics at *BG* 1.48.5-7: **Equitum milia erant sex, totidem numero pedites velocissimi ac fortissimi, quos ex omni copia singulos suae salutis causa delegerant; cum his in proeliis versabantur. Ad eos se equites recipiebant: hi, si quid erat durius, concurrebant; si quis graviore vulnere accepto equo deciderat, circumsistebant; si quo erat longius prodeundum aut celerius recipiendum, tanta erat horum exercitatione celeritas ut iubis equorum sublevati cursum adaequarent.**

inter equites: Prepositional phrase, **inter** with the accusative here means "among" (*OLD* **inter** 1).

proeliari: Complementary infinitive after **consuessent** (A.G. 456).

insidiarum causa: A preceding genitive with the ablative of **causa** means "for the sake of" A (A.G. 359.b and 404.c). **insidiarum**: The noun is always plural (A.G. 101).

eo ... quo: Two correlative adverbs meaning "to that place ... whither" (*OLD* **eo2** 1 and **quo1** 3.b).

quo ... arbitraretur: Relative clause; a subordinate clause in indirect discourse takes the subjunctive (A.G. 278.b and 580). **quo**: Relative adverb (*OLD* **quo1** 3.b). **arbitraretur**: The main verb of the subordinate clause (A.G. 278.b). Imperfect subjunctive; the tense of the subjunctive is in secondary sequence and follows the rule for sequence of tense after **cognovit** (A.G. 482-85). The pronoun **is**, with **Vercingetorigem** as the antecedent, is understood as the subject (A.G. 271.a).

nostros ... venturos (esse): Accusative/infinitive construction in indirect discourse after **arbitraretur** (A.G. 577 ff.). **nostros**: Plural, masculine, accusative possessive pronoun used substantively to denote a special class (A.G. 302.d). **venturos (esse)**: Supply **esse** to form the future active infinitive (A.G. 187). The tense of the infinitive in indirect discourse is relative to that of the verb of saying (A.G. 584).

postero die: Ablative of *time when* (A.G. 423.1). **die**: The noun **dies** is normally masculine gender (A.G. 97.a).

pabulatum: The supine in **-um** is used after a verb of motion (**venturos (esse)**) to express purpose (A.G. 509).

(18.2-3) Quibus rebus cognitis media nocte (3) silentio profectus ad hostium castra mane pervenit.

ad, *to, towards.*
cognosco, -gnoscere, -gnovi, cognitus, *learn, ascertain, recognize.*
mane, *in the morning.*
nox, noctis, f., *night.*

proficiscor, -ficisci, -fectus, *set out, depart, proceed.*
res, rei, f., *matter, affair, event.*

castra, -orum, n., pl., *camp, encampment.*
hostis, -is, m., *enemy, foe*; pl., *the enemy.*
medius, -a, -um, *in the middle, midst, middle, mid-.*
pervenio, -venire, -veni, -ventus, *come to, reach, arrive.*
qui, quae, quod, *who, which, what.*
silentium, -i, m., *silence, stillness.*

Quibus rebus cognitis: Ablative absolute (A.G. 419-20). **Quibus**: Plural, feminine, ablative relative pronoun (A.G. 305). The antecedent is **rebus** in its own clause (adjectival use) (A.G. 307.b). The relative does not introduce a relative clause but is a connecting relative; at the beginning of a clause the pronoun is often best rendered by a personal or demonstrative pronoun, with or without *and* (A.G. 308.f). **cognitis**: The perfect tense of the participle represents the action as completed at the time indicated by the tense of the main verb (A.G. 489).

media nocte: Ablative of *time when* (A.G. 423.1). **media**: The adjective designates not what object, but what part of it is meant (A.G. 293).

silentio: Ablative of manner without the preposition **cum** (A.G. 412.b).

profectus: Nominative, perfect, deponent participle used as a predicate, where in English a phrase or a subordinate clause would be more normal (A.G. 496). The pronoun **is**, with **Caesar** as the antecedent, is understood. Nominative subject (A.G. 339).

ad hostium castra: Accusative of *place to which* with the preposition **ad** (A.G. 426.2). **hostium**: Possessive genitive with **castra** (A.G. 343).

mane: Adverb (A.G. 320-21).

pervenit: The main verb of the main clause (A.G. 278.b).

(18.3-4) Illi celeriter per exploratores adventu Caesaris cognito carros impedimentaque sua in artiores silvas abdiderunt, copias (4) omnis in loco edito atque aperto instruxerunt.

abdo, -dere, -didi, -ditus, *put away, remove, conceal.*
apertus, -a, um, *open, exposed, unprotected.*
atque, *and.*
carrus, -i, m., *cart, wagon.*
cognosco, -gnoscere, -gnovi, cognitus, *learn, ascertain, recognize.*
editus, -a, -um, *elevated, high.*
ille, illae, illud, *that; he, she, it.*
in, *within, inside; in.*

adventus, -us, m., *coming, approach, arrival.*
artus, -a, -um, comp. **-ior**, *dense, deep.*
Caesar, -aris, m., *Caesar.*
celeriter, *quickly, speedily, at once, immediately.*
copiae, -arum, f., pl., *forces, troops.*
explorator, -oris, m., *spy, scout.*
impedimenta, -orum, n., pl., *heavy baggage, baggage.*
instruo, -struere, -struxi, -structus, *draw up, form.*

locus, -i, m., *place, location, position.*
per, *by* (means of), *through.*
silvae, -arum, f., pl., *wooded parts* or *region.*

omnis, -e, *all.*
-que, *and.*
suus, -a, -um, *their*, with or without *own.*

Illi: Plural, masculine, nominative demonstrative pronoun used substantively (A.G. 296.2). The antecedent is **hostium** (A.G. 297.e). The pronoun marks a change in subject to one previously mentioned (**hostium**) (A.G. 601.d). Nominative subject of **abdiderunt ... instruxerunt** (A.G. 339).
celeriter: Adverb (A.G. 214.b and 320-21).
per exploratores adventu Caesaris cognito: Ablative absolute (A.G. 419-20). **per exploratores**: Prepositional phrase, the personal agent, when considered as instrument or means, is often expressed by **per** with the accusative meaning "by" (means of) (A.G. 405.b). **Caesaris**: Possessive genitive with **adventu** (A.G. 343). See Appendix A. **cognito**: The perfect tense of the participle represents the action as completed at the time indicated by the tense of the main verb (A.G. 489).
carros impedimentaque sua: Two accusative direct objects of **abdiderunt** (A.G. 387). **sua**: Plural, neuter, accusative possessive pronoun used as an adjective with **impedimenta** (A.G. 302). **-que**: The enclitic conjunction connects the two accusative nouns (A.G. 324.a).
in artiores silvas: Accusative of *place to which* with the preposition **in** (A.G. 426.2). **artiores**: Comparative adjective (A.G. 124). **silvas**: The plural of the noun means "wooded parts or regions" (*OLD* silva 1).
abdiderunt: The main verb of the coordinate clause **Illi ... abdiderunt** (A.G. 278.a).
copias omnis: Accusative direct object of **instruxerunt** (A.G. 387). **omnis**: Accusative plural adjective; **-is** for **-es** is the regular form in i-stem adjectives (A.G. 114.a and 116).
in loco edito atque aperto: Ablative of *place where* with the preposition **in** (locative ablative) (A.G. 426.3). **atque**: The conjunction connects the two adjectives modifying **loco** and means "and" (*OLD* atque 12). Two adjectives belonging to the same noun are regularly connected by a conjunction (A.G. 323.d).
instruxerunt: The main verb of the coordinate clause **copias ... instruxerunt** (A.G. 278.a). Notice the asyndeton between the two main verbs **abdiderunt ... instruxerunt** (A.G. 323.b).

(18.4) **Qua re nuntiata Caesar celeriter sarcinas conferri, arma expediri iussit.**

arma, -orum, n., *arms, weapons.*
celeriter, *quickly, speedily, at once, immediately.*

expedio, -pedire, -pedivi, -peditus, *get ready, make ready.*

nuntio, -are, -avi, -atus, *announce, report.*
res, rei, f., *matter, affair, event.*

Caesar, -aris, m., *Caesar.*
confero, -ferre, -tuli, collatus, *bring together, gather, collect.*
iubeo, iubere, iussi, iussus, *order, give orders, bid, command.*
qui, quae, quod, *who, which, what.*
sarcinae, -arum, f., pl., *baggage, packs.*

Qua re nuntiata: Ablative absolute (A.G. 419-20). **qua**: Singular, feminine, ablative relative pronoun (A.G. 305). The antecedent is **re** in its own clause (adjectival use) (A.G. 307.b). The relative does not introduce a relative clause but is a connecting relative; at the beginning of a clause the pronoun is often best rendered by a personal or demonstrative pronoun, with or without *and* (A.G. 308.f).
nuntiata: The perfect tense of the participle represents the action as completed at the time indicated by the tense of the main verb (A.G. 489).
Caesar: Nominative subject (A.G. 339). See Appendix A.
celeriter: Adverb (A.G. 214.b and 320-21).
sarcinas conferri, arma expediri: Two subject accusative/infinitive constructions after **iussit**. The construction is equivalent to a substantive clause of purpose (A.G. 563.a). Notice the asyndeton construction (A.G. 323.b). **sarcinas**: "Besides his personal belongings, each soldier carried his share of the picks, spades, baskets, etc., used in entrenching the camp; cooking utensils; and several days' ration of grain, which seems to have been apportioned out only twice a month. All this, weighing from thirty to forty-five pounds, was made into a pack (*sarcina*), and strapped on a forked stick; this the soldier carried on his shoulder. While thus encumbered the soldiers were said to be **impediti**. If the army was attacked on the march the packs were stacked in one place under guard, and the soldiers were then **expediti**." (Walker, 25)
iussit: The main verb of the main clause (A.G. 278.b).

(19.1) **Collis erat leniter ab infimo acclivis.**

ab, *at.*
collis, -is, m., *hill, height, elevation.*
leniter, *mildly, gently, slightly.*

acclivis, -e, *sloping, up-hill, rising.*
infimum, -i, n., *foot, bottom.*
sum, esse, fui, futurus, *be.*

Collis: Nominative subject (A.G. 339).
erat: The main verb of the simple sentence (A.G. 278.1).
leniter: Adverb (A.G. 214.b and 320-21).
ab infimo: Ablative of *position* with the preposition **ab** (A.G. 429.b). **infimo**: Singular, neuter, ablative adjective used substantively (A.G. 288). The neuter singular of the adjective **infimus** means "the lowest part, base" (*OLD* infimus 1.c).
acclivis: Singular, masculine, nominative predicate adjective modifying **Collis** after **erat** (A.G. 283-84).

(19.1-2) Hunc ex omnibus fere partibus palus difficilis atque impedita cingebat, non (2) latior pedibus quinquaginta.

atque, *and.*

difficilis, -e, *difficult, impracticable, perilous.*
fere, *almost, nearly.*
impeditus, -a, -um, *hard to reach, inaccessible.*
non, *not.*
palus, -udis, f., *marsh, swamp, bog, morass.*
pes, pedis, m., *foot,* = .9708 of the English foot.

cingo, cingere, cinxi, cinctus, *surround, enclose, encircle.*
ex, *on.*
hic, haec, hoc, *this; he, she, it.*
latus, -a, -um, comp. -ior, *broad, wide.*
omnis, -e, *all.*
pars, partis, f., *side.*
quinquaginta, *fifty.*

Hunc: Singular, masculine, accusative demonstrative pronoun used substantively (A.G. 296.2). The antecedent is **collis** (A.G. 297.e). Accusative direct object of **cingebat** (A.G. 387).
ex omnibus fere partibus: Ablative of *position* with the preposition **ex** (A.G. 429.b). **fere:** Adverb (A.G. 320-21).
palus difficilis atque impedita ... (latior): Nominative subject (A.G. 339). **atque:** The conjunction connects the two adjectives modifying **palus** and means "and" (*OLD* **atque** 12). Two adjectives belonging to the same noun are regularly connected by a conjunction (A.G. 323.d).
cingebat: The main verb of the simple sentence (A.G. 278.1).
non: Adverb modifying **latior**; the negative precedes the word it especially effects (A.G. 217.e, 320-21, and 599.a).
latior pedibus quinquaginta: Ablative of comparison; the comparative adjective followed by the ablative signifies "than" (A.G. 406). **latior:** Nominative comparative adjective modifying **palus** (A.G. 124). **quinquaginta:** Indeclinable cardinal number used as an adjective modifying **pedibus** (A.G. 132-35).

(19.2-3) Hoc se colle interruptis pontibus Galli fiducia loci continebant, generatimque distributi in civitates omnia vada ac +saltus+ eius paludis obtinebant, sic animo parati ut, si eam paludem Romani perrumpere conarentur, haesitantis premerent ex loco supe(3)riore;

ac, *and.*
civitas, -tatis, f., *state, nation.*
conor, -ari, -atus, endeavor, *attempt, undertake, try.*
distribuo, -tribuere, -tribui, -tributus, *distribute, divide, assign.*
fiducia, -ae, f., *trust, reliance, confidence.*
generatim, *by peoples, by tribes, nation by nation.*
hic, haec, hoc, *this; he, she, it.*
interrupo, -rumpere, -rupi, -ruptus, *break down, destroy.*
locus, -i, m., *place, location, position.*
omnis, -e, *all.*
paro, -are, -avi, -atus, *prepare, make ready, resolve.*
pons, pontis, m., *bridge.*
-que, *and.*
saltus, -us, m., *narrow pass, ravine, thicket.*
sic, *so, in this way, thus, with this intent.*
superior, -or, -us, *higher, upper, superior.*
vadum, -i, n., *ford.*

animus, -i, m., *mind, temper, spirit, resolution.*
collis, -is, m., *hill, height, elevation.*
contineo, -tinere, -tinui, -tentus, *hold back, keep, retain, shut in.*
ex, *from.*
Galli, -orum, m., *the Gauls.*
haesito, -are, -avi, -atus, *stick fast, remain fixed.*
in, *in accordance with, according to.*
is, ea, id, *he, she, it; that, this.*
obtineo, -tinere, -tinui, -tentus, *hold fast, retain, keep, hold.*
palus, -udis, f., *marsh, swamp, bog, morass.*
perrumpo, -rumpere, -rupi, -ruptus, *break, burst, or make a way through.*
premo, -ere, pressi, pressus, *harass, oppress.*
Romani, -orum, m., pl., *the Romans.*
si, *if.*
sui, sibi, se, or sese, nom. wanting, *themselves.*
ut, *so that.*

Hoc ... colle: Ablative of *place where* without a preposition (429.2). **hoc:** Singular, masculine, ablative demonstrative pronoun used as an adjective modifying **colle** (A.G. 296.1 and a).
se: Plural, masculine, accusative direct reflexive pronoun (A.G. 300.1). The antecedent is **Galli**, the subject of **continebant** (A.G. 299). Accusative direct object of **continebant** (A.G. 387).
interruptis pontibus: Ablative absolute (A.G. 419-20). **interruptis:** The perfect tense of the participle represents the action as completed at the time indicated by the tense of the main verb (A.G. 489).
Galli: Nominative subject of **continebant** (A.G. 339). See Appendix A.
fiducia loci: Ablative of quality (descriptive ablative) with a genitive modifier (A.G. 415). **loci:** Objective genitive (A.G. 348).
continebant: The main verb of the coordinate clause **Hoc ... continebant** (A.G. 278.a).
generatimque: Adverb (A.G. 215.2 and 320-21). **-que:** The enclitic conjunction connects the two main verbs **continebant ... obtinebant** (A.G. 324.a).
distributi: Nominative, perfect, passive participle used as a predicate, where in English a phrase or a subordinate clause would be more normal (A.G. 496). The pronoun **ei**, with **Galli** as the antecedent, is understood. Nominative subject of **obtinebant** (A.G. 339).
in civitates: Prepositional phrase, **in** with the accusative expressing manner here means "in accordance with" (*OLD* **in** 18).
omnia vada ac +saltus+: Two accusative direct objects of **obtinebant** (A.G. 387). **ac:** The conjunction connects the two accusative

nouns **vada** ... **saltus** and means "and" (*OLD* **atque** 12). **saltus**: "Places in the bog grown over with bushes and underbrush, by which the Romans might attempt to cross." (Kelsey, 406)

eius paludis: Possessive genitive with both **vada** and **saltus** (A.G. 343). **eius**: Singular, feminine, genitive demonstrative pronoun used as an adjective modifying **paludis** (A.G. 296.1 and a).

obtinebant: The main verb of the coordinate clause **generatimque ... superiore** (A.G. 278.a).

sic animo parati: Compare with sic animo paratos at 19.5.

sic: Adverb (A.G. 217.c and 320-21).

animo: Ablative of *place where* without a preposition (A.G. 429.3).

parati: Nominative, perfect, passive participle used as a predicate, where in English a phrase or a subordinate clause would be more normal (A.G. 496). The pronoun **ei**, with **Galli** as the antecedent, is understood. Nominative subject of **obtinebant** (A.G. 339).

ut si ... conarentur ... premerent: A subordinate conditional statement (A.G. 512.c). The apodosis, as a purpose clause dependent on **parati**, takes the subjunctive and the protasis, as a clause subordinate to a subjunctive clause, also takes the subjunctive (attraction) (A.G. 512.c and 593).

ut ... premerent: The apodosis of the conditional statement (A.G. 512.c). The conjunction **ut** ("so that") with the subjunctive forms a substantive clause of purpose which is used as the object of **parati** denoting an action directed toward the future (A.G. 563).

premerent: The main verb of the subordinate clause (A.G. 278.b). Imperfect subjunctive; the tense of the subjunctive is in secondary sequence and follows the rules for the sequence of tense after **obtinebant** (A.G. 482-4). The pronoun **ipsi**, with **Galli** as the antecedent, is understood as the subject (A.G. 271.a).

si ... conarentur: The conjunction **si** ("if") with the subjunctive forms the protasis of the conditional statement (A.G. 512). A clause dependent on a subjunctive clause (**ut ... premerent**) takes the subjunctive when regarded as an integral part of that clause (attraction) (A.G. 593). **conarentur**: The main verb of the subordinate clause (A.G. 278.b). Imperfect subjunctive; the tense of the subjunctive is in secondary sequence and follows the rules for the sequence of tense after **obtinebant** (A.G. 482-4).

eam paludem: Accusative direct object of the infinitive **perrumpere** (A.G. 387 and 451.3). **eam**: Singular, feminine, accusative demonstrative pronoun used as an adjective modifying **paludem** (A.G. 296.1 and a).

Romani: Nominative subject (A.G. 339).

perrumpere: Complementary infinitive after **conarentur** (A.G. 456 and 563.e).

haesitantis: Plural, masculine, accusative present participle used substantively (A.G. 494.a). The pronoun **eos**, with **Romani** as the antecedent, is understood (A.G. 288.b). Accusative plural; **-is** for **-es** is the regular form of the present participle (A.G. 117-18). Accusative direct object of **premerent** (A.G. 387). An iterative form of **haereo** (A.G. 263.2).

ex loco superiore: Ablative of *place from which* with the preposition **ex** (A.G. 426.1). **superiore**: Defective comparative adjective (A.G. 130.b).

(19.3-4) **ut qui propinquitatem loci videret paratos prope aequo Marte ad dimicandum existimaret, qui iniquitatem condicionis perspiceret inani simulatione sese ostentare (4) cognosceret.**

ad, *for, in order to, for the purpose of, in.*
cognosco, -gnoscere, -gnovi, cognitus, *know, recognize.*
dimico, -are, -avi, -atus, *fight, contend, struggle.*
inanis, -e, *vain, useless.*
locus, -i, m., *place, location, position.*
ostento, -are, -avi, -atus, (with se), *show off.*

perspicio, -spicere, -spexi, -spectus, *perceive, observe, ascertain.*
propinquitas, -atis, f., *nearness, vicinity.*
simulatio, -onis, f., *pretence, shamming, deceit.*

ut, *so that.*

aequus, -a, -um, *equal.*
condicio, -onis, f., *position, situation.*
existimo, -are, -avi, -atus, *think, consider, judge.*
iniquitas, -atis, f., *unfavorableness, unfairness.*
Mars, Martis, m., *Mars*, (by metonymy), *battle, contest.*
paro, -are, -avi, -atus, *prepare, make ready, make ready for.*
prope, *near, nearly, almost.*
qui, quae, quod, *whoever, anyone who, if anyone.*
sui, sibi, se, or **sese**, nom. wanting, *they*, with or without *themselves.*
video, videre, visi, visus, *perceive, observe, see.*

ut qui ... videret ... existimaret (**ut**) **qui ... perspiceret ... cognosceret**: A double subordinate disguised conditional statement (A.G. 521).

ut qui ... videret ... existimaret: The first subordinate disguised conditional statement (A.G. 512.c, 519, and 521). The apodosis, as a result clause dependent on **obtinebant**, takes the subjunctive and the protasis, as a clause subordinate to a subjunctive clause, also takes the subjunctive (attraction) (A.G. 512.c, 519, 521, and 593).

ut ... existimaret: The apodosis of the conditional statement (A.G. 512.c). The conjunction **ut** ("so that") with the subjunctive forms a clause of result dependent on **obtinebant** (A.G. 537.1). **existimaret**: The main verb of the subordinate clause (A.G. 278.b). Imperfect subjunctive; the tense of the subjunctive is in secondary sequence and follows the rules for the sequence of tense after **obtinebant** (A.G. 482-4). The pronoun **is**, with **qui** as the antecedent, is understood as the subject (A.G. 271.a).

qui ... videret: The protasis of the conditional statement (A.G. 519). Relative clause; a clause dependent on a subjunctive clause (**ut ... existimaret**) takes the subjunctive when regarded as an integral part of that clause (attraction) (A.G. 303 and 593). **qui**: Singular, masculine, nominative relative pronoun with indefinite force used substantively (= **si quis**) (A.G. 148-49, esp. 149.b Note) (*OLD* **quil** 15.b). Nominative subject (A.G. 339). **videret**: The main verb of the subordinate clause (A.G. 278.b). Imperfect subjunctive; the tense of the subjunctive is in secondary sequence and follows the rules for the sequence of tense after **obtinebant** (A.G. 482-4).

propinquitatem: Accusative direct object of **videret** (A.G. 387).

loci: Possessive genitive with **propinquitatem** (A.G. 343).

(Romanos et Gallos) paratos (esse): Accusative/infinitive construction in indirect discourse after **existimaret** (A.G. 577 ff.). Supply **Romanos et Gallos** as the accusative subject. **paratos (esse)**: Supply **esse** to form the perfect, passive, infinitive (A.G. 184). The tense of the infinitive in indirect discourse is relative to that of the verb of saying (A.G. 584).

prope: Adverb (A.G. 320-21).

aequo Marte: Ablative of manner with a limiting adjective (A.G. 412). **Marte**: The noun means "battle, contest" by metonymy (A.G. 641). "'equal battle conditions' is *aequo Marte* - Mars, the god of war, is a common Latin metonym for battle. Caesar is careful here to explain why the Gauls only *appear* to be brave, and to counter their specious courage with the genuine enthusiasm of the Romans in a way which reflects well upon himself also." (Hammond, 238)

ad dimicandum: The preposition **ad** with the accusative gerund denotes purpose (A.G. 506). **dimicandum**: Singular, neuter, accusative gerund (A.G. 501-02).

(ut) qui ... perspiceret ... cognosceret: The second subordinate disguised conditional statement (A.G. 512.c, 519, and 521). The apodosis, as a result clause dependent on **obtinebant**, takes the subjunctive and the protasis, as a clause subordinate to a subjunctive clause, also takes the subjunctive (attraction) (A.G. 512.c, 519, 521, and 593).

(ut) ... cognosceret: The apodosis of the conditional statement (A.G. 512.c). The conjunction **ut** ("so that") with the subjunctive forms a clause of result dependent on **obtinebant** (A.G. 537.1). **cognosceret**: The main verb of the subordinate clause (A.G. 278.b). Imperfect subjunctive; the tense of the subjunctive is in secondary sequence and follows the rules for the sequence of tense after **obtinebant** (A.G. 482-4). The pronoun **is**, with **qui** as the antecedent, is understood as the subject (A.G. 271.a).

qui ... perspiceret: The protasis of the conditional statement (A.G. 519). Relative clause; a clause dependent on a subjunctive clause ((**ut**) ... **cognosceret**) takes the subjunctive when regarded as an integral part of that clause (attraction) (A.G. 303 and 593). **qui**: Singular, masculine, nominative relative pronoun with indefinite force used substantively (= **si quis**) (A.G. 148-49, esp. 149.b Note) (*OLD* **qui1** 15.b). Nominative subject (A.G. 339). **perspiceret**: The main verb of the subordinate clause (A.G. 278.b). Imperfect subjunctive; the tense of the subjunctive is in secondary sequence and follows the rules for the sequence of tense after **obtinebant** (A.G. 482-4).

iniquitatem: Accusative direct object of **perspiceret** (A.G. 387).

condicionis: Possessive genitive with **iniquitatem** (A.G. 343).

inani simulatione: Ablative of manner with a limiting adjective (A.G. 412). "'with mere parade' spoken contemptuously. Caesar intimates, rather ungraciously, that the Gauls knew that they were safe from all attack where they were, and that they were simply showing themselves off." (Kelsey, 406)

sese: Plural, masculine, accusative direct reflexive pronoun (A.G. 300.1). The antecedent is **Gallos**, the supplied subject of **ostentare** (A.G. 299). Reduplicated form of **se** (A.G. 144.b Note 1).

(Gallos) ostentare: Accusative/infinitive construction in indirect discourse after **cognosceret** (A.G. 577 ff.). Supply the noun **Gallos** as the accusative subject. **ostentare**: Present infinitive; the tense of the infinitive in indirect discourse is relative to that of the verb of saying (A.G. 584).

(19.4-6) Indignantis milites Caesar, quod conspectum suum hostes perferre possent tantulo spatio interiecto, et signum proeli exposcentis edocet quanto detrimento et quot virorum fortium morte necesse sit constare victoriam;

Caesar, -aris, m., *Caesar.*	**conspectus, -us**, m., *sight, view, presence.*
consto, -stare, -stiti, -staturus, *cost, stand at, be dependent* or *determined.*	**detrimentum, -i**, n., *loss, damage, injury, repulse, defeat.*
edoceo, -docere, -docui, -doctus, *instruct, inform, tell.*	**et**, *and.*
exposco, -poscere, -poposci, -----, *earnestly request, demand.*	**fortis, -e**, *strong, brave, courageous, valiant.*
hostis, -is, m., *enemy, foe*; pl., *the enemy.*	**indignor, -ari, -atus**, *be indignant, be offended.*
intericio, -icere, -ieci, -iectus, (pass), *intervening.*	**miles, -itis**, m., *soldier, foot-solider.*
mors, mortis, f., *death.*	**necesse**, n., *necessary, unavoidable, inevitable.*
perfero, -ferre, -tuli, -latus, *endure.*	**possum, posse, potui, -----**, *be able.*
proelium, -i, n., *battle, combat, engagement.*	**quantus, -a, -um**, *how great, how much, how large.*
quod, *because, since, for, as.*	**quot**, *how many.*
signum, -i, n., *signal.*	**spatium, -i**, n., *space, distance.*
sum, esse, fui, futurus, *be.*	**suus, -a, -um**, *their.*
tantulus, -a, -um, *so very small, so slight, so trivial.*	**victoria, -ae**, f., *victory.*
vir, viri, m., *man.*	

Indignantis milites ... exposcentis: Accusative direct object of **edocet** (A.G. 387). **Indignantis ... exposcentis**: Two present participles used as adjectives modifying **milites** (A.G. 494). Accusative plural; **-is** for **-es** is the regular form of the present participle (A.G. 117-18).

Caesar: Nominative subject of **edocet** (A.G. 339). See Appendix A.

quod ... possent: Causal clause dependent on **Indignantis**, the conjunction **quod** ("because" (as they said)) takes the subjunctive when the reason is given on the authority of another (informal indirect discourse) (A.G. 540.2 and 592). **possent**: The main verb of the subordinate clause (A.G. 278.b). Imperfect subjunctive; the tense of the subjunctive is in secondary sequence after the historical present **edocet** (A.G. 482-85, esp. 485.e).

conspectum suum: Accusative direct object of the infinitive **perferre** (A.G. 387 and 451.3). **suum**: Singular, masculine, accusative possessive pronoun used as an adjective modifying **conspectum** (A.G. 302).

hostes: Nominative subject (A.G. 339).

perferre: Complementary infinitive after **possent** (A.G. 456).

tantulo spatio interiecto: Ablative absolute (A.G. 419-20). **tantulo**: The adjective is formed from the adjective **tantus** with the diminutive ending **-ulus** (A.G. 243). **interiecto**: The perfect tense of the participle represents the action as completed at the time indicated by the tense of the main verb (A.G. 489).

et: The conjunction connects the two present participles **Indignantis ... exposcentis** (A.G. 324.a).

signum: Accusative direct object of the participle **exposcentis** (A.G. 387 and 488).

proeli: Objective genitive with **signum** (A.G. 348). The singular genitive of nouns in **-ium** ended, until the Augustan Age, in a single **-i** (A.G. 49.b).

edocet: The main verb of the main clause (A.G. 278.b). The historical present, giving vividness to the narrative, is present in Chapter 19 (A.G. 469). This usage, common in all languages, comes from imagining past events as going on before our eyes (*repraesentatio*) (A.G. 469 Note).

quanto ... quot ... necesse sit: A double indirect question with the subjunctive; the phrase is the object of **edocet** (A.G. 573-75).

quanto: See below. **quot**: See below. **necesse sit**: Impersonal verb, the following infinitive phrase forms the subject (A.G. 208.c).

necesse: Singular, neuter, nominative adjective used in the predicate position after **sit** as an indeclinable noun (A.G. 103.a Note 1 and 283-84). **sit**: The main verb of the subordinate clause (A.G. 278.b). Present subjunctive; the tense of the subjunctive is normally in secondary sequence after the historical present **edocet** (A.G. 575). Here it is in primary sequence through *repraesentatio* (A.G. 485.e and 585.b Note).

quanto detrimento: Ablative of price after **constare** (A.G. 416). **quanto**: Interrogative adjective modifying **detrimento** (*OLD* **quantus** 1).

et: The conjunction connects the two interrogatives **quanto ... quot** (A.G. 324.a).

quot ... morte: Ablative of price after **constare** (A.G. 416). **quot**: Indeclinable interrogative adjective (*OLD* **quot**).

virorum fortium: Possessive genitive with **morte** (A.G. 343).

constare victoriam: The infinitive phrase functions as the subject of the impersonal verb **necesse sit** (A.G. 454). **victoriam**: Accusative subject of the infinitive (A.G. 397.e).

(19.5-6) **(5) quos cum sic animo paratos videat ut nullum pro sua laude periculum recusent, summae se iniquitatis condemnari de(6)bere, nisi eorum vitam sua salute habeat cariorem.**

animus, -i, m., *mind, temper, resolution, spirit.*
condemno, -are, -avi, -atus, *condemn, find guilty of.*
cum, *since, seeing that.*
habeo, habere, habui, habitus, *consider, reckon, hold.*

is, ea, id, *he, she, it; that, this.*
nisi, *if not, unless, except.*
paro, -are, -avi, -atus, *prepare, make ready.*
pro, *on behalf of.*
recuso, -are, -avi, -atus, *refuse, make refusal, decline.*
sic, *so, in this way, thus, with this intent.*

summus, -a, -um, *utmost, greatest.*
ut, *so that.*
vita, -ae, f., *life.*

carus, -a, -um, comp. **-ior**, *dear, precious, valued.*
condicio, -onis, f., *condition, position, situation.*
debeo, debere, debui, debitus, *ought, must, should.*
iniquitas, -atis, f., *injustice, unfairness, unreasonableness.*
laus, laudis, f., *praise, fame, glory, commendation.*
nullus, -a, -um, *no, not any.*
periculum, -i, n., *risk, danger, hazard.*
qui, quae, quod, *who, which, what.*
salus, -utis, f., *welfare, safety.*
sui, sibi, se, or **sese**, nom. wanting, *he, with or without himself.*
suus, -a, -um, *his, with or without own.*
video, videre, visi, visus, *perceive, observe, see.*

quos ... paratos (esse): Accusative/infinitive construction in indirect discourse after **videat** (A.G. 577 ff). **quos**: Plural, masculine, accusative relative pronoun used substantively (A.G. 305). The antecedent is **milites** (A.G. 307). The relative does not introduce a relative clause but is a connecting relative; at the beginning of a clause the pronoun is often best rendered by a personal or demonstrative pronoun, with or without *and* (A.G. 308.f). **paratos (esse)**: Supply **esse** to form the perfect, passive infinitive (A.G. 184). The tense of the infinitive in indirect discourse is relative to that of the verb of saying (A.G. 584).

cum ... videat: Causal clause; the relative adverb **cum** ("since") with the subjunctive forms a clause expressing cause (A.G. 549).

videat: The main verb of the subordinate clause (A.G. 278.b). Present subjunctive; the tense of the subjunctive is normally in secondary sequence after the historical present **edocet** (A.G. 482-85). Here it is in primary sequence through *repraesentatio* (A.G. 485.e and 585.b Note). The pronoun **is**, with **Caesar** as the antecedent, is understood as the subject (A.G. 271.a).

sic animo paratos: Compare **sic animo parati** at 19.2.

sic: Adverb (A.G. 217.c and 320-21).

animo: Ablative of *place where* without a preposition (A.G. 429.3).

ut ... recusent: The conjunction **ut** ("so that") with the subjunctive forms a substantive clause of purpose which is used as the object of **paratos (esse)** denoting an action directed toward the future (A.G. 563). **recusent**: The main verb of the subordinate clause (A.G. 278.b). Present subjunctive; the tense of the subjunctive is normally in secondary sequence after the historical present **edocet** (A.G. 482-85). Here it is in primary sequence through *repraesentatio* (A.G. 485.e and 585.b Note). The pronoun **ei**, with **quos** (**milites**) as the antecedent, is understood as the subject (A.G. 271.a).

nullum ... periculum: Accusative direct object of **recusent** (A.G. 387).

pro sua laude: Prepositional phrase, **pro** with the ablative here means "on behalf of" (*OLD* **pro1** 3). **sua**: Singular, feminine, ablative reflexive pronoun used as an adjective modifying **laude** (A.G. 302).

summae ... iniquitatis: Genitive of charge after **condemnari**, an infinitive of condemning (A.G. 352). **summae**: Defective superlative adjective (A.G. 130.b).

se ... debere ... nisi ... habeat: Conditional statement in indirect discourse after **edocet** (A.G. 589). The protasis, as a dependent clause, is in the subjunctive and the apodosis, as the principal clause, is in the infinitive (A.G. 589).

se ... debere: The apodosis of the conditional statement (A.G. 589.2). Accusative/infinitive construction in indirect discourse after **edocet** (A.G. 577 ff.). **se**: Singular, masculine, accusative direct reflexive pronoun (A.G. 300.1). The antecedent is **Caesar**, the subject of **edocet** (A.G. 299). **debere**: Present infinitive; the tense of the infinitive in indirect discourse is relative to that of the verb of saying (A.G. 584).

condemnari: Complementary infinitive after **debere** (A.G. 456).

nisi ... habeat: The conjunction **nisi** ("unless") with the subjunctive forms the protasis of a conditional statement in indirect discourse (A.G. 589.1). **nisi**: With **nisi** the protasis is stated as universally true except in the single case supposed, in which case it is (impliedly) not true (A.G. 512.a Note and 525.a.1). **habeat**: The main verb of the subordinate clause (A.G. 278.b). Present subjunctive; the tense of the subjunctive is normally in secondary sequence after the historical present **edocet** (A.G. 482-85). Here it is in primary sequence through *repraesentatio* (A.G. 485.e and 585.b Note). The pronoun **is**, with **Caesar** as the antecedent, is understood as the subject (A.G. 271.a).

eorum: Plural, masculine, genitive demonstrative pronoun used substantively (A.G. 296.2). The antecedent is **milites** (A.G. 297.e). Possessive genitive with **vitam** (A.G. 343 Note).

vitam ... cariorem: Accusative direct object of **habeat** (A.G. 387). **cariorem**: Comparative adjective (AG. 124).

(cariorem) sua salute: Ablative of comparison; the comparative degree is followed by the ablative signifying "than" (A.G. 406). **sua**: Singular, feminine, ablative reflexive pronoun used as an adjective modifying **salute** (A.G. 302).

(19.6) Sic milites consolatus eodem die reducit in castra reliquaque quae ad oppugnationem pertinebant oppidi administrare instituit.

ad, *to*.

castra, -orum, n., pl., *camp, encampment.*

conspectus, -us, m., *sight, view, presence.*
idem, eadem, idem, *the same.*
instituo, -stituere, -stitui, -stitutus, *undertake, commence, begin.*
oppidum, -i, n., *fortified town, city.*
pertineo, -tinere, -tinui, -----, *pertain to, concern, belong to, have to do with.*
qui, quae, quod, *who, which, what.*

reliqua, -orum, n., pl., *the remaining things.*

administro, -are, -avi, -atus, *arrange for, get ready.*
consolor, -ari, -atus, *comfort, cheer, console, encourage.*
dies, -ei, m. and f., *day.*
in, *into.*
miles, -itis, m., *soldier, foot-solider.*
oppugnatio, -onis, f., *assault, attack, sieging.*
-que, *and.*
reduco, -ducere, -duxi, -ductus, *lead back, conduct back.*
sic, *so, in this way, thus.*

Sic: Adverb (A.G. 217.c and 320-21).

milites: Accusative direct object of the participle **consolatus** (A.G. 387 and 488).

consolatus: Nominative, perfect, deponent participle used as a predicate, where in English a phrase or a subordinate clause would be more normal (A.G. 496). The pronoun **is**, with **Caesar** as the antecedent, is understood. Nominative subject (A.G. 339).

eodem die: Ablative of *time when* (A.G. 423.1). **eodem**: Singular, masculine, ablative demonstrative pronoun used as an adjective modifying **die** (A.G. 296.1 and a). **die**: The noun **dies** is normally masculine gender (A.G. 97.a).

reducit: The main verb of the coordinate clause **Sic ... castra** (A.G. 278.a). The pronoun **eos**, with **milites** as the antecedent, is understood as the accusative direct object (A.G. 387).

in castra: Accusative of *place to which* with the preposition **in** (A.G. 426.2).

reliquaque: Plural, neuter, accusative adjective used substantively (A.G. 288). Accusative direct object of the infinitive **administrare** (A.G. 387 and 451.3). **-que**: The enclitic conjunction connects the two main verbs **reducit ... instituit** (A.G. 324.a).

quae ... oppidi: Relative clause (A.G. 303). **quae**: Plural, neuter, nominative relative pronoun used substantively (A.G. 305). The antecedent is **reliqua** (A.G. 307). Nominative subject (A.G. 339). **oppidi**: See below.

ad oppugnationem ... oppidi: Prepositional phrase, **ad** with the accusative here means "to" (*OLD* ad 24.c). **oppidi**: Objective genitive with **oppugnationem** (A.G. 348).

pertinebant: The main verb of the subordinate clause (A.G. 278.b).

administrare: Complementary infinitive after **instituit** (A.G. 456).

instituit: The main verb of the coordinate clause **reliquaque ... instituit** (A.G. 278.a). The pronoun **is**, with **consolatus (Caesar)** as the antecedent, is understood as the subject (A.G. 271.a).

2.C CHAPTERS 20-21: VERCINGETORIX IS CHARGED WITH TREASON AND HIS SUCCESSFUL SELF-DEFENSE; CONTINGENTS ARE SELECTED FOR THE DEFENSE OF AVARICUM

(20.1-2) Vercingetorix, cum ad suos redisset, proditionis insimulatus, quod castra propius Romanos movisset, quod cum omni equitatu discessisset, quod sine imperio tantas copias reliquisset, quod eius discessu Romani tanta opportunitate (2) et celeritate venissent;

ad, *to*.
celeritas, -tatis, f., *speed, quickness, swiftness, rapidity, despatch.*

castra, -orum, n., pl., *camp, encampment.*
copiae, -arum, f., pl., *forces, troops.*

cum, *after, when; with.*

discessus, -us, m., *departure, going away.*
et, *and.*
insimulo, -are, -avi, -atus, *charge with, accuse of.*
moveo, movere, movi, motus, *move.*
opportunitas, -atis, f., *advantage.*
prope, comp. **-ius,** *near.*
redeo, -ire, -ii, -itus, *go back, return.*
Romani, -orum, m., pl., *the Romans.*
sui, -orum, m., pl., *his men,* with or without *own.*
venio, venire, veni, ventus, *come.*

discedo, -cedere, -cessi, -cessurus, *go away, depart, leave.*
equitatus, -us, m., *cavalry.*
imperium, -i, n., *command, control, military authority.*
is, ea, id, *he, she, it; that, this.*
omnis, -e, *all.*
proditio, -onis, f., *a betraying, treachery.*
quod, *because, since, for, as.*
relinquo, -linquere, -liqui, -lictus, *leave, leave behind.*
sine, *without.*
tantus, -a, -um, *so great, so large, such.*
Vercingetorix, -igis, m., *Vercingetorix.*

Vercingetorix ... insimulatus: Nominative subject of **respondit** at 20.3 (A.G. 339). **Vercingetorix**: See Appendix A. **insimulatus**: Nominative, perfect, passive, participle used as a predicate, where in English a phrase or a subordinate clause would be more normal (A.G. 496). The charges arise from the events of Chapters 18-19

cum ... redisset: Temporal clause; the relative adverb **cum** ("after, when") with the pluperfect subjunctive describes the circumstances that preceded the action of the main verb (A.G. 546). **redisset**: The main verb of the subordinate clause (A.G. 278.b). Contracted form of **redivisset** (A.G. 181.b). The pronoun **is**, with **Vercingetorix** as the antecedent, is understood as the subject (A.G. 271.a).

ad suos: Prepositional phrase, **ad** with the accusative here means "to" (*OLD* **ad** 1). **suos**: Plural, masculine, accusative possessive pronoun used substantively to denote a special class (A.G. 302.d).

proditionis: Genitive of charge after **insimulat**, a participle of accusing (A.G. 352).

quod ... quod ... quod ... quod: The repetition of words at the beginning of successive clauses is anaphora (A.G. 641).

quod ... movisset: Causal clause; the conjunction **quod** ("because" (as they said)) takes the subjunctive when the reason is given on the authority of another (informal indirect discourse) (A.G. 540.2 and 592). **movisset**: The main verb of the subordinate clause (A.G. 278.b). Pluperfect subjunctive; the tense of the subjunctive is in secondary sequence and follows the rules for the sequence of tense after **respondit** (A.G. 482-85). The pronoun **is**, with **Vercingetorix** as the antecedent, is understood as the subject (A.G. 271.a).

castra: Accusative direct object of **movisset** (A.G.. 387).

propius Romanos: The comparative adverb **propius** is here used as a preposition with the accusative and means "nearer" (A.G. 432.a).

quod ... discessisset: Causal clause; the conjunction **quod** ("because" (as they said)) takes the subjunctive when the reason is given on the authority of another (informal indirect discourse) (A.G. 540.2 and 592). **discessisset**: The main verb of the subordinate clause (A.G. 278.b). Pluperfect subjunctive; the tense of the subjunctive is in secondary sequence and follows the rules for the sequence of tense after **respondit** (A.G. 482-85). The pronoun **is**, with **Vercingetorix** as the antecedent, is understood as the subject (A.G. 271.a).

cum omni equitatu: Ablative of accompaniment with the preposition **cum** (A.G. 413).

quod ... reliquisset: Causal clause; the conjunction **quod** ("because" (as they said)) takes the subjunctive when the reason is given on the authority of another (informal indirect discourse) (A.G. 540.2 and 592). **reliquisset**: The main verb of the subordinate clause (A.G. 278.b). Pluperfect subjunctive; the tense of the subjunctive is in secondary sequence and follows the rules for the sequence of tense after **respondit** (A.G. 482-85). The pronoun **is**, with **Vercingetorix** as the antecedent, is understood as the subject (A.G. 271.a).

sine imperio: Prepositional phrase, **sine** with the ablative here means "without the accompaniment of" (*OLD* **sine** 1). "i.e. *sine imperatore*; Vercingetorix had left his army temporarily without placing anyone in command." (Kelsey, 406)

tantas copias: Accusative direct object of **reliquisset** (A.G. 387).

quod ... venissent: Causal clause; the conjunction **quod** ("because" (as they said)) takes the subjunctive when the reason is given on the authority of another (informal indirect discourse) (A.G. 540.2 and 592). **venissent**: The main verb of the subordinate clause (A.G. 278.b). Pluperfect subjunctive; the tense of the subjunctive is in secondary sequence and follows the rules for the sequence of tense after **respondit** (A.G. 482-85). The pronoun **is**, with **Vercingetorix** as the antecedent, is understood as the subject (A.G. 271.a).

Romani: Nominative subject (A.G. 339).

eius: Singular, masculine, genitive demonstrative pronoun used substantively (A.G. 296.2). The antecedent is **Vercingetorix** (A.G. 297.e). Possessive genitive with **discessu** (A.G. 343). Here the indirect reflexive possessive adjective **suo** is not used as the subordinate clause does not express the words or thoughts of the main subject (A.G. 300.a).

discessu: Ablative of *time when* (A.G. 423.1).

tanta opportunitate et celeritate: Two ablatives of manner with a limiting adjective (A.G. 412). **tanta**: The adjective should be construed with both **opportunitate** and **celeritate** but agrees in number with only the nearest noun (A.G. 286.a). **et**: The conjunction connects the two ablative nouns (A.G. 324.a).

(20.2-3) non haec omnia fortuito aut sine consilio accidere potuisse; regnum illum Galliae malle (3) Caesaris concessu quam ipsorum habere beneficio:

accido, -cidere, -cidi, -----, *happen, occur, come to pass.*
beneficium, -i, n., *kindness, favor.*
concessus, -us, m., *permission, leave.*
fortuito, *by chance.*
habeo, habere, habui, habitus, *have, hold.*
ille, illae, illud, *that; he, she, it.*

aut, *or.*
Caesar, -aris, m., *Caesar.*
consilium, -i, n., *consultation, plan, design.*
Gallia, -ae, f., *Gaul.*
hic, haec, hoc, *this; he, she, it.*
ipse, -a, -um, *he, they,* with or without *himself,*

malo, malle, malui, -----, *prefer, choose rather, had rather.*
omnis, -e, *all.*
quam, (*rather*) *than.*
sine, *without.*

themselves.
non, *not.*
possum, posse, potui, -----, *be able.*
regnum, -i, n., *kingship, sovereignty, absolute authority.*

non: Adverb; when **non** is especially emphatic it begins the clause (A.G. 217.e, 320-21, and 599.a).

haec omnia ... potuisse: Accusative/infinitive construction in indirect discourse (A.G. 577 ff.). The verb of saying is not expressed, but implied in the general drift of the sentence (A.G. 580.a). **haec**: Plural, neuter, accusative demonstrative pronoun used substantively meaning "these things" (A.G. 296.2). The antecedent is the four previous charges (A.G. 297.e). **potuisse**: Perfect infinitive; the tense of the infinitive in indirect discourse is relative to that of the verb of saying (A.G. 584).

fortuito: Adverb (A.G. 320-21).

aut: The conjunction connects the adverb and prepositional phrase (A.G. 324.e). Normally, the conjunction excludes the alternative but this distinction is not always observed (A.G. 324.e).

sine consilio: Prepositional phrase, **sine** with the ablative here means "with" (*OLD* **sine** 1).

accidere: Complementary infinitive after **potuisse** (A.G. 456).

regnum ... beneficio: This clause can be written in full (approximating English word order) as: **illum malle habere regnum Galliae concessu Caesaris quam habere regnum Galliae beneficio ipsorum.**

regnum: Accusative direct object of the infinitive **habere** (A.G. 387 and 451.3).

illum ... malle: Accusative/infinitive construction in indirect discourse (A.G. 577 ff.). The verb of saying is not expressed, but implied in the general drift of the sentence (A.G. 580.a). **illum**: Singular, masculine, accusative demonstrative pronoun used substantively (A.G. 296.2). The antecedent is **Vercingetorix** (A.G. 297.e). **malle**: Present infinitive; the tense of the infinitive in indirect discourse is relative to that of the verb of saying (A.G. 584).

Galliae: Objective genitive with **regnum** (A.G. 348). See Appendix A.

Caesaris: Possessive genitive with **concessu** (A.G. 343). See Appendix A.

concessu: Ablative of means (A.G. 409).

quam: A relative adverb after **malle** meaning "(rather) than" comparing **concessu** and **beneficio** (*OLD* **quam** 9.b). The two things being compared are put in the same case (A.G. 407).

ipsorum: Plural, masculine, genitive demonstrative pronoun used substantively (A.G. 296.2). The antecedent is **suos** (the Gauls who are charging Vercingetorix) (A.G. 297.e). Possessive genitive with **beneficio** (A.G. 343 Note). The demonstrative pronoun (referring to the subject of the unexpressed verb of saying, i.e. the Gauls) is here used instead of the indirect reflexive adjective **suo** (modifying **beneficio**) because the reference could be confused with the subject of the main clause (**Vercingetorix**) (A.G. 300.b).

habere: Complementary infinitive after **malle** (A.G. 456).

beneficio: Ablative of means (A.G. 409).

(20.3) **tali modo accusatus ad haec respondit:**

accuso, -are, -avi, -atus, *reproach, accuse.*
hic, haec, hoc, *this; he, she, it.*
respondeo, -spondere, -spondi, -sponsus, *answer, reply.*

ad, *in reply to.*
modus, -i, m., *manner, fashion, style.*
talis, -e, *such.*

tali modo: Ablative of manner with a limiting adjective (A.G. 412.b).

accusatus: Nominative, perfect, passive, participle used as a predicate, where in English a phrase or a subordinate clause would be more normal (A.G. 496). Carry down **Vercingetorix ... insimulatus** from 20.1. Nominative subject (A.G. 339).

ad haec: Prepositional phrase, **ad** with the accusative here means "in reply to" (*OLD* **ad** 29). **haec**: Plural, neuter, accusative demonstrative pronoun used substantively meaning "these things" (A.G. 296.2). The antecedent is the charges outlined above (A.G. 297.e).

respondit: The main verb of the main clause (A.G. 278.b). The verb introduces indirect discourse through **videantur** at 20.8.

quod ... milites: This speech (20.3-9), a mixture of both indirect and direct discourse, is classified by Murphy as forensic (C. Murphy, 122 and Note 3).

(20.3-4) **quod castra movisset, factum inopia pabuli, etiam ipsis hortantibus; quod propius Romanos accessisset, persuasum loci opportunitate qui +se (4) ipsum+ munitione defenderet;**

accedo, -cedere, -cessi, -cessurus, *come to, draw near, approach.*
defendo, -fendere, -fensi, -fensus, *defend, guard, protect.*
facio, facere, feci, factus, *bring about, make, do.*

inopia, -ae, f., *want, lack, need, scarcity.*

locus, -i, m., *place, location, position.*
munitio, -onis, f., *fortification, intrenchment, defenses.*
pabulum, -i, n., *fodder.*

castra, -orum, n., pl., *camp, encampment.*
etiam, *even.*
hortor, -ari, -atus, *urge, encourage, exhort, incite, press.*
ipse, -a, -um, *he, they,* with or without *himself, themselves; alone, just.*
moveo, movere, movi, motus, *move.*
opportunitas, -atis, f., *favorable situation, advantage.*
persuadeo, -suadere, -suasi, -suasus, *convince,*

prope, comp. **-ius**, *near*.
quod, *as to*, or *with regard to, the fact that*.
sui, sibi, se, or **sese**, nom. wanting, *himself, itself*.

persuade, prevail upon.
qui, quae, quod, *who, which, what*.
Romani, -orum, m., pl., *the Romans*.

quod ... movisset: The conjunction **quod** ("as to, or with regard to, the fact that") introduces a subordinate clause which is grammatically unrelated to the main sentence (A.G. 572) (*OLD* **quod** 6). This construction would normally take the indicative when the statement is regarded as fact (A.G. 572). Here the subordinate clause takes the subjunctive as it expresses the thought of some other person than the writer or speaker (informal indirect discourse ("as they said")) (A.G. 592). **movisset**: The main verb of the subordinate clause (A.G. 278.b). Pluperfect subjunctive; the tense of the subjunctive is in secondary sequence and follows the rules for the sequence of tense after **respondit** (A.G. 482-85). The pronoun **is**, with **Vercingetorix** as the antecedent, is understood as the subject (A.G. 271.a).
castra: Accusative direct object of **movisset** (A.G. 387).
(id) factum (esse): Accusative/infinitive construction in indirect discourse after **respondit** (A.G. 577 ff.). Supply the pronoun **id** as the accusative subject (A.G. 318.c). **factum (esse)**: Supply **esse** to form the perfect, passive infinitive (A.G. 188). Impersonal use of the passive verb (A.G. 208.d). The tense of the infinitive in indirect discourse is relative to that of the verb of saying (A.G. 584).
inopia: Ablative of cause without a preposition (A.G. 404).
pabuli: Objective genitive with **inopia** (A.G. 348).
etiam: Adverb (A.G. 320-21 and 322.a). The adverb normally proceeds the emphatic word (A.G. 322.a).
ipsis hortantibus: Ablative of cause without a preposition (A.G. 404). **ipsis**: Plural, masculine, ablative demonstrative pronoun used substantively (A.G. 296.2). The antecedent is **ipsorum** (A.G. 298.1). The pronoun is here emphatic (A.G. 298.d.1). **hortantibus**: Present participle used as an adjective modifying **ipsis** (A.G. 494).
quod ... accessisset: The conjunction **quod** ("as to , or with regard to, the fact that") introduces a subordinate clause which is grammatically unrelated to the main sentence (A.G. 572) (*OLD* **quod** 6). This construction would normally take the indicative when the statement is regarded as fact (A.G. 572). Here the subordinate clause takes the subjunctive as it expresses the thought of some other person than the writer or speaker (informal indirect discourse) (A.G. 592). **accessisset**: The main verb of the subordinate clause (A.G. 278.b). Pluperfect subjunctive; the tense of the subjunctive is in secondary sequence and follows the rules for the sequence of tense after **respondit** (A.G. 482-85). The pronoun **is**, with **Vercingetorix** as the antecedent, is understood as the subject (A.G. 271.a).
propius Romanos: The comparative adverb **propius** is here used as a preposition with the accusative and means "nearer" (A.G. 432.a).
(id ei) persuasum (esse): Accusative/infinitive construction in indirect discourse after **respondit** (A.G. 577 ff.). Supply the pronoun **id** as the accusative subject (A.G. 318.c). Supply the pronoun **ei**, with **Vercingetorix** as the antecedent, as the dative indirect object (A.G. 367). **persuasum (esse)**: Supply **esse** to form the perfect, passive infinitive (A.G. 185). Impersonal use of the intransitive passive infinitive (A.G. 208.d). The tense of the infinitive in indirect discourse is relative to that of the verb of saying (A.G. 584).
loci: Possessive genitive with **opportunitate** (A.G. 343).
opportunitate: Ablative of cause without a preposition (A.G. 404).
qui ... defenderet: Relative clause; a subordinate clause in indirect discourse takes the subjunctive (A.G. 303 and 580). **qui**: Singular, masculine, nominative relative pronoun used substantively (A.G. 305). The antecedent is **loci** (A.G. 307). Nominative subject (A.G. 339). **defenderet**: The main verb of the subordinate clause (A.G. 278.b). Imperfect subjunctive; the tense of the subjunctive is in secondary sequence and follows the rules for the sequence of tense after **respondit** (A.G. 482-85).
+se ipsum+: Accusative direct object of **defenderet** (A.G. 387). "Bentley suggests *ipse sine munitione*, which gives the sense implied." (Edwards, 408) **se**: Singular, masculine, accusative direct reflexive pronoun (A.G. 300.1). The antecedent is **qui**, the subject of **defenderet** (A.G. 299). **ipsum**: Singular, masculine, accusative demonstrative pronoun used as an adjective modifying **se** meaning "alone, just" (A.G. 296.1 and a and 298.c Note 1).
munitione: Ablative of means (A.G. 409).

(20.4-5) equitum vero operam neque in loco palustri desiderari debuisse et illic fuisse utilem (5) quo sint profecti.

debeo, debere, debui, debitus, *ought, must, should*.

eques, -itis, m., *rider, horseman, cavalryman, trooper*.
illic, *there, in that place*.
locus, -i, m., *place, location, position*.
opera, -ae, f., *service, aid, assistance*.
proficiscor, -ficisci, -fectus, *set out, depart, proceed*.
sum, esse, fui, futurus, *be*.
vero, *in truth, indeed, in fact, truly, certainly*.

desidero, -are, -avi, -atus, *wish for, want, long for, miss*.
et, *and*.
in, *in, at*.
neque, *nor*.
paluster, -tris, -tre, *marshy, swampy*.
quo, *in the place to which, where*.
utilis, -e, *useful, serviceable*.

equitum: Possessive genitive with **operam** (A.G. 346.a.1).
vero ... neque: The combination of adverbs means "nor in truth, nor indeed" (*OLD* **neque** 9.b). **vero**: The adverb is postpositive (A.G. 599.b).
operam ... debuisse: Accusative/infinitive construction in indirect discourse after **respondit** (A.G. 577 ff.). **debuisse**: Perfect infinitive; the tense of the infinitive in indirect discourse is relative to that of the verb of saying (A.G. 584).
in loco palustri: Ablative of *place where* with the preposition **in** (locative ablative) (A.G. 426.3).

desiderari: Complementary infinitive after **debuisse** (A.G. 456).
et: The conjunction connects the two infinitive clauses **debuisse ... fuisse** (A.G. 324.a).
illic: Adverb (A.G. 217.a and 320-21).
(equitem) fuisse: Accusative/infinitive construction in indirect discourse after **respondit** (A.G. 577 ff.). The noun **equitem**, used as a collective singular meaning "cavalry", is understood as the subject (*OLD* **eques** 2.b).
utilem: Singular, masculine, accusative predicate adjective modifying the supplied **equitem** after **fuisse** (A.G. 283-84).
quo sint profecti: Relative clause; a subordinate clause in indirect discourse takes the subjunctive (A.G. 279.a and 580). **quo**: Relative adverb correlative to **illic** meaning "in the place to which" (*OLD* **quo1** 3.b). **sint profecti**: The main verb of the subordinate clause (A.G. 278.b). Perfect subjunctive; the tense of the subjunctive would normally be secondary sequence after the perfect verb **respondit** (A.G. 482-4). Here, it is the primary sequence through *repraesentatio* (A.G. 585.b Note). The pronoun **ei**, with **equitum** as the antecedent, is understood as the subject (A.G. 271.a).

(20.5) **Summam imperi se consulto nulli discedentem tradidisse, ne is multitudinis studio ad dimicandum impelleretur; cui rei propter animi mollitiem studere omnis videret, quod diutius laborem ferre non possent.**

ad, *for, in order to, for the purpose of.*
consulto, *on purpose, designedly, purposely.*
discedo, -cedere, -cessi, -cessurus, *go away, depart, leave.*
fero, ferre, tuli, latus, *bear, endure, suffer.*

imperium, -i, n., *command, order, military authority.*
labor, -oris, m., *toil, exertion, labor.*
mollities, -ei, f., *weakness, irresolution.*
non, *not.*
omnes, -ium, m., pl., *all men, all.*
propter, *on account of, in consequence of.*
quod, *because, since, for, as.*
studeo, -ere, -ui, -----, *be eager for, eagerly desire.*
sui, sibi, se, or **sese**, nom. wanting, *he*, with or without *himself.*

trado, -dere, -didi, -ditus, *hand over, give up, deliver, surrender.*

animus, -i, m., *courage, spirit, temper, resolution.*
dimico, -are, -avi, -atus, *fight, contend, struggle.*
diu, comp. **diutius**, *long, for a long time.*
impello, -pellere, -puli, -pulsus, *urge, drive on, incite, impel.*
is, ea, id, *he, she, it; that, this.*
multitudo, -inis, f., *multitude, crowd.*
ne, *lest.*
nullus, -i, m., *no one, nobody.*
possum, posse, potui, -----, *be able.*
qui, quae, quod, *who, which, what.*
res, rei, f., *object, outcome.*
studium, -i, n., *zeal, eagerness, energy, enthusiasm.*
summa, -ae, f., *general management, control, administration.*
video, videre, visi, visus, *perceive, observe, see.*

Summam: Accusative direct object of the transitive infinitive **tradidisse** (A.G. 387 and 451.3). From the noun **summa, -ae**, f..
imperi: Partitive genitive with **Summam** (A.G. 346.a.1). The singular genitive of nouns in -ium ended, until the Augustan Age, in a single -i (A.G. 49.b).
se ... discedentem ... tradidisse: Accusative/infinitive construction in indirect discourse after **respondit** (A.G. 577 ff.). **se**: Singular, masculine, accusative direct reflexive pronoun (A.G. 300.1). The antecedent is **Vercingetorix**, the subject of **respondit** (A.G. 299).
discedentem: Present participle used as an adjective modifying **se** (A.G. 494). **tradidisse**: Perfect infinitive; the tense of the infinitive in indirect discourse is relative to that of the verb of saying (A.G. 584).
consulto: Adverb (A.G. 320-21).
nulli: Singular, masculine, dative adjective used substantively (A.G. 288). The noun **viro** is understood (A.G. 288.b). Dative indirect object of the transitive infinitive **tradidisse** (A.G. 362). The dative singular ending of **nullus** is -i (A.G. 113).
(veritum) ne ... impelleretur: The conjunction **ne** ("lest") with the subjunctive forms a substantive clause of fearing (A.G. 564). Here the verb, **veritum** (**vereor, vereri, veritus sum**, *fear, dread, be afraid of*), must be supplied in the form of a participle modifying **se**, the accusative subject of **tradidisse** (A.G. 491). **impelleretur**: The main verb of the subordinate clause (A.G. 278.b). Imperfect subjunctive; the tense of the subjunctive is in secondary sequence and follows the rules for the sequence of tense after **respondit** (A.G. 482-85).
is: Singular, masculine, nominative demonstrative pronoun used substantively (A.G. 296.2). The antecedent is **nulli** (A.G. 297.e). Nominative subject (A.G. 339).
multitudinis: Possessive genitive with **studio** (A.G. 343 Note).
studio: Ablative of cause without a preposition (A.G. 404).
ad dimicandum: The preposition **ad** with the accusative gerund denotes purpose (A.G. 506). **dimicandum**: Singular, neuter, accusative gerund (A.G. 501-02).
cui ... videret: Relative clause; a subordinate clause in indirect discourse takes the subjunctive (A.G. 303 and 580). **cui**: See below.
videret: The main verb of the subordinate clause (A.G. 278.b). Imperfect subjunctive; the tense of the subjunctive is in secondary sequence and follows the rules for the sequence of tense after **respondit** (A.G. 482-85 and 585). The pronoun **is**, with **Vercingetorix** as the antecedent, is understood as the subject (A.G. 271.a).
cui rei: Dative indirect object of the intransitive infinitive **studere** (A.G. 368.3). **cui**: Singular, feminine, dative relative pronoun (A.G. 305). The pronoun agrees with **rei** in its own clause (adjectival use) (A.G. 306).
propter animi mollitiem: Prepositional phrase, **propter** with the accusative here means "as a result or consequence of, in view of, because of" (*OLD* **propter** 3). Critognatus also charges the Gauls with a lack of fortitude at 77.5 with the same phrase: **Animi est ista mollitia**. **animi**: Possessive genitive with **mollitiem** (A.G. 343 Note).
studere omnis: Accusative/infinitive construction in indirect discourse after **videret** (A.G. 577 ff.). **studere**: Present infinitive; the tense of the infinitive in indirect discourse is relative to that of the verb of saying (A.G. 584). **omnis**: Plural, masculine, accusative

adjective used substantively (A.G. 288). **-is** for **-es** is the regular form in i-stem adjectives (A.G. 114.a and 116).

quod ... possent: Causal clause; the conjunction **quod** ("because") would normally take the indicative when the reason is given on the authority of the writer or speaker (A.G. 540.1). Here **quod** takes the subjunctive as a subordinate clause in indirect discourse after **respondit** (A.G. 580). **possent**: The main verb of the subordinate clause (A.G. 278.b). Imperfect subjunctive; the tense of the subjunctive is in secondary sequence and follows the rules for the sequence of tense after **respondit** (A.G. 482-85 and 585). The pronoun **ei**, with **omnis** as the antecedent, is understood as the subject (A.G. 271.a).

diutius: Irregular comparative adverb (A.G. 218.a and 320-21).

laborem: Accusative direct object of the infinitive **ferre** (A.G. 387 and 451.3).

ferre: Complementary infinitive after **possent** (A.G. 456).

non: Adverb, the adverb generally precedes the verb if it belongs to no one word in particular (A.G. 217.e, 320-21, and 599.a).

(20.6) **(6) Romani si casu intervenerint, fortunae, si alicuius indicio vocati, huic habendam gratiam, quod et paucitatem eorum ex loco superiore cognoscere et virtutem despicere potuerint, qui dimicare non ausi turpiter se in castra receperint.**

aliquis, aliqua, aliquid, *some one, any one, anybody, something, anything.*
castra, -orum, n., pl., *camp, encampment.*
cognosco, -gnoscere, -gnovi, cognitus, *learn, ascertain, recognize.*
dimico, -are, -avi, -atus, *fight, contend, struggle.*
ex, *from.*
gratia, -ae, f., *kindly feeling, esteem, regard.*
hic, haec, hoc, *this; he, she, it.*
indicium, -i, n., *information, disclosure.*

is, ea, id, *he, she, it; that, this.*
non, *not.*
possum, posse, potui, -----, *be able.*
quod, *because, since, for, as.*

Romani, -orum, m., pl., *the Romans.*
sui, sibi, se, or **sese**, nom. wanting, *themselves.*
turpiter, *basely, disgracefully, shamefully, dishonorably.*

voco, -are, -avi, -atus, *call, summon.*

audeo, audere, ausus sum, *venture, dare, risk.*
casu, *by chance.*
despicio, -spicere, -spexi, -spectus, *despise, disdain.*
et ... et, *both ... and.*
fortuna, -ae, f., *luck, fate, fortune, good fortune.*
habeo, habere, habui, habitus, *feel.*
in, *into.*
intervenio, -venire, -veni, -ventus, *arrive, come on the scene.*
locus, -i, m., *place, location, position.*
paucitas, -atis, f., *fewness, small number.*
qui, quae, quod, *who, which, what.*
recipio, -cipere, -cepi, -ceptus, (with **se**), *turn back, retire.*
si, *if.*
superior, -or, -us, *higher, upper, superior.*
virtus, -utis, f., *manliness, courage, bravery, valor, prowess.*

Romani ... gratiam: This clause can be rewritten in full as follows: **si Romani casu intervenerint, fortunae habendam (esse) gratiam, si (Romani) alicuius indicio vocati (erint), huic habendam (esse) gratiam.**

Romani: Nominative subject of **intervenerint ... vocati (erint)** (A.G. 339).

si ... intervenerint ... si ... vocati (erint) ... habendam gratiam (esse): A double conditional statement in indirect discourse after **respondit** (A.G. 589). The protasis, as a dependent clause, is in the subjunctive and the apodosis, as the principal clause, is in the infinitive (A.G. 589).

si ... intervenerint: The conjunction **si** ("if") with the subjunctive forms the protasis of a conditional statement in indirect discourse (A.G. 589.1). **intervenerint**: The main verb of the subordinate clause (A.G. 278.b). Perfect subjunctive; the tense of the subjunctive would normally be secondary sequence after the perfect verb **respondit** (A.G. 482-4). Here, it is the primary sequence through *repraesentatio* (A.G. 585.b Note).

casu: Adverb (A.G. 320-21).

fortunae: The first dative indirect object of the phrase **habendam (esse) gratiam** (A.G. 367 Note 2).

si ... vocati (erint): The conjunction **si** ("if") with the subjunctive forms the apodosis of a conditional statement in indirect discourse (A.G. 589.1). **vocati (erint)**: The main verb of the subordinate clause (A.G. 278.b). Supply **erint** to form the perfect, passive subjunctive (A.G. 184). Perfect subjunctive; the tense of the subjunctive would normally be secondary sequence after the perfect verb **respondit** (A.G. 482-4). Here, it is the primary sequence through *repraesentatio* (A.G. 585.b Note).

alicuius: Singular, masculine, genitive indefinite pronoun used substantively (A.G. 151.e). Possessive genitive with **indicio** (A.G. 343).

indicio: Ablative of cause without a preposition (A.G. 404).

huic: Singular, masculine, dative demonstrative pronoun used substantively (A.G. 296.2). The antecedent is **alicuius** (A.G. 297.e). The second dative indirect object of the phrase **habendam (esse) gratiam** (A.G. 367 Note 2).

habendam (esse) gratiam: The apodosis of the conditional statement (A.G. 589.2). Accusative/infinitive construction in indirect discourse after **respondit** (A.G. 577 ff.). **habendam (esse)**: Supply **esse** to form the second periphrastic (passive) present infinitive with the gerundive implying necessity (A.G. 194.b and 196). The tense of the infinitive in indirect discourse is relative to that of the verb of saying (A.G. 584). **habendam gratiam**: The phrase **gratiam habere** is an idiom that means "to feel grateful" (*OLD* **gratia** 4.b).

quod ... potuerint: Causal clause; the conjunction **quod** ("because") would normally take the indicative when the reason is given on the authority of the writer or speaker (A.G. 540.1). Here **quod** takes the subjunctive as a subordinate clause in indirect discourse after **respondit** (A.G. 580). **potuerint**: The main verb of the subordinate clause (A.G. 278.b). Perfect subjunctive; the tense of the subjunctive would normally be secondary sequence after the perfect verb **respondit** (A.G. 482-4). Here, it is the primary sequence through *repraesentatio* (A.G. 585.b Note). The pronoun **ipsi**, (those at the council), is understood as the subject (A.G. 271.a).

et ... et: The repeated conjunction connects the two infinitives **cognoscere ... despicere** and means "both ... and" (A.G. 323.e).

paucitatem: Accusative direct object of the infinitive **cognoscere** (A.G. 387 and 451.3).

eorum: Plural, masculine, genitive demonstrative pronoun used substantively (A.G. 296.2). The antecedent is **Romani** (A.G. 297.e). Possessive genitive with **paucitatem** (A.G. 343 Note).

ex loco superiore: Ablative of *place from which* with the preposition **ex** (A.G. 426.1). **superiore**: Defective comparative adjective (A.G. 130.b).

cognoscere: Complementary infinitive after **potuerint** (A.G. 456).

virtutem: Accusative direct object of the infinitive **despicere** (A.G. 387 and 451.3).

despicere: Complementary infinitive after **potuerint** (A.G. 456).

qui ... ausi ... receperint: Relative clause; a subordinate clause in indirect discourse takes the subjunctive (A.G. 303 and 580). **qui ... ausi**: Nominative subject (A.G. 339). **qui**: Plural, masculine, nominative relative pronoun used substantively (A. G. 305). The antecedent is **eorum** (A.G. 307). **ausi**: Nominative, perfect, semi-deponent participle used as a predicate, where in English a phrase or a subordinate clause would be more normal (A.G. 192 and 496). **receperint**: The main verb of the subordinate clause (A.G. 278.b). Perfect subjunctive; the tense of the subjunctive would normally be secondary sequence after the perfect verb **respondit** (A.G. 482-4). Here, it is the primary sequence through *repraesentatio* (A.G. 585.b Note).

dimicare: Complementary infinitive after the participle **ausi** (A.G. 456 and 488).

non: Adverb modifying **ausi**; the negative precedes the word it especially effects (A.G. 217.e, 320-21, and 599.a).

turpiter: Adverb (A.G. 214.b and 320-21).

se: Plural, masculine, accusative direct reflexive pronoun (A.G. 300.1). The antecedent is **qui**, the subject of **receperint** (A.G. 299). Accusative direct object of **receperint** (A.G. 387). The verb **recipere** used reflexively means "to turn back, retire" (*OLD* **recipio** 12).

in castra: Accusative of *place to which* with the preposition **in** (A.G. 426.2).

(20.7) (7) Imperium se ab Caesare per proditionem nullum desiderare, quod habere victoria posset quae iam esset sibi atque omnibus Gallis explorata:

atque, *and.*	**ab**, *from.*
Caesar, -aris, m., *Caesar.*	**desidero, -are, -avi, -atus**, *wish for, want, long for.*
exploratus, -a, -um, *established, certain, settled, sure.*	**Galli, -orum**, m., *the Gauls.*
habeo, habere, habui, habitus, *have.*	**iam**, *already, now, presently.*
imperium, -i, n., *command, control, dominion, military authority.*	**nullus, -a, -um**, *no, not any.*
omnis, -e, *all.*	**per**, *as a result of, by reason of, through.*
possum, posse, potui, -----, *be able.*	**proditio, -onis**, f., *a betraying, treachery.*
qui, quae, quod, *who, which, what.*	**sui, sibi, se**, or **sese**, nom. wanting, *he*, with or without *himself, himself.*
sum, esse, fui, futurus, *be.*	**victoria, -ae**, f., *victory.*

Imperium ... nullum: Accusative direct object of the infinitive **desiderare** (A.G. 387 and 451.3).

se ... desiderare: Accusative/infinitive construction in indirect discourse after **respondit** (A.G. 577 ff.). **se**: Singular, masculine, accusative direct reflexive pronoun (A.G. 300.1). The antecedent is **Vercingetorix**, the subject of **respondit** (A.G. 299). **desiderare**: Present infinitive; the tense of the infinitive in indirect discourse is relative to that of the verb of saying (A.G. 584).

ab Caesare: Ablative of source with the preposition **ab** (A.G. 403.1). **Caesare**: See Appendix A.

per proditionem: Prepositional phrase, **per** with the accusative here means "as a result of, by reason of, through" (*OLD* **per** 13).

quod ... posset: Relative clause; a subordinate clause in indirect discourse takes the subjunctive (A.G. 303 and 580). **quod**: Singular, neuter, accusative relative pronoun used substantively (A.G. 305). The antecedent is **Imperium** (A.G. 307). Accusative direct object of the infinitive **habere** (A.G. 387 and 451.3). **posset**: The main verb of the subordinate clause (A.G. 278.b). Imperfect subjunctive; the tense of the subjunctive is in secondary sequence and follows the rules for the sequence of tense after **respondit** (A.G. 482-85). The pronoun **is**, with **Vercingetorix** as the antecedent, is understood as the subject (A.G. 271.a).

habere: Complementary infinitive after **posset** (A.G. 456).

victoria: Ablative of means (A.G. 409).

quae ... esset ... explorata: Relative clause; a subordinate clause in indirect discourse takes the subjunctive (A.G. 303 and 580). **quae**: Singular, feminine, nominative relative pronoun used substantively (A.G. 305). The antecedent is **victoria** (A.G. 307). Nominative subject (A.G. 339). **esset**: The main verb of the subordinate clause (A.G. 278.b). Imperfect subjunctive; the tense of the subjunctive is in secondary sequence and follows the rules for the sequence of tense after **respondit** (A.G. 482-85). **explorata**: Singular, feminine, nominative predicate adjective modifying **quae** after **esset** (A.G. 283-84).

iam: Adverb (A.G. 215.6, 217.b and 320-21).

sibi atque omnibus Gallis: Two datives of reference; the dative in this construction is often called the dative of advantage as denoting the person for whose benefit the action is performed (A.G. 376). **sibi**: Singular, masculine, dative indirect reflexive pronoun (A.G. 300.2). The antecedent is **Vercingetorix**, the subject of **respondit** (A.G. 299). **atque**: The conjunction connects the two dative pronoun and noun and means "and" (*OLD* **atque** 12). **Gallis**: See Appendix A.

(20.7-8) quin etiam ipsis remittere, si sibi magis honorem tribuere quam ab se salutem accipere vide(8)antur.

ab, *from.*	**accipio, -cipere, -cepi, -ceptus**, *take to one's self,*

honor, -oris, m., *honor, esteem, respect, dignity.*
magis, *more, rather.*
quin etiam, *moreover, yes, and -, and furthermore.*

salus, -utis, f., *welfare, safety, deliverance.*
sui, sibi, se, or sese, nom. wanting, *he,* with or without *himself.*

videor, videri, visus sum, *seem to oneself, suppose* or *imagine that.*

receive, accept.
ipse, -a, -um, *he, they.*
quam, (*rather*) *than.*
remitto, -mittere, -misi, -missus, *give back, return,*
restore.
si, *if.*
tribuo, -ere, -ui, -utus, *assign, ascribe, allot, give,*
concede.

quin etiam: The two adverbs taken together mean " (in weakened sense, adding a new point, a new item in an enumeration) yes, and -, and furthermore" (*OLD* quin 3.a).
ipsis: Plural, masculine, dative demonstrative pronoun used substantively (A.G. 296.2 and 298.d). The antecedent is Gallis (A.G. 298). Dative indirect object of the transitive infinitive remittere (A.G. 362 and 451.3). The pronoun is here emphatic (A.G. 298.d.1).
remittere si ... videantur: Conditional statement in indirect discourse after respondit (A.G. 589). The protasis, as a dependent clause, is in the subjunctive and the apodosis, as the principal clause, is in the infinitive (A.G. 589).
(se imperium) remittere: The apodosis of the conditional statement (A.G. 589.2). Accusative/infinitive construction in indirect discourse after respondit (A.G. 577 ff.). In order to fill the ellipsis, carry down from above se and imperium. se: Singular, masculine, accusative direct reflexive pronoun used as the subject of the infinitive (A.G. 300.1). The antecedent is Vercingetorix, the subject of respondit (A.G. 299). imperium: Supply the noun as the accusative direct object of the infinitive (A.G. 387 and 451.3).
remittere: Present infinitive; the tense of the infinitive in indirect discourse is relative to that of the verb of saying (A.G. 584). Notice how vivid the present tense is rather than a future infinitive.
si ... videantur: The conjunction si ("if") with the subjunctive forms the protasis of a conditional statement in indirect discourse (A.G. 589.1). videantur: The main verb of the subordinate clause (A.G. 278.b). Present subjunctive; the tense of the subjunctive would normally be secondary sequence after the perfect verb respondit (A.G. 482-4). Here, it is the primary sequence through *repraesentatio* (A.G. 585.b Note). The pronoun ei, with ipsis as the antecedent, is understood as the subject (A.G. 271.a).
sibi: Singular, masculine, dative indirect reflexive pronoun (A.G. 300.2). The antecedent is Vercingetorix, the subject of respondit (A.G. 299). Dative indirect object of the transitive infinitive tribuere (A.G. 362).
magis: Adverb (A.G. 320-21).
honorem: Accusative direct object of the transitive infinitive tribuere (A.G. 387 and 451.3).
(ipsos) tribuere: Accusative/infinitive construction in indirect discourse after videantur (A.G. 577 ff.). Supply the pronoun ipsos, with ei the supplied subject of videantur as the antecedent, as the accusative subject. tribuere: Present infinitive; the tense of the infinitive in indirect discourse is relative to that of the verb of saying (A.G. 584).
quam ... (ipsos) accipere: Relative clause (A.G. 279.a). quam: Relative adverb meaning "than" after the comparison implied in magis (*OLD* quam 8). Supply the pronoun ipsos, with ei the supplied subject of videantur as the antecedent, as the accusative subject. accipere: The infinitive construction is regularly continued after a comparative with quam in indirect discourse rather than switching to the subjunctive in the dependent clause (A.G. 583.c).
ab se: Ablative of source with the preposition ab (A.G. 403.1). se: Singular, masculine, ablative indirect reflexive pronoun (A.G. 300.2). The antecedent is Vercingetorix, the subject of respondit (A.G. 299).
salutem: Accusative direct object of the infinitive accipere (A.G. 387 and 451.3).

(20.8-9) 'Haec ut intellegatis,' inquit 'a me sincere pronun(9)tiari, audite Romanos milites.'

a(b), *by.*
ego, mei, *I, me.*
inquam, inquis, inquit, *say.*

miles, -itis, m., *soldier, foot-solider.*

Romanus, -a, -um, *Roman.*
ut, *so that.*

audio, -ire, -ivi or -ii, -itus, *hear, listen to.*
hic, haec, hoc, *this; he, she, it.*
intellego, -legere, -lexi, -lectus, *understand, perceive,*
ascertain.
pronuntio, -are, -avi, -atus, *tell openly, declare,*
announce.
sincere, *frankly, honestly.*

Haec ... pronuntiari: Accusative/infinitive construction in indirect discourse after intellegatis (A.G. 577.ff.). Haec: Plural, neuter, accusative demonstrative pronoun used substantively meaning "these things" (A.G. 296.2). The antecedent is Vercingetorix's reply to the accusations described above (A.G. 297.e). pronuntiari: Present infinitive; the tense of the infinitive in indirect discourse is relative to that of the verb of saying (A.G. 584).
ut intellegatis: The conjunction ut ("so that") with the subjunctive forms a final (purpose) clause dependent on audite (A.G. 531.1).
intellegatis: The main verb of the subordinate clause (A.G. 278.b). Present subjunctive; the tense of the subjunctive is in primary sequence and follows the rules for the sequence of tense after audite (A.G. 482-85). The personal pronoun vos is understood as the subject but is not expressed except for distinction or emphasis (A.G. 295.a).
inquit: The main verb of the main clause (A.G. 278.b). The historical present, giving vividness to the narrative, is present in Chapter 20 (A.G. 469). This usage, common in all languages, comes from imagining past events as going on before our eyes (*repraesentatio*) (A.G. 469 Note). The verb inquit is used only in *oratio recta* introducing direct speech (A.G. 206.b and 578). It is always used parenthetically, following one or more words (A.G. 599.c). Siedler counts 5 uses of direct speech with inquit in Book 7 (Siedler, 46).

The pronoun **is**, with **Vercingetorix** as the antecedent, is understood as the subject (A.G. 271.a). "In 20 when Vercingetorix refutes a charge of treason, Caesar alternates between direct and indirect quotation, breaking into direct speech to expose the Gaul's dishonorable ruse with captured Roman slaves; it is clearly more effective to quote Vercingetorix's unprincipled use of the word 'sincerity' than to supply the word 'insincerity' in a third-person description of the action." (Kahn, 253) Kahn notes that "in effect his characters are what they do and not what he says about them." (Kahn, 251)

a me: Ablative of agent with the preposition **a(b)** (A.G. 405). **me**: Singular, masculine, ablative personal pronoun used substantively (A.G. 143 and 295).

sincere: Adverb (A.G. 214.a and 320-21).

audite: The main verb of the main clause (A.G. 278.b). Plural imperative (A.G. 187). The present tense in *oratio recta* after **inquit** denotes an action as now taking place (A.G. 578). Therefore, the tense in *oratio recta* is the true present and not the historical present (A.G. 465.2). The personal pronoun **vos** is understood as the subject but is not expressed except for distinction or emphasis (A.G. 295.a). Siedler counts 7 uses of the imperative in Book 7 (none by Caesar himself) (Siedler, 46).

Romanos milites: Accusative direct object of **audite** (A.G. 387).

(20.9-10) **Producit servos, quos in pabulatione paucis ante diebus exceperat et fame vinculisque (10) excruciaverat.**

ante, *before, prior.*	**dies**, **-ei**, m. and f., *day.*
et, *and.*	**excipio**, **-cipere**, **-cepi**, **-ceptus**, *cut off, catch.*
excrucio, **-are**, **-avi**, **-atus**, *torment, torture.*	**fames**, **-is**, f., *hunger, starvation.*
in, *engaged* or *occupied in.*	**pabulatio**, **-onis**, f., *foraging, getting fodder.*
paucus, **-a**, **-um**, *few.*	**produco**, **-ducere**, **-duxi**, **-ductus**, *bring out, lead forth.*
-que, *and.*	**qui**, **quae**, **quod**, *who, which, what.*
servus, **-i**, m., *slave.*	**vinculum**, **-i**, n., *chain, bond, fetters.*

Producit: The main verb of the main clause (A.G. 278.b). Verb first in the emphatic position. Here it marks the end of the direct discourse (A.G. 598.d). The pronoun **is**, with **Vercingetorix** as the antecedent, is understood as the subject (A.G. 271.a). See also the similar ruse by Litaviccus at 38.4-6.

servos: Accusative direct object of **Producit** (A.G. 387). Slaves included "the officer's servants and tent-servants (*calones*), as well as the drivers and muleteers with the heavy baggage (muliones)." (Kelsey, 24)

quos ... exceperat ... excruciaverat: Relative clause (A.G. 303). **quos**: Plural, masculine, accusative relative pronoun used substantively (A.G. 305). The antecedent is **servos** (A.G. 307). Accusative direct object of **exceperat** and **excruciaverat** (A.G. 387).

exceperat ... excruciaverat: The main verbs of the subordinate clause (A.G. 278.b). The pronoun **is**, with **Vercingetorix** as the antecedent, is understood as the subject of both verbs (A.G. 271.a). The pluperfect tense of the verbs denotes an action completed in past time (A.G. 477).

in pabulatione: Prepositional phrase, **in** with the ablative here means "engaged or occupied in" (*OLD* **in** 39).

paucis ante diebus: The ablative with the adverb here expresses distance of time before ("before, by a few days") (A.G. 424.f). **ante**: Adverb (A.G. 320-21 and 433.1).

et: The conjunction connects the two main verbs in the relative clause **exceperat ... excruciaverat** (A.G. 324.a).

fame: Ablative of means (A.G. 409).

vinculisque: Ablative of instrument (A.G. 409). **-que**: The enclitic conjunction connects the two ablative nouns (A.G. 324.a).

(20.10-11) **Hi iam ante edocti quae interrogati pronuntiarent, milites se esse legionarios dicunt; fame atque inopia adductos clam ex castris exisse, si quid frumenti aut (11) pecoris in agris reperire possent;**

adduco, **-ducere**, **-duxi**, **-ductus**, *induce, prevail upon, influence.*	**ager**, **-ri**, m., *land* (under cultivation), *field*, pl., *the country.*
ante, *before, previously.*	**atque**, *and.*
aut, *or.*	**castra**, **-orum**, n., pl., *camp, encampment.*
clam, *secretly.*	**dico**, **dicere**, **dixi**, **dictus**, *say.*
edoceo, **-docere**, **-docui**, **-doctus**, *teach carefully, instruct, inform, tell.*	**ex**, *from, out of.*
exeo, **-ire**, **-ivi**, or **-ii**, **-itus**, *go forth, go out, withdraw, leave.*	**fames**, **-is**, f., *hunger, starvation.*
frumentum, **-i**, n., *grain.*	**hic**, **haec**, **hoc**, *this; he, she, it.*
iam, *already.*	**in**, *in.*
inopia, **-ae**, f., *want, lack, need, scarcity.*	**interrogo**, **-are**, **-avi**, **-atus**, *ask, question.*
legionarius, **-a**, **-um**, *of a legion, legionary.*	**miles**, **-itis**, m., *soldier, foot-solider.*
pecus, **-oris**, n., *cattle.*	**possum**, **posse**, **potui**, **-----**, *be able.*
pronuntio, **-are**, **-avi**, **-atus**, *tell openly, declare, announce.*	**quis**, **-----**, **quid**, (inter.) *who? what?*
quis, **-----**, **quid**, (indef.) *anyone, anything.*	**reperio**, **-perire**, **repperi**, **repertus**, *find, discover, obtain, procure.*
si, *to see if, in case, on the off-chance that.*	**sui**, **sibi**, **se**, or **sese**, nom. wanting, *they*, with or without *themselves.*
sum, **esse**, **fui**, **futurus**, *be.*	

Hi ... edocti: Nominative subject of **dicunt** (A.G. 339). **Hi**: Plural, masculine, nominative demonstrative pronoun used substantively

(A.G. 296.2). The antecedent is **servos** (A.G. 297.e). **edocti**: Nominative, perfect, passive, participle used as a predicate, where in English a phrase or a subordinate clause would be more normal (A.G. 496).

iam: Adverb (A.G. 215.6, 217.b and 320-21).

ante: Adverb (A.G. 320-21 and 433.1).

quae ... pronuntiarent: Indirect question with the subjunctive; the phrase is the object of the participle **edocti** (A.G. 573-75). **quae**: Plural, neuter, accusative interrogative pronoun used substantively meaning "what things" (A.G. 148). Accusative direct object of **pronuntiarent** (A.G. 387). **pronuntiarent**: The main verbs of the subordinate clause (A.G. 278.b). Imperfect subjunctive; the tense of the subjunctive is in secondary sequence and follows the rules for the sequence of tense for indirect questions after the historical present **dicunt** (A.G. 485.e and 575).

interrogati: Nominative, perfect, passive, participle used as a predicate, where in English a phrase or a subordinate clause would be more normal (A.G. 496). The pronoun **ei**, with **Hi** (**servi**) as the antecedent, is understood. Nominative subject (A.G. 339).

milites se esse legionarios: Accusative/infinitive construction in indirect discourse after **dicunt** (A.G. 577 ff.). **milites ... legionarios**: Predicate accusative after **esse** (A.G. 283-84). **se**: Plural, masculine, accusative direct reflexive pronoun (A.G. 300.1). The antecedent is **Hi**, the subject of **dicunt** (A.G. 299). Accusative subject of the infinitive (A.G. 397.e). **esse**: Present infinitive; the tense of the infinitive in indirect discourse is relative to that of the verb of saying (A.G. 584).

dicunt: The main verb of the main clause (A.G. 278.b).

fame atque inopia: Two ablatives of cause without a preposition (A.G. 404.b). **atque**: The conjunction connects the two ablative nouns and means "and" (*OLD* **atque** 12).

adductos ... exisse: Accusative/infinitive construction in indirect discourse after **dicunt** (A.G. 577 ff.). **adductos**: Accusative, perfect, passive, participle used as a predicate, where in English a phrase or a subordinate clause would be more normal (A.G. 496). Carry down **se** from above as the pronoun. **exisse**: Perfect infinitive; the tense of the infinitive in indirect discourse is relative to that of the verb of saying (A.G. 584). A contracted form of **exivisse** (A.G. 181.a).

clam: Adverb (A.G. 320-21).

ex castris: Ablative of *place from which* with the preposition **ex** (A.G. 426.1).

si ... possent: The conjunction **si** with the subjunctive forms the protasis of a conditional statement without an apodosis meaning "to see if, in case, on the off-chance that" (*OLD* **si** 11). **possent**: The main verb of the subordinate clause (A.G. 278.b). Imperfect subjunctive; the tense of the subjunctive is in secondary sequence after the historical present tense of **dicunt** (A.G. 482-85, esp. 485.e). The pronoun **ipsi**, with **Hi** (**servi**) as the antecedent, is understood as the subject (A.G. 271.a).

quid: Singular, neuter, accusative indefinite pronoun used substantively (A.G. 149). The indefinite pronoun **quis**, -----, **quid** is used after **si** (A.G. 310.a). Accusative direct object of the infinitive **reperire** (A.G 387 and 451.3).

frumenti aut pecoris: Two partitive genitives after **quid** (A.G. 346.a.3). **aut**: The conjunction connects the two nouns and excludes the alternative (A.G. 324.e).

in agris: Ablative of *place where* with the preposition **in** (locative ablative) (A.G. 426.3).

reperire: Complementary infinitive after **possent** (A.G. 456).

(20.11-12) simili omnem exercitum inopia premi nec iam vires sufficere cuiusquam nec ferre operis laborem posse;

exercitus, -us, m., *army*.

inopia, -ae, f., *want, lack, need, scarcity*.

nec iam ... nec, *and no longer ... nor*.

opus, operis, n., *work, labor, toil*.

premo, -ere, pressi, pressus, (in the pass.), *be hard pressed, weighed down, oppressed*.

similis, -e, *like, similar*.

vires, -ium, f., pl., *physical powers, strength*.

fero, ferre, tuli, latus, *bear, endure, suffer*.

labor, -oris, m., *toil, exertion, labor*.

omnis, -e, *all, the whole*.

possum, posse, potui, -----, *be able*.

quisquam, -----, quidquam, *anyone, anything*.

sufficio, -ficere, -feci, -fectus, *suffice, hold out*.

simili ... inopia: Ablative of manner with a limiting adjective (A.G. 412).

omnem exercitum ... premi: Accusative/infinitive construction in indirect discourse after **dicunt** (A.G. 577 ff.). **premi**: Present infinitive; the tense of the infinitive in indirect discourse is relative to that of the verb of saying (A.G. 584).

nec iam ... nec: The repeated conjunctions mean "and no longer ... nor", connecting the two complementary infinitives **sufficere ... ferre** (*OLD* **neque** 7). **nec iam**: The adverb **iam** with a negative adverb **nec** means A (no) longer (A.G. 322.b).

vires ... posse: Accusative/infinitive construction in indirect discourse after **dicunt** (A.G. 577 ff.). **posse**: Present infinitive; the tense of the infinitive in indirect discourse is relative to that of the verb of saying (A.G. 584).

sufficere: Complementary infinitive after **posse** (A.G. 456).

cuiusquam: Singular, masculine, genitive indefinite pronoun used substantively (A.G. 151.d). Possessive genitive with **vires** (A.G. 343 Note).

ferre: Complementary infinitive after **posse** (A.G. 456).

operis: Objective genitive with **laborem** (A.G. 348). From the noun **opus**, not **opera**.

laborem: Accusative direct object of the infinitive **ferre** (A.G. 387 and 451.3).

(quemquam) posse: Accusative/infinitive construction in indirect discourse after **dicunt** (A.G. 577 ff). Supply **quemquam** as the second subject accusative of **posse** as **vires** can not with sense be carried on as the subject with the second infinitive **ferre**.

quemquam: Singular, masculine, accusative indefinite pronoun used substantively picking up on the previous pronoun **cuiusquam** (A.G. 151.d).

(20.11-12) itaque statuisse imperatorem, si nihil in oppugnatione oppidi profecissent, triduo exercitum de(12)ducere.

deduco, -ducere, -duxi, -ductus, *lead away, lead off, withdraw.*
imperator, -oris, m., *commander-in-chief, commander, general.*
itaque, *and so, in consequence, and thus, accordingly, therefore.*
oppidum, -i, n., *fortified town, city.*
proficio, -ficere, -feci, -fectus, *effect, gain, accomplish.*
statuo, -uere, -ui, -utus, *determine, resolve.*

exercitus, -us, m., *army.*
in, *in.*
nihil, n., *nothing.*
oppugnatio, -onis, f., *storming, assault, attack, siege.*
si, *if.*
triduum, -i, n., *space of three days, three days.*

itaque: An adverb expressing the result of the previous ideas meaning "and so, in consequence" (*OLD* **itaque** 1). The adverb stands in the first position (A.G. 599.b).

statuisse imperatorem: Accusative/infinitive construction in indirect discourse after **dicunt** (A.G. 577 ff). **statuisse:** Perfect infinitive; the tense of the infinitive in indirect discourse is relative to that of the verb of saying (A.G. 584). **imperatorem:** = **Caesarem**.

si ... profecissent ... deducere: A subordinate conditional statement (A.G. 512.c). The apodosis is an infinitive equivalent to a substantive clause of purpose dependent on **statuisse**, and the protasis, as a clause subordinate to an infinitive equivalent to a subjunctive clause, also takes the subjunctive (attraction) (A.G. 512.c and 593).

si ... profecissent: The conjunction **si** ("if") with the subjunctive forms the protasis of a conditional statement in indirect discourse (A.G. 589.1). **profecissent:** The main verbs of the subordinate clause (A.G. 278.b). Pluperfect subjunctive; the tense of the subjunctive is in secondary sequence after the historical present tense of **dicunt** (A.G. 482-85, esp. 485.e). The pluperfect tense of the subjunctive is here standing for a future perfect in direct discourse (A.G. 484.c). The future perfect tense denotes action completed (at the time referred to), and hence is represented in the subjunctive by the pluperfect tense in secondary sequence (A.G. 484.c). The pronoun **ei**, with the men implied in **exercitum** as the antecedent, is understood as the subject (A.G. 271.a).

nihil: Accusative indeclinable noun, used only as nominative and accusative singular (A.G. 103.a). Accusative direct object of **profecissent** (A.G. 387).

in oppugnatione oppidi: Prepositional phrase, **in** with the ablative here means "in" (given circumstances) (*OLD* **in** 40). **oppidi:** Objective genitive with **oppugnatione** (A.G. 348).

triduo: Ablative of *time when* (A.G. 423.1).

exercitum: Accusative direct object of the infinitive **deducere** (A.G. 387 and 451.3).

deducere: The apodosis of the conditional statement (A.G. 589.2). Complementary infinitive after **statuisse**. The infinitive is equivalent to a substantive clause of purpose (A.G. 456 and 563.d).

(20.12) 'Haec,' inquit 'a me,' Vercingetorix, 'beneficia habetis, quem proditionis insimulatis;

a(b), *from.*
ego, mei, *I, me.*
hic, haec, hoc, *this; he, she, it.*
insimulo, -are, -avi, -atus, *charge with, accuse of.*
qui, quae, quod, *who, which, what.*

beneficium, -i, n., *service, benefit.*
habeo, habere, habui, habitus, *have, hold, possess.*
inquam, inquis, inquit, *say.*
proditio, -onis, f., *a betraying, treachery.*
Vercingetorix, -igis, m., *Vercingetorix.*

Haec ... beneficia: Accusative direct object of **habetis** (A.G. 387). **Haec:** Plural, neuter, accusative demonstrative pronoun used as an adjective modifying **beneficia** (A.G. 296.1 and a).

inquit: The main verb of the main clause (A.G. 278.b). The verb **inquit** is used only in *oratio recta* introducing direct speech (A.G. 206.b and 578). It is always used parenthetically, following one or more words (A.G. 599.c). Siedler counts 5 uses of direct speech with **inquit** in Book 7 (Siedler, 46).

a me: Ablative of source with the preposition **a(b)** (A.G. 403.1). **me:** Singular, masculine, ablative personal pronoun used substantively (A.G. 143 and 295).

Vercingetorix: Nominative subject of the previous verb **inquit** (A.G. 339). See Appendix A.

habetis: The main verb of the main clause (A.G. 278.b). The present tense in *oratio recta* after **inquit** denotes an action as now taking place (A.G. 578). Therefore, the tense in *oratio recta* is the true present and not the historical present (A.G. 465.2). The personal pronoun **vos** is understood as the subject but is not expressed except for distinction or emphasis (A.G. 295.a).

quem ... insimulatis: Relative clause (A.G. 303). **quem:** Singular, masculine, accusative relative pronoun used substantively (A.G. 305). The antecedent is **Vercingetorix** (A.G. 307). Accusative direct object of **insimulatis** (A.G. 387). **insimulatis:** The main verb of the subordinate clause (A.G. 278.b). The personal pronoun **vos** is understood as the subject but is not expressed except for distinction or emphasis (A.G. 295.a).

proditionis: Genitive of charge after **insimulatis**, a verb of accusing (A.G. 352).

(20.12) cuius opera sine vestro sanguine tantum exercitum victorem fame consumptum videtis; quem turpiter se ex fuga recipientem ne qua civitas suis finibus recipiat a me provisum est.'

a(b), *by.*
consumo, -sumere, -sumpsi, -sumptus, *waste, exhaust, destroy.*
ex, *after.*
fames, -is, f., *hunger, starvation.*

civitas, -tatis, f., *state, nation.*
ego, mei, *I, me.*
exercitus, -us, m., *army.*
fines, -ium, m., pl., *borders,* hence *territory, country,*

fuga, -ae, f., *flight.*
opera, -ae, f., *effort, work, pains.*

qui, quae, quod, *who, which, what.*
recipio, -cipere, -cepi, -ceptus, (with se), *recover; receive, admit.*
sine, *without.*
suus, -a, -um, *her,* with or without *own.*
turpiter, *basely, disgracefully, shamefully, dishonorably.*
victor, -oris, m., (as adj.), *victorious, triumphant.*

land.
ne, *so that ... not.*
provideo, -videre, -vidi, -visus, *foresee, provide for, look out for.*
quis, -----, quid, *any;* (as adj., qui, quae, or qua, quod).
sanguis, -inis, m., *blood.*
sui, sibi, se, or sese, nom. wanting, *himself.*
tantus, -a, -um, *so great, so large, such.*
vester, -tra, -trum, *your, yours.*
video, videre, visi, visus, *perceive, observe, see.*

cuius: Singular masculine, genitive relative pronoun used substantively (A.G. 305). The antecedent is **Vercingetorix** (A.G. 297.d). Possessive genitive with **opera** (A.G. 343 Note). The relative does not introduce a relative clause but is a connecting relative; at the beginning of a clause the pronoun is often best rendered by a personal or demonstrative pronoun, with or without *and* (A.G. 308.f). **opera**: Ablative of means (A.G. 409).

sine vestro sanguine: Prepositional phrase, **sine** with the ablative here means "with" (*OLD sine* 1). **vestro**: Singular, masculine, ablative possessive pronoun used as an adjective modifying **sanguine** (A.G. 302).

tantum exercitum victorem ... consumptum: Accusative direct object of **videtis** (A.G. 387). **victorem**: A noun used as an adjective modifying **exercitum** (A.G. 321.c). **consumptum**: Accusative, perfect, passive, participle used as an adjective modifying **exercitum** (A.G. 494).

fame: Ablative of cause without a preposition after the participle **consumptum** (A.G. 404).

videtis: The main verb of the simple sentence (A.G. 278.1). The personal pronoun **vos** is understood as the subject but is not expressed except for distinction or emphasis (A.G. 295.a).

quem ... recipientem: Accusative direct object of **recipiat** (A.G. 387). **quem**: Singular, masculine, accusative relative pronoun used substantively (A.G. 305). The antecedent is **exercitum** (A.G. 307). The relative does not introduce a relative clause but is a connecting relative; at the beginning of a clause the pronoun is often best rendered by a personal or demonstrative pronoun, with or without *and* (A.G. 308.f). **recipientem**: Present participle used as an adjective modifying **quem** (A.G. 494.a).

turpiter: Adverb modifying **recipientem** (A.G. 214.b and 320-21).

se: Singular, masculine, accusative indirect reflexive pronoun (A.G. 300.2). The antecedent is **quem**, the direct object of **recipiat** (A.G. 299). Accusative direct object of the participle **recipientem** (A.G. 387 and 488). **se ... recipientem**: The verb **recipere** with the reflexive **se** in Book 7 usually means "to retreat" (*OLD repicio* 12), here it means "to recover" (*OLD recipio* 14).

ex fuga: Prepositional phrase, **ex** with the ablative here means "after" (*OLD ex* 9). This refers to the (supposed) withdrawal which will take place in three days.

ne ... recipiat: The conjunction **ne** ("so that ... not") with the subjunctive forms a negative substantive clause of purpose (A.G. 563). The clause functions as the subject of the impersonal verb **provisum est**; a substantive clause used as the object of a verb becomes the subject when the verb is put into the passive (A.G. 566). **recipiat**: The main verb of the subordinate clause (A.G. 278.b). Present subjunctive; the tense of the subjunctive would normally be secondary sequence after the perfect verb **provisum est** (A.G. 482-4). Here, it is the primary sequence through *repraesentatio* (A.G. 585.b Note).

qua civitas: Nominative subject (A.G. 339). **qua**: Singular, feminine, ablative indefinite pronoun used as an adjective modifying **civitas** (A.G. 149). The indefinite pronoun **quis, -----, quid** (qui, quae, or qua, quod when used adjectively) is used after **ne** (A.G. 310.a).

suis finibus: Ablative of *place where* without a preposition (A.G. 429.2). **suis**: Plural, masculine, ablative possessive pronoun used as an adjective modifying **finibus** (A.G. 302).

a me: Ablative of agent with the preposition **a(b)** after the passive verb **provisum est** (A.G. 405). **me**: Singular, masculine, ablative personal pronoun used substantively (A.G. 143 and 295).

provisum est: Impersonal use of the verb (A.G. 208.c). The previous negative purpose clause functions as the subject; a substantive clause used as the object of a verb becomes the subject when the verb is put in the passive (A.G. 566).

(21.1) Conclamat omnis multitudo et suo more armis concrepat, quod facere in eo consuerunt cuius orationem approbant:

approbo, -are, -avi, -atus, *approve, favor.*
conclamo, -are, -avi, -atus, *cry out loud together, shout, cry out.*
consuesco, -suescere, -suevi, -suetus, *form a habit, be accustomed, be wont.*
facio, facere, feci, factus, *do.*
is, ea, id, *he, she, it; that, this.*
multitudo, -inis, f., *multitude, crowd.*
oratio, -onis, f., *speech, words, address.*
suus, -a, -um, *her,* with or without *own.*

arma, -orum, n., *arms, weapons.*
concrepo, -are, -ui, -itus, *rattle, clash.*
et, *and.*
in, *in the matter of, for.*
mos, moris, m., *custom, way, wont, practice.*
omnis, -e, *all, the whole.*
qui, quae, quod, *who, which, what.*

Conclamat: The main verb of the coordinate clause **Conclamat ... multitudo** (A.G. 278.a). Verb first in the emphatic position. Here it marks the end of the direct discourse (A.G. 598.d). The historical present, giving vividness to the narrative, is present in Chapter 21 (A.G. 469). This usage, common in all languages, comes from imagining past events as going on before our eyes (*repraesentatio*) (A.G. 469 Note).

omnis multitudo: Nominative subject of **Conclamat ... concrepat** (A.G. 339).

et: The conjunction connects the two main verbs **Conclamat** ... **concrepat** (A.G. 324.a).

suo more: Ablative of specification (A.G. 418). **suo**: Singular, masculine, ablative possessive pronoun used as an adjective modifying **more** (A.G. 302).

armis: Ablative of instrument (A.G. 409).

concrepat: The main verb of the coordinate clause **suo** ... **approbant** (A.G. 278.a). "The early Germans also at their war-councils expressed approval by beating with their spears upon their shields; see Tac. Germ. 11." (Kelsey, 406) "see also Livy 28.29." (Hammond, 238)

quod ... consuerunt: Relative clause (A.G. 303). **quod**: Singular, neuter, accusative relative pronoun used substantively (A.G. 305). The antecedent is the previous method of showing approval (A.G. 307.d Note). Accusative direct object of the infinitive **facere** (A.G. 387 and 451.3). **consuerunt**: The main verb of the subordinate clause (A.G. 278.b). Contracted form of **consueverunt** (A.G. 181.a). A prefect form with present force (A.G. 476). The noun **Galli** (in general) is understood as the subject (A.G. 271.a).

facere: Complementary infinitive after **consuerunt** (A.G. 456).

in eo: Prepositional phrase, **in** with the ablative here means "in the matter of" (*OLD* **in** 42). **eo**: Singular, masculine, ablative demonstrative pronoun used substantively (A.G. 296.2). The pronoun functions as a correlative to the relative clause **cuius** ... **approbant** (A.G. 297.d).

cuius ... approbant: Relative clause (A.G. 303). **cuius**: Singular masculine, genitive relative pronoun used substantively (A.G. 305). The antecedent is **eo** (A.G. 297.d). Possessive genitive with **orationem** (A.G. 343 Note). **approbant**: The main verb of the subordinate clause (A.G. 278.b). The pronoun **ei**, with **Galli** the supplied subject of **consuerunt** as the antecedent, is understood as the subject (A.G. 271.a).

orationem: Accusative direct object of **approbant** (A.G. 387).

(21.1) **summum esse Vercingetorigem ducem nec de eius fide dubitandum nec maiore ratione bellum administrari posse.**

administro, -are, -avi, -atus, *execute, manage, carry on, administer.*	**bellum, -i**, n., *war.*
de, *about, concerning.*	**dubito, -are, -avi, -atus**, *be uncertain, doubt.*
dux, ducis, m., *leader, general, commander.*	**fides, -is**, f., *good faith, fidelity, loyalty.*
is, ea, id, *he, she, it; that, this.*	**maior, -or, -us**, *more skillful, greater.*
nec ... nec, *neither ... nor.*	**possum, posse, potui, -----**, *be able.*
ratio, -onis, f., *plan, method, way.*	**sum, esse, fui, futurus**, *be.*
summus, -a, -um, *best, greatest, very great.*	**Vercingetorix, -igis**, m., *Vercingetorix.*

summum esse Vercingetorigem ducem: Accusative/infinitive construction in indirect discourse (A.G. 577 ff.). The verb of saying is not expressed, but implied in the general drift of the sentence (A.G. 580.a). **summum ... ducem**: Predicate accusative after **esse** (A.G. 284). **summum**: Defective superlative adjective (A.G. 130.b). **esse**: Present infinitive; the tense of the infinitive in indirect discourse is relative to that of the verb of saying (A.G. 584). **Vercingetorigem**: Accusative subject of the infinitive (A.G. 397.e). "The ingenious ruse of Vercingetorix had turned the fickle Gauls at once; they were now as much in favor of him as a few hours previous they had been against him." (Kelsey, 406) See Appendix A.

nec ... nec: The repeated conjunction means "neither ... nor", connecting the two infinitives **dubitandum** (esse) ... **posse** (*OLD* **neque** 7).

de eius fide: Prepositional phrase, **de** with the ablative meaning "concerning, about" (*OLD* **de** 12). **eius**: Singular, masculine, genitive demonstrative pronoun used substantively (A.G. 296.2). The antecedent is **Vercingetorigem** (A.G. 297.e). Possessive genitive with **fide** (A.G. 343).

(id) dubitandum (esse): Accusative/infinitive construction in indirect discourse (A.G. 577 ff.). The verb of saying is not expressed, but implied in the general drift of the sentence (A.G. 580.a). **dubitandum (esse)**: Supply **esse** to form the second periphrastic (passive) present infinitive with the gerundive implying necessity (A.G. 194.b and 196). The tense of the infinitive in indirect discourse is relative to that of the verb of saying (A.G. 584). Impersonal use of the verb (A.G. 208.d). Supply **id** as the subject (A.G. 318.c).

maiore ratione: Ablative of manner with a limiting adjective (A.G. 412). **maiore**: Irregular comparative adjective (A.G. 129).

bellum ... posse: Accusative/infinitive construction in indirect discourse (A.G. 577 ff.). The verb of saying is not expressed, but implied in the general drift of the sentence (A.G. 580.a). **posse**: Present infinitive; the tense of the infinitive in indirect discourse is relative to that of the verb of saying (A.G. 584).

administrari: Complementary infinitive after **posse** (A.G. 456).

(21.2-3) **(2) Statuunt ut X milia hominum delecta ex omnibus copiis in (3) oppidum mittantur, nec solis Biturigibus communem salutem committendam censent, quod penes eos, si id oppidum retinuissent, summam victoriae constare intellegebant.**

Bituriges, -um, m., pl., *the Bituriges.*	**censeo, -ere, -ui, -us**, *think, hold, judge.*
committo, -mittere, -misi, -missus, *intrust, commit.*	**communis, -e**, *common, in common, public, general.*
consto, -stare, -stiti, -staturus, *remain, lie.*	**copiae, -arum**, f., pl., *forces, troops.*
deligo, -ligere, -legi, -lectus, *choose, select, pick out.*	**ex**, *from.*
homo, hominis, m., *man, person.*	**in**, *into.*
intellego, -legere, -lexi, -lectus, *understand, see clearly, perceive.*	**is, ea, id**, *he, she, it; that, this.*
milia, -um, n., pl., *thousand, thousands.*	**mitto, mittere, misi, missus**, *send.*
nec, *and ... not.*	**omnis, -e**, *all.*

oppidum, -i, n., *fortified town, city.*
quod, *because, since, for, as.*
salus, -utis, f., *welfare, safety, deliverance.*
solus, -a, -um, *only, alone.*

statuo, -uere, -ui, -utus, *determine, resolve.*
victoria, -ae, f., *victory.*

penes, *in the hands of, in the power of.*
retineo, -tinere, -tinui, -tentus, *hold.*
si, *if.*
summa, -ae, f., *crowning stage, culmination, completion.*
ut, *so that.*
X, in expression of number, = *10.*

Statuunt: The main verb of the coordinate clause **Statuunt ... mittantur** (A.G. 278.a). The verb comes in the first position when the idea in it is emphatic (A.G. 598.d). Here it marks the end of the indirect discourse (A.G. 589.d). The pronoun **ei**, with the leaders present at the council as the antecedent, is understood as the subject (A.G. 271.a).

ut ... mittantur: The conjunction **ut** ("so that") with the subjunctive forms a substantive clause of purpose which is used as the object of **Statuunt** denoting an action directed toward the future (A.G. 563 and 580.d.2). **mittantur**: The main verb of the subordinate clause (A.G. 278.b). Present subjunctive; the tense of the subjunctive is normally in secondary sequence after the historical present **Statuunt** (A.G. 482-85). Here it is in primary sequence through *repraesentatio* (A.G. 485.e and 585.b Note).

X milia ... delecta: Nominative subject (A.G. 339). **X**: Roman numeral used as an adjective modifying **milia** (A.G. 133). **milia**: Nominative plural; in the plural **mille** declines as a neuter noun (A.G. 134.d). **delecta**: Nominative, perfect, passive participle used as a predicate, where in English a phrase or a subordinate clause would be more natural (A.G. 496).

hominum: Partitive genitive with **milia** (A.G. 346.a.2).

ex omnibus copiis: Ablative of source with the preposition **ex** after the adjective **delecta** (A.G. 403.1).

in oppidum: Accusative of *place to which* with the preposition **in** (A.G. 426.2). **oppidum**: = **Avaricum**.

nec: The conjunction joins a negative clause (**solis ... intellegebant**) to a preceding positive one (**Statuunt ... oppidum**) and means "and ... not" (*OLD* **neque** 3).

solis Biturigibus: Dative indirect object of the passive infinitive **committendam** (**esse**), verbs which in the active voice take the accusative and dative retain the dative when used in the passive (A.G. 365). **Biturigibus**: See Appendix A.

communem salutem committendam (**esse**): Accusative/infinitive construction in indirect discourse after **censent** (A.G. 577 ff.).

committendam (**esse**): Supply **esse** to form the second periphrastic (passive) present infinitive with the gerundive implying necessity (A.G. 194.b and 196). The tense of the infinitive in indirect discourse is relative to that of the verb of saying (A.G. 584).

censent: The main verb of the coordinate clause **solis ... intellegebant** (A.G. 278.a). The pronoun **ei**, with the leaders present at the council as the antecedent, is understood as the subject (A.G. 271.a).

quod ... intellegebant: Causal clause; the conjunction **quod** ("because") normally takes the indicative when the reason is given on the authority of the writer or speaker (A.G. 540.1). Here, as a dependent clause in indirect statement after **censent**, it should take the subjunctive (A.G. 580). However, a subordinate clause merely explanatory, or containing statements which are regarded as true independently of the quotation, takes the indicative (A.G. 583). **intellegebant**: The main verb of the subordinate clause (A.G. 278.b). The pronoun **ei**, with the leaders present at the council as the antecedent, is understood as the subject (A.G. 271.a).

penes eos: Prepositional phrase, **penes** with the accusative here means "in the hands of" (*OLD* **penes** 3). **eos**: Plural, masculine, accusative demonstrative pronoun used substantively (A.G. 296.2). The antecedent is **Biturigibus** (A.G. 297.e). "Caesar indicates that the Gallic position is being undermined by internal rivalries. Many editors adopt the inferior reading *paene in eo*, and thus the meaning that the Gauls expected the outcome of the war to depend on their holding Avaricum." (Hammond, 238)

si ... retinuissent ... constare: Conditional statement in indirect discourse after **intellegebant** (A.G. 589). The protasis, as a dependent clause, is in the subjunctive and the apodosis, as the principal clause, is in the infinitive (A.G. 589).

si ... retinuissent: The conjunction **si** ("if") with the subjunctive forms the protasis of a conditional statement in indirect discourse (A.G. 589.1). **retinuissent**: The main verb of the subordinate clause (A.G. 278.b). Pluperfect subjunctive; the tense of the subjunctive is in secondary sequence and follows the rules for the sequence of tense after **intellegebant** (A.G. 482-85 and 585). The pluperfect tense of the subjunctive is here standing for a future perfect in direct discourse (A.G. 484.c). The future perfect tense denotes action completed (at the time referred to), and hence is represented in the subjunctive by the pluperfect tense in secondary sequence (A.G. 484.c). The pronoun **ei**, with **Biturigibus** as the antecedent, is understood as the subject (A.G. 271.a).

id oppidum: Accusative direct object of **retinuissent** (A.G. 387). **id**: Singular, neuter, accusative demonstrative pronoun used as an adjective modifying **oppidum** (A.G. 296.1 and a). **oppidum**: = **Avaricum**.

summam ... constare: The apodosis of the conditional statement (A.G. 589.2). Accusative/infinitive construction in indirect discourse after **intellegebant** (A.G. 577 ff.). **summam**: From the noun **summa, -ae**, f.. **constare**: Present infinitive; the tense of the infinitive in indirect discourse is relative to that of the verb of saying (A.G. 584).

victoriae: Partitive genitive with **summam** (A.G. 346.a.1).

2.D CHAPTER 22: THE SIEGE OF AVARICUM RESUMES; THE GAULS MOUNT A SPIRITIED DEFENSE

(22.1-2) **Singulari militum nostrorum virtuti consilia cuiusque modi Gallorum occurrebant, ut est summae genus sollertiae atque ad omnia imitanda et efficienda quae ab quoque (2) traduntur aptissimum.**

ab, *by.*
aptus, -a, um, sup. **-issimus**, *fitted, adapted, suitable.*
consilium, -i, n., *measure, design, policy.*

et, *and.*
genus, -oris, n., *race.*

ad, *for, at, in.*
atque, *and.*
efficio, -ficere, -feci, -fectus, *accomplish, produce, make, construct.*
Galli, -orum, m., *the Gauls.*
imitor, -ari, -atus, *copy, imitate.*

miles, -itis, m., *soldier, foot-solider.*
noster, -tra, -trum, *our, our own.*

omnia, -ium, n., *all things, everything.*
quisque, quaeque, quidque, (pron.), *each one, everyone, anyone.*
singularis, -e, *singular, matchless, extraordinary.*
sum, esse, fui, futurus, *be.*
trado, -dere, -didi, -ditus, *pass on, teach, impart.*
virtus, -utis, f., *manliness, courage, bravery, valor, vigor, energy, effort.*

modus, -i, m., *manner, fashion, style.*
occurro, -currere, -curri or -cucurri, -cursurus, *match, offset.*
qui, quae, quod, *who, which, what.*
quisque, quaeque, quodque, (adj.), *every, each.*
sollertia, -ae, f., *skill, cleverness, versatility.*
summus, -a, -um, *utmost, greatest, very great.*
ut, *as.*

Singulari ... virtuti: Dative indirect object of the compound verb **occurrebant** (A.G. 370).
militum nostrorum: Possessive genitive with **virtuti** (A.G. 343). **nostrorum:** Plural, masculine, genitive possessive pronoun used as an adjective modifying **militum** (A.G. 302).
consilia: Nominative subject (A.G. 339).
cuiusque modi: Genitive of quality with **consilia** (A.G. 345). **cuiusque:** Singular, masculine, genitive indefinite (universal) pronoun used as an adjective modifying **modi** (A.G. 151.g).
Gallorum: Possessive genitive with **consilia** (A.G. 343). See Appendix A.
occurrebant: The main verb of the main clause (A.G. 278.b).
ut est ... aptissimum: The relative adverb **ut** ("as") with the indicative introduces a parenthetical remark (*OLD* **ut** 12). **est:** The main verb of the subordinate clause (A.G. 278.b). The present tense is not the historical present but denotes a state as now existing in present time (A.G. 465.1). The verb **sum** in the sense of "exist" makes a complete predicate without a predicate noun or adjective ("it is ..."). It is then called the substantive verb and regularly comes first (A.G. 284.b and 598.c). **aptissimum:** See below.
summae ... sollertiae: Genitive of quality with **genus** (A.G. 345). **summae:** Defective superlative adjective (A.G. 130.b).
genus: Nominative subject (A.G. 339).
atque: The conjunction connects the genitive modifier **summae ... sollertiae** and the adjective **aptissimum** (notice the change in construction), both modifying **genus** (A.G. 324.b).
ad omnia imitanda et efficienda: The preposition **ad** with the accusative substantive adjective and two gerundives denotes purpose or end after **aptissimum** (A.G. 385.a). **omnia:** Plural, neuter, nominative adjective used substantively (A.G. 288). **imitanda et efficienda:** Two plural, neuter, accusative gerundives used as adjectives modifying **omnia** denoting necessity, obligation or propriety (A.G. 500.1). **et:** The conjunction connects the two gerundives (A.G. 324.a). Two adjectives belonging to the same noun are regularly connected by a conjunction (A.G. 323.d).
quae ... traduntur: Relative clause (A.G. 303). **quae:** Plural, neuter, nominative relative pronoun used substantively (A.G. 305). The antecedent is **omnia** (A.G. 307). Nominative subject (A.G. 339). **traduntur:** The main verb of the subordinate clause (A.G. 278.b). The present tense is not the historical present but denotes a state as now existing in present time (A.G. 465.1).
ab quoque: Ablative of agent with the preposition **ab** after the passive verb **traduntur** (A.G. 405). **quoque:** Singular, masculine, ablative, indefinite (universal) pronoun used substantively (A.G. 151.g). The pronoun usually means "each one or everyone", but here it must be translated "anyone".
aptissimum: Singular, neuter, nominative superlative predicate adjective modifying **genus** (A.G. 124 and 285.2).

(22-2-3) Nam et laqueis falces avertebant, quas cum destinaverant tormentis introrsus reducebant, et aggerem cuniculis subtrahebant, eo scientius quod apud eos magnae sunt ferrariae atque omne genus cuniculorum (3) notum atque usitatum est.

agger, -eris, m., *rampart, ramp.*
atque, *and.*
cum, *when.*
destino, -are, -avi, -atus, *make fast, bind, stay.*
et ... et, *both ... and.*
ferraria, -ae, f., *iron mine.*
introrsus, *within, inside.*
laqueus, -i, m., *noose.*
nam, *for.*
omnis, -e, *every.*
quod, *because, since, for, as.*
scienter, comp. -ius, *expertly, skillfully, knowingly.*

sum, esse, fui, futurus, *be.*
usitatus, -a, -um, *common, familiar.*

apud, *in the country of, among.*
averto, -tere, -ti, -sus, *turn away, turn aside, avert.*
cuniculus, -i, m., *underground passage, mine.*
eo, *so much (the more).*
falx, falcis, f., *sickle-shaped hook.*
genus, -oris, n., *type, kind.*
is, ea, id, *he, she, it; that, this.*
magnus, -a, -um, *great, large.*
notus, -a, -um, *known, familiar.*
qui, quae, quod, *who, which, what.*
reduco, -ducere, -duxi, -ductus, *draw back.*
subtraho, -trahere, -traxi, -tractus, *take away, draw out, remove.*
tormentum, -i, n., *windlass.*

Nam: Causal conjunction (A.G. 223.a.3).
et ... et: The repeated conjunction means "both ... and", connecting the two main verbs **avertebant ... subtrahebant** (A.G. 323.e).
laqueis: Ablative of instrument (A.G. 409).
falces: Accusative direct object of **avertebant** (A.G. 387). "'*facles murales*, strong poles, to one end of which was fastened a heavy point for prying, with a hook for pulling stones out of the enemy's wall; whether they were usually worked by hand or by machinery is not known. In this case the Gauls caught hold of the *falces* with nooses, turned them aside, and having gotten a firm grip on them,

drew them over inside the walls by means of windlasses (*tormentis*)." (Kelsey, 407)

avertebant: The main verb of the coordinate clause **laqueis ... reducebant** (A.G. 278.a). The pronoun **ei**, with **Gallorum** as the antecedent, is understood as the subject (A.G. 271.a).

quas ... reducebant: Relative clause (A.G. 303). **quas**: Plural, feminine, accusative relative pronoun used substantively (A.G. 305). The antecedent is **falces** (A.G. 307). Accusative direct object of **reducebant** (A.G. 387). **reducebant**: The main verb of the subordinate clause (A.G. 278.b). The pronoun **ei**, with **Gallorum** as the antecedent, is understood as the subject (A.G. 271.a).

cum destinaverant: Temporal clause; the relative adverb **cum** ("when") with the pluperfect indicative defines the time at which the action of the main verb occurred (A.G. 545). **destinaverant**: The main verb of the subordinate clause (A.G. 278.b). The pronoun **ei**, with **Gallorum** as the antecedent, is understood as the subject (A.G. 271.a).

tormentis: Ablative of instrument (A.G. 409).

introrsus: Adverb (A.G. 320-21).

aggerem: Accusative direct object of **subtrahebant** (A.G. 387).

cuniculis: Ablative of instrument (A.G. 409). "Before the introduction of gunpowder, tunneling and mining of a wall, or tower, was carried out as followed: Under cover of mantlets a gallery was driven under its foundations, and a chamber excavated, the roof of which was shored up with pit props. The chamber was then filled with combustibles which, on being ignited, consumed the props; the roof then caved in and the structure above it collapsed. To frustrate this, the defenders resorted to countermining. According to Appian, when, in 72 B.C., Lucullus laid siege to Themiscyra, its inhabitants cut openings from above into the tunnels, 'and thrust bears and other wild animals and swarms of bees into them against his workers'." (Fuller, 93)

subtrahebant: The main verb of the coordinate clause **aggerem ... est** (A.G. 278.a). The pronoun **ei**, with **Gallorum** as the antecedent, is understood as the subject (A.G. 271.a).

eo scientius: Ablative of degree of difference with a comparative adverb meaning "the more expertly" (A.G. 414 Note). **eo**: Singular, neuter, ablative demonstrative pronoun used as an adverb and meaning "so much" (the more) (*OLD* eo3 2). **scientius**: Comparative adverb (A.G. 218).

quod ... sunt ... est: Causal clause; the conjunction **quod** ("because") takes the indicative when the reason is given on the authority of the writer or speaker (A.G. 540.1). **sunt ... est**: The main verbs of the subordinate clause (A.G. 278.b). The present tense is not the historical present but denotes a state as now existing in present time (A.G. 465.1).

apud eos: Prepositional phrase, **apud** with the accusative here means "in the country of" (*OLD* apud 5). **eos**: Plural, masculine, accusative demonstrative pronoun used substantively (A.G. 296.2). The antecedent is **Gallorum** (A.G. 297.e).

magnae: Plural, feminine, nominative predicate adjective modifying **ferrariae** after **sunt** (A.G. 283-84).

ferrariae: Nominative subject (A.G. 339).

atque: The conjunction connects the two main verbs in the causal clause **sunt ... est** (A.G. 324.b).

omne genus: Nominative subject (A.G. 339).

cuniculorum: Partitive genitive with **genus** (A.G. 346.a.1).

notum: Singular, neuter, nominative predicate adjective modifying **genus** after **est** (A.G. 283-84).

atque: The conjunction connects the two adjectives **notum ... usitatum** (A.G. 324.b). Two adjectives belonging to the same noun are regularly connected by a conjunction (A.G. 323.d).

usitatum: Singular, neuter, nominative predicate adjective modifying **genus** after **est** (A.G. 283-84).

(22.3) **Totum autem murum ex omni parte turribus contabulaverant atque has coriis intexerant.**

atque, *and.*	**autem**, *moreover.*
contabulo, -are, -avi, -atus, *cover.*	**corium, -i**, n., *thick skin, hide.*
ex, *on.*	**hic, haec, hoc**, *this; he, she, it.*
intego, -tegere, -texi, -tectus, *cover, cover over.*	**murus, -i**, m., *wall, rampart.*
omnis, -e, *every.*	**pars, partis**, f., *side.*
totus, -a, -um, *the whole of, all.*	**turris, -is**, f., *tower.*

Totum ... murum: Accusative direct object **contabulaverant** (A.G. 387).

autem: Postpositive conjunction (A.G. 324.j and 599.b).

ex omni parte: Ablative of *position* with the preposition **ex** (A.G. 429.b).

turribus: Ablative of means (A.G. 409). "The towers were built of wood, and two or more stories in height above the wall." (Kelsey, 407) "It is not clear why the Gauls built towers all along their walls, as Caesar was not encircling their town (7.17)." (Hammond, 238)

contabulaverant: The main verb of the coordinate clause **Totum ... contabulaverant** (A.G. 278.a). The pronoun **ei**, with **Gallorum** as the antecedent, is understood as the subject (A.G. 271.a). Although the pluperfect tense is normally used in subordinate clauses, its use as a main verb is frequent. The pluperfect tense of the verb denotes an action completed in past time (A.G. 477).

atque: The conjunction connects the two main verbs **contabulaverant ... intexerant** (A.G. 324.b).

has: Plural, feminine, accusative demonstrative pronoun used substantively (A.G. 296.2). The antecedent is **turribus** (A.G. 297.e). Accusative direct object of **intexerant** (A.G. 387).

coriis: Ablative of instrument (A.G. 409). "The hides were put on to protect the towers against the firebrands of the besiegers." (Kelsey, 407)

intexerant: The main verb of the coordinate clause **has ... intexerant** (A.G. 278.a). The pronoun **ei**, with **Gallorum** as the antecedent, is understood as the subject (A.G. 271.a). Although the pluperfect tense is normally used in subordinate clauses, its use as a main verb is frequent. The pluperfect tense of the verb denotes an action completed in past time (A.G. 477).

(22.4-5) **(4)** Tum crebris diurnis nocturnisque eruptionibus aut aggeri ignem inferebant aut milites occupatos in opere adoriebantur et nostrarum turrium altitudinem, quantum has cotidianus agger expresserat, commissis suarum turrium **(5)** malis adaequabant et apertos cuniculos praeusta et praeacuta materia et pice fervefacta et maximi ponderis saxis morabantur moenibusque appropinquare prohibebant.

adaequo, -are, -avi, -atus, *make equal to, bring up to a level with.*
agger, -eris, m., *rampart, ramp.*
aperio, -perire, -perui, -pertus, *open.*

aut ... aut, *either ... or.*

cotidianus, -a, -um, *daily.*
cuniculus, -i, m., *underground passage, mine.*
eruptio, -onis, f., *a bursting forth, sally, sortie.*
exprimo, -primere, -pressi, -pressus, *raise, increase.*

hic, haec, hoc, *this; he, she, it.*
in, *engaged or occupied in.*
malus, -i, m., *upright pole, beam, mast.*
maximus, -a, -um, *greatest, very great, largest, very large.*
moenia, -ium, n., pl., *walls, fortifications.*
nocturnus, -a, -um, *by night, of night.*
occupo, -are, -avi, -atus, *engage, occupy.*
pix, picis, f., *pitch.*
praeacutus, -a, -um, *sharpened at the end, sharpened, pointed.*
prohibeo, -hibere, -hibui, -hibitus, *prevent, hinder.*
-que, *and.*
suus, -a, -um, *their,* with or without *own.*
turris, -is, f., *tower.*

adorior, -oriri, -ortus, *attack, assail, assault.*
altitudo, -onis, f., *height, depth.*
appropinquo, -are, -avi, -atus, *approach, come near, draw near.*
committo, -mittere, -misi, -missus, *join, bring together, connect.*
creber, -bra, -brum, *numerous, frequent.*
diurnus, -a, -um, *of the day, by day.*
et, *and.*
fervefacio, -facere, -feci, -factus, *make hot, heat, make red-hot.*
ignis, -is, m., *fire.*
infero, -ferre, intuli, illatus, *throw upon, apply, set.*
materia, -ae, f., *timber, wood.*
miles, -itis, m., *soldier, foot-solider.*
moror, -ari, -atus, *hinder, delay, impede.*
noster, -tra, -trum, *our, our own.*
opus, operis, n., *work, labor.*
pondus, ponderis, n., *heaviness, weight.*
praeustus, -a, -um, *burnt at the end* (to make it hard).
quantum, *to what extent.*
saxum, -i, n., *stone, rock.*
tum, *then, at that time.*

Tum ... prohibebat: The basic structure of this sentence is: **aut ... inferebant aut ... adoriebantur et ... adaequabant et ... morabantur -que ... prohibebant.**
Tum: Adverb (A.G. 217.b and 320-21).
crebris diurnis nocturnisque eruptionibus: Ablative of *time within which* (A.G. 423.1). **-que:** The enclitic conjunction connects the two adjectives **diurnis nocturnis** (A.G. 324.a). Two adjectives belonging to the same noun are regularly connected by a conjunction (A.G. 323.d).**aut ... aut:** The double connective introduces two logically exclusive alternatives (**inferebant ... adoriebantur**) and means "either ... or" (*OLD* **aut** 1).
aggeri: Dative indirect object of the transitive verb **inferebant** (A.G. 362)
ignem: Accusative direct object of the transitive verb **inferebant** (A.G. 387).
inferebant: The main verb of the coordinate clause **Tum ... inferebant** (A.G. 278.a). The pronoun **ei,** with **Gallorum** as the antecedent, is understood as the subject (A.G. 271.a).
milites occupatos: Accusative direct object of **adoriebantur** (A.G. 387). **occupatos:** Accusative, perfect, passive, participle used as a predicate, where in English a phrase or a subordinate clause would be more normal (A.G. 496).
in opere: Prepositional phrase, **in** with the ablative here means "engaged or occupied in" (*OLD* **in** 39).
adoriebantur: The main verb of the coordinate clause **milites ... adoriebantur** (A.G. 278.a). The pronoun **ei,** with **Gallorum** as the antecedent, is understood as the subject (A.G. 271.a).
et: The conjunction connects the main verbs **adoriebantur ... adaequabant** (A.G. 324.a).
nostrarum turrium: Possessive genitive with **altitudinem** (A.G. 343). **nostrarum:** Plural, feminine, genitive possessive pronoun used as an adjective modifying **turrium** (A.G. 302).
altitudinem: Accusative direct object of **adaequabant** (A.G. 387).
quantum ... expresserat: Relative clause (A.G. 279.a). **quantum:** Relative adverb meaning "to what extent" (*OLD* **quantum2** B.2).
expresserat: The main verb of the subordinate clause (A.G. 278.b). The pluperfect tense of the verb denotes an action completed in past time (A.G. 477).
has: Plural, feminine, accusative demonstrative pronoun used substantively (A.G. 296.2). The antecedent is **turrium** (A.G. 297.e). Accusative direct object of **expresserat** (A.G. 387).
cotidianus agger: Nominative subject (A.G. 339).
commissis ... malis: Ablative of means (A.G. 409). "'by building up between the cornerposts of their towers.' When the Gauls erected a tower on the walls they left the upright posts at the corners at full length, projecting above the stories at first built; the height could readily be increased, as circumstances might demand, by laying crosspieces above, between these corner-posts already in position." (Kelsey, 407) **commissis:** Ablative, perfect, passive, participle used as a predicate, where in English a phrase or a subordinate clause would be more normal (A.G. 496).
suarum turrium: Possessive genitive with **malis** (A.G. 343). **suarum:** Plural, feminine, genitive possessive pronoun used as an adjective modifying **turrium** (A.G. 302). **malis:** From the noun **malus, -i,** m. meaning "pole, beam" (*OLD* **malus3** 1).
adaequabant: The main verb of the coordinate clause **nostrarum ... adaequabant** (A.G. 278.a). The pronoun **ei,** with **Gallorum** as

the antecedent, is understood as the subject (A.G. 271.a).

et: The conjunction connects the two verbs **adaequabant ... morabantur** (A.G. 324.a).

apertos cuniculos: Accusative direct object of **morabantur** (A.G. 387). **apertos**: Accusative, perfect, passive participle used as a predicate, where in English a phrase or a subordinate clause would be more normal (A.G. 496).

praeusta et praeacuta materia: Ablative of instrument (A.G. 409). **et**: The conjunction connects the two adjective modifying **materia** (A.G. 324.a). Two adjectives belonging to the same noun are regularly connected by a conjunction (A.G. 323.d).

et: The conjunction connects the ablatives **materia ... pice** (A.G. 324.a).

pice fervefacta: Ablative of instrument (A.G. 409). **fervefacta**: Ablative, perfect, passive, participle used as an adjective modifying **pice** (A.G. 494).

et: The conjunction connects the two ablative nouns **pice** and **saxis** (A.G. 324.a).

saxis: Ablative of instrument (A.G. 409).

maximi ponderis: Genitive of quality with **saxis** (A.G. 345). **maximi**: Irregular superlative adjective (A.G. 129).

morabantur: The main verb of the coordinate clause **apertos ... morabantur** (A.G. 278.a). The pronoun **ei**, with **Gallorum** as the antecedent, is understood as the subject (A.G. 271.a).

moenibusque: Dative indirect object of the intransitive infinitive **appropinquare** (A.G. 370 and 451.3). **-que**: The enclitic conjunction connects the two main verbs **morabantur ... prohibebant** (A.G. 324.a). The conjunction is used to connect the last member of a series (A.G. 323.c.3).

(nostros) appropinquare: Subject accusative with the infinitive after **prohibebant** (A.G. 558.b Note). Supply **nostros** ("our men") as the accusative subject.

prohibebant: The main verb of the coordinate clause **moenibusque ... prohibebant** (A.G. 278.a). The pronoun **ei**, with **Gallorum** as the antecedent, is understood as the subject (A.G. 271.a).

2.E CHAPTER 23: A DESCRIPTION OF THE CONSTRUCTION OF GALLIC WALLS

(23.1) **Muri autem omnes Gallici hac fere forma sunt.**

autem, *and now*, *moreover*.
forma, -ae, f., *shape, form*.
hic, haec, hoc, *this*; *he, she, it*.
omnis, -e, *all*.

fere, *for the most part, as a rule, usually, generally*.
Gallicus, -a, -um, *of Gaul, Gallic*.
murus, -i, m., *wall*.
sum, esse, fui, futurus, *be*.

Muri ... omnes Gallici: Nominative subject (A.G. 339).

autem: Postpositive conjunction (A.G. 324.j and 599.b).

hac ... forma: Ablative of quality (descriptive ablative) with an adjective modifier (A.G. 415). **hac**: Singular, feminine, ablative demonstrative pronoun used as an adjective modifying **forma** (A.G. 296.1 and a).

fere: Adverb (A.G. 320-21).

sunt: The main verb of the simple sentence (A.G. 278.1). The present tense in this chapter is not the historical present but denotes the action as now existing in present time (A.G. 465.1).

(23.1-2) **Trabes directae perpetuae in longitudinem paribus intervallis di(2)stantes inter se binos pedes in solo collocantur.**

bini, -ae, -a, *two each*.
directus, -a, -um, *standing at right angles*.

in, *in, in respect to*; *on*.
intervallum, -i, n., *interval, space, distance*.

par, paris, *like, similar, same, equal*.

pes, pedis, m., *foot*, = .9708 of the English foot.
sui, sibi, se, or **sese**, nom. wanting, *each other, themselves*.

colloco, -are, -avi, -atus, *place, set, post, station*.
disto, -are, -----, -----, *stand apart, be separated, be distant*.
inter, *between*.
longitudo, -inis, f., *length*, (with **in**), *lengthwise, longitudinally*.
perpetuus, -a, -um, *placed at regular intervals throughout the length*.
solum, -i, n., *lowest part, ground*.
trabs, trabis, f., *beam, timber*.

This sentence can be rewritten as: **in solo trabes collocantur, directae, perpetuae in longitudinem paribus intervallis, distantes inter se binos pedes** and literally translated as "on the ground beams are located, standing at right angles, placed lengthwise at equal intervals, separated from each other by the extent of two feet each."

Trabes directae perpetuae ... distantes: Nominative subject (A.G. 339). **directae perpetuae**: Two predicate adjectives modifying **Trabes** (A.G. 285.2). Two adjectives belonging to the same noun are regularly connected by a conjunction, but not here (A.G. 323.d). **directae**: The adjective here has the specialized meaning of "standing at right angles" (*OLD* **directus** 2). **perpetuae**: The adjective here has the specialized meaning of "placed at regular intervals throughout the length of anything" (*OLD* **perpetuus** 1.b). **distantes**: Present participle used as an adjective modifying **Trabes** (A.G. 494.a).

in longitudinem: Prepositional phrase, **in** with the accusative of **longitudo** means "lengthwise, longitudinally" (*OLD* **longitudo** 1.c).

paribus intervallis: Ablative of *place where* after **collocantur** (A.G. 430).

inter se: Prepositional phrase, **inter** with the accusative reflexive pronoun here expresses distance apart and means "between" (*OLD* **inter** 1 9.c). **se**: Plural, feminine, accusative direct reflexive pronoun (A.G. 300.1). The antecedent is **Trabes** (A.G. 299).

binos pedes: Accusative of *extent of space* (A.G. 425). **binos**: Distributive numeral used as an adjective (A.G. 136-37).

in solo: Ablative of *place where* with the preposition **in** (locative ablative) (A.G. 426.3).
collocantur: The main verb of the simple sentence (A.G. 278.1).

(23.2-3) Hae revinciuntur introrsus et multo aggere vestiuntur; ea autem quae diximus intervalla grandibus in fronte saxis (3) effarciuntur.

agger, -eris, m., *dirt, rubble, earth.*	**autem**, *and now, moreover.*
dico, dicere, dixi, dictus, *say.*	**effarcio, -ire, -----, effertus**, *stop up, fill.*
et, *and.*	**frons, frontis**, f., *front, face, façade.*
grandis, -e, *large, great.*	**hic, haec, hoc**, *this; he, she, it.*
in, *on.*	**intervallum, -i**, n., *interval, space, distance.*
introrsus, *within, inside.*	**is, ea, id**, *he, she, it; that, this.*
multus, -a, -um, *much, considerable, extensive.*	**qui, quae, quod**, *who, which, what.*
revincio, -vincire, -vinxi, -vinctus, *bind back, bind, fasten.*	**saxum, -i**, n., *stone, rock.*
vestio, -ire, -ivi, -itus, *cover.*	

Hae: Plural, feminine, nominative demonstrative pronoun used substantively (A.G. 296.2). The antecedent is **Trabes** (A.G. 297.e). Nominative subject of **revinciuntur ... vestiuntur** (A.G. 339).
revinciuntur: The main verb of the coordinate clause **Hae ... introrsus** (A.G. 278.a).
introrsus: Adverb (A.G. 320-21).
et: The conjunction connects the two main verbs **revinciuntur ... vestiuntur** (A.G. 324.a).
multo aggere: Ablative of means (A.G. 409). **aggere**: The noun here does not mean the usual "rampart", but "material for a mound, dirt, rubble" (*OLD* **agger** 1).
vestiuntur: The main verb of the coordinate clause **multo ... vestiuntur** (A.G. 278.a).
ea ... intervalla: Nominative subject (A.G. 339). **ea**: Plural, neuter, nominative demonstrative pronoun used as an adjective modifying **intervalla** (A.G. 296.1 and a).
autem: Postpositive conjunction (A.G. 324.j and 599.b).
quae diximus: Relative clause (A.G. 303). For the reference see immediately above at 23.1-2. **quae**: Plural, neuter, accusative relative pronoun used substantively (A.G. 305). The antecedent is **intervalla** (A.G. 307). Accusative direct object of **diximus** (A.G. 387). **diximus**: The main verb of the subordinate clause (A.G. 278.b). The personal pronoun **nos** is understood as the subject but is not expressed except for distinction or emphasis (A.G. 295.a). In Book 7, Caesar refers to himself only in the third person, either in the singular or occasionally in the plural (see **Caesar** at 1.1). Siedler counts 11 uses of the first person plural in Book 7 (Siedler, 46). These uses are at 17.1, 23.2, 25.1, 37.1, 48.1, 58.4, 70.1, 76.1, 79.2, 83.8, and 85.4.
grandibus ... saxis: Ablative of means or instrument (A.G. 409).
in fronte: Ablative of *place where* with the preposition **in** (locative ablative) (A.G. 426.3).
effarciuntur: The main verb of the main clause (A.G. 278.b).

(23.3-4) His collocatis et coagmentatis alius insuper ordo additur, ut idem illud intervallum servetur neque inter se contingant trabes sed paribus intermissae spatiis (4) singulae singulis saxis interiectis arte contineantur.

addo, -dere, -didi, -ditus, *add, join, lay on.*	**alius, -a, -ud**, *another.*
arte, *closely, tightly.*	**coagmento, -are, -avi, -atus**, *fasten together, connect.*
colloco, -are, -avi, -atus, *place, set.*	**contineo, -tinere, -tinui, -tentus**, *hold back, keep, retain.*
contingo, -tingere, -tigi, -tactus, *touch, extend to, reach.*	**et**, *and.*
hic, haec, hoc, *this; he, she, it.*	**idem, eadem, idem**, *the same.*
ille, illae, illud, *that; he, she, it.*	**insuper**, *above, on top.*
inter, *with, to.*	**intericio, -icere, -ieci, -iectus**, *place between, put between.*
intermitto, -mittere, -misi, -missus, *leave unoccupied, leave vacant.*	**intervallum, -i**, n., *interval, space, distance.*
neque, *and ... not.*	**ordo, -inis**, m., *layer.*
par, paris, *like, similar, same, equal.*	**saxum, -i**, n., *stone, rock.*
sed, *but.*	**servo, -are, -avi, -atus**, *keep, maintain, retain.*
singuli, -ae, -a, *separate, single.*	**spatium, -i**, n., *space, distance.*
sui, sibi, se, or **sese**, nom. wanting, *each other, one another.*	**trabs, trabis**, f., *beam, timber.*
ut, *so that.*	

His collocatis et coagmentatis: Ablative absolute (A.G. 419-20). **His**: Plural, feminine, ablative demonstrative pronoun used substantively (A.G. 296.2). The antecedent is **trabes** (A.G. 297.e). **collocatis ... coagmentatis**: The perfect tense of the participles represents the action as completed at the time indicated by the tense of the main verb (A.G. 489). **et**: The conjunction connects the two ablative participles (A.G. 324.a). Two adjectives belonging to the same noun are regularly connected by a conjunction (A.G. 323.d).
alius ... ordo: Nominative subject (A.G. 339).
insuper: Adverb (A.G. 320-21).

additur: The main verb of the main clause (A.G. 278.b).

ut ... servetur ... contingant ... contineantur: The conjunction **ut** ("so that") with the subjunctive forms a clause of result dependent on **additur** (A.G. 537.1). **servetur ... contingant ... contineantur**: The main verbs of the subordinate clause (A.G. 278.b). Present subjunctives; the tense of the subjunctives is in primary sequence and follows the rules for the sequence of tense after **additur** (A.G. 482-85).

idem illud intervallum: Nominative subject (A.G. 339). **idem**: Singular, neuter, nominative demonstrative pronoun used as an adjective modifying **intervallum** (A.G. 296.1 and a and 298.c). **illud**: Singular, neuter, nominative demonstrative pronoun used as an adjective modifying **intervallum** (A.G. 296.1 and a).

neque: The conjunction here joins the two verbs in the result clause **servetur ... contingant** and means "and ... not" (*OLD* **neque** 3).

inter se: Prepositional phrase, **inter** with the accusative reflexive pronoun here expresses mutual contact and means "with or to each other" (*OLD* **inter**1 15). **se**: Plural, feminine, accusative direct reflexive pronoun (A.G. 300.1). The antecedent is **trabes** (A.G. 299).

trabes: Nominative subject of **contingant ... contineantur** (A.G. 339). The subject is in the last position (A.G. 597.b).

sed: Coordinate conjunction connecting the two verbs in the result clause **contingant ... contineantur** (A.G. 324.d).

spatiis singulae singulis saxis: Notice the 's' alliteration (A.G. 641).

paribus ... spatiis: Ablative of degree of difference after **intermissae**; when distance is considered as degree of difference, it is put in the ablative (A.G. 425.b).

intermissae ... singulae: Nominative subject (A.G. 339). **intermissae**: Nominative, perfect, passive, participle used as a predicate, where in English a phrase or a subordinate clause would be more normal (A.G. 496). **singulae**: Distributive numeral used substantively (A.G. 136-37 and 288). The noun **trabes** is understood (A.G. 288.b).

singulis saxis interiectis: Ablative of means (A.G. 409). **singulis**: Distributive numeral used as an adjective modifying **saxis** (A.G. 136-37). **interiectis**: Ablative, perfect, passive, participle used as a predicate, where in English a phrase or a subordinate clause would be more normal (A.G. 496).

arte: Adverb (A.G. 214.a and 320-21).

(23.4-5) Sic deinceps omne opus contexitur, dum iusta muri altitudo (5) expleatur.

altitudo, -onis, f., *height, depth.*	**contexo, -texere, -texui, -textus**, *bind together, join.*
deinceps, *one after the other, in succession, in turn.*	**dum**, *until.*
expleo, -plere, -plevi, -pletus, *fill up, fill full, fill out, complete.*	**iustus, -a, -um**, *proper, suitable, due.*
murus, -i, m., *wall, rampart.*	**omnis, -e**, *the whole.*
opus, operis, n., *work, structure.*	**sic**, *so, in this way, thus.*

Sic: Adverb (A.G. 217.c and 320-21).

deinceps: Adverb (A.G. 217.b and 320-21).

omne opus: Nominative subject (A.G. 339).

contexitur: The main verb of the main clause (A.G. 278.b).

dum ... expleatur: Temporal clause; the conjunction **dum** ("until") takes the present subjunctive (A.G. 553). **expleatur**: The main verb of the subordinate clause (A.G. 278.b).

iusta ... altitudo: Nominative subject (A.G. 339).

muri: Possessive genitive with **altitudo** (A.G. 343).

(23.5) Hoc cum in speciem varietatemque opus deforme non est, alternis trabibus ac saxis quae rectis lineis suos ordines servant, tum ad utilitatem et defensionem urbium summam habet opportunitatem, quod et ab incendio lapis et ab ariete materia defendit, quae perpetuis trabibus pedes quadragenos plerumque introrsus revincta neque perrumpi neque distrahi potest.

ab, *from.*	**ac**, *and.*
ad, *for the purpose of, to be used for.*	**alternus, -a, -um**, *in turn, alternate.*
aries, -ietis, m., *battering-ram.*	**cum ... tum**, *not only ----- but also, both ----- and.*
defendo, -fendere, -fensi, -fensus, *defend, guard, protect.*	**defensio, -onis**, f., *defense.*
deformis, -e, *ugly, unsightly.*	**distraho, -trahere, -traxi, -tractus**, *wrench asunder, pull apart.*
et, *and*; **et ... et**, *both ... and.*	**habeo, habere, habui, habitus**, *have.*
hic, haec, hoc, *this*; *he, she, it.*	**in**, *in reference to, respecting, regarding.*
incendium, -i, n., *fire, conflagration.*	**introrsus**, *within, inside.*
lapis, -idis, m., *stone.*	**linea, -ae**, f., *line.*
materia, -ae, f., *timber, wood.*	**neque ... neque**, *neither ... nor.*
non, *not.*	**opportunitas, -atis**, f., *fitness, advantage, suitableness.*
opus, operis, n., *work, structure.*	**ordo, -inis**, m., *layer.*
perpetuus, -a, -um, *placed at regular intervals throughout the length.*	**perrumpo, -rumpere, -rupi, -ruptus**, *break or burst through.*
pes, pedis, m., *foot*, = .9708 of the English foot.	**plerumque**, *commonly, generally, usually, for the most part.*
possum, posse, potui, -----, *be able.*	**quadrageni, -ae, -a**, *forty each, forty in each case.*

-que, *and.*

quod, *because, since, for, as.*

revincio, -vincire, -vinxi, -vinctus, *bind back, bind, fasten.*

servo, -are, -avi, -atus, *keep, maintain, retain.*

sum, esse, fui, futurus, *be.*

suus, -a, -um, *their,* with or without *own,* i.e. *proper.*

tum (with cum), *both ----- and, not only ----- but also.*

utilitas, -atis, f., *advantage, service, benefit.*

qui, quae, quod, *who, which, what.*

rectus, -a, -um, *straight, direct.*

saxum, -i, n., *stone, rock.*

species, -iei, f., *sight, show, appearance.*

summus, -a, -um, *utmost, greatest, very great.*

trabs, trabis, f., *beam, timber.*

urbs, urbis, f., *city.*

varietas, -atis, f., *variety, diversity.*

Hoc ... opus: Nominative subject of est ... habet (A.G. 339). Hoc: Singular, neuter, nominative demonstrative pronoun used as an adjective modifying opus (A.G. 296.1 and a).

cum ... tum: A relative and demonstrative adverb used correlatively as conjunctions meaning "not only ... but also" (A.G. 323.g).

cum ... est: Relative clause (A.G. 279.a). est: The main verb of the subordinate clause (A.G. 278.b).

in speciem varietatemque: Prepositional phrase, in with the accusative here means "in reference to, respecting, regarding" (*OLD* in 17). -que: The enclitic conjunction connects the two accusative nouns in the prepositional phrase (A.G. 324.a).

deforme: Singular, neuter, nominative predicate adjective modifying opus after est (A.G. 283-84).

non: Adverb, the adverb generally precedes the verb if it belongs to no one word in particular (A.G. 217.e, 320-21, and 599.a).

alternis trabibus ac saxis: Two ablatives of quality (descriptive ablative) with an adjective modifier (A.G. 415). ac: The conjunction connects the two ablative nouns and means "and" (*OLD* atque 12).

quae ... servant: Relative clause (A.G. 303). quae: Plural, neuter, nominative relative pronoun used substantively (A.G. 305). The antecedent is trabibus ac saxis, agreeing in gender with the nearest noun, saxis (A.G. 305.a). Nominative subject (A.G. 387).

servant: The main verb of the subordinate clause (A.G. 278.b).

rectis lineis: Ablative of quality (descriptive ablative) with an adjective modifier (A.G. 415). The phrase recta linea means "in a straight line" (*OLD* linea 2.b).

suos ordines: Accusative direct object of servant (A.G. 387). suos: Plural, masculine, accusative possessive pronoun used as an adjective modifying ordines (A.G. 302). Here suus means "proper" (*OLD* suus 12).

tum: See above at cum.

ad utilitatem et defensionem urbium: Prepositional phrase, ad with the accusative here denotes purpose meaning "for the purpose of, to be used for" (*OLD* ad 44). et: The conjunction connects the two accusative nouns in the prepositional phrase (A.G. 324.a).

urbium: Objective genitive with defensionem (A.G. 348).

summam ... opportunitatem: Accusative direct object of habet (A.G. 387). summam: Irregular superlative adjective (A.G. 130.b). habet: The main verb of the main clause (A.G. 278.b).

quod ... defendit: Causal clause; the conjunction quod ("because") takes the indicative when the reason is given on the authority of the writer or speaker (A.G. 540.1). defendit: The main verb of the subordinate clause (A.G. 278.b). Two singular subjects normally take a verb in the plural (A.G. 317). Here, the verb is singular as the two subjects (lapis ... materia) are connected by disjunctives (et ... et) (A.G. 317.b). The noun urbem is understood as the accusative direct object.

et ... et: The repeated conjunctions mean "both ... and", connecting the two nominative nouns lapis ... materia (A.G. 323.e).

ab incendio: Ablative of separation with the preposition ab after defendit (A.G. 402).

lapis: First nominative subject of defendit (A.G. 339).

ab ariete: Ablative of separation with the preposition ab after defendit (A.G. 402). ariete: "The ram (*aries*), *par excellence* 'the siege gun' of antiquity, was a beam which resembled a ship's mast crowned with an iron head or beak; it was worked either from within a large penthouse, or, as already described, from the ground floor of a moveable tower. It was swung from chains suspended from the roof of its shelter, and when required to span an intervening ditch or moat, was sometimes over 100 feet in length. Appian records that, in 149 B.C., the Romans used a ram against Carthage which required 6,000 men to bring it into action." (Fuller, 93)

materia: Second nominative subject of defendit (A.G. 339).

quae ... potest: Relative clause (A.G. 303). quae: See below. potest: The main verb of the subordinate clause (A.G. 278.b).

quae ... revincta: Nominative subject (A.G. 339). quae: Singular, feminine, nominative relative pronoun used substantively (A.G. 305). The antecedent is materia (A.G. 307). revincta: Nominative, perfect, passive, participle used as a predicate, where in English a phrase or a subordinate clause would be more normal (A.G. 496).

perpetuis trabibus: Ablative of means (A.G. 409).

pedes quadragenos: Accusative of *extent of space* (A.G. 425). quadragenos: Distributive numeral used as an adjective (A.G. 136-37).

plerumque: Adverb modifying pedes (A.G. 320-21).

introrsus: Adverb modifying revincta (A.G. 320-21).

neque ... neque: The repeated conjunction means "neither ... nor", connecting the two complementary infinitives (*OLD* neque 7).

perrumpi: Complementary infinitive after potest (A.G. 456).

distrahi: Complementary infinitive after potest (A.G. 456).

2.F CHAPTERS 24-28: THE SIEGE OF AVARICUM CONTINUES; THE GAULS RESIST BRAVELY; AVARICUM IS TAKEN AND SACKED, THE INHABITANTS ARE PUT TO THE SWORD IN A FEARFUL SLAUGHTER

(24.1-2) His tot rebus impedita oppugnatione milites, cum toto tempore frigore et assiduis imbribus tardarentur, tamen continenti labore omnia haec superaverunt et diebus XXV aggerem latum pedes CCCXXX, altum pedes LXXX ex(2)struxerunt.

agger, -eris, m., *rampart, ramp.*
assiduus, -a, -um, *continuous, constant, incessant.*
continens, -entis, *continuous, uninterrupted, continual.*
dies, -ei, m. and f., *day.*
exstruo, -struere, -struxi, -structus, *rear, build, make.*
hic, haec, hoc, *this; he, she, it.*
impedio, -pedire, -pedivi, -peditus, *hinder, obstruct.*
labor, -oris, m., *toil, exertion, labor.*
miles, -itis, m., *soldier, foot-solider.*
oppugnatio, -onis, f., *assault, attack, siege.*
res, rei, f., *matter, affair, event, circumstance.*
tamen, *yet, still, for all that, nevertheless, however.*
tempus, -oris, n., *time.*
totus, -a, -um, *the whole of, the entire.*
X, in expression of number, = *10.*

altus, -a, -um, *high, tall.*
C, in expression of number, = *100.*
cum, *although.*
et, *and.*
frigus, frigoris, n., *cold, cold weather.*
imber, imbris, m., *rain, rain storm.*
L, in expression of number, *50.*
latus, -a, -um, *broad, wide.*
omnis, -e, *all.*
pes, pedis, m., *foot,* = .9708 of the English foot.
supero, -are, -avi, -atus, *surmount, overcome.*
tardo, -are, -avi, -atus, *check, impede, hinder.*
tot, *so many.*
V, in expression of number, = *5.*

His tot rebus impedita oppugnatione: Ablative absolute (A.G. 419-20). **His tot rebus**: Ablative of cause without a preposition (A.G. 404). This refers back to the difficulties described in Chapter 22. **His**: Plural, feminine, ablative demonstrative pronoun used as an adjective modifying **rebus** (A.G. 296.1 and a). **tot**: Indeclinable adjective modifying **rebus** (*OLD* tot). **impedita**: The perfect tense of the participle represents the action as completed at the time indicated by the tense of the main verb (A.G. 489).
milites: Nominative subject of **superaverunt ... exstruxerunt** (A.G. 339).
cum ... tardarentur: Concessive clause, the relative adverb **cum** ("although") with the subjunctive here forms a concessive clause (A.G. 549). **tardarentur**: The main verb of the subordinate clause (A.G. 278.b). Imperfect subjunctive; the tense of the subjunctive is in secondary sequence and follows the rules for the sequence of tense after **superaverunt** (A.G. 482-85). The pronoun **ei**, with **milites** as the antecedent, is understood as the subject (A.G. 271.a).
toto tempore: Ablative expressing *duration of time* (A.G. 424.b).
frigore et assiduis imbribus: Two ablatives of cause without a preposition (A.G. 404). **et**: The conjunction connects the two ablative nouns (A.G. 324.a).
tamen: Adverb, correlative to the previous concessive clause meaning "nevertheless" (*OLD* tamen 3). The adverb is often postpositive, but not here (A.G. 320-21 and 324.j).
continenti labore: Ablative of means (A.G. 409). **continenti**: Present participle of **contineo** used as an adjective modifying **labore** (A.G. 494). Participles used as adjectives regularly end in -i in the ablative singular (A.G. 121.a.2).
omnia haec: Accusative direct object of **superaverunt** (A.G. 387). **haec**: Plural, neuter, accusative demonstrative pronoun used substantively meaning "these things" (A.G. 296.2). The antecedent is the difficulties mentioned above in Chapter 22 (A.G. 297.e).
superaverunt: The main verb of the coordinate clause **His ... superaverunt** (A.G. 278.a).
et: The conjunction connects the two main verbs **superaverunt ... exstruxerunt** (A.G. 324.a).
diebus XXV: Ablative of *time within which* (A.G. 423.1). **XXV**: Roman numeral used as an adjective (A.G. 133).
aggerem latum ... altum: Accusative direct object of **exstruxerunt** (A.G. 387). **latum ... altum**: Two predicate adjectives modifying **aggerem** (A.G. 285.2). "The greatness of the dimensions given has led some to doubt whether the figures are correct; but in view of the number of men which Caesar now had at his command, there is nothing improbable in the statement of the text as it stands. We are not told how long the agger was." (Kelsey, 408)
pedes CCCXXX: Accusative of *extent of space* with **aggerem latum** (A.G. 425). **CCCXXX**: Roman numeral used as an adjective (A.G. 133).
pedes LXXX: Accusative of *extent of space* with **aggerem ... altum** (A.G. 425). **LXXX**: Roman numeral used as an adjective (A.G. 133).
exstruxerunt: The main verb of the coordinate clause **diebus ... exstruxerunt** (A.G. 278.a).

(24.2-3) **Cum is murum hostium paene contingeret et Caesar ad opus consuetudine excubaret militesque hortaretur ne quod omnino tempus ab opere intermitteretur, paulo ante tertiam vigiliam est animadversum fumare (3) aggerem, quem cuniculo hostes succenderant;**

ab, *from.*
agger, -eris, m., *rampart, ramp.*
ante, *before.*
consuetudo, -inis, f., *habit, practice, custom, usage.*

cum, *when, while.*
et, *and.*

fumo, -are, -----, -----, *smoke.*

hostis, -is, m., *enemy, foe*; pl., *the enemy.*

is, ea, id, *he, she, it; that, this.*

ad, *at, near, beside.*
animadverto, -tere, -ti, -sus, *notice, observe, perceive.*
Caesar, -aris, m., *Caesar.*
contingo, -tingere, -tigi, -tactus, *touch, extend to, reach.*
cuniculus, -i, m., *underground passage, mine.*
excubo, -cubare, -cubui, -cubitus, *lie out of doors, keep watch, keep guard.*
hortor, -ari, -atus, *urge, encourage, exhort, incite, press.*
intermitto, -mittere, -misi, -missus, *leave off, discontinue, interrupt.*
miles, -itis, m., *soldier, foot-solider.*

murus, -i, m., *wall, rampart.*
omnino, (after a neg.), *at all.*

paene, *almost, nearly.*
-que, *and.*
quis, -----, quid, *any;* (as adj., qui, quae, or qua, quod).

tempus, -oris, n., *time.*
vigilia, -ae, f., *watch.*

ne, *so that ... not.*
opus, operis, n., *works, line of works, fortification; work, labor.*
paulo, *a little, just a little.*
qui, quae, quod, *who, which, what.*
succendo, -cendere, -cendi, -census, *set on fire, set fire to.*
tertius, -a, um, *third.*

Cum ... contingeret ... excubaret ... hortaretur: Temporal clause; the relative adverb **cum** ("when, while") with the imperfect subjunctive describes the circumstances that accompanied the action of the main verb (A.G. 546). **contingeret ... excubaret ... hortaretur:** The main verbs of the subordinate clause (A.G. 278.b).
is: Singular, masculine, nominative demonstrative pronoun used substantively (A.G. 296.2). The antecedent is **aggerem** (A.G. 297.e). Nominative subject (A.G. 339).
murum: Accusative direct object of **contingeret** (A.G. 387).
hostium: Possessive genitive with **murum** (A.G. 343).
paene: Adverb (A.G. 217.c and 320-21).
et: The conjunction connects the two verbs **contingeret ... excubaret** (A.G. 324.a).
Caesar: Nominative subject of **excubaret ... hortaretur** (A.G. 339). See Appendix A.
ad opus: Prepositional phrase, **ad** with the accusative here means "at, near, beside" (*OLD* **ad** 13).
consuetudine: Ablative of specification (A.G. 418).
militesque: Accusative direct object of **hortaretur** (A.G. 387). **-que:** The enclitic conjunction connects the two verbs **excubaret ... hortaretur** (A.G. 324.a).
ne ... intermitteretur: The conjunction **ne** ("so that ... not") with the subjunctive forms a negative substantive clause of purpose which is used as the object of **hortaretur** denoting an action directed toward the future (A.G. 563). **intermitteretur:** The main verb of the subordinate clause (A.G. 278.b). Imperfect subjunctive; the tense of the subjunctive is in secondary sequence and follows the rules for the sequence of tense after **hortaretur** (A.G. 482-85).
quod ... tempus: Nominative subject (A.G. 339). **quod:** Singular, neuter, nominative indefinite pronoun used as an adjective modifying **tempus** (A.G. 149). The indefinite **quis, -----, quid** (**qui, quae,** or **qua, quod** when used adjectively) is used after **ne** (A.G. 310.a).
omnino: Adverb (A.G. 320-21).
ab opere: Ablative of separation with the preposition **ab** after **intermitteretur** (A.G. 401).
paulo: Adverb (A.G. 320-21).
ante tertiam vigiliam: Prepositional phrase, **ante** with the accusative here means "before" (*OLD* **ante2** 5). **tertiam:** Declinable ordinal number used as an adjective modifying **vigiliam** (A.G. 132-35). The third watch runs from midnight to 3 A.M.
est animadversum: The main verb of the main clause (A.G. 278.b). Impersonal use of the passive verb (A.G. 208.c). The following infinitive phrase functions as the subject (A.G. 454).
fumare ... succenderant: The infinitive phrase with a dependent clause is the subject of the passive verb **est animadversum** (A.G. 454).
fumare aggerem: A subject accusative with the infinitive functions as the subject of the passive verb **est animadversum** (A.G. 454).
quem ... succenderant: Relative clause (A.G. 303). **quem:** Singular, masculine, accusative relative pronoun used substantively (A.G. 305). The antecedent is **aggerem** (A.G. 307). Accusative direct object of **succenderant** (A.G. 387). **succenderant:** The main verb of the subordinate clause (A.G. 278.b). The pluperfect tense of the verb denotes an action completed in past time (A.G. 477).
cuniculo: Ablative of means (A.G. 409).
hostes: Nominative subject (A.G. 339).

(24.3-4) **eodemque tempore toto muro clamore sublato, duabus portis ab (4) utroque latere turrium eruptio fiebat.**

ab, *from.*
duo, -ae, -o, *two.*
fio, fieri, factus, *take place, happen, come about, come to pass.*
latus, -eris, n., *side, flank.*
porta -ae, f., *city gate.*
tempus, -oris, n., *time.*
totus, -a, -um, *the whole of, the entire.*
utrerque, -traque, -trumque, *each, both.*

clamor, -oris, m., *outcry, clamor, noise, din.*
eruptio, -onis, f., *a bursting forth, sally, sortie.*
idem, eadem, idem, *the same.*
murus, -i, m., *wall, rampart.*
-que, *and, now.*
tollo, tollere, sustuli, sublatus, *lift up, raise.*
turris, -is, f., *tower.*

eodemque tempore toto muro clamore sublato: Ablative absolute (A.G. 419-20). **eodemque tempore:** Ablative of *time when* (A.G. 423.1). **eodem:** Singular, neuter, ablative demonstrative pronoun used as an adjective modifying **tempore** (A.G. 296.1 and a). **-que:** The enclitic here begins the sentence and means "and, now" (*OLD* **-que** 4). **toto muro:** Ablative of *place where* without a preposition (A.G. 429.2). **clamore sublato:** The noun, participle element of the ablative absolute (A.G. 419-20). **sublato:** The perfect tense of the participle represents the action as completed at the time indicated by the tense of the main verb (A.G. 489).
duabus portis: Ablative of *way by which* without a preposition (A.G. 429.a). **duabus:** Declinable cardinal number used as an

adjective (A.G. 132-35).

ab utroque latere turrium: Ablative of *position* with the preposition **ab** (A.G. 429.b). **turrium**: Partitive genitive with **latere** (A.G. 346.a.1).

eruptio: Nominative subject (A.G. 339).

fiebat: The main verb of the main clause (A.G. 278.b).

(24.4-5) Alii faces atque aridam materiam de muro in aggerem eminus iaciebant, picem reliquasque res quibus ignis excitari potest fundebant, ut quo primum curreretur aut cui rei ferretur auxi(5)lium vix ratio iniri posset.

agger, -eris, m., *rampart, ramp.*

aridus, -a, -um, *dry.*

aut, *or.*

curro, -ere, cucurri, -sum, *run, hurry, hasten.*

eminus, *at a distance, from afar.*

fax, facis, f., *torch, firebrand.*

fundo, fundere, fudi, fusus, *pour.*

ignis, -is, m., *fire.*

ineo, -ire, -ivi, or **-ii, -itus**, *enter upon, begin, form.*

murus, -i, m., *wall, rampart.*

possum, posse, potui, -----, *be able.*

-que, *and.*

quis, -----, quid, *who? what?* (as adj., **qui, quae, quod**).

ratio, -onis, f., *plan of action.*

res, rei, f., *thing; affair, situation.*

vix, *scarcely, barely.*

alii, -orum, m., *other persons, others.*

atque, *and.*

auxilium, -i, n., *help, aid, assistance, relief.*

de, *down from* (a higher position).

excito, -are, -avi, -atus, *kindle.*

fero, ferre, tuli, latus, *bear, carry, bring.*

iacio, iacere, ieci, iactus, *throw, cast, hurl.*

in, *onto.*

materia, -ae, f., *material, stuff, timber, wood.*

pix, picis, f., *pitch.*

primum, *first, before everything else, in the first place.*

qui, quae, quod, *who, which, what.*

quo, *where.*

reliquus, -a, -um, *remaining, the rest.*

ut, *so that.*

Alii: Plural, masculine, nominative pronoun used substantively meaning "other persons, others" (*OLD* **alius2** 1). Nominative subject of **iaciebant ... fundebant** (A.G. 339). These men are in contrast to those making the sortie from the gates.

faces atque aridam materiam: Two accusative direct objects of **iaciebant** (A.G. 387). **atque**: The conjunction connects the two accusative nouns and means "and" (*OLD* **atque** 12).

de muro: Prepositional phrase, **de** with the ablative here means Adown from (a higher position) (*OLD* **de** 1.b).

in aggerem: Accusative of *place to which* with the preposition **in** (A.G. 426.2).

eminus: Adverb (A.G. 320-21).

iaciebant: The main verb of the coordinate clause **Alii ... iaciebant** (A.G. 278.a).

picem reliquasque res: Two accusative direct objects of **fundebant** (A.G. 387). **-que**: The enclitic conjunction connects the two accusative nouns (A.G. 324.a).

quibus ... potest: Relative clause (A.G. 303). **quibus**: Plural, feminine, ablative relative pronoun used substantively (A.G. 305). The antecedent is **picem reliquasque res** (A.G. 307.b). Ablative of means (A.G. 409). **potest**: The main verb of the subordinate clause (A.G. 278.b). The present tense amid the imperfect tenses is not the historical present but denotes the action as now existing in present time (A.G. 465.1).

ignis: Nominative subject (A.G. 339).

excitari: Complementary infinitive after **potest** (A.G. 456).

fundebant: The main verb of the coordinate clause **picem ... posset** (A.G. 278.a). Notice the asyndeton between the two main verbs **iaciebant ... fundebant** (A.G. 323.b).

ut ... posset: The conjunction **ut** ("so that") with the subjunctive forms a clause of result dependent on **fundebant** (A.G. 537.1).

posset: The main verb of the subordinate clause (A.G. 278.b). Imperfect subjunctive; the tense of the subjunctive is in secondary sequence and follows the rules for the sequence of tense after **fundebant** (A.G. 482-85).

quo ... (id) curreretur: Indirect question with the subjunctive; the phrase is in apposition to the noun **ratio** (A.G. 573-75). **quo**: Interrogative adverb meaning "where" (*OLD* **quo1** 1). **curreretur**: The main verb of the subordinate clause (A.G. 278.b). Imperfect subjunctive; the tense of the subjunctive is in secondary sequence and follows the rules for the sequence of tense for indirect questions after **fundebant** (A.G. 575). Impersonal use of the verb (A.G. 208.d). Supply **id** as the subject (A.G. 318.c).

primum: Adverb (A.G. 214.d, 320-21, and 322.d).

aut: The conjunction connects the two indirect questions and excludes the alternative (A.G. 324.e).

cui ... auxilium: Indirect question with the subjunctive; the phrase is the object of **ratio iniri posset** (A.G. 573-75). **cui**: See below.

auxilium: Nominative subject of the previous verb **ferretur** (A.G. 339).

cui rei: Dative indirect object of the passive verb **ferretur**, verbs which in the active voice take the accusative and dative retain the dative when used in the passive (A.G. 365). **cui**: Singular, feminine, dative interrogative pronoun used as an adjective modifying **rei** (A.G. 148.b).

ferretur: The main verb of the subordinate clause (A.G. 278.b). Imperfect subjunctive; the tense of the subjunctive is in secondary sequence and follows the rules for the sequence of tense for indirect questions after **fundebant** (A.G. 575).

vix: Adverb (A.G. 217.c and 320-21).

ratio: Nominative subject (A.G. 339).

iniri: Complementary infinitive after **posset** (A.G. 456).

(24.5) **Tamen, quod instituto Caesaris semper duae legiones pro castris excubabant pluresque partitis temporibus erant in opere, celeriter factum est ut alii eruptionibus resisterent alii turres reducerent aggeremque interscinderent, omnis vero ex castris multitudo ad restinguendum concurreret.**

ad, *for, in order to, for the purpose of.*
alii ... alii, **-orum**, m., pl., *some ... others.*
castra, **-orum**, n., pl., *camp, encampment.*
concurro, **-currere**, **-cucurri** or **-curri**, **-cursus**, *run together, run up, rush.*
eruptio, **-onis**, f., *a bursting forth, sally, sortie.*
excubo, **-cubare**, **-cubui**, **-cubitus**, *lie out of doors, keep watch, keep guard.*
in, *engaged* or *occupied in.*
interscindo, **-scindere**, **-scidi**, **-scisus**, *cut through, divide by cutting.*
multitudo, **-inis**, f., *multitude, crowd.*
opus, **operis**, n., *work, labor.*
plures, **-ium**, m., *more, quite a number, several.*
-que, *and.*
reduco, **-ducere**, **-duxi**, **-ductus**, *draw back, drag back.*

restinguo, **-stinguere**, **-stinxi**, **-stinctus**, *put out* or *extinguish the flames.*
sum, **esse**, **fui**, **futurus**, *be.*
tempus, **-oris**, n., *time.*
ut, *so that.*

agger, **-eris**, m., *rampart, ramp.*
Caesar, **-aris**, m., *Caesar.*
celeriter, *quickly, speedily, at once, immediately.*
duo, **-ae**, **-o**, *two.*
ex, *from, out of.*
facio, **facere**, **feci**, **factus**, *do.*
institutum, **-i**, n., *plan, practice, custom.*
legio, **-onis**, f., *legion.*
omnis, **-e**, *all of, the whole.*
partior, **partiri**, **partitus**, (part. in a pass. sense), *divided.*
pro, *in front of, before.*
quod, *because, since, for, as.*
resisto, **-sistere**, **-stiti**, **-----**, *resist, oppose, withstand, offer resistance.*
semper, *always, constantly.*
tamen, *yet, still, for all that, nevertheless, however.*
turris, **-is**, f., *tower.*
vero, *but, but indeed, however.*

Tamen: Adverb, normally postpositive but not here (A.G. 320-21 and 324.j).
quod ... excubabant ... erant ... opere: Causal clause; the conjunction **quod** ("because") takes the indicative when the reason is given on the authority of the writer or speaker (A.G. 540.1). **excubabant ... erant**: The main verbs of the subordinate clause (A.G. 278.b).
opere: See below.
instituto: Ablative of specification (A.G. 418).
Caesaris: Possessive genitive with **instituto** (A.G. 343). See Appendix A.
semper: Adverb (A.G. 217.b and 320-21).
duae legiones: Nominative subject (A.G. 339). **duae**: Declinable cardinal number used as an adjective (A.G. 132-35).
pro castris: Prepositional phrase, **pro** with the ablative here means "in front of, before" (*OLD* **pro1** 1).
pluresque: Plural, masculine, nominative adjective used substantively (A.G. 288). Supply **milites** as the noun (A.G. 288.b). Irregular comparative adjective (A.G. 129). **-que**: The enclitic conjunction connects the two main verbs in the causal clause **excubabant ... erant** (A.G. 324.a).
partitis temporibus: Ablative absolute (A.G. 419-20). **partitis**: Deponent participle with passive force (A.G. 190.f). The perfect tense of the participle represents the action as completed at the time indicated by the tense of the main verb (A.G. 489).
in opere: Prepositional phrase, **in** with the ablative here means "engaged or occupied in" (*OLD* **in** 39). The prepositional phrase is in the predicate position after **erant** (A.G. 272).
celeriter: Adverb (A.G. 214.b and 320-21).
factum est: The main verb of the main clause (A.G. 278.b). Impersonal use of the verb (A.G. 208.c). The substantive clause of result **ut ... concurreret** functions as the subject (A.G. 567-69). When **facio** is used in the passive, the object clause becomes the subject (A.G. 567).
ut ... resisterent ... reducerent ... interscinderent ... concurreret: The conjunction **ut** ("so that") with the subjunctive here forms a substantive clause of result which is the subject of the passive verb (**factum est**) denoting the accomplishment of an effort (A.G. 569.1). **resisterent ... reducerent ... interscinderent ... concurreret**: The main verbs of the subordinate clause (A.G. 278.b). Imperfect subjunctives; the tense of the subjunctive is in secondary sequence and follows the rules for the sequence of tense after **factum est** (A.G. 482-85). Notice the asyndeton between the two main verbs **interscinderent ... concurreret** (A.G. 323.b).
alii ... alii: Two nominative subjects (A.G. 339). Plural, masculine, nominative pronouns used substantively; the repeated pronoun **alius** means "some ... others" (A.G. 315.a). The first is the subject of **resisterent**, the second is the subject of **reducerent ... interscinderent**.
eruptionibus: Dative indirect object of the intransitive verb **resisterent** (A.G. 367).
turris: Accusative direct object of **reducerent** (A.G. 387). Accusative plural noun; **-is** for **-es** is the regular form in i-stem nouns (A.G. 65-7 and 74.c).
aggeremque: Accusative direct object of **interscinderent** (A.G. 387). "They cut the agger in two to prevent the spreading of the flames through the entire length of the structure. It was constructed largely of timber." (Kelsey, 409) **-que**: The enclitic conjunction connects the two verbs in the purpose clause **reducerent ... interscinderent** (A.G. 324.a).
omnis ... multitudo: Nominative subject (A.G. 339).
vero: Adverb, postpositive position (A.G. 320-21 and 599.b).
ex castris: Ablative of *place from which* with the preposition **ex** (A.G. 426.1).
ad restinguendum: The preposition **ad** with the accusative gerund denotes purpose (A.G. 506). **restinguendum**: Singular, neuter, accusative gerund (A.G. 501-02).

(25.1) **Cum in omnibus locis, consumpta iam reliqua parte noctis, pugnaretur semperque hostibus spes victoriae** redintegraretur, eo magis quod deustos pluteos turrium videbant nec facile adire apertos ad auxiliandum animadvertebant, semperque ipsi recentes defessis succederent omnemque Galliae salutem in illo vestigio temporis positam arbitrarentur, accidit inspectantibus nobis quod dignum memoria visum praetereundum non existimavimus.

accido, -cidere, -cidi, -----, (imp.), *it happens, occurs, turns out.*
adeo, -ire, -ivi, or -ii, -itus, *go to, approach.*
apertus, -i, m., *exposed soldiers, unprotected soldiers.*
auxilior, -ari, -atus, *render aid, assist, help.*

cum, *when, while.*
deuro, -uere, -ussi, -ustus, *burn up, consume.*
eo, (with comp.), *the, all the.*
facile, *easily, readily, with no trouble.*
hostis, -is, m., *enemy, foe;* pl., *the enemy.*
ille, illae, illud, *that; he, she, it.*
inspecto, -are, -----, -----, *look at.*
loca, -orum, n., pl., *places, positions.*
memoria, -ae, f., *memory, recollection, remembrance.*
non, *not.*
nox, noctis, f., *night.*
pars, partis, f., *part, portion.*
pono, ponere, posui, positus, *place, put.*
pugno, -are, -avi, -atus, *fight, combat, engage.*
qui, quae, quod, *who, which, what.*
recentes, -ium, m., pl., *those who were fresh, the unwearied.*

reliquus, -a, -um, *remaining, the rest.*
semper, *always, ever, constantly.*
succedo, -cedere, -cessi, -cessurus, *succeed, take the place of, relieve.*
turris, -is, f., *tower.*
victoria, -ae, f., *victory.*
videor, videri, visus sum, *be seen, seem, appear.*

ad, *for, in order to, for the purpose of.*
animadverto, -tere, -ti, -sus, *notice, observe, perceive.*
arbitror, -ari, -atus, *think, suppose, consider, believe.*
consumo, -sumere, -sumpsi, -sumptus, *spend, pass, consume.*
defessi, -orum, m., pl., *the exhausted, weary men.*
dignus, -a, -um, *worthy, worth, deserving.*
existimo, -are, -avi, -atus, *think, consider, judge.*
Gallia, -ae, f., *Gaul.*
iam, *already, by this time.*
in, *in.*
ipse, -a, -um, *for their own part.*
magis, *more.*
nec, *and ... not.*
nos, nostrum, *we, us.*
omnis, -e, *all.*
pluteus, -i, *breastwork.*
praetereo, -ire, -ivi, or -ii, -itus, *pass over.*
-que, *and.*
quod, *because, since, for, as.*
redintegro, -are, -avi, -atus, *restore, renew, refresh, revive.*
salus, -utis, f., *welfare, safety, deliverance.*
spes, -ei, f., *hope, expectation.*
tempus, -oris, n., *time.*
vestigium, -i, n., *moment, instant.*
video, videre, visi, visus, *perceive, observe, see.*

Cum ... (id) pugnaretur ... redintegraretur ... succederent ... arbitrarentur: Temporal clause; **cum** ("when, while") with the imperfect subjunctive describes the circumstances that accompanied the action of the main verb (A.G. 546). **pugnaretur** ... **redintegraretur ... succederent ... arbitrarentur**: The main verbs of the subordinate clause (A.G. 278.b). **pugnaretur**: Impersonal use of the intransitive passive verb (A.G. 208.d). Supply **id** as the subject (A.G. 318.c).
in omnibus locis: Ablative of *place where* with the preposition **in** (locative ablative) (A.G. 426.3).
consumpta iam reliqua parte noctis: Ablative absolute (A.G. 419-20). **consumpta**: The perfect tense of the participle represents the action as completed at the time indicated by the tense of the main verb (A.G. 489). **iam**: Adverb (A.G. 215.6, 217.b and 320-21).
noctis: Partitive genitive with **parte** (A.G. 346.a.1).
semperque: Adverb (A.G. 217.b and 320-21). **-que**: The enclitic conjunctions connects the two verbs in the temporal clause **pugnaretur ... redintegraretur** (A.G. 324.a).
hostibus: Dative of reference; the dative in this construction is often called the dative of advantage as denoting the person for whose benefit the action is performed (A.G. 376).
spes: Nominative subject (A.G. 339).
victoriae: Objective genitive with **spes** (A.G. 348).
eo magis quod ... videbant ... animadvertebant: Causal clause; the conjunction **quod** ("because") normally takes the indicative when the reason is given on the authority of the writer or speaker (A.G. 540.1). Here, the clause is dependent on a subjunctive clause (**cum ... redintegraretur**) and so should take the subjunctive (attraction) (A.G. 593). But a dependent clause may be closely connected grammatically with a subjunctive clause and still take the indicative if it is not regarded as a necessary logical part of that clause. The use of the indicative emphasizes the fact, as true independently of the statement contained in the subjunctive clause (A.G. 593.a). **eo magis**: The two adverbs used in conjunction mean "so much more" (*OLD* eo3 2). **videbant ... animadvertebant**: The main verbs of the subordinate clause (A.G. 278.b). The pronoun **ei**, with **hostibus** as the antecedent, is understood as the subject of both verbs (A.G. 271.a).
deustos (esse) pluteos: Accusative/infinitive construction in indirect discourse after **videbant** (A.G. 577 ff.). **deustos (esse)**: Supply **esse** to form the perfect, passive infinitive (A.G. 186). The tense of the infinitive in indirect discourse is relative to that of the verb of saying (A.G. 584). **pluteos**: "The mantlet (*pluteus*) was a large shield constructed of hurdlework or planks, and sometimes of cable mats, or mattresses, suspended on a frame. It resembled a huge snowplow mounted on wheels, and was pushed forward by men in rear of it." (Fuller, 92)
turrium: Partitive genitive with **pluteos** (A.G. 346.a.1).
nec: The conjunction qualifies the single word **facile** rather than a whole clause and means "and ... not" (*OLD* neque 4.c).
facile: Adverb formed from the neuter accusative adjective (A.G. 214.d and 320-21).
adire apertos: Accusative/infinitive construction in indirect discourse after **animadvertebant** (A.G. 577 ff.). **adire**: The tense of the

infinitive in indirect discourse is relative to that of the verb of saying (A.G. 584). **apertos**: Plural, masculine, accusative adjective used substantively (A.G. 288). The noun **milites** is understood (A.G. 288.b). These men are exposed due to the burning of the towers.

ad auxiliandum: The preposition **ad** with the accusative gerund denotes purpose (A.G. 506). **auxiliandum**: Singular, neuter, accusative gerund (A.G. 501-02).

semperque: Adverb (A.G. 217.b and 320-21). **-que**: The enclitic conjunctions connects the two verbs in the temporal clause **redintegraretur ... succederent** (A.G. 324.a).

ipsi recentes: Nominative subject of **succederent ... arbitrarentur** (A.G. 339). **ipsi**: Plural, masculine, nominative demonstrative pronoun used as an adjective (A.G. 296.1 and a). The pronoun marks a transition and means "for their own part" (*OLD* **ipse** 3). The antecedent is **hostibus** (A.G. 298.1). **recentes**: Plural, masculine, nominative adjective used substantively (A.G. 288).

defessis: Plural, masculine, dative adjective used substantively (A.G. 288). The noun **militibus** is understood (A.G. 288.b). Dative indirect object of the intransitive use of **succederent** (A.G. 367.c).

omnemque ... salutem ... positam (esse): Accusative/infinitive construction in indirect discourse after **arbitrarentur** (A.G. 577 ff.). **-que**: The enclitic conjunctions connects the two verbs in the temporal clause **succederent ... arbitrarentur** (A.G. 324.a). **positam (esse)**: Supply **esse** to form the perfect, passive infinitive (A.G. 186). The tense of the infinitive in indirect discourse is relative to that of the verb of saying (A.G. 584).

Galliae: Possessive genitive with **salutem** (A.G. 343). See Appendix A.

in illo vestigio temporis: Prepositional phrase, **in** with the ablative here means "in" (expressing an abstract location) (*OLD* **in** 26). **illo**: Singular, neuter, ablative demonstrative pronoun used as an adjective modifying **vestigio** (A.G. 296.1 and a). **temporis**: Partitive genitive with **vestigio** (A.G. 346.a.1).

accidit: The main verb of the main clause (A.G. 278.b). Impersonal use of the verb, supply **id** as the subject (A.G. 207).

inspectantibus nobis: Dative indirect object of the intransitive use of **accidit** (A.G. 366). **inspectantibus**: Dative, present, active, participle used as a predicate, where in English a phrase or a subordinate clause would be more normal (A.G. 496). An iterative form of **inspicio** (A.G. 263.2). **nobis**: Plural, masculine, dative personal pronoun used substantively (A.G.143 and 295).

quod ... existimavimus: Relative clause (A.G. 303). **quod**: See below. **existimavimus**: The main verb of the subordinate clause (A.G. 278.b). The personal pronoun **nos** is understood as the subject but is not expressed except for distinction or emphasis (A.G. 295.a). In Book 7, Caesar refers to himself only in the third person, either in the singular or occasionally in the plural (see **Caesar** at 1.1). Siedler counts 11 uses of the first person plural in Book 7 (Siedler, 46). These uses are at 17.1, 23.2, 25.1, 37.1, 48.1, 58.4, 70.1, 76.1, 79.2, 83.8, and 85.4.

quod dignum ... visum praetereundum (esse): Accusative/infinitive construction in indirect discourse after **existimavimus** (A.G. 577 ff.). **quod**: Singular, neuter, accusative relative pronoun used substantively (A.G. 305). The antecedent is omitted, supply **id** (A.G. 307.d Note). **dignum (esse)**: Singular, neuter, accusative, predicate adjective modifying **quod** after **visum** (A.G. 283). A predicate adjective after a complementary infinitive takes the case of the subject of the main verb (A.G. 283 and 458). Supply **esse** as the complementary infinitive after **visum**. **visum**: Perfect, deponent participle used as an adjective modifying **quod** (A.G. 494). **praetereundum (esse)**: Supply **esse** to form the second periphrastic (passive) present infinitive with the gerundive implying necessity (A.G. 194.b and 196). The tense of the infinitive in indirect discourse is relative to that of the verb of saying (A.G. 584).

memoria: Ablative object of the adjective **dignum** (A.G. 418.b).

non: Adverb, the adverb generally precedes the verb if it belongs to no one word in particular (A.G. 217.e, 320-21, and 599.a).

Quidam ... factus: This is a vivid description of the noble character of the Gallic enemy. This can be conveniently compared to their fickleness at 7.22. "This is certainly the type of behavior which marks the 'noble savage' character type off from the barbarian: constancy, bravery, and loyalty to liberty over personal safety. These soldiers are similar to Roman soldiers and exhibit qualities which defy expectation." (Mannetter, 38).

(25.2) (2) Quidam ante portam oppidi Gallus per manus sebi ac picis traditas glaebas in ignem e regione turris proiciebat: scorpione ab latere dextro traiectus exanimatusque concidit.

ab, *on.*
ante, *before, in front of.*
dexter, -tra, -trum, *right.*
exanimo, -are, -avi, -atus, *kill.*
glaeba, -ae, f., *lump. mass.*
in, *into, onto.*
manus, -us, f., *hand.*
per, (with **manus**), *from hand to hand.*
porta -ae, f., *city gate.*
-que, *and.*

regio, -onis, f., *region, direction.*
sebum, -i, n., *fat, tallow.*
traicio, -icere, -ieci, -iectus, *strike through, pierce, transfix.*

ac, *and.*
concido, -cidere, -cidi, *fall down, fall.*
e(x), (with **regio**), *directly opposite.*
Gallus, -i, m., *a Gaul.*
ignis, -is, m., *fire.*
latus, -eris, n., *side, flank.*
oppidum, -i, n., *fortified town, city.*
pix, picis, f., *pitch.*
proicio, -icere, -ieci, -iectus, *fling, cast, throw down.*
quidam, qauedam, quiddam, *a certain one, a certain something.*
scorpio, -onis, m., *a scorpion, scorpion.*
trado, -dere, -didi, -ditus, *hand over, deliver.*
turris, -is, f., *tower.*

Quidam ... Gallus: Nominative subject of **proiciebat** (A.G. 339). **Quidam**: Singular, masculine, nominative indefinite pronoun used as an adjective modifying **Gallus** (A.G. 151.c).

ante portam oppidi: Prepositional phrase, **ante** with the accusative here means "before" (*OLD* **ante2** 5). **oppidi**: Partitive genitive with **portam** (A.G. 346.a.1).

per manus: Prepositional phrase, **per** with the accusative plural of **manus** means "from hand to hand" (*OLD* **manus1** 18.b).

sebi ac picis: Two genitives of material with **glaebas** (A.G. 344). **ac**: The conjunction connects the two genitive nouns and means "and" (*OLD* **atque** 12).

traditas glaebas: Accusative direct object of **proiciebat** (A.G. 387). **traditas**: Accusative, perfect, passive, participle used as a predicate, where in English a phrase or a subordinate clause would be more normal (A.G. 496).

in ignem: Accusative of *place to which* with the preposition **in** (A.G. 426.2).

e regione turris: Prepositional phrase, **e(x)** with the ablative of **regio** means "directly opposite" with the genitive (*OLD* **regio** 2.a). **e**: The preposition **ex** may be used before vowels and consonants but only before vowels does the preposition lose the consonant 'x' and legthen the quantity of 'ĕ' to 'ē' (*OLD* **ex**). **turris**: Possessive genitive with **regione** (A.G. 343).

proiciebat: The main verb of the coordinate clause **Quidam ... proiciebat** (A.G. 278.a).

scorpione: Ablative of instrument (A.G. 409). "The scorpio was a small catapult." (Walker, 36)

ab latere dextro: Ablative of *position* with the preposition **ab** (A.G. 429.b).

traiectus exanimatusque: Two nominative, perfect, passive, participle used as a predicate, where in English a phrase or a subordinate clause would be more normal (A.G. 496). The pronoun **is**, with **Gallus** as the antecedent, is understood. Nominative subject (A.G. 339). **-que**: The enclitic conjunction connects the two participles (A.G. 324.a).

concidit: The main verb of the coordinate clause **scorpione ... concidit** (A.G. 278.a). Notice the asyndeton between the two main verbs **proiciebat ... concidit** (A.G. 323.b).

(25.3-4) **(3) Hunc ex proximis unus iacentem transgressus eodem illo munere fungebatur; eadem ratione ictu scorpionis exani(4)mato alteri successit tertius et tertio quartus;**

alter, -era, -erum, *the second*.	**et**, *and*.
ex, *from the number of, from among, of*.	**exanimo, -are, -avi, -atus**, *kill*.
fungor, fungi, functus, *discharge, perform, do*.	**hic, haec, hoc**, *this; he, she, it*.
iaceo, -iacere, iacui, -----, *lie dead*.	**ictus, -us**, m., *blow, stroke*.
idem, eadem, idem, *the same*.	**ille, illae, illud**, *that; he, she, it*.
munus, -eris, n., *duty, service, function*.	**proximus, -i**, m., *the nearest man, the next man*.
quartus, -a, -um, *fourth*.	**ratio, -onis**, f., *manner, method, fashion, way*.
scorpio, -onis, m., *a scorpion, scorpion*.	**succedo, -cedere, -cessi, -cessurus**, *succeed, take the place of*.
tertius, -a, um, *third*.	**transgredior, -gredi, -gressus**, *go over, pass over, go across, cross*.
unus, -a, -um, *one*.	

Hunc ex proximis unus iacentem transgressus: Notice the interlocking word order (A.G. 589.h).

Hunc ... iacentem: Accusative direct object of the deponent participle **transgressus** (A.G. 387 and 488). **Hunc**: Singular, masculine, accusative demonstrative pronoun used substantively (A.G. 296.2). The antecedent is **Gallus** (A.G. 297.e). **iacentem**: Present participle used as an adjective modifying **Hunc** (A.G. 494).

ex proximis: Prepositional phrase after **unus**, **ex** with the ablative instead of the partitive genitive means "from the number of, from among, of". Cardinal numbers regularly take the ablative with **ex** instead of the partitive genitive (A.G. 346.c) (*OLD* **ex** 17).

proximis: Plural, masculine, ablative superlative adjective used substantively (A.G. 288). The noun **Gallis** is understood (A.G. 288.b). Defective superlative adjective (A.G. 130.a).

unus ... transgressus: Nominative subject (A.G. 339). **unus**: Declinable cardinal number used substantively (A.G. 132-35). The pronoun **is**, with **Gallus** as the antecedent, is understood. **transgressus**: Nominative, perfect, deponent, participle used as a predicate, where in English a phrase or a subordinate clause would be more normal (A.G. 496).

eodem illo munere: Ablative direct object of the deponent verb **fungebatur** (A.G. 410). **eodem**: Singular, neuter, ablative demonstrative pronoun used as an adjective modifying **munere** (A.G. 296.1 and a). **illo**: Singular, neuter, ablative demonstrative pronoun used as an adjective modifying **munere** (A.G. 296.1 and a).

fungebatur: The main verb of the simple sentence (A.G. 278.1).

eadem ratione: Ablative of manner with a limiting adjective (A.G. 412). **eadem**: Singular, feminine, ablative demonstrative pronoun used as an adjective modifying **ratione** (A.G. 296.1 and a).

ictu: Ablative of cause without a preposition (A.G. 404).

scorpionis: Objective genitive with **ictu** (A.G. 348).

exanimato alteri: Dative indirect object of the intransitive use of **successit** (A.G. 367.c). **exanimato**: Dative, perfect, passive, participle used as a predicate, where in English a phrase or a subordinate clause would be more normal (A.G. 496). **alteri**: The dative singular of **alter** ends in **-i** (A.G. 113).

successit: The main verb of the coordinate clause **eadem ... successit** (A.G. 278.a).

tertius: Declinable ordinal numeral used substantively (A.G. 132-35). The pronoun **is**, with **Gallus** as the antecedent, is understood. Nominative subject of the previous verb **successit** (A.G. 339).

et: The conjunction connects the clause **eadem ... tertius** with the elliptical clause **tertio quartus** (A.G. 324.a).

tertio quartus: An ellipsis for **ictu scorpionis exanimato tertio successit quartus** (A.G. 640). **tertio**: Dative declinable ordinal numeral used substantively (A.G. 132-35). Dative indirect object of the intransitive use of **successit** (A.G. 367.c). The noun **Gallo** is understood (A.G. 288.b). **quartus**: Declinable ordinal numeral used substantively (A.G. 132-35). The pronoun **is**, with **Gallus** as the antecedent, is understood. Nominative subject (A.G. 339).

(25.4) **nec prius ille est a propugnatoribus vacuus relictus locus quam restincto aggere atque omni ex parte summotis hostibus finis est pugnandi factus.**

a(b), *by.*
atque, *and in fact, and even.*
finis, -is, m., *end.*

hostis, -is, m., *enemy, foe*; pl., *the enemy.*
locus, -i, m., *place, location, position, station.*
omnis, -e, *every.*
prius ... quam, *before, sooner than.*
pugno, -are, -avi, -atus, *fight, combat, engage.*

restinguo, -stinguere, -stinxi, -stinctus, *put out, extinguish.*

vacuus, -a, -um, *empty, clear, free, vacant, unoccupied.*

agger, -eris, m., *rampart, ramp.*
ex, *from.*
fio, fieri, factus, *take place, happen, come about, come to pass.*
ille, illae, illud, *that; he, she, it.*
nec, *and ... not.*
pars, partis, f., *part, region, district, direction, side.*
propugnator, -oris, m., *defender, combatant.*
relinquo, -linquere, -liqui, -lictus, *leave, leave behind, desert, abandon.*
summoveo, -movere, -movi, -motus, *drive back, remove.*

nec ... factus: "Caesar states this with admiration of the courage exhibited." (Kelsey, 409) Indeed, it is hard not to be moved by such a display of selfless courage.
nec: The conjunction joins a negative clause to a preceding positive one and means "and ... not" (*OLD* **neque** 3).
prius: Construe **prius** with **quam** below.
ille ... locus: Nominative subject (A.G. 339). **ille**: Singular, masculine, nominative demonstrative pronoun used as an adjective modifying **locus** (A.G. 296.1 and a).
est ... relictus: The main verb of the main clause (A.G. 278.b). The perfect passive verb is here split (tmesis) (A.G. 640).
a propugnatoribus: Ablative of agent with the preposition **a(b)** after the passive verb **est ... relictus** (A.G. 405).
vacuus: Singular, masculine, nominative predicate adjective modifying **locus** after **est ... relictus** (A.G. 283).
(prius) ... quam ... est ... factus: Temporal clause; **(prius) ... quam** ("before") with the perfect indicative states a fact in past time (A.G. 551.a). **(prius) ... quam**: The conjunction is here split (tmesis) (A.G. 640). **est ... factus**: The main verb of the subordinate clause (A.G. 278.b). The perfect passive verb is here split (tmesis) (A.G. 640).
restincto aggere: Ablative absolute (A.G. 419-20). **restincto**: The perfect tense of the participle represents the action as completed at the time indicated by the tense of the main verb (A.G. 489).
atque: The conjunction connects the two ablative absolutes and strengthens the first "and in fact, and even" (A.G. 324.b) (*OLD* **atque** 4).
omni ex parte summotis hostibus: Ablative absolute (A.G. 419-20). **omni ex parte**: Ablative of separation with the preposition **ex** after **summotis** (A.G. 401). **ex**: A monosyllabic preposition is often placed between a noun and its adjective (A.G. 599.d.2).
summotis: The perfect tense of the participle represents the action as completed at the time indicated by the tense of the main verb (A.G. 489).
finis est pugnandi factus: Interlocking word order (A.G. 589.h).
finis: Nominative subject (A.G. 339).
pugnandi: Singular, neuter, genitive gerund (A.G. 501-02). Subjective genitive with **finis** (A.G. 504).

(26.1-2) **Omnia experti Galli, quod res nulla successerat, postero die consilium ceperunt ex oppido profugere, hortante et (2) iubente Vercingetorige.**

capio, capere, cepi, captus, *form, adopt.*
dies, -ei, m. and f., *day.*
ex, *from, out of.*
Galli, -orum, m., *the Gauls.*
iubeo, iubere, iussi, iussus, *order, give orders, bid, command.*
omnia, -ium, n., *all things, everything.*
posterus, -a, -um, *following, the next.*
quod, *because, since, for, as.*
succedo, -cedere, -cessi, -cessurus, *prosper, succeed.*

consilium, -i, n., *plan, scheme.*
et, *and then.*
experior, -periri, -pertus, *put to the test, try.*
hortor, -ari, -atus, *urge, encourage, exhort, press.*
nullus, -a, -um, *no, not any.*
oppidum, -i, n., *fortified town, city.*
profugio, -fugere, -fugi, -----, *flee, escape.*
res, rei, f., *outcome, circumstance.*
Vercingetorix, -igis, m., *Vercingetorix.*

Omnia: Plural, neuter, accusative adjective used substantively (A.G. 288). Accusative direct object of the deponent participle **experti** (A.G. 387 and 488).
experti Galli: Nominative subject of **ceperunt** (A.G. 339). **experti**: Nominative, perfect, deponent, participle used as a predicate, where in English a phrase or a subordinate clause would be more normal (A.G. 496). **Galli**: See Appendix A.
quod ... successerat: Causal clause; the conjunction **quod** ("because") takes the indicative when the reason is given on the authority of the writer or speaker (A.G. 540.1). **successerat**: The main verb of the subordinate clause (A.G. 278.b). The pluperfect tense of the verb denotes an action completed in past time (A.G. 477).
res nulla: Nominative subject (A.G. 339).

110

postero die: Ablative of *time when* (A.G. 423.1). die: The noun dies is normally masculine gender (A.G. 97.a).
consilium ceperunt: The phrase consilium capere is an idiom that means "to adopt or form a plan" (*OLD* capio 9.e).
consilium: Accusative direct object of ceperunt (A.G. 387).
ceperunt: The main verb of the main clause (A.G. 278.b).
ex oppido: Ablative of *place from which* with the preposition ex (A.G. 426.1).
profugere: Complementary infinitive after consilium ceperunt (A.G. 456 and 563.d). The infinitive is equivalent to a substantive clause of purpose (A.G. 563.d).
hortante et iubente Vercingetorige: Ablative absolute with two present participles (A.G. 419-20). Notice that he must be doing this through envoys as he is not present in the city. hortante et iubente: The participle ends in -e rather than -i in the ablative singular when used in an ablative absolute (A.G. 121.2). Here the present participle denotes an action continued in the present but begun in the past (A.G. 490.1). et: The conjunction connects the two present participles and adds a subsequent or consequent event and means "and then" (*OLD* et 16). Two adjectives belonging to the same noun are regularly connected by a conjunction (A.G. 323.d).
Vercingetorige: See Appendix A.

(26.2-3) Id silentio noctis conati non magna iactura suorum sese effecturos sperabant, propterea quod neque longe ab oppido castra Vercingetorigis aberant et palus, quae perpetua intercedebat, Romanos ad inse(3)quendum tardabat.

ab, *from.*

ad, *for, in order to, for the purpose of.*
conor, -ari, -atus, *endeavor, attempt, undertake, try.*

iactura, -ae, f., *loss, sacrifice, cost.*

intercedo, -ere, -cessi, -cessus, *come between, intervene, be between.*
longe, *at a distance, far.*
neque ... et, *while not ... (yet) at the same time.*
nox, noctis, f., *night.*
palus, -udis, f., *marsh, swamp, bog, morass.*
propterea, *for this reason, therefore.*
quod, *because, since, for, as.*
silentium, -i, m., *silence, stillness.*
sui, sibi, se, or sese, nom. wanting, *they*, with or without *themselves.*
tardo, -are, -avi, -atus, *check, delay, impede, hinder.*

Vercingetorix, -igis, m., *Vercingetorix.*

absum, -esse, afui, -futurus, *be distant, be absent, be away from.*
castra, -orum, n., pl., *camp, encampment.*
efficio, -ficere, -feci, -fectus, *accomplish, make, bring to pass.*
insequor, -sequi, -secutus, *follow up, pursue, follow in pursuit.*
is, ea, id, *he, she, it, that, this.*
magnus, -a, -um, *great, large.*
non, *not.*
oppidum, -i, n., *fortified town, city.*
perpetuus, -a, -um, *continuous, unbroken, entire.*
qui, quae, quod, *who, which, what.*
Romani, -orum, m., pl., *the Romans.*
spero, -are, -avi, -atus, *hope, expect.*
sui, -orum, m., pl., *their men*, with or without *own.*
timor, -oris, m., *fear, dread, apprehension, alarm, timidity.*

Id: Singular, neuter, accusative demonstrative pronoun used substantively (A.G. 296.2). The antecedent is the idea of flight above (A.G. 297.e). Accusative direct object of the deponent participle conati (A.G. 387 and 488) and the infinitive effecturos (esse) (A.G. 387 and 451.3).
silentio: Ablative of *time within which* (A.G. 423.1)
noctis: Partitive genitive with silentio (A.G. 346.a.1).
conati ... effecturos (esse): A disguised conditional statement in indirect discourse after sperabant (A.G. 521 and 589). Normally, the protasis, as a dependent clause, is in the subjunctive and the apodosis, as the principal clause, is in the infinitive (A.G. 589). Here, the deponent participle takes the place of the protasis (A.G. 521).
conati: The participle functions as the protasis of the conditional statement (= si ei conati esset A.G. 496 and 521). Nominative, perfect, deponent, participle used as a predicate, where in English a phrase or a subordinate clause would be more normal (A.G. 496). The pronoun ei, with Galli as the antecedent, is understood. Nominative subject of sperabant (A.G. 339).
non: Adverb modifying magna; the negative precedes the word it especially effects (A.G. 217.e, 320-21, and 599.a).
magna iactura: Ablative of manner with a limiting adjective (A.G. 412).
suorum: Plural, masculine, genitive possessive pronoun used substantively to denote a special class (A.G. 302.d). Objective genitive with iactura (A.G. 348).
sese effecturos (esse): The apodosis of the conditional statement (A.G. 589.2). Accusative/infinitive construction in indirect discourse after sperabant (A.G. 577 ff.). sese: Plural, masculine, accusative direct reflexive pronoun (A.G. 300.1). The antecedent is conati, the subject of sperabant (A.G. 299). Reduplicated form of se (A.G. 144.b Note 1). effecturos (esse): Supply esse to form the future, active infinitive (A.G. 188). The tense of the infinitive in indirect discourse is relative to that of the verb of saying (A.G. 584).
sperabant: The main verb of the main clause (A.G. 278.b).
propterea: Adverb (A.G. 217.c and 320-21).
quod ... aberant ... tardabat: Causal clause; the conjunction quod ("because") normally takes the indicative when the reason is given on the authority of the writer or speaker (A.G. 540.1). Here, as a dependent clause in indirect statement after sperabant, it should take the subjunctive (A.G. 580). However, a subordinate clause merely explanatory, or containing statements which are regarded as true independently of the quotation, takes the indicative (A.G. 583). aberant ... tardabat: The main verbs of the subordinate clause (A.G. 278.b).
neque ... et: The combination of conjunctions means Awhile not ... (yet) at the same time (*OLD* neque 8).

longe: Adverb (A.G. 214.a and 320-21).

ab oppido: Ablative of separation with the preposition **ab** after the compound verb **aberant** (A.G. 402).

castra: Nominative subject (A.G. 339).

Vercingetorigis: Possessive genitive with **castra** (A.G. 343). See Appendix A.

palus: Nominative subject (A.G. 339).

quae ... intercedebat: Relative clause (A.G. 303). **quae**: Singular, feminine, nominative relative pronoun used substantively (A.G. 305). The antecedent is **palus** (A.G. 307). Nominative subject (A.G. 339). **intercedebat**: The main verb of the subordinate clause (A.G. 278.b).

perpetua: Singular, feminine, nominative adjective modifying the pronoun **quae** but used to qualify the action of the verb, and so has the force of an adverb (A.G. 290).

Romanos: Accusative direct object of **tardabat** (A.G. 387).

ad insequendum: The preposition **ad** with the accusative gerund denotes purpose (A.G. 506). **insequendum**: Singular, neuter, accusative gerund (A.G. 501-02).

(26.3-4) **Iamque hoc facere noctu apparabant, cum matres familiae repente in publicum procurrerunt flentesque proiectae ad pedes suorum omnibus precibus petierunt ne se et communis liberos hostibus ad supplicium dederent, quos ad capiendam fugam naturae et (4) virium infirmitas impediret.**

ad, *at; for; for, in order to, for the purpose of.*

capio, capere, cepi, captus, *take.*

cum, *when.*

et, *and.*

familia, -ae, f., *household, family,* (pl. with **matres**) *matrons.*

fuga, -ae, f., *flight.*

hostis, -is, m., *enemy, foe*; pl., *the enemy.*

impedio, -pedire, -pedivi, -peditus, *hinder, obstruct.*

infirmitas, -atis, f., *weakness, feebleness.*

mater, -tris, f., *mother,* (with **familiae**) *matrons.*

ne, *so that ... not.*

omnis, -e, *all.*

peto, petere, petivi, and **petii, petitus**, *seek, ask, request.*

procurro, -currere, -cucurri or **-curri, -cursum**, *run, hasten, or rush forward.*

publicum, -i, n., *open, street, public place.*

qui, quae, quod, *who, which, what.*

silentium, -i, m., *silence, stillness.*

supplicium, -i, n., *punishment, death-penalty, execution.*

vires, -ium, f., *physical powers, strength.*

apparo, -are, -avi, -atus, *prepare, make ready, get ready.*

communis, -e, *common, in common.*

dedo, -dere, -didi, -ditus, *give up, surrender.*

facio, facere, feci, factus, *do.*

fleo, flere, flevi, fletus, *weep, shed tears, cry.*

hic, haec, hoc, *this; he, she, it.*

iam, *already, now.*

in, *into.*

liberi, -orum, m., pl., *children.*

natura, -ae, f., *nature, character.*

noctu, *by night, at night, in the night.*

pes, pedis, m., *foot.*

prex, precis, f., *prayer, entreaty, supplication.*

proicio, -icere, -ieci, -iectus, *lie outstretched* or *prone.*

-que, *and, now.*

repente, *suddenly.*

sui, sibi, se, or **sese**, nom. wanting, *them* with or without *-selves.*

sui, -orum, m., pl., *their men* (i.e., husbands), with or without *own.*

Iamque: Adverb (A.G. 215.6, 217.b and 320-21). **-que**: The enclitic conjunction here begins the sentence introducing a fresh situation and means "and, now" (*OLD* **-que** 4).

hoc: Singular, neuter, ablative demonstrative pronoun used substantively (A.G. 296.2). The antecedent is the idea of flight expressed above (A.G. 297.e). Accusative direct object of the infinitive **facere** (A.G. 387 and 451.3).

facere: Complementary infinitive after **apparabant** (A.G. 456).

noctu: Adverb (ablative or locative of **noctus, fourth-declension variant of nox*) (*OLD* **noctu**) (A.G. 320-21).

apparabant: The main verb of the main clause (A.G. 278.b). The pronoun **ei**, with **conati** (**Galli**) as the antecedent, is understood as the subject (A.G. 271.a).

cum ... procurrerunt ... petierunt: Temporal clause; when the principle action is expressed in the form of a temporal clause with the relative adverb **cum** ("when"), and the definition of time becomes the main clause, **cum** takes the indicative. This use is called *cum inversum* (A.G. 546.a). **procurrerunt ... petierunt**: The main verbs of the subordinate clause (A.G. 278.b). **petierunt**: A contracted form of **petiverunt** (A.G. 181.b).

matres: Nominative subject (A.G. 339). Women are not well represented in Book 7: for **matres familiae** see 26.3, 47.5, and 48.3; for **mulier** see 28.4, 47.5; for **uxor** see 66.7 and 78.3-4. For women in the *BG* see 1.3.5, 1.9.3, 1.18.6-7, 2.26.4, 1.29.1, 1.50.4, 1.53.4-5, 2.13.3, 2.16.4, 2.28.1, 4.14.5, 4.19.2, 5.14.4, 6.19.1, 6.19.3.

familiae: Partitive genitive with **matres** (A.G. 346.a.1).

repente: Adverb (A.G. 214.a and 320-21).

in publicum: Prepositional phrase, **in** with the accusative of **publicum** means "into the open, into the streets" (*OLD* **publicum** 5).

flentesque: Nominative, present, active, participle used as an adjective modifying **matres** (A.G. 494). **-que**: The enclitic conjunction connects the two verbs in the temporal clause **procurrerunt ... petierunt** (A.G. 324.a).

proiectae: Nominative, perfect, passive, participle used as an adjective modifying **matres** (A.G. 494). The passive participle of the verb **proicere** can have the active meaning "lying outstretched or prone" (*OLD* **proicio** 5.c).

ad pedes suorum: Prepositional phrase, **ad** with the accusative here means "at" (*OLD* **ad** 13). **suorum**: Plural, masculine, genitive possessive pronoun used substantively to denote a special class (A.G. 302.d). Possessive genitive with **pedes** (A.G. 343).

omnibus precibus: Ablative of means (A.G. 409).

ne ... dederent: The conjunction **ne** ("so that ... not") with the subjunctive forms a negative substantive clause of purpose which is used as the object of **petierunt** denoting an action directed toward the future (A.G. 563). **dederent**: The main verb of the subordinate clause (A.G. 278.b). Imperfect subjunctive; the tense of the subjunctive is in secondary sequence and follows the rules for the sequence of tense after **petierunt** (A.G. 482-85). The pronoun **ei**, with **Galli** as the antecedent, is understood as the subject (A.G. 271.a).

se et communis liberos: Two accusative direct objects of the transitive verb **dederent** (A.G. 387). **se**: Plural, feminine, accusative indirect reflexive pronoun (A.G. 300.2). The antecedent is **matres familiae**, the subject of **petierunt** (A.G. 299). **et**: The conjunction connects the two accusative nouns (A.G. 324.a). **communis**: Accusative plural adjective modifying **liberos**; **-is** for **-es** is the regular form in i-stem adjectives (A.G. 114.a and 115).

hostibus: Dative indirect object of the transitive verb **dederent** (A.G. 362).

ad supplicium: Prepositional phrase, **ad** with the accusative here means "for" (*OLD* **ad** 40).

quos ... impediret: Relative clause; a clause dependent on a subjunctive clause (**ne ... dederent**) takes the subjunctive when regarded as an integral part of that clause (attraction) (A.G. 303 and 593). **quos**: Plural, masculine, accusative relative pronoun used substantively (A.G. 305). The antecedent is **se et communis liberos**, agreeing in gender with the nearest noun (A.G. 305.a and 307). Accusative direct object of **impediret** (A.G. 387). **impediret**: The main verb of the subordinate clause (A.G. 278.b). Imperfect subjunctive; the tense of the subjunctive is in secondary sequence and follows the rules for the sequence of tense after **petierunt** (A.G. 482-85).

ad capiendam fugam: The preposition **ad** with the accusative gerundive and noun denotes purpose (A.G. 506). **capiendam**: Singular, feminine, accusative gerundive used as an adjective modifying **fugam** denoting necessity, obligation or propriety (A.G. 500.1).

naturae et virium: Two objective genitives after **infirmitas** (A.G. 348). **et**: The conjunction connects the two genitive nouns (A.G. 324.a).

infirmitas: Nominative subject (A.G.339).

(26.4-5) Ubi eos in sententia perstare viderunt, quod plerumque in summo periculo timor misericordiam non recipit, conclamare et significare de (5) fuga Romanis coeperunt.

coepi, -isse, coeptus, *begin, start, commence.*

de, *about, concerning.*
fuga, -ae, f., *flight.*
is, ea, id, *he, she, it; that, this.*
non, *not.*
persto, -stare, -steti, -staturus, *stand firmly, persist.*

quod, *because, since, for, as.*
Romani, -orum, m., pl., *the Romans.*
significo, -are, -avi, -atus, *show by signs, show, intimate, indicate.*
timor, -oris, m., *fear, dread, apprehension, alarm, timidity.*
video, videre, visi, visus, *perceive, observe, see.*

conclamo, -are, -avi, -atus, *cry out loud together, shout, cry out.*
et, *and.*
in, *in.*
misericordia, -ae, f., *pity, compassion, mercy.*
periculum, -i, n., *risk, danger, hazard.*
plerumque, *commonly, generally, usually, for the most part.*
recipio, -cipere, -cepi, -ceptus, *admit, allow.*
sententia, -ae, f., *opinion, view, notion.*
summus, -a, -um, *utmost, greatest, very great.*
ubi, *when.*

Ubi ... viderunt: Temporal clause; the relative adverb **ubi** ("when") with the indicative introduces a subordinate clause (A.G. 543). **viderunt**: The main verb of the subordinate clause (A.G. 278.b). The pronoun **eae**, with **matres familiae** as the antecedent, is understood as the subject (A.G. 271.a).

eos ... perstare: Accusative/infinitive construction in indirect discourse after **viderunt** (A.G. 577 ff.). **eos**: Plural, masculine, accusative demonstrative pronoun used substantively (A.G. 296.2). The antecedent is **suorum** (Galli) (A.G. 297.e). **perstare**: The tense of the infinitive in indirect discourse is relative to that of the verb of saying (A.G. 584).

in sententia: Prepositional phrase, **in** with the ablative here means "in" (expressing an abstract location) (*OLD* **in** 26).

quod ... recipit: A gnomic statement. Craig categorizes this general statement as one "whose application is as wide as human nature." (Craig, 109)

quod ... recipit: Causal clause; the conjunction **quod** ("because") takes the indicative when the reason is given on the authority of the writer or speaker (A.G. 540.1). **recipit**: The main verb of the subordinate clause (A.G. 278.b). The present tense here is not the historical present but the gnomic present which refers to no particular time, but denotes a general truth (A.G. 465.3).

plerumque: Adverb (A.G. 320-21).

in summo periculo: Prepositional phrase, **in** with the ablative here means "in" (expressing an abstract location) (*OLD* **in** 26). **summo**: Defective superlative adjective modifying **periculo** (A.G. 130.b).

timor: Nominative subject (A.G. 339).

misericordiam: Accusative direct object of **recipit** (A.G. 387).

non: Adverb, the adverb generally precedes the verb if it belongs to no one word in particular (A.G. 217.e, 320-21, and 599.a).

conclamare et significare: Two complementary infinitives after **coeperunt** (A.G. 456). **et**: The conjunction connects the two infinitives (A.G. 324.a).

de fuga: Prepositional phrase, **de** with the ablative here means "about, concerning" (*OLD* **de** 12). The prepositional phrase stands as the direct object of **significare**, a transitive infinitive used absolutely (A.G. 389).

Romanis: Dative indirect object of the transitive infinitive **significare** (the prepositional phrase **de fuga** functions as the direct object) (A.G. 362).

coeperunt: The main verb of the main clause (A.G. 278.b). The pronoun **eae**, with **matres familiae** as the antecedent, is understood as the subject (A.G. 271.a).

(26.5) **Quo timore perterriti Galli ne ab equitatu Romanorum viae praeoccuparentur consilio destiterunt.**

ab, *by.*
desisto, -sistere, -stiti, -stitus, *leave off, stop, give up.*
Galli, -orum, m., *the Gauls.*
perterreo, -terrere, -----, -territus, *greatly alarm, frighten, terrify, dismay.*
qui, quae, quod, *who, which, what.*
timor, -oris, m., *fear, dread, apprehension, alarm, timidity.*

consilium, -i, n., *plan, scheme, design.*
equitatus, -us, m., *cavalry.*
ne, *lest, that.*
praeoccupo, -are, -avi, -atus, *take possession of beforehand.*
Romani, -orum, m., pl., *the Romans.*
via, -ae, f., *way, road.*

Quo timore: Ablative of cause without a preposition (A.G. 404). **Quo**: Singular, masculine, ablative relative pronoun (A.G. 305). The antecedent is **timore** in its own clause (adjectival use) (A.G. 307.b). The relative does not introduce a relative clause but is a connecting relative; at the beginning of a clause the pronoun is often best rendered by a personal or demonstrative pronoun, with or without *and* (A.G. 308.f).

perterriti Galli: Nominative subject of **destiterunt** (A.G. 339). **perterriti**: Nominative, perfect, passive, participle used as a predicate, where in English a phrase or a subordinate clause would be more normal (A.G. 496). **Galli**: See Appendix A.

ne ... praeoccuparentur: The conjunction **ne** ("lest, that") with the subjunctive forms a substantive clause of fearing dependent on **perterriti** (A.G. 564). **praeoccuparentur**: The main verb of the subordinate clause (A.G. 278.b). Imperfect subjunctive; the tense of the subjunctive is in secondary sequence and follows the rules for the sequence of tense after **destiterunt** (A.G. 482-85).

ab equitatu Romanorum: Ablative of agent with the preposition **ab** after the passive verb **praeoccuparentur** (A.G. 405).

Romanorum: Partitive genitive with **equitatu** (A.G. 346.a.1).

viae: Nominative subject (A.G. 339).

consilio: Ablative of separation without a preposition after the compound verb **destiterunt** (A.G. 402).

destiterunt: The main verb of the main clause (A.G. 278.b).

(27.1-2) **Postero die Caesar, promota turri perfectisque operibus quae facere instituerat, magno coorto imbre, non inutilem hanc ad capiendum consilium tempestatem arbitratus est, quod paulo incautius custodias in muro dispositas videbat, suosque languidius in opere versari iussit et quid fieri (2) vellet ostendit;**

ad, *for, in order to, for the purpose of.*
Caesar, -aris, m., *Caesar.*
consilium, -i, n., *plan, scheme.*
custodia, -ae, f., *guard, watch.*
dispono, -ponere, -posui, -positus, *set in various places, station, post.*
facio, facere, feci, factus, *bring about, make, do.*

hic, haec, hoc, *this; he, she, it.*
in, *on; in.*
instituo, -stituere, -stitui, -stitutus, *undertake, commence, begin.*
iubeo, iubere, iussi, iussus, *order, give orders, bid, command.*
magnus, -a, -um, *great, large.*
non, *not.*

ostendo, -tendere, -tendi, -tentus, *point out, set forth, declare.*
perficio, -ficere, -feci, -fectus, *finish, complete.*
promoveo, -movere, -movi, -motus, *move forward, push forward.*
qui, quae, quod, *who, which, what.*
quod, *because, since, for, as.*
tempestas, -tatis, f., *stormy weather, bad weather, storm.*
volo, velle, volui, *wish, desire, intend.*

video, videre, visi, visus, *perceive, observe, see.*

arbitror, -ari, -atus, *think, suppose, consider, believe.*
capio, capere, cepi, captus, *form.*
coorior, -oriri, -ortus, *rise, spring up.*
dies, -ei, m. and f., *day.*
et, *and.*
fio, fieri, factus, *take place, happen, come about, come to pass.*
imber, imbris, m., *rain, rain storm.*
incaute, comp. **-ius**, *carelessly.*
inutilis, -e, *disadvantageous.*
languide, comp. **-ius**, *in a weak manner, feebly.*
murus, -i, m., *wall, rampart.*
opus, operis, n., *works, line of works, fortification; work, labor.*
paulo, *somewhat more.*
posterus, -a, -um, *following, the next.*
-que, *and.*
quis, -----, quid, *who? what?*
sui, -orum, m., pl., *his men*, with or without *own.*
turris, -is, f., *tower.*
versor, -ari, -atus, *be occupied, engaged, employed, busy.*

Postero die: Ablative of *time when* (A.G. 423.1). **die**: The noun **dies** is normally masculine gender (A.G. 97.a).

Caesar: Nominative subject of **arbitratus est ... iussit ... ostendit** (A.G. 339). See Appendix A.

promota turri: Ablative absolute (A.G. 419-20). **promota**: The perfect tense of the participle represents the action as completed at the time indicated by the tense of the main verb (A.G. 489).

perfectis ... instituerat: Ablative absolute with a dependent clause.

perfectisque operibus: Ablative absolute (A.G. 419-20). **perfectis**: The perfect tense of the participle represents the action as completed at the time indicated by the tense of the main verb (A.G. 489). **-que**: The enclitic conjunction connects the two ablative absolutes (A.G. 324.a).

quae ... instituerat: Relative clause (A.G. 303). **quae**: Plural, neuter, accusative relative pronoun used substantively (A.G. 305). The antecedent is **operibus** (A.G. 307). Accusative direct object of the infinitive **facere** (A.G. 387 and 451.3). **instituerat**: The main verb of the subordinate clause (A.G. 278.b). The pronoun **is**, with **Caesar** as the antecedent, is understood as the subject (A.G. 271.a). The pluperfect tense of the verb denotes an action completed in past time (A.G. 477).

facere: Complementary infinitive after **instituerat** (A.G. 456).

magno coorto imbre: Ablative absolute (A.G. 419-20). **coorto**: The perfect tense of the participle represents the action as completed at the time indicated by the tense of the main verb (A.G. 489).

non inutilem: A litotes, a statement is made emphatic by denying its contrary (A.G. 326.c).

non: Adverb modifying **inutilem**; the negative precedes the word it especially effects (A.G. 217.e, 320-21, and 599.a).

inutilem hanc ... tempestatem (esse): Accusative/infinitive construction in indirect discourse after **arbitratus est** (A.G. 577 ff.).

inutilem: Singular, feminine, accusative predicate adjective modifying **tempestatem** after the supplied infinitive **esse** (A.G. 283-84). The adjective is a compound of the adverbial prefix **in-** (meaning *not*) and **utilis** (A.G. 267.d.1). **hanc**: Singular, feminine, accusative demonstrative pronoun used as an adjective modifying **tempestatem** (A.G. 297.1 and a). **esse**: Supply **esse** as the infinitive.

ad capiendum consilium: The preposition **ad** with the accusative gerundive and noun denotes purpose (A.G. 506). **capiendum consilium**: The phrase **consilium capere** is an idiom that means "to adopt or form a plan" (*OLD* capio 9.e). **capiendum**: Singular, neuter, accusative gerundive used as an adjective modifying **consilium** denoting necessity, obligation or propriety (A.G. 500.1).

arbitratus est: The main verb of the coordinate clause **Postero ... videbat** (A.G. 278.a).

quod ... videbat: Causal clause; the conjunction **quod** ("because") takes the indicative when the reason is given on the authority of the writer or speaker (A.G. 540.1). **videbat**: The main verb of the subordinate clause (A.G. 278.b). The pronoun **is**, with **Caesar** as the antecedent, is understood as the subject (A.G. 271.a).

paulo: Adverb; **paulo** with a comparative adverb means "somewhat more" (*OLD* paul(l)o 2.a).

incautius: Comparative adverb (A.G. 218 and 320-21).

custodias ... dispositas (esse): Accusative/infinitive construction in indirect discourse after **videbat** (A.G. 577 ff.). **dispositas (esse)**: Supply **esse** to form the perfect, passive infinitive (A.G. 186). The tense of the infinitive in indirect discourse is relative to that of the verb of saying (A.G. 584).

in muro: Ablative of *place where* with the preposition **in** (locative ablative) (A.G. 426.3).

suosque. ... versari: Subject accusative with the infinitive after **iussit**. The construction is equivalent to a substantive clause of purpose (A.G. 563.a). **suos**: Plural, masculine, accusative possessive pronoun used substantively to denote a special class (A.G. 302.d). **-que**: The enclitic conjunction connects the two verbs **arbitratus est ... iussit** (A.G. 324.a). **versari**: Present infinitive; the tense of the infinitive in indirect discourse is relative to that of the verb of saying (A.G. 584).

languidius: Comparative adverb (A.G. 218 and 320-21).

in opere: Prepositional phrase, **in** with the ablative here means "in" (expressing an abstract location) (*OLD* in 26).

iussit: The main verb of the coordinate clause **suosque ... iussit** (A.G. 278.a).

et: The conjunction connects the two main verbs **iussit ... ostendit** (A.G. 324.a).

quid ... vellet: Indirect question with the subjunctive; the phrase is the object of **ostendit** (A.G. 573-75). **quid**: See below. **vellet**: The main verb of the subordinate clause (A.G. 278.b). Imperfect subjunctive; the tense of the subjunctive is in secondary sequence and follows the rules for the sequence of tense for indirect questions after **ostendit** (A.G. 575). The pronoun **is**, with **Caesar** as the antecedent, is understood as the subject (A.G. 271.a).

quid fieri: Subject accusative with the infinitive after **vellet**. The construction is equivalent to a substantive clause of purpose (A.G. 563.b.2). **quid**: Singular, neuter, accusative interrogative pronoun used substantively (A.G. 148).

ostendit: The main verb of the coordinate clause **quid ... ostendit** (A.G. 278.a).

(27.2) legionibusque extra castra intra vineas in occulto expeditis, cohortatus ut aliquando pro tantis laboribus fructum victoriae perciperent eis qui primi murum ascendissent praemia proposuit militibusque signum dedit.

aliquando, *at length, finally, now at last.*

castra, -orum, n., pl., *camp, encampment.*

do, dare, dedi, datus, *give.*

extra, *outside, beyond.*

in, *in.*

is, ea, id, *he, she, it; that, this.*

legio, -onis, f., *legion.*

murus, -i, m., *wall.*

percipio, -cipere, -cepi, -ceptus, *get, secure.*

primus, -a, -um, *first.*

propono, -ponere, -posui, -positus, *put forward, present, propose.*

qui, quae, quod, *who, which, what.*

tantus, -a, -um, *so great, so large, such.*

ascendo, -scendere, -scendi, -scensus, *ascend, climb, mount, scale.*

cohortor, -ari, -atus, *encourage, urge, exhort, address.*

expedio, -pedire, -pedivi, -peditus, *get ready, make ready.*

fructus, -us, m., *advantage, gain, enjoyment, reward.*

intra, *within, inside.*

labor, -oris, m., *toil, exertion, labor.*

miles, -itis, m., *soldier, foot-solider.*

occultum, -i, n., *hiding, concealment.*

praemium, -i, n., *reward, recompense.*

pro, *as a reward for, in return for.*

-que, *and, now; and.*

signum, -i, n., *signal.*

ut, *so that.*

vinea, -ae, f., *arbor-shed, vinea.*   victoria, -ae, f., *victory.*

legionibusque extra castra intra vineas in occulto expeditis: Ablative absolute (A.G. 419-20). **-que**: The enclitic here begins the sentence and means "and, now" (*OLD* -que 4). **extra ... intra ... in**: Three consecutive prepositional phrases. **extra castra**: Prepositional phrase, **extra** with the accusative here means "outside" (*OLD* extra 6). **intra vineas**: Prepositional phrase, **intra** with the accusative here means "within, inside" (*OLD* intra 1). **in occulto**: Prepositional phrase, **in** with the singular, neuter, ablative of the adjective **occultus** means "in hiding or concealment" (*OLD* occultus 5). **expeditis**: The perfect tense of the participle represents the action as completed at the time indicated by the tense of the main verb (A.G. 489).

cohortatus: Nominative, perfect, deponent, participle used as a predicate, where in English a phrase or a subordinate clause would be more normal (A.G. 496). The pronoun **is**, with **Caesar** as the antecedent, is understood. Nominative subject of **proposuit ... dedit** (A.G. 339).

ut ... perciperent: The conjunction **ut** ("so that") with the subjunctive forms a substantive clause of purpose which is used as the object of the participle **cohortatus** denoting an action directed toward the future (A.G. 563). **perciperent**: The main verb of the subordinate clause (A.G. 278.b). Imperfect subjunctive; the tense of the subjunctive is in secondary sequence and follows the rules for the sequence of tense after **proposuit** (A.G. 482-85). The pronoun **eae**, with **legionibus** as the antecedent, is understood as the subject (A.G. 271.a).

aliquando: Adverb (A.G. 217.b and 320-21).

pro tantis laboribus: Prepositional phrase, **pro** with the ablative here means "as a reward for, in return for" (*OLD* pro 10).

fructum: Accusative direct object of the transitive verb **perciperent** (A.G. 387)

victoriae: Partitive genitive with **fructum** (A.G. 346.a.1).

eis: Plural, masculine, dative demonstrative pronoun used substantively (A.G. 296.2). The pronoun is correlative to the relative clause **qui ... ascendissent** (A.G. 297.d). Dative indirect object of the transitive verb **proposuit** (A.G. 362).

qui ... ascendissent: A relative clause of characteristic; a relative clause with the subjunctive is often used to indicate a characteristic of the antecedent (A.G. 535). **qui**: Plural, masculine, nominative relative pronoun used substantively (A. G. 305). The antecedent is **eis** (A.G. 307). Nominative subject (A.G. 339). **ascendissent**: The main verb of the subordinate clause (A.G. 278.b). Pluperfect subjunctive; the tense of the subjunctive is in secondary sequence and follows the rules for the sequence of tense after **proposuit** (A.G. 482-85). The pluperfect tense of the subjunctive is here standing for a future perfect (A.G. 484.c). The future perfect tense denotes action completed (at the time referred to), and hence is represented in the subjunctive by the pluperfect tense in secondary sequence (A.G. 484.c).

primi: Declinable ordinal number used as an adjective modifying **qui** (A.G. 132-35).

murum: Accusative direct object of **ascendissent** (A.G. 387).

praemia: Accusative direct object of **proposuit** (A.G. 387). "Sometimes Caesar gave money realized from the sale of booty (*praemium*); ... As other rewards (*praemia*), the commander could make special gifts (*dona*), such as the familiar disk-shaped decorations of metal, for the breast (*phalerae*); chains (*torques*); rings for the arms (*armillae*); little silver or gold spears (*hostae purae*) or shields (*parmae purae*); and sacrificial bowls (*paterae sacrificiales*)." (Kelsey, 27) (For a full discussion see Watson, 114-117)

proposuit: The main verb of the coordinate clause **legionibusque ... proposuit** (A.G. 278.a).

militibusque: Dative indirect object of the transitive verb **dedit** (A.G. 362). **-que**: The enclitic conjunction connects the two main verbs **proposuit ... dedit** (A.G. 324.a).

signum: Accusative direct object of the transitive verb **dedit** (A.G. 387).

dedit: The main verb of the coordinate clause **militibusque ... dedit** (A.G. 278.a).

(27.3) **(3) Illi subito ex omnibus partibus evolaverunt murumque celeriter compleverunt.**

celeriter, *quickly, speedily, at once, immediately.*   compleo, -plere, -plevi, -pletus, *fully occupy, fill full.*
evolo, -are, -avi, -atus, *fly forth, rush out, dash out.*   ex, *from, out of.*
ille, illae, illud, *that; he, she, it.*   murus, -i, m., *wall.*
omnis, -e, *all.*   pars, partis, f., *part, region, district, direction, side.*
-que, *and.*   subito, *suddenly, on a sudden.*

Illi: Plural, masculine, nominative demonstrative pronoun used substantively (A.G. 296.2). The antecedent is **militibus** (A.G. 297.e). Nominative subject of **evolaverunt ... compleverunt** (A.G. 339). The pronoun marks a change in subject to one previously mentioned (**militibus**) (A.G. 601.d).

subito: Adverb (A.G. 320-21).

ex omnibus partibus: Ablative of *place from which* with the preposition **ex** (A.G. 426.1).

evolaverunt: The main verb of the coordinate clause **Illi ... evolaverunt** (A.G. 278.a).

murumque: Accusative direct object of **compleverunt** (A.G. 387). **-que**: The enclitic conjunction connects the two main verbs **evolaverunt ... compleverunt** (A.G. 324.a).

celeriter: Adverb (A.G. 214.b and 320-21).

compleverunt: The main verb of the coordinate clause **murumque ... compleverunt** (A.G. 278.a).

(28.1-2) **Hostes re nova perterriti, muro turribusque deiecti in foro ac locis patentioribus cuneatim constiterunt hoc animo ut, si qua ex parte obviam [contra] veniretur, acie instructa (2) depugnarent.**

ac, *and.*   acies, -ei, f., *battle line, line.*

animus, **-i**, m., *purpose, intention, resolve.*

contra, *opposite, in opposition.*
deicio, **-icere**, **-ieci**, **-iectus**, *throw down, cast down, dislodge, rout.*
ex, *on.*
hic, **haec**, **hoc**, *this; he, she, it.*
in, *in.*
loca, **-orum**, n., pl., *places.*
novus, **-a**, **-um**, *new, fresh, strange.*
pars, **partis**, f., *part, region, district, direction, side.*
perterreo, **-terrere**, **-----**, **-territus**, *greatly alarm, frighten, terrify, dismay.*
quis, **-----**, **quid**, *any;* (as adj., **qui**, **quae**, or **qua**, **quod**).
si, *if.*
ut, *so that.*

consisto, **-sistere**, **-stiti**, **-stitus**, *take a position, take a stand, stand, stop.*
cuneatim, *in the form of a wedge.*
depugno, **-are**, **-avi**, **-atus**, *fight decisively.*
forum, **-i**, n., *market-place, forum.*
hostis, **-is**, m., *enemy, foe;* pl., *the enemy.*
instruo, **-struere**, **-struxi**, **-structus**, *draw up, form.*
murus, **-i**, m., *wall.*
obviam, *towards, against.*
patens, **-entis**, comp. **-ior**, *open, accessible.*
-que, *and.*
res, **rei**, f., *situation, circumstance.*
turris, **-is**, f., *tower.*
venio, **venire**, **veni**, **ventus**, *come.*

Hostes ... perterriti ... deiecti: Nominative subject of **constiterunt** (A.G. 339). **perterriti ... deiecti:** Two nominative, perfect, passive, participles used as a predicate, where in English a phrase or a subordinate clause would be more normal (A.G. 496). Note the asyndeton between the two participles (A. G. 323.b).
re nova: Ablative of cause without a preposition (A.G. 404).
muro turribusque: Two ablatives of separation without a preposition after the compound participle **deiecti** (A.G. 402). **-que:** The enclitic conjunction connects the two ablative nouns (A.G. 324.a).
in foro ac locis patentioribus: Ablative of *place where* with the preposition **in** (locative ablative) (A.G. 426.3). **ac:** The conjunction connects the two ablative nouns and means "and" (*OLD* **atque** 12). **patentioribus:** The comparative degree of the present participle used as an adjective modifying **locis** (A.G. 494.a).
cuneatim: Adverb (A.G. 320-21).
constiterunt: The main verb of the main clause (A.G. 278.b).
hoc animo: Ablative of manner with a limiting adjective (A.G. 412). The phrase is correlative to the following purpose clause (A.G. 531.1 Note 1). **hoc:** Singular, masculine, ablative demonstrative pronoun used as an adjective modifying **animo** (A.G. 296.1 and a).
ut si ... veniretur ... depugnarent: A subordinate conditional statement (A.G. 512.c). The apodosis, as a purpose clause after **constiterunt** and correlative to **hoc animo**, takes the subjunctive and the protasis, as a clause subordinate to a subjunctive clause, also takes the subjunctive (attraction) (A.G. 512.c and 593).
ut ... depugnarent: The apodosis of the conditional statement (A.G. 512.c). The conjunction **ut** ("so that") with the subjunctive forms a final (purpose) clause correlative to **hoc animo** (A.G. 531.1 and Note 1). **depugnarent:** The main verb of the subordinate clause (A.G. 278.b). Imperfect subjunctive; the tense of the subjunctive is in secondary sequence and follows the rules for the sequence of tense after **constiterunt** (A.G. 482-85). The pronoun **ei**, with **Hostes** as the antecedent, is understood as the subject (A.G. 271.a).
si ... (id) veniretur: The conjunction **si** ("if") with the subjunctive forms the protasis of the conditional statement (A.G. 512). A clause dependent on a subjunctive clause (**ut ... depugnarent**) takes the subjunctive when regarded as an integral part of that clause (attraction) (A.G. 593). **veniretur:** The main verb of the subordinate clause (A.G. 278.b). Imperfect subjunctive; the tense of the subjunctive is in secondary sequence and follows the rules for the sequence of tense after **constiterunt** (A.G. 482-85). Impersonal use of the passive verb (A.G. 208.d). Supply **id** as the subject (A.G. 318.c).
qua ex parte: Ablative of *position* with the preposition **ex** (A.G. 429.b). **qua:** Singular, feminine, ablative indefinite pronoun used as an adjective modifying **parte** (A.G. 149). The indefinite pronoun **quis**, **-----**, **quid** (**qui**, **quae**, or **qua**, **quod** when used adjectively) is used after **si** (A.G. 310.a). **ex:** A monosyllabic preposition is often placed between a noun and its adjective (A.G. 599.d.2).
obviam: Adverb, used with a verb of motion (**veniretur**) (A.G. 320-21). The phrase **obviam veniri** is an idiom that means "an advance is made" (*Lewis*, **obviam**).
[contra]: Adverb (A.G. 320-21).
acie instructa: Ablative absolute (A.G. 419-20). **instructa:** The perfect tense of the participle represents the action as completed at the time indicated by the tense of the main verb (A.G. 489).

(28.2-4) Ubi neminem in aequum locum sese demittere sed toto undique muro circumfundi viderunt, veriti ne omnino spes fugae tolleretur, abiectis armis ultimas (3) oppidi partis continenti impetu petiverunt, parsque ibi, cum angusto exitu portarum se ipsi premerent, a militibus, pars iam egressa portis ab equitibus est interfecta; nec fuit (4) quisquam qui praedae studeret.

a(b), *by.*
aequus, **-a**, **-um**, *level, even, flat.*
arma, **-orum**, n., *arms, weapons.*

continens, **-entis**, *continuous, uninterrupted, continual.*
demitto, **-mittere**, **-misi**, **-misus**, *let down, lower.*

eques, **-itis**, m., *rider, horseman, cavalryman, trooper.*
fuga, **-ae**, f., *flight.*
ibi, *in that place, there.*
in, *to, into.*

abicio, **-icere**, **-ieci**, **-iectus**, *throw away, throw down.*
angustus, **-a**, **-um**, *contracted, narrow, close.*
circumfundo, **-fundere**, **-fudi**, **fusus**, *surround, encircle, hem in.*
cum, *when, while.*
egredior, **-gredi**, **-gressus**, *go out, go forth, come forth, leave.*
exitus, **-us**, m., *passage.*
iam, *already, by this time.*
impetus, **-us**, m., *attack, assault, onset, charge.*
interficio, **-ficere**, **-feci**, **-fectus**, *slay, kill.*

ipse, -a, -um, *he, they*, with or without *himself, themselves*.
miles, -itis, m., *soldier, foot-solider*.
ne, *lest, that*.
nemo, acc. **neminem**, m., *no man, no one, nobody*.
oppidum, -i, n., *fortified town, city*.
peto, petere, petivi, and **petii, petitus**, *make for, try to reach, seek*.
praeda, -ae, f., *booty, spoil, plunder*.
-que, *and*.
quisquam, -----, quidquam, *anyone, anything, any*.
spes, -ei, f., *hope*   .
sui, sibi, se, or **sese**, nom. wanting, *himself, each other, one another*.
tollo, tollere, sustuli, sublatus, *remove, take away, abolish, do away with*.
ubi, *when*.
undique, *on all sides, everywhere*.
video, videre, visi, visus, *perceive, observe, see*.

locus, -i, m., *place, location, spot, area*.
murus, -i, m., *wall*.
nec, *and ... not*.
omnino, *all together, wholly, entirely, utterly*.
pars, partis, f., *part, region, district, side*; *part*.
porta -ae, f., *city gate*.
premo, -ere, pressi, pressus, *press, crowd*.
qui, quae, quod, *who, which, what*.
sed, *but in fact*.
studeo, -ere, -ui, -----, *be eager for, eagerly desire*.
sum, esse, fui, futurus, *be*.
totus, -a, -um, *the whole of, the entire*.
ultimus, -a, -um, *furthest, most distant, most remote*.
vereor, -eri, -itus, *fear, be afraid of*.

Ubi ... viderunt: Temporal clause; the relative adverb **ubi** ("when") with the indicative introduces a subordinate clause (A.G. 543). **viderunt**: The main verb of the subordinate clause (A.G. 278.b). The pronoun **ei**, with **Hostes** as the antecedent, is understood as the subject (A.G. 271.a).

neminem ... demittere: Accusative/infinitive construction in indirect discourse after **viderunt** (A.G. 577 ff.). **neminem**: Singular, masculine, accusative indefinite pronoun used substantively (A.G. 314.1). **demittere**: Present infinitive; the tense of the infinitive in indirect discourse is relative to that of the verb of saying (A.G. 584).

in aequum locum: Accusative of *place to which* with the preposition **in** (A.G. 426.2). Where the Gauls were awaiting the Romans.

sese: Singular, masculine, accusative direct reflexive pronoun (A.G. 300.1). The antecedent is **neminem**, the subject of the infinitive **demittere** (A.G. 299). Accusative direct object of the infinitive **demittere** (A.G. 387 and 451.3). Reduplicated form of **se** (A.G. 144.b Note 1).

sed: Coordinate conjunction (A.G. 324.d).

toto ... muro: Ablative of *place where* without a preposition (A.G. 429.2).

undique: Adverb (A.G. 217.a and 320-21).

(se) circumfundi: Accusative/infinitive construction in indirect discourse after **viderunt** (A.G. 577 ff.). Supply the direct reflexive pronoun **se**, with **Hostes** as the antecedent, as the accusative subject of the infinitive. **circumfundi**: Present infinitive; the tense of the infinitive in indirect discourse is relative to that of the verb of saying (A.G. 584).

veriti ne ... tolleretur: The conjunction **ne** ("lest, that") with the subjunctive forms a substantive clause of fearing (A.G. 564). **veriti**: Nominative, perfect, deponent participle used as a predicate, where in English a phrase or a subordinate clause would be more normal (A.G. 496). The pronoun **ei**, with **Hostes** as the antecedent, is understood. Nominative subject of **petiverunt** (A.G. 339). **tolleretur**: The main verb of the subordinate clause (A.G. 278.b). Imperfect subjunctive; the tense of the subjunctive is in secondary sequence and follows the rules for the sequence of tense after **petiverunt** (A.G. 482-85).

omnino: Adverb (A.G. 320-21).

spes: Nominative subject (A.G. 339).

fugae: Objective genitive with **spes** (A.G. 348).

abiectis armis: Ablative absolute (A.G. 419-20). **abiectis**: The perfect tense of the participle represents the action as completed at the time indicated by the tense of the main verb (A.G. 489).

ultimas ... partis: Accusative direct object of **petiverunt** (A.G. 387). **ultimas**: Defective superlative adjective (A.G. 130.a). The adjective designates not what object, but what part of it is meant (A.G. 293). **partis**: Accusative plural noun, **-is** for **-es** is the regular form in mixed i-stem nouns (A.G. 71-2).

oppidi: Partitive genitive with **partis** (A.G. 346.a.1).

continenti impetu: Ablative of manner with a limiting adjective (A.G. 412). **continenti**: Present participle of **contineo** used as an adjective modifying **impetu** (A.G. 494). Participles used as adjectives regularly end in -i in the ablative singular (A.G. 121.a.2).

petiverunt: The main verb of the coordinate clause **Ubi ... petiverunt** (A.G. 278.a).

parsque: First nominative subject of **interfecta est** (A.G. 339). **-que**: The enclitic conjunction connects the two verbs **petiverunt ... interfecta est** (A.G. 324.a).

ibi: Adverb (A.G. 215.5 and 320-21).

cum ... premerent: Temporal clause; the relative adverb **cum** ("when, while") with the imperfect subjunctive describes the circumstances that accompanied the action of the main verb (A.G. 546). **premerent**: The main verb of the subordinate clause (A.G. 278.b).

angusto exitu: Ablative of *place where* without a preposition (A.G. 429.2).

portarum: Partitive genitive with **exitu** (A.G. 346.a.1).

se: Plural, masculine, accusative direct pronoun used reciprocally and meaning "each other, one another" (A.G. 300.1) (*OLD* se 8). The antecedent is **ipsi**, the subject of **premerent** (A.G. 299). Accusative direct object of **premerent** (A.G. 387).

ipsi: Plural, masculine, nominative demonstrative pronoun used substantively (A.G. 296.2). The antecedent is **hostes** (A.G. 298.1). Nominative subject (A.G. 339). The pronoun is here emphatic (A.G. 298.d.1).

a militibus: Ablative of agent with the preposition **a(b)** with the passive verb **est interfecta** (A.G. 405).

pars ... egressa: Second nominative subject of **interfecta est** (A.G. 339). **egressa**: Nominative, perfect, deponent, participle used as a predicate, where in English a phrase or a subordinate clause would be more normal (A.G. 496).

iam: Adverb (A.G. 215.6, 217.b and 320-21).

portis: Ablative of separation without a preposition after the compound participle **egressa** (A.G. 402).

ab equitibus: Ablative of agent with the preposition **ab** with the passive verb **est interfecta** (A.G. 405).

interfecta est: The main verb of the coordinate clause **parsque ... interfecta est** (A.G. 278.a). Two singular subjects normally take a verb in the plural (A.G. 317). Here they are considered as a single whole and so the verb is singular (A.G. 317.b).

nec: The conjunction joins a negative clause to a preceding positive one and means "and ... not" (*OLD* **neque** 3).

fuit: The main verb of the main clause (A.G. 278.b). The verb **sum** in the sense of "exist" makes a complete predicate without a predicate noun or adjective ("was there ..."). It is then called the substantive verb and regularly comes first (A.G. 284.b and 598.c).

quisquam: Singular, masculine, nominative indefinite pronoun used substantively (A.G. 151.d). Nominative subject (A.G. 339).

qui ... studeret: A relative clause of characteristic; a relative clause with the subjunctive is often used to indicate a characteristic of the antecedent (A.G. 535). **qui**: Singular, masculine, nominative relative pronoun used substantively (A.G. 305). The antecedent is **quisquam** (A.G. 307). Nominative subject (A.G. 339). **studeret**: The main verb of the subordinate clause (A.G. 278.b). Imperfect subjunctive; the tense of the subjunctive is in secondary sequence and follows the rules for the sequence of tense after **fuit** (A.G. 482-85).

praedae: Dative indirect object of the intransitive verb **studeret** (A.G. 368.3).

(28.4-5) Sic et Cenabi caede et labore operis incitati non aetate confectis, non mulieribus, (5) non infantibus pepercerunt.

aetas, -tatis, f., *old age*.
Cenabum, -i, n., *Cenabum*.
et ... et, *both ... and*.
infans, -antis, m., or f., *child, infant*.
mulier, -eris, f., *woman*.
opus, operis, n., *work, labor, toil, siege-work*.

sic, *so, in this way, thus*.

caedes, -is, f., *killing, slaughter, murder, massacre*.
conficio, -ficere, -feci, -fectus, *wear out, exhaust*.
incito, -are, -avi, -atus, *rouse, stir up, excite*.
labor, -oris, m., *toil, exertion, fatigue, labor*.
non, *not*.
parco, parcere, peperci, and **parsi, parsus**, *spare, give quarter to*.

Sic: Adverb (A.G. 217.c and 320-21).

et ... et: The repeated conjunction means "both ... and", connecting the ablative nouns **caede ... labore** (A.G. 323.e).

Cenabi: Locative case of the city name **Cenabum, -i**, n. (A.G. 49.a). See Appendix A.

caede ... labore: Two ablatives of cause after **incitati** (A.G. 404).

operis: Objective genitive with **labore** (A.G. 348).

incitati: Nominative, perfect, passive, participle used as a predicate, where in English a phrase or a subordinate clause would be more normal (A.G. 496). The noun **Romani** is understood. Nominative subject of **pepercerunt** (A.G. 339).

non ... non ... non: The repetition of words at the beginning of successive clauses is anaphora (A.G. 641). "Caesar uses triple anaphora of *non* to highlight this fierce vengeance, rather than attempt to conceal it. Killing people who might have been sold into slavery for profit is meant to show the disinterested nature of the soldier's revenge." (Hammond, 238)

non: Adverb; when **non** is especially emphatic it begins the clause (A.G. 217.e, 320-21, and 599.a).

aetate: Ablative of cause without a preposition after **confectis** (A.G. 404).

confectis ... mulieribus ... infantibus: Three dative indirect objects of the intransitive use of the verb **pepercerunt** (A.G. 367).

confectis: Plural, masculine, dative, perfect, passive participle used substantively (A.G. 494.a). The noun **hominibus** is understood.

non: Adverb; the negative precedes the word it especially effects (**mulieribus**) (A.G. 217.e, 320-21, and 599.a).

non: Adverb; the negative precedes the word it especially effects (**infantibus**) (A.G. 217.e, 320-21, and 599.a).

pepercerunt: The main verb of the simple sentence (A.G. 278.1). "A more horrible slaughter is not recorded in history." (Kelsey, 409)

(28.5-6) Denique ex omni numero, qui fuit circiter milium XL, vix DCCC, qui primo clamore audito se ex oppido eiecerunt, incolumes ad Vercingetori(6)gem pervenerunt.

ad, *to*.
C, in expression of number, = *100*.
clamor, -oris, m., *outcry, loud call, shout, din*.
denique, *at last, finally*.
ex, *from the number of, from among, of, from, out of*.
L, in expression of number, *50*.
numerus, -i, m., *number*.
oppidum, -i, n., *fortified town, city*.
primus, -a, -um, *first*.
sui, sibi, se, or **sese**, nom. wanting, *themselves*.
Vercingetorix, -igis, m., *Vercingetorix*.
X, in expression of number, = *10*.

audio, -ire, -ivi or **-ii, -itus**, *hear*.
circiter, *about*.
D, in expression of number, = *500*.
eicio, -icere, -ieci, -iectus, (with **se**), *rush forth*.
incolumis, -e, *safe, unharmed, uninjured, unhurt*.
milia, -um, n., pl., *thousand, thousands*.
omnis, -e, *the whole*.
pervenio, -venire, -veni, -ventus, *come to, reach*.
qui, quae, quod, *who, which, what*.
sum, esse, fui, futurus, *be*.
vix, *scarcely, barely*.

Denique: Adverb (A.G. 320-21).

ex omni numero: Prepositional phrase with **DCCC**, **ex** with the ablative instead of the partitive genitive means "from the number of, from among, of". Cardinal numbers (here the Roman numeral **DCCC**) regularly take the ablative with **ex** instead of the partitive genitive (A.G. 346.c) (*OLD* **ex** 17).

qui ... XL: Relative clause (A.G. 303). **qui**: Singular, masculine, nominative relative pronoun used substantively (A.G. 305). The antecedent is **numero** (A.G. 307). Nominative subject (A.G. 339). **XL**: See below.

fuit: The main verb of the subordinate clause (A.G. 278.b).

circiter: Adverb (A.G. 320-21).

milium XL: Possessive genitive (predicate genitive); the possessive genitive often stands in the predicate, connected to its noun (**qui**) by a verb (**fuit**) (A.G. 343.b). **milium**: Genitive plural; in the plural **mille** declines as a neuter noun (A.G. 134.d). **XL**: Roman numeral used as an adjective modifying **milium** (A.G. 133).

vix: Adverb (A.G. 217.c and 320-21).

DCCC: Nominative subject of **pervenerunt** (A.G. 339). Roman numeral used substantively as a cardinal number (A.G. 133). The noun **homines** is understood (A.G. 288).

qui ... eiecerunt: Relative clause (A.G. 303). **qui**: Plural, masculine, nominative relative pronoun used substantively (A.G. 305). The antecedent is **DCCC** (A.G. 307). Nominative subject (A.G. 339). **eiecerunt**: The main verb of the subordinate clause (A.G. 278.b).

primo clamore audito: Ablative absolute (A.G. 419-20). **primo**: Declinable ordinal number used as an adjective modifying **clamore** (A.G. 132-35). **audito**: The perfect tense of the participle represents the action as completed at the time indicated by the tense of the main verb (A.G. 489).

se: Plural, masculine, accusative direct reflexive pronoun (A.G. 300.1). The antecedent is **qui**, the subject of **eiecerunt** (A.G. 299). Accusative direct object of **eiecerunt** (A.G. 387).

ex oppido: Ablative of *place from which* with the preposition **ex** (A.G. 426.1).

incolumes: Plural, masculine, nominative adjective modifying **DCCC** but used to qualify the action of the verb, and so has the force of an adverb (A.G. 290).

ad Vercingetorigem: Prepositional phrase, **ad** with the accusative here means "to" (*OLD* **ad** 1). **Vercingetorigem**: See Appendix A.

pervenerunt: The main verb of the main clause (A.G. 278.b).

(28.6) Quos ille multa iam nocte silentio ex fuga excepit veritus ne qua in castris ex eorum concursu et misericordia vulgi seditio oriretur, ut procul in via dispositis familiaribus suis principibusque civitatum disparandos deducendosque ad suos curaret, quae cuique civitati pars castrorum ab initio obvenerat.

ab, *from, since.*
castra, -orum, n., pl., *camp, encampment.*
concursus, -us, m., *running together, rushing about.*

deduco, -ducere, -duxi, -ductus, *lead away, lead off, withdraw.*
dispono, -ponere, -posui, -positus, *set in various places, station, post.*
ex, *immediately after, following on; from, because of.*
fuga, -ae, f., *flight.*

iam, *already, by this time, previously.*
in, *in; on.*
is, ea, id, *he, she, it; that, this.*
multus, -a, -um, *late at.*
nox, noctis, f., *night.*
orior, oriri, ortus, *rise.*
princeps, -ipis, m., *head man, leader, chief, prince.*
-que, *and.*
quis, -----, quid, *any;* (as adj., **qui, quae,** or **qua, quod**).

seditio, -onis, f., *revolt, sedition.*
sui, -orum, m., pl., *his men*, with or without *own.*
ut, *so that.*
via, -ae, f., *way, road.*

ad, *to.*
civitas, -tatis, f., *state, nation.*
curo, -are, -avi, -atus, *take care, provide for, superintend, arrange.*
disparo, -are, -avi, -atus, *divide, separate.*
et, *and.*
excipio, -cipere, -cepi, -ceptus, *take in.*
familiaris, -is, m., *intimate friend, confidant, companion.*
ille, illae, illud, *that; he, she, it.*
initium, -i, n., *beginning, commencement.*
misericordia, -ae, f., *pity, compassion, mercy.*
ne, *lest, that.*
obvenio, -venire, -veni, -ventus, *fall to the lot of, fall to.*
pars, partis, f., *part, section, district, side.*
procul, *at a distance, from afar, far off.*
qui, quae, quod, *who, which, what.*
quisque, quaeque, quidque, *each,* (as adj., **quisque, quaeque, quodque**)
silentium, -i, m., *silence, stillness.*
suus, -a, -um, *his*, with or without *own.*
vereor, -eri, -itus, *fear, be afraid of.*
vulgus, -i, n., *common people, mass, multitude, crowd.*

Quos: Plural, masculine, accusative relative pronoun used substantively (A.G. 305). The antecedent is **DCCC** (A.G. 307). Accusative direct object of **excepit** (A.G. 387). The relative does not introduce a relative clause but is a connecting relative; at the beginning of a clause the pronoun is often best rendered by a personal or demonstrative pronoun, with or without *and* (A.G. 308.f).

ille: Singular, masculine, nominative demonstrative pronoun used substantively (A.G. 296.2). The antecedent is **Vercingetorigem** (A.G. 297.e). Nominative subject (A.G. 339). The pronoun marks a change in subject to one previously mentioned (**Vercingetorigem**) (A.G. 601.d).

multa ... nocte: Ablative of *time when* meaning "late at night" (A.G. 423.1) (*OLD* **multus** 5).

iam: Adverb (A.G. 215.6, 217.b and 320-21).

silentio: Ablative of manner (A.G. 412.b).

ex fuga: Prepositional phrase, **ex** with the ablative here means "immediately after, following on" (*OLD* **ex** 10).

excepit: The main verb of the main clause (A.G. 278.b).

veritus ne ... oriretur: The conjunction **ne** ("lest, that") with the subjunctive forms a substantive clause of fearing (A.G. 564).
veritus: The nominative, perfect, deponent participle used as a predicate modifying **ille**, where in English a phrase or a subordinate clause would be more normal (A.G. 496). Nominative subject (A.G. 339). **oriretur**: The main verb of the subordinate clause (A.G. 278.b). Imperfect subjunctive; the tense of the subjunctive is in secondary sequence and follows the rules for the sequence of tense **excepit** (A.G. 482-85).
qua ... seditio: Nominative subject (A.G. 339). **qua**: Singular, feminine, ablative indefinite pronoun used as an adjective modifying **seditio** (A.G. 149). The indefinite **quis, -----, quid** (**qui, quae,** or **qua, quod** when used adjectively) is used after **ne** (A.G. 310.a).
in castris: Ablative of *place where* with the preposition **in** (locative ablative) (A.G. 426.3).
ex eorum concursu et misericordia vulgi: Two ablatives of source with the preposition **ex** (A.G. 403.1). **eorum**: Plural, masculine, genitive demonstrative pronoun used substantively (A.G. 296.2). The antecedent is **DCCC** (A.G. 297.e). Possessive genitive with **concursu** (A.G. 343). **et**: The conjunction connects the two ablative nouns in the prepositional phrase (A.G. 324.a). **vulgi**: Possessive genitive with **misericordia** (A.G. 343).
ut ... curaret: The conjunction **ut** ("so that") with the subjunctive forms a final (purpose) clause dependent on **excepit** (A.G. 531.1).
curaret: The main verb of the subordinate clause (A.G. 278.b). Imperfect subjunctive; the tense of the subjunctive is in secondary sequence and follows the rules for the sequence of tense after **excepit** (A.G. 482-85). The pronoun **is**, with **ille** (**Vercingetorix**) as the antecedent, is understood as the subject (A.G. 271.a). The pronoun **eos**, with **quos** (**DCCC**) as the antecedent, is understood as the direct object.
procul in via dispositis familiaribus suis principibusque civitatum: Ablative absolute (A.G. 419-20). **procul**: Adverb (A.G. 320-21). **in via**: Ablative of *place where* with the preposition **in** (locative ablative) (A.G. 426.3). **dispositis**: The perfect tense of the participle represents the action as completed at the time indicated by the tense of the main verb (A.G. 489). **suis**: Plural, masculine, ablative possessive pronoun used as an adjective modifying **familiaribus** (A.G. 302). **-que**: The enclitic conjunction connects the two ablative nouns **familiaribus ... principibus** (A.G. 324.a). **civitatum**: Partitive genitive with **principibus** (A.G. 346.a.1).
(eos) disparandos deducendosque: Two plural, masculine, accusative gerundives used as adjectives modifying **eos**, the supplied object of **curaret** (A.G. 500.1). A gerundive in agreement with the object of **curaret** express purpose (A.G. 500.4).
ad suos: Prepositional phrase, **ad** with the accusative here means "to" (*OLD* **ad** 1). **suos**: Plural, masculine, accusative possessive pronoun used substantively to denote a special class (A.G. 302.d).
quae ... obvenerat: Relative clause; a clause dependent on a subjunctive clause (**ut ... curaret**) normally takes the subjunctive (attraction) (A.G. 303 and 593). However, when a dependent clause is not regarded as a necessary logical part of the clause, the indicative is used. The indicative serves to emphasize the fact, as true independently of the statement contained in the subjunctive clause (A.G. 593.a Note 1). **quae**: See below. **obvenerat**: The main verb of the subordinate clause (A.G. 278.b). The pluperfect tense of the verb denotes an action completed in past time (A.G. 477).
quae ... pars: Nominative subject (A.G. 339). **quae**: Singular, feminine, nominative relative pronoun (A.G. 305). The antecedent is **pars** in its own clause (adjectival use) (A.G. 307.b).
cuique civitati: Dative indirect object of the compound verb **obvenerat** (A.G. 370). **cuique**: Singular, feminine, dative indefinite pronoun used as an adjective modifying **civitati** (A.G. 151.g).
castrorum: Partitive genitive with **pars** (A.G. 346.a.1).
ab initio: Prepositional phrase, **ab** with the ablative singular of **initium** means "from the beginning" (*OLD* **initium** 1.c).

2.G CHAPTERS 29-31: VERCINGETORIX RALLIES THE GAULS AFTER THE DEFEAT AT AVARICUM; HE LEVIES FRESH REINFORCEMENTS

(29.1-2) Postero die concilio convocato, consolatus cohortatusque est ne se admodum animo demitterent, ne perturbarentur (2) incommodo.

admodum, *fully, completely, entirely.*
cohortor, -ari, -atus, *encourage, urge, exhort, address.*
consolor, -ari, -atus, *comfort, cheer, console, encourage.*

demitto, -mittere, -misi, -misus, (with **se animo**), *become dispirited, lose heart.*
incommodum, -i, n., *misfortune, disaster, injury, defeat.*
perturbo, -are, -avi, -atus, *disturb greatly, throw into confusion, disorder.*
-que, *and.*

animus, -i, m., *mind, heart, spirit, resolution.*
concilium, -i, n., *meeting, assembly, council.*
convoco, -are, -avi, -atus, *call together, summon, assemble.*
dies, -ei, m. and f., *day.*

ne, *so that ... not.*
posterus, -a, -um, *following, the next.*
sui, sibi, se, or **sese**, nom. wanting, *themselves.*

Postero die concilio convocato: Ablative absolute (A.G. 419-20). Kahn claims that the council scene functions as a substitute for choral odes between major episodes. (Kahn, 251) See also 1.4, 14.1, 63.5-6, 75.1, and 89.1. **Postero die**: Ablative of *time when* (A.G. 423.1). **die**: The noun **dies** is normally masculine gender (A.G. 97.a). **convocato**: The perfect tense of the participle represents the action as completed at the time indicated by the tense of the main verb (A.G. 489).
concilio convocato, consolatus cohortatusque: Notice the alliteration of the letter 'c' (A.G. 641).
consolatus cohortatusque est: The main verbs of the main clause (A.G. 278.b). Two perfect, deponent, indicative verbs sharing **est** (= **consolatus est et cohortatus est**) (A.G. 187-88). For the same construction see 62.7 and 80.7. The pronoun **is**, with **ille** (**Vercingetorix**) from 28.6 as the antecedent, is understood as the subject of both verbs (A.G. 271.a). **-que**: The enclitic conjunction connects the two participle elements of the main verbs (A.G. 324.a).
ne ... ne: The repetition of words at the beginning of successive clauses is anaphora (A.G. 641). Note the asyndeton between the two clauses (A. G. 323.b).

ne ... demitterent: The conjunction **ne** ("so that ... not") with the subjunctive forms a negative substantive clause of purpose which is used as the object of the verb **cohortatur est** denoting an action directed toward the future (A.G. 563). **demitterent**: The main verb of the subordinate clause (A.G. 278.b). Imperfect subjunctive; the tense of the subjunctive is in secondary sequence and follows the rules for the sequence of tense after **cohortatus est** (A.G. 482-85). The pronoun **ei**, with those attending the council as the antecedent, is understood as the subject (A.G. 271.a).

se ... animo demitterent: The phrase **se ... animo demittere** is an idiom that means "to become dispirited" (*OLD* **demitto** 11).

se: Plural, masculine, accusative direct reflexive pronoun (A.G. 300.1). The antecedent is the pronoun **ei**, the supplied subject of **demitterent** (A.G. 299). Accusative direct object of **demitterent** (A.G. 387).

admodum: Adverb (A.G. 320-21).

animo: Ablative of *place where* without a preposition (A.G. 429.2).

ne perturbarentur: The conjunction **ne** ("so that ... not") with the subjunctive forms a negative substantive clause of purpose which is used as the object of the verb **cohortatur est** denoting an action directed toward the future (A.G. 563). **perturbarentur**: The main verb of the subordinate clause (A.G. 278.b). Imperfect subjunctive; the tense of the subjunctive is in secondary sequence and follows the rules for the sequence of tense after **cohortatus est** (A.G. 482-85). The pronoun **ei**, with those attending the council as the antecedent, is understood as the subject (A.G. 271.a).

incommodo: Ablative of cause without a preposition (A.G. 404).

Non ... sustinerent. The remainder of the chapter is a speech in indirect discourse after an unexpressed verb of saying (A.G. 580.a). Murphy classifies this speech as deliberative (C. Murphy, 122).

(29.2-3) Non virtute neque in acie vicisse Romanos sed artificio quodam et scientia oppugnationis, cuius rei (3) fuerint ipsi imperiti.

acies, -ei, f., *engagement, battle.*
et, *and.*

in, *in.*

neque, *nor.*
oppugnatio, -onis, f., *siege, assault, attack.*
quidam, qauedam, quiddam, *a certain, some,* (as adj., **quidam, qauedam, quoddam**).
Romani, -orum, m., pl., *the Romans.*
sed, *but.*
vinco, vincere, vici, victus, *conquer, overcome, defeat, subdue.*

artificium, -i, n., *trick, craft, cunning.*
imperitus, -a, -um, *inexperienced, unskilled, unacquainted.*
ipse, -a, -um, *he, they,* with or without *himself, themselves.*
non, *not.*
qui, quae, quod, *who, which, what.*
res, rei, f., *matter, business, matter.*

scientia, -ae, f., *knowledge, skill, science.*
sum, esse, fui, futurus, *be.*
virtus, -utis, f., *manliness, courage, bravery, valor.*

non ... neque: The general negation of **non** is not destroyed by **neque** introducing a coordinate member (A.G. 327.3).

non: Adverb; when **non** is especially emphatic it begins the clause (A.G. 217.e, 320-21, and 599.a).

virtute: Ablative of means (A.G. 409).

neque: The conjunction continues after **non** with negative force and means "nor" (*OLD* **neque** 6).

in acie: Ablative of *place where* with the preposition **in** (locative ablative) (A.G. 426.3).

vicisse Romanos: Accusative/infinitive construction in indirect discourse (A.G. 577 ff.). The verb of saying is not expressed, but implied in the general drift of the sentence (A.G. 580.a). **vicisse**: Perfect infinitive; the tense of the infinitive in indirect discourse is relative to that of the verb of saying (A.G. 584).

sed: Coordinate conjunction (A.G. 324.a).

artificio quodam et scientia: Two ablatives of means (A.G. 409). **quodam**: Singular, neuter, ablative indefinite pronoun used as an adjective modifying **artificio** (A.G. 151.c). **et**: The conjunction connects the two ablative nouns (A.G. 324.a).

oppugnationis: Objective genitive with **scientia** (A.G. 348).

cuius ... fuerint: Relative clause; a subordinate clause in indirect discourse takes the subjunctive (A.G. 303 and 580). **cuius**: See below. **fuerint**: The main verb of the subordinate clause (A.G. 278.b). Perfect subjunctive; the tense of the subjunctive is normally in secondary sequence after an unexpressed verb of saying (A.G. 482-84). Here it is in primary sequence through *repraesentatio* (A.G. 585.b Note).

cuius rei: Objective genitive with the adjective **imperiti** (A.G. 349). **cuius**: Singular, feminine, genitive relative pronoun (A.G. 305). The antecedent is **rei** in its own clause (adjectival use) (A.G. 307.a).

ipsi: Plural, masculine, nominative demonstrative pronoun used substantively (A.G. 296.2). The antecedent is **ei** (the members of the council), the supplied subject of **perturbarentur** (A.G. 298.1). Nominative subject (A.G. 339). The pronoun is here emphatic (A.G. 298.d.1).

imperiti: Plural, masculine, nominative predicate adjective modifying **ipsi** after **fuerint** (A.G. 285.2).

(29.3-4) Errare, si qui in bello omnis secundos (4) rerum proventus exspectent.

bellum, -i, n., *war, warfare.*
exspecto, -are, -avi, -atus, *expect.*
omnis, -e, *all.*

erro, -are, -avi, -atus, *be mistaken, in error.*
in, *in.*
proventus, -us, m., *result, issue, outcome.*

quis, -----, quid, (with **si**), *whoever, anyone who.*
secundus, -a, -um, *favorable.*

res, rei, f., *matter, affair, event, circumstance.*
si, *if.*

Errare, si ... exspectent: Conditional statement in indirect discourse (A.G. 589). The verb of saying is not expressed, but implied in the general drift of the sentence (A.G. 580.a). The protasis, as a dependent clause, is in the subjunctive and the apodosis, as the principal clause, is in the infinitive (A.G. 589).
(eos) Errare: The apodosis of the conditional statement (A.G. 589.2). Accusative/infinitive construction in indirect discourse (A.G. 577 ff.). The verb of saying is not expressed, but implied in the general drift of the sentence (A.G. 580.a). Supply the pronoun **eos**, correlative to the following indefinite pronoun **qui**, as the accusative subject of the infinitive. **Errare**: Present infinitive; the tense of the infinitive in indirect discourse is relative to that of the verb of saying (A.G. 584).
si ... exspectent: The conjunction **si** ("if") with the subjunctive forms the protasis of a conditional statement in indirect discourse (A.G. 589.1). **exspectent**: The main verb of the subordinate clause (A.G. 278.b). Present subjunctive; the tense of the subjunctive is normally in secondary sequence after an unexpressed verb of saying (A.G. 482-84). Here it is in primary sequence through *repraesentatio* (A.G. 585.b Note).
qui: Plural, masculine, nominative indefinite pronoun used substantively (A.G. 149). The indefinite **quis, -----, quid** is used after **si** (A.G. 310.a). Nominative subject (A.G. 339).
in bello: Prepositional phrase, **in** with the ablative here means "in" (expressing an abstract location) (*OLD* in 26).
omnis secundos rerum proventus (esse): Accusative/infinitive construction in indirect discourse after **exspectent** (A.G. 577 ff.).
omnis: Plural, masculine, accusative attributive adjective modifying **proventus** (A.G. 285.1). **-is** for **-es** is the regular form in i-stem adjectives (A.G. 114.a and 116). **secundos**: Plural, masculine, accusative predicate adjective modifying **proventus** after the supplied infinitive **esse** (A.G. 285.2). **rerum**: Objective genitive with **proventus** (A.G. 348). **esse**: Supply **esse** as the infinitive.

(29.4-5) Sibi numquam placuisse Avaricum defendi, cuius rei testis ipsos haberet; sed factum imprudentia Biturigum et nimia obsequentia reliquorum uti (5) hoc incommodum acciperetur.

accipio, -cipere, -cepi, -ceptus, *take to one's self, receive, suffer, bear.*
Bituriges, -um, m., pl., *the Bituriges.*

et, *and.*
habeo, habere, habui, habitus, *have.*
imprudentia, -ae, f., *lack of foresight, indiscretion, ignorance, imprudence.*
ipse, -a, -um, *he, they*, with or without *himself, themselves.*
numquam, *never.*
placeo, placere, placui, placitus, (imper.), *it seems good, be acceptable.*
reliqui, -orum, m., pl., *the rest.*
sed, *but.*
testis, -is, m., *witness.*

Avaricum, -i, n., *Avaricum.*
defendo, -fendere, -fensi, -fensus, *defend, guard, protect.*
facio, facere, feci, factus, *bring about, make, do.*
hic, haec, hoc, *this; he, she, it.*
incommodum, -i, n., *misfortune, disaster, injury, defeat.*
nimius, -a, -um, *excessive, too great.*
obsequentia, -ae, f., *compliance, obsequiousness.*
qui, quae, quod, *who, which, what.*
res, rei, f., *fact.*
sui, sibi, se, or **sese**, nom. wanting, *himself.*
uti, *so that.*

Sibi: Singular, masculine, dative indirect reflexive pronoun (A.G. 300.2). The antecedent is **ille** (**Vercingetorix**) at 28.6 (A.G. 299). Dative indirect object of the intransitive infinitive **placuisse** (A.G. 367).
numquam: Adverb (A.G. 217.b and 320-21).
placuisse: Impersonal infinitive construction in indirect discourse (A.G. 577 ff.). The verb of saying is not expressed, but implied in the general drift of the sentence (A.G. 580.a). Impersonal use of the verb (A.G. 208.c). The following infinitive phrase functions as the subject (A.G. 454). Perfect infinitive; the tense of the infinitive in indirect discourse is relative to that of the verb of saying (A.G. 584).
Avaricum defendi: The infinitive phrase functions as the subject of the impersonal infinitive **placuisse** (A.G. 454). **Avaricum**: Subject accusative of the infinitive (A.G. 455.2). See Appendix A.
cuius ... haberet: Relative clause; a subordinate clause in indirect discourse takes the subjunctive (A.G. 303 and 580). **cuius**: See below. **haberet**: The main verb of the subordinate clause (A.G. 278.b). Imperfect subjunctive; the tense of the subjunctive is in secondary sequence and follows the rules for the sequence of tense after the unexpressed verb of saying (A.G. 585). The pronoun **is**, with **ille** (**Vercingetorix**) as the antecedent, is understood as the subject (A.G. 271.a).
cuius rei: Objective genitive with **testis** (A.G. 348). **cuius**: Singular, feminine, genitive relative pronoun (A.G. 305). The antecedent is **rei** in its own clause (adjectival use) (A.G. 307.a).
testis: An accusative noun in apposition to the substantive pronoun **ipsos** ("as witnesses") (A.G. 282). Accusative plural noun; **-is** for **-es** is the regular form in i-stem nouns (A.G. 65-67 and 74.c).
ipsos: Plural, masculine, accusative demonstrative pronoun used substantively (A.G. 296.2). The antecedent is **ei** (the members of the council), the supplied subject of **perturbarentur** (A.G. 298.1). Accusative direct object of **haberet** (A.G. 387). The pronoun is here emphatic (A.G. 298.d.1).
sed: Coordinate conjunction (A.G. 324.d).
factum (esse): Impersonal infinitive construction in indirect discourse (A.G. 577 ff.). The verb of saying is not expressed, but implied in the general drift of the sentence (A.G. 580.a). Impersonal use of the verb (A.G. 208.c). The following substantive clause of result **uti ... acciperetur** functions as the subject (A.G. 567-69). When **facio** is used in the passive, the object clause becomes the subject (A.G. 567). **factum (esse)**: Supply **esse** to form the perfect, passive infinitive (A.G. 188). The tense of the infinitive in indirect discourse is relative to that of the verb of saying (A.G. 584).

imprudentia ... et nimia obsequentia: Two ablatives of cause (A.G. 404). **et**: The conjunction connects the two ablative nouns **imprudentia ... obsequentia** (A.G. 324.a).

Biturigum: Possessive genitive of the tribe name **Bituriges** with **imprudentia** (A.G. 343). See Appendix A.

reliquorum: Plural, masculine, genitive adjective used substantively (A.G. 288). The noun **triborum** is understood (A.G. 288.b). Possessive genitive with **obsequentia** (A.G. 343).

uti ... acciperetur: The conjunction **uti** ("so that") with the subjunctive here forms a substantive clause of result which is the subject of the passive verb **factum (esse)** denoting the accomplishment of an effort (A.G. 569.1). **acciperetur**: The main verb of the subordinate clause (A.G. 278.b). Imperfect subjunctive; the tense of the subjunctive is in secondary sequence and follows the rules for the sequence of tense after the unexpressed verb of saying (A.G. 482-85).

hoc incommodum: Nominative subject (A.G. 339). **hoc**: Singular, neuter, nominative demonstrative pronoun used as an adjective modifying **incommodum** (A.G. 296.1 and a).

(29.5-6) **Id tamen se celeriter (6) maioribus commodis sanaturum.**

celeriter, *quickly, speedily, at once, immediately.*
is, ea, id, *he, she, it; that, this.*
sano, -are, -avi, -atus, *make good, remedy.*

tamen, *yet, still, for all that, nevertheless, however.*

commodum, -i, n., *advantage, profit.*
maior, -or, -us, *greater, larger,*
sui, sibi, se, or **sese**, nom. wanting, *he*, with or without *himself.*

Id: Singular, neuter, accusative demonstrative pronoun used substantively (A.G. 296.2). The antecedent is **incommodum** (A.G. 297.e). Accusative direct object of the infinitive **sanaturum (esse)** (A.G. 387 and 451.3).

tamen: Adverb, postpositive (A.G. 320-21 and 324.j).

se ... sanaturum (esse): Accusative/infinitive construction in indirect discourse (A.G. 577 ff.). The verb of saying is not expressed, but implied in the general drift of the sentence (A.G. 580.a). **se**: Singular, masculine, accusative direct reflexive pronoun (A.G. 300.1). The antecedent is **ille (Vercingetorix)**, the subject of the unexpressed verb of saying (A.G. 299). **sanaturum (esse)**: Supply **esse** to form the future, active infinitive (A.G. 184). The tense of the infinitive in indirect discourse is relative to that of the verb of saying (A.G. 584).

celeriter: Adverb (A.G. 214.b and 320-21).

maioribus commodis: Ablative of means (A.G. 409). **maioribus**: Irregular comparative adjective (A.G. 129).

(29.6-7) **Nam quae ab reliquis Gallis civitates dissentirent, has sua diligentia adiuncturum atque unum consilium totius Galliae effecturum, cuius consensui ne orbis quidem terrarum possit obsistere; idque se prope iam effectum habere.**

ab, *from.*
atque, *and then.*
consensus, -us, m., *united opinion, concord, unanimity.*
diligentia, -ae, f., *care, diligence.*

efficio, -ficere, -feci, -fectus, *accomplish, produce, make, construct.*
Gallia, -ae, f., *Gaul.*
hic, haec, hoc, *this; he, she, it.*
is, ea, id, *he, she, it; that, this.*
ne ... quidem, *not even.*
orbis terrarum, orbis terrarum, m., f., pl., *the world.*
prope, *near, nearly, almost.*
qui, quae, quod, *who, which, what.*
sui, sibi, se, or **sese**, nom. wanting, *he*, with or without *himself.*
terra, -ae, f., see **orbis**.
unus, -a, -um, *one.*

adiungo, -iungere, -iunxi, -iunctus, *add, unite.*
civitas, -tatis, f., *state, nation.*
consilium, -i, n., *plan, design, policy.*
dissentio, -sentire, -sensi, -sensus, *differ in opinion, disagree.*
Galli, -orum, m., *the Gauls.*
habeo, habere, habui, habitus, *have.*
iam, *already, now.*
nam, *for.*
obsisto, -sistere, -stiti, -stitus, *resist, withstand.*
possum, posse, potui, -----, *be able.*
-que, *and, now.*
reliquus, -a, -um, *remaining, the rest.*
suus, -a, -um, *his*, with or without *own.*
totus, -a, -um, *the whole of, all.*

Nam: Conjunction, here explanatory meaning "for" (*OLD* **nam** 2).

quae ... dissentirent: Relative clause; a subordinate clause in indirect discourse takes the subjunctive (A.G. 303 and 580). **quae**: See below. **dissentirent**: The main verb of the subordinate clause (A.G. 278.b). Imperfect subjunctive; the tense of the subjunctive is in secondary sequence after the unexpressed verb of saying (A.G. 585).

quae ... civitates: Nominative subject (A.G. 339). **quae**: Plural, feminine, nominative relative pronoun (A.G. 305). The antecedent is **civitates** in its own clause (adjectival use) (A.G. 307.a).

ab reliquis Gallis: Ablative of separation with the preposition **ab** after the compound verb **dissentirent** (A.G. 402). **Gallis**: See Appendix A.

has: Plural, feminine, accusative demonstrative pronoun used substantively (A.G. 296.2). The antecedent is **civitates** (A.G. 297.e). Accusative direct object of the infinitive **adiuncturum (esse)** (A.G. 387 and 451.3).

sua diligentia: Ablative of means (A.G. 409). **sua**: Singular, feminine, ablative reflexive pronoun used as an adjective (A.G. 302).

(se) adiuncturum (esse): Accusative/infinitive construction in indirect discourse (A.G. 577 ff.). The verb of saying is not expressed, but implied in the general drift of the sentence (A.G. 580.a). Carry down **se** as the accusative subject. **adiuncturum (esse)**: Supply esse to form the future, active infinitive (A.G. 186). The tense of the infinitive in indirect discourse is relative to that of the verb of saying (A.G. 584).

atque: The conjunction connects the two infinitives **adiuncturum (esse)** ... **effecturum (esse)** and means "and then" (*OLD atque* 7).

unum consilium: Accusative direct object of the infinitive **effecturum (esse)** (A.G. 387 and 451.3). **unum**: Declinable cardinal number used as an adjective (A.G. 132-35).

totius Galliae: Objective genitive with **consilium** (A.G. 348). **totius**: -ius is the regular genitive singular ending for the adjective **totus** (A.G. 113). **Galliae**: See Appendix A.

(se) effecturum (esse): Accusative/infinitive construction in indirect discourse (A.G. 577 ff.). The verb of saying is not expressed, but implied in the general drift of the sentence (A.G. 580.a). Carry down **se** as the accusative subject. **effecturum (esse)**: Supply esse to form the future, active infinitive (A.G. 188). The tense of the infinitive in indirect discourse is relative to that of the verb of saying (A.G. 584).

cuius ... possit ... obsistere: Relative clause; a subordinate clause in indirect discourse takes the subjunctive (A.G. 303 and 580).

cuius: Singular, feminine, genitive relative pronoun used substantively (A.G. 305). The antecedent is **Galliae** (A.G. 307). Possessive genitive with **consensui** (A.G. 343). **possit**: The main verb of the subordinate clause (A.G. 278.b). Present subjunctive; the tense of the subjunctive is normally in secondary sequence after an unexpressed verb of saying (A.G. 482-84). Here it is in primary sequence through *repraesentatio* (A.G. 585.b Note). **obsistere**: Complementary infinitive after **possit** (A.G. 456).

consensui: Dative indirect object of the intransitive infinitive **obsistere** (A.G. 366).

ne ... quidem: The negative adverb with the particle means "not even" (*OLD* ne1 6). The emphatic word must stand between **ne** and **quidem** (A.G. 322.f).

orbis: Nominative subject (A.G. 339).

terrarum: Partitive genitive with **orbis** (A.G. 346.a.1).

idque ... effectum: Accusative direct object of the infinitive **habere** (A.G. 387and 451.3). Singular, neuter, accusative demonstrative pronoun used substantively (A.G. 296.2). The antecedent is the previous idea of the unification of Gaul (A.G. 297.e). **-que**: At the beginning of a sentence, the enclitic conjunction can introduce a further point in an argument and mean "and, now" (*OLD* -que1 4).

effectum: Singular, neuter, accusative perfect passive participle used as a predicate, where in English a phrase or a subordinate clause would be more normal (A.G. 496). The perfect participle with **habeo** has almost the same meaning as a perfect active, but denotes the continued effect of the action of the verb (A.G. 497.b). "**effectum habere**: translate as if *effecisse*." (Kelsey, 410)

se ... habere: Accusative/infinitive construction in indirect discourse (A.G. 577 ff.). The verb of saying is not expressed, but implied in the general drift of the sentence (A.G. 580.a). **se**: Singular, masculine, accusative demonstrative pronoun used substantively (A.G. 296.2). The antecedent is **ille (Vercingetorix)** (A.G. 299). **habere**: Present infinitive; the tense of the infinitive in indirect discourse is relative to that of the verb of saying (A.G. 584).

prope: Adverb (A.G. 320-21).

iam: Adverb (A.G. 215.6, 217.b and 320-21).

(29.7) Interea aequum esse ab eis communis salutis causa impetrari ut castra munire instituerent, quo facilius repentinos hostium impetus sustinerent.

ab, *from.*
castra, -orum, n., pl., *camp, encampment.*

communis, -e, *common, in common, public, general.*
hostis, -is, m., *enemy, foe*; pl., *the enemy.*
impetus, -us, m., *attack, assault, onset, charge.*

interea, *in the meantime, meanwhile.*
munio, -ire, -ivi, -itus, *fortify, protect, secure.*

repentinus, -a, -um, *sudden, hasty, unexpected.*
sum, esse, fui, futurus, *be.*

ut, *so that.*

aequus, -a, -um, *right.*
causa, -ae, f., abl. with the gen., *for the sake of, on account of.*
facile, comp. -ius, *easily, readily, with no trouble.*
impetro, -are, -avi, -atus, *obtain by request* or *entreaty.*
instituo, -stituere, -stitui, -stitutus, *undertake, commence, begin.*
is, ea, id, *he, she, it; that, this.*
quo, *so that* (by that degree), *in order that, that, that thereby.*
salus, -utis, f., *welfare, safety, deliverance.*
sustineo, -tinere, -tinui, -tentus, *hold out, bear, endure, withstand.*

Interea: Adverb, marks a passage to a new subject (*OLD interea* c).

aequum esse: Impersonal infinitive construction in indirect discourse (A.G. 577 ff.). The verb of saying is not expressed, but implied in the general drift of the sentence (A.G. 580.a). Impersonal verb, the following infinitive phrase forms the subject (A.G. 208.c).

aequum: Singular, neuter, accusative predicate adjective after **esse** meaning "it is right" (A.G. 282-84) (*OLD aequus1* 6). **esse**: Present infinitive; the tense of the infinitive in indirect discourse is relative to that of the verb of saying (A.G. 584).

ab eis communis salutis causa impetrari: The infinitive phrase (with the dependent clause **ut ... instituerent**) functions as the subject of the impersonal verb **aequum esse** (A.G. 454).

ab eis: Ablative of source with the preposition **ab** after the passive infinitive **impetrari** (A.G. 403.1). **eis**: Plural, masculine, ablative demonstrative pronoun used substantively (A.G. 296.2). The antecedent is **ipsos** (the members of the council) (A.G. 297.e).

communis salutis causa: A preceding genitive with the ablative of **causa** means "for the sake of" A (A.G. 359.b and 404.c).

impetrari: The infinitive functions as the subject of the impersonal verb **aequum esse** (A.G. 454). Impersonal use of the passive infinitive (A.G. 208.c). The following purpose clause functions as the subject; a substantive clause used as the object of a verb becomes the subject when the verb is put in the passive (A.G. 566).

ut ... instituerent: The conjunction **ut** ("so that") with the subjunctive forms a substantive clause of purpose (A.G. 563). The clause functions as the subject of the impersonal infinitive **impetrari**; a substantive clause used as the object of a verb becomes the subject when the verb is put into the passive (A.G. 566). **instituerent**: The main verb of the subordinate clause (A.G. 278.b). Imperfect subjunctive; the tense of the subjunctive is in secondary sequence after the unexpressed verb of saying (A.G. 585). Supply the pronoun **ei**, with **eis** (the members of the council) as the antecedent, as the subject (A.G. 271.a).

castra: Accusative direct object of the infinitive **munire** (A.G. 387 and 451.3).

munire: Complementary infinitive after **instituerent** (A.G. 456).

quo facilius ... sustinerent: Relative clause of purpose, the ablative **quo** (= **ut eo**) is used as a conjunction in a final (purpose) clause with the subjunctive (A.G. 531.a). **quo**: In a final clause with a comparative, the conjunction means "so that by that degree" (*OLD* quo2 3.b). **facilius**: Comparative adverb (A.G. 218 and 320-21). **sustinerent**: The main verb of the subordinate clause (A.G. 278.b). Imperfect subjunctive; the tense of the subjunctive is in secondary sequence after the unexpressed verb of saying (A.G. 585). Supply the pronoun **ei**, with **eis** (the members of the council) as the antecedent, as the subject (A.G. 271.a).

repentinos ... impetus: Accusative direct object of **sustinerent** (A.G. 387).

hostium: Objective genitive with **impetus** (A.G. 348).

(30.1) **Fuit haec oratio non ingrata Gallis, et maxime, quod ipse animo non defecerat tanto accepto incommodo neque se in occultum abdiderat et conspectum multitudinis fugerat;**

abdo, -dere, -didi, -ditus, *remove, conceal.*
animus, -i, m., *courage, heart, spirit, resolution.*
deficio, -ficere, -feci, -fectus, (with **animo**) *to lose heart.*
fugio, fugere, fugi, -----, *avoid, shun.*
hic, haec, hoc, *this*; *he, she, it.*
incommodum, -i, n., *misfortune, disaster, injury, defeat.*
ipse, -a, -um, *he, they,* with or without *himself, themselves.*
multitudo, -inis, f., *multitude, crowd.*
non, *not.*
oratio, -onis, f., *speech, words, address.*
sui, sibi, se, or sese, nom. wanting, *himself.*
tantus, -a, -um, *so great, so large, such.*

accipio, -cipere, -cepi, -ceptus, *receive, suffer, bear.*
conspectus, -us, m., *sight, view, presence.*
et, *and.*
Galli, -orum, m., *the Gauls.*
in, *into.*
ingratus, -a, -um, *unacceptable, unpleasing.*
maxime, *especially, chiefly.*
neque, *nor.*
occultum, -i, n., *hiding, concealment.*
quod, *because, since, for, as.*
sum, esse, fui, futurus, *be.*

Fuit: The main verb of the main clause (A.G. 278.b). The verb comes in the first position when the idea in it is emphatic (A.G. 598.d). Here it marks the end of the indirect discourse (A.G. 589.d).

haec oratio: Nominative subject (A.G. 339). **haec**: Singular, feminine, nominative demonstrative pronoun used as an adjective modifying **oratio** (A.G. 296.1 and a).

non ingrata: A litotes, a statement is made emphatic by denying its contrary (A.G. 326.c).

non: Adverb modifying **ingrata**; the negative precedes the word it especially effects (A.G. 217.e, 320-21, and 599.a).

ingrata: Singular, feminine, nominative predicate adjective modifying **oratio** after **fuit** (A.G. 283).

Gallis: Dative after the adjective **ingrata** (A.G. 384). See Appendix A.

et maxime: The combination means "and especially" (*OLD* et 10.b). **et**: Conjunction (A.G. 324.a). **maxime**: Irregular superlative adverb (A.G. 218.a and 320-21).

quod ... defecerat ... abdiderat ... fugerat: Causal clause; the conjunction **quod** ("because") takes the indicative when the reason is given on the authority of the writer or speaker (A.G. 540.1). Note here that Caesar is reporting what he thinks, not the Gauls, otherwise the verbs would be in the subjunctive in implied indirect discourse. **defecerat ... abdiderat ... fugerat**: The main verbs of the subordinate clause (A.G. 278.b). The pluperfect tense of the verbs denotes an action completed in past time (A.G. 477).

ipse: Singular, masculine, nominative demonstrative pronoun used substantively (A.G. 296.2 and 298.d). The antecedent is **ille** (**Vercingetorix**) at 28.6 (A.G. 298). Nominative subject of **defecerat ... abdiderat ... fugerat** (A.G. 339). The pronoun is here emphatic (A.G. 298.d.1).

animo: Ablative of separation without a preposition after the compound verb **defecerat** (A.G. 402).

non: Adverb, the adverb generally precedes the verb if it belongs to no one word in particular (A.G. 217.e, 320-21, and 599.a).

tanto accepto incommodo: Ablative absolute (A.G. 419-20). **accepto**: The perfect tense of the participle represents the action as completed at the time indicated by the tense of the main verb (A.G. 489).

neque: The conjunction continues after **non** and means "nor" (*OLD* neque 6).

se: Singular, masculine, accusative direct reflexive pronoun (A.G. 300.1). The antecedent is **ipse** (**Vercingetorix**), the subject of **abdiderat** (A.G. 299). Accusative direct object of **abdiderat** (A.G. 387).

in occultum: Prepositional phrase, **in** with the singular, neuter, accusative of the adjective **occultus** means "into hiding or concealment" (*OLD* occultus 5).

et: The conjunction connects the two verbs **abdiderat ... fugerat** and the general negation of the preceding **neque** is not destroyed (A.G. 324.a).

conspectum: Accusative direct object of **fugerat** (A.G. 387).

multitudinis: Possessive genitive with **conspectum** (A.G. 343).

(30.2-3) **(2) plusque animo providere et praesentire existimabatur, quod re integra primo incendendum Avaricum, post**

deserendum (3) censuerat.

animus, -i, m., *mind.*
censeo, -ere, -ui, -us, *think, hold, judge.*
et, *and.*
incendo, -cendere, -cendi, -census, *set on fire, burn.*
plus, *more.*
praesentio, -sentire, -sensi, -sensus, *perceive beforehand.*
provideo, -videre, -vidi, -visus, *foresee, provide for, look out for.*
quod, *because, since, for, as.*

Avaricum, -i, n., *Avaricum.*
desero, -serere, -serui, -sertus, *leave, abandon, desert.*
existimo, -are, -avi, -atus, *think, consider, judge.*
integer, -ra, -rum, *undecided.*
post, *afterwards.*
primo, *at first, in the first place.*
-que, *and, now.*
res, rei, f., *matter, affair, event.*

plusque: Adverb (A.G. 320-21). **-que**: The enclitic here begins the sentence and means "and, now" (*OLD* -que 4).
animo: Ablative of *place where* without a preposition (A.G. 429.3).
providere et praesentire: Two infinitives without a subject accusative in indirect discourse after the passive use of **existimabatur** (A.G. 577 ff. and 582). **et**: The conjunction connects the two infinitives (A.G. 324.a).
existimabatur: The main verb of the main clause (A.G. 278.b). The pronoun **is**, with **ipse** (**Vercingetorix**) as the antecedent, is understood as the subject (A.G. 271.a).
quod ... censuerat: Causal clause; the conjunction **quod** ("because") takes the indicative when the reason is given on the authority of the writer or speaker (A.G. 540.1). For the reference see Chapter 15. **censuerat**: The main verb of the subordinate clause (A.G. 278.b). The pronoun **is**, with **ipse** (**Vercingetorix**) as the antecedent, is understood as the subject (A.G. 271.a). The pluperfect tense of the verb denotes an action completed in past time (A.G. 477).
re integra: Ablative absolute with an adjective (**integra**) taking the place of a participle (there is no participle for "being") (A.G. 419.a-20).
primo ... post: Two adverbs (A.G. 320-21). **primo** means "at first", as opposed to **post** "afterwards", giving prominence to the difference in time (A.G. 322.d).
incendendum (esse) Avaricum: Accusative/infinitive construction in indirect discourse after **censuerat** (A.G. 577 ff.). **incendendum (esse)**: Supply **esse** to form the second periphrastic (passive) present infinitive with the gerundive implying necessity (A.G. 194.b and 196). The tense of the infinitive in indirect discourse is relative to that of the verb of saying (A.G. 584). **Avaricum**: See Appendix A.
deserendum (esse Avaricum): Accusative/infinitive construction in indirect discourse after **censuerat** (A.G. 577 ff.). **deserendum (esse)**: Supply **esse** to form the second periphrastic (passive) present infinitive with the gerundive implying necessity (A.G. 194.b and 196). The tense of the infinitive in indirect discourse is relative to that of the verb of saying (A.G. 584). Carry down **Avaricum** as the accusative subject.

(30.3-4) Itaque ut reliquorum imperatorum res adversae auctoritatem minuunt, sic huius ex contrario dignitas incom(4)modo accepto in dies augebatur.

accipio, -cipere, -cepi, -ceptus, *receive, suffer, bear.*
auctoritas, -tatis, f., *prestige, authority, power.*

contrarius, -a, -um, *contrary.*
dignitas, -tatis, f., *greatness, rank, reputation.*
hic, haec, hoc, *this; he, she, it.*

in, (with dies), *daily, as the days proceed.*
itaque, *and so, in consequence, accordingly, therefore.*
reliquus, -a, -um, *other, the rest.*
ut ... sic, *while ... yet.*

adversus, -a, -um, *unfavorable, adverse, unsuccessful.*
augeo, augere, auxi, auctus, *increase, enlarge, augment, add to.*
dies, -ei, m. and f., *day.*
ex, *to, on.*
imperator, -oris, m., *commander-in-chief, commander, general.*
incommodum, -i, n., *misfortune, disaster, injury, defeat.*
minuo, -uere, -ui, -utus, *lessen, diminish, reduce.*
res, rei, f., *condition, circumstance, affair.*

Itaque: An adverb expressing the result of the previous ideas meaning "and so, in consequence" (*OLD* itaque 1). The adverb stands in the first position (A.G. 599.b).
ut ... sic: Two adverbs used correlatively to mean Awhile ... yet (A.G. 323.g).
reliquorum imperatorum: Possessive genitive with **auctoritatem** (A.G. 343).
res adversae: Nominative subject (A.G. 339).
auctoritatem: Accusative direct object of **minuunt** (A.G. 387). **Auctoritas** is the "unofficial, informal power held by individuals or groups as a result of previous distinguished actions. Syme defines the term as the ability to bring about one's wishes without resorting either to violence or legislation. In modern terms, the word approximates the colloquial clout. (Rubel, James S. *Caesar and the Crisis of the Roman Aristocracy: A Civil War Reader*. University of Oklahoma Press, 1994. Page 3)
minuunt: The main verb of the coordinate clause **Itaque ... minuunt** (A.G. 278.a).
huius: Singular, masculine, genitive demonstrative pronoun used substantively (A.G. 296.2). The antecedent is **ipse** (**Vercingetorix**) (A.G. 297.e). Possessive genitive with **dignitas** (A.G. 343).
ex contrario: Prepositional phrase, **ex** with the singular, neuter, ablative of the adjective **contrarius** means "to the contrary, in contradiction" (*OLD* contrarius 3).
dignitas: Nominative subject (A.G. 339). "*Dignitas* is the expression of an individual's public value or self-worth; this sense of 'status', 'honor', or 'respect' cannot be precisely measured, but it is manifested in the degree to which an individual is accorded respect

by his peers and to which he claims to distinction and eminence are recognized, even by his opponents. It arises from the nobility of one's birth, from the glory of one's deeds, and from the continued exercise of political influence through magistracies or in the Senate. (Rubel, James S. *Caesar and the Crisis of the Roman Aristocracy: A Civil War Reader*. University of Oklahoma Press, 1994. Page 3)

incommodo accepto: Ablative absolute (A.G. 419-20). **accepto**: The perfect tense of the participle represents the action as completed at the time indicated by the tense of the main verb (A.G. 489).

in dies: Prepositional phrase, **in** with the accusative plural of **dies** means "daily, as the days proceed" (*OLD* dies 3.b). **dies**: The noun **dies** is normally masculine gender (A.G. 97.a).

augebatur: The main verb of the coordinate clause **sic**... **augebatur** (A.G. 278.a).

(30.4) **Simul in spem veniebant eius adfirmatione de reliquis adiungendis civitatibus; primumque eo tempore Galli castra munire instituerunt, et sic sunt animo consternati homines insueti laboris ut omnia quae imperarentur sibi patienda existimarent.**

adfirmatio, -onis, f., *assertion, assurance.*
animus, -i, m., *mind.*
civitas, -tatis, f., *state, nation.*

de, *about, concerning.*
existimo, -are, -avi, -atus, *think, consider, judge.*
homo, hominis, m., *man, person.*
in, *into.*

insuetus, -a, -um, *unaccustomed.*
labor, -oris, m., *toil, exertion, labor.*
omnia, -ium, n., *all things, everything.*
primum, *first, before everything else, in the first place.*
qui, quae, quod, *who, which, what.*
sic, *so, thus.*
spes, -ei, f., *hope, expectation.*
tempus, -oris, n., *time, occasion, circumstance.*
venio, venire, veni, ventus, *come.*

adiungo, -iungere, -iunxi, -iunctus, *add, unite.*
castra, -orum, n., pl., *camp, encampment.*
consterno, -are, -avi, -atus, *thrown into confusion, be confounded, shocked.*
et, *and.*
Galli, -orum, m., *the Gauls.*
impero, -are, -avi, -atus, *command, order.*
instituo, -stituere, -stitui, -stitutus, *undertake, commence, begin.*
is, ea, id, *he, she, it; that, this.*
munio, -ire, -ivi, -itus, *fortify, protect, secure.*
patior, pati, passus, *suffer, bear, endure.*
-que, *and, now.*
reliquus, -a, -um, *remaining, the rest.*
simul, *at the same time, at once.*
sui, sibi, se, or **sese**, nom. wanting, *themselves.*
ut, *so that.*

Simul: Adverb (A.G. 320-21).

in spem: Prepositional phrase, **in** with the accusative here means "into" (a state or condition) (*OLD* in 2).

veniebant: The main verb of the simple sentence (A.G. 278.1). The pronoun **ei**, with **Gallis** as the antecedent, is understood as the subject (A.G. 271.a).

eius: Singular, masculine, genitive demonstrative pronoun used substantively (A.G. 296.2). The antecedent is **huius (Vercingetorix)** (A.G. 297.e). Possessive genitive with **adfirmatione** (A.G. 343).

adfirmatione: Ablative of cause without a preposition (A.G. 404).

de reliquis adiungendis civitatibus: Prepositional phrases, **de** with the ablative here means "about, concerning" (*OLD* de 12).

adiungendis: Plural, feminine, ablative of the gerundive modifying **civitatibus** used after the preposition **de** (A.G. 507.3).

primumque ... instituerunt: "Vercingetorix wisely adopted the Roman method of encampment, as he had previously adopted the cavalry tactics of the Germans." (Kelsey, 410)

primumque: Adverb (A.G. 214.d and 320-21). **-que**: The enclitic here begins the sentence and means "and, now" (*OLD* -que 4).

eo tempore: Ablative of *time when* (A.G. 423.1). **eo**: Singular, neuter, ablative demonstrative pronoun used as an adjective modifying **tempore** (296.1 and a).

Galli: Nominative subject (A.G. 339). See Appendix A.

castra: Accusative direct object of the infinitive **munire** (A.G. 387 and 451.3).

munire: Complementary infinitive after **instituerunt** (A.G. 387).

instituerunt: The main verb of the coordinate clause **primumque**... **instituerunt** (A.G. 278.a).

et: The conjunction connects the two verbs **instituerunt ... sunt ... consternati** (A.G. 324.a).

sic: Adverb correlative to the result clause **ut ... existimarent** (A.G. 217.c, 320-21 and 537 Note 2).

animo: Ablative of *place where* without a preposition (A.G. 429.3).

sunt ... consternati: The main verb of the coordinate clause **sic**... **existimarent** (A.G. 278.a). The perfect passive verb is here split (tmesis) (A.G. 640). The verb means "thrown into confusion, confounded, shocked" (*OLD* consterno2 1). The Budé and Loeb texts read **sunt ... confirmati**, meaning "encouraged, rendered confident" (*OLD* confirmo 3), which fits the context much better. The pronoun **ei**, with **Galli** as the antecedent, is understood as the subject (A.G. 271.a).

homines: A nominative noun in apposition to **ei**, the supplied subject of **sunt ... consternati** (A.G. 282).

insueti: Plural, masculine, nominative predicate adjective modifying **homines** (A.G. 285.2).

laboris: Objective genitive with the adjective **insueti** (A.G. 349.a).

(sic) ... ut ... existimarent: The conjunction **ut** ("so that") with the subjunctive forms a clause of result dependent on **sunt ... consternati** (A.G. 537.1). **existimarent**: The main verb of the subordinate clause (A.G. 278.b). Imperfect subjunctive; the tense of the subjunctive is in secondary sequence and follows the rules for the sequence of tense after **sunt ... consternati** (A.G. 482-85). The pronoun **ei**, with **Galli** as the antecedent, is understood as the subject (A.G. 271.a).

omnia patienda (esse): Accusative/infinitive construction in indirect discourse after **existimarent** (A.G. 577 ff.). **omnia:** Plural, neuter, accusative adjective used substantively (A.G. 288). **patienda (esse):** Supply **esse** to form the second periphrastic (passive) present infinitive with the gerundive implying necessity (A.G. 194.b and 196). The tense of the infinitive in indirect discourse is relative to that of the verb of saying (A.G. 584).

quae imperarentur: Relative clause; a subordinate clause in indirect discourse takes the subjunctive (A.G. 303 and 580). **quae:** Plural, neuter, nominative relative pronoun used substantively (A.G. 305). The antecedent is **omnia** (A.G. 307). Nominative subject (A.G. 339). **imperarentur:** The main verb of the subordinate clause (A.G. 278.b). Imperfect subjunctive; the tense of the subjunctive is in secondary sequence and follows the rules for the sequence of tense after **sunt ... consternati** (A.G. 482-85).

sibi: Plural, masculine, dative indirect reflexive pronoun (A.G. 300.2). The antecedent is **Galli**, the subject of **existimarent** (A.G. 299). Dative of agent after the second periphrastic infinitive **patienda (esse)** (A.G. 374.a).

(31.1-2) Nec minus quam est pollicitus Vercingetorix animo laborabat ut reliquas civitates adiungeret, atque eas donis (2) pollicitationibusque alliciebat.

adiungo, -iungere, -iunxi, -iunctus, *add, unite.*
animus, -i, m., *zeal, enthusiasm.*
civitas, -tatis, f., *state, nation.*
is, ea, id, *he, she, it; that, this.*
minus, *less.*
pollicitatio, -onis, f., *offer, promise.*
quam, *than.*
reliquus, -a, -um, *remaining, the rest.*
Vercingetorix, -igis, m., *Vercingetorix.*

allicio, -licere, -lexi, -lectus, *attract, allure.*
atque, *and.*
donum, -i, n., *gift, present.*
laboro, -are, -avi, -atus, *make effort, labor, strive.*
nec, *and ... not.*
polliceor, -liceri, -lictus, *promise, offer.*
-que, *and.*
ut, *so that.*

Nec ... pollicitus: Relative clause (A.G. 279.a). **Nec:** The conjunction qualifies the single word **minus** rather than a whole clause and means "and ... not" (*OLD* **neque** 4.c). **pollicitus:** See below.

minus quam: The comparative adverb **minus** is followed by **quam** and means "less than" (A.G. 218.a and 407). **minus:** Defective comparative adverb (A.G. 218.a and 320-21). **quam:** Relative adverb (*OLD* **quam** 8).

est pollicitus: The main verb of the subordinate clause (A.G. 278.b). The pronoun **is**, with the following noun **Vercingetorix** as the antecedent, is understood as the subject (A.G. 271.a).

Vercingetorix: Nominative subject (A.G. 339). See Appendix A.

animo: Ablative of manner without the preposition **cum** (A.G. 412). Here, **animus** means "zeal, enthusiasm" (*OLD* **animus** 8.d).

laborabat: The main verb of the coordinate clause **Nec ... adiungeret** (A.G. 278.a).

ut ... adiungeret: The conjunction **ut** ("so that") with the subjunctive forms a final (purpose) clause (A.G. 531.1). **adiungeret:** The main verb of the subordinate clause (A.G. 278.b). Imperfect subjunctive; the tense of the subjunctive is in secondary sequence and follows the rules for the sequence of tense after **laborabat** (A.G. 482-85). The pronoun **is**, with **Vercingetorix** as the antecedent, is understood as the subject (A.G. 271.a).

reliquas civitates: Accusative direct object of **adiungeret** (A.G. 387).

atque: The conjunction connects the two main verbs **laborabat ... alliciebat** and means "and" (*OLD* **atque** 12).

eas: Plural, feminine, accusative demonstrative pronoun used substantively (A.G. 296.2). The antecedent is **civitates** (A.G. 297.e). Accusative direct object of **alliciebat** (A.G. 387).

donis pollicitationibusque: Two ablatives of means (A.G. 409). **-que:** The enclitic conjunction connects the two ablative nouns (A.G. 324.a).

alliciebat: The main verb of the coordinate clause **eas ... alliciebat** (A.G. 278.a). The pronoun **is**, with **Vercingetorix** as the antecedent, is understood as the subject (A.G. 271.a).

(31.2-3) Huic rei idoneos homines deligebat quorum quisque aut oratione subdola aut amicitia (3) facillime capere posset.

amicitia, -ae, f., *friendship, alliance.*
capio, capere, cepi, captus, *seduce, win over.*
facile, sup. -lime, *easily, readily, with no trouble.*
homo, hominis, m., *man.*
oratio, -onis, f., *speech, words, address, plea.*
qui, quae, quod, *who, which, what.*
res, rei, f., *matter, affair, business.*

aut ... aut, *either ... or.*
deligo, -ligere, -legi, -lectus, *choose, select, pick out.*
hic, haec, hoc, *this; he, she, it.*
idoneus, -a, -um, *suitable, fit, capable.*
possum, posse, potui, -----, *be able.*
quisque, -----, quidque, *each one, each thing.*
subdolus, -a, -um, *crafty, cunning.*

Huic rei: Dative after the adjective **idoneos** (A.G. 384). **Huic:** Singular, feminine, dative demonstrative pronoun used as an adjective modifying **rei** (A.G. 296.1 and a).

idoneos homines: Accusative direct object of **deligebat** (A.G. 387).

deligebat: The main verb of the main clause (A.G. 278.b). The pronoun **is**, with **Vercingetorix** as the antecedent, is understood as the subject (A.G. 271.a).

quorum ... posset: A relative clause of characteristic; a relative clause with the subjunctive is often used to indicate a characteristic of the antecedent (A.G. 535). **quorum:** Plural, masculine, genitive demonstrative pronoun used substantively (A.G. 296.2). The antecedent is **homines** (A.G. 297.e). Partitive genitive with **quisque** (A.G. 346.d). **posset:** The main verb of the subordinate clause

(A.G. 278.b). Imperfect subjunctive; the tense of the subjunctive is in secondary sequence and follows the rules for the sequence of tense after **deligebat** (A.G. 482-85).

quisque: Singular, masculine, nominative indefinite pronoun used substantively (A.G. 151.g). Nominative subject (A.G. 339).

aut ... aut: The double connective introduces two logically exclusive alternatives meaning "either ... or" (*OLD* **aut** 1).

oratione subdola: Ablative of means (A.G. 409).

amicitia: Ablative of means (A.G. 409).

facillime: Superlative adverb (A.G. 218 and 320-21).

capere: Complementary infinitive after **posset** (A.G. 456). The pronoun **eas**, with **reliquas civitates** as the antecedent, is understood as the accusative direct object of the infinitive.

(31.3-4) **Qui Avarico expugnato refugerant, (4) armandos vestiendosque curat; simul, ut deminutae copiae redintegrarentur, imperat certum numerum militum civitatibus, quem et quam ante diem in castra adduci velit, sagittariosque omnis, quorum erat permagnus numerus in Gallia, conquiri et ad se mitti iubet.**

ad, *to.*

ante, *before.*
Avaricum, -i, n., *Avaricum.*
certus, -a, -um, *fixed, definite.*
conquiro, -quirere, -quisivi, -quisitus, *seek out, hunt up, bring together.*
curo, -are, -avi, -atus, *take care, provide for, superintend, arrange.*

dies, -ei, m. and f., *day.*
expugno, -are, -avi, -atus, *storm, take by assault, capture.*
impero, -are, -avi, -atus, *levy, draft, demand.*
iubeo, iubere, iussi, iussus, *order, give orders, bid, command.*
mitto, mittere, misi, missus, *send.*
omnis, -e, *all.*
-que, *and.*
quis, -----, quid, *who? what?; who? what?* (as adj., **qui, quae, quod**).
refugio, -fugere, -fugi, -----, *flee away, escape.*
simul, *at the same time.*
sum, esse, fui, futurus, *be.*
volo, velle, volui, *wish, desire, mean, intend.*

adduco, -ducere, -duxi, -ductus, *lead* or *bring to, bring up, lead.*
armo, -are, -avi, -atus, *provide with weapons, arm.*
castra, -orum, n., pl., *camp, encampment.*
civitas, -tatis, f., *state, nation.*
copiae, -arum, f., pl., *forces, troops.*
deminuo, -minuere, -minui, -minutus, *lessen, make smaller.*
et, *and.*
Gallia, -ae, f., *Gaul.*
in, *into; in.*
miles, -itis, m., *soldier, foot-solider.*
numerus, -i, m., *number.*
permagnus, -a, -um, *very large, very great.*
qui, quae, quod, *who, which, what.*
redintegro, -are, -avi, -atus, *replenish.*
sagittarius, -i, m., *archer, bowman.*
sui, sibi, se, or **sese**, nom. wanting, *himself.*
ut, *so that.*
vestio, -ire, -ivi, -itus, *clothe.*

Qui ... refugerant: Relative clause (A.G. 303). **Qui**: Plural, masculine, nominative relative pronoun used substantively (A.G. 305). The indefinite antecedent is omitted, supply **eos** (A.G. 307.c). Nominative subject (A.G. 339). **refugerant**: The main verb of the subordinate clause (A.G. 278.b). The pluperfect tense of the verb denotes an action completed in past time (A.G. 477).

Avarico expugnato: Ablative absolute (A.G. 419-20). For the reference see 15-28, esp. 28.5-6. **Avarico**: See Appendix A.

expugnato: The perfect tense of the participle represents the action as completed at the time indicated by the tense of the main verb (A.G. 489).

(eos) armandos vestiendosque: Two plural, masculine, accusative gerundives used as adjectives modifying **eos**, the supplied object of **curat** (A.G. 500.1). A gerundive in agreement with the object of **curaret** expresses purpose (A.G. 500.4). Supply **eos**, the supplied antecedent of **Qui**, as the object of **curat**. **-que**: The enclitic conjunction connects the two gerundives (A.G. 324.a). Two adjectives belonging to the same noun are regularly connected by a conjunction (A.G. 323.d).

curat: The main verb of the main clause (A.G. 278.b). The historical present, giving vividness to the narrative, is present in Chapter 31 (A.G. 469). This usage, common in all languages, comes from imagining past events as going on before our eyes (*repraesentatio*) (A.G. 469 Note). The pronoun **is**, with **Vercingetorix** as the antecedent, is understood as the subject (A.G. 271.a).

simul: Adverb (A.G. 320-21).

ut ... redintegrarentur: The conjunction **ut** ("so that") with the subjunctive forms a substantive clause of purpose which is used as the object of **imperat** denoting an action directed toward the future (A.G. 563). **redintegrarentur**: The main verb of the subordinate clause (A.G. 278.b). Imperfect subjunctive; the tense of the subjunctive is in secondary sequence after the historical present **imperat** (A.G. 482-85, esp. 485.e).

deminutae copiae: Nominative subject (A.G. 339). **deminutae**: Nominative, perfect, passive, participle used as a predicate, where in English a phrase or a subordinate clause would be more normal (A.G. 496).

imperat: The main verb of the coordinate clause **simul ... velit** (A.G. 278.a). The pronoun **is**, with **Vercingetorix** as the antecedent, is understood as the subject (A.G. 271.a).

simul: Adverb (A.G. 320-21).

certum numerum: Accusative direct object of the normally intransitive verb **imperat** (A.G. 369 and 387).

militum: Partitive genitive with **numerum** (A.G. 346.a.1).

civitatibus: Dative indirect object of the normally intransitive verb **imperat** (A.G. 369).

quem et quam ante diem ... velit: A double indirect question with the subjunctive; the phrase is in apposition to **numerum**, the direct object of **imperat** (A.G. 573-75). **quem**: See below. **et**: The conjunction connects the two interrogatives (A.G. 324.a). **quam ante diem**: Prepositional phrase, **ante** with the accusative here means "before" (*OLD* **ante2** 5). **quam**: Singular, feminine, accusative interrogative pronoun used as an adjective modifying **diem** (A.G. 148). **ante**: A monosyllabic preposition is often placed between a noun and its adjective (A.G. 599.d.2). **diem**: The noun **dies** is sometimes feminine in the singular, especially in phrases indicating a fixed time (A.G. 97.a). **velit**: The main verb of the subordinate clause (A.G. 278.b). Present subjunctive; the tense of the subjunctive is normally in secondary sequence after the historical present **imperat** (A.G. 575). Here it is in primary sequence through *repraesentatio* (A.G. 485.e and 585.b Note). The pronoun **is**, with **Vercingetorix** as the antecedent, is understood as the subject (A.G. 271.a).

simul: Adverb (A.G. 320-21).

quem ... adduci: Subject accusative with the infinitive after **velit**. The construction is equivalent to a substantive clause of purpose (A.G. 563.b.2). **quem**: Singular, masculine, accusative interrogative pronoun used substantively (A.G. 148). The pronoun is in apposition to **numerum** (A.G. 282).

in castra: Accusative of *place to which* with the preposition **in** (A.G. 426.2).

sagittariosque omnis ... conquiri ... mitti: A subject accusative with two infinitives after **iubet**. The construction is equivalent to a substantive clause of purpose (A.G. 563.a). **-que**: The enclitic conjunction connects the two main verbs **imperat ... iubet** (A.G. 324.a). **omnis**: Plural, masculine, accusative attributive adjective modifying **sagittarios** (A.G. 285.1). **-is** for **-es** is the regular form in i-stem adjectives (A.G. 114.a and 116).

quorum ... Gallia: Relative clause (A.G. 303). **quorum**: Plural, masculine, genitive demonstrative pronoun used substantively (A.G. 296.2). The antecedent is **sagittarios** (A.G. 297.e). Partitive genitive with **numerus** (A.G. 346.a). **Gallia**: See below.

erat: The main verb of the subordinate clause (A.G. 278.b). The verb **sum** in the sense of "exist" makes a complete predicate without a predicate noun or adjective ("there was ..."). It is then called the substantive verb and regularly comes first (A.G. 284.b and 598.c).

permagnus numerus: Nominative subject (A.G. 339). **permagnus**: The adverbial prefix **per-**, modifying an adjective, means "very" (A.G. 267.d.1).

in Gallia: Ablative of *place where* with the preposition **in** (locative ablative) (A.G. 426.3). **Gallia**: See Appendix A.

et: The conjunction connects the two infinitives **conquiri ... mitti** (A.G. 324.a).

ad se: Prepositional phrase, **ad** with the accusative here means "to" (*OLD* ad 1). **se**: Singular, masculine, accusative indirect reflexive pronoun (A.G. 300.2). The antecedent is **is** (**Vercingetorix**), the supplied subject of **iubet** (A.G. 299).

iubet: The main verb of the coordinate clause **sagittariosque ... iubet** (A.G. 278.a). The pronoun **is**, with **Vercingetorix** as the antecedent, is understood as the subject (A.G. 271.a).

simul: Adverb (A.G. 320-21).

(31.4-5) His rebus celeriter id quod (5) Avarici deperierat expletur.

Avaricum, -i, n., *Avaricum*.	**celeriter**, *quickly, speedily, at once, immediately*.
depereo, -ire, -ii, -iturus, *be lost*.	**expleo, -plere, -plevi, -pletus**, *fill up, fill full, fill out, complete*.
hic, haec, hoc, *this; he, she, it*.	**is, ea, id**, *he, she, it; that, this*.
qui, quae, quod, *who, which, what*.	**res, rei**, f., *measure*.

His rebus: Ablative of means (A.G. 409). **His**: Plural, feminine, ablative demonstrative pronoun used as an adjective modifying **rebus** (A.G. 296.1 and a).

celeriter: Adverb (A.G. 214.b and 320-21).

id: Singular, neuter, nominative demonstrative pronoun used substantively (A.G. 296.2). The pronoun is correlative to the relative clause **quod ... deperierat** (A.G. 297.d). Nominative subject of **expletur** (A.G. 339).

quod ... deperierat: Relative clause (A.G. 303). **quod**: Singular, neuter, nominative relative pronoun used substantively (A.G. 305). The antecedent is **id** (A.G. 297.e). Nominative subject (A.G. 339). **deperierat**: The main verb of the subordinate clause (A.G. 278.b). The pluperfect tense of the verb denotes an action completed in past time (A.G. 477).

Avarici: Locative case of the city name **Avaricum -i**, n. (A.G. 49.a). See Appendix A.

expletur: The main verb of the main clause (A.G. 278.b).

(31.5) Interim Teutomatus, Olloviconis filius, rex Nitiobrigum, cuius pater ab senatu nostro amicus erat appellatus, cum magno equitum suorum numero et quos ex Aquitania conduxerat ad eum pervenit.

ab, *by*.	**ad**, *to*.
amicus, -i, m., *a friend of the Roman state, ally*.	**appello, -are, -avi, -atus**, *name*.
Aquitania, -ae, f., *Aquitania*.	**conduco, -ducere, -duxi, -ductus**, *bring together, collect, hire*.
cum, *with*.	**eques, -itis**, m., *rider, horseman, cavalryman, trooper*.
et, *and*.	**ex**, *from, out of*.
filius, -i, m., *son*.	**interim**, *in the mean time, meanwhile*.
is, ea, id, *he, she, it; that, this*.	**magnus, -a, -um**, *great, large*.
Nitiobriges, -um, m., pl., *the Nitiobriges*.	**noster, -tra, -trum**, *our, our own*.
numerus, -i, m., *number*.	**Ollovico, -onis**, m., *Ollovico*.
pater, -tris, m., *father*.	**pervenio, -venire, -veni, -ventus**, *come to, reach*.
qui, quae, quod, *who, which, what*.	**rex, regis**, m., *king, ruler, chieftain*.
senatus, -us, m., *senate*.	**suus, -a, -um**, *his, with or without own*.

Teutomatus, -i, m., *Teutomatus.*

Interim: Adverb (A.G. 320-21).
Teutomatus: Nominative subject of **pervenit** (A.G. 339). See Appendix A.
Olloviconis: Possessive genitive with **filius** (A.G. 343). See Appendix A.
filius: A nominative noun in apposition to the proper noun **Teutomatus** (A.G. 282).
Nitiobrigum: Partitive genitive of the tribe name **Nitiobriges** with **rex** (A.G. 346.a.1). See Appendix A.
rex: A nominative noun in apposition to the proper noun **Teutomatus** (A.G. 282). See the note on **rex** at 4.5.
cuius ... erat appellatus: Relative clause (A.G. 303). **cuius**: Singular, masculine, genitive relative pronoun used substantively (A.G. 305). The antecedent is **Teutomatus** (A.G. 307). Possessive genitive with **pater** (A.G. 343). **erat appellatus**: The main verb of the subordinate clause (A.G. 278.b). The pluperfect tense of the verb denotes an action completed in past time (A.G. 477).
pater: Nominative subject (A.G. 339).
ab senatu nostro: Ablative of agent with the preposition **ab** after the passive verb **erat appellatus** (A.G. 405). **nostro**: Singular, masculine, ablative possessive pronoun used as an adjective modifying **senatu** (A.G. 302).
amicus: Predicate nominative after the verb **erat appellatus** (A.G. 284). Here, **amicus** means A (as title accorded to foreign kings) a friend of the Roman state (*OLD* **amicus2** 4).
cum magno equitum suorum numero: Ablative of accompaniment with the preposition **cum** (A.G. 413). **equitum suorum**: Partitive genitive with **numero** (A.G. 346.a.1). **suorum**: Plural, masculine, genitive possessive pronoun used as an adjective modifying **equitum** (A.G. 302).
et: The conjunction connects the prepositional phrase and the relative clause (A.G. 324.a).
quos ... conduxerat: Relative clause (A.G. 303). **quos**: Plural, masculine, accusative relative pronoun used substantively (A.G. 305). The antecedent is omitted; supply (**cum**) **eis** (A.G. 307.c). Accusative direct object of **conduxerat** (A.G. 387). **conduxerat**: The main verb of the subordinate clause (A.G. 278.b). The pronoun **is**, with **Teutomatus** as the antecedent, is understood as the subject (A.G. 271.a). The pluperfect tense of the verb denotes an action completed in past time (A.G. 477).
ex Aquitania: Ablative of source with the preposition **ex** (A.G. 403.1). **Aquitania**: See Appendix A.
ad eum: Prepositional phrase, **ad** with the accusative here means "to" (*OLD* **ad** 1). **eum**: Singular, masculine, accusative demonstrative pronoun used substantively (A.G. 296.2). The antecedent is **Vercingetorix** at 31.1 (A.G. 297.e).
pervenit: The main verb of the main clause (A.G. 278.b).

2.H CHAPTERS 32-33: A CIVIL WAR AMONG THE AEDUI IS PREVENTED BY CAESAR
(32.1-2) Caesar Avarici compluris dies commoratus summamque ibi copiam frumenti et reliqui commeatus nactus exercitum (2) ex labore atque inopia reficit.

atque, *and.*
Caesar, -aris, m., *Caesar.*
commoror, -ari, -atus, *stay, linger, remain, stop.*
copia, -ae, f., *quantity, abundance, supply, plenty.*
et, *and.*
exercitus, -us, m., *army.*
ibi, *in that place, there.*
labor, -oris, m., *toil, exertion, labor.*

-que, *and.*
reliquus, -a, -um, *remaining, the rest.*

Avaricum, -i, n., *Avaricum.*
commeatus, -us, m., *supplies, provisions.*
complures, -a and -ia, *several, a number of, many.*
dies, -ei, m. and f., *day.*
ex, *after.*
frumentum, -i, n., *grain.*
inopia, -ae, f., *want, lack, need, scarcity.*
naniscor, -cisci, nactus, and nanctus, *come upon, find, obtain, get, secure.*
reficio, -ficere, -feci, -fectus, *refresh.*
summus, -a, -um, *greatest, very great.*

Caesar ... commoratus ... nactus: Nominative subject (A.G. 339). **Caesar**: See Appendix A. **commoratus ... nactus**: Two nominative perfect, deponent, participles used as predicates, where in English a phrase or a subordinate clause would be more normal (A.G. 496).
Avarici: Locative case of the city name **Avaricum -i**, n. (A.G. 49.a). See Appendix A.
compluris dies: Accusative of *time how long* (A.G. 423.2). **compluris**: Plural, masculine, accusative comparative adjective, a compound of **plus** (A.G. 120). **-is** for **-es** is an allowable accusative ending for comparative adjectives (A.G. 120-21.c). **dies**: The noun **dies** is normally masculine gender (A.G. 97.a).
summamque ... copiam: Accusative direct object of the participle **nactus** (A.G. 387 and 488). **summam**: Irregular superlative adjective (A.G. 130.b). **-que**: The enclitic conjunction connects the two participles **commoratus ... nactus** (A.G. 324.a).
ibi: Adverb (A.G. 215.5 and 320-21).
frumenti et reliqui commeatus: Two partitive genitives with **copiam** (A.G. 346.a.1). **et**: The conjunction connects the two genitive nouns **frumenti ... commeatus** (A.G. 324.a).
exercitum: Accusative direct object of **refecit** (A.G. 387).
ex labore atque inopia: Prepositional phrase, **ex** with the ablative here means "after" (*OLD* **ex** 9). **atque**: The conjunction connects the two ablative nouns in the prepositional phrase and means "and" (*OLD* **atque** 12).
reficit: The main verb of the simple sentence (A.G. 278.1). The historical present, giving vividness to the narrative, is present in Chapter 32 (A.G. 469). This usage, common in all languages, comes from imagining past events as going on before our eyes (*repraesentatio*) (A.G. 469 Note).

132

(32.2-3) Iam prope hieme confecta, cum ipso anni tempore ad gerendum bellum vocaretur et ad hostem proficisci constituisset, sive eum ex paludibus silvisque elicere sive obsidione premere posset, legati ad eum principes Aeduorum veniunt oratum ut maxime neces(3)sario tempore civitati subveniat:

ad, *for, in order to, for the purpose of, against, to.*
annus, -i, m., *year.*
civitas, -tatis, f., *state, nation.*
constituo, -stituere, -stitui, -stitutus, *resolve upon, determine, decide.*
elicio, -licere, -licui, -----, *entice forth, bring out, draw out.*
ex, *from, out of.*
hiems, hiemis, f., *winter.*
iam , *already, now.*
is, ea, id, *he, she, it; that, this.*
maxime, *chiefly, especially.*

obsidio, -onis, f., *siege, blockade.*
palus, -udis, f., *marsh, swamp, bog, morass.*
princeps, -ipis, m., *head man, leader, chief, prince.*
proficiscor, -ficisci, -fectus, *set out, depart, proceed.*
-que, *and.*
sive ... sive, (*to see*) *whether ... or.*

tempus, -oris, n., *time.*
venio, venire, veni, ventus, *come.*

Aedui, -orum, m., pl., *the Aedui.*
bellum, -i, n., *war, warfare.*
conficio, -ficere, -feci, -fectus, *wear out, exhaust.*
cum, *when, while; after, when.*
et, *and.*
gero, gerere, gessi, gestus, *carry on, wage.*
hostis, -is, m., *enemy, foe; pl., the enemy.*
ipse, -a, -um, *the very.*
legatus, -i, m., *envoy, ambassador.*
necessarius, -a, -um, *needful, necessary, urgent, pressing.*
oro, -are, -avi, -atus, *plead, beg, entreat.*
possum, posse, potui, -----, *be able.*
premo, -ere, pressi, pressus, *press, harass, oppress.*
prope, *near, nearly, almost.*
silva, -arum, f., pl., *wooded parts* or *region.*
subvenio, -venire, -veni, -ventus, *come to the help* or *rescue of, assist, render assistance.*
ut, *so that.*
voco, -are, -avi, -atus, *call, summon.*

Iam prope hieme confecta: Ablative absolute (A.G. 419-20). **Iam**: Adverb (A.G. 215.6, 217.b and 320-21). **prope**: Adverb (A.G. 320-21). **confecta**: The perfect tense of the participle represents the action as completed at the time indicated by the tense of the main verb (A.G. 489).

cum ... vocaretur ... constituisset: Temporal clause with two subjunctive verbs, the first consists of the relative adverb **cum** ("when, while") with the imperfect subjunctive describing the circumstances that accompanied the action of the main verb (A.G. 546); the second consists of the relative adverb **cum** ("after, when") with the pluperfect subjunctive describing the circumstances that preceded the action of the main verb (A.G. 546). **vocaretur ... constituisset**: The main verbs of the subordinate clause (A.G. 278.b). The pronoun **is**, with **Caesar** as the antecedent, is understood as the subject of both verbs (A.G. 271.a).

ipso ... tempore: Ablative of *time when* (A.G. 423.1). **ipso**: Singular, neuter, ablative demonstrative pronoun used as an adjective modifying **tempore** (A.G. 296.1 and a). The intensive pronoun can be used with a noun for the sake of emphasis and means "The very (A.G. 298.c).

anni: Partitive genitive with **tempore** (A.G. 346.a.1).

ad gerendum bellum: The preposition **ad** with the accusative gerundive and noun denotes purpose (A.G. 506). **gerendum**: Singular, neuter, accusative gerundive used as an adjective modifying **bellum** denoting necessity, obligation or propriety (A.G. 500.1).

et: The conjunction connects the two verbs in the temporal clause **vocaretur ... constituisset** (A.G. 324.a).

ad hostem: Prepositional phrase, **ad** with the accusative here means "against" (*OLD* **ad** 2).

proficisci: Complementary infinitive after **constituisset** (A.G. 456 and 563.d). The infinitive is equivalent to a substantive clause of purpose (A.G. 563.d).

sive ... sive ... posset: Subordinate clause; a dependent clause takes the subjunctive when it is depending on an infinitive (**proficisci**) which is equivalent to a subjunctive clause and regarded as an integral part of that clause (attraction) (A.G. 278.b and 593). **sive ... sive**: The two conjunctions without an expressed question mean A(to see) whether ... or and connect the two complementary infinitives **elicere ... premere** (*OLD* **sive** 7). **posset**: The main verb of the subordinate clause (A.G. 278.b). Imperfect subjunctive; the tense of the subjunctive is in secondary sequence and follows the rules for the sequence of tense after **constituisset** (A.G. 482-85). The pronoun **is**, with **Caesar** as the antecedent, is understood as the subject (A.G. 271.a).

eum: Singular, masculine, accusative demonstrative pronoun used substantively (A.G. 296.2). The antecedent is **hostem** (A.G. 297.e). Accusative direct object of the infinitive **elicere** (A.G. 387 and 451.3).

ex paludibus silvisque: Ablative of *place from which* with the preposition **ex** (A.G. 426.1). **silvis**: The plural of the noun means "wooded parts or regions" (*OLD* **silva** 1). **-que**: The enclitic conjunction connects the two ablative nouns in the prepositional phrase (A.G. 324.a).

elicere: Complementary infinitive after **posset** (A.G. 456).

obsidione: Ablative of means (A.G. 409).

premere: Complementary infinitive after **posset** (A.G. 456). Carry down **eum** as the accusative direct object of the infinitive.

legati: Nominative subject (A.G. 339).

ad eum: Prepositional phrase, **ad** with the accusative here means "to" (*OLD* **ad** 1). **eum**: Singular, masculine, accusative demonstrative pronoun used substantively (A.G. 296.2). The antecedent is **Caesar** (A.G. 297.e).

principes: A nominative noun in apposition to **legati** (A.G. 282).

Aeduorum: Partitive genitive with **principes** (A.G. 346.a.1). See Appendix A.

veniunt: The main verb of the main clause (A.G. 278.b).

oratum: The supine in **-um** is used after a verb of motion (**veniunt**) to express purpose (A.G. 509).

ut ... subveniat: The conjunction ut ("so that") with the subjunctive forms a substantive clause of purpose which is used as the object of the supine oratum denoting an action directed toward the future (A.G. 563). subveniat: The main verbs of the subordinate clause (A.G. 278.b). Present subjunctive; the tense of the subjunctive is normally in secondary sequence after the historical present veniunt (A.G. 482-85). Here it is in primary sequence through *repraesentatio* (A.G. 485.e and 585.b Note). The pronoun is, with Caesar as the antecedent, is understood as the subject (A.G. 271.a).

maxime: Irregular superlative adverb (A.G. 218.a and 320-21).

necessario tempore: Ablative of *time when* (A.G. 423.1).

civitati: Dative indirect object of the intransitive compound verb subveniat (A.G. 370).

summo ... auctoritate (32.3-6): The remainder of Chapter 32 is in indirect discourse after an unexpressed verb of saying (A.G. 580.a).

(32.3-4) summo esse in periculo rem, quod, cum singuli magistratus antiquitus creari atque regiam potestatem annum obtinere consuessent, duo magistratum gerant et se uterque eorum legibus creatum esse (4) dicat.

annus, -i, m., *year.*

atque, *and.*

creo, -are, -avi, -atus, *choose, elect, appoint.*

dico, dicere, dixi, dictus, *say.*

et, *and.*

in, *in.*

lex, legis, f., *law, enactment, decree.*

obtineo, -tinere, -tinui, -tentus, *hold fast, retain, keep, hold.*

potestas, -tatis, f., *power, authority, lordship.*

regius, -a, -um, *kingly, royal.*

singuli, -ae, -a, *single.*

sum, esse, fui, futurus, *be.*

uterque, -traque, -trumque, *each, each one, both.*

antiquitus, *in former times, long ago, anciently.*

consuesco, -suescere, -suevi, -suetus, *be accustomed.*

cum, *although, while.*

duo, -ae, -o, *two.*

gero, gerere, gessi, gestus, *carry out, perform, exercise.*

is, ea, id, *he, she, it; that, this.*

magistratus, -us, m., *one holding a magistracy, magistrate; magistracy, civil office.*

periculum, -i, n., *risk, danger, hazard.*

quod, *because, since, for, as.*

res, rei, f., *state, government, affair, matter.*

sui, sibi, se, or sese, nom. wanting, *he,* with or without *himself.*

summus, -a, -um, *highest, greatest, very great.*

summo ... in periculo: Prepositional phrase, in with the ablative here means "in" (given circumstances) (*OLD* in 40). The prepositional phrase is in the predicate position after esse (A.G. 272). summo: Defective superlative adjective (A.G. 130.b).

esse ... rem: Accusative/infinitive construction in indirect discourse (A.G. 577 ff.). The verb of saying is not expressed, but implied in the general drift of the sentence (A.G. 580.a). esse: Present infinitive; the tense of the infinitive in indirect discourse is relative to that of the verb of saying (A.G. 584).

quod ... gerant ... dicat: Causal clause; the conjunction quod ("because") would normally take the indicative when the reason is given on the authority of the writer or speaker (A.G. 540.1). Here quod takes the subjunctive as a subordinate clause in indirect discourse after the unexpressed verb of saying (A.G. 580). gerant ... dicat: The main verbs of the subordinate clause (A.G. 278.b). Present subjunctives; the tense of the subjunctive is normally in secondary sequence after an unexpressed verb of saying (A.G. 482-85). Here it is in primary sequence through *repraesentatio* (A.G. 485.e and 585.b Note).

cum ... consuessent: Concessive clause, the relative adverb cum ("although, while") with the subjunctive here forms a concessive clause (A.G. 549). consuessent: The main verb of the subordinate clause (A.G. 278.b). Pluperfect subjunctive; the tense of the subjunctive is in secondary sequence after the unexpressed verb of saying (A.G. 482-85). Contracted form of consuevisset (A.G. 181.a).

singuli magistratus: Nominative subject (A.G. 339). singuli: Distributive numeral used as an adjective (A.G. 136-37). magistratus ... magistratum: Notice that both meanings of the noun (the person holding the office and the office itself) are used in this sentence.

antiquitus: Adverb (A.G. 320-21).

creari: Complementary infinitive after consuessent (A.G. 456).

atque: The conjunction connects the two complementary infinitives and means "and" (*OLD* atque 12).

regiam potestatem: Accusative direct object of the infinitive obtinere (A.G. 387 and 451.3).

annum: Accusative of *extent of time* (A.G. 423.2).

obtinere: Complementary infinitive after consuessent (A.G. 456).

duo: Declinable cardinal numeral used substantively (A.G. 132-35). The noun principes is understood. Nominative subject (A.G. 339).

magistratum: Accusative direct object of gerant (A.G. 387).

et: The conjunction connects the two verbs in the causal clause gerant ... dicat (A.G. 324.a).

se ... creatum esse: Accusative/infinitive construction in indirect discourse after dicat (A.G. 577 ff.). se: Singular, masculine, accusative direct reflexive pronoun (A.G. 300.1). The antecedent is uterque, the subject of dicat (A.G. 299). creatum esse: Perfect infinitive; the tense of the infinitive in indirect discourse is relative to that of the verb of saying (A.G. 584).

uterque: Nominative subject (A.G. 339).

eorum: Plural, masculine, genitive demonstrative pronoun used substantively (A.G. 296.2). The antecedent is duo (A.G. 297.e). Partitive genitive with uterque (A.G. 346.a.2).

legibus: Ablative of means (A.G. 409).

(32.4-5) Horum esse alterum Convictolitavem, florentem et inlustrem adulescentem; alterum Cotum, antiquissima familia natum atque ipsum hominem summae potentiae et magnae cognationis, cuius frater Valetiacus proximo anno eundem (5) magistratum gesserit.

adulescens, -entis, m., *young man, youth.*
annus, -i, m., *year.*
atque, *and.*
Convictolitavis, -is, m., *Convictolitavis.*
et, *and.*
florens, -entis, *influential.*
gero, gerere, gessi, gestus, *carry out, perform, exercise.*
homo, hominis, m., *man, person.*
inlustris, -e, *prominent, distinguished.*

magistratus, -us, m., *magistracy, civil office.*
nascor, nasci, natus, *be born, produced.*
proximus, -a, -um, *nearest, next, last.*
sum, esse, fui, futurus, *be.*
Valetiacus, -i, m., *Valetiacus.*

alter ... alter, -i, m., *the one ... the other.*
antiquus, -a, -um, sup. **-issimus**, *old, ancient.*
cognatio, -onis, f., *family connections.*
Cotus, -i, m., *Cotus.*
familia, -ae, f., *family.*
frater, -tris, m., *brother.*
hic, haec, hoc, *this; he, she, it.*
idem, eadem, idem, *the same.*
ipse, -a, -um, *he, they*, with or without *himself, themselves.*
magnus, -a, -um, *great, large.*
potentia, -ae, f., *might, power, influence.*
qui, quae, quod, *who, which, what.*
summus, -a, -um, *highest, greatest, very great.*

Horum: Plural, masculine, genitive demonstrative pronoun used substantively (A.G. 296.2). The antecedent is **duo** (A.G. 297.e). Partitive genitive with **alterum** (A.G. 346.a.2).
esse alterum Convictolitavem: Accusative/infinitive construction in indirect discourse (A.G. 577 ff.). The verb of saying is not expressed, but implied in the general drift of the sentence (A.G. 580.a). **esse**: Present infinitive; the tense of the infinitive in indirect discourse is relative to that of the verb of saying (A.G. 584). **alterum**: Singular, masculine, accusative pronoun is the accusative subject of **esse** (A.G. 397.e). **alterum ... (alterum)**: The pronouns, when used correlatively, mean "the one ... the other" (A.G. 315.a). **Convictolitavem**: Accusative predicate noun after the infinitive **esse** (A.G. 283-4). See Appendix A.
florentem et inlustrem adulescentem: An accusative noun phrase in apposition to the proper noun **Convictolitavem** (A.G. 282). **florentem et inlustrem**: Two attributive adjectives modifying **adulescentem** (A.G. 285.1). **et**: The conjunction connects the two adjectives (A.G. 324.a). Two adjectives belonging to the same noun are regularly connected by a conjunction (A.G. 323.d).
(esse) alterum Cotum: Accusative/infinitive construction in indirect discourse (A.G. 577 ff.). The verb of saying is not expressed, but implied in the general drift of the sentence (A.G. 580.a). Carry down **esse** as the infinitive. **alterum**: Singular, masculine, accusative pronoun is the accusative subject of the supplied infinitive **esse** (A.G. 397.e). **Cotum**: Accusative predicate noun after the infinitive **esse** (A.G. 283-4). See Appendix A.
antiquissima familia: Ablative of source without a preposition after **natum** (A.G. 403.a). **antiquissima**: Superlative adjective (A.G. 124).
natum: Accusative perfect, deponent, participle used as a predicate modifying **Cotum**, where in English a phrase or a subordinate clause would be more normal (A.G. 496).
atque: The conjunction connects the two accusatives **natum ... hominem** which modify **Cotum** and means "and" (*OLD* **atque** 12).
ipsum hominem: An accusative noun phrase in apposition to the proper noun **Cotum** (A.G. 282). **ipsum**: Singular, masculine, accusative demonstrative pronoun used as an adjective modifying **hominem** meaning "himself" (A.G. 296.1 and a and 298.c).
summae potentiae et magnae cognationis: Two genitives of quality with **hominem** (A.G. 345). **summae**: Defective superlative adjective (A.G. 130.b). **et**: The conjunction connects the two genitive nouns (A.G. 324.a).
cuius ... gesserit: Relative clause; a subordinate clause in indirect discourse takes the subjunctive (A.G. 303 and 580). **cuius**: Singular, masculine, genitive relative pronoun used substantively (A.G. 305). The antecedent is **Cotum** (A.G. 307). Possessive genitive with **frater** (A.G. 343). **gesserit**: The main verb of the subordinate clause (A.G. 278.b). Perfect subjunctive; the tense of the subjunctive is normally in secondary sequence after an unexpressed verb of saying (A.G. 482-84). Here it is in primary sequence through *repraesentatio* (A.G. 585.b Note).
frater: Nominative subject (A.G. 339).
Valetiacus: A nominative proper noun in apposition to **frater** (A.G. 282). See Appendix A.
proximo anno: Ablative of *time when* (A.G. 423.1). **proximo**: Defective superlative adjective (A.G. 130.a).
eundem magistratum: Accusative direct object of **gesserit** (A.G. 387). **eundem**: Singular, masculine, accusative demonstrative pronoun used as an adjective modifying **magistratum** (A.G. 296.1 and a).

(32.5-6) Civitatem esse omnem in armis; divisum senatum, divisum populum, suas cuiusque eorum (6) clientelas.

arma, -orum, n., *arms.*
clientelae, -arum, f., pl., *following of clients.*
in, *bearing, under.*
omnis, -e, *the whole of.*
quisque, -----, quidque, *each one, each thing.*
sum, esse, fui, futurus, *be.*

civitas, -tatis, f., *state, nation.*
divido, -videre, -visi, -visus, *separate, divide.*
is, ea, id, *he, she, it; that, this.*
populus, -i, m., *people, nation.*
senatus, -us, m., *council of elders, senate.*
suus, -a, -um, *his*, with or without *own.*

Civitatem esse omnem: Accusative/infinitive construction in indirect discourse (A.G. 577 ff.). The verb of saying is not expressed,

but implied in the general drift of the sentence (A.G. 580.a). **esse**: Present infinitive; the tense of the infinitive in indirect discourse is relative to that of the verb of saying (A.G. 584). **omnem**: Attributive adjective modifying **Civitatem** (A.G. 285.1).
in armis: Prepositional phrase, **in** with the ablative here means "bearing" (*OLD* **in** 36.b). The prepositional phrase is in the predicate position after **esse** (A.G. 272).
divisum (esse) senatum: Accusative/infinitive construction in indirect discourse (A.G. 577 ff.). The verb of saying is not expressed, but implied in the general drift of the sentence (A.G. 580.a). **divisum (esse)**: Supply **esse** to form the perfect, passive infinitive (A.G. 188). The tense of the infinitive in indirect discourse is relative to that of the verb of saying (A.G. 584).
divisum (esse) populum: Accusative/infinitive construction in indirect discourse (A.G. 577 ff.). The verb of saying is not expressed, but implied in the general drift of the sentence (A.G. 580.a). **divisum (esse)**: Supply **esse** to form the perfect, passive infinitive (A.G. 188). The tense of the infinitive in indirect discourse is relative to that of the verb of saying (A.G. 584).
suas cuiusque eorum clientelas (esse): This phrase has the same meaning as **quisque eorum suas clientelas habebat**.
suas ... clientelas (esse): Accusative/infinitive construction in indirect discourse (A.G. 577 ff.). The verb of saying is not expressed, but implied in the general drift of the sentence (A.G. 580.a). **suas**: Plural, feminine, accusative possessive pronoun used as an adjective modifying **clientelas** (A.G. 302). Supply **esse** as the infinitive.
cuiusque: Singular, masculine, genitive indefinite (universal) pronoun used substantively (A.G. 151.g) (*OLD* **quisque** 1). Possessive genitive (predicate genitive); the possessive genitive often stands in the predicate, connected to its noun (**clientelas**) by a verb (**esse**) (A.G. 343.b).
eorum: Plural, masculine, genitive demonstrative pronoun used substantively (A.G. 296.2). The antecedent is **Convictolitavem ... Cotum** (A.G. 297.e). Partitive genitive with **cuiusque** (A.G. 346.a.2).

(32.6) Quod si diutius alatur controversia, fore uti pars cum parte civitatis confligat. Id ne accidat, positum in eius diligentia atque auctoritate.

accido, -cidere, -cidi, -----, *happen, occur, turn out.*

atque, *and.*
civitas, -tatis, f., *state, nation.*
controversia, -ae, f., *dispute, debate, controversy, quarrel.*
diligentia, -ae, f., *care, diligence.*
in, *in.*
ne, *so that ... not.*
pono, ponere, posui, positus, *place, put.*
si, *if.*
uti, *so that.*

alo, alere, alui, altus or **alitus,** *nourish, maintain, keep, foster.*
auctoritas, -tatis, f., *influence, weight, authority.*
confligo, -fligere, -flixi, -flictus, *contend, fight.*
cum, *with.*
diu, comp. **diutius,** *long, for a long time.*
is, ea, id, *he, she, it; that, this.*
pars, partis, f., *part, side.*
quod, *but, and, now.*
sum, esse, fui, futurus, *be.*

Quod si: The combination means Abut if, and if, now if (A.G. 324.d). **Quod**: The relative adverb is used as a connective particle, referring to what precedes (*OLD* **quod** 1). **si**: Conjunction (*OLD* **si**).
si ... alatur ... fore: Conditional statement in indirect discourse (A.G. 589). The verb of saying is not expressed, but implied in the general drift of the sentence (A.G. 580.a). The protasis, as a dependent clause, is in the subjunctive and the apodosis, as the principal clause, is in the infinitive (A.G. 589).
si ... alatur: The conjunction **si** ("if") with the subjunctive forms the protasis of a conditional statement in indirect discourse (A.G. 589.1). **alatur**: The main verb of the subordinate clause (A.G. 278.b). Present subjunctive; the tense of the subjunctive is normally in secondary sequence after an unexpressed verb of saying (A.G. 482-84). Here it is in primary sequence through *repraesentatio* (A.G. 585.b Note).
diutius: Irregular comparative adverb (A.G. 218.a and 320-21).
controversia: Nominative subject (A.G. 339). The subject is in the last position (A.G. 597.b).
fore uti ... confligat: The apodosis of the conditional statement (A.G. 589.2). Accusative/infinitive construction in indirect discourse (A.G. 577 ff.). The verb of saying is not expressed, but implied in the general drift of the sentence (A.G. 580.a). **fore uti** with a clause of result as subject is used instead of the future infinitive active or passive (A.G. 569.a). **fore**: Future active infinitive of **sum** (A.G. 170.a). The tense of the infinitive in indirect discourse is relative to that of the verb of saying (A.G. 584). **uti ... confligat**: A substantive clause of result with the conjunction **uti** ("so that") is used as the accusative subject of **fore** (A.G. 569.a). **confligat**: The main verb of the subordinate clause (A.G. 278.b). Present subjunctive; the tense of the subjunctive is normally in secondary sequence after an unexpressed verb of saying (A.G. 482-84). Here it is in primary sequence through *repraesentatio* (A.G. 585.b Note).
pars: Nominative subject (A.G. 339).
cum parte: Ablative of accompaniment with the preposition **cum**, words of contention (**confligat**) require **cum** (A.G. 413.b).
civitatis: Partitive genitive with both **pars** and **parte** (A.G. 346.a.1).
Id: Singular, neuter, nominative demonstrative pronoun used substantively (A.G. 296.2). The antecedent is the idea of civil war immediately above (A.G. 297.e). Nominative subject of **accidat** (A.G. 339).
ne accidat: The conjunction **ne** ("so that ... not") with the subjunctive forms a negative purpose clause dependent on **positum (esse)** (A.G. 531.1). **accidat**: The main verb of the subordinate clause (A.G. 278.b). Present subjunctive; the tense of the subjunctive is normally in secondary sequence after an unexpressed verb of saying (A.G. 482-84). Here it is in primary sequence through *repraesentatio* (A.G. 585.b Note).
(id) ... positum (esse): Accusative/infinitive construction in indirect discourse (A.G. 577 ff.). The verb of saying is not expressed, but implied in the general drift of the sentence (A.G. 580.a). **positum (esse)**: Supply **esse** to form the perfect, passive infinitive (A.G.

186). The tense of the infinitive in indirect discourse is relative to that of the verb of saying (A.G. 584). Impersonal use of the passive verb (A.G. 208.d). Supply **id** (i.e., the entire matter) as the subject (A.G. 318.c).

in eius diligentia atque auctoritate: Prepositional phrase, **in** with the ablative here means "in" (expressing an abstract location) (*OLD* **in** 26). **eius**: Singular, masculine, genitive demonstrative pronoun used substantively (A.G. 296.2). The antecedent is **Caesar** (A.G. 297.e). Possessive genitive with both **diligentia** and **auctoritate** (A.G. 343). **atque**: The conjunction connects the two ablative nouns in the prepositional phrase and means "and" (*OLD* **atque** 12). **auctoritate**: See note on **auctoritatem** at 30.3.

(33.1-3) Caesar, etsi a bello atque hoste discedere detrimentosum esse existimabat, tamen non ignorans quanta ex dissensionibus incommoda oriri consuessent, ne tanta et tam coniuncta populo Romano civitas, quam ipse semper aluisset omnibusque rebus ornasset, ad vim atque arma descenderet atque ea pars quae minus sibi confideret auxilia a Vercingeto(2)rige arcesseret, huic rei praevertendum existimavit et, quod legibus Aeduorum eis qui summum magistratum obtinerent excedere ex finibus non liceret, ne quid de iure aut de legibus eorum deminuisse videretur, ipse in Aeduos proficisci statuit senatumque omnem et quos inter controversia esset **(3)** ad se Decetiam evocavit.

a(b), *from.*
Aedui, -orum, m., pl., *the Aedui.*

arcesso, -sere, -sivi, -situs, *send for, summon.*
atque, *and.*
auxilia, -orum, n., *auxiliaries, auxiliary troops, allied forces.*
Caesar, -aris, m., *Caesar.*
confido, -fidere, -fisus sum, *believe, be confident.*

consuesco, -suescere, -suevi, -suetus, *be accustomed.*

de, *about, concerning.*
deminuo, -minuere, -minui, -minutus, *lessen, make smaller.*

detrimentosus, -a, -um, *hurtful, detrimental.*

dissensio, -onis, f., *difference of opinion, disagreement.*
etsi, *although, though, even if.*

ex, *from, out of.*

existimo, -are, -avi, -atus, *think, consider, judge.*

hic, haec, hoc, *this; he, she, it.*
ignoro, -are, -avi, -atus, *be ignorant.*
incommodum, -i, n., *misfortune, disaster, injury, defeat.*
ipse, -a, -um, *he, they*, with or without *himself, themselves.*
ius, iuris, n., *right, authority.*
licet, licere, licuit, and licitum est, (imper.), *it is allowed, lawful, permitted.*
minus, *less.*
non, *not.*
omnis, -e, *all; the whole.*
orno, -are, -avi, -atus, *honor, dignify.*
populus, -i, m., *people, nation.*
proficiscor, -ficisci, -fectus, *set out, depart, proceed.*
-que, *and.*
quis, -----, quid, *anyone, anything.*
res, rei, f., *matter, affair.*
semper, *always, ever, constantly.*
statuo, -uere, -ui, -utus, *determine, resolve.*

sum, esse, fui, futurus, *be.*
tam, *so very.*
tantus, -a, -um, *so great, so large, such.*
videor, videri, visus sum, *be seen, seem, appear.*

ad, *to.*
alo, alere, alui, altus or **alitus**, *nourish, maintain, keep, foster.*
arma, -orum, n., *arms, weapons.*
aut, *or.*
bellum, -i, n., *war.*
civitas, -tatis, f., *state, nation.*
coniungo, -iungere, -iunxi, -iunctus, *join together, unite, join.*
controversia, -ae, f., *dispute, debate, controversy, quarrel.*
Decetia, -ae, f., *Decetia.*
descendo, -scendere, -scendi, -scensus, *resort* or *stoop to.*
discedo, -cedere, -cessi, -cessurus, *go away, depart, leave.*
et, *and.*
evoco, -are, -avi, -atus, *call out, call forth, call, summon.*
excedo, -cedere, -cessi, -cessurus, *go out, leave, withdraw, depart.*
fines, -ium, m., pl., *borders*, hence *territory, country, land.*
hostis, -is, m., *enemy, foe.*
in, *into the country of, towards.*
inter, *among.*
is, ea, id, *he, she, it; that, this.*
lex, legis, f., *law, enactment, decree.*
magistratus, -us, m., *magistracy, civil office.*
ne, *so that ... not.*
obtineo, -tinere, -tinui, -tentus, *retain, keep, hold.*
orior, oriri, ortus, *rise, arise, spring from.*
pars, partis, f., *side, party, faction.*
praeverto, -vertere, -verti, -----, *attend to first.*
quantus, -a, -um, *how great, how much, how large.*
qui, quae, quod, *who, which, what.*
quod, *because, since, for, as.*
Romanus, -a, -um, *Roman.*
senatus, -us, m., *council of elders, senate.*
sui, sibi, se, or **sese**, nom. wanting, (*herself*) *itself, himself.*
summus, -a, -um, *highest.*
tamen, *yet, still, for all that, nevertheless, however.*
Vercingetorix, -igis, m., *Vercingetorix.*
vis, acc. **vim**, abl. **vi**, *force, violence.*

This is a rare periodic sentence in Book 7 (A.G. 600-01).

Caesar ... ignorans ... ipse ... ipse: Nominative subject (A.G. 339). **Caesar ... ignorans**: Nominative subject of **existimavit**. **Caesar**: See Appendix A. **ignorans**: Nominative present participle used as an adjective modifying **Caesar** (A.G. 494). **ipse**: Nominative subject of **aluisset ... ornasset**. See below. **ipse**: Nominative subject of **statuit ... evocavit**. See below.

etsi ... tamen: A conjunction and adverb introducing correlative clauses meaning "although ... nevertheless" (*OLD* **etsi** 2 and **tamen** 3).

etsi ... existimabat: Concessive clause; the conjunction **etsi** ("although") with the indicative forms a concessive clause (A.G. 527).

existimabat: The main verb of the subordinate clause (A.G. 278.b). The pronoun **is**, with **Caesar** as the antecedent, is understood as the subject (A.G. 271.a).

a bello atque hoste discedere: The infinitive phrase functions as the subject of the impersonal verb **detrimentosum esse** (A.G. 454).

a bello atque hoste: Ablative of separation with the preposition **a(b)** after the compound infinitive **discedere** (A.G. 402). **atque**: The conjunction connects the two ablative nouns in the prepositional phrase and means "and" (*OLD* **atque** 12).

detrimentosum esse: Accusative/infinitive construction in indirect discourse after **existimabat** (A.G. 577 ff.). Impersonal use of the verb (A.G. 207.c). The previous infinitive phrase functions as the subject (A.G. 454). **detrimentosum**: Singular, neuter, accusative predicate accusative adjective after **esse** (A.G. 283-84).

tamen: Adverb, normally postpositive but not here (A.G. 320-21 and 324.j).

non: Adverb modifying the participle **ignorans**, the negative precedes the word it especially effects (A.G. 217.e, 320-21, and 599.a).

quanta ... incommoda ... consuessent: Indirect question with the subjunctive; the phrase is the object of the present participle **ignorans** (A.G. 573-75). **quanta ... incommoda**: Nominative subject (A.G. 339). **quanta**: Interrogative adjective (*OLD* **quantus** 1).

consuessent: The main verb of the subordinate clause (A.G. 278.b). Pluperfect subjunctive; the tense of the subjunctive is in secondary sequence and follows the rules for the sequence of tense after **existimavit** (A.G. 575). Contracted form of **consuevisset** (A.G. 181.a).

ex dissensionibus: Ablative of source with the preposition **ex** (A.G. 403.1).

oriri: Complementary infinitive after **consuessent** (A.G. 456).

ne ... descenderet ... arcesseret: The conjunction **ne** ("so that ... not") with the subjunctive forms a substantive clause of purpose (A.G. 563). The clause functions as the subject of the impersonal infinitive **praevertendum (esse)**; a substantive clause used as the object of a verb becomes the subject when the verb is put into the passive (A.G. 566). **descenderet ... arcesseret**: The main verbs of the subordinate clause (A.G. 278.b). Imperfect subjunctives; the tense of the subjunctives is in secondary sequence and follows the rules for sequence of tense after **existimavit** (A.G. 482-85).

tanta et tam coniuncta ... civitas: Nominative subject of **descenderet** (A.G. 339). **et**: The conjunction connects the two adjectives modifying **civitas** (A.G. 324.a). Two adjectives belonging to the same noun are regularly connected by a conjunction (A.G. 323.d).

tam: Adverb modifying **coniuncta** (A.G. 215.2 and 320-21). **coniuncta**: Nominative, perfect, passive participle used as a predicate where in English a phrase or a subordinate clause would be more natural (A.G. 496).

populo Romano: Ablative of accompaniment without **cum** after **coniuncta** (A.G. 413.a Note). This expression has an invariable word order (A.G. 598.k).

quam ... aluisset ... ornasset: Relative clause; a clause dependent on a subjunctive clause (**ne ... descenderet**) takes the subjunctive when regarded as an integral part of that clause (attraction) (A.G. 593). **quam**: Singular, feminine, accusative relative pronoun used substantively (A.G. 305). The antecedent is **civitas** (A.G. 307). Accusative direct object of both verbs **aluisset ... ornasset** (A.G. 387).

aluisset ... ornasset: The main verbs of the subordinate clause (A.G. 278.b). Pluperfect subjunctives; the tense of the subjunctives is in secondary sequence and follows the rules for sequence of tense after **existimavit** (A.G. 482-85). The pronoun **is**, with **Caesar** as the antecedent, is understood as the subject of both verbs (A.G. 271.a). **ornasset**: Contracted form of **ornavisset** (A.G. 181.a).

ipse: Singular, masculine, nominative demonstrative pronoun used substantively (A.G. 296.2 and 298.d). The antecedent is **Caesar** (A.G. 298). Nominative subject of **aluisset ... ornasset** (A.G. 339). The pronoun is here emphatic (A.G. 298.d.1).

semper: Adverb (A.G. 217.b and 320-21).

omnibusque rebus: Ablative of specification (A.G. 418). **-que**: The enclitic conjunction connects the two verbs in the relative clause **aluisset ... ornasset** (A.G. 324.a).

ad vim atque arma: Prepositional phrase, **ad** with the accusative here means "to" (*OLD* **ad** 6). **atque**: The conjunction connects the two accusative nouns in the prepositional phrase and means "and" (*OLD* **atque** 12).

atque: The conjunction connects the two verbs in the negative purpose clause **descenderet ... arcesseret** (A.G. 324.b).

ea pars: Nominative subject of **arcesseret** (A.G. 339). **ea**: Singular, feminine, nominative demonstrative pronoun used as an adjective modifying **pars** (A.G. 296.1 and a). The pronoun functions as a correlative to the relative clause **quae ... confideret** (A.G. 297.d).

quae ... confideret: Relative clause; a clause dependent on a subjunctive clause (**ne ... arcesseret**) takes the subjunctive when regarded as an integral part of that clause (attraction) (A.G. 593). **quae**: Singular, feminine, nominative relative pronoun used substantively (A.G. 305). The antecedent is **pars** (A.G. 307). Nominative subject (A.G. 339). **confideret**: The main verb of the subordinate clause (A.G. 278.b). Imperfect subjunctive; the tense of the subjunctive is in secondary sequence and follows the rules for sequence of tense after **existimavit** (A.G. 482-85).

minus: Defective comparative adverb (A.G. 218.a and 320-21).

sibi: Singular, feminine, dative direct reflexive pronoun (A.G. 300.1). The antecedent is **pars**, the subject of **confideret** (A.G. 299). Dative indirect object of the intransitive verb **confideret** (A.G. 367). The literal translation, "herself", should be rendered in English by the gender neutral "itself".

auxilia: Accusative direct object of **arcesseret** (A.G. 387). In the plural the noun means "auxiliaries" (A.G. 107).

a Vercingetorige: Ablative of source with the preposition **a(b)** (A.G. 403.1). **Vercingetorige**: See Appendix A.

huic rei: Dative indirect object of the compound infinitive **praevertendum (esse)** (A.G. 370). When intransitive verbs that govern the dative are used impersonally in the passive the dative is retained (A.G. 372). **huic**: Singular, feminine, dative demonstrative pronoun used as an adjective modifying **rei** (A.G. 296.1 and a).

praevertendum (esse): Accusative/infinitive construction in indirect discourse after **existimavit** (A.G. 577 ff.). **praevertendum**

(**esse**): Supply **esse** to form the second periphrastic (passive) present infinitive with the gerundive implying necessity (A.G. 194.b and 196). The tense of the infinitive in indirect discourse is relative to that of the verb of saying (A.G. 584). Impersonal use of the infinitive (A.G. 208.c). The preceeding negative purpose clause (**ne ... descenderet ... arcesseret**) functions as the subject; a substantive clause used as the object of a verb becomes the subject when the verb is put in the passive (A.G. 566).

existimavit: The main verb of the coordinate clause **Caesar ... existimavit** (A.G. 278.a).

et: The conjunction connects the main verbs **existimavit ... statuit** (A.G. 324.a).

quod ... liceret: Causal clause; the conjunction **quod** ("because") normally takes the indicative when the reason is given on the authority of the writer or speaker (A.G. 540.1). Here **quod** takes the subjunctive as a subordinate clause depending on an infinitive (**proficisci**) which is equivalent to a subjunctive clause and regarded as an integral part of that clause (attraction) (A.G. 593). **liceret**: The main verb of the subordinate clause (A.G. 278.b). Imperfect subjunctive; the tense of the subjunctive is in secondary sequence and follows the rules for the sequence of tense after **statuit** (A.G. 482-85). Impersonal use of the verb (A.G. 208.c). The following infinitive phrase **excedere ex finibus** functions as the subject (A.G. 454).

legibus: Ablative of cause without a preposition (A.G. 404).

Aeduorum: Possessive genitive with **legibus** (A.G. 343). See Appendix A.

eis: Plural, masculine, dative demonstrative pronoun used substantively (A.G. 296.2). The pronoun is correlative to the relative clause **qui ... obtinerent** (A.G. 297.d). Dative indirect object of **liceret** (A.G. 368.1).

qui ... obtinerent: Relative clause; a clause dependent on a subjunctive clause (**quod ... liceret**) takes the subjunctive when regarded as an integral part of that clause (attraction) (A.G. 593). **qui**: Plural, masculine, nominative relative pronoun used substantively (A.G. 305). The antecedent is **eis** (A.G. 307). Nominative subject (A.G. 339). **obtinerent**: The main verb of the subordinate clause (A.G. 278.b). Imperfect subjunctive; the tense of the subjunctive is in secondary sequence and follows the rules for the sequence of tense after **statuit** (A.G. 482-85).

summum magistratum: Accusative direct object of **obtinerent** (A.G. 387). **summum**: Defective superlative adjective (A.G. 130.b).

excedere ex finibus: The infinitive phrase functions as the subject of the impersonal verb **liceret** (A.G. 454). **ex finibus**: Ablative of *place from which* with the preposition **ex** (A.G. 426.1).

non: Adverb, the adverb generally precedes the verb if it belongs to no one word in particular (A.G. 217.e, 320-21, and 599.a).

ne ... videretur: The conjunction **ne** ("so that ... not") with the subjunctive forms a negative purpose clause dependent on **proficisci statuit** (A.G. 531.1). **videretur**: The main verb of the subordinate clause (A.G. 278.b). Imperfect subjunctive; the tense of the subjunctive is in secondary sequence and follows the rules for the sequence of tense after **statuit** (A.G. 482-85). The pronoun **is**, with **ipse (Caesar)** as the antecedent, is understood as the subject (A.G. 271.a).

quid: Singular, neuter, accusative indefinite pronoun used substantively (A.G. 149). The indefinite **quis, -----**, **quid** is used after **ne** (A.G. 310.a). Accusative direct object of the infinitive **deminuisse** (A.G 387 and 451.3).

de iure aut de legibus eorum: Prepositional phrases, **de** with the ablative here means "about, concerning" (*OLD* **de** 12). **aut**: The conjunction connects the two prepositional phrases and excludes the alternative (A.G. 324.e). **eorum**: Plural, masculine, genitive demonstrative pronoun used substantively (A.G. 296.2). The antecedent is **Aeduorum** (A.G. 297.e). Possessive genitive with **legibus** (A.G. 343).

deminuisse: Complementary infinitive after **videretur** (A.G. 456).

ipse: Singular, masculine, nominative demonstrative pronoun used substantively (A.G. 296.2 and 298.d). The antecedent is **Caesar** (A.G. 298). Nominative subject of **statuit ... evocavit** (A.G. 339). The pronoun is here emphatic (A.G. 298.d.1).

in Aeduos: Accusative of *place to which* with the preposition **in** ("into the country of") (A.G. 426.2). **Aeduos**: See Appendix A.

proficisci: Complementary infinitive after **statuit** (A.G. 456 and 563.d). The infinitive is equivalent to a substantive clause of purpose (A.G. 563.d).

statuit: The main verb of the coordinate clause **quod ... statuit** (A.G. 278.a).

senatumque omnem: Accusative direct object of **evocavit** (A.G. 387). **-que**: The enclitic conjunction connects the two main verbs **statuit ... evocavit** (A.G. 324.a).

et: The conjunction connects the two accusatives **senatum ... quos** (A.G. 324.a).

quos inter ... esset: A relative clause of characteristic; a relative clause with the subjunctive is often used to indicate a characteristic of the antecedent (A.G. 535). **quos**: Plural, masculine, accusative relative pronoun used substantively (A.G. 305). The antecedent is omitted, supply **eos** (A.G. 307.c). **quos inter**: Prepositional phrase, **inter** with the accusative here means "among" (*OLD* **inter1** 1). The preposition **inter** occasionally follows its noun (A.G. 435). The prepositional phrase is in the predicate position after **esset** (A.G. 272). **esset**: The main verb of the subordinate clause (A.G. 278.b). Imperfect subjunctive; the tense of the subjunctive is in secondary sequence and follows the rules for the sequence of tense after **evocavit** (A.G. 482-85).

controversia: Nominative subject (A.G. 339).

ad se: Prepositional phrase, **ad** with the accusative here means "to" (*OLD* **ad** 1). **se**: Singular, masculine, accusative direct reflexive pronoun (A.G. 300.1). The antecedent is **ipse (Caesar)**, the subject of **evocavit** (A.G. 299).

Decetiam: Accusative of *place to which* without a preposition (city name) (A.G. 427.2). See Appendix A.

evocavit: The main verb of the coordinate clause **senatumque ... evocavit** (A.G. 278.a).

(33-3) **Cum prope omnis civitas eo convenisset, docereturque paucis clam convocatis alio loco, alio tempore atque oportuerit fratrem a fratre renuntiatum, cum leges duo ex una familia vivo utroque non solum magistratus creari vetarent sed etiam in senatu esse prohiberent, Cotum imperium deponere coegit;**

a(b), *by.*

atque, *than.*

clam, *secretly.*

alius, -a, -ud, *another.*

civitas, -tatis, f., *state, nation.*

cogo, cogere, coegi, coactus, *compel, force, oblige.*

convenio, -venire, -veni, -ventus, *come together, assemble.*

Cotus, -i, m., *Cotus.*
cum, *after, when; when, while; although.*
doceo, docere, docui, doctus, *inform, point out, state.*
eo, *thither, there.*
ex, *from, out of.*
frater, -tris, m., *brother.*
in, *in.*
locus, -i, m., *place, location.*

non, *not.*
oportet, oportere, oportuit, (imper.), *it is proper.*
prohibeo, -hibere, -hibui, -hibitus, *prevent, hinder.*
-que, *and.*
sed, *but.*
solum, *only.*
tempus, -oris, n., *time.*
uterque, -traque, -trumque, *each, both.*
vivus, -a, -um, *living, alive.*

convoco, -are, -avi, -atus, *call together, summon, assemble.*
creo, -are, -avi, -atus, *choose, elect, appoint.*
depono, -ponere, -posui, -positus, *give up, resign.*
duo, -ae, -o, *two.*
etiam, *even.*
familia, -ae, f., *family.*
imperium, -i, n., *command, control.*
lex, legis, f., *law, enactment, decree.*
magistratus, -us, m., *one holding a magistracy, magistrate.*
omnis, -e, *the whole.*
pauci, -orum, m., pl., *a few men, only a few men.*
prope, *nearly, almost.*
renuntio, -are, -avi, -atus, *declare elected.*
senatus, -us, m., *council of elders, senate.*
sum, esse, fui, futurus, *be.*
unus, -a, -um, *one.*
veto, -are, -ui, -itus, *not allow, not permit.*

Cum ... convenisset ... docereturque: Temporal clause with two subjunctive verbs; the first consists of the relative adverb cum ("after, when") with the pluperfect subjunctive describing the circumstances that preceded the action of the main verb (A.G. 546); the second consists of the relative adverb cum ("when, while") with the imperfect subjunctive describing the circumstances that accompanied the action of the main verb (A.G. 546). convenisset ... doceretur: The main verbs of the subordinate clause (A.G. 278.b). doceretur: The pronoun is, with Caesar as the antecedent, is understood as the subject (A.G. 271.a). -que: The enclitic conjunction connects the two main verbs in the temporal clause (A.G. 324.a).
prope: Adverb (A.G. 320-21).
omnis civitas: Nominative subject of convenisset (A.G. 339).
eo: Adverb (A.G. 217.a and 320-21). The adverb eo normally stands outside the cum clause, as at 6.2, 7.5, 9.5, 55.4, and 61.1, but not here.
paucis ... oportuerit: Ablative absolute with a dependent clause.
paucis clam convocatis: Ablative absolute (A.G. 419-20). paucis: Plural, masculine, ablative adjective used substantively (A.G. 288). The noun principibus is understood (A.G. 288.b). clam: Adverb (A.G. 320-21). convocatis: The perfect tense of the participle represents the action as completed at the time indicated by the tense of the main verb (A.G. 489).
alio loco: Ablative of *place where* without a preposition (A.G. 429.1-2).
alio tempore: Ablative of *time when* (A.G. 423.1).
(alio) ... (alio) ... atque oportuerit: Subordinate clause; a clause dependent on a subjunctive clause (cum ... doceretur) takes the subjunctive when regarded as an integral part of that clause (attraction) (A.G. 278.b and 593). alio ... alio ... atque: The adjective alius followed by the conjunction atque forms a subordinate clause meaning "other than" (A.G. 407.d). oportuerit: The main verb of the subordinate clause (A.G. 278.b). Perfect subjunctive; the tense of the subjunctive would normally be secondary sequence after the imperfect verb doceretur (A.G. 482-4). Here, it is the primary sequence through *repraesentatio* (A.G. 585.b Note). Impersonal use of the verb, supply id as the subject (*OLD* oportet).
fratrem ... renuntiatum (esse): Accusative/infinitive construction in indirect discourse after doceretur (A.G. 577 ff.). fratrem: This is Cotus. renuntiatum (esse): Supply esse to form the perfect, passive infinitive (A.G. 184). The tense of the infinitive in indirect discourse is relative to that of the verb of saying (A.G. 584).
a fratre: Ablative of agent with the preposition a(b) after the passive infinitive renuntiatum (esse) (A.G. 405). fratre: This is Valetiacus.
cum ... vetarent ... prohiberent: Concessive clause, cum ("although") with the subjunctive forms a concessive clause (A.G. 549). "The excellence of this regulation throws light upon the political advancement of the Aedui." (Kelsey, 411) vetarent ... prohiberent: The main verbs of the subordinate clause (A.G. 278.b). Imperfect subjunctives; the tense of the subjunctives is in secondary sequence and follows the rules for the sequence of tense after doceretur (A.G. 482-85).
leges: Nominative subject of vetarent ... prohiberent (A.G. 387). "The Celtic communities were moving away from a system of hereditary 'kingships' towards an oligarchical pattern of annually elected magistrates, usually in pairs, called *vergobret*, with an advisory council of notables. The system was remarkably similar to that of Rome itself." (Sherwin-White, 41). At *BG* 1.5-6 Caesar remarks of the Vergobret that in his Diviciaco et Lisco, qui summo magistratui praeerant quem Vergobretum appellant Aedui, qui creatur annuus et vitae necisque in suos habet potestatem ... .
duo ... creari: Subject accusative with the infinitive after vetarent. The construction is equivalent to a substantive clause of purpose (A.G. 563.a). duo: Declinable cardinal number used substantively (A.G. 132-35). The noun principes is understood. The normal form of the accusative is duos, the form in -o being a remnant of the dual number (A.G. 134.b).
ex una familia: Ablative of source with the preposition ex (A.G. 403.1). una: Declinable cardinal number used as an adjective modifying familia (A.G. 132-35).
vivo utroque: Ablative absolute with an adjective (vivo) taking the place of a participle (there is no participle for "being") (A.G. 419.a-20).

non solum ... sed etiam: The correlative phrases mean "not only ... but even" (*OLD* solum2 2.b). **non**: Adverb (A.G. 217.e, 320-21, and 599.a). **solum**: Adverb (*OLD* solum2 2). **sed**: Coordinate conjunction (A.G. 324.d). **etiam**: Adverb (A.G. 320-21 and 322.a)
magistratus: Accusative direct object of the infinitive **creari** (A.G. 387 and 451.3).
in senatu: Ablative of *place where* with the preposition **in** (locative ablative) (A.G. 426.3). The prepositional phrase is in the predicate position after **esse** (A.G. 272).
(duo ex una familia) esse: Subject accusative with the infinitive after **prohiberent** (A.G. 558.b Note). Carry down **duo ex una familia** to fill in the ellipsis.
Cotum ... deponere: Subject accusative with the infinitive after **coegit**. The construction is equivalent to a substantive clause of purpose (A.G. 563.a Note). **Cotum**: See Appendix A.
imperium: Accusative direct object of the infinitive **deponere** (A.G. 387 and 451.3).
coegit: The main verb of the main clause (A.G. 278.b). The pronoun **is**, with **Caesar** as the antecedent, is understood as the subject (A.G. 271.a).

(33-3) Convictolitavem, qui per sacerdotes more civitatis intermissis magistratibus esset creatus, potestatem obtinere iussit.

civitas, -tatis, f., *state, nation.*
creo, -are, -avi, -atus, *choose, elect, appoint.*

iubeo, iubere, iussi, iussus, *order, give orders, bid, command.*
mos, moris, f., *custom, way, wont, practice.*

per, *by* (means of), *through.*
qui, quae, quod, *who, which, what.*

Convictolitavis, -is, m., *Convictolitavis.*
intermitto, -mittere, -misi, -missus, *leave off, discontinue, interrupt.*
magistratus, -us, m., *magistracy, civil office.*
obtineo, -tinere, -tinui, -tentus, *hold fast, retain, keep, hold.*
potestas, -tatis, f., *power, authority, lordship.*
sacerdos, -dotis, m., *priest.*

Convictolitavem ... obtinere: Subject accusative with the infinitive after **iussit**. The construction is equivalent to a substantive clause of purpose (A.G. 563.a). **Convictolitavem**: See Appendix A.
qui ... esset creatus: Relative clause; the relative clause takes the subjunctive as a subordinate clause depending on an infinitive (**obtinere**) which is equivalent to a subjunctive clause and regarded as an integral part of that clause (attraction) (A.G. 593). **qui**: Singular, masculine, nominative relative pronoun used substantively (A.G. 305). The antecedent is **Convictolitavem** (A.G. 307). Nominative subject (A.G. 339). **esset creatus**: The main verb of the subordinate clause (A.G. 278.b). Pluperfect subjunctive; the tense of the subjunctive is in secondary sequence and follows the rules for the sequence of tense after **iussit** (A.G. 482-83).
per sacerdotes: Prepositional phrase, the personal agent, when considered as instrument or means, is often expressed by **per** with the accusative meaning "by" (means of) (A.G. 405.b). **sacerdotes**: "The Druids had great influence. Above the individual, above the state, as endowed with authority from the unseen world they awed into submission the fierce spirit of a people that acknowledged no other control. They alone had knowledge; from generation to generation they handed down by word of mouth a body of doctrines about the universe and life. Believing in the transmigration of souls, they exhorted men not to fear death, since immortality must follow. To the Druids was intrusted the administration of justice. Whoso obeyed not their decrees was ever after treated as an outcast. Once a year Druids from all parts of Gaul met in the land of the Carnutes, and settled difficulties between states as well as individuals. In Caesar's time the great stronghold of Druidism, however, was not Gaul but Britain." (Kelsey, 41-42) For a description of the Druid class see *BG* 6.13-14, 16-18, and 21.
more: Ablative of specification (A.G. 418).
civitatis: Possessive genitive with **more** (A.G. 343).
intermissis magistratibus: Ablative absolute (A.G. 419-20). **intermissis**: The perfect tense of the participle represents the action as completed at the time indicated by the tense of the main verb (A.G. 489). "'in case of vacancies in the magistracy'; properly the interval between the going out of one magistrate and the inauguration of his successor. As a rule, the retiring Vergobret appointed his successor; since Valetiacus had unlawfully chosen his brother to the office, the Druids, by virtue of the right they had to fill the magistracy in case of vacancy, proceeded to nominate and install Convictolitavis, treating the appointment of Cotus as null and void. Possibly Caesar has not told the whole truth in regard to the matter. It seems probable that the division of parties among the Aedui was on question of loyalty to himself; at any rate, a number of the Aedui soon joined the rebellion against him." (Kelsey, 411)
potestatem: Accusative direct object of the infinitive **obtinere** (A.G. 387 and 451.3).
iussit: The main verb of the main clause (A.G. 278.b). The pronoun **is**, with **Caesar** as the antecedent, is understood as the subject (A.G. 271.a). Convictolitavis will not prove to be the pro-Roman puppet ruler which no doubt Caesar was hoping he would be. He will be one of the main leaders of the Aedui in the eventual rebellion against Rome.

PART 3: THE SIEGE OF GERGOVIA; THE ROMANS ARE REPULSED WITH SIGNIFICANT LOSSES (7.34-52)

3.A CHAPTERS 34-36: CAESAR DIVIDES HIS ARMY WITH LABIENUS; HE SENDS LABIENUS NORTH WHILE HE CROSSES THE ALLIER RIVER AND BEGINS THE SIEGE OF GERGOVIA
(34.1-2) Hoc decreto interposito, cohortatus Aeduos ut controversiarum ac dissensionis obliviscerentur atque omnibus omissis his rebus huic bello servirent, eaque quae meruissent praemia ab se devicta Gallia exspectarent, equitatumque omnem et peditum milia X sibi celeriter mitterent quae in praesidiis rei frumentariae causa disponeret, exer(2)citum in duas partis divisit:

ab, *from.*

ac, *and.*

Aedui, -orum, m., pl., *the Aedui.*
bellum, -i, n., *war, warfare.*

celeriter, *quickly, speedily, at once, immediately.*
controversia, -ae, f., *dispute, debate, controversy, quarrel.*
devinco, -vincere, -vici, -victus, *conquer completely, subdue, overcome.*

dissensio, -onis, f., *difference of opinion, disagreement.*
duo, -ae, -o, *two.*
et, *and.*
exspecto, -are, -avi, -atus, *expect.*

Gallia, -ae, f., *Gaul.*
in, *into; in.*

is, ea, id, *he, she, it; that, this.*
milia, -um, n., pl., *thousand, thousands.*
obliviscor, -livisci, -litus, *forget.*
omnis, -e, *all.*
pedites, -um, m., pl., *infantry.*
praesidium, -i, n., *garrison, fortress.*
qui, quae, quod, *who, which, what.*

servio, -ire, -ivi, -itus, *devote one's self to.*
ut, *so that.*

atque, *and.*
causa, -ae, f., abl. with the gen., *for the sake of, on account of.*
cohortor, -ari, -atus, *encourage, urge, exhort, address.*
decretum, -i, n., *decree, decision.*
dispono, -ponere, -posui, -positus, *set in various places, station, post.*
divido, -videre, -visi, -visus, *separate, divide.*
equitatus, -us, m., *cavalry.*
exercitus, -us, m., *army.*
frumentarius, -a, -um, *having to do with grain or supplies.*
hic, haec, hoc, *this; he, she, it.*
interpono, -ponere, -posui, -positus, *interpose, put forward, present.*
mereo, -ere, -ui, -itus, *deserve, be entitled to, merit.*
mitto, mittere, misi, missus, *send.*
omitto, -mittere, -misi, -missus, *lay aside.*
pars, partis, f., *part.*
praemium, -i, n., *reward, recompense.*
-que, *and.*
res, rei, f., *matter, affair;* (with **frumentaria**) *supply of grain, supplies.*
sui, sibi, se, or **sese**, nom. wanting, *himself.*
X, in expression of number, = *10.*

Hoc decreto interposito: Ablative absolute (A.G. 419-20). **Hoc**: Singular, neuter, ablative demonstrative pronoun used as an adjective modifying **decreto** (A.G. 296.1 and a). **interposito**: The perfect tense of the participle represents the action as completed at the time indicated by the tense of the main verb (A.G. 489).
cohortatus: Nominative perfect, deponent, participle used as a predicate, where in English a phrase or a subordinate clause would be more normal (A.G. 496). The pronoun **is**, with **Caesar** from 33.1 as the antecedent, is understood. Nominative subject of **divisit** (A.G. 339).
Aeduos: Accusative direct object of the participle **cohortatus** (A.G. 387 and 488). See Appendix A.
ut ... obliviscerentur ... servirent ... exspectarent ... mitterent: The conjunction **ut** ("so that") with the subjunctive forms a substantive clause of purpose which is used as the object of the participle **cohortatus** denoting an action directed toward the future (A.G. 563). **obliviscerentur ... servirent ... exspectarent ... mitterent**: The main verbs of the subordinate clause (A.G. 278.b). Imperfect subjunctives; the tense of the subjunctives is in secondary sequence and follows the rules for the sequence of tense after **divisit** (A.G. 482-85). The pronoun **ei**, with **Aeduos** as the antecedent, is understood as the subject of the four verbs.
controversiarum ac dissensionis: Two genitive objects of **obliviscerentur**, a verb of forgetting (A.G. 350.a). **ac**: The conjunction connects the two genitive nouns and means "and" (*OLD* **atque** 12).
atque: The conjunction connects the two verbs in the purpose clause **obliviscerentur ... servirent** and means "and" (*OLD* **atque** 12).
omnibus omissis his rebus: Ablative absolute (A.G. 419-20). **his**: Plural, feminine, ablative demonstrative pronoun used as an adjective modifying **rebus** (A.G. 296.1 and a). **omissis**: The perfect tense of the participle represents the action as completed at the time indicated by the tense of the main verb (A.G. 489).
huic bello: Dative indirect object of the intransitive verb **servirent** (A.G. 366). **huic**: Singular, neuter, dative demonstrative pronoun used as an adjective modifying **bello** (A.G. 296.1 and a).
eaque ... praemia: Accusative direct object of **exspectarent** (A.G. 387). **ea**: Plural, neuter, accusative demonstrative pronoun used as an adjective modifying **praemia** (A.G. 296.1 and a). The pronoun functions as a correlative to the relative clause **quae meruissent** (A.G. 297.d). **-que**: The enclitic conjunction connects the two verbs in the purpose clause **servirent ... expectarent** (A.G. 324.a).
quae meruissent: Relative clause; a clause dependent on a subjunctive clause (**ut ... exspectarent**) takes the subjunctive when regarded as an integral part of that clause (attraction) (A.G. 303 and 593). **quae**: Plural, neuter, accusative relative pronoun used substantively (A.G. 305). The antecedent is **ea** (A.G. 307). Accusative direct object of **meruissent** (A.G. 387). **meruissent**: The main verb of the subordinate clause (A.G. 278.b). Pluperfect subjunctive; the tense of the subjunctive is in secondary sequence and follows the rules for the sequence of tense after **divisit** (A.G. 482-85). The pronoun **ei**, with **Aeduos** as the antecedent, is understood as the subject (A.G. 271.a).
ab se: Ablative of source with the preposition **ab** (A.G. 403.1). **se**: Singular, masculine, accusative indirect reflexive pronoun (A.G. 300.2). The antecedent is **cohortatus** (**Caesar**), the subject of **divisit** (A.G. 299).
devicta Gallia: Ablative absolute (A.G. 419-20). **devicta**: The perfect tense of the participle represents the action as completed at the time indicated by the tense of the main verb (A.G. 489). **Gallia**: See Appendix A.
equitatumque omnem et peditum milia X: Two accusative direct objects of the transitive verb **mitterent** (A.G. 387). **-que**: The enclitic conjunction connects the two verbs in the purpose clause **exspectarent ... mitterent** (A.G. 324.a). **et**: The conjunction connects the two accusative nouns **equitatum ... milia** (A.G. 324.a). **peditum**: Partitive genitive with **milia** (A.G. 346.a.2). **milia**: Accusative plural; in the plural **mille** declines as a neuter noun (A.G. 134.d). **X**: Roman numeral used as an adjective modifying **milia** (A.G. 133).

sibi: Singular, masculine, dative indirect reflexive pronoun (A.G. 300.2). The antecedent is **cohortatus (Caesar)**, the subject of **divisit** (A.G. 299). Dative indirect object of the transitive verb **mitterent** (A.G. 362).

celeriter: Adverb (A.G. 214.b and 320-21).

quae ... disponeret: A relative clause of purpose is introduced by a relative pronoun and takes the subjunctive (A.G. 531.2). **quae**: Plural, neuter, accusative relative pronoun used substantively (A.G. 305). The antecedent is **equitatumque omnem et peditum milia X**, agreeing with the nearest neuter plural noun (A.G. 305.a). Accusative direct object of **disponeret** (A.G. 387). The relative is here equivalent to **ut ea** (A.G. 531.2 Note). **disponeret**: The main verb of the subordinate clause (A.G. 278.b). Imperfect subjunctive; The tense of the subjunctive is in secondary sequence and follows the rules for the sequence of tense after **divisit** (A.G. 482-85). The pronoun **is**, with **cohortatus (Caesar)** as the antecedent, is understood as the subject (A.G. 271.a).

in praesidiis: Ablative of *place where* with the preposition **in** (locative ablative) (A.G. 426.3).

rei frumentariae causa: A preceding genitive with the ablative of **causa** means "for the sake of" (A.G. 359.b and 404.c). Although Caesar here claims that these troops will see limited duty, they will be used in the assualt on the camps at Gergovia.

exercitum: Accusative direct object of **divisit** (A.G. 387).

in duas partis: Prepositional phrase, **in** with the accusative here means "into" (*OLD* **in** 2). **duas**: Declinable cardinal number used as an adjective modifying **partis** (A.G. 132-35). **partis**: Accusative plural noun, **-is** for **-es** is the regular form in mixed i-stem nouns (A.G. 71-2).

divisit: The main verb of the main clause (A.G. 278.b). The pronoun **is**, with **cohortatus (Caesar)** as the antecedent, is understood as the subject (A.G. 271.a). Fuller remarks of this decision that "Caesar opened his Gergovia campaign by dividing his army. His penalty was his repulse." (Fuller, 145) It does seem to be a very ill-conceived strategy at this stage in the war. Gergovia was a strong base of power for Vercingetorix as his family had resided there at the beginning of the rebellion (see Chapter 4) and the Aedui were at best volatile allies. However, Caesar had divided his army before and often relied on a small force, for example, in BG 3 he divided his army into four parts while deep in the territory of the Belgae and again divided his army in Book 4, taking only two legions with him on his first expedition to Britain.

(34.2-3) quattuor legiones in Senones Parisiosque Labieno ducendas dedit, sex ipse in Arvernos ad oppidum Gergoviam secundum flumen Elaver duxit; (3) equitatus partem illi attribuit, partem sibi reliquit.

ad, *to, towards.*	**Arverni, -orum**, m., pl., *the Arverni.*
attribuo, -uere, -ui, -utus, *assign, allot, turn over to.*	**do, dare, dedi, datus,** *give, give over.*
duco, ducere, duxi, ductus, *lead.*	**Elaver, Elaveris,** n., *the Elaver river.*
equitatus, -us, m., *cavalry.*	**flumen, -inis,** n., *stream, river.*
Gergovia, -ae, f., *Gergovia.*	**ille, illae, illud,** *that; he, she, it.*
in, *into the country of, against.*	**ipse, -a, -um,** *he, they,* with or without *himself, themselves.*
Labienus, -i, m., *Labienus.*	**legio, -onis,** f., *legion.*
oppidum, -i, n., *fortified town, city.*	**Parisii, -orum,** m., pl., *the Parisii.*
pars, partis, f., *part, portion.*	**quattuor,** *four.*
-que, *and.*	**relinquo, -linquere, -liqui, -lictus,** *leave, leave remaining.*
secundum, *along, next to, by the side of.*	**Senones, -um,** m., pl., *the Senones.*
sex, *six.*	**sui, sibi, se,** or **sese,** nom. wanting, *himself.*

quattuor legiones ... ducendas: Accusative direct object of the transitive verb **dedit** (A.G. 387). The 7th, 8th, 12th, and one unnamed legion. **quattuor**: Indeclinable cardinal number used as an adjective modifying **legiones** (A.G. 132-35). **ducendas**: Plural, feminine, accusative gerundive used as an adjective modifying **legiones** and implying necessity (A.G. 500.1).

in Senones Parisiosque: Accusative of *place to which* with the preposition **in** ("into the country of") (A.G. 426.2). **Senones**: See Appendix A. **Parisios**: See Appendix A. **-que**: The enclitic conjunction connects the two accusative nouns in the prepositional phrase (A.G. 324.a).

Labieno: Dative indirect object of the transitive verb **dedit** (A.G. 362). See Chapters 57-62 for Labienus' campaign. See Appendix A.

dedit: The main verb of the coordinate clause **quattuor ... dedit** (A.G. 278.a). The pronoun **is**, with **cohortatus (Caesar)** as the antecedent, is understood as the subject (A.G. 271.a).

sex: Accusative direct object of **duxit** (A.G. 387). The 8th, 10th, 13th, and three unnamed legions. **sex**: Indeclinable cardinal number used substantively (A.G. 132-35). The noun **legiones** is understood.

ipse: Singular, masculine, nominative demonstrative pronoun used substantively (A.G. 296.2 and 298.d). The antecedent is **cohortatus (Caesar)** (A.G. 298). Nominative subject of **duxit** (A.G. 339). The pronoun **ipse** distinguishes the principle person **(Caesar)** from a subordinate person **(Labieno)** (A.G. 298.3).

in ... ad ... secundum: Three consecutive prepositional phrases.

in Arvernos: Accusative of *place to which* with the preposition **in** ("into the country of") (A.G. 426.2). **Arvernos**: See Appendix A.

ad oppidum Gergoviam: Accusative of *place to which* with the preposition **ad** (A.G. 426.2). **Gergoviam**: A proper noun in apposition to **oppidum** (A.G. 282). See Appendix A.

secundum flumen Elaver: Prepositional phrase, **secundum** with the accusative means "along" (*OLD* **secundum2** 2). **Elaver**: An accusative proper noun in apposition to **flumen** (A.G. 282). See Appendix A.

duxit: The main verb of the coordinate clause **sex ... duxit** (A.G. 278.a).

equitatus: Partitive genitive with **partem** (A.G. 346.a.1).

partem: Accusative direct object of the transitive verb **attribuit** (A.G. 387).

illi: Singular, masculine, dative demonstrative pronoun used substantively (A.G. 296.2). The antecedent is **Labieno** (A.G. 297.e). Dative indirect object of the transitive verb **attribuit** (A.G. 362).

attribuit: The main verb of the coordinate clause **equitatus ... attribuit** (A.G. 278.a). The pronoun **is**, with **ipse (Caesar)** as the antecedent, is understood as the subject (A.G. 271.a).

(equitatus) partem: Accusative direct object of the transitive verb **reliquit** (A.G. 387). Carry down **equitatus** as the partitive genitive.

sibi: Singular, masculine, dative direct reflexive pronoun (A.G. 300.1). The antecedent is **ipse (Caesar)**, the subject of **reliquit** (A.G. 299). Dative indirect object of the transitive verb **reliquit** (A.G. 362).

reliquit: The main verb of the coordinate clause **partem ... reliquit** (A.G. 278.a). The pronoun **is**, with **ipse (Caesar)** as the antecedent, is understood as the subject (A.G. 271.a).

(34.3) **Qua re cognita Vercingetorix omnibus interruptis eius fluminis pontibus ab altera fluminis parte iter facere coepit.**

ab, *on.*
coepi, -isse, coeptus, *begin, start, commence.*

facio, facere, feci, factus, *make.*
interrupo, -rumpere, -rupi, -ruptus, *break down, destroy.*
iter, itineris, n., *march, journey.*
pars, partis, f., *side.*
qui, quae, quod, *who, which, what.*
Vercingetorix, -igis, m., *Vercingetorix.*

alter, -era, -erum, *the other.*
cognosco, -gnoscere, -gnovi, cognitus, *learn, ascertain, recognize.*
flumen, -inis, n., *stream, river.*
is, ea, id, *he, she, it; that, this.*
omnis, -e, *all.*
pons, pontis, m., *bridge.*
res, rei, f., *matter, affair, event.*

Qua re cognita: Ablative absolute (A.G. 419-20). **Qua**: Singular, feminine, ablative relative pronoun (A.G. 305). The antecedent is **re** in its own clause (adjectival use) (A.G. 307.b). The relative does not introduce a relative clause but is a connecting relative; at the beginning of a clause the pronoun is often best rendered by a personal or demonstrative pronoun, with or without *and* (A.G. 308.f).

cognita: The perfect tense of the participle represents the action as completed at the time indicated by the tense of the main verb (A.G. 489).

Vercingetorix: Nominative subject (A.G. 339). See Appendix A.

omnibus interruptis eius fluminis pontibus: Ablative absolute (A.G. 419-20). **interruptis**: The perfect tense of the participle represents the action as completed at the time indicated by the tense of the main verb (A.G. 489). **eius fluminis**: Possessive genitive with **pontibus** (A.G. 343). **eius**: Singular, neuter, genitive demonstrative pronoun used as an adjective modifying **fluminis** (A.G. 296.1 and a). This is the river **Elaver** mentioned at 34.2 above.

ab altera fluminis parte: Ablative of *position* with the preposition **ab** (A.G. 429.b). **fluminis**: Partitive genitive with **parte** (A.G. 346.a). "Vercingetorix was on the west side of the Allier (Elaver). Caesar, leaving Decize (Decetia) marched along the east bank in the direction of Gergovia, which he could not reach without crossing the stream." (Kelsey, 411)

iter: Accusative direct object of the infinitive **facere** (A.G. 387 and 451.3). The phrase **iter facere** is an idiom that means "to march or travel" (*OLD* **iter** 1.b).

facere: Complementary infinitive after **coepit** (A.G. 456).

coepit: The main verb of the main clause (A.G. 278.b).

(35.1-2) **Cum uterque utrimque exisset exercitus, in conspectu fereque e regione castris castra ponebant, dispositis exploratoribus (2) necubi effecto ponte Romani copias traducerent.**

castra, -orum, n., pl., *camp, encampment.*
copiae, -arum, f., pl., *forces, troops*
dispono, -ponere, -posui, -positus, *set in various places, station, post.*
e(x), *direct opposite.*

exercitus, -us, m., *army.*
fere, *almost, nearly, for the most part.*
necubi, *that nowhere, lest anywhere.*
pons, pontis, m., *bridge.*
regio, -onis, f., *region, territory.*
traduco, -ducere, -duxi, -ductus, *lead across, bring over, bring across.*
utrimque, *on both sides.*

conspectus, -us, m., *sight, view, presence.*
cum, *after, when.*
efficio, -ficere, -feci, -fectus, *produce, make, construct.*
exeo, -ire, -ivi, or -ii, -itus, *go forth, go out, withdraw, leave.*
explorator, -oris, m., *spy, scout.*
in, *in.*
pono, ponere, posui, positus, *place, put.*
-que, *and.*
Romani, -orum, m., pl., *the Romans.*
uterque, -traque, -trumque, *each, both.*

Cum ... exisset: Temporal clause; the relative adverb **cum** ("after, when") with the pluperfect subjunctive describes the circumstances that preceded the action of the main verb (A.G. 546). **exisset**: The main verb of the subordinate clause (A.G. 278.b). Contracted form of **exivisset** (A.G. 181.b).

uterque ... exercitus: Nominative subject (A.G. 339).

utrimque: Adverb (A.G. 320-21).

in conspectu: Prepositional phrase, **in** with the ablative here means "in" (an area defined by the range of the senses) (*OLD* **in** 24.b).

fereque: Adverb (A.G. 320-21). **-que**: The enclitic conjunction connects the two prepositional phrases (A.G. 324.a).

e regione castris: Prepositional phrase, **e(x)** with the ablative of **regio** and the dative means "directly opposite the camp" (*OLD* **regio** 2.b). This is the only use in Book 7 of this phrase with the dative. Compare the same expression with the genitive at 25.2, 35.3, 36.5, 58.6, 61.5. **castris**: Dative of reference (A.G. 377).

castra: Accusative direct object of **ponebant** (A.G. 387).

ponebant: The main verb of the main clause (A.G. 278.b). The nouns **Romani et Galli** are understood as the subject (A.G. 271.a).

dispositis ... traducerent: Ablative absolute with a dependent clause.

dispositis exploratoribus: Ablative absolute (A.G. 419-20). **dispositis**: The perfect tense of the participle represents the action as completed at the time indicated by the tense of the main verb (A.G. 489).

necubi ... traducerent: The adverb **necubi** with the subjunctive forms a negative purpose clause (A.G. 531.1). **necubi**: Adverb meaning "lest at any place, that nowhere" (*OLD* **necubi**). **traducerent**: The main verb of the subordinate clause (A.G. 278.b). Imperfect subjunctive; the tense of the subjunctive is in secondary sequence and follows the rules for the sequence of tense **ponebant** (A.G. 482-85).

effecto ponte: Ablative absolute (A.G. 419-20). **effecto**: The perfect tense of the participle represents the action as completed at the time indicated by the tense of the main verb (A.G. 489).

Romani: Nominative subject (A.G. 339).

copias: Accusative direct object of **traducerent** (A.G. 387).

(35.2-3) Erat in magnis Caesari difficultatibus res, ne maiorem aestatis partem flumine impediretur, quod non fere ante autumnum (3) Elaver vado transiri solet.

aestas, -tatis, f., *summer*.	**ante**, *before*.
autumnus, -i, m., *autumn*.	**Caesar, -aris**, m., *Caesar*.
difficultas, -tatis, f., *difficulty, trouble*.	**Elaver, Elaveris**, n., *the Elaver river*.
fere, *for the most part, as a rule, usually, generally*.	**flumen, -inis**, n., *stream, river*.
impedio, -pedire, -pedivi, -peditus, *hinder, obstruct*.	**in**, *in*.
magnus, -a, -um, *great, considerable*.	**maior, -or, -us**, *greater, larger*.
ne, *lest, that*.	**non**, *not*.
pars, partis, f., *part, portion*.	**quod**, *because, since, for, as*.
res, rei, f., *matter, affair, business, affair*.	**soleo, -ere, -itus sum**, *be accustomed*.
sum, esse, fui, futurus, *be*.	**transeo, -ire, -ivi, or -ii, -itus**, *go over, go across, pass over, cross over*.

vadum, -i, n., *ford*.

Erat: The main verb of the main clause (A.G. 278.b). Verb first in the emphatic position (A.G. 598.d).

in magnis ... difficultatibus: Prepositional phrase, **in** with the ablative here means "in" (given circumstances) (*OLD* **in** 40). The prepositional phrase is in the predicate position after **Erat** (A.G. 272). **difficultatibus**: The plural noun implies numerous difficulties.

Caesari: Dative of reference; the dative in this construction is often called the dative of disadvantage as denoting the person to whose prejudice the action is performed (A.G. 376). See Appendix A.

res: Nominative subject (A.G. 339).

(verito) ne ... impediretur: The conjunction **ne** ("lest") with the subjunctive forms a substantive clause of fearing. Here the verb of fearing, **verito** (**vereor, vereri, veritus sum**, *fear, dread, be afraid of*), must be supplied in the form of a participle modifying **Caesari** (A.G. 564). **impediretur**: The main verb of the subordinate clause (A.G. 278.b). Imperfect subjunctive; the tense of the subjunctive is in secondary sequence and follows the rules for the sequence of tense after **Erat** (A.G. 482-85). The pronoun **is**, with **Caesari** as the antecedent, is understood as the subject (A.G. 271.a).

maiorem ... partem: Accusative of *extent of time* (A.G. 423.2). **maiorem**: Irregular comparative adjective (A.G. 129).

aestatis: Partitive genitive with **partem** (A.G. 346.a.1).

flumine: Ablative of cause without a preposition (A.G. 404). "Swollen by the melting of the snow upon the mountains." (Kelsey, 411-12)

quod ... solet: Causal clause; the conjunction **quod** ("because") normally takes the subjunctive when it is dependent on a subjunctive clause (**ne ... impediretur**) (attraction) (A.G. 593). However, when a dependent clause is not regarded as a necessary logical part of the clause, the indicative is used. The indicative serves to emphasize the fact, as true independently of the statement contained in the subjunctive clause (A.G. 593.a Note 1). **solet**: The main verb of the subordinate clause (A.G. 278.b). The present tense is not the historical present but denotes a state as now existing in present time (A.G. 465.1).

non: Adverb modifying **fere**, the negative precedes the word it especially effects (A.G. 217.e, 320-21, and 599.a). **fere**: Adverb (A.G. 320-21).

ante autumnum: Prepositional phrase, **ante** with the accusative here means "before" (*OLD* **ante2** 5).

Elaver: Nominative subject (A.G. 339). See Appendix A.

vado: Ablative of means (A.G. 409). "The Allier is now almost everywhere fordable in summer, apparently on account of the filling up of the river-bed." (Kelsey, 412)

transiri: Complementary infinitive after **solet** (A.G. 456).

(35.3-4) Itaque, ne id accideret, silvestri loco castris positis e regione unius eorum pontium quos Vercingetorix rescindendos curaverat, postero die cum (4) duabus legionibus in occulto restitit;

accido, -cidere, -cidi, -----, *happen, occur, turn out.*
cum, *with.*

dies, -ei, m. and f., *day.*
e(x), *directly opposite.*
is, ea, id, *he, she, it; that, this.*
legio, -onis, f., *legion.*
ne, *so that ... not.*
pono, ponere, posui, positus, *place, put.*
posterus, -a, -um, *following, the next.*
regio, -onis, f., *region, territory.*

resisto, -sistere, -stiti, -----, *remain, stay.*
unus, -a, -um, *one.*

castra, -orum, n., pl., *camp, encampment.*
curo, -are, -avi, -atus, *take care, provide for, superintend, arrange.*
duo, -ae, -o, *two.*
in, *in.*
itaque, *and so, in consequence, accordingly, therefore.*
locus, -i, m., *place, location, position.*
occultum, -i, n., *hiding, concealment.*
pons, pontis, m., *bridge.*
qui, quae, quod, *who, which, what.*
rescindo, -scindere, -scidi, -scissus, *cut down, break up, destroy.*
silvestris, -e, *covered with woods, wooded, woody.*
Vercingetorix, -igis, m., *Vercingetorix.*

Itaque: An adverb expressing the result of the previous ideas meaning "and so, in consequence" (*OLD* **itaque** 1). The adverb stands in the first position (A.G. 599.b).

ne ... accideret: The conjunction **ne** ("so that ... not") with the subjunctive forms a negative purpose clause (A.G. 531.1). **accideret**: The main verb of the subordinate clause (A.G. 278.b). Imperfect subjunctive; the tense of the subjunctive is in secondary sequence and follows the rules for the sequence of tense after **restitit** (A.G. 482-85).

id: Singular, neuter, nominative demonstrative pronoun used substantively (A.G. 296.2). The antecedent is the idea of being blocked by the river (A.G. 297.e). Nominative subject (A.G. 339).

silvestri ... curaverat: Ablative absolute with a dependent clause.

silvestri loco castris positis e regione unius eorum pontium: Ablative absolute (A.G. 419-20).

silvestri loco: Ablative of *place where* without a preposition (A.G. 429.1-2).

castris positis: The noun, participle element of the ablative absolute (A.G. 419-20). **positis**: The perfect tense of the participle represents the action as completed at the time indicated by the tense of the main verb (A.G. 489).

e regione unius eorum pontium: Prepositional phrase, **e(x)** with the ablative or **regio** and the genitive means "directly opposite one of those bridges" (*OLD* **regio** 2.a). **unius**: Singular, masculine, genitive cardinal number used substantively (A.G. 132-35). The noun **pontis** is understood. Possessive genitive with **regione** (A.G. 343). **-ius** is the regular genitive singular ending for the adjective **unus** (A.G. 113). **eorum pontium**: Partitive genitive with **unius** (A.G. 346.a.2). **eorum**: Plural, masculine, genitive demonstrative pronoun used as an adjective modifying **pontium** (A.G. 296.1 and a). The pronoun functions as a correlative to the relative clause **quos ... curaverat** (A.G. 297.d).

quos ... curaverat: Relative clause (A.G. 303). For the reference see 34.3. **quos**: See below. **curaverat**: The main verb of the subordinate clause (A.G. 278.b). The pluperfect tense of the verb denotes an action completed in past time (A.G. 477).

quos ... rescindendos: Accusative direct object of **curaverat** (A.G. 387). **quos**: Plural, masculine, accusative relative pronoun used substantively (A.G. 305). The antecedent is **eorum pontium** (A.G. 307). **rescindendos**: Plural, masculine, accusative gerundive used as an adjective modifying **quos**, the direct object of **curaverat** (A.G. 500.1). A gerundive in agreement with the object of **curaverat** expresses purpose (A.G. 500.4).

Vercingetorix: Nominative subject (A.G. 339). See Appendix A.

postero die: Ablative of *time when* (A.G. 423.1). **die**: The noun **dies** is normally masculine gender (A.G. 97.a).

cum duabus legionibus: Ablative of accompaniment with the preposition **cum** (A.G. 413). **duabus**: Declinable cardinal number used as an adjective modifying **legionibus** (A.G. 132-35).

in occulto: Prepositional phrase, **in** with the neuter, singular, ablative of the adjective **occultus** means "in hiding or concealment" (*OLD* **occultus** 5).

restitit: The main verb of the main clause (A.G. 278.b). The pronoun **is**, with **Caesari** at 35.2 as the antecedent, is understood as the subject (A.G. 271.a).

(35.4) **reliquas copias cum omnibus impedimentis, ut consueverat, misit, apertis quibusdam cohortibus, uti numerus legionum constare videretur.**

aperio, -perire, -perui, -pertus, *open.*

consto, -stare, -stiti, -staturus, *be full, remain the same.*
copiae, -arum, f., pl., *forces, troops.*
impedimenta, -orum, n., pl., *heavy baggage, baggage.*
mitto, mittere, misi, missus, *send.*
omnis, -e, *all.*
reliquus, -a, -um, *remaining, the rest.*
uti, *so that.*

cohors, -hortis, f., *cohort, company,* (the tenth part of a legion).
consuesco, -suescere, -suevi, -suetus, *be accustomed.*
cum, *with.*
legio, -onis, f., *legion.*
numerus, -i, m., *number.*
quidam, quaedam, quiddam, *a certain, certain, some.*
ut, *as.*
videor, videri, visus sum, *be seen, seem, appear.*

reliquas copias: Accusative direct object of **misit** (A.G. 387).

cum omnibus impedimentis: Ablative of accompaniment with the preposition **cum** (A.G. 413).

ut consueverat: The relative adverb **ut** ("as") with the indicative introduces a parenthetical remark (*OLD* **ut** 12). **consueverat**: The main verb of the subordinate clause (A.G. 278.b). The pronoun **is**, with **Caesari** at 35.2 as the antecedent, is understood as the subject (A.G. 271.a). The pluperfect tense of the verb denotes an action completed in past time (A.G. 477).

misit: The main verb of the main clause (A.G. 278.b). The pronoun **is**, with **Caesari** at 35.2 as the antecedent, is understood as the subject (A.G. 271.a).

apertis ... videretur: Ablative absolute with a dependent clause.

apertis quibusdam cohortibus: Ablative absolute (A.G. 419-20). **apertis**: The perfect tense of the participle represents the action as completed at the time indicated by the tense of the main verb (A.G. 489). **quibusdam**: Plural, feminine, ablative indefinite pronoun used as an adjective modifying **cohortibus** (A.G. 151.c).

uti ... videretur: The conjunction **uti** ("so that") with the subjunctive forms a final (purpose) clause (A.G. 531.1). **videretur**: The main verb of the subordinate clause (A.G. 278.b). Imperfect subjunctive; the tense of the subjunctive is in secondary sequence and follows the rules for the sequence of tense after **misit** (A.G. 482-85).

numerus: Nominative subject (A.G. 339).

legionum: Partitive genitive with **numerus** (A.G. 346.a.1).

constare: Complementary infinitive after **videretur** (A.G. 456). "'to be full.' From the six legions with him Caesar seems to have chosen out 20 cohorts (= 2 legions); he then arranged the remaining 40 cohorts so that on the march they presented the appearance of 6 full legions, and sent them on in the direction that he had been following." (Kelsey, 412)

(35.5-6) **(5) His quam longissime possent progredi iussis, cum iam ex diei tempore coniecturam ceperat in castra perventum, isdem sublicis, quarum pars inferior integra remanebat, (6) pontem reficere coepit.**

capio, capere, cepi, captus, *form, adopt, take.*	**castra, -orum**, n., pl., *camp, encampment.*
coepi, -isse, coeptus, *begin, start, commence.*	**coniectura, -ae**, f., *conjecture, guess.*
cum, *when.*	**dies, -ei**, m. and f., *day.*
ex, *from.*	**hic, haec, hoc**, *this; he, she, it.*
iam, *now, already, at this time, at present.*	**idem, eadem, idem**, *the same.*
in, *into.*	**inferus, -a, -um**, comp. -ior, *low.*
integer, -ra, -rum, *untouched, whole, undamaged.*	**iubeo, iubere, iussi, iussus**, *order, give orders, bid, command.*
longe, sup. -issime, (with **quam**), *far.*	**pars, partis**, f., *part, portion.*
pervenio, -venire, -veni, -ventus, *come to, arrive at, reach.*	**pons, pontis**, m., *bridge.*
possum, posse, potui, -----, *be able.*	**progredior, -gredi, -gressus**, *advance, go forward, proceed.*
quam, as ---- *as possible.*	**qui, quae, quod**, *who, which, what.*
reficio, -ficere, -feci, -fectus, *repair, refit.*	**remaneo, -manere, -mansi, -----**, *remain, continue to be.*
sublica, -ae, f., *pile.*	**tempus, -oris**, n., *time.*

His quam longissime possent progredi iussis: Ablative absolute (A.G. 419-20). **His ... iussis**: The noun, participle element of the ablative absolute (A.G. 419-20). **His**: Plural, feminine, ablative demonstrative pronoun used substantively (A.G. 296.2). The antecedent is **copias** (A.G. 297.e). **iussis**: The perfect tense of the participle represents the action as completed at the time indicated by the tense of the main verb (A.G. 489). **progredi**: Complementary infinitive after the passive participle **iussis**. The construction is equivalent to a substantive clause of purpose (A.G. 563.a). **quam longissime possent**: Relative clause; a clause dependent on an infinitive equivalent to a subjunctive clause (**progredi**) will itself take the subjunctive if regarded as an integral part of that clause (attraction) (A.G. 279.a and 593). **quam**: The relative adverb with the superlative denotes the highest possible degree "as far as possible" (A.G. 291.c) (*OLD* **quam** 7). **longissime**: Superlative adverb (A.G. 218 and 320-21). **possent**: The main verb of the subordinate clause (A.G. 278.b). Imperfect subjunctive; the tense of the subjunctive is in secondary sequence and follows the rules for the sequence of tense after **coepit** (A.G. 482-85). The pronoun **eae**, with **his** (**copiae**) as the antecedent, is understood as the subject (A.G. 271.a).

cum ... ceperat: Temporal clause; the relative adverb **cum** ("when") with the pluperfect indicative defines the time at which the action of the main verb occurred (A.G. 545). **ceperat**: The main verb of the subordinate clause (A.G. 278.b). The pronoun **is**, with **Caesari** at 35.2 as the antecedent, is understood as the subject (A.G. 271.a).

iam: Adverb (A.G. 215.6, 217.b and 320-21).

ex diei tempore: Prepositional phrase, **ex** with the ablative here means "from" (*OLD* **ex** 14.c). **diei**: Partitive genitive with **tempore** (A.G. 346.a.1).

coniecturam: Accusative direct object of **ceperat** (A.G. 387).

in castra: Accusative of *place to which* with the preposition **in** (A.G. 426.2).

(id) perventum (esse): Impersonal infinitive construction in indirect discourse after **coniecturam ceperat** (A.G. 577 ff.). **perventum (esse)**: Supply **esse** to form the perfect, passive infinitive (A.G. 187). The tense of the infinitive in indirect discourse is relative to that of the verb of saying (A.G. 584). Impersonal use of the intransitive passive verb (A.G. 208.d). Supply the pronoun **id** as the accusative subject (A.G. 318.c). "I.e., that the legions had gone about the usual distance of a day's march, and had halted to encamp. Vercingetorix, following along on the other side of the river, would naturally encamp too, leaving the coast clear for Caesar and the two legions that had stayed back to build the bridge. Thus Caesar's ruse succeeded perfectly. Vercingetorix had not yet learned to keep scouts in the rear." (Kelsey, 412)

isdem sublicis: Ablative of *place where* without a preposition (A.G. 429.2). **isdem**: Plural, feminine, ablative demonstrative pronoun used as an adjective modifying **sublicis** (A.G. 296.1 and a). A variant form of **eisdem** (A.G. 146).

quarum ... remanebat: Relative clause (A.G. 303). **quarum**: Plural, feminine, genitive relative pronoun used substantively A.G. 305). The antecedent is **sublicis** (A.G. 307). Partitive genitive with **pars** (A.G. 346.a.1). **remanebat**: The main verb of the subordinate clause (A.G. 278.b).

pars inferior: Nominative subject (A.G. 339). "The piles had not been destroyed below the water line." (Kelsey, 412) **inferior**: Defective comparative adverb (A.G. 130.b).

integra: Singular, feminine, nominative predicate adjective modifying **pars** after **remanebat** (A.G. 283).

pontem: Accusative direct object of the infinitive **reficere** (A.G. 387 and 451.3).

reficere: Complementary infinitive after **coepit** (A.G. 456).

coepit: The main verb of the main clause (A.G. 278.b). The pronoun **is**, with **Caesari** at 35.2 as the antecedent, is understood as the subject (A.G. 271.a).

(35.6-7) Celeriter effecto opere legionibusque traductis et loco castris idoneo delecto, reliquas (7) copias revocavit.

castra, -orum, n., pl., *camp, encampment.*
copiae, -arum, f., pl., *forces, troops.*
efficio, -ficere, -feci, -fectus, *accomplish, finish, complete.*
idoneus, -a, -um, *suitable, convenient, fit, capable.*
locus, -i, m., *place, location, position.*
-que, *and.*
revoco, -are, -avi, -atus, *call back, recall.*

celeriter, *quickly, speedily, at once, immediately.*
deligo, -ligere, -legi, -lectus, *choose, select, pick out.*
et, *and.*
legio, -onis, f., *legion.*
opus, operis, n., *work.*
reliquus, -a, -um, *remaining, the rest.*
traduco, -ducere, -duxi, -ductus, *lead across, bring over, bring across.*

effecto ... traductis ... delecto: The three successive ablative absolutes give a sense of rapidity to the succession of events.

Celeriter effecto opere: Ablative absolute (A.G. 419-20). **Celeriter**: Adverb (A.G. 214.b and 320-21). **effecto**: The perfect tense of the participle represents the action as completed at the time indicated by the tense of the main verb (A.G. 489).

legionibusque traductis: Ablative absolute (A.G. 419-20). **-que**: The enclitic conjunction connects the first two ablative absolutes (A.G. 324.a). **traductis**: The perfect tense of the participle represents the action as completed at the time indicated by the tense of the main verb (A.G. 489).

et: The conjunction connects the first two connected ablative absolutes with the third (A.G. 324.a).

loco castris idoneo delecto: Ablative absolute (A.G. 419-20). **castris**: Dative with the adjective **idoneo** (A.G. 384). **delecto**: The perfect tense of the participle represents the action as completed at the time indicated by the tense of the main verb (A.G. 489).

reliquas copias: Accusative direct object of **revocavit** (A.G. 387).

revocavit: The main verb of the main clause (A.G. 278.b). The pronoun **is**, with **Caesari** at 35.2 as the antecedent, is understood as the subject (A.G. 271.a).

(35.7) Vercingetorix re cognita, ne contra suam voluntatem dimicare cogeretur, magnis itineribus antecessit.

antecedo, -cedere, -cessi, -----, *go in advance, precede.*

cogo, cogere, coegi, coactus, *compel, force, oblige.*
dimico, -are, -avi, -atus, *fight, contend, struggle.*
magnus, -a, -um, *forced.*
res, rei, f., *matter, affair, event.*
Vercingetorix, -igis, m., *Vercingetorix.*

cognosco, -gnoscere, -gnovi, cognitus, *learn, ascertain, recognize.*
contra, *against, in spite of.*
iter, itineris, n., *march.*
ne, *so that ... not.*
suus, -a, -um, *his*, with or without *own.*
voluntas, -atis, f., *will, wish, inclination, desire.*

Vercingetorix: Nominative subject of **antecessit** (A.G. 339). See Appendix A.

re cognita: Ablative absolute (A.G. 419-20). **cognita**: The perfect tense of the participle represents the action as completed at the time indicated by the tense of the main verb (A.G. 489).

ne ... cogeretur: The conjunction **ne** ("so that ... not") with the subjunctive forms a negative purpose clause (A.G. 531.1). **cogeretur**: The main verb of the subordinate clause (A.G. 278.b). Imperfect subjunctive; the tense of the subjunctive is in secondary sequence and follows the rules for the sequence of tense after **antecessit** (A.G. 482-85). The pronoun **is**, with **Vercingetorix** as the antecedent, is understood as the subject (A.G. 271.a).

contra suam voluntatem: Prepositional phrase, **contra** with the accusative here means "against" (*OLD* contra 16). **suam**: Singular, feminine, accusative possessive pronoun used as an adjective modifying **voluntatem** (A.G. 302).

dimicare: Complementary infinitive after **cogeretur** (A.G. 456).

magnis itineribus: Ablative of manner with a limiting adjective (A.G. 412). The phrase **magna itinera** is an idiom for "forced marches" (*OLD* magnus 1.c). These were 20-25 miles a day.

antecessit: The main verb of the main clause (A.G. 278.b).

(36.1) Caesar ex eo loco quintis castris Gergoviam pervenit equestrique eo die proelio levi facto, perspecto urbis situ, quae posita in altissimo monte omnis aditus difficilis habebat, de expugnatione desperavit;

148

aditus, -us, m., *approach, access, way of approach, means of access.*
Caesar, -aris, m., *Caesar.*

de, *about, concerning.*

dies, -ei, m. and f., *day.*
equester, -tris, -tre, *of cavalry, cavalry-.*
expugnatio, -onis, f., *storming, assault.*
Gergovia, -ae, f., *Gergovia.*
in, *on.*
levis, -e, *unimportant.*
mons, montis, m., *mountain, elevation, height.*
perspicio, -spicere, -spexi, -spectus, *perceive, observe, ascertain.*

pono, ponere, posui, positus, pass., often *be situated.*
-que, *and.*
quintus, -a, -um, *fifth.*
urbs, urbis, f., *city.*

altus, -a, -um, sup. -issimus, *high.*
castra, -orum, n., pl., *a night-encampment on a march, a day's march.*
despero, -are, -avi, -atus, *give up hope of, despair of, have no hope of.*
difficilis, -e, *difficult, hard.*
ex, *from.*
facio, facere, feci, factus, *bring about, make, do.*
habeo, habere, habui, habitus, *have.*
is, ea, id, *he, she, it; that, this.*
locus, -i, m., *place, location, position.*
omnis, -e, *of every kind, all sorts.*
pervenio, -venire, -veni, -ventus, *come to, arrive at, reach.*
proelium, -i, n., *battle, combat, engagement.*
qui, quae, quod, *who, which, what.*
situs, -us, m., *situation, site.*

Caesar: Nominative subject of **pervenit ... desperavit** (A.G. 339). See Appendix A.
ex eo loco: Ablative of *place from which* with the preposition **ex** (A.G. 426.1). "The place where Caesar had encamped, after crossing the Allier." (Kelsey, 412) **eo**: Singular, masculine, ablative demonstrative pronoun used as an adjective modifying **loco** (A.G. 296.1 and a).
quintis castris: Ablative of *time when* (A.G. 423.1). **quintis**: Declinable ordinal number used as an adjective (A.G. 132-35). **castris**: Here **castra** means "a night-encampment on a march; hence, a day's march" (*OLD* **castra** 4). "'In five marches,' 'on the fifth day,' a camp being taken as a measure of time, because at the close of each day's march a camp was fortified. Vercingetorix was already at Gergovia when Caesar came." (Kelsey, 412)
Gergoviam: Accusative of *place to which* without a preposition (city name) (A.G. 427.2). See Appendix A.
pervenit: The main verb of the coordinate clause **Caesar ... pervenit** (A.G. 278.a).
equestrique eo die proelio levi facto: Ablative absolute (A.G. 419-20). **-que**: The enclitic conjunction connects the two main verbs **pervenit ... desperavit** (A.G. 324.a). **eo die**: Ablative of *time when* (A.G. 423.1). **eo**: Singular, masculine, ablative demonstrative pronoun used as an adjective modifying **die** (A.G. 296.1 and a). **die**: The noun **dies** is normally masculine gender (A.G. 97.a). **facto**: The perfect tense of the participle represents the action as completed at the time indicated by the tense of the main verb (A.G. 489).
perspecto ... habebat: Ablative absolute with a dependent clause. Notice the asyndeton between the two ablative absolutes (A.G. 323.b).
perspecto urbis situ: Ablative absolute (A.G. 419-20). "Gergovia lay on a high plateau, accessible only from the south and southeast, and by a narrow projection on the western slope of the Risolle Heights." (Kelsey, 412) **perspecto**: The perfect tense of the participle represents the action as completed at the time indicated by the tense of the main verb (A.G. 489). **urbis**: Possessive genitive with **situ** (A.G. 343).
quae ... habebat: Relative clause (A.G. 303). **quae**: See below. **habebat**: The main verb of the subordinate clause (A.G. 278.b).
quae posita: Nominative subject (A.G. 339). **quae**: Singular, feminine, nominative relative pronoun used substantively (A.G. 305). The antecedent is **urbis** (A.G. 307). **posita**: Nominative, perfect, passive, participle used as a predicate, where in English a phrase or a subordinate clause would be more normal (A.G. 496).
in altissimo monte: Ablative of *place where* with the preposition **in** (locative ablative) (A.G. 426.3). **altissimo**: Superlative adjective (A.G. 124).
omnis aditus difficilis: Accusative direct object of **habebat** (A.G. 387). **omnis**: -is for -es is the regular form in i-stem adjectives (A.G. 114.a and 116). **difficilis**: Plural, masculine, accusative attributive adjective modifying **aditus** (A.G. 285.1). -is for -es is the regular form in i-stem adjectives (A.G. 114.a and 116).
de expugnatione: Prepositional phrase, **de** with the ablative here means "about, concerning" (*OLD* **de** 12).
desperavit: The main verb of the coordinate clause **equestrique ... desperavit** (A.G. 278.a).

(36.1) **de obsessione non prius agendum constituit quam rem frumentariam expedisset.**

ago, agere, egi, actus, *do, pursue, attempt.*

de, *about, concerning.*

frumentarius, -a, -um, *having to do with grain* or *supplies.*
obsessio, -onis, f., *siege.*
res, rei, f., (with **frumentaria**) *supply of grain, supplies.*

constituo, -stituere, -stitui, -stitutus, *establish, resolve upon, determine.*
expedio, -pedire, -pedivi, -peditus, *get ready, make ready.*
non, *not.*
prius ... quam, *before, sooner than.*

de obsessione: Prepositional phrase, **de** with the ablative here means "about, concerning" (*OLD* **de** 12).
non: Adverb modifying **agendum**, the negative precedes the word it especially effects (**prius** is connected with **quam** below) (A.G. 217.e, 320-21, and 599.a).

prius: Construe **prius** with **quam** below.

(id) agendum (esse): A subject accusative with the infinitive after **constituit** (A.G. 563.d). The construction is equivalent to a substantive clause of purpose (A.G. 563.d). **agendum (esse)**: Supply **esse** to form the second periphrastic (passive) present infinitive with the gerundive implying necessity (A.G. 194.b and 196). The tense of the infinitive in indirect discourse is relative to that of the verb of saying (A.G. 584). Impersonal use of the intransitive passive verb (A.G. 208.d). Supply **id** as the subject (A.G. 318.c).

constituit: The main verb of the main clause (A.G. 278.b). The pronoun **is**, with **Caesar** as the antecedent, is understood as the subject (A.G. 271.a).

(prius) ... quam ... expedisset: Temporal clause; a dependent clause in indirect discourse takes the subjunctive (A.G. 580). In direct discourse, **prius quam** ("before") with the imperfect subjunctive is common when the subordinate clause implies purpose or expectancy in the past (A.G. 551.b). The pluperfect subjunctive is rare, except as here where it is in indirect discourse by sequence of tense for the future perfect indicative (A.G. 484.c and 551.b Note 1). **prius ... quam**: The conjunction is here split (tmesis) (A.G. 434 and 640). **expedisset**: The main verb of the subordinate clause (A.G. 278.b). Pluperfect subjunctive; the tense of the subjunctive is in secondary sequence and follows the rules for the sequence of tense after **constituit** (A.G. 585). The pluperfect tense of the subjunctive is here standing for a future perfect in direct discourse (A.G. 484.c). The future perfect tense denotes action completed (at the time referred to), and hence is represented in the subjunctive by the pluperfect tense in secondary sequence (A.G. 484.c). A contracted form of **expedivisset** (A.G. 181.a). The pronoun **is**, with **Caesar** as the antecedent, is understood as the subject (A.G. 271.a).

rem frumentariam: Accusative direct object of **expedisset** (A.G. 387).

(36.2-3) (2) At Vercingetorix, castris prope oppidum positis, mediocribus circum se intervallis separatim singularum civitatum copias collocaverat atque omnibus eius iugi collibus occupatis, qua (3) despici poterat, horribilem speciem praebebat;

at, *but, however, on the other hand.*
castra, -orum, n., pl., *camp, encampment.*
civitas, -tatis, f., *state, nation.*
colloco, -are, -avi, -atus, *place, set, station.*
despicio, -spicere, -spexi, -spectus, *look down.*
intervallum, -i, n., *interval, space, distance.*
iugum, -i, n., *ridge, summit, chain.*
occupo, -are, -avi, -atus, *seize, take possession of, fill, occupy.*
oppidum, -i, n., *fortified town, city.*
possum, posse, potui, -----, *it can be done* or *happen, it is possible.*

prope, *near.*
separatim, *separately, apart.*
species, -iei, f., *sight, show, appearance.*
Vercingetorix, -igis, m., *Vercingetorix.*

atque, *and.*
circum, *round about* (but not necessarily encircling).
collis, -is, m., *hill, height, elevation.*
copiae, -arum, f., pl., *forces, troops.*
horribilis, -e, *dread-inspiring, horrible.*
is, ea, id, *he, she, it; that, this.*
mediocris, -cre, *moderate, short.*
omnis, -e, *all.*
pono, ponere, posui, positus, *place, put.*
praebeo, -ere, praebui, praebitus, *exhibit, manifest, show.*
qua, *where, in which part.*
singuli, -ae, -a, *separate, single, each.*
sui, sibi, se, or **sese**, nom. wanting, *himself.*

At: Conjunction, expressing a contrast between two persons and meaning Abut, however, on the other hand (*OLD* **at** 1).

Vercingetorix: Nominative subject of **collocaverat ... praebebat** (A.G. 339). See Appendix A.

castris prope oppidum positis: Ablative absolute (A.G. 419-20). "On a terrace of rock south of the town and at the top only a few feet below the level of the plateau; ... Vercingetorix had thus an extremely favorable position." (Kelsey, 412) **prope oppidum**: Prepositional phrase, **prope** with the accusative here means "near" (*OLD* **prope** B.9). **positis**: The perfect tense of the participle represents the action as completed at the time indicated by the tense of the main verb (A.G. 489).

mediocribus ... intervallis: Distance, when considered as degree of difference, is put in the ablative. The phrase is dependent on **separatim**. (A.G. 425.b).

circum se: Prepositional phrase, **circum** with the accusative here means Around about (but not necessarily encircling) (*OLD* **circum2** 3). **se**: Singular, masculine, accusative direct reflexive pronoun (A.G. 300.1). The antecedent is **Vercingetorix**, the subject of **collocaverat** (A.G. 299).

separatim: Adverb (A.G. 215.2 and 320-21).

singularum civitatum: Partitive genitive with **copias** (A.G. 346.a.1). **singularum**: Declinable distributive numeral used as an adjective (A.G. 136-37).

copias: Accusative direct object of **collocaverat** (A.G. 387).

collocaverat: The main verb of the coordinate clause **At ... collocaverat** (A.G. 278.a). Although the pluperfect tense is normally used in subordinate clauses, its use as a main verb is frequent. The pluperfect tense of the verb denotes an action completed in past time (A.G. 477).

atque: The conjunction connects the two main verbs **collocaverat ... praebebat** and means "and" (*OLD* **atque** 12).

omnibus ... poterat: Ablative absolute with a dependent clause.

omnibus eius iugi collibus occupatis: Ablative absolute (A.G. 419-20). **eius iugi**: Partitive genitive with **collibus** (A.G. 346.a.1).

eius: Singular, neuter, genitive demonstrative pronoun used as an adjective modifying **iugi** (A.G. 296.1 and a). **occupatis**: The perfect tense of the participle represents the action as completed at the time indicated by the tense of the main verb (A.G. 489).

qua ... (id) poterat: Relative clause (A.G. 279.a). **qua**: Relative adverb meaning "in which part, where" (*OLD* **qua** B.4). **poterat**: The main verb of the subordinate clause (A.G. 278.b). Impersonal use of the verb, supply **id** as the subject (A.G. 271.a). When used impersonally with the passive infinitive, **posse** means "it can be done or happen, it is possible" (*OLD* **possum** 6.b).

despici: Complementary infinitive after **poterat** (A.G. 456).

horribilem speciem: Accusative direct object of **praebebat** (A.G. 387). "On account of the number and impregnable position of the Gallic troops." (Kelsey, 412)
praebebat: The main verb of the coordinate clause **omnibus ... praebebat** (A.G. 278.a).

(36.3-4) principesque earum civitatum quos sibi ad consilium capiendum delegerat prima luce cotidie ad se convenire iubebat, seu quid (4) communicandum seu quid administrandum videretur;

ad, *for, in order to, for the purpose of, to.*

capio, capere, cepi, captus, *form, adopt.*
communico, -are, -avi, -atus, *communicate, impart.*
convenio, -venire, -veni, -ventus, *come together, assemble.*
deligo, -ligere, -legi, -lectus, *choose, select, pick out.*
iubeo, iubere, iussi, iussus, *order, give orders, bid, command.*
primus, -a, -um, *first.*
-que, *and, now.*
quis, -----, quid, *anyone, anything.*
sui, sibi, se, or **sese,** nom. wanting, *himself.*

administro, -are, -avi, -atus, *execute, manage, carry on, administer.*
civitas, -tatis, f., *state, nation.*
consilium, -i, n., *plan, design, policy.*
cotidie, *daily, every day.*
is, ea, id, *he, she, it, that, this.*
lux, lucis, f., *light,* (with **prima**), *daybreak.*
princeps, -ipis, m., *head man, leader, chief, prince.*
qui, quae, quod, *who, which, what.*
seu ... seu, (to see) *whether ... or.*
videor, videri, visus sum, *be regarded, seem, appear.*

principesque ... convenire: A subject accusative with the infinitive after **iubebat**. The construction is equivalent to a substantive clause of purpose (A.G. 563.a). **-que**: The enclitic here begins the sentence and means "and, now" (*OLD* **-que** 4).
earum civitatum: Partitive genitive with **principes** (A.G. 346.a.1). **earum**: Plural, feminine, genitive demonstrative pronoun used as an adjective modifying **civitatum** (A.G. 296.1 and a).
quos ... delegerat: Relative clause (A.G. 303). **quos**: Plural, masculine, accusative relative pronoun used substantively (A.G. 305). The antecedent is **principes** (A.G. 307). Accusative direct object of **delegerat** (A.G. 387). **delegerat**: The main verb of the subordinate clause (A.G. 278.b). The pronoun **is**, with **Vercingetorix** as the antecedent, is understood as the subject (A.G. 271.a). The pluperfect tense of the verb denotes an action completed in past time (A.G. 477).
sibi: Singular, masculine, dative direct reflexive pronoun (A.G. 300.1). The antecedent is **is** (**Vercingetorix**), the supplied subject of **delegerat** (A.G. 299). Dative of reference; the dative in this construction is often called the dative of advantage as denoting the person for whose benefit the action is performed (A.G. 376).
ad consilium capiendum: The preposition **ad** with the accusative noun and gerundive denotes purpose (A.G. 506). **consilium capiendum**: The phrase **consilium capere** is an idiom that means "to adopt or form a plan" (*OLD* **capio** 9.e). **capiendum**: Singular, neuter, accusative gerundive used as an adjective modifying **consilium** denoting necessity, obligation or propriety (A.G. 500.1).
prima luce: Ablative of *time when* (A.G. 423.1). **prima**: Declinable ordinal number used as an adjective (A.G. 132-35).
cotidie: Adverb (A.G. 217.b and 320-21).
ad se: Prepositional phrase, **ad** with the accusative here means "to" (*OLD* **ad** 1). **se**: Singular, masculine, accusative indirect reflexive pronoun (A.G. 300.2). The antecedent is **is** (**Vercingetorix**), the supplied subject of **iubebat** (A.G. 299).
iubebat: The main verb of the main clause (A.G. 278.b). The pronoun **is**, with **Vercingetorix** as the antecedent, is understood as the subject (A.G. 271.a).
seu ... seu ... videretur: A double indirect question with the subjunctive without an expressed question (A.G. 573-76). **seu ... seu**: The repetition of the conjunction means "(to see) whether ... or (*OLD* **sive** 7). **videretur**: The main verb of the subordinate clause (A.G. 278.b). Imperfect subjunctive; the tense of the subjunctive is in secondary sequence and follows the rules for the sequence of tense for indirect question after **iubebat** (A.G. 575).
quid: Singular, neuter, nominative indefinite pronoun used substantively (A.G. 148). Nominative subject (A.G. 339).
communicandum (esse): Singular, neuter, nominative gerundive used as a predicate adjective modifying **quid** after the supplied infinitive **esse** and implying necessity. A predicate adjective after a complementary infinitive takes the case of the subject of the main verb (A.G. 283, 458, and 500.1). Supply **esse** as the complementary infinitive after **videretur**.
quid: Singular, neuter, nominative indefinite pronoun used substantively (A.G. 148). Nominative subject (A.G. 339).
administrandum (esse): Singular, neuter, nominative gerundive used as a predicate adjective modifying **quid** after the supplied infinitive **esse** and implying necessity. A predicate adjective after a complementary infinitive takes the case of the subject of the main verb (A.G. 283-84, 458, and 500.1). Supply **esse** as the complementary infinitive after **videretur**.

(36.4-5) neque ullum fere diem intermittebat quin equestri proelio interiectis sagittariis quid in quoque esset animi ac virtutis (5) suorum periclitaretur.

ac, *and.*
dies, -ei, m. and f., *day.*
fere, *almost, nearly.*
intericio, -icere, -ieci, -iectus, *be interspersed, intermingled, place between.*
neque, *and ... not.*
proelium, -i, n., *battle, combat, engagement.*
quis, -----, quid, *who? what?*
sagittarius, -i, m., *archer, bowman.*
sui, -orum, m., pl., *his men,* with or without *own.*

animus, -i, m., *zeal, enthusiasm.*
equester, -tris, -tre, *of cavalry, cavalry-.*
in, *in.*
intermitto, -mittere, -misi, -missus, *let pass, omit.*
periclitor, -ari, -atus, *try, prove, make trial of, test.*
quin, *but that, that.*
quisque, -----, quidque, *each one, each thing.*
sum, esse, fui, futurus, *be.*
ullus, -a, -um, *any.*

virtus, -utis, f., *manliness, courage, bravery, valor, prowess.*

neque: The conjunction qualifies the single word **ullum** rather than a whole clause and means "and ... not" (*OLD* **neque** 4.c).

ullum ... diem: Accusative direct object of **intermittebat** (A.G. 387). **diem**: The noun **dies** is normally masculine gender (A.G. 97.a).

fere: Adverb (A.G. 320-21).

intermittebat: The main verb of the main clause (A.G. 278.b). The pronoun **is**, with **Vercingetorix** as the antecedent, is understood as the subject (A.G. 271.a).

quin ... periclitaretur: Subordinate clause; the conjunction **quin** (Abut that) with the subjunctive is used after **neque ... intermittebat** (A.G. 278.b and 558). **periclitaretur**: The main verb of the subordinate clause (A.G. 278.b). Imperfect subjunctive; the tense of the subjunctive is in secondary sequence and follows the rules for the sequence of tense after **intermittebat** (A.G. 482-85). The pronoun **is**, with **Vercingetorix** as the antecedent, is understood as the subject (A.G. 271.a).

equestri proelio: Ablative of *place where* without a preposition (A.G. 429.2).

interiectis sagittariis: Ablative absolute (A.G. 419-20). **interiectis**: The perfect tense of the participle represents the action as completed at the time indicated by the tense of the main verb (A.G. 489).

quid ... suorum: This clause can be rewritten in English word order as **quid animi ac virtutis esset in quoque suorum**.

quid ... suorum: Indirect question with the subjunctive; the phrase is the object of **periclitaretur** (A.G. 573-75). **quid**: Singular, neuter, nominative interrogative pronoun used substantively (A.G. 148). Nominative subject (A.G. 339). **suorum**: Plural, masculine, genitive possessive pronoun used substantively to denote a special class (A.G. 302.d). Partitive genitive with **quoque** (A.G. 346.a.1).

in quoque: Prepositional phrase, **in** with the ablative here means "in" (expressing an abstract location) (*OLD* **in** 26). The prepositional phrase is in the predicate position after **esset** (A.G. 272). **quoque**: Singular, masculine, ablative, indefinite (universal) pronoun used substantively (A.G. 151.g).

esset: The main verb of the subordinate clause (A.G. 278.b). Imperfect subjunctive; the tense of the subjunctive is in secondary sequence and follows the rules for the sequence of tense for indirect questions after **intermittebat** (A.G. 575).

animi ac virtutis: Two partitive genitives with **quid** (A.G. 346.a.3). **ac**: The conjunction connects the two genitive nouns and means "and" (*OLD* **atque** 12).

(36.5-6) Erat e regione oppidi collis sub ipsis radicibus montis egregie munitus atque ex omni parte circumcisus;

atque, *and.*	**circumcisus, -a, -um**, *cut off, inaccessible, steep.*
collis, -is, m., *hill, height, elevation.*	**egregie**, *remarkably well, admirably, splendidly.*
e(x), *directly opposite; on.*	**ipse, -a, -um**, *the very.*
mons, montis, m., *mountain, elevation, height.*	**munitus, -a, -um**, *fortified, protected, secure.*
omnis, -e, *every.*	**oppidum, -i**, n., *fortified town, city.*
pars, partis, f., *side.*	**radix, -icis**, f., *root, foot, base.*
regio, -onis, f., *region, territory.*	**sub**, *at the foot of, below.*
sum, esse, fui, futurus, *be.*	

Erat: The main verb of the main clause (A.G. 278.b). The verb **sum** in the sense of "exist" makes a complete predicate without a predicate noun or adjective ("there was ..."). It is then called the substantive verb and regularly comes first (A.G. 284.b and 598.c).

e regione oppidi: Prepositional phrase, **e(x)** with the ablative of **regio** means "directly opposite" with the genitive (*OLD* **regio** 2.a).

oppidi: Possessive genitive with **regione** (A.G. 343).

collis ... munitus ... circumcisus: Nominative subject (A.G. 339).

sub ipsis radicibus montis: Prepositional phrase, **sub** with the ablative here means "at the foot of, below" (*OLD* **sub** 6). **ipsis**: Plural, feminine, ablative demonstrative pronoun used as an adjective modifying **radicibus** and meaning "The very (A.G. 296.1 and a and 298 Note 1). **montis**: Partitive genitive with **radicibus** (A.G. 346.a.1). **egregie**: Adverb (A.G. 214.a and 320-21).

atque: The conjunction connects the two participles **munitus ... circumcisus** and means "and" (*OLD* **atque** 12). Two adjectives belonging to the same noun are regularly connected by a conjunction (A.G. 323.d).

ex omni parte: Ablative of *position* with the preposition **ex** (A.G. 429.b).

(36.5-6) quem si tenerent nostri, et aquae magna parte (6) et pabulatione libera prohibituri hostis videbantur.

aqua, -ae, f., *water.*	**et ... et**, *both ... and.*
hostis, -is, m., *enemy, foe*; pl., *the enemy.*	**liber, -era, -erum**, *unimpeded, unrestricted.*
magnus, -a, -um, *great, large.*	**nostri, -orum**, m., pl., *our men, our side.*
pabulatio, -onis, f., *foraging, getting fodder.*	**pars, partis**, f., *part, portion.*
prohibeo, -hibere, -hibui, -hibitus, *prevent, hinder.*	**qui, quae, quod**, *who, which, what.*
si, *if.*	**teneo, tenere, tenui, -----**, *take possession of, seize.*
videor, videri, visus sum, *seem to oneself, suppose* or *imagine that.*	

quem: Singular, masculine, accusative relative pronoun used substantively (A.G. 305). The antecedent is **collis** (A.G. 307). Accusative direct object of **tenerent** (A.G. 387). The relative does not introduce a relative clause but is a connecting relative; at the beginning of a clause the pronoun is often best rendered by a personal or demonstrative pronoun, with or without *and* (A.G. 308.f).

si tenerent ...videbantur: Mixed conditional statement, the protasis (imperfect subjunctive) is from a contrary to fact, present time condition (A.G. 514 C.1). The apodosis (imperfect indicative) is from a simple, past time condition (A.G. 514.A.2).

si tenerent: The conjunction **si** ("if") with the imperfect subjunctive forms the protasis of the conditional statement (A.G. 514 C.1).

tenerent: The main verb of the subordinate clause (A.G. 278.b).

nostri: Plural, masculine, nominative possessive pronoun used substantively to denote a special class (A.G. 302.d). Nominative subject of **tenerent** (A.G. 339). The subject is in the last position (A.G. 597.b).

et ... et: The repeated conjunction connects the two ablative nouns and means "both ... and" (A.G. 323.e).

aquae: Partitive genitive with **parte** (A.G. 346.a.1).

magna parte: Ablative of separation after the future participle **prohibituri** (A.G. 401).

pabulatione libera: Ablative of separation after the future participle **prohibituri** (A.G. 401).

prohibituri (esse): Nominative, future, active participle used as a predicate adjective modifying **ei**, the supplied subject of **videbantur** (A.G. 283 and 495). A predicate adjective after a complementary infinitive takes the case of the subject of the main verb (A.G. 283-84 and 458). Supply **esse** as the complementary infinitive after **videbantur**.

The future participle used in simple agreement with a substantive expresses likelihood or certainty (A.G. 499.1).

hostis: Accusative direct object of the participle **prohibituri** (A.G. 387 and 488). Accusative plural noun; **-is** for **-es** is the regular form in i-stem nouns (A.G. 65-67 and 74.c).

videbantur: The main verb of the apodosis of the conditional statement (A.G. 514.A.2). The main verb of the main clause (A.G. 278.b). The pronoun **ei**, with **nostri** as the antecedent, is understood as the subject (A.G. 271.a).

(36.6) Sed is locus praesidio ab his, non nimis firmo tamen, tenebatur.

ab, *by*.
hic, haec, hoc, *this*; *he, she, it*.
locus, -i, m., *place, location, position*.
non, *not*.
sed, *but*.
teneo, tenere, tenui, -----, *hold, keep*.

firmus, -a, -um, *strong, firm*.
is, ea, id, *he, she, it*; *that, this*.
nimis, *very, overly, too*.
praesidium, -i, n., *guard, garrison*.
tamen, *yet, still, for all that, nevertheless, however*.

Sed: Coordinate conjunction (A.G. 324.d).

is locus: Nominative subject (A.G. 339). **is**: Singular, masculine, nominative demonstrative pronoun used as an adjective modifying **locus** (A.G. 296.1 and a).

praesidio ... firmo: Ablative of means after **tenebatur** (A.G. 409).

ab his: Ablative of agent with the preposition **ab** after the passive verb **tenebatur** (A.G. 409). **his**: Plural, masculine, ablative demonstrative pronoun used substantively (A.G. 296.2). The antecedent is **hostis** (A.G. 297.e).

non nimis: The two adverbs taken together mean "not very, none too" (*OLD* nimis 2). **non**: Adverb modifying **nimis**, the negative precedes the word it especially effects (A.G. 217.e, 320-21, and 599.a). **nimis**: Adverb (A.G. 320-21).

tamen: Adverb, postpositive (A.G. 320-21 and 324.j). "In spite of the fact that this hill was guarded by the enemy." (Kelsey, 413)

tenebatur: The main verb of the simple sentence (A.G. 278.1).

(36.7) (7) Silentio noctis Caesar ex castris egressus, prius quam subsidio ex oppido veniri posset deiecto praesidio, potitus loco duas ibi legiones collocavit, fossamque duplicem duodenum pedum a maioribus castris ad minora perduxit, ut tuto ab repentino hostium incursu etiam singuli commeare possent.

a(b), *from*.
Caesar, -aris, m., *Caesar*.
colloco, -are, -avi, -atus, *place, set*.
deicio, -icere, -ieci, -iectus, *dislodge, rout*.
duodeni, -ae, -a, *twelve each*.
egredior, -gredi, -gressus, *go out, go forth, come forth, leave*.
ex, *from, out of*.
hostis, -is, m., *enemy, foe*; pl., *the enemy*.
incursus, -us, m., *assault, attack*.
locus, -i, m., *place, location, position*.
minor, -or, -ius, *smaller, lesser*.
oppidum, -i, n., *fortified town, city*.

pes, pedis, m., *foot*, = .9708 of the English foot.

potior, potiri, potitus, *obtain possession of, become master of, acquire*.
prius quam, *before, sooner than*.
repentinus, -a, -um, *sudden, unexpected*.
singuli, -ae, -a, *one at a time, individual*.
tuto, *in safety, safely, secretly*.
venio, venire, veni, ventus, *come*.

ad, *to*.
castra, -orum, n., pl., *camp, encampment*.
commeo, -are, -avi, -atus, *go to and fro*.
duo, -ae, -o, *two*.
duplex, -icis, *twofold, double*.
etiam, *even*.
fossa, -ae, f., *ditch, trench, intrenchment, fosse*.
ibi, *in that place, there*.
legio, -onis, f., *legion*.
maior, -or, -us, *greater, larger*.
nox, noctis, f., *night*.
perduco, -ducere, -duxi, -ductus, *extend, construct, make*.
possum, posse, potui, -----, *it can be done* or *happen, it is possible*.
praesidium, -i, n., *guard, garrison*.
-que, *and*.
silentium, -i, m., *silence, stillness*.
subsidium, -i, n., *support, relief, reinforcement, help*.
ut, *so that*.

Silentio: Ablative of *time when* (A.G. 423.1).

noctis: Partitive genitive with **Silentio** (A.G. 346.a.1).

Caesar ... egressus ... potitus: Nominative subject of **collocavit ... perduxit** (A.G. 339). **Caesar**: See Appendix A. **egressus** ...

potitus: Two nominative perfect, deponent, participles used as predicates, where in English a phrase or a subordinate clause would be more normal (A.G. 496).

ex castris: Ablative of *place from which* with the preposition **ex** (A.G. 426.1).

prius quam ... (id) posset: Temporal clause; the conjunction **prius quam** ("before") with the imperfect subjunctive denotes action which did not take place (A.G. 551.b). **posset**: The main verb of the subordinate clause (A.G. 278.b). Impersonal use of the verb, supply **id** as the subject (A.G. 271.a). When used impersonally with the passive infinitive, **posse** means "it can be done or happen, it is possible" (*OLD* **possum** 6.b).

subsidio: Dative of the purpose or end. The dative of an abstract noun is used to show that for which a thing serves or which it accomplishes (A.G. 382.1).

ex oppido: Ablative of *place from which* with the preposition **ex** (A.G. 426.1).

veniri: Complementary infinitive after **posset** (A.G. 456).

deiecto praesidio: Ablative absolute (A.G. 419-20). **deiecto**: The perfect tense of the participle represents the action as completed at the time indicated by the tense of the main verb (A.G. 489).

loco: Ablative direct object of the deponent participle **potitus** (A.G. 410).

duas ... legiones: Accusative direct object of **collocavit** (A.G. 387). **duas**: Declinable cardinal number used as an adjective (A.G. 132-35).

ibi: Adverb (A.G. 215.5 and 320-21).

collocavit: The main verb of the coordinate clause **Silentio ... collocavit** (A.G. 278.a).

fossamque duplicem: Accusative direct object of **perduxit** (A.G. 387). **fossam**: "The size of the trench (**fossa**) varied, but was usually about nine feet wide and seven deep. The earth, dug out with spades and carried in baskets, was piled up just inside the trench to make a wall (**vallum**)." (Walker, 29) **-que**: The enclitic conjunction connects the two main verbs **collocavit ... perduxit** (A.G. 324.a). **duplicem**: Multiplicative numeral used as an adjective with **fossam** (A.G. 139).

duodenum pedum: Genitive of quality (measure) with **fossam** (A.G. 345.b). **duodenum**: Declinable distributive numeral used as an adjective (A.G. 136-37).

a maioribus castris: Ablative of *place from which* with the preposition **ab** (A.G. 426.1). **maioribus**: Irregular comparative adjective (A.G. 129).

ad minora: Accusative of *place to which* with the preposition **ad** (A.G. 426.2). "As this contained two legions, in the large camp there must have been four legions beside the auxiliaries and cavalry." (Kelsey, 413) **minora**: Irregular comparative adjective used substantively (A.G. 129 and 288). The noun **castra** is understood (A.G. 288.b).

perduxit: The main verb of the coordinate clause **fossamque ... possent** (A.G. 278.a).

ut ... possent: The conjunction **ut** ("so that") with the subjunctive forms a clause of result (A.G. 537.1). **possent**: The main verb of the subordinate clause (A.G. 278.b). Imperfect subjunctive; the tense of the subjunctive is in secondary sequence and follows the rules for the sequence of tense after **perduxit** (A.G. 482-85).

tuto: Adverb (A.G. 320-21).

ab repentino hostium incursu: Prepositional phrase, **ab** with the ablative here means "from" and is dependent on the adverb **tuto** (cf. the ablative of separation after adjectives (A.G. 402.a)) (*OLD* **ab** 7.b). **hostium**: Possessive genitive with **incursu** (A.G. 343).

etiam: Adverb (A.G. 320-21 and 322.a). The adverb normally proceeds the emphatic word (A.G. 322.a).

singuli: Distributive numeral used substantively (A.G. 136-37). The noun **milites** is understood. Nominative subject (A.G. 339).

commeare: Complementary infinitive after **possent** (A.G. 456).

3.B CHAPTERS 37-43: THE FIRST DEFECTION OF THE AEDUI AND THEIR SUBSEQUENT REPENTENCE

The defection of the Aedui is a complex story. Here, it begins with Convictolitavis, the Vergobret, being bribed by the Arverni and recruiting Litaviccus and his brothers to join him in revolt (37). Litaviccus lies to his army of 10,000 foot-soldiers and cavalry, causing a revolt and then sends messages through the state of the Aedui urging rebellion (38). The Aeduan Eporedorix informs Caesar of the mutiny (39). Caesar recovers the Aeduan army with the help of Eporedorix and Viridomarus; Litaviccus flees to Gergovia (40). Caesar sends messages to the Aedui that he has their army in his power and he has spared them (41). The Aedui act on the messages from Litaviccus (sent at 38) and proceed into open revolt (42). The messages come from Caesar (sent at 41) and they repent publicly, but privately they plot rebellion (43). After the loss at Gergovia, Eporedorix and Viridomarus ask to return to the Aedui in order to counter the seditious Litaviccus and keep the state loyal; Caesar does not believe them but allows them to depart anyway (54). When Eporedorix and Viridomarus learn that Litaviccus has been received at Bibracte, that Convictolitavis and many senators were joining him, and that the state was officially seeking peace and friendship from Vercingetorix, they join the rebellion and sacked Noviodunum (55). Finally, Caesar announces that **Defectione Aeduorum cognita bellum augetur** (63.1).

(37.1) **Dum haec ad Gergoviam geruntur, Convictolitavis Aeduus, cui magistratum adiudicatum a Caesare demonstravimus, sollicitatus ab Arvernis pecunia cum quibusdam adulescentibus colloquitur; quorum erat princeps Litaviccus atque eius fratres, amplissima familia nati adulescentes.**

a(b), *by*.

adiudico, -are, -avi, -atus, *award, adjudge.*

Aeduus, -i, m., *an Aeduan.*

Arverni, -orum, m., pl., *the Arverni.*

ad, *at.*

adulescens, -entis, m., *young man, youth.*

amplus, -a, -um, sup. **-issimus**, *distinguished.*

atque, *and.*

Caesar, -aris, m., *Caesar.*
Convictolitavis, -is, m., *Convictolitavis.*
demonstro, -are, -avi, -atus, *point out, show, say, mention, explain.*
familia, -ae, f., *family.*
Gergovia, -ae, f., *Gergovia.*
hic, haec, hoc, *this; he, she, it.*
Litaviccus, -i, m., *Litaviccus.*
nascor, nasci, natus, *be born.*
princeps, -ipis, m., *head man, leader, chief, prince.*
quidam, quaedam, quiddam, *a certain, certain, some.*
sum, esse, fui, futurus, *be.*

colloquor, -loqui, -locutus, *talk with, hold a conference.*
cum, *with.*
dum, *while.*
frater, -tris, m., *brother.*
gero, gerere, gessi, gestus, *carry out, perform, do.*
is, ea, id, *he, she, it; that, this.*
magistratus, -us, m., *magistracy, civil office.*
pecunia, -ae, f., *money, wealth.*
qui, quae, quod, *who, which, what.*
sollicito, -are, -avi, -atus, *incite, tamper with, tempt.*

Dum ... geruntur: Temporal clause; the conjunction **dum** ("when, while") with the present indicative denotes continued action in past time (A.G. 556). **geruntur:** The main verb of the subordinate clause (A.G. 278.b).

haec: Plural, neuter, nominative demonstrative pronoun used substantively (A.G. 296.2). The antecedent is the actions described above in Chapter 36 (A.G. 297.e). Nominative subject (A.G. 339).

ad Gergoviam: Prepositional phrase, with all names of places *at*, meaning *near* (not *in*), is expressed by **ad** with the accusative (A.G. 428.d). **Gergoviam:** See Appendix A.

Convictolitavis ... sollicitatus: Nominative subject of **colloquitur** (A.G. 339). **Convictolitavis:** See Appendix A. **sollicitatus:** Nominative, perfect, passive, participle used as a predicate, where in English a phrase or a subordinate clause would be more normal (A.G. 496).

Aeduus: A nominative noun in apposition to the proper noun **Convictolitavis** (A.G. 282).

cui ... demonstravimus: Relative clause (A.G. 303). See Chapters 32-33 for the reference. **cui:** Singular, masculine, dative relative pronoun used substantively (A.G. 305). The antecedent is **Convictolitavis** (A.G. 307). Dative indirect object of the passive infinitive **adiudicatum (esse)**, verbs which in the active voice take the accusative and dative retain the dative when used in the passive (A.G. 365). **demonstravimus:** The main verb of the subordinate clause (A.G. 278.b). The personal pronoun **nos** is understood as the subject but is not expressed except for distinction or emphasis (A.G. 295.a). In Book 7, Caesar refers to himself only in the third person, either in the singular or occasionally in the plural (see **Caesar** at 1.1). Siedler counts 11 uses of the first person plural in Book 7 (Siedler, 46). These uses are at 17.1, 23.2, 25.1, 37.1, 48.1, 58.4, 70.1, 76.1, 79.2, 83.8, and 85.4.

magistratum adiudicatum (esse): Accusative/infinitive construction in indirect discourse after **demonstravimus** (A.G. 577 ff.).

adiudicatum (esse): Supply **esse** to form the perfect, passive infinitive (A.G. 184). The tense of the infinitive in indirect discourse is relative to that of the verb of saying (A.G. 584).

a Caesare: Ablative of agent with the preposition **a(b)** after the passive infinitive **adiudicatum (esse)** (A.G. 405). **Caesare:** See Appendix A.

ab Arvernis: Ablative of source with the preposition **ab** (A.G. 403.1). **Arvernis:** See Appendix A.

pecunia: Ablative of means (A.G. 409).

cum quibusdam adulescentibus: Ablative of accompaniment with the preposition **cum** (A.G. 413). **quibusdam:** Plural, masculine, ablative indefinite pronoun used as an adjective modifying **adulescentibus** (A.G. 151.c and 296.1 and a).

colloquitur: The main verb of the main clause (A.G. 278.b). The historical present, giving vividness to the narrative, is present in Chapter 37 (A.G. 469). This usage, common in all languages, comes from imagining past events as going on before our eyes (*repraesentatio*) (A.G. 469 Note).

quorum: Plural, masculine, genitive demonstrative pronoun used substantively (A.G. 296.2). The antecedent is **adulescentibus** (A.G. 297.e). Partitive genitive with **princeps** (A.G. 346.a.1). The relative does not introduce a relative clause but is a connecting relative; at the beginning of a clause the pronoun is often best rendered by a personal or demonstrative pronoun, with or without *and* (A.G. 308.f).

erat: The main verb of the main clause (A.G. 278.b). Two or more subjects (**Litaviccus ... fratres**) normally take a verb in the plural (A.G. 317). However, when a verb belongs to two or more subjects separately, it often agrees with one (**Litaviccus**) and is understood with the others (A.G. 317.c).

princeps: Nominative subject (A.G. 339).

Litaviccus: Singular, masculine, nominative noun in the predicate position after **erat** (A.G. 283-84). See Appendix A.

atque: The conjunction connects the two nominative nouns **Litaviccus ... fratres** and means "and" (*OLD* **atque** 12).

eius: Singular, masculine, genitive demonstrative pronoun used substantively (A.G. 296.2). The antecedent is **Litaviccus** (A.G. 297.e). Possessive genitive with **fratres** (A.G. 343).

fratres: Plural, masculine, nominative noun in the predicate position after **erat** (A.G. 283). The brothers are otherwise unnamed.

amplissima familia: Ablative of source without a preposition after the participle **nati** (A.G. 403.a). **amplissima:** Superlative adjective (A.G. 124).

nati: Nominative, perfect, deponent, participle used as a predicate modifying **adulescentes**, where in English a phrase or a subordinate clause would be more normal (A.G. 496).

adulescentes: A nominative noun in apposition to **fratres** (A.G. 288).

(37.2-3) **(2) Cum his praemium communicat hortaturque [eos] ut se libe(3)ros et imperio natos meminerint.**

communico, -are, -avi, -atus, *share together, share with, divide with.*
et, *and.*
hortor, -ari, -atus, *urge, encourage, exhort, incite, press.*

cum, *with.*
hic, haec, hoc, *this; he, she, it.*
imperium, -i, n., *command, military authority.*

is, ea, id, *he, she, it; that, this.*
memini, -isse, *remember, bear in mind.*
praemium, -i, n., *bribe.*
sui, sibi, se, or sese, nom. wanting, *they,* with or without *themselves.*

liber, -era, -erum, *free, independent.*
nascor, nasci, natus, *be born.*
-que, *and.*
ut, *so that.*

Cum his: Ablative of accompaniment with the preposition **cum** (A.G. 413). **his**: Plural, masculine, ablative demonstrative pronoun used substantively (A.G. 296.2). The antecedent is **Litaviccus ... fratres** (A.G. 297.e).
praemium: Accusative direct object of **communicat** (A.G. 387). This is the money given to Convictolitavis by the Arverni at 37.1.
communicat: The main verb of the coordinate clause **Cum ... communicat** (A.G. 278.a). The pronoun **is**, with **Convictolitavis** as the antecedent, is understood as the subject (A.G. 271.a).
hortaturque: The main verb of the coordinate clause **hortaturque ... meminerint** (A.G. 278.a). The pronoun **is**, with **Convictolitavis** as the antecedent, is understood as the subject (A.G. 271.a). **-que**: The enclitic conjunction connects the two main verbs (A.G. 324.a).
[eos]: Plural, masculine, accusative demonstrative pronoun used substantively (A.G. 296.2). The antecedent is **Litaviccus ... fratres** (A.G. 297.e). Accusative direct object of **hortatur** (A.G. 387).
ut ... meminerint: The conjunction **ut** ("so that") with the subjunctive forms a substantive clause of purpose which is used as the object of the verb **hortatur** denoting an action directed toward the future (A.G. 563). **meminerint**: The main verb of the subordinate clause (A.G. 278.b). Perfect subjunctive; the tense of the subjunctive is normally in secondary sequence after the historical present **hortatur** (A.G. 482-85). Here it is in primary sequence through *repraesentatio* (A.G. 485.e and 585.b Note). Perfect tense with present force (A.G. 205). The pronoun **ei**, with **his** (**Litaviccus ... fratres**) as the antecedent, is understood as the subject (A.G. 271.a).
se ... natos (esse): Accusative/infinitive construction in indirect discourse after **meminerint** (A.G. 577 ff.). **se**: Plural, masculine, accusative direct reflexive pronoun (A.G. 300.1). The antecedent is **ei (Litaviccus ... fratres)**, the supplied subject of **meminerint** (A.G. 299). **natos (esse)**: Supply **esse** to form the perfect, deponent infinitive (A.G. 190). The tense of the infinitive in indirect discourse is relative to that of the verb of saying (A.G. 584).
liberos: Plural, masculine, accusative, predicate adjective modifying **se** after **natos (esse)** (A.G. 283).
et: The conjunction connects the adjective **liberos** and the noun **imperio** (A.G. 324.a).
imperio: Dative of the purpose or end. The dative of an abstract noun (**imperio**) is used to show that for which a thing serves or which it accomplishes (A.G. 382.1).

Unam ... veniant: Murphy classifies this speech in indirect discourse as deliberative (C. Murphy, 122).

(37.3) Unam esse Aeduorum civitatem quae certissimam Galliae victoriam distineat; eius auctoritate reliquas contineri;

Aedui, -orum, m., pl., *the Aedui.*
certus, -a, -um, sup. -issimus, *certain, definite, undoubted.*
contineo, -tinere, -tinui, -tentus, *hold back, keep, retain.*
Gallia, -ae, f., *Gaul.*
qui, quae, quod, *who, which, what.*
sum, esse, fui, futurus, *be.*
victoria, -ae, f., *victory.*

auctoritas, -tatis, f., *influence, weight, authority.*
civitas, -tatis, f., *state, nation.*
distineo, -tinere, -tinui, -tentus, *hinder, delay.*
is, ea, id, *he, she, it; that, this.*
reliquus, -a, -um, *remaining, the rest.*
unus, -a, -um, *only one, only, single, sole.*

Unam esse ... civitatem: Accusative/infinitive construction in indirect discourse (A.G. 577 ff.). The verb of saying is not expressed, but implied in the general drift of the sentence (A.G. 580.a). **Unam**: Singular, feminine, accusative declinable cardinal number used as a predicate adjective modifying **civitatem** after **esse** (A.G. 132-35 and 283-84). **esse**: Present infinitive; the tense of the infinitive in indirect discourse is relative to that of the verb of saying (A.G. 584).
Aeduorum: Possessive genitive with **civitatem** (A.G. 343). See Appendix A.
quae ... distineat: Relative clause; a subordinate clause in indirect discourse takes the subjunctive (A.G. 303 and 580). **quae**: Singular, feminine, nominative relative pronoun used substantively (A.G. 305). The antecedent is **civitatem** (A.G. 307). Nominative subject (A.G. 339). **distineat**: The main verb of the subordinate clause (A.G. 278.b). Present subjunctive; the tense of the subjunctive is normally in secondary sequence after an unexpressed verb of saying (A.G. 482-84). Here it is in primary sequence through *repraesentatio* (A.G. 585.b Note).
certissimam ... victoriam: Accusative direct object of **distineat** (A.G. 387). **certissimam**: Superlative adjective (A.G. 124).
Galliae: Possessive genitive with **victoriam** (A.G. 343). See Appendix A.
eius: Singular, feminine, genitive demonstrative pronoun used substantively (A.G. 296.2). The antecedent is **civitatem** (A.G. 297.e). Possessive genitive with **auctoritate** (A.G. 343).
auctoritate: Ablative of means (A.G. 409).
reliquas contineri: Accusative/infinitive construction in indirect discourse (A.G. 577 ff.). The verb of saying is not expressed, but implied in the general drift of the sentence (A.G. 580.a). **reliquas**: Plural, feminine, accusative, adjective used substantively (A.G. 288). The noun **civitates** is understood (A.G. 288.b). **contineri**: Present infinitive; the tense of the infinitive in indirect discourse is relative to that of the verb of saying (A.G. 584).

(37.3-4) qua traducta, locum consis(4)tendi Romanis in Gallia non fore.

consisto, -sistere, -stiti, -stitus, *take a position, take a stand, stay, remain.*
in, *in.*

Gallia, -ae, f., *Gaul.*
locus, -i, m., *place, location, position.*

non, *not*.
Romani, -orum, m., pl., *the Romans*.
traduco, -ducere, -duxi, -ductus, *transfer, remove, turn*.

qui, quae, quod, *who, which, what*.
sum, esse, fui, futurus, *be*.

qua traducta ... fore: A disguised conditional statement in indirect discourse (A.G. 521 and 589). The verb of saying is not expressed, but implied in the general drift of the sentence (A.G. 580.a). Normally, the protasis, as a dependent clause, is in the subjunctive and the apodosis, as the principal clause, is in the infinitive (A.G. 589). Here, the ablative absolute takes the place of the protasis (A.G. 521).

qua traducta: An ablative absolute standing as the protasis of the conditional statement (= **si ea traducta esset** A.G. 484.c) (A.G. 420.4 and 521.a). **qua**: Singular, feminine, ablative relative pronoun used substantively (A.G. 305). The antecedent is **civitatem** (A.G. 307). The relative does not introduce a relative clause but is a connecting relative; at the beginning of a clause the pronoun is often best rendered by a personal or demonstrative pronoun, with or without *and* (A.G. 308.f).

locum ... fore: The apodosis of the conditional statement (A.G. 589.2). Accusative/infinitive construction in indirect discourse (A.G. 577 ff.). The verb of saying is not expressed, but implied in the general drift of the sentence (A.G. 580.a). **fore**: Future active infinitive of **sum** (A.G. 170.a). The tense of the infinitive in indirect discourse is relative to that of the verb of saying (A.G. 584).

consistendi: Singular, neuter, genitive gerund (A.G. 501-02). Objective genitive with **locum** (A.G. 504).

Romanis: Dative of possession with **fore** (A.G. 373).

in Gallia: Ablative of *place where* with the preposition **in** (locative ablative) (A.G. 426.3). **Gallia**: See Appendix A.

non: Adverb, the adverb generally precedes the verb if it belongs to no one word in particular (A.G. 217.e, 320-21, and 599.a).

(37.4) Esse non nullo se Caesaris beneficio adfectum, sic tamen ut iustissimam apud eum causam obtinuerit; sed plus communi libertati tribuere.

adficio, -ficere, -feci, -fectus, *benefit, move, influence, treat*.
beneficium, -i, n., *kindness, favor, service, benefit*.
causa, -ae, f., *case, suit*.
is, ea, id, *he, she, it; that, this*.
libertas, -atis, f., *freedom, liberty, independence*.
nullus, -a, -um, *no, not any*.
plus, -ris, n., *more*.
sic ... ut, *only to the extent that*.

tamen, *yet, still, for all that, nevertheless, however*.

apud, *before*.
Caesar, -aris, m., *Caesar*.
communis, -e, *common, in common, public, general*.
iustus, -a, -um, sup. **-issimus**, *just, rightful, fair*.
non, *not*.
obtineo, -tinere, -tinui, -tentus, *win*.
sed, *but*.
sui, sibi, se, or **sese**, nom. wanting, *he*, with or without *himself*.
tribuo, -ere, -ui, -utus, *pay regard* to, *put value on*.

Esse ... se ... adfectum: Accusative/infinitive construction in indirect discourse (A.G. 577 ff.). The verb of saying is not expressed, but implied in the general drift of the sentence (A.G. 580.a). **se**: Singular, masculine, accusative direct reflexive pronoun (A.G. 300.1). The antecedent is **Convictolitavis**, the subject of the unexpressed verb of saying (A.G. 299). **Esse ... adfectum**: The perfect, passive infinitive is here split (tmesis) (A.G. 640). The tense of the infinitive in indirect discourse is relative to that of the verb of saying (A.G. 584).

non nullo: A litotes, a statement is made emphatic by denying its contrary (A.G. 326.c).

non: Adverb modifying **nullo**, the negative precedes the word it especially effects (A.G. 217.e, 320-21, and 599.a).

nullo ... beneficio: Ablative of means (A.G. 409).

Caesaris: Objective genitive with **beneficio** (A.G. 348). See Appendix A.

sic ... ut ... obtinuerit: The adverb **sic** and conjunction **ut** ("only to the extent that") with the subjunctive introduces a subordinate clause where the main clause (**Esse ... adfectum**) represents a concession with which the **ut** clause is contrasted (*OLD* **ut** 34). Indeed, he must concede some benefit from Caesar as he had made Convictolitavis Vergobret. See Chapters 32-33 for the reference.

obtinuerit: The main verb of the subordinate clause (A.G. 278.b). Perfect subjunctive; the tense of the subjunctive is normally in secondary sequence after an unexpressed verb of saying (A.G. 482-84). Here it is in primary sequence through *repraesentatio* (A.G. 585.b Note). The pronoun **is**, with **Convictolitavis** as the antecedent, is understood as the subject (A.G. 271.a).

tamen: Adverb, postpositive (A.G. 320-21 and 324.j).

iustissimam ... causam: Accusative direct object of **obtinuerit** (A.G. 387). **iustissimam**: Superlative adjective (A.G. 124).

apud eum: Prepositional phrase, **apud** with the accusative here means "before" (*OLD* **apud** 8.b). **eum**: Singular, masculine, accusative demonstrative pronoun used substantively (A.G. 296.2). The antecedent is **Caesaris** (A.G. 297.e).

sed: Coordinate conjunction (A.G. 324.d).

plus: Singular, neuter, accusative comparative adjective used substantively; the neuter singular of the adjective is used only as a noun (A.G. 120.c). Accusative direct object of the transitive infinitive **tribuere** (A.G. 320-21).

communi libertati: Dative indirect object of the transitive infinitive **tribuere** (A.G. 362). **libertati**: For the theme of liberty in Book 7, see **liberius** at 1.3.

(se) tribuere: Accusative/infinitive construction in indirect discourse (A.G. 577 ff.). The verb of saying is not expressed, but implied in the general drift of the sentence (A.G. 580.a). Carry down **se** as the accusative subject. **tribuere**: Present infinitive; the tense of the infinitive in indirect discourse is relative to that of the verb of saying (A.G. 584).

(37.5-6) (5) Cur enim potius Aedui de suo iure et de legibus ad Caesarem (6) disceptatorem quam Romani ad Aeduos veniant?

ad, *to*.
Caesar, -aris, m., *Caesar*.
de, *about, concerning*.
enim, *for, for in fact, and in fact*.
ius, iuris, n., *right, justice, authority*.
potius ... quam, *rather than*.
suus, -a, -um, *their*, with or without *own*.

Aedui, -orum, m., pl., *the Aedui*.
cur, *why?*.
disceptator, -oris, m., *arbitrator, umpire, judge*.
et, *and*.
lex, legis, f., *law, enactment, decree*.
Romani, -orum, m., pl., *the Romans*.
venio, venire, veni, ventus, *come*.

Cur ... veniant: A question in indirect discourse; a real question, asking for an answer, is generally put in the subjunctive (A.G. 586).
cur: Interrogative adverb (A.G. 333). veniant: The main verb of the simple sentence (A.G. 278.1). Present subjunctive; the tense of the subjunctive is normally in secondary sequence after an unexpressed verb of saying (A.G. 482-84 and 585). Here it is in primary sequence through *repraesentatio* (A.G. 585.b Note).
enim: Postpositive conjunction (A.G. 324.j and 599.b).
potius: Construe with quam below.
Aedui: First nominative subject of veniant (A.G. 339). See Appendix A.
de suo iure et de legibus: Two prepositional phrases, de with the ablative here means "about, concerning" (*OLD* de 12). suo: Singular, neuter, ablative possessive pronoun used as an adjective modifying iure (A.G. 302). et: The conjunction connects the two prepositional phrases (A.G. 324.a).
ad Caesarem: Prepositional phrase, ad with the accusative here means "to" (*OLD* ad 1). Caesarem: See Appendix A.
disceptatorem: An accusative noun in apposition to the proper noun Caesarem (A.G. 282).
(potius) ... quam: The combination of adverbs means "rather than" (*OLD* potius 1).
Romani: Second nominative subject of veniant (A.G. 339).
ad Aeduos: Prepositional phrase, ad with the accusative here means "to" (*OLD* ad 1). Aeduos: See Appendix A.

(37.6-7) Celeriter adulescentibus et oratione magistratus et praemio deductis, cum se vel principes eius consili fore profiterentur, ratio perficiendi quaerebatur, quod civitatem temere ad suscipien(7)dum bellum adduci posse non confidebant.

ad, *for, in order to, for the purpose of*.

adulescens, -entis, m., *young man, youth*.
celeriter, *quickly, speedily, at once, immediately*.
confido, -fidere, -fisus sum, *believe, be confident*.
cum, *since, seeing that*.
et ... et, *both ... and*.
magistratus, -us, m., *one holding a magistracy, magistrate*.
oratio, -onis, f., *speech, words, address*.

possum, posse, potui, -----, *be able*.
princeps, -ipis, m., *head man, leader, chief, prince*.

quaero, -ere, quaesivi, quaesitus, *look for, seek*.
ratio, -onis, f., *manner, plan, procedure*.

sum, esse, fui, futurus, *be*.

temere, *blindly, rashly*.

adduco, -ducere, -duxi, -ductus, *induce, prevail upon, influence*.
bellum, -i, n., *war, warfare*.
civitas, -tatis, f., *state, nation*.
consilium, -i, n., *plan, design, policy*.
deduco, -ducere, -duxi, -ductus, *seduce, entice*.
is, ea, id, *he, she, it; that, this*.
non, *not*.
perficio, -ficere, -feci, -fectus, *finish, complete, perform, carry out*.
praemium, -i, n., *bribe*.
profiteor, -fiteri, -fessus, *declare openly, avow; offer, promise*.
quod, *because, since, for, as*.
sui, sibi, se, or sese, nom. wanting, *they*, with or without *themselves*.
suscipio, -ere, -cepi, -ceptus, *undertake, assume, begin, enter upon*.
vel, *even, assuredly, certainly*.

Celeriter adulescentibus et oratione magistratus et praemio deductis: Ablative absolute (A.G. 419-20). Celeriter: Adverb (A.G. 214.b and 320-21). adulescentibus: These are Litaviccus, his brothers, and a few select young men. et ... et: The repetition of the conjunction connects the two ablative nouns and means "both ... and" (A.G. 323.e). oratione ... praemio: Two ablatives of means (A.G. 409). praemio: This is the money given to Convictolitavis by the Arverni at 37.1. magistratus: Possessive genitive with oratione (A.G. 343). This is Convictolitavis. deductis: The perfect tense of the participle represents the action as completed at the time indicated by the tense of the main verb (A.G. 489). Kahn here sees "the vacillation of the Aeduans as an example of the fickleness, selfishness, and treachery of the Gauls." (Kahn, 254)
cum ... profiterentur: Causal clause; the relative adverb cum ("since") with the subjunctive forms a clause expressing cause (A.G. 549) (*OLD* cum2 6). profiterentur: The main verb of the subordinate clause (A.G. 278.b). Imperfect subjunctive; the tense of the subjunctive is in secondary sequence and follows the rules for the sequence of tense after quaerebatur (A.G. 482-85). The pronoun ei, with adulescentibus as the antecedent, is understood as the subject (A.G. 271.a).
se ... principes ... fore: Accusative/infinitive construction in indirect discourse after profiterentur (A.G. 577 ff.). se: Plural, masculine, accusative direct reflexive pronoun (A.G. 300.1). The antecedent is ei (adulescentes), the supplied subject of profiterentur (A.G. 299). fore: Future active infinitive of sum (A.G. 170.a). The tense of the infinitive in indirect discourse is relative to that of the verb of saying (A.G. 584). principes: Plural, masculine, accusative predicate noun after fore (A.G. 283-84).
vel: The intensifying particle introduces what might be thought an extreme position and means "even" (*OLD* vel 5).
eius: Either: singular, masculine, genitive demonstrative pronoun used substantively (A.G. 296.2). The antecedent is Convictolitavis

(A.G. 297.e). Possessive genitive with **consili** (A.G. 343). Or: Singular, neuter, genitive demonstrative pronoun used as an adjective modifying **consili** (A.G. 296.1 and a).

consili: Objective genitive with **principes** (A.G. 348.b). The singular genitive of nouns in **-ium** ended, until the Augustan Age, in a single **-i** (A.G. 49.b).

ratio: Nominative subject (A.G. 339).

perficiendi: Singular, neuter, genitive gerund (A.G. 501-02). Objective genitive with **ratio** (A.G. 504).

quaerebatur: The main verb of the main clause (A.G. 278.b).

quod ... confidebant: Causal clause; the conjunction **quod** ("because") takes the indicative when the reason is given on the authority of the writer or speaker (A.G. 540.1). **confidebant**: The main verb of the subordinate clause (A.G. 278.b). The pronoun **ei**, with **adulescentibus** as the antecedent, is understood as the subject (A.G. 271.a).

civitatem ... posse: Accusative/infinitive construction in indirect discourse after **confidebant** (A.G. 577 ff.). **posse**: Present infinitive; the tense of the infinitive in indirect discourse is relative to that of the verb of saying (A.G. 584). The present infinitive **posse** often has a future sense in indirect discourse (A.G 584.b).

temere: Adverb (A.G. 320-21).

ad suscipiendum bellum: The preposition **ad** with the accusative gerundive and noun denotes purpose (A.G. 506). **suscipiendum**: Singular, neuter, accusative gerundive used as an adjective modifying **bellum** denoting necessity, obligation or propriety (A.G. 500.1).

adduci: Complementary infinitive after **posse** (A.G. 456).

non: Adverb, the adverb generally precedes the verb if it belongs to no one word in particular (A.G. 217.e, 320-21, and 599.a).

(37.7) Placuit, uti Litaviccus decem illis milibus quae Caesari ad bellum mitterentur praeficeretur atque ea ducenda curaret, fratresque eius ad Caesarem praecurrerent.

ad, *for the purpose of, to be used for; to.*
bellum, -i, n., *war, warfare.*
curo, -are, -avi, -atus, *take care, provide for, superintend, arrange.*
duco, ducere, duxi, ductus, *lead.*
ille, illae, illud, *that; he, she, it.*
Litaviccus, -i, m., *Litaviccus.*
mitto, mittere, misi, missus, *send.*

praecurro, -currere, -cucurri or **-curri, -----**, *hasten in advance.*

-que, *and.*
uti, *so that.*

atque, *and.*
Caesar, -aris, m., *Caesar.*
decem, *ten.*
frater, -tris, m., *brother.*
is, ea, id, *he, she, it; that, this.*
milia, -um, n., pl., *thousand, thousands.*
placeo, placere, placui, placitus, (imper.), *it is agreed or determined.*
praeficio, -ficere, -feci, -fectus, *place over, place in command of.*
qui, quae, quod, *who, which, what.*

Placuit: The main verb of the main clause (A.G. 278.b). Verb first in the emphatic position (A.G. 589.d). Impersonal use of the verb (A.G. 208.c). The following result clause functions as the subject (A.G. 569.2).

ut ... praeficeretur ... curaret ... praecurrerent: The conjunction **ut** ("so that") with the subjunctive is here a substantive clause of result which is used as the subject of the impersonal verb **Placuit** (A.G. 561.a Note 2 and 569.2). **praeficeretur ... curaret ... praecurrerent**: The main verbs of the subordinate clause (A.G. 278.b). Imperfect subjunctive; the tense of the subjunctives is in secondary sequence and follows the rules for the sequence of tense after **Placuit** (A.G. 482-85).

Litaviccus: Nominative subject of **praeficeretur ... curaret** (A.G. 339). See Appendix A.

decem illis milibus: Dative indirect object of the passive verb **praeficeretur**, verbs which in the active voice take the accusative and dative retain the dative when used in the passive (A.G. 365). See Chapter 34 for the reference. **decem**: Indeclinable cardinal number used as an adjective modifying **milibus** (A.G. 132-35). **illis**: Plural, neuter, dative demonstrative pronoun used as an adjective modifying **milibus** (A.G. 296.1 and a). **milibus**: Ablative plural; in the plural **mille** declines as a neuter noun (A.G. 134.d).

quae ... mitterentur: Relative clause; a clause dependent on a subjunctive clause (**ut ... praeficeretur**) takes the subjunctive when regarded as an integral part of that clause (attraction) (A.G. 303 and 593). **quae**: Plural, neuter, nominative relative pronoun used substantively (A.G. 305). The antecedent is **milibus** (A.G. 297.e). Nominative subject (A.G. 339). **mitterentur**: The main verb of the subordinate clause (A.G. 278.b). Imperfect subjunctive; the tense of the subjunctive is in secondary sequence and follows the rules for the sequence of tense after **Placuit** (A.G. 482-85).

Caesari: Dative indirect object of the passive verb **mitterentur**, verbs which in the active voice take the accusative and dative retain the dative when used in the passive (A.G. 365). See Appendix A.

ad bellum: Prepositional phrase, **ad** with the accusative here denotes purpose meaning "for the purpose of, to be used for" (*OLD* **ad** 44).

atque: The conjunction connects the two verbs in the purpose clause **praeficeretur ... curaret** and means "and" (*OLD* **atque** 12).

ea ducenda: Accusative direct object of **curaret** (A.G. 387). **ea**: Plural, neuter, accusative demonstrative pronoun used substantively (A.G. 296.2). The antecedent is **milibus** (A.G. 297.e). **ducenda**: Plural, neuter, accusative gerundive used as an adjective modifying **ea**, the direct object of **curaret** (A.G. 500.1). A gerundive in agreement with the object of **curaret** expresses purpose (A.G. 500.4).

fratresque: Nominative subject (A.G. 339). "These were trying to win over to the scheme of revolt the Aeduan contingent already serving under Caesar." (Kelsey, 413) **-que**: The enclitic conjunction connects the two verbs in the purpose clause **curaret ... praecurrerent** (A.G. 324.a). The conjunction is used to connect the last member of a series (A.G. 323.c.3).

eius: Singular, masculine, genitive demonstrative pronoun used substantively (A.G. 296.2). The antecedent is **Litaviccus** (A.G. 297.e). Possessive genitive with **fratres** (A.G. 343).

ad Caesarem: Prepositional phrase, **ad** with the accusative here means "to" (*OLD* **ad** 1). **Caesarem**: See Appendix A.

(37.7) **Reliqua qua ratione agi placeat constituunt.**

ago, agere, egi, actus, *do, accomplish, perform.*

placeo, placere, placui, placitus, (imper.), *it seems good.*
ratio, -onis, f., *plan of action, plan, way.*

constituo, -stituere, -stitui, -stitutus, *establish, resolve upon, determine.*
quis, -----, quid, *who? what?* (as adj., **qui, quae, quod**).
reliqua, -orum, n., pl., *the remaining things.*

Reliqua: Plural, neuter, accusative adjective used substantively (A.G. 288). Accusative direct object of **constituunt** (A.G. 387).
qua ... placeat: Indirect question with the subjunctive; the phrase is in apposition to **reliqua**, the object of **constituunt** (A.G. 573-75). **qua**: See below. **placeat**: The main verb of the subordinate clause (A.G. 278.b). Present subjunctive; the tense of the subjunctive is normally in secondary sequence after the historical present **constituunt** (A.G.575). Here it is in primary sequence through *repraesentatio* (A.G. 485.e and 585.b Note). Impersonal use of the verb (A.G. 208.c). The previous infinitive functions as the subject (A.G. 454).
qua ratione: Ablative of manner with a limiting adjective (A.G. 412). **qua**: Singular, feminine, ablative interrogative pronoun used as an adjective modifying **ratione** (A.G. 148.b).
agi: The infinitive functions as the subject of the impersonal verb **placeat** (A.G. 454).
constituunt: The main verb of the main clause (A.G. 278.b). The pronoun **ei**, with **adulescentibus** as the antecedent, is understood as the subject (A.G. 271.a).

(38.1-2) **Litaviccus accepto exercitu, cum milia passuum circiter XXX a Gergovia abesset, convocatis subito militibus lacri(2)mans:**

a(b), *from.*

accipio, -cipere, -cepi, -ceptus, *take to one's self, receive, accept.*
convoco, -are, -avi, -atus, *call together, summon, assemble.*
exercitus, -us, m., *army.*
lacrimo, -are, -avi, -atus, *shed tears, weep.*
miles, -itis, m., *soldier, foot-solider.*
passus, -us, m., *step, pace,* = 4 feet, 10 ¼ inches.
X, in expression of number, = *10.*

absum, -esse, afui, -futurus, *be distant, be absent* or *away from.*
circiter, *about.*
cum, *when, while.*
Gergovia, -ae, f., *Gergovia.*
Litaviccus, -i, m., *Litaviccus.*
milia, -um, n., pl., *thousand, thousands.*
subito, *suddenly, on a sudden.*

Litaviccus ... lacrimans: Nominative subject of **inquit** below (A.G. 339). **Litaviccus**: See Appendix A. **lacrimans**: Present participle used as an adjective modifying **Litaviccus** (A.G. 494).
accepto exercitu: Ablative absolute (A.G. 419-20). **accepto**: The perfect tense of the participle represents the action as completed at the time indicated by the tense of the main verb (A.G. 489). "The 10,000 soldiers intended for Caesar." (Kelsey, 413)
cum ... abesset: Temporal clause; the relative adverb **cum** ("when, while") with the imperfect subjunctive describes the circumstances that accompanied the action of the main verb (A.G. 546). **abesset**: The main verb of the subordinate clause (A.G. 278.b). The pronoun **is**, with **Litaviccus** as the antecedent, is understood as the subject (A.G. 271.a).
milia passuum circiter XXX: Accusative of *extent of space* (A.G. 425). **milia**: Accusative plural; in the plural **mille** declines as a neuter noun (A.G. 134.d). **passuum**: Partitive genitive with **milia** (A.G. 346.a.2). **circiter**: Adverb (A.G. 320-21). **XXX**: Roman numeral used as an adjective modifying **milia** (A.G. 133).
a Gergovia: Ablative of separation with the preposition **a(b)** with the compound verb **abesset** (A.G. 402). **Gergovia**: See Appendix A.
convocatis subito militibus: Ablative absolute (A.G. 419-20). **convocatis**: The perfect tense of the participle represents the action as completed at the time indicated by the tense of the main verb (A.G. 489). **subito**: Adverb (A.G. 320-21).

(38.2) **'quo proficiscimur,' inquit, 'milites?**

inquam, inquis, inquit, *say.*
proficiscor, -ficisci, -fectus, *set out, depart, proceed.*

miles, -itis, m., *soldier, foot-solider.*
quo, *where.*

quo ... pronuntiare ... Quasi ... interficiamus: This speech, classified by Murphy as deliberative, is one of two speeches that are direct discourse throughout (the other is at 7.77). Murphy contends that "The interesting point about both these speeches is the fact that Caesar couldn't have heard either one of them; his information about them came from someone else, presumably deserters or prisoners. Caesar therefore means us to understand that he is not giving the exact words of those speakers; he is, in fact, doing what later historians are to do with his material: i.e., he takes the substance of what was said and puts it into good rhetorical form. It may be that there is no more compelling reason for this than a simple desire for variety; but it may also be that Caesar is dropping a hint to future historians as to how to handle the speeches in his *Commentaries*." (C. Murphy, 122, 125).

quo ... milites?: An example of a rhetorical question in direct speech (A.G. 330).
quo: Interrogative adverb meaning "where" (*OLD* **quo1** 1).

proficiscimur: The main verb of the simple sentence (A.G. 278.1). The personal pronoun **nos** is understood as the subject but is not expressed except for distinction or emphasis (A.G. 295.a). The present tense in *oratio recta* after **inquit** denotes an action as now taking place (A.G. 578). Therefore, the tense in *oratio recta* is the true present and not the historical present (A.G. 465.2).

inquit: The main verb of the main clause (A.G. 278.b). **inquit** is used only in *oratio recta* introducing direct speech (A.G. 206.b and 578). It is always used parenthetically, following one or more words (A.G. 599.c). Siedler counts 5 uses of direct speech with **inquit** in Book 7 (Siedler, 46). The historical present, giving vividness to the narrative, is present in Chapter 38 (A.G. 469). This usage, common in all languages, comes from imagining past events as going on before our eyes (*repraesentatio*) (A.G. 469 Note).

milites: Vocative case (A.G. 38.a).

(38.2-3) Omnis noster equitatus, omnis nobilitas interiit; principes civitatis, Eporedorix et Viridomarus, insimulati proditionis ab Romanis (3) indicta causa interfecti sunt.

ab, *by*.
civitas, -tatis, f., *state, nation*.
equitatus, -us, m., *cavalry*.
indictus, -a, -um, *without the case's having been pleaded, without a hearing*.
intereo, -ire, -ii, -iturus, *perish, be destroyed, die*.
nobilitas, -tatis, f., *nobility, nobles, men of rank*.
omnis, -e, *all of, the whole of*.
proditio, -onis, f., *a betraying, treachery*.
Viridomarus, -i, m., *Viridomarus*.

causa, -ae, f., *case, suit*.
Eporedorix, -igis, m., *Eporedorix*.
et, *and*.
insimulo, -are, -avi, -atus, *charge with, accuse of*.
interficio, -ficere, -feci, -fectus, *slay, kill*.
noster, -tra, -trum, *our, our own*.
princeps, -ipis, m., *head man, leader, chief, prince*.
Romani, -orum, m., pl., *the Romans*.

Omnis noster equitatus, omnis nobilitas: Two nominative subjects (A.G. 339). **Omnis ... omnis**: The repetition of words at the beginning of successive clauses is anaphora (A.G. 641). **noster**: Singular, masculine, nominative possessive pronoun used as an adjective modifying **equitatus** (A.G. 302). Notice the asyndeton between the two nouns (A.G. 323.b).

interiit: The main verb of the simple sentence (A.G. 278.1). Two singular subjects normally take a verb in the plural (A.G. 317). Here they are considered as a single whole and so the verb is singular (A.G. 317.b). Contracted form of **interivit** (A.G. 181.b).

principes ... insimulati: Nominative subject (A.G. 339). **insimulati**: Nominative, perfect, passive, participle used as a predicate, where in English a phrase or a subordinate clause would be more normal (A.G. 496).

civitatis: Partitive genitive with **principes** (A.G. 346.a.1).

Eporedorix et Viridomarus: Two nominative proper nouns in apposition to **principes** (A.G. 282). "Both favorites of Caesar, though afterwards traitors to his cause; Litaviccus was lying." (Kelsey, 413) **Eporedorix**: See Appendix A. **et**: The conjunction connects the two nominative nouns (A.G. 324.a). **Viridomarus**: See Appendix A.

proditionis: Genitive of charge after **insimulati**, a participle of accusing (A.G. 352).

ab Romanis: Ablative of agent with the preposition **ab** after the passive participle **insimulati** or the passive verb **interfecti sunt** (A.G. 405).

indicta causa: Ablative of manner with a limiting adjective (A.G. 412). In legal use, the phrase **indicta causa** means "without a hearing" (*OLD* **indictus** 1.b).

interfecti sunt: The main verb of the simple sentence (A.G. 278.1).

(38.3) Haec ab ipsis cognoscite, qui ex ipsa caede fugerunt: nam ego fratribus atque omnibus meis propinquis interfectis dolore prohibeor quae gesta sunt pronuntiare.'

ab, *from*.
caedes, -is, f., *killing, slaughter, murder, massacre*.
dolor, -oris, m., *grief, distress, vexation*.
ex, *from, out of*.
fugio, fugere, fugi, -----, *escape*.
hic, haec, hoc, *this; he, she, it*.
ipse, -a, -um, *he, they,* with or without *himself, themselves; itself, the very*.
nam, *for*.
prohibeo, -hibere, -hibui, -hibitus, *prevent, hinder*.

propinqui, -orum, m., pl., *relatives, kinfolk*.

atque, *and*.
cognosco, -gnoscere, -gnovi, cognitus, *learn, ascertain*.
ego, mei, *I, me*.
frater, -tris, m., *brother*.
gero, gerere, gessi, gestus, *carry out, perform, do*.
interficio, -ficere, -feci, -fectus, *slay, kill*.
meus, -a, -um, *my*.
omnis, -e, *all*.
pronuntio, -are, -avi, -atus, *tell openly, declare, announce*.
qui, quae, quod, *who, which, what*.

Haec: Plural, neuter, accusative demonstrative pronoun used substantively meaning "these things" (A.G. 296.2). The antecedent is the alleged murder of the cavalry, nobility, and Eporedorix and Viridomarus (A.G. 297.e). Accusative direct object of **cognoscite** (A.G. 387).

ab ipsis: Ablative of source with the preposition **ab** (A.G. 403.1). **ipsis**: Plural, masculine, ablative demonstrative pronoun used substantively (A.G. 296.2 and 298.d). The pronoun is correlative to the following relative clause **qui ... fugerunt** (A.G. 298). The pronoun is here emphatic (A.G. 298.d.1).

cognoscite: The main verb of the main clause (A.G. 278.b). Plural imperative (A.G. 186). Siedler counts 7 uses of the imperative in Book 7 (none by Caesar himself) (Siedler, 46). The personal pronoun **vos** is understood as the subject but is not expressed except for distinction or emphasis (A.G. 295.a).

qui ... fugerunt: Relative clause (A.G. 303). **qui**: Plural, masculine, nominative relative pronoun used substantively (A.G. 305). The antecedent is **ipsis** (A.G. 307). Nominative subject (A.G. 339). **fugerunt**: The main verb of the subordinate clause (A.G. 278.b). **ex ipsa caede**: Ablative of *place from which* with the preposition **ex** (A.G. 426.1). **ipsa**: Singular, feminine, ablative demonstrative pronoun used as an adjective modifying **caede** and meaning "itself" or "The very (A.G. 296.1 and a and 298.c).

nam: Causal conjunction (A.G. 223.a.3).

ego: Singular, masculine, nominative personal pronoun used substantively for emphasis (A.G. 143 and 295.a). Nominative subject (A.G. 339).

fratribus atque omnibus meis propinquis interfectis: Ablative absolute (A.G. 419-20). **atque**: The conjunction connects the two nouns in the ablative absolute **fratribus ... propinquis** and means "and" (*OLD* **atque** 12). **meis**: Plural, masculine, ablative possessive pronoun used as an adjective modifying **propinquis** and understood with **fratribus** (A.G. 302). **propinquis**: Plural, masculine, ablative adjective used substantively (A.G. 288) (*OLD* **propinquus** 4.b). **interfectis**: The perfect tense of the participle represents the action as completed at the time indicated by the tense of the main verb (A.G. 489).

dolore: Ablative of cause without a preposition (A.G. 404).

prohibeor: The main verb of the main clause (A.G. 278.b).

quae gesta sunt: Relative clause (A.G. 303). **quae**: Plural, neuter, nominative relative pronoun used substantively (A.G. 305). The indefinite antecedent is omitted, supply **ea** (A.G. 307.c and 451.3). Nominative subject (A.G. 339). **gesta sunt**: The main verb of the subordinate clause (A.G. 278.b).

pronuntiare: Infinitive without a subject accusative after **prohibeor** (A.G. 558.b Note).

(38.3-5) **Producuntur ei, quos ille edocuerat (4) quae dici vellet, atque eadem quae Litaviccus pronuntia(5)verat multitudini exponunt:**

atque, *and.*	**dico, dicere, dixi, dictus**, *say.*
edoceo, -docere, -docui, -doctus, *teach carefully, instruct, inform, tell.*	**expono, -ponere, -posui, -positus**, *set forth, state, explain.*
idem, eadem, idem, *the same.*	**ille, illae, illud**, *that; he, she, it.*
is, ea, id, m., *he, she, it; that, this.*	**Litaviccus, -i**, m., *Litaviccus.*
multitudo, -inis, f., *multitude, crowd.*	**produco, -ducere, -duxi, -ductus**, *bring out, lead forth.*
pronuntio, -are, -avi, -atus, *tell openly, declare, announce.*	**qui, quae, quod**, *who, which, what.*
quis, -----, quid, *who? what?*	**volo, velle, volui**, *wish, desire, mean, intend.*

Producuntur: The main verb of the coordinate clause **Producuntur ... vellet** (A.G. 278.a). Verb first in the emphatic position. Here it marks the end of the direct discourse (A.G. 589.d). The direct speech is interrupted until 38.7. "A ruse like that of Vercingetorix, 7.20.8-12." (Kelsey, 413)

ei: Plural, masculine, nominative demonstrative pronoun used substantively (A.G. 296.2). The pronoun is correlative to the relative clause **quos ... edocuerat** (A.G. 297.d). Nominative subject of **Producuntur ... exponunt** (A.G. 339).

quos ... edocuerat: Relative clause (A.G. 303). **quos**: Plural, masculine, accusative relative pronoun used substantively (A.G. 305). The antecedent is **ei** (A.G. 307). Accusative direct object of **edocuerat** (A.G. 387 and 396). **edocuerat**: The main verb of the subordinate clause (A.G. 278.b). The pluperfect tense of the verb denotes an action completed in past time (A.G. 477).

ille: Singular, masculine, nominative demonstrative pronoun used substantively (A.G. 296.2). The antecedent is **Litaviccus** (A.G. 297.e). Nominative subject (A.G. 339). The pronoun marks a change in subject to one previously mentioned (**Litaviccus**) (A.G. 601.d).

quae ... vellet: Indirect question with the subjunctive; the phrase is the object of **edocuerat** (A.G. 573-75). This phrase is the secondary object of the verb **edocuerat** (**quos** is the primary object) (A.G. 396). **quae**: See below. **vellet**: The main verb of the subordinate clause (A.G. 278.b). Imperfect subjunctive; the tense of the subjunctive is in secondary sequence and follows the rules for the sequence of tense for indirect questions after **edocuerat** (A.G. 575). The pronoun **is**, with **ille** (**Litaviccus**) as the antecedent, is understood as the subject (A.G. 271.a).

quae dici: Subject accusative with the infinitive after **vellet**. The construction is equivalent to a substantive clause of purpose (A.G. 563.b.2). **quae**: Plural, neuter, accusative interrogative pronoun used substantively meaning "what things" (A.G. 148).

atque: The conjunction connects the two main verbs **Producuntur ... exponunt** and means "and" (A.G. 324.a).

eadem: Plural, neuter, accusative demonstrative pronoun used substantively meaning "The same things (A.G. 296.2). The antecedent is the alleged murder of the cavalry, nobility, and Eporedorix and Viridomarus (A.G. 297.e). Accusative direct object of the transitive verb **exponunt** (A.G. 387).

quae ... pronuntiaverat: Relative clause (A.G. 303). **quae**: Plural, neuter, accusative relative pronoun used substantively (A.G. 305). The antecedent is **eadem** (A.G. 307). Accusative direct object of **pronuntiaverat** (A.G. 387). **pronuntiaverat**: The main verb of the subordinate clause (A.G. 278.b). The pluperfect tense of the verb denotes an action completed in past time (A.G. 477).

Litaviccus: Nominative subject (A.G. 339). See Appendix A.

multitudini: Dative indirect object of the transitive verb **exponunt** (A.G. 362).

exponunt: The main verb of the coordinate clause **eadem ... exponunt** (A.G. 278.a).

(38.5-6) **[multos] equites Aeduorum interfectos, quod collocuti cum Arvernis dicerentur; ipsos se inter multitudinem militum occultasse, atque ex media caede (6) fugisse.**

Aedui, -orum, m., pl., *the Aedui.*	**Arverni, -orum**, m., pl., *the Arverni.*

atque, *and.*
colloquor, -loqui, -locutus, *talk with,* hold a conference, hold a parley.
dico, dicere, dixi, dictus, *say.*
ex, *from, out of.*
inter, *among.*
ipse, -a, -um, *he, they,* with or without *himself, themselves.*
miles, -itis, m., *soldier, foot-solider.*
multus, -a, -um, *many.*
quod, *because, since, for, as.*

caedes, -is, f., *killing, slaughter, murder, massacre.*
cum, *with.*
eques, -itis, m., *rider, horseman, cavalryman, trooper.*
fugio, fugere, fugi, -----, *escape.*
interficio, -ficere, -feci, -fectus, *slay, kill.*
medius, -a, -um, *in the middle, midst, middle, mid-.*
multitudo, -inis, f., *great number, multitude, crowd.*
occulto, -are, -avi, -atus, *hide, conceal, keep secret.*
sui, sibi, se, or sese, nom. wanting, *themselves.*

[multos] equites ... interfectos (esse): Accusative/infinitive construction in indirect discourse after exponunt (A.G. 577 ff.).
interfectos (esse): Supply esse to form the perfect, passive, infinitive (A.G.188). The tense of the infinitive in indirect discourse is relative to that of the verb of saying (A.G. 584).
Aeduorum: Possessive genitive with equites (A.G. 343). See Appendix A.
quod ... dicerentur: Causal clause; the conjunction quod ("because") normally takes the indicative when the reason is given on the authority of the writer or speaker (A.G. 540.1). Here quod takes the subjunctive as a subordinate clause in indirect discourse (A.G. 580). dicerentur: The main verb of the subordinate clause (A.G. 278.b). Imperfect subjunctive; the tense of the subjunctive is in secondary sequence and follows the rules for the sequence of tense after the historical present exponunt (A.G. 482-85, esp. 485.e). The pronoun ei, with equites as the antecedent, is understood as the subject (A.G. 271.a).
collocuti (esse): Nominative/infinitive (personal construction) in indirect discourse after the passive verb of saying dicerentur (A.G. 577 ff. and 582). collocuti: Nominative, perfect, deponent participle agreeing in case with the subject of dicerentur rather than the more normal accusative in indirect discourse (A.G. 582). Supply esse as the infinitive.
cum Arvernis: Ablative of accompaniment with the preposition cum (A.G. 413). Arvernis: See Appendix A.
ipsos ... occultasse: Accusative/infinitive construction in indirect discourse after exponunt (A.G. 577 ff.). ipsos: Plural, masculine, accusative demonstrative pronoun used substantively (A.G. 298.d). The pronoun is here emphatic (A.G. 298.d.1). The pronoun is here used in place of the direct pronoun se in order to avoid confusion (A.G. 298.e and 300.b). occultasse: Perfect infinitive; the tense of the infinitive in indirect discourse is relative to that of the verb of saying (A.G. 584). A contracted form of occultavisse (A.G. 181.a).
se: Plural, masculine, accusative direct reflexive pronoun (A.G. 300.1). The antecedent is ipsos, the subject of occultasse (A.G. 299). Accusative direct object of the infinitive occultasse (A.G. 387 and 451.3).
inter multitudinem militum: Prepositional phrase, inter with the accusative here means "among" (*OLD* inter1 1). militum: Partitive genitive with multitudinem (A.G. 346.a.1).
atque: The conjunction connects the two infinitives occultasse ... fugisse and means "and" (*OLD* atque 12).
ex media caede: Ablative of *place from which* with the preposition ex (A.G. 426.1). media: The adjective designates not what object, but what part of it is meant (A.G. 293).
(ipsos) fugisse: Accusative/infinitive construction in indirect discourse after exponunt (A.G. 577 ff.). Carry down ipsos as the accusative subject. fugisse: Perfect infinitive; the tense of the infinitive in indirect discourse is relative to that of the verb of saying (A.G. 584).

(38.6-7) Conclamant Aedui et Litaviccum obsecrant ut (7) sibi consulat.

Aedui, -orum, m., pl., *the Aedui.*

consulo, -sulere, -sului, -sultus, *have regard for, look out for.*
Litaviccus, -i, m., *Litaviccus.*
sui, sibi, se, or sese, nom. wanting, *them,* with or without *-selves.*

conclamo, -are, -avi, -atus, *cry out loud together, shout, cry out.*
et, *and.*
obsecro, -are, -avi, -atus, *beseech, implore, beg.*
ut, *so that.*

Conclamant: The main verb of the coordinate clause Conclamant Aedui (A.G. 278.a). Verb first in the emphatic position. Here it marks the end of the indirect discourse (A.G. 589.d).
Aedui: Nominative subject of Conclamant ... obsecrant (A.G. 339). See Appendix A.
et: The conjunction connects the two main verbs Conclamant ... obsecrant (A.G. 324.a).
Litaviccum: Accusative direct object of obsecrant (A.G. 387). See Appendix A.
obsecrant: The main verb of the coordinate clause Litaviccum ... consulat (A.G. 278.a).
ut ... consulat: The conjunction ut ("so that") with the subjunctive is here a substantive clause of purpose which is used as the object of obsecrant denoting an action directed toward the future (A.G. 563). consulat: The main verb of the subordinate clause (A.G. 278.b). Present subjunctive; the tense of the subjunctive is normally in secondary sequence after the historical present obsecrant (A.G. 482-85). Here it is in primary sequence through *repraesentatio* (A.G. 485.e and 585.b Note). The pronoun is, with Litaviccum as the antecedent, is understood as the subject (A.G. 271.a).
sibi: Plural, masculine, dative indirect reflexive pronoun (A.G. 300.2). The antecedent is Aedui, the subject of obsecrant (A.G. 299). Dative indirect object of the intransitive use of the verb consulat (A.G. 367.b).

(38.7-8) 'Quasi vero,' inquit ille, 'consilii sit res, ac non necesse sit nobis Gergoviam contendere et cum (8) Arvernis nosmet coniungere.

ac, *and.*

Arverni, -orum, m., pl., *the Arverni.*

coniungo, -iungere, -iunxi, -iunctus, *join together, unite, join.*
contendo, -tendere, -tendi, -tentus, *hasten, make haste, push forward.*
egomet, nosmet, *myself, ourselves.*
Gergovia, -ae, f., *Gergovia.*
inquam, inquis, inquit, *say.*
non, *not.*
quasi, *as if.*
sum, esse, fui, futurus, *be.*

consilium, -i, n., *consultation, deliberation.*
cum, *with.*
et, *and.*
ille, illae, illud, *that; he, she, it.*
necesse, n., *necessary, unavoidable, inevitable.*
nos, nostrum, *we, us.*
res, rei, f., *matter, affair.*
vero, *in truth, in fact, truly, certainly.*

Direct speech is again resumed through 38.9.

Quasi ... sit ... necesse sit: A clause of comparison (conclusion omitted); the clause is introduced by the comparative particle **quasi** ("as if") and takes the present subjunctive (A.G. 524). **sit ... sit**: The main verbs of the subordinate clause (A.G. 278.b). **necesse sit**: Impersonal verb, the following infinitive phrases form the subject (A.G. 208.c). **necesse**: Singular, neuter, nominative adjective used in the predicate position after **sit** as an indeclinable noun (A.G. 103.a Note 1 and 283-84).
vero: Adverb, postpositive position (A.G. 320-21 and 599.b).
inquit: The main verb of the main clause (A.G. 278.b). The verb **inquit** is used only in *oratio recta* introducing direct speech (A.G. 206.b and 578). It is always used parenthetically, following one or more words (A.G. 599.c). Siedler counts 5 uses of direct speech with **inquit** in Book 7 (Siedler, 46).
ille: Singular, masculine, nominative demonstrative pronoun used substantively (A.G. 296.2). The antecedent is **Litaviccum** (A.G. 297.e). Nominative subject of **inquit** (A.G. 339). The pronoun marks a change in subject to one previously mentioned (**Litaviccum**) (A.G. 601.d).
consili: Possessive genitive (predicate genitive); the possessive genitive often stands in the predicate, connected to its noun (**res**) by a verb (**sit**) (A.G. 343.b). The singular genitive of nouns in **-ium** ended, until the Augustan Age, in a single **-i** (A.G. 49.b).
res: Nominative subject (A.G. 339).
ac: The conjunction connects the two verbs in the clause of comparison **sit ... sit** and means "and" (*OLD atque* 12).
non: Adverb modifying **necesse**, the negative precedes the word it especially effects (A.G. 217.e, 320-21, and 599.a).
nobis: Plural, masculine, dative personal pronoun used substantively (A.G. 143 and 295). Dative indirect object of the phrase **necesse sit** (A.G. 366.a).
Gergoviam contendere: The infinitive phrase functions as the subject of the impersonal verb **necesse sit** (A.G. 454).
Gergoviam: Accusative of *place to which* without a preposition (city name) (A.G. 427.2). See Appendix A.
et: The conjunction connects the two infinitives **contendere ... coniungere** (A.G. 324.a).
cum Arvernis nosmet coniungere: The infinitive phrase functions as the subject of the impersonal verb **necesse sit** (A.G. 454).
cum Arvernis: Ablative of accompaniment with the preposition **cum** (A.G. 413). **Arvernis**: See Appendix A.
nosmet: Plural, masculine, accusative reflexive pronoun (A.G. 144.a). Accusative direct object of the infinitive **coniungere** (A.G. 387 and 451.3). **-met**: The enclitic ending on reflexive pronouns makes an emphatic form (A.G. 144 Note 1).

(38.8) An dubitamus quin nefario facinore admisso Romani iam ad nos interficiendos concurrant?

ad, *in order to, for the purpose of.*
an, *can it really be that ..., or indeed.*

dubito, -are, -avi, -atus, *be uncertain, doubt.*
iam, *already, now.*
nefarius, -a, -um, *execrable, atrocious, abominable, nefarious.*
quin, *that, but that.*

admitto, -mittere, -misi, -missus, *commit.*
concurro, -currere, -cucurri or -curri, -cursus, *rush, hurry, come together.*
facinus, -oris, n., *misdeed, crime.*
interficio, -ficere, -feci, -fectus, *slay, kill.*
nos, nostrum, *we, us.*
Romani, -orum, m., pl., *the Romans.*

An: Particle, introduces direct questions usually with the notion of surprise, indignation, etc. meaning "can it really be that ..." (*OLD an* 1).
dubitamus: The main verb of the main clause (A.G. 278.b). The personal pronoun **nos** is understood as the subject but is not expressed except for distinction or emphasis (A.G. 295.a). The present tense in *oratio recta* after **inquit** denotes an action as now taking place (A.G. 578). Therefore, the tense in *oratio recta* is the true present and not the historical present (A.G. 465.2).
quin ... concurrant: Subordinate clause; the conjunction **quin** ("that") with the subjunctive is used after **dubitamus** (A.G. 278.b and 558.a). **concurrant**: The main verb of the subordinate clause (A.G. 278.b). Present subjunctive; the tense of the subjunctive is in primary sequence and follows the rules for the sequence of tense after **dubitamus** (A.G. 482-85).
nefario facinore admisso: Ablative absolute (A.G. 419-20). **admisso**: The perfect tense of the participle represents the action as completed at the time indicated by the tense of the main verb (A.G. 489).
Romani: Nominative subject (A.G. 339).
iam: Adverb (A.G. 215.6, 217.b and 320-21).
ad nos interficiendos: The preposition **ad** with the accusative pronoun and gerundive denotes purpose (A.G. 506). **nos**: Plural, masculine, accusative personal pronoun used substantively (A.G. 142-43). **interficiendos**: Plural, masculine, accusative gerundive used as an adjective modifying **nos** denoting necessity, obligation or propriety (A.G. 500.1).

(38.8-9) Proinde, si quid in nobis animi est, persequamur eorum mortem qui indignissime interierunt, atque hos (9) latrones

interficiamus.'

animus, -i, m., *courage, spirit, temper, resolution.*
hic, haec, hoc, *this; he, she, it.*
indigne, sup. -issime, *unworthily, shamefully.*
interficio, -ficere, -feci, -fectus, *slay, kill.*
latro, -onis, m., *freebooter, robber.*
nos, nostrum, *we, us.*
proinde, *hence, therefore, and so.*
quis, -----, quid, *anyone, anything.*
sum, esse, fui, futurus, *be.*

atque, *and.*
in, *in.*
intereo, -ire, -ii, -iturus, *perish, be destroyed, die.*
is, ea, id, *he, she, it; that, this.*
mors, mortis, f., *death.*
persequor, -sequi, -secutus, *avenge.*
qui, quae, quod, *who, which, what.*
si, *if.*

Proinde: Adverb, when used in exhortations it means "so then, accordingly" (*OLD* **proinde** 3.a).

si ... est, persequamur ... interficiamus: A simple, present time conditional statement (present indicative in the protasis, two hortatory subjunctives in the apodosis) (A.G. 514.a.1).

si ... est: The conjunction **si** ("if") with the present indicative forms the protasis of the conditional statement (A.G. 514.a.1). **est**: The main verb of the subordinate clause (A.G. 278.b).

quid: Singular, neuter, nominative indefinite pronoun used substantively (A.G. 149). The indefinite **quis, -----, quid** is used after **si** (A.G. 310.a). Nominative subject (A.G. 339).

in nobis: Prepositional phrase, **in** with the ablative here means "in" (expressing an abstract location) (*OLD* **in** 26). **nobis**: Plural, masculine, ablative personal pronoun used substantively (A.G. 143 and 295). The prepositional phrase is in the predicate position after **est** (A.G. 272).

animi: Partitive genitive with **quid** (A.G. 346.a.3).

persequamur ... interficiamus: The main verbs of the main clause (A.G. 278.b). Hortatory subjunctives; the two verbs are the main verbs of the apodosis of the conditional statement (A.G. 439 and 515.a). The personal pronoun **nos** is understood as the subject of both verbs but is not expressed except for distinction or emphasis (A.G. 295.a).

eorum: Plural, masculine, genitive demonstrative pronoun used substantively (A.G. 296.2). The pronoun is correlative to the relative clause **qui ... interierunt** (A.G. 297.d). Possessive genitive with **mortem** (A.G. 343).

mortem: Accusative direct object of **persequamur** (A.G. 387).

qui ... interierunt: Relative clause (A.G. 303). **qui**: Plural, masculine, nominative relative pronoun used substantively (A.G. 305). The antecedent is **eorum** (A.G. 307). Nominative subject (A.G. 339). **interierunt**: The main verb of the subordinate clause (A.G. 278.b). Contracted form of **interiverunt** (A.G. 181.b).

indignissime: Superlative adverb (A.G. 218 and 320-21).

atque: The conjunction connects the two hortatory subjunctives in the apodosis and means "and" (*OLD* **atque** 12).

hos latrones: Accusative direct object of **interficiamus** (A.G. 387). **hos**: Plural, masculine, accusative demonstrative pronoun used as an adjective modifying **latrones** (A.G. 296.1 and a). He can be imagined as pointing at them.

(38.9) Ostendit civis Romanos, qui eius praesidi fiducia una erant; magnum numerum frumenti commeatusque diripit, ipsos crudeliter excruciatos interficit.

civis, -is, m., *citizen.*
crudeliter, *cruelly, with cruelty, fiercely.*
excrucio, -are, -avi, -atus, *torment, torture.*
frumentum, -i, n., *grain.*
ipse, -a, -um, *he, they.*
magnus, -a, -um, *great, large.*
ostendo, -tendere, -tendi, -tentus, *show, display.*
-que, *and.*
Romanus, -a, -um, *Roman.*
una, *in the same place, together, in company.*

commeatus, -us, m., *supplies, provisions.*
diripio, -ripere, -ripui, -reptus, *plunder, pillage.*
fiducia, -ae, f., *trust, reliance, confidence, assurance.*
interficio, -ficere, -feci, -fectus, *slay, kill.*
is, ea, id, *he, she, it; that, this.*
numerus, -i, m., *amount.*
praesidium, -i, n., *protection.*
qui, quae, quod, *who, which, what.*
sum, esse, fui, futurus, *be.*

Ostendit ... diripit ... interficit ... (dimittit ... permovit ... hortatur): Note the asyndeton construction with the main verbs (A.G. 323.b). The pronoun **is**, with **ille** (**Litaviccus**) as the antecedent, is understood as the subject of all six verbs (A.G. 271.a).

Ostendit: The main verb of the main clause (A.G. 278.b). Verb first in the emphatic position. Here it marks the end of the direct discourse (A.G. 589.d).

civis Romanos: Accusative direct object of **Ostendit** (A.G. 387). "These, relying on the protection of the Aedui, were probably conveying to Caesar the supplies mentioned in the next line." (Kelsey, 413) **civis**: Accusative plural noun; **-is** for **-es** is the regular form in i-stem nouns (A.G. 65-7 and 74.c).

qui ... erant: Relative clause (A.G. 303). **qui**: Plural, masculine, nominative relative pronoun used substantively (A.G. 305). The antecedent is **civis** (A.G. 307). Nominative subject (A.G. 339). **erant**: The main verb of the subordinate clause (A.G. 278.b).

eius: Singular, masculine, genitive demonstrative pronoun used substantively (A.G. 296.2). The antecedent is **ille** (**Litaviccus**) (A.G. 297.e). Possessive genitive with **praesidi** (A.G. 343).

praesidi fiducia: Ablative of quality (descriptive ablative) with a genitive modifier (A.G. 415). **praesidi**: Objective genitive with **fiducia** (A.G. 348.b). The singular genitive of nouns in **-ium** ended, until the Augustan Age, in a single **-i** (A.G. 49.b).

una: Adverb (A.G. 320-21). The adverb is in the predicate position after **erant** (A.G. 272).

magnum numerum: Accusative direct object of **diripit** (A.G. 387).

frumenti commeatusque: Two partitive genitives with **numerum** (A.G. 346.a.1). **-que**: The enclitic conjunction connects the two genitive nouns (A.G. 324.a).

diripit: The main verb of the simple sentence (A.G. 278.1).

ipsos ... excruciatos: Accusative direct object of **interficit** (A.G. 387). **ipsos**: Plural, masculine, accusative demonstrative pronoun used substantively (A.G. 296.2 and 298.d). The antecedent is **civis Romanos** (A.G. 298). The pronoun is here emphatic (A.G. 298.d.1). **excruciatos**: Accusative, perfect, passive, participle used as a predicate, where in English a phrase or a subordinate clause would be more normal (A.G. 496).

crudeliter: Adverb (A.G. 214.b and 320-21).

interficit: The main verb of the simple sentence (A.G. 278.1).

(38.10) **(10) Nuntios tota civitate Aeduorum dimittit, eodem mendacio de caede equitum et principum permovet; hortatur ut simili ratione atque ipse fecerit suas iniurias persequantur.**

Aedui, -orum, m., pl., *the Aedui.*
caedes, -is, f., *killing, slaughter, murder, massacre.*
de, *about, concerning.*

eques, -itis, m., *rider, horseman, cavalryman, trooper.*
facio, facere, feci, factus, *do.*

idem, eadem, idem, *the same.*
ipse, -a, -um, *he, they*, with or without *himself, themselves.*
nuntius, -i, m., *message, tidings.*

persequor, -sequi, -secutus, *avenge, proceed against.*
ratio, -onis, f., *manner, method, fashion, way.*
suus, -a, -um, *their*, with or without *own.*
ut, *so that.*

atque, *as.*
civitas, -tatis, f., *state, nation.*
dimitto, -mittere, -misi, -missus, *send in different directions, send about.*
et, *and.*
hortor, -ari, -atus, *urge, encourage, exhort, incite, press.*
iniuria, -ae, f., *wrong, outrage, injustice, injury.*
mendacium, -i, n., *lie, falsehood.*
permoveo, -movere, -movi, -motus, *deeply move, alarm, influence.*
princeps, -ipis, m., *head man, leader, chief, prince.*
similis, -e, *like, similar.*
totus, -a, -um, *the whole, all, all the, entire.*

Nuntios: Accusative direct object of **dimittit** (A.G. 387).

tota civitate: Ablative of *place where* without a preposition, here meaning "throughout" (in the whole of) (A.G. 429.2).

Aeduorum: Possessive genitive with **civitate** (A.G. 343). See Appendix A.

dimittit: The main verb of the coordinate clause **Nuntios ... dimittit** (A.G. 278.a).

eodem mendacio: Ablative of means (A.G. 409). **eodem**: Singular, neuter, ablative demonstrative pronoun used as an adjective modifying **mendacio** (A.G. 296.1 and a).

de caede equitum et principum: Prepositional phrases, **de** with the ablative here means "about, concerning" (*OLD* de 12). **equitum et principum**: Two possessive genitives with **caede** (A.G. 343). **et**: The conjunction connects the two genitive nouns (A.G. 324.a).

permovit: The main verb of the coordinate clause **eodem ... pervenit** (A.G. 278.a). The pronoun **eos**, with **Aeduorum** as the antecedent, is understood as the accusative direct object.

hortatur: The main verb of the main clause (A.G. 278.b).

ut ... persequantur: The conjunction **ut** ("so that") with the subjunctive forms a substantive clause of purpose which is used as the object of the verb **hortatur** denoting an action directed toward the future (A.G. 563). **persequantur**: The main verb of the subordinate clause (A.G. 278.b). Present subjunctive; the tense of the subjunctive is normally in secondary sequence after the historical present **hortatur** (A.G. 482-85). Here it is in primary sequence through *repraesentatio* (A.G. 485.e and 585.b Note). The pronoun **ei**, with **Aeduorum** as the antecedent, is understood as the subject (A.G. 271.a).

simili ratione: Ablative of manner with a limiting adjective (A.G. 412.b)

(simili) ... atque ... fecerit: Subordinate clause; a clause dependent on a subjunctive clause (**ut ... persequantur**) takes the subjunctive when regarded as an integral part of that clause (attraction) (A.G. 593). **(simili) ... atque**: An adjective of likeness (**simili**) is followed by the conjunction **atque** meaning "as" (A.G. 384 Note 2). **fecerit**: The main verb of the subordinate clause (A.G. 278.b). Perfect subjunctive; the tense of the subjunctive is normally in secondary sequence after the historical present **hortatur** (A.G. 482-85). Here it is in primary sequence through *repraesentatio* (A.G. 485.e and 585.b Note).

ipse: Singular, masculine, nominative demonstrative pronoun used substantively (A.G. 296.2 and 298.d). The antecedent is **ille** (**Litaviccus**) (A.G. 298). Nominative subject (A.G. 339). The pronoun is here emphatic (A.G. 298.d.1).

suas iniurias: Accusative direct object of **persequantur** (A.G. 387). **suas**: Plural, feminine, accusative possessive pronoun used as an adjective modifying **iniurias** (A.G. 302).

(39.1-2) **Eporedorix Aeduus, summo loco natus adulescens et summae domi potentiae, et una Viridomarus, pari aetate et gratia sed genere dispari, quem Caesar ab Diviciaco sibi traditum ex humili loco ad summam dignitatem perduxerat, in equitum numero convenerant nominatim ab (2) eo evocati.**

ab, *by.*
adulescens, -entis, m., *young man, youth.*

ad, *to.*
Aeduus, -i, m., *an Aeduan.*

aetas, -tatis, f., *age.*
convenio, -venire, -veni, -ventus, *come together, gather, meet.*
dispar, -paris, *unequal, unlike, different.*
domus, -us, f., *house, home.*
eques, -itis, m., *rider, horseman, cavalryman, trooper.*
evoco, -are, -avi, -atus, *call out, call forth, call, summon.*
genus, -oris, n., *birth, descent, family.*
humilis, -e, *mean, poor, humble, insignificant.*
is, ea, id, *he, she, it; that, this.*
nascor, nasci, natus, *be born.*
numerus, -i, m., *number, company.*
perduco, -ducere, -duxi, -ductus, *lead, bring, conduct, raise.*
qui, quae, quod, *who, which, what.*
sui, sibi, se, or sese, nom. wanting, *himself.*
trado, -dere, -didi, -ditus, *commend, intrust.*
Viridomarus, -i, m., *Viridomarus.*

Caesar, -aris, m., *Caesar.*
dignitas, -tatis, f., *greatness, rank, reputation.*
Diviciacus, -i, m., *Diviciacus.*
Eporedorix, -igis, m., *Eporedorix*
et, *and.*
ex, *from, out of.*
gratia, -ae, f., *influence.*
in, *in.*
locus, -i, m., *place, position, rank.*
nominatim, *by name.*
par, paris, *like, similar, same, equal.*
potentia, -ae, f., *might, power, influence.*
sed, *but.*
summus, -a, -um, *highest, greatest, very great.*
una, *together with.*

Eporedorix: First nominative subject of **convenerant** (A.G. 339). See Appendix A.
Aeduus: A nominative noun in apposition to the proper noun **Eporedorix** (A.G. 282).
summo loco: Ablative of source after the participle **natus** (A.G. 403.a). **summo:** Defective superlative adjective (A.G. 130.b).
natus: Nominative, perfect, deponent, participle used as a predicate modifying **adulescens**, where in English a phrase or a subordinate clause would be more normal (A.G. 496).
adulescens: A nominative noun in apposition to the proper noun **Eporedorix** (A.G. 282).
et: The conjunction connects the nominative phrase **summo ... natus** with the following genitive phrase **summae ... potentiae**, both modifying **adulescens** (A.G. 324.a).
summae ... potentiae: Genitive of quality modifying **adulescens** (A.G. 345). **summae:** Defective superlative adjective (A.G. 130.b).
domi: Locative case of the noun **domus, -us,** f. (A.G. 427.3).
et: The conjunction connects the two nominative nouns **Eporedorix ... Viridomarus** (A.G. 324.a).
una: Adverb (A.G. 320-21).
Viridomarus: Second nominative subject of **convenerant** (A.G. 339). See Appendix A.
pari aetate et gratia sed genere dispari: Three ablatives of quality (descriptive ablative) with adjective modifiers (A.G. 415). **pari:** The adjective should be construed with both ablative nouns **aetate ... gratia** but agrees in number with only the nearest noun (A.G. 286.a). **et:** The conjunction connects the first two ablative nouns **aetate ... gratia** (A.G. 324.a). **sed:** Coordinate conjunction connecting the third ablative noun **genere** (A.G. 324.d).
quem ... perduxerat: Relative clause (A.G. 303). **quem:** See below. **perduxerat:** The main verb of the subordinate clause (A.G. 278.b). The pluperfect tense of the verb denotes an action completed in past time (A.G. 477).
quem ... traditum: Accusative direct object of **perduxerat** (A.G. 387). **quem:** Singular, masculine, accusative relative pronoun used substantively (A.G. 305). The antecedent is **Viridomarus** (A.G. 307). **traditum:** Accusative, perfect, passive, participle used as a predicate, where in English a phrase or a subordinate clause would be more normal (A.G. 496).
Caesar: Nominative subject (A.G. 339). See Appendix A.
ab Diviciaco: Ablative of agent with the preposition **ab** after the passive participle **traditum** (A.G. 405). **Diviciaco:** See Appendix A.
sibi: Singular, masculine, dative direct reflexive pronoun (A.G. 300.1). The antecedent is **Caesar**, the subject of **perduxerat** (A.G. 299). Dative indirect object of the passive participle **traditum**, verbs which in the active voice take the accusative and dative retain the dative when used in the passive (A.G. 365).
ex humili loco: Ablative of source with the preposition **ex** (A.G. 403.1).
ad summam dignitatem: Prepositional phrase; ad with the accusative here means "to" (expressing progress towards or attainment of a condition, situation, etc.) (*OLD* ad 5). **summam:** Defective superlative adjective (A.G. 130.b).
in equitum numero: Prepositional phrase, in with the ablative here means "in" (expressing an abstract location) (*OLD* in 26).
equitum: Partitive genitive with **numero** (A.G. 346.a.1).
convenerant: The main verb of the main clause (A.G. 278.b). Plural verb with two singular subjects (A.G. 317). Although the pluperfect tense is normally used in subordinate clauses, its use as a main verb is frequent. Here the pluperfect denotes an action completed in past time (A.G. 477).
nominatim: Adverb (A.G. 320-21).
ab eo: Ablative of agent with the preposition **ab** after the passive participle **evocati** (A.G. 405). **eo:** Singular, masculine, ablative demonstrative pronoun used substantively (A.G. 296.2). The antecedent is **Caesar** (A.G. 297.e).
evocati: Nominative, perfect, passive, participle used as a predicate, where in English a phrase or a subordinate clause would be more normal (A.G. 496). Here the plural participle modifies the two singular nouns **Eporedorix ... Viridomarus** (A.G. 286.a).

(39.2-3) **His erat inter se de principatu contentio, et in illa magistratuum controversia alter pro Convictolitavi, (3) alter pro Coto summis opibus pugnaverant.**

alter ... alter, -i, m., *the former ... the latter.*

controversia, -ae, f., *dispute, debate, controversy, quarrel.*

contentio, -onis, f., *struggle, fight, contest, dispute, controversy.*

Convictolitavis, -is, m., *Convictolitavis.*

Cotus, -i, m., *Cotus.*
et, *and.*
ille, illae, illud, *that; he, she, it.*
inter, *among.*

opes, -um, f., pl., *resources, means, wealth, influence, strength.*

pro, *on behalf of.*
sui, sibi, se, or sese, nom. wanting, *each other, one another.*
summus, -a, -um, *highest, greatest, very great.*

de, *about, concerning.*
hic, haec, hoc, *this; he, she, it.*
in, *in.*
magistratus, -us, m., *one holding a magistracy, magistrate.*
principatus, -us, m., *chief authority, headship, leadership.*
pugno, -are, -avi, -atus, *fight, combat, engage.*
sum, esse, fui, futurus, *be.*

His: Plural, masculine, dative demonstrative pronoun used substantively (A.G. 296.2). The antecedent is **Eporedorix ... Viridomarus** (A.G. 297.e). Dative of possession after **erat** (A.G. 373).
erat: The main verb of the coordinate clause **His ... contentio** (A.G. 278.a).
inter se: Prepositional phrase, **inter** with the accusative reciprocal pronoun here means "with or to each other" (*OLD* **inter**1 15). **se**: Plural, masculine, accusative pronoun used reciprocally and meaning "each other, one another" (A.G. 300.1) (*OLD* **se** 8). The antecedent is **His**, the subject of **erant** (A.G. 299). The reciprocal pronoun is often without reference to the grammatical subject (*OLD* **se** 8).
de principatu: Prepositional phrases, **de** with the ablative here means "about, concerning" (*OLD* **de** 12).
contentio: Nominative subject (A.G. 339).
et: The conjunction connects the two main verbs **erat ... pugnaverant** (A.G. 324.a).
in illa magistratuum controversia: Prepositional phrase, **in** with the ablative here means "during" (*OLD* **in** 35.a). **illa**: Singular, feminine, ablative demonstrative pronoun used as an adjective modifying **controversia** (A.G. 296.1 and a). For the reference see Chapter 33. **magistratuum**: Objective genitive with **controversia** (A.G. 348). These magistrates were **Convictolitavis** and **Cotus**.
alter ... alter: Two singular, masculine, nominative pronouns used substantively (A.G. 286.2). The antecedents are **Eporedorix ... Viridomarus** (A.G. 297.e). The pronouns, when used correlatively, mean "the former ... the latter" (*OLD* **alter**2 5). Nominative subjects (A.G. 339).
pro Convictolitavi: Prepositional phrase, **pro** with the ablative here means "on behalf of" (*OLD* **pro**1 3). **Convictolitavi**: See Appendix A.
pro Coto: Prepositional phrase, **pro** with the ablative here means "on behalf of" (*OLD* **pro**1 3). **Coto**: See Appendix A.
summis opibus: Ablative of manner with a limiting adjective (A.G. 412). **summis**: Defective superlative adjective (A.G. 130.b).
pugnaverant: The main verb of the coordinate clause **in ... pugnaverant** (A.G. 278.a). Plural verb with two singular subjects (A.G. 317). Although the pluperfect tense is normally used in subordinate clauses, its use as a main verb is frequent. Here the pluperfect denotes an action completed in past time (A.G. 477).

(39.3) **Ex his Eporedorix cognito Litavicci consilio media fere nocte rem ad Caesarem defert;**

ad, *to.*
cognosco, -gnoscere, -gnovi, cognitus, *learn, ascertain, recognize.*
defero, -ferre, -tuli, -latus, *report, announce.*
ex, *from the number of, from among, of.*
hic, haec, hoc, *this; he, she, it.*
medius, -a, -um, *in the middle, midst, middle, mid-.*
res, rei, f., *matter, affair.*

Caesar, -aris, m., *Caesar.*
consilium, -i, n., *plot, plan, design, scheme.*
Eporedorix, -igis, m., *Eporedorix.*
fere, with words denoting time, *about.*
Litaviccus, -i, m., *Litaviccus*
nox, noctis, f., *night.*

Ex his: Prepositional phrase, **ex** with the ablative here indicates a partitive sense "from the number of, from among, of" (*OLD* **ex** 16). Here **ex** with the ablative is used instead of the partitive genitive (A.G. 346.c). **his**: Plural, masculine, ablative demonstrative pronoun used substantively (A.G. 296.2). The antecedent is **Eporedorix ... Viridomarus** (A.G. 297.e).
Eporedorix: Nominative subject (A.G. 339). See Appendix A.
cognito Litavicci consilio: Ablative absolute (A.G. 419-20). **cognito**: The perfect tense of the participle represents the action as completed at the time indicated by the tense of the main verb (A.G. 489). **Litavicci**: Possessive genitive with **consilio** (A.G. 343). See Appendix A.
media ... nocte: Ablative of *time when* (A.G. 423.1). **media**: The adjective designates not what object, but what part of it is meant (A.G. 293).
fere: Adverb (A.G. 320-21).
rem: Accusative direct object of **defert** (A.G. 387).
ad Caesarem: Prepositional phrase, **ad** with the accusative here means "to" (*OLD* **ad** 1). **Caesarem**: See Appendix A.
defert: The main verb of the main clause (A.G. 278.b). The historical present, giving vividness to the narrative, is present in Chapter 39 (A.G. 469). This usage, common in all languages, comes from imagining past events as going on before our eyes (*repraesentatio*) (A.G. 469 Note). Eporedorix's loyalty here is understandable as Caesar had sided in the dispute with Convictolitavis, Eporedorix's patron. He is at this time unaware that Convictolitavis is a major mover of the rebellion.

(39.3) **orat ne patiatur civitatem pravis adulescentium consiliis ab amicitia populi Romani deficere;**

ab, *from, away from.*
amicitia, -ae, f., *friendship, alliance.*
consilium, -i, n., *plot, plan, design, scheme.*
ne, *so that ... not.*
patior, pati, passus, *permit, allow.*
pravus, -a, -um, *bad, wicked.*

adulescens, -entis, m., *young man, youth.*
civitas, -tatis, f., *state, nation.*
deficio, -ficere, -feci, -fectus, *fall away, revolt, rebel.*
oro, -are, -avi, -atus, *plead, beg, entreat.*
populus, -i, m., *people, nation.*
Romanus, -a, -um, *Roman.*

orat: The main verb of the main clause (A.G. 278.b). The pronoun **is**, with **Eporedorix** as the antecedent, is understood as the subject (A.G. 271.a).

ne patiatur ... deficere: The conjunction **ne** ("so that ... not") with the subjunctive is here a negative substantive clause of purpose which is used as the object of **orat** denoting an action directed toward the future (A.G. 563). **patiatur**: The main verb of the subordinate clause (A.G. 278.b). Present subjunctive; the tense of the subjunctive is normally in secondary sequence after the historical present **orat** (A.G. 482-85). Here it is in primary sequence through *repraesentatio* (A.G. 485.e and 585.b Note). The pronoun **is**, with **Caesarem** as the antecedent, is understood as the subject (A.G. 271.a). **deficere**: See below.

civitatem ... deficere: A subject accusative with the infinitive after **patiatur**. The construction is equivalent to a substantive clause of purpose (A.G. 563.c).

pravis ... consiliis: Ablative of cause without a preposition (A.G. 404).

adulescentium: Possessive genitive with **consiliis** (A.G. 343).

ab amicitia populi Romani: Ablative of separation with the preposition **ab** after the compound verb **deficere** (A.G. 402). **populi Romani**: Possessive genitive with **amicitia** (A.G. 343). This expression has an invariable word order (A.G. 598.k).

(39.3) quod futurum provideat, si se tot hominum milia cum hostibus coniunxerint, quorum salutem neque propinqui neglegere neque civitas levi momento aestimare posset.

aestimo, -are, -avi, -atus, *reckon, regard, consider.*
coniungo, -iungere, -iunxi, -iunctus, *join together, unite, join.*
homo, hominis, m., *man, person.*
levis, -e, *light, slight.*
momentum, -i, n., *importance, account.*

neque ... neque, *neither ... nor.*
propinqui, -orum, m., pl., *relatives, kinfolk.*

qui, quae, quod, *who, which, what.*
si, *if.*
sum, esse, fui, futurus, *be.*

civitas, -tatis, f., *state, nation.*
cum, *with.*
hostis, -is, m., *enemy, foe*; pl., *the enemy.*
milia, -um, n., pl., *thousand, thousands.*
neglego, -legere, -lexi, -lectus, *disregard, be indifferent to, neglect.*
possum, posse, potui, -----, *be able.*
provideo, -videre, -vidi, -visus, *foresee, perceive in advance.*
salus, -utis, f., *welfare, safety, deliverance.*
sui, sibi, se, or **sese**, nom. wanting, *themselves.*
tot, *so many.*

quod ... provideat: Relative clause; a clause dependent on a subjunctive clause (**ne ... patiatur**) takes the subjunctive when regarded as an integral part of that clause (attraction) (A.G. 303 and 593). **quod**: See below. **provideat**: The main verb of the subordinate clause (A.G. 278.b). Present subjunctive; the tense of the subjunctive is normally in secondary sequence after the historical present **orat** (A.G. 482-85). Here it is in primary sequence through *repraesentatio* (A.G. 485.e and 585.b Note). The pronoun **is**, with **Eporedorix** as the antecedent, is understood as the subject (A.G. 271.a).

quod futurum (esse) ... si ... coniunxerint: Conditional statement in indirect discourse after **provideat** (A.G. 589). The protasis, as a dependent clause, is in the subjunctive and the apodosis, as the principal clause, is in the infinitive (A.G. 589).

quod futurum (esse): The apodosis of the conditional statement (A.G. 589.2). Accusative/infinitive construction in indirect discourse after **provideat** (A.G. 577 ff.). **quod**: Singular, neuter, accusative relative pronoun used substantively (A.G. 305). The antecedent is omitted, supply **id** (A.G. 307.d Note). **futurum (esse)**: Supply **esse** to form the future infinitive of **sum** (A.G. 170). The tense of the infinitive in indirect discourse is relative to that of the verb of saying (A.G. 584).

si ... coniunxerint: The conjunction **si** ("if") with the subjunctive forms the protasis of a conditional statement in indirect discourse (A.G. 589.1). **coniunxerint**: The main verb of the subordinate clause (A.G. 278.b). Perfect subjunctive; the tense of the subjunctive is normally in secondary sequence after the historical present **orat** (A.G. 482-85). Here it is in primary sequence through *repraesentatio* (A.G. 485.e and 585.b Note). The perfect tense of the subjunctive is here standing for a future perfect in direct discourse (A.G. 484.c). The future perfect tense denotes action completed (at the time referred to), and hence is represented in the subjunctive by the perfect tense in primary sequence (A.G. 484.c).

se: Plural, neuter, accusative direct reflexive pronoun (A.G. 300.1). The antecedent is **milia**, the subject of **coniunxerint** (A.G. 299). Accusative direct object of **coniunxerint** (A.G. 387).

tot ... milia: Nominative subject (A.G. 339). **tot**: Indeclinable adjective modifying **milia** (*OLD* tot). **milia**: Nominative plural; in the plural **mille** declines as a neuter noun (A.G. 134.d).

hominum: Partitive genitive with **milia** (A.G. 346.a.2).

cum hostibus: Ablative of accompaniment with the preposition **cum** (A.G. 413).

quorum ... posset: Relative clause; a clause dependent on a subjunctive clause (**si ... coniunxerint**) takes the subjunctive when regarded as an integral part of that clause (attraction) (A.G. 303 and 593). **quorum**: Plural, masculine, genitive demonstrative pronoun used substantively (A.G. 296.2). The antecedent is **hominum** (A.G. 297.e). Possessive genitive with **salutem** (A.G. 343). **posset**: The main verb of the subordinate clause (A.G. 278.b). Imperfect subjunctive; the tense of the subjunctive is in secondary sequence and follows the rules for sequence of tense after the historical present **orat** (A.G. 482-85, esp. 485.e). Two or more singular subjects normally take a verb in the plural (A.G. 317). However, when a verb belongs to two or more subjects separately, it often agrees with one (**civitas**) and is understood with the others (**propinqui**) (A.G. 317.c).

salutem: Accusative direct object of the infinitive **neglegere** (A.G. 387 and 451.3).

neque ... neque: The repeated conjunction means "neither ... nor" and connects the two infinitives (*OLD* **neque** 7).

propinqui: Plural, masculine, nominative adjective used substantively (A.G. 288). First nominative subject of the singular verb **posset** (A.G. 339).

neglegere: Complementary infinitive after **posset** (A.G. 456).

civitas: Second nominative subject of **posset** (A.G. 339).

levi momento: Ablative of value after **aestimare** (*OLD* **aestimo** 3.b).

aestimare: Complementary infinitive after **posset** (A.G. 456). Supply the pronoun **eam**, with **salutem** as the antecedent, as the accusative direct object.

(40.1-2) **Magna adfectus sollicitudine hoc nuntio Caesar, quod semper Aeduorum civitati praecipue indulserat, nulla interposita dubitatione legiones expeditas quattuor equitatumque (2) omnem ex castris educit;**

adficio, -ficere, -feci, -fectus, *afflict, trouble, fill.*
Caesar, -aris, m., *Caesar.*
civitas, -tatis, f., *state, nation.*
educo, -ducere, -duxi, -ductus, *lead out, lead forth.*
ex, *from, out of.*
hic, haec, hoc, *this; he, she, it.*
interpono, -ponere, -posui, -positus, *allow.*
magnus, -a, -um, *great.*
nuntius, -i, m., *message, tidings.*
praecipue, *especially, specially, particularly.*
-que, *and.*
semper, *always, ever, constantly.*

Aedui, -orum, m., pl., *the Aedui.*
castra, -orum, n., pl., *camp, encampment.*
dubitatio, -onis, f., *doubt, hesitation.*
equitatus, -us, m., *cavalry.*
expeditus, -a, -um, *light-armed, without baggage.*
indulgeo, -dulgere, -dulsi, -dultus, *be kind to, favor.*
legio, -onis, f., *legion.*
nullus, -a, -um, *no, not any.*
omnis, -e, *all.*
quattuor, *four.*
quod, *because, since, for, as.*
sollicitudo, -inis, f., *anxiety, apprehension.*

Magna ... sollicitudine: Ablative of manner with a limiting adjective (A.G. 412).

adfectus ... Caesar: Nominative subject of **educit** (A.G. 339). **adfectus**: Nominative, perfect, passive, participle used as a predicate, where in English a phrase or a subordinate clause would be more normal (A.G. 496). **Caesar**: See Appendix A.

hoc nuntio: Ablative of cause without a preposition (A.G. 404). **hoc**: Singular, masculine, ablative demonstrative pronoun used as an adjective modifying **nuntio** (A.G. 296.1 and a).

quod ... indulserat: Causal clause; the conjunction **quod** ("because") takes the indicative when the reason is given on the authority of the writer or speaker (A.G. 540.1). **indulserat**: The main verb of the subordinate clause (A.G. 278.b). The pronoun **is**, with **Caesar** as the antecedent, is understood as the subject (A.G. 271.a). The pluperfect denotes an action completed in past time (A.G. 477).

semper: Adverb (A.G. 217.b and 320-21).

Aeduorum: Possessive genitive with **civitati** (A.G. 343). See Appendix A.

civitati: Dative indirect object of the intransitive verb **indulserat** (A.G. 367).

praecipue: Adverb (A.G. 214.a and 320-21).

nulla interposita dubitatione: Ablative absolute (A.G. 419-20). **interposita**: The perfect tense of the participle represents the action as completed at the time indicated by the tense of the main verb (A.G. 489).

legiones expeditas quattuor equitatumque omnem: Two accusative direct objects of **educit** (A.G. 387). **quattuor**: Indeclinable cardinal number used as an adjective modifying **legiones** (A.G. 132-35). **-que**: The enclitic conjunction connects the two accusative nouns **legiones ... equitatum** (A.G. 324.a).

ex castris: Ablative of *place from which* with the preposition **ex** (A.G. 426.1).

educit: The main verb of the main clause (A.G. 278.b). The historical present, giving vividness to the narrative, is present in Chapter 40 (A.G. 469). This usage, common in all languages, comes from imagining past events as going on before our eyes (*repraesentatio*) (A.G. 469 Note).

(40.2-3) **nec fuit spatium tali tempore ad contrahenda castra, quod res posita in celeritate videbatur; (3) C. Fabium legatum cum legionibus duabus castris praesidio relinquit.**

ad, *for, in order to, for the purpose of.*
castra, -orum, n., pl., *camp, encampment.*

contraho, -trahere, -traxi, -tractus, *draw in, contract, make smaller.*
duo, -ae, -o, *two.*
legatus, -i, m., *lieutenant, lieutenant-general.*
nec, *and ... not.*

praesidium, -i, n., *guard, garrison, protection.*
relinquo, -linquere, -liqui, -lictus, *leave, leave behind.*

C. Fabius, -i, m., *Gaius Fabius.*
celeritas, -tatis, f., *speed, quickness, swiftness, rapidity, despatch.*
cum, *with.*
in, *on.*
legio, -onis, f., *legion.*
pono, ponere, posui, positus, (pass., often) *be dependent, depend.*
quod, *because, since, for, as.*
res, rei, f., *matter, affair.*

spatium, -i, n., *space, time, leisure, opportunity.*
talis, -e, *such.*
videor, videri, visus sum, *seem, appear.*

sum, esse, fui, futurus, *be.*
tempus, -oris, n., *time.*

nec: The conjunction **nec** joins a negative clause to a preceding positive one and means "and ... not" (*OLD* **neque** 3).
fuit: The main verb of the main clause (A.G. 278.b). The verb **sum** in the sense of "exist" makes a complete predicate without a predicate noun or adjective ("was there …"). It is then called the substantive verb and regularly comes first (A.G. 284.b and 598.c).
spatium: Nominative subject (A.G. 339).
tali tempore: Ablative of *time when* (A.G. 423.1).
ad contrahenda castra: The preposition **ad** with the accusative gerundive and noun denotes purpose (A.G. 506). "To reduce the size of the camp so that it could be defended by the two legions left behind; for Caesar had but six legions at Gergovia, four having been sent with Labienus to the north." (Kelsey, 414) **contrahenda**: Plural, neuter, accusative gerundive used as an adjective modifying **castra** denoting necessity, obligation or propriety (A.G. 500.1).
quod ... videbatur: Causal clause; the conjunction **quod** ("because") takes the indicative when the reason is given on the authority of the writer or speaker (A.G. 540.1). **videbatur**: The main verb of the subordinate clause (A.G. 278.b).
res: Nominative subject (A.G. 339).
posita (esse): Singular, feminine, nominative predicate adjective modifying **res** after the supplied infinitive **esse**. A predicate adjective after a complementary infinitive takes the case of the subject of the main verb (A.G. 283-84 and 458). Supply **esse** as the complementary infinitive after **videbatur**.
in celeritate: Prepositional phrase, **in** with the ablative here means "on" (expressing an abstract location) (*OLD* **pono** 23.b).
C. Fabium: Accusative direct object of **relinquit** (A.G. 387). See Appendix A. **C.**: Abbreviated form of the praenomen **Gaius** (A.G. 108.c).
legatum: An accusative noun in apposition to the proper noun **Fabium** (A.G. 282).
cum legionibus duabus: Ablative of accompaniment with the preposition **cum** (A.G. 413). **duabus**: Declinable cardinal number used as an adjective modifying **legionibus** (A.G. 132-35).
castris praesidio: Dative of the purpose or end (double dative). The dative of an abstract noun (**praesidio**) is used to show that for which a thing serves or which it accomplishes, with another dative of the person or thing affected (**castris**) (A.G. 382.1).
relinquit: The main verb of the simple sentence (A.G. 278.1). The pronoun **is**, with **Caesar** as the antecedent, is understood as the subject (A.G. 271.a).

(40.3-4) Fratres Litavicci, cum comprehendi iussis(4)set, paulo ante reperit ad hostes fugisse.

ad, *to.*
comprehendo, -hendere, -hendi, -hensus, *seize, lay hold of, arrest, capture.*
frater, -tris, m., *brother.*
hostis, -is, m., *enemy, foe*; pl., *the enemy.*

Litaviccus, -i, m., *Litaviccus.*
reperio, -perire, repperi, repertus, *find, discover, ascertain, learn.*

ante, *before, previously.*
cum, *after, when.*
fugio, fugere, fugi, -----, *flee, run away, make off.*
iubeo, iubere, iussi, iussus, *order, give orders, bid, command.*
paulo, *by a little, just a little.*

Fratres ... fugisse: Accusative/infinitive construction in indirect discourse after **reperit** (A.G. 577 ff.). **fugisse**: The tense of the infinitive in indirect discourse is relative to that of the verb of saying (A.G. 584).
Litavicci: Possessive genitive with **Fratres** (A.G. 343). See Appendix A.
cum ... iussisset: Temporal clause; the relative adverb **cum** ("after, when") with the pluperfect subjunctive describes the circumstances that preceded the action of the main verb (A.G. 546). **iussisset**: The main verb of the subordinate clause (A.G. 278.b). The pronoun **is**, with **Caesar** as the antecedent, is understood as the subject (A.G. 271.a).
(eos) comprehendi: Subject accusative with the infinitive after **iussisset**. The construction is equivalent to a substantive clause of purpose (A.G. 563.a). Supply the pronoun **eos**, with **Fratres** as the antecedent, as the accusative subject.
paulo: Adverb (A.G. 320-21).
ante: Adverb (A.G. 320-21 and 433.1).
reperit: The main verb of the main clause (A.G. 278.b). The pronoun **is**, with **Caesar** as the antecedent, is understood as the subject (A.G. 271.a).
ad hostis: Prepositional phrase, **ad** with the accusative here means "to" (*OLD* **ad** 1). **hostis**: Accusative plural noun; **-is** for **-es** is the regular form in i-stem nouns (A.G. 65-67 and 74.c).

(40.4) Adhortatus milites ne necessario tempore itineris labore permoveantur, cupidissimis omnibus progressus milia passuum XXV, agmen Aeduorum conspicatus immisso equitatu iter eorum moratur atque impedit;

adhortor, -ari, -atus, *encourage, rally, exhort, rouse, urge.*
agmen, -minis, n., *army on the march, marching column, line of march.*
conspicor, -ari, -atus, *catch sight of, see, observe.*
equitatus, -us, m., *cavalry.*
impedio, -pedire, -pedivi, -peditus, *obstruct, hinder, detain, delay.*
iter, itineris, n., *journey, march.*

Aedui, -orum, m., pl., *the Aedui.*
atque, *and then.*
cupidus, -a, -um, sup. **-issimus**, *desirous, eager.*
immitto, -mittere, -misi, -missus, *send against.*
is, ea, id, *he, she, it; that, this.*
labor, -oris, m., *toil, exertion, labor.*

miles, -itis, m., *soldier, foot-solider.*
moror, -ari, -atus, *hinder, delay, impede.*
necessarius, -a, -um, *critical.*
passus, -us, m., *step, pace,* = 4 feet, 10 ¼ inches.

progredior, -gredi, -gressus, *advance, go forward, proceed.*
V, in expression of number, = 5.

milia, -um, n., pl., *thousand, thousands.*
ne, *so that ... not.*
omnes, -ium, m., pl., *all men, all.*
permoveo, -movere, -movi, -motus, *disturb, be discouraged.*
tempus, -oris, n., *time.*
X, in expression of number, = 10.

Adhortatus ... progressus ... conspicatus: Nominative subject of **moratur ... impedit** (A.G. 339). Three nominative, perfect, deponent, participle used as a predicate, where in English a phrase or a subordinate clause would be more normal (A.G. 496). The pronoun **is**, with **Caesar** from 40.1 as the antecedent, is understood. Notice the asyndeton construction between the three participles (A.G. 323.b).
milites: Accusative direct object of the participle **Adhortatus** (A.G. 387 and 488).
ne ... permoveantur: The conjunction **ne** ("so that ... not") with the subjunctive forms a negative substantive clause of purpose which is used as the object of the participle **Adhortatus** denoting an action directed toward the future (A.G. 563). **permoveantur**: The main verb of the subordinate clause (A.G. 278.b). Present subjunctive; the tense of the subjunctive is normally in secondary sequence after the historical present **moratur** (A.G. 482-85). Here it is in primary sequence through *repraesentatio* (A.G. 485.e and 585.b Note). The pronoun **ei**, with **milites** as the antecedent, is understood as the subject (A.G. 271.a).
necessario tempore: Ablative of *time when* (A.G. 423.1).
itineris: Objective genitive with **labore** (A.G. 348).
labore: Ablative of cause without a preposition (A.G. 404).
cupidissimis omnibus: Ablative absolute with an adjective (**cupidissimis**) taking the place of a participle (there is no participle for "being") (A.G. 419.a-20). **cupidissimis**: Superlative adjective (A.G. 124). **omnibus**: Plural, masculine, ablative, adjective used substantively (A.G. 288). These are the four legions and cavaly.
milia passuum XXV: Accusative of *extent of space* (A.G. 425). **milia**: Accusative plural; in the plural **mille** declines as a neuter noun (A.G. 134.d). **passuum**: Partitive genitive with **milia** (346.2). **XXV**: Roman numeral used as an adjective modifying **milia** (A.G. 133).
agmen: Accusative direct object of the participle **conspicatus** (A.G. 387 and 488).
Aeduorum: Possessive genitive with **agmen** (A.G. 343). See Appendix A.
immisso equitatu: Ablative absolute (A.G. 419-20). **immisso**: The perfect tense of the participle represents the action as completed at the time indicated by the tense of the main verb (A.G. 489).
iter: Accusative direct object of both verbs **moratur ... impedit** (A.G. 387).
eorum: Plural, masculine, genitive demonstrative pronoun used substantively (A.G. 296.2). The antecedent is **Aeduorum** (A.G. 297.e). Possessive genitive with **iter** (A.G. 343).
moratur: The main verb of the coordinate clause **Adhortatus ... moratur** (A.G. 278.a).
atque: The conjunction connects the two main verbs **moratur ... impedit** and means "and then" (*OLD* atque 7).
impedit: The main verb of the coordinate clause **impedit** (A.G. 278.a).

(40.4-5) interdicitque omnibus ne quemquam (5) interficiant.

interdico, -dicere, -dixi, -dictus, *enjoin, command.*
ne, *so that ... not.*
-que, *and yet, at the same time.*

interficio, -ficere, -feci, -fectus, *slay, kill.*
omnes, -ium, m., pl., *all men, all.*
quisquam, -----, quidquam, *anyone, anything, any.*

interdicitque: The main verb of the main clause (A.G. 278.b). The pronoun **is**, with **Caesar** as the antecedent, is understood as the subject (A.G. 271.a). **-que**: The enclitic conjunction connects terms which show a slight contrast (**impedit interdicit**) and means "and yet, at the same time" (*OLD* -que 8).
omnibus: Plural, masculine, dative, adjective used substantively (A.G. 288). Dative indirect object of the transitive verb **interdicit** (the following substantive clause functions as the direct object) (A.G. 364 Note 1).
ne ... interficiant: The conjunction **ne** ("so that ... not") with the subjunctive forms a negative substantive clause of purpose which is used as the object of **interdicit** denoting an action directed toward the future (A.G. 563). **interficiant**: The main verb of the subordinate clause (A.G. 278.b). Present subjunctive; the tense of the subjunctive is normally in secondary sequence after the historical present **interdicit** (A.G. 482-85). Here it is in primary sequence through *repraesentatio* (A.G. 485.e and 585.b Note). The pronoun **ei**, with **omnibus** as the antecedent, is understood as the subject (A.G. 271.a).
quemquam: Singular, masculine, accusative indefinite pronoun used substantively (A.G. 151.d). Accusative direct object of **interficiant** (A.G. 387).

(40.5-6) Eporedorigem et Viridomarum, quos illi interfectos existimabant, inter equites versari suosque appellare (6) iubet.

appello, -are, -avi, -atus, *address, call upon.*
eques, -itis, m., *rider, horseman, cavalryman, trooper.*
existimo, -are, -avi, -atus, *think, consider, judge.*
inter, *among.*
iubeo, iubere, iussi, iussus, *order, give orders, bid, command.*

Eporedorix, -igis, m., *Eporedorix.*
et, *and.*
ille, illae, illud, *that; he, she, it.*
interficio, -ficere, -feci, -fectus, *slay, kill.*
-que, *and.*

qui, quae, quod, *who, which, what.*
versor, -ari, -atus, *move about.*

sui, -orum, m., pl., *their men*, with or without *own.*
Viridomarus, -i, m., *Viridomarus.*

Eporedorigem et Viridomarum ... versari ... appellare: Two subject accusatives with two infinitives after **iubet.** The construction is equivalent to a substantive clause of purpose (A.G. 563.a). **Eporedorigem:** See Appendix A. **et:** The conjunction connects the two accusative nouns (A.G. 324.a). **Viridomarum:** See Appendix A.

quos ... existimabant: Relative clause; a clause dependent on an infinitive (**versari**) which is equivalent to a subjunctive clause normally takes the subjunctive (attraction) (A.G. 303 and 593). However, when a dependent clause is not regarded as a necessary logical part of the clause, the indicative is used. The indicative serves to emphasize the fact, as true independently of the statement contained in the subjunctive clause (A.G. 593.a Note 1). **quos:** See below. **existimabant:** The main verb of the subordinate clause (A.G. 278.b).

quos ... interfectos (esse): Accusative/infinitive construction in indirect discourse after **existimabant** (A.G. 577 ff.). **quos:** Plural, masculine, accusative relative pronoun used substantively (A.G. 305). The antecedent is **Eporedorigem et Viridomarum** (A.G. 307). **interfectos (esse):** Supply **esse** to form the perfect, passive, infinitive (A.G. 188). The tense of the infinitive in indirect discourse is relative to that of the verb of saying (A.G. 584).

illi: Plural, masculine, nominative demonstrative pronoun used substantively (A.G. 296.2). The antecedent is **Aeduorum** (i.e., the 10,000 soldiers and the cavalry under Litaviccus on the way to Caesar) (A.G. 297.e). Nominative subject (A.G. 339). The pronoun marks a change in subject to one previously mentioned (**Aeduorum**) (A.G. 601.d).

inter equites: Prepositional phrase, **inter** with the accusative here means "among" (*OLD* inter1 1).

suosque: Plural, masculine, accusative possessive pronoun used substantively to denote a special class (A.G. 302.d). Accusative direct object of the infinitive **appellare** (A.G. 387 and 451.3). **-que:** The enclitic conjunction connects the two infinitives (A.G. 324.a).

iubet: The main verb of the main clause (A.G. 278.b). The pronoun **is**, with **Caesar** as the antecedent, is understood as the subject (A.G. 271.a).

(40.6-7) His cognitis et Litavicci fraude perspecta Aedui manus tendere et deditionem significare et proiectis armis (7) mortem deprecari incipiunt.

Aedui, -orum, m., pl., *the Aedui.*
cognosco, -gnoscere, -gnovi, cognitus, *recognize, perceive, identify.*
deprecor, -ari, -atus, *pray to be delivered from, beg to escape.*
fraus, fraudis, f., *deception, imposition.*
incipio, -cipere, -cepi, -ceptus, *begin, commence, undertake.*
manus, -us, f., *hand.*
perspicio, -spicere, -spexi, -spectus, *perceive, observe, ascertain.*
significo, -are, -avi, -atus, *show by signs, show, intimate, indicate.*

arma, -orum, n., pl., *arms, armor, weapons.*
deditio, -onis, f., *surrender.*
et, *and.*
hic, haec, hoc, *this; he, she, it.*
Litaviccus, -i, m., *Litaviccus.*
mors, mortis, f., *death.*
proicio, -icere, -ieci, -iectus, *fling, cast, throw down.*
tendo, tendere, tetendi, tentus, *and* tensus, *stretch, extend.*

His cognitis: Ablative absolute (A.G. 419-20). **His:** Plural, masculine, ablative demonstrative pronoun used substantively (A.G. 296.2). The antecedent is **Eporedorigem et Viridomarum** (A.G. 297.e). **cognitis:** The perfect tense of the participle represents the action as completed at the time indicated by the tense of the main verb (A.G. 489).

et: The conjunction connects the two ablative absolutes (A.G. 324.a).

Litavicci fraude perspecta: Ablative absolute (A.G. 419-20). **Litavicci:** Possessive genitive with **fraude** (A.G. 343). See Appendix A. **perspecta:** The perfect tense of the participle represents the action as completed at the time indicated by the tense of the main verb (A.G. 489).

Aedui: Nominative subject (A.G. 339). See Appendix A.

manus: Accusative direct object of the infinitive **tendere** (A.G. 387 and 451.3).

tendere: Complementary infinitive after **incipiunt** (A.G. 456).

et: The conjunction connects the two infinitives **tendere ... significare** (A.G. 324.a).

deditionem: Accusative direct object of the infinitive **significare** (A.G. 387 and 451.3).

significare: Complementary infinitive after **incipiunt** (A.G. 456).

et: The conjunction connects the two infinitives **significare ... deprecari** (A.G. 324.a).

proiectis armis: Ablative absolute (A.G. 419-20). **proiectis:** The perfect tense of the participle represents the action as completed at the time indicated by the tense of the main verb (A.G. 489).

mortem: Accusative direct object of the infinitive **deprecari** (A.G. 387 and 451.3).

deprecari: Complementary infinitive after **incipiunt** (A.G. 456).

incipiunt: The main verb of the main clause (A.G. 278.b).

(40.7) Litaviccus cum suis clientibus, quibus more Gallorum nefas est etiam in extrema fortuna deserere patronos, Gergoviam profugit.

cliens, -entis, m., *retainer, dependant, client, adherent.*
desero, -serere, -serui, -sertus, *leave, abandon, desert.*
extremus, -a, -um, *last, extreme, at the end.*
Galli, -orum, m., *the Gauls.*

cum, *with.*
etiam, *even.*
fortuna, -ae, f., *ill-luck, misfortune, adversity.*
Gergovia, -ae, f., *Gergovia.*

in, *in*.
mos, moris, f., *custom, way, wont, practice*.
patronus, -i, m., *protector, patron*.
qui, quae, quod, *who, which, what*.
suus, -a, -um, *his*, with or without *own*.

Litaviccus, -i, m., *Litaviccus*.
nefas, n., *wrong, not permitted*.
profugio, -fugere, -fugi, -----, *flee, escape*.
sum, esse, fui, futurus, *be*.

Litaviccus: Nominative subject (A.G. 339). See Appendix A.
cum suis clientibus: Ablative of accompaniment with the preposition **cum** (A.G. 413). **suis**: Plural, masculine, ablative possessive pronoun used as an adjective modifying **clientibus** (A.G. 302).
quibus ... patronos: Relative clause (A.G. 303). **quibus**: Plural, masculine, dative relative pronoun used substantively (A.G. 305). The antecedent is **clientibus** (A.G. 307). Dative indirect object of the phrase **nefas est** (A.G. 366.a). **patronos**: See below.
more: Ablative of specification (A.G. 418).
Gallorum: Possessive genitive with **more** (A.G. 343). See Appendix A.
nefas est: The main verb of the subordinate clause (A.G. 278.b). Impersonal verb, the following infinitive phrase functions as the subject (A.G. 208.c). **nefas**: Nominative indeclinable noun used in the predicate position (A.G. 103.a Note 1). **est**: The main verb of the subordinate clause (A.G. 278.b). The present tense is not the historical present but denotes a state as now existing in present time (A.G. 465.2).
etiam in extrema fortuna deserere patronos: The infinitive phrase functions as the subject of the impersonal verb **nefas est** (A.G. 454). **etiam**: Adverb modifying the adjective **extrema** (A.G. 320-21 and 322.a). The adverb normally proceeds the emphatic word (A.G. 322.a). **in extrema fortuna**: Prepositional phrase, **in** with the ablative here means "in, amid" (certain circumstances) (*OLD* in 40). **patronos**: Accusative direct object of the infinitive **deserere** (A.G. 387 and 451.3).
Gergoviam: Accusative of *place to which* without a preposition (city name) (A.G. 427.2). See Appendix A.
profugit: The main verb of the main clause (A.G. 278.b).

(41.1-2) Caesar, nuntiis ad civitatem Aeduorum missis qui suo beneficio conservatos docerent quos iure belli interficere potuisset, tribusque horis noctis exercitui ad quietem datis, (2) castra ad Gergoviam movit.

ad, *to; for, for the purpose of, towards, to the neighborhood of*.
bellum, -i, n., *war, warfare*.
Caesar, -aris, m., *Caesar*.
civitas, -tatis, f., *state, nation*.
do, dare, dedi, datus, *give, give over*.
exercitus, -us, m., *army*.
hora, -ae, f., *hour*.
ius, iuris, n., *laws*.
moveo, movere, movi, motus, *move*.
nuntius, -i, m., *messenger, courier*.
-que, *and*.
quies, -etis, f., *rest, repose, quiet*.
tres, tria, trium, *three*.

Aedui, -orum, m., pl., *the Aedui*.
beneficium, -i, n., *kindness, favor*.
castra, -orum, n., pl., *camp, encampment*.
conservo, -are, -avi, -atus, *save, spare, preserve*.
doceo, docere, docui, doctus, *inform, point out, state*.
Gergovia, -ae, f., *Gergovia*.
interficio, -ficere, -feci, -fectus, *slay, kill*.
mitto, mittere, misi, missus, *send*.
nox, noctis, f., *night*.
possum, posse, potui, -----, *be able*.
qui, quae, quod, *who, which, what*.
suus, -a, -um, *his*, with or without *own*.

Caesar: Nominative subject of **movit** (A.G. 339). See Appendix A.
nuntiis ... potuisset: Ablative absolute with dependent clauses. Much has been made of Caesar's policy of clemency, especially in the civil war. Whatever his motives for sparing fellow Romans during the civil war, when granting clemency to Gallic enemies, there is always an admitted political goal to be achieved (i.e., see the treatment of the Aedui and Arverni captives at Chapters 89-90). For a full treatment see Coulter.
nuntiis ad civitatem Aeduorum missis: Ablative absolute (A.G. 419-20). **ad civitatem Aeduorum**: Accusative of *place to which* with the preposition **ad** (A.G. 426.2). **Aeduorum**: Possessive genitive with **civitatem** (A.G. 343). See Appendix A. **missis**: The perfect tense of the participle represents the action as completed at the time indicated by the tense of the main verb (A.G. 489).
qui ... docerent: A relative clause of purpose is introduced by a relative pronoun and takes the subjunctive (A.G. 531.2). **qui**: Plural, masculine, nominative relative pronoun used substantively (A.G. 305). The antecedent is **nuntiis** (A.G. 307). Nominative subject (A.G. 339). The relative is here equivalent to **ut ei** (A.G. 531.2 Note). **docerent**: The main verb of the subordinate clause (A.G. 278.b). Imperfect subjunctive; the tense of the subjunctive is in secondary sequence after the historical present **movit** (A.G. 482-85, esp. 485.e).
suo beneficio: Ablative of cause without a preposition (A.G. 404). **suo**: Singular, neuter, ablative possessive pronoun used as an adjective modifying **beneficio** (A.G. 302).
(eos) conservatos (esse): Accusative/infinitive construction in indirect discourse after **docerent** (A.G. 577 ff). Supply the pronoun **eos** (the 10,000 Aeduan soldiers and cavalry), correlative to the following relative clause, as the accusative subject. **conservatos (esse)**: Supply **esse** to form the perfect, passive infinitive (A.G. 184). The tense of the infinitive in indirect discourse is relative to that of the verb of saying (A.G. 584).
quos ... potuisset: Relative clause; a clause dependent on a subjunctive clause (**qui ... docerent**) takes the subjunctive when regarded as an integral part of that clause (attraction) (A.G. 303 and 593). **quos**: Plural, masculine, accusative relative pronoun used substantively (A.G. 305). The antecedent is the supplied pronoun **eos** (A.G. 307). Accusative direct object of the infinitive **interficere** (A.G. 387 and 451.3). **potuisset**: The main verb of the subordinate clause (A.G. 278.b). Pluperfect subjunctive; the tense of the

subjunctive is in secondary sequence after the historical present **movit** (A.G. 482-85, esp. 485.e). The pronoun **is**, with **Caesar** as the antecedent, is understood as the subject (A.G. 271.a).

iure: Ablative of specification (A.G. 418).

belli: Partitive genitive with **iure** (A.G. 346.a.1).

interficere: Complementary infinitive after **potuisset** (A.G. 456).

tribusque horis noctis exercitui ad quietem datis: Ablative absolute (A.G. 419-20). **tribus**: Declinable cardinal number used as an adjective modifying **horis** (A.G. 132-35). **-que**: The enclitic conjunction connects the two ablative absolutes (A.G. 324.a). **noctis**: Partitive genitive with **horis** (A.G. 346.a.1). **exercitui**: Dative indirect object of the passive participle **datis**, verbs which in the active voice take the accusative and dative retain the dative when used in the passive (A.G. 365). **ad quietem**: Prepositional phrase, **ad** with the accusative here denotes purpose meaning "for the purpose of" (*OLD* **ad** 44). **datis**: The perfect tense of the participle represents the action as completed at the time indicated by the tense of the main verb (A.G. 489).

castra: Accusative direct object of **movit** (A.G. 387). "Caesar had encamped after having received the submission of the Aedui." (Kelsey, 414)

ad Gergoviam: Accusative of *place to which* with the preposition **ad**; **ad** with the name of a town means "towards, to the neighborhood of" (A.G. 428.a). Gergoviam: See Appendix A.

movit: The main verb of the main clause (A.G. 278.b). The historical present, giving vividness to the narrative, is present in Chapter 41 (A.G. 469). This usage, common in all languages, comes from imagining past events as going on before our eyes (*repraesentatio*) (A.G. 469 Note).

(41.2) Medio fere itinere equites a Fabio missi quanto res in periculo fuerit exponunt.

a(b), *by.*

expono, -ponere, -posui, -positus, *set forth, state, explain.*

fere, *almost, nearly.*

iter, itineris, n., *journey, march.*

mitto, mittere, misi, missus, *send.*

quantus, -a, -um, *how great, how much, how large.*

sum, esse, fui, futurus, *be.*

eques, -itis, m., *rider, horseman, cavalryman, trooper.*

Fabius, -i, m., *Fabius.*

in, *in.*

medius, -a, -um, *in the middle, midst, middle, mid-.*

periculum, -i, n., *risk, danger, hazard.*

res, rei, f., *matter, condition, circumstance.*

Medio ... itinere: Ablative of *place where* without a preposition (A.G. 429.1-2). **Medio**: The adjective designates not what object, but what part of it is meant (A.G. 293).

fere: Adverb (A.G. 320-21).

equites ... missi: Nominative subject (A.G. 339). **missi**: Nominative, perfect, passive, participle used as a predicate, where in English a phrase or a subordinate clause would be more normal (A.G. 496).

a Fabio: Ablative of agent with the preposition **a(b)** after the perfect participle **missi** (A.G. 405). **Fabio**: See Appendix A.

quanto ... fuerit: Indirect question with the subjunctive; the phrase is the object of **exponunt** (A.G. 573-75). **quanto**: See below.

fuerit: The main verb of the subordinate clause (A.G. 278.b). Perfect subjunctive; the tense of the subjunctive is normally in secondary sequence after the historical present **exponunt** (A.G. 575). Here it is in primary sequence through *repraesentatio* (A.G. 485.e and 585.b Note).

res: Nominative subject (A.G. 339).

quanto ... in periculo: Prepositional phrase, **in** with the ablative here means "in (given circumstances) (*OLD* **in** 40). The prepositional phrase is in the predicate position after **fuerit** (A.G. 272).

exponunt: The main verb of the main clause (A.G. 278.b).

(41.2-3) Summis copiis castra oppugnata demonstrant, cum crebro integri defessis succederent nostrosque assiduo labore defatigarent, quibus propter magnitudinem castrorum perpetuo (3) esset isdem in vallo permanendum.

assiduus, -a, -um, *continuous, constant, incessant.*

copiae, -arum, f., pl., *forces, troops.*

cum, *since, seeing that.*

defessi, -orum, m., pl., *the exhausted, weary men.*

idem, eadem, idem, *the same.*

integri, -orum, m., pl., *those who were unexhausted, fresh men.*

magnitudo, -inis, f., *greatness, extent.*

oppugno, -are, -avi, -atus, *attack, assault, storm, besiege.*

perpetuo, *continuously, constantly.*

-que, *and.*

succedo, -cedere, -cessi, -cessurus, *succeed, take the place of, relieve.*

vallum, -i, n., *rampart, wall, intrenchment.*

castra, -orum, n., pl., *camp, encampment.*

crebro, *frequently, often, in quick succession.*

defatigo, -are, -avi, -atus, *tire out, exhaust, fatigue.*

demonstro, -are, -avi, -atus, *point out, show, say, explain.*

in, *on.*

labor, -oris, m., *toil, exertion, labor.*

nostri, -orum, m., pl., *our men, our side.*

permaneo, -manere, -mansi, -mansurus, *continue, stay, remain.*

propter, *as a result* or *consequence of, in view of, because of.*

qui, quae, quod, *who, which, what.*

summus, -a, -um, *greatest in amount, the maximum amount of.*

Summis copiis: Ablative of manner with a limiting adjective (A.G. 412). **Summis**: Defective superlative adjective (A.G. 130.b). The adjective here means "greatest in amount, maximum, the greatest amount of" (*OLD* **summus** 8).

castra oppugnata (esse): Accusative/infinitive construction in indirect discourse after **demonstrant** (A.G. 577 ff.). **oppugnata (esse)**: Supply **esse** to form the perfect, passive infinitive (A.G. 184). The tense of the infinitive in indirect discourse is relative to that of the verb of saying (A.G. 584).

demonstrant: The main verb of the main clause (A.G. 278.b). The pronoun **ei**, with **equites** as the antecedent, is understood as the subject (A.G. 271.a).

cum ... succederent ... defatigarent: Causal clause; the relative adverb **cum** ("since") with the subjunctive forms a clause expressing cause (A.G. 549). **succederent ... defatigarent**: The main verbs of the subordinate clause (A.G. 278.b). Imperfect subjunctive; the tense of the subjunctive is in secondary sequence after the historical present **demonstrant** (A.G. 482-85, esp. 485.e).

crebro: Adverb (A.G. 214.e and 320-21).

integri: Plural, masculine, nominative, adjective used substantively (A.G. 288). The noun **Galli** is understood (A.G. 288.b). Nominative subject of **succederent ... defatigarent** (A.G. 339).

defessis: Plural, masculine, dative, adjective used substantively (A.G. 288). The noun **Gallis** is understood (A.G. 288.b). Dative indirect object of the compound verb **succederent** (A.G. 370).

nostrosque: Plural, masculine, accusative possessive pronoun used substantively to denote a special class (A.G. 302.d). Accusative direct object of **defatigarent** (A.G. 387). **-que**: The enclitic conjunction connects the two verbs in the temporal clause (A.G. 324.a).

assiduo labore: Ablative of means (A.G. 409).

quibus ... (id) esset ... permanendum: Relative clause; a clause dependent on a subjunctive clause (**cum ... defatigarent**) takes the subjunctive when regarded as an integral part of that clause (attraction) (A.G. 303 and 593). (It is also a subordinate clause in indirect discourse). **quibus**: Plural, masculine, dative relative pronoun used substantively (A.G. 305). The antecedent is **nostros** (A.G. 307). Dative of agent after the second periphrastic verb **esset ... permanendum** (A.G. 374.a). **esset ... permanendum**: The main verb of the subordinate clause (A.G. 278.b). Imperfect subjunctive; the tense of the subjunctive is in secondary sequence after the historical present **demonstrant** (A.G. 482-85, esp. 485.e). Second periphrastic (passive) imperfect subjunctive implying necessity (A.G. 194.b and 196). Impersonal use of the intransitive verb (A.G. 208.d). Supply **id** as the subject (A.G. 318.c).

propter magnitudinem castrorum: Prepositional phrase, **propter** with the accusative here means "as a result or consequence of, in view of, because of" (*OLD* **propter** 3). **castrorum**: Possessive genitive with **magnitudinem** (A.G. 343).

perpetuo: Adverb (A.G. 320-21).

isdem: Plural, masculine, dative demonstrative pronoun used as an adjective modifying **quibus** (A.G. 426.1 and a). A variant form of **eisdem** (A.G. 146).

in vallo: Ablative of *place where* with the preposition **in** (locative ablative) (A.G. 426.3).

(41.3-4) Multitudine sagittarum atque omnis generis telorum multos vulneratos; ad haec (4) sustinenda magno usui fuisse tormenta.

ad, *for, in order to, for the purpose of.*
genus, generis, n., *kind, type.*
magnus, -a, -um, *great.*
multitudo, -inis, f., *great number.*
sagitta, -ae, f., *arrow.*
sustineo, -tinere, -tinui, -tentus, *bear, endure, withstand.*
tormentum, -i, n., *torsion-hurlers, engines of war, artillery.*
vulnero, are, -avi, -atus, *wound, hurt.*

atque, *and.*
hic, haec, hoc, *this; he, she, it.*
multi, -orum, m., pl. *many men.*
omnis, -e, *all, every.*
sum, esse, fui, futurus, *be.*
telum, -i, n., *dart, spear.*
usus, -us, m., *advantage, profit, benefit.*

Multitudine: Ablative of means after the passive verb **vulneratos (esse)** (A.G. 409).

sagittarum atque ... telorum: Two partitive genitives with **Multitudine** (A.G. 346.a.1). **atque**: The conjunction connects the two genitive nouns **sagittarum ... telorum** and means "and" (*OLD* **atque** 12).

omnis generis: Genitive of quality with **telorum** (A.G. 345).

multos vulneratos (esse): Accusative/infinitive construction in indirect discourse after **demonstrant** (A.G. 577 ff.). **multos**: Plural, masculine, accusative adjective used substantively (A.G. 288). The noun **Romanos** is understood (A.G. 288.b). **vulneratos (esse)**: Supply **esse** to form the perfect, passive infinitive (A.G. 184). The tense of the infinitive in indirect discourse is relative to that of the verb of saying (A.G. 584).

ad haec sustinenda: The preposition **ad** with the accusative pronoun and gerundive denotes purpose (A.G. 506). **haec**: Plural, neuter, accusative demonstrative pronoun used substantively (A.G. 296.2). The antecedent is the assaults on the camp described immediately above (A.G. 297.e). **sustinenda**: Plural, neuter, accusative gerundive used as an adjective modifying **haec** denoting necessity, obligation or propriety (A.G. 500.1).

magno usui: Dative of the purpose or end. The dative of an abstract noun (**usui**) is used to show that for which a thing serves or which it accomplishes (A.G. 382.1).

fuisse tormenta: Accusative/infinitive construction in indirect discourse after **demonstrant** (A.G. 577 ff.). **fuisse**: Perfect infinitive; the tense of the infinitive in indirect discourse is relative to that of the verb of saying (A.G. 584). **tormenta**: "Caesar had with him engines of war, the purpose of which corresponded to that of modern artillery. They were too heavy and clumsy to be of much service in battle: hence their chief use was in siege operations. The general name **tormenta** is derived from **torqueo**, to twist and was applied to them because the propelling force was obtained by twisting a stick between two tightly stretched horse-hair ropes." (Walker, 35)

(41.4) Fabium discessu eorum duabus relictis portis obstruere ceteras pluteosque vallo addere et se in posterum diem similemque casum apparare.

addo, -dere, -didi, -ditus, *add, join, lay on.*

casus, -us, m., *chance, fortune, event, misfortune.*
discessus, -us, m., *departure, going away.*
duo, -ae, -o, *two.*
Fabius, -i, m.., *Fabius.*
is, ea, id, *he, she, it; that, this.*
pluteus, -i, *breastwork.*
posterus -a, -um, *the next, the following.*
relinquo, -linquere, -liqui, -lictus, *leave, permit to remain, let remain.*
sui, sibi, se, or **sese**, nom. wanting, *he*, with or without *himself.*

apparo, -are, -avi, -atus, *prepare, make ready, get ready.*
ceteri, -ae, -a, *the rest, all the others, the others.*
dies, -ei, m. and f., *day.*
et, *and.*
in, *for.*
obstruo, -struere, -struxi, -structus, *block up, stop up.*
porta -ae, f., *gate, entrance, passage.*
-que, *and.*
similis, -e, *like, similar.*
vallum, -i, n., *rampart, wall, intrenchment.*

Fabium ... obstruere: Accusative/infinitive construction in indirect discourse after **demonstrant** (A.G. 577 ff.). **Fabium**: See Appendix A. **obstruere**: Present infinitive; the tense of the infinitive in indirect discourse is relative to that of the verb of saying (A.G. 584).

obstruere ... addere ... apparare: "The present tense implies that the messengers left Fabius engaged in the work." (Kelsey, 414)

discessu: Ablative of *time when* (A.G. 423.1).

eorum: Plural, masculine, genitive demonstrative pronoun used substantively (A.G. 296.2). The antecedent is the men implied in **copiis** at 41.2 (i.e., the Gauls) (A.G. 297.e). Possessive genitive with **discessu** (A.G. 343).

duabus relictis portis: Ablative absolute (A.G. 419-20). **duabus**: Declinable cardinal number used as an adjective modifying **portis** (A.G. 132-35). **relictis**: The perfect tense of the participle represents the action as completed at the time indicated by the tense of the main verb (A.G. 489).

ceteras: Plural, feminine, accusative adjective used substantively (A.G. 288). The noun **portas** is understood (A.G. 288.b). Accusative direct object of the infinitive **obstruere** (A.G. 387 and 451.3).

pluteosque: Accusative direct object of the transitive infinitive **addere** (A.G. 387 and 451.3). **-que**: The enclitic conjunction connects the two infinitives **obstruere ... addere** (A.G. 324.a).

vallo: Dative indirect object of the transitive infinitive **addere** (A.G. 362).

(eum) ... addere: Accusative/infinitive construction in indirect discourse after **demonstrant** (A.G. 577 ff.). The pronoun **eum**, with **Fabium** as the antecedent, is understood as the accusative subject. **addere**: Present infinitive; the tense of the infinitive in indirect discourse is relative to that of the verb of saying (A.G. 584).

et: The conjunction connects the two infinitives **addere ... apparare** (A.G. 324.a).

se: Singular, masculine, accusative direct reflexive pronoun (A.G. 300.1). The antecedent is **eum** (**Fabius**), the supplied accusative subject of the infinitive **obstruere** (A.G. 299). Accusative direct object of the infinitive **apparare** (A.G. 387 and 451.3).

in posterum diem similemque casum: Prepositional phrase, **in** with the accusative here means "for" (*OLD* **in** 23.a). **diem**: The noun **dies** is normally masculine gender (A.G. 97.a). **-que**: The enclitic conjunction connects the two accusative nouns in the prepositional phrase **diem ... casum** (A.G. 324.a).

(eum) ... apparare: Accusative/infinitive construction in indirect discourse after **demonstrant** (A.G. 577 ff.). The pronoun **eum**, with **Fabium** as the antecedent, is understood as the accusative subject. **apparare**: Present infinitive; the tense of the infinitive in indirect discourse is relative to that of the verb of saying (A.G. 584).

(41.4) His rebus cognitis, Caesar summo studio militum ante ortum solis in castra pervenit.

ante, *before.*
castra, -orum, n., pl., *camp, encampment.*

hic, haec, hoc, *this; he, she, it.*
miles, -itis, m., *soldier, foot-solider.*
pervenio, -venire, -veni, -ventus, *come to, arrive at, reach.*

sol, -is, m., *the sun.*
summus, -a, -um, *utmost, greatest, very great.*

Caesar, -aris, m., *Caesar.*
cognosco, -gnoscere, -gnovi, cognitus, *learn, ascertain, recognize.*
in, *to, into.*
ortus, -us, m., *rising.*
res, rei, f., *matter, affair, condition, circumstance, affair.*
studium, -i, n., *zeal, eagerness, energy, enthusiasm.*

His rebus cognitis: Ablative absolute (A.G. 419-20). **His**: Plural, feminine, ablative demonstrative pronoun used as an adjective modifying **rebus** (A.G. 426.1 and a). **cognitis**: The perfect tense of the participle represents the action as completed at the time indicated by the tense of the main verb (A.G. 489).

Caesar ... pervenit: "Caesar had learned of the defection stirred up by Litaviccus about midnight (7.39.3); he started with his troops immediately (7.40.1-2) and marched 25 miles (7.40.4-5); after three hours rest he brought his force back again reaching Gergovia before sunrise. His men had marched 50 Roman miles in less than 28 hours." (Kelsey, 414)

Caesar: Nominative subject (A.G. 339). See Appendix A.

summo studio: Ablative of means (A.G. 409). **summo**: Defective superlative adjective (A.G. 130.b).

militum: Objective genitive with **studio** (A.G. 348).

ante ortum solis: Prepositional phrase, **ante** with the accusative here means "before" (*OLD* **ante2** 5). **solis**: Possessive genitive with **ortum** (A.G. 343).

in castra: Accusative of *place to which* with the preposition **in** (A.G. 426.2).

pervenit: The main verb of the main clause (A.G. 278.b).

(42.1-2) **Dum haec ad Gergoviam geruntur, Aedui primis nuntiis ab Litavicco acceptis nullum sibi ad cognoscendum spatium (2) relinquunt.**

ab, *from.*
ad, *at, in the neighborhood of, for, in order to, for the purpose of.*
cognosco, -gnoscere, -gnovi, cognitus, *learn, examine, investigate.*
Gergovia, -ae, f., *Gergovia.*
hic, haec, hoc, *this; he, she, it.*
nullus, -a, -um, *no, not any.*
primus, -a, -um, *first.*
spatium, -i, n., *time, opportunity, space.*

accipio, -cipere, -cepi, -ceptus, *receive, accept.*
Aedui, -orum, m., pl., *the Aedui.*
dum, *while.*
gero, gerere, gessi, gestus, *carry out, perform, do.*
Litaviccus, -i, m., *Litaviccus.*
nuntius, -i, m., *message, tidings.*
relinquo, -linquere, -liqui, -lictus, *leave.*
sui, sibi, se, or **sese**, nom. wanting, *themselves.*

Dum ... geruntur: Temporal clause; the conjunction **dum** ("when, while") with the present indicative denotes continued action in past time (A.G. 556). **geruntur**: The main verb of the subordinate clause (A.G. 278.b).

haec: Plural, neuter, nominative demonstrative pronoun used substantively (A.G. 296.2). The antecedent is Caesar's recovery of the Aedui (A.G. 297.e). Nominative subject (A.G. 339).

ad Gergoviam: Accusative of *place to which* with the preposition **ad**; **ad** with the name of a town means "at" (i.e. in the neighborhood of) (A.G. 428.a). **Gergoviam**: See Appendix A.

Aedui: Nominative subject (A.G. 339). I.e., those back home, not the 10,000 soldiers and horsemen. See Appendix A.

primis nuntiis ab Litavicco acceptis: Ablative absolute (A.G. 419-20). **primis**: Declinable ordinal number used as an adjective modifying **nuntiis** (A.G. 132-35). **ab Litavicco**: Ablative of source with the preposition **ab** (A.G. 403.1). **Litavicco**: See Appendix A. **acceptis**: The perfect tense of the participle represents the action as completed at the time indicated by the tense of the main verb (A.G. 489). Litaviccus sends these messages at 38.10.

nullum ... spatium: Accusative direct object of **relinquunt** (A.G. 387).

sibi: Plural, masculine, dative direct reflexive pronoun (A.G. 300.1). The antecedent is **Aedui**, the subject of **relinquunt** (A.G. 299). Dative of reference; the dative in this construction is often called the dative of advantage as denoting the person for whose benefit the action is performed (A.G. 376).

ad cognoscendum: The preposition **ad** with the accusative gerund denotes purpose (A.G. 506). **cognoscendum**: Singular, neuter, accusative gerund (A.G. 501-02).

relinquunt: The main verb of the main clause (A.G. 278.b). The historical present, giving vividness to the narrative, is present in Chapter 42 (A.G. 469). This usage, common in all languages, comes from imagining past events as going on before our eyes (*repraesentatio*) (A.G. 469 Note).

(42.2-3) **Impellit alios avaritia, alios iracundia et temeritas quae maxime illi hominum generi est innata, ut levem (3) auditionem habeant pro re comperta.**

alii ... alii, -orum, m., *some ... others.*
avaritia, -ae, f., *greed, avarice, covetousness.*
et, *and.*
habeo, habere, habui, habitus, *hold, treat, regard.*
ille, illae, illud, *that; he, she, it.*

innatus, -a, -um, *native, inborn, innate, inherent, natural.*
levis, -e, *baseless, unfounded.*
pro, *as.*
res, rei, f., *fact, reality.*
temeritas, -tatis, f., *rashness, hastiness.*

auditio, -onis, f., *report, rumor, hearsay.*
compertus, -a, -um, *ascertain, proved.*
genus, generis, n., *race.*
homo, hominis, m., *man, person.*
impello, -pellere, -puli, -pulsus, *urge, drive on, incite, impel.*
iracundia, -ae, f., *anger, passion.*
maxime, *very greatly, exceedingly, chiefly, especially.*
qui, quae, quod, *who, which, what.*
sum, esse, fui, futurus, *be.*
ut, *so that.*

Impellit: The main verb of the main clause (A.G. 278.b). The verb comes in the first position when the idea in it is emphatic (A.G. 598.d). Two or more singular subjects normally take a verb in the plural (A.G. 317). However, when a verb belongs to two or more subjects separately, it often agrees with one (**avaritia**) and is understood with the others (**iracundia et temeritas**) (A.G. 317.c).

alios ... alios: Plural, masculine, accusative pronouns used substantively; the repeated pronoun **alius** means "some ... others" (A.G. 315.a). Accusative direct objects of **Impellit** (A.G. 387).

avaritia ... iracundia et temeritas: Three nominative subjects (A.G. 339). **et**: The conjunction connects the final two nominative nouns (A.G. 324.a). While **avaritia** applies to some, **iracundia** to others, the final member, **temeritas**, applies to all.

quae ... innata: Relative clause (A.G. 303). **quae**: Singular, feminine, nominative relative pronoun used substantively (A.G. 305). The antecedent is **temeritas** (A.G. 307). Nominative subject (A.G. 339). **innata**: Singular, feminine, nominative predicate adjective modifying **quae** after **est** (A.G. 283-84).

maxime: Irregular superlative adverb (A.G. 218.a and 320-21).

illi ... generi: Dative with the participle **innata** (A.G. 383-84). **illi**: Singular, neuter, dative demonstrative pronoun used as an adjective modifying **generi** (A.G. 296.1 and a).

hominum: Partitive genitive with **generi** (A.G. 346.a.1).

est: The main verb of the subordinate clause (A.G. 278.b). The present tense is not the historical present but denotes a state as now existing in present time (A.G. 465.2).

ut ... habeant: The conjunction **ut** ("so that") with the subjunctive forms a clause of result (A.G. 537.1). **habeant**: The main verb of the subordinate clause (A.G. 278.b). Present subjunctive; the tense of the subjunctive is in primary sequence and follows the rules for the sequence of tense after **est** (A.G. 482-85). The pronoun **ei**, with **hominum** as the antecedent, is understood as the subject (A.G. 271.a).

levem auditionem: Accusative direct object of **habeant** (A.G. 387).

pro re comperta: Prepositional phrase, **pro** with the ablative here means "as" (*OLD* **pro1** 9). **re comperta**: The phrase **res comperta** is an idiom that means "reliable information, a certainty" (*OLD* **competus**).

(42.3-4) Bona civium Romanorum diripiunt, caedes faciunt, in servitutem abstra(4)hunt.

abstraho, -trahere, -traxi, -tractus, *drag off* or *away, take away by force.*
caedes, -is, f., *killing, slaughter, murder, massacre.*
diripio, -ripere, -ripui, -reptus, *ravage, plunder, pillage.*
in, *into.*
servitus, -tutis, f., *slavery, bondage, subjection.*

bona, -orum, n., pl., *possessions, property, goods.*
civis, -is, m., *citizen.*
facio, facere, feci, factus, *make.*
Romanus, -a, -um, *Roman.*

Bona: Plural, masculine, accusative adjective used substantively meaning "possessions, property" (A.G. 107 and 288) (*OLD* **bonum** 8). Accusative direct object of **diripiunt** (A.G. 387).

civium Romanorum: Possessive genitive with **bona** (A.G. 343).

diripiunt ... faciunt ... abstrahunt: The asyndeton construction lends rapidity to the actions described (A.G. 323.b). The pronoun **ei**, with **Aedui** as the antecedent, is understood as the subject of all three verbs (A.G. 271.a).

diripiunt: The main verb of the coordinate clause **Bona ... diripiunt** (A.G. 278.a).

caedes: Accusative direct object of **faciunt** (A.G. 387).

faciunt: The main verb of the coordinate clause **caedes faciunt** (A.G. 278.a).

in servitutem: Prepositional phrase, **in** with the accusative here means "into" (a state or condition) (*OLD* **in** 2).

abstrahunt: The main verb of the coordinate clause **in ... abstrahunt** (A.G. 278.a). Supply the pronoun **eos**, with **civium** as the antecedent, as the accusative direct object.

(42.4-5) Adiuvat rem proclinatam Convictolitavis plebemque ad furorem impellit, ut facinore admisso ad sanitatem (5) reverti pudeat.

ad, *to.*
admitto, -mittere, -misi, -missus, *commit.*
facinus, -oris, n., *misdeed, crime.*
impello, -pellere, -puli, -pulsus, *urge, drive on, incite, impel.*
proclino, -are, -avi, -atus, *to unbalance, cause to totter.*
-que, *and.*
revertor, -verti, -versus, *return, come back, go back.*
ut, *so that.*

adiuvo, -iuvare, -iuvi, -iutus, *further, sustain, support.*
Convictolitavis, -is, m., *Convictolitavis.*
furor, -oris, m., *outrage, madness, fury.*
plebs, plebis, f., *the common folk, the common people, the populace.*
pudet, pudere, puduit, or **puditum est**, (imper.), *it makes ashamed.*
res, rei, f., *situation.*
sanitas, -tatis, f., *soundness of mind, good sense.*

Adiuvat ... Convictolitavis: The reversal of the normal word order (subject first, verb last) is called hyperbaton (A.G. 596) (Gotoff, 6-10).

Adiuvat: The main verb of the coordinate clause **Adiuvat ... Convictolitavis** (A.G. 278.a). The verb comes in the first position when the idea in it is emphatic (A.G. 598.d).

rem proclinatam: Accusative direct object of **Adiuvat** (A.G. 387). The noun **rem** here means "situation" and **proclinatam**, a perfect, passive participle, means "unbalanced" (OLD **res** 17 and **proclino** 1.c); taken together the literal phrase "unbalanced situation" means "crisis".

Convictolitavis: Nominative subject of **Adiuvat ... impellit** (A.G. 339). The subject is in the last position in its clause (A.G. 597.b). See Appendix A.

plebemque: Accusative direct object of **impellit** (A.G. 387). **plebem**: Note that the rebellion has spread from just the leaders who stand to profit to the general populace. **-que**: The enclitic conjunction connects the two main verbs **Adiuvat ... impellit** (A.G. 324.a).

ad furorem ... ad sanitatem: Notice the nice juxtaposition of the two prepositional phrases of opposite meaning.

ad furorem: Prepositional phrase, **ad** with the accusative here expresses the attainment of a condition and means "to" (*OLD* **ad** 5).

impellit: The main verb of the coordinate clause **plebemque ... pudeat** (A.G. 278.a).

ut ... pudeat: The conjunction **ut** ("so that") with the subjunctive forms a final (purpose) clause (A.G. 531.1). **pudeat**: The main verb of the subordinate clause (A.G. 278.b). Present subjunctive; the tense of the subjunctive is normally in secondary sequence after the historical present **impellit** (A.G. 482-85). Here it is in primary sequence through *repraesentatio* (A.G. 485.e and 585.b Note).

Impersonal verb, the previous infinitive phrase functions as the subject (A.G. 208.c).

facinore admisso: Ablative absolute (A.G. 419-20). **admisso**: The perfect tense of the participle represents the action as completed at the time indicated by the tense of the main verb (A.G. 489).

ad sanitatem reverti: The infinitive phrase functions as the subject of the impersonal verb **pudeat** (A.G. 354.c and 454).

ad sanitatem: Prepositional phrase, **ad** with the accusative here expresses the attainment of a condition and means "to" (*OLD* **ad** 5).

(42.5) **M. Aristium, tribunum militum, iter ad legionem facientem fide data ex oppido Cabillono educunt: idem facere cogunt eos, qui negotiandi causa ibi constiterant.**

ad, *to, towards.*
causa, -ae, f., abl. with the gen., *for the sake of, on account of.*
consisto, -sistere, -stiti, -stitus, *stay, remain, settle.*
educo, -ducere, -duxi, -ductus, *lead out, lead forth.*
facio, facere, feci, factus, *make; do.*
ibi, *in that place, there.*
is, ea, id, *he, she, it; that, this.*
legio, -onis, f., *legion.*
miles, -itis, m., *soldier, foot-solider.*
oppidum, -i, n., *fortified town, city.*
tribunus, -i, m., *tribune.*

Cabillonum, -i, n., *Cabillonum.*
cogo, cogere, coegi, coactus, *compel, force, oblige.*
do, dare, dedi, datus, *give, offer, furnish, grant.*
ex, *from, out of.*
fides, -ei, f, *pledge of good faith, promise.*
idem, eadem, idem, *the same.*
iter, itineris, n., *journey, march.*
M. Aristius, -i, m., *Marcus Aristius.*
negotior, -ari, -atus, *transact business.*
qui, quae, quod, *who, which, what.*

M. Aristium ... facientem: Accusative direct object of **educunt** (A.G. 387). **M. Aristium**: See Appendix A. **M.**: Abbreviated form of the praenomen **Marcus** (A.G. 108.c). **facientem**: Present participle used as an adjective modifying **Aristium** (A.G. 494).

tribunum: A noun in apposition to the proper noun **Aristium** (A.G. 282).

militum: Possessive genitive with **tribunum** (A.G. 343).

iter: Accusative direct object of the present participle **facientem** (A.G. 387 and 488). The phrase **iter facere** is an idiom that means "to march or travel" (*OLD* **iter** 1.b).

ad legionem: Accusative of *place to which* with the preposition **ad** (A.G. 426.2). "Probably going to join his legion at Gergovia. Aristius seems to have been accompanied by a detachment of soldiers, and probably the traders put themselves under his protection." (Kelsey, 415)

fide data: Ablative absolute (A.G. 419-20). **data**: The perfect tense of the participle represents the action as completed at the time indicated by the tense of the main verb (A.G. 489). The breaking of a explicit promise reinforces the fickle nature of the 'barbarian' character type of the Gauls (see Chapter 2).

ex oppido: Ablative of *place from which* with the preposition **ex** (A.G. 426.1).

Cabillono: An ablative proper noun in apposition to **oppido** (A.G. 282). See Appendix A.

educunt: The main verb of the main clause (A.G. 278.b). The pronoun **ei**, with **Aedui** as the antecedent, is understood as the subject (A.G. 271.a).

idem: Singular, neuter, accusative demonstrative pronoun used substantively (A.G. 296.2). The antecedent is the idea of the departure of Aristius (A.G. 298). Accusative direct object of the infinitive **facere** (A.G. 387 and 451.3). "I.e., to leave Cabillonum at once. The number of traders at Châlon must have been considerable." (Kelsey, 415)

facere ... eos: Subject accusative with the infinitive after **cogunt**. The construction is equivalent to a substantive clause of purpose (A.G. 563.a Note). **eos**: Plural, masculine, accusative demonstrative pronoun used substantively (A.G. 296.2). The pronoun is correlative to the relative clause **qui ... constiterant** (A.G. 297.d).

cogunt: The main verb of the main clause (A.G. 278.b). The pronoun **ei**, with **Aedui** as the antecedent, is understood as the subject (A.G. 271.a).

qui ... constiterant: Relative clause (A.G. 303). **qui**: Plural, masculine, nominative relative pronoun used substantively (A.G. 305). The antecedent is **eos** (A.G. 307). Nominative subject (A.G. 339). **constiterant**: The main verb of the subordinate clause (A.G. 278.b). The pluperfect denotes an action completed in past time (A.G. 477).

negotiandi causa: The genitive gerund with the ablative of **causa** expresses purpose (A.G. 504.b). "The Romans in Gallic cities were chiefly engaged in loaning money, in buying grain and other commodities, and in farming revenues." (Kelsey, 401) **negotiandi**: Singular, neuter, genitive gerund (A.G. 501-02).

ibi: Adverb (A.G. 215.5 and 320-21).

(42.6) **(6) Hos continuo *in* itinere adorti omnibus impedimentis exuunt; repugnantis diem noctemque obsident; multis utrimque interfectis maiorem multitudinem ad arma concitant.**

ad, *to.*
arma, -orum, n., pl., *arms, weapons.*
continuo, *forthwith, immediately, at once.*
exuo, -uere, -ui, -utus, *strip, strip off, despoil, deprive.*
impedimenta, -orum, n., pl., *heavy baggage, baggage.*
interficio, -ficere, -feci, -fectus, *slay, kill.*
maior, -or, -us, *greater, larger, bigger.*
multitudo, -inis, f., *multitude, crowd.*

adorior, -oriri, -ortus, *fall upon, attack, assail.*
concito, -are, -avi, -atus, *rouse, stir up, excite, provoke.*
dies, -ei, m. and f., *day.*
hic, haec, hoc, *this; he, she, it.*
in, *on.*
iter, itineris, n., *road, route.*
multi, -orum, m., pl., *many men.*
nox, noctis, f., *night.*

obsideo, -sidere, -sedi, -sessus, *besiege, blockade.*
-que, *and.*
utrimque, *on both sides.*

omnis, -e, *all.*
repugno, -are, -avi, -atus, *resist, oppose.*

Hos: Plural, masculine, accusative demonstrative pronoun used substantively (A.G. 296.2). The antecedent is **eos** (the Roman traders) (A.G. 297.e). Accusative direct object of the participle **adorti** (A.G. 387 and 488).
continuo: Adverb (A.G. 320-21).
in itinere: Ablative of *place where* with the preposition **in** (locative ablative) (A.G. 426.3).
adorti: Nominative, perfect, deponent, participle used as a predicate, where in English a phrase or a subordinate clause would be more normal (A.G. 496). The pronoun **ei**, with **Aedui** from 42.1 as the antecedent, is understood. Nominative subject (A.G. 339).
omnibus impedimentis: Ablative of separation after **exuunt** (A.G. 364 and 402).
exuunt: The main verb of the simple sentence (A.G. 278.1).
repugnantis: Plural, masculine, accusative present participle used substantively (A.G. 494.a). The noun **Romanos** is understood (A.G. 288.b). Accusative plural; **-is** for **-es** is the regular form of the present participle (A.G. 117-18). Accusative direct object of **obsident** (A.G. 387).
diem noctemque: Accusative of *time how long* (A.G. 423.2). **-que**: The enclitic conjunction connects the two accusative nouns (A.G. 324.a).
obsident: The main verb of the simple sentence (A.G. 278.1). The pronoun **ei**, with **adorti** (**Aedui**) as the antecedent, is understood as the subject (A.G. 271.a).
multis utrimque interfectis: Ablative absolute (A.G. 419-20). **utrimque**: Adverb (A.G. 320-21). **multis**: Plural, masculine, ablative adjective used substantively (A.G. 288). **interfectis**: The perfect tense of the participle represents the action as completed at the time indicated by the tense of the main verb (A.G. 489).
maiorem multitudinem: Accusative direct object of **concitant** (A.G. 387). **maiorem**: Irregular comparative adjective (A.G. 129).
ad arma: Prepositional phrase, **ad** with the accusative here means "to" (an act or policy) (*OLD* ad 6).
concitant: The main verb of the main clause (A.G. 278.b). The pronoun **ei**, with **adorti** (**Aedui**) as the antecedent, is understood as the subject (A.G. 271.a).

(43.1-3) Interim nuntio allato omnis eorum milites in potestate (2) Caesaris teneri, concurrunt ad Aristium; nihil publico factum consilio demonstrant; quaestionem de bonis direptis decernunt, Litavicci fratrumque bona publicant, legatos ad (3) Caesarem sui purgandi gratia mittunt.

ad, *to.*
Aristius, -i, m., *Aristius.*
Caesar, -aris, m., *Caesar.*

consilium, -i, n., *plan, design, scheme.*
decerno, -cernere, -crevi, -cretus, *resolve upon, decree.*

diripio, -ripere, -ripui, -reptus, *ravage, plunder, pillage.*
frater, -tris, m., *brother.*
in, *in.*
is, ea, id, *he, she, it; that, this.*
Litaviccus, -i, m., *Litaviccus.*
mitto, mittere, misi, missus, *send.*
nuntius, -i, m., *message, tidings.*
potestas, -tatis, f., *power.*
publicus, -a, -um, *of the state, public.*
quaestio, -onis, f. *inquiry, examination, investigation.*
sui, sibi, se, or **sese**, nom. wanting, *themselves.*

affero, -ferre, attuli, allatus, *bring, convey, deliver.*
bona, -orum, n., pl., *possessions, property, goods.*
concurro, -currere, -cucurri or **-curri, -cursus**, *run together, run up, rush.*
de, *about, concerning.*
demonstro, -are, -avi, -atus, *point out, show, say, mention, explain.*
facio, facere, feci, factus, *bring about, make, do.*
gratia, -ae, f., (abl. with the gen.) *for the sake of.*
interim, *in the mean time, meanwhile.*
legatus, -i, m., *envoy, ambassador.*
miles, -itis, m., *soldier, foot-solider.*
nihil, n., *nothing.*
omnis, -e, *all.*
publico, -are, -avi, -atus, *confiscate.*
purgo, -are, -avi, -atus, *free from blame, excuse, clear.*
-que, *and.*
teneo, tenere, tenui, -----, *hold fast, hold, keep.*

Interim ... teneri: Ablative absolute with a dependent clause.
Interim: Adverb (A.G. 320-21).
nuntio allato: Ablative absolute (A.G. 419-20). **allato**: The perfect tense of the participle represents the action as completed at the time indicated by the tense of the main verb (A.G. 489).
omnis milites ... teneri: Accusative/infinitive construction in indirect discourse (A.G. 577 ff.). The verb of saying is not expressed, but implied in the ablative absolute **nuntio allato** (A.G. 580.a). **omnis**: Plural, masculine, accusative attributive adjective with **milites** (A.G. 285.1). **-is** for **-es** is the regular form in i-stem adjectives (A.G. 114.a and 116). **teneri**: Present infinitive; the tense of the infinitive in indirect discourse is relative to that of the verb of saying (A.G. 584).
eorum: Plural, masculine, genitive demonstrative pronoun used substantively (A.G. 296.2). The antecedent is **Aedui** at 42.1 (A.G. 297.e). Possessive genitive with **milites** (A.G. 343).
in potestate Caesaris: Prepositional phrase, **in** with the ablative here means "in" (a specified case or condition) (*OLD* in 37).
Caesaris: Possessive genitive with **potestate** (A.G. 343). See Appendix A.
concurrunt ... demonstrant... decernunt ... publicant ... mittunt: The pronoun **ei**, with the leaders of the Aedui who have received the messages as the antecedent, is understood as the subject of all five verbs (A.G. 271.a). The asyndeton construction lends rapidity to

the actions described (A.G. 323.b). For another rapid succession of main verbs see 11.9.

concurrunt: The main verb of the main clause (A.G. 278.b). The historical present, giving vividness to the narrative, is present in Chapter 43 (A.G. 469). This usage, common in all languages, comes from imagining past events as going on before our eyes (*repraesentatio*) (A.G. 469 Note).

ad Aristium: Prepositional phrase, **ad** with the accusative here means "to" (*OLD* **ad** 1). **Aristium**: See Appendix A.

nihil ... factum (esse): Accusative/infinitive construction in indirect discourse after **demonstrant** (A.G. 577 ff.). **nihil**: Accusative indeclinable noun, used only as nominative and accusative singular (A.G. 103.a). **factum (esse)**: Supply **esse** to form the perfect, passive infinitive (A.G. 188). The tense of the infinitive in indirect discourse is relative to that of the verb of saying (A.G. 584).

publico ... consilio: Ablative of manner with a limiting adjective (A.G. 412).

demonstrant: The main verb of the main clause (A.G. 278.b).

quaestionem: Accusative direct object of **decernunt** (A.G. 387).

de bonis direptis: Prepositional phrases, **de** with the ablative here means "about, concerning" (*OLD* **de** 12). **bonis**: Plural, neuter, ablative adjective used substantively meaning "possessions, property" (A.G. 107 and 288) (*OLD* **bonum** 8). **direptis**: Ablative, perfect, passive, participle used as an adjective modifying **bonis** (A.G. 494).

decernunt: The main verb of the simple sentence (A.G. 278.1).

Litavicci fratrumque: Two possessive genitives with **bona** (A.G. 343). **Litavicci**: See Appendix A. **-que**: The enclitic conjunction connects the two genitive nouns (A.G. 324.a).

bona: Plural, neuter, accusative adjective used substantively meaning "possessions, property" (A.G. 107 and 288) (*OLD* **bonum** 8). Accusative direct object of **publicant** (A.G. 387).

publicant: The main verb of the simple sentence (A.G. 278.1).

legatos: Accusative direct object of **mittunt** (A.G. 387).

ad Caesarem: Prepositional phrase, **ad** with the accusative here means "to" (*OLD* **ad** 1). **Caesarem**: See Appendix A.

sui purgandi gratia: The genitive of the pronoun and gerund/gerundive with the ablative **gratia** expresses purpose (A.G. 504.b). This is an irregular construction with **gratia**. **sui**: Genitive direct reflexive pronoun used substantively (A.G. 144 and 300.1). **purgandi**: If the substantive is a personal or reflexive pronoun, an irregular construction is used, **mei, tui, sui, nostri,** or **vestri** with a genitive in -i (sometimes called gerund, sometimes gerundive), regardless of gender and number. Thus, **sui purgandi gratia** means "for the sake of" clearing themselves. The usual gerund construction would be **se purgandi gratia**; the gerundive construction **sui purgandorum gratia**. (Walker, 526, 291.a). For parallel constructions with **causa** and the objective genitive see 50.2 and 80.9.

mittunt: The main verb of the simple sentence (A.G. 278.1).

(43.3) Haec faciunt reciperandorum suorum causa;

causa, -ae, f., abl. with the gen., *for the sake of, on account of.*
hic, haec, hoc, *this*; *he, she, it.*
sui, -orum, m., pl., *their men*, with or without *own.*

facio, facere, feci, factus, *bring about, make, do.*
recipero, -are, -avi, -atus, *recover, regain, get back.*

Haec: Plural, neuter, accusative demonstrative pronoun used substantively meaning "these things" (A.G. 296.2). The antecedent is the repentance of the **Aedui** described immediately above (A.G. 297.e). Accusative direct object of **faciunt** (A.G. 387).

faciunt: The main verb of the simple sentence (A.G. 278.1). The pronoun **ei**, with **Aedui** as the antecedent, is understood as the subject (A.G. 271.a).

reciperandorum suorum causa: The genitive of the gerundive and pronoun with the ablative **causa** expresses purpose (A.G. 504.b).

suorum: Plural, masculine, genitive possessive pronoun used substantively to denote a special class (A.G. 300.1 and 302.d).

reciperandorum: Plural, masculine, genitive gerundive used as an adjective modifying **suorum** denoting necessity, obligation or propriety (A.G. 500.1).

(43.3) sed contaminati facinore et capti compendio ex direptis bonis, quod ea res ad multos pertinebat, timore poenae exterriti consilia clam de bello inire incipiunt civitatesque reliquas legationibus sollicitant.

ad, *to.*
bona, -orum, n., pl., *possessions, property, goods.*
civitas, -tatis, f., *state, nation.*
compendium, -i, n., *profit, gain.*
contamino, -are, -avi, -atus, *taint, pollute.*
diripio, -ripere, -ripui, -reptus, *ravage, plunder, pillage.*
ex, *from.*
facinus, -oris, n., *misdeed, crime.*

ineo, -ire, -ivi, or **-ii, -itus**, *enter upon, begin, form.*
legatio, -onis, f., *deputation, embassy, envoys.*
pertineo, -tinere, -tinui, -----, *pertain to, concern, have to do with.*
-que, *and.*
reliquus, -a, -um, *remaining, the rest.*
sed, *but.*

bellum, -i, n., *war, warfare.*
capio, capere, cepi, captus, *seduce, win over.*
clam, *secretly.*
consilium, -i, n., *plan, plot, design, scheme.*
de, *about, concerning.*
et, *and.*
exterreo, -ere, -ui, -itus, *frighten, strike with terror.*
incipio, -cipere, -cepi, -ceptus, *begin, commence, undertake.*
is, ea, id, *he, she, it; that, this.*
multi, -orum, m., pl., *many men.*
poena, -ae, f., *punishment, penalty.*
quod, *because, since, for, as.*
res, rei, f., *situation, event, affair.*
sollicito, -are, -avi, -atus, *instigate, urge, incite, tamper with, tempt.*

timor, -oris, m., *fear, dread, apprehension, alarm, timidity.*

sed: Coordinate conjunction (A.G. 324.d).

contaminati ... capti ... exterriti: Three nominative, perfect, passive, participle used as a predicate, where in English a phrase or a subordinate clause would be more normal (A.G. 496). The pronoun **ei**, with the leaders of the Aedui as the antecedent, is understood. Nominative subject of **incipiunt ... sollicitant** (A.G. 339).

facinore: Ablative of cause without a preposition (A.G. 404).

et: The conjunction connects the two perfect participles (A.G. 324.a).

compendio: Ablative of cause without a preposition (A.G. 404).

ex direptis bonis: Prepositional phrase, **ex** with the ablative here indicates the source from which a thing is obtained and means "from" (*OLD* **ex** 14). **direptis**: Ablative, perfect, passive, participle used as an adjective modifying **bonis** (A.G. 494). **bonis**: Plural, neuter, ablative adjective used substantively meaning "possessions, property" (A.G. 107 and 288) (*OLD* **bonum** 8).

quod ... pertinebat: Causal clause; the conjunction **quod** ("because") takes the indicative when the reason is given on the authority of the writer or speaker (A.G. 540.1). **pertinebat**: The main verb of the subordinate clause (A.G. 278.b).

ea res: Nominative subject (A.G. 339). "The profit accruing from the booty." (Kelsey, 415) **ea**: Singular, feminine, nominative demonstrative pronoun used as an adjective modifying **res** (A.G. 296.1 and a).

ad multos: Prepositional phrase, **ad** with the accusative here means "to" (*OLD* **ad** 28). **multos**: Plural, masculine, accusative adjective used substantively (A.G. 288). The noun **Aeduos** is understood (A.G. 288.b).

timore ... sollicitant: This secret plotting, while openly submitting to Aristius, reinforces the fickle nature of the 'barbarian' character type of the Gauls (see Chapter 2).

timore: Ablative of cause without a preposition (A.G. 404).

poenae: Objective genitive with **timore** (A.G. 348).

consilia: Accusative direct object of the infinitive **inire** (A.G. 387 and 451.3). The phrase **consilium inire** is an idiom that means "to deliberate" (*OLD* **consilium** 1) or "to form a plan or plot" (*OLD* **ineo** 7.b). Notice that the noun is here plural, implying numerous plots.

clam: Adverb (A.G. 320-21).

de bello: Prepositional phrase, **de** with the ablative here means "about, concerning" (*OLD* **de** 12).

inire: Complementary infinitive after **incipiunt** (A.G. 456).

incipiunt: The main verb of the coordinate clause **sed ... incipiunt** (A.G. 278.a).

civitatesque reliquas: Accusative direct object of **sollicitant** (A.G. 387). **-que**: The enclitic conjunction connects the two main verbs **incipiunt ... sollicitant** (A.G. 324.a).

legationibus: Ablative of means (A.G. 405.b Note 1 and 409).

sollicitant: The main verb of the coordinate clause **civitatesque ... sollicitant** (A.G. 278.a).

(43.4) **(4) Quae tametsi Caesar intellegebat, tamen quam mitissime potest legatos appellat:**

appello, -are, -avi, -atus, *address.*

intellego, -legere, -lexi, -lectus, *understand, see clearly, perceive.*

mitissime, *very gently, very kindly.*

quam, *as ----- as possible.*

tamen, *yet, still, for all that, nevertheless, however.*

Caesar, -aris, m., *Caesar.*

legatus, -i, m., *envoy, ambassador.*

possum, posse, potui, -----, *be able.*

qui, quae, quod, *who, which, what.*

tametsi, *although, though.*

Quae: Plural, neuter, accusative relative pronoun used substantively to mean "and these things" (A.G. 288 and 305). The antecedent is omitted but it refers to the actions of the **Aedui** described immediately above (A.G. 307.c). Accusative direct object of **intellegebat** (A.G. 387). The relative does not introduce a relative clause but is a connecting relative; at the beginning of a clause the pronoun is often best rendered by a personal or demonstrative pronoun, with or without *and* (A.G. 308.f).

tametsi ... intellegebat ... (tamen): Concessive clause, **tametsi** with the indicative means "even though" and is correlative to **tamen** in the main clause meaning "nevertheless" (A.G. 527) (*OLD* **tametsi** 1 and **tamen** 1). **intellegebat**: The main verb of the subordinate clause (A.G. 278.b).

Caesar: Nominative subject (A.G. 339). See Appendix A.

tamen: Adverb, normally postpositive but not here (A.G. 320-21 and 324.j).

quam mitissime potest: Relative clause (A.G. 279.a). **quam**: The relative adverb with the superlative denotes the highest possible degree "as gently as possible" (A.G. 291.c) (*OLD* **quam** 7). **mitissime**: Superlative adverb (A.G. 218 and 320-21). **potest**: The main verb of the subordinate clause (A.G. 278.b). The pronoun **is**, with **Caesar** as the antecedent, is understood as the subject (A.G. 271.a).

legatos: Accusative direct object of **appellat** (A.G. 387).

appellat: The main verb of the main clause (A.G. 278.b). The pronoun **is**, with **Caesar** as the antecedent, is understood as the subject (A.G. 271.a).

(43.4-5) **nihil se propter inscientiam levitatemque vulgi gravius de civitate iudicare neque de sua in (5) Aeduos benevolentia deminuere.**

Aedui, -orum, m., pl., *the Aedui.*

civitas, -tatis, f., *state, nation.*

benevolentia, -ae, f., *good-will, kindly feeling, friendship.*

de, *with regard to, in the matter of, from.*

deminuo, -minuere, -minui, -minutus, *take away.*
in, *towards.*
iudico, -are, -avi, -atus, *judge, decide, think.*
neque, *and ... not.*
propter, *as a result* or *consequence of, in view of, because of, on account of.*
sui, sibi, se, or **sese,** nom. wanting, *he,* with or without *himself.*
vulgus, -i, n., *common people, mass, multitude, crowd.*

graviter, comp. **-ius,** *severely, seriously.*
inscientia, -ae, f., *ignorance, lack of knowledge.*
levitas, -atis, f., *fickleness, instability.*
nihil, n., *nothing.*
-que, *and.*
suus, -a, -um, *his,* with or without *own.*

nihil: Accusative direct object of the infinitive **iudicare** (A.G. 387 and 451.3). Indeclinable noun, used only as nominative and accusative singular (A.G. 103.a).
se ... iudicare: Accusative/infinitive construction in indirect discourse (A.G. 577 ff.). The verb of saying is not expressed, but implied in the verb **appellat** (A.G. 580.a). **se:** Singular, masculine, accusative direct reflexive pronoun (A.G. 300.1). The antecedent is **Caesar,** the subject of the unexpressed verb of saying (A.G. 299). **iudicare:** Present infinitive; the tense of the infinitive in indirect discourse is relative to that of the verb of saying (A.G. 584).
propter inscientiam levitatemque vulgi: Prepositional phrase, **propter** with the accusative here means "as a result or consequence of, in view of, because of" (*OLD* **propter** 3). **-que:** The enclitic conjunction connects the two accusative nouns in the prepositional phrase (A.G. 324.a). **vulgi:** Possessive genitive to be construed with both accusative nouns (A.G. 343).
gravius: Comparative adverb (A.G. 218 and 320-21).
de civitate: Prepositional phrase, **de** with the ablative here means "with regard to, in the matter" (*OLD* **de** 13).
neque: The conjunction here joins a negative clause to a preceding positive one and means "and ... not" (*OLD* **neque** 3).
de sua ... benevolentia: Prepositional phrase, **de** with the ablative here means "from" (*OLD* **de** 7). **sua:** Singular, feminine, ablative reflexive pronoun used as an adjective modifying **benevolentia** (A.G. 302). The prepositional phrase functions as the object of the infinitive **deminuere** used absolutely (A.G. 389).
in Aeduos: Prepositional phrase, **in** with the accusative here indicates the person towards whom feelings are directed and means "towards" (*OLD* **in** 11). **Aeduos:** See Appendix A.
(eas) deminuere: Accusative/infinitive construction in indirect discourse (A.G. 577 ff.). The verb of saying is not expressed, but implied in the verb **appellat** (A.G. 580.a). The pronoun **eas,** with **inscientiam levitatemque vulgi** as the antecedent, is understood as the accusative subject. **deminuere:** Present infinitive; the tense of the infinitive in indirect discourse is relative to that of the verb of saying (A.G. 584). The infinitive is here used absolutely; a transitive verb may often be used absolutely, i.e. without any object expressed, where the verb does not cease to be transitive because the object is left indefinite, as we see by adding **quid,** *what*? (**sua benevolentia**) (A.G. 273 Note 2). Present infinitive; the tense of the infinitive in indirect discourse is relative to that of the verb of saying (A.G. 584).

(43.5) Ipse maiorem Galliae motum exspectans, ne ab omnibus civitatibus circumsisteretur, consilia inibat quem ad modum ab Gergovia discederet ac rursus omnem exercitum contraheret, ne profectio nata ab timore defectionis similis fugae videretur.

ab, *by; from.*
circumsisto, -sistere, -steti, or **-stiti, -----,** *surround.*
civitas, -tatis, f., *state, nation.*
contraho, -trahere, -traxi, -tractus, *gather together, unite.*
discedo, -cedere, -cessi, -cessurus, *go away, depart, leave.*
exspecto, -are, -avi, -atus, *expect.*
Gallia, -ae, f., *Gaul.*
ineo, -ire, -ivi, or **-ii, -itus,** *enter upon, begin, form.*

maior, -or, -us, *greater, larger, bigger.*
nascor, nasci, natus, *be born.*
omnis, -e, *all; the whole, entire.*
quem ad modum, *in what way, how.*
similis, -e, *like, similar.*
videor, videri, visus sum, *seem, appear.*

ac, *and.*
civitas, -tatis, f., *state, nation.*
consilium, -i, n., *plan, plot, design, scheme.*
defectio, -onis, f., *revolt, rebellion.*
exercitus, -us, m., *army.*
fuga, -ae, f., *flight.*
Gergovia, -ae, f., *Gergovia.*
ipse, -a, -um, *he, they,* with or without *himself, themselves.*
motus, -us, m., *disturbance, revolt, uprising.*
ne, *so that ... not.*
profectio, -onis, f., *departure, setting out.*
rursus, *again, anew.*
timor, -oris, m., *fear, dread.*

Ipse ... exspectans: Nominative subject of **inibat** (A.G. 339). **Ipse:** Singular, masculine, nominative demonstrative pronoun used substantively (A.G. 296.2 and 298.d). The antecedent is **Caesar.** The pronoun is emphatic and emphasizes the end of the indirect discourse (A.G. 298.d.1). **exspectans:** Present participle used as an adjective modifying **Ipse** (A.G. 494).
maiorem ... motum: Accusative direct object of the participle **exspectans** (A.G. 387 and 488). **maiorem:** Irregular comparative adjective (A.G. 129).
Galliae: Locative case of **Gallia, -ae,** f. (A.G. 43.c). See Appendix A.
ne ... circumsisteretur: The conjunction **ne** ("so that ... not") with the subjunctive forms a negative purpose clause dependent on **consilia inibat** (A.G. 531.1). **circumsisteretur:** The main verb of the subordinate clause (A.G. 278.b). Imperfect subjunctive; the tense of the subjunctive is in secondary sequence and follows the rules for the sequence of tense after **inibat** (A.G. 482-85). The pronoun **is,** with **Caesar** as the antecedent, is understood as the subject (A.G. 271.a).
ab omnibus civitatibus: Ablative of agent with the preposition **ab** with the passive verb **circumsisteretur** (A.G. 405).
consilia: Accusative direct object of **inibat** (A.G. 387). The phrase **consilium inire** is an idiom that means "to deliberate" (*OLD*

consilium 1) or "to form a plan or plot" (*OLD* **ineo** 7.b). Notice that the noun is here plural, implying numerous plans.

inibat: The main verb of the main clause (A.G. 278.b).

quem ad modum ... discederet ... contraheret: Indirect question in apposition to the noun **consilia** (A.G. 573-75). **quem ad modum**: Interrogative adverb written as three words (*OLD* **quemadmodum**). **discederet ... contraheret**: The main verbs of the subordinate clause (A.G. 278.b). Imperfect subjunctives; the tense of the subjunctives is in secondary sequence and follows the rules for the sequence of tense for indirect questions after **inibat** (A.G. 575). The pronoun **is**, with **Caesar** as the antecedent, is understood as the subject of both verbs (A.G. 271.a). **discederet**: S. E. Stevens does not accept that Caesar's aim was a simple "prestige" success that would allow him to leave, but that "he wanted to capture Gergovia." (Stevens, 16-17)

ab Gergovia: Ablative of *place from which* with the preposition **ab**; when **ab** is used with a city name it means "from the vicinity of" (A.G. 428.a). **Gergovia**: See Appendix A.

ac: The conjunction connects the two verbs in the indirect question and means "and" (*OLD* **atque** 12).

rursus: Adverb (A.G. 216 and 320-21).

omnem exercitum: Accusative direct object of **contraheret** (A.G. 387). Caesar had split his army with Labienus at 7.34.

ne ... videretur: The conjunction **ne** ("so that ... not") with the subjunctive forms a negative purpose clause (A.G. 531.1). **videretur**: The main verb of the subordinate clause (A.G. 278.b). Imperfect subjunctive; the tense of the subjunctive is in secondary sequence and follows the rules for the sequence of tense after **inibat** (A.G. 482-85).

profectio nata: Nominative subject (A.G. 339). **nata**: Perfect, deponent participle used as a predicate, where in English a phrase or a subordinate clause would be more normal (A.G. 496).

ab timore defectionis: Ablative of source with the preposition **ab** after the participle **nata** (A.G. 403.1). **defectionis**: Objective genitive with **timore** (A.G. 348).

similis (esse): Singular, feminine, nominative predicate adjective modifying **profectio** after **videretur** (A.G. 283). A predicate adjective after a complementary infinitive takes the case of the subject of the main verb (A.G. 283-84 and 458). Supply **esse** as the complementary infinitive after **videretur**.

fugae: Objective genitive with **similis** (A.G. 385.c.2).

3.C CHAPTERS 44-51: THE BREAKDOWN OF MILITARY DISCIPLINE AND THE REPULSE OF THE ROMAN ARMY AT GERGOVIA; NEARLY 700 SOLDIERS ARE LOST IN ONE BATTLE

(44.1) **Haec cogitanti accidere visa est facultas bene rei gerendae.**

accido, -cidere, -cidi, -----, *come, occur.*
cogito, -are, -avi, -atus, *think about, consider, intend, purpose, plan.*
gero, gerere, gessi, gestus, *carry out, perform, do.*
res, rei, f., *matter, affair, situation, event.*

bene, *well, successfully.*
facultas, -atis, f., *ability, opportunity, chance.*
hic, haec, hoc, *this; he, she, it.*
videor, videri, visus sum, *seem, appear.*

Haec: Plural, neuter, accusative demonstrative pronoun used substantively meaning "these things" (A.G. 296.2). The antecedent is the idea of departure described immediately above (A.G. 297.e). Accusative direct object of the participle **cogitanti** (A.G. 387 and 488).

cogitanti: Singular, masculine, dative present participle used substantively (A.G. 494.a). The noun **Caesari** is understood (288.b). Dative indirect object of the intransitive infinitive **accidere** (A.G. 366 and 451.3). Here the present participle denotes an action continued in the present but begun in the past (A.G. 490.1).

accidere: Complementary infinitive after **visa est** (A.G. 456).

visa est: The main verb of the simple sentence (A.G. 278.1).

facultas: Nominative subject (A.G. 339).

bene: Adverb (A.G. 320-21).

rei gerendae: Objective genitive with **facultas** (A.G. 348). **gerendae**: Gerundive used as an adjective modifying **rei** (A.G. 500.1). The phrase **rem gerere** is an idiom that means "to deal with a business" (*OLD* **gero** 9).

(44.1-2) **Nam cum in minora castra operis perspiciendi causa venisset, animadvertit collem, qui ab hostibus tenebatur, nudatum hominibus, qui superioribus diebus vix prae multitudine (2) cerni poterat.**

ab, *by.*
castra, -orum, n., pl., *camp, encampment.*

cerno, cernere, -----, -----, *discern, see, perceive.*
cum, *after, when.*
homo, hominis, m., *man, person.*
in, *into.*
multitudo, -inis, f., *great number, multitude, crowd.*
nudo, -are, -avi, -atus, *expose, leave unprotected.*
perspicio, -spicere, -spexi, -spectus, *inspect, survey.*
prae, *for, because of.*
superior, -or, -us, *former, earlier, previous.*
venio, venire, veni, ventus, *come.*

animadverto, -tere, -ti, -sus, *notice, observe, perceive.*
causa, -ae, f., abl. with the gen., *for the sake of, for the purpose of.*
collis, -is, m., *hill, height, elevation.*
dies, -ei, m. and f., *day.*
hostis, -is, m., *enemy, foe;* pl., *the enemy.*
minor, -or, -ius, *smaller, less.*
nam, *for.*
opus, operis, n., *works, line of works, fortification.*
possum, posse, potui, -----, *be able.*
qui, quae, quod, *who, which, what.*
teneo, tenere, tenui, -----, *hold, keep.*
vix, *scarcely, barely.*

Nam: Causal conjunction (A.G. 223.a.3).

cum ... venisset: Temporal clause; the relative adverb **cum** ("after, when") with the pluperfect subjunctive describes the circumstances that preceded the action of the main verb (A.G. 546). **venisset**: The main verb of the subordinate clause (A.G. 278.b). The pronoun **is**, with **cogitanti** (**Caesar**) as the antecedent, is understood as the subject (A.G. 271.a).

in minora castra: Accusative of *place to which* with the preposition **in** (A.G. 426.2). **minora**: Irregular comparative adjective (A.G. 129).

operis perspiciendi causa: The genitive of the noun and gerundive with the ablative **causa** expresses purpose (A.G. 504.b). **perspiciendi**: Singular, neuter, genitive gerundive used as an adjective modifying **operis** denoting necessity, obligation or propriety (A.G. 500.1).

animadvertit: The main verb of the main clause (A.G. 278.b). The historical present, giving vividness to the narrative, is present in Chapter 44 (A.G. 469). This usage, common in all languages, comes from imagining past events as going on before our eyes (*repraesentatio*) (A.G. 469 Note). The pronoun **is**, with **cogitanti** (**Caesar**) as the antecedent, is understood as the subject (A.G. 271.a).

collem ... nudatum (esse): Accusative/infinitive construction in indirect discourse after **animadvertit** (A.G. 577 ff.). **nudatum (esse)**: Supply **esse** to form the perfect, passive infinitive (A.G. 184). The tense of the infinitive in indirect discourse is relative to that of the verb of saying (A.G. 584).

qui ... tenebatur: Relative clause; a dependent clause in indirect discourse normally takes the subjunctive unless it is merely explanatory or contains statements which are regarded as true independently of the quotation in which case it takes the indicative (A.G. 303, 580 and 583). **qui**: Singular, masculine, nominative relative pronoun used substantively (A.G. 305). The antecedent is **collem** (A.G. 307). Nominative subject (A.G. 339). **tenebatur**: The main verb of the subordinate clause (A.G. 278.b).

ab hostibus: Ablative of agent with the preposition **ab** after the passive verb **tenebatur** (A.G. 405).

hominibus: Ablative of separation without a preposition after **nudatum (esse)** (A.G. 402.a).

qui ... poterat: Relative clause; a dependent clause in indirect discourse normally takes the subjunctive unless it is merely explanatory or contains statements which are regarded as true independently of the quotation in which case it takes the indicative (A.G. 303, 580 and 583). **qui**: Singular, masculine, nominative relative pronoun used substantively (A.G. 305). The antecedent is **collem** (A.G. 307). Nominative subject (A.G. 339). **poterat**: The main verb of the subordinate clause (A.G. 278.b).

superioribus diebus: Ablative of *time when* (A.G. 423.1). **superioribus**: Defective comparative adjective (A.G. 130.b).

vix: Adverb (A.G. 217.c and 320-21).

prae multitudine: Prepositional phrase, **prae** with the ablative here means "for, because of" (*Lewis* **2. prae**).

cerni: Complementary infinitive after **poterat** (A.G. 456).

(44.2) **Admiratus quaerit ex perfugis causam, quorum magnus ad eum cotidie numerus confluebat.**

ad, *to.*
causa, -ae, f., *reason, cause.*
cotidie, *daily, every day.*
is, ea, id, *he, she, it; that, this.*
numerus, -i, m., *number, amount.*
quaero, -ere, quaesivi, quaesitus, *ask, inquire, make inquiry.*

admiror, -ari, -atus, *wonder at, be surprised at.*
confluo, -fluere, -fluxi, -----, *flock together, assemble.*
ex, *from.*
magnus, -a, -um, *great, large.*
perfuga, -ae, m., *deserter.*
qui, quae, quod, *who, which, what.*

Admiratus: Nominative, perfect, deponent, participle used as a predicate, where in English a phrase or a subordinate clause would be more normal (A.G. 496). The pronoun **is**, with **cogitanti** (**Caesar**) as the antecedent, is understood. Nominative subject (A.G. 339). **quaerit**: The main verb of the main clause (A.G. 278.b).

ex perfugis: Ablative of source with the preposition **ex** (A.G. 403.1).

causam: Accusative direct object of **quaerit** (A.G. 387).

quorum ... confluebat: Relative clause (A.G. 303). **quorum**: Plural, masculine, genitive demonstrative pronoun used substantively (A.G. 296.2). The antecedent is **perfugis** (A.G. 297.e). Partitive genitive with **numerus** (A.G. 346.a.1). **confluebat**: The main verb of the subordinate clause (A.G. 278.b).

magnus ... numerus: Nominative subject (A.G. 339).

ad eum: Prepositional phrase, **ad** with the accusative here means "to" (*OLD* **ad** 1). **eum**: Singular, masculine, accusative demonstrative pronoun used substantively (A.G. 296.2). The antecedent is **cogitanti** (**Caesar**) (A.G. 297.e).

cotidie: Adverb (A.G. 217.b and 320-21).

(44.3-4) **(3) Constabat inter omnis quod iam ipse Caesar per exploratores cognoverat, dorsum esse eius iugi prope aequum, sed hunc silvestrem et angustum, qua esset aditus ad alteram (4) partem oppidi;**

ad, *to.*

aequus, -a, -um, *level, even, flat.*
angustus, -a, -um, *contracted, narrow, close.*
cognosco, -gnoscere, -gnovi, cognitus, *become acquainted with, learn.*

dorsum, -i, n., *top, ridge.*
explorator, -oris, m., *spy, scout.*
iam, *already, by this time.*

aditus, -us, m., *approach, access, way of approach, means of access.*
alter, -era, -erum, *the other.*
Caesar, -aris, m., *Caesar.*
consto, -stare, -stiti, -staturus, (imper.), *it is agreed, there is agreement.*
et, *and.*
hic, haec, hoc, *this; he, she, it.*
inter, *among.*

ipse, -a, -um, *himself.*
iugum, -i, n., *ridge, summit, chain.*
oppidum, -i, n., *fortified town, city.*
per, *by* (means of), *through.*
qua, *where.*
sed, *but.*
sum, esse, fui, futurus, *be.*

is, ea, id, *he, she, it; that, this.*
omnes, -ium, m., pl., *all men, all.*
pars, partis, f., *part, side.*
prope, *nearly.*
qui, quae, quod, *who, which, what.*
silvestris, -e, *covered with woods, wooded, woody.*

Constabat: The main verb of the main clause (A.G. 278.b). Impersonal use of the verb, supply **id** as the subject (A.G. 207). The impersonal use means "it is agreed, there is agreement" (*OLD* **consto** 9.c). The verb comes in the first position when the idea in it is emphatic (A.G. 598.d).

inter omnis: Prepositional phrase, **inter** with the accusative here means "among" (indicating a group in which a common attitude, opinion, practice, etc. exists) (*OLD* **inter1** 4.a). **omnis**: Plural, masculine, accusative adjective used substantively (A.G. 288). **-is** for **-es** is the regular form in i-stem adjectives (A.G. 114.a and 116). These are the deserters (**perfugis**) mentioned above. Notice that the deserters inform Caesar of two things: first, the physical description which has already been collaborated by Caesar's scouts (**dorsum ... oppidi**); second, what the Gauls thought and planned (**huic .... evocatos**) which is new information not previously reported by the scouts to Caesar.

quod ... oppidi: Relative clause with dependent clauses.

quod ... cognoverat: Relative clause (A.G. 303). **quod**: Singular, neuter, accusative relative pronoun used substantively (A.G. 305). The antecedent is omitted, supply **id**, the supplied subject of **Constabat** (A.G. 307.d Note). Accusative direct object of **cognoverat** (A.G. 387). **cognoverat**: The main verb of the subordinate clause (A.G. 278.b). The pluperfect denotes an action completed in past time (A.G. 477).

iam: Adverb (A.G. 215.6, 217.b and 320-21).

ipse Caesar: Nominative subject (A.G. 339). **ipse**: Singular, masculine, nominative demonstrative pronoun used as an intensifying adjective modifying **Caesar** meaning "himself" (A.G. 296.1 and a and 298.c). **Caesar**: See Appendix A.

per exploratores: Prepositional phrase, the personal agent, when considered as instrument or means, is often expressed by **per** with the accusative meaning "by" (means of) (A.G. 405.b).

dorsum esse ... aequum: Accusative/infinitive construction in indirect discourse after **cognoverat** (A.G. 577 ff.). **esse**: Present infinitive; the tense of the infinitive in indirect discourse is relative to that of the verb of saying (A.G. 584). **aequum**: Singular, neuter, accusative, predicate adjective modifying **dorsum** after **esse** (A.G. 283-84).

eius iugi: Partitive genitive with **dorsum** (A.G. 346.a.1). **eius**: Singular, neuter, genitive demonstrative pronoun used as an adjective modifying **iugi** (A.G. 296.1 and a).

prope: Adverb (A.G. 320-21).

sed: Coordinate conjunction (A.G. 324.d).

hunc (esse) silvestrem et angustum: Accusative/infinitive construction in indirect discourse after **cognoverat** (A.G. 577 ff.). Supply **esse** as the infinitive. **hunc**: Singular, masculine, accusative demonstrative pronoun used substantively (A.G. 296.2). The antecedent is **collem** at 44.1 (A.G. 297.e). **silvestrem et angustum**: Two singular, masculine, accusative predicate adjectives modifying **hunc** after the supplied **esse** (A.G. 283-84). **et**: The conjunction connects the two adjectives (A.G. 324.a). Two adjectives belonging to the same noun are regularly connected by a conjunction (A.G. 323.d).

qua ... oppidi: Relative clause; a subordinate clause in indirect discourse takes the subjunctive (A.G. 279.a and 580). **qua**: Relative adverb meaning "where" (*OLD* **qua** 4). **oppidi**: See below.

esset: The main verb of the subordinate clause (A.G. 278.b). Imperfect subjunctive; the tense of the subjunctive is in secondary sequence and follows the rules for the sequence of tense after **cognoverat** (A.G. 482-85). The verb **sum** in the sense of "exist" makes a complete predicate without a predicate noun or adjective ("there was ..."). It is then called the substantive verb and regularly comes first (A.G. 284.b and 598.c).

aditus: Nominative subject (A.G. 339).

ad alteram partem oppidi: Accusative of *place to which* with the preposition **ad** (A.G. 426.2). **oppidi**: Partitive genitive with **partem** (A.G. 346.a.1).

(44.4) vehementer huic illos loco timere nec iam aliter sentire, uno colle ab Romanis occupato, si alterum amisissent, quin paene circumvallati atque omni exitu et pabulatione interclusi viderentur:

ab, *by.*
alter, -i, m., *the second, next, other.*
atque, *and.*

collis, -is, m., *hill, height, elevation.*
exitus, -us, m., *a going out, egress.*
iam, *now, at this time, at present.*
intercludo, -cludere, -clusi, -clusus, *shut off, block up, blockade.*
nec, *and ... not.*

omnis, -e, *all, every.*
paene, *almost, nearly.*

aliter, *otherwise, differently.*
amitto, -mittere, -misi, -missus, *lose.*
circumvallo, -are, -avi, -atus, *surround with a rampart, blockade, invest.*
et, *and.*
hic, haec, hoc, *this; he, she, it.*
ille, illae, illud, *that; he, she, it.*
locus, -i, m., *place, position.*
occupo, -are, -avi, -atus, *seize, take possession of, fill, occupy.*
pabulatio, -onis, f., *foraging, getting fodder.*
quin, *than, that, but that.*

Romani, -orum, m., pl., *the Romans.*
si, *if.*

unus, -a, -um, *one.*
videor, videri, visus sum, *seem, appear.*

sentio, sentire, sensi, sensus, *feel, think.*
timeo, -ere, -ui, -----, *have fear, be afraid, be apprehensive.*
vehementer, *vigorously, violently, exceedingly.*

vehementer: Adverb (A.G. 214.b and 320-21).
huic ... loco: Dative indirect object of the intransitive use of the infinitive timere (A.G. 367.c and 451.3). huic: Singular, masculine, dative demonstrative pronoun used as an adjective modifying loco (A.G. 296.1 and a).
illos ... timere: Accusative/infinitive construction in indirect discourse (A.G. 577 ff.). The verb of saying is not expressed, but implied in the phrase Constabat inter omnis (A.G. 580.a). illos: Plural, masculine, accusative demonstrative pronoun used substantively (A.G. 296.2). The antecedent is hostibus at 44.1 (A.G. 297.e). timere: Present infinitive; the tense of the infinitive in indirect discourse is relative to that of the verb of saying (A.G. 584). "Now that one hill had been lost, if Caesar should get possession of another he might extend his line of works along the whole south side of the city, thus shutting the Gauls off from their main water supply and from foraging in the plain." (Kelsey, 415)
nec: The conjunction joins a negative clause to a preceding positive one and means "and ... not" (*OLD* neque 3).
iam: Adverb (A.G. 215.6, 217.b and 320-21).
aliter: Adverb with quin (A.G. 320-21) (*OLD* aliter 2).
(illos) sentire: Accusative/infinitive construction in indirect discourse (A.G. 577 ff.). The verb of saying is not expressed, but implied in the phrase Constabat inter omnis (A.G. 580.a). Carry down the pronoun illos as the accusative subject. sentire: Present infinitive; the tense of the infinitive in indirect discourse is relative to that of the verb of saying (A.G. 584).
uno colle ab Romanis occupato: Ablative absolute (A.G. 419-20). See 36.5-7 for the taking of the first hill. uno: Declinable cardinal number used as an adjective modifying colle (A.G. 132-35). ab Romanis: Ablative of agent with the preposition ab after the passive participle occupato (A.G. 405). occupato: The perfect tense of the participle represents the action as completed at the time indicated by the tense of the main verb (A.G. 489).
si ... amisissent ... quin viderentur: A subordinate conditional statement in indirect statement after sentire (A.G. 512.c). The apodosis, as a subordinate quin clause, takes the subjunctive rather than the infinitive and the protasis, as a clause subordinate to a subjunctive clause, also takes the subjunctive (A.G. 512.c and 589).
si ... amisissent: The conjunction si ("if") with the subjunctive forms the protasis of a conditional statement in indirect discourse (A.G. 589.1). amisissent: The main verb of the subordinate clause (A.G. 278.b). Pluperfect subjunctive; the tense of the subjunctive is in secondary sequence and follows the rules for the sequence of tense after Constabat (A.G. 482-85). The pluperfect tense of the subjunctive is here standing for a future perfect in direct discourse (A.G. 484.c). The future perfect tense denotes action completed (at the time referred to), and hence is represented in the subjunctive by the pluperfect tense in secondary sequence (A.G. 484.c). The pronoun ei, with illos as the antecedent, is understood as the subject (A.G. 271.a).
alterum: Singular, masculine, accusative adjective used substantively (A.G. 288). The noun collem is understood (A.G. 288.b). The adjective here is in a series after the cardinal number uno and means "The second, the next" (*OLD* alter1 3.d). Accusative direct object of amisissent (A.G. 387).
quin ... viderentur: The apodosis of the conditional statement is here a dependent clause (A.G. 512.c). Subordinate clause; the conjunction quin ("than") with the subjunctive is used after aliter sentire (A.G. 278.b and 558). viderentur: The main verb of the subordinate clause (A.G. 278.b). Imperfect subjunctive; the tense of the subjunctive is in secondary sequence and follows the rules for the sequence of tense after Constabat (A.G. 482-85). The pronoun ei, with illos as the antecedent, is understood as the subject (A.G. 271.a).
paene: Adverb (A.G. 217.c and 320-21).
circumvallati ... interclusi (esse): Two plural, masculine, nominative, perfect, passive participle used as a predicate adjectives modifying ei, the supplied subject, after viderentur (A.G. 283-84). A predicate adjective after a complementary infinitive takes the case of the subject of the main verb (A.G. 283-84, 458, and 500.1). Supply esse as the complementary infinitive after viderentur.
atque: The conjunction connects the two participles and means "and" (*OLD* atque 12).
omni exitu et pabulatione: Two ablatives of separation without a preposition after the passive participle interclusi (A.G. 401). et: The conjunction connects the two ablative nouns (A.G. 324.a).

(44.4) ad hunc muniendum omnis a Vercingetorige evocatos.

a(b), *by.*
evoco, -are, -avi, -atus, *call out, call forth, call, summon.*
munio, -ire, -ivi, -itus, *fortify, protect, secure.*
Vercingetorix, -igis, m., *Vercingetorix.*

ad, *for, in order to, for the purpose of.*
hic, haec, hoc, *this; he, she, it.*
omnes, -ium, m., pl., *all men, all.*

ad hunc muniendum: The preposition ad with the accusative pronoun and gerundive denotes purpose (A.G. 506). hunc: Singular, masculine, accusative demonstrative pronoun used substantively (A.G. 296.2). The antecedent is alterum (collis) (A.G. 297.e).
muniendum: Singular, masculine, accusative gerundive used as an adjective modifying hunc denoting necessity, obligation or propriety (A.G. 500.1).
omnis ... evocatos (esse): Accusative/infinitive construction in indirect discourse (A.G. 577 ff.). The verb of saying is not expressed, but implied in the phrase Constabat inter omnis (A.G. 580.a). omnis: Plural, masculine, accusative adjective used substantively (A.G. 288). -is for -es is the regular form in i-stem adjectives (A.G. 114.a and 116). evocatos (esse): Supply esse to form the perfect,

passive infinitive (A.G. 184). The tense of the infinitive in indirect discourse is relative to that of the verb of saying (A.G. 584).

a Vercingetorige: Ablative of agent with the preposition **a(b)** after the passive verb **evocatos (esse)** (A.G. 405). **Vercingetorige**: See Appendix A.

(45.1-2) Hac re cognita, Caesar mittit compluris equitum turmas eo de media nocte. Imperat his ut paulo tumultuosius (2) omnibus locis pervagentur.

Caesar, -aris, m., *Caesar.*

complures, -a and **-ia**, *several, a number of, many.*
eo, *thither, there.*
hic, haec, hoc, *this; he, she, it.*
loca, -orum, n., pl., *places.*
mitto, mittere, misi, missus, *send.*
omnis, -e, *all.*
pervagor, -ari, -atus, *roam about.*
tumultuose, comp. **-ius**, *with bustling, with confusion.*
ut, *so that.*

cognosco, -gnoscere, -gnovi, cognitus, *learn, ascertain, recognize.*
de, *immediately after, following.*
eques, -itis, m., *rider, horseman, cavalryman, trooper.*
impero, -are, -avi, -atus, *command, order.*
medius, -a, -um, *in the middle, midst, middle, mid-.*
nox, noctis, f., *night.*
paulo, *somewhat more.*
res, rei, f., *situation, event, affair.*
turma, -ae, f., *troop, squadron.*

Hac re cognita: Ablative absolute (A.G. 419-20). **Hac**: Singular, feminine, ablative demonstrative pronoun used as an adjective modifying **re** (A.G. 296.1 and a). **cognita**: The perfect tense of the participle represents the action as completed at the time indicated by the tense of the main verb (A.G. 489).
Caesar: Nominative subject (A.G. 339). See Appendix A.
mittit: The main verb of the main clause (A.G. 278.b). The historical present, giving vividness to the narrative, is present in Chapter 45 (A.G. 469). This usage, common in all languages, comes from imagining past events as going on before our eyes (*repraesentatio*) (A.G. 469 Note). "Toward the point which the Gauls were engaged in fortifying, ... By seeming to concentrate his forces against this position, Caesar drew the attention of the enemy from his real design, the seizing of their camp." (Kelsey, 415)
compluris ... turmas: Accusative direct object of **mittit** (A.G. 387). **compluris**: Plural, masculine, accusative comparative adjective, a compound of **plus** (A.G. 120). **-is** for **-es** is an allowable accusative ending for comparative adjectives (A.G. 120-21.c). **turmas**: "The cavalry was divided into squads (*turma*), of about 30 horsemen; ... probably the squad contained three decuries (*decuriae*), of ten men each, under the command of decurions (*decuriones*). The higher officers were called cavalry perfects (*praefecti equitum*)." (Walker, 24)
equitum: Partitive genitive with **turmas** (A.G. 346.a.1).
eo: Adverb (A.G. 217.a and 320-21).
de media nocte: Prepositional phrase, **de** with the ablative here means "immediately after, following" (*OLD* de 4.b). **media**: The adjective designates not what object, but what part of it is meant (A.G. 293).
Imperat: The main verb of the main clause (A.G. 278.b). The verb comes in the first position when the idea in it is emphatic (A.G. 598.d). The pronoun **is**, with **Caesar** as the antecedent, is understood as the subject (A.G. 271.a).
his: Plural, masculine, dative demonstrative pronoun used substantively (A.G. 296.2). The antecedent is **equitum** (A.G. 297.e). Dative indirect object of the normally intransitive verb **Imperat** (A.G. 367).
ut ... pervagentur: The conjunction **ut** ("so that") with the subjunctive is here a substantive clause of purpose which is used as the object of **Imperat** denoting an action directed toward the future (A.G. 563). **pervagentur**: The main verb of the subordinate clause (A.G. 278.b). Present subjunctive; the tense of the subjunctive is normally in secondary sequence after the historical present **Imperat** (A.G. 482-85). Here it is in primary sequence through *repraesentatio* (A.G. 485.e and 585.b Note). The pronoun **ei**, with **his** (**equites**) as the antecedent, is understood as the subject (A.G. 271.a).
paulo: Adverb; **paulo** with a comparative adverb means "somewhat more" (*OLD* paul(l)o 2.a).
tumultuosius: Comparative adverb (A.G. 218 and 320-21).
omnibus locis: Ablative of *place where* without a preposition (A.G. 429.1-2).

(45.2-3) Prima luce magnum numerum impedimentorum ex castris mulorumque produci deque his stramenta detrahi mulionesque cum cassidibus equitum specie (3) ac simulatione collibus circumvehi iubet.

ac, *and.*
castra, -orum, n., pl., *camp, encampment.*
collis, -is, m., *hill, height, elevation.*
de, *from.*

eques, -itis, m., *rider, horseman, cavalryman, trooper.*
hic, haec, hoc, *this; he, she, it.*
iubeo, iubere, iussi, iussus, *order, give orders, bid, command.*
magnus, -a, -um, *great, large.*
mulus, -i, m., *mule.*
primus, -a, -um, *first.*
-que, *and.*

cassis, -idis, f., *helmet.*
circumvehor, -vehi, -vectus, *ride around.*
cum, *with.*
detraho, -trahere, -traxi, -tractus, *take off, take away, remove.*
ex, *from, out of.*
impedimenta, -orum, n., pl., *baggage animals.*
lux, lucis, f., *light*, (with **prima**), *daybreak.*
mulio, -onis, m., *muleteer, mule-driver.*
numerus, -i, m., *number.*
produco, -ducere, -duxi, -ductus, *bring out, lead forth.*
simulatio, -onis, f., *pretense, guise.*

species, -iei, f., *semblance, pretense, appearance.*   stramentum, -i, n., *pack-saddle.*

Prima luce: Ablative of *time when* (A.G. 423.1). **Prima**: Declinable ordinal number used as an adjective (A.G. 132-35).

magnum numerum ... produci: Subject accusative with the infinitive after **iubet**. The construction is equivalent to a substantive clause of purpose (A.G. 563.a).

impedimentorum ... mulorumque: Two partitive genitives with **numerum** (A.G. 346.a.1). **impedimentorum**: Here the noun **impedimentorum** means "baggage animals" and not the usual meaning in the *BG* of "baggage" (*OLD* **impedimentum** 3.b). **-que**: The enclitic conjunction connects the two genitive nouns (A.G. 324.a).

ex castris: Ablative of *place from which* with the preposition **ex** (A.G. 426.1).

deque his: Prepositional phrase, **de** with the ablative here means "from" (*OLD* **de** 2). **-que**: The enclitic conjunction connects the two infinitives **produci ... detrahi** (A.G. 324.a). **his**: Plural, masculine, ablative demonstrative pronoun used substantively (A.G. 296.2). The antecedent is **impedimentorum ... mulorumque** (A.G. 297.e). Masculine gender is assigned to the pronoun following the rules for the agreement of predicate adjectives (A.G. 287.3).

stramenta detrahi: A subject accusative with the infinitive after **iubet**. The construction is equivalent to a substantive clause of purpose (A.G. 563.a). **stramenta**: "'pack-saddles,' used only for the conveyance of burdens and not adapted for riding." (Kelsey, 415)

mulionesque ... circumvehi: A subject accusative with the infinitive after **iubet**. The construction is equivalent to a substantive clause of purpose (A.G. 563.a). **-que**: The enclitic conjunction connects the two infinitives **detrahi ... circumvehi** (A.G. 324.a).

cum cassidibus: Ablative of accompaniment with the preposition **cum** (A.G. 413). **cassidibus**: "A helmet of metal (*cassis* or *galea*), ornamented with a crest (*crista*)." (Kelsey, 28)

equitum specie ac simulatione: Two ablatives of manner with a limiting genitive (A.G. 412). **equitum**: Objective genitive with both nouns (A.G. 348). **ac**: The conjunction connects the two ablative nouns and means "and" (*OLD* **atque** 12).

collibus: Ablative of *place where* without a preposition (A.G. 429.1).

iubet: The main verb of the main clause (A.G. 278.b). The pronoun **is**, with **Caesar** as the antecedent, is understood as the subject (A.G. 271.a).

(45.3-4) His paucos addit equites qui latius ostentationis causa vagarentur. Longo (4) circuitu easdem omnis iubet petere regiones.

addo, -dere, -didi, -ditus, *add, join.*

circuitus, -us, m., *circuit, way around, winding path.*
hic, haec, hoc, *this; he, she, it.*
iubeo, iubere, iussi, iussus, *order, give orders, bid, command.*
longus, -a, -um, *long, extended, distant.*
ostentatio, -onis, f., *display, show.*
peto, petere, petivi, and petii, petitus, *make for, try to reach, seek.*
regio, -onis, f., *region, territory.*

causa, -ae, f., abl. with the gen., *for the sake of, for the purpose of.*
eques, -itis, m., *rider, horseman, cavalryman, trooper.*
idem, eadem, idem, *the same.*
late, comp. -ius, *widely, broadly, extensively.*
omnis, -e, *all.*
paucus, -a, -um, *few.*
qui, quae, quod, *who, which, what.*
vagor, -ari, -atus, *wander, wander about, rove, rove about.*

His: Plural, masculine, dative demonstrative pronoun used substantively (A.G. 296.2). The antecedent is **impedimentorum ... mulorumque** (A.G. 297.e). Dative indirect object of the transitive verb **addit** (A.G. 387). Masculine gender is assigned to the pronoun following the rules for the agreement of predicate adjectives (A.G. 287.3).

paucos ... equites: Accusative direct object of the transitive verb **addit** (A.G. 387).

addit: The main verb of the main clause (A.G. 278.b). The pronoun **is**, with **Caesar** as the antecedent, is understood as the subject (A.G. 271.a).

qui ... vagarentur: A relative clause of purpose is introduced by a relative pronoun and takes the subjunctive (A.G. 531.2). **qui**: Plural, masculine, nominative relative pronoun used substantively (A.G. 305). The antecedent is **equites** (A.G. 307). Nominative subject (A.G. 339). The relative is here equivalent to **ut ei** (A.G. 531.2 Note). **vagarentur**: The main verb of the subordinate clause (A.G. 278.b). Imperfect subjunctive; the tense of the subjunctive is in secondary sequence after the historical present **addit** (A.G. 482-85, esp. 485.e).

latius: Comparative adverb (A.G. 218 and 320-21).

ostentationis causa: A preceding genitive with the ablative of **causa** means "for the sake of" A (A.G. 359.b and 404.c).

Longo circuitu: Ablative of *way by which* without a preposition (A.G. 429.a).

easdem ... regiones: Accusative direct object of the infinitive **petere** (A.G. 387 and 451.3). **easdem**: Plural, feminine, accusative demonstrative pronoun used as an adjective modifying **regiones** (A.G. 296.1 and a).

omnis ... petere: A subject accusative with the infinitive after **iubet**. The construction is equivalent to a substantive clause of purpose (A.G. 563.a). **omnis**: Plural, masculine, accusative adjective used substantively (A.G. 288). **-is** for **-es** is the regular form in i-stem adjectives (A.G. 114.a and 116). This refers to both **muliones** and **equites**.

iubet: The main verb of the main clause (A.G. 278.b). The pronoun **is**, with **Caesar** as the antecedent, is understood as the subject (A.G. 271.a). Notice that for the sake of variation the verb **iubet** is not in the last position as it had been in the previous sentence.

(45.4) Haec procul ex oppido videbantur, ut erat a Gergovia despectus in castra, neque tanto spatio certi quid esset explorari poterat.

a(b), *from.*
certum, -i, n., *certainty.*
ex, *from.*
Gergovia, -ae, f., *Gergovia.*
in, *in the direction of, towards.*
oppidum, -i, n., *fortified town, city.*
procul, *at a distance, from afar, far off.*
spatium, -i, n., *space, distance.*
tantus, -a, -um, *so great, so large, such.*
videor, videri, visus sum, *be seen.*

castra, -orum, n., pl., *camp, encampment.*
despectus, -us, m., *a looking down, view, prospect.*
exploro, -are, -avi, -atus, *spy out, reconnoiter.*
hic, haec, hoc, *this; he, she, it.*
neque, *but ... not.*
possum, posse, potui, -----, *be able.*
quis, -----, quid, *who? what?*
sum, esse, fui, futurus, *be.*
ut, *as.*

Haec: Plural, neuter, nominative demonstrative pronoun used substantively meaning "these things" (A.G. 296.2). The antecedent is the actions described immediately above (A.G. 297.e). Nominative subject (A.G. 339).
procul: Adverb (A.G. 320-21).
ex oppido: Prepositional phrase, **ex** with the ablative here means "from" (indicating the point at or from which an action is performed) (*OLD* ex 7).
videbantur: The main verb of the coordinate clause **Haec ... castra** (A.G. 278.a).
ut erat ... castra: The relative adverb **ut** ("as") with the indicative introduces a parenthetical remark (*OLD* ut 12). **erat**: The main verb of the subordinate clause (A.G. 278.b). The verb **sum** in the sense of "exist" makes a complete predicate without a predicate noun or adjective ("there was ..."). It is then called the substantive verb and regularly comes first (A.G. 284.b and 598.c). The present tense is not the historical present but denotes a state as now existing in present time (A.G. 465.1). **castra**: See below.
a Gergovia: Prepositional phrase, **a(b)** with the ablative here means "from" (expressing the physical position from which an action is performed) (*OLD* ab 16). **Gergovia**: See Appendix A.
despectus: Nominative subject (A.G. 339).
in castra: Prepositional phrase, **in** with the accusative here means "in the direction of, towards" (*OLD* in 15).
neque: The conjunction here joins a negative clause to a preceding positive one implying a contrast and means Abut ... not (*OLD* neque 5). The negative portion modifies **poterat**.
tanto spatio: Ablative absolute with an adjective (**tanto**) taking the place of a participle (there is no participle for "being") (A.G. 419.a-20).
certi quid esset: Indirect question with the subjunctive; the phrase is the subject of **poterat** (A.G. 573-75). **certi**: Partitive genitive with **quid** (A.G. 346.a.3). **quid**: Singular, neuter, nominative interrogative pronoun used substantively (A.G. 148). Nominative subject (A.G. 339). **esset**: The main verb of the subordinate clause (A.G. 278.b). Imperfect subjunctive; the tense of the subjunctive follows the rules for the sequence of tense for indirect questions after **poterat** (A.G. 575). The verb **sum** in the sense of "exist" makes a complete predicate without a predicate noun or adjective ("there was ..."). It is then called the substantive verb and regularly comes first (A.G. 284.b and 598.c). The phrase **quid certi esset**, which literally means "what of certainty there was" is an idiom that means "what was really going on." (Kelsey, 20)
explorari: Complementary infinitive after **poterat** (A.G. 456).
poterat: The main verb of the coordinate clause **tanto ... poterat** (A.G. 278.a).

(45.5-6) **(5) Legionem unam eodem iugo mittit et paulum progressam (6) inferiore constituit loco silvisque occultat.**

constituo, -stituere, -stitui, -stitutus, *station, draw up, bring to a halt, stop.*
inferior, -ior, -ius, *lower, inferior.*
iugum, -i, n., *ridge, summit.*
locus, -i, m., *place, position.*
occulto, -are, -avi, -atus, *hide, conceal, keep secret.*
progredior, -gredi, -gressus, *advance, go forward, proceed.*
silvae, -arum, f., pl., *wooded parts* or *region.*

et, *and.*
idem, eadem, idem, *the same.*
legio, -onis, f., *legion.*
mitto, mittere, misi, missus, *send.*
paulum, *a little, somewhat.*
-que, *and.*
unus, -a, -um, *one.*

Legionem unam: Accusative direct object of **mittit** (A.G. 387). **unam**: Declinable cardinal number used as an adjective (A.G. 132-35).
eodem iugo: Dative indirect object of the transitive verb **mittit** (A.G. 363). **eodem**: Singular, neuter, ablative demonstrative pronoun used as an adjective modifying **iugo** (A.G. 296.1 and a).
mittit: The main verb of the coordinate clause **Legionem ... mittit** (A.G. 278.a). The pronoun **is**, with **Caesar** as the antecedent, is understood as the subject (A.G. 271.a).
et: The conjunction connects the two main verbs **mittit ... constituit** (A.G. 324.a).
paulum: Adverb (A.G. 320-21).
progressam: Accusative perfect, deponent, participle used as a predicate, where in English a phrase or a subordinate clause would be more normal (A.G. 496). The pronoun **eam**, with **legionem** as the antecedent, is understood. Accusative direct object of **constituit** (A.G. 387).
inferiore ... loco: Ablative of *place where* without a preposition (A.G. 429.1-2). **inferiore**: Defective comparative adjective (A.G. 130.a).
constituit: The main verb of the coordinate clause **paulum ... loco** (A.G. 278.a). The pronoun **is**, with **Caesar** as the antecedent, is

understood as the subject (A.G. 271.a).

silvisque: Ablative of *place where* without a preposition (A.G. 429.1). **silvis**: The plural of the noun means "wooded parts or regions" (*OLD* silva 1). **-que**: The enclitic conjunction connects the final verb in the series **constituit ... occultat** (A.G. 323.c.3).

occultat: The main verb of the coordinate clause **silvisque occultat** (A.G. 278.a). The pronoun **is**, with **Caesar** as the antecedent, is understood as the subject (A.G. 271.a). Supply the pronoun **eam**, with **legionem** as the antecedent, as the accusative direct object (A.G. 387).

(45.6-7) Augetur Gallis suspicio atque omnes illo ad munitionem copiae tradu(7)cuntur.

ad, *for, in order to, for the purpose of.*	**atque**, *and.*
augeo, augere, auxi, auctus, *increase, enlarge, augment, add to.*	**copiae, -arum**, f., pl., *forces, troops.*
Galli, -orum, m., *the Gauls.*	**illo**, *thither, to that place.*
munitio, -onis, f., *a fortifying, building of fortifications.*	**omnis, -e**, *all.*
suspicio, -onis, f., *suspicion, mistrust.*	**traduco, -ducere, -duxi, -ductus**, *lead across, bring over, bring across.*

Augetur ... suspicio: The reversal of the normal word order (subject first, verb last) is called hyperbaton (A.G. 596) (Gotoff, 6-10).
Augetur: The main verb of the coordinate clause **Augetur ... suspicio** (A.G. 278.a). The verb comes in the first position when the idea in it is emphatic (A.G. 598.d).
Gallis: Dative of reference, the dative is often used to qualify a whole idea (**augetur ... suspicio**) instead of the possessive genitive modifying one word (**suspicio**) (A.G. 376-77). See Appendix A.
suspicio: Nominative subject (A.G. 339). The subject is in the last position (A.G. 597.b).
atque: The conjunction connects the two main verbs **Augetur ... traducuntur** and means "and" (*OLD* atque 12).
omnes ... copiae: Nominative subject (A.G. 339). These are the Gallic troops. Caesar's ruse to draw off troops is working.
illo: Adverb (A.G. 320-21).
ad munitionem: Prepositional phrase, **ad** with the accusative here denotes purpose meaning "for the purpose of" (*OLD* ad 44).
traducuntur: The main verb of the coordinate clause **omnes ... traducuntur** (A.G. 278.a).

(45.7-8) Vacua castra hostium Caesar conspicatus, tectis insignibus suorum occultatisque signis militaribus raros milites qui ex oppido animadverterentur ex maioribus (8) castris in minora traducit;

animadverto, -tere, -ti, -sus, *notice, observe, perceive.*	**Caesar, -aris**, m., *Caesar.*
castra, -orum, n., pl., *camp, encampment.*	**conspicor, -ari, -atus**, *catch sight of, see, observe.*
ex, *from; from, out of.*	**hostis, -is**, m., *enemy, foe*; pl., *the enemy.*
in, *into.*	**insigne, -is**, n., *decoration.*
maior, -or, -us, *greater, larger, bigger.*	**miles, -itis**, m., *soldier, foot-solider.*
militaris, -e, *military.*	**minor, -or, -ius**, *smaller, less.*
occulto, -are, -avi, -atus, *hide, conceal, keep secret.*	**oppidum, -i**, n., *fortified town, city.*
-que, *and.*	**qui, quae, quod**, *who, which, what.*
rarus, -a, -um, *few, scattered, in small parties.*	**signum, -i**, n., *standard.*
sui, -orum, m., pl., *his men, with or without* own.	**tego, tegere, texi, tectus**, *hide, conceal, protect.*
traduco, -ducere, -duxi, -ductus, *lead across, bring over, bring across.*	**vacuus, -a, -um**, *empty, vacant, unoccupied.*

Vacua castra (esse): Accusative/infinitive construction in indirect discourse after **conspicatus** (A.G. 577 ff.). Supply **esse** as the infinitive. **Vacua**: Plural, neuter, accusative predicate adjective modifying **castra** after the supplied infinitive **esse** (A.G. 283-84).
hostium: Possessive genitive with **castra** (A.G. 343).
Caesar conspicatus: Nominative subject of **traducit** (A.G. 339). **Caesar**: See Appendix A. **conspicatus**: Nominative, perfect, passive, participle used as a predicate, where in English a phrase or a subordinate clause would be more normal (A.G. 496).
tectis insignibus suorum: Ablative absolute (A.G. 419-20). **tectis**: The perfect tense of the participle represents the action as completed at the time indicated by the tense of the main verb (A.G. 489). **insignibus**: "The exact reference is unclear. The Latin may perhaps refer to the crests on their helmets, or to some other symbol by which they could be quickly identified as Romans." (Hammond, 226) A... particularly the crests, which were taken off from the helmets on the march. In battle it was important that the crests be in place, for by differences of these in form and color the different legions and cohorts could be distinguished." (Kelsey, 310) **suorum**: Plural, masculine, genitive possessive pronoun used substantively to denote a special class (A.G. 302.d). Possessive genitive with **insignibus** (A.G. 343).
occultatisque signis militaribus: Ablative absolute (A.G. 419-20). **occultatis**: The perfect tense of the participle represents the action as completed at the time indicated by the tense of the main verb (A.G. 489). **-que**: The enclitic conjunction connects the two ablative absolutes (A.G. 324.a).
raros milites: Accusative direct object of **traducit** (A.G. 387).
qui ... animadverterentur: A relative clause of characteristic; a relative clause with the subjunctive is often used to indicate a characteristic of the antecedent (A.G. 535). The variant reading in the Loeb and Budé texts of **ne** for **qui** makes this a negative clause of purpose and better fits the sense. **qui**: Plural, masculine, nominative relative pronoun used substantively (A.G. 305). The antecedent is **milites** (A.G. 307). Nominative subject (A.G. 339). **animadverterentur**: The main verb of the subordinate clause (A.G. 278.b). Imperfect subjunctive; the tense of the subjunctive is in secondary sequence after the historical present **traducit** (A.G. 482-85,

esp. 485.e).

ex oppido: Prepositional phrase, **ex** with the ablative here means "from" (indicating the point at or from which an action is performed) (*OLD* **ex** 7).

ex maioribus castris: Ablative of *place from which* with the preposition **ex** (A.G. 426.1). **maioribus**: Irregular comparative adjective (A.G. 129).

in minora: Accusative of *place to which* with the preposition **in** (A.G. 426.2). **minora**: Irregular comparative adjective used substantively (A.G. 129 and 288). The noun **castra** is understood (A.G. 288.b). This smaller camp had been constructed and connected to the larger one at 36.7.

traducit: The main verb of the main clause (A.G. 278.b).

(45.8) legatisque, quos singulis legionibus praefecerat, quid fieri velit ostendit:

fio, fieri, factus, *take place, happen, come about.*
legio, -onis, f., *legion.*

praeficio, -ficere, -feci, -fectus, *place over, appoint to command.*
qui, quae, quod, *who, which, what.*
singuli, -ae, -a, *separate, individual.*

legatus, -i, m., *lieutenant, lieutenant-general.*
ostendo, -tendere, -tendi, -tentus, *point out, set forth, declare.*
-que, *and, now.*
quis, -----, quid, *who? what?*
volo, velle, volui, *wish, desire, mean, intend.*

legatisque: Dative indirect object of the transitive verb **ostendit** (A.G. 362). **-que**: The enclitic here begins the sentence, introducing a further point, and means "and, now" (*OLD* **-que** 4).

quos ... praefecerat: Relative clause (A.G. 303). **quos**: Plural, masculine, accusative relative pronoun used substantively (A.G. 305). The antecedent is **legatis** (A.G. 307). Accusative direct object of the transitive verb **praefecerat** (A.G. 387). **praefecerat**: The main verb of the subordinate clause (A.G. 278.b). The pronoun **is**, with **Caesar** as the antecedent, is understood as the subject (A.G. 271.a). The pluperfect denotes an action completed in past time (A.G. 477).

singulis legionibus: Dative indirect object of the transitive verb **praefecerat** (A.G. 362). **singulis**: Distributive numeral used as an adjective (A.G. 136).

quid ... velit: Indirect question with the subjunctive; the phrase is the object of **ostendit** (A.G. 573-75). **quid**: See below. **velit**: The main verb of the subordinate clause (A.G. 278.b). Present subjunctive; the tense of the subjunctive is normally in secondary sequence after the historical present **ostendit** (A.G. 575). Here it is in primary sequence through *repraesentatio* (A.G. 485.e and 585.b Note). The pronoun **is**, with **Caesar** as the antecedent, is understood as the subject (A.G. 271.a).

quid fieri: Subject accusative with the infinitive after **velit**. The construction is equivalent to a substantive clause of purpose (A.G. 563.b.2). **quid**: Singular, neuter, accusative interrogative pronoun used substantively (A.G. 148).

ostendit: The main verb of the main clause (A.G. 278.b). The pronoun **is**, with **Caesar** as the antecedent, is understood as the subject (A.G. 271.a).

(45.8-9) in primis monet ut contineant milites, ne studio pugnandi aut spe praedae (9) longius progrediantur;

aut, *or.*

in primis, *especially, above all.*
miles, -itis, m., *soldier, foot-solider.*
ne, *so that ... not.*
progredior, -gredi, -gressus, *advance, go forward, proceed.*
spes, -ei, f., *hope, expectation.*
ut, *so that.*

contineo, -tinere, -tinui, -tentus, *hold back, check, retain.*
longius, *further.*
moneo, -ere, -ui, -itus, *advise, warn, remind, admonish.*
praeda, -ae, f., *booty, spoil, plunder.*
pugno, -are, -avi, -atus, *fight, combat, engage.*
studium, -i, n., *zeal, eagerness, enthusiasm.*

in ... proeli. (45.8-10) The soldiers will be reminded of these orders in Chapter 52 after they fail to obey them. See the note on **id ... proposuerat** at 47.1.

in primis: Adverbial phrase, originally a prepositional phrase, **in** with the ablative plural of **primus** means "especially, above all" (*OLD* **imprimis** 1).

monet: The main verb of the main clause (A.G. 278.b). The pronoun **is**, with **Caesar** as the antecedent, is understood as the subject (A.G. 271.a).

ut contineant milites: The conjunction **ut** ("so that") with the subjunctive is here a substantive clause of purpose which is used as the object of the participle **monet** denoting an action directed toward the future (A.G. 563). **contineant**: The main verb of the subordinate clause (A.G. 278.b). Present subjunctive; the tense of the subjunctive is normally in secondary sequence after the historical present **monet** (A.G. 482-85). Here it is in primary sequence through *repraesentatio* (A.G. 485.e and 585.b Note). The pronoun **ei**, with **legatis** as the antecedent, is understood as the subject (A.G. 271.a). **milites**: Accusative direct object of **contineant** (A.G. 387).

ne ... progrediantur: The conjunction **ne** ("so that ... not") with the subjunctive forms a negative purpose clause (A.G. 531.1).

progrediantur: The main verb of the subordinate clause (A.G. 278.b). Present subjunctive; the tense of the subjunctive is normally in secondary sequence after the historical present **monet** (A.G. 482-85). Here it is in primary sequence through *repraesentatio* (A.G. 485.e and 585.b Note). The pronoun **ei**, with **milites** as the antecedent, is understood as the subject (A.G. 271.a).

studio: Ablatives of cause without a preposition (A.G. 404).

pugnandi: Singular, neuter, genitive gerund (A.G. 501-02). Objective genitive after **studio** (A.G. 504).
aut: The conjunction connects the two ablative nouns and excludes the alternative (A.G. 324.e).
spe: Ablatives of cause without a preposition (A.G. 404).
praedae: Objective genitive with **spe** (A.G. 504).
longius: Comparative adverb (A.G. 218 and 320-21). The comparative degree here denotes a considerable or excessive degree of the quality meaning "too" (A.G. 291.a).

(45.9-10) **quid iniquitas loci habeat incommodi proponit: hoc una celeritate posse mutari; occasionis (10) esse rem, non proeli.**

celeritas, -tatis, f., *speed, quickness, swiftness, rapidity.*
hic, haec, hoc, *this; he, she, it.*
iniquitas, -atis, f., *unfavorableness.*
muto, -are, -avi, -atus, *change, remedy, alter.*
occasio, -onis, f., *dash, raid, surprise.*
proelium, -i, n., *battle, combat, engagement.*

quis, -----, quid, *who? what?*
sum, esse, fui, futurus, *be.*

habeo, habere, habui, habitus, *have, exhibit, produce.*
incommodum, -i, n., *disadvantage, detriment.*
locus, -i, m., *place, position, location, terrain.*
non, *not.*
possum, posse, potui, -----, *be able.*
propono, -ponere, -posui, -positus, *point out, declare, set forth.*
res, rei, f., *situation, event, affair.*
unus, -a, -um, *alone.*

quid ... habeat: Indirect question with the subjunctive; the phrase is the object of **proponit** (A.G. 573-75). **quid**: Singular, neuter, accusative interrogative pronoun used substantively (A.G. 148). Accusative direct object of **habeat** (A.G. 387). **habeat**: The main verb of the subordinate clause (A.G. 278.b). Present subjunctive; the tense of the subjunctive is normally in secondary sequence after the historical present **proponit** (A.G. 575). Here it is in primary sequence through *repraesentatio* (A.G. 485.e and 585.b Note).
iniquitas: Nominative subject (A.G. 339).
loci: Possessive genitive with **iniquitas** (A.G. 343).
incommodi: Partitive genitive with **quid** (346.3).
proponit: The main verb of the main clause (A.G. 278.b). The pronoun **is**, with **Caesar** as the antecedent, is understood as the subject (A.G. 271.a).
hoc ... posse: Accusative/infinitive construction in indirect discourse (A.G. 577 ff.). The verb of saying is not expressed, but implied in the general drift of the sentence (A.G. 580.a). **hoc**: Singular, neuter, ablative demonstrative pronoun used substantively (A.G. 296.2). The antecedent is either the idea of uneven terrain immediately above or **incommodi** (A.G. 297.e). **posse**: Present infinitive; the tense of the infinitive in indirect discourse is relative to that of the verb of saying (A.G. 584).
una celeritate: Ablative of means (A.G. 409). **una**: Declinable cardinal number used as an adjective and here meaning "alone" (A.G. 132-35) (*OLD* **unus** 7).
mutari: Complementary infinitive after **posse** (A.G. 456).
occasionis: Possessive genitive; the possessive genitive often stands in the predicate, connected to its noun (**rem**) by a verb (**esse**) (predicate genitive) (A.G. 343.b).
esse rem: Accusative/infinitive construction in indirect discourse (A.G. 577 ff.). The verb of saying is not expressed, but implied in the general drift of the sentence (A.G. 580.a). **esse**: Present infinitive; the tense of the infinitive in indirect discourse is relative to that of the verb of saying (A.G. 584).
non proeli: Ellipsis of **non proeli esse rem** (A.G. 640).
non: Adverb modifying **proeli**, the negative precedes the word it especially effects (A.G. 217.e, 320-21, and 599.a). **proeli**: Possessive genitive paralleling **occasionis**; the possessive genitive often stands in the predicate, connected by its noun by a verb (predicate genitive) (A.G. 343.b). The singular genitive of nouns in **-ium** ended, until the Augustan Age, in a single **-i** (A.G. 49.b). "Caesar's purpose was not to hold the Gallic encampment but simply to raid it, thinking that after a successful dash of this sort he could withdraw from the siege with his credit good." (Kelsey, 416)

(45.10) **His rebus expositis signum dat et ab dextra parte alio ascensu eodem tempore Aeduos mittit.**

ab, *on.*
alius, -a, -ud, *another.*
dexter, -tra, -trum, *right.*
et, *and.*

hic, haec, hoc, *this; he, she, it.*
mitto, mittere, misi, missus, *send.*
res, rei, f., *matter, affair, thing, condition.*
tempus, -oris, n., *time.*

Aedui, -orum, m., pl., *the Aedui.*
ascensus, -us, m., *ascent, way up, approach.*
do, dare, dedi, datus, *give.*
expono, -ponere, -posui, -positus, *set forth, state, explain.*
idem, eadem, idem, *the same.*
pars, partis, f., *side.*
signum, -i, n., *signal.*

His rebus expositis: Ablative absolute (A.G. 419-20). **His**: Plural, feminine, ablative demonstrative pronoun used as an adjective modifying **rebus** (A.G. 296.1 and a). **expositis**: The perfect tense of the participle represents the action as completed at the time indicated by the tense of the main verb (A.G. 489).
signum: Accusative direct object of **dat** (A.G. 387).
dat: The main verb of the coordinate clause **His ... dat** (A.G. 278.a). The pronoun **is**, with **Caesar** as the antecedent, is understood as

the subject (A.G. 271.a).

et: The conjunction connects the two main verbs **dat** ... **mittit** (A.G. 324.a).

ab ... **mittit**: Stevens believes that this action proves that Caesar was attempting an all out assault on Gergovia: "According to Caesar an essential factor in his attempt not on Gergovia, we remember, but to obtain a prestige success at Gergovia, was the employment of 10,000 Aedui on his right flank. Can we believe that if the state had been in open revolt, murdering Roman citizens wherever they could be found (which is what Caesar says), he would have used so many troops whose temper must have become so unreliable simply in the hope of a prestige success? He would have risked the annihilation of his legions." (Stevens, 16-17) For the muster of these soldiers see 34.1. Although there Caesar states that they would be of limited use (**milia X** ... **quae in praesidiis rei frumentariae causa disponeret** ...), the need for troops after the splitting of his army with Labienus must have made him change his mind.

ab dextra parte: Ablative of *position* with the preposition **ab** (A.G. 429.b). "The Aedui were to march from the east while the legions attacked from the south." (Hammond, 238)

alio ascensu: Ablative of *way by which* without a preposition (A.G. 429.a).

eodem tempore: Ablative of *time when* (A.G. 423.1). **eodem**: Singular, neuter, ablative demonstrative pronoun used as an adjective modifying **tempore** (A.G. 296.1 and a).

Aeduos: Accusative direct object of **mittit** (A.G. 387). See Appendix A.

mittit: The main verb of the coordinate clause **ab** ... **mittit** (A.G. 278.a). The pronoun **is**, with **Caesar** as the antecedent, is understood as the subject (A.G. 271.a).

Chapters 46-51: Compare John Keegan's critique of Caesarian battle narrative to these six chapters. None of his critiques (disjunctive movement, uniformity of behavior, simplified characterization, and simplified motivation) are valid for this narrative section. (Keegan, 61-72, esp. 64 and Mannetter, Chapter 5).

(46.1-2) Oppidi murus a planitie atque initio ascensus recta regione, si nullus anfractus intercederet, mille CC passus (2) aberat:

a(b), *from, away from.*

anfractus, -us, m., *curve, bend.*
atque, *and.*
initium, -i, n., *beginning, commencement.*
mille, *a thousand.*
nullus, -a, -um, *no, not any.*
passus, -us, m., *step, pace,* = 4 feet, 10 ¼ inches.
rectus, -a, -um, *straight, direct.*

si, *if.*

absum, -esse, afui, -futurus, *be distant, be absent* or *away from.*
ascensus, -us, m., *ascent, way up, approach.*
C, in expression of number, = *100.*
intercedo, -cedere, -cessi, -cessurus, *lie between.*
murus, -i, m., *wall, rampart.*
oppidum, -i, n., *fortified town, city.*
planities, -ei, f., *level ground, plain.*
regio, -onis, f., *direction, line,* (with **recta**), *in the direct line, as the crow flies.*

oppidi: Possessive genitive with **murus** (A.G. 343).

murus: Nominative subject (A.G. 339).

a planitie atque initio ascensus: Ablative of separation with the preposition **a(b)** after the compound verb **aberat** (A.G. 402). **atque**: The conjunction connects the two ablative nouns in the prepositional phrase and means "and" (*OLD* **atque** 12). **ascensus**: Possessive genitive with **initio** (A.G. 343).

recta regione: Ablative of manner with a limiting adjective (A.G. 412).

si ... intercederet ... aberat: Mixed conditional statement; the protasis (imperfect subjunctive) is from a contrary to fact, present time condition (A.G. 514.C.1). The apodosis (imperfect indicative) is from a simple, past time condition (A.G. 514.A.2).

si ... intercederet: The conjunction **si** ("if") with the subjunctive forms the protasis of a conditional statement (A.G. 514.C.1).

intercederet: The main verb of the subordinate clause (A.G. 278.b).

nullus anfractus: Nominative subject (A.G. 339).

mille CC passus: Accusative of *extent of space* (A.G. 425). **mille**: In the singular **mille** is an indeclinable adjective modifying **passus** (A.G. 134.d). **CC**: Roman numeral used as an adjective modifying **passus** (A.G. 133).

aberat: The protasis of the conditional statement (A.G. 514.A.2). The main verb of the main clause (A.G. 278.b).

(46.2-3) quidquid huc circuitus ad molliendum clivum acces(3)serat, id spatium itineris augebat.

accedo, -cedere, -cessi, -cessurus, *be added.*
augeo, augere, auxi, auctus, *increase, enlarge, augment, add to.*
clivus, -i, m., *slope, declivity.*
is, ea, id, *he, she, it; that, this.*
mollio, -ire, -ivi, -itus, *make easier.*
spatium, -i, n., *space, distance.*

ad, *for, in order to, for the purpose of.*
circuitus, -us, m., *circuit, way around, winding path.*
huc, *to this amount* or *total.*
iter, itineris, n., *road, route.*
quisquis, quaequae, quidquid, *whoever, whatever.*

quidquid ... accesserat: Relative clause (A.G. 279.a). **quidquid**: Singular, neuter, nominative indefinite relative pronoun used substantively (A.G. 151.b). Nominative subject (A.G. 339). **accesserat**: The main verb of the subordinate clause (A.G. 278.b). The pluperfect denotes an action completed in past time (A.G. 477).

huc: Adverb; **huc** with a verb of adding (**accesserat**) means "to this amount or total" (*OLD* **huc** 3).

circuitus: Partitive genitive with **quidquid** (A.G. 346.a.3).

ad molliendum clivum: The preposition **ad** with the accusative gerundive and noun expresses purpose (A.G. 506). **molliendum**: Singular, neuter, accusative gerundive used as an adjective modifying **clivum** denoting necessity, obligation or propriety (A.G. 500.1).

id: Singular, neuter, nominative demonstrative pronoun used substantively (A.G. 296.2). The antecedent is **quidquid** (A.G. 297.e). Nominative subject (A.G. 339).

spatium: Accusative direct object of **augebat** (A.G. 387).

itineris: Possessive genitive with **spatium** (A.G. 343).

augebat: The main verb of the main clause (A.G. 278.b).

(46.3-4) **A medio fere colle in longitudinem, ut natura montis ferebat, ex grandibus saxis sex pedum murum qui nostrum impetum tardaret praeduxerant Galli atque inferiore omni spatio vacuo relicto superiorem partem collis usque ad murum oppidi densissimis (4) castris compleverant.**

a(b), *on, at.*

castra, -orum, n., pl., *camp, encampment.*

compleo, -plere, -plevi, -pletus, *fully occupy, fill full.*

ex, *of, out of, from.*

fero, ferre, tuli, latus, *suggest, allow, permit.*

grandis, -e, *large, great.*

in, *in, in respect to.*

longitudo, -inis, f., *length,* (with in), *lengthwise, longitudinally.*

mons, montis, m., *mountain, elevation, height.*

natura, -ae, f., *nature, character, natural features.*

omnis, -e, *the whole, the entire.*

pars, partis, f., *part, portion.*

praeduco, -ducere, -duxi, -ductus, *to construct along a line in front.*

relinquo, -linquere, -liqui, -lictus, *leave.*

sex, *six.*

superior, -or, -us, *higher, upper, superior.*

usque ad, *all the way to, as far as.*

vacuus, -a, -um, *empty, clear, free, vacant, unoccupied.*

atque, *and.*

collis, -is, m., *hill, height, elevation.*

densus, -a, -um, sup. -issimus, *closely packed, dense, crowded.*

fere, *almost, nearly.*

Galli, -orum, m., *the Gauls.*

impetus, -us, m., *attack, assault, onset, charge.*

inferior, -ior, -ius, *lower, inferior.*

medius, -a, -um, *in the middle, midst, middle, mid-.*

murus, -i, m., *wall, rampart.*

nos, nostrum, *we, us.*

oppidum, -i, n., *fortified town, city.*

pes, pedis, m., *foot,* = .9708 of the English foot.

qui, quae, quod, *who, which, what.*

saxum, -i, n., *stone, rock.*

spatium, -i, n., *space, area.*

tardo, -are, -avi, -atus, *check, delay, impede, hinder.*

ut, *as.*

A medio fere colle: Ablative of *position* with the preposition **A(b)** (A.G. 429.b). **medio**: The adjective designates not what object, but what part of it is meant (A.G. 293). **fere**: Adverb (A.G. 320-21).

in longitudinem: Prepositional phrase, **in** with the accusative of **longitudo** means "lengthwise, longitudinally" (*OLD* **longitudo** 1.c).

ut ... ferebat: The relative adverb **ut** ("as") with the indicative introduces a parenthetical remark (*OLD* **ut** 12). **ferebat**: The main verb of the subordinate clause (A.G. 278.b). The verb **ferre** here means "to suggest" (*OLD* **fero** 31).

natura: Nominative subject (A.G. 339).

montis: Possessive genitive with **natura** (A.G. 343).

ex grandibus saxis: Ablative of material with the preposition **ex** (A.G. 403.2).

sex pedum: Genitive of quality (measure) with **murum** (A.G. 345.b). **sex**: Indeclinable cardinal number used as an adjective (A.G. 132-35).

murum: Accusative direct object of **praeduxerant** (A.G. 387).

qui ... tardaret: A relative clause of purpose is introduced by a relative pronoun and takes the subjunctive (A.G. 531.2). **qui**: Singular, masculine, nominative relative pronoun used substantively (A.G. 305). The antecedent is **murum** (A.G. 307). Nominative subject (A.G. 339). The relative is here equivalent to **ut is** (A.G. 531.2 Note). **tardaret**: The main verb of the subordinate clause (A.G. 278.b). Imperfect subjunctive; the tense of the subjunctive is in secondary sequence and follows the rules for the sequence of tense after **praeduxerant** (A.G. 482-85).

nostrum: First person, plural, genitive personal pronoun (A.G. 142-43). The form of the genitive of the personal pronoun is really the genitive of the possessive and so here is used substantively to denote a special class (A.G. 143.b Note and 302.d). Objective genitive with **impetum**, the form **nostri** is normally objective and **nostrum** partitive, but not always (A.G. 295.b, esp. Note 1).

impetum: Accusative direct object of **tardaret** (A.G. 387). See also **ad nostrum auxilium** at 77.7.

praeduxerant: The main verb of the coordinate clause **A ... Galli** (A.G. 278.a). Although the pluperfect tense is normally used in subordinate clauses, its use as a main verb is frequent. Here the pluperfect denotes an action completed in past time (A.G. 477).

Galli: Nominative subject of the preceding verb **praeduxerant** and **compleverant** (A.G. 339). See Appendix A.

atque: The conjunction connects the two main verbs **praeduxerant ... compleverant** and means "and" (*OLD* **atque** 12).

inferiore omni spatio vacuo relicto: Ablative absolute (A.G. 419-20). **inferiore**: Defective comparative adjective (A.G. 130.a).

vacuo: Singular, neuter, ablative predicate adjective modifying **spatio** after **relicto** (A.G. 283). **relicto**: The perfect tense of the participle represents the action as completed at the time indicated by the tense of the main verb (A.G. 489).

superiorem partem: Accusative direct object of **compleverant** (A.G. 387). **superiorem**: Defective comparative adjective (A.G. 130.b).

collis: Partitive genitive with **partem** (A.G. 346.a.1).

usque ad murum oppidi: Prepositional phrase, **usque ad** with the accusative means "all the way to, right up to, as far as" (A.G. 432.b) (*OLD* usque 1). **usque:** Adverb (A.G. 320-21 and 432.b). **oppidi:** Possessive genitive with **murum** (A.G. 343).

densissimis castris: Ablative of means after **compleverant** (A.G. 409.a). **densissimis:** Superlative adjective (A.G. 124).

compleverant: The main verb of the coordinate clause **inferiore ... compleverant** (A.G. 278.a). Although the pluperfect tense is normally used in subordinate clauses, its use as a main verb is frequent. The pluperfect denotes an action completed in past time (A.G. 477). Here the pluperfect denotes an action completed in past time (A.G. 477).

(46.4-5) Milites dato signo celeriter ad munitionem perveniunt eamque transgressi trinis castris potiun(5)tur;

ad, *to, towards.*
celeriter, *quickly, speedily, at once, immediately.*
is, ea, id, *he, she, it; that, this.*
munitio, -onis, f., *works of fortifications, intrenchment, defenses.*

potior, potiri, potitus, *obtain possession of, become master of, obtain.*
signum, -i, n., *signal.*

trini, -ae, -a, *three.*

castra, -orum, n., pl., *camp, encampment.*
do, dare, dedi, datus, *give.*
miles, -itis, m., *soldier, foot-solider.*
pervenio, -venire, -veni, -ventus, *come to, arrive at, reach.*
-que, *and.*
transgredior, -gredi, -gressus, *go over, pass over, go across, cross.*

Milites: Nominative subject (A.G. 339).

dato signo: Ablative absolute (A.G. 419-20). **dato:** The perfect tense of the participle represents the action as completed at the time indicated by the tense of the main verb (A.G. 489).

celeriter: Adverb (A.G. 214.b and 320-21).

ad munitionem: Accusative of *place to which* with the preposition **ad** (A.G. 426.2).

perveniunt: The main verb of the coordinate clause **Milites ... perveniunt** (A.G. 278.a). The historical present, giving vividness to the narrative, is present in Chapter 46 (A.G. 469). This usage, common in all languages, comes from imagining past events as going on before our eyes (*repraesentatio*) (A.G. 469 Note).

eamque: Singular, feminine, accusative demonstrative pronoun used substantively (A.G. 296.2). The antecedent is **munitionem** (A.G. 297.e). Accusative direct object of the participle **transgressi** (A.G. 387 and 488). **-que:** The enclitic conjunction connects the two main verbs **perveniunt ... potiuntur** (A.G. 324.a).

transgressi: Nominative, perfect, passive, participle used as a predicate, where in English a phrase or a subordinate clause would be more normal (A.G. 496). The pronoun **ei**, with **milites** as the antecedent, is understood. Nominative subject (A.G. 339).

trinis castris: Ablative direct object of the deponent verb **potiuntur** (A.G. 410). **trinis:** A distributive number used in place of a cardinal number (A.G. 136-37). A distributive is used instead of a cardinal number to express simple number when a noun plural in form but singular in meaning is used in a plural sense (**castris**) (A.G. 137.b).

potiuntur: The main verb of the coordinate clause **eamque ... potiuntur** (A.G. 278.a).

(46.4) ac tanta fuit in castris capiendis celeritas ut Teutomatus, rex Nitiobrigum, subito in tabernaculo oppressus, ut meridie conquieverat, superiore corporis parte nudata, vulnerato equo vix se ex manibus praedantium militum eriperet.

ac, *and in fact, and what is more, and indeed.*

castra, -orum, n., pl., *camp, encampment.*

conquiesco, -ere, -quievi, -quietus, *take one's rest, rest, repose.*
equus, -i, m., *horse.*

ex, *from, out of.*
manus, -us, f., *hand.*
miles, -itis, m., *soldier, foot-solider.*
nudo, -are, -avi, -atus, *expose, leave unprotected.*

pars, partis, f., *part, portion.*
rex, regis, m., *king, ruler, chieftain.*
sui, sibi, se, or sese, nom. wanting, *himself.*
superior, -or, -us, *upper.*
tantus, -a, -um, *so great, so large, such.*
ut, *so that; as soon as, when, just as.*
vulnero, are, -avi, -atus, *wound, hurt.*

capio, capere, cepi, captus, *take, get, seize, capture, occupy.*
celeritas, -tatis, f., *speed, quickness, swiftness, rapidity, despatch.*
corpus, -oris, n., *body.*
eripio, -ripere, -ripui, -reptus, (with **se**), *escape, rescue one's self.*
in, *in.*
meridies, -ei, m., *mid-day.*
Nitiobriges, -um, m., pl., *Nitiobriges.*
opprimo, -primere, -pressi, -pressus, *take by suprise, suprise, fall upon.*
praedor, -ari, -atus, *obtain booty, pillage, plunder.*
subito, *suddenly, on a sudden.*
sum, esse, fui, futurus, *be.*
tabernaculum, -i, n., *tent, hut.*
Teutomatus, -i, m., *Teutomatus.*
vix, *scarcely, barely.*

ac: The conjunction, beginning an emphatic sentence, means "and in fact, and what is more, and indeed" (*OLD* atque 2).

tanta: Singular, feminine, nominative predicate adjective modifying **celeritas** after **fuit** (A.G. 283-84). The adjective is correlative to the following result clause (A.G. 217.c, 320-21 and 537 Note 2).

fuit: The main verb of the main clause (A.G. 278.b).

in castris capiendis: Prepositional phrase, **in** with the ablative here means "in" (given circumstances) (*OLD* **in** 40). **capiendis**: Plural, neuter, ablative gerundive modifying **castris** after the preposition **in** (A.G. 507.3).

celeritas: Nominative subject (A.G. 339).

(tanta) ... ut ... eriperet: The conjunction **ut** ("so that") with the subjunctive forms a clause of result (A.G. 537.1). **eriperet**: The main verb of the subordinate clause (A.G. 278.b). Imperfect subjunctive; the tense of the subjunctive is in secondary sequence and follows the rules for the sequence of tense after **fuit** (A.G. 482-85).

Teutomatus ... oppressus: Nominative subject (A.G. 339). **Teutomatus**: See Appendix A. **oppressus**: Nominative, perfect, passive, participle used as a predicate, where in English a phrase or a subordinate clause would be more normal (A.G. 496).

rex: A noun in apposition to the proper noun **Teutomatus** (A.G. 282). See the note on **rex** at 4.5.

Nitiobrigum: Partitive genitive of the tribe name **Nitiobriges** with **rex** (A.G. 346.a.1). See Appendix A.

subito: Adverb (A.G. 320-21).

in tabernaculo: Ablative of *place where* with the preposition **in** (locative ablative) (A.G. 426.3).

ut ... conquieverat: Temporal clause; the relative adverb **ut** ("as soon as, when") with the pluperfect indicative introduces a subordinate clause. The pluperfect tense denotes an action completed in past time (*OLD* **ut** 26) (A.G. 543.a). A clause dependent on a subjunctive clause (**ut ... eriperet**) normally takes the subjunctive (attraction) (A.G. 303 and 593). However, when a dependent clause is not regarded as a necessary logical part of the clause, the indicative is used. The indicative serves to emphasize the fact, as true independently of the statement contained in the subjunctive clause (A.G. 593.a Note 1). **conquieverat**: The main verb of the subordinate clause (A.G. 278.b). The pronoun **is**, with **Teutomatus** as the antecedent, is understood as the subject (A.G. 271.a).

meridie: Ablative of *time when* (A.G. 423.1).

superiore corporis parte nudata: Ablative absolute (A.G. 419-20). "explained by *ut ... conquieverat*." (Kelsey, 416) **superiore**: Defective comparative adjective (A.G. 130.b). **corporis**: Partitive genitive with **parte** (A.G. 346.a.1). **nudata**: The perfect tense of the participle represents the action as completed at the time indicated by the tense of the main verb (A.G. 489).

vulnerato equo: Ablative absolute (A.G. 419-20). **vulnerato**: The perfect tense of the participle represents the action as completed at the time indicated by the tense of the main verb (A.G. 489). The asyndeton between the two ablative absolutes lends a sense of rapidity to the actions described (A.G. 323.b).

vix: Adverb (A.G. 217.c and 320-21).

se: Singular, masculine, accusative direct reflexive pronoun (A.G. 300.1). The antecedent is **Teutomatus**, the subject of **eriperet** (A.G. 299). Accusative direct object of **eriperet** (A.G. 387). **se ... eriperet**: The verb **eripere** used reflexively means "to escape" (*OLD* **eripio** 5.b).

ex manibus praedantium militum: Prepositional phrase; **ex** with the ablative here means "from" (*OLD* **ex**). **praedantium militum**: Possessive genitive with **manibus** (A.G. 343). **praedantium**: Plural, masculine, genitive present participle used as an adjective modifying **militum** (A.G. 494.a).

(47.1-2) Consecutus id quod animo proposuerat Caesar receptui cani iussit legionique decimae, quacum erat +concionatus+, (2) signa constituit;

animus, -i, m., *mind*.

cano, canere, cecini, *sound*.

concionatus, *make a speech*, or *immediately* (see below).

-cum, *with*.

is, ea, id, *he, she, it; that, this*.

legio, -onis, f., *legion*.

-que, *and*.

receptus, -us, m., *retreat*.

Caesar, -aris, m., *Caesar*.

constituo, -stituere, -stitui, -stitutus, *station, draw up, bring to a halt*.

consequor, -sequi, -secutus, *obtain, secure, gain*.

decimus, -a, -um, *tenth*.

iubeo, iubere, iussi, iussus, *order, give orders, bid, command*.

propono, -ponere, -posui, -positus, *put forward, present, propose*.

qui, quae, quod, *who, which, what*.

signum, -i, n., *standard*.

Consecutus ... Caesar: Nominative subject of **iussit ... constituit** (A.G. 339). **Consecutus**: Nominative, perfect, deponent, participle used as a predicate, where in English a phrase or a subordinate clause would be more normal (A.G. 496). **Caesar**: See Appendix A.

id ... proposuerat: Stevens believes that "Caesar was not in the least satisfied, as he asks us to believe, with the capture of three empty camps outside the town-walls. He did not want a prestige success; he wanted to capture Gergovia. ... and then he blames his soldiers for over-confidence (blame which soldiers would be proud to take), because he did not get it." (Stevens, 17) Kelsey holds an opposing view: "It has been maintained that Caesar does not tell the truth in regard to his intentions in making this assault; that he seriously planned by a daring attempt, when the enemy had been drawn off by a feint, to capture the city; but that, having failed in this, he passed the matter over as a mere dash, the purpose of which was simply to humble the enemy and encourage his own men. This view does not seem plausible, because of the nature of the instructions given before the battle (see Chap. 45). About these Caesar would hardly have ventured to falsify, for the reason that, when the memoirs were given to the world, the lieutenants placed in command of the legions were still living, and Caesar knew that they might bring any untruth at once to the public notice. After the Gallic War several of Caesar's lieutenants became his bitterest enemies." (Kelsey, 416-17) "*Caesar ... intended*: a controversial claim, which many scholars have seen as an attempt to disguise the failure of his manœuvre. The question is whether 'what he intended' implies the completion of the entire manœuvre, or its successful progress *up to that point*. Thus far, nothing of military significance has been achieved, so it is more likely that Caesar wants the reader to assume that he is about to regroup half-way through a planned manœuvre. He does not explain, however, what he would have done next if discipline had not broken down at this point; a he is careful to distance himself from blame by inserting at an earlier point the information that he warned his officers not to let this happen (7.45). This is then picked up in the aftermath of battle (7.52)." (Hammond, 240)

id: Singular, neuter, accusative demonstrative pronoun used substantively (A..G. 296.2). The pronoun is correlative to the relative clause **quod ... proposuerat** (A.G. 297.d). Accusative direct object of the deponent participle **Consecutus** (A.G. 387 and 488).

quod ... proposuerat: Relative clause (A.G. 303). For the reference see Chapter 45. **quod**: Singular, neuter, accusative relative pronoun used substantively (A.G. 305). The antecedent is **id** (A.G. 297.e). Accusative direct object of **proposuerat** (A.G. 387).

proposuerat: The main verb of the subordinate clause (A.G. 278.b). The pronoun **is**, with **Consecutus (Caesar)** as the antecedent, is understood as the subject (A.G. 271.a). The pluperfect denotes an action completed in past time (A.G. 477).

animo: Ablative of *place where* without a preposition (A.G. 429.3).

receptui: Dative of purpose with **cani** (A.G. 382.2).

(id) cani: Impersonal passive infinitive after **iussit**. The construction is equivalent to a substantive clause of purpose (A.G. 208.d and 563.a). Supply **id** as the accusative subject (A.G. 318.c). The phrase **receptui cani** means "The retreat to be sounded (*OLD* **cano** 6.e).

iussit: The main verb of the coordinate clause **Consecutus ... iussit** (A.G. 278.a).

legionique decimae: Dative of reference; the dative in this construction is often called the dative of advantage as denoting the person for whose benefit the action is performed (A.G. 376). **decimae**: Declinable ordinal number used as an adjective (A.G. 132-35). **-que**: The enclitic conjunction connects the two main verbs **iussit ... constituit** (A.G. 324.a).

quacum erat +concionatus+: Relative clause (A.G. 303). **quacum**: Ablative of accompaniment with the preposition **cum** (A.G. 413). **qua**: Singular, feminine, ablative relative pronoun used substantively (A.G. 305). The antecedent is **legioni** (A.G. 307). **-cum**: The preposition **cum** ("with") is joined enclitically with the ablative (A.G. 150.d). **erat**: The main verb of the subordinate clause (A.G. 278.b). The pronoun **is**, with **Caesar** as the antecedent, is understood as the subject (A.G. 271.a). **+concionatus+**: The word is corrupt. The Budé here changes the 'c' to 't' (for **contionor, -atus**, "to make a speech, harangue, address") and reads: ... **decimae, quacum erat, contionatus signa** ... . The Loeb renders the word an adverb (**continuo**, "immediately, without delay") and reads: ... **decimae, quacum erat, continuo signa** ... . Both change the punctuation to make **quacum erat** ("with which he was") a separate clause.

signa: Accusative direct object of the transitive verb **constituit** (A.G. 387). "Each maniple was provided with a standard (*signum*), a pole crowned with a twist of hay would appear to have been the earliest type; it was used by the maniple commander to transmit orders by signal and to rally his men. ... Further, the standard of the maniple of each cohort became the standard of the cohort, and to encourage morale Marius gave each legion an eagle of silver as the legionary standard; it was carried by the *aquilifer*. It symbolized the majesty of the legion, and its loss in battle sometimes entailed the legion's disbandment." (Fuller, 78 and 81)

constituit: The main verb of the coordinate clause **legionique ... constituit** (A.G. 278.a).

(47.2-3) ac reliquarum legionum milites, non exaudito sono tubae, quod satis magna valles intercedebat, tamen ab tribunis militum legatisque, ut erat a Caesare prae(3)ceptum, retinebantur.

ab, a(b), *by*.
Caesar, -aris, m., *Caesar*.

intercedo, -cedere, -cessi, -cessurus, *lie between*.
legio, -onis, f., *legion*.
miles, -itis, m., *soldier, foot-solider*.
praecipio, -cipere, -cepi, -ceptus, *order, direct, instruct*.
quod, *because, since, for, as*.
retineo, -tinere, -tinui, -tentus, *detain, keep back*.
sonus, -i, m., *sound*.
tribunus, -i, m., *tribune*.
ut, *as*.

ac, *and yet*.
exaudio, -dire, -divi, -ditus, *hear distinctly, hear plainly*.
legatus, -i, m., *lieutenant, lieutenant-general*.
magnus, -a, -um, *great, large*.
non, *not*.
-que, *and*.
reliquus, -a, -um, *remaining, the rest*.
satis, *moderately, rather*.
tamen, *yet, still, for all that, nevertheless, however*.
tuba, -ae, f., *trumpet*.
valles, -is, f., *valley*.

ac: The conjunction here has a adversative sense and means "and yet" (*OLD* **atque** 9).

reliquarum legionum: Partitive genitive with **milites** (A.G. 346.a.1).

milites: Nominative subject of **retinebantur** (A.G. 339).

non ... intercedebat: Ablative absolute with a dependent clause.

non exaudito sono tubae: Ablative absolute (A.G. 419-20). The ablative absolute here takes the place of a concessive clause ("although") which is made clearer by the adversative particle **tamen** ("nevertheless") in the main clause (A.G. 420.3). **non**: Adverb, the adverb generally precedes the verb if it belongs to no one word in particular (A.G. 217.e, 320-21, and 599.a). **exaudito**: The perfect tense of the participle represents the action as completed at the time indicated by the tense of the main verb (A.G. 489). **tubae**: Possessive genitive with **sono** (A.G. 343). "The trumpet (*tuba*), about three feet long, with a funnel-shaped opening; it had a deep tone." (Kelsey, 31)

quod ... intercedebat: Causal clause; the conjunction **quod** ("because") takes the indicative when the reason is given on the authority of the writer or speaker (A.G. 540.1). **intercedebat**: The main verb of the subordinate clause (A.G. 278.b).

satis: Adverb modifying **magna** (A.G. 320-21).

magna valles: Nominative subject (A.G. 339). "A depression in the slope ... Caesar with the tenth legion was on the east side of this, the other legions on the west side." (Kelsey, 417)

tamen: Adverb, normally postpositive but not here (A.G. 320-21 and 324.j).

ab tribunis militum legatisque: Two ablatives of agent with the preposition **ab** after the passive verb **retinebantur** (A.G. 405).

militum: Possessive genitive with **tribunis** (A.G. 343). **-que**: The enclitic conjunction connects the two ablative nouns in the prepositional phrase (A.G. 324.a).

ut (id) erat ... praeceptum: The relative adverb **ut** ("as") with the indicative introduces a parenthetical remark (*OLD* **ut** 12). For the reference see 45.8-9. **erat ... praeceptum**: The main verb of the subordinate clause (A.G. 278.b). Impersonal use of the passive verb (A.G. 208.d). Supply **id** as the subject (A.G. 318.c). The pluperfect passive verb is here split (tmesis) (A.G. 640). The pluperfect denotes an action completed in past time (A.G. 477).

a Caesare: Ablative of agent with the preposition **a(b)** with the passive verb **erat ... praeceptum** (A.G. 405). **Caesare**: See Appendix A.

retinebantur: The main verb of the main clause (A.G. 278.b). Conative imperfect; the imperfect tense here denotes an action as attempted (A.G. 471.c). This attempt will prove unsuccessful in the next sentence.

(47.3-4) Sed elati spe celeris victoriae et hostium fuga et superiorum temporum secundis proeliis nihil adeo arduum sibi esse existimaverunt quod non virtute consequi possent, neque finem prius sequendi fecerunt quam (4) muro oppidi portisque appropinquarunt.

adeo, *so.*

arduus, -a, -um, *difficult.*

consequor, -sequi, -secutus, *obtain, secure, gain.*

et, *and.*
facio, facere, feci, factus, *bring about, make.*
fuga, -ae, f., *flight.*
murus, -i, m., *wall, rampart.*
nihil, n., *nothing.*
oppidum, -i, n., *fortified town, city.*
possum, posse, potui, -----, *be able.*
proelium, -i, n., *battle, combat, engagement.*
qui, quae, quod, *who, which, what.*
sed, *but.*
spes, -ei, f., *hope, expectation.*
sum, esse, fui, futurus, *be.*
tempus, -oris, n., *time.*
virtus, -utis, f., *courage, bravery, vigor, energy, effort.*

appropinquo, -are, -avi, -atus, *approach, come near, draw near.*
celer, -eris, -ere, *quick, swift, sudden.*
effero, -ferre, extuli, elatus, *puff up, elate; lift up, pull up.*
existimo, -are, -avi, -atus, *think, consider, judge.*
finis, -is, m., *end.*
hostis, -is, m., *enemy, foe;* pl., *the enemy.*
neque, *and ... not.*
non, *not.*
porta -ae, f., *city gate.*
prius ... quam, *before, sooner than.*
-que, *and.*
secundus, -a, -um, *propitious, fortunate, favorable.*
sequor, -qui, -cutus, *follow, follow after, pursue.*
sui, sibi, se, or **sese**, nom. wanting, *themselves.*
superior, -or, -us, *former, earlier, previous.*
victoria, -ae, f., *victory.*

Sed: Coordinate conjunction (A.G. 324.d).

elati: Plural, masculine, nominative adjective used substantively (A.G. 288). The pronoun **ei**, with **milites** as the antecedent, is understood. Nominative subject of **existimaverunt ... fecerunt** (A.G. 339). The adjective **elatus** foreshadows doom as Caesar only applies it to those who will soon suffer disaster. "Caesar is rarely defeated, and this adjective helps to foreshadow the unusual negative result." (Mannetter, 134-35).

spe: Ablative of cause without a preposition after **elati** (A.G. 404).

celeris victoriae: Objective genitive with **spe** (A.G. 348).

et: The conjunction connects the two ablative nouns **spe ... fuga** (A.G. 324.a).

hostium: Possessive genitive with **fuga** (A.G. 343).

fuga: Ablative of cause without a preposition after **elati** (A.G. 404).

et: The conjunction connects the two ablative nouns **fuga ... proeliis** (A.G. 324.a).

superiorum temporum: Genitive of quality (measure) with **proeliis** (A.G. 345.b and 417). **superiorum**: Defective comparative adjective (A.G. 130.b).

secundis proeliis: Ablative of cause without a preposition after **elati** (A.G. 404).

nihil ... arduum ...esse: Accusative/infinitive construction in indirect discourse after **existimaverunt** (A.G. 577 ff.). **nihil**: Indeclinable accusative noun, used only as nominative and accusative singular (A.G. 103.a). **arduum**: Singular, neuter, accusative predicate adjective modifying **nihil** after **esse** (A.G. 283-84). **esse**: Present infinitive; the tense of the infinitive in indirect discourse is relative to that of the verb of saying (A.G. 584).

adeo: Adverb (A.G. 320-21).

sibi: Plural, masculine, dative indirect reflexive pronoun (A.G. 300.2). The antecedent is **milites**, the subject of **existimaverunt** (A.G. 299). Dative after the adjective **arduum** (A.G. 383).

existimaverunt: The main verb of the coordinate clause **Sed ... possent** (A.G. 278.a).

(adeo) ... quod ... possent: A relative clause of result is introduced by a relative pronoun and takes the subjunctive (A.G. 537.2). **adeo**: Adverb modifying **arduum** and correlative to the result clause (A.G. 217.c, 320-21 and 537 Note 2). **quod**: Singular, neuter, accusative relative pronoun used substantively (A.G. 305). The antecedent is **nihil** (A.G. 307). The relative is here equivalent to **ut id** (A.G. 537.2). Accusative direct object of the infinitive **consequi** (A.G. 387 and 451.3). **possent**: The main verb of the subordinate clause (A.G. 278.b). Imperfect subjunctive; the tense of the subjunctive is in secondary sequence and follows the rules for the sequence of tense after **existimaverunt** (A.G. 482-85). The pronoun **ei**, with **elati (milites)** as the antecedent, is understood as the subject (A.G. 271.a).

non: Adverb; when **non** is especially emphatic it begins the clause (A.G. 217.e, 320-21, and 599.a).

virtute: Ablative of means (A.G. 409).

consequi: Complementary infinitive after **possent** (A.G. 456).

neque: The conjunction here joins a negative clause to a preceding positive one (**Sed** ... **possent**) and means "and ... not" (*OLD* **neque** 3).

finem: Accusative direct object of **fecerunt** (A.G. 387).

prius: Construe with **quam** below.

sequendi: Singular, neuter, genitive gerund (A.G. 501-02). Objective genitive with **finem** (A.G. 504).

fecerunt: The main verb of the coordinate clause **finem** ... **appropinquarunt** (A.G. 278.a).

(prius) ... quam ... appropinquarunt: Temporal clause; **prius** ... **quam** with the perfect indicative states a fact in past time. The perfect indicative in this construction is regular when the main clause is negative and the main verb (**fecerunt**) is in an historical tense (A.G. 551.a). **prius ... quam**: The conjunction is here split (tmesis) (A.G. 640). **appropinquarunt**: The main verb of the subordinate clause (A.G. 278.b). A contracted form of **appropinquaverunt** (A.G. 181.a). The pronoun **ei**, with **elati** (**milites**) as the antecedent, is understood as the subject (A.G. 271.a).

muro ... portisque: Two dative indirect objects of the intransitive verb **appropinquarunt** (A.G. 366). **-que**: The enclitic conjunction connects the two dative nouns (A.G. 324.a).

oppidi: Possessive genitive with **muro** (A.G. 343).

(47.4-5) Tum vero ex omnibus urbis partibus orto clamore, qui longius aberant repentino tumultu perterriti, cum hostem intra portas esse (5) existimarent, sese ex oppido eiecerunt.

absum, -esse, afui, -futurus, *be distant, be absent* or *away from.*
cum, *since, seeing that.*

ex, *from, out of.*
hostis, -is, m., *enemy, foe.*
longius, *further, at a distance.*
oppidum, -i, n., *fortified town, city.*
pars, partis, f., *part, portion, side.*

porta -ae, f., *city gate.*
repentinus, -a, -um, *sudden, hasty, unexpected.*
sum, esse, fui, futurus, *be.*
tumultus, -us, m., *disturbance, confusion, disorder, uproar.*
vero, *indeed, in fact.*

clamor, -oris, m., *outcry, clamor, noise, din.*
eicio, -icere, -ieci, -iectus, *throw out, cast out, thrust out, expel.*
existimo, -are, -avi, -atus, *think, consider, judge.*
intra, *within, inside.*
omnis, -e, *all, every.*
orior, oriri, ortus, *rise, arise.*
perterreo, -terrere, -----, -territus, *greatly alarm, frighten, terrify, dismay.*
qui, quae, quod, *who, which, what.*
sui, sibi, se, or **sese**, nom. wanting, *themselves.*
tum, *then, thereupon.*
urbs, urbis, f., *city.*

Tum vero ex omnibus urbis partibus orto clamore: Ablative absolute (A.G. 419-20). **Tum**: Adverb (A.G. 271.b and 320-21).

vero: Adverb, postpositive position (A.G. 320-21 and 599.b). **ex omnibus urbis partibus**: Ablative of *place from which* with the preposition **ex** (A.G. 426.1). **urbis**: Partitive genitive with **partibus** (A.G. 346.a.1). **orto**: The perfect tense of the participle represents the action as completed at the time indicated by the tense of the main verb (A.G. 489).

qui ... aberant: Relative clause (A.G. 303). **qui**: Plural, masculine, nominative relative pronoun used substantively (A.G. 305). The antecedent is omitted, supply **ei** (A.G. 307.c). Nominative subject (A.G. 339).

longius: Comparative adverb (A.G. 218 and 320-21).

aberant: The main verb of the subordinate clause (A.G. 278.b).

repentino tumultu: Ablative of cause without a preposition after **perterriti** (A.G. 404).

perterriti: Nominative, perfect, passive, participle used as a predicate, where in English a phrase or a subordinate clause would be more normal (A.G. 496). The pronoun **ei**, the supplied antecedent of **qui**, is understood. Nominative subject of **eiecerunt** (A.G. 339).

cum ... existimarent: Causal clause; the relative adverb **cum** ("since") with the subjunctive forms a clause expressing cause (A.G. 549). **existimarent**: The main verb of the subordinate clause (A.G. 278.b). Imperfect subjunctive; the tense of the subjunctive is in secondary sequence and follows the rules for the sequence of tense after **eiecerunt** (A.G. 482-85). The pronoun **ei**, with **perterriti** as the antecedent, is understood as the subject (A.G. 271.a).

hostem intra portas esse: Accusative/infinitive construction in indirect discourse after **existimarent** (A.G. 577 ff.). **hostem**: This is the Romans. **intra portas**: Prepositional phrase, **intra** with the accusative here means "within, inside" (*OLD* **intra** A.1). The prepositional phrase is in the predicate position after **esse** (A.G. 272). **esse**: Present infinitive; the tense of the infinitive in indirect discourse is relative to that of the verb of saying (A.G. 584).

sese: Plural, masculine, accusative direct reflexive pronoun (A.G. 300.1). The antecedent is **perterriti**, the subject of **eiecerunt** (A.G. 299). Accusative direct object of **eiecerunt** (A.G. 387). Reduplicated form of **se** (A.G. 144.b Note 1).

ex oppido: Ablative of *place from which* with the preposition **ex** (A.G. 426.1).

eiecerunt: The main verb of the main clause (A.G. 278.b).

(47.5-7) Matres familiae de muro vestem argentumque iactabant, et pectore nudo prominentes passis manibus obtestabantur Romanos ut sibi parcerent neu, sicut Avarici fecissent, ne a mulieribus quidem (6) atque infantibus abstinerent:

a(b), *from.*

abstineo, -tinere, -tinui, -tentus, (with **ab**), *to keep*

argentum, -i, n., *silver-ware.*
Avaricum, -i, n., *Avaricum.*
et, *and.*

facio, facere, feci, factus, *bring about, make, do.*
infans, -antis, m., or f., *child, infant.*
manus, -us, f., *hand.*
mulier, -eris, f., *woman.*
ne ... quidem, *not even.*
nudus, -a, -um, *naked, bare.*
pando, pandere, pandi, passus, *spread out.*

pectus, -oris, n., *breast.*

-que, *and.*
sicut, *just as, as.*
ut, *so that.*

one's hands off.
atque, *and.*
de, *down from.*
familia, -ae, f., *household, family,* (pl. with **matres**) *matrons.*
iacto, -are, -avi, -atus, *throw, cast.*
intercedo, -cedere, -cessi, -cessurus, *lie between.*
mater, -tris, f., *mother,* (with **familiae**) *matrons.*
murus, -i, m., *wall, rampart.*
neu, *and that ... not, and not, nor.*
obtestor, -ari, -atus, *implore, adjure.*
parco, parcere, peperci, and parsi, parsus, *spare, give quarter to.*
promineo, -minere, -minui, -----, *bend forward, lean forward, reach out.*
Romani, -orum, m., pl., *the Romans.*
sui, sibi, se, or sese, nom. wanting, *them.*
vestis, -is, f., *clothing.*

Matres: Nominative subject (A.G. 339).
familiae: Partitive genitive with **Matres** (A.G. 346.a.1).
de muro: Prepositional phrase, **de** with the ablative here means Adown from (a higher position) (*OLD* **de** 1.b).
vestem argentumque: Two accusative direct objects of **iactabant** (A.G. 387). **-que**: The enclitic conjunction connects the two accusative nouns (A.G. 324.a).
iactabant: The main verb of the coordinate clause **Matres ... iactabant** (A.G. 278.a).
et: The conjunction connects the two main verbs **iactabant ... obtestabantur** (A.G. 324.a).
pectore nudo: Ablative of quality (descriptive ablative) with an adjective modifier (A.G. 415).
prominentes: Nominative, present participle used as a predicate, where in English a phrase or a subordinate clause would be more normal (A.G. 496). The pronoun **eae**, with **Matres** as the antecedent, is understood. Nominative subject (A.G. 339).
passis manibus: Ablative absolute (A.G. 419-20). **passis**: The perfect tense of the participle represents the action as completed at the time indicated by the tense of the main verb (A.G. 489).
obtestabantur: The main verb of the coordinate clause **pectore ... abstinerent** (A.G. 278.a).
Romanos: Accusative direct object of **obtestabantur** (A.G. 387).
ut ... parcerent ... neu ... abstinerent: The conjunction **ut** ("so that") with the subjunctive is here a substantive clause of purpose which is used as the object of **obtestabantur** denoting an action directed toward the future (A.G. 563). **parcerent ... abstinerent**: The main verbs of the subordinate clause (A.G. 278.b). Imperfect subjunctive; the tense of the subjunctives is in secondary sequence and follows the rules for the sequence of tense after **obtestabantur** (A.G. 482-85). The pronoun **ei**, with **Romanos** as the antecedent, is understood as the subject of both verbs (A.G. 271.a). **neu**: After **ut**, the conjunction **neu** adds a negative purpose clause to a positive one and means "and that ... not" (*OLD* neve 2).
sibi: Plural, feminine, dative indirect reflexive pronoun (A.G. 300.1). The antecedent is **matres**, the subject of **obtestabantur** (A.G. 299). Dative indirect object of **parcerent**, a verb of sparing (A.G. 367).
sicut ... fecissent: Subordinate clause (A.G. 278.b). A clause dependent on a subjunctive clause (**neu ... abstinerent**) takes the subjunctive when regarded as an integral part of that clause (attraction) (A.G. 593). **sicut**: Conjunction (*OLD* sicut 2). **fecissent**: The main verb of the subordinate clause (A.G. 278.b). Pluperfect subjunctive; the tense of the subjunctive is in secondary sequence and follows the rules for the sequence of tense after **obtestabantur** (A.G. 482-85). The pronoun **ei**, with **Romanos** as the antecedent, is understood as the subject (A.G. 271.a).
Avarici: Locative case of the city name **Avaricum, -i,** n. (A.G. 49.a). See Chapter 28 for the sack of **Avaricum** and the indiscriminate slaughter that ensued. See Appendix A.
ne ... quidem: The negative adverb with the particle means "not even" (*OLD* ne1 6). The emphatic word must stand between **ne** and **quidem** (A.G. 322.f).
a mulieribus ... atque infantibus: Two ablatives of separation with the preposition **a(b)** after the intransitive compound verb **abstinerent** (A.G. 402). **atque**: The conjunction connects the two ablative nouns in the prepositional phrase and means "and" (*OLD* atque 12).

(47.6-7) **non nullae de muro per manus (7) demissae sese militibus tradebant.**

de, *down from.*
manus, -us, f., *hand.*
murus, -i, m., *wall, rampart.*
non, *not.*
sui, sibi, se, or sese, nom. wanting, *themselves.*

demitto, -mittere, -misi, -misus, *let down.*
miles, -itis, m., *soldier, foot-solider.*
nulla, -ae, f., *no one, nobody.*
per, (with **manus**), *from hand to hand.*
trado, -dere, -didi, -ditus, *hand over, give up, deliver, surrender.*

non nullae: A litotes, a statement is made emphatic by denying its contrary (A.G. 326.c). **non**: Adverb modifying **nullae**, the negative precedes the word it especially effects (A.G. 217.e, 320-21, and 599.a).

nullae ... demissae: Nominative subject (A.G. 339). **nullae**: Plural, feminine, nominative adjective used substantively (A.G. 288). The noun pair **matres familiae** is understood (A.G. 288.b). **demissae**: Nominative, perfect, passive, participle used as a predicate, where in English a phrase or a subordinate clause would be more normal (A.G. 496).

de muro: Prepositional phrase, **de** with the ablative here means Adown from (a higher position) (*OLD* **de** 1.b).

per manus: Prepositional phrase, **per** with the accusative plural of **manus** means "from hand to hand" (*OLD* **manus1** 18.b).

sese: Plural, feminine, accusative direct reflexive pronoun (A.G. 300.1). The antecedent is **nullae**, the subject of **tradebant** (A.G. 299). Accusative direct object of the transitive verb **tradebant** (A.G. 387). Reduplicated form of **se** (A.G. 144.b Note 1).

militibus: Dative indirect object of the transitive verb **tradebant** (A.G. 362).

tradebant: The main verb of the simple sentence (A.G. 278.1).

(47.7) L. Fabius, centurio legionis VIII., quem inter suos eo die dixisse constabat excitari se Avaricensibus praemiis neque commissurum ut prius quisquam murum ascenderet, tris suos nactus manipularis atque ab his sublevatus murum ascendit:

ab, *by*.

atque, *and*.

centurio, -onis, m., *centurion*.

consto, -stare, -stiti, -staturus, (imper.), *it is agreed, there is agreement*.

dies, -ei, m. and f., *day*.

hic, haec, hoc, *this*; *he, she, it*.

inter, *among*.

L. Fabius, -i, m., *Lucius Fabius*.

manipularis, -is, m., *soldier of a maniple, fellow-manipular*.

naniscor, -cisci, nactus, and **nanctus**, *come upon, find, get hold of*.

praemium, -i, n., *reward, recompense*.

qui, quae, quod, *who, which, what*.

sublevo, -are, -avi, -atus, *lift up, support, hold up*.

sui, -orum, m., pl., *his men*, with or without *own*.

ut, *so that*.

ascendo, -scendere, -scendi, -scensus, *ascend, climb, mount, scale*.

Avaricensis, -e, *of Avaricum, at Avericum*.

committo, -mittere, -misi, -missus, *bring about, allow, cause to happen*.

dico, dicere, dixi, dictus, *say*.

excito, -are, -avi, -atus, *stir up, rouse, animate*.

I, in expression of number, *1*.

is, ea, id, *he, she, it; that, this*.

legio, -onis, f., *legion*.

murus, -i, m., *wall, rampart*.

neque, *and ... not*.

prius, *before, sooner, earlier*.

quisquam, -----, quidquam, *anyone, anything, any*.

sui, sibi, se, or **sese**, nom. wanting, *he*, with or without *himself*.

tres, tria, trium, *three*.

V, in expression of number, *= 5*.

L. Fabius ... nactus ... sublevatus: Nominative subject of **ascendit** (A.G. 339). **L. Fabius**: See Appendix A. **L.**: Abbreviated form of the praenomen **Lucius** (A.G. 108.c). **nactus**: Nominative perfect, deponent, participle used as a predicate, where in English a phrase or a subordinate clause would be more normal (A.G. 496). **sublevatus**: Nominative perfect, passive, participle used as a predicate, where in English a phrase or a subordinate clause would be more normal (A.G. 496).

centurio: A nominative noun in apposition to the proper noun **Fabius** (A.G. 282).

legionis VIII.: Partitive genitive with **centurio** (A.G. 346.a.1). **VIII.**: Roman numeral used as an adjective (A.G. 133). Collins notes that only five individuals are singled out for criticism in the *BG* and Fabius is one of them: AL. Fabius, the centurion, is portrayed as the victim of his own greed and rashness." (Collins, 940) Caesar seems to be thinking specifically of him when he says at 52.1: **Postero die Caesar contione advocata temeritatem cupiditatemque militum reprehendit**. Notice how the character of this centurion compares with that of M. Petronius at 50.4-6, who gives his life for his men. In the *BG*, centurions are almost always paradigms of Roman military virtue. See especially Publius Sextius Baculus at 2.25, 3.5, and 6.38; Titus Pullo and Lucius Vorenus at 5.44; and the unnamed centurions at 6.40

quem ... ascenderet: Relative clause with dependent clauses.

quem ... (id) constabat: Relative clause (A.G. 303). **quem**: See below. **constabat**: The main verb of the subordinate clause (A.G. 278.b). Impersonal use of the verb, supply **id** as the subject (A.G. 207). The impersonal use means "it is agreed, there is agreement" (*OLD* **consto** 9.c).

quem ... dixisse: Accusative/infinitive construction in indirect discourse after **constabat** (A.G. 577 ff.). **quem**: Singular, masculine, accusative relative pronoun used substantively (A.G. 305). The antecedent is **Fabius** (A.G. 307). **dixisse**: Perfect infinitive; the tense of the infinitive in indirect discourse is relative to that of the verb of saying (A.G. 584).

inter suos: Prepositional phrase, **inter** with the accusative here means "among" (*OLD* **inter1** 1). **suos**: Plural, masculine, accusative possessive pronoun used substantively to denote a special class (A.G. 302.d).

eo die: Ablative of *time when* (A.G. 423.1). **eo**: Singular, masculine, ablative demonstrative pronoun used as an adjective modifying **die** (A.G. 296.1 and a). **die**: The noun **dies** is normally masculine gender (A.G. 97.a).

excitari se: Accusative/infinitive construction in indirect discourse after **dixisse** (A.G. 577 ff.). **excitari**: Present infinitive; the tense of the infinitive in indirect discourse is relative to that of the verb of saying (A.G. 584). **se**: Singular, masculine, accusative direct reflexive pronoun (A.G. 300.1). The antecedent is **quem**, the subject of the first accusative/infinitive construction (A.G. 299).

Avaricensibus praemiis: Ablative of cause without a preposition (A.G. 404). **Avaricensibus**: An adjective denoting *belonging to* or *coming from* of the city name **Avaricum** (A.G. 249.2). "'Gained at Avaricum,' which Caesar permitted his men to sack with all manner of atrocities." (Kelsey, 417) For the sack of Avaricum see 27.2 and 28.2-5.

neque: The conjunction here joins a negative clause to a preceding positive one (**excitari se**) and means "and ... not" (*OLD* **neque** 3).

(se) commissurum (esse): Accusative/infinitive construction in indirect discourse after **dixisse** (A.G. 577 ff.). Carry down **se** as the accusative subject. **commissurum (esse)**: Supply **esse** to form the future, active, infinitive (A.G. 186). The tense of the infinitive in indirect discourse is relative to that of the verb of saying (A.G. 584).

ut ... ascenderet: The conjunction **ut** ("so that") with the subjunctive is here a substantive clause of purpose which is used as the object of **commissurum (esse)** denoting an action directed toward the future (A.G. 563). **ascenderet**: The main verb of the subordinate clause (A.G. 278.b). Imperfect subjunctive; the tense of the subjunctive is in secondary sequence and follows the rules for the sequence of tense after **constabat** (A.G. 482-85).

prius: Adverb (A.G. 320-21).

quisquam: Singular, masculine, nominative indefinite pronoun used substantively (A.G. 151.d). Nominative subject (A.G. 339).

murum: Accusative direct object of **ascenderet** (A.G. 387).

tris suos: Accusative direct object of the deponent participle **nactus** (A.G. 387 and 488). **tris**: Declinable cardinal number used as an adjective modifying **suos** (A.G. 132-35). **-is** for **-es** is an alternative accusative plural ending (A.G. 134.b). **suos**: Plural, masculine, accusative possessive pronoun used substantively to denote a special class (A.G. 302.d).

manipularis: An accusative noun in apposition to the pronoun **suos** (A.G. 282). Accusative plural noun; **-is** for **-es** is the regular form in i-stem nouns (A.G. 65-67 and 74.c).

atque: The conjunction connects the two participles and means "and" (*OLD* atque 12).

ab his: Ablative of agent with the preposition **ab** with the passive participle **sublevatus** (A.G. 405). **his**: Plural, masculine, ablative demonstrative pronoun used substantively (A.G. 296.2). The antecedent is **suos** (A.G. 297.e).

murum: Accusative direct object of **ascendit** (A.G. 387).

ascendit: The main verb of the main clause (A.G. 278.b).

(47.7) hos ipse rursus singulos exceptans in murum extulit.

effero, -ferre, extuli, elatus, *lift up, pull up.*
hic, haec, hoc, *this; he, she, it.*
ipse, -a, -um, *he, they*, with or without *himself, themselves.*
rursus, *in turn.*

excepto, -are, -avi, -atus, *catch up, take hold of.*
in, *onto.*
murus, -i, m., *wall, rampart.*
singuli, -ae, -a, *one by one, one at a time.*

hos ipse rursus singulos exceptans: Interlocking word order (A.G. 589.h).

hos ... singulos: Accusative direct object of the participle **exceptans** (A.G. 387 and 488). **hos**: Plural, masculine, accusative demonstrative pronoun used substantively (A.G. 296.2). The antecedent is **suos** (A.G. 297.e). **singulos**: Distributive numeral used as an adjective (A. G. 136-37).

ipse ... exceptans: Nominative subject (A.G. 339). **ipse**: Singular, masculine, nominative demonstrative pronoun used substantively (A.G. 296.2 and 298.d). The antecedent is **Fabius** (A.G. 298). The pronoun is here emphatic (A.G. 298.d.1). **exceptans**: Present participle used as an adjective modifying **ipse** (A.G. 494).

rursus: Adverb (A.G. 216 and 320-21).

in murum: Accusative of *place to which* with the preposition **in** (A.G. 426.2).

extulit: The main verb of the simple sentence (A.G. 278.1). For Fabius' eventual fate see 50.3-4.

(48.1-2) Interim ei qui ad alteram partem oppidi, ut supra demonstravimus, munitionis causa convenerant, primo exaudito clamore, inde etiam crebris nuntiis incitati oppidum a Romanis teneri, praemissis equitibus magno cursu eo con(2)tenderunt.

a(b), *by.*
alter, -era, -erum, *the other.*

clamor, -oris, m., *outcry, clamor, noise, din.*

convenio, -venire, -veni, -ventus, *come together, assemble.*
cursus, -us, m., *speed.*

eo, *thither, there.*
etiam, *also, even.*

incito, -are, -avi, -atus, *rouse, stir up, excite.*
interim, *in the mean time, meanwhile.*
magnus, -a, -um, *great, full.*
nuntius, -i, m., *message, tidings.*
pars, partis, f., *part, portion, side.*

primo, *at first, in the first place.*
Romani, -orum, m., pl., *the Romans.*
teneo, tenere, tenui, -----, *take possession of, seize, hold, keep.*

ad, *at.*
causa, -ae, f., abl. with the gen., *for the sake of, for the purpose of.*
contendo, -tendere, -tendi, -tentus, *hasten, make haste, push forward.*
creber, -bra, -brum, *numerous, frequent.*
demonstro, -are, -avi, -atus, *point out, show, say, mention, explain.*
eques, -itis, m., *rider, horseman, cavalryman, trooper.*
exaudio, -dire, -divi, -ditus, *hear distinctly, hear plainly.*
inde, *next, then, after that.*
is, ea, id, *he, she, it; that, this.*
munitio, -onis, f., *a fortifying, building of fortifications.*
oppidum, -i, n., *fortified town, city.*
praemitto, -mittere, -misi, -missus, *send forward, send on in advance.*
qui, quae, quod, *who, which, what.*
supra, *before, previously.*
ut, *as.*

Interim: Adverb (A.G. 320-21).

ei ... incitati: Nominative subject of **contenderunt** (A.G. 339). **ei**: Plural, masculine, nominative demonstrative pronoun used substantively (A.G. 296.2). The pronoun is correlative to the relative clause **qui ... convenerant** (A.G. 297.d). The noun **Galli** is understood. **incitati**: Nominative, perfect, passive, participle used as a predicate, where in English a phrase or a subordinate clause would be more normal (A.G. 496).

qui ... convenerant: Relative clause (A.G. 303). **qui**: Plural, masculine, nominative relative pronoun used substantively (A. G. 305). The antecedent is **ei** (A.G. 307). Nominative subject (A.G. 339). **convenerant**: The main verb of the subordinate clause (A.G. 278.b). The pluperfect denotes an action completed in past time (A.G. 477).

ad alteram partem oppidi: Prepositional phrase, **ad** with the accusative here means "at" (*OLD* **ad** 13). **oppidi**: Partitive genitive with **partem** (A.G. 346.a.1).

ut ... demonstravimus: The relative adverb **ut** ("as") with the indicative introduces a parenthetical remark (*OLD* **ut** 12). For the reference see 45.6. **demonstravimus**: The main verb of the subordinate clause (A.G. 278.b). The personal pronoun **nos** is understood as the subject but is not expressed except for distinction or emphasis (A.G. 295.a). In Book 7, Caesar refers to himself only in the third person, either in the singular or occasionally in the plural (see **Caesar** at 1.1). Siedler counts 11 uses of the first person plural in Book 7 (Siedler, 46). These uses are at 17.1, 23.2, 25.1, 37.1, 48.1, 58.4, 70.1, 76.1, 79.2, 83.8, and 85.4.

supra: Adverb (A.G. 320-21).

munitionis causa: A preceding genitive with the ablative of **causa** means "for the sake of" A (A.G. 359.b and 404.c).

primo ... inde: Two adverbs (A.G. 217.a and 320-21). **primo** means "at first", as opposed to **inde** "next, then" (*OLD* **primo** 1) (*OLD* **inde** 5).

primo exaudito clamore: Ablative absolute (A.G. 419-20). **primo**: See above. **exaudito**: The perfect tense of the participle represents the action as completed at the time indicated by the tense of the main verb (A.G. 489).

etiam: Adverb (A.G. 320-21 and 322.a). The adverb normally proceeds the emphatic word (A.G. 322.a).

crebris nuntiis: Ablative of cause without a preposition after the passive participle **incitati** (A.G. 404).

oppidum ... teneri: Accusative/infinitive construction in indirect discourse (A.G. 577.ff). The verb of saying is not expressed, but implied in the phrase **crebris nuntiis** (A.G. 580.a). **teneri**: Present infinitive; the tense of the infinitive in indirect discourse is relative to that of the verb of saying (A.G. 584).

a Romanis: Ablative of agent with the preposition **a(b)** after the passive infinitive **teneri** (A.G. 405).

praemissis equitibus: Ablative absolute (A.G. 419-20). **praemissis**: The perfect tense of the participle represents the action as completed at the time indicated by the tense of the main verb (A.G. 489).

magno cursu: Ablative of manner with a limiting adjective (A.G. 412).

eo: Adverb (A.G. 217.a and 320-21).

contenderunt: The main verb of the main clause (A.G. 278.b).

(48.2) Eorum ut quisque primus venerat, sub muro consistebat suorumque pugnantium numerum augebat.

augeo, augere, auxi, auctus, *increase, enlarge, augment, add to.*

is, ea, id, *he, she, it; that, this.*
numerus, -i, m., *number.*
pugno, -are, -avi, -atus, *fight, combat, engage.*
quisque, -----, quidque, *each one, each thing.*
sui, -orum, m., pl., *his men,* with or without *own.*
venio, venire, veni, ventus, *come.*

consisto, -sistere, -stiti, -stitus, *stop, halt, take a position, make a stand.*
murus, -i, m., *wall, rampart.*
primus, -a, -um, *first.*
-que, *and.*
sub, *under, near to, close to, at the foot of.*
ut, *as soon as, when.*

Eorum: Plural, masculine, genitive demonstrative pronoun used substantively (A.G. 296.2). The antecedent is **ei** (A.G. 297.e). Partitive genitive with **quisque** (A.G. 346.a.1).

ut ... venerat: Subordinate clause; the relative adverb **ut** ("as soon as, when") with the pluperfect indicative forms a temporal clause (A.G. 287.b). The pluperfect tense emphasizes the fact that the action expressed in the **ut** clause was completed before the action in the main clause (*OLD* **ut** 26.b). **venerat**: The main verb of the subordinate clause (A.G. 278.b).

quisque primus: Nominative subject of (A.G. 339). **quisque**: Singular, masculine, nominative indefinite pronoun used substantively (A.G. 151.g). **primus**: Declinable ordinal number used as an adjective (A.G. 132-35). The adjective modifies the pronoun **quisque** but is used to qualify the action of the verb, and so has the force of an adverb (A.G. 290).

sub muro: Prepositional phrase, **sub** with the ablative here means "at the foot of, below" (*OLD* **sub** 6).

consistebat: The main verb of the coordinate clause **Eorum ... consistebat** (A.G. 278.a). The pronoun **is**, with **quisque** as the antecedent, is understood as the subject (A.G. 271.a).

suorumque pugnantium: Partitive genitive with **numerum** (A.G. 346.a.1). **suorumque**: Plural, masculine genitive possessive pronoun used substantively to denote a special class (A.G. 302.d). **-que**: The enclitic conjunction connects the two main verbs **consistebat ... augebat** (A.G. 324.a). **pugnantium**: Present participle used as an adjective modifying **suorum** (A.G. 494.a).

numerum: Accusative direct object of **augebat** (A.G. 387).

augebat: The main verb of the coordinate clause **suorumque ... augebat** (A.G. 278.a). The pronoun **is**, with **quisque** as the antecedent, is understood as the subject (A.G. 271.a).

(48.3-4) (3) Quorum cum magna multitudo convenisset, matres familiae, quae paulo ante Romanis de muro manus tendebant, suos obtestari et more Gallico passum capillum ostentare liberos(4)que in conspectum proferre coeperunt.

ante, *before, previously.*

capillus, -i, m., *hair of the head, hair.*

coepi, -isse, coeptus, *begin, start, commence.*
convenio, -venire, -veni, -ventus, *come together, assemble.*
de, *from.*
familia, -ae, f., *household, family,* (pl. with matres) *matrons.*
in, *into.*
magnus, -a, -um, *great, large.*
mater, -tris, f., *mother,* (with familiae) *matrons.*
multitudo, -inis, f., *multitude, crowd.*
obtestor, -ari, -atus, *implore, adjure.*
pando, pandere, pandi, passus, *spread out.*
profero, -ferre, -tuli, -latus, *bring out, bring forth.*
qui, quae, quod, *who, which, what.*
sui, -orum, m., pl., *their men,* with or without *own.*

conspectus, -us, m., *sight, view, presence.*
cum, *after, when.*
et, *and.*
Gallicus, -a, -um, *of Gaul, Gallic.*
liberi, -orum, m., pl., *children.*
manus, -us, f., *hand.*
mos, moris, f., *custom, way, wont, practice.*
murus, -i, m., *wall, rampart.*
ostento, -are, -avi, -atus, *display, show.*
paulo, *by a little, just a little.*
-que, *and.*
Romani, -orum, m., pl., *the Romans.*
tendo, tendere, tetendi, tentus, and tensus, *stretch, extend.*

Quorum: Plural, masculine, genitive demonstrative pronoun used substantively (A.G. 296.2). The antecedent is suorum (A.G. 297.e). Partitive genitive with multitudo (A.G. 346.a.1). The relative does not introduce a relative clause but is a connecting relative; at the beginning of a clause the pronoun is often best rendered by a personal or demonstrative pronoun, with or without *and* (A.G. 308.f).

cum ... convenisset: Temporal clause; the relative adverb cum ("after, when") with the pluperfect subjunctive describes the circumstances that preceded the action of the main verb (A.G. 546). convenisset: The main verb of the subordinate clause (A.G. 278.b).

magna multitudo: Nominative subject (A.G. 339).

matres familiae: Nominative subject of coeperunt (A.G. 339). familiae: Partitive genitive (A.G. 346.a.1).

quae ... tendebant: Relative clause (A.G. 303). quae: Plural, feminine, nominative relative pronoun used substantively (A.G. 305). The antecedent is matres (A.G. 307). Nominative subject (A.G. 339). tendebant: The main verb of the subordinate clause (A.G. 278.b).

paulo: Adverb (A.G. 320-21).

ante: Adverb (A.G. 320-21 and 433.1).

Romanis: Dative indirect object of the transitive verb tendebant (A.G. 362).

de muro: Prepositional phrase, de with the ablative here means "from" (*OLD de* 2).

manus: Accusative direct object of the transitive verb tendebant (A.G. 387).

suos: Plural, masculine, accusative possessive pronoun used substantively to denote a special class (A.G. 302.d). Accusative direct object of the infinitive obtestari (A.G. 387 and 451.3).

obtestari: Complementary infinitive after coeperunt (A.G. 456).

et: The conjunction connects the two infinitives obtestari ... ostentare (A.G. 324.a).

more Gallico: Ablative of manner with a limiting adjective (A.G. 412).

passum capillum: Accusative direct object of the infinitive ostentare (A.G. 387 and 451.3). passum: Singular, masculine, accusative, perfect, passive participle used as an adjective (A.G. 494.a).

ostentare: Complementary infinitive after coeperunt (A.G. 456).

liberosque: Accusative direct object of the infinitive proferre (A.G. 387 and 451.3). -que: The enclitic conjunction connects the last infinitive in the series ostentare ... proferre (A.G. 323.c.3).

in conspectum: Prepositional phrase, in with the accusative here means "into" (an area defined by a range of the senses) (*OLD in* 1.b).

proferre: Complementary infinitive after coeperunt (A.G. 456). "The women of the ancient Germans also placed themselves and their children in sight of their husbands and fathers, in order to inspire greater courage. Cf. 1.51.3 and Tac. Germ. 7." (Kelsey, 417)

coeperunt: The main verb of the main clause (A.G. 278.b).

(48.4) **Erat Romanis nec loco nec numero aequa contentio; simul et cursu et spatio pugnae defatigati non facile recentis atque integros sustinebant.**

aequus, -a, -um, *fair, equal, advantageous.*
contentio, -onis, f., *struggle, fight, contest, dispute, controversy.*
defatigo, -are, -avi, -atus, *tire out, exhaust, fatigue.*
facile, *easily, readily, with no trouble.*

locus, -i, m., *place, position.*
non, *not.*
pugna, -ae, f., *fight, combat, battle.*

Romani, -orum, m., pl., *the Romans.*
spatium, -i, n., *duration, length.*
sustineo, -tinere, -tinui, -tentus, *bear, endure, withstand.*

atque, *and.*
cursus, -us, m., *speed.*
et ... et, *both ... and.*
integri, -orum, m., pl., *those who were unexhausted, fresh men.*
nec ... nec, *neither ... nor.*
numerus, -i, m., *number.*
recentes, -ium, m., pl., *those who were fresh, unwearied men.*
simul, *at the same time, at once.*
sum, esse, fui, futurus, *be.*

Erat: The main verb of the simple sentence (A.G. 278.1). The verb sum in the sense of "exist" makes a complete predicate without a

predicate noun or adjective ("there was …"). It is then called the substantive verb and regularly comes first (A.G. 284.b and 598.c).
Romanis: Dative of reference; the dative in this construction is often called the dative of advantage as denoting the person for whose benefit the action is performed (A.G. 376).
nec … nec: The repeated conjunction connects the two ablative nouns and means "neither … nor" (*OLD* **neque** 7).
loco … numero: Two ablatives of specification (A.G. 418).
aequa contentio: Nominative subject (A.G. 339).
simul: Adverb (A.G. 320-21).
et … et: The repeated conjunction means "both … and" and connects the two ablative nouns (A.G. 323.e).
cursu … spatio: Two ablatives of cause after the passive participle **defatigati** (A.G. 404).
pugnae: Possessive genitive with **spatio** (A.G. 343).
defatigati: Nominative, perfect, passive, participle used as a predicate, where in English a phrase or a subordinate clause would be more normal (A.G. 496). The pronoun **ei**, with **Romanis** as the antecedent, is understood (A.G. 288.d). Nominative subject (A.G. 339).
non: Adverb modifying **facile**, the negative precedes the word it especially effects (A.G. 217.e, 320-21, and 599.a).
facile: Adverb formed from the neuter accusative adjective (A.G. 214.d and 320-21).
recentis atque integros: Two accusative direct objects of **sustinebant** (A.G. 387). **recentis**: Plural, masculine, accusative adjective used substantively (A.G. 288). The noun **Gallos** is understood (A.G. 288.d). Accusative plural adjective; **-is** for **-es** is the regular form for a one termination adjective (A.G. 117-18). **atque**: The conjunction connects the two accusative adjectives and means "and" (*OLD* **atque** 12). **integros**: Plural, masculine, accusative adjective used substantively (A.G. 288). The noun **Gallos** is understood (A.G. 288.d).
sustinebant: The main verb of the simple sentence (A.G. 278.1).

(49.1-2) Caesar, cum iniquo loco pugnari hostiumque augeri copias videret, praemetuens suis ad T. Sextium legatum, quem minoribus castris praesidio reliquerat, misit, ut cohortis ex castris celeriter educeret et sub infimo colle ab dextro latere hostium constitueret, ut, si nostros loco depulsos vidisset, (2) quo minus libere hostes insequerentur terreret.

ab, *on*.
augeo, augere, auxi, auctus, *increase, enlarge, augment, add to*.
castra, -orum, n., pl., *camp, encampment*.
cohors, -hortis, f., *cohort, company*, (the tenth part of a legion).
consisto, -sistere, -stiti, -status, *stop, halt, take a position, make a stand*.
cum, *since, seeing that*.
dexter, -tra, -trum, *right*.
et, *and*.
hostis, -is, m., *enemy, foe*; pl., *the enemy*.
iniquus, -a, -um, *uneven, sloping, unfavorable, disadvantageous*.

latus, -eris, n., *side, flank*.
libere, *freely, without hindrance*.
minor, -or, -ius, *smaller, less*.
nostri, -orum, m., pl., *our men, our side*.

praesidium, -i, n., *guard, garrison, protection*.
-que, *and*.
quo minus, *that not*, often best translated by *from* with a participle.
si, *if*.
sui, -orum, m., pl., *his men*, with or without *own*.
terreo, -ere, -ui, -itus, *deter, frighten*.
video, videre, visi, visus, *perceive, observe, see*.

ad, *to*.
Caesar, -aris, m., *Caesar*.
celeriter, *quickly, speedily, at once, immediately*.
collis, -is, m., *hill, height, elevation*.
copiae, -arum, f., pl., *forces, troops*.
depello, -pellere, -puli, -pulsus, *drive away, dislodge*.
educo, -ducere, -duxi, -ductus, *lead out, lead forth*.
ex, *from, out of*.
infimus, -a, -um, *lowest, at the bottom*.
insequor, -sequi, -secutus, *follow up, pursue, follow in pursuit*.
legatus, -i, m., *lieutenant, lieutenant-general*.
locus, -i, m., *place, position*.
mitto, mittere, misi, missus, *send*.
praemetuo, -ere, -----, -----, *be apprehensive, be anxious*.
pugno, -are, -avi, -atus, *fight, combat, engage*.
qui, quae, quod, *who, which, what*.
relinquo, -linquere, -liqui, -lictus, *leave, leave behind*.
sub, *at the foot of, below*.
T. Sextius, -i, m., *Titus Sextius*.
ut, *so that*.

Caesar … praemetuens: Nominative subject of **misit** (A.G. 339). **Caesar**: See Appendix A. **praemetuens**: Present participle used as an adjective modifying **Caesar** (A.G. 494.a).
cum … videret: Causal clause; the relative adverb **cum** ("since") with the subjunctive forms a clause expressing cause (A.G. 549).
videret: The main verb of the subordinate clause (A.G. 278.b). Imperfect subjunctive; the tense of the subjunctive is in secondary sequence and follows the rules for the sequence of tense after **misit** (A.G. 482-85). The pronoun **is**, with **Caesar** as the antecedent, is understood as the subject (A.G. 271.a).
iniquo loco: Ablative of *place where* without a preposition (A.G. 429.1-2).
(id) pugnari: Impersonal infinitive construction in indirect discourse after **videret** (A.G. 577 ff.). Impersonal use of the infinitive (A.G. 208.d). Supply **id** as the subject (A.G. 318.c). Present infinitive; the tense of the infinitive in indirect discourse is relative to that of the verb of saying (A.G. 584).
hostiumque: Partitive genitive with **copias** (A.G. 346.a.1). **-que**: The enclitic conjunction connects the two infinitives **pugnari** … **augeri** (A.G. 324.a).
augeri copias: Accusative/infinitive construction in indirect discourse after **videret** (A.G. 577 ff.). **augeri**: Present infinitive; the tense of the infinitive in indirect discourse is relative to that of the verb of saying (A.G. 584).

suis: Plural, masculine, dative possessive pronoun used substantively to denote a special class (A.G. 302.d). Dative indirect object of the intransitive use of the participle **praemetuens** (A.G. 367.c).

ad T. Sextium legatum: Prepositional phrase, **ad** with the accusative here means "to" with **misit** (A.G. 363) (*OLD* **ad** 1). **T. Sextium**: See Appendix A. **T.**: Abbreviated form of the praenomen **Titus** (A.G. 108.c). **legatum**: An accusative noun in apposition to the proper noun **Sextium** (A.G. 282).

quem ... reliquerat: Relative clause (A.G. 303). **quem**: Singular, masculine, accusative relative pronoun used substantively (A.G. 305). The antecedent is **Sextium** (A.G. 307). Accusative direct object of **reliquerat** (A.G. 387). **reliquerat**: The main verb of the subordinate clause (A.G. 278.b). The pronoun **is**, with **Caesar** as the antecedent, is understood as the subject (A.G. 271.a). The pluperfect denotes an action completed in past time (A.G. 477).

minoribus castris praesidio: Dative of the purpose or end (double dative). The dative of an abstract noun (**praesidio**) is used to show that for which a thing serves or which it accomplishes, with another dative of the person or thing affected (**minoribus castris**) (A.G. 382.1). **minoribus**: Irregular comparative adjective (A.G. 129).

misit: The main verb of the main clause (A.G. 278.b).

ut ... educeret ... constitueret: The conjunction **ut** ("so that") with the subjunctive forms a final (purpose) clause dependent upon **misit** (A.G. 531.1). **educeret ... constitueret**: The main verbs of the subordinate clause (A.G. 278.b). Imperfect subjunctives; the tense of the subjunctives is in secondary sequence and follows the rules for the sequence of tense after **misit** (A.G. 482-85). The pronoun **is**, with **Sextium** as the antecedent, is understood as the subject of both verbs (A.G. 271.a).

cohortis: Accusative direct object of **educeret** (A.G. 387). Accusative plural noun, **-is** for **-es** is the regular form in mixed i-stem nouns (A.G. 71-2).

ex castris: Ablative of *place from which* with the preposition **ex** (A.G. 426.1).

celeriter: Adverb (A.G. 214.b and 320-21).

et: The conjunction connects the two verbs in the purpose clause (A.G. 324.a).

sub infimo colle: Prepositional phrase, **sub** with the ablative here means "at the foot of, below" (*OLD* **sub** 6).

ab dextro latere hostium: Ablative of *position* with the preposition **ab** (A.G. 429.b). **hostium**: Possessive genitive with **latere** (A.G. 343).

ut, si ... vidisset ... terreret: A subordinate conditional statement (A.G. 512.c). The apodosis, as a purpose clause dependent on **constitueret**, takes the subjunctive and the protasis, as a clause subordinate to a subjunctive clause, also takes the subjunctive (attraction) (A.G. 512.c and 593).

ut ... terreret: The apodosis of the conditional statement (A.G. 512.c). The conjunction **ut** ("so that") with the subjunctive forms a final (purpose) clause dependent upon **constitueret** (A.G. 531.1). **terreret**: The main verb of the subordinate clause (A.G. 278.b). Imperfect subjunctive; the tense of the subjunctive is in secondary sequence and follows the rules for the sequence of tense after **misit** (A.G. 482-4). The pronoun **is**, with **Sextium** as the antecedent, is understood as the subject (A.G. 271.a).

si ... vidisset: The protasis of the conditional statement (A.G. 512.a). A clause dependent on a subjunctive clause (**ut ... terreret**) takes the subjunctive when regarded as an integral part of that clause (attraction) (A.G. 593). **vidisset**: The main verb of the subordinate clause (A.G. 278.b). Pluperfect subjunctive; the tense of the subjunctive is in secondary sequence and follows the rules for the sequence of tense after **misit** (A.G. 482-85). The pluperfect tense of the subjunctive is here standing for a future perfect in direct discourse (A.G. 484.c). The future perfect tense denotes action completed (at the time referred to), and hence is represented in the subjunctive by the pluperfect tense in secondary sequence (A.G. 484.c). The pronoun **is**, with **Sextium** as the antecedent, is understood as the subject (A.G. 271.a).

nostros... depulsos (esse): Accusative/infinitive construction in indirect discourse after **vidisset** (A.G. 577 ff.). **nostros**: Plural, masculine, accusative possessive pronoun used substantively to denote a special class (A.G. 302.d). **depulsos (esse)**: Supply **esse** to form the perfect, passive infinitive (A.G. 186). The tense of the infinitive in indirect discourse is relative to that of the verb of perceiving (A.G. 584).

loco: Ablative of separation without a preposition after the compound verb **depulsos (esse)** (A.G. 402).

quo minus ... insequerentur: A verb of hindering (**terreret**) takes the subjunctive with the conjunction **quo minus** ("that not") (A.G. 558.b). **quo minus**: Conjunction written as two words (*OLD* **quominus**). **Quominus** is really a phrase (**quo minus**), and the dependent constructions which it introduces have their origin in the relative clause of purpose with **quo** and a comparative (see 531.a) (A.G. 557). **insequerentur**: The main verb of the subordinate clause (A.G. 278.b). Imperfect subjunctive; the tense of the subjunctive is in secondary sequence and follows the rules for the sequence of tense after **misit** (A.G. 482-4).

libere: Adverb (A.G. 214.a and 320-21).

hostes: Nominative subject (A.G. 339).

(49.2) Ipse paulum ex eo loco cum legione progressus, ubi constiterat, eventum pugnae exspectabat.

consisto, -sistere, -stiti, -stitus, *stop, halt, take a position, make a stand.*
eventus, -us, m., *outcome, issue, result.*
exspecto, -are, -avi, -atus, *wait to see, wait for, await.*

is, ea, id, *he, she, it; that, this.*
locus, -i, m., *place, position.*
progredior, -gredi, -gressus, *advance, go forward, proceed.*
ubi, *where.*

cum, *with.*
ex, *from.*
ipse, -a, -um, *he, they*, with or without *himself, themselves.*
legio, -onis, f., *legion.*
paulum, *a little, somewhat.*
pugna, -ae, f., *fight, combat, battle.*

Ipse ... progressus: Nominative subject (A.G. 339). **Ipse**: Singular, masculine, nominative demonstrative pronoun used substantively

208

(A.G. 296.2 and 298.d). The antecedent is **Caesar** (A.G. 298). The pronoun distinguishes the principle person (**Caesar**) from a subordinate person (**Sextium**) (A.G. 298.3). **progressus**: Nominative, perfect, deponent participle used as a predicate, where in English a phrase or a subordinate clause would be more normal (A.G. 496).

paulum: Adverb (A.G. 320-21).

ex eo loco: Ablative of *place from which* with the preposition **ex** (A.G. 402 and 426.1). **eo**: Singular, masculine, ablative demonstrative pronoun used as an adjective modifying **loco** (A.G. 296.1 and a).

cum legione: Ablative of accompaniment with the preposition **cum** (A.G. 413). Caesar is with the tenth legion.

ubi constiterat: Relative clause; the relative adverb **ubi** ("in the place in which, where") with the indicative forms a subordinate clause correlative to the previous **eo** (A.G. 278.b) (*OLD* **ubi** 5). For the reference see 47.1-2. **constiterat**: The main verb of the subordinate clause (A.G. 278.b). The pronoun **is**, with **Ipse** (**Caesar**) as the antecedent, is understood as the subject (A.G. 271.a). The pluperfect denotes an action completed in past time (A.G. 477).

eventum: Accusative direct object of **exspectabat** (A.G. 387).

pugnae: Possessive genitive with **eventum** (A.G. 343).

exspectabat: The main verb of the main clause (A.G. 278.b).

(50.1-2) Cum acerrime comminus pugnaretur, hostes loco et numero, nostri virtute confiderent, subito sunt Aedui visi ab latere nostris aperto, quos Caesar ab dextra parte alio (2) ascensu manus distinendae causa miserat.

ab, *on.*

Aedui, -orum, m., pl., *the Aedui.*
apertus, -a, um, *open, exposed, unprotected.*
Caesar, -aris, m., *Caesar.*

comminus, *hand to hand, at close quarters.*

cum, *when, while.*
distineo, -tinere, -tinui, -tentus, *delay, hinder, engage, divert.*
hostis, -is, m., *enemy, foe*; pl., *the enemy.*
locus, -i, m., *place, position.*
mitto, mittere, misi, missus, *send.*
numerus, -i, m., *number.*
pugno, -are, -avi, -atus, *fight, combat, engage.*
subito, *suddenly, on a sudden.*
virtus, -utis, f., *manliness, courage, bravery, valor, prowess.*

acerriter, sup. **acerrimme**, *sharply, fiercely, with vigor, courageously.*
alius, -a, -ud, *another.*
ascensus, -us, m., *ascent, way up, approach.*
causa, -ae, f., abl. with the gen., *for the sake of, for the purpose of.*
confido, -fidere, -fisus sum, *trust, rely upon, have confidence in.*
dexter, -tra, -trum, *right.*
et, *and.*
latus, -eris, n., *side, flank.*
manus, -us, f., *band, force.*
nostri, -orum, m., pl., *our men, our side.*
pars, partis, f., *side.*
qui, quae, quod, *who, which, what.*
video, videre, visi, visus, *perceive, observe, see.*

Cum ... (id) pugnaretur ... confiderent: Temporal clause; the relative adverb **cum** ("when, while") with the imperfect subjunctive describes the circumstances that accompanied the action of the main verb (A.G. 546). **pugnaretur ... confiderent**: The main verbs of the subordinate clause (A.G. 278.b). Notice the asyndeton construction between the two verbs in the temporal clause (A.G. 323.b).

pugnaretur: Impersonal use of the intransitive passive verb (A.G. 208.d). Supply **id** as the subject (A.G. 318.c).

acerrime: Superlative adverb (A.G. 218 and 320-21).

comminus: Adverb (A.G. 320-21).

hostes: First nominative subject of **confiderent** (A.G. 339).

loco et numero: Two dative indirect objects of the intransitive verb **confiderent**, a verb of trusting (A.G. 367). **et**: The conjunction connects the two dative nouns (A.G. 324.a).

nostri: Plural, masculine, nominative possessive pronoun used substantively to denote a special class (A.G. 302.d). Second nominative subject of **confiderent** (A.G. 339).

virtute: Dative indirect object of the intransitive verb **confiderent**, a verb of trusting (A.G. 367).

subito: Adverb (A.G. 320-21).

sunt ... visi: The main verb of the main clause (A.G. 278.b). The perfect passive verb is here split (tmesis) (A.G. 640).

Aedui: Nominative subject (A.G. 339). These are the 10,000 requisitioned at 34.1, recovered from mutiny at Chapter 40, and in this battle sent to attack the Gauls at 45.10. See Appendix A.

ab latere nostris aperto: Ablative of *position* with the preposition **ab** (A.G. 429.b). **nostris**: Plural, masculine dative possessive pronoun used substantively to denote a special class (A.G. 302.d). Dative of reference, the dative is often used to qualify a whole idea (**ab latere ... aperto**) instead of the possessive genitive modifying one word (**latere**) (A.G. 376-77).

quos ... miserat: Relative clause (A.G. 303). For the reference see 45.10. **quos**: Plural, masculine, accusative relative pronoun used substantively (A.G. 305). The antecedent is **Aedui** (A.G. 307). Accusative direct object of **miserat** (A.G. 387). **miserat**: The main verb of the subordinate clause (A.G. 278.b). The pluperfect denotes an action completed in past time (A.G. 477).

Caesar: Nominative subject (A.G. 339). See Appendix A.

ab dextra parte: Ablative of *position* with the preposition **ab** (A.G. 429.b).

alio ascensu: Ablative of *way by which* without a preposition (A.G. 429.a).

manus distinendae causa: The genitive of the noun and gerundive with the ablative **causa** expresses purpose (A.G. 504.b). **manus**: This is the enemy forces. **distinendae**: Singular, feminine, genitive gerundive used as an adjective modifying **manus** denoting necessity, obligation or propriety (A.G. 500.1).

(50.2-3) **Hi similitudine armorum vehementer nostros perterruerunt ac, tametsi dextris umeris exsertis animadvertebantur, quod insigne +pacatum+ esse consuerat, tamen id ipsum sui fallendi causa milites (3) ab hostibus factum existimabant.**

ab, *by.*
animadverto, -tere, -ti, -sus, *notice, observe, perceive.*
causa, -ae, f., abl. with the gen., *for the sake of, for the purpose of.*

dexter, -tra, -trum, *right.*
exsero, -serere, -serui, -sertus, *thrust out, bare.*
fallo, fallere, fefelli, falsus, *deceive, cheat.*
hostis, -is, m., *enemy, foe*; pl., *the enemy.*
ipse, -a, -um, *the very.*
miles, -itis, m., *soldier, foot-solider.*
pacatus, -a, -um, *peaceful.*

qui, quae, quod, *who, which, what.*
sui, sibi, se, or **sese**, nom. wanting, *them*, with or without *-selves.*
tamen, *yet, still, for all that, nevertheless, however.*
umerus, -i, m., *shoulder.*

ac, *and.*
arma, -orum, n., pl., *arms, armor, weapons.*
consuesco, -suescere, -suevi, -suetus, *be accustomed, be wont.*
existimo, -are, -avi, -atus, *think, consider, judge.*
facio, facere, feci, factus, *bring about, make, do.*
hic, haec, hoc, *this; he, she, it.*
insigne, -is, n., *sign, mark, token, indication.*
is, ea, id, *he, she, it; that, this.*
nostri, -orum, m., pl., *our men, our side.*
perterreo, -terrere, -----, -territus, *greatly alarm, frighten, terrify, dismay.*
similitudo, -inis, f., *likeness, resemblance, similarity.*
sum, esse, fui, futurus, *be.*
tametsi, *although, though.*
vehementer, *vigorously, violently, exceedingly.*

Hi: Plural, masculine, nominative demonstrative pronoun used substantively (A.G. 296.2). The antecedent is **Aedui** (A.G. 297.e). Nominative subject (A.G. 339).
similitudine: Ablative of cause without a preposition (A.G. 404).
armorum: Possessive genitive with **similitudine** (A.G. 343).
vehementer: Adverb (A.G. 214.b and 320-21).
nostros: Plural, masculine, accusative possessive pronoun used substantively to denote a special class (A.G. 302.d). Accusative direct object of **perterruerunt** (A.G. 387).
perterruerunt: The main verb of the coordinate clause **Hi ... perterruerunt** (A.G. 278.a).
ac: The conjunction connects the two main verbs **perterruerunt ... existimabant** and means "and" (*OLD* **atque** 12).
tametsi ... tamen: Correlative clauses meaning "even though ... nevertheless" (*OLD* **etsi** 2 and **tamen** 3).
tametsi ... animadvertebantur: Concessive clause; the conjunction **tametsi** ("even though") takes the indicative (A.G. 527.c).
animadvertebantur: The main verb of the subordinate clause (A.G. 278.b). The pronoun **ei**, with **Hi** (**Aedui**) as the antecedent, is understood as the subject (A.G. 271.a).
dextris umeris exsertis (esse): Ablative of quality (descriptive ablative) with an adjective modifier (A.G. 415). **exsertis**: Perfect, passive, participle used as an adjective modifying **umeris** (A.G. 494). Supply **esse** as the infinitive after the passive use of the verb of perception (**animadvertebantur**) (A.G. 582).
quod ... consuerat: Relative clause (A.G. 303). **quod**: See below. **consuerat**: The main verb of the subordinate clause (A.G. 278.b). Contracted form of **consueverat** (A.G. 181.a). The pluperfect denotes an action completed in past time (A.G. 477).
quod insigne: Nominative subject (A.G. 339). "As the dress and armor of the Aedui were Gallic, the mistake of the panic-stricken soldiers in supposing them enemies was a natural one." (Kelsey 417). **quod**: Singular, neuter, nominative relative pronoun (A.G. 305). The pronoun agrees with the adjective **insigne** in its own clause (adjectival use) (A.G. 306).
+pacatum+: Singular, neuter, nominative predicate adjective modifying **insigne** after **esse**. A predicate adjective after a complementary infinitive takes the case of the subject of the main verb (A.G. 283-84 and 458).
esse: Complementary infinitive after **consuerat** (A.G. 454).
tamen: Adverb, normally postpositive but not here (A.G. 320-21 and 324.j).
id ipsum ... factum (esse): Accusative/infinitive construction in indirect discourse after **existimabant** (A.G. 577 ff.). **id**: Singular, neuter, accusative demonstrative pronoun used substantively meaning "this thing" (A.G. 296.2). The antecedent is the uncovered right shoulders of the Aedui (A.G. 297.e). **ipsum**: Singular, neuter, accusative demonstrative pronoun used as an intensive adjective modifying **id** meaning "very" (A.G. 296.1 and a and 298.c). **factum (esse)**: Supply **esse** to form the perfect, passive infinitive (A.G. 188). The tense of the infinitive in indirect discourse is relative to that of the verb of saying (A.G. 584).
sui fallendi causa: The genitive of the pronoun and gerund/gerundive with the ablative **causa** expresses purpose (A.G. 504.b). This is an irregular construction with **causa**. **sui**: Genitive indirect reflexive pronoun used substantively (A.G. 144 and 300.2). **fallendi**: If the substantive is a personal or reflexive pronoun, an irregular construction is used, **mei, tui, nostri**, or **vestri** with a genitive in **-i** (sometimes called gerund, sometimes gerundive), regardless of gender and number. Thus, **sui fallendi causa** means "for the sake of" deceiving them. The usual gerund would be **se fallendi causa**; the gerundive **sui fallendorum causa**. (Walker, 526, 291.a). For parallel constructions with **causa/gratia** and the objective genitive see 43.3 and 80.9.
milites: Nominative subject (A.G. 339).
ab hostibus: Ablative of agent with the preposition **ab** after the passive infinitive **factum (esse)** (A.G. 405).
existimabant: The main verb of the coordinate clause **tametsi ... existimabant** (A.G. 278.a).

(50.3-4) **Eodem tempore L. Fabius centurio quique una murum ascenderant, circum(4)venti atque interfecti muro praecipitabantur.**

ascendo, -scendere, -scendi, -scensus, *ascend, climb, mount, scale.*
centurio, -onis, m., *centurion.*

idem, eadem, idem, *the same.*
L. Fabius, -i, m., *Lucius Fabius.*
praecipito, -are, -avi, -atus, *hurl headlong, fling down.*
qui, quae, quod, *who, which, what.*
una, *together, at the same time.*

atque, *and then.*
circumvenio, -venire, -veni, -ventus, *surround, encompass.*
interficio, -ficere, -feci, -fectus, *slay, kill.*
murus, -i, m., *wall, rampart.*
-que, *and.*
tempus, -oris, n., *time.*

Eodem tempore: Ablative of *time when* (A.G. 423.1). **Eodem**: Singular, neuter, ablative demonstrative pronoun used as an adjective modifying **tempore** (A.G. 296.1 and a).
L. Fabius: Nominative subject (A.G. 339). See Appendix A. **L.**: Abbreviated form of the praenomen **Lucius** (A.G. 108.c).
centurio: A nominative noun in apposition to the proper noun **Fabius** (A.G. 282).
quique ... ascenderant: Relative clause (A.G. 303). For the reference see 47.7. **qui**: Plural, masculine, nominative relative pronoun used substantively (A.G. 305). The antecedent is omitted, supply **ei** (A.G. 307.c). Nominative subject (A.G. 339). **-que**: The enclitic conjunction connects the two nominatives **Fabius ... qui** (A.G. 324.a). **ascenderant**: The main verb of the subordinate clause (A.G. 278.b). The pluperfect denotes an action completed in past time (A.G. 477).
una: Adverb (A.G. 320-21).
murum: Accusative direct object of **ascenderant** (A.G. 387).
circumventi atque interfecti: Two nominative, perfect, passive, participles used as a predicate, where in English a phrase or a subordinate clause would be more normal (A.G. 496). Here the plural participles modify the singular noun **Fabius** and the plural pronoun **ei**, the supplied antecedent of **qui** (A.G. 286.a). **atque**: The conjunction connects the two participles and means "and then" (*OLD* **atque** 7).
muro: Ablative of separation without a preposition (A.G. 401).
praecipitabantur: The main verb of the main clause (A.G. 278.b).

(50.4) M. Petronius, eiusdem legionis centurio, cum portas excidere conatus esset, a multitudine oppressus ac sibi desperans multis iam vulneribus acceptis, manipularibus suis, qui illum secuti erant, 'Quoniam,' inquit, 'me una vobiscum servare non possum, vestrae quidem certe vitae prospiciam, quos cupiditate gloriae adductus in periculum deduxi.

a(b), *by.*
accipio, -cipere, -cepi, -ceptus, *receive, suffer, bear.*

centurio, -onis, m., *centurion.*
conor, -ari, -atus, *endeavor, attempt, undertake, try.*
cum, *after, when.*
deduco, -ducere, -duxi, -ductus, *lead, conduct, bring.*

excido, -cidere, -cidi, -cisus, *raze, demolish, destroy.*
iam, *already.*
ille, illae, illud, *that; he, she, it.*
inquam, inquis, inquit, *say.*
M. Petronius, -i, m., *Marcus Petronius.*

mei, mihi, me, me, nom. wanting, *myself.*
multus, -a, -um, *many.*
opprimo, -primere, -pressi, -pressus, *overwhelm, crush, destroy.*
porta -ae, f., *city gate.*
prospicio, -spicere, -spexi, -spectus, *provide for, look out for.*
quidem, *indeed, at least.*
sequor, -qui, -cutus, *follow, follow after.*
sui, sibi, se, or sese, nom. wanting, *himself.*
una, *together with.*
vita, -ae, f., *life.*
vulnus, -eris, n., *wound.*

ac, *and.*
adduco, -ducere, -duxi, -ductus, *induce, prevail upon, influence.*
certe, *at least, at any rate.*
-cum, *with.*
cupiditas, -tatis, f., *ardent desire, longing, eagerness.*
despero, -are, -avi, -atus, *give up hope of, despair of, have no hope of.*
gloria, -ae, f., *glory, fame, renown.*
idem, eadem, idem, *the same.*
in, *into.*
legio, -onis, f., *legion.*
manipularis, -is, m., *soldier of a maniple, fellow-manipular.*
multitudo, -inis, f., *great number, multitude, crowd.*
non, *not.*
periculum, -i, n., *risk, danger, hazard.*
possum, posse, potui, -----, *be able.*
qui, quae, quod, *who, which, what.*
quoniam, *since, seeing that, because.*
servo, -are, -avi, -atus, *save.*
suus, -a, -um, *his, with or without own.*
vester, -tra, -trum, *your, yours.*
vos, vestrum, *thou, you.*

M. Petronius ... oppressus ... desperans: Nominative subject of **inquit** (A.G. 339). The actions of Petronius are juxtaposed to those of Lucius Fabius to highlight the proper conduct for a centurion. "surely for the Roman reader one of the most emotive and appealing *exempla virtutis* in *GW*. The manner of his self-sacrifice, enhanced by the attribution of direct speech, underlies the moral superiority of the Romans at the time of their most serious defeat." (Hammond, 240). **M. Petronius**: See Appendix A. **M.**: Abbreviated form of the praenomen **Marcus** (A.G. 108.c). **oppressus ... desperans**: Notice the tense change in the participles. The perfect tense signifies completed action, the present tense signifies action in progress (A.G. 489). **oppressus**: Nominative, perfect, passive, participle used as a predicate, where in English a phrase or a subordinate clause would be more normal (A.G. 496). **desperans**: Present participle used as an adjective modifying **Petronius** (A.G. 494.a).

eiusdem legionis: Partitive genitive with **centurio** (A.G. 346.a.1). "The VIIIth." (Kelsey, 417) **eiusdem**: Singular, feminine, genitive demonstrative pronoun used as an adjective modifying **legionis** (A.G. 296.1 and a). The same as Lucius Fabius.

centurio: A nominative noun in apposition to the proper noun **Petronius** (A.G. 282).

cum ... conatus esset: Temporal clause; the relative adverb **cum** ("after, when") with the pluperfect subjunctive describes the circumstances that preceded the action of the main verb (A.G. 546). **conatus esset**: The main verb of the subordinate clause (A.G. 278.b).

portas: Accusative direct object of the infinitive **excidere** (A.G. 387 and 451.3).

excidere: Complementary infinitive after **conatus esset** (A.G. 456 and 563.e).

a multitudine: Ablative of agent with the preposition **a(b)** after the passive participle **oppressus** (A.G. 405).

ac: The conjunction connects the two participles **oppressus ... desperans** and means "and" (*OLD* **atque** 12).

sibi: Singular, masculine, dative direct reflexive pronoun (A.G. 299 and 300.1). The antecedent is **Petronius**, the subject of **inquit** (A.G. 299). Dative indirect object of the intransitive participle **desperans** (A.G. 367.b).

multis iam vulneribus acceptis: Ablative absolute (A.G. 419-20). **iam**: Adverb (A.G. 215.6, 217.b and 320-21). **acceptis**: The perfect tense of the participle represents the action as completed at the time indicated by the tense of the main verb (A.G. 489).

manipularibus suis: Dative indirect object of the transitive verb **inquit** (the quotation stands as the accusative direct object) (A.G. 362). **suis**: Plural, masculine, dative possessive pronoun used as an adjective modifying **manipularibus** (A.G. 302).

qui ... secuti erant: Relative clause (A.G. 303). **qui**: Plural, masculine, nominative relative pronoun used substantively (A. G. 305). The antecedent is **manipularibus** (A.G. 307). Nominative subject (A.G. 339). **secuti erant**: The main verb of the subordinate clause (A.G. 278.b). The pluperfect denotes an action completed in past time (A.G. 477).

illum: Singular, masculine, accusative demonstrative pronoun used substantively (A.G. 296.2). The antecedent is **Petronius** (A.G. 297.e). Accusative direct object of **secuti erant** (A.G. 387).

Quoniam ... consulite ... Frustra ... recipite (50.4-5 and 50.6): This speech in direct discourse is not treated by Murphy as a speech proper (C. Murphy Note 5).

Quoniam ... possum: Causal clause; the conjunction **quoniam** ("seeing as") takes the indicative (A.G. 540 Note 1). **possum**: The main verb of the subordinate clause (A.G. 278.b). The present tense in *oratio recta* after **inquit** denotes an action as now taking place (A.G. 578). Therefore, the tense in *oratio recta* is the true present and not the historical present (A.G. 465.2). The personal pronoun **ego** is understood as the subject but is not expressed except for distinction or emphasis (A.G. 295.a).

inquit: The main verb of the main clause (A.G. 278.b). The verb **inquit** is used only in *oratio recta* introducing direct speech (A.G. 206.b and 578). It is always used parenthetically, following one or more words (A.G. 599.c). The historical present, giving vividness to the narrative, is present in Chapter 50 (A.G. 469). This usage, common in all languages, comes from imagining past events as going on before our eyes (*repraesentatio*) (A.G. 469 Note). Siedler counts 5 uses of direct speech with **inquit** in Book 7 (Siedler, 46).

me: Singular, masculine, accusative reflexive pronoun (A.G. 144). Accusative direct object of the infinitive **servare** (A.G. 387 and 451.3).

una: Adverb (A.G. 320-21).

vobiscum: Ablative of accompaniment with the preposition **cum** (A.G. 413). **vos**: Plural, masculine, ablative personal pronoun used substantively (A.G. 143 and 295). **-cum**: The preposition **cum** ("with") is joined enclitically with the ablative (A.G. 143.f).

servare: Complementary infinitive after **possum** (A.G. 456).

non: Adverb, the adverb generally precedes the verb if it belongs to no one word in particular (A.G. 217.e, 320-21, and 599.a).

vestrae ... vitae: Dative indirect object of the intransitive verb **prospiciam** (A.G. 367.c). **vestrae**: Singular, feminine, dative possessive pronoun used as an adjective modifying **vitae** (A.G. 302).

quidem: Particle, placed directly after the word it emphasizes (**vestrae**) (*OLD* **quidem**).

certe: Adverb (A.G. 214.a and 320-21).

prospiciam: The main verb of the main clause (A.G. 278.b). This is the future tense, not the subjunctive (A.G. 188). The personal pronoun **ego** is understood as the subject but is not expressed except for distinction or emphasis (A.G. 295.a).

quos ... deduxi: Relative clause (A.G. 303). **quos**: Plural, masculine, accusative relative pronoun used substantively (A.G. 305). The antecedent is implied in **vobis** (A.G. 306.b). Accusative direct object of **deduxi** (A.G. 387). **deduxi**: The main verb of the subordinate clause (A.G. 278.b).

cupiditate: Ablative of cause without a preposition with the passive participle **adductus** (A.G. 404).

gloriae: Objective genitive with **cupiditate** (A.G. 348).

adductus: Nominative, perfect, passive, participle used as a predicate, where in English a phrase or a subordinate clause would be more normal (A.G. 496). The personal pronoun **ego** is understood but is not expressed except for distinction or emphasis (A.G. 295.a). Nominative subject of **deduxi** (A.G. 339).

in periculum: Prepositional phrase, **in** with the accusative here means "into" (a state or condition) (*OLD* **in** 2).

(50.4-5) **Vos data facul(5)tate vobis consulite.'**

consulo, -sulere, -sului, -sultus, *have regard for, look out for.*	**do, dare, dedi, datus**, *give.*
facultas, -atis, f., *ability, opportunity, chance.*	**vos, vestrum**, (personal pronoun), *thou, you.*
vestrum (-i), vobis, vos, vobis, nom. wanting, (reflexive pronoun), *yourself.*	

Vos: Plural, masculine, nominative personal pronoun used substantively (A.G. 143 and 295). Nominative subject of **consulite** (A.G. 339). The personal pronoun is not normally expressed except for distinction or emphasis (A.G. 295.a).

data facultate: Ablative absolute (A.G. 419-20). **data**: The perfect tense of the participle represents the action as completed at the time indicated by the tense of the main verb (A.G. 489).

vobis: Plural, masculine, dative reflexive pronoun (A.G. 144 and 299.a). Dative indirect object of the intransitive verb **consulite** (A.G. 367.c).

consulite: The main verb of the main clause (A.G. 278.b). Plural imperative (A.G. 186). Siedler counts 7 uses of the imperative in Book 7 (none by Caesar himself) (Siedler, 46).

(50.5) Simul in medios hostis irrupit duobusque interfectis reliquos a porta paulum summovit.

a(b), *from.*
hostis, -is, m., *enemy, foe*; pl., *the enemy.*
interficio, -ficere, -feci, -fectus, *slay, kill.*

medius, -a, -um, *in the middle, midst, middle, mid-.*
porta -ae, f., *city gate.*
reliqui, -orum, m., pl., *the rest.*
summoveo, -movere, -movi, -motus, *drive back, remove.*

duo, -ae, -o, *two.*
in, *into.*
irrumpo, -rumpere, -rupi, -ruptus, *break into, burst into, rush in.*
paulum, *a little, somewhat.*
-que, *and.*
simul, *at the same time, at once.*

Simul: Adverb (A.G. 320-21).
in medios hostis: Accusative of *place to which* with the preposition **in** (A.G. 426.2). **medios**: The adjective designates not what object, but what part of it is meant (A.G. 293). **hostis**: Accusative plural noun; **-is** for **-es** is the regular form in i-stem nouns (A.G. 65-67 and 74.c).
irrupit: The main verb of the coordinate clause **Simul ... irrupit** (A.G. 278.a). The pronoun **is**, with **adductus** (**Petronius**) as the antecedent, is understood as the subject (A.G. 271.a).
duobusque interfectis: Ablative absolute (A.G. 419-20). **duobusque**: Declinable cardinal number used substantively (A.G. 132-35). The noun **militibus** is understood (A.G. 288.b). **-que**: The enclitic conjunction connects the two main verbs **irrupit ... summovit** (A.G. 324.a). **interfectis**: The perfect tense of the participle represents the action as completed at the time indicated by the tense of the main verb (A.G. 489).
reliquos: Plural, masculine, accusative adjective used substantively (A.G. 288). The noun **milites** is understood (A.G. 288.b). Accusative direct object of **summovit** (A.G. 387).
a porta: Ablative of *place from which* with the preposition **a(b)** (A.G. 426.1).
paulum: Adverb (A.G. 320-21).
summovit: The main verb of the coordinate clause **duobusque ... summovit** (A.G. 278.a). The pronoun **is**, with **adductus** (**Petronius**) as the antecedent, is understood as the subject (A.G. 271.a).

(50.6) (6) Conantibus auxiliari suis, 'Frustra,' inquit, 'meae vitae subvenire conamini, quem iam sanguis viresque deficiunt.

auxilior, -ari, -atus, *render aid, assist, help.*
deficio, -ficere, -feci, -fectus, *fail, begin to be lacking, be exhausted.*
iam, *already, now.*
meus, -a, -um, *my, mine.*
qui, quae, quod, *who, which, what.*
subvenio, -venire, -veni, -ventus, *come to the help* or *rescue of, assist.*
vires, -ium, f., *physical powers, strength.*

conor, -ari, -atus, *endeavor, attempt, undertake, try.*
frustra, *in vain, with out effect, for nothing.*
inquam, inquis, inquit, *say.*
-que, *and.*
sanguis, -inis, m., *blood.*
sui, -orum, m., pl., *his men*, with or without *own.*
vita, -ae, f., *life.*

Conantibus ... suis: Dative indirect object of the transitive verb **inquit** (the quotation stands as the accusative direct object) (A.G. 362). **Conantibus**: Present participle used as an adjective modifying **suis** (A.G. 494). **suis**: Plural, masculine, dative possessive pronoun used substantively to denote a special class (A.G. 302.d).
auxiliari: Complementary infinitive after the participle **Conantibus** (A.G. 456 and 563.e).
Frustra: Adverb (A.G. 320-21).
inquit: The main verb of the main clause (A.G. 278.b). The verb **inquit** is used only in *oratio recta* introducing direct speech (A.G. 206.b and 578). It is always used parenthetically, following one or more words (A.G. 599.c). Siedler counts 5 uses of direct speech with **inquit** in Book 7 (Siedler, 46). The pronoun **is**, with **adductus** (**Petronius**) as the antecedent, is understood as the subject (A.G. 271.a).
meae vitae: Dative indirect object of the intransitive infinitive **subvenire** (A.G. 367). **meae**: Singular, feminine, dative possessive pronoun used as an adjective modifying **vitae** (A.G. 302).
subvenire: Complementary infinitive after **conamini** (A.G. 456 and 563.e).
conamini: The main verb of the main clause (A.G. 278.b). The present tense in *oratio recta* after **inquit** denotes an action as now taking place (A.G. 578). Therefore, the tense in *oratio recta* is the true present and not the historical present (A.G. 465.2). The personal pronoun **vos** is understood as the subject but is not expressed except for distinction or emphasis (A.G. 295.a).
quem ... deficiunt: Relative clause (A.G. 303). **quem**: Singular, masculine, accusative relative pronoun used substantively (A.G. 305). The antecedent is **Petronius** implied in **meae** (A.G. 306.b). Accusative direct object of **deficiunt** (A.G. 387). **deficiunt**: The main verb of the subordinate clause (A.G. 278.b).
iam: Adverb (A.G. 215.6, 217.b and 320-21).
sanguis viresque: Two nominative subjects (A.G. 339). **-que**: The enclitic conjunction connects the two nominative nouns (A.G. 324.a).

(50.6) **Proinde abite, dum est facultas, vosque ad legionem recipite.'**

abeo, -ire, -ii, -iturus, *go away, depart.*
dum, *while, as long as.*
legio, -onis, f., *legion.*
-que, *and.*
sum, esse, fui, futurus, *be.*

ad, *to.*
facultas, -atis, f., *ability, opportunity, chance.*
proinde, *hence, therefore, and so.*
recipio, -cipere, -cepi, -ceptus, (with vos), *return.*
vestrum (-i), vobis, vos, vobis, nom. wanting, *yourself.*

Proinde: Adverb, when used in exhortations it means "so then, accordingly" (*OLD* proinde 3.a).
abite: The main verb of the coordinate clause **Proinde ... facultas** (A.G. 278.a). Plural imperative (A.G. 203). Siedler counts 7 uses of the imperative in Book 7 (none by Caesar himself) (Siedler, 46). The personal pronoun **vos** is understood as the subject but is not expressed except for distinction or emphasis (A.G. 295.a).
dum ... facultas: Temporal clause; the conjunction **dum** (Awhile) takes the present indicative (A.G. 555). **facultas**: Nominative subject (A.G. 339).
est: The main verb of the subordinate clause (A.G. 278.b). The verb **sum** in the sense of "exist" makes a complete predicate without a predicate noun or adjective ("there is ..."). It is then called the substantive verb and regularly comes first (A.G. 284.b and 598.c).
vosque: Plural, masculine, accusative reflexive pronoun (A.G. 144 and 299.a). Accusative direct object of **recipite** (A.G. 387). **-que**: The enclitic conjunction connects the two imperatives (A.G. 324.a).
ad legionem: Accusative of *place to which* with the preposition **ad** (A.G. 426.2).
recipite: The main verb of the coordinate clause **vosque ... recipite** (A.G. 278.a). Plural imperative (A.G. 188). Siedler counts 7 uses of the imperative in Book 7 (none by Caesar himself) (Siedler, 46). **vos ... recipite**: The verb **recipere** used reflexively means "to return" (*OLD* recipio 12). The personal pronoun **vos** is understood as the subject but is not expressed except for distinction or emphasis (A.G. 295.a).

(50.6) **Ita pugnans post paulo concidit ac suis saluti fuit.**

ac, *and yet.*
ita, *in this way, so, thus.*
post, *afterwards.*
salus, -utis, f., *preservation, safety, deliverance.*
sui, -orum, m., pl., *his men*, with or without *own.*

concido, -cidere, -cidi, *fall down, fall, perish, be slain.*
paulo, *by a little, just a little.*
pugno, -are, -avi, -atus, *fight, combat, engage.*
sum, esse, fui, futurus, *be.*

Ita: Adverb (A.G. 217.c and 320-21).
pugnans: Nominative, present participle used as a predicate, where in English a phrase or a subordinate clause would be more normal (A.G. 496). The pronoun **is**, with **adductus (Petronius)** as the antecedent, is understood. Nominative subject of **concidit ... fuit** (A.G. 339).
post: Adverb (A.G. 320-21).
paulo: Adverb (A.G. 320-21).
concidit: The main verb of the coordinate clause **Ita ... concidit** (A.G. 278.a).
ac: The conjunction connects the two main verbs **concidit ... fuit** and has an adversative sense meaning "and yet" (*OLD* atque 9).
suis saluti: Dative of the purpose or end (double dative). The dative of an abstract noun (**saluti**) is used to show that for which a thing serves or which it accomplishes, with another dative of the person or thing affected (**suis**). The verb is usually a form of **sum** (**fuit**) (A.G. 382.1). **suis**: Plural, masculine, dative possessive pronoun used substantively to denote a special class (A.G. 302.d).
fuit: The main verb of the coordinate clause **suis ... fuit** (A.G. 278.a).

(51.1) **Nostri, cum undique premerentur, XLVI centurionibus amissis deiecti sunt loco.**

amitto, -mittere, -misi, -missus, *lose.*
cum, *since, because, in view of the fact that.*
I, in expression of number, *1.*
locus, -i, m., *place, position.*
premo, -ere, pressi, pressus, *press, harass, oppress.*

V, in expression of number, = *5.*

centurio, -onis, m., *centurion.*
deicio, -icere, -ieci, -iectus, *dislodge, rout.*
L, in expression of number, *50.*
nostri, -orum, m., pl., *our men, our side.*
undique, *from all sides, from all parts, on all sides, everywhere.*

X, in expression of number, = *10.*

Nostri: Plural, masculine, nominative possessive pronoun used substantively to denote a special class (A.G. 302.d). Nominative subject (A.G. 339).
cum ... premerentur: Causal clause; the relative adverb **cum** ("since") with the subjunctive forms a clause expressing cause (A.G. 549). **premerentur**: The main verb of the subordinate clause (A.G. 278.b). Imperfect subjunctive; the tense of the subjunctive is in secondary sequence and follows the rules for the sequence of tense after **deiecti sunt** (A.G. 482-85). The pronoun **ei**, with **Nostri** as the antecedent, is understood as the subject (A.G. 271.a).
undique: Adverb (A.G. 217.a and 320-21).
XLVI centurionibus amissis: Ablative absolute (A.G. 419-20). **XLVI**: Roman numeral used as an adjective modifying

centurionibus (A.G. 133). **amissis**: The perfect tense of the participle represents the action as completed at the time indicated by the tense of the main verb (A.G. 489).

deiecti sunt: The main verb of the main clause (A.G. 278.b).

loco: Ablative of separation without a preposition after the compound verb **deiecti sunt** (A.G. 402).

(51.1-2) Sed intolerantius Gallos insequentis legio decima tardavit, quae pro subsidio paulo (2) aequiore loco constiterat.

aequus, -a, -um, comp. **-ior**, *level, even, flat.*

decimus, -a, -um, *tenth.*

insequor, -sequi, -secutus, *follow up, pursue, follow in pursuit.*

legio, -onis, f., *legion.*

paulo, *somewhat.*

qui, quae, quod, *who, which, what.*

subsidium, -i, n., *support, relief, reinforcement.*

consisto, -sistere, -stiti, -stitus, *stop, halt, take a position, make a stand.*

Galli, -orum, m., *the Gauls.*

intoleranter, comp. **-ius**, *immoderately, insupportably, excessively.*

locus, -i, m., *place, position.*

pro, *in the capacity of.*

sed, *but.*

tardo, -are, -avi, -atus, *check, delay, impede, hinder.*

Sed: Coordinate conjunction (A.G. 324.d).

intolerantius: Comparative adverb modifying **insequentis** (A.G. 218 and 320-21). The comparative degree here denotes a considerable or excessive degree of the quality meaning "too" (A.G. 291.a).

Gallos insequentis: Accusative direct object of **tardavit** (A.G. 387). **Gallos**: See Appendix A. **insequentis**: Present participle used as an adjective modifying **Gallos** (A.G. 494). Accusative plural; **-is** for **-es** is the regular form of the present participle (A.G. 117-18).

legio decima: Nominative subject (A.G. 339). **decima**: Declinable ordinal number used as an adjective (A.G. 132-35).

tardavit: The main verb of the main clause (A.G. 278.b).

quae ... constiterat: Relative clause (A.G. 303). For the reference see 47.1-2. **quae**: Singular, feminine, nominative relative pronoun used substantively (A.G. 305). The antecedent is **legio** (A.G. 307). Nominative subject (A.G. 339). **constiterat**: The main verb of the subordinate clause (A.G. 278.b). The pluperfect denotes an action completed in past time (A.G. 477).

pro subsidio: Prepositional phrase, **pro** with the ablative here means "in the capacity of" (*OLD* pro1 8).

paulo aequiore loco: Ablative of *place where* without a preposition (A.G. 429.1-2). **paulo**: Adverb modifying **aequiore**; with a comparative adjective **paulo** means "somewhat" (A.G. 320-21) (*OLD* paul(l)o 2.a). **aequiore**: Comparative adjective (A.G. 124).

(51.2-3) Hanc rursus XIII. legionis cohortes exceperunt, quae ex castris minoribus eductae cum (3) T. Sextio legato ceperant locum superiorem.

capio, capere, cepi, captus, *take, get, seize, capture, occupy.*

cohors, -hortis, f., *cohort, company*, (the tenth part of a legion).

educo, -ducere, -duxi, -ductus, *lead out, lead forth.*

excipio, -cipere, -cepi, -ceptus, *come next to, succeed, follow.*

I, in expression of number, *1.*

legio, -onis, f., *legion.*

minor, -or, -ius, *smaller, less.*

rursus, *in turn.*

T. Sextius, -i, m., *Titus Sextius.*

castra, -orum, n., pl., *camp, encampment.*

cum, *with.*

ex, *from, out of.*

hic, haec, hoc, *this; he, she, it.*

legatus, -i, m., *lieutenant, lieutenant-general.*

locus, -i, m., *place, position.*

qui, quae, quod, *who, which, what.*

superior, -or, -us, *higher, upper, superior.*

X, in expression of number, = *10.*

Hanc: Singular, feminine, accusative demonstrative pronoun used substantively (A.G. 296.2). The antecedent is **legio decima** (A.G. 297.e). Accusative direct object of **exceperunt** (A.G. 387).

rursus: Adverb (A.G. 216 and 320-21).

XIII. legionis: Partitive genitive with **cohortes** (A.G. 346.a.1). **XIII.**: Roman numeral used as an adjective modifying **legionis** (A.G. 133).

cohortes: Nominative subject (A.G. 339).

exceperunt: The main verb of the main clause (A.G. 278.b).

quae ... superiorem: Relative clause (A.G. 303). **quae**: See below. **superiorem**: See below.

quae ... eductae: Nominative subject (A.G. 339). **quae**: Plural, feminine, nominative relative pronoun used substantively (A.G. 305). The antecedent is **cohortes** (A.G. 307). **eductae**: Nominative, perfect, passive, participle used as a predicate, where in English a phrase or a subordinate clause would be more normal (A.G. 496).

ex castris minoribus: Ablative of *place from which* with the preposition **ex** (A.G. 426.1). **minoribus**: Irregular comparative adjective (A.G. 129).

cum T. Sextio legato: Ablative of accompaniment with the preposition **cum** (A.G. 413). **T. Sextio**: See Appendix A. **T.**: Abbreviated form of the praenomen **Titus** (A.G. 108.c). **legato**: A noun in apposition to the proper noun **Sextio** (A.G. 282).

ceperant: The main verb of the subordinate clause (A.G. 278.b). The pluperfect denotes an action completed in past time (A.G. 477).

locum superiorem: Accusative direct object of **ceperant** (A.G. 387). **superiorem**: Defective comparative adjective (A.G. 130.b).

(51.3-4) Legiones, ubi primum planitiem attigerunt, infestis contra hostis signis (4) constiterunt.

attingo, -tingere, -tigi, -tactus, *touch upon, touch, reach.*

contra, *against, to meet.*
infestus, -a, -um, *on the offensive, hostile, threatening.*
planities, -ei, f., *level ground, plain.*
signum, -i, n., *standard.*

consisto, -sistere, -stiti, -status, *stop, halt, take a position, make a stand.*
hostis, -is, m., *enemy, foe;* pl., *the enemy.*
legio, -onis, f., *legion.*
primum, *first, before everything else, in the first place.*
ubi, *when,* (with **primum**), *as soon as, the moment that.*

Legiones: Nominative subject (A.G. 339). "Driven by the Gauls down the entire ascent leading to the town; once on level ground, however, and supported by the Xth and XIIIth legions, they turned and drove back their pursuers." (Kelsey, 418)
ubi primum ... attigerunt: Temporal clause; the relative adverb **ubi** with the indicative and the adverb **primum** means "as soon as, the moment that" introducing a subordinate clause (A.G. 279.a and 543) (*OLD* ubi 9.b). **primum**: Adverb (A.G. 214.d, 320-21, and 322.d). **attigerunt**: The main verb of the subordinate clause (A.G. 278.b). The pronoun **eae**, with **Legiones** as the antecedent, is understood as the subject (A.G. 271.a).
planitiem: Accusative direct object of **attigerunt** A.G. 387).
infestis contra hostis signis: Ablative absolute with an adjective (**infestis**) taking the place of a participle (there is no participle for "being") (A.G. 419.a-20). **infestis**: The adjective with **signis** indicates attack (*OLD* infestus 3.b). **contra hostis**: Prepositional phrase, **contra** with the accusative here means "against, to meet" (*OLD* contra 15). **hostis**: Accusative plural noun; **-is** for **-es** is the regular form in i-stem nouns (A.G. 65-67 and 74.c).
constiterunt: The main verb of the main clause (A.G. 278.b).

(51.4) Vercingetorix ab radicibus collis suos intra munitiones reduxit.

ab, *from.*
intra, *inside of, within.*

radix, -icis, f., *root, foot, base.*

sui, -orum, m., pl., *his men,* with or without *own.*

collis, -is, m., *hill, height, elevation.*
munitio, -onis, f., *works of fortifications, intrenchment, defenses.*
reduco, -ducere, -duxi, -ductus, *lead back, conduct back.*
Vercingetorix, -igis, m., *Vercingetorix.*

Vercingetorix: Nominative subject (A.G. 339). See Appendix A.
ab radicibus collis: Ablative of *place from which* with the preposition **ab** (A.G. 402 and 426.1). **collis**: Partitive genitive with **radicibus** (A.G. 346..a.1).
suos: Plural, masculine, accusative possessive pronoun used substantively to denote a special class (A.G. 302.d). Accusative direct object of **reduxit** (A.G. 387).
intra munitiones: Prepositional phrase, **intra** with the accusative here means "within" (*OLD* intra 1).
reduxit: The main verb of the simple sentence (A.G. 278.1).

(51.4) Eo die milites sunt paulo minus septingenti desiderati.

desidero, -are, -avi, -atus, *be missing, be lost.*
is, ea, id, *he, she, it; that, this.*
minus, *less than.*
septingenti, -ae, -a, *seven hundred.*

dies, -ei, m. and f., *day.*
miles, -itis, m., *soldier, foot-solider.*
paulo, *by a little, just a little.*

Eo die: Ablative of *time when* (A.G. 423.1). **Eo**: Singular, masculine, ablative demonstrative pronoun used as an adjective modifying **die** (A.G. 296.1 and a). **die**: The noun **dies** is normally masculine gender (A.G. 97.a).
milites: Nominative subject (A.G. 339).
sunt ... desiderati: The main verb of the simple sentence (A.G. 278.1). The perfect passive verb is here split (tmesis) (A.G. 640).
paulo: Adverb modifying **minus** (A.G. 320-21).
minus: Defective comparative adverb modifying **septingenti** (A.G. 218.a and 320-21).
septingenti: Plural, masculine, nominative declinable cardinal number used as an adjective with **milites** (A.G. 132-35 and 339). After the comparative **minus** without **quam**, a word of number can be used without a change of case (here, the nominative is retained rather than the ablative of comparison) (A.G. 407.c).

3.D CHAPTER 52: CAESAR REPRIMANDS HIS SOLDIERS FOR THEIR LACK OF DISCIPLINE
(52.1-2) Postero die Caesar contione advocata temeritatem cupiditatemque militum reprehendit, quod sibi ipsi iudicavissent quo procedendum aut quid agendum videretur neque signo recipiendi dato constitissent neque a tribunis militum (2) legatisque retineri potuissent.

a(b), *by.*
ago, agere, egi, actus, *do, accomplish, perform.*
Caesar, -aris, m., *Caesar.*
contio, -onis, f., *assembly, meeting.*
dies, -ei, m. and f., *day.*

advoco, -are, -avi, -atus, *call, summon.*
aut, *or.*
consisto, -sistere, -stiti, -status, *stop, halt.*
cupiditas, -tatis, f., *avarice.*
do, dare, dedi, datus, *give.*

216

ipse, -a, -um, *he, they,* with or without *himself, themselves.*
legatus, -i, m., *lieutenant, lieutenant-general.*
neque, *and ... not.*
possum, posse, potui, -----, *be able.*
-que, *and.*
quo, *where.*
recipio, -cipere, -cepi, -ceptus, *withdraw.*

retineo, -tinere, -tinui, -tentus, *detain, keep back, hold.*
sui, sibi, se, or sese, nom. wanting, *themselves.*
tribunus, -i, m., *tribune.*

iudico, -are, -avi, -atus, *judge, decide, determine.*
miles, -itis, m., *soldier, foot-solider.*
posterus, -a, -um, *the following, the next.*
procedo, -cedere, -cessi, -----, *advance, go forward.*
quis, -----, quid, *who? what?*
quod, *because, since, for, as.*
reprehendo, -hendere, -hendi, -hensus, *criticize, blame, find fault with.*
signum, -i, n., *signal.*
temeritas, -tatis, f., *rashness, hastiness.*
videor, videri, visus sum, *seem, appear.*

Postero die: Ablative of *time when* (A.G. 423.1). **die**: The noun **dies** is normally masculine gender (A.G. 97.a).
Caesar: Nominative subject (A.G. 339). See Appendix A.
contione advocata: Ablative absolute (A.G. 419-20). "the assembly (*contio*) is a masterpiece of rhetoric, in which criticism of the soldiers' failure is offset against stylistically highlighted evocations of their bravery (e.g. by the triple anaphora of *non*; or casting in the form of a quasi-*praeteritio*: 'However admirable ...')." (Hammond, 240) **advocata**: The perfect tense of the participle represents the action as completed at the time indicated by the tense of the main verb (A.G. 489).
temeritatem cupiditatemque: Two accusative direct objects of **reprehendit** (A.G. 387).
militum: Possessive genitive with both **temeritatem cupiditatemque** (A.G. 343). **-que**: The enclitic conjunction connects the two accusative nouns (A.G. 324.a).
reprehendit: The main verb of the main clause (A.G. 278.b). The tense is perfect (A.G. 473).
quod ... iudicavissent ... constitissent ... potuissent: Causal clause; the conjunction **quod** ("because") takes the subjunctive when the reason is given on the authority of another (informal indirect discourse) (A.G. 540.2 and 592.3). **iudicavissent ... constitissent ... potuissent**: The main verbs of the subordinate clause (A.G. 278.b). Pluperfect subjunctives; the tense of the subjunctives is in secondary sequence and follows the rules for the sequence of tense after **reprehendit** (A.G. 482-85).
sibi: Plural, masculine, dative direct reflexive pronoun (A.G. 299 and 300.1). The antecedent is **ipsi**, the subject of **iudicavissent** (A.G. 299). Dative of reference; the dative in this construction is often called the dative of advantage as denoting the person for whose benefit the action is performed (A.G. 376).
ipsi: Plural, masculine, nominative demonstrative pronoun used substantively (A.G. 296.2 and 298.d). The antecedent is **militum** (A.G. 298). Nominative subject of **iudicavissent ... constitissent ... potuissent** (A.G. 339). The pronoun is here emphatic (A.G. 298.d.1).
quo (id) procedendum (esse) ... videretur: Indirect question with the subjunctive; the phrase is the object of **iudicavissent** (A.G. 573-75). **quo**: Interrogative adverb meaning "where" (*OLD* quo1 1). **procedendum**: Singular, neuter, nominative gerundive used as a predicate adjective modifying the supplied subject **id** after **videretur** and implying necessity. A predicate adjective after a complementary infinitive takes the case of the subject of the main verb (A.G. 283-84, 458 and 500.1). Supply **esse** as the complementary infinitive. **videretur**: The main verb of the subordinate clause (A.G. 278.b). Imperfect subjunctive; the tense of the subjunctive is in secondary sequence and follows the rules for the sequence of tense for indirect questions after **reprehendit** (A.G. 575). Impersonal use, supply the pronoun **id** as the subject (*OLD* video 23).
aut: The conjunction connects the two indirect questions and excludes the alternative (A.G. 324.e).
quid agendum (esse) videretur: Indirect question with the subjunctive; the phrase is the object of **iudicavissent** (A.G. 573-75). **quid**: Singular, neuter, nominative interrogative pronoun used substantively (A.G. 148). Nominative subject (A.G. 339). **agendum**: Singular, neuter, nominative gerundive used as a predicate adjective modifying **quid** after **videretur** and implying necessity. A predicate adjective after a complementary infinitive takes the case of the subject of the main verb (A.G. 283-84, 458 and 500.1). Supply **esse** as the complementary infinitive. **videretur**: The main verb of the subordinate clause (A.G. 278.b). Imperfect subjunctive; the tense of the subjunctive is in secondary sequence and follows the rules for the sequence of tense for indirect questions after **reprehendit** (A.G. 575). Compare the construction at 36.3.
neque ... neque: The repeated conjunction here joins two negative clauses (**constitissent ... potuissent**) to a preceding positive one and means "and ... not" (*OLD* neque 3).
signo recipiendi dato: Ablative absolute (A.G. 419-20). **recipiendi**: Singular, neuter, genitive gerund (A.G. 501-02). Objective genitive with **signo** (A.G. 504). **dato**: The perfect tense of the participle represents the action as completed at the time indicated by the tense of the main verb (A.G. 489).
a tribunis militum legatisque: Ablative of agent with the preposition **ab** after the passive infinitive **retineri** (A.G. 405). **militum**: Possessive genitive with **tribunis** (A.G. 343). **-que**: The enclitic conjunction connects the two ablative nouns in the prepositional phrase (A.G. 324.a).
retineri: Complementary infinitive after **potuissent** (A.G. 456).

(52.2-3) **Exposuit quid iniquitas loci posset, quid ipse ad Avaricum sensisset, cum sine duce et sine equitatu deprehensis hostibus exploratam victoriam dimisisset ne parvum modo detrimentum in contentione (3) propter iniquitatem loci accideret;**

accido, -cidere, -cidi, -----, *come to pass, occur, take place.*
Avaricum, -i, n., *Avaricum.*
cum, *when.*

ad, *at, near.*
contentio, -onis, f., *struggle, fight, contest.*
deprehendo, -hendere, -hendi, -hensus, *catch, seize, suprise.*

detrimentum, -i, n., *loss, damage, injury, repulse, reverse, defeat.*

dux, ducis, m., *leader, general, commander.*
et, *and.*
expono, -ponere, -posui, -positus, *set forth, state, explain.*
in, *in.*
ipse, -a, -um, *he, they,* with or without *himself, themselves.*
modo, *even.*
parvus, -a, -um, *small, trifling, insignificant.*
propter, *as a result* or *consequence of, in view of, because of.*
sentio, sentire, sensi, sensus, *feel, think, know.*
victoria, -ae, f., *victory.*

dimitto, -mittere, -misi, -missus, *give up, relinquish, forsake.*
equitatus, -us, m., *cavalry.*
exploratus, -a, -um, *established, certain, settled, sure.*
hostis, -is, m., *enemy, foe;* pl., *the enemy.*
iniquitas, -atis, f., *unfavorableness.*
locus, -i, m., *place, position, location, terrain.*
ne, *so that ... not.*
possum, posse, potui, -----, *have power* or *efficacy.*
quis, -----, quid, *to what extent; who? what?*
sine, *without the accompaniment of.*

Exposuit: The main verb of the main clause (A.G. 278.b). The verb introduces indirect statement through the end of Chapter 52. The pronoun **is**, with **Caesar** as the antecedent, is understood as the subject (A.G. 271.a).

quid ... desiderare: This speech in indirect discourse is classified by Charles Murphy as a military address (C. Murphy, 122). Murphy states that this speech, together with that at *BG* 1.40, "might serve as models for anyone who wish to know how to reprimand an army without destroying its morale." (C. Murphy, 123) Paul Murphy notes that the theme in this speech is **continentia**, "self-control, especially at **non ... desiderare**." (P. Murphy, 242).

quid ... posset: Indirect question with the subjunctive; the phrase is the object of **Exposuit** (A.G. 573-75). **quid**: Singular, neuter, accusative interrogative pronoun (A.G. 148). The pronoun is used as a cognate accusative with **posset** and means "to what extent" (A.G. 390.c) (*OLD* quis115). **posset**: The main verb of the subordinate clause (A.G. 278.b). Imperfect subjunctive; the tense of the subjunctive is in secondary sequence and follows the rules for the sequence of tense tenses for indirect questions after **Exposuit** (A.G. 575). Here **posse** without a complementary infinitive means A(of things, natural forces, etc.) to have power or efficacy (*OLD* possum 8.b).

iniquitas loci: Notice that this phrase is mentioned three times in fifteen lines, at 52.2, 52.3, and 53.1. Mark Williams does not believe that word repetitions in Caesar are due to inability or carelessness, but that he has had a reason for writing as he did (Williams, 217-219). It could be that here Caesar is anticipating his critiques and driving home the point that the general has not just here learned the tactical disadvantage of an unfavorable position, but has long known it and specifically devised his strategy around this fact. **iniquitas**: Nominative subject (A.G. 339).
loci: Possessive genitive with **iniquitas** (A.G. 343).

quid ... sensisset: Indirect question with the subjunctive; the phrase is the object of **Exposuit** (A.G. 573-75). **quid**: Singular, neuter, accusative interrogative pronoun used substantively (A.G. 148). Accusative direct object of **sensisset** (A.G. 387). **sensisset**: The main verb of the subordinate clause (A.G. 278.b). Pluperfect subjunctive; the tense of the subjunctive is in secondary sequence and follows the rules for the sequence of tense tenses for indirect questions after **Exposuit** (A.G. 575).
ipse: Singular, masculine, nominative demonstrative pronoun used substantively (A.G. 296.2 and 298.d). The antecedent is **Caesar** (A.G. 298). Nominative subject (A.G. 339). The pronoun is here emphatic (A.G. 298.d.1).
ad Avaricum: Prepositional phrase, with all names of places *at*, meaning *near* (not *in*), is expressed by **ad** with the accusative (A.G. 428.d). For the reference see Chapter 19. **Avaricum**: See Appendix A.
cum ... dimisisset: Temporal clause; the relative adverb **cum** ("when") with the pluperfect subjunctive describes the circumstances that preceded the action of the main verb (A.G. 546). **dimisisset**: The main verb of the subordinate clause (A.G. 278.b). The pronoun **is**, with **ipse** (**Caesar**) as the antecedent, is understood as the subject (A.G. 271.a).
sine duce et sine equitatu deprehensis hostibus: Ablative absolute (A.G. 419-20). **sine ... sine**: The needless repetition of the preposition gives emphasis. **sine duce**: Prepositional phrase, **sine** with the ablative means "without the accompaniment of" (*OLD* **sine** 1). **et**: The conjunction connects the two prepositional phrases (A.G. 324.a). **sine equitatu**: Prepositional phrase, **sine** with the ablative means "without the accompaniment of" (*OLD* **sine** 1). **deprehensis**: The perfect tense of the participle represents the action as completed at the time indicated by the tense of the main verb (A.G. 489).
exploratam victoriam: Accusative direct object of **dimisisset** (A.G. 387). "Caesar was not so sure about the victory at the time. Cf. Chap. 19." (Kelsey, 418)
ne ... accideret: The conjunction **ne** ("so that ... not") with the subjunctive forms a negative purpose clause (A.G. 531.1). **accideret**: The main verb of the subordinate clause (A.G. 278.b). Imperfect subjunctive; the tense of the subjunctive is in secondary sequence and follows the rules for the sequence of tense tenses after **Exposuit** (A.G. 482-85).
parvum ... detrimentum: Nominative subject (A.G. 339).
modo: Adverb (A.G. 320-21).
in contentione: Prepositional phrase, **in** with the ablative here means "in" (expressing an abstract location) (*OLD* **in** 26).
propter iniquitatem loci: Prepositional phrase, **propter** with the accusative here means "as a result or consequence of, in view of, because of" (*OLD* **propter** 3). **iniquitatem loci**: This phrase is mentioned three times in fifteen lines, at 52.2, 52.3, and 53.1. **loci**: Possessive genitive with **iniquitatem** (A.G. 343).

(52.3-4) **quanto opere eorum animi magnitudinem admiraretur, quos non castrorum munitiones, non altitudo montis, non murus oppidi tardare potuisset, tanto opere licentiam arrogantiamque reprehendere, quod plus se quam imperatorem de victoria atque (4) exitu rerum sentire existimarent;**

admiror, -ari, -atus, *admire.*

altitudo, -onis, f., *height.*

animus, -i, m., *courage, spirit, temper, resolution.*
atque, *and.*
de, *about, concerning.*
exitus, -us, m., *issue, result, outcome.*

is, ea, id, *he, she, it; that, this.*
magnitudo, -inis, f., *greatness.*
munitio, -onis, f., *works of fortifications, intrenchment, defenses.*
non, *not.*
plus, *more.*
quam, *than.*
-que, *and.*
quod, *because, since, for, as.*

res, rei, f., *event, affair.*
sui, sibi, se, or **sese**, nom. wanting, *they*, with or without *themselves.*
tardo, -are, -avi, -atus, *check, delay, impede, hinder.*

arrogantia, -ae, f., *presumption, arrogance, insolence.*
castra, -orum, n., pl., *camp, encampment.*
existimo, -are, -avi, -atus, *think, consider, judge.*
imperator, -oris, m., *commander-in-chief, commander, general.*
licentia, -ae, f., *presumption.*
mons, montis, m., *mountain, elevation, height.*
murus, -i, m., *wall, rampart.*
oppidum, -i, n., *fortified town, city.*
possum, posse, potui, -----, *be able.*
quanto opere, *in what degree, as much as.*
qui, quae, quod, *who, which, what.*
reprehendo, -hendere, -hendi, -hensus, *criticize, blame, find fault with.*
sentio, sentire, sensi, sensus, *feel, think, know.*
tanto opere, *to such a degree, so much.*
victoria, -ae, f., *victory.*

quanto opere ... tanto opere: A relative adverb correlative to a demonstrative adverb meaning "in what degree ... to such a degree" (A.G. 152) (*OLD* quantopere 2). **quanto opere**: The adverb is written as two words (*OLD* quantopere). **tanto opere**: The adverb is written as two words (*OLD* tantopere).

quanto opere ... admiraretur: Relative clause; a subordinate clause in indirect discourse takes the subjunctive (A.G. 279.a and 580). **admiraretur**: The main verb of the subordinate clause (A.G. 278.b). Imperfect subjunctive; the tense of the subjunctive is in secondary sequence and follows the rules for the sequence of tense tenses after **Exposuit** (A.G. 482-85). The pronoun **is**, with **ipse** (Caesar) as the antecedent, is understood as the subject (A.G. 271.a).

eorum: Plural, masculine, genitive demonstrative pronoun used substantively (A.G. 296.2). The pronoun is correlative to the relative clause **quos ... potuisset** (A.G. 297.d). Possessive genitive with **animi** (A.G. 343).

animi magnitudinem: This phrase is repeated at 52.5.

animi: Possessive genitive with **magnitudinem** (A.G. 343). The noun **animus** here means "courage or spirit" (*OLD* animus 13).

magnitudinem: Accusative direct object of **admiraretur** (A.G. 387).

quos ... potuisset: Relative clause; a subordinate clause in indirect discourse takes the subjunctive (A.G. 303 and 580). **quos**: Plural, masculine, accusative relative pronoun used substantively (A.G. 305). The antecedent is **eorum** (A.G. 307). Accusative direct object of the infinitive **tardare** (A.G. 387 and 451.3). **potuisset**: The main verb of the subordinate clause (A.G. 278.b). Pluperfect subjunctive; the tense of the subjunctive is in secondary sequence and follows the rules for the sequence of tense tenses after **Exposuit** (A.G. 482-85). Two or more singular subjects (and even one plural) normally take a verb in the plural (A.G. 317). However, when a verb belongs to two or more subjects separately, it often agrees with one (**murus**) and is understood with the others (**munitiones ... altitudo**) (A.G. 317.c).

non ... non ... non: Three adverbs, the negative precedes the word it especially effects (A.G. 217.e, 320-21, and 599.a). The repetition of a word at the beginning of successive clauses is anaphora (A.G. 641). Note the asyndeton construction with the remaining clauses (A.G. 323.b).

castrorum: Possessive genitive with **munitiones** (A.G. 343).

munitiones: First nominative subject of **potuisset** (A.G. 339).

altitudo: Second nominative subject of **potuisset** (A.G. 339).

montis: Possessive genitive with **altitudo** (A.G. 343).

murus: Third nominative subject of **potuisset** (A.G. 339).

oppidi: Possessive genitive with **murus** (A.G. 343).

tardare: Complementary infinitive after **potuisset** (A.G. 456).

licentiam arrogantiamque: Two accusative direct objects of the infinitive **reprehendere** (A.G. 387 and 451.3). **-que**: The enclitic conjunction connects the two accusative nouns (A.G. 324.a).

(se) reprehendere: Accusative/infinitive construction in indirect discourse after **Exposuit** (A.G. 577 ff.). Supply **se** as the singular, masculine, accusative direct reflexive pronoun as the accusative subject. The antecedent is **is** (Caesar), the supplied subject of **Exposuit** (A.G. 299). **reprehendere**: Present infinitive; the tense of the infinitive in indirect discourse is relative to that of the verb of saying (A.G. 584).

quod ... existimarent: Causal clause; the conjunction **quod** ("because") would normally take the indicative when the reason is given on the authority of the writer or speaker (A.G. 540.1). Here **quod** takes the subjunctive as a subordinate clause in indirect discourse after **Exposuit** (A.G. 580). **existimarent**: The main verb of the subordinate clause (A.G. 278.b). Imperfect subjunctive; the tense of the subjunctive is in secondary sequence and follows the rules for the sequence of tense tenses after **Exposuit** (A.G. 482-85). The pronoun **ipsi**, with **eorum** (**milites**) as the antecedent, is understood as the subject (A.G. 271.a).

plus: Construe with **quam** below.

se ... sentire: Accusative/infinitive construction in indirect discourse after **existimarent** (A.G. 577 ff.). **se**: Plural, masculine, accusative direct reflexive pronoun (A.G. 300.1). The antecedent is **ipsi**, the supplied subject of **existimarent** (A.G. 299). **sentire**: Present infinitive; the tense of the infinitive in indirect discourse is relative to that of the verb of saying (A.G. 584).

(plus) ... quam imperatorem: The comparative adverb **plus** is followed by the relative adverb **quam**, meaning "more than", and compares two things in the same case (**se ... imperatorem**) (A.G. 407) (*OLD* plus2). **imperatorem**: = **Caesar**.

de victoria atque exitu rerum: Prepositional phrase, **de** with the ablative here means "about, concerning" (*OLD* **de** 12). **atque**: The conjunction connects the two ablative nouns in the prepositional phrase and means "and" (*OLD* **atque** 12). **rerum**: Possessive genitive with **exitu** (A.G. 343).

(52.4) nec minus se ab milite modestiam et continentiam quam virtutem atque animi magnitudinem desiderare.

ab, *from.*
atque, *and.*
desidero, -are, -avi, -atus, *require, demand, expect.*
magnitudo, -inis, f., *greatness.*
minus, *less.*
nec, *no.*
sui, sibi, se, or **sese**, nom. wanting, *he*, with or without *himself.*

animus, -i, m., *courage, spirit, temper, resolution.*
continentia, -ae, f., *self-restraint, moderation.*
et, *and.*
miles, -itis, m., *soldier, foot-solider.*
modestia, -ae, f., *self-control, subordination.*
quam, *than.*
virtus, -utis, f., *courage, bravery, valor, prowess, vigor, energy, effort.*

This is a terse formulation of the virtues of a Roman soldier.

nec minus: Construe with **quam** below.
se ... desiderare: Accusative/infinitive construction in indirect discourse after **Exposuit** (A.G. 577 ff.). **se**: Singular, masculine, accusative direct reflexive pronoun (A.G. 300.1). The antecedent is **is** (**Caesar**), the supplied subject of **Exposuit** (A.G. 299).
ab milite: Ablative of source with the preposition **ab** (A.G. 403.1).
modestiam et continentiam: Two accusative direct objects of the infinitive **desiderare** (A.G. 387 and 451.3). **et**: The conjunction connects the two accusative nouns (A.G. 324.a).
(nec minus) ... quam: The comparative adverb **minus** is followed by the relative adverb **quam**, meaning "less than", and compares two things in the same case (**modestiam et continentiam ... virtutem atque ... magnitudinem**) (A.G. 218.a and 407). **nec**: The conjunction qualifies the single word **minus** rather than a whole clause and means "no" (*OLD* **neque** 4.c).
virtutem atque ... magnitudinem: Two accusative direct objects of the infinitive **desiderare** (A.G. 387 and 451.3). **atque**: The conjunction connects the two accusative nouns and means "and" (*OLD* **atque** 12).
animi magnitudinem: This phrase is repeated at 52.4.
animi: Possessive genitive with **magnitudinem** (A.G. 343).

PART 4: THE FINAL ROMAN VICTORY AT ALESIA (7.53-90)

4.A CHAPTER 53: CAESAR STABILIZES MORALE BY OFFERING BATTLE; INCONCLUSIVE CAVALRY ENGAGEMENTS ENSUE ON TWO CONSECUTIVE DAYS; CAESAR DEPARTS AND CROSSES THE ELAVER RIVER
(53.1) Hac habita contione et ad extremam orationem confirmatis militibus, ne ob hanc causam animo permoverentur neu quod iniquitas loci attulisset id virtuti hostium tribuerent, eadem de profectione cogitans, quae ante senserat legiones ex castris eduxit aciemque idoneo loco constituit.

acies, -ei, f., *line of battle, line.*
adfero, -ferre, attuli, allatus, *produce, cause, occasion.*
ante, *before, previously.*
causa, -ae, f., *reason, cause.*
confirmo, -are, -avi, -atus, *encourage.*

contio, -onis, f., *assembly, meeting.*
educo, -ducere, -duxi, -ductus, *lead out, lead forth.*
ex, *from, out of.*
habeo, habere, habui, habitus, *hold, deliver, make.*
hostis, -is, m., *enemy, foe*; pl., *the enemy.*
idoneus, -a, -um, *suitable, fit.*
is, ea, id, *he, she, it; that, this.*
locus, -i, m., *place, position, location, terrain.*
ne, *so that ... not.*
ob, *because of, on account of.*
permoveo, -movere, -movi, -motus, *deeply move, alarm, influence.*
-que, *and.*
sentio, sentire, sensi, sensus, *feel, think, know.*

ad, *at.*
animus, -i, m., *mind.*
castra, -orum, n., pl., *camp, encampment.*
cogito, -are, -avi, -atus, *intend, purpose, plan.*
constituo, -stituere, -stitui, -stitutus, *station, place, establish.*
de, *about, concerning.*
et, *and.*
extremus, -a, -um, *end of, the last part of.*
hic, haec, hoc, *this; he, she, it.*
idem, eadem, idem, *the same.*
iniquitas, -atis, f., *unfavorableness.*
legio, -onis, f., *legion.*
miles, -itis, m., *soldier, foot-solider.*
neu, *nor, and not, and that not.*
oratio, -onis, f., *speech, words, address.*
profectio, -onis, f., *departure, setting out.*
qui, quae, quod, *who, which, what.*
tribuo, -ere, -ui, -utus, *assign, ascribe, allot, give, concede.*

virtus, -utis, f., *manliness, courage, bravery, valor, prowess.*

Hac habita contione: Ablative absolute (A.G. 419-20). **Hac**: Singular, feminine, ablative demonstrative pronoun used as an adjective modifying **contione** (A.G. 296.1 and a). **habita**: The perfect tense of the participle represents the action as completed at the time indicated by the tense of the main verb (A.G. 489).
et: The conjunction connects the two ablative absolutes (A.G. 324.a).

ad ... tribuerent: Ablative absolute with a dependent clause.

ad extremam orationem confirmatis militibus: Ablative absolute (A.G. 419-20). **ad extremam orationem**: Prepositional phrase, **ad** with the accusative here means "at", indicating time (*OLD* **ad** 21.b). **extremam**: The adjective designates not what object, but what part of it is meant, "end of, the last part of" (A.G. 293) (*OLD* **extremus** 3.b). **confirmatis**: The perfect tense of the participle represents the action as completed at the time indicated by the tense of the main verb (A.G. 489). When the verb **confirmare** is followed by a negative purpose clause, it means "to encourage" (a person not to do something) (*OLD* **confirmo** 3).

ne ... permoverentur neu ... tribuerent: The conjunction **ne** ("so that ... not") with the subjunctive forms a negative purpose clause dependent on **confirmatis** (A.G. 531.1). **permoverentur ... tribuerent**: The main verbs of the subordinate clause (A.G. 278.b). Imperfect subjunctives; the tense of the subjunctives is in secondary sequence and follows the rules for the sequence of tense after **eduxit** (A.G. 482-85). The pronoun **ei**, with **militibus** as the antecedent, is understood as the subject of both verbs (A.G. 271.a). **neu**: The conjunction adds an alternative in a negative purpose clause and means "nor" (*OLD* **neve** 1).

ob hanc causam: Prepositional phrase, **ob** with the accusative means "because of" (*OLD* **causa** 9.d). **hanc**: Singular, feminine, accusative demonstrative pronoun used as an adjective modifying **causam** (A.G. 297.1 and a).

animo: Ablative of *place where* without a preposition (A.G. 429.3).

quod ... attulisset: Relative clause; a clause dependent on a subjunctive clause (**neu ... tribuerent**) takes the subjunctive when regarded as an integral part of that clause (attraction) (A.G. 303 and 593). **quod**: Singular, neuter, accusative relative pronoun used substantively (A.G. 305). The antecedent is the following pronoun **id** (A.G. 297.e). **attulisset**: The main verb of the subordinate clause (A.G. 278.b). Pluperfect subjunctive; the tense of the subjunctive is in secondary sequence and follows the rules for the sequence of tense after **eduxit** (A.G. 482-85).

iniquitas loci: Notice that this phrase is mentioned three times in fifteen lines, at 52.2, 52.3, and 53.1.

iniquitas: Nominative subject (A.G. 339).

loci: Possessive genitive with **iniquitas** (A.G. 343).

id: Singular, neuter, accusative demonstrative pronoun used substantively (A..G. 296.2). The pronoun is correlative to the previous relative clause **quod ... attulisset** (A.G. 297.d). Accusative direct object of the transitive verb **tribuerent** (A.G. 387).

virtuti: Dative indirect object of the transitive verb **tribuerent** (A.G. 362).

hostium: Possessive genitive with **virtuti** (A.G. 343).

eadem: Plural, neuter, accusative demonstrative pronoun used substantively meaning "The same things (A.G. 296.2). The pronoun is correlative to the relative clause **quae ... senserat** (A.G. 297.d). Accusative direct object of the participle **cogitans** (A.G. 387 and 488).

de profectione: Prepositional phrase, **de** with the ablative here means "about" (*OLD* **de** 12).

cogitans: Singular, masculine, nominative present participle used as a predicate, where in English a phrase or a subordinate clause would be more normal (A.G. 496). The pronoun **is**, with **Caesar** from 52.1 as the antecedent, is understood. Nominative subject of **eduxit ... constituit** (A.G. 339).

quae ... senserat: Relative clause (A.G. 303). For the reference see 43.5. **quae**: Plural, neuter, accusative relative pronoun used substantively (A.G. 305). The antecedent is **eadem** (A.G. 307). Accusative direct object of **senserat** (A.G. 387). **senserat**: The main verb of the subordinate clause (A.G. 278.b). The pronoun **is**, with **cogitans** (**Caesar**) as the antecedent, is understood as the subject (A.G. 271.a). The pluperfect denotes an action completed in past time (A.G. 477).

ante: Adverb (A.G. 320-21 and 433.1).

legiones: Accusative direct object of **eduxit** (A.G. 387).

ex castris: Ablative of *place from which* with the preposition **ex** (A.G. 426.1).

eduxit: The main verb of the coordinate clause **Hac ... eduxit** (A.G. 278.a).

aciemque: Accusative direct object of **constituit** (A.G. 387). **-que**: The enclitic conjunction connects the two main verbs **eduxit ... constituit** (A.G. 324.a).

idoneo loco: Ablative of *place where* without a preposition (A.G. 429.1-2). "Caesar wished to entice the Gauls into a general engagement, in which they would be at a great disadvantage. Vercingetorix, however, was wise enough to avoid a regular battle." (Kelsey, 418)

constituit: The main verb of the coordinate clause **aciemque ... constituit** (A.G. 278.a).

(53.2-3) **(2) Cum Vercingetorix nihilo minus in aequum locum descenderet, levi facto equestri proelio atque secundo in castra (3) exercitum reduxit.**

aequus, -a, -um, *level, even, flat.*
castra, -orum, n., pl., *camp, encampment.*
descendo, -scendere, -scendi, -scensus, *come down, descend.*
exercitus, -us, m., *army.*
in, *into.*
locus, -i, m., *place, position.*
proelium, -i, n., *battle, combat, engagement.*

secundus, -a, -um, *second, favorable.*

atque, *and then, and in fact.*
cum, *although.*
equester, -tris, -tre, *of cavalry, cavalry-.*
facio, facere, feci, factus, *make.*
levis, -e, *not vigorously contested, minor, light, slight.*
nihilo minus, *none the less.*
reduco, -ducere, -duxi, -ductus, *lead back, conduct back.*
Vercingetorix, -igis, m., *Vercingetorix.*

Cum ... reduxit: "some scholars are puzzled that Caesar did not engage with Vercingetorix (and even amend the text to state that the latter did *not* come down on to level ground, to explain this 'failure'). It is clear, however, that Caesar's intention was merely to restore his troops' morale and 'face', rather than attempt a final resolution at such an unpropitious moment." (Hammond, 240) The Budé text is amended and here reads **Cum Vercingetorix nihilo minus *intra munitiones remaneret neque* in aequum** ... .

Cum ... descenderet: Concessive clause; the relative adverb **cum** ("although") with the subjunctive forms a concessive clause (A.G. 549). **descenderet**: The main verb of the subordinate clause (A.G. 278.b). Imperfect subjunctive; the tense of the subjunctive is in secondary sequence and follows the rules for the sequence of tense after **reduxit** (A.G. 482-85).

Vercingetorix: Nominative subject (A.G. 339). See Appendix A.

nihilo minus: Adverb written as two words (A.G. 320-21) (*OLD* **nihilominus**).

in aequum locum: Accusative of *place to which* with the preposition **in** (A.G. 426.2).

levi facto equestri proelio atque secundo: Ablative absolute (A.G. 419-20). **levi**: The adjective here means "not vigorously contested, minor" (*OLD* **levis** 9.b). **facto**: The perfect tense of the participle represents the action as completed at the time indicated by the tense of the main verb (A.G. 489). **atque secundo**: This phrase may mean two things: 1) An ellipsis of **levi facto equestri proelio secundo** "and then" a second brief cavalry battle occurred (A.G. 640). **atque**: The conjunction here means "and then" (*OLD* **atque** 7). **secundo**: Declinable ordinal number used as an adjective meaning "second" (*OLD* **secundus1** 5); or 2) **secundo** is an adjective modifying **proelio** connected by **atque** and meaning "and in fact favorable". **atque**: The conjunction means "and in fact" (*OLD* **atque** 2). **secundo**: Attributive adjective meaning "favorable" (*OLD* **secundus1** 4).

in castra: Accusative of *place to which* with the preposition **in** (A.G. 426.2).

exercitum: Accusative direct object of **reduxit** (A.G. 387).

reduxit: The main verb of the main clause (A.G. 278.b). The pronoun **is**, with **cogitans (Caesar)** as the antecedent, is understood as the subject (A.G. 271.a).

(53.3-4) Cum hoc idem postero die fecisset, satis ad Gallicam ostentationem minuendam militumque animos confirmandos factum existimans in Aeduos movit (4) castra.

ad, *for, in order to, for the purpose of.*	**Aedui, -orum**, m., pl., *the Aedui.*
animus, -i, m., *courage, spirit, temper, resolution, mind.*	**castra, -orum**, n., pl., *camp, encampment.*
confirmo, -are, -avi, -atus, *reassure, encourage.*	**cum**, *after, when.*
dies, -ei, m. and f., *day.*	**existimo, -are, -avi, -atus**, *think, consider, judge.*
facio, facere, feci, factus, *make, do.*	**Gallicus, -a, -um**, *of Gaul, Gallic.*
hic, haec, hoc, *this; he, she, it.*	**idem, eadem, idem**, *the same.*
in, *into the country of.*	**miles, -itis**, m., *soldier, foot-solider.*
minuo, -uere, -ui, -utus, *lessen, diminish, reduce.*	**moveo, movere, movi, motus**, *move.*
ostentatio, -onis, f., *display, show.*	**posterus, -a, -um**, *following, the next.*
-que, *and.*	**satis**, n., indeclinable, *enough.*

Cum ... fecisset: Temporal clause; the relative adverb **cum** ("after, when") with the pluperfect subjunctive describes the circumstances that preceded the action of the main verb (A.G. 546). **fecisset**: The main verb of the subordinate clause (A.G. 278.b). The pronoun **is**, with **cogitans (Caesar)** as the antecedent, is understood as the subject (A.G. 271.a).

hoc idem: Accusative direct object of **fecisset** (A.G. 339). **hoc**: Singular, neuter, accusative demonstrative pronoun used substantively (A.G. 296.2). The antecedent is the idea contained in the sentence **cum ... reduxit** above (A.G. 297.e). **idem**: Singular, neuter, accusative demonstrative pronoun used as an adjective modifying **hoc** (A.G. 296.1 and a and 298).

postero die: Ablative of *time when* (A.G. 423.1). **die**: The noun **dies** is normally masculine gender (A.G. 97.a).

satis ... factum (esse): Accusative/infinitive construction in indirect discourse after **existimans** (A.G. 577 ff.). "These words hardly conceal the fact that the siege of Gergovia resulted in a serious reverse." (Kelsey, 418). **factum (esse)**: Supply **esse** to form the perfect, passive infinitive (A.G. 188). The tense of the infinitive in indirect discourse is relative to that of the verb of saying (A.G. 584).

ad Gallicam ostentationem minuendam: The preposition **ad** with an accusative noun and gerundive denotes purpose (A.G. 506). **minuendam**: Singular, feminine, accusative gerundive used as an adjective modifying **ostentationem** denoting necessity, obligation or propriety (A.G. 500.1).

(ad) militumque animos confirmandos: The preposition **ad** with an accusative noun and gerundive denotes purpose (A.G. 506). **militum**: Possessive genitive with **animos** (A.G. 343). **-que**: The enclitic conjunction connects the two gerundive phrases after **ad** (A.G. 324.a). **confirmandos**: Plural, masculine, accusative gerundive used as an adjective modifying **animos** denoting necessity, obligation or propriety (A.G. 500.1).

existimans: Singular, masculine, nominative present participle used as a predicate, where in English a phrase or a subordinate clause would be more normal (A.G. 496). The pronoun **is**, with **Caesar** from 52.1 as the antecedent, is understood. Nominative subject (A.G. 339).

in Aeduos: Accusative of *place to which* with the preposition **in** ("into the country of") (A.G. 426.2). **Aeduos**: See Appendix A.

movit: The main verb of the main clause (A.G. 278.b).

castra: Accusative direct object of **movit** (A.G. 387).

(53.4) Ne tum quidem insecutis hostibus, tertio die ad flumen Elaver pontis reficit eoque exercitum traducit.

ad, *at.*	**dies, -ei**, m. and f., *day.*
Elaver, Elaveris, n., *the Elaver river.*	**eo**, *thither, there.*
exercitus, -us, m., *army.*	**flumen, -inis**, n., *flowing water, current, stream, river.*
hostis, -is, m., *enemy, foe*; pl., *the enemy.*	**insequor, -sequi, -secutus**, *follow up, pursue, follow in pursuit.*

ne ... quidem, *not even*.
-que, *and*.
tertius, -a, um, *third*.

tum, *then*.

pons, pontis, m., *bridge*.
reficio, -ficere, -feci, -fectus, *repair, refit*.
traduco, -ducere, -duxi, -ductus, *lead across, bring over, bring across*.

Ne tum quidem insecutis hostibus: Ablative absolute (A.G. 419-20). Caesar seems genuinely shocked that Vercingetorix does not pursue him and this statement is critical of Vercingetorix. Caesar would never have allowed a demoralized enemy to escape so easily but would have dogged and crushed a retreating army. Vercingetorix had a large cavalry force at his command which he could have used with a devastating effect. Vercingetorix here allows Caesar the opportunity to depart and eventually reunite his army with Labienus' troops. **Ne ... quidem**: The negative adverb with the particle means "not even" (*OLD* **ne1** 6). The emphatic word must stand between **ne** and **quidem** (A.G. 322.f). **tum**: Adverb (A.G. 271.b and 320-21). **insecutis**: The perfect tense of the participle represents the action as completed at the time indicated by the tense of the main verb (A.G. 489).

tertio die: Ablative of *time when* (A.G. 423.1). **tertio**: Ordinal number used as an adjective (A.G. 132-35). **die**: The noun **dies** is normally masculine gender (A.G. 97.a).

ad flumen Elaver: Prepositional phrase, **ad** with the accusative here means "at" (*OLD* **ad** 13). **Elaver**: Accusative proper noun in apposition to **flumen** (A.G. 282). See Appendix A.

pontis: Accusative direct object of **reficit** (A.G. 387). Accusative plural noun, **-is** for **-es** is the regular form in mixed i-stem nouns (A.G. 71-2).

reficit: The main verb of the coordinate clause **Ne ... reficit** (A.G. 278.a). The historical present, giving vividness to the narrative, is present in Chapter 53 (A.G. 469). This usage, common in all languages, comes from imagining past events as going on before our eyes (*repraesentatio*) (A.G. 469 Note). The pronoun **is**, with **existimans (Caesar)** as the antecedent, is understood as the subject (A.G. 271.a).

eoque: Adverb (A.G. 217.a and 320-21). **-que**: The enclitic conjunction connects the two main verbs **reficit ... traducit** (A.G. 324.a). **exercitum**: Accusative direct object of **traducit** (A.G. 387).

traducit: The main verb of the coordinate clause **eoque ... traducit** (A.G. 278.a). The pronoun **is**, with **existimans (Caesar)** as the antecedent, is understood as the subject (A.G. 271.a).

4.B CHAPTER 54: CAESAR ALLOWS VIRIDOMARUS AND EPOREDORIX THE AEDUANS TO DEPART, DESPITE HIS MISTRUST OF THEM

Chapters 54-55: Kahn notes that Caesar "juxtaposes in Book 7 the actions of the Romans and the Gauls implicitly to expose the differences between the antagonists. Thus in ... 54-55 he counterposes examples of Roman clemency and beneficence with incidents of Aeduan brutality and faithlessness." (Kahn, 253)

(54.1-2) Ibi a Viridomaro atque Eporedorige Aeduis appellatus discit cum omni equitatu Litaviccum ad sollicitandos Aeduos profectum: opus esse ipsos antecedere ad confirmandam (2) civitatem.

a(b), *by*.
Aedui, -orum, m., pl., *the Aedui*.
antecedo, -cedere, -cessi, -----, *go in advance, precede*.
atque, *and*.
confirmo, -are, -avi, -atus, *confirm in loyalty*.
disco, discere, didici, -----, *learn*.
equitatus, -us, m., *cavalry*.
ipse, -a, -um, *he, they*, with or without *himself, themselves*.
omnis, -e, *all*.
proficiscor, -ficisci, -fectus, *set out, depart, proceed*.
sum, esse, fui, futurus, *be*.

ad, *for, in order to, for the purpose of*.
Aeduus, -i, m., *an Aeduan*.
appello, -are, -avi, -atus, *address*.
civitas, -tatis, f., *state, nation*.
cum, *with*.
Eporedorix, -igis, m., *Eporedorix*.
ibi, *in that place, there*.
Litaviccus, -i, m., *Litaviccus*.
opus, operis, n., *need, necessity, requisite*.
sollicito, -are, -avi, -atus, *incite, tamper with, tempt*.
Viridomarus, -i, m., *Viridomarus*.

Ibi: Adverb (A.G. 215.5 and 320-21). "On the east side of the Elaver (Allier), in the territory of the Aedui." (Kelsey, 418)

a Viridomaro ... Eporedorige Aeduis: Ablative of agent with the preposition **a(b)** after the passive participle **appellatus** (A.G. 405). **Viridomaro**: See Appendix A. **atque**: The conjunction connects the two ablative nouns and means "and" (*OLD* **atque** 12). **Eporedorix**: See Appendix A. **Aeduis**: A plural, ablative noun in apposition to the two singular proper nouns **Viridomaro** and **Eporedorige** (A.G. 282).

appellatus: Nominative, perfect, passive, participle used as a predicate, where in English a phrase or a subordinate clause would be more normal (A.G. 496). The pronoun **is**, with **Caesar** from 52.1 as the antecedent, is understood. Nominative subject (A.G. 339). **discit**: The main verb of the main clause (A.G. 278.b). The historical present, giving vividness to the narrative, is present in Chapter 54 (A.G. 469). This usage, common in all languages, comes from imagining past events as going on before our eyes (*repraesentatio*) (A.G. 469 Note).

cum omni equitatu: Ablative of accompaniment with the preposition **cum** (A.G. 413).

Litaviccum ... profectum (esse): Accusative/infinitive construction in indirect discourse after **discit** (A.G. 577 ff.). **Litaviccum**: See Appendix A. **profectum (esse)**: Supply **esse** to form the perfect, deponent infinitive (A.G. 190). The tense of the infinitive in indirect discourse is relative to that of the verb of saying (A.G. 584)

ad sollicitandos Aeduos: The preposition **ad** with the accusative gerundive and noun expresses purpose (A.G. 506). **sollicitandos**:

Plural, masculine, accusative gerundive used as an adjective modifying **Aeduos** denoting necessity, obligation or propriety (A.G. 500.1). **Aeduos:** See Appendix A.

opus ... civitatem: "Viridomarus and Eporedorix were going to turn traitors to Caesar, and wished for an excuse to get away from him." (Kelsey, 418)

opus esse: Impersonal accusative/infinitive construction in indirect discourse (A.G. 577 ff.). The verb of saying is not expressed, but implied in the general drift of the sentence (A.G. 580.a). **opus:** Singular, neuter, accusative predicate noun after **esse** (A.G. 283-83). The following infinitive phrase functions as the accusative subject (A.G. 208.c) (*OLD* **opus** 13). **esse:** Present infinitive; the tense of the infinitive in indirect discourse is relative to that of the verb of saying (A.G. 584). The phrase **opus esse** is an idiom that means "it is needed or requisite" (*OLD* **opus** 13).

ipsos antecedere ad confirmandam civitatem: The infinitive phrase functions as the subject of the impersonal verb **opus esse** (A.G. 454). **ipsos:** Plural, masculine, accusative demonstrative pronoun used substantively (A.G. 296.2 and 298.d). The antecedent is **Viridomaro ... Eporedorige** (A.G. 298). Accusative subject of the infinitive (A.G. 397.e and 455.2). The pronoun is here emphatic (A.G. 298.d.1).

ad confirmandam civitatem: The preposition **ad** with the accusative gerundive and noun expresses purpose (A.G. 506).

confirmandam: Singular, feminine, accusative gerundive used as an adjective modifying **civitatem** denoting necessity, obligation or propriety (A.G. 500.1).

(54.2-3) Etsi multis iam rebus perfidiam Aeduorum perspectam habebat atque horum discessu admaturari defectionem civitatis existimabat, tamen eos retinendos non constituit, ne aut inferre iniuriam videretur aut dare timoris (3) aliquam suspicionem.

admaturo, -are, -----, -----, *hasten.*
aliqui, aliqua, aliquod, *some, any.*
aut ... aut, *either ... or.*
constituo, -stituere, -stitui, -stitutus, *establish, resolve upon, determine.*
discessus, -us, m., *departure, going away.*
etsi, *although, though.*
habeo, habere, habui, habitus, *have, hold, regard, think.*
iam, *already, previous.*
iniuria, -ae, f., *wrong, outrage, injustice, injury.*
multus, -a, -um, *many.*
non, *not.*
perspicio, -spicere, -spexi, -spectus, *perceive, observe, ascertain.*
retineo, -tinere, -tinui, -tentus, *detain, keep back, hold.*
tamen, *yet, still, for all that, nevertheless, however.*

Aedui, -orum, m., pl., *the Aedui.*
atque, *and.*
civitas, -tatis, f., *state, nation.*
defectio, -onis, f., *revolt, rebellion.*
do, dare, dedi, datus, *give, allow.*
existimo, -are, -avi, -atus, *think, consider, judge.*
hic, haec, hoc, *this; he, she, it.*
infero, -ferre, intuli, illatus, *inflict.*
is, ea, id, *he, she, it; that, this.*
ne, *so that ... not.*
perfidia, -ae, f., *faithlessness, bad faith, treachery.*
res, rei, f., *matter, event, affair.*
suspicio, -onis, f., *suspicion, suggestion.*
timor, -oris, m., *fear, dread, apprehension, alarm, timidity.*

videor, videri, visus sum, *seem, appear.*

Etsi ... tamen: The conjunction and adverb form correlative clauses meaning "although ... nevertheless" (*OLD* **etsi2** and **tamen** 3).

Etsi ... habebat ... existimabat: Concessive clause; the conjunction **etsi** ("although") takes the indicative (A.G. 527.c). **habebat ... existimabat:** The main verbs of the subordinate clause (A.G. 278.b). The pronoun **is**, with **appellatus** (**Caesar**) as the antecedent, is understood as the subject (A.G. 271.a).

multis ... rebus: Ablative of source without a preposition (A.G. 403.1).

iam: Adverb (A.G. 215.6, 217.b and 320-21).

perfidiam ... perspectam: Accusative direct object of **habebat** (A.G. 387). **perspectam:** Singular, feminine, accusative perfect passive participle used as a predicate, where in English a phrase or a subordinate clause would be more normal (A.G. 496). The perfect participle with **habeo** has almost the same meaning as a perfect active, but denotes the continued effect of the action of the verb (A.G. 497.b). "**perspectam habebat:** translate as if *perspexerat*." (Kelsey, 418)

Aeduorum: Possessive genitive with **perfidiam** (A.G. 343). See Appendix A.

atque: The conjunction connects the two main verbs in the concessive clause (A.G. 324.a).

horum: Plural, masculine, genitive demonstrative pronoun used substantively (A.G. 296.2). The antecedent is **Viridomaro ... Eporedorige** (A.G. 297.e). Possessive genitive with **discessu** (A.G. 343).

discessu: Ablative of *time when* (A.G. 423.1).

admaturari defectionem civitatis: Stevens claims that this "is sheer nonsense. The *defectio* had already happened; according to Caesar himself, while the siege of Gergovia was going on, the chief magistrate of the Aedui, the Vergobret, was leading the massacre of Roman citizens." (Stevens, 17)

admaturari defectionem: Accusative/infinitive construction in indirect discourse after **existimabat** (A.G. 577 ff.). **admaturari:** Present infinitive; the tense of the infinitive in indirect discourse is relative to that of the verb of saying (A.G. 584).

civitatis: Possessive genitive with **defectionem** (A.G. 343).

tamen: Adverb, normally postpositive but not here (A.G. 320-21 and 324.j).

eos retinendos (esse): A subject accusative with the infinitive after **constituit** (A.G. 563.d). The construction is equivalent to a substantive clause of purpose (A.G. 563.d). **eos:** Plural, masculine, accusative demonstrative pronoun used substantively (A.G. 296.2). The antecedent is **Viridomaro ... Eporedorige** (A.G. 297.e). **retinendos (esse):** Supply **esse** to form the second periphrastic (passive) present infinitive with the gerundive implying necessity (A.G. 194.b and 196).

non: Adverb, the adverb generally precedes the verb if it belongs to no one word in particular (A.G. 217.e, 320-21, and 599.a).

constituit: The main verb of the main clause (A.G. 278.b). The pronoun **is**, with **appellatus** (**Caesar**) as the antecedent, is understood as the subject (A.G. 271.a).

ne ... videretur: The conjunction **ne** ("so that ... not") with the subjunctive forms a negative purpose clause (A.G. 531.1). **videretur**: The main verb of the subordinate clause (A.G. 278.b). Imperfect subjunctive; the tense of the subjunctive is in secondary sequence and follows the rules for the sequence of tense after **constituit** (A.G. 482-85). The pronoun **is**, with **appellatus** (**Caesar**) as the antecedent, is understood as the subject (A.G. 271.a).

aut ... aut: The double connective introduces two logically exclusive alternatives and means "either ... or" (*OLD* **aut** 1).

inferre: Complementary infinitive after **videretur** (A.G. 456).

iniuriam: Accusative direct object of the infinitive **inferre** (A.G. 387 and 451.3).

dare: Complementary infinitive after **videretur** (A.G. 456).

timoris: Objective genitive with **suspicionem** (A.G. 348).

aliquam suspicionem: Accusative direct object of the infinitive **dare** (A.G. 387 and 451.3).

(54.3-4) **Discedentibus his breviter sua in Aeduos merita exposuit: quos et quam humilis accepisset, compulsos in oppida, multatos agris, omnibus ereptis sociis, imposito stipendio, obsidibus summa cum contumelia (4) extortis, et quam in fortunam quamque in amplitudinem deduxisset, ut non solum in pristinum statum redissent sed omnium temporum dignitatem et gratiam antecessisse viderentur.**

accipio, -cipere, -cepi, -ceptus, *receive, take under protection.*

ager, -ri, m., *land* (under cultivation), *field, lands, territory.*

antecedo, -cedere, -cessi, -----, *surpass, excel.*

compello, -pellere, -puli, -pulsus, *drive, force.*

cum, *with.*

dignitas, -tatis, f., *greatness, rank, reputation.*

eripio, -ripere, -ripui, -reptus, *take away, snatch away.*

expono, -ponere, -posui, -positus, *set forth, state, explain.*

fortuna, -ae, f., *lot, fate, chance, fortune.*

hic, haec, hoc, *this; he, she, it.*

impono, -ponere, -posui, -positus, *put on, put, impose.*

meritum, -i, n., *desert, merit, service.*

non, *not.*

omnis, -e, *all.*

pristinus, -a, -um, *former, previous, earlier.*

-que, *and.*

redeo, -ire, -ii, -itus, *go back, return.*

socii, -orum, m., pl., *allies.*

status, -us, m., *position, situation, condition.*

summus, -a, -um, *utmost, greatest, very great.*

tempus, -oris, n., *time.*

videor, videri, visus sum, *seem, appear.*

Aedui, -orum, m., pl., *the Aedui.*

amplitudo, -onis, f., *greatness, dignity.*

breviter, *briefly, with few words, concisely.*

contumelia, -ae, f., *insult, abuse, indignity, violence.*

deduco, -ducere, -duxi, -ductus, *lead, conduct, bring.*

discedo, -cedere, -cessi, -cessurus, *go away, depart, leave.*

et, *and.*

extorqueo, -torquere, -torsi, -tortus, *force from, take from.*

gratia, -ae, f., *influence.*

humilis, -e, *mean, poor, humble, insignificant.*

in, *towards; into.*

multo, -are, -avi, -atus, *deprive of.*

obses, -idis, m. and f., *hostage.*

oppidum, -i, n., *fortified town, city.*

quam, *how.*

quis, -----, quid, *who? what?; who? what? (as adj., **qui, quae, quod**).*

sed, *but.*

solum, *only.*

stipendium, -i, n., *tribute.*

suus, -a, -um, *his, with or without own.*

ut, *so that.*

Discedentibus his: Dative indirect object of the transitive verb **exposuit** (A.G. 362). **Discedentibus**: Present participle used as an adjective modifying **his** (A.G. 494). **his**: Plural, masculine, dative demonstrative pronoun used substantively (A.G. 296.2). The antecedent is **Viridomaro ... Eporedorige** (A.G. 297.e).

breviter: Adverb (A.G. 214.b and 320-21).

sua ... merita: Accusative direct object of the transitive verb **exposuit** (A.G. 387). **sua**: Plural, neuter, accusative reflexive pronoun used as an adjective modifying **merita** (A.G. 302).

in Aeduos: Prepositional phrase, **in** with the accusative here means "towards", indicating the person towards whom feelings are directed (*OLD* **in** 11). **Aeduos**: See Appendix A.

exposuit: The main verb of the main clause (A.G. 278.b). The pronoun **is**, with **appellatus** (**Caesar**) as the antecedent, is understood as the subject (A.G. 271.a).

quos ... viderentur: Murphy classifies this speech in indirect discourse as deliberative (C. Murphy, 122). Kahn notes that here Caesar defends his imperialist ambitions in Gaul (contra Critognatus in 77); "he reminds them how Gaul had been wracked with internecine strife before the Roman conquerors had brought prosperity and tranquility." (Kahn, 253).

quos ... extortis: The first indirect question with modifying clauses.

quos et quam humilis accepisset: A double indirect question with the subjunctive; the phrase is in apposition to **Aeduos** (A.G. 573-75). **quos**: Plural, masculine, accusative interrogative pronoun used substantively (A.G. 148). The pronoun is in apposition to **Aeduos** (A.G. 282). Accusative direct object of **accepisset** (A.G. 387). **et**: The conjunction connects the two interrogatives introducing the indirect questions (A.G. 324.a). **quam humilis**: For the reference see 1.31 and 6.12. **quam**: The interrogative adverb modifies **humilis** and represents an original exclamation meaning "how!" (*OLD* **quam** 1.b-2). **humilis**: Plural, masculine, accusative adjective used as an attributive adjective modifying **quos** (A.G. 283.1). Accusative plural adjective; **-is** for **-es** is the regular form in i-stem adjectives (A.G. 114.a and 116). **accepisset**: The main verb of the subordinate clause (A.G. 278.b). Pluperfect subjunctive; the tense of the subjunctive is in secondary sequence and follows the rules for the sequence of tense for indirect questions after **exposuit** (A.G. 575). The pronoun **is**, with **appellatus (Caesar)** as the antecedent, is understood as the subject (A.G. 271.a).

compulsos ... multatos ... omnibus ... imposito ... obsidibus: Notice how the asyndeton construction between the clauses reinforces the idea of the piling up of the Aedui's woes (A.G. 323.b).

compulsos: Accusative, perfect, passive, participle used as a predicate modifying **quos**, where in English a phrase or a subordinate clause would be more normal (A.G. 496).

in oppida: Accusative of *place to which* with the preposition **in** (A.G. 426.2).

multatos: Accusative, perfect, passive, participle used as a predicate modifying **quos**, where in English a phrase or a subordinate clause would be more normal (A.G. 496).

agris: Ablative of separation after **multatos** (A.G. 401).

omnibus ereptis sociis: Ablative absolute (A.G. 419-20). **ereptis**: The perfect tense of the participle represents the action as completed at the time indicated by the tense of the main verb (A.G. 489).

imposito stipendio: Ablative absolute (A.G. 419-20). **imposito**: The perfect tense of the participle represents the action as completed at the time indicated by the tense of the main verb (A.G. 489).

obsidibus summa cum contumelia extortis: Ablative absolute (A.G. 419-20). **summa cum contumelia**: Ablative of manner with the preposition **cum** (A.G. 412). **summa**: Defective superlative adjective (A.G. 130.b). **cum**: A monosyllabic preposition is often placed between a noun and its adjective (A.G. 599.d.2). **extortis**: The perfect tense of the participle represents the action as completed at the time indicated by the tense of the main verb (A.G. 489).

et: The conjunction connects the two indirect questions (A.G. 324.a).

quam in fortunam quamque in amplitudinem deduxisset: A double indirect question with the subjunctive; the phrase is in apposition to **Aeduos** (A.G. 573-75). **quam in fortunam**: Prepositional phrase, **in** with the accusative here means "into" (a state or condition) (*OLD* **in** 2). **quam**: Singular, feminine, accusative interrogative pronoun used as an adjective modifying **fortunam** (A.G. 148.b). **in**: A monosyllabic preposition is often placed between a noun and its adjective (A.G. 599.d.2). **quamque in amplitudinem**: Prepositional phrase, **in** with the accusative here means "into" (a state or condition) (*OLD* **in** 2). **quam**: Singular, feminine, accusative interrogative pronoun used as an adjective modifying **amplitudinem** (A.G. 148.b). **-que**: The enclitic conjunction connects the two interrogatives introducing the indirect question (A.G. 324.a). **in**: A monosyllabic preposition is often placed between a noun and its adjective (A.G. 599.d.2). **deduxisset**: The main verb of the subordinate clause (A.G. 278.b). Pluperfect subjunctive; the tense of the subjunctive is in secondary sequence and follows the rules for the sequence of tense for indirect questions after **exposuit** (A.G. 575). The pronoun **is**, with **appellatus (Caesar)** as the antecedent, is understood as the subject (A.G. 271.a). Supply **eos**, with **Aeduos** as the antecedent, as the accusative direct object.

ut ... redissent ... viderentur: The conjunction **ut** ("so that") with the subjunctive forms a clause of result (A.G. 537.1). **redissent ... viderentur**: The main verb of the subordinate clause (A.G. 278.b). Pluperfect and imperfect subjunctives; the tense of the subjunctives is in secondary sequence and follows the rules for the sequence of tense after **exposuit** (A.G. 482-85). Notice the switch in the tenses of the subjunctive. The pronoun **ei**, with **Aeduos** as the antecedent, is understood as the subject of both verbs (A.G. 271.a).

non solum ... sed: The correlatives mean "not only ... but also" (*OLD* **solum2** 2). **non**: Adverb (A.G. 217.e, 320-21, and 599.a). **solum**: Adverb (A.G. 320-21). **sed**: Coordinate conjunction (A.G. 324.d).

in pristinum statum: Prepositional phrase, **in** with the accusative here means "into" (a state or condition) (*OLD* **in** 2).

omnium temporum: Genitive of quality (measure) with both **dignitatem ... gratiam** (A.G. 345.b and 417).

dignitatem et gratiam: Two accusative direct objects of the infinitive **antecessisse** (A.G. 387 and 451.3). **et**: The conjunction connects the two accusative nouns (A.G. 324.a).

antecessisse: Complementary infinitive after **viderentur** (A.G. 456).

(54.4) **His datis mandatis eos ab se dimisit.**

ab, *from.*	**dimitto, -mittere, -misi, -missus**, *dismiss, send off.*
do, dare, dedi, datus, *give, give over.*	**hic, haec, hoc**, *this; he, she, it.*
is, ea, id, *he, she, it; that, this.*	**mandatum, -i**, n., *order, command, instruction.*
sui, sibi, se, or **sese**, nom. wanting, *himself.*	

His datis mandatis: Ablative absolute (A.G. 419-20). **His**: Plural, neuter, ablative demonstrative pronoun used as an adjective modifying **mandatis** (A.G. 296.1 and a). **datis**: The perfect tense of the participle represents the action as completed at the time indicated by the tense of the main verb (A.G. 489). **mandatis**: "Points which Caesar gave Viridomarus and Eporedorix to understand they were to use with their fellow-countrymen." (Kelsey, 419)

eos: Plural, masculine, accusative demonstrative pronoun used substantively (A.G. 296.2). The antecedent is **Viridomaro ... Eporedorige** (A.G. 297.e). Accusative direct object of **dimisit** (A.G. 387). Presumably they took the 10,000 Aeduan soldiers with them as Caesar does not mention them again in his service and describes one of them, the captured Cavarillus at 67.7, as **qui post defectionem Litavicci pedestribus copiis praefuerat**.

ab se: Ablative of separation with the preposition **ab** after the compound verb **dimisit** (A.G. 402). **se**: Singular, masculine, ablative direct reflexive pronoun (A.G. 300.1). The antecedent is **is (Caesar)**, the supplied subject of **dimisit** (A.G. 299).

dimisit: The main verb of the main clause (A.G. 278.b). The pronoun **is**, with **appellatus (Caesar)** as the antecedent, is understood as the subject (A.G. 271.a).

226

4.C CHAPTER 55: THE SECOND REVOLT OF THE AEDUI; THE SACK OF NOVIODUNUM
(55.1-2) **Noviodunum erat oppidum Aeduorum ad ripas Ligeris (2) opportuno loco positum.**

ad, *at*.
Liger, -eris, m., *the Loire River*.
Noviodunum, -i, n., *Noviodunum*.
opportunus, -a, -um, *favorable, opportune*.
ripa, -ae, f., *bank of a stream*.

Aedui, -orum, m., pl., *the Aedui*.
locus, -i, m., *place, position*.
oppidum, -i, n., *fortified town, city*.
pono, ponere, posui, positus, pass., often *be situated*.
sum, esse, fui, futurus, *be*.

Noviodunum: Nominative subject (A.G. 339). Notice that there are two cities by this name. This one (of the Aedui) is mentioned only in this chapter. The other (of the Bituriges) is mentioned at 7.12 and 7.14. "This town Caesar had made his permanent base of supplies." (Kelsey, 419) See Appendix A.
erat: The main verb of the simple sentence (A.G. 278.1).
oppidum: Predicate nominative after **erat** (A.G. 283-84).
Aeduorum: Possessive genitive with **oppidum** (A.G. 343). See Appendix A.
ad ripas Ligeris: Prepositional phrase, **ad** with the accusative here means "at" (*OLD* **ad** 13). **Ligeris**: Partitive genitive with **ripas** (A.G. 346.a). See Appendix A.
opportuno loco: Ablative of *place where* without a preposition (A.G. 429.1-2).
positum: Nominative perfect, passive, participle used as an adjective modifying **oppidum** (A.G. 494.a).

(55.2-3) **Huc Caesar omnis obsides Galliae, frumentum, pecuniam publicam, suorum atque (3) exercitus impedimentorum magnam partem contulerat;**

atque, *and*.
confero, -ferre, -tuli, collatus, *bring together, gather, collect, convey*.
frumentum, -i, n., *grain*.
huc, *hither, here, to this place*.
magnus, -a, -um, *great, large*.
omnis, -e, *all*.
pecunia, -ae, f., *money, property*.
suus, -a, -um, *his*, with or without *own*.

Caesar, -aris, m., *Caesar*.
exercitus, -us, m., *army*.
Gallia, -ae, f., *Gaul*.
impedimenta, -orum, n., pl., *heavy baggage, baggage*.
obses, -idis, m. and f., *hostage*.
pars, partis, f., *part, portion*.
publicus, -a, -um, *of the state, public*.

Huc ... (huc): The repetition of words at the beginning of successive clauses is anaphora (A.G. 641).
Huc: Adverb (A.G. 217.a and 320-21).
Caesar: Nominative subject (A.G. 339). See Appendix A.
omnis obsides ... frumentum, pecuniam publicam, ... magnam partem: Four accusative direct objects of **contulerat** (A.G. 387). Notice the asyndeton construction (A.G. 323.b). **omnis**: Accusative plural adjective modifying **obsides**; **-is** for **-es** is the regular form in i-stem adjectives (A.G. 114.a and 116). **pecuniam publicam**: "The military chest." (Kelsey, 419)
Galliae: Partitive genitive with **obsides** (A.G. 346.a). See Appendix A.
suorum: Plural, masculine genitive possessive pronoun used as an adjective modifying **impedimentorum** (A.G. 302.).
atque: The conjunction connects the two genitive modifiers of **impedimentorum** and means "and" (*OLD* **atque** 12).
exercitus: Possessive genitive with **impedimentorum** (A.G. 343).
impedimentorum: Partitive genitive with **partem** (A.G. 346.a.1).
contulerat: The main verb of the simple sentence (A.G. 278.1). Although the pluperfect tense is normally used in subordinate clauses, its use as a main verb is frequent. The pluperfect denotes an action completed in past time (A.G. 477).

(55.3-4) **huc magnum numerum equorum huius belli causa in Italia (4) atque Hispania coemptum miserat.**

atque, *and*.
causa, -ae, f., abl. with the gen., *for the sake of, for the purpose of*.
equus, -i, m., *horse*.
Hispania, -ae, f., *Spain*.
in, *in*.
magnus, -a, -um, *great, large*.
numerus, -i, m., *number*.

bellum, -i, n., *war, warfare*.
coemo, -emere, -emi, -emptus, *buy up, purchase*.
hic, haec, hoc, *this*; *he, she, it*.
huc, *hither, here, to this place*.
Italia, -ae, f., *Italy*.
mitto, mittere, misi, missus, *send*.

huc: Adverb (A.G. 217.a and 320-21).
magnum numerum ... coemptum: Accusative direct object of **miserat** (A.G. 387). **coemptum**: Accusative perfect, passive, participle used as a predicate modifying **numerum**, where in English a phrase or a subordinate clause would be more normal (A.G. 496).
equorum: Partitive genitive with **numerum** (A.G. 346.a.1).
huius belli causa: A preceding genitive with the ablative of **causa** means "for the sake of" A (A.G. 359.b and 404.c). **huius**: Singular, neuter, genitive demonstrative pronoun used as an adjective modifying **belli** (A.G. 296.1 and a).

in Italia atque Hispania: Ablative of *place where* with the preposition in (locative ablative) (A.G. 426.3). Italia: See Appendix A.
atque: The conjunction connects the two ablative nouns in the prepositional phrase and means "and" (*OLD* atque 12). Hispania: See Appendix A.
miserat: The main verb of the simple sentence (A.G. 278.1). The pronoun is, with Caesar as the antecedent, is understood as the subject (A.G. 271.a). Although the pluperfect tense is normally used in subordinate clauses, its use as a main verb is frequent. The pluperfect denotes an action completed in past time (A.G. 477).

(55.4-5) Eo cum Eporedorix Viridomarusque venissent et de statu civitatis cognovissent, Litaviccum Bibracte ab Aeduis receptum, quod est oppidum apud eos maximae auctoritatis, Convictolitavem magistratum magnamque partem senatus ad eum convenisse, legatos ad Vercingetorigem de pace et amicitia concilianda publice missos, non praetermittendum tantum commodum existima(5)verunt.

ab, *by.*
Aedui, -orum, m., pl., *the Aedui*
apud, *in the opinion* or *estimation of, in the eyes of, with.*
Bibracte, -is, n. *Bibracte.*
cognosco, -gnoscere, -gnovi, cognitus, *learn, ascertain, recognize.*

concilio, -are, -avi, -atus, *bring about, procure, acquire, gain, win.*

Convictolitavis, -is, m., *Convictolitavis.*
de, *about; about, concerning.*
Eporedorix, -igis, m., *Eporedorix.*
existimo, -are, -avi, -atus, *think, consider, judge.*
legatus, -i, m., *envoy, ambassador.*
magistratus, -us, m., *one holding a magistracy, magistrate.*
maximus, -a, -um, *greatest, very great.*
non, *not.*
pars, partis, f., *part, portion.*
praetermitto, -mittere, -misi, -missus, *pass over, let slip, allow to go by.*
-que, *and.*
recipio, -cipere, -cepi, -ceptus, *take back, receive, admit.*
status, -us, m., *attitude, situation, condition, state.*
tantus, -a, -um, *so great, so large, such.*
Vercingetorix, -igis, m., *Vercingetorix.*

ad, *to.*
amicitia, -ae, f., *friendship, alliance.*
auctoritas, -tatis, f., *prestige, authority, power.*
civitas, -tatis, f., *state, nation.*
commodum, -i, n., *convenient opportunity, favorable condition.*
convenio, -venire, -veni, -ventus, *come together, gather.*
cum, *after, when.*
eo, *thither, there.*
et, *and.*
is, ea, id, *he, she, it; that, this.*
Litaviccus, -i, m., *Litaviccus.*
magnus, -a, -um, *great, large.*
mitto, mittere, misi, missus, *send.*
oppidum, -i, n., *fortified town, city.*
pax, pacis, f., *peace.*
publice, *in the name of the state, as a state, publicly.*
qui, quae, quod, *who, which, what.*
senatus, -us, m., *council of elders, senate.*
sum, esse, fui, futurus, *be.*
venio, venire, veni, ventus, *come.*
Viridomarus, -i, m., *Viridomarus.*

Eo: Adverb (A.G. 217.a and 320-21). The adverb eo normally stands outside the cum clause, as at 6.2, 7.5, 9.5, 33.3 and 61.1.
cum ... venissent ... cognovissent ... missos: Temporal clause; the relative adverb cum ("after, when") with the pluperfect subjunctive describes the circumstances that preceded the action of the main verb (A.G. 546). Caesar here characterizes Eporedorix and Viridomarus as loyal to himself but overcome by the circumstances which they find back home. venissent ... cognovissent: The main verbs of the subordinate clause (A.G. 278.b). missos: See below.
Eporedorix Viridomarusque: Two nominative subjects (A.G. 339). Eporedorix: See Appendix A. Viridomarus: See Appendix A. -que: The enclitic conjunction connects the two nominative nouns (A.G. 324.a).
et: The conjunction connects the two main verbs in the temporal clause (A.G. 324.a).
de statu civitatis: Prepositional phrase, de with the ablative here means "about" (*OLD* de 12). civitatis: Possessive genitive (A.G. 343).
Litaviccum ... receptum ... Convictolitavem ... convenisse ...legatos ... missos: Notice the asyndeton between the three accusative/infinitive constructions after cognovissent (A.G. 323.b).
Litaviccum ... receptum (esse): Accusative/infinitive construction in indirect discourse after cognovissent (A.G. 577 ff.).
Litaviccum: See Appendix A. receptum (esse): Supply esse to form the perfect, passive infinitive (A.G. 188). The tense of the infinitive in indirect discourse is relative to that of the verb of saying (A.G. 584).
Bibracte: Locative case of the city name Bibracte, -is, n. (A.G. 80). See Appendix A.
ab Aeduis: Ablative of agent with the preposition ab after the passive infinitive receptum (esse) (A.G. 405). Aeduis: See Appendix A.
quod ... auctoritatis: Relative clause; a dependent clause in indirect discourse normally takes the subjunctive unless it is merely explanatory or contains statements which are regarded as true independently of the quotation in which case it takes the indicative (A.G. 303, 580 and 583). quod: Singular, neuter, nominative relative pronoun used substantively (A.G. 305). The antecedent is Bibracte (A.G. 307). Nominative subject (A.G. 339). auctoritatis: See below.
est: The main verb of the subordinate clause (A.G. 278.b). The present tense is not the historical present but denotes a state as now existing in present time (A.G. 465.2).
oppidum: Singular, neuter, nominative predicate noun after est (A.G. 283-84).
apud eos: Prepositional phrase, apud with the accusative here means "in the opinion or estimation of, in the eyes of, with" (*OLD* apud 12). eos: Plural, masculine, accusative demonstrative pronoun used substantively (A.G. 296.2). The antecedent is Aeduis (A.G. 297.e).

maximae auctoritatis: Genitive of quality with **oppidum** (A.G. 345). **maximae**: Irregular superlative adjective (A.G. 129).

Convictolitavem ... magnamque partem ... convenisse: Accusative/infinitive construction in indirect discourse after **cognovissent** (A.G. 577 ff.). **Convictolitavem**: See Appendix A. **-que**: The enclitic conjunction connects the two accusative subjects (A.G. 324.a). **convenisse**: Perfect infinitive; the tense of the infinitive in indirect discourse is relative to that of the verb of saying (A.G. 584).

magistratum: An accusative noun in apposition to the proper noun **Convictolitavem** (A.G. 282).

senatus: Partitive genitive with **partem** (A.G. 346.a.1).

ad eum: Prepositional phrase, **ad** with the accusative here means "to" (*OLD* **ad** 1). **eum**: Singular, masculine, accusative demonstrative pronoun used substantively (A.G. 296.2). The antecedent is **Litaviccum** (A.G. 297.e).

legatos ... missos (esse): Accusative/infinitive construction in indirect discourse after **cognovissent** (A.G. 577 ff.). **missos (esse)**: Supply **esse** to form the perfect, passive infinitive (A.G. 186). The tense of the infinitive in indirect discourse is relative to that of the verb of saying (A.G. 584).

ad Vercingetorigem: Prepositional phrase, **ad** with the accusative here means "to" (*OLD* **ad** 1). **Vercingetorigem**: See Appendix A.

de pace et amicitia concilianda: Prepositional phrase, **de** with the ablative here means "about, concerning" (*OLD* **de** 12). **et**: The conjunction connects the two ablative nouns in the prepositional phrase (A.G. 324.a). **concilianda**: Singular, feminine, ablative gerundive modifying **amicitia** after the preposition **de** (A.G. 500 and 507.3). The adjective should be construed with both ablative nouns but agrees in number with only the nearest noun (A.G. 286.a).

publice: Adverb (A.G. 214.a and 320-21).

non: Adverb modifying **praetermittendum**, the negative precedes the word it especially effects (A.G. 217.e, 320-21, and 599.a).

praetermittendum (esse) tantum commodum: Accusative/infinitive construction in indirect discourse after **existimaverunt** (A.G. 577 ff.). **praetermittendum (esse)**: Supply **esse** to form the second periphrastic (passive) present infinitive with the gerundive implying necessity (A.G. 194.b and 196). The tense of the infinitive in indirect discourse is relative to that of the verb of saying (A.G. 584).

existimaverunt: The main verb of the main clause (A.G. 278.b). The pronoun **ei**, with **Eporedorix Viridomarus** as the antecedent, is understood as the subject (A.G. 271.a).

(55.5-6) **Itaque interfectis Novioduni custodibus quique eo negotiandi causa convenerant, pecuniam atque equos (6) inter se partiti sunt;**

atque, *and.*

convenio, -venire, -veni, -ventus, *come together, gather.*
eo, *thither, there.*
inter, *among.*
itaque, *and so, in consequence, accordingly, therefore.*
Noviodunum, -i, n., *Noviodunum.*
pecunia, -ae, f., *money, property.*
qui, quae, quod, *who, which, what.*

causa, -ae, f., abl. with the gen., *for the sake of, for the purpose of.*
custos, -todis, m., *guard, keeper, watch.*
equus, -i, m., *horse.*
interficio, -ficere, -feci, -fectus, *slay, kill.*
negotior, -ari, -atus, *transact business.*
partior, partiri, partitus, *divide, divide up.*
-que, *and.*
sui, sibi, se, or **sese**, nom. wanting, *themselves.*

Itaque: An adverb expressing the result of the previous ideas meaning "and so, in consequence" (*OLD* **itaque** 1). The adverb stands in the first position (A.G. 599.b).

interfectis ... convenerant: Ablative absolute with a dependent clause.

interfectis Novioduni custodibus: Ablative absolute (A.G. 419-20). **interfectis**: The perfect tense of the participle represents the action as completed at the time indicated by the tense of the main verb (A.G. 489). **Novioduni**: Locative case of the city name **Noviodunum, -i**, n. (A.G. 49.a). See Appendix A.

quique ... convenerant: Relative clause (A.G. 303). **quique**: Plural, masculine, nominative relative pronoun used substantively (A. G. 305). The antecedent is omitted, supply **eis** (with **interfectis** to form a second ablative absolute) (A.G. 307.c). **-que**: The enclitic conjunction connects the ablative absolute and the relative clause (A.G. 324.a). **convenerant**: The main verb of the subordinate clause (A.G. 278.b). The pluperfect denotes an action completed in past time (A.G. 477).

eo: Adverb (A.G. 217.a and 320-21).

negotiandi causa: The genitive gerund with the ablative of **causa** expresses purpose (A.G. 504.b). "The Romans in Gallic cities were chiefly engaged in loaning money, in buying grain and other commodities, and in farming revenues." (Kelsey, 401) **negotiandi**: Singular, neuter, genitive gerund (A.G. 501-02).

pecuniam atque equos: Two accusative direct objects of **partiti sunt** (A.G. 387). **atque**: The conjunction connects the two accusative nouns and means "and" (*OLD* **atque** 12).

inter se: Prepositional phrase, **inter** with the accusative reflexive pronoun here means "among themselves" (*OLD* **inter1** 14). **se**: Plural, masculine, accusative direct reflexive pronoun (A.G. 300.1). The antecedent is **ei** (**Eporedorix Viridomarus**), the supplied subject of **partiti sunt** (A.G. 299).

partiti sunt: The main verb of the main clause (A.G. 278.b). The pronoun **ei**, with **Eporedorix Viridomarus** as the antecedent, is understood as the subject (A.G. 271.a).

(55.6-7) **obsides civitatum Bibracte ad magi(7)stratum deducendos curaverunt;**

ad, *to.*
civitas, -tatis, f., *state, nation.*

Bibracte, -is, n. *Bibracte.*
curo, -are, -avi, -atus, *take care, provide for,*

deduco, -ducere, -duxi, -ductus, *lead, conduct, bring.*

obses, -idis, m. and f., *hostage.*

superintend, arrange.

magistratus, -us, m., *one holding a magistracy, magistrate.*

obsides ... deducendos: Accusative direct object of **curaverunt** (A.G. 387). **deducendos:** Plural, masculine, accusative gerundive used as an adjective modifying **obsides**, the direct object of **curaverunt** (A.G. 500.1). A gerundive in agreement with the object of **curaverunt** expresses purpose (A.G. 500.4).

obsides civitatum: "Held by Caesar as pledges of loyalty. The capture of these by the Aedui had much to do with hastening the spread of the rebellion." (Kelsey, 419)

civitatum: Partitive genitive with **obsides** (A.G. 346.a).

Bibracte: Locative case of the city name **Bibracte, -is,** n. (A.G. 80). This is where Litaviccus, Convictolitavis, and part of the senate had gone at 55.4. See Appendix A.

ad magistratum: Prepositional phrase, **ad** with the accusative here means "to" (*OLD* **ad** 1). This is Convictolitavis.

curaverunt: The main verb of the simple sentence (A.G. 278.1). The pronoun **ei,** with **Eporedorix Viridomarus** as the antecedent, is understood as the subject (A.G. 271.a).

(55.7-8) oppidum, quod a se teneri non posse iudicabant, ne cui esset usui Romanis, incende(8)runt;

a(b), *by.*
iudico, -are, -avi, -atus, *judge, decide, think.*
non, *not.*
possum, posse, potui, -----, *be able.*
quis, -----, quid, *any;* (as adj., **qui, quae,** or **qua, quod**).
sui, sibi, se, or **sese,** nom. wanting, *themselves.*
teneo, tenere, tenui, -----, *hold, keep.*

incendo, -cendere, -cendi, -census, *set on fire, burn.*
ne, *so that ... not.*
oppidum, -i, n., *fortified town, city.*
qui, quae, quod, *who, which, what.*
Romani, -orum, m., pl., *the Romans.*
sum, esse, fui, futurus, *be.*
usus, -us, m., *advantage, profit, benefit.*

oppidum: Accusative direct object of **incenderunt** (A.G. 387). This is Noviodunum.

quod ... iudicabant: Relative clause (A.G. 303). **quod:** See below. **iudicabant:** The main verb of the subordinate clause (A.G. 278.b). The pronoun **ei,** with **Eporedorix Viridomarus** as the antecedent, is understood as the subject (A.G. 271.a).

quod ... posse: Accusative/infinitive construction in indirect discourse after **iudicabant** (A.G. 577 ff.). **quod:** Singular, neuter, accusative relative pronoun used substantively (A.G. 305). The antecedent is **oppidum** (A.G. 297.e). **posse:** Present infinitive; the tense of the infinitive in indirect discourse is relative to that of the verb of saying (A.G. 584).

a se: Ablative of agent with the preposition **a(b)** after the passive infinitive **teneri** (A.G. 405). **se:** Plural, masculine, ablative indirect reflexive pronoun (A.G. 300.2). The antecedent is **ei (Eporedorix Viridomarus),** the supplied subject of **iudicabant** (A.G. 299).

teneri: Complementary infinitive after **posse** (A.G. 456).

non: Adverb modifying **posse,** the negative precedes the word it especially effects (A.G. 217.e, 320-21, and 599.a).

ne ... esset ... Romanis: The conjunction **ne** ("so that ... not") with the subjunctive forms a negative purpose clause (A.G. 531.1). **esset:** The main verb of the subordinate clause (A.G. 278.b). Imperfect subjunctive; the tense of the subjunctive is in secondary sequence and follows the rules for the sequence of tense after **incenderunt** (A.G. 482-85). The pronoun **id,** with **oppidum** as the antecedent, is understood as the subject (A.G. 271.a). **Romanis:** See below.

cui ... usui Romanis: Dative of the purpose or end (double dative). The dative of an abstract noun (**cui ... usui**) is used to show that for which a thing serves or which it accomplishes, with another dative of the person or thing affected (**Romanis**). The verb is usually a form of **sum** (**esset**) (A.G. 382.1). **cui:** Singular, masculine, dative indefinite pronoun used as an adjective modifying **usui** (A.G. 148-49). The indefinite **quis, -----, quid** (**qui, quae,** or **qua, quod** when used adjectively) is used after **ne** (A.G. 310.a).

incenderunt: The main verb of the main clause (A.G. 278.b). The pronoun **ei,** with **Eporedorix Viridomarus** as the antecedent, is understood as the subject (A.G. 271.a).

(55.8-9) frumenti quod subito potuerunt navibus avexerunt, (9) reliquum flumine atque incendio corruperunt.

atque, *and.*
corrumpo, -rumpere, -rupi, -ruptus, *spoil, destroy, ruin.*
frumentum, -i, n., *grain.*
navis, -is, f., *ship, vessel.*
qui, quae, quod, *as much (of) as, whatever.*
subito, *suddenly, on a sudden.*

aveho, -vehere, -vexi, -vectus, *carry off, carry away.*
flumen, -inis, n., *flowing water, current, stream, river.*
incendium, -i, n., *fire, conflagration.*
possum, posse, potui, -----, *be able to do, be capable of.*
reliquus, -a, -um, *remaining, the rest.*

frumenti ... potuerunt: Relative clause (A.G. 303). **frumenti:** Partitive genitive with **quod** (A.G. 346.a.3). **potuerunt:** The main verb of the subordinate clause (A.G. 278.b). When the verb **posse** is used with an accusative but not with an infinitive it means "to be able to do, be capable of" (*OLD* **possum** 7). The pronoun **ei,** with **Eporedorix Viridomarus** as the antecedent, is understood as the subject (A.G. 271.a).

quod: Singular, neuter, accusative relative pronoun used substantively (A.G. 305). The pronoun is used as a cognate accusative with **potuerunt** (A.G. 390.c). When the neuter singular is used with a partitive genitive, it means "as much (of) as, whatever" (*OLD* **qui1** 16)

subito: Adverb (A.G. 320-21).

frumenti ... potuerunt: Kelsey suggests supplying the complementary infinitive **avexere** with **potuerunt**, which would make **quod** the accusative direct object of the infinitive. (Kelsey, 419)

navibus: Ablative of means (A.G. 409).

avexerunt: The main verb of the coordinate clause **frumenti ... avexerunt** (A.G. 278.a). The pronoun **ei**, with **Eporedorix Viridomarus** as the antecedent, is understood as the subject (A.G. 271.a).

reliquum: Singular, neuter, accusative adjective used substantively (A.G. 288). The noun **frumentum** is understood (A.G. 288.b). Accusative direct object of **corruperunt** (A.G. 387).

flumine atque incendio: Two ablatives of instrument (A.G. 409). **atque**: The conjunction connects the two ablative nouns and means "and" (*OLD* **atque** 12).

corruperunt: The main verb of the coordinate clause **reliquum ... corruperunt** (A.G. 278.a). The pronoun **ei**, with **Eporedorix Viridomarus** as the antecedent, is understood as the subject (A.G. 271.a). **avexerunt ... corruperunt**: Notice the asyndeton construction between the clauses (A.G. 323.b).

(55.9-10) **Ipsi ex finitimis regionibus copias cogere, praesidia custodiasque ad ripas Ligeris disponere equitatumque omnibus locis iniciendi timoris causa ostentare coeperunt, si ab re frumentaria Romanos excludere [aut adductos inopia ex provincia (10) expellere] possent.**

ab, *from.*

adduco, -ducere, -duxi, -ductus, *induce, persuade, move.*

causa, -ae, f., abl. with the gen., *for the sake of, for the purpose of.*

cogo, cogere, coegi, coactus, *collect, summon, bring together.*

custodia, -ae, f., *guard, watch.*

equitatus, -us, m., *cavalry.*

excludo, -cludere, -clusi, -clusus, *shut off, shut out, hinder, prevent.*

finitimus, -a, -um, *bordering on, neighboring, adjoining.*

inicio, -icere, -ieci, -iectus, *strike into.*

ipse, -a, -um, *he, they*, with or without *himself, themselves.*

loca, -orum, n., pl., *places.*

ostento, -are, -avi, -atus, *display, show.*

praesidium, -i, n., *guard, garrison.*

-que, *and.*

res, rei, f., (with **frumentaria**) *supply of grain, supplies.*

Romani, -orum, m., pl., *the Romans.*

timor, -oris, m., *fear, dread, apprehension, alarm.*

ad, *at.*

aut, *or.*

coepi, -isse, coeptus, *begin, start, commence.*

copiae, -arum, f., pl., *forces, troops.*

dispono, -ponere, -posui, -positus, *distribute, station, post.*

ex, *from, out of.*

expello, -pellere, -puli, -pulsus, *drive out, drive away, remove, expel.*

frumentarius, -a, -um, *having to do with grain or supplies.*

inopia, -ae, f., *want, lack, need, scarcity.*

Liger, -eris, m., *the Loire River.*

omnis, -e, *all.*

possum, posse, potui, -----, *be able.*

provincia, -ae, f., *province, subject territory.*

regio, -onis, f., *region, territory.*

ripa, -ae, f., *bank of a stream.*

si, *to see if, in case, on the off-chance that.*

Ipsi: Plural, masculine, nominative demonstrative pronoun used substantively (A.G. 296.2 and 298.d). The antecedent is **Eporedorix Viridomarus** (A.G. 298). Nominative subject of **coeperunt** (A.G. 339). The pronoun is here emphatic (A.G. 298.d.1).

ex finitimis regionibus: Ablative of source with the preposition **ex** (A.G. 403.1).

copias: Accusative direct object of the infinitive **cogere** (A.G. 387 and 451.3).

cogere: Complementary infinitive after **coeperunt** (A.G. 456).

praesidia custodiasque: Two accusative direct objects of the infinitive **disponere** (A.G. 387 and 451.3). **-que**: The enclitic conjunction connects the two accusative nouns (A.G. 324.a).

ad ripas Ligeris: Prepositional phrase, **ad** with the accusative here means "at" (*OLD* **ad** 13). **Ligeris**: Partitive genitive with **ripas** (A.G. 346.a). See Appendix A.

disponere: Complementary infinitive after **coeperunt** (A.G. 456). Notice the asyndeton construction between the two infinitives **cogere ... disponere** (A.G. 323.b).

equitatumque: Accusative direct object of the infinitive **ostentare** (A.G. 387 and 451.3). **-que**: The enclitic conjunction is used with the last infinitive in the series **disponere ... ostentare** (A.G. 323.c.3).

omnibus locis: Ablative of *place where* without a preposition (A.G. 429.1-2).

iniciendi timoris causa: The genitive of the gerundive and noun with the ablative of **causa** expresses purpose (A.G. 504.b). **iniciendi**: Singular, masculine, genitive gerundive used as an adjective modifying **timoris** denoting necessity, obligation or propriety (A.G. 500.1).

ostentare: Complementary infinitive after **coeperunt** (A.G. 456).

coeperunt: The main verb of the main clause (A.G. 278.b).

si ... possent: The conjunction **si** with the subjunctive forms the protasis of a contrary to fact, present time conditional statement without an apodosis meaning "to see if, in case, on the off-chance that" (A.G. 514.C.1) (*OLD* **si** 11). **possent**: The main verb of the subordinate clause (A.G. 278.b). Imperfect subjunctive; the tense of the subjunctive is in secondary sequence and follows the rules for the sequence of tense after **coeperunt** (A.G. 482-85). The pronoun **ei**, with **Ipsi** (**Eporedorix Viridomarus**)as the antecedent, is understood as the subject (A.G. 271.a).

ab re frumentaria: Ablative of separation with the preposition **ab** after the compound infinitive **excludere** (A.G. 402).

Romanos: Accusative direct object of the infinitive **excludere** (A.G. 387 and 451.3).

excludere: Complementary infinitive after **possent** (A.G. 456).

[aut: The conjunction connects the two infinitives and excludes the alternative (A.G. 324.e).

adductos: Accusative direct object of the infinitive **expellere** (A.G. 387 and 451.3). Accusative, perfect, passive, participle used as a predicate, where in English a phrase or a subordinate clause would be more normal (A.G. 496). The pronoun **eos**, with **Romanos** as the antecedent, is understood.

inopia: Ablative of cause without a preposition (A.G. 404).

ex provincia: Ablative of *place from which* with the preposition **ex** (A.G. 426.1). **provincia**: See Appendix A.

expellere]: Complementary infinitive after **possent** (A.G. 456).

(55.10) **Quam ad spem multum eos adiuvabat quod Liger ex nivibus creverat, ut omnino vado non posse transiri videretur.**

ad, *with a view to achieving, acquiring,* or *bringing about, for.*
cresco, crescere, crevi, cretus, *become swollen.*
is, ea, id, *he, she, it; that, this.*
multum, *much, by far, greatly.*
non, *not.*
possum, posse, potui, -----, *be able.*
quod, *the fact* or *circumstances that.*
transeo, -ire, -ivi, or **-ii, -itus,** *go over, go across, pass over, cross over.*
vadum, -i, n., *ford.*

adiuvo, -iuvare, -iuvi, -iutus, *help, aid, assist, support.*
ex, *from.*
Liger, -eris, m., *the Loire River.*
nix, nivis, f., *snow.*
omnino, *all together, in general.*
qui, quae, quod, *who, which, what.*
spes, -ei, f., *hope, expectation.*
ut, *so that.*
videor, videri, visus sum, *seem, appear.*

Quam ad spem: Prepositional phrase, **ad** with the accusative here means "with a view to achieving, acquiring, or bringing about, for" (*OLD* **ad** 45). **Quam**: Singular, feminine, accusative relative pronoun (A.G. 305). The antecedent is **spem** in its own clause (adjectival use) (A.G. 305.a). The relative does not introduce a relative clause but is a connecting relative; at the beginning of a clause the pronoun is often best rendered by a personal or demonstrative pronoun, with or without *and* (A.G. 308.f). **ad**: A monosyllabic preposition is often placed between a noun and its adjective (A.G. 599.d.2).

multum: Adverb (214.d and 320-21).

eos: Plural, masculine, accusative demonstrative pronoun used substantively (A.G. 296.2). The antecedent is **Eporedorix Viridomarus** (A.G. 297.e). Accusative direct object of **adiuvabat** (A.G. 387).

adiuvabat: The main verb of the main clause (A.G. 278.b). Impersonal use of the verb, the clause **quod ... creverat** (with the dependent clause **ut ... videretur**) functions as the subject (A.G. 208.c) (*OLD* **adiuuo** 3.b).

quod ... creverat: The conjunction **quod** ("The fact or circumstances that) with the indicative here forms a substantive clause which function as the subject of **adiuvabat** (A.G. 561.a and 572 Note) (*OLD* **quod** 4). **creverat**: The main verb of the subordinate clause (A.G. 278.b). The pluperfect denotes an action completed in past time (A.G. 477).

Liger: Nominative subject (A.G. 339). See Appendix A.

ex nivibus: Ablative of source with the preposition **ex** (A.G. 403.1). "The melting of the snow on the mountains. It was now harvest-time (July)." (Kelsey, 419)

ut ... videretur: The conjunction **ut** ("so that") with the subjunctive forms a clause of result (A.G. 537.1). **videretur**: The main verb of the subordinate clause (A.G. 278.b). Imperfect subjunctive; the tense of the subjunctive is in secondary sequence and follows the rules for the sequence of tense after **adiuvabat** (A.G. 482-85). The pronoun **is**, with **Liger** as the antecedent, is understood as the subject (A.G. 271.a).

omnino: Adverb (A.G. 320-21).

vado: Ablative of means (A.G. 409).

non: Adverb modifying **posse**, the negative precedes the word it especially effects (A.G. 217.e, 320-21, and 599.a).

posse: Complementary infinitive after **videretur** (A.G. 456).

transiri: Complementary infinitive after the infinitive **posse** (A.G. 456).

4.D CHAPTER 56: CAESAR REJECTS FLIGHT TO THE PROVINCE, CROSSES THE LOIRE RIVER, AND MOVES INTO THE TERRITORY OF THE SENONES

(56.1-2) **Quibus rebus cognitis Caesar maturandum sibi censuit, si esset in perficiendis pontibus periclitandum, ut prius (2) quam essent maiores eo coactae copiae dimicaret.**

Caesar, -aris, m., *Caesar.*
cognosco, -gnoscere, -gnovi, cognitus, *learn, ascertain, recognize.*

copiae, -arum, f., pl., *forces, troops.*
eo, *thither, there.*
maior, -or, -us, *greater, larger, bigger.*
perficio, -ficere, -feci, -fectus, *finish, complete.*

pons, pontis, m., *bridge.*
qui, quae, quod, *who, which, what.*
si, *if.*

censeo, -ere, -ui, -us, *think, hold, judge.*
cogo, cogere, coegi, coactus, *collect, summon, bring together.*
dimico, -are, -avi, -atus, *fight, contend, struggle.*
in, *in.*
maturo, -are, -avi, -atus, *hurry, hasten.*
periclitor, -ari, -atus, *try, make an attempt, venture, run a risk.*
prius quam, *before, sooner than.*
res, rei, f., *matter, event, affair.*
sui, sibi, se, or **sese,** nom. wanting, *himself.*

ut, *so that*.

Quibus rebus cognitis: Ablative absolute (A.G. 419-20). **Quibus**: Plural, feminine, ablative relative pronoun (A.G. 305). The antecedent is **rebus** in its own clause (adjectival use) (A.G. 307.b). The relative does not introduce a relative clause but is a connecting relative; at the beginning of a clause the pronoun is often best rendered by a personal or demonstrative pronoun, with or without *and* (A.G. 308.f). **cognitis**: The perfect tense of the participle represents the action as completed at the time indicated by the tense of the main verb (A.G. 489).

Caesar: Nominative subject (A.G. 339). See Appendix A.

maturandum (esse) ... si esset ... periclitandum: Conditional statement in indirect discourse after **censuit** (A.G. 589). The protasis, as a dependent clause, is in the subjunctive and the apodosis, as the principal clause, is in the infinitive (A.G. 589).

(id) maturandum (esse): The apodosis of the conditional statement (A.G. 589.2). Accusative/infinitive construction in indirect discourse after **censuit** (A.G. 577 ff.). **maturandum (esse)**: Supply **esse** to form the second periphrastic (passive) present infinitive with the gerundive implying necessity (A.G. 194.b and 196). The tense of the infinitive in indirect discourse is relative to that of the verb of saying (A.G. 584). Impersonal use of the intransitive verb (A.G. 208.d). Supply **id** as the subject (A.G. 318.c).

sibi: Singular, masculine, dative indirect reflexive pronoun (A.G. 300.2). The antecedent is **Caesar**, the subject of **censuit** (A.G. 299). Dative of agent with the gerundive **maturandum** (A.G. 374).

censuit: The main verb of the main clause (A.G. 278.b).

si (id) esset ... periclitandum: The conjunction **si** ("if") with the subjunctive forms the protasis of a conditional statement in indirect discourse (A.G. 589.1). "Haste was necessary in order to get across to the north side of the Liger before the enemy should have gathered greater forces to prevent his crossing. Retreat to the Province was out of the question; he must push to the north, and effect a junction with Labienus at all hazards." (Kelsey, 419) **esset ... periclitandum**: Second periphrastic (passive) imperfect subjunctive implying necessity (A.G. 194.b and 196). The main verb of the subordinate clause (A.G. 278.b). Imperfect subjunctive; the tense of the subjunctive is in secondary sequence and follows the rules for the sequence of tense after **censuit** (A.G. 482-85). The verb is here split (tmesis) (A.G. 640). Impersonal use of the intransitive verb (A.G. 208.d). Supply **id** as the subject (A.G. 318.c).

in perficiendis pontibus: Prepositional phrase, **in** with the ablative here means "in" (*OLD* in 40). **perficiendis**: Plural, masculine, ablative gerundive modifying **pontibus** after the preposition **in** (A.G. 500 and 507.3).

ut ... dimicaret: The conjunction **ut** ("so that") with the subjunctive forms a final (purpose) clause (A.G. 531.1). **dimicaret**: The main verb of the subordinate clause (A.G. 278.b). Imperfect subjunctive; the tense of the subjunctive is in secondary sequence and follows the rules for the sequence of tense after **censuit** (A.G. 482-4). The pronoun **is**, with **Caesar** as the antecedent, is understood as the subject (A.G. 271.a).

prius quam essent ... coactae: Temporal clause; a dependent clause in indirect discourse takes the subjunctive (A.G. 580). In direct discourse, **prius quam** ("before") with the imperfect subjunctive is common when the subordinate clause implies purpose or expectancy in the past (A.G. 551.b). The pluperfect subjunctive is rare, except as here where it is in indirect discourse by sequence of tense for the future perfect indicative (A.G. 484.c and 551.b Note 1). **essent ... coactae**: The main verb of the subordinate clause (A.G. 278.b). Pluperfect subjunctive; the tense of the subjunctive is in secondary sequence and follows the rules for the sequence of tense after **censuit** (A.G. 482-85). The pluperfect tense of the subjunctive is here standing for a future perfect in direct discourse (A.G. 484.c). The future perfect tense denotes action completed (at the time referred to), and hence is represented in the subjunctive by the pluperfect tense in secondary sequence (A.G. 484.c). The pluperfect, passive verb is here split (tmesis) (A.G. 640).

essent maiores eo coactae copiae: Notice the interlocking word order (A.G. 598.h).

maiores ... copiae: Nominative subject (A.G. 339). **maiores**: Irregular comparative adjective (A.G. 129).

eo: Adverb (A.G. 217.a and 320-21).

(56.2-3) **Nam, ut commutato consilio iter in provinciam converteret, ut ne metu quidem necessario faciendum existimabat, cum infamia atque indignitas rei et oppositus mons Cevenna viarumque difficultas impediebat, tum maxime quod abiuncto Labieno atque eis legionibus quas una miserat (3) vehementer timebat.**

abiungo, -iungere, -iunxi, -iunctus, *cut off*.

Cevenna, -ae, f., *the Cevennes*.

consilium, -i, n., *plan, design*.

cum ... tum, *not only ... but also*.

et, *and*.

facio, facere, feci, factus, *do*.

in, *into*.

infamia, -ae, f., *discredit, disgrace, dishonor*.

iter, itineris, n., *line of march, march, road, route*.

legio, -onis, f., *legion*.

metus, -us, m., *fear, apprehension*.

mons, montis, m., *mountain, mountain-range, elevation, height*.

ne ... quidem, *not even*.

oppositus -a, -um, *laying in the way*.

-que, *and*.

atque, *and*.

commuto, -are, -avi, -atus, *change, wholly change, alter*.

converto, -vertere, -verti, -versus, *turn, turn back, reverse*.

difficultas, -tatis, f., *difficulty, trouble*.

existimo, -are, -avi, -atus, *think, consider, judge*.

impedio, -pedire, -pedivi, -peditus, *hinder, obstruct*.

indignitas, -atis, f., *unworthiness, disgracefulness, shamefulness*.

is, ea, id, *he, she, it; that, this*.

Labienus, -i, m., *Labienus*.

maxime, *very greatly, exceedingly, chiefly, especially*.

mitto, mittere, misi, missus, *send*.

nam, *for*.

necessario, *of necessity, unavoidably*.

provincia, -ae, f., *the province*.

qui, quae, quod, *who, which, what*.

quod, *because, since, for, as.*
timeo, -ere, -ui, -----, *have fear, be afraid, be apprehensive.*
ut, *so that; how.*
via, -ae, f., *way, road.*

res, rei, f., *matter, affair.*
una, *together.*
vehementer, *vigorously, exceedingly.*

Nam: The particle is put before an interrogative adverb (the second **ut**) in lively or impatient questions (*OLD* **nam** 7).

ut ... converteret: The conjunction **ut** ("so that") with the subjunctive forms a substantive clause of result (A.G. 567). The clause functions as the subject of the impersonal verb **faciendum (esse)**; a substantive clause used as the object of a verb becomes the subject when the verb is put into the passive (A.G. 569.1). **converteret**: The main verb of the subordinate clause (A.G. 278.b). Imperfect subjunctive; the tense of the subjunctive is in secondary sequence and follows the rules for the sequence of tense for indirect questions after **existimabat** (A.G. 575). The pronoun **is**, with **Caesar** as the antecedent, is understood as the subject (A.G. 271.a).

commutato consilio: Ablative absolute (A.G. 419-20). **commutato**: The perfect tense of the participle represents the action as completed at the time indicated by the tense of the main verb (A.G. 489).

iter: Accusative direct object of **converteret** (A.G. 387).

in provinciam: Accusative of *place to which* with the preposition **in** (A.G. 426.2). **provinciam**: See Appendix A.

ut ... faciendum (esset): Indirect question with the subjunctive; the phrase is the object of **existimabat** (A.G. 573-75). **ut**: Interrogative adverb meaning "how" (*OLD* **ut** 1.b). **faciendum (esset)**: Supply **esset** to form the second periphrastic (passive) imperfect subjunctive implying necessity (A.G. 194.b and 196). The main verb of the subordinate clause (A.G. 278.b). Imperfect subjunctive; the tense of the subjunctive is in secondary sequence and follows the rules for the sequence of tense for indirect questions after **existimabat** (A.G. 575). Impersonal use of the intransitive verb (A.G. 208.c). The previous substantive clause of result functions as the subject (A.G. 569.1)

ne ... quidem: The negative adverb with the particle means "not even" (*OLD* **ne1** 6). The emphatic word must stand between **ne** and **quidem** (A.G. 322.f).

metu: Ablative of cause without a preposition (A.G. 404.b).

necessario: Adverb (A.G. 320-21).

existimabat: The main verb of the main clause (A.G. 278.b). The pronoun **is**, with **Caesar** as the antecedent, is understood as the subject (A.G. 271.a).

cum ... tum: A relative and demonstrative adverb used correlatively as conjunctions meaning "not only ... but also" (A.G. 323.g).

infamia atque indignitas ... et oppositus mons ... -que difficultas: Four nominative subjects (A.G. 339). **atque**: The conjunction is used to connect the pair of similar words **infamia** and **indignitas** and means "and" (*OLD* **atque** 10). **et**: The conjunction connects the two nominative nouns **indignitas** ... **mons** (A.G. 324.a). **-que**: The enclitic conjunction is used with the last member of the series **mons ... difficultas** (A.G. 323.c.3).

rei: Possessive genitive with both **infamia** and **indignitas** (A.G. 343).

Cevenna: A nominative proper noun in apposition to **mons** (A.G. 282). Caesar had battled the elements on this mountain range in the beginning of the campaign season in Chapter 8. See Appendix A.

viarum: Possessive genitive with **difficultas** (A.G. 343).

impediebat: The main verb of the coordinate clause **cum ... impediebat** (A.G. 278.a). Two or more singular subjects normally take a verb in the plural (A.G. 317). However, when a verb belongs to two or more subjects separately, it often agrees with one (**difficultas**) and is understood with the others (A.G. 317.c).

tum maxime (impediebatur): **tum**: Adverb (A.G. 271.b and 320-21). **maxime**: Irregular superlative adverb (A.G. 218.a and 320-21). Supply **impediebatur** as the main verb in the coordinate clause **tum ... timebat** with the pronoun **is** (**Caesar**) as the subject (A.G. 278.a).

quod ... timebat: Causal clause; the conjunction **quod** ("because") takes the indicative when the reason is given on the authority of the writer or speaker (A.G. 540.1). **timebat**: The main verb of the subordinate clause (A.G. 278.b). The pronoun **is**, with **Caesar** as the antecedent, is understood as the subject (A.G. 271.a).

abiuncto Labieno atque eis legionibus: Two dative indirect objects of the intransitive verb **timebat** (A.G. 367.c). **abiuncto**: Dative perfect, passive, participle used as a predicate modifying **Labieno**, where in English a phrase or a subordinate clause would be more normal (A.G. 496). **Labieno**: See Appendix A. **atque**: The conjunction connects the two dative nouns and means "and" (*OLD* **atque** 12). **eis**: Plural, feminine, dative demonstrative pronoun used as an adjective modifying **legionibus** (A.G. 296.1 and a). The pronoun functions as a correlative to the relative clause **quas ... miserat** (A.G. 297.d).

quas ... miserat: Relative clause (A.G. 303). For the reference see 34.2. **quas**: Plural, feminine, accusative relative pronoun used substantively (A.G. 305). The antecedent is **legionibus** (A.G. 307). Accusative direct object of **miserat** (A.G. 387). **miserat**: The main verb of the subordinate clause (A.G. 278.b). The pronoun **is**, with **Caesar** as the antecedent, is understood as the subject (A.G. 271.a). The pluperfect denotes an action completed in past time (A.G. 477).

una: Adverb (A.G. 320-21).

vehementer: Adverb (A.G. 214.b and 320-21).

(56.3-5) **Itaque admodum magnis diurnis nocturnisque itineribus confectis contra omnium opinionem (4) ad Ligerim venit, vadoque per equites invento pro rei necessitate opportuno, ut bracchia modo atque umeri ad sustinenda arma liberi ab aqua esse possent, disposito equitatu qui vim fluminis refringeret atque hostibus primo (5) aspectu perturbatis, incolumem exercitum traduxit;**

ab, *from, out of.*
admodum, *quite, very.*

ad, *to; for, in order to, for the purpose of.*
aqua, -ae, f., *water.*

arma, -orum, n., pl., *arms, armor, weapons.*
atque, *and.*
conficio, -ficere, -feci, -fectus, *complete, finish, accomplish, do.*
dispono, -ponere, -posui, -positus, *set in various places, distribute, station, post.*
eques, -itis, m., *rider, horseman, cavalryman, trooper.*
exercitus, -us, m., *army.*
hostis, -is, m., *enemy, foe*; pl., *the enemy.*
invenio, -venire, -veni, -ventus, *find, discover.*
iter, itineris, n., *march.*
Liger, -eris, m., *the Loire River.*
modo, *only, merely.*
nocturnus, -a, -um, *by night, of night.*
opinio, -onis, f., *idea, belief, notion.*
per, *by* (means of).

possum, posse, potui, -----, *be able.*
pro, *considering.*
qui, quae, quod, *who, which, what.*
res, rei, f., *situation, event, affair.*
sustineo, -tinere, -tinui, -tentus, *hold up.*

umerus, -i, m., *shoulder.*
vadum, -i, n., *ford.*
vis, acc. **vim**, abl. **vi**, *strength, force.*

aspectus, -us, m., *appearance, sight, look.*
bracchium, -i, n., *arm, forearm.*
contra, *contrary to.*
diurnus, -a, -um, *of the day, by day.*

equitatus, -us, m., *cavalry.*
flumen, -inis, n., *flowing water, current, stream, river.*
incolumis, -e, *safe, unharmed, uninjured, unhurt.*
itaque, *and so, in consequence, accordingly, therefore.*
liber, -era, -erum, *free, unimpeded.*
magnus, -a, -um, *long.*
necessitas, -tatis, f., *necessity, need.*
omnes, -ium, m., pl., *all men, all.*
opportunus, -a, -um, *fit, suitable.*
perturbo, -are, -avi, -atus, *disturb greatly, disorder, confuse.*
primus, -a, -um, *first.*
-que, *and.*
refringo, -fringere, -fregi, -fractus, *break.*
sum, esse, fui, futurus, *be.*
traduco, -ducere, -duxi, -ductus, *lead across, bring over.*
ut, *so that.*
venio, venire, veni, ventus, *come.*

Itaque: An adverb expressing the result of the previous ideas meaning "and so, in consequence" (*OLD* itaque 1). The adverb stands in the first position (A.G. 599.b).

admodum magnis diurnis nocturnisque itineribus confectis: Ablative absolute (A.G. 419-20). **admodum**: An adverb modifying **magnis** (A.G. 320-21). **-que**: The enclitic conjunction is used to join opposites which form a complementary pair, here the adjectives **diurnis nocturnis** (*OLD* -que 1.b). Two adjectives belonging to the same noun are regularly connected by a conjunction (A.G. 323.d). **confectis**: The perfect tense of the participle represents the action as completed at the time indicated by the tense of the main verb (A.G. 489).

contra omnium opinionem: Prepositional phrase, **contra** with the accusative here means "contrary to" (*OLD* contra 22). Once again in a tight spot Caesar relies on speed to seize the initiative. **omnium**: Plural, masculine, genitive adjective used substantively (A.G. 288). Possessive genitive with **opinionem** (A.G. 343).

ad Ligerim: Accusative of *place to which* with the preposition **ad** (A.G. 426.2). **Ligerim**: The accusative singular of the third declension masculine i-stem noun **Liger** ends in **-im**, not **-em** (A.G. 73-75, esp. 74.d and 75.a.1). See Appendix A.

venit: The main verb of the coordinate clause **Itaque ... venit** (A.G. 278.a). The pronoun **is**, with **Caesar** as the antecedent, is understood as the subject (A.G. 271.a).

invento ... disposito ... perturbatis: Notice how the three consecutive ablative absolutes gives the impression of rapidity to the events.

vadoque ... possent: Ablative absolute with a dependent clause.

vadoque per equites invento pro rei necessitate opportuno: Ablative absolute (A.G. 419-20). **-que**: The enclitic conjunction connects the two main verbs **venit ... traduxit** (A.G. 324.a). **per equites**: Prepositional phrase, the personal agent, when considered as instrument or means, is often expressed by **per** with the accusative meaning "by" (means of) (A.G. 405.b). **invento**: The perfect tense of the participle represents the action as completed at the time indicated by the tense of the main verb (A.G. 489). **pro rei necessitate**: Prepositional phrase, **pro** with the ablative here means "considering" (*OLD* pro 13). "Though under ordinary circumstances dangerous and impracticable." (Kelsey, 419) **rei**: Possessive genitive with **necessitate** (A.G. 343). **opportuno**: Singular, neuter, ablative, predicate adjective modifying **vado** after **invento** (A.G. 283).

ut ... possent: The conjunction **ut** ("so that") with the subjunctive forms a clause of result (A.G. 537.1). **possent**: The main verb of the subordinate clause (A.G. 278.b). Imperfect subjunctive; the tense of the subjunctive is in secondary sequence and follows the rules for the sequence of tense after **traduxit** (A.G. 482-85).

bracchia ... umeri: Two nominative subjects (A.G. 339).

modo: Adverb (A.G. 320-21).

atque: The conjunction connects the two nominative subjects and means "and" (*OLD* atque 12).

ad sustinenda arma: The preposition **ad** with the accusative gerundive and noun expresses purpose (A.G. 506). **sustinenda**: Plural, neuter, accusative gerundive used as an adjective modifying **arma** denoting necessity, obligation or propriety (A.G. 500.1).

liberi: Plural, masculine, nominative predicate adjective modifying both **bracchia** and **umeri** after **esse** (A.G. 283-84). A predicate adjective after a complementary infinitive takes the case of the subject of the main verb (A.G. 458). When a predicate adjective modifies two nouns of different genders, the adjective may agree with the nearest noun (**umeri**), if the nouns form one connected idea (A.G. 287.2).

ab aqua: Ablative of separation with the preposition **ab** after the adjective **liberi** (A.G. 402.a).

esse: Complementary infinitive after **possent** (A.G. 456).

disposito ... refringeret: Ablative absolute with a dependent clause.

disposito equitatu: Ablative absolute (A.G. 419-20). **disposito**: The perfect tense of the participle represents the action as completed at the time indicated by the tense of the main verb (A.G. 489). "By stationing the cavalry in a compact line across the stream, the force of the current was broken, so that the infantry could keep their footing in the deep water while marching over." (Kelsey, 419) Notice the asyndeton construction between the ablative absolutes **vado ... invento ... disposito ... equitatu** (A.G. 323.b).

qui ... refringeret: A relative clause of purpose is introduced by a relative pronoun and takes the subjunctive (A.G. 531.2). **qui**: Singular, masculine, nominative relative pronoun used substantively (A.G. 305). The antecedent is **equitatu** (A.G. 307). Nominative subject (A.G. 339). The relative is here equivalent to **ut is** (A.G. 531.2 Note). **refringeret**: The main verb of the subordinate clause (A.G. 278.b). Imperfect subjunctive; the tense of the subjunctive is in secondary sequence and follows the rules for the sequence of tense after **traduxit** (A.G. 482-85).

vim: Accusative direct object of **refringeret** (A.G. 387).

fluminis: Possessive genitive with **vim** (A.G. 343).

atque: The conjunction connects the two ablative absolutes **disposito equitatu ... hostibus ... perturbatis** and means "and" (*OLD* **atque** 12).

hostibus primo aspectu perturbatis: Ablative absolute (A.G. 419-20). **primo aspectu**: Ablative of cause without a preposition (A.G. 404). **primo**: Declinable ordinal number used as an adjective (A.G. 132-35). **perturbatis**: The perfect tense of the participle represents the action as completed at the time indicated by the tense of the main verb (A.G. 489).

incolumem exercitum: Accusative direct object of **traduxit** (A.G. 387). **incolumem**: Singular, masculine, accusative adjective modifying the noun **exercitum** but used to qualify the action of the verb, and so has the force of an adverb (A.G. 290).

traduxit: The main verb of the coordinate clause **vadoque ... traduxit** (A.G. 278.a). The pronoun **is**, with **Caesar** as the antecedent, is understood as the subject (A.G. 271.a).

(56.5) frumentumque in agris et pecoris copiam nactus, repleto his rebus exercitu iter in Senones facere instituit.

ager, -ri, m., *land* (under cultivation), *field*; pl., *the country*.	**copia, -ae**, f., *quantity, abundance, supply*.
et, *and*.	**exercitus, -us**, m., *army*.
facio, facere, feci, factus, *make*.	**frumentum, -i**, n., *grain*.
hic, haec, hoc, *this*; *he, she, it*.	**in**, *in*; *into the country of, against*.
instituo, -stituere, -stitui, -stitutus, *undertake, commence, begin*.	**iter, itineris**, n., *march, journey*.
naniscor, -cisci, nactus, and **nanctus**, *come upon, find, obtain, get, secure*.	**pecus, -oris**, n., *cattle*.
-que, *and, now*.	**repleo, -plere, -plevi, -pletus**, *supply amply*.
res, rei, f., *supply, thing*.	**Senones, -um**, m., pl., *the Senones*.

frumentumque: Accusative direct object of the participle **nactus** (A.G. 387 and 488). **-que**: The enclitic conjunction begins the sentence, introducing a fresh situation, and means "and, now" (*OLD* **-que** 4).

in agris: Ablative of *place where* with the preposition **in** (locative ablative) (A.G. 426.3).

et: The conjunction connects the two accusative nouns **frumentum ... copiam** (A.G. 324.a).

pecoris: Partitive genitive with **copiam** (A.G. 346.a.1).

copiam: Accusative direct object of the participle **nactus** (A.G. 387 and 488).

nactus: Nominative perfect, deponent, participle used as a predicate, where in English a phrase or a subordinate clause would be more normal (A.G. 496). The pronoun **is**, with **Caesar** as the antecedent, is understood. Nominative subject (A.G. 339).

repleto his rebus exercitu: Ablative absolute (A.G. 419-20). **repleto**: The perfect tense of the participle represents the action as completed at the time indicated by the tense of the main verb (A.G. 489). **his rebus**: Ablative of means (A.G. 409). **his**: Plural, feminine, ablative demonstrative pronoun used as an adjective modifying **rebus** (A.G. 296.1 and a).

iter: Accusative direct object of the infinitive **facere** (A.G. 387 and 451.3). The phrase **iter facere** is an idiom that means "to march or travel" (*OLD* **iter** 1.b).

in Senones: Accusative of *place to which* with the preposition **in** ("into the country of") (A.G. 426.2). **Senones**: See Appendix A.

facere: Complementary infinitive after **instituit** (A.G. 456).

instituit: The main verb of the main clause (A.G. 278.b).

4.E CHAPTERS 57-62: LABIENUS CAPTURES METIOSEDUM, DEFEATS CAMULOGENUS, THEN ESCAPES TO AGEDINCUM AND REJOINS CAESAR

The Latin in this subsection is stylistically simple, with a homogenous vocabulary, lack of indirect discourse, speeches, uses of the subjunctive, etc. Adcock remarks that "when he is describing the doings of his lieutenants the style is, in general, less emphatic, less vigorous, though even in these ... there is a more dramatic treatment of the situation. ... On the whole, though, the operations of the legati are described so that the military quality of their actions, their consilia, so far as these are their own and not Caesar's at one remove, can be appraised, but that is all." (Adcock, 73-74).

(57.1) Dum haec apud Caesarem geruntur, Labienus eo supplemento, quod nuper ex Italia venerat, relicto Agedinci, ut esset impedimentis praesidio, cum IIII legionibus Lutetiam proficiscitur.

Agedincum, -i, n., *Agedincum*.	**apud**, *under the command of*.
Caesar, -aris, m., *Caesar*.	**cum**, *with*.
dum, *while*.	**ex**, *from, out of*.
gero, gerere, gessi, gestus, *carry out, perform, do*.	**hic, haec, hoc**, *this*; *he, she, it*.

I, in expression of number, *1*.
is, ea, id, *he, she, it; that, this.*
Labienus, -i, m., *Labienus.*
Lutetia, -ae, f., *Lutetia.*
praesidium, -i, n., *guard, protection.*
qui, quae, quod, *who, which, what.*
sum, esse, fui, futurus, *be.*
ut, *so that.*

impedimenta, -orum, n., pl., *heavy baggage, baggage.*
Italia, -ae, f., *Italy.*
legio, -onis, f., *legion.*
nuper, *lately, recently.*
proficiscor, -ficisci, -fectus, *set out, depart, proceed.*
relinquo, -linquere, -liqui, -lictus, *leave, leave behind.*
supplementum, -i, n., *reinforcement, reinforcements.*
venio, venire, veni, ventus, *come.*

Dum ... geruntur: Temporal clause; the conjunction **dum** ("when, while") with the present indicative denotes continued action in past time (A.G. 556). **geruntur**: The main verb of the subordinate clause (A.G. 278.b).

haec: Plural, neuter, nominative demonstrative pronoun used substantively (A.G. 296.2). The antecedent is the actions described since the army was split at 34.2 (A.G. 297.e). Nominative subject (A.G. 339).

apud Caesarem: Prepositional phrase, **apud** with the accusative here means "under the command of" (*OLD* **apud** 4.c). **Caesarem**: See Appendix A.

Labienus: Nominative subject of **proficiscitur** (A.G. 339). Kahn notes that Caesar "demonstrates how his lieutenant employs Caesarian tactics, treats his troops with similar tact and commands equal loyalty. Labienus's vicissitudes intensify the impression of Roman desperation at this stage of the war and help to magnify the wonder of the subsequent victory." (Kahn, 254) See Appendix A.

eo ... praesidio: Ablative absolute with dependent clauses.

eo supplemento quod nuper ex Italia venerat, relicto Agedinci: Ablative absolute (A.G. 419-20). **eo**: Singular, neuter, ablative demonstrative pronoun used as an adjective modifying **supplemento** (A.G. 296.1 and a). The pronoun functions as a correlative to the relative clause **quod ... venerat** (A.G. 297.d). **quod ... venerat**: Relative clause (A.G. 303). **quod**: Singular, neuter, nominative relative pronoun used substantively (A.G. 305). The antecedent is **supplemento** (A.G. 297.e). Nominative subject (A.G. 339). **venerat**: The main verb of the subordinate clause (A.G. 278.b). The pluperfect denotes an action completed in past time (A.G. 477). **nuper**: Adverb (A.G. 320-21). **ex Italia**: Ablative of *place from which* with the preposition **ex** (A.G. 426.1). **Italia**: See Appendix A. **relicto**: The perfect tense of the participle represents the action as completed at the time indicated by the tense of the main verb (A.G. 489). **Agedinci**: Locative of the city name **Agedincum, -i.**, n. (A.G. 49.a). See Appendix A.

ut ... esset ... praesidio: The conjunction **ut** ("so that") with the subjunctive forms a final (purpose) clause (A.G. 531.1). **esset**: The main verb of the subordinate clause (A.G. 278.b). Imperfect subjunctive; the tense of the subjunctive is in secondary sequence after the historical present **proficiscitur** (A.G. 482-85, esp. 485.e). The pronoun **id**, with **supplementum** as the antecedent, is understood as the subject (A.G. 271.a). **praesidio**: See below.

impedimentis praesidio: Dative of the purpose or end (double dative). The dative of an abstract noun (**praesidio**) is used to show that for which a thing serves or which it accomplishes, with another dative of the person or thing affected (**impedimentis**). The verb is usually a form of **sum** (**esset**) (A.G. 382.1).

cum IIII legionibus: Ablative of accompaniment with the preposition **cum** (A.G. 413). **IIII**: Roman numeral used as an adjective modifying **legionibus** (A.G. 133).

Lutetiam: Accusative of *place to which* without a preposition (city name) (A.G. 427.2). An island city on the Seine river, now Paris. See Appendix A.

proficiscitur: The main verb of the main clause (A.G. 278.b). The historical present, giving vividness to the narrative, is present in Chapter 57 (A.G. 469). This usage, common in all languages, comes from imagining past events as going on before our eyes (*repraesentatio*) (A.G. 469 Note).

(57.1-2) Id est oppidum Parisiorum, quod positum est (2) in insula fluminis Sequanae.

flumen, -inis, n., *flowing water, current, stream, river.*
insula, -ae, f., *island.*
oppidum, -i, n., *fortified town, city.*
pono, ponere, posui, positus, pass., often *be situated.*
Sequana, -ae, f., *the Sequana river.*

in, *on.*
is, ea, id, *he, she, it; that, this.*
Parisii, -orum, m., pl., *the Parisii.*
qui, quae, quod, *who, which, what.*
sum, esse, fui, futurus, *be.*

Id: Singular, neuter, nominative demonstrative pronoun used substantively (A.G. 296.2). Although the antecedent is **Lutetiam**, the gender agrees with **oppidum** in its own clause (A.G. 297.e). Nominative subject (A.G. 339).

est: The main verb of the main clause (A.G. 278.b). The present tense is not the historical present but denotes a state as now existing in present time (A.G. 465.2).

oppidum: Singular, neuter, nominative predicate noun after **est** (A.G. 283-84).

Parisiorum: Possessive genitive of the tribe name **Parisii** with **oppidum** (A.G. 343). See Appendix A.

quod ... Sequanae: Relative clause (A.G. 303). **quod**: Singular, neuter, nominative, relative pronoun used substantively (A.G. 305). The antecedent is **oppidum** (A.G. 307). Nominative subject (A.G. 339). **Sequanae**: See below.

positum: Nominative perfect, passive, participle used as a predicate adjective modifying **quod** after **est** (A.G. 495).

est: The main verb of the subordinate clause (A.G. 278.b). The present tense is not the historical present but denotes a state as now existing in present time (A.G. 465.2).

in insula fluminis Sequanae: Ablative of *place where* with the preposition **in** (locative ablative) (A.G. 426.3). **fluminis Sequanae**: Partitive genitive with **insula** (A.G. 346.a). **Sequanae**: A genitive proper noun in apposition to **fluminis** (A.G. 282). The modern name is the Seine river. See Appendix A.

(57.2) Cuius adventu ab hostibus cognito, magnae ex finitimis civitatibus copiae convenerunt.

ab, *by.*

civitas, -tatis, f., *state, nation.*

convenio, -venire, -veni, -ventus, *come together, gather.*
ex, *from.*

hostis, -is, m., *enemy, foe*; pl., *the enemy.*
qui, quae, quod, *who, which, what.*

adventus, -us, m., *coming, approach, arrival.*

cognosco, -gnoscere, -gnovi, cognitus, *learn, ascertain, recognize.*
copiae, -arum, f., pl., *forces, troops.*
finitimus, -a, -um, *bordering on, neighboring, adjoining.*
magnus, -a, -um, *great, large.*

Cuius adventu ab hostibus cognito: Ablative absolute (A.G. 419-20). **Cuius**: Singular, masculine, genitive relative pronoun used substantively (A.G. 305). The antecedent is **Labienus** (A.G. 307). Possessive genitive with **adventu** (A.G. 343). The relative does not introduce a relative clause but is a connecting relative; at the beginning of a clause the pronoun is often best rendered by a personal or demonstrative pronoun, with or without *and* (A.G. 308.f). **ab hostibus**: Ablative of agent with the preposition **ab** after the passive participle **cognito** (A.G. 405). **cognito**: The perfect tense of the participle represents the action as completed at the time indicated by the tense of the main verb (A.G. 489).
magnae ... copiae: Nominative subject (A.G. 339).
ex finitimis civitatibus: Ablative of source with the preposition **ex** (A.G. 426.1).
convenerunt: The main verb of the main clause (A.G. 278.b).

(57.3-4) (3) Summa imperi traditur Camulogeno Aulerco, qui prope confectus aetate tamen propter singularem scientiam rei (4) militaris ad eum est honorem evocatus.

ad, *for, to.*
Aulercus, -i, m., *an Aulercan.*
conficio, -ficere, -feci, -fectus, *wear out, exhaust.*

honor, -oris, m., *honor, office, post.*
is, ea, id, *he, she, it; that, this.*
prope, *near, nearly, almost.*

qui, quae, quod, *who, which, what.*
scientia, -ae, f., *knowledge, skill.*
summa, -ae, f., *general management, control, administration.*
trado, -dere, -didi, -ditus, *hand over, give up, deliver.*

aetas, -tatis, f., *age.*
Camulogenus, -i, m., *Camulogenus.*
evoco, -are, -avi, -atus, *call out, call forth, call, summon.*
imperium, -i, n., *command, control, military authority.*
militaris, -e, *military.*
propter, *as a result* or *consequence of, in view of, because of.*
res, rei, f., (with **militaris**), *military affairs* or *practice.*
singularis, -e, *singular, matchless, extraordinary.*
tamen, *yet, still, for all that, nevertheless, however.*

Summa: Nominative subject (A.G. 339). From the noun **summa, -ae**, f..
imperi: Partitive genitive with **summa** (A.G. 346.a.1). The singular genitive of nouns in **-ium** ended, until the Augustan Age, in a single **-i** (A.G. 49.b).
traditur: The main verb of the main clause (A.G. 278.b).
Camulogeno: Dative indirect object of the passive verb **traditur**, verbs which in the active voice take the accusative and dative retain the dative when used in the passive (A.G. 365). See Appendix A.
Aulerco: A dative noun in apposition to the proper noun **Camulogeno** (A.G. 282).
qui ... est ... evocatus: Relative clause (A.G. 303). **qui**: Singular, masculine, nominative relative pronoun used substantively (A. G. 305). The antecedent is **Camulogeno** (A.G. 307). Nominative subject (A.G. 339). **est ... evocatus**: The main verb of the subordinate clause (A.G. 278.b). The perfect passive verb is here split (tmesis) (A.G. 640).
prope: Adverb (A.G. 320-21).
confectus: Nominative perfect, passive, participle used as a predicate modifying **qui**, where in English a phrase or a subordinate clause would be more normal. The participle is equivalent to a clause of concession correlative to the following adverb **tamen** and has the meaning "although" (A.G. 496).
aetate: Ablative of cause without a preposition (A.G. 404).
tamen: Adverb, normally postpositive but not here (A.G. 320-21 and 324.j).
propter singularem scientiam rei militaris: Prepositional phrase, **propter** with the accusative here means "as a result or consequence of, in view of, because of" (*OLD* **propter** 3). **rei militaris**: Objective genitive with **scientiam** (A.G. 348). The phrase **res militaris** means "military affairs or practice" (*OLD* **militaris** 1.c).
ad eum est honorem evocatus: Notice the interlocking word order (A.G. 598.h).
ad eum ... honorem: Prepositional phrase, **ad** with the accusative here means "for" (*OLD* **ad** 41). **eum**: Singular, masculine, accusative demonstrative pronoun used as an adjective modifying **honorem** (A.G. 296.1 and a).

(57.4) Is cum animadvertisset perpetuam esse paludem quae influeret in Sequanam atque illum omnem locum magnopere impediret, hic consedit nostrosque transitu prohibere instituit.

animadverto, -tere, -ti, -sus, *notice, observe, perceive.*
consido, -sidere, -sedi, -sessus, *halt, encamp.*
hic, *here, at this place.*
impedio, -pedire, -pedivi, -peditus, *hinder, obstruct.*
influo, -fluere, -fluxi, -fluxus, *flow into, flow.*

is, ea, id, *he, she, it; that, this.*
magnopere, *very much, greatly.*
omnis, -e, *whole, entire.*
perpetuus, -a, -um, *continuous, unbroken.*
-que, *and.*
Sequana, -ae, f., *the Sequana river.*
transitus, -us, m., *going over, crossing over, crossing.*

atque, *and.*
cum, *after, when.*
ille, illae, illud, *that; he, she, it.*
in, *into.*
instituo, -stituere, -stitui, -stitutus, *undertake, commence, begin.*
locus, -i, m., *place, position.*
nostri, -orum, m., pl., *our men, our side.*
palus, -udis, f., *marsh, swamp, bog, morass.*
prohibeo, -hibere, -hibui, -hibitus, *prevent, hinder.*
qui, quae, quod, *who, which, what.*
sum, esse, fui, futurus, *be.*

Is: Singular, masculine, nominative demonstrative pronoun used substantively (A.G. 296.2). The antecedent is **Camulogeno** (A.G. 297.e). Nominative subject of **animadvertisset ... consedit ... instituit** (A.G. 339).
cum animadvertisset ... impediret: Temporal clause; the relative adverb **cum** ("after, when") with the pluperfect subjunctive describes the circumstances that preceded the action of the main verb (A.G. 546). **animadvertisset**: The main verb of the subordinate clause (A.G. 278.b). **impediret**: See below.
perpetuam esse paludem: Accusative/infinitive construction in indirect discourse after **animadvertisset** (A.G. 577 ff.). **perpetuam ... paludem**: "This 'continuous marsh' probably lay along the little stream Essonne, extending back from its junction with the Seine. On the north side of it the Gauls were securely posted." (Kelsey, 419) **perpetuam**: Singular, feminine, accusative predicate adjective modifying **paludem** after **esse** (A.G. 283-84). **esse**: Present infinitive; the tense of the infinitive in indirect discourse is relative to that of the verb of saying (A.G. 584).
quae influeret ... impediret: Relative clause; a clause dependent on a subjunctive clause (**cum ... animadvertisset**) takes the subjunctive when regarded as an integral part of that clause (attraction) (A.G. 303 and 593). (It is also a subordinate clause in indirect discourse). **quae**: Singular, feminine, nominative relative pronoun used substantively (A.G. 305). The antecedent is **paludem** (A.G. 307). Nominative subject of **influeret ... impediret** (A.G. 339). **influeret ... impediret**: The main verbs of the subordinate clause (A.G. 278.b). Imperfect subjunctives; the tense of the subjunctives is in secondary sequence and follows the rules for the sequence of tense after **animadvertisset** (A.G. 482-85 and 585).
in Sequanam: Accusative of *place to which* with the preposition **in** (A.G. 426.2). **Sequanam**: See Appendix A.
atque: The conjunction connects the two main verbs in the relative clause and means "and" (*OLD* atque 12).
illum omnem locum: Accusative direct object of **impediret** (A.G. 387). **illum**: Singular, masculine, accusative demonstrative pronoun used as an adjective modifying **locum** (A.G. 296.1 and a).
magnopere: Adverb (A.G. 320-21).
hic: Adverb (A.G. 217.a and 320-21).
consedit: The main verb of the coordinate clause **Is ... consedit** (A.G. 278.a).
nostrosque: Plural, masculine, accusative possessive pronoun used substantively to denote a special class (A.G. 302.d). Accusative direct object of the infinitive **prohibere** (A.G. 387). **-que**: The enclitic conjunction connects the two main verbs **consedit ... instituit** (A.G. 324.a).
transitu: Ablative of separation without a preposition after **prohibere** (A.G. 401).
prohibere: Complementary infinitive after **instituit** (A.G. 456).
instituit: The main verb of the coordinate clause **nostrosque ... instituit** (A.G. 278.a).

(58.1-2) Labienus primo vineas agere, cratibus atque aggere (2) paludem explere atque iter munire conabatur.

agger, -eris, m., *material for a mound* (earth, timber), *earth.*
atque, *and.*
crates, -is, f., *wicker-work, hurdle, fascine, bundle of brushwood.*
iter, itineris, n., *road.*
munio, -ire, -ivi, -itus, *construct.*
primo, *at first, in the first place.*

ago, agere, egi, actus, *move forward, press forward.*
conor, -ari, -atus, endeavor, *attempt, undertake, try.*
expleo, -plere, -plevi, -pletus, *fill up, fill full, stuff.*
Labienus, -i, m., *Labienus.*
palus, -udis, f., *marsh, swamp, bog, morass.*
vinea, -ae, f., *arbor-shed, vinea.*

Labienus: Nominative subject (A.G. 339). See Appendix A.
primo: Adverb (A.G. 217.b, 320-21, and 322.d).
vineas ... explere: "Labienus proposed, under cover of *vineae*, to build a causeway over the marsh in the face of the enemy, throwing in fascines and earth as if filling up the moat of a besieged city." (Kelsey, 420) It is amazing that a Roman general would consider such a massive project as a normal procedure. Even today, with modern equipment, one does not contemplate filling in a marsh without much thought and preparation. It is a testament to the fortitude of the Roman soldier and the methodical planning of their superiors that this could even be considered.
vineas: Accusative direct object of the infinitive **agere** (A.G. 387 and 451.3).
agere: Complementary infinitive after **conabatur** (A.G. 456 and 563.e).
cratibus atque aggere: Two ablatives of means after **explere** (A.G. 409.a). **atque**: The conjunction connects the two ablative nouns and means "and" (*OLD* atque 12). **aggere**: The noun here does not mean the usual "rampart", but "material for a mound (dirt),

rubble" (*OLD* **agger** 1).

paludem: Accusative direct object of the infinitive **explere** (A.G. 387 and 451.3).

explere: Complementary infinitive after **conabatur** (A.G. 456 and 563.e). **agere ... explere**: Notice the asyndeton construction between the first two infinitives (A.G. 323.b).

atque: The conjunction connects the two infinitives **explere ... munire** and means "and" (*OLD* **atque** 12).

iter: Accusative direct object of the infinitive **munire** (A.G. 387 and 451.3).

munire: Complementary infinitive after **conabatur** (A.G. 456 and 563.e).

conabatur: The main verb of the simple sentence (A.G. 278.1).

(58.2-3) Postquam id difficilius fieri animadvertit, silentio e castris tertia vigilia egressus eodem quo venerat itinere Metiosedum (3) pervenit.

animadverto, -tere, -ti, -sus, *notice, observe, perceive.*	**castra, -orum**, n., pl., *camp, encampment.*
difficulter, comp. **difficilius**, *difficult, with difficulty.*	**egredior, -gredi, -gressus**, *go out, go forth, come forth, leave.*
e(x), *from, out of.*	**fio, fieri, factus**, *be made, be done, become.*
idem, eadem, idem, *the same.*	**is, ea, id**, *he, she, it; that, this.*
iter, itineris, n., *road, route.*	**Metiosedum, -i**, n., *Metiosedum.*
pervenio, -venire, -veni, -ventus, *come to, arrive at, reach.*	**postquam**, *after, when.*
qui, quae, quod, *who, which, what.*	**silentium, -i**, m., *silence, stillness.*
tertius, -a, um, *third.*	**venio, venire, veni, ventus**, *come.*
vigilia, -ae, f., *watch.*	

Postquam ... animadvertit: Subordinate clause; the conjunction **postquam** ("after") with the perfect indicative forms a temporal clause (A.G. 543). "The implication is that the difficulty arose less from the attacks of the enemy than from the yielding nature of the marsh." (Kelsey, 420) **animadvertit**: The main verb of the subordinate clause (A.G. 278.b). The pronoun **is**, with **Labienus** as the antecedent, is understood as the subject (A.G. 271.a).

id ... fieri: Accusative/infinitive construction in indirect discourse after **animadvertit** (A.G. 577 ff.). **id**: Singular, neuter, accusative demonstrative pronoun used substantively (A.G. 296.2). The antecedent is the filling in of the marsh (A.G. 297.e). **fieri**: Present infinitive; the tense of the infinitive in indirect discourse is relative to that of the verb of saying (A.G. 584).

difficilius: Comparative adverb (A.G. 218 and 320-21). The comparative degree here denotes a considerable or excessive degree of the quality meaning "too" (A.G. 291.a).

silentio: Ablative of manner (A.G. 412.b).

e castris: Ablative of *place from which* with the preposition **e(x)** (A.G. 426.1).

tertia vigilia: Ablative of *time when* (A.G. 423.1). **tertia**: Ordinal number used as an adjective (A.G. 132-35). "The third watch runs from midnight to 3 A.M..

egressus: Nominative perfect, deponent, participle used as a predicate, where in English a phrase or a subordinate clause would be more normal (A.G. 496). The pronoun **is**, with **Labienus** as the antecedent, is understood. Nominative subject (A.G. 339).

eodem ... pervenit: "Labienus had come from Agedincum along the left bank of the Seine as far as the Essonne. Not being able to cross this, he marched back the way he had come as far as Melun, there passed over to the east side of the Seine, and followed the course of the river down to Paris unhindered." (Kelsey, 420)

eodem quo venerat itinere: He backtracked.

eodem ... itinere: Ablative of *way by which* without a preposition (A.G. 429.a). **eodem**: Singular, neuter, ablative demonstrative pronoun used as an adjective modifying **itinere** (A.G. 296.1 and a).

quo venerat: Relative clause (A.G. 303). **quo**: Singular, neuter, ablative relative pronoun used substantively (A.G. 305). The antecedent is **itinere** (A.G. 307). Ablative of *way by which* without a preposition (A.G. 429.a). **venerat**: The main verb of the subordinate clause (A.G. 278.b). The pronoun **is**, with **egressus** (**Labienus**) as the antecedent, is understood as the antecedent. The pluperfect denotes an action completed in past time (A.G. 477).

Metiosedum: Accusative of *place to which* without a preposition (city name) (A.G. 427.2). See Appendix A.

pervenit: The main verb of the main clause (A.G. 278.b).

(58.3-4) Id est oppidum Senonum, in insula Sequanae (4) positum, ut paulo ante de Lutetia diximus.

ante, *before, previously.*	**de**, *about, concerning.*
dico, dicere, dixi, dictus, *say.*	**in**, *on.*
insula, -ae, f., *island.*	**is, ea, id**, *he, she, it; that, this.*
Lutetia, -ae, f., *Lutetia.*	**oppidum, -i**, n., *fortified town, city.*
paulo, *by a little, just a little.*	**pono, ponere, posui, positus**, pass., often *be situated.*
Senones, -um, m., pl., *the Senones.*	**Sequana, -ae**, f., *the Sequana river.*
sum, esse, fui, futurus, *be.*	**ut**, *as.*

Id: Singular, neuter, nominative demonstrative pronoun used substantively (A.G. 296.2). The antecedent is **Metiosedum** (A.G. 297.e). Nominative subject (A.G. 339).

est: The main verb of the main clause (A.G. 278.b). The present tense is not the historical present but denotes a state as now existing in present time (A.G. 465.1).

oppidum: Singular, neuter, nominative predicate noun after **est** (A.G. 283-84).

Senonum: Possessive genitive with **oppidum** of the tribe name **Senones** (A.G. 343). See Appendix A.

in insula Sequanae: Ablative of *place where* with the preposition **in** (locative ablative) (A.G. 426.3). **Sequanae**: Partitive genitive with **insula** (A.G. 346.a). See Appendix A.

positum: Nominative perfect, passive, participle used as an adjective modifying **oppidum** (A.G. 494.a).

ut ... diximus: The relative adverb **ut** ("as") with the indicative introduces a parenthetical remark (*OLD* **ut** 12). For the reference see 57.1-2. **diximus**: The main verb of the subordinate clause (A.G. 278.b). The personal pronoun **nos** is understood as the subject but is not expressed except for distinction or emphasis (A.G. 295.a). In Book 7, Caesar refers to himself only in the third person, either in the singular or occasionally in the plural (see **Caesar** at 1.1). Siedler counts 11 uses of the first person plural in Book 7 (Siedler, 46). These uses are at 17.1, 23.2, 25.1, 37.1, 48.1, 58.4, 70.1, 76.1, 79.2, 83.8, and 85.4.

paulo: Adverb (A.G. 320-21).

ante: Adverb (A.G. 320-21 and 433.1).

de Lutetia: Prepositional phrase, **de** with the ablative here means "about, concerning" (*OLD* **de** 12). **Lutetia**: See Appendix A.

(58.4-5) Deprehensis navibus circiter quinquaginta celeriterque coniunctis atque eo militibus iniectis et rei novitate perterritis oppidanis, quorum magna pars erat ad bellum evocata, sine contentione (5) oppido potitur.

ad, *for, for the purpose of.*
bellum, -i, n., *war.*
circiter, *about.*

contentio, -onis, f., *struggle, fight, contest, dispute, controversy.*
eo, *thither, there.*
evoco, -are, -avi, -atus, *call out, call forth, call, summon.*
magnus, -a, -um, *great, large.*
navis, -is, f., *ship, vessel.*
oppidani, -orum, m., pl., *townspeople, inhabitants of the town.*
pars, partis, f., *part, portion.*

potior, potiri, potitus, *obtain possession of, become master of.*
qui, quae, quod, *who, which, what.*
res, rei, f., *matter, affair, event.*

atque, *and.*
celeriter, *quickly, speedily, at once, immediately.*
coniungo, -iungere, -iunxi, -iunctus, *join together, unite, join.*
deprehendo, -hendere, -hendi, -hensus, *seize.*
et, *and.*
inicio, -icere, -ieci, -iectus, *place on, put on.*
miles, -itis, m., *soldier, foot-solider.*
novitas, -tatis, f., *novelty, newness, strangeness.*
oppidum, -i, n., *fortified town, city.*
perterreo, -terrere, -----, -territus, *greatly alarm, frighten, terrify, dismay.*
-que, *and.*
quinquaginta, *fifty.*
sine, *without.*

Deprehensis ... navibus ... –que ... coniunctis ... atque ... militibus iniectis ... et ... perterritis oppidanis: Notice how the three consecutive ablative absolutes gives the impression of rapidity to the events

Deprehensis navibus circiter quinquaginta celeriterque coniunctis: Ablative absolute (A.G. 419-20). **Deprehensis ... coniunctis**: The perfect tense of the participles represents the action as completed at the time indicated by the tense of the main verb (A.G. 489). **circiter**: Adverb (A.G. 320-21). **quinquaginta**: Indeclinable cardinal number used as an adjective modifying **navibus** (A.G. 132-35). **celeriter**: Adverb (A.G. 214.b and 320-21). **-que**: The enclitic conjunction connects the two participles **Deprehensis ... coniunctis** modifying **navibus** (A.G. 324.a). Two adjectives belonging to the same noun are regularly connected by a conjunction (A.G. 323.d). **atque**: The conjunction connects the first and second ablative absolutes and means "and" (*OLD* **atque** 12).

eo militibus iniectis: Ablative absolute (A.G. 419-20). **eo**: Adverb (A.G. 217.a and 320-21). **iniectis**: The perfect tense of the participle represents the action as completed at the time indicated by the tense of the main verb (A.G. 489).

et: The conjunction connects the second and third ablative absolutes (A.G. 324.a).

rei novitate perterritis oppidanis: Ablative absolute (A.G. 419-20). **rei**: Possessive genitive with **novitate** (A.G. 343). **novitate**: Ablative of cause without a preposition (A.G. 404). **perterritis**: The perfect tense of the participle represents the action as completed at the time indicated by the tense of the main verb (A.G. 489).

quorum ... erat ... evocata: Relative clause (A.G. 303). **quorum**: Plural, masculine, genitive relative pronoun used substantively (A.G. 305). The antecedent is **oppidanis** (A.G. 307). Partitive genitive with **pars** (A.G. 346.a.1). **erat ... evocata**: The main verb of the subordinate clause (A.G. 278.b). The pluperfect denotes an action completed in past time (A.G. 477). The pluperfect passive verb is here split (tmesis) (A.G. 640).

magna pars: Nominative subject (A.G. 339).

ad bellum: Prepositional phrase, **ad** with the accusative here implies purpose and means "for, for the purpose of" (*OLD* **ad** 44).

sine contentione: Prepositional phrase, **sine** with the ablative means "with" (*OLD* **sine** 1).

oppido: Ablative direct object of the deponent verb **potitur** (A.G. 410).

potitur: The main verb of the main clause (A.G. 278.b). The historical present, giving vividness to the narrative, is present in Chapter 58 (A.G. 469). This usage, common in all languages, comes from imagining past events as going on before our eyes (*repraesentatio*) (A.G. 469 Note). The pronoun **is**, with **egressus** (**Labienus**) as the antecedent, is understood as the antecedent.

(58.5-6) Refecto ponte, quem superioribus diebus hostes resciderant, exercitum traducit et secundo flumine (6) ad Lutetiam iter facere coepit.

ad, *to, towards.*

coepi, -isse, coeptus, *begin, start, commence.*

dies, -ei, m. and f., *day*.
exercitus, -us, m., *army*.
flumen, -inis, n., *stream, river*.
iter, itineris, n., *march, journey*.
pons, pontis, m., *bridge*.
reficio, -ficere, -feci, -fectus, *repair, refit*.

secundus, -a, -um, *moving with, traveling with, down*.
traduco, -ducere, -duxi, -ductus, *lead across, bring over, bring across*.

et, *and*.
facio, facere, feci, factus, *make*.
hostis, -is, m., *enemy, foe*; pl., *the enemy*.
Lutetia, -ae, f., *Lutetia*.
qui, quae, quod, *who, which, what*.
rescindo, -scindere, -scidi, -scissus, *cut down, break up, destroy*.
superior, -or, -us, *former, earlier, previous*.

Refecto ... resciderant: Ablative absolute with a dependent clause.
Refecto ponte: Ablative absolute (A.G. 419-20). **Refecto**: The perfect tense of the participle represents the action as completed at the time indicated by the tense of the main verb (A.G. 489). "Across the Seine at Melun." (Kelsey, 420)
quem ... resciderant: Relative clause (A.G. 303). **quem**: Singular, masculine, accusative relative pronoun used substantively (A.G. 305). The antecedent is **ponte** (A.G. 307). Accusative direct object of **resciderant** (A.G. 387). **resciderant**: The main verb of the subordinate clause (A.G. 278.b). The pluperfect denotes an action completed in past time (A.G. 477).
superioribus diebus: Ablative of *time when* (A.G. 423.1). **superioribus**: Defective comparative adjective (A.G. 130.b).
hostes: Nominative subject (A.G. 339).
exercitum: Accusative direct object of **traducit** (A.G. 387).
traducit: The main verb of the coordinate clause **Refecto ... traducit** (A.G. 278.a). The pronoun **is**, with **egressus (Labienus)** as the antecedent, is understood as the antecedent.
et: The conjunction connects the two main verbs **traducit ... coepit** (A.G. 324.a).
secundo flumine: Ablative of *way by which* without a preposition (A.G. 429.a). The phrase **secundo flumine** means "travelling with the current, downstream" (*OLD secundus*1 2).
ad Lutetiam: Accusative of *place to which* with the preposition **ad**; **ad** with the name of a town denotes "towards, to the neighborhood of" (A.G. 428.a). **Lutetiam**: See Appendix A.
iter: Accusative direct object of the infinitive **facere** (A.G. 387 and 451.3). The phrase **iter facere** is an idiom that means "to march or travel" (*OLD* **iter** 1.b).
facere: Complementary infinitive after **coepit** (A.G. 456).
coepit: The main verb of the coordinate clause **secundo ... coepit** (A.G. 278.a). The pronoun **is**, with **egressus (Labienus)** as the antecedent, is understood as the antecedent.

(58.6) **Hostes, re cognita ab eis qui Metiosedo fugerant, Lutetiam incendi pontisque eius oppidi rescindi iubent;**

ab, *from*.

fugio, fugere, fugi, -----, *flee, run away, make off*.
incendo, -cendere, -cendi, -census, *set on fire, burn*.
iubeo, iubere, iussi, iussus, *order, give orders, bid, command*.
Metiosedum, -i, n., *Metiosedum*.
pons, pontis, m., *bridge*.
qui, quae, quod, *who, which, what*.
rescindo, -scindere, -scidi, -scissus, *cut down, break up, destroy*.

cognosco, -gnoscere, -gnovi, cognitus, *learn, ascertain, recognize*.
hostis, -is, m., *enemy, foe*; pl., *the enemy*.
is, ea, id, *he, she, it; that, this*.
Lutetia, -ae, f., *Lutetia*.
oppidum, -i, n., *fortified town, city*.
-que, *and*.
res, rei, f., *situation, affair, matter*.

Hostes: Nominative subject of **iubent** (A.G. 339).
re ... fugerant: Ablative absolute with a dependent clause.
re cognita ab eis: Ablative absolute (A.G. 419-20). **cognita**: The perfect tense of the participle represents the action as completed at the time indicated by the tense of the main verb (A.G. 489). **ab eis**: Ablative of source with the preposition **ab** (A.G. 403.1). **eis**: Plural, masculine, ablative demonstrative pronoun used substantively (A.G. 296.2). The pronoun is correlative to the relative clause **qui ... fugerant** (A.G. 297.d).
qui ... fugerant: Relative clause (A.G. 303). **qui**: Plural, masculine, nominative relative pronoun used substantively (A. G. 305). The antecedent is **eis** (A.G. 307). Nominative subject (A.G. 339). **fugerant**: The main verb of the subordinate clause (A.G. 278.b). The pluperfect denotes an action completed in past time (A.G. 477).
Metiosedo: Ablative of *place from which* without a preposition (city name) (A.G. 427.1). See Appendix A.
Lutetiam incendi: Subject accusative with the infinitive after **iubent**. The construction is equivalent to a substantive clause of purpose (A.G. 563.a). **Lutetiam**: See Appendix A.
pontisque ... rescindi: A subject accusative with the infinitive after **iubent**. The construction is equivalent to a substantive clause of purpose (A.G. 563.a). **pontis**: Accusative plural noun, -is for -es is the regular form in mixed i-stem nouns (A.G. 71-2). -que: The enclitic conjunction connects the two infinitives **incendi ... rescindi** (A.G. 324.a).
eius oppidi: Possessive genitive with **pontis** (A.G. 343). **eius**: Singular, neuter, genitive demonstrative pronoun used as an adjective modifying **oppidi** (A.G. 296.1 and a).
iubent: The main verb of the main clause (A.G. 278.b).

(58.6) **ipsi profecti a palude ad ripas Sequanae e regione Lutetiae contra Labieni castra considunt.**

a(b), *from, out of.*
castra, -orum, n., pl., *camp, encampment.*
contra, *directed at, facing.*
ipse, -a, -um, *he, they,* with or without *himself, themselves.*
Lutetia, -ae, f., *Lutetia.*
proficiscor, -ficisci, -fectus, *set out, depart, proceed.*
ripa, -ae, f., *bank* (of a stream).

ad, *to, towards.*
consido, -sidere, -sedi, -sessus, *halt, encamp.*
e(x), *directly opposite.*
Labienus, -i, m., *Labienus.*
palus, -udis, f., *marsh, swamp, bog, morass.*
regio, -onis, f., *region, territory.*
Sequana, -ae, f., *the Sequana river.*

ipsi profecti: Nominative subject of **considunt** (A.G. 339). **ipsi**: Plural, masculine, nominative demonstrative pronoun used substantively (A.G. 296.2 and 298.d). The antecedent is **hostes** (A.G. 298). The pronoun is here emphatic (A.G. 298.d.1). **profecti**: Nominative perfect, deponent, participle used as a predicate, where in English a phrase or a subordinate clause would be more normal (A.G. 496).
a ... ad ... e ... contra: Four prepositional phrases in a row. The first two go with **profecti** and the second two with **considunt**.
a palude: Ablative of *place from which* with the preposition **a(b)** (A.G. 426.1).
ad ripas Sequanae: Accusative of *place to which* with the preposition **ad** (A.G. 426.2). **Sequanae**: Partitive genitive with **ripas** (A.G. 346.a). See Appendix A.
e regione Lutetiae: Prepositional phrase, **e(x)** with the ablative of **regio** means "directly opposite" with the genitive (*OLD* regio 2.a). **Lutetiae**: Possessive genitive with **regione** (A.G. 343). See Appendix A.
contra Labieni castra: Prepositional phrase, **contra** with the accusative here means "directed at, facing" (*OLD* contra 13). **Labieni**: Possessive genitive with **castra** (A.G. 343). See Appendix A.
consadunt: The main verb of the simple sentence (A.G. 278.1).

(59.1-2) Iam Caesar a Gergovia discessisse audiebatur, iam de Aeduorum defectione et secundo Galliae motu rumores adferebantur, Gallique in colloquiis interclusum itinere et Ligere Caesarem inopia frumenti coactum in provinciam (2) contendisse confirmabant.

a(b), *from the vicinity of.*
Aedui, -orum, m., pl., *the Aedui.*
Caesar, -aris, m., *Caesar.*
colloquium, -i, n., *conference, interview.*
contendo, -tendere, -tendi, -tentus, *hasten, make haste, push forward.*
defectio, -onis, f., *revolt, rebellion.*

et, *and.*
Galli, -orum, m., *the Gauls.*
Gergovia, -ae, f., *Gergovia.*
in, *in; to, into, towards.*
intercludo, -cludere, -clusi, -clusus, *shut off, cut off, block up, blockade.*
Liger, -eris, m., *the Loire River.*
provincia, -ae, f., *the province.*
rumor, -oris, m., *report.*

adfero, -ferre, attuli, allatus, *bring, convey, deliver.*
audio, -ire, -ivi or -ii, -itus, *hear.*
cogo, cogere, coegi, coactus, *compel, force, oblige.*
confirmo, -are, -avi, -atus, *assert, declare.*
de, *about, concerning.*
discedo, -cedere, -cessi, -cessurus, *go away, depart, leave.*
frumentum, -i, n., *grain.*
Gallia, -ae, f., *Gaul.*
iam ... iam, *first ... then.*
inopia, -ae, f., *want, lack, need, scarcity.*
iter, itineris, n., *road, route, march.*
motus, -us, m., *disturbance, revolt, uprising.*
-que, *and.*
secundus, -a, -um, *favorable, propitious, fortunate.*

Iam ... iam: The repetition of the adverb means "first ... then" (*OLD* iam 1.d).
Caesar: Nominative subject of **audiebatur** (A.G. 339). See Appendix A.
a Gergovia: Ablative of *place from which* with the preposition **a(b)**; when **ab** is used with a city name it means "from the vicinity of" (A.G. 428.a). **Gergovia**: See Appendix A.
discessisse: Infinitive without a subject accusative in indirect discourse after the passive verb **audiebatur** (A.G. 577 ff. and 582).
audiebatur: The main verb of the coordinate clause **Iam ... audiebatur** (A.G. 278.a).
de Aeduorum defectione et secundo Galliae motu: Prepositional phrase, **de** with the ablative here means "about, concerning" (*OLD* de 12). **Aeduorum**: Possessive genitive with **defectione** (A.G. 343). See Appendix A. **et**: The conjunction connects the two ablative nouns in the prepositional phrase (A.G. 324.a). **secundo**: "favorable" from the Gallic viewpoint. **Galliae**: Locative case of **Gallia, -ae**, f. (A.G. 43.c). See Appendix A.
rumores: Nominative subject of **adferebantur** (A.G. 339). Here, the noun **rumor** does not have the pejorative sense of "rumour, gossip" (*OLD* rumor 2), but means "a report or rumour of some particular occurrence" (*OLD* rumor 3).
adferebantur: The main verb of the coordinate clause **iam ... adferebantur** (A.G. 278.a).
Gallique: Nominative subject of **confirmabant** (A.G. 339). **Galli**: See Appendix A. **-que**: The enclitic conjunction connects the two main verbs **adferebantur ... confirmabant** (A.G. 324.a).
in colloquiis: Prepositional phrase, **in** with the ablative here means "in" (expressing an abstract location) (*OLD* in 26). "i.e. probably between Gallic cavalry, serving with the Romans, and their own countrymen." (Edwards, 463)
interclusum ... Caesarem ... coactum ... contendisse: Accusative/infinitive construction in indirect discourse after **confirmabant** (A.G. 577 ff.). **interclusum ... coactum**: Two accusative perfect, passive, participles used as a predicate modifying **Caesarem**, where in English a phrase or a subordinate clause would be more normal (A.G. 496). Normally a conjunction connects two adjectives modifying one noun but here there is asyndeton (A.G. 323.d and 323.b). **Caesarem**: See Appendix A. **contendisse**: Perfect

infinitive; the tense of the infinitive in indirect discourse is relative to that of the verb of saying (A.G. 584).

itinere et Ligere: Two ablatives of separation without a preposition after **interclusum** (A.G. 401). **et**: The conjunction connects the two ablative nouns (A.G. 324.a). **Ligere**: See Appendix A.

inopia: Ablative of cause without a preposition after **coactum** (A.G. 404).

frumenti: Objective genitive with **inopia** (A.G. 348).

in provinciam: Accusative of *place to which* with the preposition **in** (A.G. 426.2). **provinciam**: See Appendix A.

confirmabant: The main verb of the coordinate clause **Gallique ... confirmabant** (A.G. 278.a).

(59.2-3) **Bellovaci autem, defectione Aeduorum cognita, qui ante erant per se infideles, manus (3) cogere atque aperte bellum parare coeperunt.**

Aedui, -orum, m., pl., *the Aedui*.	**ante**, *before, previously*.
aperte, *openly, clearly, manifestly*.	**atque**, *and*.
autem, *but, however*.	**Bellovaci, -orum**, m., pl., *the Bellovaci*.
bellum, -i, n., *war, warfare*.	**coepi, -isse, coeptus**, *begin, start, commence*.
cognosco, -gnoscere, -gnovi, cognitus, *learn, ascertain, recognize*.	**cogo, cogere, coegi, coactus**, *bring together, collect, gather, assemble*.
defectio, -onis, f., *revolt, rebellion*.	**infidelis, -e**, *unfaithful, faithless*.
manus, -us, f., *band, force*.	**paro, -are, -avi, -atus**, *prepare, make ready, make ready for*.
per, (with **se**), *on their own account*.	**qui, quae, quod**, *who, which, what*.
sui, sibi, se, or **sese**, nom. wanting, *themselves*.	**sum, esse, fui, futurus**, *be*.

Bellovaci: Nominative subject of **coeperunt** (A.G. 339). See Appendix A.

autem: Postpositive conjunction (A.G. 324.j and 599.b).

defectione Aeduorum cognita: Ablative absolute (A.G. 419-20). **Aeduorum**: Possessive genitive with **defectione** (A.G. 343). See Appendix A. **cognita**: The perfect tense of the participle represents the action as completed at the time indicated by the tense of the main verb (A.G. 489).

qui ... infideles: Relative clause (A.G. 303). **qui**: Plural, masculine, nominative relative pronoun used substantively (A. G. 305). The antecedent is **Bellovaci** (A.G. 307). Nominative subject (A.G. 339). **infideles**: Plural, masculine, nominative predicate adjective modifying **qui** after **erant** (A.G. 285.2). The adverbial prefix **in-**, modifying an adjective, means "not" (A.G. 267.d.1).

ante ... per se: The point here is that previously the Bellovaci had had a long history of warfare against the Romans alone; now they are more than willing to join a general uprising, but on their own terms (see 75.5)

ante: Adverb (A.G. 320-21 and 433.1).

erant: The main verb of the subordinate clause (A.G. 278.b).

per se: Prepositional phrase, **per** with the accusative **se** means "on their own account" (*OLD* **per** 11). **se**: Plural, masculine, accusative direct reflexive pronoun (A.G. 300.1). The antecedent is **qui**, the subject of **erant** (A.G. 299).

manus: Accusative direct object of the infinitive **cogere** (A.G. 387 and 451.3).

cogere: Complementary infinitive after **coeperunt** (A.G. 456).

atque: The conjunction connects the two infinitives and means "and" (*OLD* **atque** 12).

aperte: Adverb (A.G. 214.a and 320-21).

bellum: Accusative direct object of the infinitive **parare** (A.G. 387 and 451.3).

parare: Complementary infinitive after **coeperunt** (A.G. 456).

coeperunt: The main verb of the main clause (A.G. 278.b).

(59.3-5) **Tum Labienus tanta rerum commutatione longe aliud sibi capiendum consilium atque antea senserat intellegebat, (4) neque iam ut aliquid adquireret proelioque hostis lacesseret sed ut incolumem exercitum Agedincum reduceret cogita(5)bat.**

adquiro, -quirere, -quisivi, -quisitus, *gain further*.	**Agedincum, -i**, n., *Agedincum*.
aliquis, aliqua, aliquid, *some one, anybody, something, anything*.	**alius, -a, -ud**, *other, another, different*.
antea, *previously, before, formerly*.	**atque**, *than*.
capio, capere, cepi, captus, *form, adopt*.	**cogito, -are, -avi, -atus**, *consider, think, plan*.
commutatio, -onis, f., *change, alteration*.	**consilium, -i**, n., *plan, design, policy*.
exercitus, -us, m., *army*.	**hostis, -is**, m., *enemy, foe*; pl., *the enemy*.
iam, *now*.	**incolumis, -e**, *safe, unharmed, uninjured, unhurt*.
intellego, -legere, -lexi, -lectus, *understand, see clearly, perceive*.	**Labienus, -i**, m., *Labienus*.
lacesso, -ere, -ivi, -itus, *provoke, assail, attack*.	**longe**, *far, by far*.
neque, *and ... not*.	**proelium, -i**, n., *battle, combat, engagement*.
-que, *and*.	**reduco, -ducere, -duxi, -ductus**, *lead back, conduct back*.
res, rei, f., *affair, circumstance*.	**sed**, *but*.
sentio, sentire, sensi, sensus, *think, deem, judge, imagine, suppose*.	**sui, sibi, se,** or **sese**, nom. wanting, *himself*.
tantus, -a, -um, *so great, so large, such*.	**tum**, *then, thereupon*.
ut, *how*.	

Tum: Adverb (A.G. 271.b and 320-21).

Labienus: Nominative subject of **intellegebat ... cogitabat** (A.G. 339). See Appendix A.

tanta rerum commutatione: Ablative absolute with an adjective (**tanta**) taking the place of a participle (there is no participle for "being") (A.G. 419.a-20). **rerum**: Objective genitive with **commutatione** (A.G. 348).

longe: Adverb (A.G. 214.a and 320-21).

aliud ... capiendum (esse) consilium: Accusative/infinitive construction in indirect discourse after **intellegebat** (A.G. 577 ff.).

capiendum consilium: The phrase **consilium capere** is an idiom that means "to adopt or form a plan" (*OLD* **capio** 9.e). **capiendum (esse)**: Supply **esse** to form the second periphrastic (passive) present infinitive with the gerundive implying necessity (A.G. 194.b and 196). The tense of the infinitive in indirect discourse is relative to that of the verb of saying (A.G. 584).

sibi: Singular, masculine, dative indirect reflexive pronoun (A.G. 300.2). The antecedent is **Labienus**, the subject of **intellegebat** (A.G. 299). Dative of agent with the gerundive **capiendum** (A.G. 374).

(aliud) ... atque ante senserat: Subordinate clause (A.G. 278.b). **(aliud) ... atque**: The adjective followed by the conjunction means "other than" (A.G. 407.d). **antea**: Adverb (A.G. 320-21). **senserat**: The main verb of the subordinate clause (A.G. 278.b). A dependent clause in indirect discourse normally takes the subjunctive unless it is merely explanatory or contains statements which are regarded as true independently of the quotation in which case it takes the indicative (A.G. 580 and 583). The pronoun **is**, with **Labienus** as the antecedent, is understood as the subject (A.G. 271.a). The pluperfect denotes an action completed in past time (A.G. 477).

intellegebat: The main verb of the coordinate clause **Tum ... intellegebat** (A.G. 278.a).

neque: The conjunction here joins a negative clause to a preceding positive one (**Tum ... intellegebat**) and means "and ... not" (*OLD* **neque** 3).

iam: Adverb (A.G. 215.6, 217.b and 320-21).

ut ... adquireret ... lacesseret: Indirect question with the subjunctive; the phrase is the object of **cogitabat** (A.G. 573-75). **ut**: Interrogative adverb meaning "how" (*OLD* **ut** 1.b). **adquireret ... lacesseret**: The main verbs of the subordinate clause (A.G. 278.b). Imperfect subjunctives; the tense of the subjunctives is in secondary sequence and follows the rules for the sequence of tense for indirect questions after **cogitabat** (A.G. 575). The pronoun **is**, with **Labienus** as the antecedent, is understood as the subject of both verbs (A.G. 271.a).

aliquid: Singular, neuter, accusative indefinite pronoun used substantively (A.G. 151.e). Accusative direct object of **adquireret** (A.G. 387).

proelioque: Ablative of means (A.G. 409). **-que**: The enclitic conjunction connects the two main verbs in the indirect question (A.G. 324.a).

hostis: Accusative direct object of **lacesseret** (A.G. 387). Accusative plural noun; **-is** for **-es** is the regular form in i-stem nouns (A.G. 65-67 and 74.c).

sed: Coordinate conjunction (A.G. 324.d).

ut ... reduceret: Indirect question with the subjunctive; the phrase is the object of **cogitabat** (A.G. 573-75). **ut**: Interrogative adverb meaning "how" (*OLD* **ut** 1.b). **reduceret**: The main verb of the subordinate clause (A.G. 278.b). Imperfect subjunctive; the tense of the subjunctive is in secondary sequence and follows the rules for the sequence of tense for indirect questions after **cogitabat** (A.G. 575). The pronoun **is**, with **Labienus** as the antecedent, is understood as the subject (A.G. 271.a).

incolumem exercitum: Accusative direct object of **reduceret** (A.G. 387). **incolumem**: Singular, masculine, accusative adjective modifying **exercitum** but used to qualify the action of the verb, and so has the force of an adverb (A.G. 290).

Agedincum: Accusative of *place to which* without a preposition (city name) (A.G. 427.2). See Appendix A.

cogitabat: The main verb of the coordinate clause **iam ... cogitabat** (A.G. 278.a).

(59.5) Namque altera ex parte Bellovaci, quae civitas in Gallia maximam habet opinionem virtutis, instabant, alteram Camulogenus parato atque instructo exercitu tenebat;

alter ... alter, -era, -erum, *the one ... the other.*	**atque**, *and.*
Bellovaci, -orum, m., pl., *the Bellovaci.*	**Camulogenus, -i**, m., *Camulogenus.*
civitas, -tatis, f., *state, nation.*	**ex**, *on.*
exercitus, -us, m., *army.*	**Gallia, -ae**, f., *Gaul.*
habeo, habere, habui, habitus, *have, hold, possess.*	**in**, *in.*
insto, -stare, -stiti, -staturus, *be near at hand, approach.*	**instruo, -struere, -struxi, -structus**, *draw up, form.*
maximus, -a, -um, *greatest, very great, largest, very large.*	**namque**, *for indeed, for truly, and (with good reason).*
opinio, -onis, f., *reputation.*	**paro, -are, -avi, -atus**, *prepare, make ready.*
pars, partis, f., *side.*	**qui, quae, quod**, *who, which, what.*
teneo, tenere, tenui, -----, *hold, keep.*	**virtus, -utis**, f., *manliness, courage, bravery, valor, prowess, vigor.*

Namque: Causal conjunction (A.G. 223.a.3).

altera ex parte ... alteram (partem): "on one side ... the other (side)"; Labienus is between the proverbial rock and a hard place.

altera ex parte: Ablative of *position* with the preposition **ex** (A.G. 429.b). **altera ... alteram**: The repeated adjective means "The one ... the other (*OLD* **alter1** 5.b). **ex**: A monosyllabic preposition is often placed between a noun and its adjective (A.G. 599.d.2).

alteram: Singular, feminine, accusative adjective used substantively (A.G. 288). The noun **partem** is understood (A.G. 288.b). Accusative direct object of **tenebat** (A.G. 387). The construction changes with the function in the sentence: **Altera ex parte** is a prepositional phrase with the intransitive verb **instabant** while **alteram** is the direct object of the transitive verb **tenebat**.

Bellovaci: Nominative subject (A.G. 339). See Appendix A.

quae ... virtutis: Relative clause (A.G. 303). **quae**: See below. **virtutis**: See below.

quae civitas: Nominative subject (A.G. 339). **quae**: Singular, feminine, nominative relative pronoun (A.G. 305). The antecedent is **civitas** in its own clause (adjectival use) (A.G. 307.b).

in Gallia: Ablative of *place where* with the preposition **in** (locative ablative) (A.G. 426.3). **Gallia**: See Appendix A.

maximam ... opinionem: Accusative direct object of **habet** (A.G. 387). **maximam**: Irregular superlative adjective modifying **opinionem** (A.G. 129).

virtutis: Objective genitive with **opinionem** (A.G. 348).

habet: The main verb of the subordinate clause (A.G. 278.b). The present tense is not the historical present but denotes a state as now existing in present time (A.G. 465.1).

instabant: The main verb of the coordinate clause **Namque ... instabant** (A.G. 278.a).

alteram: See above.

Camulogenus: Nominative subject (A.G. 339). See Appendix A.

parato atque instructo exercitu: Ablative absolute (A.G. 419-20). **parato ... instructo**: The perfect tense of the participles represents the action as completed at the time indicated by the tense of the main verb (A.G. 489). **atque**: The conjunction connects the two participles in the ablative absolute and means "and" (*OLD* **atque** 12). Two adjectives belonging to the same noun are regularly connected by a conjunction (A.G. 323.d).

tenebat: The main verb of the coordinate clause **alteram ... tenebat** (A.G. 278.a).

(59.5-6) **tum legiones a praesidio atque impedimentis interclusas maxi(6)mum flumen distinebat.**

a(b), *from.*

distineo, -tinere, -tinui, -tentus, *keep apart, cut off, separate.*

impedimenta, -orum, n., pl., *heavy baggage, baggage.*

legio, -onis, f., *legion.*

praesidium, -i, n., *guard, garrison.*

atque, *and.*

flumen, -inis, n., *flowing water, current, stream, river.*

intercludo, -cludere, -clusi, -clusus, *shut off, cut off, block up, blockade.*

maximus, -a, -um, *greatest, very great, largest, very large.*

tum, *then, thereupon, besides*

tum: Adverb (A.G. 271.b and 320-21).

legiones ... interclusas: Accusative direct object of **distinebat** (A.G. 387). **interclusas**: Accusative perfect, passive, participle used as a predicate, where in English a phrase or a subordinate clause would be more normal (A.G. 496).

a praesidio atque impedimentis: Ablative of separation with the preposition **a(b)** after **interclusas** (A.G. 401). These were left by Labienus at Agedincum at 57.1. **atque**: The conjunction connects the two ablative nouns in the prepositional phrase and means "and" (*OLD* **atque** 12).

maximum flumen: Nominative subject (A.G. 339). "The Seine; Labienus was on the east side, while Agedincum lay to the southwest of the river." (Kelsey, 420) **maximum**: Irregular superlative adjective (A.G. 129).

distinebat: The main verb of the simple sentence (A.G. 278.1).

(59.6) **Tantis subito difficultatibus obiectis ab animi virtute auxilium petendum videbat.**

ab, *from.*

auxilium, -i, n., *help, aid, assistance, relief.*

obicio, -icere, -ieci, -iectus, *put in the way, present.*

subito, *suddenly, on a sudden.*

video, videre, visi, visus, *see, perceive, understand.*

animus, -i, m., *courage, spirit, temper, resolution, mind.*

difficultas, -tatis, f., *difficulty, trouble.*

peto, petere, petivi, and petii, petitus, *seek, get, secure.*

tantus, -a, -um, *so great, so large, such.*

virtus, -utis, f., *strength, vigor, effort.*

Tantis subito difficultatibus obiectis: Ablative absolute (A.G. 419-20). **subito**: Adverb (A.G. 320-21). **obiectis**: The perfect tense of the participle represents the action as completed at the time indicated by the tense of the main verb (A.G. 489).

ab animi virtute: Ablative of source with the preposition **ab** (A.G. 403.1). **animi**: Partitive genitive with **virtute** (A.G. 346.a.1). The noun **animus** here means "courage or spirit" (*OLD* **animus** 13).

auxilium petendum (esse): Accusative/infinitive construction in indirect discourse after **videbat** (A.G. 577 ff.). **petendum (esse)**: Supply **esse** to form the second periphrastic (passive) present infinitive with the gerundive implying necessity (A.G. 194.b and 196). The tense of the infinitive in indirect discourse is relative to that of the verb of saying (A.G. 584).

videbat: The main verb of the main clause (A.G. 278.b). The pronoun **is**, with **Labienus** as the antecedent, is understood as the subject (A.G. 271.a).

(60.1-2) **Sub vesperum consilio convocato, cohortatus ut ea quae imperasset diligenter industrieque administrarent, navis quas Metiosedo deduxerat singulas equitibus Romanis attribuit et prima confecta vigilia IIII milia passuum secundo flumine (2) silentio progredi ibique se exspectari iubet.**

administro, -are, -avi, -atus, *execute, manage, carry on, administer.*

cohortor, -ari, -atus, *encourage, urge, exhort, address.*

attribuo, -uere, -ui, -utus, *assign, allot, turn over to.*

conficio, -ficere, -feci, -fectus, *wear out, finish.*

consilium, -i, n., *deliberation, gathering for deliberation, council.*

deduco, -ducere, -duxi, -ductus, *lead, bring.*
eques, -itis, m., *knight, one of the equestrian order.*
exspecto, -are, -avi, -atus, *wait for, await.*
I, in expression of number, *1.*
impero, -are, -avi, -atus, *command, order.*
is, ea, id, *he, she, it; that, this.*

Metiosedum, -i, n., *Metiosedum.*
navis, -is, f., *ship, vessel.*
primus, -a, -um, *first, the first.*

-que, *and.*
Romanus, -a, -um, *Roman.*
silentium, -i, m., *silence.*
sub, *towards.*
ut, *so that.*
vigilia, -ae, f., *watch.*

convoco, -are, -avi, -atus, *call together, summon, assemble.*
diligenter, *carefully, industriously, diligently.*
et, *and.*
flumen, -inis, n., *stream, river.*
ibi, *in that place, there.*
industrie, *diligently.*
iubeo, iubere, iussi, iussus, *order, give orders, bid, command.*
milia, -um, n., pl., *thousand, thousands.*
passus, -us, m., *step, pace,* = 4 feet, 10 ¼ inches.
progredior, -gredi, -gressus, *advance, go forward, proceed.*
qui, quae, quod, *who, which, what.*
secundus, -a, -um, *moving with, traveling with, down.*
singuli, -ae, -a, *one to each.*
sui, sibi, se, or sese, nom. wanting, *himself.*
vesper, -eri, and -eris, m., *evening.*

Sub vesperum consilio convocato: Ablative absolute (A.G. 419-20). **Sub vesperum**: Prepositional phrase, **sub** with the accusative here means "towards" (A.G. 424.e). **convocato**: The perfect tense of the participle represents the action as completed at the time indicated by the tense of the main verb (A.G. 489).

cohortatus: Nominative perfect, deponent, participle used as a predicate, where in English a phrase or a subordinate clause would be more normal (A.G. 496). The pronoun **is**, with **Labienus** as the antecedent, is understood. Nominative subject of **attribuit** ... **iubet** (A.G. 339).

ut ... administrarent: Labienus' plan is as follows: He sends all his ships silently downstream four miles to wait for him; five cohorts he leaves as a guard for the camp; five noisy cohorts he sends upstream with the baggage and some small boats; he himself silently leads three legions downstream to meet up with the boats. The Gauls in Chapter 61 believe that his army has been split into three in order to flee. Actually, Labienus was using a 'divide and conquer' strategy. The troops and boats sent upstream were to be noisy in order to draw off the greatest amount of troops possible and the boats going downstream were to be quiet in order to cross the legions over while maintaining an element of surprise. This plan allowed the three legions under his command to cross the river unopposed and annihilate Camulogenus' reduced army. If the Gauls had concentrated their troops and attacked the three divisions one at a time, the Romans would have had little hope of escape. Once again, the Gauls *assumed* what the case was and assumed incorrectly.

ut ... administrarent: The conjunction **ut** ("so that") with the subjunctive is here a substantive clause of purpose which is used as the object of the participle **cohortatus** denoting an action directed toward the future (A.G. 563). **administrarent**: The main verb of the subordinate clause (A.G. 278.b). Imperfect subjunctive; the tense of the subjunctive is in secondary sequence after the historical present **attribuit** (A.G. 482-85, esp. 485.e). The pronoun **ei**, with the Roman leaders present at the council as the antecedent, is understood as the subject (A.G. 271.a).

ea: Plural, neuter, accusative demonstrative pronoun used substantively meaning "those things" (A.G. 296.2). The pronoun is correlative to the relative clause **quae imperasset** (A.G. 297.d). The accusative direct object of **administrarent** (A.G. 387).

quae imperasset: Relative clause; a clause dependent on a subjunctive clause (**ut ... administrarent**) takes the subjunctive when regarded as an integral part of that clause (attraction) (A.G. 303 and 593). **quae**: Plural, neuter, accusative relative pronoun used substantively (A.G. 305). The antecedent is **ea** (A.G. 307). Accusative direct object of the normally intransitive verb **imperasset** (A.G. 369 and 387). **imperasset**: The main verb of the subordinate clause (A.G. 278.b). Pluperfect subjunctive; the tense of the subjunctive is in secondary sequence and follows the rules for the sequence of tense after the historical present **attribuit** (A.G. 482-85, esp. 485.e). A contracted form of **imperavissent** (A.G. 181.a). The pronoun **is**, with **cohortatus** (**Labienus**) as the antecedent, is understood as the subject (A.G. 271.a).

diligenter: Adverb (A.G. 214.b and 320-21).

industrieque: Adverb (A.G. 214.a and 320-21). **-que**: The enclitic conjunction connects the nearly synonymous adverbs and means "and" (*OLD* -que 1.c).

navis ... singulas: Accusative direct object of the transitive verb **attribuit** (A.G. 387). **navis**: Accusative plural noun; **-is** for **-es** is the regular form in i-stem nouns (A.G. 65-67 and 74.c). **singulas**: Distributive numeral used as an adjective (A. G. 136-37).

quas ... deduxerat: Relative clause (A.G. 303). **quas**: Plural, feminine, accusative relative pronoun used substantively (A.G. 305). The antecedent is **navis** (A.G. 307). Accusative direct object of **deduxerat** (A.G. 387). **deduxerat**: The main verb of the subordinate clause (A.G. 278.b). The pronoun **is**, with **cohortatus** (**Labienus**) as the antecedent, is understood as the subject (A.G. 271.a). The pluperfect denotes an action completed in past time (A.G. 477).

Metiosedo: Ablative of *place from which* without a preposition (city name) (A.G. 427.1). See Appendix A.

equitibus Romanis: Dative indirect object of the transitive verb **attribuit** (A.G. 362). "These knights were officers waiting for an appointment in the army." (Kelsey, 420)

attribuit: The main verb of the coordinate clause **Sub ... attribuit** (A.G. 278.a). The historical present, giving vividness to the narrative, is present in Chapter 60 (A.G. 469). This usage, common in all languages, comes from imagining past events as going on before our eyes (*repraesentatio*) (A.G. 469 Note).

et: The conjunction connects the two main verbs **attribuit ... iubet** (A.G. 324.a).

prima confecta vigilia: Ablative absolute (A.G. 419-20). **prima**: Declinable ordinal number used as an adjective modifying **vigilia** (A.G. 132-35). The first watch runs until 9 o'clock. **confecta**: The perfect tense of the participle represents the action as completed at the time indicated by the tense of the main verb (A.G. 489).

IIII milia passuum: Accusative of *extent of space* (A.G. 425). **IIII**: Roman numeral used as an adjective modifying **milia** (A.G. 133). **milia**: Accusative plural; in the plural **mille** declines as a neuter noun (A.G. 134.d). **passuum**: Partitive genitive with **milia** (346.2).

secundo flumine: Ablative of *way by which* without a preposition (A.G. 429.a). The phrase **secundo flumine** means "downstream" (*OLD* secundus1 2).

silentio: Ablative of manner (A.G. 412.b).

(eos) progredi: A subject accusative with the infinitive after **iubet**. The construction is equivalent to a substantive clause of purpose (A.G. 563.a). Supply the pronoun **eos**, with **equitibus Romanis** as the antecedent, as the accusative subject.

ibique: Adverb (A.G. 215.5 and 320-21). **-que**: The enclitic conjunction connects the two infinitives (A.G. 324.a).

se ... exspectari: A subject accusative with the infinitive after **iubet**. The construction is equivalent to a substantive clause of purpose (A.G. 563.a). **se**: Singular, masculine, accusative direct reflexive pronoun (A.G. 300.1). The antecedent is **cohortatus (Labienus)**, the subject of **iubet** (A.G. 299).

iubet: The main verb of the coordinate clause **prima ... iubet** (A.G. 278.a).

(60.2-3) Quinque cohortis, quas minime firmas ad dimicandum esse existi(3)mabat, castris praesidio relinquit;

ad, *for, at, in.*	**castra, -orum**, n., pl., *camp, encampment.*
cohors, -hortis, f., *cohort, company*, (the tenth part of a legion).	**dimico, -are, -avi, -atus**, *fight, contend, struggle.*
existimo, -are, -avi, -atus, *think, consider, judge.*	**firmus, -a, -um**, *strong, firm, steadfast.*
minime, *least, not at all.*	**praesidium, -i**, n., *guard, garrison, protection.*
qui, quae, quod, *who, which, what.*	**quinque**, *five.*
relinquo, -linquere, -liqui, -lictus, *leave, leave behind.*	**sum, esse, fui, futurus**, *be.*

Quinque cohortis: Accusative direct object of **relinquit** (A.G. 387). Labienus splits the legion exactly in half. **Quinque**: Indeclinable cardinal number used as an adjective (A.G. 132-35). **cohortis**: Accusative plural noun, -is for -es is the regular form in mixed i-stem nouns (A.G. 71-2).

quas ... existimabat: Relative clause (A.G. 303). **quas**: See below. **existimabat**: The main verb of the subordinate clause (A.G. 278.b). The pronoun **is**, with **cohortatus (Labienus)** as the antecedent, is understood as the subject (A.G. 271.a).

quas ... firmas ... esse: Accusative/infinitive construction in indirect discourse after **existimabat** (A.G. 577 ff.). **quas**: Plural, feminine, accusative relative pronoun used substantively (A.G. 305). The antecedent is **cohortis** (A.G. 307). **firmas**: Plural, feminine, accusative predicate adjective modifying **quas** after **esse** (A.G. 283-84). **esse**: Present infinitive; the tense of the infinitive in indirect discourse is relative to that of the verb of saying (A.G. 584).

minime: Defective superlative adverb modifying **firmas** (A.G. 218.a).

ad dimicandum: Prepositional phrase, **ad** with the gerund here means "for, at, in" (*OLD* ad 42.b). **dimicandum**: Singular, neuter, accusative gerund (A.G. 501-02).

castris praesidio: Dative of the purpose or end (double dative). The dative of an abstract noun (**praesidio**) is used to show that for which a thing serves or which it accomplishes, with another dative of the person or thing affected (**castris**) (A.G. 382.1).

relinquit: The main verb of the main clause (A.G. 278.b). The pronoun **is**, with **cohortatus (Labienus)** as the antecedent, is understood as the subject (A.G. 271.a).

(60.3-4) quinque eiusdem legionis reliquas de media nocte cum omnibus impedimentis adverso (4) flumine magno tumultu proficisci imperat.

adversus, -a, -um, *adverse, up.*	**cum**, *with.*
de, *about.*	**flumen, -inis**, n., *stream, river.*
idem, eadem, idem, *the same.*	**impedimenta, -orum**, n., pl., *heavy baggage, baggage.*
impero, -are, -avi, -atus, *command, order.*	**legio, -onis**, f., *legion.*
magnus, -a, -um, *great, large, loud.*	**medius, -a, -um**, *in the middle, midst, middle, mid-.*
nox, noctis, f., *night.*	**omnis, -e**, *all.*
proficiscor, -ficisci, -fectus, *set out, depart, proceed.*	**quinque**, *five.*
reliquus, -a, -um, *remaining, the rest.*	**tumultus, -us**, m., *disturbance, confusion, disorder, uproar.*

quinque ... reliquas ... proficisci: A subject accusative with the infinitive after **imperat**. The construction is equivalent to a substantive clause of purpose (A.G. 563.a Note). **quinque**: Indeclinable cardinal number used as an adjective modifying **reliquas** (A.G. 132-35). **reliquas**: Plural, feminine, accusative adjective used substantively (A.G. 288). Carry down **cohortis** from above as the noun (A.G. 288.b).

eiusdem legionis: Partitive genitive with **reliquas** (A.G. 346.a.1). **eiusdem**: Singular, feminine, genitive demonstrative pronoun used as an adjective modifying **legionis** (A.G. 296.1 and a).

de media nocte: Prepositional phrase, **de** with the ablative here means "immediately after" (*OLD* de 4.b). **media**: The adjective designates not what object, but what part of it is meant (A.G. 293).

cum omnibus impedimentis: Ablative of accompaniment with the preposition **cum** (A.G. 413).

adverso flumine: Ablative of *way by which* without a preposition (A.G. 429.a). The phrase **adverso flumine** means "upstream" (*OLD* adversus1 6).

magno tumultu: Ablative of manner with a limiting adjective (A.G. 412).

imperat: The main verb of the main clause (A.G. 278.b). The pronoun **is**, with **cohortatus (Labienus)** as the antecedent, is understood as the subject (A.G. 271.a).

(60.4) Conquirit etiam lintres: has magno sonitu remorum incitatas in eandem partem mittit.

conquiro, -quirere, -quisivi, -quisitus, *seek out, hunt up, bring together.*
hic, haec, hoc, *this; he, she, it.*
in, *into, to, towards.*

linter, -tris, f., *boat, skiff.*
mitto, mittere, misi, missus, *send.*
remus, -i, m., *oar.*

etiam, *also, even.*
idem, eadem, idem, *the same.*
incito, -are, -avi, -atus, *drive, drive forward, set in rapid motion.*
magnus, -a, -um, *great, large, loud.*
pars, partis, f., *region, district, direction.*
sonitus, -us, m., *noise, sound.*

Conquirit ... lintres: The reversal of the normal word order (subject first, verb last) is called hyperbaton (A.G. 596) (Gotoff, 6-10).

Conquirit: The main verb of the simple sentence (A.G. 278.1). Verb first in the emphatic position (A.G. 589.d). The pronoun **is**, with **cohortatus (Labienus)** as the antecedent, is understood as the subject (A.G. 271.a).

etiam: Adverb (A.G. 320-21 and 322.a). The adverb normally proceeds the emphatic word (A.G. 322.a).

lintres: Accusative direct object of **Conquirit** (A.G. 387).

has ... incitatas: Accusative direct object of **mittit** (A.G. 387). **has**: Plural, feminine, accusative demonstrative pronoun used substantively (A.G. 296.2). The antecedent is **lintres** (A.G. 297.e). **incitatas**: Accusative perfect, passive, participle used as a predicate, where in English a phrase or a subordinate clause would be more normal (A.G. 496).

magno sonitu: Ablative of manner with a limiting adjective (A.G. 412).

remorum: Objective genitive with **sonitu** (A.G. 348).

in eandem partem: Accusative of *place to which* with the preposition **in** (A.G. 426.2). That is, upstream with the second half of the split legion. **eandem**: Singular, feminine, accusative demonstrative pronoun used as an adjective modifying **partem** (A.G. 296.1 and a).

mittit: The main verb of the simple sentence (A.G. 278.1). The pronoun **is**, with **cohortatus (Labienus)** as the antecedent, is understood as the subject (A.G. 271.a).

(60.4) Ipse post paulo silentio egressus cum tribus legionibus eum locum petit, quo navis appelli iusserat.

appello, -pellere, -puli, -pulsus, *bring in, put in, land.*
egredior, -gredi, -gressus, *go out, go forth, come forth, leave.*

is, ea, id, *he, she, it; that, this.*

legio, -onis, f., *legion.*
navis, -is, f., *ship, vessel.*
peto, petere, petivi, and **petii, petitus**, *make for, try to reach, seek.*
quo, *to which place, where.*
tres, tria, trium, *three.*

cum, *with.*
ipse, -a, -um, *he, they*, with or without *himself, themselves.*
iubeo, iubere, iussi, iussus, *order, give orders, bid, command.*
locus, -i, m., *place, position.*
paulo, *by a little, just a little.*
post, *after.*
silentium, -i, m., *silence.*

Ipse ... egressus: Nominative subject (A.G. 339). **Ipse**: Singular, masculine, nominative demonstrative pronoun used substantively (A.G. 296.2 and 298.d). The antecedent is **cohortatus (Labienus)** (A.G. 298). The pronoun distinguishes the principal personage (**Labienus**) from the subordinate persons (**equitibus Romanis**) (A.G. 298.d.3). **egressus**: Nominative perfect, deponent, participle used as a predicate, where in English a phrase or a subordinate clause would be more normal (A.G. 496).

post: Adverb (A.G. 320-21).

paulo: Adverb (A.G. 320-21).

silentio: Ablative of manner (A.G. 412.b).

cum tribus legionibus: Ablative of accompaniment with the preposition **cum** (A.G. 413). These are the 7th, 8th, and 12th legions. The number of the legion which Labienus has split is not disclosed in the narrative. **tribus**: Declinable cardinal number used as an adjective modifying **legionibus** (A.G. 132-35).

eum locum: Accusative direct object of **petit** (A.G. 387). **eum**: Singular, masculine, accusative demonstrative pronoun used as an adjective modifying **locum** (A.G. 296.1 and a).

petit: The main verb of the main clause (A.G. 278.b).

quo ... iusserat: Relative clause (A.G. 279.a). For the reference see 60.1-2. **quo**: Relative adverb meaning "to which place" (*OLD* quo1 3). **iusserat**: The main verb of the subordinate clause (A.G. 278.b). The pronoun **is**, with **Ipse (Labienus)** as the antecedent, is understood as the subject (A.G. 271.a). The pluperfect denotes an action completed in past time (A.G. 477).

navis appelli: A subject accusative with the infinitive after **iusserat**. The construction is equivalent to a substantive clause of purpose

(A.G. 563.a). i.e., downstream. **navis**: Accusative plural noun; **-is** for **-es** is the regular form in i-stem nouns (A.G. 65-67 and 74.c).

(61.1) Eo cum esset ventum, exploratores hostium, ut omni fluminis parte erant dispositi, inopinantes, quod magna subito erat coorta tempestas, a nostris opprimuntur;

a(b), *by.*
cum, *after, when.*

eo, *thither, there.*
flumen, -inis, n., *stream, river.*
inopinans, -antis, *not expecting, unaware, off one's guard.*
nostri, -orum, m., pl., *our men, our side.*
opprimo, -primere, -pressi, -pressus, *overwhelm, crush, destroy.*
quod, *because, since, for, as.*
tempestas, -tatis, f., *stormy weather, bad weather, a storm.*
venio, venire, veni, ventus, *come.*

coorior, -oriri, -ortus, *rise, spring up.*
dispono, -ponere, -posui, -positus, *distribute, station, post.*
explorator, -oris, m., *spy, scout.*
hostis, -is, m., *enemy, foe*; pl., *the enemy.*
magnus, -a, -um, *great, large.*
omnis, -e, *every.*
pars, partis, f., *part, portion, side.*
subito, *suddenly, on a sudden.*
ut, *as soon as, when.*

Eo: Adverb (A.G. 217.a and 320-21). The adverb **eo** normally stands outside the **cum** clause, as at 6.2, 7.5, 9.5, 33.3 and 61.1.
cum (id) esset ventum: Temporal clause; the relative adverb **cum** ("after, when") with the pluperfect subjunctive describes the circumstances that preceded the action of the main verb (A.G. 546). **esset ventum**: The main verb of the subordinate clause (A.G. 278.b). Impersonal use of the verb (A.G. 208.d). Supply **id** as the subject (A.G. 318.c).
exploratores: Nominative subject of **opprimuntur** (A.G. 339).
hostium: Partitive genitive with **exploratores** (A.G. 346.a.1).
ut ... erant dispositi: Temporal clause; the relative adverb **ut** with the pluperfect indicative means "as soon as, when" (A.G. 543). The pluperfect emphasizes the fact that the action expressed in the **ut** clause was completed before the action expressed in the main clause (*OLD* **ut** 26.c). **erant dispositi**: The main verb of the subordinate clause (A.G. 278.b). The pronoun **ei**, with **exploratores** as the antecedent, is understood as the subject (A.G. 271.a).
omni ... parte: Ablative of *place where* without a preposition (A.G. 429.1-2).
fluminis: Partitive genitive with **parte** (A.G. 346.a.1).
inopinantes: Plural, masculine, nominative predicate adjective modifying **exploratores** (A.G. 285).
quod ... erat coorta tempestas: Causal clause; the conjunction **quod** ("because") takes the indicative when the reason is given on the authority of the writer or speaker (A.G. 540.1). **erat coorta**: The main verb of the subordinate clause (A.G. 278.b). The pluperfect denotes an action completed in past time (A.G. 477). **tempestas**: See below.
magna ... tempestas: Nominative subject (A.G. 339). **tempestas**: The subject is in the last position (A.G. 597.b).
subito: Adverb (A.G. 320-21).
a nostris: Ablative of agent with the preposition **a(b)** after the passive verb **opprimuntur** (A.G. 405). **nostris**: Plural, masculine, ablative possessive pronoun used substantively to denote a special class (A.G. 302.d).
opprimuntur: The main verb of the main clause (A.G. 278.b). The historical present, giving vividness to the narrative, is present in Chapter 61 (A.G. 469). This usage, common in all languages, comes from imagining past events as going on before our eyes (*repraesentatio*) (A.G. 469 Note).

(61.2-3) (2) exercitus equitatusque equitibus Romanis administrantibus, (3) quos ei negotio praefecerat celeriter transmittitur.

administro, -are, -avi, -atus, *control, guide, superintend, direct.*
eques, -itis, m., *knight, one of the equestrian order.*
exercitus, -us, m., *army.*
negotium, -i, n., *business, enterprise.*

-que, *and.*
Romanus, -a, -um, *Roman.*

celeriter, *quickly, speedily, at once, immediately.*
equitatus, -us, m., *cavalry.*
is, ea, id, *he, she, it; that, this.*
praeficio, -ficere, -feci, -fectus, *place over, appoint to command.*
qui, quae, quod, *who, which, what.*
transmitto, -mittere, -misi, -missus, *send across, send over.*

exercitus equitatusque: Two nominative subjects (A.G. 339). **-que**: The enclitic conjunction connects the two nominative nouns (A.G. 324.a).
equitibus Romanis administrantibus: Ablative absolute (A.G. 419-20). **administrantibus**: The present participle represents the action as in progress at the time indicated by the tense of the main verb (A.G. 489).
quos ... praefecerat: Relative clause (A.G. 303). **quos**: Plural, masculine, accusative relative pronoun used substantively (A.G. 305). The antecedent is **equitibus** (A.G. 307). Accusative direct object of the transitive verb **praefecerat** (A.G. 387). **praefecerat**: The main verb of the subordinate clause (A.G. 278.b). The pronoun **is**, with **Ipse (Labienus)** as the antecedent, is understood as the subject (A.G. 271.a). The pluperfect denotes an action completed in past time (A.G. 477).
ei negotio: Dative indirect object of the transitive verb **praefecerat** (A.G. 362). **ei**: Singular, neuter, dative demonstrative pronoun used as an adjective modifying **negotio** (A.G. 296.1 and a).
celeriter: Adverb (A.G. 214.b and 320-21).
transmittitur: The main verb of the main clause (A.G. 278.b). Two singular subjects (**exercitus equitatusque**) normally take a verb

in the plural (A.G. 317). Here they are considered as a single whole and so the verb is singular (A.G. 317.b). "Across the Seine, not far below the Gallic camp." (Kelsey, 420)

(61.3) Uno fere tempore sub lucem hostibus nuntiatur in castris Romanorum praeter consuetudinem tumultuari et magnum ire agmen adverso flumine sonitumque remorum in eadem parte exaudiri et paulo infra milites navibus transportari.

adversus, -a, -um, *adverse, up.*

castra, -orum, n., pl., *camp, encampment.*
eo, ire, ivi, or **ii, iturus,** *go, pass, march, advance.*
exaudio, -dire, -divi, -ditus, *hear distinctly, hear plainly.*
flumen, -inis, n., *stream, river.*
idem, eadem, idem, *the same.*
infra, *below.*
magnus, -a, -um, *great, large.*
navis, -is, f., *ship, vessel.*
pars, partis, f., *region, district, direction.*
praeter, *out of line with, contrary to.*
remus, -i, m., *oar.*
sonitus, -us, m., *noise, sound.*
tempus, -oris, n., *time.*

tumultuor, -ari, -atus, also **-o, -are,** (pass., imper.), *there is disorder.*

agmen, -minis, n., *army on the march, marching column, line of march.*
consuetudo, -inis, f., *habit, practice, custom.*
et, *and.*
fere, *nearly,* with words denoting time, *about.*
hostis, -is, m., *enemy, foe;* pl., *the enemy.*
in, *in.*
lux, lucis, f., *daybreak.*
miles, -itis, m., *soldier, foot-solider.*
nuntio, -are, -avi, -atus, *announce, report.*
paulo, *by a little, just a little.*
-que, *and.*
Romani, -orum, m., pl., *the Romans.*
sub, *just before.*
transporto, -are, -avi, -atus, *carry over, convey across, transport.*
unus, -a, -um, *one, same.*

Uno ... tempore: Ablative of *time when* (A.G. 423.1). **Uno**: Declinable cardinal number used as an adjective modifying **tempore** (A.G. 132-35).
fere: Adverb (A.G. 320-21).
sub lucem: Prepositional phrase, **sub** with the accusative here expresses an idiomatic expression of time meaning "just before" (A.G. 424.e) (*OLD* **sub** 23).
hostibus: Dative indirect object of the passive verb **nuntiatur**, verbs which in the active voice take the accusative and dative retain the dative when used in the passive (A.G. 365).
(id) nuntiatur: The main verb of the simple sentence (A.G. 278.1). Impersonal use of the intransitive verb (A.G. 208.d and 582). Supply **id** as the subject (A.G. 318.c).
in castris Romanorum: Ablative of *place where* with the preposition **in** (locative ablative) (A.G. 426.3). **Romanorum**: Possessive genitive with **castris** (A.G. 343).
praeter consuetudinem: Prepositional phrase, **praeter** with the accusative here means "out of line with, contrary to" (*OLD* **praeter** 3).
tumultuari: Infinitive without a subject accusative in indirect discourse after the passive verb **nuntiatur** (A.G. 577 ff., esp. 582).
tumultuari: Impersonal, deponent infinitive with a passive meaning (A.G. 190.f) (*OLD* **tumultuor** 1). A passive verb is often used impersonally without a subject expressed or understood (A.G. 318.c). Present infinitive; the tense of the infinitive in indirect discourse is relative to that of the verb of saying (A.G. 584).
et: The conjunction connects the two infinitives **tumultuari ... ire** (A.G. 324.a).
magnum ire agmen: Accusative/infinitive construction in indirect discourse after **nuntiatur** (A.G. 577 ff., esp. 582). **ire**: Present infinitive; the tense of the infinitive in indirect discourse is relative to that of the verb of saying (A.G. 584).
adverso flumine: Ablative of *way by which* without a preposition (A.G. 429.a). The phrase **adverso flumine** means "upstream" (*OLD* **adversus1** 6).
sonitumque ... exaudiri: Accusative/infinitive construction in indirect discourse after **nuntiatur** (A.G. 577 ff., esp. 582). **-que**: The enclitic conjunction connects the two infinitives **ire ... exaudiri** (A.G. 324.a). **exaudiri**: Present infinitive; the tense of the infinitive in indirect discourse is relative to that of the verb of saying (A.G. 584).
remorum: Objective genitive with **sonitum** (A.G. 348).
in eadem parte: Ablative of *place where* with the preposition **in** (locative ablative) (A.G. 426.3). **eadem**: Singular, feminine, ablative demonstrative pronoun used as an adjective modifying **parte** (A.G. 296.1 and a).
et: The conjunction connects the two infinitives **exaudiri ... transportari** (A.G. 324.a).
paulo: Adverb (A.G. 320-21).
infra: Adverb (A.G. 320-21).
milites ... transportari: Accusative/infinitive construction in indirect discourse after **nuntiatur** (A.G. 577 ff., esp. 582).
transportari: Present infinitive; the tense of the infinitive in indirect discourse is relative to that of the verb of saying (A.G. 584).
navibus: Ablative of means or instrument (A.G. 409).

(61.4-5) (4) Quibus rebus auditis, quod existimabant tribus locis transire legiones atque omnis perturbatos defectione Aeduorum fugam parare, suas quoque copias in tris partis distribu(5)erunt.

Aedui, -orum, m., pl., *the Aedui.*
audio, -ire, -ivi or **-ii, -itus,** *hear.*

atque, *and.*
copiae, -arum, f., pl., *forces, troops.*

defectio, -onis, f., *revolt, rebellion.*

existimo, -are, -avi, -atus, *think, consider, judge.*
in, *into.*
loca, -orum, n., pl., *places.*
paro, -are, -avi, -atus, *prepare, make ready, make ready for.*
perturbo, -are, -avi, -atus, *disturb greatly, throw into confusion.*
quod, *because, since, for, as.*
res, rei, f., *matter, affair, event.*
transeo, -ire, -ivi, or -ii, -itus, *go over, go across, pass over, cross over.*

distribuo, -tribuere, -tribui, -tributus, *distribute, divide, apportion.*
fuga, -ae, f., *flight.*
legio, -onis, f., *legion.*
omnes, -ium, m., pl., *all men, all.*
pars, partis, f., *part, portion, share.*
qui, quae, quod, *who, which, what.*
quoque, *also, too.*
suus, -a, -um, *their,* with or without *own.*
tres, tria, trium, *three.*

Quibus rebus auditis: Ablative absolute (A.G. 419-20). **Quibus**: Plural, feminine, ablative relative pronoun (A.G. 305). The antecedent is **rebus** in its own clause (adjectival use) (A.G. 307.b). The relative does not introduce a relative clause but is a connecting relative; at the beginning of a clause the pronoun is often best rendered by a personal or demonstrative pronoun, with or without *and* (A.G. 308.f). **auditis**: The perfect tense of the participle represents the action as completed at the time indicated by the tense of the main verb (A.G. 489).
Quod existimabant ... parare: Causal clause; the conjunction **quod** ("because") takes the indicative when the reason is given on the authority of the writer or speaker (A.G. 540.1). **existimabant**: The main verb of the subordinate clause (A.G. 278.b). The pronoun **ei**, with **hostibus** as the antecedent, is understood as the subject (A.G. 271.a). **parare**: See below.
tribus locis: Ablative of *place where* without a preposition (A.G. 429.1-2). **tribus**: Declinable cardinal number used as an adjective (A.G. 132-35).
transire legiones: Accusative/infinitive construction in indirect discourse after **existimabant** (A.G. 577 ff.). **transire**: Present infinitive; the tense of the infinitive in indirect discourse is relative to that of the verb of saying (A.G. 584).
atque: The conjunction connects the two infinitives **transire ... parare** and means "and" (*OLD* atque 12).
omnis perturbatos ... parare: Accusative/infinitive construction in indirect discourse after **existimabant** (A.G. 577 ff.). **omnis**: Plural, masculine, accusative adjective used substantively (A.G. 288). Accusative plural adjective; -is for -es is the regular form in i-stem adjectives (A.G. 114.a and 116). **perturbatos**: Accusative perfect, passive, participle used as a predicate, where in English a phrase or a subordinate clause would be more normal (A.G. 496). **parare**: Present infinitive; the tense of the infinitive in indirect discourse is relative to that of the verb of saying (A.G. 584).
defectione: Ablative of cause without a preposition with **perturbatos** (A.G. 404).
Aeduorum: Possessive genitive with **defectione** (A.G. 343). See Appendix A.
fugam: Accusative direct object of the infinitive **parare** (A.G. 387 and 451.3).
suas ... copias: Accusative direct object of **distribuerunt** (A.G. 387). **suas**: Plural, feminine, accusative possessive pronoun used as an adjective modifying **copias** (A.G. 302).
quoque: Adverb (A.G. 320-21). The adverb follows the emphatic word (A.G. 322.a).
in tris partis: Prepositional phrase, **in** with the accusative here means "into" (*OLD* in 2). **tris**: Declinable cardinal number used as an adjective modifying **partis** (A.G. 132-35). -is for -es is an alternative accusative plural ending (A.G. 134.b). **partis**: Accusative plural noun, -is for -es is the regular form in mixed i-stem nouns (A.G. 71-2).
distribuerunt: The main verb of the main clause (A.G. 278.b). The pronoun **ei**, with **hostibus** as the antecedent, is understood as the subject (A.G. 271.a).

(61.5) Nam praesidio e regione castrorum relicto et parva manu Metiosedum versus missa, quae tantum progrediatur quantum naves processissent, reliquas copias contra Labienum duxerunt.

castra, -orum, n., pl., *camp, encampment.*
copiae, -arum, f., pl., *forces, troops.*
et, *and.*
Labienus, -i, m., *Labienus.*
Metiosedum, -i, n., *Metiosedum.*
nam, *for.*
parvus, -a, -um, *small, trifling, insignificant.*
procedo, -cedere, -cessi, -----, *advance, go forward.*

quantum, *to which, as.*
regio, -onis, f., *region, territory.*
reliquus, -a, -um, *remaining, the rest.*
versus, *towards, in the direction of.*

contra, *against, to meet.*
duco, ducere, duxi, ductus, *lead.*
e(x), *directly opposite.*
manus, -us, f., *band, force.*
mitto, mittere, misi, missus, *send.*
navis, -is, f., *ship, vessel.*
praesidium, -i, n., *guard, garrison.*
progredior, -gredi, -gressus, *advance, go forward, proceed.*
qui, quae, quod, *who, which, what.*
relinquo, -linquere, -liqui, -lictus, *leave, leave behind.*
tantum, *to such an extent, only so much, so far.*

Nam: Causal conjunction (A.G. 223.a.3).
praesidio e regione castrorum relicto: Ablative absolute (A.G. 419-20). **e regione castrorum**: Prepositional phrase, e(x) with the ablative of **regio** means "directly opposite" with the genitive (*OLD* regio 2.a). **castrorum**: Possessive genitive with **regione** (A.G. 343). **relicto**: The perfect tense of the participle represents the action as completed at the time indicated by the tense of the main verb (A.G. 489).
et: The conjunction connects the two ablative absolutes (A.G. 324.a).

parva ... processissent: Ablative absolute with dependent clauses.

parva manu Metiosedum versus missa: Ablative absolute (A.G. 419-20). **Metiosedum versus**: Prepositional phrase, **versus** is an adverb, used with prepositional force, placed after the accusative noun and means "towards" (A.G. 435) (*OLD* **versus2** 2).

Metiosedum: See Appendix A. **missa**: The perfect tense of the participle represents the action as completed at the time indicated by the tense of the main verb (A.G. 489).

quae ... progrediatur: A relative clause of purpose is introduced by a relative pronoun and takes the subjunctive (A.G. 531.2). **quae**: Singular, feminine, nominative relative pronoun used substantively (A.G. 305). The antecedent is **manu** (A.G. 307). Nominative subject (A.G. 339). The relative is here equivalent to **ut ea** (A.G. 531.2 Note). **progrediatur**: The main verb of the subordinate clause (A.G. 278.b). Present subjunctive; the tense of the subjunctive is normally in secondary sequence after the perfect tense **duxerunt** (A.G. 482-85). Here it is in primary sequence through *repraesentatio* (A.G. 485.e and 585.b Note). The Budé text adopts the reading **progrederetur** which follows the normal (secondary) sequence of tense and matches **processissent**.

tantum ... quantum: Correlatives meaning "to such an extent ... (to the extent) to which" (*OLD* **tantum** 7, **quantum2** 2). **tantum**: Adverbial use of the accusative pronoun (*OLD* **tantum** 7).

quantum ... processissent: Relative clause; a clause dependent on a subjunctive clause (**quae ... progrediatur**) takes the subjunctive when regarded as an integral part of that clause (attraction) (A.G. 279.a and 593). **quantum**: Relative adverb (*OLD* **quantum2** 2).

processissent: The main verb of the subordinate clause (A.G. 278.b). Pluperfect subjunctive; the tense of the subjunctive is in secondary sequence and follows the rules for the sequence of tense after **duxerunt** (A.G. 482-85). The pluperfect tense of the subjunctive is here standing for a future perfect tense (A.G. 484.c). The future perfect tense denotes action completed (at the time referred to), and hence is represented in the subjunctive by the pluperfect tense in secondary sequence (A.G. 484.c).

naves: Nominative subject (A.G. 339). "The lintres of 60.4, which were being rowed up-stream with great noise." (Kelsey, 421) **reliquas copias**: Accusative direct object of **duxerunt** (A.G. 387).

contra Labienum: Prepositional phrase, **contra** with the accusative here means "against, to meet" (*OLD* **contra** 15). **Labienum**: See Appendix A.

duxerunt: The main verb of the main clause (A.G. 278.b). The pronoun **ei**, with **hostibus** as the antecedent, is understood as the subject (A.G. 271.a). "The Gauls heard the uproar in the Roman camp, learned that a detachment was going up the river, and were informed by scouts of the approach of Labienus from below. Accordingly they separated their forces into three divisions, one of which went up-stream, another mounted guard on the bank of the Seine opposite the Roman camp, and a third went to meet Labienus. Thus the ruse of Labienus was successful in scattering the forces of the enemy, though not in taking them on the rear by surprise as he had perhaps intended." (Kelsey, 421)

(62.1-2) Prima luce et nostri omnes erant transportati et hostium (2) acies cernebatur.

acies, -ei, f., *line, army in battle array.*
et ... et, *both ... and.*
lux, lucis, f., *light*, (with **prima**), *daybreak.*
omnis, -e, *all.*
transporto, -are, -avi, -atus, *carry over, convey across, transport.*

cerno, cernere, -----, -----, *discern, see, perceive.*
hostis, -is, m., *enemy, foe*; pl., *the enemy.*
nostri, -orum, m., pl., *our men, our side.*
primus, -a, -um, *first.*

Prima luce: Ablative of *time when* (A.G. 423.1). **Prima**: Ordinal number used as an adjective (A.G. 132-35).

et ... et: The repeated conjunction means "both ... and", connecting the two main verbs **erant transportati ... cernebatur** (A.G. 323.e).

nostri omnes: Nominative subject (A.G. 339). "Labienus with three legions and the cavalry; five cohorts had remained at the camp, and the remaining five of the same legion had gone up-stream." (Kelsey, 421) **nostri**: Plural, masculine, nominative possessive pronoun used substantively to denote a special class (A.G. 302.d).

erant transportati: The main verb of the coordinate clause **Prima ... transportati** (A.G. 278.a). Although the pluperfect tense is normally used in subordinate clauses, its use as a main verb is frequent. The pluperfect denotes an action completed in past time (A.G. 477).

acies: Nominative subject (A.G. 339). "The division of the enemy that had marched down-stream from their camp." (Kelsey, 421) **hostium**: Possessive genitive with **acies** (A.G. 343).

cernebatur: The main verb of the coordinate clause **hostium ... cernebatur** (A.G. 278.a). Note the change from the pluperfect (**erant transportati**) to the imperfect tense.

(62.2-3) Labienus milites cohortatus ut suae pristinae virtutis et secundissimorum proeliorum retinerent memoriam atque ipsum Caesarem, cuius ductu saepe numero hostis superassent, praesentem adesse existimarent, (3) dat signum proeli.

adsum, -esse, affui, -----, *be at hand, be present.*
Caesar, -aris, m., *Caesar.*
do, dare, dedi, datus, *give.*
et, *and.*
hostis, -is, m., *enemy, foe*; pl., *the enemy.*
Labienus, -i, m., *Labienus.*
miles, -itis, m., *soldier, foot-solider.*
praesens, -entis, *in person.*
proelium, -i, n., *battle, combat, engagement.*

atque, *and.*
cohortor, -ari, -atus, *encourage, urge, exhort, address.*
ductus, -us, m., *lead, generalship, command.*
existimo, -are, -avi, -atus, *think, consider, judge.*
ipse, -a, -um, *himself.*
memoria, -ae, f., *memory, recollection, remembrance.*
numero, *quickly, rapidly.*
pristinus, -a, -um, *former, previous, earlier.*
qui, quae, quod, *who, which, what.*

retineo, -tinere, -tinui, -tentus, *retain, keep, maintain, uphold.*
secundus, -a, -um, sup. -issimus, *propitious, fortunate, favorable.*
suus, -a, -um, *their,* with or without *own.*
ut, *so that.*

saepe, *often, frequently.*
signum, -i, n., *signal.*
supero, -are, -avi, -atus, *surmount, overcome.*
virtus, -utis, f., *courage, bravery, valor, prowess.*

Labienus ... proeli: Stevens notes that "even the great Labienus, who realizes in a crisis that in the absence of his *imperator* the strength of character on which he must rely on is his own, twice advises his troops (he is the only *legatus* who is allowed a reported speech) to fight as though the imperator were at hand." (Stevens, 7-8)
Labienus ... cohortatus: Nominative subject of **dat** (A.G. 339). **Labienus:** See Appendix A. **cohortatus:** Nominative perfect, deponent, participle used as a predicate, where in English a phrase or a subordinate clause would be more normal (A.G. 496).
milites: Accusative direct object of the participle **cohortatus** (A.G. 387 and 488).
ut ... retinerent ... existimarent: The conjunction **ut** ("so that") with the subjunctive is here a substantive clause of purpose which is used as the object of the participle **cohortatus** denoting an action directed toward the future (A.G. 563). **retinerent ... existimarent:** The main verbs of the subordinate clause (A.G. 278.b). Imperfect subjunctives; the tense of the subjunctives is in secondary sequence and follows the rules for the sequence of tense after the historical present **dat** (A.G. 482-85, esp. 485.e). The pronoun **ei**, with **milites** as the antecedent, is understood as the subject of both verbs (A.G. 271.a).
suae pristinae virtutis et secundissimorum proeliorum: Two objective genitives with **memoriam** (A.G. 348). **suae:** Singular, feminine, genitive possessive pronoun used as an adjective modifying **virtutis** (A.G. 302). **et:** The conjunction connects the two genitive nouns **virtutis ... proeliorum** (A.G. 324.a). **secundissimorum:** Superlative adjective modifying **proeliorum** (A.G. 124).
memoriam: Accusative direct object of **retinerent** (A.G. 387).
atque: The conjunction connects the two main verbs in the purpose clause and means "and" (*OLD* atque 12).
ipsum Caesarem ... praesentem adesse: Accusative/infinitive construction in indirect discourse after **existimarent** (A.G. 577 ff.). **ipsum:** Singular, masculine, accusative demonstrative pronoun used as an adjective modifying **Caesarem** meaning "himself" (A.G. 296.1 and a and 298.c). **Caesarem:** See Appendix A. **praesentem:** Singular, masculine, accusative predicate adjective modifying **Caesarem**, when used as a predicate adjective it means "in person" (A.G. 283) (*OLD* preasens 1). **adesse:** Present infinitive; the tense of the infinitive in indirect discourse is relative to that of the verb of saying (A.G. 584).
cuius ... superassent: Relative clause; a clause dependent on a subjunctive clause (**ut ... existimarent**) takes the subjunctive when regarded as an integral part of that clause (attraction) (A.G. 303 and 593). **cuius:** Singular, masculine, genitive relative pronoun used substantively (A.G. 305). The antecedent is **Caesarem** (A.G. 307). Possessive genitive with **ductu** (A.G. 343). **superassent:** The main verb of the subordinate clause (A.G. 278.b). Pluperfect subjunctive; the tense of the subjunctive is in secondary sequence and follows the rules for the sequence of tense after the historical present **dat** (A.G. 482-85, esp. 485.e). A contracted form of **superavissent** (A.G. 181.a). The pronoun **ei**, with **milites** as the antecedent, is understood as the subject (A.G. 271.a).
ductu: Ablative of manner with a limiting adjective (**cuius**) (A.G. 418).
saepe: Adverb (A.G. 217.b and 320-21).
numero: Adverb (A.G. 320-21).
hostis: Accusative direct object of **superassent** (A.G. 387). Accusative plural noun; **-is** for **-es** is the regular form in i-stem nouns (A.G. 65-67 and 74.c).
dat: The main verb of the main clause (A.G. 278.b). The historical present, giving vividness to the narrative, is present in Chapter 62 (A.G. 469). This usage, common in all languages, comes from imagining past events as going on before our eyes (*repraesentatio*) (A.G. 469 Note).
signum: Accusative direct object of **dat** (A.G. 387).
proeli: Objective genitive with **signum** (A.G. 348). The singular genitive of nouns in **-ium** ended, until the Augustan Age, in a single **-i** (A.G. 49.b).

(62.3-4) Primo concursu ab dextro cornu, ubi septima legio constiterat, hostes pelluntur atque in fugam (4) coiciuntur;

ab, *on.*
concursus, -us, m., *onset, charge, running together.*
consisto, -sistere, -stiti, -stitus, *stop, halt, take a position, make a stand.*
dexter, -tra, -trum, *right.*
hostis, -is, m., *enemy, foe*; pl., *the enemy.*
legio, -onis, f., *legion.*
primus, -a, -um, *first.*
ubi, *where.*

atque, *and.*
coicio, -icere, -ieci, -iectus, *put, throw.*
cornu, -us, n., *wing, flank.*
fuga, -ae, f., *flight.*
in, *into.*
pello, pellere, pepuli, pulsus, *rout, put to flight, defeat.*
septimus, -a, -um, *the seventh.*

Primo concursu: Ablative of *time when* (A.G. 423.1). **Primo:** Declinable ordinal number used as an adjective (A.G. 132-35).
ab dextro cornu: Ablative of *position* with the preposition **ab** (A.G. 429.b).
ubi ... constiterat: Relative clause; the relative adverb **ubi** ("where") with the indicative forms a subordinate clause (A.G. 279.a).
constiterat: The main verb of the subordinate clause (A.G. 278.b). The pluperfect denotes an action completed in past time (A.G. 477).
septima legio: Nominative subject (A.G. 339). **septima:** Declinable ordinal number used as an adjective (A.G. 132-35).
hostes: Nominative subject of **pelluntur ... coiciuntur** (A.G. 339).
pelluntur ... coiciuntur ... (resistebant ... dabat): Notice the switch in tense and voice between the description of the Gauls on the right and left flanks: passive historical present when losing on the right, active imperfect when winning on the left. Compare the use of

the active and passive voices at 11.2, 12.4, 12.5 and 89.3-5.

pelluntur: The main verb of the coordinate clause **Primo ... pelluntur** (A.G. 278.a).

atque: The conjunction connects the two main verbs **pelluntur ... coiciuntur** and means "and" (*OLD* **atque** 12).

in fugam: Prepositional phrase, **in** with the accusative here means "into" (a state or condition) (*OLD* **in** 2).

coiciuntur: The main verb of the coordinate clause **in ... coiciuntur** (A.G. 278.a).

(62.4-5) ab sinistro, quem locum duodecima legio tenebat, cum primi ordines hostium transfixi telis concidissent, tamen acerrime reliqui resistebant nec dabat suspici(5)onem fugae quisquam.

ab, *on.*

concido, -cidere, -cidi, *fall down, fall, perish, be slain.*
do, dare, dedi, datus, *give, offer.*
fuga, -ae, f., *flight.*
legio, -onis, f., *legion.*
nec, *and ... not.*
primus, -a, -um, *the first.*
quisquam, -----, quidquam, *anyone, anything, any.*
resisto, -sistere, -stiti, -----, *resist, oppose, withstand, offer resistance.*
suspicio, -onis, f., *faint indication, trace, suggestion.*
telum, -i, n., *dart, spear.*
transfigo, -figere, -fixi, -fixus, *pierce through, transfix.*

acriter, sup. **acerrime**, *sharply, fiercely, with vigor, courageously.*
cum, *although.*
duodecimus, -a, -um, *the twelfth.*
hostis, -is, m., *enemy, foe*; pl., *the enemy.*
locus, -i, m., *place, position.*
ordo, -inis, m., *rank, order, company.*
qui, quae, quod, *who, which, what.*
reliqui, -orum, m., pl., *the remaining ranks.*
sinister, -tra, -trum, *left.*
tamen, *yet, still, for all that, nevertheless, however.*
teneo, tenere, tenui, -----, *hold, keep.*

ab sinistro: Ablative of *position* with the preposition **ab** (A.G. 429.b). **sinistro**: Singular, neuter, ablative adjective used substantively (A.G. 288). The noun **cornu** is understood (A.G. 288.b).

quem ... tenebat: Relative clause (A.G. 303). **quem**: See below. **tenebat**: The main verb of the subordinate clause (A.G. 278.b).

quem locum: Accusative direct object of **tenebat** (A.G. 387). **quem**: Singular, masculine, accusative relative pronoun (A.G. 305). The antecedent is **locum** in its own clause (adjectival use) rather than **sinistro** (**cornu**) (A.G. 307.b).

duodecima legio: Nominative subject (A.G. 339). **duodecima**: Declinable ordinal number used as an adjective (A.G. 132-35).

cum ... concidissent: Concessive clause, the relative adverb **cum** ("although") with the subjunctive here forms a concessive clause (A.G. 549). **concidissent**: The main verb of the subordinate clause (A.G. 278.b). Pluperfect subjunctive; the tense of the subjunctive is in secondary sequence and follows the rules for the sequence of tense after **resistebant** (A.G. 482-85).

primi ordines ... transfixi: Nominative subject (A.G. 339). **primi**: Declinable ordinal number used as an adjective modifying **ordines** (A.G. 132-35). **transfixi**: Nominative perfect, passive, participle used as a predicate modifying **ordines**, where in English a phrase or a subordinate clause would be more normal (A.G. 496).

hostium: Partitive genitive with **ordines** (A.G. 346.a.1).

telis: Ablative of instrument after the passive participle **transfixi** (A.G. 409).

tamen: Adverb correlative to the preceding concessive clause, normally postpositive but not here (A.G. 320-21 and 324.j).

acerrime: Superlative adverb (A.G. 218 and 320-21).

reliqui: Plural, masculine, nominative adjective used substantively (A.G. 288). The noun **ordines** is understood (A.G. 288.b). Nominative subject (A.G. 339).

resistebant: The main verb of the coordinate clause **ab ... resistebant** (A.G. 278.a).

nec: The conjunction joins a negative clause to a preceding positive one and means "and ... not" (*OLD* **neque** 3).

dabat ... quisquam: The reversal of the normal word order (subject first, verb last) is called hyperbaton (A.G. 596) (Gotoff, 6-10).

dabat: The main verb of the coordinate clause **dabat ... quisquam** (A.G. 278.a). Verb first in the emphatic position (A.G. 589.d).

suspicionem: Accusative direct object of **dabat** (A.G. 387).

fugae: Objective genitive with **suspicionem** (A.G. 348).

quisquam: Singular, masculine, nominative indefinite pronoun used substantively (A.G. 151.d). Nominative subject (A.G. 339). The subject is in the last position (A.G. 597.b). "Emphatic by position." (Kelsey, 421)

(62.5-6) Ipse dux hostium Camulogenus (6) suis aderat atque eos cohortabatur.

adsum, -esse, affui, -----, *be at hand, be present.*
Camulogenus, -i, m., *Camulogenus.*
dux, ducis, m., *leader, general, commander.*
ipse, -a, -um, *himself.*
sui, -orum, m., pl., *his men*, with or without *own.*

atque, *and.*
cohortor, -ari, -atus, *encourage, urge, exhort, address.*
hostis, -is, m., *enemy, foe*; pl., *the enemy.*
is, ea, id, *he, she, it; that, this.*

Ipse dux: Nominative subject (A.G. 339). **Ipse**: Singular, masculine, nominative demonstrative pronoun used as an intensifying adjective modifying **dux** meaning "himself" (A.G. 296.1 and a and 298.c).

hostium: Partitive genitive with **dux** (A.G. 346.a.1).

Camulogenus: A nominative proper noun in apposition to **dux** (A.G. 282). See Appendix A.

suis: Plural, masculine, dative possessive pronoun used substantively to denote a special class (A.G. 302.d). Dative of reference; the dative in this construction is often called the dative of advantage as denoting the person for whose benefit the action is performed (A.G.

376).

aderat: The main verb of the coordinate clause **Ipse ... aderat** (A.G. 278.a).

atque: The conjunction connects the two main verbs **aderat ... cohortabatur** and means "and" (*OLD* **atque** 12).

eos: Plural, masculine, accusative demonstrative pronoun used substantively (A.G. 296.20. The antecedent is **suis** (A.G. 297.e). Accusative direct object of **cohortabatur** (A.G. 387).

cohortabatur: The main verb of the coordinate clause **eos cohortabatur** (A.G. 278.a).

(62.6-7) **At incerto etiam nunc exitu victoriae, cum septimae legionis tribunis esset nuntiatum quae in sinistro cornu gererentur, post tergum hostium (7) legionem ostenderunt signaque intulerunt.**

at, *however, but.*	**cornu, -us**, n., *wing, flank.*
cum, *after, when.*	**etiam**, *even.*
exitus, -us, m., *issue, event, outcome.*	**gero, gerere, gessi, gestus**, *carry out, perform, do.*
hostis, -is, m., *enemy, foe*; pl., *the enemy.*	**in**, *on.*
incertus, -a, -um, *undecided.*	**infero, -ferre, intuli, illatus**, (with **signa**), *advance.*
legio, -onis, f., *legion.*	**nunc**, *now.*
nuntio, -are, -avi, -atus, *announce, report.*	**ostendo, -tendere, -tendi, -tentus**, *show, display.*
post, *behind.*	**-que**, *and.*
quis, -----, quid, *who? what?*	**septimus, -a, -um**, *the seventh.*
signum, -i, n., *standard.*	**sinister, -tra, -trum**, *left.*
tergum, -i, n., *back*, (with **post**), *in the rear.*	**tribunus, -i**, m., *tribune.*
victoria, -ae, f., *victory.*	

At: Conjunction, expressing a contrast with the preceding statement, meaning "however, but" (A.G. 324.d) (*OLD* **at** 3).

incerto etiam nunc exitu victoriae: Ablative absolute with an adjective (**incerto**) taking the place of a participle (there is no participle for "being") (A.G. 419.a-20). **etiam**: Adverb (A.G. 320-21 and 322.a). The adverb normally proceeds the emphatic word (A.G. 322.a). **nunc**: Adverb (A.G. 320-21 and 322.b). **victoriae**: Partitive genitive with **exitu** (A.G. 346.a).

cum ... esset nuntiatum: Temporal clause; the relative adverb **cum** ("after, when") with the pluperfect subjunctive describes the circumstances that preceded the action of the main verb (A.G. 546). **esset nuntiatum**: The main verb of the subordinate clause (A.G. 278.b). Impersonal use of the intransitive verb (A.G. 208.c). The following indirect question functions as the subject (A.G. 573).

septimae legionis: Possessive genitive with **tribunis** (A.G. 343). **septimae**: Declinable ordinal number used as an adjective (A.G. 132-35).

tribunis: Dative indirect object of the passive verb **esset nuntiatum**, verbs which in the active voice take the accusative and dative retain the dative when used in the passive (A.G. 365 and 369.a).

quae ... gererentur: Indirect question with the subjunctive; the phrase is the subject of the impersonal verb **esset nuntiatum** (A.G. 573-75). **quae**: Plural, neuter, nominative interrogative pronoun used substantively meaning "what things" (A.G. 148). Nominative subject (A.G. 339). **gererentur**: The main verb of the subordinate clause (A.G. 278.b). Imperfect subjunctive; the tense of the subjunctive is in secondary sequence and follows the rules for the sequence of tense for indirect questions after **esset nuntiatum** (A.G. 575).

in sinistro cornu: Ablative of *place where* with the preposition **in** (locative ablative) (A.G. 426.3).

post tergum hostium: Prepositional phrase, **post** with the accusative here means "behind" (*OLD* **post2** 1). "The VIIIth legion made a flank movement and turned the enemy's rear." (Kelsey, 421) **hostium**: Possessive genitive with **tergum** (A.G. 343).

legionem: Accusative direct object of **ostenderunt** (A.G. 387).

ostenderunt: The main verb of the coordinate clause **At ... ostenderunt** (A.G. 278.a). The pronoun **ei**, with **tribunis** as the antecedent, is understood as the subject (A.G. 271.a).

signaque: Accusative direct object of **intulerunt** (A.G. 387). **-que**: The enclitic conjunction connects the two main verbs **ostenderunt ... intulerunt** (A.G. 324.a).

intulerunt: The main verb of the coordinate clause **signaque intulerunt** (A.G. 278.a). The pronoun **ei**, with **tribunis** as the antecedent, is understood as the subject (A.G. 271.a).

(62.7) **Ne eo quidem tempore quisquam loco cessit, sed circumventi omnes interfectique sunt. Eandem fortunam tulit Camulogenus.**

Camulogenus, -i, m., *Camulogenus.*	**cedo, cedere, cessi, cessurus**, *withdraw, retreat, yield.*
circumvenio, -venire, -veni, -ventus, *surround, encompass.*	**fero, ferre, tuli, latus**, *bear, endure, suffer.*
fortuna, -ae, f., *lot, fate, chance, fortune.*	**idem, eadem, idem**, *the same.*
interficio, -ficere, -feci, -fectus, *slay, kill.*	**is, ea, id**, *he, she, it; that, this.*
locus, -i, m., *place, position.*	**ne ... quidem**, *not even.*
omnes, -ium, m., pl., *all men, all.*	**-que**, *and.*
quisquam, -----, quidquam, *anyone, anything, any.*	**sed**, *but.*
tempus, -oris, n., *time.*	

Ne ... quidem: The negative adverb with the particle means "not even" (*OLD* **ne1** 6). The emphatic word must stand between **ne** and **quidem** (A.G. 322.f).

eo ... tempore: Ablative of *time when* (A.G. 423.1). **eo**: Singular, neuter, ablative demonstrative pronoun used as an adjective modifying **tempore** (A.G. 296.1 and a).

quisquam: Singular, masculine, nominative indefinite pronoun used substantively (A.G. 151.d). Nominative subject (A.G. 339).

loco: Ablative of separation without a preposition after **cessit** (A.G. 401).

cessit: The main verb of the coordinate clause **Ne ... cessit** (A.G. 278.a).

sed: Coordinate conjunction (A.G. 324.d).

circumventi ... interfectique sunt: The main verbs of the coordinate clause **circumventi ... sunt** (A.G. 278.a). Two perfect, passive indicative verbs sharing **sunt** (= **circumventi sunt et interfecti sunt**) (A.G. 187-88). **-que**: The enclitic conjunction connects the two participle elements of the main verbs (A.G. 324.a). For the same construction see 29.1 and 80.7.

omnes: Plural, masculine, nominative adjective used substantively (A.G. 288). Nominative subject (A.G. 339).

Eandem fortunam: Accusative direct object of **tulit** (A.G. 387). **Eandem**: Singular, feminine, accusative demonstrative pronoun used as an adjective modifying **fortunam** (A.G. 296.1 and a).

tulit: The main verb of the simple sentence (A.G. 278.1).

Camulogenus: Nominative subject (A.G. 339). The subject is in the last position (A.G. 597.b). See Appendix A.

(62.8-9) **(8) At ei qui praesidio contra castra Labieni erant relicti, cum proelium commissum audissent, subsidio suis ierunt collemque ceperunt, neque nostrorum militum victorum (9) impetum sustinere potuerunt.**

at, *but, but on the other hand.*
capio, capere, cepi, captus, *take, get, seize, capture, occupy, take possession of.*
collis, -is, m., *hill, height, elevation.*
contra, *directed at, facing.*
eo, ire, ivi, or ii, iturus, *go, march, move, advance.*
is, ea, id, *he, she, it; that, this.*
miles, -itis, m., *soldier, foot-solider.*
noster, -tra, -trum, *our, our own.*
praesidium, -i, n., *guard, garrison, protection.*
-que, *and.*
relinquo, -linquere, -liqui, -lictus, *leave, leave behind.*
sustineo, -tinere, -tinui, -tentus, *bear, endure, withstand.*
victor, -oris, m., (as adj.), *victorious, triumphant.*

audio, -ire, -ivi or -ii, -itus, *hear.*
castra, -orum, n., pl., *camp, encampment.*
committo, -mittere, -misi, -missus, *join, begin.*
cum, *after, when.*
impetus, -us, m., *attack, assault, onset, charge.*
Labienus, -i, m., *Labienus.*
neque, *and yet ... not, but ... not.*
possum, posse, potui, -----, *be able.*
proelium, -i, n., *battle, combat, engagement.*
qui, quae, quod, *who, which, what.*
subsidium, -i, n., *support, relief, reinforcement, help.*
sui, -orum, m., pl., *their men*, with or without *own.*

At: Conjunction introducing a change of subject (A.G. 324.d) (*OLD* **at** 2).

ei: Plural, masculine, nominative demonstrative pronoun used substantively (A.G. 296.2). The pronoun is correlative to the relative clause **qui ... erant relicti** (A.G. 297.d). Nominative subject of **audissent ... ierunt ... ceperunt ... potuerunt**. (A.G. 339).

qui ... erant relicti: Relative clause (A.G. 303). For the reference see 61.5. **qui**: Plural, masculine, nominative relative pronoun used substantively (A. G. 305). The antecedent is **ei** (A.G. 307). Nominative subject (A.G. 339). **erant relicti**: The main verb of the subordinate clause (A.G. 278.b). The pluperfect denotes an action completed in past time (A.G. 477).

praesidio: Dative of the purpose or end. The dative of an abstract noun (**praesidio**) is used to show that for which a thing serves or which it accomplishes (A.G. 382.1).

contra castra Labieni: Prepositional phrase, **contra** with the accusative here means "directed at, facing" (*OLD* **contra** 13). **Labieni**: Possessive genitive with **castra** (A.G. 343). See Appendix A.

cum ... audissent: Temporal clause; the relative adverb **cum** ("after, when") with the pluperfect subjunctive describes the circumstances that preceded the action of the main verb (A.G. 546). **audissent**: The main verb of the subordinate clause (A.G. 278.b). A contracted form of **audivissent** (A.G. 181.a).

proelium commissum (esse): Accusative/infinitive construction in indirect discourse after **audissent** (A.G. 577 ff.). **commissum (esse)**: Supply **esse** to form the perfect, passive infinitive (A.G. 186). The tense of the infinitive in indirect discourse is relative to that of the verb of saying (A.G. 584).

subsidio suis: Dative of the purpose or end (double dative). The dative of an abstract noun (**subsidio**) is used to show that for which a thing serves or which it accomplishes, with another dative of the person or thing affected (**suis**) (A.G. 382.1). **suis**: Plural, masculine, dative possessive pronoun used substantively to denote a special class (A.G. 302.d).

ierunt: The main verb of the coordinate clause **At ... ierunt** (A.G. 278.a).

collemque: Accusative direct object of **ceperunt** (A.G. 387). **-que**: The enclitic conjunction connects the two main verbs **ierunt ... ceperunt** (A.G. 324.a).

ceperunt: The main verb of the coordinate clause **collemque ceperunt** (A.G. 278.a).

neque: The conjunction here implies a contrast "and yet ... not, but ... not" (*OLD* **neque** 5).

nostrorum militum victorum: Possessive genitive with **impetum** (A.G. 343). **nostrorum**: Plural, masculine, genitive possessive pronoun used as an adjective modifying **militum** (A.G. 302). **victorum**: A genitive plural noun used as an adjective modifying **militum** (A.G. 321.c).

impetum: Accusative direct object of the infinitive **sustinere** (A.G. 387 and 451.3).

sustinere: Complementary infinitive with **potuerunt** (A.G. 456).

potuerunt: The main verb of the coordinate clause **nostrorum ... potuerunt** (A.G. 278.a).

(62.9-10) Sic cum suis fugientibus permixti, quos non silvae montesque texerunt, ab equitatu (10) sunt interfecti.

ab, *by.*	cum, *with.*
equitatus, -us, m., *cavalry.*	fugio, fugere, fugi, -----, *flee, run away, make off.*
interficio, -ficere, -feci, -fectus, *slay, kill.*	mons, montis, m., *mountain, elevation, height.*
non, *not.*	permisceo, -miscere, -miscui, -mixtus, *mingle, mix.*
-que, *and.*	qui, quae, quod, *who, which, what.*
sic, *so, thus.*	silvae, -arum, f., pl., *wooded parts* or *region.*
sui, -orum, m., pl., *their men*, with or without *own.*	tego, tegere, texi, tectus, *hide, conceal, protect, shelter.*

Sic: Adverb (A.G. 217.c and 320-21).

cum suis fugientibus: Ablative of accompaniment with the preposition **cum** (A.G. 413). **suis**: Plural, masculine, ablative possessive pronoun used substantively to denote a special class (A.G. 302.d). **fugientibus**: Present participle used as an adjective modifying **suis** (A.G. 494).

permixti: Nominative perfect, passive, participle used as a predicate, where in English a phrase or a subordinate clause would be more normal (A.G. 496). Carry down **ei** (the Gauls who have come to the aid of the routed Gauls) as the pronoun. Nominative subject (A.G. 339). **quos ... texerunt**: Relative clause (A.G. 303). **quos**: Plural, masculine, accusative indefinite pronoun used substantively (A.G. 305). The antecedent is **suis ... permixti** (A.G. 307). Accusative direct object of **texerunt** (A.G. 387). **texerunt**: The main verb of the subordinate clause (A.G. 278.b).

non: Adverb; when **non** is especially emphatic it begins the clause (A.G. 217.e, 320-21, and 599.a).

silvae montesque: Two nominative subjects (A.G. 339). **silvae**: The plural of the noun means "wooded parts or regions" (*OLD* **silva** 1). **-que**: The enclitic conjunction connects the two nominative nouns (A.G. 324.a).

ab equitatu: Ablative of agent with the preposition **ab** after the passive verb **sunt interfecti** (A.G. 405).

sunt interfecti: The main verb of the main clause (A.G. 278.b).

(62.10) Hoc negotio confecto Labienus revertitur Agedincum, ubi impedimenta totius exercitus relicta erant: inde die III. cum omnibus copiis ad Caesarem pervenit.

ad, *to.*	Agedincum, -i, n., *Agedincum.*
Caesar, -aris, m., *Caesar.*	conficio, -ficere, -feci, -fectus, *complete, finish, accomplish, do.*
copiae, -arum, f., pl., *forces, troops.*	cum, *with.*
dies, -ei , m. and f., *day.*	exercitus, -us, m., *army.*
hic, haec, hoc, *this; he, she, it.*	I, in expression of number, *1.*
impedimenta, -orum, n., pl., *heavy baggage, baggage.*	inde, *after that, then.*
Labienus, -i, m., *Labienus.*	negotium, -i, n., *business, enterprise.*
omnis, -e, *all.*	pervenio, -venire, -veni, -ventus, *come to, arrive at, reach.*
relinquo, -linquere, -liqui, -lictus, *leave, leave behind.*	revertor, -verti, -versus, *return, come back, go back.*
totus, -a, -um, *the whole, all, all the, entire.*	ubi, *where.*

Hoc negotio confecto: Ablative absolute (A.G. 419-20). **Hoc**: Singular, neuter, ablative demonstrative pronoun used as an adjective modifying **negotio** (A.G. 296.1 and a). **confecto**: The perfect tense of the participle represents the action as completed at the time indicated by the tense of the main verb (A.G. 489).

Labienus: Nominative subject (A.G. 339). See Appendix A.

revertitur: The main verb of the main clause (A.G. 278.b).

Agedincum: Accusative of *place to which* without a preposition (city name) (A.G. 427.2). See Appendix A.

ubi ... relicta erant: Relative clause; the relative adverb **ubi** ("where") with the indicative forms a subordinate clause (A.G. 279.a).

relicta erant: The main verb of the subordinate clause (A.G. 278.b). The pluperfect denotes an action completed in past time (A.G. 477).

impedimenta: Nominative subject (A.G. 339).

totius exercitus: Possessive genitive with **impedimenta** (A.G. 343). **totius**: -ius is the regular genitive singular ending for the adjective **totus** (A.G. 113).

inde: Adverb (A.G. 217.a and 320-21).

die III.: Ablative of *time when* (A.G. 423.1). **die**: The noun **dies** is normally masculine gender (A.G. 97.a). **III.**: Roman numeral used as an adjective (A.G. 133).

cum omnibus copiis: Ablative of accompaniment with the preposition **cum** (A.G. 413).

ad Caesarem: Prepositional phrase, **ad** with the accusative here means "to" (*OLD* **ad** 1). **Caesarem**: See Appendix A. "Caesar had been marching to the north of the Loire, and met Labienus probably near Joigny, on the Yonne." (Kelsey, 421)

pervenit: The main verb of the simple sentence (A.G. 278.1). The pronoun **is**, with **Labienus** as the antecedent, is understood as the subject (A.G. 271.a)

4.F CHAPTERS 63-64: THE REBELLION SPREADS; THE AEDUI DEMAND ULTIMATE CONTROL BUT VERCINGETORIX IS ELECTED LEADER; THE GAULS AGAIN ADOPT A SCORCHED-EARTH POLICY

258

(63.1) **Defectione Aeduorum cognita bellum augetur.**

Aedui, -orum, m., pl., *the Aedui.*

bellum, -i, n., *war.*

defectio, -onis, f., *revolt, rebellion.*

augeo, augere, auxi, auctus, *increase, enlarge, augment, add to.*

cognosco, -gnoscere, -gnovi, cognitus, *learn, ascertain, recognize.*

Defectione ... augetur: Caesar ignores the possibility that his defeat at Gergovia is also a cause of the spread of the uprising. This would seem to be a greater cause than the defection of the Aedui as Caesar's air of invincibility had certainly been damaged.
Defectione Aeduorum cognita: Ablative absolute (A.G. 419-20). **Aeduorum:** Possessive genitive with **Defectione** (A.G. 343). See Appendix A. **cognita:** The perfect tense of the participle represents the action as completed at the time indicated by the tense of the main verb (A.G. 489). This final defection of Caesar's allies is the turning point for the unification of Gallic resistance.
bellum: Nominative subject (A.G. 339).
augetur: The main verb of the main clause (A.G. 278.b). The historical present, giving vividness to the narrative, is present in Chapter 63 (A.G. 469). This usage, common in all languages, comes from imagining past events as going on before our eyes (*repraesentatio*) (A.G. 469 Note).

(63.1-4) **Legationes (2) in omnis partis circummittuntur; quantum gratia, auctoritate, pecunia valent ad sollicitandas civitates nituntur; (3) nacti obsides quos Caesar apud eos deposuerat, horum (4) supplicio dubitantis territant.**

ad, *for, in order to, for the purpose of.*

auctoritas, -tatis, f., *prestige, authority, power.*
circummitto, -mittere, -misi, -missus, *send around.*
depono, -ponere, -posui, -positus, *place, put.*

gratia, -ae, f., *influence.*
in, *into.*
legatio, -onis, f., *deputation, embassy, envoys.*

nitor, niti, nixus, and **nisus,** *strive, endeavor.*
omnis, -e, *all.*
pecunia, -ae, f., *money, property.*
qui, quae, quod, *who, which, what.*

supplicium, -i, n., *punishment, death-penalty, execution.*
valeo, -ere, -ui, -iturus, *have power, influence,* or *weight.*

apud, *in the keeping of, in the care or custody of, in the hands of.*
Caesar, -aris, m., *Caesar.*
civitas, -tatis, f., *state, nation.*
dubito, -are, -avi, -atus, *waver, be irresolute, hesitate, delay.*
hic, haec, hoc, *this; he, she, it.*
is, ea, id, *he, she, it; that, this.*
naniscor, -cisci, nactus, and **nanctus,** *come upon, find, obtain, get hold of.*
obses, -idis, m. and f., *hostage.*
pars, partis, f., *region, district, direction.*
quantum, *to what extent* or *degree.*
sollicito, -are, -avi, -atus, *instigate, urge, incite, tamper with, tempt.*
territo, -are, -----, -----, *frighten greatly, terrify.*

Legationes: Nominative subject (A.G. 339).
in omnis partis: Accusative of *place to which* with the preposition **in** A.G. 426.2). **omnis:** Accusative plural adjective; **-is** for **-es** is the regular form in i-stem adjectives (A.G. 114.a and 116). **partis:** Accusative plural noun; **-is** and **-es** are both forms in mixed i-stem nouns (A.G. 71).
circummittuntur: The main verb of the simple sentence (A.G. 278.1).
quantum ... valent: Relative clause (A.G. 279.a). **quantum:** Relative adverb meaning "to what extent, degree" (*OLD* **quantum2** 2).
valent: The main verb of the subordinate clause (A.G. 278.b). The pronoun **ei**, with **Legationes** as the antecedent, is understood as the subject (A.G. 271.a).
gratia, auctoritate, pecunia: Three ablatives of specification (A.G. 418). Notice the asyndeton construction (A.G. 323.b).
ad sollicitandas civitates: The preposition **ad** with the accusative gerundive and noun expresses purpose (A.G. 506). **sollicitandas:** Plural, feminine, accusative gerundive used as an adjective modifying **civitates** denoting necessity, obligation or propriety (A.G. 500.1).
nituntur: The main verb of the main clause (A.G. 278.b). The pronoun **ei**, with **Legationes** as the antecedent, is understood as the subject (A.G. 271.a).
nacti: Nominative perfect, deponent, participle used as a predicate, where in English a phrase or a subordinate clause would be more normal (A.G. 496). The pronoun **eae**, with **Legationes** as the antecedent, is understood. Nominative subject (A.G. 339).
obsides: Accusative direct object of the participle **nacti** (A.G. 387 and 488).
quos ... deposuerat: Relative clause (A.G. 303). **quos:** Plural, masculine, accusative relative pronoun used substantively (A.G. 305). The antecedent is **obsides** (A.G. 307). Accusative direct object of **deposuerat** (A.G. 387). **deposuerat:** The main verb of the subordinate clause (A.G. 278.b). The pluperfect denotes an action completed in past time (A.G. 477).
Caesar: Nominative subject (A.G. 339). See Appendix A.
apud eos: Prepositional phrase, **apud** with the accusative here means "in the keeping of, in the care or custody of, in the hands of" (*OLD* **apud** 9). **eos:** Plural, masculine, accusative demonstrative pronoun used substantively (A.G. 296.2). The antecedent is **Aeduorum** (A.G. 297.e). See Chapter 55 for the taking of the Gallic hostages at Noviodunum and their removal to Bibracte.
horum: Plural, masculine, genitive demonstrative pronoun used substantively (A.G. 296.2). The antecedent is **obsides** (A.G. 297.e).

Objective genitive with **supplicio** (A.G. 348).

supplicio: Ablative of means (A.G. 409).

dubitantis: Plural, masculine, accusative present participle used substantively (A.G. 494.a). Accusative plural; **-is** for **-es** is the regular form of the present participle (A.G. 117-18). Accusative direct object of **territant** (A.G. 387).

territant: The main verb of the main clause (A.G. 278.b). Iterative form of **terreo** (A.G. 263.2).

(63.4) Petunt a Vercingetorige Aedui ut ad se veniat rationesque belli gerendi communicet.

a(b), *from.*	**ad**, *to.*
Aedui, -orum, m., pl., *the Aedui.*	**bellum, -i**, n., *war, warfare.*
communico, -are, -avi, -atus, *communicate, impart.*	**gero, gerere, gessi, gestus**, *carry on, wage.*
peto, petere, petivi, and **petii, petitus**, *seek, get, secure.*	**-que**, *and.*
ratio, -onis, f., *plan.*	**sui, sibi, se**, or **sese**, nom. wanting, *them,* with or without *-selves.*
ut, *so that.*	**venio, venire, veni, ventus**, *come.*
Vercingetorix, -igis, m., *Vercingetorix.*	

Petunt ... Aedui: The reversal of the normal word order (subject first, verb last) is called hyperbaton (A.G. 596) (Gotoff, 6-10).

Petunt: The main verb of the main clause (A.G. 278.b). Verb first in the emphatic position (A.G. 589.d).

a Vercingetorige: Ablative of source with the preposition **a(b)** after **Petunt** (A.G. 403.1). **Vercingetorige**: See Appendix A.

Aedui: Nominative subject (A.G. 339). The subject is in the last position (A.G. 597.b). See Appendix A.

ut ... veniat ... communicet: The conjunction **ut** ("so that") with the subjunctive is here a substantive clause of purpose which is used as the object of the verb **Petunt** denoting an action directed toward the future (A.G. 563). **veniat ... communicet**: The main verbs of the subordinate clause (A.G. 278.b). Present subjunctives; the tense of the subjunctives is normally in secondary sequence after the historical present **Petunt** (A.G. 482-85). Here it is in primary sequence through *repraesentatio* (A.G. 485.e and 585.b Note). The pronoun **is**, with **Vercingetorige** as the antecedent, is understood as the subject of both verbs (A.G. 271.a).

ad se: Prepositional phrase, **ad** with the accusative here means "to" (*OLD* **ad** 1). **se**: Plural, masculine, accusative indirect reflexive pronoun (A.G. 300.2). The antecedent is **Aedui**, the subject of **Petunt** (A.G. 299).

rationesque: Accusative direct object of **communicet** (A.G. 387). **-que**: The enclitic conjunction connects the two main verbs in the purpose clause (A.G. 324.a).

belli gerendi: Objective genitive with **rationes** (A.G. 348). **gerendi**: Singular, neuter, genitive gerundive used as an adjective modifying **belli** (A.G. 500.1).

(63.5-6) (5) Re impetrata contendunt ut ipsis summa imperi tradatur et re in controversiam deducta totius Galliae concilium (6) Bibracte indicitur.

Bibracte, -is, n. *Bibracte.*	**concilium, -i**, n., *meeting, assembly, council.*
contendo, -tendere, -tendi, -tentus, *demand, insist.*	**controversia, -ae**, f., *dispute, debate, controversy, quarrel.*
deduco, -ducere, -duxi, -ductus, *divert, reduce, bring, draw out.*	**et**, *and.*
Gallia, -ae, f., *Gaul.*	**imperium, -i**, n., *command, control, military authority.*
impetro, -are, -avi, -atus, *accomplish, gain, grant.*	**in**, *into.*
indico, -dicere, -dixi, -dictus, *convoke, call, appoint.*	**ipse, -a, -um**, *he, they,* with or without *himself, themselves.*
res, rei, f., *object, case, request.*	**summa, -ae**, f., *general management, control, administration.*
totus, -a, -um, *the whole, all, all the, entire.*	**trado, -dere, -didi, -ditus**, *hand over, give up, deliver.*
ut, *so that.*	

Re impetrata: Ablative absolute (A.G. 419-20). Notice that Vercingetorix values an alliance with the Aedui high enough to go to them but yet does not buckle to pressure from them and allow them the leadership position. **impetrata**: The perfect tense of the participle represents the action as completed at the time indicated by the tense of the main verb (A.G. 489).

contendunt: The main verb of the coordinate clause **Re ... tradatur** (A.G. 278.a). The pronoun **ei**, with **Aedui** as the antecedent, is understood as the subject (A.G. 271.a).

ut ... tradatur: The conjunction **ut** ("so that") with the subjunctive is here a substantive clause of purpose which is used as the object of **contendunt** denoting an action directed toward the future (A.G. 563). **tradatur**: The main verbs of the subordinate clause (A.G. 278.b). Present subjunctive; the tense of the subjunctive is normally in secondary sequence after the historical present **contendunt** (A.G. 482-85). Here it is in primary sequence through *repraesentatio* (A.G. 485.e and 585.b Note).

ipsis: Plural, masculine, dative demonstrative pronoun used substantively (A.G. 296.2 and 298.d). The antecedent is **Aedui** (A.G. 298). Dative indirect object of the passive verb **tradatur**, verbs which in the active voice take the accusative and dative retain the dative when used in the passive (A.G. 365 and 369.a). Here the demonstrative pronoun is used for emphasis instead of the indirect reflexive pronoun **sibi** (A.G. 300.b).

summa: Nominative subject (A.G. 339). From the noun **summa, -ae**, f..

imperi: Partitive genitive with **summa** (A.G. 346.a.1). The singular genitive of nouns in **-ium** ended, until the Augustan Age, in a single -i (A.G. 49.b).

et: The conjunction connects the two main verbs **contendunt ... indicitur** (A.G. 324.a).

re in controversiam deducta: Ablative absolute (A.G. 419-20). **in controversiam**: Prepositional phrase, **in** with the accusative here means "into" (a state or condition) (*OLD* **in** 2). **deducta**: The perfect tense of the participle represents the action as completed at the time indicated by the tense of the main verb (A.G. 489).

totius Galliae concilium Bibracte indicitur: Kahn claims that the council scene functions as a substitute for choral odes between major episodes. (Kahn, 251) See also 1.4, 14.1, 29.1, 75.1, and 89.1.

totius Galliae: Objective genitive with **concilium** (A.G. 348). **totius**: -ius is the regular genitive singular ending for the adjective **totus** (A.G. 113). **Galliae**: See Appendix A.

concilium: Nominative subject (A.G. 339).

Bibracte: Locative case of the city name **Bibracte, -is**, n. (A.G. 80). See Appendix A.

indicitur: The main verb of the coordinate clause **re ... indicitur** (A.G. 278.a).

(63.6-7) Eodem conveniunt undique frequentes. Multitudinis suffragiis res permittitur: ad unum omnes (7) Vercingetorigem probant imperatorem.

ad unum, *without exeption, to a man.*

eodem, *to the same place.*
imperator, -oris, m., *commander-in-chief, commander, general.*
omnes, -ium, m., pl., *all men, all.*

probo, -are, -avi, -atus, *approve.*
suffragium, -i, n., *vote.*
Vercingetorix, -igis, m., *Vercingetorix.*

convenio, -venire, -veni, -ventus, *come together, gather.*
frequens, -entis, *in large numbers, crowded, thronging.*
multitudo, -inis, f., *multitude, crowd.*
permitto, -mittere, -misi, -missus, *refer to, give over, commit.*
res, rei, f., *matter, affair*
undique, *from all sides, from all parts.*

Eodem: Adverb (A.G. 217.a and 320-21).

conveniunt: The main verb of the simple sentence (A.G. 278.1).

undique: Adverb (A.G. 217.a and 320-21).

frequentes: Plural, masculine, nominative adjective used substantively (A.G. 288). The noun **Galli** is understood (A.G. 288.b). Nominative subject (A.G. 339).

Multitudinis suffragiis: It is interesting how democratic the election process was; the Gauls actually vote for a common leader. This is a rare instance of the Gallic leadership in agreement, and even here, as we see below, the Aedui are disgruntled.

Multitudinis: Possessive genitive with **suffragiis** (A.G. 343).

suffragiis: Dative indirect object of the passive verb **permittitur**, verbs which in the active voice take the accusative and dative retain the dative when used in the passive (A.G. 365).

permittitur: The main verb of the simple sentence (A.G. 278.1). The verb **permittere** in the passive here means "to be referred to" (*OLD* **permitto** 4).

ad unum: Prepositional phrase, **ad** with the accusative of **unus** is an idiom that means "without exeption, to a man" (*OLD* **unus** 2.b). It does not seem likely that the Aedui contingent voted for Vercingetorix as they were seeking the hegemony for themselves.

omnes: Plural, masculine, nominative adjective used substantively (A.G. 288). Nominative subject (A.G. 339).

Vercingetorigem: Accusative direct object of **probant** (A.G. 387). See Appendix A.

probant: The main verb of the simple sentence (A.G. 278.1).

imperatorem: A predicate accusative noun with the proper noun **Vercingetorigem** after **probant** (A.G. 392-93). "a title with official Roman connotations, much more ominous than the title of 'leader' (*dux*) given to e.g. Camulogenus (7.62)." (Hammond, 241) Vercingetorix had been chosen rex by the Arverni and given the imperium by the initially rebellious states in Chapter 4. Now he is named imperator.

(63.7-8) Ab hoc concilio Remi, Lingones, Treveri afuerunt: illi, quod amicitiam Romanorum sequebantur; Treveri, quod aberant longius et ab Germanis premebantur, quae fuit causa quare toto (8) abessent bello et neutris auxilia mitterent.

ab, *from; by.*

amicitia, -ae, f., *friendship, alliance.*

bellum, -i, n., *war, warfare.*
concilium, -i, n., *meeting, assembly, council.*
Germani, -orum, m., pl., *the Germans.*
ille, illae, illud, *the former.*
longius, *far.*
neutri, -orum, m., pl., *neither side.*
quare, *why, wherefore.*
quod, *because, since, for, as.*
Romani, -orum, m., pl., *the Romans.*

absum, -esse, afui, -futurus, *be absent* or *away from; be distant.*
auxilia, -orum, n., *auxiliary troops, auxiliaries, allied forces.*
causa, -ae, f., *reason, cause.*
et, *and.*
hic, haec, hoc, *this; he, she, it.*
Lingones, -um, m., pl., *the Lingones.*
mitto, mittere, misi, missus, *send.*
premo, -ere, pressi, pressus, *press, harass, oppress.*
qui, quae, quod, *who, which, what.*
Remi, -orum, m., pl., *the Remi.*
sequor, -qui, -cutus, *hold to, maintain.*

sum, esse, fui, futurus, *be.*
Treveri, -orum, m., pl., *the Treveri.*

totus, -a, -um, *the whole, all, all the, entire.*

Ab hoc concilio: Ablative of separation with the preposition **ab** after **afuerunt** (A.G. 402). **hoc**: Singular, neuter, ablative demonstrative pronoun used as an adjective modifying **concilio** (A.G. 296.1 and a).

Remi, Lingones, Treveri: Three nominative subjects (A.G. 339). Notice the asyndeton construction (A.G. 323.b). See Appendix A for each tribe.

afuerunt: The main verb of the simple sentence (A.G. 278.1).

illi (afuerunt): Plural, masculine, nominative demonstrative pronoun used substantively (A.G. 296.2). The antecedent is **Remi, Lingones**, meaning "The former (A.G. 297.b). Nominative subject (A.G. 339). Supply **afuerunt** as the main verb of the main clause.

quod ... sequebantur: Causal clause; the conjunction **quod** ("because") takes the indicative when the reason is given on the authority of the writer or speaker (A.G. 540.1). **sequebantur**: The main verb of the subordinate clause (A.G. 278.b). The pronoun **ei**, with **illi** (**Remi, Lingones**) as the antecedent, is understood as the subject (A.G. 271.a).

amicitiam: Accusative direct object of **sequebantur** (A.G. 387).

Romanorum: Objective genitive with **amicitiam** (A.G. 348).

Treveri (afuerunt): Nominative subject (A.G. 339). Supply **afuerunt** as the main verb of the main clause. See Appendix A.

quod aberant ... premebantur: Causal clause; the conjunction **quod** ("because") takes the indicative when the reason is given on the authority of the writer or speaker (A.G. 540.1). **aberant ... premebantur**: The main verbs of the subordinate clause (A.G. 278.b). The pronoun **ei**, with **Treveri** as the antecedent, is understood as the subject of both verbs (A.G. 271.a).

longius: Comparative adverb (A.G. 218 and 320-21). The comparative degree here denotes a considerable or excessive degree of the quality meaning "too" (A.G. 291.a).

et: The conjunction connects the two main verbs **aberant ... premebantur** (A.G. 324.a).

ab Germanis: Ablative of agent with the preposition **ab** after the passive verb **premebantur** (A.G. 405). **Germanis**: See Appendix A.

quae ... causa: Relative clause (A.G. 303). **quae**: Singular, feminine, nominative relative pronoun used substantively (A.G. 305). The antecedent is the clause **quod aberant ... premebantur** but the relative agrees with the predicate noun **causa** in its own clause (A.G. 306). Nominative subject (A.G. 339). **causa**: Singular, feminine, nominative predicate noun after **fuit** (A.G. 283-84).

fuit: The main verb of the subordinate clause (A.G. 278.b).

quare ... abessent ... mitterent: Indirect question with the subjunctive; the phrase is in apposition to **causa** (A.G. 573-75). **quare**: Interrogative adverb meaning "why" (*OLD* quare A.2). **abessent ... mitterent**: The main verbs of the subordinate clause (A.G. 278.b). Imperfect subjunctives; the tense of the subjunctives is in secondary sequence and follows the rules for the sequence of tense for indirect questions after **fuit** (A.G. 575). The pronoun **ei**, with **Treveri** as the antecedent, is understood as the subject of both verbs (A.G. 271.a).

toto ... bello: Ablative of separation without a preposition after the compound verb **abessent** (A.G. 402). Kelsey suggests "abl. of time, 'in the entire war'." (Kelsey, 422)

et: The conjunction connects the two main verbs in the indirect question (A.G. 324.a)

neutris: Plural, masculine, dative adjective used substantively meaning "to neither side" (A.G. 288) (*OLD* neuter 1.b). Dative indirect object of the transitive verb **mitterent** (A.G. 362).

auxilia: Accusative direct object of the transitive verb **mitterent** A.G. 387).

(63.8-9) **Magno dolore Aedui ferunt se deiectos principatu, queruntur fortunae commutationem et Caesaris indulgentiam in se requirunt; neque tamen suscepto bello suum consilium ab reliquis (9) separare audent.**

ab, *from.*
audeo, audere, ausus sum, *venture, dare, risk.*
Caesar, -aris, m., *Caesar.*
consilium, -i, n., *policy.*
deicio, -icere, -ieci, -iectus, *remove, depose, oust.*
et, *and.*
fortuna, -ae, f., *luck, lot, fate, chance, fortune.*
indulgentia, -ae, f., *favor, kindness.*
neque, *and yet ... not, but ... not.*

queror, queri, questus, *complain, lament.*
requiro, -quirere, -quisivi, -quisitus, *miss, wish back again.*

sui, sibi, se, or sese, nom. wanting, *they,* with or without *themselves.*
suus, -a, -um, *their,* with or without *own.*

Aedui, -orum, m., pl., *the Aedui.*
bellum, -i, n., *war, warfare.*
commutatio, -onis, f., *change, alteration.*
defectio, -onis, f., *revolt, rebellion.*
dolor, -oris, m., *grief, distress, vexation.*
fero, ferre, tuli, latus, *bear, endure, suffer.*
in, *towards, to, for.*
magnus, -a, -um, *great, abundant, considerable.*
principatus, -us, m., *chief authority, headship, leadership.*
reliqui, -orum, m., pl., *the rest.*
separo, -are, -avi, -atus, *consider separately, distinguish.*
suscipio, -cipere, -cepi, -ceptus, *undertake, take up.*
tamen, *yet, still, for all that, nevertheless, however.*

Magno dolore: Ablative of manner with a limiting adjective (A.G. 412).

Aedui: Nominative subject of **ferunt** (A.G. 339). See Appendix A.

ferunt: The main verb of the coordinate clause **Magno ... principatu** (A.G. 278.a).

se deiectos (esse): Accusative/infinitive construction in indirect discourse (A.G. 577 ff.). The verb of saying is not expressed, but implied in the phrase **Magno dolore ... ferunt**; here **dolore** implies a thought, and this thought is added in the form of indirect discourse (A.G. 580.a). **se**: Plural, masculine, accusative direct reflexive pronoun (A.G. 300.1). The antecedent is **Aedui**, the subject of **ferunt** (A.G. 299). **deiectos (esse)**: Supply **esse** to form the perfect, passive infinitive (A.G. 188). The tense of the infinitive in indirect discourse is relative to that of the verb of saying (A.G. 584).

principatu: Ablative of separation without a preposition after the compound infinitive **deiectos (esse)** (A.G. 402).

queruntur: The main verb of the coordinate clause **queruntur ... commutationem** (A.G. 278.a). The verb comes in the first position when the idea in it is emphatic (A.G. 598.d). Notice the asyndeton construction between the two verbs **ferunt ... queruntur** (A.G. 323.b). The pronoun **ei**, with **Aedui** as the antecedent, is understood as the subject (A.G. 271.a).

fortunae: Objective genitive with **commutationem** (A.G. 348).

commutationem: Accusative direct object of **queruntur** (A.G. 387).

et: The conjunction connects the two main verbs **queruntur ... requirunt** (A.G. 324.a).

Caesaris: Possessive genitive with **indulgentiam** (A.G. 343). See Appendix A.

indulgentiam: Accusative direct object of **requirunt** (A.G. 387).

in se: Prepositional phrase, **in** with the accusative here means "towards, to, for" (*OLD* **in** 11). **se**: Plural, masculine, accusative direct reflexive pronoun (A.G. 300.1). The antecedent is **ei** (**Aedui**), the supplied subject of **requirunt** (A.G. 299).

requirunt: The main verb of the coordinate clause **Caesaris ... requirunt** (A.G. 278.a). The pronoun **ei**, with **Aedui** as the antecedent, is understood as the subject (A.G. 271.a).

neque: The conjunction here implies a contrast "and yet ... not, but ... not" (*OLD* **neque** 5).

tamen: Adverb, postpositive (A.G. 320-21 and 324.j).

suscepto bello: Ablative absolute (A.G. 419-20). **suscepto**: The perfect tense of the participle represents the action as completed at the time indicated by the tense of the main verb (A.G. 489).

suum consilium: Accusative direct object of the infinitive **separare** (A.G. 387 and 451.3). **suum**: Singular, masculine, accusative possessive pronoun used as an adjective modifying **consilium** (A.G. 302).

ab reliquis: Ablative of separation with the preposition **ab** after the infinitive **separare** (A.G. 401). **reliquis**: Plural, masculine, ablative adjective used substantively (A.G. 288). The noun **Gallis** is understood (A.G. 288.b).

separare: Complementary infinitive after **audent** (A.G. 456).

audent: The main verb of the coordinate clause **tamen ... audent** (A.G. 278.a). The pronoun **ei**, with **Aedui** as the antecedent, is understood as the subject (A.G. 271.a).

(63.9) Inviti summae spei adulescentes Eporedorix et Viridomarus Vercingetorigi parent.

adulescens, -entis, m., *young man, youth.*
et, *and.*
pareo, parere, parui, -----, *obey, submit to, be subject to.*
summus, -a, -um, *utmost, greatest, very great.*
Viridomarus, -i, m., *Viridomarus.*

Eporedorix, -igis, m., *Eporedorix.*
invitus, -a, -um, *unwilling, reluctant.*
spes, -ei, f., *promise, expectation.*
Vercingetorix, -igis, m., *Vercingetorix.*

Inviti ... adulescentes: Nominative subject (A.G. 339). **Inviti**: Plural, masculine, nominative adjective modifying **adulescentes**, but used to qualify the action of the verb, and so has the force of an adverb (A.G. 290).

summae spei: Genitive of quality (descriptive genitive) with **adulescentes** (A.G. 345). **summae**: Defective superlative adjective (A.G. 130.b).

Eporedorix et Viridomarus: Two proper nouns in apposition to **adulescentes** (A.G. 282). **Eporedorix**: See Appendix A. **et**: The conjunction connects the two nouns (A.G. 324.a). **Viridomarus**: See Appendix A.

Vercingetorigi: Dative indirect object of the intransitive verb **parent** (A.G. 367). See Appendix A.

parent: The main verb of the simple sentence (A.G. 278.1).

(64.1-2) Ipse imperat reliquis civitatibus obsides +denique+ ei rei constituit +diem; huc+ omnis equites XV milia numero celeriter (2) convenire iubet:

celeriter, *quickly, speedily, at once, immediately.*
constituo, -stituere, -stitui, -stitutus, *establish, resolve upon, determine.*

denique, *at last, finally.*
eques, -itis, m., *rider, horseman, cavalryman, trooper.*
impero, -are, -avi, -atus, *levy, draft, demand.*

is, ea, id, *he, she, it; that, this.*

milia, -um, n., pl., *thousand, thousands.*
obses, -idis, m. and f., *hostage.*
reliquus, -a, -um, *remaining, the rest.*
V, in expression of number, = 5.

civitas, -tatis, f., *state, nation.*
convenio, -venire, -veni, -ventus, *come together, gather.*
dies, -ei, m. and f., *day.*
huc, *hither, here, to this place.*
ipse, -a, -um, *he, they, with or without himself, themselves.*
iubeo, iubere, iussi, iussus, *order, give orders, bid, command.*
numerus, -i, m., (in abl.), in *number, in all.*
omnis, -e, *all.*
res, rei, f., *matter, event, affair.*
X, in expression of number, = 10.

Ipse: Singular, masculine, nominative demonstrative pronoun used substantively (A.G. 296.2 and 298.d). The antecedent is **Vercingetorigi** (A.G. 298). Nominative subject (A.G. 339). The pronoun distinguishes the principal personage (**Vercingetorix**) from the subordinate persons (**Eporedorix** ... **Viridomarus**) (A.G. 298.d.3).

imperat ... constituit ... iubet: Once again, as at 4.7-8, upon being given authority, Vercingetorix does not hesitate to wield it.

imperat: The main verb of the coordinate clause **Ipse ... obsides** (A.G. 278.a). The historical present, giving vividness to the narrative, is present in Chapter 64 (A.G. 469). This usage, common in all languages, comes from imagining past events as going on before our eyes (*repraesentatio*) (A.G. 469 Note).

reliquis civitatibus: Dative indirect object of the normally intransitive verb **imperat** (A.G. 369 and 387).

obsides: Accusative direct object of the normally intransitive verb **imperat** (A.G. 369 and 387).

+denique+: Adverb (A.G. 320-21).

ei rei: Dative indirect object of the transitive verb **constituit** (A.G. 362). **ei**: Singular, feminine, dative demonstrative pronoun used as an adjective modifying **rei** (A.G. 296.1 and a).

constituit: The main verb of the coordinate clause **denique ... diem** (A.G. 278.a). The pronoun **is**, with **Ipse** (**Vercingetorix**) as the antecedent, is understood as the subject (A.G. 271.a).

+diem: Accusative direct object of the transitive verb **constituit** (A.G. 387). **diem**: The noun **dies** is normally masculine gender (A.G. 97.a).

huc+: Adverb (A.G. 217.a and 320-21).

omnis equites ... convenire: A subject accusative with the infinitive after **iubet**. The construction is equivalent to a substantive clause of purpose (A.G. 563.a). **omnis**: Accusative adjective; **-is** for **-es** is the regular form in i-stem adjectives (A.G. 114.a and 116).

XV milia: Accusative plural phrase in apposition to **omnis equites** (A.G. 282).

numero: Ablative of specification (A.G. 418). In the ablative singular, with a number, **numerus** means "in number, in all" (*OLD* **numerus** 1.b).

celeriter: Adverb (A.G. 214.b and 320-21).

iubet: The main verb of the main clause (A.G. 278.b). The pronoun **is**, with **Ipse** (**Vercingetorix**) as the antecedent, is understood as the subject (A.G. 271.a).

(64.2-3) peditatu quem antea habuerit se fore contentum dicit, neque fortunam temptaturum aut in acie dimicaturum sed, quoniam abundet equitatu, perfacile esse factu frumentationibus pabulationibusque Romanos prohi(3)bere;

abundo, -are, -avi, -----, *abound in, be well provided with.*
antea, *previously, before, formerly.*
contentus, -a, -um, *satisfied, content.*
dimico, -are, -avi, -atus, *fight, contend, struggle.*
facio, facere, feci, factus, *do.*
frumentatio, -onis f., *expedition in quest of supplies, foraging.*
in, *in.*
pabulatio, -onis, f., *foraging, getting fodder.*
perfacilis, -e, *very easy, not at all difficult.*
-que, *and.*
quoniam, *since, seeing that, because.*
Romani, -orum, m., pl., *the Romans.*
sui, sibi, se, or **sese,** nom. wanting, *he,* with or without *himself.*
tempto, -are, -avi, -atus, *put to trial, put to test.*

acies, -ei, f., *battle.*
aut, *or.*
dico, dicere, dixi, dictus, *say.*
equitatus, -us, m., *cavalry.*
fortuna, -ae, f., *luck, fate, chance, fortune.*
habeo, habere, habui, habitus, *have, hold, possess.*
neque, *and ... not.*
peditatus, -us, m., *infantry.*
prohibeo, -hibere, -hibui, -hibitus, *prevent, hinder.*
qui, quae, quod, *who, which, what.*
resido, -sidere, -sedi, -----, *settle down, subside.*
sed, *but.*
sum, esse, fui, futurus, *be.*

peditatu: Locative ablative after **contentum** (A.G. 431.a).

quem ... habuerit: Relative clause; a subordinate clause in indirect discourse takes the subjunctive (A.G. 303 and 580). **quem**: Singular, masculine, accusative relative pronoun used substantively (A.G. 305). The antecedent is **peditatu** (A.G. 307). Accusative direct object of **habuerit** (A.G. 387). **habuerit**: The main verb of the subordinate clause (A.G. 278.b). Perfect subjunctive; the tense of the subjunctive is normally in secondary sequence after the historical present **dicit** (A.G. 482-85). Here it is in primary sequence through *repraesentatio* (A.G. 485.e and 585.b Note). The pronoun **is**, with **Ipse** (**Vercingetorix**) as the antecedent, is understood as the subject (A.G. 271.a).

antea: Adverb (A.G. 216 Note and 320-21).

se fore contentum: Accusative/infinitive construction in indirect discourse after **dicit** (A.G. 577 ff.). **se**: Singular, masculine, accusative direct reflexive pronoun (A.G. 300.1). The antecedent is **is** (**Vercingetorix**), the supplied subject of **dicit** (A.G. 299). **fore**: Future active infinitive of **sum** (A.G. 170.a). The tense of the infinitive in indirect discourse is relative to that of the verb of saying (A.G. 584). **contentum**: Singular, masculine, accusative predicate adjective modifying **se** after **fore** (A.G. 283-84).

dicit: The main verb of the main clause (A.G. 278.b). The verb introduces indirect speech through 64-4. The pronoun **is**, with **Ipse** (**Vercingetorix**) as the antecedent, is understood as the subject (A.G. 271.a).

neque: The conjunction here joins a negative clause to a preceding positive one and means "and ... not" (*OLD* **neque** 3).

fortunam: Accusative direct object of the infinitive **temptaturum** (esse) (A.G. 387 and 451.3).

(se) temptaturum (esse): Accusative/infinitive construction in indirect discourse after **dicit** (A.G. 577 ff.). Carry down **se** from above as the accusative pronoun. **temptaturum (esse)**: Supply **esse** to form the future, active infinitive (A.G. 184). The tense of the infinitive in indirect discourse is relative to that of the verb of saying (A.G. 584).

aut: The conjunction connects the two accusative/infinitive constructions and excludes the alternative (A.G. 324.e).

in acie: Ablative of *place where* with the preposition **in** (locative ablative) (A.G. 426.3).

(se) dimicaturum (esse): Accusative/infinitive construction in indirect discourse after **dicit** (A.G. 577 ff.). Carry down **se** from above as the accusative pronoun. **dimicaturum (esse)**: Supply **esse** to form the future, active infinitive (A.G. 184). The tense of the infinitive in indirect discourse is relative to that of the verb of saying (A.G. 584).

sed: Coordinate conjunction (A.G. 324.d).

quoniam abundet equitatu: Causal clause; the conjunction **quoniam** ("since") introduces a reason given on the authority of the writer or speaker and normally takes the indicative (A.G. 540.a). Here **quoniam** takes the subjunctive as it is a dependent clause in indirect discourse after **dicit** (A.G. 580). **abundet**: The main verb of the subordinate clause (A.G. 278.b). Present subjunctive; the tense of the subjunctive is normally in secondary sequence after the historical present **dicit** (A.G. 482-85). Here it is in primary sequence through *repraesentatio* (A.G. 485.e and 585.b Note). The pronoun **is**, with **Ipse (Vercingetorix)** as the antecedent, is understood as the subject (A.G. 271.a). **equitatu**: Ablative of means with **abundet** (A.G. 409.a).

perfacile esse: Accusative/infinitive construction in indirect discourse after **dicit** (A.G. 577 ff.). Impersonal verb, the following infinitive phrase forms the subject (A.G. 208.c and 454). **perfacile**: Singular, neuter, accusative predicate adjective after **esse** (A.G. 284-85). The adverbial prefix **per-**, modifying an adjective, means "very" (A.G. 267.d.1). **esse**: Present infinitive; the tense of the infinitive in indirect discourse is relative to that of the verb of saying (A.G. 584).

factu: A supine in **-u** after **perfacile** meaning "a very easy thing to do" (A.G. 510 Note 2).

frumentationibus pabulationibusque Romanos prohibere: The infinitive phrase functions as the accusative subject of the impersonal verb **perfacile esse** (A.G. 454).

frumentationibus pabulationibusque: Two ablatives of separation without a preposition after **prohibere** (A.G. 401). **-que**: The enclitic conjunction connects the two ablative nouns (A.G. 324.a). Siedler calls this combination of words "interesting because of their 'Rock 'n Roll'." (Siedler, 30).

Romanos: Accusative direct object of the infinitive **prohibere** (A.G. 387 and 451.3).

(64.3-4) aequo modo animo sua ipsi frumenta corrumpant aedificiaque incendant, qua rei familiaris iactura perpetuum (4) imperium libertatemque se consequi videant.

aedificium, -i, n., *building.*
animus, -i, m., *mind, spirit, temper.*
corrumpo, -rumpere, -rupi, -ruptus, *spoil, destroy, ruin.*
frumentum, -i, n., *grain;* pl., *crops of grain, grain-crops.*
imperium, -i, n., *sovereignty, empire, dominion.*
ipse, -a, -um, *he, they,* with or without *himself, themselves.*
modo, *only, but.*
-que, *and.*
res, rei, f., *property, possessions, estate.*
suus, -a, -um, *their,* with or without *own.*

aequus, -a, -um, *patient, calm, resigned, tranquil.*
consequor, -sequi, -secutus, *obtain, secure, gain.*
familiaris, -e, *private.*
iactura, -ae, f., *loss, sacrifice, cost.*
incendo, -cendere, -cendi, -census, *set on fire, burn.*
libertas, -atis, f., *freedom, liberty, independence.*
perpetuus, -a, -um, *perpetual, lasting, permanent.*
qui, quae, quod, *who, which, what.*
sui, sibi, se, or **sese**, nom. wanting, *they,* with or without *themselves.*
video, videre, visi, visus, *see, perceive, understand.*

aequo modo animo sua ipsi frumenta corrumpant: Notice the interlocking word order (A.G. 598.h).

aequo ... animo: Ablative of quality (descriptive ablative) with an adjective modifier (A.G. 415). The phrase is an idiom that means "with calmness, patience, or resignation" (*OLD* **aequus**, 8.a).

modo: Adverb (A.G. 320-21).

sua ... frumenta: Accusative direct object of **corrumpant** (A.G. 387). **sua**: Plural, neuter, accusative reflexive pronoun used as an adjective modifying **frumenta** (A.G. (A.G. 302).

ipsi: Plural, masculine, nominative demonstrative pronoun used substantively (A.G. 296.2 and 298.d). The antecedent is **omnes** (those being addressed at the council) at 63.6 (A.G. 298). Nominative subject (A.G. 339). The pronoun is here emphatic (A.G. 298.d.1).

corrumpant: The main verb of the coordinate clause **aequo ... corrumpant** (A.G. 278.a). Present subjunctive; a hortatory subjunctive (jussive) in indirect discourse after **dicit** remains in the subjunctive rather than the infinitive even though it is an independent clause in indirect discourse (A.G. 577 and 588.a).

aedificiaque: Accusative direct object of **incendant** (A.G. 387). **-que**: The enclitic conjunction connects the two hortatory subjunctive verbs (A.G. 324.a).

incendant: The main verb of the coordinate clause **aedificiaque ... videant** (A.G. 278.a). Present subjunctive; a hortatory subjunctive (jussive) in indirect discourse after **dicit** remains in the subjunctive rather than the infinitive even though it is an independent clause in indirect discourse (A.G. 577 and 588.a). "Vercingetorix was consistently carrying out the policy that he had proposed at the outset." (Kelsey, 422)

qua ... videant: A relative clause of purpose is introduced by a relative pronoun and takes the subjunctive (A.G. 531.2). This clause is dependent on the idea contained in both verbs **corrumpant ... incendant**. **qua**: See below. **videant**: The main verb of the subordinate clause (A.G. 278.b). Present subjunctive; the tense of the subjunctive is normally in secondary sequence after the historical present **dicit** (A.G. 482-85). Here it is in primary sequence through *repraesentatio* (A.G. 485.e and 585.b Note). The pronoun **ei**, with **ipsi** (those present at the council) as the antecedent, is understood as the subject (A.G. 271.a).

qua ... iactura: Ablative of means (A.G. 409). **qua**: Singular, feminine, ablative relative pronoun (A.G. 305). The antecedent is **iactura** in its own clause (adjectival use) (A.G. 307.b). The pronoun is here equivalent to **ut ea** (A.G. 531.2).

rei familiaris: Objective genitive with **iactura** (A.G. 348). The phrase **res familiaris** means "one's private property" (*OLD* **familiaris** 1.c).

perpetuum imperium libertatemque: Two accusative direct objects of the infinitive **consequi** (A.G. 387 and 451.3). **perpetuum**: The adjective should be construed with both **imperium** and **libertatem**, but agrees in gender and number with only the nearest noun

(A.G. 286.a). **libertatem**: For the theme of liberty in Book 7, see **liberius** at 1.3. **-que**: The enclitic conjunction connects the two accusative nouns (A.G. 324.a).

se consequi: Accusative/infinitive construction in indirect discourse after **videant** (A.G. 577 ff.). **se**: Plural, masculine, accusative direct reflexive pronoun (A.G. 300.1). The antecedent is **ei (ipsi)**, the supplied subject of **videant** (A.G. 299). **consequi**: Present infinitive; the tense of the infinitive in indirect discourse is relative to that of the verb of saying (A.G. 584). "The present is more vivid than the future, which might have been expected." (Kelsey, 422)

(64.4-5) His constitutis rebus, Aeduis Segusiavisque, qui sunt finitimi provinciae, decem milia peditum imperat; huc addit equites (5) octingentos.

addo, -dere, -didi, -ditus, *add, join.*
constituo, -stituere, -stitui, -stitutus, *establish, resolve upon, determine.*
eques, -itis, m., *rider, horseman, cavalryman, trooper.*
hic, haec, hoc, *this; he, she, it.*
impero, -are, -avi, -atus, *levy, draft, demand.*
octingenti, -ae, -a, *eight hundred.*
provincia, -ae, f., *the province.*
qui, quae, quod, *who, which, what.*
Segusiavi, -orum, m., pl., *the Segusiavi.*

Aedui, -orum, m., pl., *the Aedui.*
decem, *ten.*
finitimi, -orum, m., pl., *neighbors, neighboring peoples.*
huc, *to this amount* or *total.*
milia, -um, n., pl., *thousand, thousands.*
pedites, -um, m., pl., *infantry.*
-que, *and.*
res, rei, f., *matter, affair.*
sum, esse, fui, futurus, *be.*

His constitutis rebus: Ablative absolute (A.G. 419-20). **His**: Plural, feminine, ablative demonstrative pronoun used as an adjective modifying **rebus** (A.G. 296.1 and a). **constitutis**: The perfect tense of the participle represents the action as completed at the time indicated by the tense of the main verb (A.G. 489).
Aeduis Segusiavisque: Two dative indirect objects of the normally intransitive verb **imperat** (A.G. 369). See Appendix A for each tribe. **-que**: The enclitic conjunction connects the two dative nouns (A.G. 324.a).
qui ... provinciae: Relative clause (A.G. 303). **qui**: Plural, masculine, nominative relative pronoun used substantively (A.G. 305). The antecedent is **Segusiavis** (A.G. 307). Nominative subject (A.G. 339). **provinciae**: Dative object of the adjective **finitimi** (A.G. 384). See Appendix A.
sunt: The main verb of the subordinate clause (A.G. 278.b). The present tense is not the historical present but denotes a state as now existing in present time (A.G. 465.1).
finitimi: Plural, masculine, nominative adjective used substantively (A.G. 288). Predicate nominative noun after **sunt** (A.G. 283-84).
decem milia: Accusative direct object of the normally intransitive verb **imperat** (A.G. 369 and 387). **decem**: Indeclinable cardinal number used as an adjective modifying **milia** (A.G. 132-35). **milia**: Accusative plural; in the plural **mille** declines as a neuter noun (A.G. 134.d).
peditum: Partitive genitive with **milia** (A.G. 346.a.2).
imperat: The main verb of the main clause (A.G. 278.b). The pronoun **is**, with **Ipse (Vercingetorix)** as the antecedent, is understood as the subject (A.G. 271.a).
huc: Adverb, with a verb of adding (**addit**) the adverb means "to this amount or total" (*OLD* **huc** 3).
addit: The main verb of the simple sentence (A.G. 278.1). The pronoun **is**, with **Ipse (Vercingetorix)** as the antecedent, is understood as the subject (A.G. 271.a).
equites octingentos: Accusative direct object of **addit** (A.G. 387). **octingentos**: Declinable cardinal number used as an adjective (A.G. 132-35).

(64.5-6) His praeficit fratrem Eporedorigis bellumque (6) inferri Allobrogibus iubet.

Allobroges, -um (acc. **Allobrogas**), m., pl., *the Allobroges.*
Eporedorix, -igis, m., *Eporedorix.*
hic, haec, hoc, *this; he, she, it.*
iubeo, iubere, iussi, iussus, *order, give orders, bid, command.*

-que, *and.*

bellum, -i, n., *war, warfare.*
frater, -tris, m., *brother.*
infero, -ferre, intuli, illatus, *make.*
praeficio, -ficere, -feci, -fectus, *place over, appoint to command.*

His: Plural, masculine, dative demonstrative pronoun used substantively (A.G. 296.2). The antecedent is **milia peditum ... equites octingentos** (A.G. 297.e). Masculine gender is assigned to the pronoun following the rules for the agreement of predicate adjectives (A.G. 287.3). Dative indirect object of the transitive verb **praeficit** (A.G. 362).
praeficit: The main verb of the coordinate clause **His ... Eporedorigis** (A.G. 278.a). The pronoun **is**, with **Ipse (Vercingetorix)** as the antecedent, is understood as the subject (A.G. 271.a).
fratrem: Accusative direct object of **praeficit** (A.G. 387). This brother is otherwise unnamed.
Eporedorigis: Possessive genitive with **fratrem** (A.G. 343). See Appendix A.
bellumque inferri: A subject accusative with the infinitive after **iubet**. The construction is equivalent to a substantive clause of purpose (A.G. 563.a). **-que**: The enclitic conjunction connects the two main verbs **praeficit ... iubet** (A.G. 324.a).
Allobrogibus: Dative indirect object of the passive infinitive **inferri**, verbs which in the active voice take the accusative and dative retain the dative when used in the passive (A.G. 365 and 451.3). See Appendix A.
iubet: The main verb of the coordinate clause **bellumque ... iubet** (A.G. 278.a). The pronoun **is**, with **Ipse (Vercingetorix)** as the

antecedent, is understood as the subject (A.G. 271.a).

(64.6-7) Altera ex parte Gabalos proximosque pagos Arvernorum in Helvios, item Rutenos Cadurcosque ad finis Volcarum Arecomicorum depopulandos (7) mittit.

ad, *for, in order to, for the purpose of.*
Arverni, -orum, m., pl., *the Arverni.*
depopulor, -ari, -atus, *lay waste, plunder.*
fines, -ium, m., pl., *borders*, hence *territory, country, land.*
Helvii, -orum, m., pl., *the Helvii.*
item, *also, further*
pagus, -i, m., *district, canton.*
proximus, -a, -um, *nearest, next.*
Ruteni, -orum, m., pl., *the Ruteni.*

alter, -era, -erum, *the other.*
Cadurci, -orum, m., pl., *the Cadurci.*
ex, *on.*
Gabali, -orum, m., pl., *the Gabali.*
in, *into the country of, against.*
mitto, mittere, misi, missus, *send.*
pars, partis, f., *side.*
-que, *and.*
Volcae Arecomici , -arum -orum, m., pl., *the Volci Arecomici.*

Altera ex parte: Ablative of *position* with the preposition **ex** meaning "on the other side" (A.G. 429.b). **ex**: A monosyllabic preposition is often placed between a noun and its adjective (A.G. 599.d.2). "On the west, reckoning from the territory of the Aedui, which for the time being Vercingetorix made his base of operations." (Kelsey, 422)
Gabalos proximosque pagos: First two accusative direct objects of **mittit** (A.G. 387). **Gabalos**: See Appendix A. **proximos**: Defective superlative adjective (A.G. 130.a). **-que**: The enclitic conjunction connects the two accusative nouns (A.G. 324.a). **Arvernorum**: Possessive genitive with **pagos** (A.G. 343). See Appendix A.
in Helvios: Accusative of *place to which* with the preposition **in** ("into the country of") (A.G. 426.2). **Helvios**: See Appendix A. **item**: Adverb (A.G. 320-21).
Rutenos Cadurcosque: Second two accusative direct objects of **mittit** (A.G. 387). See Appendix A for each tribe. **-que**: The enclitic conjunction connects the two accusative nouns (A.G. 324.a).
ad finis Volcarum Arecomicorum depopulandos: The preposition **ad** with the accusative noun and gerundive expresses purpose (A.G. 506). **finis**: Accusative plural noun; **-is** for **-es** is the regular form in i-stem nouns (A.G. 65-7 and 74.c). **Volcarum Arecomicorum**: Possessive genitive with **finis** (A.G. 343). See Appendix A. **depopulandos**: Plural, masculine, accusative gerundive used as an adjective modifying **finis** denoting necessity, obligation or propriety (A.G. 500.1).
mittit: The main verb of the simple sentence (A.G. 278.1). The pronoun **is**, with **Ipse (Vercingetorix)** as the antecedent, is understood as the subject (A.G. 271.a).

(64.7-8) Nihilo minus clandestinis nuntiis legationibusque Allobrogas sollicitat, quorum mentis nondum ab superiore (8) bello resedisse sperabat.

ab, *because of, as a result of.*

bellum, -i, n., *war, warfare.*
legatio, -onis, f., *deputation, embassy, envoys.*
nihilo minus, *just as much, no less.*
nuntius, -i, m., *message.*
qui, quae, quod, *who, which, what.*
sollicito, -are, -avi, -atus, *urge, incite, tamper with, tempt.*
superior, -or, -us, *former, earlier, previous.*

Allobroges, -um (acc. **Allobrogas**), m., pl., *the Allobroges.*
clandestinus, -a, -um, *secret, hidden.*
mens, mentis, f., *attitude of mind, feeling.*
nondum, *not yet.*
-que, *and.*
resido, -sidere, -sedi, -----, *settle down, subside.*
spero, -are, -avi, -atus, *hope, expect.*

Nihilo minus: Adverb written as two words (A.G. 320-21) (*OLD* **nihilominus**).
clandestinis nuntiis legationibusque: Two ablatives of means (A.G. 409). **clandestinis**: The adjective should be construed with both **nuntiis** and **legationibus** (A.G. 286.a). **-que**: The enclitic conjunction connects the two ablative nouns (A.G. 324.a).
Allobrogas: Accusative direct object of **sollicitat** (A.G. 387). The masculine, accusative, plural ending of the tribe **Allobrox** is **-as**. See Appendix A.
sollicitat: The main verb of the main clause (A.G. 278.b). The pronoun **is**, with **Ipse (Vercingetorix)** as the antecedent, is understood as the subject (A.G. 271.a).
quorum ... sperabat: Relative clause (A.G. 303). **quorum**: Plural, masculine, genitive relative pronoun used substantively (A.G. 305). The antecedent is **Allobrogas** (A.G. 307). Possessive genitive with **mentis** (A.G. 343). **sperabat**: The main verb of the subordinate clause (A.G. 278.b). The pronoun **is**, with **Ipse (Vercingetorix)** as the antecedent, is understood as the subject (A.G. 271.a).
mentis ... resedisse: Accusative/infinitive construction in indirect discourse after **sperabat** (A.G. 577 ff.). **mentis**: Accusative plural noun, **-is** for **-es** is the regular form in mixed i-stem nouns (A.G. 71-2). **resedisse**: Perfect infinitive; the tense of the infinitive in indirect discourse is relative to that of the verb of saying (A.G. 584).
nondum: Adverb (A.G. 217.b and 320-21).
ab superiore bello: Prepositional phrase, **ab** with the ablative here means "because of, as a result of" (*OLD* **ab** 15). **superiore**: Defective comparative adjective (A.G. 130.b). See *BG* 1.6 for the other reference to this war in 61 BC. "The uprising of the Allobroges in B.C. 61, for which they had been terribly punished by the Romans. Vercingetorix hoped that their old hatred of the

Romans had not died out." (Kelsey, 422)

(64.8) Horum principibus pecunias, civitati autem imperium totius provinciae pollicetur.

autem, *moreover.*
hic, haec, hoc, *this; he, she, it.*

pecunia, -ae, f., *money, property.*
princeps, -ipis, m., *head man, leader, chief, prince.*
totus, -a, -um, *the whole, all, all the, entire.*

civitas, -tatis, f., *state, nation.*
imperium, -i, n., *control, government, dominion, military authority.*
polliceor, -liceri, -lictus, *promise, offer.*
provincia, -ae, f., *the province.*

Horum: Plural, masculine, genitive demonstrative pronoun used substantively (A.G. 296.2). The antecedent is **Allobrogas** (A.G. 297.e). Partitive genitive with **principibus** (A.G. 346.a.1).
principibus: First dative indirect object of the transitive verb **pollicetur** (A.G. 362).
pecunias: First accusative direct object of the transitive verb **pollicetur** (A.G. 387).
civitati: Second dative indirect object of the transitive verb **pollicetur** (A.G. 362).
autem: Postpositive conjunction (A.G. 324.j and 599.b).
imperium: Second accusative direct object of the transitive verb **pollicetur** (A.G. 387).
totius provinciae: Objective genitive with **imperium** (A.G. 348). **totius**: -ius is the regular genitive singular ending for the adjective **totus** (A.G. 113). **provinciae**: See Appendix A.
pollicetur: The main verb of the simple sentence (A.G. 278.1). The pronoun **is**, with **Ipse** (**Vercingetorix**) as the antecedent, is understood as the subject (A.G. 271.a).

4.G CHAPTER 65: CAESAR PROCURES GERMAN HORSEMEN
(65.1-2) Ad hos omnis casus provisa erant praesidia cohortium duarum et XX, quae ex ipsa coacta provincia ab L. (2) Caesare legato ad omnis partis opponebantur.

ab, *by.*
casus, -us, m., *chance, fortune, event.*

cohors, -hortis, f., *cohort, company*, (the tenth part of a legion).
et, *and.*
hic, haec, hoc, *this; he, she, it.*
L. Caesar, -aris, m., *Lucius Caesar.*
omnis, -e, *all.*

pars, partis, f., *district, region, side, point.*
provincia, -ae, f., *province.*

qui, quae, quod, *who, which, what.*

ad, *in preparation for, in expectation of, to deal with; at.*
cogo, cogere, coegi, coactus, *levy, collect, gather, assemble.*
duo, -ae, -o, *two.*
ex, *from, out of.*
ipse, -a, -um, (*herself*), *itself.*
legatus, -i, m., *lieutenant, lieutenant-general.*
oppono, -ponere, -posui, -positus, *place before, set against, oppose.*
praesidium, -i, n., *guard, garrison.*
provideo, -videre, -vidi, -visus, *make available in advance, provide, supply.*
X, in expression of number, = *10.*

Ad hos omnis casus: Prepositional phrase, **ad** with the accusative here means "in preparation for, in expecation of, to deal with" (*OLD* **ad** 32). **hos**: Plural, masculine, accusative demonstrative pronoun used as an adjective modifying **casus** (A.G. 296.1 and a). **omnis**: Accusative adjective; -is for -es is the regular form in i-stem adjectives (A.G. 114.a and 116).
provisa erant ... opponebantur: Notice the switch in tenses. These garrisons had been provided and were being set in position.
provisa erant: The main verb of the main clause (A.G. 278.b). Although the pluperfect tense is normally used in subordinate clauses, its use as a main verb is frequent. The pluperfect denotes an action completed in past time (A.G. 477).
praesidia: Nominative subject (A.G. 339).
cohortium duarum et XX: Partitive genitive with **praesidia** (A.G. 346.a.1). **duarum**: Declinable cardinal number used as an adjective modifying **cohortium** (A.G. 132-35). **et**: The conjunction here connects the cardinal number and Roman numeral (A.G. 135.a and 324.a). **XX**: Roman numeral used as an adjective modifying **cohortium** (A.G. 133).
quae ... opponebantur: Relative clause (A.G. 303). **quae**: See below. **opponebantur**: The main verb of the subordinate clause (A.G. 278.b).
quae ... coacta: Nominative subject (A.G. 339). **quae**: Plural, neuter, nominative relative pronoun used substantively (A.G. 305). The antecedent is **praesidia** (A.G. 307). **coacta**: Nominative perfect, passive, participle used as a predicate, where in English a phrase or a subordinate clause would be more normal (A.G. 496).
ex ipsa ... provincia: Ablative of *place from which* with the preposition **ex** (A.G. 426.1). **ipsa**: Singular, feminine, ablative demonstrative pronoun used as an adjective modifying **provincia** meaning "itself" (i.e. not from Gaul) (A.G. 296.1 and a and 298.c). The literal translation, "herself", should be rendered in English by the gender neutral "itself". **provincia**: See Appendix A.
ab L. Caesare legato: Ablative of agent with the preposition **ab** after the passive participle **coacta** (A.G. 405). **L. Caesare**: See Appendix A. **L.**: Abbreviated form of the praenomen **Lucius** (A.G. 108.c). **legato**: An ablative noun in apposition to the proper noun **Caesare** (A.G. 282).
ad omnis partis: Prepositional phrase, **ad** with the accusative here means "at" (*OLD* **ad** 13). **omnis**: Accusative adjective; -is for -es is the regular form in i-stem adjectives (A.G. 114.a and 116). **partis**: Accusative plural noun, -is for -es is the regular form in mixed i-

stem nouns (A.G. 71-2).

(65.2-3) Helvii sua sponte cum finitimis proelio congressi pelluntur et C. Valerio Donnotauro, Caburi filio, principe civitatis, compluribusque aliis interfectis intra oppida ac muros compel(3)luntur.

ac, *and.*
C. Valerius Donnotaurus, -i, m., *Gaius Valerius Donnotaurus.*
civitas, -tatis, f., *state, nation.*
complures, -a and **-ia**, *several, a number of, many.*

cum, *with.*
filius, -i, m., *son.*
Helvii, -orum, m., pl., *the Helvii.*
intra, *within.*
oppidum, -i, n., *fortified town, city.*
princeps, -ipis, m., *head man, leader, chief, prince.*
-que, *and.*
suus, -a, -um, *their, with or without own.*

alii, -orum, m., pl., *others.*
Caburus, -i, m., *Gaius Valerius Caburus.*
compello, -pellere, -puli, -pulsus, *drive, force.*
congredior, -gredi, -gressus, *join battle, engage, contend.*
et, *and.*
finitimi, -orum, m., pl., *neighbors, neighboring peoples.*
interficio, -ficere, -feci, -fectus, *slay, kill.*
murus, -i, m., *wall, rampart.*
pello, pellere, pepuli, pulsus, *rout, put to flight, defeat.*
proelium, -i, n., *battle, combat, engagement.*
(spons), spontis, f., *freewill, accord, motion, impulse.*

Helvii ... congressi: Nominative subject of **pelluntur ... compelluntur** (A.G. 339). **Helvii**: See Appendix A. **congressi**: Nominative perfect, deponent participle used as a predicate, where in English a phrase or a subordinate clause would be more normal (A.G. 496).
sua sponte: Ablative of manner with a limiting adjective (A.G. 412). **sua**: Singular, feminine, ablative possessive pronoun used as an adjective modifying **sponte** (A.G. 302). **sponte**: The noun is only used in the genitive (rare) and ablative singular (A.G. 103.c.2). The phrase **sua sponte** is an idiom that means "of their own accord, without prompting, voluntarily" (*OLD* **(spons)** 2).
cum finitimis: Ablative of accompaniment with the preposition **cum**, words of contention (**congressi**) require **cum** (A.G. 413.b).
finitimis: Plural, masculine, ablative adjective used substantively (A.G. 288).
proelio: Ablative of *place where* without a preposition (A.G. 429.3).
pelluntur: The main verb of the coordinate clause **Helvii ... pelluntur** (A.G. 278.a). The historical present, giving vividness to the narrative, is present in Chapter 65 (A.G. 469). This usage, common in all languages, comes from imagining past events as going on before our eyes (*repraesentatio*) (A.G. 469 Note).
et: The conjunction connects the two main verbs **pelluntur ... compelluntur** (A.G. 324.a).
C. Valerio Donnotauro, Caburi filio, principe civitatis compluribusque aliis interfectis: Ablative absolute (A.G. 419-20). **C. Valerio Donnotauro**: See Appendix A. **C.**: Abbreviated form of the praenomen **Gaius** (A.G. 108.c). **Caburi**: Possessive genitive with **filio** (A.G. 343). See Appendix A. **filio**: An ablative noun in apposition to the proper noun **Valerio** (A.G. 282). **principe**: An ablative noun in apposition to the proper noun **Valerio** (A.G. 282). **civitatis**: Partitive genitive with **principe** (A.G. 346.a). **aliis**: Plural, masculine, ablative, pronoun used substantively meaning "others" (*OLD* **alius2** 1). **-que**: The enclitic conjunction connects the two substantives in the ablative absolute **Valerio ... compluribus** (A.G. 324.a). **interfectis**: The perfect tense of the participle represents the action as completed at the time indicated by the tense of the main verb (A.G. 489).
intra oppida ac muros: Prepositional phrase, **intra** with the accusative here means "within" (*OLD* **intra** 1). **ac**: The conjunction connects the two accusative nouns in the prepositional phrase and means "and" (*OLD* **atque** 12).
compelluntur: The main verb of the coordinate clause **C. ... compelluntur** (A.G. 278.a).

(65.3-4) Allobroges crebris ad Rhodanum dispositis praesi(4)diis magna cum cura et diligentia suos finis tuentur.

ad, *at.*
creber, -bra, -brum, *numerous, frequent.*
cura, -ae, f., *care, attention.*
dispono, -ponere, -posui, -positus, *set in various places, distribute, station, post.*
fines, -ium, m., pl., *borders,* hence *territory, country, land.*
praesidium, -i, n., *guard, garrison.*
suus, -a, -um, *their, with or without own.*

Allobroges, -um, m., pl., *the Allobroges.*
cum, *with.*
diligentia, -ae, f., *care, diligence.*
et, *and.*

magnus, -a, -um, *great, considerable.*
Rhodanus, -i, m., *the Rhone river.*
tueor, tueri, -----, *maintain, guard, protect, defend.*

Allobroges: Nominative subject (A.G. 339). See Appendix A.
crebris ad Rhodanum dispositis praesidiis: Ablative absolute (A.G. 419-20). **ad Rhodanum**: Prepositional phrase, with all names of places *at*, meaning *near* (not *in*), is expressed by **ad** with the accusative (A.G. 428.d). **Rhodanum**: See Appendix A. **dispositis**: The perfect tense of the participle represents the action as completed at the time indicated by the tense of the main verb (A.G. 489).
magna cum cura et diligentia: Ablative of manner with the preposition **cum** (A.G. 412). **magna**: The adjective should be construed with both **cura** and **diligentia** but agrees in number with only the nearest noun (A.G. 286.a). **cum**: A monosyllabic preposition is often placed between a noun and its adjective (A.G. 599.d.2). **et**: The conjunction connects the two ablative nouns in the prepositional phrase (A.G. 324.a).
suos finis: Accusative direct object of **tuentur** (A.G. 387). **suos**: Plural, masculine, accusative possessive pronoun used as an adjective modifying **finis** (A.G. 302). **finis**: Accusative plural noun; **-is** for **-es** is the regular form in i-stem nouns (A.G. 65-7 and 74.c).

tuentur: The main verb of the main clause (A.G. 278.b).

(65.4-5) **Caesar, quod hostis equitatu superiores esse intellegebat et interclusis omnibus itineribus nulla re ex provincia atque Italia sublevari poterat, trans Rhenum in Germaniam mittit ad eas civitates quas superioribus annis pacaverat equitesque ab his arcessit et levis armaturae pedites, qui inter eos proeliari (5) consuerant.**

ab, *from.*
annus, -i, m., *year.*
armatura, -ae, f., *armor, equipment.*
Caesar, -aris, m., *Caesar.*
consuesco, -suescere, -suevi, -suetus, *be accustomed.*
equitatus, -us, m., *cavalry.*
ex, *from, out of.*
hic, haec, hoc, *this; he, she, it.*
in, *into.*

inter, *among, amid.*

is, ea, id, *he, she, it; that, this.*
iter, itineris, n., *road, route.*
mitto, mittere, misi, missus, *send.*
omnis, -e, *all.*
pedites, -um, m., pl., *infantry.*
proelior, -ari, -atus, *fight, join battle, engage in battle.*
-que, *and.*
quod, *because, since, for, as.*
Rhenus, -i, m., *the Rhine river.*
sum, esse, fui, futurus, *be.*

trans, *across.*

ad, *to.*
arcesso, -sere, -sivi, -situs, *send for, summon.*
atque, *and.*
civitas, -tatis, f., *state, nation.*
eques, -itis, m., *rider, horseman, cavalryman, trooper.*
et, *and.*
Germania, -ae, f., *Germany.*
hostis, -is, m., *enemy, foe;* pl., *the enemy.*
intellego, -legere, -lexi, -lectus, *understand, see clearly, perceive.*
intercludo, -cludere, -clusi, -clusus, *shut off, cut off, blockade, hinder.*
Italia, -ae, f., *Italy.*
levis, -e, *light.*
nullus, -a, -um, *no, not any.*
paco, -are, -avi, -atus, *pacify, subdue.*
possum, posse, potui, -----, *be able.*
provincia, -ae, f., *the province.*
qui, quae, quod, *who, which, what.*
res, rei, f., *way, manner.*
sublevo, -are, -avi, -atus, *relieve, assist, aid, support.*
superior, -or, -us, *superior, stronger; former, earlier, previous.*

Caesar: Nominative subject of **mittit** ... **arcessit** (A.G. 339). See Appendix A.

quod ... intellegebat ... poterat: Causal clause; the conjunction **quod** ("because") takes the indicative when the reason is given on the authority of the writer or speaker (A.G. 540.1). **intellegebat ... poterat**: The main verbs of the subordinate clause (A.G. 278.b). The pronoun **is**, with **Caesar** as the antecedent, is understood as the subject of both verbs (A.G. 271.a).

hostis ... superiores esse: Accusative/infinitive construction in indirect discourse after **intellegebat** (A.G. 577 ff.). **hostis**: Accusative plural noun; **-is** for **-es** is the regular form in i-stem nouns (A.G. 65-67 and 74.c). **superiores**: Plural, masculine, accusative defective comparative adjective in the predicate position modifying **hostis** after **esse** (A.G. 130.b and 283-84). **esse**: Present infinitive; the tense of the infinitive in indirect discourse is relative to that of the verb of saying (A.G. 584).

equitatu: Ablative of specification after **superiores** (A.G. 418).

et: The conjunction connects the two main verbs in the causal clause (A.G. 324.a).

interclusis omnibus itineribus: Ablative absolute (A.G. 419-20). **interclusis**: The perfect tense of the participle represents the action as completed at the time indicated by the tense of the main verb (A.G. 489).

nulla re: Ablative of means with the passive infinitive **sublevari** (A.G. 409).

ex provincia atque Italia: Ablative of source with the preposition **ex** (A.G. 403.1). **provincia**: See Appendix A. **atque**: The conjunction connects the two ablative nouns in the prepositional phrase and means "and" (*OLD* atque 12). **Italia**: See Appendix A. **sublevari**: Complementary infinitive after **poterat** (A.G. 456).

trans Rhenum: Prepositional phrase, **trans** with the accusative here means "across" (*OLD* trans 1). **Rhenum**: See Appendix A.

in Germaniam: Accusative of *place to which* with the preposition **in** (A.G. 426.2). **Germaniam**: See Appendix A.

mittit: The main verb of the coordinate clause **Caesar ... pacaverat** (A.G. 278.a).

ad eas civitates: Accusative of *place to which* with the preposition **ad** (A.G. 426.2). **eas**: Plural, feminine, accusative demonstrative pronoun used as an adjective modifying **civitates** (A.G. 296.1 and a). The pronoun functions as a correlative to the relative clause **quas ... pacaverat** (A.G. 297.d). "The Ubii were friendly to Caesar; what other German states are referred to it is impossible to determine." (Kelsey, 422)

quas ... pacaverat: Relative clause (A.G. 303). For Caesar's dealings with the Germans see *BG* 1.30-53, 4.1-19, and 6.9-10, 21-28. **quas**: Plural, feminine, accusative relative pronoun used substantively (A.G. 305). The antecedent is **civitates** (A.G. 307). Accusative direct object of **pacaverat** (A.G. 387). **pacaverat**: The main verb of the subordinate clause (A.G. 278.b). The pronoun **is**, with **Caesar** as the antecedent, is understood as the subject (A.G. 271.a). The pluperfect denotes an action completed in past time (A.G. 477).

superioribus annis: Ablative of *time when* (A.G. 423.1). **superioribus**: Defective comparative adjective (A.G. 130.b).

equitesque: Accusative direct object of **arcessit** (A.G. 387). **-que**: The enclitic conjunction connects the two main verbs **mittit** ... **arcessit** (A.G. 324.a).

ab his: Ablative of source with the preposition **ab** (A.G. 403.1). **his**: Plural, feminine, ablative demonstrative pronoun used substantively (A.G. 296.2). The antecedent is **civitates** (A.G. 297.e).

arcessit: The main verb of the coordinate clause **equitesque ... consuerant** (A.G. 278.a). Third conjugation iterative verbs end in -esso (A.G. 263.2.b).

et: The conjunction connects the two accusative nouns **equites ... pedites** (A.G. 324.a).

levis armaturae: Genitive of quality (descriptive genitive) with **pedites** (A.G. 345). "Besides the legions, a Roman army contained bodies of infantry and cavalry drawn from allied and subject peoples, or hired outright from independent nations (*auxilia*). These in some cases retained their native dress, equipment, and mode of fighting, in others were armed and trained after the Roman fashion. To the former class belong the light-armed troops (*milites levis armaturae*), including especially the slingers and bowmen. In the Gallic war Caesar availed himself of the help of slingers from the Balearic Islands, bowmen from Crete and Numidia, and light-armed German troops. He utilized also contingents from Illyricum and from the Gallic states that he subdued. In 52 B.C. he had a force of ten thousand Aeduans. Caesar, as other Roman writers, is generally not careful to state the exact number of auxiliary troops; they were regarded as relatively unimportant. The officers of the auxiliaries, both infantry and cavalry, were Romans." (Kelsey, 23)

pedites: Accusative direct object of **arcessit** (A.G. 387).

qui ... consuerant: Relative clause (A.G. 303). **qui**: Plural, masculine, nominative relative pronoun used substantively (A.G. 305). The antecedent is **pedites** (A.G. 307). Nominative subject (A.G. 339). **consuerant**: The main verb of the subordinate clause (A.G. 278.b). Contracted form of **consueverant** (A.G. 181.a). The pluperfect denotes an action in indefinite time, but prior to some past time referred to (A.G. 477).

inter eos: Prepositional phrase, **inter** with the accusative here means "among, amid" (*OLD* **inter1** 1). **eos**: Plural, masculine, accusative demonstrative pronoun used substantively (A.G. 296.2). The antecedent is **equites** (A.G. 297.e).

proeliari: Complementary infinitive after **consuerant** (A.G. 456). For a description of these tactics see **inter equites proeliari** at 18.1.

(65.5) Eorum adventu, quod minus idoneis equis utebantur, a tribunis militum reliquisque [sed et] equitibus Romanis atque evocatis equos sumit Germanisque distribuit.

a(b), *from.*
atque, *and.*

eques, -itis, m., *rider, horseman, cavalryman, trooper.*
et, *and.*
Germani, -orum, m., pl., *the Germans.*
is, ea, id, *he, she, it; that, this.*
minus, *less.*
quod, *because, since, for, as.*
Romanus, -a, -um, *Roman.*
sumo, sumere, sumpsi, sumptus, *take, appropriate.*
utor, uti, usus, *use, employ, have.*

adventus, -us, m., *coming, arrival.*
distribuo, -tribuere, -tribui, -tributus, *distribute, divide, assign, apportion.*
equus, -i, m., *horse.*
evocatus, -i, m., *reenlisted veteran.*
idoneus, -a, -um, *suitable, fit, capable.*
miles, -itis, m., *soldier, foot-solider.*
-que, *and.*
reliquus, -a, -um, *remaining, the rest.*
sed, *but.*
tribunus, -i, m., *tribune.*

Eorum: Plural, masculine, genitive demonstrative pronoun used substantively (A.G. 296.2). The antecedent is **equites** (A.G. 297.e). Possessive genitive with **adventu** (A.G. 343).

adventu: Ablative of *time when* (A.G. 423.1).

quod ... utebantur: Causal clause; the conjunction **quod** ("because") takes the indicative when the reason is given on the authority of the writer or speaker (A.G. 540.1). **utebantur**: The main verb of the subordinate clause (A.G. 278.b). The pronoun **ei**, with **Eorum** (**equites**) as the antecedent, is understood as the subject (A.G. 271.a).

minus: Defective comparative adverb modifying **idoneis** (A.G. 218.a, 291.c Note 2, and 320-21).

idoneis equis: Ablative direct object of the deponent verb **utebantur** (A.G. 410). "The German horses, though hardy, were small and scraggy." (Kelsey, 422-23)

a tribunis militum reliquisque [sed et] equitibus Romanis atque evocatis: Three ablatives of separation with the preposition **a(b)** after **sumit** (A.G. 401). **militum**: Possessive genitive with **tribunis** (A.G. 343). **-que**: The enclitic conjunction connects the two ablative nouns in the prepositional phrase **tribunis ... equitibus** (A.G. 324.a). **[sed et]**: Sense necessitates the deletion of these two words. **atque**: The conjunction connects the two ablative nouns in the prepositional phrase **equitibus ... evocatis** and means "and" (*OLD* **atque** 12). **evocatis**: "Below the centurions, but ranking above the common soldiers, were the privileged soldiers, who were relieved from picket-duty as well as work on fortifications and other manual labor. Such were the veteran volunteers (*evocati*), soldiers who had served their full time but had re-enlisted at the general's request." (Kelsey, 26)

equos: Accusative direct object of **sumit** (A.G. 387).

sumit: The main verb of the coordinate clause **Eorum ... sumit** (A.G. 278.a). The pronoun **is**, with **Caesar** as the antecedent, is understood as the subject (A.G. 271.a).

Germanisque: Dative indirect object of the transitive verb **distribuit** (A.G. 362). **Germanis**: See Appendix A. **-que**: The enclitic conjunction connects the two main verbs **sumit ... distribuit** (A.G. 324.a).

distribuit: The main verb of the coordinate clause **Germanisque distribuit** (A.G. 278.a). The pronoun **is**, with **Caesar** as the antecedent, is understood as the subject (A.G. 271.a). The pronoun **eos**, with **equos** as the antecedent, is understood as the direct object.

4.H CHAPTERS 66-68: THE GALLIC CAVALRY ATTACKS THE ROMANS ON THE MARCH AND ARE BEATEN BY THE GERMAN CAVALRY; THE GALLIC ARMY FLEES TO ALESIA

(66.1) Interea, dum haec geruntur, hostium copiae ex Arvernis equitesque qui toti Galliae erant imperati conveniunt.

Arverni, -orum, m., pl., *the Arverni.*

copiae, -arum, f., pl., *forces, troops.*
eques, -itis, m., *rider, horseman, cavalryman, trooper.*
Gallia, -ae, f., *Gaul.*
hic, haec, hoc, *this; he, she, it.*
impero, -are, -avi, -atus, *levy, draft, demand.*
-que, *and.*
totus, -a, -um, *the whole, all, all the, entire.*

convenio, -venire, -veni, -ventus, *come together, gather.*
dum, *while.*
ex, *from.*
gero, gerere, gessi, gestus, *carry out, perform, do.*
hostis, -is, m., *enemy, foe;* pl., *the enemy.*
interea, *in the meantime, meanwhile.*
qui, quae, quod, *who, which, what.*

Interea: Adverb, marks the passage to a new subject (*OLD* **interea** c).
dum ... geruntur: Temporal clause; the conjunction **dum** ("when, while") with the present indicative denotes continued action in past time (A.G. 556). **geruntur**: The main verb of the subordinate clause (A.G. 278.b).
haec: Plural, neuter, nominative demonstrative pronoun used substantively (A.G. 296.2). The antecedent is the actions described in Chapter 65 (A.G. 297.e).
hostium: Partitive genitive with **copiae** (A.G. 346.a.1).
copiae: Nominative subject (A.G. 339). These are the 10,000 levied at 64.4-5.
ex Arvernis: Ablative of source with the preposition **ex** (A.G. 403.1). **Arvernis**: See Appendix A.
equitesque: Nominative subject (A.G. 339). These are the 800 levied at 64.4-5. **-que**: The enclitic conjunction connects the two nominative nouns (A.G. 324.a).
qui ... erant imperati: Relative clause (A.G. 303). For the reference see 64.4-5. **qui**: Plural, masculine, nominative relative pronoun used substantively (A.G. 305). The antecedent is **equites** (A.G. 307). Nominative subject (A.G. 339). **erant imperati**: The main verb of the subordinate clause (A.G. 278.b). The pluperfect denotes an action completed in past time (A.G. 477).
toti Galliae: Dative indirect object of the passive verb **erant imperati** (A.G. 369.a). Some verbs ordinarily intransitive may have an accusative of the direct object along with the dative of the indirect object (A.G. 369); with the passive voice this dative may be retained (A.G. 369.a). **toti**: -i is the regular dative singular ending for the adjective **totus** (A.G. 113). **Galliae**: See Appendix A.
conveniunt: The main verb of the main clause (A.G. 278.b). The historical present, giving vividness to the narrative, is present in Chapter 66 (A.G. 469). This usage, common in all languages, comes from imagining past events as going on before our eyes (*repraesentatio*) (A.G. 469 Note).

(66.2-3) (2) Magno horum coacto numero, cum Caesar in Sequanos per extremos Lingonum finis iter faceret quo facilius subsidium provinciae ferri posset, circiter milia passuum X ab Romanis (3) trinis castris Vercingetorix consedit;

ab, *from, away from.*
castra, -orum, n., pl., *camp, encampment.*
cogo, cogere, coegi, coactus, *bring together, collect, gather, assemble.*

consido, -sidere, -sedi, -sessus, *halt, encamp.*
extremus, -a, -um, *outermost, farthest.*
facio, facere, feci, factus, *make.*
fines, -ium, m., pl., *borders*, hence *territory, country, land.*
in, *into the country of.*
Lingones, -um, m., pl., *the Lingones.*
milia, -um, n., pl., *thousand, thousands.*
passus, -us, m., *step, pace*, = 4 feet, 10 ¼ inches.
possum, posse, potui, -----, *be able.*
quo, *so that* (by that degree), *in order that, that, that thereby.*
Sequani, -orum, m., pl., *the Sequani.*
trini, -ae, -a, *three.*
X, in expression of number, = *10.*

Caesar, -aris, m., *Caesar.*
circiter, *about.*
conclamo, -are, -avi, -atus, *cry out loud together, shout, cry out.*
cum, *when, while.*
facile, comp. **-ius**, *easily, readily, with no trouble.*
fero, ferre, tuli, latus, *bring.*
hic, haec, hoc, *this; he, she, it.*
iter, itineris, n., *march, journey.*
magnus, -a, -um, *great, large.*
numerus, -i, m., *number, amount.*
per, *through.*
provincia, -ae, f., *the province.*
Romani, -orum, m., pl., *the Romans.*
subsidium, -i, n., *support, relief, reinforcement, help.*
Vercingetorix, -igis, m., *Vercingetorix.*

Magno horum coacto numero: Ablative absolute (A.G. 419-20). **horum**: Plural, masculine, genitive demonstrative pronoun used substantively (A.G. 296.2). The antecedent is **copiae** and **equites**, agreeing in gender with **equites** (A.G. 297.e). Partitive genitive with **numero** (A.G. 346.a.1). **coacto**: The perfect tense of the participle represents the action as completed at the time indicated by the tense of the main verb (A.G. 489).
cum ... faceret ... posset: Temporal clause; the relative adverb **cum** ("when, while") with the imperfect subjunctive describes the circumstances that accompanied the action of the main verb (A.G. 546). **faceret**: The main verb of the subordinate clause (A.G. 278.b). **posset**: See below.
Caesar: Nominative subject (A.G. 339). See Appendix A.
in Sequanos: Accusative of *place to which* with the preposition **in** ("into the country of") (A.G. 426.2). **Sequanos**: See Appendix A.
per extremos Lingonum finis: Prepositional phrase, **per** with the accusative here means "through" (*OLD* **per** 1). **extremos**: Defective superlative adjective (A.G. 130.b). **Lingonum**: Possessive genitive of the tribe name **Lingones** with **finis** (A.G. 343). See

Appendix A. **finis**: Accusative plural noun; **-is** for **-es** is the regular form in i-stem nouns (A.G. 65-7 and 74.c).
iter: Accusative direct object of **faceret** (A.G. 387). The phrase **iter facere** is an idiom that means "to march or travel" (*OLD* **iter** 1.b).
quo facilius ... posset: Final clause; the ablative **quo** (= **ut eo**) is used as a conjunction in a final (purpose) clause with the subjunctive (A.G. 531.a). **quo**: In a final clause with a comparative, the conjunction means "so that by that degree" (*OLD* **quo2** 3.b). **facilius**: Comparative adverb (A.G. 218 and 320-21). **posset**: The main verb of the subordinate clause (A.G. 278.b). Imperfect subjunctive; the tense of the subjunctive is in secondary sequence and follows the rules for the sequence of tense after **faceret** (A.G. 482-85). The pronoun **is**, with **Caesar** as the antecedent, is understood as the subject (A.G. 271.a).
subsidium: Nominative subject (A.G. 339).
provinciae: Dative indirect object of the passive infinitive **ferri**; verbs which in the active voice take the accusative and dative retain the dative when used in the passive (A.G. 365). See Appendix A.
ferri: Complementary infinitive after **posset** (A.G. 456).
circiter milia passuum X: Accusative of *extent of space* (A.G. 425). **circiter**: Adverb (A.G. 320-21). **milia**: Accusative plural; in the plural **mille** declines as a neuter noun (A.G. 134.d). **passuum**: Partitive genitive with **milia** (346.2). **X**: Roman numeral used as an adjective modifying **milia** (A.G. 133).
ab Romanis: Prepositional phrase, **ab** with the ablative here expresses distance and means "from, away from" (*OLD* **ab** 4).
trinis castris: Ablative of *place where* without a preposition (A.G. 429.1-2). **trinis**: Distributive numeral used as an adjective (A.G. 136-37). A distributive is used instead of a cardinal number to express simple number when a noun plural in form but singular in meaning is used in a plural sense (**castris**) (A.G. 137.b).
Vercingetorix: Nominative subject (A.G. 339). See Appendix A.
consedit: The main verb of the main clause (A.G. 278.b).

(66.3) convocatisque ad concilium praefectis equitum venisse tempus victoriae demonstrat: fugere in provinciam Romanos Galliaque excedere:

ad, *to.*
convoco, -are, -avi, -atus, *call together, summon, assemble.*

eques, -itis, m., *rider, horseman, cavalryman, trooper.*

fugio, fugere, fugi, -----, *flee, run away, make off.*
in, *into, towards.*
provincia, -ae, f., *the province.*
Romani, -orum, m., pl., *the Romans.*
venio, venire, veni, ventus, *come.*

concilium, -i, n., *meeting, assembly, council.*
demonstro, -are, -avi, -atus, *point out, show, say, mention, explain.*
excedo, -cedere, -cessi, -cessurus, *go out, leave, withdraw, depart.*
Gallia, -ae, f., *Gaul*
praefectus, -i, m., *prefect, cavalry captain.*
-que, *and, now.*
tempus, -oris, n., *time.*
victoria, -ae, f., *victory.*

convocatisque ... futurum (66.3-7): C. Murphy classifies this speech as military address (**contio**) and notes that it performs "The function of preparing the reader for the coming strategy and tactics of the Gauls." (C. Murphy, 122-123).
convocatisque ad concilium praefectis equitum: Ablative absolute (A.G. 419-20). **convocatis**: The perfect tense of the participle represents the action as completed at the time indicated by the tense of the main verb (A.G. 489). **-que**: The enclitic conjunction here begins the sentence introducing a fresh situation and means "and, now" (*OLD* **-que** 4). **ad concilium**: Accusative of *place to which* with the preposition **ad** (A.G. 426.2). **equitum**: Partitive genitive with **praefectis** (A.G. 346.a.1).
venisse tempus: Accusative/infinitive construction in indirect discourse after **demonstrat** (A.G. 577 ff). **venisse**: Perfect infinitive; the tense of the infinitive in indirect discourse is relative to that of the verb of saying (A.G. 584).
victoriae: Objective genitive with **tempus** (A.G. 348).
demonstrat: The main verb of the main clause (A.G. 278.b). The pronoun **is**, with **Vercingetorix** as the antecedent, is understood as the subject (A.G. 271.a).
fugere ... Romanos: Accusative/infinitive construction in indirect discourse after **demonstrat** (A.G. 577 ff.). **fugere**: Present infinitive; the tense of the infinitive in indirect discourse is relative to that of the verb of saying (A.G. 584).
in provinciam: Accusative of *place to which* with the preposition **in** (A.G. 426.2). **provinciam**: See Appendix A.
Galliaque: Ablative of separation without a preposition after the compound verb **excedere** (A.G. 402). **Gallia**: See Appendix A. **-que**: The enclitic conjunction connects the two infinitives **fugere ... excedere** (A.G. 324.a).
(eos) ... excedere: Accusative/infinitive construction in indirect discourse after **demonstrat** (A.G. 577 ff.). Supply the pronoun **eos**, with **Romanos** as the antecedent, as the accusative subject. **excedere**: Present infinitive; the tense of the infinitive in indirect discourse is relative to that of the verb of saying (A.G. 584).

(66.4-5) (4) id sibi ad praesentem obtinendam libertatem satis esse, ad reliqui temporis pacem atque otium parum profici: maioribus enim coactis copiis reversuros neque finem bellandi (5) facturos.

ad, *towards the attainment of, for.*
bello, -are, -avi, -atus, *wage war, carry on war, fight.*

copiae, -arum, f., pl., *forces, troops.*
facio, facere, feci, factus, *make.*

atque, *and.*
cogo, cogere, coegi, coactus, *bring together, collect, gather, assemble.*
enim, *for, for in fact, and in fact.*
finis, -is, m., *end.*

is, ea, id, *he, she, it; that, this.*
maior, -or, -us, *greater, larger, bigger.*
obtineo, -tinere, -tinui, -tentus, *win, gain, get possession of.*
pax, pacis, f., *peace.*
praesens, -entis, *present, existing.*

reliquus, -a, -um, *remaining, the rest.*
satis, *enough.*
sum, esse, fui, futurus, *be.*

libertas, -atis, f., *freedom, liberty, independence.*
neque, *and ... not.*
otium, -i, n., *rest, quiet.*
parum, *too little, not enough.*
proficio, -ficere, -feci, -fectus, *effect, gain, accomplish, be useful.*
revertor, -verti, -versus, *return, come back, go back.*
sui, sibi, se, or **sese,** nom. wanting, *in his opinion.*
tempus, -oris, n., *time.*

id ... satis esse: Accusative/infinitive construction in indirect discourse after **demonstrat** (A.G. 577 ff.). **id:** Singular, neuter, accusative demonstrative pronoun used substantively (A..G. 296.2). The antecedent is the idea of the Romans leaving (A.G. 297.e). **satis:** An adverb in the predicate position after **esse** (A.G. 283-84 and 321.d) (*OLD* **satis** B.8). **esse:** Present infinitive; the tense of the infinitive in indirect discourse is relative to that of the verb of saying (A.G. 584).

sibi: Singular, masculine, dative indirect reflexive pronoun (A.G. 300.2). The antecedent is **is** (**Vercingetorix**), the subject of **demonstrat** (A.G. 299). Dative of person judging, a weakened variety of the dative of reference. The dative is used of the person from whose point of view an opinion is stated and means "in his opinion" (A.G. 378).

ad praesentem obtinendam libertatem: Prepositional phrase, **ad** with the accusative here denotes purpose and means "towards the attainment of, for" (*OLD* **ad** 43). **obtinendam:** Singular, feminine, accusative gerundive used as an adjective modifying **libertatem** denoting necessity, obligation or propriety (A.G. 500.1). **libertatem:** For the theme of liberty in Book 7, see **liberius** at 1.3.

ad reliqui temporis pacem atque otium: Prepositional phrase, **ad** with the accusative here denotes purpose and means "towards the attainment of, for" (*OLD* **ad** 43). **reliqui temporis:** Genitive of quality (measure) with both **pacem** and **otium** (A.G. 345.b and 417). **atque:** The conjunction connects the two accusative nouns in the prepositional phrase and means "and" (*OLD* **atque** 12).

(id) parum (esse): Accusative/infinitive construction in indirect discourse after **demonstrat** (A.G. 577 ff.). Carry down **id ... esse** to fill in the ellipsis with **parum** so that the construction is equivalent to **id ... satis esse** above (A.G. 640). **parum:** An adverb in the predicate position after the supplied infinitive **esse** (A.G. 283-84 and 321.d) (*OLD* **parum** 1).

profici: Complementary infinitive after **(id) parum (esse)** (A.G. 456).

maioribus enim coactis copiis: Ablative absolute (A.G. 419-20). **maioribus:** Irregular comparative adjective (A.G. 129). **enim:** Postpositive conjunction (A.G. 324.j and 599.b). **coactis:** The perfect tense of the participle represents the action as completed at the time indicated by the tense of the main verb (A.G. 489).

(eos) ... reversuros (esse): Accusative/infinitive construction in indirect discourse after **demonstrat** (A.G. 577 ff.). Supply the pronoun **eos**, with **Romanos** as the antecedent, as the accusative subject. **reversuros (esse):** Supply **esse** to form the future, active infinitive (A.G. 186). The tense of the infinitive in indirect discourse is relative to that of the verb of saying (A.G. 584).

nec: The conjunction joins a negative clause to a preceding positive one and means "and ... not" (*OLD* **neque** 3).

finem bellandi: Accusative direct object of the infinitive **facturos (esse)** (A.G. 387 and 451.3). **bellandi:** Singular, neuter, genitive gerund (A.G. 501-02). Objective genitive with **finem** (A.G. 504).

(eos) ... facturos (esse): Accusative/infinitive construction in indirect discourse after **demonstrat** (A.G. 577 ff.). Supply the pronoun **eos**, with **Romanos** as the antecedent, as the accusative subject. **facturos (esse):** Supply **esse** to form the future, active infinitive (A.G. 188). The tense of the infinitive in indirect discourse is relative to that of the verb of saying (A.G. 584).

(66.5) Proinde agmine impeditos adoriantur: si pedites suis auxilium ferant atque in eo morentur, iter facere non posse;

adorior, -oriri, -ortus, *fall upon, attack, assail.*
atque, *and.*
facio, facere, feci, factus, *make.*
impeditus, -i, m., *soldier encumbered with baggage.*
is, ea, id, *he, she, it; that, this.*
moror, -ari, -atus, *tarry, delay, linger.*
pedites, -um, m., pl., *infantry.*
proinde, *so then, accordingly, hence, therefore, and so.*
sui, -orum, m., pl., *their men,* with or without *own.*

agmen, -minis, n., *march, line of march.*
auxilium, -i, n., *help, aid, assistance, relief.*
fero, ferre, tuli, latus, *bear, carry, render.*
in, *in.*
iter, itineris, n., *march, journey.*
non, *not.*
possum, posse, potui, -----, *be able.*
si, *if.*

Proinde: Adverb, when used in exhortations it means "so then, accordingly" (*OLD* **proinde** 3.a).

agmine: Ablative of *place where* without a preposition (A.G. 429.1).

impeditos: Plural, masculine, accusative adjective used substantively (A.G. 288). The noun **Romanos** is understood (A.G. 288.b). Accusative direct object of **adoriantur** (A.G. 387).

adoriantur: The main verb of the main clause (A.G. 278.b). Present subjunctive; a hortatory subjunctive (jussive) in indirect discourse after **demonstrat** remains in the subjunctive rather than the infinitive even though it is an independent clause in indirect discourse (A.G. 577 and 588.a). The pronoun **ipsi**, with **praefectis equitum** (those present at the council) at 66.3 as the antecedent, is understood as the subject (A.G. 271.a).

si ... iri (66.5-6): "Vercingetorix proposed to attack the Romans on the march. If the Roman infantry, thus caught at a disadvantage, should attempt to protect the baggage-train, their retreat would be hindered; if they should leave the baggage to its fate and try to protect themselves, they would be cut off from their supplies. Either alternative, Vercingetorix reckoned, would in the end put complete victory within his grasp." (Kelsey, 423)

si ... ferant ... morentur ... posse: Conditional statement in indirect discourse after **demonstrat** (A.G. 589). The protasis, as a dependent clause, is in the subjunctive and the apodosis, as the principal clause, is in the infinitive (A.G. 589).

si ... ferant ... morentur: The conjunction **si** ("if") with the subjunctive forms the protasis of a conditional statement in indirect discourse (A.G. 589.1). **ferant ... morentur**: The main verbs of the subordinate clause (A.G. 278.b). Present subjunctives; the tense of the subjunctives is normally in secondary sequence after the historical present **demonstrat** (A.G. 482-85). Here it is in primary sequence through *repraesentatio* (A.G. 485.e and 585.b Note).

pedites: Nominative subject (A.G. 339).

suis: Plural, masculine, dative possessive pronoun used substantively to denote a special class (A.G. 302.d). Dative indirect object of the transitive verb **ferant** (A.G. 362).

auxilium: Accusative direct object of the transitive verb **ferant** (A.G. 387).

atque: The conjunction connects the two verbs in the protasis and means "and" (*OLD* atque 12).

in eo morentur: The phrase **in eo morari** is an idiom that means "to waste time on, delay over" (*OLD* moror 7.b).

in eo: Prepositional phrase; **in** with the ablative here means "in" (expressing an abstract location) (*OLD* in 26). **eo**: Singular, neuter, ablative demonstrative pronoun used substantively (A.G. 296.2). The antecedent is **auxilium** (A.G. 297.e).

iter: Accusative direct object of the infinitive **facere** (A.G. 387 and 451.3). The phrase **iter facere** is an idiom that means "to march or travel" (*OLD* iter 1.b).

facere: Complementary infinitive after **posse** (A.G. 456).

non: Adverb, the adverb generally precedes the verb if it belongs to no one word in particular (A.G. 217.e, 320-21, and 599.a).

(eos) posse: The apodosis of the conditional statement (A.G. 589.2). Accusative/infinitive construction in indirect discourse after **demonstrat** (A.G. 577 ff.). Supply the pronoun **eos**, with **Romanos** as the antecedent, as the accusative subject. **posse**: Present infinitive; the tense of the infinitive in indirect discourse is relative to that of the verb of saying (A.G. 584). The present infinitive **posse** often has a future sense (A.G. 584.b).

(66.5-6) si, id quod magis futurum confidat, relictis impedimentis suae saluti consulant, et usu rerum necessariarum et (6) dignitate spoliatum iri.

confido, -fidere, -fisus sum, *be confident, be assured*

dignitas, -tatis, f., *dignity, honor, reputation.*
impedimenta, -orum, n., pl., *heavy baggage, baggage.*
magis, *more, rather.*
qui, quae, quod, *who, which, what.*
res, rei, f., *goods, possessions.*
si, *if.*
sum, esse, fui, futurus, *be.*
usus, -us, m., *advantage, profit, benefit.*

consulo, -sulere, -sului, -sultus, *have regard for, look out for.*
et ... et, *both ... and.*
is, ea, id, *he, she, it; that, this.*
necessarius, -a, -um, *needful, necessary, critical.*
relinquo, -linquere, -liqui, -lictus, *leave, leave behind.*
salus, -utis, f., *preservation, safety, deliverance.*
spolio, -are, -avi, -atus, *strip, despoil.*
suus, -a, -um, *their,* with or without *own.*

si ... consulant ... spoliatum iri: Conditional statement in indirect discourse after **demonstrat** (A.G. 589). The protasis, as a dependent clause, is in the subjunctive and the protasis, as the principal clause, is in the infinitive (A.G. 589).

si ... consulant: The conjunction **si** ("if") with the subjunctive forms the protasis of a conditional statement in indirect discourse (A.G. 589.1). **consulant**: The main verb of the subordinate clause (A.G. 278.b). Present subjunctive; the tense of the subjunctive is normally in secondary sequence after the historical present **demonstrat** (A.G. 482-85). Here it is in primary sequence through *repraesentatio* (A.G. 485.e and 585.b Note). The pronoun **ei**, with **Romanos** as the antecedent, is understood as the subject (A.G. 271.a).

(facientes) id: Supply the participle **facientes** as an adjective modifying **ei**, the supplied subject of **consulant**. **id**: Singular, neuter, accusative demonstrative pronoun used substantively (A.G. 296.2). The pronoun functions as a correlative to the relative clause **quod ... confidat** (A.G. 297.d). Accusative direct object of the supplied participle **facientes** (A.G. 387 and 488).

quod ... confidat: Relative clause; a clause dependent on a subjunctive clause (**si ... consulant**) takes the subjunctive when regarded as an integral part of that clause (attraction) (A.G. 303 and 593). Vercingetorix will prove to be wrong about this. **quod**: See below.

confidat: The main verb of the subordinate clause (A.G. 278.b). Present subjunctive; the tense of the subjunctive is normally in secondary sequence after the historical present **demonstrat** (A.G. 482-85). Here it is in primary sequence through *repraesentatio* (A.G. 485.e and 585.b Note). The pronoun **is**, with **Vercingetorix** as the antecedent, is understood as the subject (A.G. 271.a).

quod ... futurum (esse): Accusative/infinitive construction in indirect discourse after **confidat** (A.G. 577 ff.). **quod**: Singular, neuter, accusative relative pronoun used substantively (A.G. 305). The antecedent is **id** (A.G. 297.e). **futurum (esse)**: Supply **esse** to form the future infinitive of **sum** (A.G. 170). The tense of the infinitive in indirect discourse is relative to that of the verb of saying (A.G. 584).

magis: Adverb (A.G. 320-21).

relictis impedimentis: Ablative absolute (A.G. 419-20). **relictis**: The perfect tense of the participle represents the action as completed at the time indicated by the tense of the main verb (A.G. 489).

suae saluti: Dative indirect object of the intransitive use of **consulant** (A.G. 367.c). **suae**: Singular, feminine, dative possessive pronoun use as an adjective modifying **saluti** (A.G. 302).

et ... et: The repeated conjunction means "both ... and", connecting the two ablative nouns (A.G. 323.e).

usu ... dignitate: Two ablatives of separation after **spoliatum iri** (A.G. 401).

rerum necessariarum: Objective genitive with **usu** (A.G. 348).

(eos) spoliatum iri: The apodosis of the conditional statement (A.G. 589.2). Accusative/infinitive construction in indirect discourse after **demonstrat** (A.G. 577 ff.). Supply the pronoun **eos**, with **Romanos** as the antecedent, as the accusative subject. **spoliatum iri**: The future passive infinitive is formed from the infinitive passive of **eo** (**iri**) and the supine in **-um** (**spoliatum**) (A.G. 193. Note and 203.a). The supine does not decline and so remains **spoliatum**, not **spoliatos**, which would agree with the supplied accusative pronoun **eos**. The tense of the infinitive in indirect discourse is relative to that of the verb of saying (A.G. 584).

(66.6) Nam de equitibus hostium quin nemo eorum progredi modo extra agmen audeat [et] ipsos quidem non debere dubitare:

agmen, -minis, n., *marching column, line of march.*
de, *with regard to, in the matter of.*
dubito, -are, -avi, -atus, *be uncertain, doubt.*
et, *and.*
hostis, -is, m., *enemy, foe*; pl., *the enemy.*

is, ea, id, *he, she, it; that, this.*
nam, *for.*
non, *not.*

quidem, *indeed, at least.*

audeo, audere, ausus sum, *venture, dare, risk.*
debeo, debere, debui, debitus, *ought, must, should.*
eques, -itis, m., *rider, horseman, cavalryman, trooper.*
extra, *to the outside of, out of.*
ipse, -a, -um, *he, they,* with or without *himself, themselves.*
modo, *only, merely.*
nemo, -----, m., *no one, nobody.*
progredior, -gredi, -gressus, *advance, go forward, proceed.*
quin, *that, but that.*

Nam ... dubitare: Adcock notes that Vercingetorix's "calculations are sound except that he does not know that Caesar has procured cavalry and light-armed troops from Germany. In chapter 67 their intervention at the right moment turns the well-laid scheme of Vercingetorix into a disaster." (Adcock, 55).
Nam: Causal conjunction (A.G. 223.a.3).
de equitibus hostium: Prepositional phrase, **de** with the ablative here means "with regard to, in the matter of" (*OLD* **de** 13). **hostium**: Partitive genitive with **equitibus** (A.G. 346.a.1).
quin ... audeat: Subordinate clause; the conjunction **quin** ("that") with the subjunctive is used after the infinitive **dubitare** (A.G. 278.b and 558.a). **audeat**: The main verb of the subordinate clause (A.G. 278.b). Present subjunctive; the tense of the subjunctive is normally in secondary sequence after the historical present **demonstrat** (A.G. 482-85). Here it is in primary sequence through *repraesentatio* (A.G. 485.e and 585.b Note).
nemo: Nominative subject (A.G. 339)
eorum: Plural, masculine, genitive demonstrative pronoun used substantively (A.G. 296.2). The antecedent is **equitibus** (A.G. 297.e). Partitive genitive with **nemo** (A.G. 346.a.1).
progredi: Complementary infinitive after **audeat** (A.G. 456).
modo: Adverb (A.G. 320-21).
extra agmen: Prepositional phrase, **extra** with the accusative here means "to the outside of, out of" (*OLD* **extra** 6.b).
[et]: Sense necessitates the deletion of the superfluous conjunction.
ipsos ... debere: Accusative/infinitive construction in indirect discourse after **demonstrat** (A.G. 577 ff.). **ipsos**: Plural, masculine, accusative demonstrative pronoun used substantively (A.G. 296.2 and 298.d). The antecedent is **praefectis equitum** (those present at the council) at 66.3 (A.G. 298). The pronoun is here emphatic (A.G. 298.d.1). **debere**: Present infinitive; the tense of the infinitive in indirect discourse is relative to that of the verb of saying (A.G. 584).
quidem: Particle, placed directly after the word it emphasizes (**ipsos**) (*OLD* **quidem**).
non: Adverb, the adverb generally precedes the verb if it belongs to no one word in particular (A.G. 217.e, 320-21, and 599.a).
dubitare: Complementary infinitive after **debere** (A.G. 456).

(66.6-7) id quo maiore faciant animo, copias se omnis pro castris habiturum et terrori hostibus (7) futurum.

animus, -i, m., *courage, spirit, temper, resolution.*
copiae, -arum, f., pl., *forces, troops.*
facio, facere, feci, factus, *do.*
hostis, -is, m., *enemy, foe*; pl., *the enemy.*
maior, -or, -us, *greater.*
pro, *in front of, before.*

sui, sibi, se, or **sese**, nom. wanting, *he,* with or without *himself.*
terror, -oris, m., *fear, dread, alarm, terror.*

castra, -orum, n., pl., *camp, encampment.*
et, *and.*
habeo, habere, habui, habitus, *convene, exhibit.*
is, ea, id, *he, she, it; that, this.*
omnis, -e, *all.*
quo, *so that* (by that degree), *in order that, that, that thereby.*
sum, esse, fui, futurus, *be.*

id: Singular, neuter, accusative demonstrative pronoun used substantively (A.G. 296.2). The antecedent is the previous idea of attacking the Romans (A.G. 297.e). Accusative direct object of **faciant** (A.G. 387).
quo maiore ... faciant animo: Final clause; the ablative **quo** (= **ut eo**) is used as a conjunction in a final (purpose) clause with the subjunctive (A.G. 531.a). **quo**: In a final clause with a comparative, the conjunction means "so that by that degree" (*OLD* **quo2** 3.b). **maiore ... animo**: Ablative of quality (descriptive ablative) with an adjective modifier (A.G. 415). **maiore**: Irregular comparative adjective (A.G. 129). **faciant**: The main verb of the subordinate clause (A.G. 278.b). Present subjunctive; the tense of the subjunctive is normally in secondary sequence after the historical present **demonstrat** (A.G. 482-85). Here it is in primary sequence through

repraesentatio (A.G. 485.e and 585.b Note). The pronoun **ipsi**, with **ipsos (praefectis equitum)** as the antecedent, is understood as the subject (A.G. 271.a).

copias ... omnis: Accusative direct object of the infinitive **habiturum (esse)** (A.G. 387 and 451.3). **omnis**: Accusative adjective; **-is** for **-es** is the regular form in i-stem adjectives (A.G. 114.a and 116).

se ... habiturum (esse): Accusative/infinitive construction in indirect discourse after **demonstrat** (A.G. 577 ff.). **se**: Singular, masculine, accusative direct reflexive pronoun (A.G. 300.1). The antecedent is **is (Vercingetorix)**, the supplied subject of **demonstrat** (A.G. 299). **habiturum (esse)**: Supply **esse** to form the future, active infinitive (A.G. 185). The tense of the infinitive in indirect discourse is relative to that of the verb of saying (A.G. 584).

pro castris: Prepositional phrase, **pro** with the ablative here means "in front of, before" (*OLD* **pro1** 1). "He would display the infantry before the camp as an inspiration to the cavalry, who were to make the attack." (Kelsey, 423)

et: The conjunction connects the two infinitives **habiturum (esse) ... futurum (esse)** (A.G. 324.a).

terrori hostibus: Dative of the purpose or end (double dative). The dative of an abstract noun (**terrori**) is used to show that for which a thing serves or which it accomplishes, with another dative of the person or thing affected (**hostibus**). The verb is normally a form of **sum (futurum (esse))** (A.G. 382.1).

(se) futurum (esse): Accusative/infinitive construction in indirect discourse after **demonstrat** (A.G. 577 ff.). Carry down **se** from above as the accusative pronoun. **futurum (esse)**: Supply **esse** to form the future active infinitive of **sum** (A.G. 170). The tense of the infinitive in indirect discourse is relative to that of the verb of saying (A.G. 584).

(66.7) Conclamant equites, sanctissimo iure iurando confirmari oportere ne tecto recipiatur, ne ad liberos, ne ad parentis, ne ad uxorem aditum habeat qui non bis per agmen hostium perequitasset.

ad, *to.*

agmen, -minis, n., *army on the march, marching column, line of march.*
conclamo, -are, -avi, -atus, *cry out loud together, shout, cry out.*
eques, -it is, m., *rider, horseman, cavalryman, trooper.*
hostis, -is, m., *enemy, foe*; pl., *the enemy.*

liberi, -orum, m., pl., *children.*
non, *not.*

parens, -entis, m. or f., *father, mother, parent.*
perequito, -are, -avi, -----, *ride through.*
recipio, -cipere, -cepi, -ceptus, *receive, admit.*
tectum, -i, n., *house.*

aditus, -us, m., *approach, access, way of approach, means of access.*
bis, *twice.*
confirmo, -are, -avi, -atus, *bind.*
habeo, habere, habui, habitus, *have.*
ius iurandum, iuris iurandi, n. (**ius** + gerundive of **iuro**), *oath.*
ne, *so that ... not.*
oportet, oportere, oportuit, (imper.), *it is necessary, it is needful.*
per, *through.*
qui, quae, quod, *who, which, what.*
sanctus, -a, -um, sup. **-issimus**, *hallowed, sacred.*
uxor, -oris, f., *wife.*

Conclamant equites: The reversal of the normal word order (subject first, verb last) is called hyperbaton (A.G. 596) (Gotoff, 6-10).
Conclamant: Verb first in the emphatic position. Here it marks the end of the indirect discourse after **demonstrat** and emphasizes the degree of approval of the Gauls (A.G. 598.d).
equites: Nominative subject (A.G. 339).
sanctissimo iure iurando confirmari: The infinitive phrase functions as the subject of the impersonal verb **oportere** (A.G. 454). "The oath given at 7.66.7. It would be interesting to know how many of them kept their vow." (Kelsey, 423) **sanctissimo iure iurando**: Ablative of means (A.G. 409). **sanctissimo**: Superlative adjective (A.G. 124). **iure iurando**: The phrase **ius iurandum** is an idiom that means "a binding formula to be sworn to, an oath" (*OLD* **ius** 5). **iurando**: Singular, neuter, ablative gerundive used as an adjective modifying **iure** denoting necessity, obligation or propriety (A.G. 500.1). **confirmari**: Impersonal use of the infinitive (A.G. 208.c). The following negative purpose clause functions as the subject; a substantive clause used as the object of a verb becomes the subject when the verb is put in the passive (A.G. 566).
oportere: Impersonal infinitive construction in indirect discourse (A.G. 577 ff.). The verb of saying is not expressed, but implied in the verb **Conclamant** (A.G. 580.a). The previous infinitive phrase functions as the subject (A.G. 208.c).
ne ... recipiatur ne ... ne ... habeat: The conjunction **ne** ("so that ... not") with the subjunctive forms a substantive clause of purpose (A.G. 563). The clause functions as the subject of the impersonal infinitive **confirmari**; a substantive clause used as the object of a verb becomes the subject when the verb is put into the passive (A.G. 566). **ne ... ne ... ne ... ne**: The repetition of words at the beginning of successive clauses is anaphora (A.G. 641). **recipiatur ... habeat**: The main verbs of the subordinate clause (A.G. 278.b). Present subjunctives; the tense of the subjunctives is normally in secondary sequence after the historical present **Conclamant** (A.G. 482-85). Here it is in primary sequence through *repraesentatio* (A.G. 485.e and 585.b Note). The pronoun **is**, correlative to the following relative clause **qui ... perequitasset**, is understood as the subject of both verbs (A.G. 271.a).
tecto: Ablative of *place where* without a preposition (A.G. 429.1).
ad liberos: Prepositional phrase, **ad** with the accusative here means "to" (*OLD* **ad** 1).
ad parentis: Prepositional phrase, **ad** with the accusative here means "to" (*OLD* **ad** 1). **parentis**: Accusative plural noun, **-is** for **-es** is the regular form in mixed i-stem nouns (A.G. 71-2).
ad uxorem: Prepositional phrase, **ad** with the accusative here means "to" (*OLD* **ad** 1).
aditum: Accusative direct object of **habeat** (A.G. 387).
qui ... perequitasset: A relative clause of characteristic; a relative clause with the subjunctive is often used to indicate a characteristic of the antecedent (this would also be subjunctive by attraction) (A.G. 535). **qui**: Singular, masculine, nominative relative pronoun

used substantively (A.G. 305). The antecedent is omitted, supply **is** (A.G. 307.c). Nominative subject (A.G. 339). **perequitasset**: The main verb of the subordinate clause (A.G. 278.b). Pluperfect subjunctive; the tense of the subjunctive is in secondary sequence after the historical present **Conclamant** (A.G. 482-85, esp. 485.e). Here the pluperfect subjunctive in a dependent clause in indirect discourse is representing the future perfect tense in direct discourse (A.G. 484.c). Contracted form of **equitavisset** (A.G. 181.a).
non: Adverb; when **non** is especially emphatic it begins the clause (A.G. 217.e, 320-21, and 599.a).
bis: Numeral adverb (A.G. 138 and 320-21).
per agmen hostium: Prepositional phrase, **per** with the accusative here means "through" (*OLD* **per** 1). **hostium**: Possessive genitive with **agmen** (A.G. 343).

(67.1-2) **Probata re atque omnibus iure iurando adactis, postero die in tris partis distributo equitatu duae se acies ab duobus lateribus ostendunt, una a primo agmine iter impedire (2) coepit.**

a, ab, *on*; *at.*
adigo, -igere, -egi, -actus, *bind by an oath, cause to take an oath.*

atque, *and.*
dies, -ei, m. and f., *day.*

duo, -ae, -o, *two.*
impedio, -pedire, -pedivi, -peditus, *hinder, obstruct.*
iter, itineris, n., *line of march, march, road, route.*

latus, -eris, n., *side, flank.*
ostendo, -tendere, -tendi, -tentus, *show, display.*
posterus, -a, -um, *following, the next.*
probo, -are, -avi, -atus, *approve.*
sui, sibi, se, or **sese**, nom. wanting, *they*, with or without *themselves.*
unus, -a, -um, *one.*

acies, -ei, f., *division.*
agmen, -minis, n., *marching column*, (with **primum**) *the van.*
coepi, -isse, coeptus, *begin, start, commence.*
distribuo, -tribuere, -tribui, -tributus, *distribute, divide, assign, apportion.*
equitatus, -us, m., *cavalry.*
in, *into.*
ius iurandum, iuris iurandi, n. (**ius** + gerundive of **iuro**), *oath.*
omnes, -ium, m., pl., *all men, all.*
pars, partis, f., *part, portion, division.*
primus, -a, -um, *first part of.*
res, rei, f., *matter, affair, course of action.*
tres, tria, gen. **trium**, *three.*

Probata re: Ablative absolute (A.G. 419-20). **Probata**: The perfect tense of the participle represents the action as completed at the time indicated by the tense of the main verb (A.G. 489).
atque: The conjunction connects the first two ablative absolutes and means "and" (*OLD* **atque** 12).
omnibus iure iurando adactis: Ablative absolute (A.G. 419-20). **omnibus**: Plural, masculine, ablative adjective used substantively (A.G. 288). **iure iurando**: Ablative of means after **adactis** (A.G. 409). The phrase **ius iurandum** means "a binding formula to be sworn to, an oath" (*OLD* **ius** 5). **iurando**: Singular, neuter, ablative gerundive used as an adjective modifying **iure** denoting necessity, obligation or propriety (A.G. 500.1). **adactis**: The perfect tense of the participle represents the action as completed at the time indicated by the tense of the main verb (A.G. 489). Perfect passive participle of **adigo** meaning "to cause (a person) to take (an oath), bind (a person) by (an oath)" (*OLD* **adigo** 9).
postero die in tris partis distributo equitatu: Ablative absolute (A.G. 419-20). **postero die**: Ablative of *time when* (A.G. 423.1). **die**: The noun **dies** is normally masculine gender (A.G. 97.a). **in tris partis**: Prepositional phrase, **in** with the accusative here means "into" (*OLD* **in** 2). **tris**: Declinable cardinal number used as an adjective modifying **partis** (A.G. 132-35). **-is** for **-es** is an alternative accusative plural ending (A.G. 134.b). **partis**: Accusative plural noun, **-is** for **-es** is the regular form in mixed i-stem nouns (A.G. 71-2). **distributo**: The perfect tense of the participle represents the action as completed at the time indicated by the tense of the main verb (A.G. 489).
duae ... acies: Nominative subject (A.G. 339). **duae**: Declinable cardinal number used as an adjective (A.G. 132-35).
se: Plural, feminine, accusative direct reflexive pronoun (A.G. 300.1). The antecedent is **acies**, the subject of **ostendunt** (A.G. 299). Accusative direct object of **ostendunt** (A.G. 387).
ab duobus lateribus: Ablative of position with the preposition **ab** (A.G. 429.b). **duobus**: Declinable cardinal number used as an adjective modifying **lateribus** (A.G. 132-35).
ostendunt: The main verb of the coordinate clause **Probata ... ostendunt** (A.G. 278.a). The historical present, giving vividness to the narrative, is present in Chapter 67 (A.G. 469). This usage, common in all languages, comes from imagining past events as going on before our eyes (*repraesentatio*) (A.G. 469 Note).
una: Cardinal number used substantively (A.G. 132-35). The noun **acies** is understood. Nominative subject (A.G. 339).
a primo agmine: Ablative of *position* with the preposition **a(b)** (A.G. 429.b). **primo**: Ordinal number used as an adjective modifying **agmine** (A.G. 132-35). The ordinal number here expresses a part of the column and means "the first part of" (*OLD* **agmen** 5.b).
iter: Accusative direct object of the infinitive **impedire** (A.G. 387 and 451.3).
impedire: Complementary infinitive after **coepit** (A.G. 456).
coepit: The main verb of the coordinate clause **una ... coepit** (A.G. 278.a). Notice the asyndeton between the two clauses (A.G. 323.b).

(67.2) **Qua re nuntiata Caesar suum quoque equitatum tripertito divisum contra hostem ire iubet.**

Caesar, -aris, m., *Caesar.*
divido, -videre, -visi, -visus, *separate, divide.*

contra, *against, to meet.*
eo, ire, ivi, or **ii, iturus**, *go, pass, march, advance.*

equitatus, -us, m., *cavalry.*
iubeo, iubere, iussi, iussus, *order, give orders, bid, command.*
qui, quae, quod, *who, which, what.*
res, rei, f., *matter, affair.*
tripertito, *in three divisions.*

hostis, -is, m., *enemy, foe.*
nuntio, -are, -avi, -atus, *announce, report.*
quoque, *also, too.*
suus, -a, -um, *his,* with or without *own.*

Qua re nuntiata: Ablative absolute (A.G. 419-20). **Qua**: Singular, feminine, ablative relative pronoun (A.G. 305). The antecedent is **re** in its own clause (adjectival use) (A.G. 307.b). The relative does not introduce a relative clause but is a connecting relative; at the beginning of a clause the pronoun is often best rendered by a personal or demonstrative pronoun, with or without *and* (A.G. 308.f). **nuntiata**: The perfect tense of the participle represents the action as completed at the time indicated by the tense of the main verb (A.G. 489).
Caesar: Nominative subject (A.G. 339). See Appendix A.
suum ... equitatum ... divisum ... ire: A subject accusative with the infinitive after **iubet**. The construction is equivalent to a substantive clause of purpose (A.G. 563.a). **suum**: Singular, masculine, accusative possessive pronoun used as an adjective modifying **equitatum** (A.G. 302). **divisum**: Accusative perfect, participle used as a predicate modifying **equitatum**, where in English a phrase or a subordinate clause would be more normal (A.G. 496).
quoque: Adverb (A.G. 320-21). The adverb follows the emphatic word (A.G. 322.a).
tripertito: Adverb (A.G. 320-21).
contra hostem: Prepositional phrase, **contra** with the accusative here means "against, to meet" (*OLD* **contra** 15).
iubet: The main verb of the main clause (A.G. 278.b).

(67.2-4) Pugnatur una (3) omnibus in partibus. Consistit agmen; impedimenta intra (4) legiones recipiuntur.

agmen, -minis, n., *army on the march, marching column.*

impedimenta, -orum, n., pl., *heavy baggage, baggage.*
intra, *within.*
omnis, -e, *all.*
pugno, -are, -avi, -atus, *fight, combat, engage.*
una, *at one and the same time, at the same time.*

consisto, -sistere, -stiti, -stitus, *stop, halt, take a position, make a stand.*
in, *in.*
legio, -onis, f., *legion.*
pars, partis, f., *part, region, district, side, direction.*
recipio, -cipere, -cepi, -ceptus, *receive, admit.*

(id) Pugnatur: The main verb of the simple sentence (A.G. 278.1). Impersonal use of a passive intransitive passive verb (A.G. 208.d). Supply **id** as the subject (.G. 318.c). The verb comes in the first position when the idea in it is emphatic (A.G. 598.d).
una: Adverb (A.G. 320-21).
omnibus in partibus: Ablative of *place where* with the preposition **in** (locative ablative) (A.G. 426.3). **in**: A monosyllabic preposition is often placed between a noun and its adjective (A.G. 599.d.2).
Consistit: The main verb of the simple sentence (A.G. 278.1). The verb comes in the first position when the idea in it is emphatic (A.G. 598.d). The pronoun **is**, with **Caesar** as the antecedent, is understood as the subject (A.G. 271.a).
agmen: Accusative direct object of **Consistit** (A.G. 387).
impedimenta: Nominative subject (A.G. 339).
intra legiones: Prepositional phrase, **intra** with the accusative here means "within" (*OLD* **intra** 1).
recipiuntur: The main verb of the simple sentence (A.G. 278.1). "Each legion protected its own baggage." (Kelsey, 424) "during the march baggage was carried between the legions, but if attack threatened, they formed up in a square and placed it in their midst." (Hammond, 241) Vercingetorix had presented two options for the Romans after they were attacked; either they stop and fight (66.5) or, as Vercingetorix thought would happen, they would leave their baggage and look to their own safety (66.5-6). He was incorrect as the Romans chose to stand and fight. It seems unlikely that, even if he had not procured cavalry from Germany, Caesar would have abandoned his baggage and fled.

(67.4) Si qua in parte nostri laborare aut gravius premi videbantur, eo signa inferri Caesar aciemque constitui iubebat;

acies, -ei, f., *line of battle, line.*
Caesar, -aris, m., *Caesar.*

eo, *thither, there.*
in, *in.*
iubeo, iubere, iussi, iussus, *order, give orders, bid, command.*

nostri, -orum, m., pl., *our men, our side.*
premo, -ere, pressi, pressus, *press, harass, oppress.*
quis, -----, quid, *any;* (as adj., **qui, quae,** or **qua, quod**).
signum, -i, n., *standard.*

aut, *or.*
constituo, -stituere, -stitui, -stitutus, *draw up, establish, form.*
graviter, comp. -ius, *severely, seriously.*
infero, -ferre, intuli, illatus, (with **signa**), *advance.*
laboro, -are, -avi, -atus, *be hard pressed, be in distress, be in danger.*
pars, partis, f., *part, region, district, direction.*
-que, *and.*
si, *if.*
videor, videri, visus sum, *seem, appear.*

Si ... videbantur ... iubebat: Conditional statement: simple condition, past time (imperfect indicative in both clause) (A.G. 514.A.2).
Si ... videbantur: The conjunction **si** ("if") with the indicative forms the protasis of the conditional statement (A.G. 512). **videbantur**:

The main verb of the subordinate clause (A.G. 278.b).

qua in parte: Ablative of *place where* with the preposition **in** (locative ablative) (A.G. 426.3). **qua**: Singular, feminine, ablative indefinite pronoun used as an adjective modifying **parte** (A.G. 149). The indefinite **quis, -----, quid** (**qui, quae,** or **qua, quod** when used adjectively) is used after **si** (A.G. 310.a). **in**: A monosyllabic preposition is often placed between a noun and its adjective (A.G. 599.d.2).

nostri: Plural, masculine, nominative possessive pronoun used substantively to denote a special class (A.G. 302.d). Nominative subject (A.G. 339).

laborare: Complementary infinitive after **videbantur** (A.G. 456).

aut: The conjunction connects the two infinitives **laborare** ... **premi**. Normally, the conjunction excludes the alternative but this distinction is not always observed (A.G. 324.e).

gravius: Comparative adverb (A.G. 218 and 320-21). The comparative degree here denotes a considerable or excessive degree of the quality meaning "too" (A.G. 291.a).

premi: Complementary infinitive after **videbantur** (A.G. 456).

eo: Adverb (A.G. 217.a and 320-21).

signa inferri: A subject accusative with the infinitive after **iubebat**. The construction is equivalent to a substantive clause of purpose (A.G. 563.a).

Caesar: Nominative subject (A.G. 339). Notice how the noun **Caesar** in the nominative, acting, is placed between the infinitives clauses, iconically right in the middle and directing the action. See Appendix A.

aciemque constitui: A subject accusative with the infinitive after **iubebat**. The construction is equivalent to a substantive clause of purpose (A.G. 563.a). **-que**: The enclitic conjunction connects the two infinitives **inferri** ... **constitui** (A.G. 324.a).

iubebat: The main verb of the apodosis of the conditional statement (A.G. 512). The main verb of the main clause (A.G. 278.b).

(67.4-5) quae res et hostis ad insequendum (5) tardabat et nostros spe auxili confirmabat.

ad, *for, in order to, for the purpose of.*
confirmo, -are, -avi, -atus, *reassure, encourage.*
hostis, -is, m., *enemy, foe*; pl., *the enemy.*

nostri, -orum, m., pl., *our men, our side.*
res, rei, f., *affair, circumstance.*
tardo, -are, -avi, -atus, *check, delay, impede, hinder.*

auxilium, -i, n., *help, aid, assistance, relief.*
et ... et, *both ... and.*
insequor, -sequi, -secutus, *follow up, pursue, follow in pursuit.*
qui, quae, quod, *who, which, what.*
spes, -ei, f., *hope, expectation.*

quae res: Nominative subject of **tardabat** ... **confirmabat** (A.G. 339). **quae**: Singular, feminine, nominative relative pronoun (A.G. 305). The antecedent is **res** in its own clause (adjectival use) (A.G. 307.b). The relative does not introduce a relative clause but is a connecting relative; at the beginning of a clause the pronoun is often best rendered by a personal or demonstrative pronoun, with or without *and* (A.G. 308.f).

et ... et: The repeated conjunction means "both ... and", connecting the two main verbs **tardabat** ... **confirmabat** (A.G. 323.e).

hostis: Accusative direct object of **tardabat** (A.G. 387). Accusative plural noun; **-is** for **-es** is the regular form in i-stem nouns (A.G. 65-67 and 74.c).

ad insequendum: The preposition **ad** with the accusative of the gerund denotes purpose (A.G. 506). **insequendum**: Singular, neuter, accusative gerund (A.G. 501-02).

tardabat: The main verb of the coordinate clause **quae** ... **tardabat** (A.G. 278.a).

nostros: Plural, masculine, accusative possessive pronoun used substantively to denote a special class (A.G. 302.d). Accusative direct object of **confirmabat** (A.G. 387).

spe: Ablative of cause without a preposition (A.G. 404).

auxili: Objective genitive with **spe** (A.G. 348). The singular genitive of nouns in **-ium** ended, until the Augustan Age, in a single **-i** (A.G. 49.b).

confirmabat: The main verb of the coordinate clause **nostros** ... **confirmabat** (A.G. 278.a).

(67.5-6) Tandem Germani ab dextro latere summum iugum nacti hostis loco depellunt; fugientis usque ad flumen, ubi Vercingetorix cum pedestribus copiis consederat, persequuntur compluris(6)que interficiunt.

ab, *on.*

consido, -sidere, -sedi, -sessus, *halt, encamp.*
cum, *with.*
dexter, -tra, -trum, *right.*
fugio, fugere, fugi, -----, *flee, run away, make off.*
hostis, -is, m., *enemy, foe*; pl., *the enemy.*
iugum, -i, n., *ridge, summit, chain.*
locus, -i, m., *place, position.*

pedester, -tris, -tre, *on foot,* (with **copiae**), *infantry.*
-que, *and.*

complures, -ium, m., pl., *several men, many men, a number of men.*
copiae, -arum, f., pl., *forces, troops.*
depello, -pellere, -puli, -pulsus, *drive away, dislodge.*
flumen, -inis, n., *stream, river.*
Germani, -orum, m., pl., *the Germans.*
interficio, -ficere, -feci, -fectus, *slay, kill.*
latus, -eris, n., *side, flank.*
naniscor, -cisci, nactus, and nanctus, *get, secure, get hold of.*
persequor, -sequi, -secutus, *follow up, pursue.*
summus, -a, -um, *highest.*

tandem, *at length, finally.*
usque ad, *all the way to, right up to, as far as.*

ubi, *where.*
Vercingetorix, -igis, m., *Vercingetorix.*

Tandem: Adverb (A.G. 320-21).
Germani ... nacti: Nominative subject (A.G. 339). **Germani**: See Appendix A. **nacti**: Nominative perfect, deponent participle used as a predicate, where in English a phrase or a subordinate clause would be more normal (A.G. 496). "To them is due the credit of having turned the tide of battle." (Kelsey, 424)
ab dextro latere: Ablative of *position* with the preposition **ab** (A.G. 429.b).
summum iugum: Accusative direct object of the participle **nacti** (A.G. 387 and 488). **summum**: Defective superlative adjective (A.G. 130.b).
hostis: Accusative direct object of **depellunt** (A.G. 387). Accusative plural noun; **-is** for **-es** is the regular accusative form in i-stem nouns (A.G. 65-67 and 74.c).
loco: Ablative of separation without a preposition after **depellunt** (A.G. 402).
depellunt: The main verb of the simple sentence (A.G. 278.1).
fugientis: Plural, masculine, accusative present participle used substantively (A.G. 494.a). Carry down **hostis** as the noun. Accusative direct object of **persequuntur** (A.G. 387). Accusative plural; **-is** for **-es** is the regular form in the present participle (A.G. 117-18).
usque ad flumen: Prepositional phrase, **usque ad** with the accusative means "all the way to, right up to, as far as" (A.G. 432.b) (*OLD* **usque** 1). **usque**: Adverb (A.G. 320-21 and 432.b).
ubi ... consederat: The relative adverb **ubi** ("where") with the indicative forms a subordinate clause (A.G. 278.b). **consederat**: The main verb of the subordinate clause (A.G. 278.b). The pluperfect denotes an action completed in past time (A.G. 477).
Vercingetorix: Nominative subject (A.G. 339). See Appendix A.
cum pedestribus copiis: Ablative of accompaniment with the preposition **cum** (A.G. 413).
persequuntur: The main verb of the coordinate clause **fugientis ... persequuntur** (A.G. 278.a). The pronoun **ei**, with **Germani** as the antecedent, is understood as the subject (A.G. 271.a).
complurisque: Plural, masculine, accusative comparative adjective used substantively meaning "several or many people", a compound of **plus** (A.G. 120) (*OLD* **complures** b). Accusative direct object of **interficiunt** (A.G. 387). **-is** for **-es** is an allowable accusative ending for comparative adjectives (A.G. 120-21.c). **-que**: The enclitic conjunction connects the two main verbs **persequuntur ... interficiunt** (A.G. 324.a).
interficiunt: The main verb of the coordinate clause **complurisque interficiunt** (A.G. 278.a). The pronoun **ei**, with **Germani** as the antecedent, is understood as the subject (A.G. 271.a).

(67.6-7) Qua re animadversa reliqui ne circum(7)irentur veriti se fugae mandant. Omnibus locis fit caedes.

animadverto, -tere, -ti, -sus, *notice, observe, perceive.*
circumeo, -ire, -ivi, or -ii, -tus, *surround, encircle.*

fuga, -ae, f., *flight.*
mando, -are, -avi, -atus, *commit, entrust, betake.*
omnis, -e, *all.*
reliqui, -orum, m., pl., *the rest.*
sui, sibi, se, or sese, nom. wanting, *themselves.*

caedes, -is, f., *killing, slaughter, murder, massacre.*
fio, fieri, factus, *take place, happen, come about, come to pass.*
loca, -orum, n., pl., *places.*
ne, *lest.*
qui, quae, quod, *who, which, what.*
res, rei, f., *matter, affair.*
vereor, -eri, -itus, *fear, be afraid of.*

Qua re animadversa: Ablative absolute (A.G. 419-20). **qua**: Singular, feminine, ablative relative pronoun (A.G. 305). The antecedent is **re** in its own clause (adjectival use) (A.G. 307.b). The relative does not introduce a relative clause but is a connecting relative; at the beginning of a clause the pronoun is often best rendered by a personal or demonstrative pronoun, with or without *and* (A.G. 308.f). **animadversa**: The perfect tense of the participle represents the action as completed at the time indicated by the tense of the main verb (A.G. 489).
reliqui ... veriti: Nominative subject of **mandant** (A.G. 339). **reliqui**: Plural, masculine, nominative adjective used substantively (A.G. 288). The noun **hostes** is understood (A.G. 288.b). **veriti**: Nominative perfect, deponent participle used as a predicate, where in English a phrase or a subordinate clause would be more normal (A.G. 496).
ne circumirentur veriti: The conjunction **ne** ("lest") with the subjunctive forms a substantive clause of fearing after **veriti** (A.G. 564). **circumirentur**: The main verb of the subordinate clause (A.G. 278.b). Imperfect subjunctive; the tense of the subjunctive is in secondary sequence and follows the rules for the sequence of tense after the historical present **mandant** (A.G. 482-85, esp. 485.e). The pronoun **ei**, with **reliqui** as the antecedent, is understood as the subject (A.G. 271.a).
se: Plural, masculine, accusative direct reflexive pronoun (A.G. 300.1). The antecedent is **reliqui**, the subject of **mandant** (A.G. 299). Accusative direct object of the transitive verb **mandant** (A.G. 387).
fugae: Dative indirect object of the transitive verb **mandant** (A.G. 362).
mandant: The main verb of the main clause (A.G. 278.b).
Omnibus ... caedes: This terse formulation of the ensuing slaughter is more powerful than a gruesome description of it as it allows the reader to fill in the details with their imagination.
Omnibus locis: Ablative of *place where* without a preposition (A.G. 429.1-2).
fit: The main verb of the simple sentence (A.G. 278.1).
caedes: Nominative subject (A.G. 339). The subject is in the last position (A.G. 597.b).

(67.7) Tres nobilissimi Aedui capti ad Caesarem perducuntur: Cotus, praefectus equitum, qui controversiam cum Convictolitavi proximis comitiis habuerat, et Cavarillus, qui post defectionem Litavicci pedestribus copiis praefuerat, et Eporedorix, quo duce ante adventum Caesaris Aedui cum Sequanis bello contenderant.

ad, *to.*
Aedui, -orum, m., pl., *the Aedui.*
ante, *before.*
Caesar, -aris, m., *Caesar.*
Cavarillus, -i, m., *Cavarillus.*
contendo, -tendere, -tendi, -tentus, *strive, fight, contend, vie.*

Convictolitavis, -is, m., *Convictolitavis.*
Cotus, -i, m., *Cotus.*
defectio, -onis, f., *revolt, rebellion.*
Eporedorix, -igis, m., *Eporedorix.*
et, *and.*
Litaviccus, -i, m., *Litaviccus.*
pedester, -tris, -tre, *on foot,* (with copiae), *infantry.*

post, *after.*
praesum, -esse, -fui, -----, *have command of, have charge of.*
qui, quae, quod, *who, which, what.*
tres, tria, trium, *three.*

adventus, -us, m., *coming, arrival.*
Aeduus, -i, m., *an Aeduan.*
bellum, -i, n., *war, warfare.*
capio, capere, cepi, captus, *take, get, seize, capture.*
comitia, -ae, f., *election.*
controversia, -ae, f., *dispute, debate, controversy, quarrel.*
copiae, -arum, f., pl., *forces, troops.*
cum, *with.*
dux, ducis, m., *leader, general, commander.*
eques, -itis, m., *rider, horseman, cavalryman, trooper.*
habeo, habere, habui, habitus, *have.*
nobilis, -e, sup. -issimus, *of high rank, noble.*
perduco, -ducere, -duxi, -ductus, *lead through, bring, conduct, convey.*
praefectus, -i, m., *prefect, cavalry captain.*
proximus, -a, -um, *last.*
Sequani, -orum, m., pl., *the Sequani.*

Tres nobilissimi Aedui capti: Nominative subject (A.G. 339). **Tres**: Declinable cardinal number used as an adjective modifying **Aedui** (A.G. 132-35). **nobilissimi**: Superlative adjective (A.G. 124). **capti**: Nominative perfect, passive, participle used as a predicate, where in English a phrase or a subordinate clause would be more normal (A.G. 496).
ad Caesarem: Prepositional phrase, **ad** with the accusative here means "to" (*OLD* ad 1). **Caesarem**: See Appendix A.
perducuntur: The main verb of the main clause (A.G. 278.b).
Cotus ... Cavarillus ... Eporedorix: Three nominative proper nouns in apposition to **Aedui** (A.G. 282.a). **Eporedorix**: This is not the Eporedorix who has been active in the revolt of the Aedui. See Appendix A for each man.
praefectus: A nominative noun in apposition to the proper noun **Cotus** (A.G. 282).
equitum: Partitive genitive with **praefectus** (A.G. 346.a.1).
qui ... habuerat: Relative clause (A.G. 303). For the conflict between Cotus and Convictolitavis over the magistracy see Chapters 32-33. **qui**: Singular, masculine, nominative relative pronoun used substantively (A.G. 305). The antecedent is **Cotus** (A.G. 307). Nominative subject (A.G. 339). **habuerat**: The main verb of the subordinate clause (A.G. 278.b). The pluperfect denotes an action completed in past time (A.G. 477).
controversiam: Accusative direct object of **habuerat** (A.G. 387).
cum Convictolitavi: Ablative of accompaniment with the preposition **cum**, words of contention (**controversiam ... habuerat**) require **cum** (A.G. 413.b). **Convictolitavi**: See Appendix A.
proximis comitiis: Ablative of *time when* (A.G. 423.1). **proximis**: Defective superlative adjective (A.G. 130.a).
et: The conjunction connects the two nominative nouns **Cotus ... Cavarillus** (A.G. 324.a).
qui ... praefuerat: Relative clause (A.G. 303). **qui**: Singular, masculine, nominative relative pronoun used substantively (A.G. 305). The antecedent is **Cavarillus** (A.G. 307). Nominative subject (A.G. 339). **praefuerat**: The main verb of the subordinate clause (A.G. 278.b). The pluperfect denotes an action completed in past time (A.G. 477).
post defectionem Litavicci: Prepositional phrase, **post** with the accusative here means "after" (*OLD* post2 3). For the reference see Chapter 37 ff.. **Litavicci**: Possessive genitive with **defectionem** (A.G. 343). See Appendix A.
pedestribus copiis: Dative indirect object of the intransitive verb **praefuerat** (A.G. 370). See the note at **eos**, 54.4.
et: The conjunction connects the two nominative nouns **Cavarillus ... Eporedorix** (A.G. 324.a).
quo ... contenderant: Relative clause (A.G. 303). **quo**: See below. **contenderant**: The main verb of the subordinate clause (A.G. 278.b). The pluperfect denotes an action completed in past time (A.G. 477).
quo duce: Ablative absolute with a relative pronoun (**quo**) taking the place of the participle (there is no participle for "being") (A.G. 419.a-20). **quo**: Singular, masculine, ablative relative pronoun (A.G. 305). The pronoun agrees with **duce** in its own clause (adjectival use) (A.G. 306).
ante adventum Caesaris: Prepositional phrase, **ante** with the accusative is here temporal and means "before" (an event) (*OLD* ante2 6). **Caesaris**: Possessive genitive with **adventum** (A.G. 343). See Appendix A.
Aedui: Nominative subject (A.G. 339).
cum Sequanis: Ablative of accompaniment with the preposition **cum**, words of contention (**bello contenderant**) require **cum** (A.G. 413.b). **Sequanis**: See Appendix A.
bello: Ablative of *place where* without a preposition (A.G. 429.3) (*OLD* contendo 8.b).

(68.1-2) Fugato omni equitatu Vercingetorix copias, ut pro castris collocaverat, reduxit protinusque Alesiam, quod est oppidum Mandubiorum, iter facere coepit celeriterque impedimenta (2) ex castris educi et se subsequi iussit.

Alesia, -ae, f., *Alesia.*
celeriter, *quickly, speedily, at once, immediately.*
colloco, -are, -avi, -atus, *place, set, post, station.*
educo, -ducere, -duxi, -ductus, *lead out, lead forth.*
et, *and.*
facio, facere, feci, factus, *make.*
impedimenta, -orum, n., pl., *heavy baggage, baggage.*
iubeo, iubere, iussi, iussus, *order, give orders, bid, command.*
omnis, -e, *all.*
pro, *in front of, before.*
-que, *and.*
reduco, -ducere, -duxi, -ductus, *lead back, conduct back.*

sui, sibi, se, or sese, nom. wanting, *him,* with or without *-self.*
ut, *as soon as, when.*

castra, -orum, n., pl., *camp, encampment.*
coepi, -isse, coeptus, *begin, start, commence.*
copiae, -arum, f., pl., *forces, troops.*
equitatus, -us, m., *cavalry.*
ex, *from, out of.*
fugo, -are, -avi, -atus, *put to flight, drive off, rout.*
iter, itineris, n., *march, journey.*
Mandubii, -orum, m., pl., *the Mandubii.*
oppidum, -i, n., *fortified town, city.*
protinus, *forthwith, at once, immediately.*
qui, quae, quod, *who, which, what.*
subsequor, -sequi, -secutus, *follow closely upon, follow after.*
sum, esse, fui, futurus, *be.*
Vercingetorix, -igis, m., *Vercingetorix.*

Stevens believes that the situation is actually the reverse of how Caesar describes it: "it is not Caesar who has trapped Vercingetorix in Alesia, but Vercingetorix who has trapped Caesar between himself in Alesia and the relieving army. ... Vercingetorix meant to trap Caesar at the holy center of Gaul - and he had done it." (Stevens, 18)

Fugato omni equitatu: Ablative absolute (A.G. 419-20). **Fugato**: The perfect tense of the participle represents the action as completed at the time indicated by the tense of the main verb (A.G. 489).

Vercingetorix: Nominative subject of **reduxit** (A.G. 339). See Appendix A.

copias: Accusative direct object of **reduxit** (A.G. 387).

ut ... collocaverat: Temporal clause; the relative adverb **ut** ("as soon as, when") with the pluperfect indicative forms a subordinate clause (A.G. 287.b). The pluperfect tense emphasizes the fact that the action expressed in the **ut** clause was completed before the action in the main clause (*OLD* ut 26.b). **collocaverat**: The main verb of the subordinate clause (A.G. 278.b). The pronoun **is**, with **Vercingetorix** as the antecedent, is understood as the subject (A.G. 271.a). The pronoun **eas**, with **copias** as the antecedent, is understood as the accusative direct object.

pro castris: Prepositional phrase, **pro** with the ablative here means "in front of, before" (*OLD* pro1 1).

reduxit: The main verb of the coordinate clause **Fugato ... reduxit** (A.G. 278.a).

protinusque: Adverb (A.G. 320-21). **-que**: The enclitic conjunction connects the two main verbs **reduxit ... coepit** (A.G. 324.a).

Alesiam: Accusative of *place to which* without a preposition (city name) (A.G. 427.2). See Appendix A.

quod ... Mandubiorum: Relative clause (A.G. 303). **quod**: Singular, neuter, nominative relative pronoun used substantively (A.G. 305). The pronoun agrees with the predicate noun **oppidum** in its own clause rather than the antecedent **Alesiam** (A.G. 306). Nominative subject (A.G. 339). **Mandubiorum**: Possessive genitive of the tribe name **Mandubii** with **oppidum** (A.G. 343). See Appendix A.

est: The main verb of the subordinate clause (A.G. 278.b). The present tense is not the historical present but denotes a state as now existing in present time (A.G. 465.1).

oppidum: Singular, neuter, nominative predicate noun after **est** (A.G. 283-84).

iter: Accusative direct object of the infinitive **facere** (A.G. 387 and 451.3). The phrase **iter facere** is an idiom that means "to march or travel" (*OLD* iter 1.b).

facere: Complementary infinitive with **coepit** (A.G. 456).

coepit: The main verb of the coordinate clause **protinusque ... coepit** (A.G. 278.a). The pronoun **is**, with **Vercingetorix** as the antecedent, is understood as the subject (A.G. 271.a).

celeriterque: Adverb (A.G. 214.b and 320-21). **-que**: The enclitic conjunction connects the two main verbs **coepit ... iussit** (A.G. 324.a).

impedimenta ... educi ... subsequi: A subject accusative with two infinitives after **iussit**. The construction is equivalent to a substantive clause of purpose (A.G. 563.a).

ex castris: Ablative of *place from which* with the preposition **ex** (A.G. 426.1).

et: The conjunction connects the two infinitives **educi ... subsequi** (A.G. 324.a).

se: Singular, masculine, accusative indirect reflexive pronoun (A.G. 300.2). The antecedent is **is** (**Vercingetorix**), the supplied subject of **iussit** (A.G. 299). Accusative direct object of the infinitive **subsequi** (A.G. 387 and 451.3).

iussit: The main verb of the coordinate clause **celeriterque ... iussit** (A.G. 278.a). The pronoun **is**, with **Vercingetorix** as the antecedent, is understood as the subject (A.G. 271.a).

(68.2-3) Caesar impedimentis in proximum collem deductis, duabus legionibus praesidio relictis secutus quantum diei tempus est passum, circiter tribus milibus hostium ex novissimo agmine interfectis altero (3) die ad Alesiam castra fecit.

ad, *at, near.*

Alesia, -ae, f., *Alesia.*
Caesar, -aris, m., *Caesar.*
circiter, *about.*
deduco, -ducere, -duxi, -ductus, *lead away, lead off, withdraw, bring.*

agmen, -minis, n., *column,* (with **novissimum**), *the rear of the column, the rear.*
alter, -era, -erum, *the next.*
castra, -orum, n., pl., *camp, encampment.*
collis, -is, m., *hill, height, elevation.*
dies, -ei, m. and f., *day.*

duo, -ae, -o, *two.*
facio, facere, feci, factus, (with **castra**), *pitch.*
impedimenta, -orum, n., pl., *heavy baggage, baggage.*
interficio, -ficere, -feci, -fectus, *slay, kill.*
milia, -um, n., pl., *thousand, thousands.*

patior, pati, passus, *permit, allow.*
proximus, -a, -um, *nearest, next.*
relinquo, -linquere, -liqui, -lictus, *leave, leave behind.*
tempus, -oris, n., *time.*

ex, *from the number of, from among, of.*
hostis, -is, m., *enemy, foe*; pl., *the enemy.*
in, *into.*
legio, -onis, f., *legion.*
novus, -a, -um, sup. -issimus, *hindmost, last, at the rear.*
praesidium, -i, n., *guard, garrison.*
quantum, *to what extent* or *degree.*
sequor, -qui, -cutus, *follow, follow after, pursue.*
tres, tria, trium, *three.*

Caesar ... secutus: Nominative subject of **fecit** (A.G. 339). **Caesar**: See Appendix A. **secutus**: Nominative perfect, deponent participle used as a predicate, where in English a phrase or a subordinate clause would be more normal (A.G. 496).
impedimentis in proximum collem deductis: Ablative absolute (A.G. 419-20). **in proximum collem**: Accusative of *place to which* with the preposition **in** (A.G. 426.2). **proximum**: Defective superlative adjective (A.G. 130.a). **deductis**: The perfect tense of the participle represents the action as completed at the time indicated by the tense of the main verb (A.G. 489).
duabus legionibus praesidio relictis: Ablative absolute (A.G. 419-20). Notice the asyndeton between the two ablative absolutes (A.G. 323.b). **duabus**: Declinable cardinal number used as an adjective modifying **legionibus** (A.G. 132-35). **praesidio**: Dative of the purpose or end. The dative of an abstract noun (**praesidio**) is used to show that for which a thing serves or which it accomplishes (A.G. 382.1). **relictis**: The perfect tense of the participle represents the action as completed at the time indicated by the tense of the main verb (A.G. 489).
quantum ... est passum: Relative clause (A.G. 279.a). **quantum**: Relative adverb meaning "to what extent, degree" (*OLD* **quantum2** B.2). **est passum**: The main verb of the subordinate clause (A.G. 278.b). Perfect tense of the deponent verb **patior** (A.G. 190).
diei: Partitive genitive with **tempus** (A.G. 346.a.1). The noun **dies** is normally masculine gender (A.G. 97.a).
tempus: Nominative subject (A.G. 339).
circiter tribus milibus hostium ex novissimo agmine interfectis: Ablative absolute (A.G. 419-20). **circiter**: Adverb (A.G. 320-21). **tribus**: Declinable cardinal number used as an adjective modifying **milibus** (A.G. 132-35). **milibus**: Ablative plural adjective used substantively; in the plural **mille** declines as a neuter noun (A.G. 134.d). **hostium**: Partitive genitive with **milibus** (A.G. 346.c). **ex novissimo agmine**: Prepositional phrase, **ex** with the ablative instead of the partitive genitive means "from the number of, from among, of" (A.G. 346.c) (*OLD* **ex** 17). **novissimo**: Superlative adjective which expresses a part of the column meaning "hindmost" (A.G. 124) (*OLD* **novissimo** 6.c). **interfectis**: The perfect tense of the participle represents the action as completed at the time indicated by the tense of the main verb (A.G. 489).
altero die: Ablative of *time when* (423.1). **die**: The noun **dies** is normally masculine gender (A.G. 97.a).
ad Alesiam: Prepositional phrase, with all names of places *at*, meaning *near* (not *in*), is expressed by **ad** with the accusative (A.G. 428.d). **Alesiam**: See Appendix A.
castra: Accusative direct object of **fecit** (A.G. 387).
fecit: The main verb of the main clause (A.G. 278.b).

(68.3) Perspecto urbis situ perterritisque hostibus, quod equitatu, qua maxime parte exercitus confidebant, erant pulsi, adhortatus ad laborem milites circumvallare instituit.

ad, *to.*

circumvallo, -are, -avi, -atus, *surround with a rampart, blockade, invest.*

equitatus, -us, m., *cavalry.*
hostis, -is, m., *enemy, foe*; pl., *the enemy.*

labor, -oris, m., *toil, exertion, labor.*
miles, -itis, m., *soldier, foot-solider.*
pello, pellere, pepuli, pulsus, *rout, put to flight, defeat.*

perterreo, -terrere, -----, -territus, *greatly alarm, frighten, terrify, dismay.*
qui, quae, quod, *who, which, what.*
situs, -us, m., *situation, site.*

adhortor, -ari, -atus, *encourage, rally, exhort, rouse, urge.*
confido, -fidere, -fisus sum, *trust, rely upon, have confidence in.*
exercitus, -us, m., *army.*
instituo, -stituere, -stitui, -stitutus, *undertake, commence, begin.*
maxime, *very greatly, exceedingly, chiefly, especially.*
pars, partis, f., *part, portion, branch.*
perspicio, -spicere, -spexi, -spectus, *perceive, observe, ascertain.*
-que, *and.*
quod, *because, since, for, as.*
urbs, urbis, f., *city.*

Perspecto urbis situ: Ablative absolute (A.G. 419-20). **Perspecto**: The perfect tense of the participle represents the action as completed at the time indicated by the tense of the main verb (A.G. 489). **urbis**: Possessive genitive with **situ** (A.G. 343).
perterritis ... pulsi: Ablative absolute with dependent clauses.
perterritisque hostibus: Ablative absolute (A.G. 419-20). **perterritis**: The perfect tense of the participle represents the action as completed at the time indicated by the tense of the main verb (A.G. 489). **-que**: The enclitic conjunction connects the two ablative absolutes (A.G. 324.a).
quod ... erant pulsi: Causal clause; the conjunction **quod** ("because") takes the indicative when the reason is given on the authority of

the writer or speaker (A.G. 540.1). For the reference see 67.2-7. **erant pulsi**: The main verb of the subordinate clause (A.G. 278.b). The pronoun ei, with **hostibus** as the antecedent, is understood as the subject (A.G. 271.a). The pluperfect denotes an action completed in past time (A.G. 477).

equitatu: Ablative of specification with **erant pulsi** (A.G. 418).

qua ... confidebant: Relative clause (A.G. 303). **qua**: See below. **confidebant**: The main verb of the subordinate clause (A.G. 278.b). The pronoun ei, with **hostibus** as the antecedent, is understood as the subject (A.G. 271.a).

qua ... parte: Locative ablative after **confidebant** without a preposition (A.G. 431 Note). **qua**: Singular, feminine, ablative relative pronoun (A.G. 305). The pronoun agrees with **parte** in its own clause rather than the antecedent **equitatu** (adjectival use) (A.G. 306).

maxime: Irregular superlative adverb (A.G. 218.a and 320-21).

exercitus: Partitive genitive with **parte** (A.G. 346.A.1).

adhortatus: Nominative perfect, deponent participle used as a predicate, where in English a phrase or a subordinate clause would be more normal (A.G. 496). The pronoun is, with **Caesar** as the antecedent, is understood. Nominative subject (A.G. 339).

ad laborem: Prepositional phrase, **ad** with the accusative here means "to" (*OLD* **ad** 28).

milites: Accusative direct object of the participle **adhortatus** (A.G. 387 and 488).

circumvallare: Complementary infinitive after **instituit** (A.G. 456). "The construction of siege-works by a besieging army was standard practice - see e.g. 7.11, 17. The scale of the circumvallation at Alesia, however, was so astonishing as to become the classic proof of Caesar's mastery of the art of generalship and command. The first. inner, line of siege-works stretched more than 10 miles (Vercingetorix got his cavalry out just in time to fetch help): a second line, even longer, was then constructed to guard the Romans from Gallic attack in the rear." (Hammond, 241)

instituit: The main verb of the main clause (A.G. 278.b).

4.I CHAPTER 69: THE SIEGE OF ALESIA BEGINS

(69.1-3) Ipsum erat oppidum Alesia in colle summo, admodum edito loco, ut nisi obsidione expugnari non posse videretur; (2) cuius collis radices duo duabus ex partibus flumina sublue(3)bant.

admodum, *quite, very.*	**Alesia, -ae**, f., *Alesia.*
collis, -is, m., *hill, height, elevation.*	**duo, -ae, -o**, *two.*
editus, -a, -um, *elevated, high.*	**ex**, *on.*
expugno, -are, -avi, -atus, *storm, take by assault, capture.*	**flumen, -inis**, n., *flowing water, current, stream, river.*
in, *on.*	**ipse, -a, -um**, *for its own part.*
locus, -i, m., *place, position.*	**nisi**, *other(wise) than, but, except.*
non, *not.*	**obsidio, -onis**, f., *siege, blockade.*
oppidum, -i, n., *fortified town, city.*	**pars, partis**, f., *side.*
possum, posse, potui, -----, *be able.*	**qui, quae, quod**, *who, which, what.*
radix, -icis, f., *root, foot, base.*	**subluo, -luere, -----, -lutus**, *wash.*
sum, esse, fui, futurus, *be.*	**summus, -a, -um**, *highest.*
ut, *so that.*	**videor, videri, visus sum**, *seem, appear.*

Ipsum ... oppidum: Nominative subject (A.G. 339). **Ipsum**: Singular, neuter, nominative demonstrative pronoun used as an adjective modifying **oppidum** (A.G. 296.1 and a). The pronoun marks a transition to the description of Alesia and means "for its own part" (*OLD* **ipse** 3).

erat: The main verb of the main clause (A.G. 278.b).

Alesia: A nominative proper noun in apposition to **oppidum** (A.G. 282). See Appendix A. "The town was situated on top of an oval elevation, a part of which is now occupied by the village of Alise-Sainte-Reine. The base of the height is washed on two sides by small streams, the Ose and Oserain, which flow near by into the Brenne. To the west, along the Brenne, a level plain, shut in by hills on the north and south, extends about three miles. On the remaining sides are ranges of heights similar to that on which the city stood. The highest point of Alesia rose about 550 feet above the beds of the brooks on each side. Excavations carried on under the direction of Napoleon III. brought to light abundant traces of Caesar's works, verifying in a remarkable way the statements in the text." (Kelsey, 424)

in colle summo: Ablative of *place where* with the preposition **in** (locative ablative) (426.3). The prepositional phrase is in the predicate position after **erat** (A.G. 272). **summo**: Defective superlative adjective (A.G. 130.b).

admodum: Adverb modifying **edito** (A.G. 320-21).

edito loco: Ablative of *place where* without a preposition (A.G. 429.1-2).

ut ... videretur: The conjunction **ut** ("so that") with the subjunctive forms a clause of result (A.G. 537.1). **videretur**: The main verb of the subordinate clause (A.G. 278.b). Imperfect subjunctive; the tense of the subjunctive is in secondary sequence and follows the rules for the sequence of tense after **erat** (A.G. 482-85). The pronoun id, with **oppidum** as the antecedent, is understood as the subject (A.G. 271.a).

nisi obsidione: Elliptical phrase without a verb (*OLD* **nisi** 6). **nisi**: The conjunction here means "other(wise) than, but, except" (*OLD* **nisi** 6). **obsidione**: Ablative of means (A.G. 409).

expugnari: Complementary infinitive after **posse** (A.G. 456).

non: Adverb modifying **posse**, the negative precedes the word it especially effects (A.G. 217.e, 320-21, and 599.a).

posse: Complementary infinitive after **videretur** (A.G. 456).

cuius collis: Possessive genitive with **radices** (A.G. 343). **cuius**: Singular, masculine, genitive relative pronoun (A.G. 305). The antecedent is both the previous **colle** and **collis** in its own clause (adjectival use) (A.G. 307.a). The relative does not introduce a relative clause but is a connecting relative; at the beginning of a clause the pronoun is often best rendered by a personal or demonstrative pronoun, with or without *and* (A.G. 308.f).

radices: Accusative direct object of **subluebant** (A.G. 387).

duabus ex partibus: Ablative of *position* with the preposition **ex** (A.G. 429.b). **duabus**: Declinable cardinal number used as an adjective modifying **partibus** (A.G. 132-35). **ex**: A monosyllabic preposition is often placed between a noun and its adjective (A.G. 599.d.2).

duo ... flumina: Nominative subject (A.G. 339). **duo**: Declinable cardinal number used as an adjective (A.G. 132-35). "The brooks Ose and Oserain." (Kelsey, 424)

subluebant: The main verb of the simple sentence (A.G. 278.1).

(69.3-5) Ante id oppidum planities circiter milia passuum (4) III in longitudinem patebat: reliquis ex omnibus partibus colles mediocri interiecto spatio pari altitudinis fastigio (5) oppidum cingebant.

altitudo, -onis, f., *height.*
cingo, cingere, cinxi, cinctus, *surround, enclose, encircle.*
collis, -is, m., *hill, height, elevation.*
fastigium, -i, n., *height, elevation, level.*
in, *in, in respect to.*

is, ea, id, *he, she, it; that, this.*

mediocris, -cre, *moderate, short.*
omnis, -e, *all.*
par, paris, *like, similar, same, equal.*
passus, -us, m., *step, pace,* = 4 feet, 10 ¼ inches.
planities, -ei, f., *level ground, plain.*
spatium, -i, n., *space, area.*

ante, *before, in front of.*
circiter, *about.*
ex, *on.*
I, in expression of number, *1.*
intericio, -icere, -ieci, -iectus, (in pass.), *intervene, interpose.*
longitudo, -inis, f., *length*, (with **in**), *lengthwise, longitudinally.*
milia, -um, n., pl., *thousand, thousands.*
oppidum, -i, n., *fortified town, city.*
pars, partis, f., *side.*
pateo, patere, patui, -----, *stretch out, extend.*
reliquus, -a, -um, *remaining, the rest.*

Ante id oppidum: Prepositional phrase, **ante** with the accusative here means "before, in front of" (*OLD* ante2 1). **id**: Singular, neuter, accusative demonstrative pronoun used as an adjective modifying **oppidum** (A.G. 296.1 and a).

planities: Nominative subject (A.G. 339).

circiter: Adverb (A.G. 320-21).

milia passuum III: Accusative of *extent of space* (A.G. 425). **milia**: Accusative plural; in the plural **mille** declines as a neuter noun (A.G. 134.d). **passuum**: Partitive genitive with **milia** (346.2). **III**: Roman numeral used as an adjective modifying **milia** (A.G. 133).

in longitudinem: Prepositional phrase, **in** with the accusative of **longitudo** means "lengthwise, longitudinally" (*OLD* longitudo 1.c).

patebat: The main verb of the simple sentence (A.G. 278.1).

reliquis ex omnibus partibus: Ablative of *position* with the preposition **ex** (A.G. 429.b). **ex**: A monosyllabic preposition is often placed between a noun and its adjective (A.G. 599.d.2).

colles: Nominative subject (A.G. 339).

mediocri interiecto spatio: Ablative absolute (A.G. 419-20). **interiecto**: The perfect tense of the participle represents the action as completed at the time indicated by the tense of the main verb (A.G. 489). "The average distance between the height of Alesia and the tops of the surrounding hills is about a mile." (Kelsey, 424)

pari ... fastigio: Ablative of quality (descriptive ablative) with an adjective modifier with **colles** (A.G. 415).

altitudinis: Genitive of specification with the adjective **pari** (A.G. 349.d).

oppidum: Accusative direct object of **cingebant** (A.G. 387).

cingebant: The main verb of the main clause (A.G. 278.b).

(69.5-6) Sub muro, quae pars collis ad orientem solem spectabat, hunc omnem locum copiae Gallorum compleverant fossamque et maceriam sex in altitudinem pedum (6) praeduxerant.

ad, *towards.*
collis, -is, m., *hill, height, elevation.*
copiae, -arum, f., pl., *forces, troops.*
fossa, -ae, f., *ditch, trench, entrenchment, fosse.*
hic, haec, hoc, *this; he, she, it.*
locus, -i, m., *place, position.*
murus, -i, m., *wall, rampart.*
orior, oriri, ortus, *rise, arise.*
pes, pedis, m., *foot,* = .9708 of the English foot.

-que, *and.*
sex, *six.*
specto, -are, -avi, -atus, *face, lie.*

altitudo, -onis, f., *height.*
compleo, -plere, -plevi, -pletus, *fully occupy, fill full.*
et, *and.*
Galli, -orum, m., *the Gauls.*
in, *to.*
maceria, -ae, f., *wall built of loose materials.*
omnis, -e, *whole, entire.*
pars, partis, f., *side.*
praeduco, -ducere, -duxi, -ductus, *to construct along a line in front.*
qui, quae, quod, *who, which, what.*
sol, -is, m., *the sun.*
sub, *at the foot of, below.*

Sub muro: Prepositional phrase, **sub** with the ablative here means "at the foot of, below" (*OLD* **sub** 6).

quae ... spectabat: Relative clause (A.G. 303). **quae**: See below. **spectabat**: The main verb of the subordinate clause (A.G. 278.b).

quae pars: Nominative subject (A.G. 339). **quae**: Singular, feminine, nominative relative pronoun (A.G. 305). The antecedent is **pars** in its own clause (adjectival use) (A.G. 307.b).

collis: Partitive genitive with **pars** (A.G. 346.a.1).

ad orientem solem: Prepositional phrase, **ad** with the accusative implies direction and here means "towards" (*OLD* **ad** 3). **orientem**: Present participle used as an adjective modifying **solem** (A.G. 494).

hunc omnem locum: Accusative direct object of **compleverant** (A.G. 387). **hunc**: Singular, masculine, accusative demonstrative pronoun used as an adjective modifying **locum** (A.G. 296.1 and a).

copiae: Nominative subject of **compleverant ... praeduxerant** (A.G. 339).

Gallorum: Partitive genitive with **copiae** (A.G. 346.a.1). See Appendix A.

compleverant: The main verb of the coordinate clause **Sub ... compleverant** (A.G. 278.a). Although the pluperfect tense is normally used in subordinate clauses, its use as a main verb is frequent. The pluperfect denotes an action completed in past time (A.G. 477).

fossamque et maceriam: Two accusative direct objects of **praeduxerant** (A.G. 387). **-que**: The enclitic conjunction connects the two main verbs **compleverant ... praeduxerant** (A.G. 324.a). **et**: The conjunction connects the two accusative nouns (A.G. 324.a).

sex in altitudinem pedum: Prepositional phrase, **in** with the accusative here means "to" (*OLD* **in** 14). **sex ... pedum**: Genitive of measure with **altitudinem** (A.G. 345.b). **sex**: Indeclinable cardinal number used as an adjective modifying **pedum** (A.G. 132-35).

praeduxerant: The main verb of the coordinate clause **fossamque ... praeduxerant** (A.G. 278.a). Although the pluperfect tense is normally used in subordinate clauses, its use as a main verb is frequent. The pluperfect denotes an action completed in past time (A.G. 477). Stevens notes that "Caesar's own narrative makes it clear that Vercingetorix had already made preparations to stand a siege." (Stevens, 17) See also 71.7.

(69.6-7) Eius munitionis quae ab Romanis institue(7)batur circuitus XI milia passuum tenebat.

ab, *by.*
I, in expression of number, *1.*

is, ea, id, *he, she, it; that, this.*
munitio, -onis, f., *fortification, works of fortifications, entrenchment.*
qui, quae, quod, *who, which, what.*
teneo, tenere, tenui, -----, *hold, contain, occupy.*

circuitus, -us, m., *circuit, way around, winding path.*
instituo, -stituere, -stitui, -stitutus, *erect, build, construct, make, begin.*
milia, -um, n., pl., *thousand, thousands.*
passus, -us, m., *step, pace,* = 4 feet, 10 ¼ inches.
Romani, -orum, m., pl., *the Romans.*
X, in expression of number, = *10.*

Eius munitionis: Possessive genitive with **circuitus** (A.G. 343). **Eius**: Singular, feminine, genitive demonstrative pronoun used as an adjective modifying **munitionis** (A.G. 296.1 and a). "Not a continuous line of works, but a series of fortified encampments, the spaces between which were guarded by frequent redoubts (*castella*)." (Kelsey, 425)

quae ... instituebatur: Relative clause (A.G. 303). **quae**: Singular, feminine, nominative relative pronoun used substantively (A.G. 305). The antecedent is **munitionis** (A.G. 307). Nominative subject (A.G. 339). **instituebatur**: The main verb of the subordinate clause (A.G. 278.b). Inceptive imperfect which denotes the action as begun meaning "were being erected" (A.G. 471.b).

ab Romanis: Ablative of agent with the preposition **ab** after the passive verb **instituebatur** (A.G. 405).

circuitus: Nominative subject (A.G. 339).

XI milia passuum: Accusative of *extent of space* after **tenebat** (A.G. 425) (*OLD* **teneo** 7). **XI**: Roman numeral used as an adjective modifying **milia** (A.G. 133). **milia**: Accusative plural; in the plural **mille** declines as a neuter noun (A.G. 134.d). **passuum**: Partitive genitive with **milia** (346.2).

tenebat: The main verb of the main clause (A.G. 278.b).

(69.7) Castra opportunis locis erant posita, ibique castella XXIII facta, quibus in castellis interdiu stationes ponebantur, ne qua subito eruptio fieret; haec eadem noctu excubitoribus ac firmis praesidiis tenebantur.

ac, *and.*
castra, -orum, n., pl., *camp, encampment.*
excubitor, -oris, m., *watchman, sentinel.*
fio, fieri, factus, *take place, happen, come about, come to pass.*
hic, haec, hoc, *this; he, she, it.*
ibi, *in that place, there.*
in, *in.*
loca, -orum, n., pl., *places.*
noctu, *by night, at night, in the night.*
pono, ponere, posui, positus, *place, put, pitch; place, put, station.*
-que, *and.*
quis, -----, quid, *any;* (as adj., **qui, quae**, or **qua, quod**).
subito, *suddenly, on a sudden.*
X, in expression of number, = *10.*

castellum, -i, n., *redoubt, fortress, stronghold.*
eruptio, -onis, f., *a bursting forth, sally, sortie.*
facio, facere, feci, factus, *make.*
firmus, -a, -um, *strong, firm, steadfast.*
I, in expression of number, *1.*
idem, eadem, idem, *the same.*
interdiu, *in the daytime, by day.*
ne, *so that ... not.*
opportunus, -a, -um, *favorable, opportune.*
praesidium, -i, n., *guard, garrison.*
qui, quae, quod, *who, which, what.*
statio, -onis, f., *outpost, picket, guard.*
teneo, tenere, tenui, -----, *hold, contain, occupy.*

Castra: Nominative subject (A.G. 339). Notice here that the noun has a plural meaning.

opportunis locis: Ablative of *place where* without a preposition (A.G. 429.1-2).

erant posita: The main verb of the coordinate clause **Castra ... posita** (A.G. 278.a). Although the pluperfect tense is normally used in subordinate clauses, its use as a main verb is frequent. The pluperfect denotes an action completed in past time (A.G. 477).

ibique: Adverb (A.G. 215.5 and 320-21). **-que**: The enclitic conjunction connects the two participles which share **erant** (**posita ... facta**) (A.G. 324.a).

castella XXIII: Nominative subject (A.G. 339). **XXIII**: Roman numeral used as an adjective (A.G. 133).

(erant) facta: The main verb of the coordinate clause **ibique ... fieret** (A.G. 278.a). Carry down **erant** to form the pluperfect passive verb (A.G. 188). Although the pluperfect tense is normally used in subordinate clauses, its use as a main verb is frequent. The pluperfect denotes an action completed in past time (A.G. 477).

quibus ... ponebantur: Relative clause (A.G. 303). **quibus**: See below. **ponebantur**: The main verb of the subordinate clause (A.G. 278.b).

quibus in castellis: Ablative of *place where* with the preposition **in** (locative ablative) (A.G. 426.3). **quibus**: Plural, neuter, ablative relative pronoun (A.G. 305). The antecedent is **castellis** in its own clause (adjectival use) (A.G. 307.a). **in**: A monosyllabic preposition is often placed between a noun and its adjective (A.G. 599.d.2).

interdiu: Adverb (A.G. 320-21).

stationes: Nominative subject (A.G. 339).

ne qua subito eruptio: Notice the similarity to the phrase **ne qua subito irruptio** at 70.2.

ne ... fieret: The conjunction **ne** ("so that ... not") with the subjunctive forms a negative purpose clause (A.G. 531.1). **fieret**: The main verb of the subordinate clause (A.G. 278.b). Imperfect subjunctive; the tense of the subjunctive is in secondary sequence and follows the rules for the sequence of tense after **(erant) facta** (A.G. 482-85).

qua ... eruptio: Nominative subject (A.G. 339). **qua**: Singular, feminine, nominative indefinite pronoun used as an adjective modifying **eruptio** (A.G. 149). The indefinite **quis, -----, quid** (**qui, quae,** or **qua, quod** when used adjectively) is used after **ne** (A.G. 310.a).

subito: Adverb (A.G. 320-21).

haec eadem: Nominative subject (A.G. 339). **haec**: Plural, neuter, nominative demonstrative pronoun used substantively (A.G. 296.2). The antecedent is **castella** (A.G. 297.e). **eadem**: Plural, neuter, nominative demonstrative pronoun used as an adjective modifying **haec** (A.G. 296.1 and a).

noctu: Adverb (ablative or locative of *noctus, fourth-declension variant of **nox**) (*OLD* **noctu**) (A.G. 320-21).

excubitoribus ac firmis praesidiis: Ablative of means after the passive verb **tenebantur** (A.G. 409). The ablative of means is often used instead of the ablative of agent, especially in military phrases (A.G. 405 Note 1). **ac**: The conjunction connects the two ablative nouns and means "and" (*OLD* **atque** 12).

tenebantur: The main verb of the simple sentence (A.G. 278.1).

4.J CHAPTERS 70-71: THE GAULS LOOSE A CAVALRY SKIRMISH; VERCINGETORIX DISMISSES HIS CAVALRY FROM ALESIA AND CHARGES THEM TO RAISE A RELIEF ARMY

(70.1) Opere instituto, fit equestre proelium in ea planitie quam intermissam collibus tria milia passuum in longitudinem patere supra demonstravimus.

collis, -is, m., *hill, height, elevation.*

equester, -tris, -tre, *of cavalry, cavalry-.*

in, *on; in, in respect to.*

intermitto, -mittere, -misi, -missus, *break, interrupt.*

longitudo, -inis, f., *length,* (with **in**) *lengthwise, longitudinally.*

opus, operis, n., *works, line of works, fortification.*

pateo, patere, patui, -----, *stretch out, extend.*

proelium, -i, n., *battle, combat, engagement.*

supra, *before, previously.*

demonstro, -are, -avi, -atus, *point out, show, say, mention, explain.*

fio, fieri, factus, *take place, happen, come about, come to pass.*

instituo, -stituere, -stitui, -stitutus, *undertake, commence, begin.*

is, ea, id, *he, she, it; that, this.*

milia, -um, n., pl., *thousand, thousands.*

passus, -us, m., *step, pace,* = 4 feet, 10 ¼ inches.

planities, -ei, f., *level ground, plain.*

qui, quae, quod, *who, which, what.*

tres, tria, trium, *three.*

Opere instituto: Ablative absolute (A.G. 419-20). **instituto**: The perfect tense of the participle represents the action as completed at the time indicated by the tense of the main verb (A.G. 489).

fit: The main verb of the main clause (A.G. 278.b). The historical present, giving vividness to the narrative, is present in Chapter 70 (A.G. 469). This usage, common in all languages, comes from imagining past events as going on before our eyes (*repraesentatio*) (A.G. 469 Note).

equestre proelium: Nominative subject (A.G. 339).

in ea planitie: Ablative of *place where* with the preposition **in** (locative ablative) (A.G. 426.3). **ea**: Singular, feminine, ablative demonstrative pronoun used as an adjective modifying **planitie** (A.G. 296.1 and a). The pronoun functions as a correlative to the relative clause **quam ... demonstravimus** (A.G. 297.d).

quam ... demonstravimus: Relative clause (A.G. 303). For the reference see 83.2-4. **quam**: See below. **demonstravimus**: The main verb of the subordinate clause (A.G. 278.b). The personal pronoun **nos** is understood as the subject but is not expressed except for distinction or emphasis (A.G. 295.a). In Book 7, Caesar refers to himself only in the third person, either in the singular or occasionally in the plural (see **Caesar** at 1.1). Siedler counts 11 uses of the first person plural in Book 7 (Siedler, 46). These uses are at 17.1, 23.2, 25.1, 37.1, 48.1, 58.4, 70.1, 76.1, 79.2, 83.8, and 85.4.

quam intermissam ... patere: Accusative/infinitive construction in indirect discourse after **demonstravimus** (A.G. 577 ff.). **quam**: Singular, feminine, accusative relative pronoun used substantively (A.G. 305). The antecedent is **planitie** (A.G. 307). **intermissam**: Accusative perfect, passive participle used as a predicate modifying **quam**, where in English a phrase or a subordinate clause would be more normal (A.G. 496).

collibus: Ablative of means with the passive participle **intermissam** (A.G. 409).

tria milia passuum: Accusative of *extent of space* (A.G. 425). **tria**: Declinable cardinal number used as an adjective modifying **milia** (A.G. 132-35). **milia**: Accusative plural; in the plural **mille** declines as a neuter noun (A.G. 134.d). **passuum**: Partitive genitive with **milia** (346.2).

in longitudinem: Prepositional phrase, **in** with the accusative of **longitudo** means "lengthwise, longitudinally" (*OLD* **longitudo** 1.c).

supra: Adverb (A.G. 320-21).

(70.1-3) **Summa vi ab utrisque con(2)tenditur. Laborantibus nostris Caesar Germanos summittit legionesque pro castris constituit, ne qua subito irruptio ab (3) hostium peditatu fiat.**

ab, *by.*

castra, -orum, n., pl., *camp, encampment.*

contendo, -tendere, -tendi, -tentus, *fight, contend, vie.*

Germani, -orum, m., pl., *the Germans.*

irruptio, -onis, f., *dash, attack.*

legio, -onis, f., *legion.*

nostri, -orum, m., pl., *our men, our side.*

pro, *in front of, before.*

quis, -----, quid, *any;* (as adj., **qui, quae,** or **qua, quod**).

summitto, -mittere, -misi, -missus, *send as reinforcement, send as support*

utrique, utrorumque, m., pl., *both sides, both forces.*

Caesar, -aris, m., *Caesar.*

constituo, -stituere, -stitui, -stitutus, *station, place, draw up.*

fio, fieri, factus, *take place, happen, come about, come to pass.*

hostis, -is, m., *enemy, foe;* pl., *the enemy.*

laboro, -are, -avi, -atus, *be hard pressed, be in distress, be in danger.*

ne, *so that ... not.*

peditatus, -us, m., *infantry.*

-que, *and.*

subito, *suddenly, on a sudden.*

summus, -a, -um, *utmost, greatest, very great.*

vis, acc. **vim**, abl. **vi**, *strength, force.*

Summa vi: Ablative of manner with a limiting adjective (A.G. 412). **Summa**: Defective superlative adjective (A.G. 130.b).

ab utrisque: Ablative of agent with the preposition **ab** after the passive verb **contenditur** (A.G. 405). **utrisque**: Plural, feminine, ablative adjective used substantively (A.G. 288). The noun **partibus** is understood (A.G. 288.b).

(id) contenditur: The main verb of the simple sentence (A.G. 278.1). Impersonal use of the intransitive passive verb (A.G. 208.d). Supply **id** as the subject (A.G. 318.c).

Laborantibus nostris: Dative indirect object of the transitive verb **summittit** (A.G. 362). **Laborantibus**: Present participle used as an adjective modifying **nostris** (A.G. 494.a). **nostris**: Plural, masculine, dative possessive pronoun used substantively to denote a special class (A.G. 302.d).

Caesar: Nominative subject of **summittit ... constituit** (A.G. 339). See Appendix A.

Germanos: Accusative direct object of **summittit** (A.G. 387). See Appendix A.

summittit: The main verb of the coordinate clause **Laborantibus ... summittit** (A.G. 278.a).

legionesque: Accusative direct object of **constituit** (A.G. 387). **-que**: The enclitic conjunction connects the two main verbs **summittit ... constituit** (A.G. 324.a).

pro castris: Prepositional phrase, **pro** with the ablative here means "in front of, before" (*OLD* **pro1** 1).

constituit: The main verb of the coordinate clause **legionesque ... constituit** (A.G. 278.a).

ne qua subito irruptio: Notice the similarity to the phrase **ne qua subito eruptio** at 69.7.

ne ... fiat: The conjunction **ne** ("so that ... not") with the subjunctive forms a negative purpose clause (A.G. 531.1). **fiat**: The main verb of the subordinate clause (A.G. 278.b). Present subjunctive; the tense of the subjunctive is normally in secondary sequence after the historical present **constituit** (A.G. 482-85). Here it is in primary sequence through *repraesentatio* (A.G. 485.e and 585.b Note).

qua ... irruptio: Nominative subject (A.G. 339). **qua**: Singular, feminine, nominative indefinite pronoun used as an adjective modifying **irruptio** (A.G. 149). The indefinite **quis, -----, quid (qui, quae,** or **qua, quod** when used adjectively) is used after **ne** (A.G. 310.a).

subito: Adverb (A.G. 320-21).

ab hostium peditatu: Ablative of agent with the preposition **ab** after the intransitive verb **fiat** (A.G. 405.a). **hostium**: Partitive genitive with **peditatu** (A.G. 346.a.1).

(70.3) **Praesidio legionum addito nostris animus augetur: hostes in fugam coniecti se ipsi multitudine impediunt atque angustioribus portis relictis coacervantur.**

addo, -dere, -didi, -ditus, *add, join.*

animus, -i, m., *courage, spirit, temper, resolution.*

augeo, augere, auxi, auctus, *increase, enlarge, augment, add to.*

coicio, -icere, -ieci, -iectus, (with **in fugam**), *put to flight.*

angustus, -a, -um, comp. **-ior,** *contracted, narrow, close.*

atque, *and.*

coacervo, -are, -avi, -atus, *crowd together.*

fuga, -ae, f., *flight.*

hostis, -is, m., *enemy, foe*; pl., *the enemy*.
in, *into*.
legio, -onis, f., *legion*.
nostri, -orum, m., pl., *our men, our side*.
praesidium, -i, n., *protection, defense, aid, assistance*.
sui, sibi, se, or sese, nom. wanting, *themselves*.

impedio, -pedire, -pedivi, -peditus, *hinder, obstruct*.
ipse, -a, -um, *themselves*.
multitudo, -inis, f., *great number, multitude, crowd*.
porta -ae, f., *gate, entrance*.
relinquo, -linquere, -liqui, -lictus, *leave, leave behind*.

Praesidio legionum addito: Ablative absolute (A.G. 419-20). **legionum:** Objective genitive with **praesidio** (A.G. 348). **addito:** The perfect tense of the participle represents the action as completed at the time indicated by the tense of the main verb (A.G. 489).
nostris: Plural, masculine dative possessive pronoun used substantively to denote a special class (A.G. 302.d). Dative of reference, the dative is often used to qualify a whole idea (**animus augetur**) instead of the possessive genitive modifying one word (**animus**) (A.G. 376-77).
animus: Nominative subject (A.G. 339).
augetur: The main verb of the main clause (A.G. 278.b).
hostes ... coniecti ... ipsi: Nominative subject of **impediunt ... coacervantur** (A.G. 339). **coniecti:** Nominative perfect, passive participle used as a predicate, where in English a phrase or a subordinate clause would be more normal (A.G. 496). **ipsi:** Plural, masculine, nominative demonstrative pronoun used as an emphatic adjective modifying **hostes** and meaning "Themselves (A.G. 298.c).
in fugam: Prepositional phrase, **in** with the accusative here means "into" (a state or condition) (*OLD* **in** 2).
se: Plural, masculine, accusative direct reflexive pronoun (A.G. 300.1). The antecedent is **hostes**, the subject of **impediunt** (A.G. 299). Accusative direct object of **impediunt** (A.G. 387).
multitudine: Ablative of cause without a preposition (A.G. 404).
impediunt: The main verb of the coordinate clause **hostes ... impediunt** (A.G. 278.a).
atque: The conjunction connects the two main verbs **impediunt ... coacervantur** and means "and" (*OLD* **atque** 12).
angustioribus portis relictis: Ablative absolute (A.G. 419-20). **angustioribus:** Comparative adjective (A.G. 124). Plural, feminine, ablative predicate adjective modifying **portis** after **relictis** (A.G. 283-84). The comparative degree here denotes a considerable or excessive degree of the quality meaning "rather or too" (A.G. 291.a). **relictis:** The perfect tense of the participle represents the action as completed at the time indicated by the tense of the main verb (A.G. 489).
coacervantur: The main verb of the coordinate clause **angustioribus ... coacervantur** (A.G. 278.a).

(70.4-5) **(4) Germani acrius usque ad munitiones sequuntur. Fit magna (5) caedes: non nulli relictis equis fossam transire et maceriam transcendere conantur.**

acriter, comp. acrius, *sharply, fiercely, with vigor, courageously*.
conor, -ari, -atus, *endeavor, attempt, undertake, try*.
et, *and*.

fossa, -ae, f., *ditch, trench, entrenchment, fosse*.
maceria, -ae, f., *wall built of loose materials*.
munitio, -onis, f., *works of fortifications, entrenchment, defenses*.
nullus, -i, m., *no one, nobody*.
sequor, -qui, -cutus, *follow, follow after, pursue*.
transeo, -ire, -ivi, or -ii, -itus, *go over, go across, pass over, cross over*.

caedes, -is, f., *killing, slaughter, murder, massacre*.
equus, -i, m., *horse*.
fio, fieri, factus, *take place, happen, come about, come to pass*.
Germani, -orum, m., pl., *the Germans*.
magnus, -a, -um, *great, large, considerable*.
non, *not*.
relinquo, -linquere, -liqui, -lictus, *leave, leave behind*.
transcendo, -scendere, -scendi, -----, *climb over*.
usque ad, *all the way to, right up to, as far as*.

Germani: Nominative subject (A.G. 339). See Appendix A.
acrius: Comparative adverb (A.G. 218 and 320-21).
usque ad munitiones: Prepositional phrase, **usque ad** with the accusative means "all the way to, right up to, as far as" (*OLD* **usque** 1) (A.G. 432.b). **usque:** Adverb (A.G. 320-21 and 432.b).
sequuntur: The main verb of the simple sentence (A.G. 278.1).
Fit ... caedes: The reversal of the normal word order (subject first, verb last) is called hyperbaton (A.G. 596) (Gotoff, 6-10).
Fit magna caedes: This phrase occurs again at 88.3. This terse formulation of the ensuing slaughter is more powerful than a gruesome description of it as it allows the reader to fill in the details with their imagination.
Fit: The main verb of the simple sentence (A.G. 278.1). The verb comes in the first position when the idea in it is emphatic (A.G. 598.d).
magna caedes: Nominative subject (A.G. 339). The subject is in the last position in the clause (A.G. 597.b).
non nulli: A litotes, a statement is made emphatic by denying its contrary (A.G. 326.c).
non: Adverb modifying **nulli**, the negative precedes the word it especially effects (A.G. 217.e, 320-21, and 599.a).
nulli: Plural, masculine, nominative adjective used substantively (A.G. 288). The noun **Galli** is understood (A.G. 288.b). Nominative subject (A.G. 339). Notice the repetition of this phrase at 70.6.
relictis equis: Ablative absolute (A.G. 419-20). **relictis:** The perfect tense of the participle represents the action as completed at the time indicated by the tense of the main verb (A.G. 489).
fossam: Accusative direct object of the infinitive **transire** (A.G. 387 and 451.3).
transire: Complementary infinitive after **conantur** (A.G. 456 and 563.e).
et: The conjunction connects the two infinitives (A.G. 324.a).

maceriam: Accusative direct object of the infinitive **transcendere** (A.G. 387 and 451.3).
transcendere: Complementary infinitive after **conantur** (A.G. 456 and 563.e).
conantur: The main verb of the main clause (A.G. 278.b).

(70.5-6) **Paulum legiones Caesar quas pro (6) vallo constituerat promoveri iubet.**

Caesar, -aris, m., *Caesar*.

iubeo, iubere, iussi, iussus, *order, give orders, bid, command*.
paulum, *a little, somewhat*.
promoveo, -movere, -movi, -motus, *move forward, push forward*.
vallum, -i, n., *rampart, wall, entrenchment*.

constituo, -stituere, -stitui, -stitutus, *station, place, draw up, bring to a halt*.
legio, -onis, f., *legion*.
pro, *in front of, before*.
qui, quae, quod, *who, which, what*.

Paulum: Adverb (A.G. 320-21).
legiones ... promoveri: A subject accusative with the infinitive after **iubet**. The construction is equivalent to a substantive clause of purpose (A.G. 563.a).
Caesar: Nominative subject of **iubet** (A.G. 339). See Appendix A.
quas ... constituerat: Relative clause (A.G. 303). For the reference see 70.2. **quas**: Plural, feminine, accusative relative pronoun used substantively (A.G. 305). The antecedent is **legiones** (A.G. 307). Accusative direct object of **constituerat** (A.G. 37).
constituerat: The main verb of the subordinate clause (A.G. 278.b). The pronoun **is**, with **Caesar** as the antecedent, is understood as the subject (A.G. 271.a). The pluperfect denotes an action completed in past time (A.G. 477).
pro vallo: Prepositional phrase, **pro** with the ablative here means "in front of, before" (*OLD* **pro** 1).
iubet: The main verb of the main clause (A.G. 278.b).

(70.6-7) **Non minus qui intra munitiones erant perturbantur Galli: veniri ad se confestim existimantes ad arma conclamant; non nulli perterriti in (7) oppidum irrumpunt.**

ad, *to*.
conclamo, -are, -avi, -atus, *cry out loud together, shout, cry out*.
existimo, -are, -avi, -atus, *think, consider, judge*.
in, *into*.
irrumpo, -rumpere, -rupi, -ruptus, *break into, burst into, rush in*.
munitio, -onis, f., *works of fortifications, entrenchment, defenses*.
nullus, -i, m., *no one, nobody*.
perterreo, -terrere, -----, -territus, *greatly alarm, frighten, terrify, dismay*.
qui, quae, quod, *who, which, what*.

sum, esse, fui, futurus, *be*.

arma, -orum, n., pl., *arms, weapons*.
confestim, *forthwith, suddenly, speedily*.
Galli, -orum, m., *the Gauls*.
intra, *within, inside*.
minus, *less*.
non, *not*.
oppidum, -i, n., *fortified town, city*.
perturbo, -are, -avi, -atus, *disturb greatly, throw into confusion, disorder*.
sui, sibi, se, or **sese**, nom. wanting, *them*, with or without *-selves*.
venio, venire, veni, ventus, *come*.

Non: Adverb modifying **minus**, the negative precedes the word it especially effects (A.G. 217.e, 320-21, and 599.a). When a negative begins a sentence it is especially emphatic (A.G. 599.a).
minus: Defective comparative adverb (A.G. 218.a and 320-21).
qui ... erant: Relative clause (A.G. 303). **qui**: Plural, masculine, nominative relative pronoun used substantively (A.G. 305). The antecedent is the following noun **Galli** (A.G. 307). Nominative subject (A.G. 339). **erant**: The main verb of the subordinate clause (A.G. 278.b).
intra munitiones: Prepositional phrase, **intra** with the accusative here means "within, inside" (*OLD* **intra** 1). The prepositional phrase is in the predicate position after **erant** (A.G. 272).
perturbantur: The main verb of the main clause (A.G. 278.b).
Galli: Nominative subject of **perturbantur** (A.G. 339). See Appendix A.
(id) veniri: Impersonal passive infinitive construction in indirect discourse after **existimantes** (A.G. 577 ff.). Impersonal use of the infinitive (A.G. 208.d). Supply **id** as the subject (A.G. 318.c). **veniri**: Present infinitive; the tense of the infinitive in indirect discourse is relative to that of the verb of saying (A.G. 584).
ad se: Prepositional phrase, **ad** with the accusative here means "to" (*OLD* **ad** 1). **se**: Plural, masculine, accusative indirect reflexive pronoun (A.G. 300.2). The antecedent is **existimantes**, the subject of **conclamant** (A.G. 299).
confestim: Adverb (A.G. 320-21).
existimantes: Nominative, present participle used as a predicate, where in English a phrase or a subordinate clause would be more normal (A.G. 496). The pronoun **ei**, with **Galli** as the antecedent, is understood. Nominative subject (A.G. 339).
ad arma: Prepositional phrase, **ad** with the accusative here means "to" (an act or policy) (*OLD* **ad** 6).
conclamant: The main verb of the main clause (A.G. 278.b).
non nulli: A litotes, a statement is made emphatic by denying its contrary (A.G. 326.c). This phrase is repeated at 70.5.
non: Adverb modifying **nulli**, the negative precedes the word it especially effects (A.G. 217.e, 320-21, and 599.a). When a negative begins a sentence it is especially emphatic (A.G. 599.a).
nulli perterriti: Nominative subject (A.G. 339). **nulli**: Plural, masculine, nominative adjective used substantively (A.G. 288). The

pronoun **ei**, with **Galli** as the antecedent, is understood. **perterriti**: Nominative, perfect, passive, participle used as a predicate, where in English a phrase or a subordinate clause would be more normal (A.G. 496).
in oppidum: Accusative of *place to which* with the preposition **in** (A.G. 426.2).
irrumpunt: The main verb of the simple sentence (A.G. 278.1).

(70.7) Vercingetorix iubet portas claudi, ne castra nudentur. Multis interfectis, compluribus equis captis Germani sese recipiunt.

capio, capere, cepi, captus, *take, get, seize, capture.*
claudo, claudere, clausi, clausus, *shut, close.*
equus, -i, m., *horse.*
interficio, -ficere, -feci, -fectus, *slay, kill.*

multi, -orum, m., pl., *many men.*
nudo, -are, -avi, -atus, *expose, leave unprotected.*
recipio, -cipere, -cepi, -ceptus, (with se), *turn back, retire.*
Vercingetorix, -igis, m., *Vercingetorix.*

castra, -orum, n., pl., *camp, encampment.*
complures, -a and **-ia**, *several, a number of, many.*
Germani, -orum, m., pl., *the Germans.*
iubeo, iubere, iussi, iussus, *order, give orders, bid, command.*
ne, *so that ... not.*
porta -ae, f., *gate, entrance.*
sui, sibi, se, or **sese**, nom. wanting, *themselves.*

Vercingetorix: Nominative subject (A.G. 339). See Appendix A.
iubet: The main verb of the main clause (A.G. 278.b).
portas claudi: A subject accusative with the infinitive after **iubet**. The construction is equivalent to a substantive clause of purpose (A.G. 563.a). **portas**: Supply **urbis**. There are Gauls on the plain amid the rout, in the camp outside the city walls but behind the wall facing the plain, and finally in the city itself. The panic starts on the plain and works successively backwards into the city like dominoes. Vercingetorix shuts up the city itself in order to prevent a complete rout.
ne ... nudentur: The conjunction **ne** ("so that ... not") with the subjunctive forms a negative purpose clause (A.G. 531.1). **nudentur**: The main verb of the subordinate clause (A.G. 278.b). Present subjunctive; the tense of the subjunctive is normally in secondary sequence after the historical present **iubet** (A.G. 482-85). Here it is in primary sequence through *repraesentatio* (A.G. 485.e and 585.b Note).
castra: Nominative subject (A.G. 339).
Multis interfectis: Ablative absolute (A.G. 419-20). **Multis**: Plural, masculine, ablative adjective used substantively meaning "many men" (A.G. 288). **interfectis**: The perfect tense of the participle represents the action as completed at the time indicated by the tense of the main verb (A.G. 489).
compluribus equis captis: Ablative absolute (A.G. 419-20). Notice the asyndeton between the two ablative absolutes (A.G. 323.b). **compluribus**: Plural, masculine, ablative comparative adjective, a compound of **plus** (A.G. 120). **captis**: The perfect tense of the participle represents the action as completed at the time indicated by the tense of the main verb (A.G. 489).
Germani: Nominative subject (A.G. 339). See Appendix A.
sese: Plural, masculine, accusative direct reflexive pronoun (A.G. 300.1). The antecedent is **Germani**, the subject of **recipiunt** (A.G. 299). Accusative direct object of **recipiunt** (A.G. 387). Reduplicated form of **se** (A.G. 144.b Note 1).
recipiunt: The main verb of the main clause (A.G. 278.b). **sese recipiunt**: The verb **recipere** used reflexively means "to turn back, retire" (*OLD* **recipio** 12). This is the second time Caesar owes the victory to the German cavalry.

(71.1-2) Vercingetorix, prius quam munitiones ab Romanis perficiantur, consilium capit omnem ab se equitatum noctu dimit(2)tere.

ab, *by, from.*
consilium, -i, n., *plan, scheme.*
equitatus, -us, m., *cavalry.*

noctu, *by night, at night, in the night.*
perficio, -ficere, -feci, -fectus, *finish, complete.*
Romani, -orum, m., pl., *the Romans.*
Vercingetorix, -igis, m., *Vercingetorix.*

capio, capere, cepi, captus, *form, adopt.*
dimitto, -mittere, -misi, -missus, *dismiss, send off.*
munitio, -onis, f., *works of fortifications, entrenchment, defenses.*
omnis, -e, *all, the entire.*
prius quam, *before, sooner than.*
sui, sibi, se, or **sese**, nom. wanting, *himself.*

Vercingetorix: Nominative subject (A.G. 339). See Appendix A.
prius quam ... perficiantur: Temporal clause; the conjunction **prius quam** ("before") with the present subjunctive refers to future time (A.G. 551.c). **perficiantur**: The main verb of the subordinate clause (A.G. 278.b).
munitiones: Nominative subject (A.G. 339).
ab Romanis: Ablative of agent with the preposition **ab** after the passive verb **perficiantur** (A.G. 405).
consilium capit: The phrase **consilium capere** is an idiom that means "to adopt or form a plan" (*OLD* **capio** 9.e).
consilium: Accusative direct object of **capit** (A.G. 387).
capit: The main verb of the main clause (A.G. 278.b). The historical present, giving vividness to the narrative, is present in Chapter 71 (A.G. 469). This usage, common in all languages, comes from imagining past events as going on before our eyes (*repraesentatio*) (A.G. 469 Note).
omnem ... equitatum: Accusative direct object of the infinitive **dimittere** (A.G. 387 and 451.3).

ab se: Ablative of separation with the preposition **ab** after the compound infinitive **dimittere** (A.G. 402). **se**: Singular, masculine, accusative direct reflexive pronoun (A.G. 300.1). The antecedent is **Vercingetorix**, the subject of **capit** (A.G. 299).
noctu: Adverb (ablative or locative of *noctus, fourth-declension variant of **nox**) (*OLD* **noctu**) (A.G. 320-21).
dimittere: Complementary infinitive after **consilium capit** (A.G. 456). "Vercingetorix now committed his fatal blunder: he set aside his harassing tactics and decided to hold Alesia until a relieving army could come to his succour." (Fuller, 150).

(71.2-3) Discedentibus mandat ut suam quisque eorum civitatem adeat omnisque qui per aetatem arma ferre possint ad (3) bellum cogant.

ad, *for, for the purpose of.*
aetas, -tatis, f., *age.*
bellum, -i, n., *war, warfare.*
cogo, cogere, coegi, coactus, *bring together, collect, gather, assemble.*

fero, ferre, tuli, latus, *bear, carry.*
mando, -are, -avi, -atus, *order, command, instruct.*
per, *as a result of, by reason of, through.*
-que, *and.*
quisque, -----, quidque, *each one, each thing.*
ut, *so that.*

adeo, -ire, -ivi, or **–ii, -itus**, *go to, approach, visit.*
arma, -orum, n., pl., *arms, armor, weapons.*
civitas, -tatis, f., *state, nation.*
discedo, -cedere, -cessi, -cessurus, *go away, depart, leave.*
is, ea, id, *he, she, it; that, this.*
omnes, -ium, m., pl., *all men, all.*
possum, posse, potui, -----, *be able.*
qui, quae, quod, *who, which, what.*
suus, -a, -um, *his*, with or without *own.*

Discedentibus: Plural, masculine, dative present participle used substantively (A.G. 494.a). The noun **equitibus** is understood (A.G. 288.b). Dative indirect object of the transitive verb **mandat** (A.G. 362).
mandat: The main verb of the main clause (A.G. 278.b). The pronoun **is**, with **Vercingetorix** as the antecedent, is understood as the subject (A.G. 271.a).
ut ... adeat ... cogant: The conjunction **ut** ("so that") with the subjunctive is here a substantive clause of purpose which is used as the object of the verb **mandat** denoting an action directed toward the future (A.G. 563). **adeat ... cogant**: The main verbs of the subordinate clause (A.G. 278.b). Present subjunctives; the tense of the subjunctives is normally in secondary sequence after the historical present **mandat** (A.G. 482-85). Here it is in primary sequence through *repraesentatio* (A.G. 485.e and 585.b Note). Notice the switch in subject between the singular **quisque** with **adeat** and the plural **cogant**. **cogant**: The pronoun **ei**, with **Discedentibus** as the antecedent, is understood as the subject (A.G. 271.a).
suam ... civitatem: Accusative direct object of **adeat** (A.G. 370.b). **suam**: Singular, feminine, accusative possessive pronoun used as an adjective modifying **civitatem** (A.G. 302).
quisque: Singular, masculine, nominative indefinite pronoun used substantively (A.G. 151.g). Nominative subject (A.G. 339).
eorum: Plural, masculine, genitive demonstrative pronoun used substantively (A.G. 296.2). The antecedent is **Discedentibus** (A.G. 297.e). Partitive genitive with **quisque** (A.G. 346.d).
omnisque: Plural, masculine, accusative adjective used substantively (A.G. 288). Accusative direct object of **cogant** (A.G. 387). Accusative adjective; **-is** for **-es** is the regular form in i-stem adjectives (A.G. 114.a and 116). **-que**: The enclitic conjunction connects the two main verbs in the purpose clause **adeat ... cogant** (A.G. 324.a).
qui ... possint: Relative clause; a clause dependent on a subjunctive clause (**ut ... cogant**) takes the subjunctive when regarded as an integral part of that clause (attraction) (A.G. 303 and 593). **qui**: Plural, masculine, nominative relative pronoun used substantively (A.G. 305). The antecedent is **omnis** (A.G. 307). Nominative subject (A.G. 339). **possint**: The main verb of the subordinate clause (A.G. 278.b). Present subjunctive; the tense of the subjunctive is normally in secondary sequence after the historical present **mandat** (A.G. 482-85). Here it is in primary sequence through *repraesentatio* (A.G. 485.e and 585.b Note).
per aetatem: Prepositional phrase, **per** with the accusative here means "as a result of, by reason of, through" (*OLD* **per** 13).
arma: Accusative direct object of the infinitive **ferre** (A.G. 387 and 451.3).
ferre: Complementary infinitive after **possint** (A.G. 456).
ad bellum: Prepositional phrase, **ad** with the accusative here implies purpose and means "for, for the purpose of" (*OLD* **ad** 44). The Gallic leadership outside Alesia does not follow this advice at 75.1 but instead assembles a smaller, more manageable, force.

(71.3) Sua in illos merita proponit obtestaturque ut suae salutis rationem habeant, neu se optime de communi libertate meritum hostibus in cruciatum dedant.

communis, -e, *common, in common, public, general.*
de, *with regard to, in the matter of.*
habeo, habere, habui, habitus, *have*, (with **ratio**), *take account of, pay regard to.*
ille, illae, illud, *that; he, she, it.*
libertas, -atis, f., *freedom, liberty, independence.*
meritum, -i, n., *merit, service, kindness, benefit.*
obtestor, -ari, -atus, *implore, adjure.*
propono, -ponere, -posui, -positus, *put forward, present.*
ratio, -onis, f., *regard, consideration, care, concern.*
sui, sibi, se, or **sese**, nom. wanting, *him*, with or without -*self.*

cruciatus, -i, m., *torture, cruelty, torment, suffering.*
dedo, -dere, -didi, -ditus, *give up, surrender.*
hostis, -is, m., *enemy, foe*; pl., *the enemy.*

in, *towards; so as to result in.*
mereor, -eri, -itus, *deserve, merit.*
neu, *and that ... not, and not, nor.*
optime, *best.*
-que, *and.*
salus, -utis, f., *welfare, safety, deliverance.*
suus, -a, -um, *his*, with or without *own.*

ut, *so that*.

Sua ...merita: Accusative direct object of **proponit** (A.G. 387). **Sua**: Plural, neuter, accusative possessive pronoun used as an adjective modifying **merita** (A.G. 302).

in illos: Prepositional phrase, **in** with the accusative here means "towards", indicating the person towards whom feelings are directed (*OLD* **in** 11). **illos**: Plural, masculine, accusative demonstrative pronoun used substantively (A.G. 296.2). The antecedent is **Discedentibus** (A.G. 297.e).

proponit: The main verb of the coordinate clause **Sua ... proponit** (A.G. 278.a). The pronoun **is**, with **Vercingetorix** as the antecedent, is understood as the subject (A.G. 271.a).

obtestaturque: The main verb of the coordinate clause **obtestaturque ... dedant** (A.G. 278.a). **obtestatur**: The pronoun **is**, with **Vercingetorix** as the antecedent, is understood as the subject (A.G. 271.a). **-que**: The enclitic conjunction connects the two main verbs (A.G. 324.a).

ut ... habeant ... neu ... dedant: The conjunction **ut** ("so that") with the subjunctive is here a substantive clause of purpose which is used as the object of the verb **obtestatur** denoting an action directed toward the future (A.G. 563). **habeant ... dedant**: The main verbs of the subordinate clause (A.G. 278.b). Present subjunctives; the tense of the subjunctives is normally in secondary sequence after the historical present **obtestatur** (A.G. 482-85). Here it is in primary sequence through *repraesentatio* (A.G. 485.e and 585.b Note). The pronoun **ei**, with **Discedentibus** as the antecedent, is understood as the subject of both verbs (A.G. 271.a). **neu**: After **ut**, the conjunction **neu** adds a negative purpose to a positive one meaning "and that ... not" (*OLD* **neve** 2)

suae salutis: Objective genitive with **rationem** (A.G. 348). **suae**: Singular, feminine, genitive possessive pronoun used as an adjective modifying **salutis** (A.G. 302).

rationem: Accusative direct object of **habeant** (A.G. 387). The phrase **rationem habere** is an idiom with the genitive meaning "to take account of, pay regard to" (*OLD* **ratio** 8.b).

se ... meritum: Accusative direct object of the transitive verb **dedant** (A.G. 387). **se**: Singular, masculine, accusative indirect reflexive pronoun (A.G. 300.2). The antecedent is **is** (**Vercingetorix**), the supplied subject of **obtestatur** (A.G. 299). **meritum**: Accusative perfect, deponent participle (from **mereor**) used as a predicate, where in English a phrase or a subordinate clause would be more normal (A.G. 496).

optime: Superlative adverb (A.G. 218 and 320-21).

de communi libertate: Prepositional phrase, **de** with the ablative here means "with regard to, in the matter of" (*OLD* **de** 13).

libertate: For the theme of liberty in Book 7, see **liberius** at 1.3.

hostibus: Dative indirect object of the transitive verb **dedant** (A.G. 362).

in cruciatum: Prepositional phrase, **in** with the accusative here implies consequence and means "so as to result in" (*OLD* **in** 20).

(71.3-4) Quod si indiligentiores fuerint, milia hominum delecta LXXX una (4) secum interitura demonstrat.

-cum, *with*.
demonstro, -are, -avi, -atus, *point out, show, say, mention, explain*.
indiligens, -entis, comp. **-ior**, *careless, heedless*.
L, in expression of number, *50*.
quod si, *but if, and if, now if*.

sum, esse, fui, futurus, *be*.

X, in expression of number, = *10*.

deligo, -ligere, -legi, -lectus, *choose, select, pick out*.
homo, hominis, m., *man, person*.
intereo, -ire, -ii, -iturus, *perish, be destroyed, die*.
milia, -um, n., pl., *thousand, thousands*.
sui, sibi, se, or **sese**, nom. wanting, *him*, with or without *-self*.
una, *at one and the same time, at the same time, together*.

Quod si: The combination means "but if, and if, now if" (A.G. 324.d). **Quod**: The relative adverb is used as a connective particle, referring to what precedes (*OLD* **quod** 1). **si**: Conjunction (*OLD* **si**).

si ... fuerint ... interitura (esse): Conditional statement in indirect discourse after **demonstrat** (A.G. 589). The protasis, as a dependent clause, is in the subjunctive and the apodosis, as the principal clause, is in the infinitive (A.G. 589).

si fuerint: The conjunction **si** ("if") with the subjunctive forms the protasis of a conditional statement in indirect discourse (A.G. 589.1). **fuerint**: The main verb of the subordinate clause (A.G. 278.b). Perfect subjunctive; the tense of the subjunctive is normally in secondary sequence after the historical present **demonstrat** (A.G. 482-85). Here it is in primary sequence through *repraesentatio* (A.G. 485.e and 585.b Note). The perfect subjunctive here stands for the future perfect in direct speech. The future perfect tense denotes action completed (at the time referred to), and hence is represented in the subjunctive by the perfect tense in primary sequence (A.G. 484.c). The pronoun **ei**, with **Discedentibus** as the antecedent, is understood as the subject (A.G. 271.a).

indiligentiores: Plural, masculine, nominative comparative adjective used in the predicate position modifying **ei**, the supplied subject, after **fuerint** (A.G. 124 and 283-84). The comparative degree here denotes a considerable or excessive degree of the quality meaning "too" (A.G. 291.a).

milia ... delecta LXXX ... interitura (esse): The apodosis of the conditional statement (A.G. 589.2). Accusative/infinitive construction in indirect discourse after **demonstrat** (A.G. 577 ff.). **milia**: Accusative plural; in the plural **mille** declines as a neuter noun (A.G. 134.d). **LXXX**: Roman numeral used as an adjective modifying **milia** (A.G. 133). **delecta**: Accusative perfect, passive participle used as a predicate modifying **milia**, where in English a phrase or a subordinate clause would be more normal (A.G. 496).

interitura (esse): Supply **esse** to form the future, active infinitive (A.G. 203). The tense of the infinitive in indirect discourse is relative to that of the verb of saying (A.G. 584).

hominum: Partitive genitive with **milia** (A.G. 346.a.2).

una: Adverb (A.G. 320-21).

secum: Ablative of accompaniment with the preposition **cum** (A.G. 413). **se**: Singular, masculine, ablative indirect reflexive pronoun (A.G. 300.2). The antecedent is **is** (**Vercingetorix**), the supplied subject of **demonstrat** (A.G. 299). **-cum**: The preposition **cum** ("with") is joined enclitically with the ablative (A.G. 143.f).

demonstrat: The main verb of the main clause (A.G. 278.b). The pronoun **is**, with **Vercingetorix** as the antecedent, is understood as the subject (A.G. 271.a).

(71.4-5) Ratione inita exigue dierum se habere XXX frumentum, sed paulo etiam longius tolerare (5) posse parcendo.

dies, **-ei**, m. and f., *day*.
exigue, *barely, hardly*.
habeo, **habere**, **habui**, **habitus**, *have, possess*.
longe, comp., **-ius**, *long*.

paulo, *by a little, just a little*.
ratio, **-onis**, f., *reckoning, calculation, account, assessment*.
sui, **sibi**, **se**, or **sese**, nom. wanting, *him*, with or without *-self*.
X, in expression of number, = *10*.

etiam, *even*.
frumentum, **-i**, n., *grain*.
ineo, **-ire**, **-ivi**, or **-ii**, **-itus**, *arrive at, determine*.
parco, **parcere**, **peperci**, and **parsi**, **parsus**, *use sparingly*.
possum, **posse**, **potui**, **-----**, *be able*.
sed, *but*.
tolero, **-are**, **-avi**, **-atus**, *endure, hold out*.

Ratione inita: Ablative absolute (A.G. 419-20). The phrase **rationem inire** means "to make a calculation, keep count" (*OLD* **ratio** 1). **inita**: The perfect tense of the participle represents the action as completed at the time indicated by the tense of the main verb (A.G. 489).

exigue: Adverb (A.G. 214.a and 320-21).

dierum ... XXX: Genitive of quality (measure) with **frumentum** (A.G. 346.a.2). **dierum**: The noun **dies** is normally masculine gender (A.G. 97.a). **XXX**: Roman numeral used as an adjective (A.G. 133).

se habere: Accusative/infinitive construction in indirect discourse after **demonstrat** (A.G. 577 ff.). **se**: Singular, masculine, accusative direct reflexive pronoun (A.G. 300.1). The antecedent is **is** (**Vercingetorix**), the supplied subject of **demonstrat** (A.G. 299). **habere**: Present infinitive; the tense of the infinitive in indirect discourse is relative to that of the verb of saying (A.G. 584).

frumentum: Accusative direct object of the infinitive **habere** (A.G. 387 and 451.3).

sed: Coordinate conjunction (A.G. 324.d).

paulo: Adverb (A.G. 320-21).

etiam: Adverb (A.G. 320-21 and 322.a). The adverb normally proceeds the emphatic word (A.G. 322.a).

longius: Comparative adverb (A.G. 218 and 320-21).

tolerare: Complementary infinitive after **posse** (A.G. 456).

(se) posse: Accusative/infinitive construction in indirect discourse after **demonstrat** (A.G. 577 ff.). Carry down **se** from above as the accusative subject. **posse**: Present infinitive; the tense of the infinitive in indirect discourse is relative to that of the verb of saying (A.G. 584). The present infinitive **posse** often has a future sense (A.G. 584.b).

parcendo: Ablative of means (A.G. 409). Singular, neuter, ablative gerund (A.G. 507.1).

(71.5) His datis mandatis, qua nostrum opus erat intermissum, secunda vigilia silentio equitatum dimittit.

dimitto, **-mittere**, **-misi**, **-missus**, *dismiss, send off*.
equitatus, **-us**, m., *cavalry*.
intermitto, **-mittere**, **-misi**, **-missus**, *leave unoccupied, leave vacant*.
noster, **-tra**, **-trum**, *our, our own*.
qua, *where*.
silentium, **-i**, m., *silence*.

do, **dare**, **dedi**, **datus**, *give*.
hic, **haec**, **hoc**, *this; he, she, it*.
mandatum, **-i**, n., *order, command, instruction*.
opus, **operis**, n., *works, line of works, fortification*.
secundus, **-a**, **-um**, *second*.
vigilia, **-ae**, f., *watch*.

His datis mandatis: Ablative absolute (A.G. 419-20). **His**: Plural, neuter, ablative demonstrative pronoun used as an adjective modifying **mandatis** (A.G. 296.1 and a). **datis**: The perfect tense of the participle represents the action as completed at the time indicated by the tense of the main verb (A.G. 489).

qua ... intermissum: Relative clause (A.G. 279.a). **qua**: Relative adverb meaning "where" (*OLD* **qua** 4). **intermissum**: Nominative, perfect, passive, participle used as a predicate adjective modifying **opus** after **erat** (A.G. 495).

nostrum opus: Nominative subject (A.G. 339). **nostrum**: Singular, neuter, nominative possessive pronoun used as an adjective modifying **opus** (A.G. 302 and 302.a).

erat: The main verb of the subordinate clause (A.G. 278.b).

secunda vigilia: Ablative of *time when* (423.1). **secunda**: Declinable ordinal number used as an adjective (A.G. 132-35). The second watch runs from 9:00 to midnight.

silentio: Ablative of manner (A.G. 412.b).

equitatum: Accusative direct object of **dimittit** (A.G. 387).

dimittit: The main verb of the main clause (A.G. 278.b). The pronoun **is**, with **Vercingetorix** as the antecedent, is understood as the subject (A.G. 271.a).

(71.6-9) (6) Frumentum omne ad se referri iubet; capitis poenam eis (7) qui non paruerint constituit; pecus, cuius magna erat

copia (8) ab Mandubiis compulsa, viritim distribuit; frumentum parce et paulatim metiri instituit; copias omnis quas pro oppido (9) collocaverat in oppidum recepit.

ab, *by.*
caput, **-itis**, n., *head*; by metonymy *life, safety.*
compello, **-pellere**, **-puli**, **-pulsus**, *collect, drive.*

copia, **-ae**, f., *quantity, abundance, supply, plenty.*
distribuo, **-tribuere**, **-tribui**, **-tributus**, *distribute, divide, assign, apportion.*
frumentum, **-i**, n., *grain.*
instituo, **-stituere**, **-stitui**, **-stitutus**, *undertake, commence, begin.*
iubeo, **iubere**, **iussi**, **iussus**, *order, give orders, bid, command.*
Mandubii, **-orum**, m., pl., *the Mandubii.*

non, *not.*
oppidum, **-i**, n., *fortified town, city.*
pareo, **parere**, **parui**, -----, *obey, submit, comply.*
pecus, **-oris**, n., *cattle.*
pro, *in front of, before.*
recipio, **-cipere**, **-cepi**, **-ceptus**, *take back, withdraw, receive, admit.*
sui, **sibi**, **se**, or **sese**, nom. wanting, *himself.*

ad, *to.*
colloco, **-are**, **-avi**, **-atus**, *place, set, post, station.*
constituo, **-stituere**, **-stitui**, **-stitutus**, *establish, resolve upon, determine, fix.*
copiae, **-arum**, f., pl., *forces, troops.*
et, *and.*
in, *into.*
is, **ea**, **id**, *he, she, it; that, this.*
magnus, **-a**, **-um**, *great, large, considerable.*
metior, **metiri**, **mensus**, *measure, measure out, distribute.*
omnis, **-e**, *all.*
parce, *sparingly.*
paulatim, *little by little, gradually.*
poena, **-ae**, f., *punishment, penalty.*
qui, **quae**, **quod**, *who, which, what.*
refero, **-ferre**, **rettuli**, **-latus**, *bring, carry, convey.*
viritim, *man by man, to each individually.*

Frumentum omne ... referri: A subject accusative with the infinitive after **iubet**. The construction is equivalent to a substantive clause of purpose (A.G. 563.a).
ad se: Prepositional phrase, **ad** with the accusative here means "to" (*OLD* **ad** 1). **se**: Singular, masculine, accusative indirect reflexive pronoun (A.G. 300.2). The antecedent is **is** (**Vercingetorix**), the supplied subject of **iubet** (A.G. 299).
iubet: The main verb of the main clause (A.G. 278.b). The pronoun **is**, with **Vercingetorix** as the antecedent, is understood as the subject (A.G. 271.a).
capitis: Genitive of charge or penalty with **poenam** (A.G. 352). Here, the noun **caput** means "one's life" as forfeit for various offenses by metonymy ("the use of the name of one thing to indicate some kindred meaning") (A.G. 641) (*OLD* **caput** 5.b).
poenam: Accusative direct object of the transitive verb **constituit** (A.G. 387).
eis: Plural, masculine, dative demonstrative pronoun used substantively (A.G. 296.2). The pronoun is correlative to the relative clause **qui ... paruerint** (A.G. 297.d). Dative indirect object of the transitive verb **constituit** (A.G. 362).
qui ... paruerint: A relative clause of characteristic; a relative clause with the subjunctive is often used to indicate a characteristic of the antecedent (A.G. 535). **qui**: Plural, masculine, nominative relative pronoun used substantively (A.G. 305). The antecedent is **eis** (A.G. 307). Nominative subject (A.G. 339). **paruerint**: The main verb of the subordinate clause (A.G. 278.b). Perfect subjunctive; the tense of the subjunctive is normally in secondary sequence after the historical present **constituit** (A.G. 482-85). Here it is in primary sequence through *repraesentatio* (A.G. 485.e and 585.b Note). The perfect subjunctive here stands for the future perfect. The future perfect tense denotes action completed (at the time referred to), and hence is represented in the subjunctive by the perfect tense (A.G. 484.c).
non: Adverb, the adverb generally precedes the verb if it belongs to no one word in particular (A.G. 217.e, 320-21, and 599.a).
constituit: The main verb of the main clause (A.G. 278.b). The pronoun **is**, with **Vercingetorix** as the antecedent, is understood as the subject (A.G. 271.a).
pecus: Accusative direct object of **distribuit** (A.G. 387).
cuius ... erat ... compulsa: Relative clause (A.G. 303). **cuius**: Singular, neuter, genitive relative pronoun used substantively (A.G. 305). The antecedent is **pecus** (A.G. 307). Partitive genitive with **copia** (A.G. 346.1.a). **erat ... compulsa**: The main verb of the subordinate clause (A.G. 278.b). The pluperfect passive verb is here split (tmesis) (A.G. 640). The pluperfect denotes an action completed in past time (A.G. 477).
magna ...copia: Nominative subject (A.G. 339).
ab Mandubiis: Ablative of agent with the preposition **ab** after the passive verb **erat ... compulsa** (A.G. 405). **Mandubiis**: See Appendix A. Alesia is a city of the Mandubii.
viritim: Adverb (A.G. 215.2 and 320-21).
distribuit: The main verb of the main clause (A.G. 278.b). The pronoun **is**, with **Vercingetorix** as the antecedent, is understood as the subject (A.G. 271.a).
frumentum: Accusative direct object of the infinitive **metiri** (A.G. 387 and 451.3).
parce: Adverb (A.G. 214.a and 320-21).
et: The conjunction connects the two adverbs (A.G. 324.a).
paulatim: Adverb (A.G. 215.2 and 320-21).
metiri: Complementary infinitive after **instituit** (A.G. 456).
instituit: The main verb of the main clause (A.G. 278.b). The pronoun **is**, with **Vercingetorix** as the antecedent, is understood as the subject (A.G. 271.a).
copias omnis: Accusative direct object of **recepit** (A.G. 387). **omnis**: Accusative adjective; **-is** for **-es** is the regular form in i-stem adjectives (A.G. 114.a and 116).
quas ... collocaverat: Relative clause (A.G. 303). **quas**: Plural, feminine, accusative relative pronoun used substantively (A.G. 305).

The antecedent is **copias** (A.G. 307). Accusative direct object of **collocaverat** (A.G. 387). **collocaverat**: The main verb of the subordinate clause (A.G. 278.b). The pronoun **is**, with **Vercingetorix** as the antecedent, is understood as the subject (A.G. 271.a). The pluperfect denotes an action completed in past time (A.G. 477).

pro oppido: Prepositional phrase, **pro** with the ablative here means "in front of, before" (*OLD* **pro1** 1).

in oppidum: Ablative of *place to which* with the preposition **in** (A.G. 426.2).

recepit: The main verb of the main clause (A.G. 278.b). The pronoun **is**, with **Vercingetorix** as the antecedent, is understood as the subject (A.G. 271.a).

(71.8-9) His rationibus auxilia Galliae exspectare et bellum parat administrare.

administro, -are, -avi, -atus, *execute, manage, carry on, administer.*

bellum, -i, n., *war, warfare.*
exspecto, -are, -avi, -atus, *wait to see, wait for, await, expect.*
hic, haec, hoc, *this; he, she, it.*
ratio, -onis, f., *procedure, method, measure, plan.*

auxilia, -orum, n., *auxiliary troops, auxiliaries, allied forces.*
et, *and.*
Gallia, -ae, f., *Gaul.*
paro, -are, -avi, -atus, *prepare, make ready.*

His rationibus: Ablative of means (A.G. 409). **His**: Plural, feminine, ablative demonstrative pronoun used as an adjective modifying **rationibus** (A.G. 296.1 and a).

auxilia: Accusative direct object of the infinitive **exspectare** (A.G. 387 and 451.3).

Galliae: Objective genitive with **auxilia** (A.G. 348).

exspectare: Complementary infinitive after **parat** (A.G. 456).

et: The conjunction connects the two infinitives (A.G. 324.a).

bellum: Accusative direct object of the infinitive **administrare** (A.G. 387 and 451.3).

parat: The main verb of the main clause (A.G. 278.b). The pronoun **is**, with **Vercingetorix**, as the antecedent, is understood as the subject (A.G. 271.a).

administrare: Complementary infinitive after **parat** (A.G. 456).

4.K CHAPTERS 72-74: A DESCRIPTION OF CAESAR'S SIEGE WORKS AT ALESIA, FIRST THOSE FACING INWARD TOWARD ALESIA AND THEN THOSE FACING OUTWARD TOWARD THE RELIEF ARMY
(72.1) Quibus rebus cognitis ex perfugis et captivis, Caesar haec genera munitionis instituit.

Caesar, -aris, m., *Caesar.*
cognosco, -gnoscere, -gnovi, cognitus, *learn, ascertain, recognize.*
ex, *from.*
hic, haec, hoc, *this; he, she, it.*

munitio, -onis, f., *works of fortifications, entrenchment, defenses.*
qui, quae, quod, *who, which, what.*

captivus, -i, m., *captive, prisoner.*
et, *and.*
genus, generis, n., *kind, type.*
instituo, -stituere, -stitui, -stitutus, *build, make ready, undertake, commence.*
perfuga, -ae, m., *deserter.*
res, rei, f., *matter, event, affair.*

Quibus rebus cognitis ex perfugis et captivis: Ablative absolute (A.G. 419-20). **quibus**: Plural, feminine, ablative relative pronoun (A.G. 305). The antecedent is **rebus** in its own clause (adjectival use) (A.G. 307.b). The relative does not introduce a relative clause but is a connecting relative; at the beginning of a clause the pronoun is often best rendered by a personal or demonstrative pronoun, with or without *and* (A.G. 308.f). **cognitis**: The perfect tense of the participle represents the action as completed at the time indicated by the tense of the main verb (A.G. 489). **ex perfugis et captivis**: Two ablatives of source with the preposition **ex** (A.G. 403.1). **et**: The conjunction connects the two ablative nouns in the prepositional phrase (A.G. 324.a).

Caesar: Nominative subject (A.G. 387).

haec genera: Accusative direct object of **instituit** (A.G. 387). **haec**: Plural, neuter, accusative demonstrative pronoun used as an adjective modifying **genera** (A.G. 296.1 and a).

munitionis: Partitive genitive with **genera** (A.G. 346.a.1).

instituit: The main verb of the main clause (A.G. 278.b).

(72.1-2) Fossam pedum XX derectis lateribus duxit, ut eius fossae solum tantundem pateret (2) quantum summae fossae labra distarent.

derectus, -a, -um, *straight up and down, perpendicular.*

duco, ducere, duxi, ductus, *dig, make.*
is, ea, id, *he, she, it; that, this.*
latus, -eris, n., *side, flank.*
pes, pedis, m., *foot,* = .9708 of the English foot.
solum, -i, n., *lowest part, bottom.*
tantundem, *to the same degree* or *extent.*
X, in expression of number, = *10.*

disto, -are, -----, -----, *stand apart, be separated, be distant.*
fossa, -ae, f., *ditch, trench, entrenchment, fosse.*
labrum, -i, n., *edge.*
pateo, patere, patui, -----, *stretch out, extend.*
quantum, *to which.*
summus, -a, -um, *the top of, the highest part of.*
ut, *so that.*

Fossam: Accusative direct object of **duxit** (A.G. 387).

pedum XX: Genitive of quality (measure) with **fossam** (A.G. 345.b). **XX**: Roman numeral used as an adjective (A.G. 133).

derectis lateribus: Ablative of quality (descriptive ablative) with an adjective modifier (A.G. 415). "'with perpendicular sides,' so that the ditch was a wide at the bottom (*solum*) as at the top. This trench extended across the level plain just west of the town between the two brooks, Ose and Oserain." (Kelsey, 425-26)

duxit: The main verb of the main clause (A.G. 278.b). The pronoun **is**, with **Caesar** as the antecedent, is understood as the subject (A.G. 271.a).

ut ... pateret: The conjunction **ut** ("so that") with the subjunctive forms a clause of result (A.G. 537.1). **pateret**: The main verb of the subordinate clause (A.G. 278.b). Imperfect subjunctive; the tense of the subjunctive is in secondary sequence and follows the rules for the sequence of tense after **duxit** (A.G. 482-85).

eius fossae: Possessive genitive with **solum** (A.G. 343). **eius**: Singular, feminine, genitive demonstrative pronoun used as an adjective modifying **fossae** (A.G. 296.1 and a).

solum: Nominative subject (A.G. 339). From the noun **solum, -i**, n. (*OLD* solum1), not the adjective **solus**.

tantundem ... quantum: Correlatives (A.G. 152). **tantundem**: Singular, neuter, accusative adjective with adverbial force meaning "to the same degree or extent" (*OLD* tantusdem 3). Cognate accusative (A.G. 390.c). **quantum**: Relative adverb correlative with **tantundem** meaning "to which" (*OLD* **quantum** B.2).

(quantum) ... distarent: Subordinate relative clause; a clause dependent on a subjunctive clause (**ut ... pateret**) takes the subjunctive when regarded as an integral part of that clause (attraction) (A.G. 279.a and 593). **distarent**: The main verb of the subordinate clause (A.G. 278.b). Imperfect subjunctive; the tense of the subjunctive is in secondary sequence and follows the rules for the sequence of tense after **duxit** (A.G. 482-85).

summae fossae: Possessive genitive with **labra** (A.G. 343). **summae**: Defective superlative adjective (A.G. 130.b). The adjective designates not what object, but what part of it is meant (A.G. 293).

labra: Nominative subject (A.G. 339).

(72.2-3) Reliquas omnis munitiones ab ea fossa passus quadringentos reduxit, id hoc consilio, quoniam tantum esset necessario spatium complexus nec facile totum opus corona militum cingeretur, ne de improviso aut noctu ad munitiones hostium multitudo advolaret aut interdiu tela in nostros operi destinatos (3) coicere possent.

ab, *from*.
advolo, -are, -avi, -atus, *fly to, hasten to, rush upon*.
cingo, cingere, cinxi, cinctus, *surround, enclose, encircle*.
complector, -plecti, -plexus, *surround, include, encompass*.
corona, -ae, f., *circle*.
destino, -are, -avi, -atus, *earmark, detail*.
fossa, -ae, f., *ditch, trench, intrenchment, fosse*.
hostis, -is, m., *enemy, foe*; pl., *the enemy*.
interdiu, *in the daytime, by day*.
miles, -itis, m., *soldier, foot-solider*.
munitio, -onis, f., *works of fortifications, intrenchment, defenses*.
nec, *and ... not*.
noctu, *by night, at night, in the night*.
omnis, -e, *all*.

passus, -us, m., *step, pace*, = 4 feet, 10 ¼ inches.
quadringenti, -ae, -a, *four hundred*.
reduco, -ducere, -duxi, -ductus, *draw back, bring back, set back*.
spatium, -i, n., *space, distance, extent, area*.
telum, -i, n., *dart, spear*.

ad, *to, towards*.
aut ... aut, *either ... or*.
coicio, -icere, -ieci, -iectus, *put, throw*.
consilium, -i, n., *plan, design*.
de improviso, *unexpectedly, suddenly, without warning*.
facile, *easily, readily, with no trouble*.
hic, haec, hoc, *this; he, she, it*.
in, *against, at*.
is, ea, id, *he, she, it; that, this*.
multitudo, -inis, f., *multitude, crowd*.
ne, *so that ... not*.
necessario, *of necessity, unavoidably*.
nostri, -orum, m., pl., *our men, our side*.
opus, operis, n., *works, line of works, fortification; work, labor*.
possum, posse, potui, -----, *be able*.
quoniam, *since, seeing that, because*.
reliquus, -a, -um, *remaining, the rest*.
tantus, -a, -um, *so great, so large, such, so extensive*.
totus, -a, -um, *the whole, all, all the, entire*.

Reliquas omnis munitiones: Accusative direct object of **reduxit** (A.G. 387). **omnis**: Accusative adjective; **-is** for **-es** is the regular form in i-stem adjectives (A.G. 114.a and 116).

ab ea fossa: Ablative of *place from which* with the preposition **ab** (A.G. 426.1). **ea**: Singular, feminine, ablative demonstrative pronoun used as an adjective modifying **fossa** (A.G. 296.1 and a).

passus quadringentos: Accusative of *extent of space* (A.G. 425). **quadringentos**: Declinable cardinal number used as an adjective (A.G. 132-35).

reduxit: The main verb of the main clause (A.G. 278.b). The pronoun **is**, with **Caesar** as the antecedent, is understood as the subject (A.G. 271.a).

(faciens) id: Supply the participle **faciens** as an adjective modifying **is**, the supplied subject of **reduxit**. **id**: Singular, neuter, accusative demonstrative pronoun used substantively (A.G. 296.2). The antecedent is the previous clause **Reliquas ... reduxit** (A.G. 297.e). Accusative direct object of the supplied participle **faciens** (A.G. 387 and 488).

hoc consilio: Ablative of manner with a limiting adjective (A.G. 412). The phrase is correlative to the following negative purpose clause **ne ... possent** (A.G. 531.1 Note 1). **hoc**: Singular, neuter, ablative demonstrative pronoun used as an adjective modifying **consilio** (A.G. 296.1 and a).

quoniam ... possent: The order of the clauses can be rewritten as: **hoc consilio ne ... advolaret ... possent ... quoniam ... cingeretur**.
quoniam ... esset ... complexus ... cingeretur: Causal clause; the conjunction **quoniam** ("since") introduces a reason given on the authority of the writer or speaker and normally takes the indicative (A.G. 540.a). Here **quoniam** takes the subjunctive as it is dependent upon the negative purpose clause which follows (**ne ... advolaret ... possent**) and is regarded as an integral part of that clause (attraction) (A.G. 593). For the same construction see also 2.2-3 (do not confuse this with **quoniam** taking the subjunctive in indirect discourse as at 64.2 and 89.2). **esset ... complexus ... cingeretur**: The main verbs of the subordinate clause (A.G. 278.b). Pluperfect and imperfect subjunctive; the tense of the subjunctives is in secondary sequence and follows the rules for the sequence of tense after **reduxit** (A.G. 482-85). Notice the switch in tense in the verbs. **esset ... complexus**: The pronoun **is**, with **Caesar** as the antecedent, is understood as the subject (A.G. 271.a). The pluperfect passive verb is here split (tmesis) (A.G. 640).
tantum... spatium: Accusative direct object of **esset ... complexus** (A.G. 387).
necessario: Adverb (A.G. 320-21).
nec: The conjunction joins a negative clause to a preceding positive one and means "and ... not" (*OLD* **neque** 3).
facile: Adverb formed from the neuter accusative adjective (A.G. 214.d and 320-21).
totum opus: Nominative subject (A.G. 339).
corona: Ablative of means (A.G. 409).
militum: Partitive genitive with **corona** (A.G. 346.a.1).
ne ... advolaret ... possent: The conjunction **ne** ("so that ... not") with the subjunctive forms a negative purpose clause (A.G. 531.1).
advolaret ... possent: The main verbs of the subordinate clause (A.G. 278.b). Imperfect subjunctives; the tense of the subjunctives is in secondary sequence and follows the rules for the sequence of tense after **reduxit** (A.G. 482-85). **possent**: The pronoun **ei**, with **hostium** as the antecedent, is understood as the subject (A.G. 271.a).
de improviso: Prepositional phrase, **de** with the ablative of **improvisus** means "unexpectedly, suddenly, without warning" (*OLD* **improvisus** 2). **improviso**: Singular, neuter, ablative of the adjective used substantively (*OLD* **improvisus** 1.b).
aut ... aut: The conjunctions connect the two main verbs in the purpose clause **advolaret ... possent** and introduce two logically exclusive alternatives, meaning "either ... or" (*OLD* **aut** 1).
noctu: Adverb (ablative or locative of *noctus, fourth-declension variant of nox) (*OLD* **noctu**) (A.G. 320-21).
ad munitiones: Accusative of *place to which* with the preposition **ad** (A.G. 426.2).
hostium: Partitive genitive with **multitudo** (A.G. 346.a.1).
multitudo: Nominative subject (A.G. 339).
interdiu: Adverb (A.G. 320-21).
tela: Accusative direct object of the infinitive **coicere** (A.G. 387 and 451.3).
in nostros operi destinatos: Prepositional phrase, **in** with the accusative here means "against, at" (*OLD* **in** 9). **nostros**: Plural, masculine, accusative possessive pronoun used substantively to denote a special class (A.G. 302.d). **operi**: Dative of purpose after the passive participle **destinatos** (A.G. 382.2). **destinatos**: Accusative perfect, passive participle used as a predicate, where in English a phrase or a subordinate clause would be more normal (A.G. 496).
coicere: Complementary infinitive after **possent** (A.G. 456).

(72.3-4) Hoc intermisso spatio duas fossas quindecim pedes latas eadem altitudine perduxit, quarum interiorem campestribus ac demissis locis aqua ex flumine (4) derivata complevit.

ac, *and*.
aqua, -ae, f., *water*.
compleo, -plere, -plevi, -pletus, *fill up, fill full*.
derivo, -are, -avi, -atus, *draw off, turn aside*.
ex, *from, out of*.
fossa, -ae, f., *ditch, trench, intrenchment, fosse*.
idem, eadem, idem, *the same*.
intermitto, -mittere, -misi, -missus, *leave vacant*.
loca, -orum, n., pl., *places*

pes, pedis, m., *foot*, = .9708 of the English foot.
quindecim, *fifteen*.

altitudo, -onis, f., *depth*.
campester, -tris, -tre, *of level ground, flat, level*.
demissus, -a, -um, *low*.
duo, -ae, -o, *two*.
flumen, -inis, n., *stream, river*.
hic, haec, hoc, *this; he, she, it*.
interior, -ius, *inner, interior*.
latus, -a, -um, *broad, wide*.
perduco, -ducere, -duxi, -ductus, *extend, construct, make*.
qui, quae, quod, *who, which, what*.
spatium, -i, n., *space, distance, extent, area*.

Hoc intermisso spatio: Ablative absolute (A.G. 419-20). **Hoc**: Singular, neuter, ablative demonstrative pronoun used as an adjective modifying **spatio** (A.G. 296.1 and a). **intermisso**: The perfect tense of the participle represents the action as completed at the time indicated by the tense of the main verb (A.G. 489).
duas fossas ... latas: Accusative direct object of **perduxit** (A.G. 387). **duas**: Declinable cardinal number used as an adjective modifying **fossas** (A.G. 132-35).
quindecim pedes: Accusative of *extent of space* (A.G. 425). **quindecim**: Indeclinable cardinal number used as an adjective (A.G. 132-35).
eadem altitudine: Ablative of quality (descriptive ablative) with an adjective modifier (A.G. 415). I.e., fifteen feet. **eadem**: Singular, feminine, ablative demonstrative pronoun used as an adjective modifying **altitudine** (A.G. 296.1 and a).
perduxit: The main verb of the main clause (A.G. 278.b). The pronoun **is**, with **Caesar** as the antecedent, is understood as the subject (A.G. 271.a).
quarum ... complevit: Relative clause (A.G. 303). **quarum**: Plural, feminine, genitive relative pronoun used substantively A.G.

305). The antecedent is **fossas** (A.G. 307). Partitive genitive with **interiorem** (A.G. 346.a.1). **complevit**: The main verb of the subordinate clause (A.G. 278.b). The pronoun **is**, with **Caesar** as the antecedent, is understood as the subject (A.G. 271.a)

interiorem: Singular, feminine, accusative adjective used substantively (A.G. 288). The noun **fossam** is understood (A.G. 288.b). Defective comparative adjective (A.G. 130.a). Accusative direct object of **complevit** (A.G. 387).

campestribus ac demissis locis: Ablative of *place where* without a preposition (A.G. 429.1-2). **ac**: The conjunction connects the two adjectives modifying **locis** and means "and" (*OLD* **atque** 12). Two adjectives belonging to the same noun are regularly connected by a conjunction (A.G. 323.d).

aqua ... derivata: Ablative of means (A.G. 409). **derivata**: Ablative perfect, passive participle used as a predicate, where in English a phrase or a subordinate clause would be more normal (A.G. 496).

ex flumine: Ablative of source with the preposition **ex** (A.G. 403.1). **flumine**: "The water was drawn from the Oserain." (Kelsey, 426)

(72.4) **Post eas aggerem ac vallum XII pedum exstruxit.**

ac, *and.*
exstruo, -struere, -struxi, -structus, *construct, build, make.*
is, ea, id, *he, she, it; that, this.*
post, *in or to the rear of, behind.*
X, in expression of number, *= 10.*

agger, -eris, m., *rampart, mole, mound, dike.*
I, in expression of number, *1.*
pes, pedis, m., *foot, = .9708 of the English foot.*
vallum, -i, n., *rampart, wall, intrenchment.*

Post eas: Prepositional phrase, **post** with the accusative here means "in or to the rear of, behind" (*OLD* **post2** 1). "Caesar describes the works from the point of view of Alesia." (Walker, 396) **eas**: Plural, feminine, accusative demonstrative pronoun used substantively (A.G. 296.2). The antecedent is **fossas** (A.G. 297.e).

aggerem ac vallum: Two accusative direct objects of **exstruxit** (A.G. 387). **aggerem**: "'Earthwork,' the line of earth thrown up on the west side of the outer trench." (Kelsey, 426) **ac**: The conjunction connects the two accusative nouns and means "and" (*OLD* **atque** 12). **vallum**: "'The palisade' erected on this earthwork, like the palisade of a camp." (Kelsey, 426)

XII pedum: Genitive of quality (measure) after **vallum** (A.G. 345.b). **XII**: Roman numeral used as an adjective (A.G. 133).

exstruxit: The main verb of the simple sentence (A.G. 278.1). The pronoun **is**, with **Caesar** as the antecedent, is understood as the subject (A.G. 271.a)

(72.4) **Huic loricam pinnasque adiecit, grandibus cervis eminentibus ad commissuras pluteorum atque aggeris qui ascensum hostium tardarent, et turris toto opere circumdedit quae pedes LXXX inter se distarent.**

ad, *in contact with, at.*
agger, -eris, m., *rampart, mole, mound, dike.*
atque, *and.*
circumdo, -dare, -dedi, -datus, *place around, set around.*
disto, -are, -----, -----, *stand apart, be separated, be distant.*
et, *and.*
hic, haec, hoc, *this; he, she, it.*
inter, *between.*
lorica, -ae, f., *breastwork.*
pes, pedis, m., *foot, = .9708 of the English foot.*
pluteus, -i, *breastwork.*
qui, quae, quod, *who, which, what.*
tardo, -are, -avi, -atus, *check, delay, impede, hinder.*
turris, -is, f., *tower.*

adicio, -icere, -ieci, -iectus, *join to, add.*
ascensus, -us, m., *ascent, way up, approach.*
cervus, -i, m., *chevaux-de-frise, stag's horns.*
commissura, -ae, f., *joint, seam, juncture.*
emineo, -minere, -minui, -----, *project, stand out.*
grandis, -e, *large, great.*
hostis, -is, m., *enemy, foe*; pl., *the enemy.*
L, in expression of number, *50.*
opus, operis, n., *works, line of works, fortification.*
pinna, -ae, f., *battlement.*
-que, *and.*
sui, sibi, se, or **sese**, nom. wanting, *themselves.*
totus, -a, -um, *the whole, all, all the, entire.*
X, in expression of number, *= 10.*

Huic: Singular, neuter, dative demonstrative pronoun used substantively (A.G. 296.2). The antecedent is **vallum** (A.G. 297.e). Dative indirect object of the transitive verb **adiecit** (A.G. 362).

loricam pinnasque: Two accusative direct objects of the transitive verb **adiecit** (A.G. 387). **loricam**: "'A breastwork,' made by weaving supple branches closely together, and put up on the exposed side of the palisade." (Kelsey, 426) **-que**: The enclitic conjunction connects the two accusative nouns (A.G. 324.a). **pinnas**: "'battlements,' made of framework covered with wickerwork (taking the place of boards), projecting above the palisade at certain intervals, and 6 to 8 feet in height above the ground. Behind these the soldiers could find shelter after having hurled their weapons over the palisade." (Kelsey, 426)

adiecit: The main verb of the coordinate clause **Huic ... tardarent** (A.G. 278.a). The pronoun **is**, with **Caesar** as the antecedent, is understood as the subject (A.G. 271.a)

grandibus cervis eminentibus: Ablative of quality (descriptive ablative) with an adjective modifier (A.G. 415). **cervis**: "'stag's-horns,' 'chevaux-de-frise,' tops of young trees, from which the foliage and twigs had been removed, leaving only the larger branches projecting from the trunk; these were planted along the earthwork at the foot of the palisade, projecting outwards over the trench and towards the town." (Kelsey, 426) **eminentibus**: Present participle used as an adjective modifying **cervis** (A.G. 494).

ad commissuras pluteorum atque aggeris: Prepositional phrase, **ad** with the accusative here means "in contact with, at" (*OLD* **ad** 15). **pluteorum atque aggeris**: Two partitive genitives with **commissuras** (A.G. 346.a). **pluteorum**: "'Parapets,' here a comprehensive term designating the woodwork above the earthwork as a whole, - including the palisade, the breastwork, and the battlements." (Kelsey, 426) **atque**: The conjunction connects the two genitive nouns and means "and" (*OLD* **atque** 12).

qui ... tardarent: A relative clause of purpose is introduced by a relative pronoun and takes the subjunctive (A.G. 531.2). **qui**: Plural, masculine, nominative relative pronoun used substantively (A.G. 305). The antecedent is **cervis** (A.G. 307). Nominative subject (A.G. 339). The relative is here equivalent to **ut ei** (A.G. 531.2 Note). **tardarent**: The main verb of the subordinate clause (A.G. 278.b). Imperfect subjunctive; the tense of the subjunctive is in secondary sequence and follows the rules for the sequence of tense after **adiecit** (A.G. 482-85).

ascensum: Accusative direct object of **tardarent** (A.G. 387).

hostium: Possessive genitive with **ascensum** (A.G. 343).

et: The conjunction connects the two main verbs **adiecit ... circumdedit** (A.G. 324.a).

turris: Accusative direct object of **circumdedit** (A.G. 387). Accusative plural noun; **-is** for **-es** is the regular form in i-stem nouns (A.G. 65-7 and 74.c).

toto opere: Ablative of *place where* without a preposition (A.G. 429.2).

circumdedit: The main verb of the coordinate clause **turris ... distarent** (A.G. 278.a). The pronoun **is**, with **Caesar** as the antecedent, is understood as the subject (A.G. 271.a)

quae ... distarent: A relative clause of result is introduced by a relative pronoun and takes the subjunctive (A.G. 537.2). **quae**: Plural, feminine, nominative relative pronoun used substantively (A.G. 305). The antecedent is **turris** (A.G. 307). The relative is here equivalent to **ut eae** (A.G. 537.2). Nominative subject (A.G. 339). **distarent**: The main verb of the subordinate clause (A.G. 278.b). Imperfect subjunctive; the tense of the subjunctive is in secondary sequence and follows the rules for the sequence of tense after **circumdedit** (A.G. 482-85).

pedes LXXX: Accusative of *extent of space* (A.G. 425). **LXXX**: Roman numeral used as an adjective (A.G. 133).

inter se: Prepositional phrase, **inter** with the accusative reflexive pronoun here expresses distance apart and means "between" (*OLD* **inter**1 9.c). **se**: Plural, feminine, accusative direct reflexive pronoun (A.G. 300.1). The antecedent is **quae** (**turris**), the subject of **distarent** (A.G. 299).

(73.1-2) Erat eodem tempore et materiari et frumentari et tantas munitiones fieri necesse deminutis nostris copiis, quae longius a castris progrediebantur: ac non numquam opera nostra Galli temptare atque eruptionem ex oppido pluribus (2) portis summa vi facere conabantur.

a(b), *from.*
atque, *and in fact, and even.*
conor, -ari, -atus, *endeavor, attempt, undertake, try.*
deminuo, -minuere, -minui, -minutus, *lessen, make smaller.*
et ... et ... et, *... and ... and.*
facio, facere, feci, factus, *make.*

frumentor, -ari, -atus, *get grain, secure supplies, forage.*
idem, eadem, idem, *the same.*
materior, -ari, -----, *procure timber, get wood.*

necesse, n., *necessary, unavoidable, inevitable.*
noster, -tra, -trum, *our, our own.*
oppidum, -i, n., *fortified town, city.*
plures, -es, -a, *quite a number, several.*
progredior, -gredi, -gressus, *advance, go forward, proceed.*
sum, esse, fui, futurus, *be.*
tantus, -a, -um, *so great, so large, such, so extensive.*

tempus, -oris, n., *time.*

ac, *and so.*
castra, -orum, n., pl., *camp, encampment.*
copiae, -arum, f., pl., *forces, troops.*
eruptio, -onis, f., *a bursting forth, sally, sortie.*
ex, *from, out of.*
fio, fieri, factus, *take place, happen, come about, come to pass.*
Galli, -orum, m., *the Gauls.*
longius, *further, longer.*
munitio, -onis, f., *works of fortifications, intrenchment, defenses.*
non, *not.*
numquam, *never.*
opus, operis, n., *works, line of works, fortification.*
porta -ae, f., *gate, entrance.*
qui, quae, quod, *who, which, what.*
summus, -a, -um, *utmost, greatest, very great.*
tempto, -are, -avi, -atus, *make an attack on, attack, assail.*
vis, acc. **vim**, abl. **vi**, f., *strength, force.*

Erat ... necesse: Impersonal verb, the following three infinitive phrases form the subject (A.G. 208.c). **Erat**: The main verb of the main clause (A.G. 278.b). **necesse**: Singular, neuter, nominative adjective used in the predicate position after **Erat** as an indeclinable noun (A.G. 103.a Note 1 and 283-84).

eodem tempore: Ablative of *time when* (A.G. 423.1). **eodem**: Singular, neuter, ablative demonstrative pronoun used as an adjective modifying **tempore** (A.G. 296.1 and a).

et ... et ... et: The repeated conjunction means "... and ... and", connecting the three infinitives (*OLD* **et** 9.b). Where there are more than two coordinate words, a conjunction, if used, is ordinarily used with all (A.G. 323.c.1).

materiari ... frumentari ... tantas munitiones fieri: The three infinitive phrases function separately as subjects of the impersonal verb **Erat ... necesse** (A.G. 454).

tantas munitiones: Accusative subject of the infinitive **fieri** (A.G. 397.e).

deminutis nostris copiis: Dative indirect object of the phrase **Erat ... necesse** (A.G. 366.a). **deminutis**: Ablative perfect, passive participle used as a predicate, where in English a phrase or a subordinate clause would be more normal (A.G. 496). **nostris**: Plural, feminine, ablative possessive pronoun used as an adjective modifying **copiis** (A.G. 302).

quae ... progrediebantur: Relative clause (A.G. 303). **quae**: Plural, feminine, nominative relative pronoun used substantively (A.G. 305). The antecedent is **copiis** (A.G. 307). Nominative subject (A.G. 339). **progrediebantur**: The main verb of the subordinate clause (A.G. 278.b).

longius: Comparative adverb (A.G. 218 and 320-21).

ab castris: Ablative of *place from which* with the preposition **ab** (A.G. 426.1).

ac: Here the conjunction introduces a subsequent event and means "and so" (*OLD* **atque** 5).

non numquam: A litotes, a statement is made emphatic by denying its contrary (A.G. 326.c).

non: Adverb modifying **numquam**, the negative precedes the word it especially effects (A.G. 217.e, 320-21, and 599.a). Adverb (A.G. 217.e, 320-21, and 599.a).

numquam: Adverb (A.G. 217.b and 320-21).

opera nostra: Accusative direct object of the infinitive **temptare** (A.G. 387 and 451.3). **nostra**: Plural, neuter, accusative possessive pronoun used as an adjective (A.G. 302).

Galli: Nominative subject (A.G. 339). See Appendix A.

temptare: Complementary infinitive after **conabantur** (A.G. 456 and 563.e).

atque: The conjunction connects the two infinitives and strengthens the first meaning "and in fact, and even" (*OLD* **atque** 4).

eruptionem: Accusative direct object of the infinitive **facere** (A.G. 387 and 451.3).

ex oppido: Ablative of *place from which* with the preposition **ex** (A.G. 426.1).

pluribus portis: Ablative of *way by which* without a preposition (A.G. 429.a). **pluribus**: Comparative adjective (A.G. 120).

summa vi: Ablative of manner with a limiting adjective (A.G. 412.b). **summa**: Defective superlative adjective (A.G. 130.b).

facere: Complementary infinitive after **conabantur** (A.G. 456 and 563.e).

conabantur: The main verb of the main clause (A.G. 278.b).

(73.2) Quare ad haec rursus opera addendum Caesar putavit, quo minore numero militum munitiones defendi possent.

ad, *to.*
Caesar, -aris, m., *Caesar.*

hic, haec, hoc, *this; he, she, it.*
minor, -or, -ius, *smaller, less.*

numerus, -i, m., *number, amount.*
possum, posse, potui, -----, *be able.*
quare, *therefore, wherefore, and for this reason.*

rursus, *on top of that, in addition, besides.*

addo, -dere, -didi, -ditus, *add.*
defendo, -fendere, -fensi, -fensus, *defend, guard, protect.*
miles, -itis, m., *soldier, foot-solider.*
munitio, -onis, f., *works of fortifications, intrenchment, defenses.*
opus, operis, n., *works, line of works, fortification.*
puto, -are, -avi, -atus, *think, consider, believe, judge.*
quo, *so that* (by that degree), *in order that, that, that thereby.*

Quare: A relative adverb introducing a fresh sentence meaning "Therefore (*OLD* **quare** 5).

ad haec ... opera: Prepositional phrase after **addendum**, **ad** with the accusative here means "to" (*OLD* **ad** 23). **haec**: Plural, neuter, accusative demonstrative pronoun used as an adjective modifying **opera** (A.G. 296.1 and a).

rursus: Adverb (A.G. 216 and 320-21).

(id) addendum (esse): Accusative/infinitive construction in indirect discourse after **putavit** (A.G. 577 ff). **addendum (esse)**: Supply **esse** to form the second periphrastic (passive) present infinitive with the gerundive implying necessity (A.G. 194.b and 196). The tense of the infinitive in indirect discourse is relative to that of the verb of saying (A.G. 584). Impersonal use of the verb (A.G. 208.d). Supply **id** as the accusative subject (A.G. 318.c).

Caesar: Nominative subject (A.G. 339). See Appendix A.

putavit: The main verb of the main clause (A.G. 278.b).

quo minore... possent: Final clause; the ablative **quo** (= **ut eo**) is used as a conjunction in a final (purpose) clause with the subjunctive (A.G. 531.a). **quo**: In a final clause with a comparative, the conjunction means "so that by that degree" (*OLD* **quo2** 3.b). **minore**: Irregular comparative adjective modifying **numero** (A.G. 129). **possent**: The main verb of the subordinate clause (A.G. 278.b). Imperfect subjunctive; the tense of the subjunctive is in secondary sequence and follows the rules for the sequence of tense after **putavit** (A.G. 482-85, esp. 485.e).

minore numero: Ablative of means after the passive infinitive **defendi** (A.G. 409).

militum: Partitive genitive with **numero** (A.G. 346.a.1).

munitiones: Nominative subject (A.G. 339).

defendi: Complementary infinitive after **possent** (A.G. 456).

(73.2-3) Itaque truncis arborum aut admodum firmis ramis abscisis atque horum delibratis ac praeacutis cacuminibus perpetuae fossae quinos (3) pedes altae ducebantur.

abscido, -cidere, -cidi, -cisus, *cut off, lop off, cut away.*
admodum, *quite, very.*
arbor, -oris, f., *tree.*
aut, *or.*
delibro, -are, -----, -atus, *strip off the bark, peel.*
firmus, -a, -um, *strong, firm, steadfast.*
hic, haec, hoc, *this; he, she, it.*

ac, *and.*
altus, -a, -um, *deep.*
atque, *and then.*
cacumen, -inis, n., *end, point.*
duco, ducere, duxi, ductus, *dig, make.*
fossa, -ae, f., *ditch, trench, intrenchment, fosse.*
itaque, *and so, in consequence, accordingly, therefore.*

perpetuus, -a, -um, *continuous, unbroken.*
praeacutus, -a, -um, *sharpened at the end, sharpened, pointed.*
ramus, -i, m., *branch, bough.*

pes, pedis, m., *foot*, = .9708 of the English foot.
quini, -ae, -a, *five each, five apiece,*
truncus, -i, m., *trunk.*

Itaque: An adverb expressing the result of the previous ideas meaning "and so, in consequence" (*OLD* **itaque** 1). The adverb stands in the first position (A.G. 599.b).

truncis arborum aut admodum firmis ramis abscisis: Ablative absolute (A.G. 419-20). **arborum**: Partitive genitive with **truncis** (A.G. 346.a.1). **aut**: The conjunction connects the two nouns in the ablative absolute and excludes the alternative (A.G. 324.e). **admodum**: Adverb modifying **firmis** (A.G. 320-21). **abscisis**: The perfect tense of the participle represents the action as completed at the time indicated by the tense of the main verb (A.G. 489).

atque: The conjunction connects the two ablative absolutes and means "and then" (*OLD* **atque** 7).

horum delibratis ac praeacutis cacuminibus: Ablative absolute (A.G. 419-20). **horum**: Plural, masculine, genitive demonstrative pronoun used substantively (A.G. 296.2). The antecedent is **ramis** (A.G. 297.e). Partitive genitive with **cacuminibus** (A.G. 346.a.1). **delibratis ... praeacutis**: The perfect tense of the participles represents the action as completed at the time indicated by the tense of the main verb (A.G. 489). **delibratis**: "The bark was peeled off in order to make them smooth and slippery, so that any one trying to step over would be able to get no firm footing on them." (Kelsey, 427) **ac**: The conjunction connects the two participles in the ablative absolute and means "and" (*OLD* **atque** 12). Two adjectives belonging to the same noun are regularly connected by a conjunction (A.G. 323.d).

perpetuae fossae ... altae: Nominative subject (A.G. 339).

quinos pedes: Accusative of *extent of space* (A.G. 425). **quinos**: Distributive numeral use as an adjective (A.G. 136-37).

ducebantur: The main verb of the main clause (A.G. 278.b).

(73.3) **Huc illi stipites demissi et ab infimo revincti, ne revelli possent, ab ramis eminebant.**

ab, *at; at, with.*
emineo, -minere, -minui, -----, *project, stick out, protrude.*
huc, *here.*
infimum, -i, n., *lower part, base, bottom.*
possum, posse, potui, -----, *be able.*
revello, -vellere, -velli, -vulsus, *pull back, tear away.*
stipes, -itis, m., *log, trunk of a tree.*

demitto, -mittere, -misi, -misus, *let down, sink.*
et, *and.*
ille, illae, illud, *that; he, she, it.*
ne, *so that ... not.*
ramus, -i, m., *branch, bough.*
revincio, -vincire, -vinxi, -vinctus, *bind, fasten.*

Huc: Adverb (A.G. 217.a and 320-21).

illi stipites ... demissi ... revincti: Nominative subject (A.G. 339). **illi**: Plural, masculine, nominative demonstrative pronoun used as an adjective modifying **stipites** (A.G. 296.1 and a). **demissi ... revincti**: Two nominative perfect participle used as a predicate, where in English a phrase or a subordinate clause would be more normal (A.G. 496). **revincti**: "'securely fastened' by attaching the lower ends to cross-pieces, which were buried in the earth when the trenches were partially filled in." (Kelsey, 427)

et: The conjunction connects the two participles (A.G. 324.a). Two adjectives belonging to the same noun are regularly connected by a conjunction (A.G. 323.d).

ab infimo: Ablative of *position* with the preposition **ab** (A.G. 429.b). **infimo**: Singular, neuter, ablative adjective used substantively to mean "The lower part, base (*OLD* **infimus** 1.c).

ne ... possent: The conjunction **ne** ("so that ... not") with the subjunctive forms a negative purpose clause (A.G. 531.1). **possent**: The main verb of the subordinate clause (A.G. 278.b). Imperfect subjunctive; the tense of the subjunctive is in secondary sequence and follows the rules for the sequence of tense after **eminebant** (A.G. 482-85). The pronoun **ei**, with **stipites** as the antecedent, is understood as the subject (A.G. 271.a).

revelli: Complementary infinitive after **possent** (A.G. 456).

ab ramis: Prepositional phrase, **ab** with the ablative here means "at, with" (expressing the point where a condition begins) (*OLD* **ab** 12). "'With the branches (only),' the other parts being in the ground." (Kelsey, 427)

eminebant: The main verb of the main clause (A.G. 278.b).

(73.4-5) **(4) Quini erant ordines coniuncti inter se atque implicati; quo qui intraverant se ipsi acutissimis vallis induebant: hos (5) cippos appellabant.**

acutus, -a, -um, sup. -issimus, *sharpened, sharp.*
atque, *and.*
coniungo, -iungere, -iunxi, -iunctus, *join together, unite, join.*
implico, -are, -avi, -atus, *interweave.*

inter, *with or to each other.*
ipse, -a, -um, *he, they,* with or without *himself, themselves.*
qui, quae, quod, *whoever, anyone who, if anyone.*
quo, *from which fact or circumstance, on account of which.*

sum, esse, fui, futurus, *be.*

appello, -are, -avi, -atus, *name, call.*
cippus, -i, m., *post, tombstone.*
hic, haec, hoc, *this; he, she, it.*
induo, -duere, -dui, -dutus, (with se), *impale, pierce, entangle.*
intro, -are, -avi, -atus, *enter, go in.*
ordo, -inis, m., *row, series.*
quini, -ae, -a, *five each, five apiece,*
sui, sibi, se, or sese, nom. wanting, *each other, one another; themselves.*
vallus, -i, m., *stake.*

Quini ... ordines: Nominative subject (A.G. 339). **Quini**: Distributive numeral used as an adjective (A.G. 136-37). Kelsey suggests this means "five rows, one in each trench." (Kelsey, 427); Walker suggests "five rows in each trench." (Walker, 397)

erant: The main verb of the simple sentence (A.G. 278.1).

coniuncti ... implicati: Two plural, masculine, nominative participles used as predicate adjectives modifying **ordines** after **erant** (A.G. 495).

inter se: Prepositional phrase, **inter** with the accusative reciprocal pronoun here means "with or to each other" (*OLD* inter1 15). **se**: Plural, masculine, accusative direct pronoun used reciprocally and meaning "each other, one another" (A.G. 300.1) (*OLD* se 8). The antecedent is **ordines**, the subject of **erant** (A.G. 299).

atque: The conjunction connects the two participles and means "and" (*OLD* atque 12).

quo: Conjunctive connecting sentences meaning "from which fact or circumstance, in consequence or on account of which, whence, whereby" (*OLD* quo2 1).

qui intraverant ... induebant: A disguised past general conditional statement (pluperfect indicative in the protasis and imperfect indicative in the apodosis) (A.G. 514.D.2.a and 521).

qui intraverant: A relative clause standing as the protasis of the conditional statement (A.G. 303, 514.D.2.a and 521.a) **qui**: Plural, masculine, nominative relative pronoun with indefinite force used substantively (= **si qui**) (A.G. 148-49, esp. 149.b Note) (*OLD* qui1 15.b). Nominative subject (A.G. 339). **intraverant**: The main verb of the subordinate clause (A.G. 278.b).

se: Plural, masculine, accusative direct reflexive pronoun (A.G. 300.1). The antecedent is **ipsi**, the subject of **induebant** (A.G. 299). Accusative direct object of the transitive verb **induebant** (A.G. 387).

ipsi: Plural, masculine, nominative demonstrative pronoun used substantively (A.G. 296.2 and 298.d). The antecedent is **qui** (A.G. 298). Nominative subject (A.G. 339). The pronoun is here emphatic (A.G. 298.d.1).

acutissimis vallis: Dative indirect object of the transitive verb **induebant** (A.G. 362) (*OLD* induo 5.b). **acutissimis**: Superlative adjective (A.G. 124). **vallis**: "Referring to the sharp, pointed branches of the *cippi*." (Kelsey, 427).

induebant: The main verb of the apodosis of the conditional statement (A.G. 514.D.2.a). The main verb of the main clause (A.G. 278.b).

hos: Plural, masculine, accusative demonstrative pronoun used substantively (A.G. 296.2). The antecedent is **stipites** (A.G. 297.e). Accusative direct object of **appellabant** (A.G. 387).

cippos: Predicate accusative noun after **appellabant** (A.G. 392-93). "Caesar's secondary defense measures are clearly innovative. His men give ironic or humorous names to them – 'gravestones' (the Latin, *cippus*, means both 'boundary marker' and 'gravestone'), 'lilies' (presumably because each pit with its projecting stake looked like such a bloom), and 'spurs' (i.e. metal objects designed to increase speed rather than, as here, forcing a halt)." (Hammond, 241)

appellabant: The main verb of the simple sentence (A.G. 278.1). The noun **milites** is understood as the subject (A.G. 271.a).

(73.5-6) Ante hos obliquis ordinibus in quincuncem dispositis scrobes tris in altitudinem pedes fodie(6)bantur paulatim angustiore ad infimum fastigio.

ad, *towards, at*.
angustus, -a, -um, comp. **-ior**, *contracted, narrow, close*.
dispono, -ponere, -posui, -positus, *set in various places, distribute*.
fodio, fodere, fodi, fossus, *dig, dig out*.
in, *so as to produce* or *result in; to*.
obliquus, -a, -um, *oblique, slanting, crosswise*.
paulatim, *little by little, gradually*.
quincunex, -uncis, f., *quincunx*.
tres, tria, trium, *three*.

altitudo, -onis, f., *depth*, (with **in**), *vertically*.
ante, *before, in front of*.
fastigium, -i, n., *descent, slope, declivity*.
hic, haec, hoc, *this; he, she, it*.
infimum, -i, n., *lowest part, base, bottom*.
ordo, -inis, m., *row, series*.
pes, pedis, m., *foot*, = .9708 of the English foot.
scrobis, -is, m., and f., *pit, wolf-pit*.

Ante hos: Prepositional phrase, **ante** with the accusative here means "before, in front of" (*OLD* ante2 1). **hos**: Plural, masculine, accusative demonstrative pronoun used substantively (A.G. 296.2). The antecedent is **cippos** (A.G. 297.e).

obliquis ordinibus in quincuncem dispositis: Ablative absolute (A.G. 419-20). **in quincuncem**: Prepositional phrase, **in** with the accusative here means "so as to produce or result in" (*OLD* in 20). **quincuncem**: A quincunx is a "pattern resembling the five spots on a dice-cube" (*OLD* quincunx 3). **dispositis**: The perfect tense of the participle represents the action as completed at the time indicated by the tense of the main verb (A.G. 489).

scrobes: Nominative subject (A.G. 339). "Pits were dug, three feet deep and small at the bottom, arranged diagonally, in eight rows, three feet apart. In these smooth stakes were set, sharpened at the upper end, but not projecting above the level of the ground more than four inches. At the bottom of the stakes earth was packed in firmly to the depth of a foot, leaving still a depth of two feet in the pits, which were concealed from view by placing brush over them. In the course of Napoleon's excavations more than 80 of these pits were brought to light, and found to correspond exactly with the description here given." (Kelsey, 427)

tris ... pedes: Accusative of *extent of space* after **scrobes** (A.G. 425). **tris**: Declinable cardinal number used as an adjective (A.G. 132-35). **-is** for **-es** is an alternative accusative plural ending (A.G. 134.b).

in altitudinem: Prepositional phrase, **in** with the accusative of **altitudo** means "vertically" (*OLD* altitudo 3).

fodiebantur: The main verb of the main clause (A.G. 278.b).

paulatim: Adverb (A.G. 320-21).

angustiore ... fastigio: Ablative of quality (descriptive ablative) with an adjective modifying **scrobes** (A.G. 415). **angustiore**: Comparative adjective (A.G. 124).

ad infimum: Prepositional phrase, **ad** with the accusative here implies direction and means "towards" (*OLD* **ad** 3). **infimum**: Singular, accusative, neuter adjective used substantively meaning "The lowest part, base (*OLD* **infimus** 1.c).

(73.6-9) The spiked pits, or 'lilies': The pits are dug three feet deep and stakes are fastened at the bottom. The bottom one foot of the pit is filled with earth. The next two feet are covered over with twigs and brush. The stakes poke out of this covering no more than four fingers.

(73.6-7) Huc teretes stipites feminis crassitudine ab summo praeacuti et praeusti demittebantur ita ut non amplius digitis quattuor (7) ex terra eminerent;

ab, *at.*
crassitudo, -inis, f., *thickness.*
digitus, -i, m., *finger's breadth.*
et, *and.*
femur, -oris, and **-inis**, n., *thigh.*
ita, *in this way, so, thus.*
praeacutus, -a, -um, *sharpened at the end, sharpened, pointed.*
quattuor, *four.*
summum, -i, n., *highest point, top.*
terra, -ae, f., *earth, ground, soil.*

amplius, *more.*
demitto, -mittere, -misi, -misus, *let down, sink.*
emineo, -minere, -minui, -----, *project, stand out.*
ex, *so as to point* or *project away from, out of.*
huc, *here.*
non, *not.*
praeustus, -a, -um, *burnt at the end* (to make it hard).
stipes, -itis, m., *log, trunk of a tree.*
teres, -etis, *well-turned, round, smooth.*
ut, *so that.*

Huc: Adverb (A.G. 217.a and 320-21).
teretes stipites ... praeacuti et praeusti: Nominative subject (A.G. 339). **praeacuti et praeusti**: Two plural, masculine, nominative predicate adjectives modifying **stipites** (A.G. 285.2). **et**: The conjunction connects the two adjectives (A.G. 387). Two adjectives belonging to the same noun are regularly connected by a conjunction (A.G. 323.d).
feminis crassitudine: Ablative of quality (descriptive ablative) with a genitive modifier after **stipites** (A.G. 415). **feminis**: Possessive genitive (A.G. 343). From the noun **femur, -inis**, n..
ab summo: Ablative of *position* with the preposition **ab** after **praeacuti** (A.G. 429.b). **summo**: Singular, neuter, ablative adjective used substantively meaning "highest point, top" (*OLD* **summus** 1.d).
demittebantur: The main verb of the main clause (A.G. 278.b).
ita ut ... eminerent: The conjunction **ut** ("so that") with the subjunctive forms a clause of result (A.G. 537.1). **ita**: Adverb modifying **demittebantur** and correlative to the result clause (A.G. 217.c and 320-21 and 537 Note 2). **eminerent**: The main verb of the subordinate clause (A.G. 278.b). Imperfect subjunctive; the tense of the subjunctive is in secondary sequence and follows the rules for the sequence of tense after **demittebantur** (A.G. 482-85). The pronoun **ei**, with **stipites** as the antecedent, is understood as the subject (A.G. 271.a).
non: Adverb modifying **amplius**, the negative precedes the word it especially effects (A.G. 217.e, 320-21, and 599.a).
amplius digitis quattuor: Ablative of comparison; the comparative degree is followed by the ablative signifying "than" (A.G. 406).
amplius: Comparative adverb modifying the verb **eminerent** (A.G. 218 and 320-21). **quattuor**: Indeclinable cardinal number used as an adjective modifying **digitis** (A.G. 132-35).
ex terra: Prepositional phrase, **ex** with the ablative here means "so as to point or project away from, out of" (*OLD* **ex** 4).

(73.7-8) simul confirmandi et stabiliendi causa singuli ab infimo solo pedes terra exculcabantur; reliqua pars scrobis ad occultandas insidias viminibus ac virgultis (8) integebatur.

ab, *from.*
ad, *for, in order to, for the purpose of.*

confirmo, -are, -avi, -atus, *strengthen.*
exculco, -are, -----, -----, *tread down, pack down by stamping.*
insidiae, -arum, f., pl., *device, trap, snare.*
occulto, -are, -avi, -atus, *hide, conceal, keep secret.*
pes, pedis, m., *foot*, = .9708 of the English foot.
scrobis, -is, m., and f., *pit, wolf-pit.*
singuli, -ae, -a, *one by one, individual.*
stabilio, -ire, -ivi, -itus, *make fast.*
vimen, -inis, n., *pliant twig, osier, withy.*

ac, *and.*
causa, -ae, f., abl. with the gen., *for the sake of, for the purpose of.*
et, *and.*
infimus, -a, -um, *lowest, at the bottom.*
intego, -tegere, -texi, -tectus, *cover, cover over.*
pars, partis, f., *part, section, division.*
reliquus, -a, -um, *remaining, the rest.*
simul, *at the same time, at once.*
solum, -i, n., *lowest part, ground.*
terra, -ae, f., *earth, ground, soil.*
virgultum, -i, n., *brushwood, brush.*

simul: Adverb (A.G. 320-21).
confirmandi et stabiliendi causa: Two genitive gerunds with the ablative of **causa** expresses purpose (A.G. 504.b). **confirmandi**: Singular, neuter, genitive gerund (A.G. 501-02). **et**: The conjunction connects the two gerunds (A.G. 324.a). **stabiliendi**: Singular, neuter, genitive gerund (A.G. 501-02).
singuli ... pedes: Nominative subject (A.G. 339). **singuli**: Distributive numeral used as an adjective (A.G. 136-37). **pedes**: The noun is plural because there are numerous pits, not just one ("feet, one apiece") (A.G. 137.a). The three foot deep pits are filled in one foot, leaving two feet.

ab infimo solo: Prepositional phrase, **ab** with the ablative here means "from" (*OLD* **ab** 4).
terra: Ablative of material (A.G. 403.2).
exculcabantur: The main verb of the simple sentence (A.G. 278.1).
reliqua pars: Nominative subject (A.G. 339). Two feet of the pit remain uncovered.
scrobis: Partitive genitive with **pars** (A.G. 346.a.1).
ad occultandas insidias: The preposition **ad** with the accusative gerundive and noun expresses purpose (A.G. 506). **occultandas**: Plural, feminine, accusative gerundive used as an adjective modifying **insidias** denoting necessity, obligation or propriety (A.G. 500.1).
viminibus ac virgultis: Ablative of means after **integebatur** (A.G. 409.a). **ac**: The conjunction connects the two ablative nouns and means "and" (*OLD* **atque** 12).
integebatur: The main verb of the simple sentence (A.G. 278.1).

(73.8-9) **Huius generis octoni ordines ducti ternos inter se pedes distabant. Id ex similitudine floris lilium (9) appellabant.**

appello, -are, -avi, -atus, *name, call.*

duco, ducere, duxi, ductus, *dig, make.*
flos, floris, m., *flower.*
hic, haec, hoc, *this; he, she, it.*
is, ea, id, *he, she, it; that, this.*
octoni, -ae, -a, *eight each.*
pes, pedis, m., *foot,* = .9708 of the English foot.
sui, sibi, se, or **sese,** nom. wanting, *themselves.*

disto, -are, -----, -----, *stand apart, be separated, be distant.*
ex, *as a result of, in consequence of.*
genus, generis, n., *kind, type.*
inter, *between.*
lilium, -i, n., *lily.*
ordo, -inis, m., *row, series.*
similitudo, -inis, f., *likeness, resemblance, similarity.*
terni, -ae, -a, *three each.*

Huius generis: Genitive of quality (descriptive genitive) with an adjective modifier with **ordines** (A.G. 345). **Huius**: Singular, neuter, genitive demonstrative pronoun used as an adjective modifying **generis** (A.G. 296.1 and a).
octoni ordines ducti: Nominative subject (A.G. 339). **octoni**: Distributive numeral used as an adjective modifying **ordines** (A.G. 136-37). **ducti**: Nominative perfect, passive participle used as a predicate, where in English a phrase or a subordinate clause would be more normal (A.G. 496).
ternos ... pedes: Accusative of *extent of space* (A.G. 425). **ternos**: Distributive numeral used as an adjective (A.G. 136-37).
inter se: Prepositional phrase, **inter** with the accusative reflexive pronoun here expresses distance apart and means "between" (*OLD* **inter**1 9.c). **se**: Plural, masculine, accusative direct reflexive pronoun (A.G. 300.1). The antecedent is **ordines**, the subject of **distabant** (A.G. 299).
distabant: The main verb of the simple sentence (A.G. 278.1).
Id: Singular, neuter, accusative demonstrative pronoun used substantively (A.G. 296.2). The antecedent is the finished pit construction (A.G. 297.e). Accusative direct object of **appellabant** (A.G. 387).
ex similitudine floris: Prepositional phrase, **ex** with the ablative here indicates cause and means "as a result of, in consequence of" (*OLD* **ex** 18). **floris**: Objective genitive with **similitudine** (A.G. 348).
lilium: Predicate accusative noun after **appellabant** (A.G. 392-93). A lily is no doubt another jest on the part of the soldiers. Compare with **cippos** above at 73.5.
appellabant: The main verb of the simple sentence (A.G. 278.1). The noun **milites** is understood as the subject (A.G. 271.a).

(73.9) **Ante haec taleae pedem longae ferreis hamis infixis totae in terram infodiebantur mediocribusque intermissis spatiis omnibus locis disserebantur; quos stimulos nominabant.**

ante, *before, in front of.*

ferreus, -a, -um, *of iron, made of iron, iron.*
hic, haec, hoc, *this; he, she, it.*
infigo, -figere, -fixi, -fixus, *fasten in.*
intermitto, -mittere, -misi, -missus, *leave unoccupied, leave vacant.*
longus, -a, -um, *long.*
nomino, -are, -avi, -atus, *name, call.*
pes, pedis, m., *foot,* = .9708 of the English foot.
qui, quae, quod, *who, which, what.*
stimulus, -i, m., *prick, spur.*
terra, -ae, f., *earth, ground, soil.*

dissero, -serere, -----, -----, *plant here and there, plant at intervals.*
hamus, -i, m., *hook.*
in, *to a point on the surface of, on to.*
infodio, -fodere, -fodi, -fossus, *bury.*
loca, -orum, n., pl., *places*
mediocris, -cre, *moderate, short.*
omnis, -e, *all.*
-que, *and.*
spatium, -i, n., *space, interval.*
talea, -ae, f., *rod, bar.*
totus, -a, -um, *the whole, all, all the, entire.*

Ante haec: Prepositional phrase, **ante** with the accusative here means "before, in front of" (*OLD* **ante**2 1). **haec**: Plural, neuter, accusative demonstrative pronoun used substantively (A.G. 296.2). The antecedent is the rows of lilies (**lilia**) built at 73.5-8 (A.G. 297.e).
taleae ... longae ... totae: Nominative subject of **infodiebantur ... disserebantur** (A.G. 339). **taleae**: "'Crow's-feet,' upright iron bars with pointed hooks projecting from the upper end, fastened to blocks of wood, which were sunk firmly in the earth." (Kelsey, 427) **totae**: Plural, feminine, nominative adjective modifying **taleae** but used to qualify the action of the verb, and so has the force of an adverb (A.G. 290).

pedem: Accusative of *extent of space* after **longae** (A.G. 425).

ferreis hamis infixis in terram: Ablative absolute (A.G. 419-20). **infixis**: The perfect tense of the participle represents the action as completed at the time indicated by the tense of the main verb (A.G. 489). **in terram**: Prepositional phrase, in with the ablative here means "to a point on the surface of, on to" (*OLD* **in** 7).

infodiebantur: The main verb of the coordinate clause **Ante ... infodiebantur** (A.G. 278.a).

mediocribusque intermissis spatiis: Ablative absolute (A.G. 419-20). **-que**: The enclitic conjunction connects the two main verbs **infodiebantur ... disserebantur** (A.G. 324.a). **intermissis**: The perfect tense of the participle represents the action as completed at the time indicated by the tense of the main verb (A.G. 489).

omnibus locis: Ablative of *place where* without a preposition (A.G. 429.1-2).

disserebantur: The main verb of the coordinate clause **mediocribusque ... disserebantur** (A.G. 278.a).

quos: Plural, masculine, accusative relative pronoun used substantively (A.G. 305). The pronoun agrees with the predicate noun **stimulos** in its own clause rather than the antecedent **taleae** (A.G. 306). Accusative direct object of **nominabant** (A.G. 387). The relative does not introduce a relative clause but is a connecting relative; at the beginning of a clause the pronoun is often best rendered by a personal or demonstrative pronoun, with or without *and* (A.G. 308.f).

stimulos: Predicate accusative noun after **nominabant** (A.G. 392-93).

nominabant: The main verb of the simple sentence (A.G. 278.1). The noun **milites** is understood as the subject (A.G. 271.a).

(74.1-2) **His rebus perfectis, regiones secutus quam potuit aequissimas pro loci natura, XIIII milia passuum complexus pares eiusdem generis munitiones, diversas ab his, contra exteriorem hostem perfecit, ut ne magna quidem multitudine, si ita accidat, +eius discessu+ munitionum praesidia circum(2)fundi possent;**

ab, *from*.

aequus, -a, -um, sup. **-issimus**, *level, even, flat*.

complector, -plecti, -plexus, *surround, include, encompass*.

discessus, -us, m., *departure, going away*.

exterior, -ior, -ius, *outer, exterior*.

hic, haec, hoc, *this*; *he, she, it*.

I, in expression of number, *1*.

is, ea, id, *he, she, it*; *that, this*.

locus, -i, m., *place*.

milia, -um, n., pl., *thousand, thousands*.

munitio, -onis, f., *works of fortifications, intrenchment, defenses*.

ne ... quidem, *not even*.

passus, -us, m., *step, pace*, = 4 feet, 10 ¼ inches.

possum, posse, potui, -----, *be able*.

pro, *in relation to, having regard to, considering*.

quidem, (with **ne**), *not even*.

res, rei, f., *project, business, operation*.

si, *if indeed*.

X, in expression of number, = *10*.

accido, -cidere, -cidi, -----, (imper.), *it happens*.

circumfundo, -fundere, -fudi, -fusus, *surround, hem in*.

contra, *directed at, facing*.

diversus, -a, -um, *facing the opposite direction*.

genus, generis, n., *kind, type*.

hostis, -is, m., *enemy, foe*.

idem, eadem, idem, *the same*.

ita, *in this way, thus*.

magnus, -a, -um, *great, large*.

multitudo, -inis, f., *multitude, crowd*.

natura, -ae, f., *nature, character, natural features*.

par, paris, *like, similar, same, equal*.

perficio, -ficere, -feci, -fectus, *finish, complete, finish constructing*.

praesidium, -i, n., *guard, garrison, fortress, redoubt*.

quam, *as ----- as possible*.

regio, -onis, f., *region, territory*.

sequor, -qui, -cutus, *follow, keep to*.

ut, *so that*.

His rebus perfectis: Ablative absolute (A.G. 419-20). **His**: Plural, feminine, ablative demonstrative pronoun used as an adjective modifying **rebus** (A.G. 296.1 and a). **perfectis**: The perfect tense of the participle represents the action as completed at the time indicated by the tense of the main verb (A.G. 489).

regiones ... aequissimas: Accusative direct object of the participle **secutus** (A.G. 387 and 488). **aequissimas**: Superlative adjective (A.G. 124).

secutus ... complexus: Nominative subject of **perfecit** (A.G. 339). Two nominative, perfect, deponent participle used as a predicate, where in English a phrase or a subordinate clause would be more normal (A.G. 496). Carry down **Caesar** from 73.2 as the noun.

quam potuit aequissimas: Relative clause (A.G. 279.a). **quam**: The relative adverb **quam** with the superlative denotes the highest possible degree "as level as possible" (A.G. 291.c) (*OLD* **quam** 7). **potuit**: The main verb of the subordinate clause (A.G. 278.b). The pronoun **is**, with **Caesar** at 73.2 as the antecedent, is understood as the subject (A.G. 271.a). **aequissimas**: Superlative adjective modifying **regiones** (A.G. 124).

pro loci natura: Prepositional phrase in the subordinate clause, **pro** with the ablative here means "in relation to, having regard to, considering" (*OLD* **pro1** 13). **loci**: Possessive genitive with **natura** (A.G. 343).

XIIII milia passuum: Accusative of *extent of space* after **complexus** (A.G. 425). **XIIII**: Roman numeral used as an adjective with **milia** (A.G. 133). **milia**: Accusative plural; in the plural **mille** declines as a neuter noun (A.G. 134.d). **passuum**: Partitive genitive with **milia** (346.2).

pares ... munitiones: Accusative direct object of **perfecit** (A.G. 387). **munitiones**: "An outer line of works, outside of the Roman encampments, for protection against the Gallic army that was coming to relieve the town." (Kelsey, 427)

eiusdem generis: Genitive of quality (descriptive genitive) with an adjective modifier with **munitiones** (A.G. 345). **eiusdem**: Singular, neuter, genitive demonstrative pronoun used as an adjective modifying **generis** (A.G. 296.1 and a).

diversas: Plural, feminine, accusative predicate adjective modifying **munitiones** (A.G. 285.2). "'Facing in the opposite direction' from the works described in the last two chapters, the purpose of which were to hem in Vercingetorix." (Kelsey, 427)

ab his: Prepositional phrase, **ab** with the ablative here means "from" (*OLD* **ab** 3.b). **his**: Plural, feminine, ablative demonstrative pronoun used substantively (A.G. 296.2). The antecedent is those fortifications just described in Chapters 72-73 (A.G. 297.e). The noun **munitionibus** is understood (A.G. 288.b).

contra exteriorem hostem: Prepositional phrase, **contra** with the accusative here means "directed at, facing" (*OLD* **contra** 13).

exteriorem: Defective comparative adjective (A.G. 130.b).

perfecit: The main verb of the main clause (A.G. 278.b).

ut ... possent: The conjunction **ut** ("so that") with the subjunctive forms a final (purpose) clause (A.G. 531.1). **possent**: The main verb of the subordinate clause (A.G. 278.b). Imperfect subjunctive; the tense of the subjunctive is in secondary sequence and follows the rules for the sequence of tense after **perfecit** (A.G. 482-85).

ne ... quidem: The negative adverb with the particle means "not even" (*OLD* **ne1** 6). The emphatic word must stand between **ne** and **quidem** (A.G. 322.f).

magna ... multitudine: Ablative of means (A.G. 409).

si ita accidat: Subordinate clause (parenthetical remark) (A.G. 278.b). **si**: The conjunction here expresses skepticism and means "if indeed" (*OLD* **si** 6.b). **ita**: Adverb (A.G. 217.c and 320-21). **accidat**: A clause dependent on a subjunctive clause (**ut ... possent**) takes the subjunctive when regarded as an integral part of that clause (attraction) (A.G. 593). The main verb of the subordinate clause (A.G. 278.b). Present subjunctive; the tense of the subjunctive is normally in secondary sequence after **perfecit** (A.G. 482-85). Here it is in primary sequence through *repraesentatio* (A.G. 485.e and 585.b Note). Impersonal use, supply **id** as the subject (A.G. 207). The pronoun **id** refers to the enemy being a great multitude (A.G. 297.e).

+eius discessu+: "the MSS includes the words 'eius discessu', which are either a senseless reference to Caesar or a hopelessly corrupt one to Vercingetorix and his cavalry. They may be a gloss on the preceding phrase, also awkward in the context ('si ita accidat': 'should the occasion arise')." (Hammond, 242) It is best to omit this phrase in the translation. **eius**: Singular, masculine (?), genitive demonstrative pronoun used substantively (A.G. 296.2). The antecedent is unknown (A.G. 297.e). Possessive genitive with **discessu** (A.G. 343). **discessu**: Ablative of *time when* (?) (A.G. 423.1).

munitionum: Objective genitive with **praesidia** (A.G. 348).

praesidia: Nominative subject (A.G. 339).

circumfundi: Complementary infinitive after **possent** (A.G. 456).

(74.2) ne autem cum periculo ex castris egredi cogatur, dierum XXX pabulum frumentumque habere omnis convectum iubet.

autem, *moreover.*
cogo, cogere, coegi, coactus, *compel, force, oblige.*

cum, *with.*
egredior, -gredi, -gressus, *go out, go forth, come forth, leave.*
frumentum, -i, n., *grain.*
iubeo, iubere, iussi, iussus, *order, give orders, bid, command.*
omnes, -ium, m., pl., *all men, all.*
periculum, -i, n., *risk, danger, hazard.*
X, in expression of number, = *10.*

castra, -orum, n., pl., *camp, encampment.*
conveho, -vehere, -vexi, -vectus, *bring together, collect, store.*
dies, -ei, m. and f., *day.*
ex, *from, out of.*
habeo, habere, habui, habitus, *have, possess.*
ne, *so that ... not.*
pabulum, -i, n., *fodder.*
-que, *and.*

ne ... cogatur: The conjunction **ne** ("so that ... not") with the subjunctive forms a negative purpose clause (A.G. 531.1). **cogatur**: The main verb of the subordinate clause (A.G. 278.b). Present subjunctive; the tense of the subjunctive is normally in secondary sequence after the historical present **iubet** (A.G. 482-85). Here it is in primary sequence through *repraesentatio* (A.G. 485.e and 585.b Note). The pronoun **is**, with **complexus** (Caesar) as the antecedent, is understood as the subject (A.G. 271.a).

autem: Postpositive conjunction (A.G. 324.j and 599.b).

cum periculo: Ablative of accompaniment with the preposition **cum** (A.G. 413).

ex castris: Ablative of *place from which* with the preposition **ex** (A.G. 426.1). "For the purpose of foraging." (Kelsey, 427)

egredi: Complementary infinitive after the passive verb **cogatur** (A.G. 456 and 566.c).

dierum XXX: Genitive of quality (measure) with **pabulum frumentumque** (A.G. 346.a.1). **XXX**: Roman numeral used as an adjective (A.G. 133). "Caesar's men suffered from want of provisions before Alesia fell; when they were fighting, half-starved, about Dyrrhachium, Caesar tells us that they consoled themselves with the thought of Alesia and Avaricum (Bel. Civ. iii., 47)." (Kelsey, 427-28) Vercingetorix also had 30 days worth of supplies at 71.4-5.

pabulum frumentumque ... convectum: Accusative direct object of the infinitive **habere** (A.G. 387 and 451.3). **-que**: The enclitic conjunction connects the two accusative nouns (A.G. 324.a). **convectum**: Accusative perfect passive participle used as a predicate, where in English a phrase or a subordinate clause would be more normal (A.G. 496). It should be construed with both **pabulum** and **frumentum** but agrees in number with only the nearest noun (A.G. 286.a). The perfect participle with **habeo** has almost the same meaning as a perfect active, but denotes the continued effect of the action of the verb (A.G. 497.b).

habere omnis: Subject accusative with the infinitive after **iubet**. The construction is equivalent to a substantive clause of purpose (A.G. 563.a). **omnis**: Plural, masculine, accusative adjective used substantively (A.G. 288). **-is** for **-es** is the regular form in i-stem adjectives (A.G. 114.a and 116).

iubet: The main verb of the main clause (A.G. 278.b). The historical present, giving vividness to the narrative, is present in Chapter 74 (A.G. 469). This usage, common in all languages, comes from imagining past events as going on before our eyes (*repraesentatio*) (A.G. 469 Note). The pronoun **is**, with **complexus** (Caesar) as the antecedent, is understood as the subject (A.G. 271.a).

4.L CHAPTERS 75-76: CATALOG OF THE RELIEF ARMY; LEADERS FOR THE RELIEF ARMY ARE CHOSEN

The catalog in Chapter 75 (75.2-4) has the informational function of providing a record of what Gallic troops were assembled before the pivotal battle of Alesia. It is certainly a valuable ethnographic source for the names of the Gallic tribes prior to the Roman conquest as Caesar mentions by name forty five tribes who have assembled for the relief of Vercingetorix inside Alesia. He also supplies the additional information of the number of troops which each tribe has sent.

By arrangement and selection of material Caesar presents the Gauls in a fashion consistent with his portrayal throughout the work; the Gauls appear as a leaderless horde. Caesar fashions the image of magnitude through the rhetorical device of asyndeton which present the tribes in an unbroken line, one next to another, a formidable array. Then, after listing some tribes in asyndeton, Caesar supplies the connective *et* and it seems as though he will use polysyndeton for the desired effect of force. However, he then drops the connective and the combination makes for a very powerful effect, as though there are so many tribes that he can not possibly retain the use of the connective: *octona Pictonibus et Turonis et Parisiis et Helvetiis;* but then: *Senonibus, Ambianis, Mediomatricis, Petrocoriis, Nerviis, Morinis, Nitiobrigibus quina milia.* This variation adds to the effect of power by increasing the flow and tempo of the elements in the catalog and thus drawing attention to the overwhelming magnitude of the Gallic contingents. This asyndeton also has a converse negative effect which Caesar draws upon, that of making the Gallic contingents into an undifferentiated mass. Caesar clearly accesses the traditional Roman fear of the northern barbarian horde which is brought on by the raw numbers and power of the enemy. A second feature of this catalog which reinforces this horde image of the Gauls is the lack of named leadership. Although Vercingetorix is mentioned by name (*ut censuit Vercingetorix*), the reference only reaffirms the split leadership among the Gauls as the council disregards the advice of their own chosen leader who is besieged in Alesia.

Notice how this catalog of Gallic contingents compares to that of the Roman troops in Chapter 90. The Roman catalog is the exact opposite: small, balanced and orderly, representing discipline and presenting Caesar as the good general, organized and in control. C.S. Saylor compares two catalogs in Virgil's *Aeneid* which are also juxtaposed: "For, although no commentator has treated them as such, the two catalogs appear designed to be thought of in conjunction, so as to express the contrasting characters of those who follow Aeneas and those who follow Turnus. The presumption elicited from the ideas already surveyed is that the catalogues will reinforce in form Latin singularity, personal color, diffusion, and disorder on the one hand and Etruscan single-mindedness, uniformity, regularity, and control under leadership of the Trojan Aeneas on the other." (Saylor, C. S. "The Magnificent Fifteen: Virgil's Catalogues of the Latin and Etruscan Forces". *CPh* 69 (1974): 249-257) The same can be said here; the two antagonists, Vercingetorix and Caesar, are defined by their respective catalogs. For a full discussion of this catalog see Mannetter, 143-158. For the Roman perception of the 'Gallic menace' see Gardner.

(75.1-2) **Dum haec apud Alesiam geruntur, Galli, concilio principum indicto, non omnis eos qui arma ferre possent, ut censuit Vercingetorix, convocandos statuunt, sed certum numerum cuique ex civitate imperandum, ne tanta multitudine confusa nec moderari nec discernere suos nec (2) frumentationem habere possent.**

Alesia, -ae, f., *Alesia.*
arma, -orum, n., pl., *arms, armor, weapons.*
certus, -a, -um, *certain, fixed, definite.*
concilium, -i, n., *meeting, assembly, council.*
convoco, -are, -avi, -atus, *call together, summon, assemble.*

dum, *while.*
fero, ferre, tuli, latus, *bear, carry.*
Galli, -orum, m., *the Gauls.*
habeo, habere, habui, habitus, *be furnished with, have, obtain.*
impero, -are, -avi, -atus, *levy, draft, demand.*
is, ea, id, *he, she, it; that, this.*
multitudo, -inis, f., *great number, multitude, crowd.*
nec ... nec ... nec, *neither ... nor ... nor.*
numerus, -i, m., *number, amount.*
possum, posse, potui, -----, *be able.*
qui, quae, quod, *who, which, what.*
sed, *but.*
sui, -orum, m., pl., *their men,* with or without *own.*
ut, *as.*

apud, *at, near, close to.*
censeo, -ere, -ui, -us, *think, hold, judge.*
civitas, -tatis, f., *state, nation.*
confundo, -fundere, -fudi, -fusus, *combine, unite.*
discerno, -cernere, -crevi, -cretus, *distinguish between, know apart.*
ex, *from.*
frumentatio, -onis f., *providing of grain, foraging.*
gero, gerere, gessi, gestus, *carry out, perform, do.*
hic, haec, hoc, *this; he, she, it.*
indico, -dicere, -dixi, -dictus, *convoke, call, appoint.*
moderor, -ari, -atus, *manage, control.*
ne, *lest, that.*
non, *not.*
omnis, -e, *all.*
princeps, -ipis, m., *head man, leader, chief, prince.*
quisque, -----, quidque, *each one, each thing.*
statuo, -uere, -ui, -utus, *determine, resolve.*
tantus, -a, -um, *so great, so large, such, so extensive.*
Vercingetorix, -igis, m., *Vercingetorix.*

Dum ... geruntur: Temporal clause; the conjunction **dum** ("when, while") with the present indicative denotes continued action in past time (A.G. 556). **geruntur:** The main verb of the subordinate clause (A.G. 278.b).
haec: Plural, neuter, nominative demonstrative pronoun used substantively (A.G. 296.2). The antecedent is the building of the fortifications described at Chapters 72-74 (A.G. 297.e). Nominative subject (A.G. 339).
apud Alesiam: Prepositional phrase, with all names of places *at,* meaning *near* (not *in*), is expressed by **apud** with the accusative (A.G. 428.d). **Alesiam:** See Appendix A.
Galli: Nominative subject of **statuunt** (A.G. 339). See Appendix A.
concilio principum indicto: Ablative absolute (A.G. 419-20). Kahn claims that the council scene functions as a substitute for choral

odes between major episodes. (Kahn, 251) See also 1.4, 14.1, 29.1, 63.5-6, and 89.1. **principum**: Objective genitive with **concilio** (A.G. 348). **indicto**: The perfect tense of the participle represents the action as completed at the time indicated by the tense of the main verb (A.G. 489).

non: Adverb; when **non** is especially emphatic it begins the clause (A.G. 217.e, 320-21, and 599.a).

omnis eos ... convocandos (esse): Subject accusative with the infinitive after **statuunt** (A.G. 563.d). The construction is equivalent to a substantive clause of purpose (A.G. 563.d). **omnis**: Accusative adjective; **-is** for **-es** is the regular form in i-stem adjectives (A.G. 114.a and 116). **eos**: Plural, masculine, accusative demonstrative pronoun used substantively (A.G. 296.2). The pronoun is correlative to the relative clause **qui ... possent** (A.G. 297.d). **convocandos (esse)**: Supply **esse** with the gerundive to form the second periphrastic (passive) present infinitive implying necessity (A.G. 194.b and 196).

qui ... possent: Relative clause; the relative clause takes the subjunctive as a subordinate clause depending on an infinitive (**convocandos (esse)**) which is equivalent to a subjunctive clause and regarded as an integral part of that clause (attraction) (A.G. 593). **qui**: Plural, masculine, nominative relative pronoun used substantively (A.G. 305). The antecedent is **eos** (A.G. 307). Nominative subject (A.G. 339). **possent**: The main verb of the subordinate clause (A.G. 278.b). Imperfect subjunctive; the tense of the subjunctive is in secondary sequence after the historical present **statuunt** (A.G. 482-85, esp. 485.e).

arma: Accusative direct object of the infinitive **ferre** (A.G. 387 and 451.3).

ferre: Complementary infinitive after **possent** (A.G. 456).

ut censuit Vercingetorix: The relative adverb **ut** ("as") with the indicative introduces a parenthetical remark (*OLD* **ut** 12). For the reference see 71.2-3. "The decision to send a fixed quota from each state, instead of all the fighting men, was wise. The total of the quota given in this chapter is 259,000. If that army could not conquer Caesar, no army of Gauls could." (Walker, 399) **censuit**: The main verb of the subordinate clause (A.G. 278.b). A clause dependent on an infinitive equivalent to a subjunctive clause (**convocandos (esse)**) normally takes the subjunctive (attraction) (A.G. 303 and 593). However, when a dependent clause is not regarded as a necessary logical part of the clause, the indicative is used. The indicative serves to emphasize the fact, as true independently of the statement contained in the subjunctive clause (A.G. 593.a Note 1). **Vercingetorix**: Nominative subject (A.G. 339). See Appendix A.

statuunt: The main verb of the main clause (A.G. 278.b). The historical present, giving vividness to the narrative, is present in Chapter 75 (A.G. 469). This usage, common in all languages, comes from imagining past events as going on before our eyes (*repraesentatio*) (A.G. 469 Note).

sed: Coordinate conjunction (A.G. 324.d).

certum numerum ... imperandum (esse): Subject accusative with the infinitive after **statuunt** (A.G. 563.d). The construction is equivalent to a substantive clause of purpose (A.G. 563.d). **imperandum (esse)**: Supply **esse** with the gerundive to form the second periphrastic (passive) present infinitive implying necessity (A.G. 194.b and 196).

cuique: Singular, masculine, dative indefinite pronoun used substantively (A.G. 151.g). Dative indirect object of the intransitive use of **imperandum**; verbs which in the active voice take the accusative and dative retain the dative when used in the passive (A.G. 365 and 367). The noun **principi** is understood.

ex civitate: Ablative of source with the preposition **ex** dependent on **certum numerum** (A.G. 426.1).

(veriti) ne ... possent: The conjunction **ne** ("lest") with the subjunctive forms a substantive clause of fearing after the supplied participle **veriti**. Here the verb of fearing, **veriti** (**vereor, vereri, veritus sum**, *fear, dread, be afraid of*), must be supplied in the form of a participle modifying **Galli** (A.G. 564). **possent**: The main verb of the subordinate clause (A.G. 278.b). Imperfect subjunctive; the tense of the subjunctive is in secondary sequence and follows the rules for the sequence of tense after the historical present tense of **statuunt** (A.G. 482-85, esp. 485.e). The pronoun **ei**, with **Galli** as the antecedent, is understood as the subject (A.G. 271.a).

tanta multitudine confusa: Ablative absolute (A.G. 419-20). **confusa**: The perfect tense of the participle represents the action as completed at the time indicated by the tense of the main verb (A.G. 489).

nec ... nec ... nec: The repeated conjunction means "neither ... nor ... nor", connecting the three infinitives (*OLD* **neque** 7.b). The repetition of words at the beginning of successive clauses is anaphora (A.G. 641).

moderari ... discernere ... habere: Three complementary infinitives after **possent** (A.G. 456).

suos: Plural, masculine, accusative possessive pronoun used substantively to denote a special class (A.G. 302.d). Accusative direct object of the infinitive **discernere** (A.G. 387 and 451.3).

frumentationem: Accusative direct object of the infinitive **habere** (A.G. 387 and 451.3).

(75.2) **Imperant Aeduis atque eorum clientibus, Segusiavis, +Ambluaretis+, Aulercis Brannovicibus, Blannoviis milia XXXV;**

Aedui, -orum, m., pl., *the Aedui.*	**Ambluareti (Ambivariti, Ambibareti), -orum**, m., pl., *the Ambluareti.*
atque, *and.*	**Aulerci Brannovices, -orum, -um**, m., *the Aulerci Brannovices.*
Blannovii, -orum, m., pl., *the Blannovii.*	**cliens, -entis**, m., *subject allies, dependants.*
impero, -are, -avi, -atus, *levy, draft, demand.*	**is, ea, id**, *he, she, it; that, this.*
milia, -um, n., pl., *thousand, thousands.*	**Segusiavi, -orum**, m., pl., *the Segusiavi.*
V, in expression of number, = *5.*	**X**, in expression of number, = *10.*

Imperant: The main verb of the simple sentence (A.G. 278.1). Verb first in the emphatic position (A.G. 589.d). "The Aquitani did not join the rebellion, nor did the Remi, Lingones, and Treveri. With these exceptions, the movement of Transalpine Gaul outside 'the Province' against Caesar seems to have been general." (Kelsey, 428) See 63.7-8 for the reasons why the Remi, Lingones, and Treveri did not join the rebellion, "Forty-two states are named in the following list." (Walker, 399)

Aeduis atque ... clientibus: Two dative indirect object of the normally intransitive verb **Imperant** (A.G. 369). **Aeduis**: See Appendix A. **atque**: The conjunction connects the two dative nouns and means "and" (*OLD* **atque** 12). **eorum**: Plural, masculine, genitive demonstrative pronoun used substantively (A.G. 296.2). The antecedent is **Aeduis** (A.G. 297.e). Possessive genitive with **clientibus** (A.G. 343).

Segusiavis, +Ambluaretis+, Aulercis Brannovicibus, Blannoviis: Four dative tribe names in apposition to **clientibus** (A.G. 282). Notice the asyndeton construction (A.G. 323.b). See Appendix A for each tribe. **Ambluaretis**: The Loeb teat reads **Ambivaretis**, the Budé text **Amb*i*uaretis**.

milia XXXV (militum): Accusative direct object of the normally intransitive verb **Imperant** (A.G. 369 and 387). **milia**: Accusative plural; in the plural **mille** declines as a neuter noun (A.G. 134.d). **XXXV**: Roman numeral used as an adjective (A.G. 133). Supply **militum** as a partitive genitive with **milia**.

(75.2-3) parem numerum Arvernis adiunctis Eleutetis, Cadurcis, Gabalis, Vellaviis, qui sub (3) imperio Arvernorum esse consuerunt;

adiungo, -iungere, -iunxi, -iunctus, *add, unite.*
Cadurci, -orum, m., pl., *the Caduci.*
Eleuteti, -orum, m., pl., *the Eleuteti.*
imperium, -i, n., *control, dominion, military authority.*
par, paris, *like, similar, same, equal.*
sub, *subject to, under.*
Vellavii, -orum, m., pl., *the Vellavii.*

Arverni, -orum, m., pl., *the Arverni.*
consuesco, -suescere, -suevi, -suetus, *be accustomed.*
Gabali, -orum, m., pl., *the Gabali.*
numerus, -i, m., *number, amount.*
qui, quae, quod, *who, which, what.*
sum, esse, fui, futurus, *be.*

parem numerum (militum): Accusative direct object of the normally intransitive verb **Imperant** (A.G. 369 and 387). Supply **militum** as a partitive genitive with **numerum**.

Arvernis adiunctis: Dative indirect object of the normally intransitive verb **Imperant** (A.G. 369). **Arvernis**: See Appendix A. **adiunctis**: Dative perfect, passive participle used as a predicate, where in English a phrase or a subordinate clause would be more normal (A.G. 496).

Eleutetis, Cadurcis, Gabalis, Vellaviis: Four dative indirect objects of the passive participle **adiunctis**; verbs which in the active voice take the accusative and dative retain the dative when used in the passive (A.G. 365 and 488). Notice the asyndeton construction (A.G. 323.b). See Appendix A for each tribe.

qui ... consuerunt: Relative clause (A.G. 303). **qui**: Plural, masculine, nominative relative pronoun used substantively (A. G. 305). The antecedent is **Eleutetis, Cadurcis, Gabalis, Vellaviis** (A.G. 307). Nominative subject (A.G. 339). **consuerunt**: The main verb of the subordinate clause (A.G. 278.b). Contracted form of **consueverunt** (A.G. 181.a).

sub imperio Arvernorum: Prepositional phrase, **sub** with the ablative here means "subject to, under" (*OLD* **sub** 15). The prepositional phrase is in the predicate position after **esse** (A.G. 272). **Arvernorum**: Possessive genitive with **imperio** (A.G. 343). **esse**: Complementary infinitive after **consuerunt** (A.G. 456). See Appendix A.

(75.3-4) Sequanis, Senonibus, Biturigibus, Santonis, Rutenis, Carnutibus duodena milia; Bellovacis decem; +totidem Lemovicibus+; octona Pictionibus et Turonis et Parisiis et Helvetiis; +Senonibus+, Ambianis, Mediomatricis, Petrocoriis, Nerviis, Morinis, Nitiobrigibus quina milia; Aulercis Cenomanis totidem; Atrebatibus ĪĪĪĪ; Veliocassis, +Lexoviis+ et Aulercis Eburo(4)vicibus terna; Rauricis et Boiis bina;

Ambiani, -orum, m., pl., *the Ambiani.*
Aulerci Cenomani, -orum, -orum, m., *the Aulerci Cenomani.*

Bellovaci, -orum, m., pl., *the Bellovaci.*
Bituriges, -um, m., pl., *the Bituriges.*
Carnutes, -um, m., pl., *the Carnutes.*
duodeni, -ae, -a, *twelve each.*
Helvetii, -orum, m., pl., *the Helvetii.*
Lemovices, -um, m., pl., *the Lemovices.*
Mediomatrici, -orum, m., pl., *the Mediomatrici.*
Morini, -orum, m., pl., *the Morini.*
Nitiobriges, -um, m., pl., *the Nitrobriges.*
Parisii, -orum, m., pl., *the Parisii.*
Pict(i)ones, -um, m., pl., *the Pictones.*
Raurici, -orum, m., pl., *the Raurici.*
Santones, -um, or Santoni, -orum, m., pl., *the Santones.*
Sequani, -orum, m., pl., *the Sequani.*
totidem, *as many, just as many, the same number of.*
Veliocasses, -um, dat. Veliocassis, m., pl., *the Veliocasses.*

Atrebas, -atis, m., *the Atrebates.*
Aulerci Eburovices, -orum, -um, m., *the Aulerci Eburovices.*
bini, -ae, -a, *two each.*
Boii, -orum, m., pl., *the Boii.*
decem, *ten.*
et ... et ... et, *... and ... and ... and.*
I, in expression of number, *1.*
Lexovii, -orum, m., pl., *the Lexovii.*
milia, -um, n., pl., *thousand, thousands.*
Nervii, -orum, m., pl., *the Nervii.*
octoni, -ae, -a, *eight each.*
Petrocorii, -orum, m., pl., *the Petrocorii.*
quini, -ae, -a, *five each.*
Ruteni, -orum, m., pl., *the Ruteni.*
Senones, -um, m., pl., *the Senones.*
terni, -ae, -a, *three each.*
Turoni, -orum, m., pl., *the Turoni.*

Sequanis, Senonibus, Biturigibus, Santonis, Rutenis, Carnutibus: Six dative indirect object of the normally intransitive verb **Imperant** (A.G. 369). Notice the asyndeton construction (A.G. 323.b). See Appendix A for each tribe.

duodena milia (militum): Accusative direct object of the normally intransitive verb Imperant (A.G. 369 and 387). duodena: Distributive numeral used as an adjective (A.G. 136-37). milia: Accusative plural; in the plural mille declines as a neuter noun (A.G. 134.d). Supply militum as a partitive genitive with milia.

Bellovacis: Dative indirect object of the normally intransitive verb Imperant (A.G. 369). See Appendix A.

decem (milia militum): Accusative direct object of the normally intransitive verb Imperant (A.G. 369 and 387). Indeclinable cardinal number used substantively (A.G. 132-35). Supply milia as the accusative noun and militum as a partitive genitive with milia.

+totidem Lemovicibus+: The Loeb text reads totidem Lemovicibus, the Budé text reads totidem Lemovicibus.

+totidem: Accusative direct object of the normally intransitive verb Imperant (A.G. 369 and 387). An indeclinable adjective used substantively meaning "as many" (A.G. 122.b) (OLD totidem 2).

Lemovicibus+: Dative indirect object of the normally intransitive verb Imperant (A.G. 369). See Appendix A.

octona (milia militum): Accusative direct object of the normally in transitive verb Imperant (A.G. 369 and 387). Distributive numeral used substantively (A.G. 136-37). Supply milia as the accusative noun and militum as a partitive genitive with milia.

Pictionibus et Turonis et Parisiis et Helvetiis: Four dative indirect objects of the normally intransitive verb Imperant (A.G. 369). See Appendix A for each tribe. Pictionibus: The Loeb text reads Pictonibus, the Budé text reads Pictonibus. et ... et ... et: The repeated conjunction means "... and ... and ... and", connecting the dative nouns (OLD et 9.b). Where there are more than two coordinate words, a conjunction, if used, is ordinarily used with all (A.G. 323.c.1). Notice the change from the asyndeton construction (A.G. 323.b).

+Senonibus+, Ambianis, Mediomatricis, Petrocoriis, Nerviis, Morinis, Nitiobrigibus: Seven dative indirect objects of the normally intransitive verb Imperant (A.G. 369). Notice the asyndeton construction (A.G. 323.b). See Appendix A for each tribe. Senonibus: Notice that this is the second time this tribe is mentioned in the catalog. The Loeb text instead reads Suessionibus, the Budé text reads [Senonibus].

quina milia (militum): Accusative direct object of the normally intransitive verb Imperant (A.G. 369 and 387). quina: Distributive numeral used as an adjective (A.G. 136-37). milia: Accusative plural; in the plural mille declines as a neuter noun (A.G. 134.d). Supply militum as a partitive genitive with milia.

Aulercis Cenomanis: Dative indirect object of the normally intransitive verb Imperant (A.G. 369). See Appendix A.

totidem: Accusative direct object of the normally intransitive verb Imperant (A.G. 369 and 387). An indeclinable adjective used substantively meaning "as many" (A.G. 122.b) (OLD totidem 2).

Atrebatibus: Dative indirect object of the normally intransitive verb Imperant (A.G. 369). See Appendix A.

IIII (militum): Accusative direct object of the normally intransitive verb Imperant (A.G. 369 and 387). Roman numeral used substantively (A.G. 133). The horizontal line over the Roman numeral indicates so many thousands (OLD mille). Supply militum as a partitive genitive.

Veliocassis, +Lexoviis+ et Aulercis Eburovicibus: Three dative indirect objects of the normally intransitive verb Imperant (A.G. 369). See Appendix A for each tribe. +Lexoviis+: The Loeb text reads Lexoviis, the Budé text reads Lexouiis. et: The conjunction connects the final two dative nouns in the series (A.G. 324.a).

terna (milia militum): Accusative direct object of the normally intransitive verb Imperant (A.G. 369 and 387). Distributive numeral used substantively (A.G. 136-37). Supply milia as the accusative noun and militum as a partitive genitive with milia.

Rauricis et Boiis: Two dative indirect objects of the normally intransitive verb Imperant (A.G. 369). Rauricis: See Appendix A. et: The conjunction connects the two dative nouns (A.G. 324.a). Boiis: See Appendix A.

bina (milia militum): Accusative direct object of the normally intransitive verb Imperant (A.G. 369 and 387). Distributive numeral used substantively (A.G. 136-37). Supply milia as the accusative noun and militum as a partitive genitive with milia.

(75.4-5) XXX milia universis civitatibus, quae Oceanum attingunt quaeque eorum consuetudine Aremoricae appellantur, quo sunt in numero Curiosolites, Redones, Ambibarii, Caletes, Osismi, Veneti, (5) +Lemovices+, Venelli.

Ambibarii, -orum, m., pl., *the Ambibarii.*
Aremoricus, -a, -um, *Aremorican.*

Caletes, -um and Caleti, -orum, m., pl., *the Caletes.*
consuetudo, -inis, f., *tradition, usage.*
in, *in.*
Lemovices, -um, m., pl., *the Lemovices.*
numerus, -i, m., *number.*
Osismi, -orum, m., pl., *the Osismi.*
qui, quae, quod, *who, which, what.*
sum, esse, fui, futurus, *be.*
Venelli, -orum, m., pl., *the Venelli.*
X, in expression of number, = *10.*

appello, -are, -avi, -atus, *name, call.*
attingo, -tingere, -tigi, -tactus, *border on, extend to, adjoin.*
civitas, -tatis, f., *state, nation.*
Curiosolites, -um, m., pl., *the Curiosolites.*
is, ea, id, *he, she, it; that, this.*
milia, -um, n., pl., *thousand, thousands.*
Oceanus, -i, m., *Ocean, the sea.*
-que, *and.*
Redones, -um, m., pl., *the Redones.*
universus, -a, -um, *all, the whole of.*
Veneti, -orum, m., pl., *the Veneti.*

XXX milia (militum): Accusative direct object of the normally intransitive verb Imperant (A.G. 369 and 387). milia: Accusative plural; in the plural mille declines as a neuter noun (A.G. 134.d). XXX: Roman numeral used as an adjective modifying milia (A.G. 133). Supply militum as a partitive genitive.

universis civitatibus: Dative indirect object of the normally intransitive verb Imperant (A.G. 369).

quae ... attingunt: Relative clause (A.G. 303). quae: Plural, feminine, nominative relative pronoun used substantively (A.G. 305). The antecedent is civitatibus (A.G. 307). Nominative subject (A.G. 339). attingunt: The main verb of the subordinate clause (A.G.

278.b).

attingunt ... appellantur ... sunt: The present tense is not the historical present but denotes a state as now existing in present time (A.G. 465.1).

Oceanum: Accusative direct object of **attingunt** (A.G. 387). See Appendix A.

quaeque ... appellantur: Relative clause (A.G. 303). **quae:** Plural, feminine, nominative relative pronoun used substantively (A.G. 305). The antecedent is **civitatibus** (A.G. 307). Nominative subject (A.G. 339). **-que:** The enclitic conjunction connects the two relative clauses (A.G. 324.a). **appellantur:** The main verb of the subordinate clause (A.G. 278.b).

eorum consuetudine: Ablative of manner with a limiting pronoun (A.G. 412). **eorum:** Plural, masculine, genitive demonstrative pronoun used substantively (A.G. 296.2). The antecedent is **Galli** at 75.1 (if it referred to the **Aremoricae** it would be **sua consuetudine**) (A.G. 297.e). Possessive genitive (A.G. 343).

Aremoricae: Plural, feminine, nominative adjective used substantively (A.G. 288). The noun **civitates** is understood (A.G. 288.b). Predicate nominative after **appellantur** (A.G. 283).

quo ... Venelli: Relative clause (A.G. 303). **quo:** See below. **Venelli:** See below.

quo ... in numero: Prepositional phrase, **in** with the ablative here means "in" (*OLD* **in** 38). **quo:** Singular, neuter, ablative relative pronoun (A.G. 305). The antecedent is **numero** in its own clause (adjectival use) (A.G. 307.b). **in:** A monosyllabic preposition is often placed between a noun and its adjective (A.G. 599.d.2). The prepositional phrase is in the predicate position after **sunt** (A.G. 272).

sunt: The main verb of the subordinate clause (A.G. 278.b).

Curiosolites, Redones, Ambibarii, Caletes, Osismi, Veneti, +Lemovices+, Venelli: Eight nominative subjects (A.G. 339). Notice the asyndeton construction (A.G. 323.b). See Appendix A for each tribe. **Lemovices:** Notice that this is the second time this tribe is mentioned in the catalog. The Loeb text reads **Lemovices**, the Budé text reads **Lemovices**. **Venelli:** The Loeb text reads **Venelli**, the Budé text reads **Vnelli**.

(75.4) Ex his Bellovaci suum numerum non compleverunt, quod se suo nomine atque arbitrio cum Romanis bellum gesturos dicebant, neque cuiusquam imperio obtemperaturos; rogati tamen ab Commio pro eius hospitio II una miserunt.

ab, *by.*
atque, *and.*
bellum, -i, n., *war, warfare.*
compleo, -plere, -plevi, -pletus, *fill up, make up, complete.*
dico, dicere, dixi, dictus, *say.*
gero, gerere, gessi, gestus, *carry on, wage.*
hospitium, -i, n., *tie of hospitality, friendship.*
imperium, -i, n., *command, military authority.*
mitto, mittere, misi, missus, *send.*
nomen, -inis, n., *account.*
numerus, -i, m., *number, quota.*
pro, *because of, on account of, out of regard for.*
quod, *because, since, for, as.*
Romani, -orum, m., pl., *the Romans.*

suus, -a, -um, *their,* with or without *own.*
una, *together, in company.*

arbitrium, -i, n., *authority.*
Bellovaci, -orum, m., pl., *the Bellovaci.*
Commius, -i, m., *Commius.*
cum, *with.*
ex, *from the number of, from among, of.*
hic, haec, hoc, *this; he, she, it.*
I, in expression of number, *1.*
is, ea, id, *he, she, it; that, this.*
neque, *and ... not.*
non, *not.*
obtempero, -are, -avi, -atus, *submit to, obey.*
quisquam, -----, quidquam, *anyone, anything, any.*
rogo, -are, -avi, -atus, *ask, request.*
sui, sibi, se, or **sese,** nom. wanting, *they,* with or without *themselves.*
tamen, *yet, still, for all that, nevertheless, however.*

Ex his: Prepositional phrase, **ex** with the ablative here indicates a partitive sense "from the number of, from among, of" (*OLD* **ex** 16). Here **ex** with the ablative is used instead of the partitive genitive (A.G. 346.c). **his:** Plural, masculine, ablative demonstrative pronoun used substantively (A.G. 296.2). The antecedent is all of the tribes listed above in the catalog (A.G. 297.e).

Bellovaci: Nominative subject (A.G. 339). The Bellovaci play no role in the remaining narrative and are only mentioned again in passing at 90.5. For the further exploits of the Bellovaci in *BG* Book 8, see 8.6-7, 12-23, 38. See Appendix A.

suum numerum: Accusative direct object of **compleverunt** (A.G. 387). **suum:** Singular, masculine, accusative possessive pronoun used as an adjective modifying **numerum** (A.G. 302).

non: Adverb, the adverb generally precedes the verb if it belongs to no one word in particular (A.G. 217.e, 320-21, and 599.a).

compleverunt: The main verb of the main clause (A.G. 278.b).

quod ... dicebant: Causal clause; the conjunction **quod** ("because") takes the indicative when the reason is given on the authority of the writer or speaker (A.G. 540.1). **dicebant:** The main verb of the subordinate clause (A.G. 278.b). The pronoun **ei**, with **Bellovaci** as the antecedent, is understood as the subject (A.G. 271.a).

se ... gesturos (esse): Accusative/infinitive construction in indirect discourse after **dicebant** (A.G. 577 ff.). **se:** Plural, masculine, accusative direct reflexive pronoun (A.G. 300.1). The antecedent is **ei** (**Bellovaci**), the supplied subject of **dicebant** (A.G. 299). **gesturos (esse):** Supply **esse** to form the future, active, infinitive (A.G. 186). The tense of the infinitive in indirect discourse is relative to that of the verb of saying (A.G. 584).

suo nomine atque arbitrio: Two ablatives of manner with a limiting adjective (A.G. 412). **suo:** Singular, neuter, ablative possessive pronoun used as an adjective modifying **nomine** (A.G. 302). The adjective should be construed with both **nomine** and **arbitrio**, agreeing in number with the nearest noun (A.G. 286.a). **atque:** The conjunction connects the two ablative nouns and means "and" (*OLD* **atque** 12).

cum Romanis: Ablative of accompaniment with the preposition **cum**, words of contention (**gesturos bellum**) require **cum** (A.G. 413.b).

bellum: Accusative direct object of the infinitive **gesturos** (**esse**) (A.G. 387 and 451.3).

neque: The conjunction here joins a negative clause to a preceding positive one and means "and ... not" (*OLD* neque 3). Here it connects the two infinitives in indirect discourse after **dicebant**.

cuiusquam: Singular, masculine, genitive indefinite pronoun used substantively (A.G. 151.d). Possessive genitive with **imperio** (A.G. 343).

imperio: Dative indirect object of **obtemperaturos** (**esse**) (A.G. 367).

(se) ... obtemperaturos (esse): Accusative/infinitive construction in indirect discourse after **dicebant** (A.G. 577 ff.). Carry down **se** from above as the accusative pronoun. **obtemperaturos (esse)**: Supply **esse** to form the future, active, infinitive (A.G. 184). The tense of the infinitive in indirect discourse is relative to that of the verb of saying (A.G. 584).

rogati: Nominative perfect passive participle used as a predicate, where in English a phrase or a subordinate clause would be more normal (A.G. 496). The pronoun **ei**, with **Bellovaci** as the antecedent, is understood. Nominative subject (A.G. 339).

tamen: Adverb, postpositive (A.G. 320-21 and 324.j).

ab Commio: Ablative of agent with the preposition **ab** after the passive participle **rogati** (A.G. 405). **Commio**: See Appendix A.

pro eius hospitio: Prepositional phrase, **pro** with the ablative here means "because of, on account of" (*OLD* pro1 17). **eius**: Singular, masculine, genitive demonstrative pronoun used substantively (A.G. 296.2). The antecedent is **Commio** (A.G. 297.e). Possessive genitive with **hospitio** (A.G. 343).

II (militum): Accusative direct object of **miserunt** (A.G. 387). Roman numeral used substantively (A.G. 133). The horizontal line over the Roman numeral indicates so many thousands (*OLD* mille). Supply **militum** as a partitive genitive.

una: Adverb (A.G. 320-21).

miserunt: The main verb of the main clause (A.G. 278.b).

(76.1) **Huius opera Commi, ut antea demonstravimus, fideli atque utili superioribus annis erat usus in Britannia Caesar; quibus ille pro meritis civitatem eius immunem esse iusserat, iura legesque reddiderat atque ipsi Morinos attribuerat.**

annus, -i, m., *year.*
atque, *and in fact, and even; and.*
Britannia, -ae, f., *Britain.*
civitas, -tatis, f., *state, nation.*
demonstro, -are, -avi, -atus, *point out, show, say, mention, explain.*
hic, haec, hoc, *this; he, she, it.*
immunis, -e, *free from taxes, unburdened.*
ipse, -a, -um, *he, they*, with or without *himself, themselves.*
iubeo, iubere, iussi, iussus, *order, give orders, bid, command.*
lex, legis, f., *law, enactment, decree.*
Morini, -orum, m., pl., *the Morini.*

pro, *as a reward for, in return for.*
qui, quae, quod, *who, which, what.*
sum, esse, fui, futurus, *be.*
ut, *as.*
utor, uti, usus, *avail one's self of.*

antea, *previously, before, formerly.*
attribuo, -uere, -ui, -utus, *assign, allot, turn over to.*
Caesar, -aris, m., *Caesar.*
Commius, -i, m., *Commius.*
fidelis, -e, *faithful, trustworthy.*
ille, illae, illud, *that; he, she, it.*
in, *in.*
is, ea, id, *he, she, it; that, this.*
ius, iuris, n., *right, justice, authority.*
meritum, -i, n., *desert, merit, service.*
opera, -ae, f., *effort, work, pains; service, aid, assistance.*
-que, *and.*
reddo, -dere, -didi, -ditus, *give back, restore, return.*
superior, -or, -us, *former, earlier, previous.*
utilis, -e, *useful, helpful.*

Huius ... Commi: Possessive genitive with **opera** (A.G. 343). **Huius**: Singular, masculine, genitive demonstrative pronoun used as an adjective modifying **Commi** (A.G. 296.1 and a). **Commi**: The singular genitive of nouns in -ius ended, until the Augustan Age, in a single -i (A.G. 49.b). See Appendix A.

opera ... fideli atque utili: Ablative direct object of the deponent verb **erat usus** (A.G. 410). **atque**: The conjunction connects the two ablative adjectives, strengthening the first term and meaning "and in fact, and even" (*OLD* atque 4). Two adjectives belonging to the same noun are regularly connected by a conjunction (A.G. 323.d).

ut ... demonstravimus: The relative adverb **ut** ("as") with the indicative introduces a parenthetical remark (*OLD* ut 12). For the reference see 4.21,35; 5.22. **demonstravimus**: The main verb of the subordinate clause (A.G. 278.b). The personal pronoun **nos** is understood as the subject but is not expressed except for distinction or emphasis (A.G. 295.a). In Book 7, Caesar refers to himself only in the third person, either in the singular or occasionally in the plural (see **Caesar** at 1.1). Siedler counts 11 uses of the first person plural in Book 7 (Siedler, 46). These uses are at 17.1, 23.2, 25.1, 37.1, 48.1, 58.4, 70.1, 76.1, 79.2, 83.8, and 85.4.

antea: Adverb (A.G. 216 Note and 320-21).

superioribus annis: Ablative of *time when* (A.G. 423.1). **superioribus**: Defective comparative adjective (A.G. 130.b).

erat usus: The main verb of the main clause (A.G. 278.b).

in Britannia: Ablative of *place where* with the preposition **in** (locative ablative) (A.G. 426.3). **Britannia**: See Appendix A.

Caesar: Nominative subject (A.G. 339). The subject is in the last position in the clause (A.G. 597.b). See Appendix A.

quibus ... attribuerat: Compare Caesar's actions with the accusations of Critognatus at 77.16.

quibus ... pro meritis: Prepositional phrase, **pro** with the ablative here means "as a reward for, in return for" (*OLD* pro 10). **quibus**: Plural, neuter, ablative relative pronoun (A.G. 305). The antecedent is **meritis** in its own clause (adjectival use) (A.G. 307.b). The relative does not introduce a relative clause but is a connecting relative; at the beginning of a clause the pronoun is often best rendered by a personal or demonstrative pronoun, with or without *and* (A.G. 308.f). **pro**: A monosyllabic preposition is often placed between a noun and its adjective (A.G. 599.d.2).

ille: Singular, masculine, nominative demonstrative pronoun used substantively (A.G. 296.2). The antecedent is **Caesar** (A.G. 297.e). Nominative subject of **iusserat ... reddiderat ... attribuerat** (A.G. 339).

civitatem ... immunem esse: A subject accusative with the infinitive after **iusserat**. The construction is equivalent to a substantive clause of purpose (A.G. 563.a). **civitatem**: The state referred to is that of the **Atrebates**. **immunem**: Singular, feminine, accusative predicate adjective modifying **civitatem** after **esse** (A.G. 283-84).

eius: Singular, masculine, genitive demonstrative pronoun used substantively (A.G. 296.2). The antecedent is **Commi** (A.G. 297.e). Possessive genitive with **civitatem** (A.G. 343).

iusserat: The main verb of the coordinate clause **quibus ... iusserat** (A.G. 278.a). Although the pluperfect tense is normally used in subordinate clauses, its use as a main verb is frequent. The pluperfect denotes an action completed in past time (A.G. 477).

iura legesque reddiderat: "This phrase is commonly used in Livy for the resumption of local government in communities in Italy or overseas that Rome had defeated, whether or not any form of province existed. It was the normal thing to restore *iura legesque*, and Caesar had no need to alter the Celtic system of local government within the tribal states by imposing any Roman forms. (Sherwin-White, 41)

iura legesque: Two accusative direct objects of **reddiderat** (A.G. 387). **-que**: The enclitic conjunction connects the two accusative nouns (A.G. 324.a).

reddiderat: The main verb of the coordinate clause **iura ... reddiderat** (A.G. 278.a). Although the pluperfect tense is normally used in subordinate clauses, its use as a main verb is frequent. The pluperfect denotes an action completed in past time (A.G. 477). Notice the asyndeton between the two main verbs **iusserat ... reddiderat** (A.G. 323.b).

atque: The conjunction connects the two main verbs **reddiderat ... attribuerat** and means "and" (*OLD* atque 12).

ipsi ... attribuerat: For the reference see *BG* 4.21.

ipsi: Singular, masculine, dative demonstrative pronoun used substantively (A.G. 296.2). The antecedent is **Commi** (A.G. 297.e). Dative indirect object of the transitive verb **attribuerat** (A.G. 362). The pronoun is here emphatic (A.G. 298.d.1).

Morinos: Accusative direct object of the transitive verb **attribuerat** (A.G. 387). See Appendix A.

attribuerat: The main verb of the coordinate clause **ipsi ... attribuerat** (A.G. 278.a). Although the pluperfect tense is normally used in subordinate clauses, its use as a main verb is frequent. The pluperfect denotes an action completed in past time (A.G. 477).

(76.2-3) **(2) Tamen tanta universae Galliae consensio fuit libertatis vindicandae et pristinae belli laudis recuperandae, ut neque beneficiis neque amicitiae memoria moverentur, omnesque (3) et animo et opibus in id bellum incumberent.**

amicitia, -ae, f., *friendship, alliance.*
bellum, -i, n., *war, warfare.*
consensio, -onis, f., *agreement, unanimity.*
Gallia, -ae, f., *Gaul.*
incumbo, -ere, incubui, incubitus, *make an effort, apply* or *exert oneself.*
laus, laudis, f., *praise, fame, glory, commendation.*
memoria, -ae, f., *memory, recollection, remembrance.*
neque ... neque, *neither ... nor.*
opes, -um, f., pl., *resources, means, strength.*
-que, *and.*
sum, esse, fui, futurus, *be.*
tantus, -a, -um, *so great, so large, such, so extensive.*
ut, *so that.*

animus, -i, m., *courage, spirit, resolution.*
beneficium, -i, n., *kindness, favor, service, benefit.*
et, *and*; **et ... et**, *both ... and.*
in, *for the needs* or *purposes of.*
is, ea, id, *he, she, it; that, this.*
libertas, -atis, f., *freedom, liberty, independence.*
moveo, movere, movi, motus, *influence, affect, move.*
omnes, -ium, m., pl., *all men, all.*
pristinus, -a, -um, *former, previous, earlier.*
recupero, -are, -avi, -atus, *get back, regain, recover.*
tamen, *yet, still, for all that, nevertheless, however.*
universus, -a, -um, *all, the whole of.*
vindico, -are, -avi, -atus, *claim, demand*

A. D. Kahn assesses Caesar's problem thus: "He had to emphasize the noble motivation impelling the Gauls, their yearning for freedom, or the war would degenerate into a mere bandit-suppression campaign and lose its high seriousness. On the other hand, he could not demean the Roman cause by depicting his troops as ruthless imperialists. Although he resolved his dilemma like a typical imperialist (freedom is only for those equipped to enjoy it), in the final speech of the book (77), he has Critognatus expose the reality behind the Roman professions of peace and civilization. Caesar's own defense is delivered to the Aeduans (54); he reminds them how Gaul had been wracked with internecine strife before the Roman conquerors had brought prosperity and tranquility. He never condemns nor even seeks to answer the Gallic insistence upon freedom as their natural right." (Kahn, 253)

Tamen: Adverb, normally postpositive but not here (A.G. 320-21 and 324.j).

tanta: Singular, feminine, nominative predicate adjective modifying **consensio** after **fuit** (A.G. 283-84). The adjective is correlative with the following result clause (A.G. 537 Note 2).

universae Galliae: Possessive genitive with **consensio** (A.G. 343). **Galliae**: See Appendix A.

consensio: Nominative subject (A.G. 339).

fuit: The main verb of the main clause (A.G. 278.b).

libertatis vindicandae: Objective genitive after **consensio** (A.G. 504). **libertatis**: For the theme of liberty in Book 7, see **liberius** at 1.3. **vindicandae**: Singular, feminine, genitive gerundive modifying **libertatis** (A.G. 500.1).

et: The conjunction connects the two gerundive phrases (A.G. 324.a).

pristinae belli: Objective genitive with **laudis** (A.G. 348).

laudis recuperandae: Objective genitive after **consensio** (A.G. 504). **recuperandae**: Singular, feminine, genitive gerundive modifying **laudis** (A.G. 500.1).

(tanta) ... **ut** ... **moverentur** ... **incumberent**: The conjunction **ut** ("so that") with the subjunctive forms a clause of result (A.G. 537.1 and Note 2). **moverentur** ... **incumberent**: The main verbs of the subordinate clause (A.G. 278.b). Imperfect subjunctives; the tense of the subjunctives is in secondary sequence and follows the rules for the sequence of tense after **fuit** (A.G. 482-85). **moverentur**: The noun **Galli** is understood as the subject (A.G. 271.a).

neque ... **neque**: The repeated conjunction means "neither ... nor", connecting the two ablative nouns (*OLD* **neque** 7).

beneficiis ... **memoria**: Two ablatives of cause without a preposition after the passive verb **moverentur** (A.G.404).

amicitiae: Objective genitive with **memoria** (A.G. 348).

omnesque: Plural, masculine, nominative adjective used substantively (A.G. 288). Nominative subject (A.G. 339). **-que**: The enclitic conjunction connects the two main verbs in the result clause (A.G. 324.a).

et ... **et**: The repeated conjunction means "both ... and", connecting the two ablative nouns (A.G. 323.e).

animo ... **opibus**: Two ablatives of means (A.G. 409).

in id bellum: Prepositional phrase, **in** with the accusative here means "for the needs or purposes of" (*OLD* **in** 22). **id**: Singular, neuter, accusative demonstrative pronoun used as an adjective modifying **bellum** (A.G. 296.1 and a).

(76.3-4) Coactis equitum VIII et peditum circiter CCXXXX, haec in Aeduorum finibus recensebantur numerusque inibatur, praefecti consti(4)tuebantur.

Aedui, -orum, m., pl., *the Aedui.*

circiter, *about.*

constituo, -stituere, -stitui, -stitutus, *appoint, establish, determine.*

et, *and.*

hic, haec, hoc, *this; he, she, it.*

in, *in.*

milia, -um, n., pl., *thousand, thousands.*

pedites, -um, m., pl., *infantry.*

-que, *and.*

V, in expression of number, = *5.*

C, in expression of number, = *100.*

cogo, cogere, coegi, coactus, *bring together, collect, gather, assemble.*

eques, -itis, m., *rider, horseman, cavalryman, trooper.*

fines, -ium, m., pl., *borders,* hence *territory, country, land.*

I, in expression of number, *1.*

ineo, -ire, -ivi, or **-ii, -itus**, *arrive at, determine.*

numerus, -i, m., *count, number.*

praefectus, -i, m., *prefect, cavalry captain.*

recenso, -ere, recensui, -----, *count, enumerate, number, survey.*

X, in expression of number, = *10*

Coactis equitum VIII milibus et peditum circiter CCXXXX milibus: Ablative absolute (A.G. 419-20). **Coactis**: The perfect tense of the participle represents the action as completed at the time indicated by the tense of the main verb (A.G. 489). **equitum**: Partitive genitive with **VIII milibus** (A.G. 346.a.2). **VIII**: Roman numeral used as an adjective modifying **milibus** (A.G. 133). **milibus**: Ablative plural; in the plural **mille** declines as a neuter noun (A.G. 134.d). **et**: The conjunction connects the two Roman numerals (A.G. 324.a). **peditum**: Partitive genitive with **CCXXXX milibus** (A.G. 346.a.2). **circiter**: Adverb (A.G. 320-21). **CCXXXX**: Roman numeral used as an adjective modifying **milibus** (A.G. 133). **miliibus**: Ablative plural; in the plural **mille** declines as a neuter noun (A.G. 134.d).

haec: Plural, feminine, nominative demonstrative pronoun used substantively (A.G. 296.2). The noun **copiae**, which encompasses both **equitum** and **peditum**, is understood. Nominative subject (A.G. 339).

in Aeduorum finibus: Ablative of *place where* with the preposition **in** (locative ablative) (A.G. 426.3). **Aeduorum**: Possessive genitive with **finibus** (A.G. 343). See Appendix A.

recensebantur: The main verb of the coordinate clause **Coactis** ... **recensebantur** (A.G. 278.a).

numerusque: Nominative subject (A.G. 339). **-que**: The enclitic conjunction connects the two main verbs **recensebantur** ... **inibatur** (A.G. 324.a).

inibatur: The main verb of the coordinate clause **numerusque inibatur** (A.G. 278.a).

praefecti: Nominative subject (A.G. 339).

constituebantur: The main verb of the coordinate clause **praefecti constituebantur** (A.G. 278.a). Notice the asyndeton between the last two verbs (A.G. 323.b).

(76.4) Commio Atrebati, Viridomaro et Eporedorigi Aeduis, Vercassivellauno Arverno, consobrino Vercingetorigis summa imperi traditur.

Aeduus, -i, m., *an Aeduan.*

Atrebas, -atis, m., *an Atrebatian.*

consobrinus, -i, m., *born of a mother's sister, cousin.*

et, *and.*

summa, -ae, f., *general management, control, administration.*

Vercassivellaunus, -i, m., *Vercassivellaunus.*

Viridomarus, -i, m., *Viridomarus.*

Arvernus, -i, m., *an Arvernian.*

Commius, -i, m., *Commius.*

Eporedorix, -igis, m., *Eporedorix.*

imperium, -i, n., *command, control, military authority.*

trado, -dere, -didi, -ditus, *hand over, give up, deliver.*

Vercingetorix, -igis, m., *Vercingetorix.*

Commio ... **Viridomaro et Eporedorigi** ... **Vercassivellauno**: Four dative indirect objects of the passive verb **traditur**; verbs which in the active voice take the accusative and dative retain the dative when used in the passive (A.G. 365). See Appendix A for each man.

Atrebati ... Aeduis ... Arverno: Notice how the nouns, which specifically designate three different traditionally rival tribes, forebodes the split in leadership among the relief army. The lack of consolidation of power has hampered the Gallic resistance to the Romans from the beginning of the war and will again surface at Alesia.

Atrebati: A dative noun in apposition to the proper noun **Commio** (A.G. 282).

et: The conjunction connects the two dative nouns **Viridomaro ... Eporedorigi** (A.G. 324.a).

Aeduis: A plural dative noun in apposition to the proper nouns **Viridomaro ... Eporedorigi** (A.G. 282).

Arverno: A dative noun in apposition to the proper noun **Vercassivellauno** (A.G. 282).

consobrino: A dative noun in apposition to the proper noun **Vercassivellauno** (A.G. 282).

Vercingetorigis: Possessive genitive with **consobrino** (A.G. 343). See Appendix A.

summa: Nominative subject (A.G. 339). From the noun **summa, -ae**, f..

imperi: Partitive genitive with **summa** (A.G. 346.a.1). The singular genitive of nouns in -**ium** ended, until the Augustan Age, in a single -**i** (A.G. 49.b).

traditur: The main verb of the simple sentence (A.G. 278.1). The historical present, giving vividness to the narrative, is present in Chapter 76 (A.G. 469). This usage, common in all languages, comes from imagining past events as going on before our eyes (*repraesentatio*) (A.G. 469 Note).

(76.4) His delecti ex civitatibus attribuuntur quorum consilio bellum administraretur.

administro, -are, -avi, -atus, *manage, carry on, administer.*	**attribuo, -uere, -ui, -utus**, *assign, allot, turn over to.*
bellum, -i, n., *war.*	**civitas, -tatis**, f., *state, nation.*
consilium, -i, n., *consultation, counsel, advice.*	**deligo, -ligere, -legi, -lectus**, *choose, select, pick out.*
ex, *from.*	**hic, haec, hoc**, *this; he, she, it.*
qui, quae, quod, *who, which, what.*	

His: Plural, masculine, dative demonstrative pronoun used substantively (A.G. 296.2). The antecedent is **Commio ... Viridomaro ... Eporedorigi ... Vercassivellauno** (A.G. 297.e). Dative indirect object of the passive verb **attribuuntur**; verbs which in the active voice take the accusative and dative retain the dative when used in the passive (A.G. 365).

delecti: Plural, masculine, nominative, perfect, passive participle used substantively meaning "chosen men, men picked out in preference to the rest" (A.G. 494.a) (*OLD* **deligo** 2). Nominative subject (A.G. 339).

ex civitatibus: Ablative of source with the preposition **ex** (A.G. 403.1).

attribuuntur: The main verb of the main clause (A.G. 278.b). "The fatal weakness of the Gauls was their inability to unite effectively. The states were so jealous of one another that they could not agree on a single commander, now that Vercingetorix was out of the question. It was bad enough to have four commanders-in-chief; but it was worse to hamper them with a council of representatives." (Walker, 400)

quorum ... administraretur: A relative clause of purpose is introduced by a relative pronoun and takes the subjunctive (A.G. 531.2).

quorum: Plural, masculine, genitive relative pronoun used substantively (A.G. 305). The antecedent is **delecti** (A.G. 307). Possessive genitive with **consilio** (A.G. 343). The relative is here equivalent to **ut eorum** (A.G. 531.2 Note). **administraretur**: The main verb of the subordinate clause (A.G. 278.b). Imperfect subjunctive; the tense of the subjunctive is in secondary sequence and follows the rules for the sequence of tense after the historical present tense of **attribuuntur** (A.G. 482-85, esp. 485.e).

consilio: Ablative of means (A.G. 409).

bellum: Nominative subject (A.G. 339).

(76.5) (5) Omnes alacres et fiduciae pleni ad Alesiam proficiscuntur, neque erat omnium quisquam qui aspectum modo tantae multitudinis sustineri posse arbitraretur, praesertim ancipiti proelio, cum ex oppido eruptione pugnaretur, foris tantae copiae equitatus peditatusque cernerentur.

ad, *towards, to the neighborhood of.*	**alacer, -cris, -cre**, *eager, ardent, spirited.*
Alesia, -ae, f., *Alesia.*	**anceps, -cipitis**, *on two fronts, both on the front and rear.*
arbitror, -ari, -atus, *think, suppose, consider, believe.*	**aspectus, -us**, m., *appearance, sight, look.*
cerno, cernere, -----, -----, *discern, see, perceive.*	**copiae, -arum**, f., pl., *forces, troops.*
cum, *when, on the ground that.*	**equitatus, -us**, m., *cavalry.*
eruptio, -onis, f., *a bursting forth, sally, sortie.*	**et**, *and.*
ex, *from, out of.*	**fiducia, -ae**, f., *self-confidence, boldness, courage, presumption.*
foris, *outside, without.*	**modo**, *even, merely.*
multitudo, -inis, f., *great number, multitude, crowd.*	**neque**, *and ... not.*
omnes, -ium, m., pl., *all men, all.*	**oppidum, -i**, n., *fortified town, city.*
peditatus, -us, m., *infantry.*	**plenus, -a, -um**, *full.*
possum, posse, potui, -----, *be able.*	**praesertim**, *especially, particularly.*
proelium, -i, n., *battle, combat, engagement.*	**proficiscor, -ficisci, -fectus**, *set out, depart, proceed.*
pugno, -are, -avi, -atus, *fight, combat, engage.*	**-que**, *and.*
qui, quae, quod, *who, which, what.*	**quisquam, -----, quidquam**, *anyone, anything, any.*
sum, esse, fui, futurus, *be.*	**sustineo, -tinere, -tinui, -tentus**, *bear, endure,*

withstand.

tantus, -a, -um, *so great, so large, such, so extensive.*

Omnes alacres et ... pleni: Nominative subject (A.G. 339). **Omnes**: Plural, masculine, nominative adjective used substantively (A.G. 288). **et**: The conjunction connects the two nominative adjectives modifying **Omnes** (A.G. 324.a). Two adjectives belonging to the same noun are regularly connected by a conjunction (A.G. 323.d).

fiduciae: Genitive with the adjective **pleni** (A.G. 409.a Note). "The noun *fiducia*, when it means 'a confident attitude with regard to an uncertainty', is thematically linked with disaster. In every instance the occurrence of the word is linked to those who are defeated." (Mannetter, 134). For *fiducia* in the *BC*, see Rowe.

ad Alesiam: Accusative of *place to which* with the preposition **ad**; **ad** with the name of a town denotes "towards, to the neighborhood of" (A.G. 428.a). **Alesiam**: See Appendix A.

proficiscuntur: The main verb of the coordinate clause **Omnes ... proficiscuntur** (A.G. 278.a).

neque: The conjunction here joins a negative clause to a preceding positive one and means "and ... not" (*OLD* **neque** 3).

erat: The main verb of the coordinate clause **erat ... cernerentur** (A.G. 278.a). The verb **sum** in the sense of "exist" makes a complete predicate without a predicate noun or adjective ("was there ..."). It is then called the substantive verb and regularly comes first (A.G. 284.b and 598.c).

omnium: Plural, masculine, genitive adjective used substantively (A.G. 288). Partitive genitive with **quisquam** (A.G. 346.a.1).

quisquam: Singular, masculine, nominative indefinite pronoun used substantively (A.G. 151.d). Nominative subject (A.G. 339).

qui ... arbitraretur: A relative clause of characteristic; a relative clause with the subjunctive is often used to indicate a characteristic of the antecedent (A.G. 535). **qui**: Singular, masculine, nominative relative pronoun used substantively (A.G. 305). The antecedent is **quisquam** (A.G. 307). Nominative subject (A.G. 339). **arbitraretur**: The main verb of the subordinate clause (A.G. 278.b). Imperfect subjunctive; the tense of the subjunctive is in secondary sequence and follows the rules for the sequence of tense after **erat** (A.G. 482-85).

aspectum ... posse: Accusative/infinitive construction in indirect discourse after **arbitraretur** (A.G. 577 ff.). **posse**: Present infinitive; the tense of the infinitive in indirect discourse is relative to that of the verb of saying (A.G. 584). The present infinitive **posse** often has a future sense (A.G. 584.b).

modo: Adverb (A.G. 320-21).

tantae multitudinis: Partitive genitive with **aspectum** (A.G. 346.a.1).

sustineri: Complementary infinitive after **posse** (A.G. 456).

praesertim: Adverb (A.G. 320-21 and 549 Note 1).

ancipiti proelio: Ablative absolute with an adjective (**ancipiti**) taking the place of the participle (there is no participle for "being") (A.G. 419.a-20). **ancipiti**: The ablative singular commonly ends in -**i** instead of -**e** in consonant stem adjectives (A.G. 121.a.3).

cum ... (id) pugnaretur ... cernerentur: Causal clause; the relative adverb **cum** ("when") with the indicative introduces an explanatory statement, and is sometimes equivalent to **quod** ("on the ground that") (A.G. 549.a). Here **cum** takes the subjunctive as it is a dependent clause in indirect discourse after **arbitraretur** (A.G. 580). **pugnaretur ... cernerentur**: The main verbs of the subordinate clause (A.G. 278.b). Imperfect subjunctives; the tense of the subjunctives is in secondary sequence and follows the rules for the sequence of tense after **erat** (A.G. 585). Here, the imperfect stands for the future tense in direct discourse (A.G. 484.b). Notice the asyndeton between the verbs (A.G. 323.b). **pugnaretur**: Impersonal use of the intransitive passive verb (A.G. 208.d). Supply **id** as the subject (A.G. 318.c).

ex oppido: Ablative of *place from which* with the preposition **ex** (A.G. 426.1).

eruptione: Ablative of means (A.G. 409).

foris: Adverb (A.G. 320-21).

tantae copiae: Nominative subject (A.G. 339).

equitatus peditatusque: Two partitive genitives with **copiae** (A.G. 346.a.1). -**que**: The enclitic conjunction connects the two genitive nouns (A.G. 324.a).

4.M CHAPTER 77: CRITOGNATUS' SPEECH INSIDE ALESIA URGING CANNIBALISM BEFORE SURRENDER

(77.1-2) At ei qui Alesiae obsidebantur, praeterita die qua auxilia suorum exspectaverant, consumpto omni frumento, inscii quid in Aeduis gereretur, concilio coacto de exitu suarum (2) fortunarum consultabant.

Aedui, -orum, m., pl., *the Aedui*

at, *but, but on the other hand.*

cogo, cogere, coegi, coactus, *bring together, collect, gather, assemble.*

consulto, -are, -avi, -atus, *deliberate, take council.*

de, *about, concerning.*

exitus, -us, m., *issue, event, outcome.*

fortuna, -ae, f., *lot, fate, chance, fortune.*

gero, gerere, gessi, gestus, *carry out, perform, do.*

inscius, -a, -um, *unknowing, not knowing, ignorant.*

obsideo, -sidere, -sedi, -sessus, *besiege, blockade.*

praetereo, -ire, -ivi, or **-ii, -itus**, *pass, go by, pass over.*

Alesia, -ae, f., *Alesia.*

auxilia, -orum, n., *auxiliary troops, auxiliaries, allied forces.*

concilium, -i, n., *meeting, assembly, council.*

consumo, -sumere, -sumpsi, -sumptus, *use up, eat up, consume.*

dies, -ei, m. and f., *day.*

exspecto, -are, -avi, -atus, *wait to see, wait for, await, expect.*

frumentum, -i, n., *grain.*

in, *among.*

is, ea, id, *he, she, it; that, this.*

omnis, -e, *all.*

qui, quae, quod, *who, which, what.*

quis, -----, quid, *who? what?*

suus, -a, -um, *their,* with or without *own.*

sui, -orum, m., pl., *their men,* with or without *own.*

At: Conjunction introducing a change of subject (A.G. 324.d) (*OLD* **at** 2).

ei: Plural, masculine, nominative demonstrative pronoun used substantively (A.G. 296.2). The pronoun is correlative to the relative clause **qui ... obsidebantur** (A.G. 297.d). Nominative subject of **exspectaverant ... consultabant** (A.G. 339).

qui ... obsidebantur: Relative clause (A.G. 303). **qui:** Plural, masculine, nominative relative pronoun used substantively (A. G. 305). The antecedent is **ei** (A.G. 307). Nominative subject (A.G. 339). **obsidebantur:** The main verb of the subordinate clause (A.G. 278.b).

Alesiae: Locative case of the city name **Alesia, -ae,** f. (A.G. 43.c). See Appendix A.

praeterita ... exspectaverant: Ablative absolute with a dependent clause.

praeterita die: Ablative absolute (A.G. 419-20). The ablative absolute is here replacing a causal clause (A.G. 420.2). **praeterita:** The perfect tense of the participle represents the action as completed at the time indicated by the tense of the main verb (A.G. 489). The perfect participle is used in an active sense (*OLD* **praetereo** 4). **die:** The noun **dies** is sometimes feminine in the singular, especially in phrases indicating a fixed time (A.G. 97.a).

qua ... exspectaverant: Relative clause (A.G. 303). Vercingetorix had told the horsemen in Chapter 71 that they could hold out for 30 days. **qua:** Singular, feminine, ablative relative pronoun used substantively (A.G. 305). The antecedent is **die** (A.G. 307). Ablative of *time when* (A.G. 423.1). **exspectaverant:** The main verb of the subordinate clause (A.G. 278.b). The pluperfect denotes an action completed in past time (A.G. 477).

auxilia: Accusative direct object of **exspectaverant** (A.G. 387).

suorum: Plural, masculine, genitive possessive pronoun used substantively to denote a special class (A.G. 302.d). Objective genitive with **auxilia** (A.G. 348).

consumpto omni frumento: Ablative absolute (A.G. 419-20). **consumpto:** The perfect tense of the participle represents the action as completed at the time indicated by the tense of the main verb (A.G. 489). Notice the asyndeton between the two ablative absolutes (A.G. 323.b).

inscii: Plural, masculine, nominative predicate adjective modifying **ei** (A.G. 285.2). Nominative subject (A.G. 339).

quid ... gereretur: Indirect question with the subjunctive; the phrase is the object of the adjective **inscii** (A.G. 573-75). **quid:** Singular, neuter, nominative interrogative pronoun used substantively (A.G. 148). Nominative subject (A.G. 339). **gereretur:** The main verb of the subordinate clause (A.G. 278.b). Imperfect subjunctive; the tense of the subjunctive is in secondary sequence and follows the rules for the sequence of tense for indirect question after **consultabant** (A.G. 575).

in Aeduis: Prepositional phrase, **in** with the ablative here means "among" (*OLD* **in** 29.b). **Alesia:** See Appendix A. "Where the army of relief had gathered." (Walker, 401)

concilio coacto: Ablative absolute (A.G. 419-20). **coacto:** The perfect tense of the participle represents the action as completed at the time indicated by the tense of the main verb (A.G. 489).

de exitu suarum fortunarum: Prepositional phrase, **de** with the ablative here means "about, concerning" (*OLD* **de** 12). **suarum fortunarum:** Possessive genitive with **exitu** (A.G. 343). **suarum:** Plural, feminine, genitive possessive pronoun used as an adjective modifying **fortunarum** (A.G. 302). **fortunarum:** The noun, when it means "what befalls or is destined to befall one, one's fate, destiny, fortunes", can be used in the plural (*OLD* **fortuna** 8).

consultabant: The main verb of the main clause (A.G. 278.b).

(77.2-3) Ac variis dictis sententiis, quarum pars deditionem, pars, dum vires suppeterent, eruptionem censebat, non praetereunda oratio Critognati videtur propter (3) eius singularem ac nefariam crudelitatem.

ac, *and thereupon; and.*

Critognatus, -i, m., *Critognatus.*

deditio, -onis, f., *surrender.*

dum, *while.*

is, ea, id, *he, she, it; that, this.*

non, *not.*

pars, partis, f., *part, party, faction.*

propter, *as a result* or *consequence of, in view of, because of.*

sententia, -ae, f., *opinion, view, notion, decision, judgment.*

suppeto, -petere, -petivi, -petitus, *hold out.*

videor, videri, visus sum, *seem, appear.*

censeo, -ere, -ui, -us, *propose, urge, argue.*

crudelitas, -tatis, f., *cruelty, barbarity.*

dico, dicere, dixi, dictus, *express.*

eruptio, -onis, f., *a bursting forth, sally, sortie.*

nefarius, -a, -um, *execrable, atrocious.*

oratio, -onis, f., *speech, words, address.*

praetereo, -ire, -ivi, or **-ii, -itus,** *pass, go by, pass over.*

qui, quae, quod, *who, which, what.*

singularis, -e, *singular, matchless, extraordinary.*

varius, -a, -um, *different, diverse, various.*

vires, -ium, f., *physical powers, strength.*

Ac: When the conjunction begins a sentence it means "and thereupon" (*OLD* **atque** 5.c).

variis dictis sententiis: Ablative absolute (A.G. 419-20). **dictis:** The perfect tense of the participle represents the action as completed at the time indicated by the tense of the main verb (A.G. 489).

quarum ... censebat: Relative clause (A.G. 303). **quarum:** Plural, feminine, genitive relative pronoun used substantively (A.G. 305). The antecedent is **sententiis** (A.G. 307). Partitive genitive with **pars** (A.G. 346.a.1). **censebat:** The main verb of the subordinate clause (A.G. 278.b). Two singular subjects (**pars ... pars**) normally take a verb in the plural (A.G. 317). Here they are considered as a single whole and so the verb is singular (A.G. 317.b).

pars: First nominative subject of **censebat** (A.G. 339).

deditionem: First accusative direct object of **censebat** (A.G. 387).

pars: Second nominative subject of **censebat** (A.G. 339).

dum ... suppeterent: Temporal clause; the conjunction **dum** (Awhile still) normally takes the indicative (*OLD* **dum2** 3). Here, **dum** (Awhile still (as they said)) takes the subjunctive since the reason is given on the authority of another (informal indirect discourse) (A.G. 592). **suppeterent**: The main verb of the subordinate clause (A.G. 278.b). Imperfect subjunctive; the tense of the subjunctive is in secondary sequence and follows the rules for the sequence of tense after **censebat** (A.G. 585).

vires: Nominative subject (A.G. 339).

eruptionem: Second accusative direct object of **censebat** (A.G. 387).

non ... crudelitatem: Adcock notes that "when one reads the speech one finds that the singular and nefarious cruelty plays a small part in it, and what one remembers is what Caesar may have meant his readers to remember - the difference between the transient raid of the Cimbri and Teutoni and the eternal yoke of iron which Rome and Caesar are placing on the necks of Gaul." (Adcock, 66).

non: Adverb modifying **praetereunda**, the negative precedes the word it especially effects (A.G. 217.e, 320-21, and 599.a).

praetereunda (esse): Singular, feminine, nominative gerundive used as a predicate adjective modifying **oratio** after **videtur** implying necessity (A.G. 283 and 500). A predicate adjective after a complementary infinitive takes the case of the subject of the main verb (A.G. 283-84, 458 and 500.1). Supply **esse** as the complementary infinitive.

oratio: Nominative subject (A.G. 339).

Critognati: Possessive genitive with **oratio** (A.G. 343). See Appendix A.

videtur: The main verb of the main clause (A.G. 278.b). The present tense is not the historical present but denotes a state as incomplete in present time (A.G. 465.2).

propter eius singularem ac nefariam crudelitatem: Prepositional phrase, **propter** with the accusative here means "as a result or consequence of, in view of, because of" (*OLD* **propter** 3). **eius**: Singular, feminine, genitive demonstrative pronoun used substantively (A.G. 296.2). The antecedent is **oratio** (A.G. 297.e). Possessive genitive with **crudelitatem** (A.G. 343). **ac**: The conjunction connects the two accusative adjectives modifying **crudelitatem** and means "and" (*OLD* **atque** 12). Two adjectives belonging to the same noun are regularly connected by a conjunction (A.G. 323.d).

(77.3-4) Hic, summo in Arvernis ortus loco et magnae habitus auctoritatis, 'nihil,' inquit 'de eorum sententia dicturus sum, qui turpissimam servitutem deditionis nomine appellant, neque hos habendos (4) civium loco neque ad concilium adhibendos censeo.

ad, *to*.	**adhibeo, -hibere, -hibui, -hibitus**, *summon, admit*.
appello, -are, -avi, -atus, *name, call*.	**Arverni, -orum**, m., pl., *the Arverni*.
auctoritas, -tatis, f., *prestige, authority, power*.	**censeo, -ere, -ui, -us**, *think, hold, judge*.
civis, -is, m., *citizen, fellow-citizen, countryman, free person*.	**concilium, -i**, n., *meeting, assembly, council*.
de, *about, concerning*.	**deditio, -onis**, f., *surrender*.
dico, dicere, dixi, dictus, *say*.	**et**, *and*.
habeo, habere, habui, habitus, *consider, account, repute, reckon*.	**hic, haec, hoc**, *this; he, she, it*.
in, *among*.	**inquam, inquis, inquit**, *say*.
is, ea, id, *he, she, it; that, this*.	**locus, -i**, m., (with gen.), *as*.
magnus, -a, -um, *great, large, considerable*.	**neque ... neque**, *neither ... nor*.
nihil, n., *nothing*.	**nomen, -inis**, n., (with gen.), *under the heading of, by way of, as*.
orior, oriri, ortus, *be born, arise, spring from*.	**qui, quae, quod**, *who, which, what*.
sententia, -ae, f., *opinion, view, notion, decision, judgment*.	**servitus, -tutis**, f., *slavery, bondage, subjection*.
summus, -a, -um, *highest, greatest, chief*.	**turpis, -e**, sup. **-issimus**, *disgraceful, shameful, base, dishonorable*.

Hic ... ortus ... habitus: Nominative subject of **inquit** (A.G. 339). **Hic**: Singular, masculine, nominative demonstrative pronoun used substantively (A.G. 296.2). The antecedent is **Critognati** (A.G. 297.e). The pronoun marks a change in subject to one previously mentioned (**Critognati**) (A.G. 601.d). **ortus**: Nominative, perfect, deponent participle used as a predicate, where in English a phrase or a subordinate clause would be more normal (A.G. 496). **habitus**: Nominative, perfect, passive participle used as a predicate, where in English a phrase or a subordinate clause would be more normal (A.G. 496). Here the verb **habere** means "consider, account, repute, reckon" (*OLD* **habeo** 24.b).

summo ... loco: Ablative of source; participles denoting birth (**ortus**) are followed by the ablative of source without a preposition (A.G. 403 and a). **summo**: Defective superlative adjective (A.G. 130.b).

in Arvernis: Prepositional phrase, **in** with the ablative here means "among" (*OLD* **in** 29.b). **Arvernis**: See Appendix A.

et: The conjunction connects the two participles **ortus ... habitus** (A.G. 324.a).

magnae ... auctoritatis: Genitive of quality (descriptive genitive) with an adjective modifier (A.G. 345).

nihil ... servitute (77.3-16): This speech, classified by Murphy as deliberative, is one of two passages that are direct discourse throughout (the other is in Chapter 38). Murphy contends that "The interesting point about both these speeches is the fact that Caesar couldn't have heard either one of them; his information about them came from someone else, presumably deserters or prisoners. Caesar therefore means us to understand that he is not giving the exact words of those speakers; he is, in fact, doing what later historians are to do with their material: i.e., he takes the substance of what was said and puts it into good rhetorical form. It may be that there is no more compelling reason for this than a simple desire for variety; but it may also be that Caesar is dropping a hint to future historians as to how to handle the speeches in his *Commentaries*." (C. Murphy, 122, 125) Sherwin-White believes that through Critognatus' critique of Roman imperial ambitions "Caesar is making his indictment of the past mistakes of Rome, and indicating the way in which he did not intend to organize his new conquests. His advice was very largely followed by his successors." (Sherwin-White, 43)

nihil ... censeo: Praeteritio.

nihil: Accusative direct object of **dicturus sum** (A.G. 387). Indeclinable noun, used only as nominative and accusative singular (A.G. 103.a).

inquit: The main verb of the main clause (A.G. 278.b). The verb **inquit** is used only in *oratio recta* introducing direct speech (A.G. 206.b and 578). It is always used parenthetically, following one or more words (A.G. 599.c). The historical present, giving vividness to the narrative, is present in Chapter 77 (A.G. 469). This usage, common in all languages, comes from imagining past events as going on before our eyes (*repraesentatio*) (A.G. 469 Note). Siedler counts 5 uses of direct speech with **inquit** in Book 7 (Siedler, 46).

de eorum sententia: Prepositional phrase, **de** with the ablative here means "about, concerning" (*OLD* **de** 12). **eorum:** Plural, masculine, genitive demonstrative pronoun used substantively (A.G. 296.2). The pronoun functions as a correlative to the relative clause **qui ... appellant** (A.G. 297.d). Possessive genitive with **sententia** (A.G. 343).

dicturus sum: The main verb of the coordinate clause **nihil ...dicturus sum** (A.G. 278.a). Present indicative of the first periphrastic (active) construction where the future active participle is combined with **sum** to denote a future or intended action (A.G. 194.a and 195). The personal pronoun **ego** is understood as the subject but is not expressed except for distinction or emphasis (A.G. 295.a). The present tense in *oratio recta* after **inquit** denotes an action as now taking place (A.G. 578). Therefore, the tense in *oratio recta* is the true present and not the historical present (A.G. 465.2).

qui ... appellant: Relative clause (A.G. 303). **qui:** Plural, masculine, nominative relative pronoun used substantively (A. G. 305). The antecedent is **eorum** (A.G. 307). Nominative subject (A.G. 339). **appellant:** The main verb of the subordinate clause (A.G. 278.b).

turpissimam servitutem: Accusative direct object of **appellant** (A.G. 387). **turpissimam:** Superlative adjective (A.G. 124). **servitutem:** Slavery is a theme in Critognatus' speech and each occurrence of **servitus** is modified by an adjective for emphasis: **turpissimam servitutem** (77.3), **perpetuae servituti** (77.10), **aeternam servitutem** (77.15), and **perpetua servitute** (77.16).

deditionis nomine: Ablative of quality (descriptive ablative) with a genitive modifier (A.G. 415). **nomine:** The noun **nomine** with the genitive means "under the heading of, by way of, as" (*OLD* **nomen** 24). **deditionis:** Appositional genitive, a limiting genitive is sometimes used instead of a noun in apposition (A.G. 343.d).

neque ... neque: The repeated conjunction means "neither ... nor", connecting the two indirect statements after **censeo** (*OLD* **neque** 7).

hos habendos (esse): Accusative/infinitive construction in indirect discourse after **censeo** (A.G. 577 ff.). **hos:** Plural, masculine, accusative demonstrative pronoun used substantively (A.G. 297.2). The antecedent is **qui** (A.G. 297.e). **habendos (esse):** Supply **esse** with the gerundive to form the second periphrastic (passive) present infinitive implying necessity (A.G. 194.b and 196). The tense of the infinitive in indirect discourse is relative to that of the verb of saying (A.G. 584).

civium loco: Ablative of quality (descriptive ablative) with a genitive modifier (A.G. 415). **civium:** Objective genitive (A.G. 348). "The Latin word, *cives*, usually indicates membership of an individual state or nation (*civitas*), but in this context must imply association with something more general and universal." (Hammond, 242) **loco:** The ablative of **locus** with the genitive means "as" (*OLD* **locus** 18.c).

(hos) adhibendos (esse): Accusative/infinitive construction in indirect discourse after **censeo** (A.G. 577 ff.). Carry down the pronoun **hos** as the accusative subject. **adhibendos (esse):** Supply **esse** with the gerundive to form the second periphrastic (passive) present infinitive implying necessity (A.G. 194.b and 196). The tense of the infinitive in indirect discourse is relative to that of the verb of saying (A.G. 584).

ad concilium: Accusative of *place to which* with the preposition **ad** (A.G. 426.2).

censeo: The main verb of the coordinate clause **neque ... censeo** (A.G. 278.a). The personal pronoun **ego** is understood as the subject but is not expressed except for distinction or emphasis (A.G. 295.a). Notice the asyndeton between the main verbs **dicturus sum ... censeo** (A.G. 323.b).

(77.4-5) Cum his mihi res sit qui eruptionem probant; quorum in consilio omnium vestrum consensu pristinae residere virtutis memoria (5) videtur.

consensus, -us, m., *united opinion, agreement, assent.*
cum, *with.*
eruptio, -onis, f., *a bursting forth, sally, sortie.*
in, *in.*
omnis, -e, *all.*
probo, -are, -avi, -atus, *approve, think highly of.*
res, rei, f., *matter, affair, business.*
sum, esse, fui, futurus, *be.*
videor, videri, visus sum, *seem, appear.*

consilium, -i, n., *advice, plan, design.*
ego, mei, *I, me, in my opinion.*
hic, haec, hoc, *this; he, she, it.*
memoria, -ae, f., *memory, recollection, remembrance.*
pristinus, -a, -um, *former, previous, earlier.*
qui, quae, quod, *who, which, what.*
resideo, -sidere, -sedi, -----, *remain behind, be left.*
vos, vestrum, *thou, you.*
virtus, -utis, f., *manliness, courage, bravery, valor, prowess.*

Cum his: Ablative of accompaniment with the preposition **cum** (A.G. 413). **his:** Plural, masculine, ablative demonstrative pronoun used substantively (A.G. 297.2). The pronoun is correlative to the relative clause **qui ... probant** (A.G. 297.d).

mihi: Singular, masculine, dative personal pronoun used substantively (A.G. 143 and 295). Dative of person judging, a weakened variety of the dative of reference. The dative is used of the person from whose point of view an opinion is stated and means "in my opinion" (A.G. 378).

res: Nominative subject (A.G. 339).

sit: The main verb of the main clause (A.G. 278.b). The hortatory subjunctive is used in the present tense to express an exhortation or command (A.G. 439).

qui ... probant: Relative clause (A.G. 303). qui: Plural, masculine, nominative relative pronoun used substantively (A.G. 305). The antecedent is his (A.G. 307). Nominative subject (A.G. 339). probant: The main verb of the subordinate clause (A.G. 278.b).

eruptionem: Accusative direct object of probant (A.G. 387).

quorum: Plural, masculine, genitive relative pronoun used substantively (A.G. 305). The antecedent is his (A.G. 307). Possessive genitive with consilio (A.G. 343). The relative does not introduce a relative clause but is a connecting relative; at the beginning of a clause the pronoun is often best rendered by a personal or demonstrative pronoun, with or without *and* (A.G. 308.f).

in consilio: Prepositional phrase, in with the ablative here means "in" (expressing an abstract location) (*OLD* in 26).

omnium vestrum consensu: Ablative of manner with a limiting adjective (A.G. 412). omnium vestrum: Possessive genitive (A.G. 343). vestrum: Second person, plural, genitive personal pronoun (A.G. 142-43). The form of the genitive of the personal pronoun is really the genitive of the possessive and so here is used substantively to denote a special class (A.G. 143.b Note and 302.d).

pristinae ... virtutis: Objective genitive after memoria (A.G. 345).

memoria: Nominative subject (A.G. 339).

residere: Complementary infinitive after videtur (A.G. 456).

videtur: The main verb of the simple sentence (A.G. 278.1).

(77.5) **Animi est ista mollitia, non virtus, paulisper inopiam ferre non posse. Qui se ultro morti offerant facilius reperiuntur quam qui dolorem patienter ferant.**

animus, -i, m., *mind, courage, spirit, temper, resolution.*
facile, comp. -ius, *easily, readily, with no trouble.*
inopia, -ae, f., *want, lack, need, scarcity.*
mollitia, -ae, f., *weakness, irresolution.*
non, *not.*

dolor, -oris, m., *grief, distress, vexation.*
fero, ferre, tuli, latus, *bear, endure, suffer.*
iste, ista, istud, *that* (in irony or scorn).
mors, mortis, f., *death.*
offero, -ferre, obtuli, oblatus, (with se), *expose one's self.*

patienter, *patiently.*
possum, posse, potui, -----, *be able.*
qui, quae, quod, *who, which, what.*
sui, sibi, se, or sese, nom. wanting, *themselves.*
ultro, *of one's own accord, voluntarily.*

paulisper, *for a short time, a little while.*
quam, *(rather) than.*
reperio, -perire, repperi, repertus, *find, discover.*
sum, esse, fui, futurus, *be.*
virtus, -utis, f., *manliness, courage, bravery, valor.*

Animi: Possessive genitive with mollitia (A.G. 343).

ista: Nominative subject (A.G. 339). Singular, feminine, nominative demonstrative pronoun used substantively (A.G. 296.2). The pronoun agrees with the predicate noun mollitia (A.G. 297.e). One would expect istud, a neuter in apposition to posse, but the pronoun is attracted to mollitia. The pronoun frequently implies antagonism or contempt (A.G. 297.c).

mollitia: First nominative predicate noun after est (A.G. 284). Animi ... mollitia: The phrase is an idiom that means "weakness of mind or character, effeminacy, cowardice" (*OLD* mollitia 6).

non virtus: An ellipsis for ista est non virtus (A.G. 640).

non: Adverb modifying virtus, the negative precedes the word it especially effects (A.G. 217.e, 320-21, and 599.a).

virtus: Second nominative predicate noun after est (A.G. 284).

paulisper: Adverb (A.G. 320-21).

inopiam: Accusative direct object of the infinitive ferre (A.G. 387 and 451.3).

ferre: Complementary infinitive after posse (A.G. 456).

non: Adverb, the adverb generally precedes the verb if it belongs to no one word in particular (A.G. 217.e, 320-21, and 599.a).

posse: The infinitive is in apposition to the pronoun ista "this, not to be able ..." (A.G. 452.2).

Qui ... offerant: A relative clause of characteristic; a relative clause with the subjunctive is often used to indicate a characteristic of the antecedent (A.G. 535). qui: Plural, masculine, nominative relative pronoun used substantively (A.G. 305). The antecedent is omitted, supply ei (A.G. 307.c). Nominative subject (A.G. 339). offerant: The main verb of the subordinate clause (A.G. 278.b). Present subjunctive; the tense of the subjunctive is in primary sequence and follows the rules for the sequence of tense after reperiuntur (A.G. 482-85).

se: Plural, masculine, accusative direct reflexive pronoun (A.G. 300.1). The antecedent is qui, the subject of offerant (A.G. 299). Accusative direct object of the transitive verb offerant (A.G. 387).

ultro: Adverb (A.G. 215.4 and 320-21).

morti: Dative indirect object of the transitive verb offerant (A.G. 362).

facilius ... quam: The comparative adverb facilius is followed by quam, meaning "easier than", and compares two things in the same case (qui ... qui) (A.G. 407) (*OLD* plus2). facilius: Comparative adverb (A.G. 218 and 320-21). quam: Relative adverb (*OLD* quam 8).

reperiuntur: The main verb of the main clause (A.G. 278.b).

qui ... ferant: A relative clause of characteristic; a relative clause with the subjunctive is often used to indicate a characteristic of the antecedent (A.G. 535). qui: Plural, masculine, nominative relative pronoun used substantively (A.G. 305). The antecedent is omitted, supply ei (A.G. 307.c). Nominative subject (A.G. 339). ferant: The main verb of the subordinate clause (A.G. 278.b). Present subjunctive; the tense of the subjunctive is in primary sequence and follows the rules for the sequence of tense after reperiuntur (A.G. 482-85).

dolorem: Accusative direct object of **ferant** (A.G. 387).

patienter: Adverb (A.G. 320-21). The phrase **patienter ferre** is an idiom that means "to tolerate" (*OLD* **patienter**).

(77.6-8) **(6) Atque ego hanc sententiam probarem (tantum apud me dignitas potest), si nullam praeterquam vitae nostrae (7) iacturam fieri viderem; sed in consilio capiendo omnem Galliam respiciamus, quam ad nostrum auxilium concitavi(8)mus.**

ad, *for, for the purpose of.*

atque, *and yet.*
capio, capere, cepi, captus, *choose, select, enter into, take up.*
consilium, -i, n., *plan, policy, strategy.*
ego, mei, *I, me.*

Gallia, -ae, f., *Gaul.*
iactura, -ae, f., *loss, sacrifice, cost.*
nos, nostrum, *we, us.*
nullus, -a, -um, *no, not any.*
possum, posse, potui, -----, *to have power, influence, importance.*
probo, -are, -avi, -atus, *approve, think highly of.*
respicio, -spicere, -spexi, -spectus, *look at, consider.*
sententia, -ae, f., *opinion, view, notion, decision, judgment.*
tantum, *this much.*

vita, -ae, f., *life.*

apud, *in the opinion* or *estimation of, in the eyes of, with.*
auxilium, -i, n., *help, aid, assistance, relief.*
concito, -are, -avi, -atus, *rouse, stir up, excite, provoke.*
dignitas, -tatis, f., *greatness, rank, reputation.*
fio, fieri, factus, *take place, happen, come about, come to pass.*
hic, haec, hoc, *this; he, she, it.*
in, *in.*
noster, -tra, -trum, *our, our own.*
omnis, -e, *all.*
praeterquam, *apart from, beyond, except.*
qui, quae, quod, *who, which, what.*
sed, *but.*
si, *if.*
video, videre, visi, visus, *see, perceive, observe, understand.*

Atque: The conjunction here has an aversive sense and means "and yet" (*OLD* **atque** 9).

ego: Singular, masculine, nominative personal pronoun used substantively (A.G. 143). Nominative subject of **probarem ... viderem** (A.G. 339). The personal pronoun is not normally expressed except, as here, for distinction or emphasis (A.G. 295.a).

hanc sententiam: Accusative direct object of **probarem** (A.G. 387). **hanc**: Singular, feminine, accusative demonstrative pronoun used as an adjective modifying **sententiam** (A.G. 297.1 and a).

probarem ... si ... viderem: Conditional statement: contrary to fact, present time (imperfect subjunctive in both clause) (A.G. 514.C.1).

probarem: The main verb of the apodosis of the conditional statement (A.G. 512). The main verb of the main clause (A.G. 278.b).

tantum ... potest: Parenthetical remark (A.G. 278.b).

tantum: Singular, neuter, accusative pronoun (neuter of **tantus**) meaning "this much" (at any rate) (*OLD* **tantum** 2.b). A cognate accusative with **potest** (A.G. 390.c).

apud me: Prepositional phrase, **apud** with the accusative here means "in the opinion or estimation of, in the eyes of, with" (*OLD* **apud** 12). **me**: Singular, masculine, accusative personal pronoun used substantively (A.G. 143 and 295).

dignitas: Nominative subject (A.G. 339).

potest: The main verb of the subordinate clause (A.G. 278.b). A clause dependent on a subjunctive clause (**probarem**) normally takes the subjunctive (attraction) (A.G. 593). However, when a dependent clause is not regarded as a necessary logical part of the clause, the indicative is used. The indicative serves to emphasize the fact, as true independently of the statement contained in the subjunctive clause (A.G. 593.a Note 1). The verb **posse**, used without a complementary infinitive, means "to have power, influence, importance" (*OLD* **possum** 8).

si ... viderem: The conjunction **si** ("if") with the subjunctive forms the protasis of the conditional statement (A.G. 512). **viderem**: The main verb of the subordinate clause (A.G. 278.b).

nullam ... iacturam fieri: Accusative/infinitive construction in indirect discourse after **viderem** (A.G. 577 ff.). **fieri**: Present infinitive; the tense of the infinitive in indirect discourse is relative to that of the verb of saying (A.G. 584).

praeterquam vitae nostrae (iacturam): The conjunction **praeterquam** ("apart from, beyond, except") introduces a syntactically conforming phrase with a slight ellipsis (*OLD* **praeterquam** 3.b). **vitae nostrae**: Objective genitive with the supplied noun **iacturam** (A.G. 348). **nostrae**: Singular, feminine, genitive possessive pronoun used as an adjective modifying **vitae** (A.G. 302). **iacturam**: Use the noun two times to fill the ellipsis (A.G. 640).

sed: Coordinate conjunction (A.G. 324.d).

in consilio capiendo: Prepositional phrase, **in** with the ablative here means "in" (given circumstances) (*OLD* **in** 40). **capiendo**: Singular, neuter, ablative gerundive modifying **consilio** used after the preposition **in** (A.G. 507.3).

omnem Galliam: Accusative direct object of **respiciamus** (A.G. 387). **Galliam**: See Appendix A. Notice that all three usages of the noun **Gallia** in Critognatus' speech are in the accusative (77.7, 77.9 and 77.16). This mirrors the fact that Gaul is not active, but reactive.

respiciamus: The main verb of the main clause (A.G. 278.b). Present subjunctive; the hortatory subjunctive (jussive) is used in the present tense to express an exhortation or command (A.G. 439). The personal pronoun **nos** is understood as the subject but is not expressed except for distinction or emphasis (A.G. 295.a).

quam ... concitavimus: Relative clause (A.G. 303). **quam**: Singular, feminine, accusative relative pronoun used substantively (A.G. 305). The antecedent is **Galliam** (A.G. 307). Accusative direct object of **concitavimus** (A.G. 387). **concitavimus**: The main verb of the subordinate clause (A.G. 278.b). The personal pronoun **nos** is understood as the subject but is not expressed except for distinction or emphasis (A.G. 295.a).

ad nostrum auxilium: Prepositional phrase, **ad** with the accusative here implies purpose and means "for, for the purpose of" (*OLD* **ad** 44). **nostrum:** First person, plural, genitive personal pronoun (A.G. 142-43). The form of the genitive of the personal pronoun is really the genitive of the possessive and so here is used substantively to denote a special class (A.G. 143.b Note and 302.d). Objective genitive with **auxilium**; the form **nostri** is normally objective and **nostrum** partitive, but not always (A.G. 295.b, esp. Note 1). See also **nostrum impetrum** at 46.3.

(77.8) Quid hominum milibus LXXX uno loco interfectis propinquis consanguineisque nostris animi fore existimatis, si paene in ipsis cadaveribus proelio decertare cogentur?

animus, -i, m., *mind, courage, spirit, temper, resolution.*
cogo, cogere, coegi, coactus, *compel, force, oblige.*
decerto, -are, -avi, -atus, *fight to a finish, fight it out, fight a decisive battle.*
homo, hominis, m., *man, person.*
interficio, -ficere, -feci, -fectus, *slay, kill.*
L, in expression of number, *50.*
milia, -um, n., pl., *thousand, thousands.*
paene, *almost, nearly.*
propinqui, -orum, m., pl., *relatives, kinfolk.*
quis, -----, quid, *who? what?*
sum, esse, fui, futurus, *be.*
X, in expression of number, = *10.*

cadaver, -eris, n., *corpse, dead body.*
consanguinei, -orum, m., pl., *kinsfolk, blood-relations.*
existimo, -are, -avi, -atus, *think, consider, judge.*
in, *on.*
ipse, -a, -um, *the very* (corpses) *themselves.*
locus, -i, m., *place, location.*
noster, -tra, -trum, *our, our own.*
proelium, -i, n., *battle, combat, engagement.*
-que, *and.*
si, *if.*
unus, -a, -um, *one.*

Quid ... fore ... si ... cogentur: Conditional statement in indirect discourse after **existimatis** (A.G. 589). The protasis, as a dependent clause, is in the subjunctive and the apodosis, as the principal clause, is in the infinitive (A.G. 589).
Quid ... fore: The apodosis of the conditional statement (A.G. 589.2). Accusative/infinitive construction in indirect discourse after **existimatis** (A.G. 577 ff.). **Quid:** Singular, neuter, accusative interrogative pronoun used substantively (A.G. 148). **fore:** Future, active infinitive of **sum** (A.G. 170.a). The tense of the infinitive in indirect discourse is relative to that of the verb of saying (A.G. 584).
hominum milibus LXXX uno loco interfectis: Ablative absolute (A.G. 419-20). **hominum:** Partitive genitive with **milibus** (A.G. 346.a.2). **milibus:** Ablative plural; in the plural **mille** declines as a neuter noun (A.G. 134.d). **LXXX:** Roman numeral used as an adjective modifying **milibus** (A.G. 133). This represents the total number of Gallic soldiers at Alesia. See 71.3-4. **uno loco:** Ablative of *place where* without a preposition (A.G. 429.1-2). **uno:** Declinable cardinal number used as an adjective (A.G. 132-35).
interfectis: The perfect tense of the participle represents the action as completed at the time indicated by the tense of the main verb (A.G. 489).
propinquis consanguineisque nostris: Two datives of possession with **fore** (A.G. 373). **propinquis:** Plural, masculine, dative adjective used substantively (A.G. 288) (*OLD* **propinquus** 4.b). **-que:** The enclitic conjunction connects the two dative nouns (A.G. 324.a). **nostris:** Plural, masculine, dative possessive pronoun used as an adjective modifying both **propinquis** and **consanguineis** (A.G. 302).
animi: Partitive genitive with **Quid** (A.G. 346.a.3).
existimatis: The main verb of the main clause (A.G. 278.b). The personal pronoun **vos** is understood as the subject but is not expressed except for distinction or emphasis (A.G. 295.a).
si ... cogentur: The conjunction **si** ("if") with the subjunctive forms the protasis of a conditional statement in indirect discourse (A.G. 589.1). **cogentur:** The main verb of the subordinate clause (A.G. 278.b). Present subjunctive; the tense of the subjunctive is in primary sequence and follows the rules for the sequence of tense after **existimatis** (A.G. 482-85). The pronoun **ei**, with **propinquis consanguineisque nostris** as the antecedent, is understood as the subject (A.G. 271.a).
paene: Adverb (A.G. 217.c and 320-21).
in ipsis cadaveribus: Ablative of *place where* with the preposition **in** (locative ablative) (A.G. 426.3). **ipsis:** Plural, neuter, ablative demonstrative pronoun used as an emphatic adjective modifying **cadaveribus** meaning "The very ... themselves (A.G. 296.1 and a and 298.c).
proelio: Ablative of *place where* without a preposition (A.G. 429.1).
decertare: Complementary infinitive after **cogentur** (A.G. 456 and 566.c).

(77.9-10) (9) Nolite hos vestro auxilio exspoliare, qui vestrae salutis causa suum periculum neglexerunt, nec stultitia ac temeritate vestra aut animi imbecillitate omnem Galliam prosternere (10) et perpetuae servituti subicere.

ac, *and.*
aut, *or.*
causa, -ae, f., abl. with the gen., *for the sake of, for the purpose of.*
exspolio, -are, -avi, -atus, *deprive, rob.*
hic, haec, hoc, *this; he, she, it.*
nec, *and ... not.*

nolo, nolle, nolui, -----, (imper. **nolite** with inf.), *do not.*

animus, -i, m., *mind, courage, spirit, temper, resolution.*
auxilium, -i, n., *help, aid, assistance.*
et, *and.*
Gallia, -ae, f., *Gaul.*
imbecillitas, -atis, f., *weakness, feebleness.*
neglego, -legere, -lexi, -lectus, *disregard, be indifferent to, neglect.*
omnis, -e, *all, the whole of.*

periculum, -i, n., *risk, danger, hazard.*
prosterno, -sternere, -stravi, -stratus, *overthrow, destroy.*
salus, -utis, f., *welfare, safety, deliverance.*
stultitia, -ae, f., *folly, lack of foresight.*
suus, -a, -um, *their,* with or without *own.*
vester, -tra, -trum, *your, yours.*

perpetuus, -a, -um, *perpetual, lasting, permanent.*
qui, quae, quod, *who, which, what.*
servitus, -tutis, f., *slavery, bondage, subjection.*
subicio, -icere, -ieci, -iectus, *make subject.*
temeritas, -tatis, f., *rashness, hastiness.*

Nolite ... exspoliare ... prosternere ... subicere: The plural prohibition (negative command) is expressed by **nolite** with the infinitive (A.G. 450.1). **Nolite**: Plural imperative of **nolle** (A.G. 199). The personal pronoun **vos** is understood as the subject but is not expressed except for distinction or emphasis (A.G. 295.a). This is the only example of a negative imperative in Book 7.
hos: Plural, masculine, accusative demonstrative pronoun used substantively (A.G. 297.2). The pronoun is correlative to the relative clause **qui ... neglexerunt** (A.G. 297.d). Accusative direct object of the infinitive **exspoliare** (A.G. 387 and 451.3).
vestro ... vestrae ... vestra: Notice how the repetition of the possessive adjective creates a direct link with the audience and makes them part of the speech.
vestro auxilio: Ablative of separation after the compound infinitive **exspoliare** (A.G. 402). **vestro**: Singular, neuter, ablative possessive pronoun used as an adjective modifying **auxilio** (A.G. 302).
qui ... neglexerunt: Relative clause (A.G. 303). **qui**: Plural, masculine, nominative relative pronoun used substantively (A. G. 305). The antecedent is **hos** (A.G. 307). Nominative subject (A.G. 339). **neglexerunt**: The main verb of the subordinate clause (A.G. 278.b).
vestrae salutis causa: A preceding genitive with the ablative of **causa** means "for the sake of" A (A.G. 359.b and 404.c). **vestrae**: Singular, feminine, genitive possessive pronoun used as an adjective modifying **salutis** (A.G. 302).
suum periculum: Accusative direct object of **neglexerunt** (A.G. 387). **suum**: Singular, neuter, accusative possessive pronoun used as an adjective modifying **periculum** (A.G. 302).
nec: The conjunction joins a negative clause to a preceding positive one and means "and ... not" (*OLD* **neque** 3). A general negation (**nolite**) is not destroyed by the conjunction **neque** introducing a coordinate member (A.G. 327.3).
stultitia ac temeritate vestra aut ... imbecillitate: Three ablatives of cause (A.G. 404). **ac**: The conjunction connects the first two ablative nouns and means "and" (*OLD* **atque** 12). **vestra**: Singular, feminine, ablative possessive pronoun used as an adjective agreeing with **temeritate**, but it should be construed with all three nouns (A.G. 286.a and 302). **aut**: The conjunction connects the first two ablative with the third and excludes the alternative (A.G. 324.e). Notice the switch in the conjunction from "and" to "or" (*OLD* **atque** 12.b).
animi: Possessive genitive with **imbecillitate** (A.G. 343).
omnem Galliam: Accusative direct object of both infinitives **prosternere ... subicere** (A.G. 387 and 451.3). **Galliam**: See Appendix A.
et: The conjunction connects the two infinitives **prosternere ... subicere** (A.G. 324.a).
perpetuae servituti: Dative indirect object of the transitive verb **subicere** (A.G. 362). **servituti**: See **servitutem** at 77.3.

(77.10-11) An, quod ad diem non venerunt, de eorum fide constantiaque dubitatis? Quid ergo? Romanos in illis ulterioribus munitionibus animine (11) causa cotidie exerceri putatis?

ad, *to, on.*
animus, -i, m., *amusement, diversion, pleasure.*

constantia, -ae, f., *firmness, resolution.*
de, *about, concerning.*
dubito, -are, -avi, -atus, *be uncertain, doubt.*
exerceo, -ercere, -ercui, -ercitus, *keep employed* or *busy, occupy.*
ille, illae, illud, *that; he, she, it.*
is, ea, id, *he, she, it; that, this.*

-ne, *?.*
puto, -are, -avi, -atus, *think, consider, believe, judge.*
quis, -----, quid, *who?, what?*
Romani, -orum, m., pl., *the Romans.*
venio, venire, veni, ventus, *come.*

an, *can it really be that, or, or indeed.*
causa, -ae, f., abl. with the gen., *for the sake of, for the purpose of.*
cotidie, *daily, every day.*
dies, -ei, m. and f., *day.*
ergo, *therefore, then.*
fides, -is, f., *good faith, fidelity, loyalty.*
in, *in.*
munitio, -onis, f., *works of fortifications, entrenchment, defenses.*
non, *not.*
-que, *and.*
quod, *because, since, for, as.*
ulterior, -ius, *farther, more remote* or *distant, outer.*

An: The particle introduces a direct question with the notion of surprise, indignation, etc. meaning "can it really be that ..." (*OLD* **an** 1) (A.G. 330.1). This is an example of a rhetorical question in direct speech (see Siedler, 46).
quod ... venerunt: Causal clause; the conjunction **quod** ("because") takes the indicative when the reason is given on the authority of the writer or speaker (A.G. 540.1). **venerunt**: The main verb of the subordinate clause (A.G. 278.b). The pronoun **ei**, with **hos** (the relief army) as the antecedent, is understood as the subject (A.G. 271.a).
ad diem: Prepositional phrase, **ad** with the accusative of **dies** expresses time and means "on the right day, promptly" (*OLD* **ad** 21.c).
diem: The noun **dies** is normally masculine gender (A.G. 97.a).
non: Adverb, the adverb generally precedes the verb if it belongs to no one word in particular (A.G. 217.e, 320-21, and 599.a).
de eorum fide constantiaque: Prepositional phrase, **de** with the ablative here means "about, concerning" (*OLD* **de** 12). **eorum**:

Plural, masculine, genitive demonstrative pronoun used substantively (A.G. 296.2). The antecedent is **hos** (the relief army) (A.G. 297.e). Possessive genitive; it should be construed with both nouns (A.G. 343). **fide constantiaque**: Compare these qualities to those he has just mentioned: **stultitia ac temeritate vestra aut animi imbecillitate**. **-que**: The enclitic conjunction connects the two ablative nouns in the prepositional phrase (A.G. 324.a).

dubitatis: The main verb of the main clause (A.G. 278.b). The personal pronoun **vos** is understood as the subject but is not expressed except for distinction or emphasis (A.G. 295.a).

Quid ergo (est)?: Supply **est** to form a rhetorical question inviting the hearer or reader to draw a conclusion (*OLD* **ergo** 2.b). **Quid**: Singular, neuter, nominative interrogative pronoun used substantively (A.G. 148). Nominative subject (A.G. 339). **ergo**: Adverb (A.G. 217.c and 320-21).

Romanos ... exerceri: Accusative/infinitive construction in indirect discourse after **putatis** (A.G. 577 ff.). **exerceri**: Present infinitive; the tense of the infinitive in indirect discourse is relative to that of the verb of saying (A.G. 584).

in illis ulterioribus munitionibus: Ablative of *place where* with the preposition **in** (locative ablative) (A.G. 426.3). **illis**: Plural, feminine, ablative demonstrative pronoun used as an adjective modifying **munitionibus** (A.G. 296.1 and a). **ulterioribus**: Defective comparative adjective (A.G. 130.a). This refers to the fortifications facing outward, towards the relief army, which are not yet complete.

animine causa: A preceding genitive with the ablative of **causa** means "for the sake of" A (A.G. 359.b and 404.c). **-ne**: An interrogative particle in direct question, attached to the emphatic word; it does not imply anything about the answer expected, though this may be clear from the context (as here) (*OLD* **-ne** 1). **animi causa**: The phrase is an idiom that means "for one's own gratification" (*OLD* **animus** 8.b).

cotidie: Adverb (A.G. 217.b and 320-21).

putatis: The main verb of the main clause (A.G. 278.b). The personal pronoun **vos** is understood as the subject but is not expressed except for distinction or emphasis (A.G. 295.a).

(77.11-12) Si illorum nuntiis confirmari non potestis omni aditu praesaepto, his utimini testibus appropinquare eorum adventum; cuius rei timore exterriti (12) diem noctemque in opere versantur. Quid ergo mei consili est?

aditus, -us, m., *approach, access, way of approach, means of access.*

appropinquo, -are, -avi, -atus, *approach, come near, draw near.*

consilium, -i, n., *counsel, advice.*

ergo, *therefore, then.*

hic, haec, hoc, *this; he, she, it.*

in, *in.*

meus, -a, -um, *my, mine.*

nox, noctis, f., *night.*

omnis, -e, *all, every.*

possum, posse, potui, -----, *be able.*

-que, *and.*

quis, -----, quid, *who?, what?*

si, *if.*

testis, -is, m., *witness.*

utor, uti, usus, *use, employ, have.*

adventus, -us, m., *coming, approach, arrival.*

confirmo, -are, -avi, -atus, *reassure, encourage.*

dies, -ei, m. and f., *day.*

exterreo, -ere, -ui, -itus, *frighten, strike with terror.*

ille, illae, illud, *that; he, she, it.*

is, ea, id, *he, she, it; that, this.*

non, *not.*

nuntius, -i, m., *message, tidings,* or *messenger, courier.*

opus, operis, n., *works, line of works, fortification.*

praesaepio, -saepsire, -saepsi, -saeptus, *fence in, block up.*

qui, quae, quod, *who, which, what.*

res, rei, f., *fact, circumstance, occurrence, situation.*

sum, esse, fui, futurus, *be.*

timor, -oris, m., *fear, dread, apprehension, alarm, timidity.*

versor, -ari, -atus, *be occupied, engaged, employed, busy.*

Si ... potestis ... utimini: Conditional statement: simple condition, present time (present indicative in the protasis, a present imperative in the apodosis) (A.G. 514.a.1 and 515.a).

si ... potestis: The conjunction **si** ("if") with the indicative forms the protasis of the conditional statement (A.G. 512 and 515).

potestis: The main verb of the subordinate clause (A.G. 278.b). The personal pronoun **vos** is understood as the subject but is not expressed except for distinction or emphasis (A.G. 295.a).

illorum: Plural, masculine, genitive demonstrative pronoun used substantively (A.G. 296.2). The antecedent is **eorum** (the relief army) (A.G. 297.e). Objective genitive with **nuntiis** (A.G. 348).

nuntiis: Ablative of means (A.G. 409).

confirmari: Complementary infinitive after **potestis** (A.G. 456).

non: Adverb, the adverb generally precedes the verb if it belongs to no one word in particular (A.G. 217.e, 320-21, and 599.a).

omni aditu praesaepto: Ablative absolute (A.G. 419-20). The ablative absolute is here replacing a causal clause (A.G. 420.2).

praesaepto: The perfect tense of the participle represents the action as completed at the time indicated by the tense of the main verb (A.G. 489).

his: Plural, masculine, ablative demonstrative pronoun used substantively (A.G. 296.2). The antecedent is **Romanos** (A.G. 297.e). Ablative direct object of the deponent verb **utimini** (A.G. 410).

utimini: The main verb of the apodosis of the conditional statement (A.G. 512 and 515). The main verb of the main clause (A.G. 278.b). Plural deponent imperative (A.G. 190). The personal pronoun **vos** is understood as the subject but is not expressed except for distinction or emphasis (A.G. 295.a). Siedler counts 7 uses of the imperative in Book 7 (none by Caesar himself) (Siedler, 46).

testibus: Plural, masculine, ablative predicate noun which describes **his** and means "as witnesses" (A.G. 283).

appropinquare ... adventum: Accusative/infinitive construction in indirect discourse (A.G. 577 ff.). The verb of saying is not expressed, but implied in the word **testibus** (A.G. 580.a). **appropinquare**: Present infinitive; the tense of the infinitive in indirect discourse is relative to that of the verb of saying (A.G. 584). **adventum**: "Emphatic by position." (Kelsey, 429)

eorum: Plural, masculine, genitive demonstrative pronoun used substantively (A.G. 296.2). The antecedent is **hos** (the relief army) (A.G. 297.e). Possessive genitive with **adventum** (A.G. 343).

cuius rei: Objective genitive with **timore** (A.G. 348). **cuius**: Singular, feminine, genitive relative pronoun (A.G. 305). The antecedent is **rei** in its own clause (adjectival use) (A.G. 307.b). The relative does not introduce a relative clause but is a connecting relative; at the beginning of a clause the pronoun is often best rendered by a personal or demonstrative pronoun, with or without *and* (A.G. 308.f).

timore: Ablative of cause without a preposition (A.G. 404).

exterriti: Nominative perfect, passive participle used as a predicate, where in English a phrase or a subordinate clause would be more normal (A.G. 496). The pronoun **ei**, with **Romanos** as the antecedent, is understood. Nominative subject (A.G. 339).

diem noctemque: Two accusatives of *extent of time* (A.G. 423.2). **diem**: The noun **dies** is normally masculine gender (A.G. 97.a). **-que**: The enclitic conjunction connects the two accusative nouns (A.G. 324.a).

in opere: Ablative of *place where* with the preposition **in** (locative ablative) (A.G. 426.3).

versantur: The main verb of the simple sentence (A.G. 278.1).

quid ergo ... est: A rhetorical question inviting the hearer or reader to draw a conclusion (*OLD* ergo 2.b). **Quid**: Singular, neuter, nominative interrogative pronoun used substantively (A.G. 148). Nominative subject (A.G. 339). **ergo**: Adverb (A.G. 217.c and 320-21).

mei consili: Partitive genitive with **Quid** (A.G. 346.a.3). **mei**: Singular, neuter, genitive possessive pronoun used as an adjective modifying **consili** (A.G. 302). **consili**: The singular genitive of nouns in **-ium** ended, until the Augustan Age, in a single **-i** (A.G. 49.b).

est: The main verb of the simple sentence (A.G. 278.1).

(77.12-13) Facere, quod nostri maiores nequaquam pari bello Cimbrorum Teutonumque fecerunt; qui in oppida compulsi ac simili inopia subacti eorum corporibus qui aetate ad bellum inutiles videbantur vitam toleraverunt **(13)** neque se hostibus tradiderunt.

ac, *and.*	**ad**, *for, in.*
aetas, -tatis, f., *age.*	**bellum, -i**, n., *war, warfare.*
Cimbri, -orum, m., pl., *the Cimbri.*	**compello, -pellere, -puli, -pulsus**, *collect, drive.*
corpus, -oris, n., *body, flesh.*	**facio, facere, feci, factus**, *do.*
hostis, -is, m., *enemy, foe*; pl., *the enemy.*	**in**, *into.*
inopia, -ae, f., *want, lack, need, scarcity.*	**inutilis, -e**, *useless, unserviceable, of no use.*
is, ea, id, *he, she, it; that, this.*	**maiores, -um**, m., pl., *forefathers, ancestors, forebears.*
nequaquam, *not at all, by no means.*	**neque**, *and ... not.*
noster, -tra, -trum, *our, our own.*	**oppidum, -i**, n., *fortified town, city.*
par, paris, *like, similar, same, equal.*	**-que**, *and.*
qui, quae, quod, *who, which, what.*	**similis, -e**, *like, similar.*
subigo, -igere, -egi, -actus, *constrain, confront.*	**sui, sibi, se**, or **sese**, nom. wanting, *themselves.*
Teutoni, -um, m., pl., *the Teutons.*	**tolero, -are, -avi, -atus**, *support, sustain, maintain.*
trado, -dere, -didi, -ditus, *hand over, give up, deliver, surrender.*	**videor, videri, visus sum**, *seem, appear.*
vita, -ae, f., *life.*	

Facere: An infinitive used in apposition to **Quid** (A.G. 452.2). Kelsey suggests supplying "*meum consilium est* to fill in the ellipsis. (Kelsey, 429)

quod ... fecerunt: Relative clause (A.G. 303). **quod**: Singular, neuter, accusative relative pronoun used substantively (A.G. 305). The antecedent is omitted, supply **id** (A.G. 307.c). Accusative direct object of **fecerunt** (A.G. 387). **fecerunt**: The main verb of the subordinate clause (A.G. 278.b).

nostri maiores: Nominative subject (A.G. 339). **nostri**: Plural, masculine, nominative possessive pronoun used as an adjective modifying **maiores** (A.G. 302). **maiores**: Irregular comparative adjective used substantively meaning "ancestors, forebears" (A.G. 129 and 291.c Note 3) (*OLD* **maior** 3.b).

nequaquam: Adverb (320-21).

pari bello: Ablative of *time when* (A.G. 423.1).

Cimbrorum Teutonumque: Two objective genitives after **bello** (A.G. 348). The genitive expresses opponents after **bellum** (*OLD* **bellum** 2.b). **Cimbrorum**: See Appendix A. **-que**: The enclitic conjunction connects the two genitive nouns (A.G. 324.a).

Teutonum: See Appendix A. In the *BG*, the **Cimbri** and **Teutoni** are always mentioned together; see *BG* 1.33, 40; 2.4, 29; 7.77. "They had ravaged Gaul and parts of Spain before they were cut off by Marius." (Kelsey, 429) "It was not Celtic tribes but Germans coming from further afield, the Cimbri and Teutoni, who in 109-101 B.C. invaded the Transalpine province, defeated three Roman armies, and finally were defeated by Marius, the Teutoni at Aix-en-Provence and the Cimbri in northern Italy at Vercellae." (Gardner, 181) Stevens claims that the use of the name here is to remind the reader that "he is not to forget the Cimbri and Teutones who are mentioned wherever relevant and even dragged into the rather tasteless speech in *oratio recta* put into the mouth of an Arvernian shut up in Alesia. Caesar has saved Rome - Cicero had made that clear - from repetitions of that alarm. And a trick can be picked up in praise not only of Marius, the family connection, but of Marius' army. Caesar is the political heir of Marius, his army the military heirs of the military machine that Marius made." (Stevens, 7) See also Ballston.

qui ... toleraverunt: Notice the desperation implied here. They are not sustaining life on the flesh of those who have died, but they are actually killing the old or young in order to eat them. This must have been an astonishingly gruesome scene.

qui ... compulsi ... subacti: Nominative subject (A.G. 339). **qui**: Plural, masculine, nominative relative pronoun used substantively (A.G. 305). The antecedent is **maiores** (A.G. 307). The relative does not introduce a relative clause but is a connecting relative; at the beginning of a clause the pronoun is often best rendered by a personal or demonstrative pronoun, with or without *and* (A.G. 308.f).

compulsi ... subacti: Two nominative perfect, passive participles used as a predicate, where in English a phrase or a subordinate clause would be more normal (A.G. 496).

in oppida: Accusative of *place to which* with the preposition **in** (A.G. 426.2).

ac: The conjunction connects the two participles and means "and" (*OLD* **atque** 12).

simili inopia: Ablative of cause without a preposition after **subacti** (A.G. 404 and b).

eorum: Plural, masculine, genitive demonstrative pronoun used substantively (A.G. 296.2). The pronoun is correlative to the relative clause **qui ... videbantur** (A.G. 297.d). Possessive genitive with **corporibus** (A.G. 343).

corporibus: Ablative of means after **vitam toleraverunt** (A.G. 409).

qui ... videbantur: Relative clause (A.G. 303). **qui**: Plural, masculine, nominative relative pronoun used substantively (A.G. 305). The antecedent is **eorum** (A.G. 307). Nominative subject (A.G. 339). **videbantur**: The main verb of the subordinate clause (A.G. 278.b).

aetate: Ablative of cause without a preposition (A.G. 404).

ad bellum: Prepositional phrase after **inutiles, ad** with the accusative here denotes purpose meaning "for, in" (*OLD* **ad** 42.b). The adjective **inutiles** can take the dative (cf. **inutiles sunt bello** at 78.1-3) but is used oftener with the accusative with the preposition **ad** to denote the purpose or end (A.G. 385.a).

inutiles (esse): Plural, masculine, nominative predicate adjective modifying **qui** after **videbantur** (A.G. 283). A predicate adjective after a complementary infinitive takes the case of the subject of the main verb (A.G. 283-84 and 458). Supply **esse** as the complementary infinitive after **videbantur**. The adjective is a compound of the adverbial prefix **in-** (meaning *not*) and **utilis** (A.G. 267.d.1).

vitam: Accusative direct object of **toleraverunt** (A.G. 387).

toleraverunt: The main verb of the coordinate clause **qui ... toleraverunt** (A.G. 278.a).

nec: The conjunction joins a negative clause to a preceding positive one and means "and ... not" (*OLD* **neque** 3).

se: Plural, masculine, accusative direct reflexive pronoun (A.G. 300.1). The antecedent is **qui**, the subject of **tradiderunt** (A.G. 299). Accusative direct object of the transitive verb **tradiderunt** (A.G. 387).

hostibus: Dative indirect object of the transitive verb **tradiderunt** (A.G. 362).

tradiderunt: The main verb of the coordinate clause **se ... tradiderunt** (A.G. 278.a).

(77.13-14) Cuius rei si exemplum non haberemus, tamen libertatis causa institui et posteris prodi (14) pulcherrimum iudicarem. Nam quid illi simile bello fuit?

bellum, -i, n., *war.*

et, *and.*
habeo, habere, habui, habitus, *be furnished with, have.*
instituo, -stituere, -stitui, -stitutus, *make, furnish, establish, institute.*
libertas, -atis, f., *freedom, liberty, independence.*
non, *not.*
prodo, -dere, -didi, -ditus, *transmit, hand down.*
qui, quae, quod, *who, which, what.*
res, rei, f., *fact, matter, affair.*
similis, -e, *like, similar.*
tamen, *yet, still, for all that, nevertheless, however.*

causa, -ae, f., abl. with the gen., *for the sake of, for the purpose of.*
exemplum, -i, n., *example, precedent.*
ille, illae, illud, *that; he, she, it.*
iudico, -are, -avi, -atus, *judge, decide, think.*
nam, *for.*
posteri, -orum, m., pl., *descendents, one's posterity.*
pulcher, -chra, -chrum, sup. **pulcherrimus,** *beautiful.*
quis, -----, quid, *who?, what?*
si, *if.*
sum, esse, fui, futurus, *be.*

Cuius rei: Objective genitive with **exemplum** (A.G. 348). **cuius**: Singular, feminine, genitive relative pronoun (A.G. 305). The antecedent is **rei** in its own clause (adjectival use) (A.G. 307.b). The relative does not introduce a relative clause but is a connecting relative; at the beginning of a clause the pronoun is often best rendered by a personal or demonstrative pronoun, with or without *and* (A.G. 308.f).

si ... haberemus ... iudicarem: Conditional statement: contrary to fact, present time (the imperfect subjunctive in both the protasis and apodosis) (A.G. 514.C.1).

si ... haberemus: The conjunction **si** ("if") with the subjunctive forms the protasis of the conditional statement (A.G. 512 and 517).

haberemus: The main verb of the subordinate clause (A.G. 278.b). The personal pronoun **nos** is understood as the subject but is not expressed except for distinction or emphasis (A.G. 295.a).

non: Adverb, the adverb generally precedes the verb if it belongs to no one word in particular (A.G. 217.e, 320-21, and 599.a).

exemplum: Accusative direct object of **haberemus** (A.G. 387).

tamen: Adverb, normally postpositive but here (A.G. 320-21 and 324.j).

libertatis causa institui: The infinitive phrase functions as the subject of the impersonal verb **pulcherrimum (esse)** (A.G. 454).

libertatis causa: A preceding genitive with the ablative of **causa** means "for the sake of" A (A.G. 359.b and 404.c). **libertatis**: Liberty is a theme in Critognatus' speech and the two occurrences of **libertas** are surrounded by the noun **servitus**: **turpissimam**

servitutem (77.3), **perpetuae servituti** (77.10), *libertatis causa* (77.13), *libertatem* (77.14), **aeternam servitutem** (77.15), and **perpetua servitute** (77.16). For the theme of liberty in Book 7, see **liberius** at 1.3.

et: The conjunction connects the two infinitive phrases (A.G. 324.a).

posteris prodi: The infinitive phrase functions as the subject of the impersonal verb **pulcherrimum (esse)** (A.G. 454). **posteris**: Plural, masculine, dative adjective used substantively to mean "descendents, one's posterity" (A.G. 288) (*OLD* **posterus** 3). Dative indirect object of the passive infinitive **prodi**; verbs which in the active voice take the accusative and dative retain the dative when used in the passive (A.G. 365).

pulcherrimum (esse): Accusative/infinitive construction in indirect discourse after **iudicarem** (A.G. 577 ff.). Supply the infinitive **esse** with the neuter adjective to form the impersonal verb (A.G. 208.c). **pulcherrimum**: Singular, neuter, accusative predicate adjective after the supplied **esse** (A.G. 284-85). Superlative adjective (A.G.124). The use of the superlative is here instructive; Critognatus does not say that cannibalism is a necessary thing, but a most beautiful thing. He is uncompromising in his resistance to the Romans.

iudicarem: The main verb of the apodosis of the conditional statement (A.G. 512 and 517). The main verb of the main clause (A.G. 278.b). The personal pronoun **ego** is understood as the subject but is not expressed except for distinction or emphasis (A.G. 295.a).

Nam: The conjunction is put before a interrogative pronoun (**quid**) in a lively or impatient question (*OLD* **nam** 7).

quid ... simile ... fuit?: The phrase means "where was the similarity?" (*OLD* **similis** 6.b). **quid**: Singular, neuter, nominative interrogative pronoun used substantively (A.G. 148). Nominative subject (A.G. 339). **simile**: Singular, neuter, nominative predicate adjective modifying **quid** after **fuit** (A.G. 283-84). **fuit**: The main verb of the simple sentence (A.G. 278.1). The perfect tense is often used in expressions containing or implying a negation, where in affirmation the imperfect would be preferred (A.G. 475.a).

illi ... bello: Dative after the adjective **simile** (A.G. 385.c.2). **illi**: Singular, neuter, dative demonstrative pronoun used as an adjective modifying **bello** (A.G. 146 and 296.1 and a). This refers back to **bello Cimbrorum Teutonumque** at 77.12 (A.G. 297.e).

(77.14) Depopulata Gallia Cimbri magnaque inlata calamitate finibus quidem nostris aliquando excesserunt atque alias terras petierunt; iura, leges, agros, libertatem nobis reliquerunt.

ager, -ri, m., *land* (under cultivation), *field, territory.*
alius, -a, -um, *other.*
calamitas, -tatis, f., *loss, damage, misfortune, disaster, defeat.*
depopulor, -ari, -atus, *lay waste, plunder, devastate.*

fines, -ium, m., pl., *borders,* hence *territory, country, land.*
infero, -ferre, intuli, illatus, *inflict, make.*
lex, legis, f., *law, enactment, decree.*
magnus, -a, -um, *great, large.*
noster, -tra, -trum, *our, our own.*

-que, *and.*
relinquo, -linquere, -liqui, -lictus, *leave, leave behind.*

aliquando, *at length, at last.*
atque, *and.*
Cimbri, -orum, m., pl., *the Cimbri.*
excedo, -cedere, -cessi, -cessurus, *go out, leave, withdraw, depart.*
Gallia, -ae, f., *Gaul.*
ius, iuris, n., *right, justice, authority.*
libertas, -atis, f., *freedom, liberty, independence.*
nos, nostrum, *we, us.*
peto, petere, petivi, and **petii, petitus,** *make for, try to reach, seek.*
quidem, *assuredly, in fact, in all events.*
terra, -ae, f., *territory, district, region.*

Depopulata Gallia: Ablative absolute (A.G. 419-20). **Depopulata**: The perfect tense of the participle represents the action as completed at the time indicated by the tense of the main verb (A.G. 489). Deponent participle with passive force (A.G. 190.f). **Gallia**: See Appendix A.

Cimbri: Nominative subject of **excesserunt ... petierunt** (A.G. 339). See Appendix A.

magnaque inlata calamitate: Ablative absolute (A.G. 419-20). **-que**: The enclitic conjunction connects the two ablative absolutes (A.G. 324.a). **inlata**: The perfect tense of the participle represents the action as completed at the time indicated by the tense of the main verb (A.G. 489).

finibus ... nostris: Ablative of separation without a preposition after the compound verb **excesserunt** (A.G. 402). **nostris**: Plural, masculine, ablative possessive pronoun used as an adjective modifying **finibus** (A.G. 302).

quidem: Adverb, here it emphasizes the whole sentence and means "assuredly, in fact, in all events" (especially in particularizing a statement as certainly valid after a more general assertion has been made) (*OLD* **quidem** 2).

aliquando: Adverb (A.G. 217.b and 320-21).

excesserunt: The main verb of the coordinate clause **Depopulata ... excesserunt** (A.G. 278.a).

atque: The conjunction connects the two main verbs **excesserunt ... petierunt** and means "and" (*OLD* **atque** 12).

alias terras: Accusative direct object of **petierunt** (A.G. 387).

petierunt: The main verb of the coordinate clause **alias ... petierunt** (A.G. 278.a). Contracted form of **petiverunt** (A.G. 181.a).

iura, leges, agros, libertatem: Four accusative direct objects of **reliquerunt** (A.G. 387). Notice the asyndeton construction (A.G. 323.b). **iura, leges**: See note on **iura legesque reddiderat** at 76.1 **libertatem**: See **libertatis** at 77.13. For the theme of liberty in Book 7, see **liberius** at 1.3.

nobis: Plural, masculine, dative personal pronoun used substantively (A.G. 143 and 295). Dative of reference; the dative in this construction is often called the dative of advantage as denoting the person for whose benefit the action is performed (A.G. 376).

reliquerunt: The main verb of the simple sentence (A.G. 278.1). The pronoun **ei**, with **Cimbri** as the antecedent, is understood as the subject (A.G. 271.a).

(77.15) (15) Romani vero quid petunt aliud aut quid volunt, nisi invidia adducti, quos fama nobilis potentisque bello

cognoverunt, horum in agris civitatibusque considere atque his aeternam iniungere servitutem?

adduco, -ducere, -duxi, -ductus, *induce, prevail upon, influence.*
ager, -ri, m., (pl.), *lands, territory, country, the country.*
atque, *and then.*
bellum, -i, n., *war, warfare.*
cognosco, -gnoscere, -gnovi, cognitus, *learn, ascertain, recognize.*

fama, -ae, f., *reputation, fame.*
in, *in.*
invidia, -ae, f., *envy, jealousy.*
nobilis, -e, *noted, renowned.*

potens, -entis, *powerful.*
qui, quae, quod, *who, which, what.*
Romani, -orum, m., pl., *the Romans.*
vero, *on the other hand, however, yet.*

aeternus, -a, -um, *everlasting, perpetual.*
alius, -a, -ud, *other, different.*
aut, *or.*
civitas, -tatis, f., *state, nation.*
consido, -sidere, -sedi, -sessus, *establish one's self, settle.*
hic, haec, hoc, *this; he, she, it.*
iniungo, -iungere, -iunxi, -iunctus, *fasten upon.*
nisi, *other(wise) than, but, except.*
peto, petere, petivi, and petii, petitus, *strive for, seek, aim at.*
-que, *and.*
quis, -----, quid, *who?, what?*
servitus, -tutis, f., *slavery, bondage, subjection.*
volo, velle, volui, *wish, desire, mean, intend.*

Romani ... servitutem: An example of a rhetorical question in direct speech (Siedler, 46).
Romani: Nominative subject of **petunt ... volunt** (A.G. 339).
vero: Here a conjunction with an adversative force meaning "on the other hand, however, yet" (*OLD* vero 7) (A.G. 324.d). The adverb **vero** is always in the postpositive position (A.G. 599.b).
quid petunt aliud: Direct question (A.G. 330-31). **quid ... aliud:** Accusative direct object of **petunt** (A.G. 387). **quid:** Singular, neuter, accusative interrogative pronoun used substantively introducing a direct question (A.G. 148 and 330.1). **petunt:** The main verb of the coordinate clause **Romani ... aliud** (A.G. 278.a).
aut: The conjunction connects the two direct questions. Normally, the conjunction excludes the alternative but this distinction is not always observed (A.G. 324.e).
quid ... servitutem: Direct question (A.G. 330-31). **quid:** Singular, neuter, accusative interrogative pronoun used substantively introducing a direct question (A.G. 148 and 330.1). Accusative direct object of **volunt** (A.G. 387). **servitutem:** See below.
volunt: The main verb of the coordinate clause **quid ... servitutem** (A.G. 278.a).
nisi: A conjunction meaning "other(wise) than, but, except" (*OLD* nisi 6).
invidia: Ablative of cause without a preposition with **adducti** (A.G. 404.b).
adducti: Nominative perfect, passive participle used as a predicate modifying **Romani**, where in English a phrase or a subordinate clause would be more normal (A.G. 496).
quos ... considere: This can be rewritten as (**quid volunt nisi) considere in agris civitatibusque horum quos ... cognoverunt.**
quos ... cognoverunt: Relative clause (A.G. 303). **quos:** Plural, masculine, accusative relative pronoun used substantively (A.G. 305). The antecedent is the following pronoun **horum**. In formal or emphatic discourse, the relative clause usually comes first and contains the antecedent noun (**nobiles potentisque**) (A.G. 308.d). Accusative direct object of **cognoverunt** (A.G. 387). **cognoverunt:** The main verb of the subordinate clause (A.G. 278.b). The pronoun **ei**, with **Romani** as the antecedent, is understood as the subject (A.G. 271.a).
fama: Ablative of specification after **nobilis** (A.G. 418).
nobilis potentisque: Two plural, masculine, accusative predicate adjectives modifying **quos** after **cognoverunt** (A.G. 285.2). **nobilis:** Accusative plural adjective; **-is** for **-es** is the regular form in i-stem adjectives (A.G. 114.a and 115 and a). **potentisque:** Accusative plural adjective; **-is** for **-es** is the regular form in the one termination adjectives (A.G. 117-18). **-que:** The enclitic conjunction connects the two accusative adjectives (A.G. 324.a). Two adjectives belonging to the same noun are regularly connected by a conjunction (A.G. 323.d).
bello: Ablative direct object of **potentis** (A.G. 410).
horum: Plural, masculine, genitive demonstrative pronoun used substantively (A.G. 296.2). The pronoun refers back to **quos** (A.G. 297.e). Possessive genitive with **agris civitatibusque** (A.G. 343).
in agris civitatibusque: Ablative of *place where* with the preposition **in** (locative ablative) (A.G. 426.3). **-que:** The enclitic conjunction connects the two ablative nouns in the prepositional phrase (A.G. 324.a).
considere: Complementary infinitive after **volunt** (A.G. 456).
atque: The conjunction connects a preliminary action (**considere**) with the main action (**iniungere**) and means "and then" (*OLD* atque 7).
his: Plural, masculine, dative demonstrative pronoun used substantively (A.G. 296.2). The antecedent is **horum** (A.G. 297.e). Dative indirect object of the transitive infinitive **iniungere** (A.G. 362).
aeternam ... servitutem: Accusative direct object of the transitive infinitive **iniungere** (A.G. 387 and 451.3). **servitutem:** See **servitutem** at 77.3.
iniungere: Complementary infinitives after **volunt** (A.G. 456).

(77.15-16) Neque enim ulla alia condicione (16) bella gesserunt.

alius, -a, -ud, *other, different.*
condicio, -onis, f., *terms, stipulation.*

bellum, -i, n., *war, warfare.*
enim, *in truth, for, for in fact, and in fact.*

gero, gerere, gessi, gestus, *carry on, wage.*
ullus, -a, -um, *any.*

neque, *nor, not.*

A terse and powerful summation of Caesar's presence and imperial aims in Gaul.

neque enim: The combination of particles means "nor in truth, for ... not" (*OLD* **neque** 9.a). **neque**: Coordinate conjunction (A.G. 223.a.1). **enim**: Postpositive particle (A.G. 599.b) (*OLD* **enim**).
ulla alia condicione: Ablative of manner with limiting adjectives (A.G. 412).
bella: Accusative direct object of **gesserunt** (A.G. 387).
gesserunt: The main verb of the simple sentence (A.G. 278.1). The pronoun **ei**, with **Romani** as the antecedent, is understood as the subject (A.G. 271.a).

(77.16) Quod si ea quae in longinquis nationibus geruntur ignoratis, respicite finitimam Galliam, quae in provinciam redacta, iure et legibus commutatis, securibus subiecta perpetua premitur servitute.'

commuto, -are, -avi, -atus, *change, wholly change, alter.*
finitimus, -a, -um, *neighboring part of, adjoining.*
gero, gerere, gessi, gestus, *carry out, perform, do.*

in, *in; into.*
ius, iuris, n., *right, justice, authority.*
longinquus, -a, -um, *far removed, remote, distant.*
perpetuus, -a, -um, *perpetual, lasting, permanent.*
provincia, -ae, f., *province, subject territory.*
quod si, *but if, and if, now if.*
respicio, -spicere, -spexi, -spectus, *look at, consider.*
servitus, -tutis, f., *slavery, bondage, subjection.*

et, *and.*
Gallia, -ae, f., *Gaul.*
ignoro, -are, -avi, -atus, *be ignorant of, not to know, be unaware.*
is, ea, id, *he, she, it; that, this.*
lex, legis, f., *law, enactment, decree.*
natio, -onis, f., *people, tribe, nation, race.*
premo, -ere, pressi, pressus, *press, oppress.*
qui, quae, quod, *who, which, what.*
redigo, -igere, -egi, -actus, *reduce, render, make.*
securis, -is, f., *axe, authority, power.*
subicio, -icere, -ieci, -iectus, *make subject.*

Quod si ... ignoratis ...respicite: Conditional statement: simple condition, present time (present indicative in the protasis, a present imperative in the apodosis) (A.G. 514.a.1 and 515.a). **Quod si**: The combination used to continue an argument and means Abut if, and if, now if (A.G. 324.d). **Quod**: The relative adverb is used as a connective particle, referring to what precedes (*OLD* **quod** 1). **si**: Conjunction (*OLD* **si**).
si ... ignoratis: The conjunction **si** ("if") with the indicative forms the protasis of the conditional statement (A.G. 512 and 515).
ignoratis: The main verb of the subordinate clause (A.G. 278.b). The personal pronoun **vos** is understood as the subject but is not expressed except for distinction or emphasis (A.G. 295.a).
ea: Plural, neuter accusative demonstrative pronoun used substantively (A.G. 296.2). The pronoun is correlative to the relative clause **quae ... geruntur** (A.G. 297.d). Accusative direct object of **ignoratis** (A.G. 387).
quae ... geruntur: Relative clause (A.G. 303). **quae**: Plural, neuter, nominative relative pronoun used substantively (A.G. 305). The antecedent is **ea** (A.G. 307). Nominative subject (A.G. 339). **geruntur**: The main verb of the subordinate clause (A.G. 278.b).
in longinquis nationibus: Ablative of *place where* with the preposition **in** (locative ablative) (A.G. 426.3). **nationibus**: Critognatus uses the term **natio** to show that Caesar's ambitions are not directed against Gaul alone, he is also aiming to subdue the Germans and Britons.
respicite: The main verb of the apodosis of the conditional statement (A.G. 512 and 515). The main verb of the main clause (A.G. 278.b). Plural imperative (A.G. 188). The personal pronoun **vos** is understood as the subject but is not expressed except for distinction or emphasis (A.G. 295.a). Siedler counts 7 uses of the imperative in Book 7 (none by Caesar himself) (Siedler, 46).
finitimam Galliam: Accusative direct object of the imperative **respicite** (A.G. 387). **Galliam**: See Appendix A.
quae ... servitute: Relative clause (A.G. 303). **quae**: See below. **servitute**: See below.
quae ... redacta ... subiecta: Nominative subject (A.G. 339). **quae**: Singular, feminine, nominative relative pronoun used substantively (A.G. 305). The antecedent is **Galliam** (A.G. 307). **redacta ... subiecta**: Two nominative, perfect, passive participles used as a predicate, where in English a phrase or a subordinate clause would be more normal (A.G. 496).
in provinciam: Prepositional phrase, **in** with the accusative here means "into" (a state or condition) (*OLD* **in** 2). **provinciam**: Here the noun **provinciam** means "province" in reference to its status and not physical location (*OLD* **provincia** 3.b).
iure et legibus commutatis: Ablative absolute (A.G. 419-20). **iure et legibus**: See the note on **iura legesque reddiderat** at 76.1. **et**: The conjunction connects the two nouns in the ablative absolute (A.G. 324.a). **commutatis**: The perfect tense of the participle represents the action as completed at the time indicated by the tense of the main verb (A.G. 489).
securibus: Dative indirect object of the passive participle **subiecta**; verbs which in the active voice take the accusative and dative retain the dative when used in the passive (A.G. 365). Here the noun **securis** is used in the plural as symbolizing Roman jurisdiction and means "an executioner's axe", especially one carried in the fasces of a Roman magistrate (*OLD* **securis** 2.c).
perpetua ... servitute: Ablative of means (A.G. 409). **servitute**: See **servitutem** at 77.3. The placement of this noun in the final position of the speech leaves a somber impression.
premitur: The main verb of the subordinate clause (A.G. 278.b).

4.N CHAPTER 78: THE MANDUBII ARE EXPELLED FROM ALESIA BUT ARE NOT RECEIVED BY CAESAR
(78.1-2) Sententiis dictis constituunt ut ei qui valetudine aut aetate inutiles sunt bello oppido excedant atque omnia prius

ex(2)periantur quam ad Critognati sententiam descendant:

ad, *to*.	**aetas, -tatis**, f., *age*.
atque, *and*.	**aut**, *or*.
bellum, -i, n., *war, warfare*.	**constituo, -stituere, -stitui, -stitutus**, *establish, resolve, determine*.
Critognatus, -i, m., *Critognatus*.	**descendo, -scendere, -scendi, -scensus**, *resort to, stoop to*.
dico, dicere, dixi, dictus, *express*.	**excedo, -cedere, -cessi, -cessurus**, *go out, leave, withdraw, depart*.
experior, -periri, -pertus, *put to the test, try*.	**inutilis, -e**, *useless, unserviceable, of no use*.
is, ea, id, *he, she, it; that, this*.	**omnia, -ium**, n., *all things, everything*.
oppidum, -i, n., *fortified town, city*.	**prius ... quam**, *before, sooner than*.
qui, quae, quod, *who, which, what*.	**sententia, -ae**, f., *opinion, view*.
sum, esse, fui, futurus, *be*.	**ut**, *so that*.
valetudo, -inis, f., *ill-health, sickness, feebleness, infirmity*.	

Sententiis dictis: Ablative absolute (A.G. 419-20). **dictis**: The perfect tense of the participle represents the action as completed at the time indicated by the tense of the main verb (A.G. 489).

constituunt: The main verb of the main clause (A.G. 278.b). The historical present, giving vividness to the narrative, is present in Chapter 78 (A.G. 469). This usage, common in all languages, comes from imagining past events as going on before our eyes (*repraesentatio*) (A.G. 469 Note). Carry down **ei** (the Gaul chieftains inside Alesia) from 77.1 as the subject (A.G. 271.a).

ut ... excedant ... experiantur: The conjunction **ut** ("so that") with the subjunctive is here a substantive clause of purpose which is used as the object of the verb **constituunt** denoting an action directed toward the future (A.G. 563). **excedant ... experiantur**: The main verbs of the subordinate clause (A.G. 278.b). Present subjunctives; the tense of the subjunctives is normally in secondary sequence after the historical present **constituunt** (A.G. 482-85). Here it is in primary sequence through *repraesentatio* (A.G. 485.e and 585.b Note). **experiantur**: Carry down **ei** (the Gaul chieftains inside Alesia) from 77.1 as the subject (A.G. 271.a).

ei: Plural, masculine, nominative demonstrative pronoun used substantively (A.G. 296.2). The pronoun is correlative to the relative clause **qui ... bello** (A.G. 297.d). Nominative subject of **excedant** (A.G. 339).

qui ... sunt bello: Relative clause; a clause dependent on a subjunctive clause (**ut ... excedant**) normally takes the subjunctive (attraction) (A.G. 303 and 593). However, when a dependent clause is not regarded as a necessary logical part of the clause, the indicative is used. The indicative serves to emphasize the fact, as true independently of the statement contained in the subjunctive clause (A.G. 593.a Note 1). **qui**: Plural, masculine, nominative relative pronoun used substantively (A. G. 305). The antecedent is **ei** (A.G. 307). Nominative subject (A.G. 339). **sunt**: The main verb of the subordinate clause (A.G. 278.b). **bello**: Dative after the adjective **inutiles** (A.G. 384). Compare the construction **ad bellum inutiles** at 77.12.

valetudine aut aetate: Two ablatives of cause without a preposition (A.G. 404). This will also include women and children at 78.3-4. **aut**: The conjunction connects the two ablative nouns and excludes the alternative (A.G. 324.e).

inutiles: Plural, masculine, nominative predicate adjective modifying **qui** after **sunt** (A.G. 283-84). The adjective is a compound of the adverbial prefix **in-** (meaning *not*) and **utilis** (A.G. 267.d.1).

oppido: Ablative of separation without a preposition after the compound verb **excedant** (A.G. 402). The city referred to is Alesia.

atque: The conjunction connects the two main verbs in the purpose clause and means "and" (*OLD* **atque** 12).

omnia ... descendant: Notice that the Gauls do not utterly reject Critognatus' repulsive plan but they will resort to cannibalism in the last resort.

omnia: Plural, neuter, accusative adjective used substantively (A.G. 288). Accusative direct object of **experiantur** (A.G. 339).

prius ... quam ... descendant: Temporal clause; the conjunction **prius quam** ("before") normally takes the present or future perfect indicative when referring to future time (A.G. 551.c). Here **prius quam** takes the subjunctive as it is dependent upon a subjunctive clause (**ut ... experiantur**) and is regarded as an integral part of that clause (attraction) (A.G. 593). **prius ... quam**: The conjunction is here split (tmesis) (A.G. 640). **descendant**: The main verbs of the subordinate clause (A.G. 278.b). Present subjunctive; the present indicative would normally be represented by the imperfect subjunctive in secondary sequence after the historical present **constituunt** (A.G. 482-85). Here it is in primary sequence through *repraesentatio* (A.G. 485.e and 585.b Note). Carry down **ei** (the Gaul chieftains inside Alesia) from 77.1 as the subject (A.G. 271.a).

ad Critognati sententiam: Prepositional phrase, **ad** with the accusative here follows a verb of resorting (**descendant**) and means "to" (an act or policy) (*OLD* **ad** 6). **Critognati**: Possessive genitive with **sententiam** (A.G. 343). See Appendix A.

(78.2-3) illo tamen tempore potius utendum consilio, si res cogat atque auxilia morentur, quam aut deditionis aut pacis subeundam (3) condicionem.

atque, *and*.	**aut ... aut**, *either ... or*.
auxilia, -orum, n., *auxiliary troops, auxiliaries, allied forces*.	**cogo, cogere, coegi, coactus**, *compel, force, oblige*.
condicio, -onis, f., *terms, stipulation*.	**consilium, -i**, n., *counsel, advice, plan, design*.
deditio, -onis, f., *surrender*.	**ille, illae, illud**, *that; he, she, it*.
moror, -ari, -atus, *hinder, delay, impede*.	**pax, pacis**, f., *peace*.
potius ... quam, *rather than*.	**res, rei**, f., *circumstance, situation*.
si, *if*.	**subeo, -ire, -ii, -itus**, *endure, submit to, accept*.

tamen, *yet, still, for all that, nevertheless, however.*
utor, uti, usus, *avail oneself of, accept, adopt.*

tempus, -oris, n., *time.*

illo ... tempore: Ablative of *time when* (A.G. 423.1). **illo**: Singular, neuter, ablative demonstrative pronoun used as an adjective modifying **tempore** (A.G. 296.1 and a).

tamen: Adverb, postpositive (A.G. 320-21 and 324.j).

potius: Construe with **quam** below.

utendum (esse) ... si ... cogat ... morentur: Conditional statement in indirect discourse (A.G. 589). The verb of saying is not expressed, but implied in the general drift of the sentence (A.G. 580.a). The protasis, as a dependent clause, is in the subjunctive and the apodosis, as the principal clause, is in the infinitive (A.G. 589).

(id) utendum (esse): The apodosis of the conditional statement (A.G. 589.2). Accusative/infinitive construction in indirect discourse after the unexpressed verb of saying (A.G. 580.a). **utendum (esse)**: Supply **esse** with the gerundive to form the second periphrastic (passive) present infinitive implying necessity (A.G. 194.b and 196). The tense of the infinitive in indirect discourse is relative to that of the verb of saying (A.G. 584). The neuter gerundive of the intransitive verb may be used impersonally in the second periphrastic conjugation (A.G. 500.3). Supply **id** as the subject (A.G. 318.c).

consilio: Ablative direct object of the deponent verb **utendum (esse)** (A.G. 410 and 500.3).

si ... cogat ... morentur: The conjunction **si** ("if") with the subjunctive forms the protasis of a conditional statement in indirect discourse (A.G. 589.1). **cogat ... morentur**: The main verbs of the subordinate clause (A.G. 278.b). Present subjunctives; the tense of the subjunctives is normally in secondary sequence after an unexpressed verb of saying (A.G. 482-84). Here it is in primary sequence through *repraesentatio* (A.G. 585.b Note).

res: Nominative subject (A.G. 339).

atque: The conjunction connects the two main verbs in the protasis and means "and" (*OLD* **atque** 12).

auxilia: Nominative subject (A.G. 339).

(potius) ... quam ... subeundam (esse) condicionem: A subordinate clause in indirect statement (A.G. 580). The infinitive construction is regularly continued after a comparative with **quam** in indirect discourse rather than switching to the subjunctive in the dependent clause (A.G. 583.c). **potius ... quam**: The conjunction is here split (tmesis) and means "rather than" (A.G. 640) (*OLD* **potius** 1). **subeundam (esse)**: Supply **esse** with the gerundive to form the second periphrastic (passive) present infinitive implying necessity (A.G. 194.b and 196). The tense of the infinitive in indirect discourse is relative to that of the verb of saying (A.G. 584). **condicionem**: Accusative subject of the infinitive **subeundam (esse)** (A.G. 459).

aut ... aut: The double connective introduces two logically exclusive alternatives, "either ... or" (*OLD* **aut** 1).

deditionis ... pacis: Two objective genitives after **condicionem** (A.G. 348).

Mandubii ... prohibebat (78.3-5): Collins states of this episode that Caesar "refused to allow the non-combatants of Alesia to pass through his lines. Of course this action was quite in accord with accepted standards of warfare, and equally severe measures are ordered by modern commanders under similar conditions. But modern commanders, writing their memoirs, commonly omit such cruelties, or try to smooth them over by explanation. The question here, as in the other cases, is not whether Caesar was justified in doing what he did, but whether he has attempted to soften or 'whitewash' it. The facts are presented nakedly, without the slightest varnish, and this is the chief difference between ancient and modern times in describing matters of this sort." (Collins, 935) It seems to me as though Caesar does whitewashes here a bit; although he mentions the episode, he does not recount the eventual gruesome fate of the Mandubii. "Caesar, brief and blunt, gives no hint of their fate. But Cassius Dio (c.AD 150-235: 40.40) states that Caesar refused to admit them both because he was short of supplies and because, expecting them to be received back into the town, he intended to increase the pressure on Alesia; instead, they died wretchedly between camp and city." (Hammond, 242) If the reader does not know this result, it would not be extrapolated from the text.

(78.3-4) Mandubii, qui eos oppido receperant, cum (4) liberis atque uxoribus exire coguntur.

atque, *and.*
cum, *with.*

is, ea, id, *he, she, it; that, this.*
Mandubii, -orum, m., pl., *the Mandubii.*
qui, quae, quod, *who, which, what.*
uxor, -oris, f., *wife.*

cogo, cogere, coegi, coactus, *compel, force, oblige.*
exeo, -ire, -ivi, or **-ii, -itus**, *go forth, go out, withdraw, leave.*
liberi, -orum, m., pl., *children.*
oppidum, -i, n., *fortified town, city.*
recipio, -cipere, -cepi, -ceptus, *receive, admit.*

Mandubii: Nominative subject (A.G. 339). See Appendix A. "The inhabitants of Alesia and those who had fled from the surrounding country into the city." (Kelsey, 429)

qui ... receperant: Relative clause (A.G. 303). The Mandubii had received Vercingetorix and his army in their city in Chapter 68. **qui**: Plural, masculine, nominative relative pronoun used substantively (A.G. 305). The antecedent is **Mandubii** (A.G. 307). Nominative subject (A.G. 339). **receperant**: The main verb of the subordinate clause (A.G. 278.b). The pluperfect denotes an action completed in past time (A.G. 477).

eos: Plural, masculine, accusative demonstrative pronoun used substantively (A.G. 296.2). The antecedent is Vercingetorix and his army inside Alesia (A.G. 297.e). Accusative direct object of **receperant** (A.G. 387).

oppido: Ablative of *place where* without a preposition (locative ablative) where there normally is one (A.G. 426.3). The city referred to is **Alesia**.

cum liberis atque uxoribus: Ablative of accompaniment with the preposition **cum** (A.G. 413). **atque**: The conjunction connects the two ablative nouns in the prepositional phrase and means "and" (*OLD* atque 12).
exire: Complementary infinitive after **coguntur** (A.G. 456 and 566.c).
coguntur: The main verb of the main clause (A.G. 278.b).

(78.4-5) Hi cum ad munitiones Romanorum accessissent, flentes omnibus precibus (5) orabant ut se in servitutem receptos cibo iuvarent.

accedo, -cedere, -cessi, -cessurus, *come to, draw near, approach.*
cibus, -i, m., *food, nourishment.*
fleo, flere, flevi, fletus, *weep, shed tears, cry.*
in, *into.*
munitio, -onis, f., *works of fortifications, entrenchment, defenses.*
oro, -are, -avi, -atus, *plead, beg, entreat.*
recipio, -cipere, -cepi, -ceptus, *receive, admit.*
servitus, -tutis, f., *slavery, bondage, subjection.*
ut, *so that.*

ad, *to.*
cum, *after, when.*
hic, haec, hoc, *this; he, she, it.*
iuvo, -are, -avi, -atus, *help, aid, assist.*
omnis, -e, *all sorts, of every kind.*
prex, precis, f., *prayer, entreaty, supplication.*
Romani, -orum, m., pl., *the Romans.*
sui, sibi, se, or sese, nom. wanting, *them.*

Hi ... flentes: Nominative subject of **orabant** (A.G. 339). **Hi**: Plural, masculine, nominative demonstrative pronoun used substantively (A.G. 296.2). The antecedent is **Mandubii** (A.G. 297.a). **flentes**: Present participle used as an adjective modifying **Hi** (A.G. 494)
cum ... accessissent: Temporal clause; the relative adverb **cum** ("after, when") with the pluperfect subjunctive describes the circumstances that preceded the action of the main verb (A.G. 546). **accessissent**: The main verb of the subordinate clause (A.G. 278.b). The pronoun **ei**, with **Hi** (**Mandubii**) as the antecedent, is understood as the subject (A.G. 271.a).
ad munitiones Romanorum: Accusative of *place to which* with the preposition **ad** (A.G. 426.2). **Romanorum**: Possessive genitive with **munitiones** (A.G. 343).
omnibus precibus: Ablative of means (A.G. 409).
orabant: The main verb of the main clause (A.G. 278.b).
ut ... iuvarent: The conjunction **ut** ("so that") with the subjunctive forms a substantive clause of purpose which is used as the object of the verb **orabant** denoting an action directed toward the future (A.G. 563). **iuvarent**: The main verb of the subordinate clause (A.G. 278.b). Imperfect subjunctive; the tense of the subjunctive is in secondary sequence and follows the rules for the sequence of tense after **orabant** (A.G. 482-85). The pronoun **ei**, with **Romanorum** as the antecedent, is understood as the subject (A.G. 271.a).
se ... receptos: Accusative direct object of **iuvarent** (A.G. 387). **se**: Plural, masculine, accusative indirect reflexive pronoun (A.G. 300.2). The antecedent is **Hi** (**Mandubii**), the subject of **orabant** (A.G. 299). **receptos**: Accusative perfect, passive participle used as a predicate, where in English a phrase or a subordinate clause would be more normal (A.G. 496).
in servitutem: Prepositional phrase, **in** with the accusative here means "into" (a state or condition) (*OLD* **in** 2).
cibo: Ablative of instrument (A.G. 409).

(78.5) At Caesar dispositis in vallo custodiis recipi prohibebat.

at, *but, but on the other hand.*
custodia, -ae, f., *guard.*
in, *on.*
recipio, -cipere, -cepi, -ceptus, *receive, admit.*

Caesar, -aris, m., *Caesar.*
dispono, -ponere, -posui, -positus, *station, post.*
prohibeo, -hibere, -hibui, -hibitus, *prevent, hinder.*
vallum, -i, n., *rampart, wall, entrenchment.*

At: Conjunction, introduces a change of subject (A.G. 324.d) (*OLD* at 2).
Caesar: Nominative subject (A.G. 339). See Appendix A.
dispositis in vallo custodiis: Ablative absolute (A.G. 419-20). **dispositis**: The perfect tense of the participle represents the action as completed at the time indicated by the tense of the main verb (A.G. 489). **in vallo**: Ablative of *place where* with the preposition **in** (locative ablative) (A.G. 426.3).
(eos) recipi: Subject accusative with the infinitive after **prohibebat** (A.G. 558.b Note). The pronoun **eos**, with **Mandubii** as the antecedent, is understood as the accusative subject.
prohibebat: The main verb of the main clause (A.G. 278.b). "The suppliants, cast out by Vercingetorix and rejected by Caesar, perished wretchedly in the spaces between the city and the Roman lines - by no means the least item in this catalog of horrors (cf. Dion Cass. XL., 40)." (Kelsey, 429)

4.O CHAPTERS 79-80: THE RELIEF ARMY ARRIVES; THE FIRST ATTEMPT AT THE RELIEF OF ALESIA; THE GERMANS REPULSE THE GAULS IN A CAVALRY ENGAGEMENT
(79.1-2) Interea Commius reliquique duces quibus summa imperi permissa erat cum omnibus copiis ad Alesiam perveniunt et colle exteriore occupato non longius mille passibus ab (2) nostris munitionibus considunt.

ab, *from.*
Alesia, -ae, f., *Alesia.*
Commius, -i, m., *Commius.*

ad, *towards, to the neighborhood of.*
collis, -is, m., *hill, height, elevation.*
consido, -sidere, -sedi, -sessus, *halt, encamp.*

copiae, -arum, f., pl., *forces, troops.*
dux, ducis, m., *leader, general, commander.*
exterior, -ior, -ius, *outer, exterior.*
interea, *in the meantime, meanwhile.*
mille, *a thousand.*

non, *not.*
occupo, -are, -avi, -atus, *seize, take possession of, fill, occupy.*
passus, -us, m., *step, pace,* = 4 feet, 10 ¼ inches.

pervenio, -venire, -veni, -ventus, *come to, arrive at, reach.*
qui, quae, quod, *who, which, what.*
summa, -ae, f., *general management, control, administration.*

cum, *with.*
et, *and.*
imperium, -i, n., *command, control, military authority.*
longius, *further.*
munitio, -onis, f., *works of fortifications, entrenchment, defenses.*
noster, -tra, -trum, *our, our own.*
omnis, -e, *all.*
permitto, -mittere, -misi, -missus, *give over, entrust, commit.*
-que, *and.*
reliquus, -a, -um, *remaining, the rest.*

Interea: Adverb, marks the passage to a new subject (*OLD* interea c).
Commius reliquique duces: Two nominative subjects of perveniunt ... considunt (A.G. 339). Commius: It is interesting that he is the only leader marked out by name, perhaps because Caesar feels his betrayal keenly due to their long association. See Appendix A.
atque: The conjunction connects the two nominative nouns and means "and" (*OLD* atque 12).
quibus ... permissa erat: Relative clause (A.G. 303). For the reference see 76.4. quibus: Plural, masculine, dative relative pronoun used substantively (A.G. 305). The antecedent is Commius reliquique duces (A.G. 307). Dative indirect object of the passive verb permissa erat; verbs which in the active voice take the accusative and dative retain the dative when used in the passive (A.G. 365).
permissa erat: The main verb of the subordinate clause (A.G. 278.b). The pluperfect denotes an action completed in past time (A.G. 477).
summa: Nominative subject (A.G. 339). From the noun summa, -ae, f..
imperi: Partitive genitive with summa (A.G. 346.a.1). The singular genitive of nouns in -ium ended, until the Augustan Age, in a single -i (A.G. 49.b).
cum omnibus copiis: Ablative of accompaniment with the preposition cum (A.G. 413).
ad Alesiam: Accusative of *place to which* with the preposition ad; ad with the name of a town denotes "towards, to the neighborhood of" (A.G. 428.a). Alesiam: See Appendix A.
perveniunt: The main verb of the coordinate clause Interea ... perveniunt (A.G. 278.a). The historical present, giving vividness to the narrative, is present in Chapter 79 (A.G. 469). This usage, common in all languages, comes from imagining past events as going on before our eyes (*repraesentatio*) (A.G. 469 Note).
et: The conjunction connects the two main verbs perveniunt ... considunt (A.G. 324.a).
colle exteriore occupato: Ablative absolute (A.G. 419-20). exteriore: Defective comparative adjective (A.G. 130.b). occupato: The perfect tense of the participle represents the action as completed at the time indicated by the tense of the main verb (A.G. 489).
non: Adverb modifying longius, the negative precedes the word it especially effects (A.G. 217.e, 320-21, and 599.a).
longius mille passibus: Ablative of comparison; the comparative degree is followed by the ablative signifying "than" (A.G. 406). longius: Comparative adverb (A.G. 218 and 320-21). mille: In the singular mille is an indeclinable adjective modifying passibus (A.G. 134.d).
ab nostris munitionibus: Ablative of *place from which* with the preposition ab (A.G. 426.1). nostris: Plural, feminine, ablative possessive pronoun used as an adjective modifying munitionibus (A.G. 302).
considunt: The main verb of the coordinate clause colle ... considunt (A.G. 278.a).

(79.2-3) **Postero die equitatu ex castris educto, omnem eam planitiem quam in longitudinem tria milia passuum patere demonstravimus complent, pedestrisque copias paulum ab eo loco abditas in locis superiori(3)bus constituunt.**

ab, *from.*
castra, -orum, n., pl., *camp, encampment.*
constituo, -stituere, -stitui, -stitutus, *station, place, draw up.*
demonstro, -are, -avi, -atus, *point out, show, say, mention, explain.*
educo, -ducere, -duxi, -ductus, *lead out, lead forth.*
ex, *from, out of.*
is, ea, id, *he, she, it; that, this.*
locus, -i, m., *place, position.*

milia, -um, n., pl., *thousand, thousands.*
passus, -us, m., *step, pace,* = 4 feet, 10 ¼ inches.
paulum, *a little, somewhat.*
planities, -ei, f., *level ground, plain.*
-que, *and.*
superior, -or, -us, *higher, upper, superior.*

abdo, -dere, -didi, -ditus, *put away, remove, conceal.*
compleo, -plere, -plevi, -pletus, *fully occupy, fill full.*
copiae, -arum, f., pl., *forces, troops.*
dies, -ei, m. and f., *day.*
equitatus, -us, m., *cavalry.*
in, *in, in respect to; in, on.*
loca, -orum, n., pl., *places*
longitudo, -inis, f., *length,* (with in), *lengthwise, longitudinally.*
omnis, -e, *whole, entire.*
pateo, patere, patui, -----, *stretch out, extend.*
pedester, -tris, -tre, *on foot,* (with copiae), *infantry.*
posterus, -a, -um, *following, the next.*
qui, quae, quod, *who, which, what.*
tres, tria, trium, *three.*

Postero die: Ablative of *time when* (A.G. 423.1). die: The noun dies is normally masculine gender (A.G. 97.a).
equitatu ex castris educto: Ablative absolute (A.G. 419-20). ex castris: Ablative of *place from which* with the preposition ex (A.G.

426.1). **educto**: The perfect tense of the participle represents the action as completed at the time indicated by the tense of the main verb (A.G. 489).

omnem eam planitiem: Accusative direct object of **complent** (A.G. 387). **eam**: Singular, feminine, accusative demonstrative pronoun used as an adjective modifying **planitiem** (A.G. 296.1. and a).

quam ... demonstravimus: Relative clause (A.G. 303). For the reference see 69.3-4. **quam**: See below. **demonstravimus**: The main verb of the subordinate clause (A.G. 278.b). The personal pronoun **nos** is understood as the subject but is not expressed except for distinction or emphasis (A.G. 295.a). In Book 7, Caesar refers to himself only in the third person, either in the singular or occasionally in the plural (see **Caesar** at 1.1). Siedler counts 11 uses of the first person plural in Book 7 (Siedler, 46). These uses are at 17.1, 23.2, 25.1, 37.1, 48.1, 58.4, 70.1, 76.1, 79.2, 83.8, and 85.4.

quam ... patere: Accusative/infinitive construction in indirect discourse after **demonstravimus** (A.G. 577 ff.). **quam**: Singular, feminine, accusative relative pronoun used substantively (A.G. 305). The antecedent is **planitiem** (A.G. 307). **patere**: Present infinitive; the tense of the infinitive in indirect discourse is relative to that of the verb of saying (A.G. 584).

in longitudinem: Prepositional phrase, **in** with the accusative of **longitudo** means "lengthwise, longitudinally" (*OLD* **longitudo** 1.c).

tria milia passuum: Accusative of *extent of space* (A.G. 425). **tria**: Declinable cardinal number used as an adjective modifying **milia** (A.G. 132-35). **milia**: Accusative plural; in the plural **mille** declines as a neuter noun (A.G. 134.d). **passuum**: Partitive genitive with **milia** (346.2).

complent: The main verb of the coordinate clause **Postero ... complent** (A.G. 278.a). The pronoun **ei**, with **Commius reliquique duces** as the antecedent, is understood as the subject (A.G. 271.a).

pedestrisque copias ... abditas: Accusative direct object of **constituunt** (A.G. 387). **pedestris**: Accusative plural adjective; -**is** for -**es** is the regular form in i-stem adjectives (A.G. 114.a and 115 and a). -**que**: The enclitic conjunction connects the two main verbs **complent ... constituunt** (A.G. 324.a). **abditas**: Perfect, passive participle used as a predicate modifying **copias**, where in English a phrase or a subordinate clause would be more normal (A.G. 496).

paulum: Adverb (A.G. 320-21).

ab eo loco: Ablative of separation with the preposition **ab** after the compound participle **abditas** (A.G. 402). **eo**: Singular, masculine, ablative demonstrative pronoun used as an adjective modifying **loco** (A.G. 296.1 and a).

in locis superioribus: Ablative of *place where* with the preposition **in** (locative ablative) (A.G. 426.3). **superioribus**: Defective comparative adjective (A.G. 130.b).

constituunt: The main verb of the coordinate clause **pedestrisque ... constituunt** (A.G. 278.a). The pronoun **ei**, with **Commius reliquique duces** as the antecedent, is understood as the subject (A.G. 271.a).

(79.3-4) Erat ex oppido Alesia despectus in campum. Concurrunt his auxiliis visis; fit gratulatio inter (4) eos atque omnium animi ad laetitiam excitantur.

ad, *to, towards*.	**Alesia, -ae**, f., *Alesia*.
animus, -i, m., *mind*.	**atque**, *and*.
auxilia, -orum, n., *auxiliary troops, auxiliaries, allied forces*.	**campus, -i**, m., *plain, open country*.
concurro, -currere, -cucurri or **-curri, -cursus**, *rush, hurry, come together*.	**despectus, -us**, m., *a looking down, view, prospect*.
ex, *from*.	**excito, -are, -avi, -atus**, *stir up, rouse*.
fio, fieri, factus, *take place, happen, come about, come to pass*.	**gratulatio, -onis**, f., *rejoicing, congratulations*.
hic, haec, hoc, *this; he, she, it*.	**in**, *in the direction of, towards*.
inter, *among*.	**is, ea, id**, *he, she, it; that, this*.
laetitia, -ae, f., *rejoicing, joy, delight*.	**omnes, -ium**, m., pl., *all men, all*.
oppidum, -i, n., *fortified town, city*.	**sum, esse, fui, futurus**, *be*.
video, videre, visi, visus, *see, perceive, observe*.	

Erat: The main verb of the simple sentence (A.G. 278.1). The verb **sum** in the sense of "exist" makes a complete predicate without a predicate noun or adjective ("there was ..."). It is then called the substantive verb and regularly comes first (A.G. 284.b and 598.c).

ex oppido Alesia: Prepositional phrase, **ex** with the ablative here means "from" (indicating the point at or from which an action is performed) (*OLD* **ex** 7). **Alesia**: An ablative proper noun in apposition to **oppido** (A.G. 282). See Appendix A.

despectus: Nominative subject (A.G. 339).

in campum: Prepositional phrase, **in** with the accusative here means "in the direction of, towards" (*OLD* **in** 15).

Concurrunt: The main verb of the main clause (A.G. 278.b). Verb first in the emphatic position (A.G. 589.d). The noun **Galli** (those inside Alesia) is understood as the subject (A.G. 271.a).

his auxiliis visis: Ablative absolute (A.G. 419-20). **his**: Plural, neuter, ablative demonstrative pronoun used as an adjective modifying **auxiliis** (A.G. 296.1 and a). **visis**: The perfect tense of the participle represents the action as completed at the time indicated by the tense of the main verb (A.G. 489).

fit: The main verb of the coordinate clause **fit ... eos** (A.G. 278.a). Verb first in the emphatic position (A.G. 589.d).

gratulatio: Nominative subject (A.G. 339).

inter eos: Prepositional phrase, **inter** with the accusative here means "among" (indicating the participants in mutual actions) (*OLD* **inter** 14). **eos**: Plural, masculine, accusative demonstrative pronoun used substantively (A.G. 296.2). The antecedent is **Galli**, the supplied subject of **Concurrunt** (A.G. 297.e).

atque: The conjunction connects the two main verbs **fit ... excitantur** and means "and" (*OLD* **atque** 12).

omnium: Plural, masculine, genitive adjective used substantively (A.G. 288). Possessive genitive with **animi** (A.G. 343).

animi: Nominative subject (A.G. 339).

ad laetitiam: Prepositional phrase, **ad** with the accusative here means "to, towards" (*OLD* ad 41). Caesar only applies emotional states to those who will soon be defeated. Compare **elati** at 47.3.

excitantur: The main verb of the coordinate clause **omnium ... excitantur** (A.G. 278.a).

(79.4) Itaque productis copiis ante oppidum considunt et proximam fossam cratibus integunt atque aggere explent seque ad eruptionem atque omnis casus comparant.

ad, *for.*

ante, *before, in front of.*
casus, -us, m., *chance, fortune, event, misfortune.*
consido, -sidere, -sedi, -sessus, *halt, station oneself.*
crates, -is, f., *wicker-work, hurdle, fascine, bundle of brushwood.*
et, *and.*
fossa, -ae, f., *ditch, trench, entrenchment, fosse.*
itaque, *and so, in consequence, accordingly, therefore.*
oppidum, -i, n., *fortified town, city.*
proximus, -a, -um, *nearest.*
sui, sibi, se, or sese, nom. wanting, *themselves.*

agger, -eris, m., *material for a mound* (earth, timber), *earth.*
atque, *and.*
comparo, -are, -avi, -atus, *prepare, make ready.*
copiae, -arum, f., pl., *forces, troops.*
eruptio, -onis, f., *a bursting forth, sally, sortie.*
expleo, -plere, -plevi, -pletus, *fill up, fill.*
intego, -tegere, -texi, -tectus, *cover, cover over.*
omnis, -e, *all.*
produco, -ducere, -duxi, -ductus, *bring out, lead forth.*
-que, *and.*

Itaque: An adverb expressing the result of the previous ideas meaning "and so, in consequence" (*OLD* itaque 1). The adverb stands in the first position (A.G. 599.b).

productis copiis: Ablative absolute (A.G. 419-20). **productis**: The perfect tense of the participle represents the action as completed at the time indicated by the tense of the main verb (A.G. 489).

ante oppidum: Prepositional phrase, **ante** with the accusative here means "before, in front of" (*OLD* ante2 1).

considunt: The main verb of the coordinate clause **Itaque ... considunt** (A.G. 278.a). The pronoun ei, with **Galli** (those inside Alesia) the supplied subject of **Concurrunt** as the antecedent, is understood as the subject (A.G. 297.e).

et: The conjunction connects the two main verbs **considunt ... integunt** (A.G. 324.a).

proximam fossam: Accusative direct object of **integunt** and **explent** (A.G. 387). "The Roman trench on the W. of Alesia mentioned at the beginning of ch. 72." (Edwards, 497) **proximam**: Defective superlative adjective (A.G. 130.a).

cratibus: Ablative of means (A.G. 409.a). "Here apparently a kind of bridge, made of interwoven boughs." (Walker, 403)

integunt: The main verb of the coordinate clause **proximam ... integunt** (A.G. 278.a). The pronoun ei, with **Galli** (those inside Alesia) the supplied subject of **Concurrunt** as the antecedent, is understood as the subject (A.G. 297.e).

atque: The conjunction connects the two main verbs **integunt ... explent** and means "and" (*OLD* atque 12).

aggere: Ablative of means (A.G. 409.a). The noun here does not mean the usual "rampart", but "material for a mound (dirt), rubble" (*OLD* agger 1).

explent: The main verb of the coordinate clause **aggere explent** (A.G. 278.a). The pronoun ei, with **Galli** (those inside Alesia) the supplied subject of **Concurrunt** as the antecedent, is understood as the subject (A.G. 297.e).

seque: Plural, masculine, accusative direct reflexive pronoun (A.G. 300.1). The antecedent is ei (**Galli**), the supplied subject of **comparant** (A.G. 299). Accusative direct object of **comparant** (A.G. 387). **-que**: The enclitic conjunction connects the final verb in the series **explent ... comparant** (A.G. 323.c.3).

ad eruptionem atque omnis casus: Prepositional phrase, **ad** with two accusatives here means "for" (*OLD* ad 40). **atque**: The conjunction connects the two accusative nouns and means "and" (*OLD* atque 12). **omnis**: Accusative plural adjective with **casus**; -is for -es is the regular form in i-stem adjectives (A.G. 114.a and 116).

comparant: The main verb of the coordinate clause **seque ... comparant** (A.G. 278.a). The pronoun ei, with **Galli** (those inside Alesia) the supplied subject of **Concurrunt** as the antecedent, is understood as the subject (A.G. 297.e).

(80.1-2) Caesar omni exercitu ad utramque partem munitionum disposito ut, si usus veniat, suum quisque locum teneat et noverit, equitatum ex castris educi et proelium committi (2) iubet.

ad, *at, on.*
castra, -orum, n., pl., *camp, encampment.*
dispono, -ponere, -posui, -positus, *station, post.*
equitatus, -us, m., *cavalry.*
ex, *from, out of.*
iubeo, iubere, iussi, iussus, *order, give orders, bid, command.*
munitio, -onis, f., *works of fortifications, entrenchment, defenses.*

omnis, -e, *the whole, all of.*
proelium, -i, n., *battle, combat, engagement.*
si, *if.*
teneo, tenere, tenui, -----, *hold, keep, occupy.*
ut, *so that.*
venio, venire, veni, ventus, *come, arise.*

Caesar, -aris, m., *Caesar.*
committo, -mittere, -misi, -missus, *join, begin.*
educo, -ducere, -duxi, -ductus, *lead out, lead forth.*
et, *and.*
exercitus, -us, m., *army.*
locus, -i, m., *station, appointed place, post.*
nosco, noscere, novi, notus, *know, be familiar with, be acquainted with.*
pars, partis, f., *part, portion, area, side.*
quisque, -----, quidque, *each one, each thing.*
suus, -a, -um, *his, with or without own.*
usus, -us, m., *need, necessity.*
uterque, -traque, -trumque, *each, both.*

Caesar: Nominative subject of **iubet** (A.G. 339). See Appendix A.

omni ... noverit: Ablative absolute with dependent clauses.

omni exercitu ad utramque partem munitionum disposito: Ablative absolute (A.G. 419-20). **exercitu**: "i.e. the infantry." (Walker, 404) **ad utramque partem munitionum**: Prepositional phrase, **ad** with the accusative here means "at, on" (*OLD* **ad** 13). **utramque partem**: "The two lines of defense, the one facing the town and the other the relieving army." (Walker, 404) **munitionum**: Partitive genitive with **partem** (A.G. 346.a.1). **disposito**: The perfect tense of the participle represents the action as completed at the time indicated by the tense of the main verb (A.G. 489).

ut si veniat ... teneat ... noverit: A subordinate conditional statement (A.G. 512.c). The apodosis, as a purpose clause dependent on **disposito**, takes the subjunctive and the protasis, as a clause subordinate to a subjunctive clause, also takes the subjunctive (attraction) (A.G. 512.c and 593).

ut ... teneat et noverit: The apodosis of the conditional statement (A.G. 512.c). The conjunction **ut** ("so that") with the subjunctive forms a final (purpose) clause dependent upon the ablative absolute **disposito** (A.G. 531.1). **teneat et noverit**: The main verbs of the subordinate clause (A.G. 278.b). Present and perfect subjunctive; the tense of the subjunctives is normally in secondary sequence after the historical present **iubet** (A.G. 482-85). Here it is in primary sequence through *repraesentatio* (A.G. 485.e and 585.b Note).

noverit: A prefect form with present force (A.G. 476). **et**: The conjunction connects the two verbs in the purpose clause (A.G. 324.a).

si ... veniat: The conjunction **si** ("if") with the subjunctive forms the protasis of the conditional statement (A.G. 512). A clause dependent on a subjunctive clause (**ut ... noverit**) takes the subjunctive when regarded as an integral part of that clause (attraction) (A.G. 593). **veniat**: The main verb of the subordinate clause (A.G. 278.b). Present subjunctive; the tense of the subjunctive is normally in secondary sequence after the historical present **iubet** (A.G. 482-85). Here it is in primary sequence through *repraesentatio* (A.G. 485.e and 585.b Note).

usus: Nominative subject (A.G. 339). The phrase **usus venire** is an idiom that means "The need arises (*OLD* **usus** 13.b).

suum ... locum: Accusative direct object of both **teneat** and **noverit** (A.G. 387). **suum**: Singular, masculine, accusative possessive pronoun used as an adjective modifying **locum** (A.G. 302).

quisque: Singular, masculine, nominative indefinite pronoun used substantively (A.G. 313). Nominative subject of **teneat ... noverit** (A.G. 339).

equitatum ... educi: A subject accusative with the infinitive after **iubet**. The construction is equivalent to a substantive clause of purpose (A.G. 563.a).

ex castris: Ablative of *place from which* with the preposition **ex** (A.G. 426.1).

et: The conjunction connects the two infinitives (A.G. 324.a).

proelium committi: A subject accusative with the infinitive after **iubet**. The construction is equivalent to a substantive clause of purpose (A.G. 563.a).

iubet: The main verb of the main clause (A.G. 278.b). The historical present, giving vividness to the narrative, is present in Chapter 80 (A.G. 469). This usage, common in all languages, comes from imagining past events as going on before our eyes (*repraesentatio*) (A.G. 469 Note).

(80.2-3) Erat ex omnibus castris, quae summum undique iugum tenebant, despectus, atque omnes milites intenti (3) pugnae proventum exspectabant.

atque, *and*.	**castra, -orum**, n., pl., *camp, encampment*.
despectus, -us, m., *a looking down, view, prospect*.	**ex**, *down from*.
exspecto, -are, -avi, -atus, *wait to see, wait for, await, expect*.	**intentus, -a, -um**, *active, eager, intent*.
iugum, -i, n., *ridge, summit*.	**miles, -itis**, m., *soldier, foot-solider*.
omnis, -e, *all parts of*.	**proventus, -us**, m., *result, issue, outcome*.
pugna, -ae, f., *fight, combat, battle*.	**qui, quae, quod**, *who, which, what*.
sum, esse, fui, futurus, *be*.	**summus, -a, -um**, *highest*.
teneo, tenere, tenui, -----, *control, watch, guard, defend, maintain*.	**undique**, *on all sides, everywhere, all around*.

Erat: The main verb of the coordinate clause **Erat ... despectus** (A.G. 278.a). The verb **sum** in the sense of "exist" makes a complete predicate without a predicate noun or adjective ("there was ..."). It is then called the substantive verb and regularly comes first (A.G. 284.b and 598.c).

ex omnibus castris: Prepositional phrase, **ex** with the ablative here means Adown from (*OLD* **ex** 5.b).

quae ... tenebant: Relative clause (A.G. 303). **quae**: Plural, neuter, nominative relative pronoun used substantively (A.G. 305). The antecedent is **castris** (A.G. 307). Nominative subject (A.G. 339). **tenebant**: The main verb of the subordinate clause (A.G. 278.b).

summum ... iugum: Accusative direct object of **tenebant** (A.G. 387). **summum**: Defective superlative adjective (A.G. 130.b).

undique: Adverb (A.G. 217.a and 320-21).

despectus: Nominative subject (A.G. 339).

atque: The conjunction connects the two main verbs **erat ... exspectabant** and means "and" (*OLD* **atque** 12).

omnes milites intenti: Nominative subject (A.G. 339). **intenti**: Plural, masculine, nominative adjective modifying **milites** but used to qualify the action of the verb, and so has the force of an adverb (A.G. 290).

pugnae: Possessive genitive with **proventum** (A.G. 343).

proventum: Accusative direct object of the verb **exspectabant** (A.G. 387).

exspectabant: The main verb of the coordinate clause **omnes ... exspectabant** (A.G. 278.a).

(80.3) Galli inter equites raros sagittarios expeditosque levis armaturae interiecerant, qui suis cedentibus auxilio succurrerent et nostrorum equitum impetus sustinerent.

armatura, -ae, f., *armor, equipment.*
cedo, cedere, cessi, cessurus, *withdraw, retreat, yield.*
et, *and.*
Galli, -orum, m., *the Gauls.*
inter, *among.*

levis, -e, *light.*
-que, *and.*
rarus, -a, -um, *few, scattered, in small parties.*
succurro, -currere, -curri, -cursus, *run to help, rush to aid, succor.*

sui, -orum, m., pl., *their men,* with or without *own.*

auxilium, -i, n., *help, aid, assistance, relief.*
eques, -itis, m., *rider, horseman, cavalryman, trooper.*
expeditus, -i, m., *light-armed soldier.*
impetus, -us, m., *attack, assault, onset, charge.*
intericio, -icere, -ieci, -iectus, *throw between, place between, put between.*
noster, -tra, -trum, *our, our own.*
qui, quae, quod, *who, which, what.*
sagittarius, -i, m., *archer, bowman.*
sustineo, -tinere, -tinui, -tentus, *bear, endure, withstand.*

For a description of this combination of foot-soldiers and cavalry see **inter equites proeliari** at 18.1.
Galli: Nominative subject (A.G. 339). See Appendix A.
inter equites: Prepositional phrase, **inter** with the accusative here means "among" (*OLD* **inter1** 1).
raros sagittarios expeditosque: Two accusative direct objects of **interiecerant** (A.G. 387). **expeditos**: Plural, masculine, accusative adjective used substantively (A.G. 288). The noun **pedites** is understood (A.G. 288.b).
levis armaturae: Genitive of quality (descriptive genitive) with **expeditos** (A.G. 345).
interiecerant: The main verb of the main clause (A.G. 278.b). Although the pluperfect tense is normally used in subordinate clauses, its use as a main verb is frequent. The pluperfect denotes an action completed in past time (A.G. 477).
qui ... succurrerent ... sustinerent: A relative clause of purpose is introduced by a relative pronoun and takes the subjunctive (A.G. 531.2). **qui**: Plural, masculine, nominative relative pronoun used substantively (A.G. 305). The antecedent is **sagittarios expeditosque** (A.G. 307). Nominative subject (A.G. 339). The relative is here equivalent to **ut ei** (A.G. 531.2 Note). **succurrerent ... sustinerent**: The main verbs of the subordinate clause (A.G. 278.b). Imperfect subjunctives; the tense of the subjunctives is in secondary sequence and follows the rules for the sequence of tense after **interiecerant** (A.G. 482-85).
suis cedentibus auxilio: Dative of the purpose or end (double dative). The dative of an abstract noun (**auxilio**) is used to show that for which a thing serves or which it accomplishes, with another dative of the person or thing affected (**suis cedentibus**) (A.G. 382.1). **suis**: Plural, masculine, dative possessive pronoun used substantively to denote a special class (A.G. 302.d). **cedentibus**: Present participle used as an adjective modifying **suis** (A.G. 494).
et: The conjunction connects the two verbs in the relative clause of purpose (A.G. 324.a).
nostrorum equitum: Possessive genitive with **impetus** (A.G. 343). **nostrorum**: Plural, masculine, genitive possessive pronoun used as an adjective modifying **equitum** (A.G. 302).
impetus: Accusative direct object of the verb **sustinerent** (A.G. 387). Notice that the plural noun indicates numerous attacks.

(80.3-4) Ab his complures de improviso vul(4)nerati proelio excedebant.

ab, *by.*

excedo, -cedere, -cessi, -cessurus, *go out, leave, withdraw, depart.*
de improviso, *unexpectedly, suddenly, without warning.*
vulnero, are, -avi, -atus, *wound, hurt.*

complures, -ium, m., pl., *several men, many men, a number of men.*
hic, haec, hoc, *this; he, she, it.*
proelium, -i, n., *battle, combat, engagement.*

Ab his: Ablative of agent with the preposition **ab** after the passive participle **vulnerati** (A.G. 405). **his**: Plural, masculine, ablative demonstrative pronoun used substantively (A.G. 296.2). The antecedent is **sagittarios expeditosque** (A.G. 297.e).
complures ... vulnerati: Nominative subject (A.G. 339). **complures**: Plural, masculine, nominative adjective used substantively (A.G. 288). Compound of the comparative adjective **plus** (A.G. 120.c). The noun **Romani** is understood (A.G. 288.b). **vulnerati**: Perfect, passive participle used as a predicate, where in English a phrase or a subordinate clause would be more normal (A.G. 496).
de improviso: Prepositional phrase, **de** with the ablative of **improvisus** means "unexpectedly, suddenly, without warning" (*OLD* **improvisus** 2). **improviso**: Singular, neuter, ablative of the adjective used substantively (*OLD* **improvisus** 1.b).
proelio: Ablative of separation without a preposition after **excedebant** (A.G. 402).
excedebant: The main verb of the simple sentence (A.G. 278.1).

(80.4-5) Cum suos pugna superiores esse Galli confiderent et nostros multitudine premi viderent, ex omnibus partibus et ei qui munitionibus continebantur et hi qui ad auxilium convenerant clamore et ululatu suorum (5) animos confirmabant.

ad, *for, for the purpose of.*
auxilium, -i, n., *help, aid, assistance, relief.*
confido, -fidere, -fisus sum, *be confident, be assured.*

contineo, -tinere, -tinui, -tentus, *keep, detain, shut in, hold.*

animus, -i, m., *mind, spirit.*
clamor, -oris, m., *outcry, loud call, shout.*
confirmo, -are, -avi, -atus, *strengthen, reassure, encourage.*
convenio, -venire, -veni, -ventus, *come together,*

gather.

cum, *when.*
ex, *from.*
hic, haec, hoc, *this; he, she, it.*
multitudo, -inis, f., *great number, multitude, crowd.*

nostri, -orum, m., pl., *our men, our side.*
pars, partis, f., *region, district, side, direction.*
pugna, -ae, f., *fight, combat, battle.*
sum, esse, fui, futurus, *be.*
sui, -orum, m., pl., *their men, with or without* own.
video, videre, visi, visus, *see, perceive, observe, understand.*

et, *and; et ... et, both ... and.*
Galli, -orum, m., *the Gauls.*
is, ea, id, *he, she, it; that, this.*
munitio, -onis, f., *works of fortifications, entrenchment, defenses.*
omnis, -e, *all.*
premo, -ere, pressi, pressus, *press, oppress.*
qui, quae, quod, *who, which, what.*
superior, -or, -us, *superior, victorious, stronger.*
ululatus, -us, m., *shouting, loud cry, shout.*

Cum ... confiderent ... viderent: Temporal clause; the relative adverb cum ("when") with the imperfect subjunctive describes the circumstances that accompanied the action of the main verb (A.G. 546). confiderent ... viderent: The main verbs of the subordinate clause (A.G. 278.b).
suos ... superiores esse: Accusative/infinitive construction in indirect discourse after confiderent (A.G. 577 ff.). suos: Plural, masculine, accusative possessive pronoun used substantively to denote a special class (A.G. 302.d). superiores: Plural, masculine, accusative predicate adjective modifying suos after esse (A.G. 283-84). Defective superlative adjective (A.G. 130.b). esse: Present infinitive; the tense of the infinitive in indirect discourse is relative to that of the verb of saying (A.G. 584).
pugna: Ablative of specification after superiores (A.G. 418) (*OLD* superior 6.b).
Galli: Nominative subject (A.G. 339). See Appendix A.
et: The conjunction connects the two verbs in the temporal clause (A.G. 324.a).
nostros ... premi: Accusative/infinitive construction in indirect discourse after viderent (A.G. 577 ff.). nostros: Plural, masculine, accusative possessive pronoun used substantively to denote a special class (A.G. 302.d). premi: Present infinitive; the tense of the infinitive in indirect discourse is relative to that of the verb of saying (A.G. 584).
multitudine: Ablative of means (A.G. 409).
ex omnibus partibus: Ablative of *place from which* with the preposition ex (A.G. 426.1).
et ... et: The repeated conjunction means "both ... and", connecting the two pronouns ei ... hi (A.G. 323.e).
ei: Plural, masculine, nominative demonstrative pronoun used substantively (A.G. 296.2). The pronoun is correlative to the relative clause qui ... continebantur (A.G. 297.d). First nominative subject of confirmabant (A.G. 339).
qui ... continebantur: Relative clause (A.G. 303). These are the Gauls in Alesia. qui: Plural, masculine, nominative relative pronoun used substantively (A.G. 305). The antecedent is ei (A.G. 307). Nominative subject (A.G. 339). continebantur: The main verb of the subordinate clause (A.G. 278.b).
munitionibus: Ablative of means (A.G. 409).
hi: Plural, masculine, nominative demonstrative pronoun used substantively (A.G. 296.2). The pronoun is correlative to the relative clause qui ... convenerant (A.G. 297.d). Second nominative subject of confirmabant (A.G. 339).
qui ... convenerant: Relative clause (A.G. 303). This is the relief army. qui: Plural, masculine, nominative relative pronoun used substantively (A.G. 305). The antecedent is hi (A.G. 307). Nominative subject (A.G. 339). convenerant: The main verb of the subordinate clause (A.G. 278.b). The pluperfect denotes an action completed in past time (A.G. 477).
ad auxilium: Prepositional phrase, ad with the accusative here implies purpose and means "for, for the purpose of" (*OLD* ad 44).
clamore et ululatu: Two ablatives of means (A.G. 409). et: The conjunction connects the two ablative nouns (A.G. 324.a).
suorum: Plural, masculine, genitive possessive pronoun used substantively to denote a special class (A.G. 302.d). Possessive genitive with animos (A.G. 343).
animos: Accusative direct object of confirmabant (A.G. 387).
confirmabant: The main verb of the main clause (A.G. 278.b).

(80.5-6) Quod in conspectu omnium res gerebatur neque recte ac turpiter factum celari poterat, utrosque et laudis cupiditas et timor ignominiae ad virtutem (6) excitabat.

ac, *and.*
celo, -are, -avi, -atus *conceal, hide, keep secret.*
cupiditas, -tatis, f., *ardent desire, longing, eagerness.*
excito, -are, -avi, -atus, *stir up, rouse.*
gero, gerere, gessi, gestus, *carry on, wage.*
in, *in.*
neque, *and ... not.*
possum, posse, potui, -----, *be able.*
recte, *nobly, excellently, rightly, well.*
timor, -oris, m., *fear, dread, apprehension.*

uterque, -traque, -trumque, *each, both.*

ad, *to, towards.*
conspectus, -us, m., *sight, view, presence.*
et ... et, *both ... and.*
factum, -i, n., *deed, action, achievement.*
ignominia, -ae, f., *disgrace, dishonor.*
laus, laudis, f., *praise, fame, glory, commendation.*
omnes, -ium, m., pl., *all men, all.*
quod, *because, since, for, as.*
res, rei, f., *affair, battle, military operation.*
turpiter, *basely, disgracefully, shamefully, dishonorably.*
virtus, -utis, f., *manliness, courage, bravery, valor, effort.*

Quod ... gerebatur ... poterat: Causal clause; the conjunction **quod** ("because") takes the indicative when the reason is given on the authority of the writer or speaker (A.G. 540.1). **gerebatur ... poterat**: The main verbs of the subordinate clause (A.G. 278.b).

in conspectu omnium: Prepositional phrase, **in** with the ablative here means "in" (an area defined by the range of the senses) (*OLD* **in** 24.b). **omnium**: Plural, masculine, genitive adjective used substantively (A.G. 288). Possessive genitive with **conspectu** (A.G. 343).

res: Nominative subject (A.G. 339).

neque: The conjunction joins a negative clause to a preceding positive one and means "and ... not" (*OLD* **neque** 3).

recte: Adverb modifying **factum** (A.G. 214.a and 320-21). The participle **factum**, when used as a noun, is regularly modified by adverbs rather than by adjectives (A.G. 321.b).

ac: The conjunction connects the two adverbs, a pair of opposites, and means "and" (*OLD* **atque** 10.b). While the Loeb text also reads **ac**, the Budé text reads **aut**.

turpiter: Adverb modifying **factum** (A.G. 214.b and 320-21). The participle **factum**, when used as a noun, is regularly modified by adverbs rather than by adjectives (A.G. 321.b).

factum: Nominative subject (A.G. 339). The perfect, passive participle of **facio** is here used as a noun (A.G. 494.a).

celari: Complementary infinitive after **poterat** (A.G. 456).

utrosque: Plural, masculine, accusative pronoun used substantively to mean "each of the two" (with reference to sets or groups of people, i.e. the Romans and Gauls) (A.G. 313) (*OLD* **uterque** 3.a). Accusative direct object of **excitabat** (A.G. 387).

et ... et: The repeated conjunction means "both ... and", connecting the two nominative nouns **cupiditas ... timor** (A.G. 323.e).

laudis: Objective genitive with **cupiditas** (A.G. 348).

cupiditas: First nominative subject of **excitabat** (A.G. 339).

timor: Second nominative subject of **excitabat** (A.G. 339).

ignominiae: Objective genitive with **timor** (A.G. 348).

ad virtutem: Prepositional phrase, **ad** with the accusative here meaning "to, towards" (*OLD* **ad** 41).

excitabat: The main verb of the main clause (A.G. 278.b). Two singular subjects normally take a verb in the plural (A.G. 317). Here, the verb is singular as the two subjects (**cupiditas** and **timor**) are connected by disjunctives (**et ... et**) (A.G. 317.b).

(80.6-7) Cum a meridie prope ad solis occasum dubia victoria pugnaretur, Germani una in parte confertis turmis (7) in hostis impetum fecerunt eosque propulerunt; quibus in fugam coiectis, sagittarii circumventi interfectique sunt.

a(b), *beginning at, from.*	**ad**, *towards.*
circumvenio, -venire, -veni, -ventus, *surround.*	**coicio, -icere, -ieci, -iectus**, *put, throw.*
confercio, -cire, -si, -tus, *pack closely together, fill densely.*	**cum**, *when, while.*
dubius, -a, -um, *doubtful, uncertain.*	**facio, facere, feci, factus**, *make.*
fuga, -ae, f., *flight.*	**Germani, -orum**, m., pl., *the Germans.*
hostis, -is, m., *enemy, foe*; pl., *the enemy.*	**impetus, -us**, m., *attack, assault, onset, charge.*
in, *in; against; into.*	**interficio, -ficere, -feci, -fectus**, *slay, kill.*
is, ea, id, *he, she, it; that, this.*	**meridies, -ei**, m., *mid-day.*
occasus, -i, m., *going down, setting.*	**pars, partis**, f., *part, side.*
prope, *near, nearly, almost.*	**propello, -pellere, -puli, -pulsus**, *drive away, put to flight, rout, defeat.*
pugno, -are, -avi, -atus, *fight, combat, engage.*	**-que**, *and.*
qui, quae, quod, *who, which, what.*	**sagittarius, -i**, m., *archer, bowman.*
sol, -is, m., *the sun.*	**turma, -ae**, f., *troop, squadron.*
unus, -a, -um, *one.*	**victoria, -ae**, f., *victory.*

Cum ... (id) pugnaretur: Temporal clause; the relative adverb **cum** ("when, while") with the imperfect subjunctive describes the circumstances that accompanied the action of the main verb (A.G. 546). **pugnaretur**: The main verb of the subordinate clause (A.G. 278.b). Impersonal use of the intransitive passive verb (A.G. 208.d). Supply **id** as the subject (A.G. 318.c).

a meridie: Prepositional phrase, **a(b)** with the ablative here expresses the earlier limit of a period of time meaning "beginning at, from" (*OLD* **ab** 11).

prope: Adverb (A.G. 320-21).

ad solis occasum: Prepositional phrase, **ad** with the accusative here means "towards" (a point in time) (*OLD* **ad** 21). **solis**: Possessive genitive with **occasum** (A.G. 343).

dubia victoria: Ablative of manner with a limiting adjective (A.G. 412).

Germani: Nominative subject of **fecerunt ... propulerunt** (A.G. 339). This is the third time that the German horsemen defeat the Gauls for Caesar. See Appendix A.

una in parte confertis turmis: Ablative absolute (A.G. 419-20). **una in parte**: Ablative of *place where* with the preposition **in** (locative ablative) (A.G. 426.3). **una**: Declinable cardinal number used as an adjective modifying **parte** (A.G. 132-35). **in**: A monosyllabic preposition is often placed between a noun and its adjective (A.G. 599.d.2). **confertis**: The perfect tense of the participle represents the action as completed at the time indicated by the tense of the main verb (A.G. 489).

in hostis: Prepositional phrase, **in** with the accusative here means "against" (*OLD* **in** 12). **hostis**: Accusative plural noun; **-is** for **-es** is the regular form in i-stem nouns (A.G. 65-67 and 74.c).

impetum: Accusative direct object of **fecerunt** (A.G. 387).

fecerunt: The main verb of the coordinate clause **Cum ... fecerunt** (A.G. 278.a).

eosque: Plural, masculine, accusative demonstrative pronoun used substantively (A.G. 296.2). The antecedent is **hostis** (A.G. 297.e).

Accusative direct object of **propulerunt** (A.G. 387). **-que**: The enclitic conjunction connects the two main verbs (A.G. 324.a).

propulerunt: The main verb of the coordinate clause **eosque propulerunt** (A.G. 278.a).

quibus in fugam coiectis: Ablative absolute (A.G. 419-20). **quibus**: Plural, masculine, ablative relative pronoun used substantively (A.G. 305). The antecedent is **eos** (A.G. 307). The relative does not introduce a relative clause but is a connecting relative; at the beginning of a clause the pronoun is often best rendered by a personal or demonstrative pronoun, with or without *and* (A.G. 308.f). **in fugam**: Prepositional phrase, **in** with the accusative here means "into" (a state or condition) (*OLD* **in** 2). **coiectis**: The perfect tense of the participle represents the action as completed at the time indicated by the tense of the main verb (A.G. 489).

sagittarii: Nominative subject (A.G. 339). The Gallic archers mentioned at 80.3. "Those among the cavalry; they had not yet learned to keep up with the horsemen after the manner of the Germans, described in Book I., Chap. 48." (Kelsey, 430)

circumventi interfectique sunt: The main verbs of the main clause (A.G. 278.b). Two perfect, passive indicative verbs sharing **sunt** (= **circumventi sunt et interfecti sunt**) (A.G. 187-88). For the same construction see 29.1 and 62.7. **-que**: The enclitic conjunction connects the two participle elements of the main verbs (A.G. 324.a).

(80.8-9) (8) Item ex reliquis partibus nostri cedentis usque in castra (9) insecuti sui colligendi facultatem non dederunt.

castra, -orum, n., pl., *camp, encampment.*
colligo, -ligere, -legi, -lectus, *gather together, come together, recover, rally.*
ex, *from, out of.*
insequor, -sequi, -secutus, *follow up, pursue, follow in pursuit.*
non, *not.*
pars, partis, f., *region, district, direction.*
sui, sibi, se, or **sese**, nom. wanting, *themselves.*

cedo, cedere, cessi, cessurus, *withdraw, retreat, yield.*
do, dare, dedi, datus, *give, offer, furnish, allow.*
facultas, -atis, f., *ability, opportunity, chance.*
item, *in a like manner, likewise.*
nostri, -orum, m., pl., *our men, our side.*
reliquus, -a, -um, *remaining, the rest.*
usque in, *up to the point of, all the way, as far as.*

Item: Adverb (A.G. 320-21).

ex reliquis partibus: Ablative of *place from which* with the preposition **ex** (A.G. 426.1).

nostri ... insecuti: Nominative subject (A.G. 339). **nostri**: Plural, masculine, nominative possessive pronoun used substantively to denote a special class (A.G. 302.d). **insecuti**: Perfect participle used as a predicate, where in English a phrase or a subordinate clause would be more normal (A.G. 496).

cedentis: Plural, masculine, accusative present participle used substantively (A.G. 494.a). The noun **hostis** is understood. Accusative direct object of the participle **insecuti** (A.G. 387 and 488). Accusative plural; **-is** for **-es** is the regular form in the present participle (A.G. 117-18).

usque in castra: Prepositional phrase, **usque in** with the accusative means "up to the point (of)" (*OLD* **usque** 7). **usque**: Adverb (A.G. 320-21 and 432.b).

sui colligendi: Objective genitive with **facultatem** (504). **colligendi**: Genitive gerund limited by a possessive pronoun **sui** rather than taking a direct object (A.G. 504.c). **sui**: Genitive reflexive pronoun limiting **colligendi** (A.G. 302). The more normal construction for the gerund would be **se colligendi facultatem**; the gerundive **sui colligendorum facultatem**. (For a parallel construction with **causa/gratia** see 43.3 and 50.2).

facultatem: Accusative direct object of **dederunt** (A.G. 387).

non: Adverb, the adverb generally precedes the verb if it belongs to no one word in particular (A.G. 217.e, 320-21, and 599.a).

dederunt: The main verb of the simple sentence (A.G. 278.1).

(80.9) At ei qui ab Alesia processerant maesti prope victoria desperata se in oppidum receperunt.

ab, *from the vicinity of, from, out of.*
at, *but, but on the other hand.*
in, *into.*
maestus, -a, -um, *sad, dejected.*
procedo, -cedere, -cessi, -----, *advance, go forward.*
qui, quae, quod, *who, which, what.*

sui, sibi, se, or **sese**, nom. wanting, *themselves.*

Alesia, -ae, f., *Alesia.*
despero, -are, -avi, -atus, *despair of.*
is, ea, id, *he, she, it; that, this.*
oppidum, -i, n., *fortified town, city.*
prope, *near, nearly, almost.*
recipio, -cipere, -cepi, -ceptus, (with se), *return, retreat.*
victoria, -ae, f., *victory.*

At: Conjunction, introduces a change of subject (A.G. 324.d) (*OLD* **at** 2).

ei ...maesti: Nominative subject (A.G. 339). **ei**: Plural, masculine, nominative demonstrative pronoun used substantively (A.G. 296.2). The pronoun is correlative to the relative clause **qui ... processerant** (A.G. 297.d). **maesti**: Plural, masculine, nominative adjective modifying **ei** but used to qualify the action of the verb, and so has the force of an adverb (A.G. 290).

qui ... processerant: Relative clause (A.G. 303). **qui**: Plural, masculine, nominative relative pronoun used substantively (A.G. 305). The antecedent is **ei** (A.G. 307). Nominative subject (A.G. 339). **processerant**: The main verb of the subordinate clause (A.G. 278.b). The pluperfect denotes an action completed in past time (A.G. 477).

ab Alesia: Ablative of *place from which* with the preposition **ab**; when **ab** is used with a city name it means "from the vicinity of" (A.G. 428.a). **Alesia**: See Appendix A.

prope victoria desperata: Ablative absolute (A.G. 419-20). **prope**: Adverb (A.G. 320-21). **desperata**: The perfect tense of the participle represents the action as completed at the time indicated by the tense of the main verb (A.G. 489).

se: Plural, masculine, accusative direct reflexive pronoun (A.G. 300.1). The antecedent is **ei**, the subject of **receperunt** (A.G. 299).

Accusative direct object of **receperunt** (A.G. 387).

in oppidum: Accusative of *place to which* with the preposition **in** (A.G. 426.2).

receperunt: The main verb of the main clause (A.G. 278.b). The verb **recipere** used reflexively means "to return" (*OLD* **recipio** 12).

4.P CHAPTERS 81-82: THE SECOND (NIGHT) ATTEMPT AT THE RELIEF OF ALESIA; THE GAULS ARE AGAIN REPULSED

(81.1-2) Uno die intermisso Galli atque hoc spatio magno cratium, scalarum, harpagonum numero effecto media nocte silentio (2) ex castris egressi ad campestris munitiones accedunt.

accedo, -cedere, -cessi, -cessurus, *come to, draw near, approach.*

atque, *and.*

castra, -orum, n., pl., *camp, encampment.*

dies, -ei, m. and f., *day.*

egredior, -gredi, -gressus, *go out, go forth, come forth, leave.*

Galli, -orum, m., *the Gauls.*

hic, haec, hoc, *this; he, she, it.*

magnus, -a, -um, *great, large.*

munitio, -onis, f., *works of fortifications, entrenchment, defenses.*

numerus, -i, m., *number, amount.*

silentium, -i, m., *silence.*

unus, -a, -um, *one.*

ad, *to, towards.*

campester, -tris, -tre, *of level ground, flat, level.*

crates, -is, f., *wicker-work, hurdle, fascine, bundle of brushwood.*

efficio, -ficere, -feci, -fectus, *produce, make, construct.*

ex, *from, out of.*

harpago, -onis, m., *grappling-iron, grappling-hook.*

intermitto, -mittere, -misi, -missus, (in pass.), *having intervened.*

medius, -a, -um, *in the middle, midst, middle, mid-.*

nox, noctis, f., *night.*

scalae, -arum, f., pl., *ladder, scaling-ladder.*

spatium, -i, n., *space, interval, time.*

Uno die intermisso: Ablative absolute (A.G. 419-20). **Uno**: Declinable cardinal number used as an adjective modifying **die** (A.G. 132-35). **die**: The noun **dies** is normally masculine gender (A.G. 97.a). **intermisso**: The perfect tense of the participle represents the action as completed at the time indicated by the tense of the main verb (A.G. 489).

Galli ... egressi: Nominative subject of **accedunt** (A.G. 339). **Galli**: This is the relief army. See Appendix A. **egressi**: Perfect, deponent participle used as a predicate, where in English a phrase or a subordinate clause would be more normal (A.G. 496). This is the exterior relief army.

atque: The conjunction connects the two ablative absolutes and means "and" (*OLD* **atque** 12).

hoc spatio magno cratium, scalarum, harpagonum numero effecto: Ablative absolute (A.G. 419-20). **hoc spatio**: Ablative of *time within which* (A.G. 423.1). **hoc**: Singular, neuter, ablative demonstrative pronoun used as an adjective modifying **spatio** (A.G. 296.1 and a). The pronoun points back to the time just mentioned at **Uno die intermisso** (A.G. 297.d). **magno**: Attributive adjective modifying **numero** (A.G. 285.1). **cratium, scalarum, harpagonum**: Three partitive genitives with **numero** (A.G. 346.a.1). Note the asyndeton construction (A.G. 323.b). **harpagonum**: "Hooks fastened to long poles, with which they intend to pull down the breastworks on the Roman ramparts." (Walker, 405) **effecto**: The perfect tense of the participle represents the action as completed at the time indicated by the tense of the main verb (A.G. 489).

media nocte: Ablative of *time when* (A.G. 423.1). **media**: The adjective designates not what object, but what part of it is meant (A.G. 293).

silentio: Ablative of manner (A.G. 412.b).

ex castris: Ablative of *place from which* with the preposition **ex** (A.G. 426.1).

ad campestris munitiones: Accusative of *place to which* with the preposition **ad** (A.G. 426.2). **campestris**: Accusative plural adjective; **-is** for **-es** is the regular form in i-stem adjectives (A.G. 114.a and 115 and a).

accedunt: The main verb of the main clause (A.G. 278.b). The historical present, giving vividness to the narrative, is present in Chapter 81 (A.G. 469). This usage, common in all languages, comes from imagining past events as going on before our eyes (*repraesentatio*) (A.G. 469 Note).

(81.2-3) Subito clamore sublato, qua significatione qui in oppido obsidebantur de suo adventu cognoscere possent, cratis proicere, fundis, sagittis, lapidibus nostros de vallo proturbare reliquaque quae ad oppugnationem pertinent parant admini(3)strare.

ad, *to.*

adventus, -us, m., *coming, approach, arrival.*

cognosco, -gnoscere, -gnovi, cognitus, *learn, ascertain, recognize.*

de, *about, concerning; from, down from.*

in, *in.*

nostri, -orum, m., pl., *our men, our side.*

oppidum, -i, n., *fortified town, city.*

paro, -are, -avi, -atus, *prepare, make ready.*

administro, -are, -avi, -atus, *administer, arrange for, get ready.*

clamor, -oris, m., *outcry, clamor, noise, din.*

crates, -is, f., *wicker-work, hurdle, fascine, bundle of brushwood.*

funda, -ae, f., *sling.*

lapis, -idis, m., *stone.*

obsideo, -sidere, -sedi, -sessus, *besiege, blockade.*

oppugnatio, -onis, f., *siege, assault, attack.*

pertineo, -tinere, -tinui, -----, *pertain to, concern, belong to, have to do with.*

possum, posse, potui, -----, *be able.*
proturbo, -are, -avi, -atus, *drive away, repulse.*
qui, quae, quod, *who, which, what.*
sagitta, -ae, f., *arrow.*
subito, *suddenly, on a sudden.*
tollo, tollere, sustuli, sublatus, *raise, send up.*

proicio, -icere, -ieci, -iectus, *fling, cast, throw down.*
-que, *and.*
reliqua, -orum, n., pl., *the remaining things.*
significatio, -onis, f., *sign, signal.*
suus, -a, -um, *their.*
vallum, -i, n., *rampart, wall, entrenchment.*

Subito ... possent: Ablative absolute with dependent clauses.
Subito clamore sublato: Ablative absolute (A.G. 419-20). **subito**: Either an adverb modifying **sublato** (A.G. 320-21) or a singular, masculine, ablative attributive adjective (from **subitus, -a, -um**) modifying **clamore** (A.G. 285.1). The adverbial use is common in Caesar; examples in *BG* Book 7 alone are at 27.3, 38.1, 46.5, 50.1, 55.8, 59.6, 61.1, 69.7, 70.2. As an adjective it is less common; see *BG* 3.7.1 and *BC* 3.8.3, 27.1, 77.1. **sublato**: The perfect tense of the participle represents the action as completed at the time indicated by the tense of the main verb (A.G. 489).
qua significatione ... possent: A relative clause of purpose is introduced by a relative pronoun and takes the subjunctive (A.G. 531.2).
qua significatione: Ablative of means (A.G. 409). **qua**: Singular, feminine, ablative relative pronoun (A.G. 305). The antecedent is **significatione** in its own clause (adjectival use) (A.G. 307.b). The relative is here equivalent to **ut ea** (A.G. 531.2 Note). **possent**: The main verb of the subordinate clause (A.G. 278.b). Imperfect subjunctive; the tense of the subjunctive is in secondary sequence and follows the rules for the sequence of tense after the historical present tense of **parant** (A.G. 482-85, esp. 485.e). The pronoun **ei** (the interior Gauls), the supplied antecedent of **qui**, is understood as the subject (A.G. 271.a).
qui ... obsidebantur: A clause dependent on a subjunctive clause (**qua ... possent**) normally takes the subjunctive (attraction) (A.G. 303 and 593). However, when a dependent clause is not regarded as a necessary logical part of the clause, the indicative is used. The indicative serves to emphasize the fact, as true independently of the statement contained in the subjunctive clause (A.G. 593.a Note 1). **qui**: Plural, masculine, nominative relative pronoun (A.G. 305). The antecedent is omitted, supply **ei** (A.G. 307.c). Nominative subject (A.G. 339). **obsidebantur**: The main verb of the subordinate clause (A.G. 278.b).
in oppido: Ablative of *place where* with the preposition **in** (locative ablative) (A.G. 426.3).
de suo adventu: Prepositional phrase, **de** with the ablative here means "about, concerning" (*OLD* **de** 12). **suo**: Singular, masculine, ablative possessive pronoun used as an adjective modifying **adventu** (A.G. 302).
cognoscere: Complementary infinitive after **possent** (A.G. 456).
cratis: Accusative direct object of the infinitive **proicere** (A.G. 387 and 451.3). Accusative plural noun; **-is** for **-es** is the regular form in i-stem nouns (A.G. 65-67 and 74.c).
proicere: Complementary infinitive after **parant** (A.G. 456). "In order to cover over the trenches." (Kelsey, 430)
fundis, sagittis, lapidibus: Three ablatives of instrument (A.G. 409). Note the asyndeton construction (A.G. 323.b).
nostros: Plural, masculine, accusative possessive pronoun used substantively to denote a special class (A.G. 302.d). Accusative direct object of the infinitive **proturbare** (A.G. 387 and 451.3).
de vallo: Ablative of *place from which* with the preposition **de** (A.G. 426.1). "The outer Roman rampart." (Kelsey, 430)
proturbare: Complementary infinitive after **parant** (A.G. 456).
reliquaque: Plural, neuter, accusative adjective used substantively (A.G. 288). Accusative direct object of the infinitive **administrare** (A.G. 387 and 451.3). **-que**: The enclitic conjunction connects the last infinitive in the series **proturbare ... administrare** (A.G. 323.c.3).
quae ... pertinent: Relative clause (A.G. 303). **quae**: Plural, neuter, nominative relative pronoun used substantively (A.G. 305). The antecedent is **reliqua** (A.G. 307). Nominative subject (A.G. 339). **pertinent**: The main verb of the subordinate clause (A.G. 278.b).
ad oppugnationem: Prepositional phrase, **ad** with the accusative here means "to" (*OLD* **ad** 41).
parant: The main verb of the main clause (A.G. 278.b). The pronoun **ei**, with **Galli** (the relief army) as the antecedent, is understood as the subject (A.G. 271.a).
administrare: Complementary infinitive after **parant** (A.G. 456).

(81.3-4) Eodem tempore clamore exaudito dat tuba signum (4) suis Vercingetorix atque ex oppido educit.

atque, *and then.*
do, dare, dedi, datus, *give.*
ex, *from, out of.*

idem, eadem, idem, *the same.*
signum, -i, n., *signal.*
tempus, -oris, n., *time.*
Vercingetorix, -igis, m., *Vercingetorix.*

clamor, -oris, m., *outcry, clamor, noise, din.*
educo, -ducere, -duxi, -ductus, *lead out, lead forth.*
exaudio, -dire, -divi, -ditus, *hear distinctly, hear plainly.*
oppidum, -i, n., *fortified town, city.*
sui, -orum, m., pl., *his men, with or without own.*
tuba, -ae, f., *trumpet.*

Eodem tempore: Ablative of *time when* (A.G. 423.1). **Eodem**: Singular, neuter, ablative demonstrative pronoun used as an adjective modifying **tempore** (A.G. 296.1 and a).
clamore exaudito: Ablative absolute (A.G. 419-20). **exaudito**: The perfect tense of the participle represents the action as completed at the time indicated by the tense of the main verb (A.G. 489).
dat ... Vercingetorix: The reversal of the normal word order (subject first, verb last) is called hyperbaton (A.G. 596) (Gotoff, 6-10).
dat: The main verb of the coordinate clause **Eodem ... Vercingetorix** (A.G. 278.a). The subject, **Vercingetorix**, follows the verb.
tuba: Ablative of instrument (A.G. 409).

signum: Accusative direct object of **dat** (A.G. 387).

suis: Plural, masculine, dative possessive pronoun used substantively used to denote a special class (A.G. 302.d). Dative indirect object of the transitive verb **dat** (A.G. 362).

Vercingetorix: Nominative subject of **dat ... educit** (A.G. 339). See Appendix A.

atque: The conjunction connects a preliminary action (**dat**) with the main action (**educit**) and means "and then" (*OLD* **atque** 7).

ex oppido: Ablative of *place from which* with the preposition **ex** (A.G. 426.1).

educit: The main verb of the coordinate clause **ex ... educit** (A.G. 278.a). The pronoun eos, with **suis** as the antecedent, is understood as the accusative direct object.

(81.4-5) **Nostri, ut superioribus diebus, ut cuique erat locus attributus, ad munitiones accedunt; fundis, librilibus sudibusque, quas in opere (5) disposuerant, ac glandibus Gallos proterrent.**

ac, *and.*

ad, *to, towards.*
dies, -ei, m. and f., *day.*

funda, -ae, f., *sling.*
glans, glandis, f., *sling-shot, bullet.*
librile, -is, n., *a weapon consisting of a stone thrown by an attached thong.*

munitio, -onis, f., *works of fortifications, entrenchment, defenses.*
opus, operis, n., *works, line of works, fortification.*
-que, *and.*
quisque, -----, quidque, *each one, each thing.*
superior, -or, -us, *former, earlier, previous.*

accedo, -cedere, -cessi, -cessurus, *come to, draw near, approach.*
attribuo, -uere, -ui, -utus, *assign, allot.*
dispono, -ponere, -posui, -positus, *set in various places, distribute.*
Galli, -orum, m., *the Gauls.*
in, *in.*
locus, -i, m., *station, appointed place, post, place, position.*
nostri, -orum, m., pl., *our men, our side.*
proterreo, -ere, -ui, -itus, *frighten away or off.*
qui, quae, quod, *who, which, what.*
sudis, -is, f., *stake, pile.*
ut, *as.*

Nostri: Plural, masculine, nominative possessive pronoun used substantively used to denote a special class (A.G. 302.d). Nominative subject of **accedunt** (A.G. 339).

ut ... ut: The second **ut** seems superfluous. The Loeb text reads **ut ... ut** but the Budé text reads **ut ... suus**, the **suus** being an adjective modifying **locus**.

ut superioribus diebus: Parenthetical remark without a verb. **ut**: Relative adverb meaning "as" (*OLD* **ut** 12). **superioribus diebus**: Ablative of *time when* (A.G. 423.1). **superioribus**: Defective comparative adjective (A.G. 130.b).

ut ... erat ... attributus: The relative adverb **ut** ("as") with the indicative introduces a parenthetical remark (*OLD* **ut** 12). **erat ... attributus**: The main verb of the subordinate clause (A.G. 278.b). The pluperfect verb is here split (tmesis) (A.G. 640). The pluperfect denotes an action completed in past time (A.G. 477).

cuique: Singular, masculine, dative indefinite pronoun used substantively (A.G. 151.g). Dative indirect object of **erat ... attributus**; verbs which in the active voice take the accusative and dative retain the dative when used in the passive (A.G. 365).

locus: Nominative subject (A.G. 339).

ad munitiones: Accusative of *place to which* with the preposition **ad** (A.G. 426.2).

accedunt: The main verb of the main clause (A.G. 278.b).

fundis, librilibus sudibusque ... ac glandibus: Four ablatives of instrument (A.G. 409). Edwards notes that "it is possible to take *fundis librilibus* together 'with one-pounder slings'." (Edwards, 498) **fundis librilibus**: "Stones weighing a pound, and attached to the end of a strap or short rope; skillfully thrown, they became a formidable means of warfare." (Kelsey, 430) **sudibus**: "Pointed stakes, burned at the end to harden the point, and used as javelins. Similar darts were made by Cicero, when, owing to the long duration of the attack on his camp, the supply of ordinary weapons gave out. See 5.40." (Kelsey, 430) **-que**: The enclitic conjunction connects the first pair of ablative nouns with the third noun (A.G. 324.a). **ac**: The conjunction connects the final ablative noun in the series and means "and" (*OLD* **atque** 12). **glandibus**: "Acorn-shaped sling-shots." (Kelsey, 430)

quas ... disposuerant: Relative clause (A.G. 303). **quas**: Plural, feminine, accusative relative pronoun used substantively (A.G. 305). The antecedent is **sudibus** (A.G. 307). Accusative direct object of **disposuerant** (A.G. 387). **disposuerant**: The main verb of the subordinate clause (A.G. 278.b). The pronoun ei, with **Nostri** as the antecedent, is understood as the subject (A.G. 271.a). The pluperfect denotes an action completed in past time (A.G. 477).

in opere: Ablative of *place where* with the preposition **in** (locative ablative) (A.G. 426.3).

Gallos: Accusative direct object of **proterrent** (A.G. 387). See Appendix A.

proterrent: The main verb of the main clause (A.G. 278.b). The pronoun ei, with **Nostri** as the antecedent, is understood as the subject (A.G. 271.a).

(81.5-6) **Prospectu tenebris adempto multa utrimque vulnera accipiuntur. Com(6)plura tormentis tela coiciuntur.**

accipio, -cipere, -cepi, -ceptus, *receive, accept.*

complures, -a and **-ia**, *several, a number of, many.*
multus, -a, -um, *many.*
telum, -i, n., *dart, spear.*

adimo, -imere, -emi, -emptus, *take away, remove, deprive.*
coicio, -icere, -ieci, -iectus, *hurl, cast, throw.*
prospectus, -us, m., *view, sight.*
tenebrae, -arum, f., pl., *darkness.*

tormentum, -i, n., *torsion-hurlers, engines of war, artillery.*
vulnus, -eris, n., *wound.*

utrimque, *on both sides.*

Prospectu tenebris adempto: Ablative absolute (A.G. 419-20). tenebris: Ablative of cause without a preposition (A.G. 404). adempto: The perfect tense of the participle represents the action as completed at the time indicated by the tense of the main verb (A.G. 489). "The attack had begun about midnight." (Kelsey, 430)
multa ... vulnera: Nominative subject (A.G. 339). "The soldiers could not parry the blows because on account of the darkness they could not see the missiles coming." (Kelsey, 430)
utrimque: Adverb (A.G. 320-21).
accipiuntur: The main verb of the main clause (A.G. 278.b).
Complura ... tela: Nominative subject (A.G. 339). Complura: Compound of the comparative adjective plus (A.G. 120.c).
tormentis: Ablative of instrument (A.G. 409).
coiciuntur: The main verb of the simple sentence (A.G. 278.1).

(81.6) At M. Antonius et C. Trebonius legati, quibus hae partes ad defendendum obvenerant, qua ex parte nostros premi intellexerant, eis auxilio ex ulterioribus castellis deductos summittebant.

ad, *for, for the purpose of.*
auxilium, -i, n., *help, aid, assistance, relief.*
castellum, -i, n., *redoubt, fortress, stronghold.*
defendo, -fendere, -fensi, -fensus, *defend, guard, protect.*
ex, *on, at; from, out of.*
intellego, -legere, -lexi, -lectus, *understand, see clearly, perceive, ascertain.*
legatus, -i, m., *lieutenant, lieutenant-general.*
nostri, -orum, m., pl., *our men, our side.*
pars, partis, f., *region, district, place.*
qui, quae, quod, *who, which, what.*

ulterior, -ius, *farther, more remote* or *distant.*

at, *but, but on the other hand.*
C. Trebonius, -i, m., *Gaius Trebonius.*
deduco, -ducere, -duxi, -ductus, *withdraw, lead, bring.*
et, *and.*
hic, haec, hoc, *this; he, she, it.*
is, ea, id, *he, she, it; that, this.*
M. Antonius, -i, m., *Marcus Antonius.*
obvenio, -venire, -veni, -ventus, *fall to the lot of, fall to.*
premo, -ere, pressi, pressus, *press, harass, oppress.*
summitto, -mittere, -misi, -missus, *send as reinforcement, send as support.*

At: Conjunction, introduces a change of subject (A.G. 324.d) (*OLD* at 2).
M. Antonius et C. Trebonius: Two nominative subjects of summittebant (A.G. 339). M. Antonius: This is the famous Marc Anthony, who will eventually assume command of one half of the Roman world upon Caesar's assassination, consort with Cleopatra, lose the civil war to Octaivan (Augustus), and be the subject of Shakespeare's *Antony and Cleopatria.* See Appendix A. M.: Abbreviated form of the praenomen Marcus (A.G. 108.c). et: The conjunction connects the two nominative nouns (A.G. 324.a). C. Trebonius: See Appendix A. C.: Abbreviated form of the praenomen Gaius (A.G. 108.c).
legati: A plural nominative noun in apposition to both proper nouns M. Antonius and C. Trebonius (A.G. 282.a).
quibus ... obvenerant: Relative clause (A.G. 303). quibus: Plural, masculine, dative relative pronoun used substantively (A.G. 305). The antecedent is M. Antonius and C. Trebonius (A.G. 307). Dative indirect object of the intransitive verb obvenerant (A.G. 366).
obvenerant: The main verb of the subordinate clause (A.G. 278.b). The pluperfect denotes an action completed in past time (A.G. 477).
hae partes: Nominative subject (A.G. 339). "The defenses in the plain." (Walker, 405) hae: Plural, feminine, nominative demonstrative pronoun used as an adjective modifying partes (A.G. 296.1 and a).
ad defendendum: The preposition ad with the accusative gerund denotes purpose (A.G. 506). defendendum: Singular, neuter, accusative gerund (A.G. 501-02).
qua ... intellexerant: Relative clause (A.G. 303). qua: See below. intellexerant: The main verb of the subordinate clause (A.G. 278.b). The pronoun ei, with M. Antonius ... C. Trebonius as the antecedent, is understood as the subject (A.G. 271.a). The pluperfect denotes an action completed in past time (A.G. 477).
qua ex parte: Ablative of *position* with the preposition ex (A.G. 429.b). qua: Singular, feminine, ablative relative pronoun (A.G. 305). The antecedent is parte in its own clause (adjectival use) (A.G. 307.b). ex: A monosyllabic preposition is often placed between a noun and its adjective (A.G. 599.d.2).
nostros premi: Accusative/infinitive construction in indirect discourse after intellexerant (A.G. 577 ff.). nostros: Plural, masculine, accusative possessive pronoun used substantively to denote a special class (A.G. 302.d). premi: Present infinitive; the tense of the infinitive in indirect discourse is relative to that of the verb of saying (A.G. 584).
eis auxilio: Dative of the purpose or end (double dative). The dative of an abstract noun (auxilio) is used to show that for which a thing serves or which it accomplishes, with another dative of the person or thing affected (eis) (A.G. 382.1). eis: Plural, masculine, dative demonstrative pronoun used substantively (A.G. 296.2). The antecedent is nostros (A.G. 297.e).
ex ulterioribus castellis: Ablative of *place from which* with the preposition ex (A.G. 426.1). Construe this with deductos.
ulterioribus: Defective comparative adjective (A.G. 130.a).
deductos: Plural, masculine, accusative, perfect, passive participle used substantively (A.G. 494.a). The noun milites is understood (A.G. 288.b). Accusative direct object of summittebant (A.G. 387).
summittebant: The main verb of the main clause (A.G. 278.b).

(82.1-2) Dum longius ab munitione aberant Galli, plus multitudine telorum proficiebant; postea quam propius successerunt,

346

aut se stimulis inopinantes induebant aut in scrobes delati transfodiebantur aut ex vallo ac turribus traiecti pilis (2) muralibus interibant.

ab, *from.*

ac, *and.*
defero, -ferre, -tuli, -latus, *fall, sink down.*
ex, *from.*
in, *into.*

inopinans, -antis, *not expecting, unaware, off one's guard.*
longius, *further, at a distance.*
munitio, -onis, f., *works of fortifications, entrenchment, defenses.*
pilum, -i, n., *javelin, pike.*
postea quam, *after.*
prope, comp. -ius, *near.*
stimulus, -i, m., *prick, spur.*

sui, sibi, se, or sese, nom. wanting, *themselves.*
traicio, -icere, -ieci, -iectus, *strike through, pierce, transfix.*

turris, -is, f., *tower.*

absum, -esse, afui, -futurus, *be distant, be absent* or *away from.*
aut ... aut ... aut, *either ... or... or.*
dum, *so long as, when, while.*
Galli, -orum, m., *the Gauls.*
induo, -duere, -dui, -dutus, (with se), *impale themselves.*
intereo, -ire, -ii, -iturus, *perish, be destroyed, die.*
multitudo, -inis, f., *great number, multitude.*
muralis, -e, *wall-,*
plus, *more.*
proficio, -ficere, -feci, -fectus, *effect, gain, accomplish.*
scrobis, -is, m., and f., *pit, wolf-pit.*
succedo, -cedere, -cessi, -cessurus, *come up, approach, advance.*
telum, -i, n., *dart, spear.*
transfodio, -fodere, -fodi, -fossus, *pierce through, thrust through, transfix.*
vallum, -i, n., *rampart, wall, entrenchment.*

Dum ... aberant: Temporal clause; the conjunction **dum** with the imperfect indicative means "so long as" (A.G. 556.a). **aberant**: The main verb of the subordinate clause (A.G. 278.b).
longius: Comparative adverb (A.G. 218 and 320-21).
ab munitione: Ablative of separation with the preposition **ab** after **aberant** (A.G. 402).
Galli: Nominative subject of **aberant** (A.G. 339). This is the exterior relief army. See Appendix A.
plus: Adverb (A.G. 320-21).
multitudine: Ablative of means (A.G. 409).
telorum: Partitive genitive with **multitudine** (A.G. 346.a.1).
proficiebant: The main verb of the main clause (A.G. 278.b). The pronoun **ei**, with **Galli** as the antecedent, is understood as the subject (A.G. 271.a).
postea quam ... successerunt: Temporal clause; the conjunction **postea quam** with the perfect indicative means "after" (A.G. 543).
successerunt: The main verb of the subordinate clause (A.G. 278.b). The pronoun **ei**, with **Galli** as the antecedent, is understood as the subject (A.G. 271.a).
propius: Comparative adverb (A.G. 218 and 320-21).
aut ... aut ... aut: The triple connective introduces three logically exclusive alternatives, "either ... or"... or (*OLD* **aut** 1). The conjunctions connect the three main verbs **induebant ... transfodiebantur ... interibant**.
se: Plural, masculine, accusative direct reflexive pronoun (A.G. 300.1). The antecedent is **inopinantes (Galli)**, the subject of **induebant** (A.G. 299). Accusative direct object of **induebant** (A.G. 387).
stimulis: Ablative of *place where* without a preposition (locative ablative) where there normally is one (A.G. 426.3). For a description of their construction see 73.9.
inopinantes: Plural, masculine, nominative, present participle used as a predicate, where in English a phrase or a subordinate clause would be more normal (A.G. 496). The pronoun **ei**, with **Galli** as the antecedent, is understood. Nominative subject (A.G. 339).
induebant: The main verb of the coordinate clause **postea ... induebant** (A.G. 278.a). The transitive verb **induo** takes the accusative of person (**se**) and ablative of thing (**stimulis**) (A.G. 364).
in scrobes: Accusative of *place to which* with the preposition **in** (A.G. 426.2). For a description of their construction see 73.5-9.
delati: Plural, masculine, nominative, perfect passive participle used as a predicate, where in English a phrase or a subordinate clause would be more normal (A.G. 496). The pronoun **ei**, with **Galli** as the antecedent, is understood. Nominative subject (A.G. 339).
transfodiebantur: The main verb of the coordinate clause **in ... transfodiebantur** (A.G. 278.a).
ex vallo ac turribus: Ablative of *place from which* with the preposition **ex** (A.G. 4266.1). **ac**: The conjunction connects the two ablative nouns in the prepositional phrase and means "and" (*OLD* **atque** 12).
traiecti: Plural, masculine, nominative, perfect passive participle used as a predicate, where in English a phrase or a subordinate clause would be more normal (A.G. 496). The pronoun **ei**, with **Galli** as the antecedent, is understood. Nominative subject (A.G. 339).
pilis muralibus: Ablative of instrument (A.G. 409). This is "a kind of pike used by defenders of fortified positions" (*OLD* **pilum2**). "Much larger and heavier than the common pikes, and suited only for hurling from an elevation." (Kelsey, 373)
interibant: The main verb of the coordinate clause **ex ... interibant** (A.G. 278.a).

(82.2-3) **Multis undique vulneribus acceptis, nulla munitione perrupta, cum lux appeteret, veriti ne ab latere aperto ex superioribus castris eruptione circumveni(3)rentur, se ad suos receperunt.**

ab, *on.*
ad, *to.*

accipio, -cipere, -cepi, -ceptus, *receive, accept.*
apertus, -a, um, *open, exposed, unprotected.*

appeto, -petere, -petivi or -petii, -petitus, *draw nigh, approach, be at hand.*
circumvenio, -venire, -veni, -ventus, *surround.*
eruptio, -onis, f., *a bursting forth, sally, sortie.*
latus, -eris, n., *side, flank.*
multus, -a, -um, *many.*

ne, *lest, that.*
perrumpo, -rumpere, -rupi, -ruptus, *break* or *burst through,*

break down, overcome.
sui, sibi, se, or sese, nom. wanting, *themselves.*
sui, -orum, m., pl., *their men,* with or without *own.*
vereor, -eri, -itus, *fear, be afraid of.*

castra, -orum, n., pl., *camp, encampment.*
cum, *when.*
ex, *from, out of.*
lux, lucis, f., *light, daylight.*
munitio, -onis, f., *works of fortifications, entrenchment, defenses.*
nullus, -a, -um, *no, not any.*
recipio, -cipere, -cepi, -ceptus, (with se), *return, retreat.*
superior, -or, -us, *higher, upper.*
undique, *from all sides, from all parts, everywhere.*
vulnus, -eris, n., *wound.*

Multis undique vulneribus acceptis: Ablative absolute (A.G. 419-20). **undique**: Adverb (A.G. 217.a and 320-21). **acceptis**: The perfect tense of the participle represents the action as completed at the time indicated by the tense of the main verb (A.G. 489).
nulla munitione perrupta: Ablative absolute (A.G. 419-20). Note the asyndeton construction between the two ablative absolutes (A.G. 323.b). **perrupta**: The perfect tense of the participle represents the action as completed at the time indicated by the tense of the main verb (A.G. 489).
cum ... appeteret: Temporal clause; the relative adverb **cum** ("when") with the imperfect subjunctive describes the circumstances that accompanied the action of the main verb (A.G. 546). **appeteret**: The main verb of the subordinate clause (A.G. 278.b).
lux: Nominative subject (A.G. 339).
veriti ne ... circumvenirentur: The conjunction **ne** ("lest") with the subjunctive forms a substantive clause of fearing after **veriti** (A.G. 564). **veriti**: Nominative, perfect, deponent participle used as a predicate, where in English a phrase or a subordinate clause would be more normal (A.G. 496). The pronoun **ei**, with **Galli** (exterior relief army) as the antecedent, is understood. Nominative subject of **receperunt** (A.G. 339). **circumvenirentur**: The main verb of the subordinate clause (A.G. 278.b). Imperfect subjunctive; the tense of the subjunctive is in secondary sequence and follows the rules for the sequence of tense after **receperunt** (A.G. 482-85). The pronoun **ei**, with **veriti** as the antecedent, is understood as the subject (A.G. 271.a).
ab latere aperto: Ablative of *position* with the preposition **ab** (A.G. 429.b).
ex superioribus castris: Ablative of *place from which* with the preposition **ex** (A.G. 426.1). "One of the main camps of the Roman legions, here referred to, lay on a height to the southward of Alesia; the other (referred to in ch. 83) on a height to the northward." (Edwards, 500-501) **superioribus**: Defective comparative adjective (A.G. 130.b).
eruptione: Ablative of means (A.G. 409).
se: Plural, masculine, accusative direct reflexive pronoun (A.G. 300.1). The antecedent is **veriti**, the subject of **receperunt** (A.G. 299). Accusative direct object of **receperunt** (A.G. 387).
ad suos: Prepositional phrase, **ad** with the accusative here means "to" (*OLD* **ad** 1). **suos**: Plural, masculine, accusative possessive pronoun used substantively to denote a special class (A.G. 302.d).
receperunt: The main verb of the main clause (A.G. 278.b). The verb **recipere** used reflexively means "to return" (*OLD* **recipio** 12).

(82.3-4) At interiores, dum ea quae a Vercingetorige ad eruptionem praeparata erant proferunt, (4) priores fossas explent, diutius in his rebus administrandis morati prius suos discessisse cognoverunt quam munitionibus appropinquarent. Ita re infecta in oppidum reverterunt.

a(b), *by.*
administro, -are, -avi, -atus, *manage, carry on, administer.*

at, *but, but on the other hand.*

discedo, -cedere, -cessi, -cessurus, *go away, depart, leave.*
dum, *when, while.*
expleo, -plere, -plevi, -pletus, *fill up, fill.*
hic, haec, hoc, *this; he, she, it.*
infectus, -a, -um, *not done, unfinished, not effected* or *achieved.*
is, ea, id, *he, she, it; that, this.*
moror, -ari, -atus, *tarry, delay, linger.*

oppidum, -i, n., *fortified town, city.*

prior, prius, *first, nearer, forward.*
profero, -ferre, -tuli, -latus, *bring out, bring forth.*
res, rei, f., *matter, affair.*
sui, -orum, m., pl., *their men,* with or without *own.*

ad, *for the purpose of.*
appropinquo, -are, -avi, -atus, *approach, come near, draw near.*
cognosco, -gnoscere, -gnovi, cognitus, *learn, ascertain, recognize.*
diu, comp. diutius, *long, for a long time.*
eruptio, -onis, f., *a bursting forth, sally, sortie.*
fossa, -ae, f., *ditch, trench, entrenchment, fosse.*
in, *in the matter of, when dealing with; into.*
interiores, -um, m., pl., *those within the city.*
ita, *in this way, thus.*
munitio, -onis, f., *works of fortifications, entrenchment, defenses.*
praeparo, -are, -avi, -atus, *make ready beforehand, prepare.*
prius ... quam, *before, sooner than.*
qui, quae, quod, *who, which, what.*
reverto, -ere, reverti, *return, come back, go back.*
Vercingetorix, -igis, m., *Vercingetorix.*

At: Conjunction, introduces a change of subject (A.G. 324.d) (*OLD* **at** 2).

interiores: Plural, masculine, nominative adjective used substantively (A.G. 288). Defective comparative adjective (A.G. 130.a). Nominative subject of **explent** (A.G. 339).

dum ... proferunt: Temporal clause; the conjunction **dum** ("when, while") with the present indicative denotes continued action in past time (A.G. 556). **proferunt**: The main verb of the subordinate clause (A.G. 278.b). The pronoun **ei**, with **interiores** as the antecedent, is understood as the subject (A.G. 271.a).

ea: Plural, neuter, accusative demonstrative pronoun used substantively (A.G. 296.2). The pronoun is correlative to the relative clause **quae ... erant** (A.G. 297.d). Accusative direct object of **proferunt** (A.G. 387).

quae ... praeparata erant: Relative clause (A.G. 303). **quae**: Plural, neuter, nominative relative pronoun used substantively (A.G. 305). The antecedent is **ea** (A.G. 307). Nominative subject (A.G. 339). **praeparata erant**: The main verb of the subordinate clause (A.G. 278.b). The pluperfect denotes an action completed in past time (A.G. 477).

a Vercingetorige: Ablative of agent with the preposition **a(b)** after the passive verb **praeparata erant** (A.G. 405). **Vercingetorige**: See Appendix A.

ad eruptionem: Prepositional phrase, **ad** with the accusative here denotes purpose meaning "for the purpose of" (*OLD* ad 44).

priores fossas: Accusative direct object of **explent** (A.G. 387). "First came the inmost trench, then two parallel trenches 400 feet west (see Chap. 72); in the intervening space were the ingenious and complicated contrivances described in Chap. 73, which well accomplished the purpose of making a simultaneous attack on Caesar's forces from both sides practically impossible." (Kelsey, 431) **priores**: Defective comparative adjective (A.G. 130.a).

explent: The main verb of the coordinate clause **At ... explent** (A.G. 278.a).

diutius: Irregular comparative adverb (A.G. 218.a and 320-21). The comparative degree here denotes a considerable or excessive degree of the quality meaning "too" (A.G. 291.a).

in his rebus administrandis: Prepositional phrase, **in** with the ablative here means "in the matter of, when dealing with" (*OLD* in 42). **his**: Plural, feminine, ablative demonstrative pronoun used as an adjective modifying **rebus** (A.G. 296.1 and a). **administrandis**: Plural, feminine, ablative gerundive modifying **rebus** after the preposition **in** (A.G. 507.3).

morati: Perfect, deponent participle used as a predicate, where in English a phrase or a subordinate clause would be more normal (A.G. 496). The pronoun **ei**, with **interiores** as the antecedent, is understood. Nominative subject of **cognoverunt** (A.G. 339).

prius: Construed with **quam** below.

suos discessisse: Accusative/infinitive construction in indirect discourse after **cognoverunt** (A.G. 577 ff.). **suos**: Plural, masculine, accusative possessive pronoun used substantively to denote a special class (A.G. 302.d). This is the relief army. **discessisse**: Perfect infinitive; the tense of the infinitive in indirect discourse is relative to that of the verb of saying (A.G. 584). The perfect infinitive here represents the pluperfect tense as the relief army had completely withdrawn by this time (A.G. 484.a).

cognoverunt: The main verb of the coordinate clause **diutius ... appropinquarent** (A.G. 278.a).

(prius) ... quam ... appropinquarent: Temporal clause; the conjunction **prius ... quam** ("before") with the imperfect subjunctive denotes action which did not take place (A.G. 551.b). **prius ... quam**: The conjunction is here split (tmesis) (A.G. 640).

appropinquarent: The main verb of the subordinate clause (A.G. 278.b). The pronoun **ei**, with **morati** (**interiores**) as the antecedent, is understood as the subject (A.G. 271.a).

munitionibus: Dative indirect object of the intransitive verb **appropinquarent** (A.G. 366).

Ita: Adverb (A.G. 217.c and 320-21).

re infecta: Ablative absolute with an adjective (**infecta**) taking the place of the participle (there is no participle for "being") (A.G. 419.a-20).

in oppidum: Accusative of *place to which* with the preposition **in** (A.G. 426.2).

reverterunt: The main verb of the main clause (A.G. 278.b). The pronoun **ei**, with **morati** (**interiores**) as the antecedent, is understood as the subject (A.G. 271.a).

4.Q CHAPTERS 83-88: THE THIRD AND FINAL ATTEMPT AT THE RELIEF OF ALESIA; THE GAULS ARE AGAIN DEFEATED; THE RELIEVING ARMY FLEES AND A GREAT SLAUGHTER ENSUES; VERCINGETORIX IS HOPELESSLY TRAPPED

Chapters 83-88: Compare John Keegan's critique of Caesarian battle narrative to these six chapters. None of his critiques (disjunctive movement, uniformity of behavior, simplified characterization, and simplified motivation) are valid for this narrative section. (Keegan, 61-72, esp. 64 and Mannetter, Chapter 5).

(83.1) Bis magno cum detrimento repulsi Galli quid agant consulunt; locorum peritos adhibent; ex his superiorum castrorum situs munitionesque cognoscunt.

adhibeo, -hibere, -hibui, -hibitus, *bring in, call in, summon, employ.*

bis, *twice.*

cognosco, -gnoscere, -gnovi, cognitus, *learn, ascertain, recognize.*

cum, *with.*

ex, *from.*

hic, haec, hoc, *this; he, she, it.*

magnus, -a, -um, *great, large.*

ago, agere, egi, actus, *do.*

castra, -orum, n., pl., *camp, encampment.*

consulo, -sulere, -sului, -sultus, *consult, deliberate, take counsel about.*

detrimentum, -i, n., *loss, damage, injury, repulse, reverse, defeat.*

Galli, -orum, m., *the Gauls.*

loca, -orum, n., pl., *places*

munitio, -onis, f., *works of fortifications, entrenchment, defenses.*

peritus, -i, m., *an expert, one familiar with.*
quis, -----, quid, *who?, what?*

situs, -us, m., *situation, site.*

-que, *and.*
repello, -pellere, repulli, repulsus, *drive back, force back, repulse.*
superior, -or, -us, *higher, upper.*

Bis: Numeral adverb (A.G. 138). For the first repulse see Chapters 79-80, for the second see Chapters 81-82.

magno cum detrimento: Ablative of manner with the preposition **cum** (A.G. 412). **cum:** A monosyllabic preposition is often placed between a noun and its adjective (A.G. 599.d.2).

repulsi Galli: Nominative subject (A.G. 339). **repulsi:** Nominative, perfect, passive participle used as a predicate, where in English a phrase or a subordinate clause would be more normal (A.G. 496). **Galli:** See Appendix A. This is the exterior relief army.

quid agant: Indirect question with the subjunctive; the phrase is the object of **consulunt** (A.G. 573-75). **quid:** Singular, neuter, accusative interrogative pronoun used substantively (A.G. 148). Accusative direct object of **agant** (A.G. 387). **agant:** The main verb of the subordinate clause (A.G. 278.b). Present subjunctive; the tense of the subjunctive is normally in secondary sequence after the historical present **consulunt** (A.G. 575). Here it is in primary sequence through *repraesentatio* (A.G. 485.e and 585.b Note). Deliberative subjunctive in an indirect question (A.G. 575.b). The pronoun **ipsi**, with **Galli** as the antecedent, is understood as the subject (A.G. 271.a).

consulunt: The main verb of the main clause (A.G. 278.b). The historical present, giving vividness to the narrative, is present in Chapter 83 (A.G. 469). This usage, common in all languages, comes from imagining past events as going on before our eyes (*repraesentatio*) (A.G. 469 Note).

locorum: Objective genitive with the adjective **peritos** (A.G. 349.a).

peritos: Plural, masculine, accusative adjective used substantively (A.G. 288). The noun **viros** is understood (A.G. 288.b). Accusative direct object of **adhibent** (A.G. 387).

adhibent: The main verb of the simple sentence (A.G. 278.1). The pronoun **ei**, with **Galli** as the antecedent, is understood as the subject (A.G. 271.a).

ex his: Ablative of source with the preposition **ex** (A.G. 403.1). **his:** Plural, masculine, ablative demonstrative pronoun used substantively (A.G. 296.2). The antecedent is **peritos** (A.G. 297.e).

superiorum castrorum: Possessive genitive construed with both nouns **situs munitionesque** (A.G. 343). **superiorum:** Defective comparative adjective (A.G. 130.b).

situs munitionesque: Two accusative direct objects of **cognoscunt** (A.G. 387). **-que:** The enclitic conjunction connects the two accusative nouns (A.G. 324.a).

cognoscunt: The main verb of the simple sentence (A.G. 278.1). The pronoun **ei**, with **Galli** as the antecedent, is understood as the subject (A.G. 271.a).

(83.1-3) Erat a septen(2)trionibus collis, quem propter magnitudinem circuitus opere circumplecti non potuerant nostri: necessarioque paene (3) iniquo loco et leniter declivi castra fecerant.

a(b), *on.*
circuitus, -us, m., *outer edge, boundary, perimeter.*

collis, -is, m., *hill, height, elevation.*
et, *and.*
iniquus, -a, -um, *uneven, sloping, unfavorable, disadvantageous.*
locus, -i, m., *place, position.*
necessario, *of necessity, unavoidably.*
nostri, -orum, m., pl., *our men, our side.*
paene, *almost, nearly.*
propter, *on account of.*
qui, quae, quod, *who, which, what.*
sum, esse, fui, futurus, *be.*

castra, -orum, n., pl., *camp, encampment.*
circumplector, -plecti, -----, *embrace, encompass, surround.*
declivis, -e, *sloping, descending.*
facio, facere, feci, factus, *(with* castra*), pitch.*
leniter, *mildly, gently, slightly.*
magnitudo, -inis, f., *greatness.*
non, *not.*
opus, operis, n., *works, line of works, fortification.*
possum, posse, potui, -----, *be able.*
-que, *and.*
septentriones, -um, m., pl., *the North.*

Erat: The main verb of the main clause (A.G. 278.b). The verb **sum** in the sense of "exist" makes a complete predicate without a predicate noun or adjective ("there was ..."). It is then called the substantive verb and regularly comes first (A.G. 284.b and 598.c).

a septentrionibus: Ablative of position with the preposition **a(b)** (A.G. 429.b).

collis: Nominative subject (A.G. 339).

quem ... nostri: Relative clause (A.G. 303). **quem:** Singular, masculine, accusative relative pronoun used substantively (A.G. 305). The antecedent is **collis** (A.G. 307). Accusative direct object of the infinitive **circumplecti** (A.G. 387 and 451.3). **nostri:** Plural, masculine, nominative possessive pronoun used substantively used to denote a special class (A.G. 302.d). Nominative subject (A.G. 339). The subject is in the last position in the clause (A.G. 597.b).

propter magnitudinem circuitus: Prepositional phrase, **propter** with the accusative here means "on account of" (*OLD* propter 4).

circuitus: Possessive genitive with **magnitudinem** (A.G. 343).

opere: Ablative of means (A.G. 409). This is the outer fortifications.

circumplecti: Complementary infinitive after **potuerant** (A.G. 456).

non: Adverb, the adverb generally precedes the verb if it belongs to no one word in particular (A.G. 217.e, 320-21, and 599.a).

potuerant: The main verb of the subordinate clause (A.G. 278.b). The pluperfect denotes an action completed in past time (A.G.

477).

necessario: Adverb with **fecerant** (A.G. 320-21).

paene: Adverb with the adjective **iniquo** (A.G. 217.c and 320-21).

iniquo loco et ... declivi: Ablative of *place where* without a preposition (A.G. 429.1-2). **iniquo loco**: "Explained by *leniter declivi*. Because the ground sloped down to its outer wall, missiles could easily be thrown into it, and a sloping mound of earth could be built up to its rampart." (Walker, 406) **et**: The conjunction connects the two adjectives modifying **loco** (A.G. 324.a). Two adjectives belonging to the same noun are regularly connected by a conjunction (A.G. 323.d).

leniter: Adverb with the adjective **declivi** (A.G. 214.b and 320-21).

castra: Accusative direct object of **fecerant** (A.G. 387).

fecerant: The main verb of the simple sentence (A.G. 278.1). The pronoun **ei**, with **nostri** as the antecedent, is understood as the subject (A.G. 271.a). Although the pluperfect tense is normally used in subordinate clauses, its use as a main verb is frequent. The pluperfect denotes an action completed in past time (A.G. 477).

(83.3-4) Haec C. Antistius Reginus et C. Caninius Rebilus legati (4) cum duabus legionibus obtinebant.

C. Antistius Reginus, -i, m., *Gaius Antistius Reginus.*	**C. Caninius Rebilus, -i**, m., *Gaius Caninius Rebilus.*
cum, *with.*	**duo, -ae, -o**, *two.*
et, *and.*	**hic, haec, hoc**, *this*; *he, she, it.*
legatus, -i, m., *lieutenant, lieutenant-general.*	**legio, -onis**, f., *legion.*
obtineo, -tinere, -tinui, -tentus, *retain, keep, hold.*	

Haec: Plural, neuter, accusative demonstrative pronoun used substantively (A.G. 296.2). The antecedent is **castra** (A.G. 297.e). Accusative direct object of **obtinebant** (A.G. 387).

C. Antistius Reginus et C. Caninius Rebilus: Two nominative subjects (A.G. 339). **C. Antistius Reginus**: See Appendix A. **C.**: Abbreviated form of the praenomen **Gaius** (A.G. 108.c). **et**: The conjunction connects the two nominative nouns (A.G. 324.a). **C. Caninius Rebilus**: See Appendix A. **C.**: Abbreviated form of the praenomen **Gaius** (A.G. 108.c).

legati: Plural nominative noun in apposition to the two singular proper nouns **C. Antistius Reginus ... C. Caninius Rebilus** (A.G. 282.a).

cum duabus legionibus: Ablative of accompaniment with the preposition **cum** (A.G. 413). "A strong garrison, to compensate for the weakness of the position." (Walker, 406) **duabus**: Declinable cardinal number used as an adjective modifying **legionibus** (A.G. 132-35).

obtinebant: The main verb of the simple sentence (A.G. 278.1).

(83.4-6) Cognitis per exploratores regionibus, duces hostium LX milia ex omni numero deligunt earum civitatum quae maximam virtutis opinio(5)nem habebant; quid quoque pacto agi placeat occulte inter se constituunt; adeundi tempus definiunt cum meridies (6) esse videatur.

adeo, -ire, -ivi, or **-ii, -itus**, *approach, advance, move up to attack.*	**ago, agere, egi, actus**, *do.*
civitas, -tatis, f., *state, nation.*	**cognosco, -gnoscere, -gnovi, cognitus**, *spy out, examine, investigate.*
constituo, -stituere, -stitui, -stitutus, *establish, resolve upon, determine.*	**cum**, *whenever.*
definio, -ire, -ivi, -itus, *define, fix, set.*	**deligo, -ligere, -legi, -lectus**, *choose, select, pick out.*
dux, ducis, m., *leader, general, commander.*	**ex**, *from the number of, from among, of.*
explorator, -oris, m., *spy, scout.*	**habeo, habere, habui, habitus**, *have, hold, possess.*
hostis, -is, m., *enemy, foe*; pl., *the enemy.*	**inter**, *between, among.*
is, ea, id, *he, she, it; that, this.*	**L**, in expression of number, *50.*
maximus, -a, -um, *greatest.*	**meridies, -ei**, m., *mid-day.*
milia, -um, n., pl., *thousand, thousands.*	**numerus, -i**, m., *body, host.*
occulte, *secretly, in secret.*	**omnis, -e**, *the whole.*
opinio, -onis, f., *reputation.*	**pactum -i**, n., *manner, way.*
per, *by* (means of), *through.*	**placeo, placere, placui, placitus**, (imper.), *it seems good.*
-que, *and.*	**qui, quae, quod**, *who, which, what.*
quis, -----, quid, *who? what?*; (as adj., **qui, quae, quod**) *who? what?*	**regio, -onis**, f., *region, territory.*
sui, sibi, se, or **sese**, nom. wanting, *themselves.*	**sum, esse, fui, futurus**, *be.*
tempus, -oris, n., *time.*	**videor, videri, visus sum**, *seem, appear.*
virtus, -utis, f., *manliness, courage, bravery, valor, prowess, vigor.*	**X**, in expression of number, *= 10.*

Cognitis per exploratores regionibus: Ablative absolute (A.G. 419-20). **Cognitis**: The perfect tense of the participle represents the action as completed at the time indicated by the tense of the main verb (A.G. 489). **per exploratores**: Prepositional phrase, the personal agent, when considered as instrument or means, is often expressed by **per** with the accusative meaning "by" (means of) (A.G. 405.b).

duces: Nominative subject (A.G. 339).

hostium: Partitive genitive with **duces** (A.G. 346.a.1).

LX milia: Accusative direct object of **deligunt** (A.G. 387). **milia**: Accusative plural; in the plural **mille** declines as a neuter noun (A.G. 134.d). **LX**: Roman numeral used as an adjective modifying **milia** (A.G. 133).

ex omni numero: Prepositional phrase, **ex** with the ablative instead of the partitive genitive means "from the number of, from among, of". Cardinal numbers (here the Roman numeral **LX**) regularly take the ablative with **ex** instead of the partitive genitive (A.G. 346.c) (*OLD* **ex** 17).

deligunt: The main verb of the main clause (A.G. 278.b).

earum civitatum: Partitive genitive with **LX** (A.G. 346.a.2). **earum**: Plural, feminine, genitive demonstrative pronoun used as an adjective modifying **civitatum** (A.G. 296.1 and a). The pronoun functions as a correlative to the relative clause **quae ... habebant** (A.G. 297.d).

quae ... habebant: Relative clause (A.G. 303). **quae**: Plural, feminine, nominative relative pronoun used substantively (A.G. 305). The antecedent is **civitatum** (A.G. 307). Nominative subject (A.G. 339). **habebant**: The main verb of the subordinate clause (A.G. 278.b). The imperfect here denotes action as continued in past time (A.G. 470).

maximam ... opinionem: Accusative direct object of **habebant** (A.G. 387). **maximam**: Irregular superlative adjective modifying **opinionem** (A.G. 129).

virtutis: Objective genitive with **opinionem** (A.G. 348).

quid quoque ... placeat: A double indirect question with the subjunctive; the phrase is the object of **constituunt** (A.G. 573-75). **quid**: See below. **quoque**: See below. **placeat**: The main verb of the subordinate clause (A.G. 278.b). Present subjunctive; the tense of the subjunctive is normally in secondary sequence after the historical present **constituunt** (A.G. 575). Here it is in primary sequence through *repraesentatio* (A.G. 485.e and 585.b Note). Impersonal use of the verb; the preceding infinitive phrase functions as the subject (A.G. 208.c).

quid quoque pacto agi: The infinitive phrase functions as the subject of the impersonal verb **placeat** (A.G. 454). **quid**: Singular, neuter, accusative interrogative pronoun used substantively (A.G. 148). Accusative subject of the infinitive **agi** (A.G. 397.e). **quoque pacto**: Ablative of means (A.G. 409). **quo**: Singular, neuter, ablative interrogative pronoun used as an adjective modifying **pacto** (A.G. 148.b). **-que**: The enclitic conjunction connects the two interrogative pronouns (A.G. 324.a).

occulte: Adverb (A.G. 214.a and 320-21).

inter se: Prepositional phrase, **inter** with the accusative reflexive pronoun here means "between, among" (*OLD* **inter**1 14). **se**: Plural, masculine, accusative direct reflexive pronoun (A.G. 300.1). The antecedent is **ei** (**duces**), the supplied subject of **constituunt** (A.G. 299).

constituunt: The main verb of the main clause (A.G. 278.b). The pronoun **ei**, with **duces** as the antecedent, is understood as the subject (A.G. 271.a).

adeundi: Singular, neuter, genitive gerund (A.G. 501-02). Objective genitive with **tempus** (A.G. 504).

tempus: Accusative direct object of **definiunt** (A.G. 387).

definiunt: The main verb of the main clause (A.G. 278.b). The pronoun **ei**, with **duces** as the antecedent, is understood as the subject (A.G. 271.a).

cum ... (id) videatur: Temporal clause; the indefinite relative adverb **cum** ("whenever") in direct discourse has the construction of the protasis (A.G. 542). The temporal clause here utilizes the subjunctive as it is in informal indirect discourse (A.G. 542 Note and 591). "Implied indirect discourse for the future; they said, in effect, 'we will attack when it shall seem, etc.'." (Walker, 406) **videatur**: The main verb of the subordinate clause (A.G. 278.b). Present subjunctive; the tense of the subjunctive is normally in secondary sequence after the historical present **definiunt** (A.G. 482-85, esp. 485.e). Here it is in primary sequence through *repraesentatio* (A.G. 485.e and 585.b Note). Impersonal use of the intransitive deponent verb (A.G. 208.d). Supply **id** as the subject (A.G. 318.c).

meridies: Singular, masculine, nominative predicate noun with **esse** after **videatur** (A.G. 283-84). A predicate noun after a complementary infinitive takes the case of the subject of the main verb (A.G. 458).

esse: Complementary infinitive after **videatur** (A.G. 456).

(83.6-7) His copiis Vercassivellaunum Arvernum, unum ex quattuor ducibus, propinquum Vercingetorigis, (7) praeficiunt.

Arvernus, -i, *an Arvernian*.	**copiae, -arum**, f., pl., *forces, troops*.
dux, ducis, m., *leader, general, commander*.	**ex**, *from the number of, from among, of*.
hic, haec, hoc, *this*; *he, she, it*.	**praeficio, -ficere, -feci, -fectus**, *place over, place in command of*.
propinquus, -i, m., *relative*.	**quattuor**, *four*.
unus, -a, -um, *one*.	**Vercassivellaunus, -i**, m., *Vercassivellaunus*.
Vercingetorix, -igis, m., *Vercingetorix*.	

His copiis: Dative indirect object of the transitive verb **praeficiunt** (A.G. 362). **His**: Plural, feminine, dative demonstrative pronoun used as an adjective modifying **copiis** (A.G. 296.1 and a).

Vercassivellaunum: Accusative direct object of the transitive verb **praeficiunt** (A.G. 387). See Appendix A.

Arvernum: An accusative noun in apposition to the proper noun **Vercassivellaunum** (A.G. 282).

unum: An accusative declinable cardinal number used substantively in apposition to the proper noun **Vercassivellaunum** (A.G. 282 and 288).

(unum) ex quattuor ducibus: Prepositional phrase, cardinal numbers regularly take the ablative with the preposition **ex** instead of the partitive genitive meaning "from the number of, from among, of" (A.G. 346.c) (*OLD* **ex** 17). **quattuor**: Indeclinable cardinal number used as an adjective modifying **ducibus** (A.G. 132-35).

propinquum: An accusative adjective used substantively in apposition to **Vercassivellaunum** (A.G. 282 and 288) (*OLD* **propinquus**

4.b).

Vercingetorigis: Possessive genitive with **propinquum** (A.G. 343). See Appendix A.

praeficiunt: The main verb of the simple sentence (A.G. 278.1). The pronoun **ei**, with **duces** as the antecedent, is understood as the subject (A.G. 271.a).

(83.7-8) Ille ex castris prima vigilia egressus prope confecto sub lucem itinere post montem se occultavit mili(8)tesque ex nocturno labore sese reficere iussit.

castra, -orum, n., pl., *camp, encampment.*

egredior, -gredi, -gressus, *go out, go forth, come forth, leave.*
ille, illae, illud, *that; he, she, it.*
iubeo, iubere, iussi, iussus, *order, give orders, bid, command.*
lux, lucis, f., *daylight.*
mons, montis, m., *mountain, elevation, height.*
occulto, -are, -avi, -atus, *hide, conceal, keep secret.*
primus, -a, -um, *first, the first.*
-que, *and.*
sub, *just before.*
vigilia, -ae, f., *watch.*

conficio, -ficere, -feci, -fectus, *complete, finish, accomplish, do.*
ex, *from, out of, from.*
iter, itineris, n., *march, journey.*
labor, -oris, m., *toil, exertion, labor.*
miles, -itis, m., *soldier, foot-solider.*
nocturnus, -a, -um, *by night, of night.*
post, *on the other* or *far side of, behind.*
prope, *near, nearly, almost.*
reficio, -ficere, -feci, -fectus, *refresh.*
sui, sibi, se, or **sese,** nom. wanting *himself, themselves.*

Ille ... egressus: Nominative subject of **occultavit ... iussit** (A.G. 339). **Ille:** Singular, masculine, nominative demonstrative pronoun used substantively (A.G. 296.2). The antecedent is **Vercassivellaunum** (A.G. 297.e). The pronoun marks a change in subject to one previously mentioned (A.G. 601.d). **egressus:** Nominative, perfect, deponent participle used as a predicate, where in English a phrase or a subordinate clause would be more normal (A.G. 496).
ex castris: Ablative of *place from which* with the preposition **ex** (A.G. 426.1).
prima vigilia: Ablative of *time when* (A.G. 423.1). **prima:** Ordinal number used as an adjective (A.G. 132-35). The first watch ends at 9:00.
prope confecto sub lucem itinere: Ablative absolute (A.G. 419-20). **prope:** Adverb (A.G. 320-21). **confecto:** The perfect tense of the participle represents the action as completed at the time indicated by the tense of the main verb (A.G. 489). **sub lucem:** Prepositional phrase, **sub** with the accusative here expresses an idiomatic expression of time meaning "just before" (A.G. 424.e) (*OLD* **sub** 23).
post montem: Prepositional phrase, **post** with the accusative here means "on the other or far side of" (*OLD* **post2** 1.b).
se: Singular, masculine, accusative direct reflexive pronoun (A.G. 300.1). The antecedent is **Ille (Vercassivellaunus),** the subject of **occultavit** (A.G. 299). Accusative direct object of **occultavit** (A.G. 387).
occultavit: The main verb of the coordinate clause **Ille ... occultavit** (A.G. 278.a).
militesque ... reficere: A subject accusative with the infinitive after **iussit.** The construction is equivalent to a substantive clause of purpose (A.G. 563.a). **-que:** The enclitic conjunction connects the two main verbs **occultavit ... iussit** (A.G. 324.a).
ex nocturno labore: Prepositional phrase, **ex** with the ablative here means "from" (expressing recovery) (*OLD* **ex** 2.c).
sese: Plural, masculine, accusative direct reflexive pronoun (A.G. 300.1). The antecedent is **milites,** the accusative subject of **reficere** (A.G. 299). Accusative direct object of the infinitive **reficere** (A.G. 387 and 451.3). Reduplicated form of **se** (A.G. 144.b Note 1).
iussit: The main verb of the coordinate clause **militesque ... iussit** (A.G. 278.a).

(83.8) Cum iam meridies appropinquare videretur, ad ea castra quae supra demonstravimus contendit; eodemque tempore equitatus ad campestris munitiones accedere et reliquae copiae pro castris sese ostendere coeperunt.

accedo, -cedere, -cessi, -cessurus, *come to, draw near, approach.*
appropinquo, -are, -avi, -atus, *approach, come near, draw near.*
castra, -orum, n., pl., *camp, encampment.*
contendo, -tendere, -tendi, -tentus, *hasten, make haste, push forward.*
cum, *when.*

equitatus, -us, m., *cavalry.*
iam, *now, at last.*
is, ea, id, *he, she, it; that, this.*
munitio, -onis, f., *works of fortifications, entrenchment, defenses.*
pro, *in front of, before.*
qui, quae, quod, *who, which, what.*
sui, sibi, se, or **sese,** nom. wanting *themselves.*
tempus, -oris, n., *time.*

ad, *to, towards.*
campester, -tris, -tre, *of level ground, flat, level.*
coepi, -isse, coeptus, *begin, start, commence.*
copiae, -arum, f., pl., *forces, troops.*
demonstro, -are, -avi, -atus, *point out, mention, explain.*
et, *and.*
idem, eadem, idem, *the same.*
meridies, -ei, m., *mid-day.*
ostendo, -tendere, -tendi, -tentus, *show, display.*
-que, *and.*
reliquus, -a, -um, *remaining, the rest.*
supra, *before, previously.*
videor, videri, visus sum, *seem, appear.*

Cum ... videretur: Temporal clause; the relative adverb **cum** ("when") with the imperfect subjunctive describes the circumstances that accompanied the action of the main verb (A.G. 546). **videretur:** The main verb of the subordinate clause (A.G. 278.b).
iam: Adverb (A.G. 215.6, 217.b and 320-21).

meridies: Nominative subject (A.G. 339).

appropinquare: Complementary infinitive after **videretur** (A.G. 456).

ad ea castra: Accusative of *place to which* with the preposition **ad** (A.G. 426.2). **ea**: Plural, neuter, accusative demonstrative pronoun used as an adjective modifying **castra** (A.G. 296.1 and a). The pronoun functions as a correlative to the relative clause **quae ... demonstravimus** (A.G. 297.d).

quae ... demonstravimus: Relative clause (A.G. 303). For the reference see 83.2-4. **quae**: Plural, neuter, accusative relative pronoun used substantively (A.G. 305). The antecedent is **castra** (A.G. 307). Accusative direct object of **demonstravimus** (A.G. 387).

demonstravimus: The main verb of the subordinate clause (A.G. 278.b). The personal pronoun **nos** is understood as the subject but is not expressed except for distinction or emphasis (A.G. 295.a). In Book 7, Caesar refers to himself only in the third person, either in the singular or occasionally in the plural (see **Caesar** at 1.1). Siedler counts 11 uses of the first person plural in Book 7 (Siedler, 46). These uses are at 17.1, 23.2, 25.1, 37.1, 48.1, 58.4, 70.1, 76.1, 79.2, 83.8, and 85.4.

supra: Adverb (A.G. 320-21).

contendit: The main verb of the coordinate clause **Cum ... contendit** (A.G. 278.a). The pronoun **is**, with **Ille** (**Vercassivellaunus**) as the antecedent, is understood as the subject (A.G. 271.a).

eodemque tempore: Ablative of *time when* (A.G. 423.1). **eodem**: Singular, neuter, ablative demonstrative pronoun used as an adjective modifying **tempore** (A.G. 296.1 and a). **-que**: The enclitic conjunction connects the two main verbs **contendit ... coeperunt** (A.G. 324.a).

equitatus: First nominative subject of **coeperunt** (A.G. 339).

ad campestris munitiones: Accusative of *place to which* with the preposition **ad** (A.G. 426.2). **campestris**: Accusative plural adjective; **-is** for **-es** is the regular form in i-stem adjectives (A.G. 114.a and 115 and a).

accedere: Complementary infinitive after **coeperunt** (A.G. 456).

et: The conjunction connects the two nominative subjects of **coeperunt** (A.G. 324.a).

reliquae copiae: Second nominative subject of **coeperunt** (A.G. 339). "They amounted to 190,000 men, less those who may have been killed in battle; but they were so poorly commanded that Caesar says nothing more of them. They probably made a feeble attack on the plain. If they had made vigorous attacks at several other points, Caesar could not have sent reinforcements to camp A. Their bad generalship saved Caesar." (Walker, 406-407).

pro castris: Prepositional phrase, **pro** with the ablative here means "in front of, before" (*OLD* **pro1** 1).

sese: Plural, feminine, accusative direct reflexive pronoun (A.G. 300.1). The antecedent is **copiae**, the subject of **coeperunt** (A.G. 299). Accusative direct object of the infinitive **ostendere** (A.G. 387 and 451.3). Reduplicated form of **se** (A.G. 144.b Note 1).

ostendere: Complementary infinitive after **coeperunt** (A.G. 456).

coeperunt: The main verb of the coordinate clause **eodemque ... coeperunt** (A.G. 278.a).

(84.1-2) Vercingetorix ex arce Alesiae suos conspicatus ex oppido egreditur; cratis, longurios, musculos, falces reliquaque (2) quae eruptionis causa paraverat profert.

Alesia, -ae, f., *Alesia.*
causa, -ae, f., abl. with the gen., *for the sake of, for the purpose of.*
crates, -is, f., *wicker-work, hurdle, fascine, bundle of brushwood.*

eruptio, -onis, f., *a bursting forth, sally, sortie.*
falx, falcis, f., *sickle-shaped hook.*
musculus, -i, m., *shed, mantlet.*
paro, -are, -avi, -atus, *prepare, make ready, make ready for.*
-que, *and.*
reliqua, -orum, n., pl., *the remaining things.*
Vercingetorix, -igis, m., *Vercingetorix.*

arx, arcis, f., *citadel, fortress, stronghold.*
conspicor, -ari, -atus, *catch sight of, see, observe.*
egredior, -gredi, -gressus, *go out, go forth, come forth, leave.*
ex, *from; from, out of.*
longurius, -i, m., *long pole.*
oppidum, -i, n., *fortified town, city.*
profero, -ferre, -tuli, -latus, *bring out, bring forth.*
qui, quae, quod, *who, which, what.*
sui, -orum, m., pl., *his men, with or without own.*

Vercingetorix ... conspicatus: Nominative subject (A.G. 339). **Vercingetorix**: See Appendix A. **conspicatus**: Nominative, perfect, deponent participle used as a predicate, where in English a phrase or a subordinate clause would be more normal (A.G. 496).

ex arce Alesiae: Prepositional phrase, **ex** with the ablative here means "from" (indicating the point at or from which an action is performed) (*OLD* **ex** 7). **Alesiae**: Possessive genitive with **arce** (A.G. 343). See Appendix A.

suos: Plural, masculine, accusative possessive pronoun used substantively to denote a special class (A.G. 302.d). Accusative direct object of the participle **conspicatus** (A.G. 387 and 488). This is the exterior relief army.

ex oppido: Ablative of *place from which* with the preposition **ex** (A.G. 426.1).

egreditur: The main verb of the simple sentence (A.G. 278.1). The historical present, giving vividness to the narrative, is present in Chapter 84 (A.G. 469). This usage, common in all languages, comes from imagining past events as going on before our eyes (*repraesentatio*) (A.G. 469 Note).

cratis, longurios, musculos, falces reliquaque: Five accusative direct objects of **profert** (A.G. 387). "Vercingetorix had adopted the Roman siege tactics and instruments." (Kelsey, 431) Notice the asyndeton construction with the first four nouns (A.G. 323.b). **cratis**: Accusative plural noun; **-is** for **-es** is the regular form in i-stem nouns (A.G. 65-67 and 74.c). **musculos**: "The **musculus** was a hut with one end open and the other end partially closed. Its roof was strong enough to withstand the shock of great stones which might be dropped upon it from the wall. It could be pushed up to the wall, and under its shelter men could dig out the foundation of the wall." (Walker, 35) "Caesar gives a detailed description of their construction at *CW* 2.10." (Hammond, 242) **falces**: "'*facles murales*,' strong poles, to one end of which was fastened a heavy point for prying, with a hook for pulling stones out of the enemy's wall;

whether they were usually worked by hand or by machinery is not known." (Kelsey, 407) **reliqua**: Plural, neuter, accusative adjective used substantively (A.G. 288). **-que**: The enclitic conjunction connects the last member in the series (A.G. 323.c.3).

quae ... paraverat: Relative clause (A.G. 303). **quae**: Plural, neuter, accusative relative pronoun used substantively (A.G. 305). The antecedent is **reliqua** (A.G. 307). Accusative direct object of **paraverat** (A.G. 387). **paraverat**: The main verb of the subordinate clause (A.G. 278.b). The pronoun **is**, with **Vercingetorix** as the antecedent, is understood as the subject (A.G. 271.a). The pluperfect denotes an action completed in past time (A.G. 477).

eruptionis causa: A preceding genitive with the ablative of **causa** means "for the sake of" A (A.G. 359.b and 404.c).

profert: The main verb of the main clause (A.G. 278.b). The pronoun **is**, with **Vercingetorix** as the antecedent, is understood as the subject (A.G. 271.a).

(84.2-3) Pugnatur uno tempore omnibus locis atque omnia temptantur: quae (3) minime visa pars firma est, huc concurritur.

atque, *and.*

firmus, -a, -um, *strong, firm, powerful.*
loca, -orum, n., pl., *places*
omnia, -ium, n., *all things, everything.*
pars, partis, f., *region, section, part, portion.*
qui, quae, quod, *who, which, what.*
tempus, -oris, n., *time.*
videor, videri, visus sum, *seem, appear.*

concurro, -currere, -cucurri or **-curri, -cursus**, *run together, come together, meet, assemble.*
huc, *hither, here, to this place.*
minime, *not at all, least.*
omnis, -e, *all.*
pugno, -are, -avi, -atus, *fight, combat, engage.*
tempto, -are, -avi, -atus, *try, attempt.*
unus, -a, -um, *one and the same.*

(id) Pugnatur: The main verb of the coordinate clause **Pugnatur ... locis** (A.G. 278.a). Verb first in the emphatic position (A.G. 589.d). Impersonal use of the intransitive passive verb (A.G. 208.d). Supply **id** as the subject (A.G. 318.c).

Pugnatur ... temptantur: Kelsey points out that this is an example of chiasmus (Kelsey, 431) (A.G. 598.f).

uno tempore: Ablative of *time when* (A.G. 423.1). **uno**: Declinable cardinal number used as an adjective (A.G. 132-35).

omnibus locis: Ablative of *place where* without a preposition (A.G. 429.1-2).

atque: The conjunction connects the two main verbs **Pugnatur ... temptantur** and means "and" (*OLD* atque 12).

omnia: Plural, neuter, nominative adjective used substantively (A.G. 288). Nominative subject (A.G. 339).

temptantur: The main verb of the coordinate clause **omnia temptantur** (A.G. 278.a).

quae ... est: Notice the interlocking word order (A.G. 598.h).

quae ... visa ... est: Relative clause (A.G. 303). **quae**: See below. **visa ... est**: The main verb of the subordinate clause (A.G. 278.b). The perfect deponent verb is here split (tmesis) (A.G. 640).

quae ... pars: Nominative subject (A.G. 339). **quae**: Singular, feminine, nominative relative pronoun (A.G. 305). The antecedent is **pars** in its own clause (adjectival use) (A.G. 307.b).

minime: Irregular superlative adverb modifying **firma** (A.G. 218.a and 320-21). A low degree of a quality is indicated by **minime** meaning "not at all" (A.G. 291.c Note 2).

firma (esse): Singular, feminine, nominative, predicate adjective modifying **pars** after the supplied infinitive **esse**. A predicate adjective after a complementary infinitive takes the case of the subject of the main verb (A.G. 283-84 and 458). Supply **esse** as the complementary infinitive after **visa ... est**.

huc: Adverb (A.G. 217.a and 320-21).

(id) concurritur: The main verb of the main clause (A.G. 278.b). Impersonal use of the intransitive passive verb (A.G. 208.d). Supply **id** as the subject (A.G. 318.c).

(84.3-4) Romanorum manus tantis munitionibus distinetur nec facile pluribus (4) locis occurrit.

distineo, -tinere, -tinui, -tentus, *divide, isolate, separate.*
loca, -orum, n., pl., *place.*
munitio, -onis, f., *works of fortifications, entrenchment, defenses.*
occurro, -currere, -curri or **-cucurri, -cursurus**, *resist, oppose, counteract.*
Romani, -orum, m., pl., *the Romans.*

facile, *easily, readily, with no trouble.*
manus, -us, f., *band, force.*
nec, *and ... not.*
plures, -es, -a, *a great number, many.*
tantus, -a, -um, *so great, so large, such, so extensive.*

Romanorum: Partitive genitive with **manus** (A.G. 346.a.1).

manus: Nominative subject of **distinetur ... occurrit** (A.G. 339).

tantis munitionibus: Ablative absolute with an adjective (**tantis**) taking the place of a participle (there is no participle for "being") (A.G. 419.a-20).

distinetur: The main verb of the coordinate clause **Romanorum ... distinetur** (A.G. 278.a).

nec: The conjunction joins a negative clause to a preceding positive one and means "and ... not" (*OLD* neque 3).

facile: Adverb formed from the neuter accusative adjective (A.G. 214.d and 320-21).

pluribus locis: Ablative of *place where* without a preposition (A.G. 429.1-2). **pluribus**: Comparative adjective (A.G. 120).

occurrit: The main verb of the coordinate clause **facile ... occurrit** (A.G. 278.a).

(84.4-5) Multum ad terrendos nostros valet clamor, qui post tergum pugnantibus exstitit, quod suum peri(5)culum in aliena vident salute constare: omnia enim plerumque quae absunt vehementius hominum mentis perturbant.

absum, -esse, afui, -futurus, *be distant, absent,* or *unseen.*
alienus, -a, -um, *another's.*
consto, -stare, -stiti, -staturus, *depend on.*
exsisto, -sistere, -stiti, -----, *spring up, arise.*
in, *in.*
multum, *much, by far, greatly.*
omnia, -ium, n., *all things, everything.*
perturbo, -are, -avi, -atus, *disturb greatly, throw into confusion.*

post, *behind.*
qui, quae, quod, *who, which, what.*
salus, -utis, f., *welfare, safety, deliverance.*
tergum, -i, n., *back,* (with post), *in the rear.*
valeo, -ere, -ui, -iturus, *be powerful, be strong.*

video, videre, visi, visus, *see, perceive, observe, understand.*

ad, *for, for the purpose of.*
clamor, -oris, m., *outcry, clamor, noise, din.*
enim, *for, for in fact, and in fact.*
homo, hominis, m., *man, person.*
mens, mentis, f., *mind.*
nostri, -orum, m., pl., *our men, our side.*
periculum, -i, n., *risk, danger, hazard.*
plerumque, *commonly, generally, usually, for the most part.*
pugno, -are, -avi, -atus, *fight, combat, engage.*
quod, *because, since, for, as.*
suus, -a, -um, *their,* with or without *own.*
terreo, -ere, -ui, -itus, *deter, frighten.*
vehementer, comp. vehementius, *vigorously, exceedingly.*

Multum: Adverb (214.d and 320-21).

ad terrendos nostros: The preposition **ad** with the accusative gerundive and possessive pronoun expresses purpose (A.G. 506).

terrendos: Plural, masculine, accusative gerundive used as an adjective modifying **nostros** denoting necessity, obligation or propriety (A.G. 500.1). **nostros:** Plural, masculine, accusative possessive pronoun used substantively to denote a special class (A.G. 302.d).

valet: The main verb of the main clause (A.G. 278.b).

clamor: Nominative subject (A.G. 339). The subject is in the last position in the clause (A.G. 597.b).

qui ... exstitit: Relative clause (A.G. 303). **qui:** Singular, masculine, nominative relative pronoun (A.G. 305). The antecedent is **clamor** (A.G. 307). Nominative subject (A.G. 339). **exstitit:** The main verb of the subordinate clause (A.G. 278.b).

post tergum: Prepositional phrase, **post** with the accusative here means "behind" (*OLD* post2 1). "The cries of combatants at the outer line of works would be heard in the rear of those defending the inner line, and vice versa." (Kelsey, 431)

pugnantibus: Plural, masculine, dative present participle used substantively (A.G. 494.a). The noun **Romanis** is understood (A.G. 288.b). Dative of reference; the dative of reference is often used to qualify a whole idea, instead of the possessive genitive modifying a single word (**tergum**) (A.G. 377).

quod ... vident: Causal clause; the conjunction **quod** ("because") takes the indicative when the reason is given on the authority of the writer or speaker (A.G. 540.1). **vident:** The main verb of the subordinate clause (A.G. 278.b). The pronoun ei, with **nostros** as the antecedent, is understood as the subject (A.G. 271.a).

suum periculum ... constare: Accusative/infinitive construction in indirect discourse after **vident** (A.G. 577 ff.). **suum:** Singular, neuter, accusative possessive pronoun used as an adjective modifying **periculum** (A.G. 302). **constare:** Present infinitive; the tense of the infinitive in indirect discourse is relative to that of the verb of saying (A.G. 584).

in aliena ... salute: Ablative of *place where* with the preposition **in** (locative ablative) (A.G. 426.3). "i.e. that, if the line were broken elsewhere, they themselves would be in peril." (Edwards, 505) **aliena:** The adjective **alienus** is commonly used in the possessive sense instead of **alius** to mean "belonging to another, another's" (A.G. 113.d and 343.a).

omnia ... perturbant: A gnomic statement. Craig categorizes this general statement "in the class of general rules which are military but have a wider application." (Craig, 107)

omnia: Plural, neuter, nominative adjective used substantively (A.G. 288). Nominative subject (A.G. 339).

enim: Postpositive conjunction (A.G. 324.j and 599.b).

plerumque: Adverb (A.G. 320-21).

quae absunt: Relative clause (A.G. 303). **quae:** Plural, neuter, nominative relative pronoun (A.G. 305). The antecedent is **omnia** (A.G. 307). Nominative subject (A.G. 339). **absunt:** The main verb of the subordinate clause (A.G. 278.b). The present tense is not the historical present but denotes a general truth (A.G. 465.3).

vehementius: Comparative adverb (A.G. 218 and 320-21).

hominum: Possessive genitive with **mentis** (A.G. 343).

mentis: Accusative direct object of **perturbant** (A.G. 387). Accusative plural noun; -**is** for -**es** is the regular form in mixed i-stem nouns (A.G. 71.3).

perturbant: The main verb of the main clause (A.G. 278.b). The present tense is not the historical present but denotes a general truth (A.G. 465.3).

(85.1-2) Caesar idoneum locum nactus quid quaque ex parte gera(2)tur cognoscit; laborantibus summittit.

Caesar, -aris, m., *Caesar.*

ex, *on, at.*
idoneus, -a, -um, *suitable, convenient.*
locus, -i, m., *place, ground, position.*
pars, partis, f., *region, district.*
quis, -----, quid, *who? what?; who? what?* (as adj., qui, quae, quod).

cognosco, -gnoscere, -gnovi, cognitus, *learn, ascertain, recognize.*
gero, gerere, gessi, gestus, *carry out, perform, do.*
laboro, -are, -avi, -atus, *make an effort, labor, strive.*
naniscor, -cisci, nactus,* and **nanctus,** *come upon, find.*
-que, *and.*
summitto, -mittere, -misi, -missus, *send as*

reinforcement, send as support.

Caesar ... nactus: Nominative subject (A.G. 339). **Caesar**: See Appendix A. **nactus**: Nominative, perfect, deponent participle used as a predicate, where in English a phrase or a subordinate clause would be more natural (A.G. 496).

idoneum locum: Accusative direct object of the participle **nactus** (A.G. 387 and 488).

quid quaque ex parte geratur: A double indirect question with the subjunctive; the phrase is the object of **cognoscit** (A.G. 573-75). **quid**: Singular, neuter, nominative interrogative pronoun used substantively (A.G. 148). Nominative subject (A.G. 339). **quaque ex parte**: Ablative of *position* with the preposition **ex** (A.G. 429.b). **quaque**: Singular, feminine, ablative interrogative pronoun used as an adjective modifying **parte** (A.G. 148). **-que**: The enclitic conjunction connects the two interrogative pronouns (A.G. 324.a). **ex**: A monosyllabic preposition is often placed between a noun and its adjective (A.G. 599.d.2). **geratur**: The main verb of the subordinate clause (A.G. 278.b). Present subjunctive; the tense of the subjunctive is normally in secondary sequence after the historical present **cognoscit** (A.G. 575). Here it is in primary sequence through *repraesentatio* (A.G. 485.e and 585.b Note).

cognoscit: The main verb of the main clause (A.G. 278.b). The historical present, giving vividness to the narrative, is present in Chapter 85 (A.G. 469). This usage, common in all languages, comes from imagining past events as going on before our eyes (*repraesentatio*) (A.G. 469 Note).

laborantibus: Plural, masculine, dative present participle used substantively (A.G. 494.a). The noun **militibus** is understood (A.G. 288.b). Dative indirect object of the transitive use of **summittit** (A.G. 366). There is no direct object; "Dr. Rice Holmes suggests the insertion of **subsidium**." (Edwards pg. 504).

summittit: The main verb of the simple sentence (A.G. 278.1). The pronoun **is**, with **Caesar** as the antecedent, is understood as the subject (A.G. 271.a).

(85.2-4) Utrisque ad animum occurrit unum esse illud tempus quo maxime contendi (3) conveniat: Galli, nisi perfregerint munitiones, de omni salute desperant; Romani, si rem obtinuerint, finem labor(4)um omnium exspectant.

ad, *to, into.*
contendo, -tendere, -tendi, -tentus, *fight, contend, vie.*
de, *about, concerning.*

exspecto, -are, -avi, -atus, *look to see, expect.*
Galli, -orum, m., *the Gauls.*
labor, -oris, m., *toil, exertion, labor.*

munitio, -onis, f., *works of fortifications, entrenchment, defenses.*
obtineo, -tinere, -tinui, -tentus, *win, gain.*

omnis, -e, *all.*
qui, quae, quod, *who, which, what.*
Romani, -orum, m., pl., *the Romans.*
si, *if.*
tempus, -oris, n., *time, occasion.*

utrique, utrorumque, m., pl., *both sides, both forces.*

animus, -i, m., *mind.*
convenio, -venire, -veni, -ventus, (imper.) *be fitting.*
despero, -are, -avi, -atus, *give up hope of, despair of, have no hope of.*
finis, -is, m., *end.*
ille, illae, illud, *that; he, she, it.*
maxime, *very greatly, exceedingly, to the greatest extent.*
nisi, *unless, if not, except.*
occurro, -currere, -curri or **-cucurri, -cursurus,** (imper.), *come into mind, occur.*
perfringo, -fringere, -fregi, -fractus, *break through.*
res, rei, f., *affair, battle, campaign, military operation.*
salus, -utis, f., *welfare, safety, deliverance.*
sum, esse, fui, futurus, *be.*
unus, -a, -um, *one in particular, one above others, one especially.*

Utrisque: Plural, masculine, dative pronoun used substantively to mean "each of the two" (with reference to sets or groups of people) (A.G. 313) (*OLD* uterque 3.a). Dative indirect object of the intransitive verb **occurrit** (A.G. 366).

ad animum: Preposition phrase, **ad** with the accusative here means "to" (*OLD* ad 24.c).

occurrit: The main verb of the main clause (A.G. 278.b). Impersonal use of the verb, supply **id** as the subject (*OLD* occurro 9).

unum esse illud tempus: Accusative/infinitive construction in indirect discourse (A.G. 577 ff.). The verb of saying is not expressed but implied in the phrase **ad animum occurrit** (A.G. 580.a). **unum**: Singular, neuter, accusative declinable cardinal number used as a predicate adjective modifying **tempus** after **esse** (A.G. 283-84). **illud**: Singular, neuter, accusative demonstrative pronoun used as an adjective modifying **tempus** (A.G. 296.1 and a). **tempus**: Accusative subject of **esse** (A.G. 397.e).

quo ... conveniat: Relative clause; a subordinate clause in indirect discourse takes the subjunctive (A.G. 303 and 580). **quo**: Singular, neuter, ablative relative pronoun used substantively (A.G. 305). The antecedent is **tempus** (A.G. 307). Ablative of *time when* (A.G. 423.1). **conveniat**: The main verb of the subordinate clause (A.G. 278.b). Present subjunctive; the tense of the subjunctive is normally in secondary sequence after the historical present **occurrit** (A.G. 482-85). Here it is in primary sequence through *repraesentatio* (A.G. 485.e and 585.b Note). Impersonal use of the verb, the following infinitive phrase forms the subject (A.G. 208.c).

maxime contendi: The infinitive phrase functions as the subject of the impersonal verb **conveniat** (A.G. 454).

maxime: Irregular superlative adverb (A.G. 218.a and 320-21).

Galli: Nominative subject of **desperant** (A.G. 339). See Appendix A.

nisi perfregerint ... desperant: Mixed conditional statement, the protasis (future perfect indicative) is from a future, more vivid condition (A.G. 514.B.1.a). The apodosis (historical present=historical perfect) is from a simple, past time condition (A.G. 514.A.2).

nisi perfregerint: The conjunction **nisi** ("unless") with the subjunctive forms the protasis of the conditional statement (A.G. 512).

nisi: With **nisi** the apodosis is stated as universally true except in the single case supposed, in which case it is (impliedly) not true (A.G. 525.a.1). **perfregerint**: The main verb of the subordinate clause (A.G. 278.b). The pronoun **ei**, with **Galli** as the antecedent, is understood as the subject (A.G. 271.a).

munitiones: Accusative direct object of **perfregerint** (A.G. 387).

de omni salute: Prepositional phrase, **de** with the ablative here means "about, concerning" (*OLD* **de** 12).

desperant: The main verb of the apodosis of the conditional statement (A.G. 512). The main verb of the main clause (A.G. 278.b).

Romani: Nominative subject of **exspectant** (A.G. 339).

si ... obtinuerint ... exspectant: Mixed conditional statement, the protasis (future perfect indicative) is from a future, more vivid condition (A.G. 514.B.1.a). The apodosis (historical present=historical perfect) is from a simple, past time condition (A.G. 514.A.2).

si ... obtinuerint: The conjunction **si** ("if") with the indicative forms the protasis of the conditional statement (A.G. 512). **obtinuerint**: The main verb of the subordinate clause (A.G. 278.b). The pronoun **ei**, with **Romani** as the antecedent, is understood as the subject (A.G. 271.a).

rem: Accusative direct object **obtinuerint** (A.G. 387). The phrase **rem obtinere** is an idiom that means "to be successful or victorious" (*OLD* **obtineo** 10).

finem: Accusative direct object of **exspectant** (A.G. 387).

laborum omnium: Objective genitive with **finem** (A.G. 348).

exspectant: The main verb of the apodosis of the conditional statement (A.G. 512). The main verb of the main clause (A.G. 278.b).

(85.4) Maxime ad superiores munitiones laboratur, quo Vercassivellaunum missum demonstravimus.

ad, *at*, *near*, *beside*.

laboro, -are, -avi, -atus, *make an effort*, *labor*, *strive*.
mitto, mittere, misi, missus, *send*.

quo, *in the place to which*, *where*.
Vercassivellaunus, -i, m., *Vercassivellaunus*.

demonstro, -are, -avi, -atus, *point out*, *show*, *say*, *mention*, *explain*.
maxime, *very greatly*, *exceedingly*, *chiefly*, *especially*.
munitio, -onis, f., *works of fortifications*, *entrenchment*, *defenses*.
superior, -or, -us, *higher*, *upper*.

Maxime: Irregular superlative adverb (A.G. 218.a and 320-21).

ad superiores munitiones: Prepositional phrase, **ad** with the accusative here means "at, near, beside" (*OLD* **ad** 13). "Millstones, broken water jars, and similar things found in the trenches seem to show that the Romans were forced to use as missiles whatever they could lay their hands on." (Walker, 407) **superiores**: Defective comparative adjective (A.G. 130.b).

(id) laboratur: The main verb of the main clause (A.G. 278.b). Impersonal use of the intransitive passive verb (A.G. 208.d). Supply **id** as the subject (A.G. 318.c).

quo ... demonstravimus: Subordinate clause (A.G. 278.b). For the reference see 83.6-7. **quo**: Adverb meaning "in the place to which" (A.G. 215.4 and 320-21) (*OLD* **quo1** 3.c). **demonstravimus**: The main verb of the subordinate clause (A.G. 278.b). The personal pronoun **nos** is understood as the subject but is not expressed except for distinction or emphasis (A.G. 295.a). In Book 7, Caesar refers to himself only in the third person, either in the singular or occasionally in the plural (see **Caesar** at 1.1). Siedler counts 11 uses of the first person plural in Book 7 (Siedler, 46). These uses are at 17.1, 23.2, 25.1, 37.1, 48.1, 58.4, 70.1, 76.1, 79.2, 83.8, and 85.4.

Vercassivellaunum missum (esse): Accusative/infinitive construction in indirect discourse after **demonstravimus** (A.G. 577 ff.).

Vercassivellaunum: See Appendix A. **missum (esse)**: Supply **esse** to form the perfect, passive infinitive (A.G. 186). The tense of the infinitive in indirect discourse is relative to that of the verb of saying (A.G. 584).

(85.4-6) Iniquum loci ad declivitatem fastigium magnum habet (5) momentum. Alii tela coiciunt, alii testudine facta subeunt; (6) defatigatis in vicem integri succedunt.

ad, *towards*.
coicio, -icere, -ieci, -iectus, *hurl*, *cast*, *throw*.

defatigo, -are, -avi, -atus, *tire out*, *exhaust*, *fatigue*.
fastigium, -i, n., *sloping side*, *slope*, *declivity*.
in vicem, *in turn*, *one after another*, *alternately*.

integri, -orum, m., pl., *those who were unexhausted*, *fresh men*.
magnus, -a, -um, *great*, *large*.
subeo, -ire, -ii, -itus, *come up*, *approach*, *go up*.

telum, -i, n., *dart*, *spear*.

alii ... alii, -orum, m., pl., *some ... others*.
declivitatas, -tatis, f., *a slope*, *declivity*, (with **ad**), *sloping downward*.
facio, facere, feci, factus, *make*, *form*.
habeo, habere, habui, habitus, *have*.
iniquus, -a, -um, *uneven*, *sloping*, *unfavorable*, *disadvantageous*.
locus, -i, m., *place*, *ground*, *position*.
momentum, -i, n., *importance*, *account*.
succedo, -cedere, -cessi, -cessurus, *succeed*, *take the place of*, *relieve*.
testudo, -inis, f., *tortoise-cover*, *testudo*.

Iniquum ... fastigium: Nominative subject (A.G. 339).

loci: Possessive genitive with **fastigium** (A.G. 343).

ad declivitatem: Prepositional phrase, **ad** with the accusative here means "towards" (*OLD* **ad** 3.b).

magnum ... momentum: Accusative direct object of **habet** (A.G. 387).

habet: The main verb of the simple sentence (A.G. 278.1).

Alii ... alii: Plural, masculine, nominative pronouns used substantively; the repeated pronoun **alius** means "some ... others" (A.G.

358

315.a). The noun **Galli** is understood with each pronoun. Nominative subjects (A.G. 339).

tela: Accusative direct object of **coiciunt** (A.G. 387).

coiciunt: The main verb of the coordinate clause **Alii ... coiciunt** (A.G. 278.a).

testudine facta: Ablative absolute (A.G. 419-20). **facta**: The perfect tense of the participle represents the action as completed at the time indicated by the tense of the main verb (A.G. 489). The testudo was "a covering formed by the soldiers' shields held above their heads and overlapping so as to ward off weapons thrown down upon them from above." (Kelsey, 112) "The Gauls evidently had shields of the Roman pattern." (Kelsey, 432)

subeunt: The main verb of the coordinate clause **alii ... subeunt** (A.G. 278.a).

defatigatis: Dative, perfect, passive participle used substantively (A.G. 494.a). The noun **Gallis** is understood (A.G. 288.b). Dative indirect object of the intransitive verb **succedunt** (A.G. 367.c).

in vicem: Adverb written as two words (320-21).

integri: Plural, masculine, nominative, adjective used substantively (A.G. 288). The noun **Galli** is understood (A.G. 288.b). Nominative subject (A.G. 339).

succedunt: The main verb of the simple sentence (A.G. 278.1).

(85.6) **Agger ab universis in munitionem coiectus et ascensum dat Gallis et ea quae in terra occultaverant Romani contegit; nec iam arma nostris nec vires suppetunt.**

ab, *by.*

arma, -orum, n., pl., *arms, armor, weapons.*
coicio, -icere, -ieci, -iectus, *hurl, cast, throw.*
do, dare, dedi, datus, *give, offer, furnish, allow.*
Galli, -orum, m., *the Gauls.*
in, *on to; in.*
munitio, -onis, f., *works of fortifications, entrenchment, defenses.*
nostri, -orum, m., pl., *our men, our side.*
qui, quae, quod, *who, which, what.*
suppeto, -petere, -petivi, -petitus, *hold out.*
universi, -orum, m., pl., *all the men together, the whole body, all together.*

agger, -eris, m., *material for a mound* (earth, timber), *earth.*
ascensus, -us, m., *ascent, way up, approach.*
contego, -tegere, -texi, -tectus, *cover, cover up.*
et ... et, *both ... and.*
iam, *now, at this time, at present.*
is, ea, id, *he, she, it; that, this.*
nec ... nec, *neither ... nor.*
occulto, -are, -avi, -atus, *hide, conceal.*
Romani, -orum, m., pl., *the Romans.*
terra, -ae, f., *earth, ground, soil.*
vires, -ium, f., *physical powers, strength.*

Agger ... coiectus: Nominative subject of **dat ... contegit** (A.G. 339). **Agger**: The noun here does not mean the usual "rampart", but "material for a mound (dirt), rubble" (*OLD* **agger** 1). "Earth was thrown over the *stimuli, scrobes*, etc.; and a sloping mound of earth was thrown against the rampart of the camp." (Walker, 408) **coiectus**: Nominative, perfect, passive participle used as a predicate, where in English a phrase or a subordinate clause would be more natural (A.G. 496).

ab universis: Ablative of agent with the preposition **ab** after the passive participle **coiectus** (A.G. 405). **universis**: Plural, masculine, ablative adjective used substantively (A.G. 288). The noun **Gallis** is understood (A.G. 288.b).

in munitionem: Prepositional phrase, **in** with the accusative here means "onto" (*OLD* **in** 7).

et ... et: The repeated conjunction means "both ... and", connecting the two verbs **dat** and **contegit** (A.G. 323.e).

ascensum: Accusative direct object of the transitive verb **dat** (A.G. 387).

dat: The main verb of the coordinate clause **Agger ... Gallis** (A.G. 278.a).

Gallis: Dative indirect object of the transitive verb **dat** (A.G. 362). See Appendix A.

ea: Plural, neuter, accusative demonstrative pronoun used substantively meaning "the things" (A.G. 296.2). The pronoun is correlative to the relative clause **quae ... Romani** (A.G. 297.d). Accusative direct object of **contegit** (A.G. 387).

quae ... Romani: Relative clause (A.G. 303). For the reference see Chapters 72-73. **quae**: Plural, neuter, accusative relative pronoun used substantively (A.G. 305). The antecedent is **ea** (A.G. 307). Accusative direct object of **occultaverant** (A.G. 387). **Romani**: Nominative subject of the previous verb **occultaverant** (A.G. 339). The subject is in the last position in the clause (A.G. 597.b).

in terra: Ablative of *place where* with the preposition **in** (locative ablative) (A.G. 426.3).

occultaverant: The main verb of the subordinate clause (A.G. 278.b). The pluperfect denotes an action completed in past time (A.G. 477).

contegit: The main verb of the coordinate clause **ea ... contegit** (A.G. 278.a).

nec ... nec: The repeated conjunction means "neither ... nor", connecting the two nominative nouns (*OLD* **neque** 7).

iam: Adverb (A.G. 215.6, 217.b and 320-21).

arma: First nominative subject of **suppetunt** (A.G. 339).

nostris: Plural, masculine, dative possessive pronoun used substantively to denote a special class (A.G. 302.d). Dative of reference; the dative of reference is often used to qualify a whole idea, instead of the possessive genitive modifying a single word (**arma** or **vires**) (A.G. 377).

vires: Second nominative subject of **suppetunt** (A.G. 339).

suppetunt: The main verb of the simple sentence (A.G. 278.1).

(86.1-3) **His rebus cognitis Caesar Labienum cum cohortibus sex (2) subsidio laborantibus mittit: imperat, si sustinere non possit, deductis cohortibus, eruptione pugnet; id, nisi (3) necessario, ne faciat.**

Caesar, -aris, m., *Caesar.*

cognosco, -gnoscere, -gnovi, cognitus, *learn of,*

cohors, -hortis, f., *cohort, company*, (the tenth part of a legion).
deduco, -ducere, -duxi, -ductus, *lead off, withdraw, bring.*
facio, facere, feci, factus, *make, do.*
impero, -are, -avi, -atus, *command, order, demand.*
Labienus, -i, m., *Labienus.*
mitto, mittere, misi, missus, *send.*
necessario, *of necessity, without option.*
non, *not.*
pugno, -are, -avi, -atus, *fight, combat, engage.*
sex, *six.*
subsidium, -i, n., *support, relief, reinforcement, help, aid.*

ascertain.
cum, *with.*
eruptio, -onis, f., *a bursting forth, sally, sortie.*
hic, haec, hoc, *this; he, she, it.*
is, ea, id, *he, she, it; that, this.*
laboro, -are, -avi, -atus, *make an effort, labor, strive.*
ne, *so that ... not.*
nisi, *other(wise) than, but, except.*
possum, posse, potui, -----, *be able.*
res, rei, f., *matter, affair.*
si, *if.*
sustineo, -tinere, -tinui, -tentus, *bear, endure, withstand.*

His rebus cognitis: Ablative absolute (A.G. 419-20). His: Plural, feminine, ablative demonstrative pronoun used as an adjective modifying rebus (A.G. 426.1 and a). cognitis: The perfect tense of the participle represents the action as completed at the time indicated by the tense of the main verb (A.G. 489).

Caesar: Nominative subject (A.G. 339). See Appendix A.

Labienum: Accusative direct object of mittit (A.G. 387). See Appendix A.

cum cohortibus sex: Ablative of accompaniment with the preposition cum (A.G. 413). sex: Indeclinable cardinal number used as an adjective modifying cohortibus (A.G. 132-35).

subsidio laborantibus: Dative of the purpose or end (double dative). The dative of an abstract noun (subsidio) is used to show that for which a thing serves or which it accomplishes, often with another dative of the person or thing affected (laborantibus) (A.G. 382.1). laborantibus: Plural, masculine, dative, present participle used substantively (A.G. 494.a). The noun militibus is understood (A.G. 288.b).

mittit: The main verb of the simple sentence (A.G. 278.1). The historical present, giving vividness to the narrative, is present in Chapter 86 (A.G. 469). This usage, common in all languages, comes from imagining past events as going on before our eyes (*repraesentatio*) (A.G. 469 Note). Fuller describes Roman tactics this way: "In brief, against their like, as well as against barbaric warriors, the techniques of the legionary battles may be summarized as follows: (1) To engage the minimum number of combatants necessary to wage the initial fight. (2) To support the fighting front with reliefs and replacements stationed immediately in rear of it. (3) To hold a reserve well outside the zone of demoralization, in order to feed the supports when required, or to clinch victory by a final assault with fresh troops." (Fuller, 91)

imperat: The main verb of the main clause (A.G. 278.b). Verb first in the emphatic position (A.G. 589.d). The pronoun is, with Caesar as the antecedent, is understood as the subject (A.G. 271.a).

si ... possit ... pugnet: A subordinate conditional statement (A.G. 512.c). The apodosis, as a substantive clause of purpose without ut dependent on imperat, takes the subjunctive and the protasis, as a clause subordinate to a subjunctive clause, also takes the subjunctive (attraction) (A.G. 512.c and 593).

si ... possit: The conjunction si ("if") with the subjunctive forms the protasis of the conditional statement (A.G. 589.1). possit: The main verb of the subordinate clause (A.G. 278.b). Present subjunctive; the tense of the subjunctive is normally in secondary sequence after the historical present imperat (A.G. 482-85). Here it is in primary sequence through *repraesentatio* (A.G. 485.e and 585.b Note). The pronoun is, with Labienum as the antecedent, is understood as the subject (A.G. 271.a).

sustinere: Complementary infinitive after possit (A.G. 456).

non: Adverb, the adverb generally precedes the verb if it belongs to no one word in particular (A.G. 217.e, 320-21, and 599.a).

deductis cohortibus: Ablative absolute (A.G. 419-20). deductis: The perfect tense of the participle represents the action as completed at the time indicated by the tense of the main verb (A.G. 489). "From the rampart." (Walker, 408)

eruptione: Ablative of means (A.G. 409). "This plan had once saved Galba under similar circumstances; III, 5 and 6." (Walker, 408)

pugnet: The main verb of the apodosis of the conditional statement (A.G. 589.2). The main verb of the subordinate clause (A.G. 278.b). Verbs of commanding (imperat) often take the subjunctive without ut (A.G. 565.a). The pronoun is, with Labienum as the antecedent, is understood as the subject (A.G. 271.a).

id: Singular, neuter, accusative demonstrative pronoun used substantively (A.G. 296.2). The antecedent is the idea of making a sortie (A.G. 297.e). Accusative direct object of faciat (A.G. 387).

nisi necessario: An elliptical phrase without a verb (*OLD* nisi 6). nisi: Here the conjunction means "other(wise) than, but, except" (*OLD* nisi 6). necessario: Adverb (A.G. 320-21).

ne faciat: The conjunction ne ("so that ... not") with the subjunctive forms a negative substantive clause of purpose which is used as the object of the verb imperat denoting an action directed toward the future (A.G. 563). faciat: The main verb of the subordinate clause (A.G. 278.b). Present subjunctive; the tense of the subjunctive is normally in secondary sequence after the historical present imperat (A.G. 482-85). Here it is in primary sequence through *repraesentatio* (A.G. 485.e and 585.b Note). The pronoun is, with Labienum as the antecedent, is understood as the subject (A.G. 271.a).

(86.3-4) Ipse adit reliquos, cohortatur ne labori succumbant; omnium superiorum dimicationum (4) fructum in eo die atque hora docet consistere.

adeo, -ire, -ivi, or -ii, -itus, *go to, approach.*
cohortor, -ari, -atus, *encourage, urge, exhort.*

atque, *and in fact, and even.*
consisto, -sistere, -stiti, -stitus, *consist in, depend on.*

dies, -ei, m. and f., *day.*
doceo, docere, docui, doctus, *inform, point out, state, tell.*
hora, -ae, f., *hour.*
ipse, -a, -um, *he, they,* with or without *himself, themselves.*
labor, -oris, m., *toil, exertion, labor.*
omnis, -e, *all.*
succumbo, -cumbere, -cubui, -----, *yield, succumb.*

dimicatio, -onis, f., *combat, engagement, encounter.*
fructus, -us, m., *result, return, reward, profit, effect.*
in, *in.*
is, ea, id, *he, she, it; that, this.*
ne, *so that ... not.*
reliqui, -orum, m., pl., *the rest.*
superior, -or, -us, *former, earlier, previous.*

Ipse: Singular, masculine, nominative demonstrative pronoun used substantively (A.G. 296.2). The antecedent is **Caesar** (A.G. 297.e). Nominative subject (A.G. 339). The pronoun distinguishes the principal personage (**Caesar**) from the subordinate person (**Labienum**) (A.G. 298.d.3).

adit: The main verb of the coordinate clause **Ipse ... reliquos** (A.G. 278.a).

reliquos: Plural, masculine, accusative adjective used substantively (A.G. 288). The noun **milites** is understood (A.G. 288.b). Accusative direct object of **adit** (A.G. 387). "Those defending the works on the plain. Caesar galloped down from his position on the hill." (Walker, 408)

cohortatur: The main verb of the coordinate clause **cohortatur ... succumbant** (A.G. 278.a). Notice the asyndeton construction between the verbs **adit ... cohortatur** (A.G. 323.b). The pronoun **is**, with **Ipse** (**Caesar**) as the antecedent, is understood as the subject (A.G. 271.a).

ne ... succumbant: The conjunction **ne** ("so that ... not") with the subjunctive forms a negative substantive clause of purpose which is used as the object of the verb **cohortatur** denoting an action directed toward the future (A.G. 563). **succumbant**: The main verb of the subordinate clause (A.G. 278.b). Present subjunctive; the tense of the subjunctive is normally in secondary sequence after the historical present **cohortatur** (A.G. 482-85). Here it is in primary sequence through *repraesentatio* (A.G. 485.e and 585.b Note). The pronoun **ei**, with **reliquos** as the antecedent, is understood as the subject (A.G. 271.a).

labori: Dative indirect object of the intransitive verb **succumbant** (A.G. 366).

omnium superiorum dimicationum: Objective genitive with **fructum** (A.G. 348). **superiorum**: Defective comparative adjective (A.G. 130.b).

fructum ... consistere: Accusative/infinitive construction in indirect discourse after **docet** (A.G. 577 ff.). **consistere**: Present infinitive; the tense of the infinitive in indirect discourse is relative to that of the verb of saying (A.G. 584).

in eo die atque hora: Ablative of *time when* with the preposition **in** (A.G. 424.a). **eo**: Singular, masculine, ablative demonstrative pronoun used as an adjective with **die** (A.G. 296.1 and a). **die**: The noun **dies** is normally masculine gender (A.G. 97.a). **atque**: The conjunction connects a word (**hora**) which strengthens or corrects the first term (**die**) and means "and in fact, and even"" (*OLD* **atque** 4).

docet: The main verb of the main clause (A.G. 278.b). The pronoun **is**, with **Ipse** (**Caesar**) as the antecedent, is understood as the subject (A.G. 271.a).

(86.4-5) Interiores, desperatis campestribus locis propter magnitudinem munitionum, loca praerupta ex ascensu temptant, huc ea quae (5) paraverant conferunt.

ascensus, -us, m., *ascent, way up, approach.*
confero, -ferre, -tuli, collatus, *bring together, gather, collect, convey.*

ex, *as a result of.*
interiores, -um, m., pl., *those within the city.*
loca, -orum, n., pl., *places*
munitio, -onis, f., *works of fortifications, entrenchment, defenses.*
praeruptus, -a, -um, *steep. precipitous.*
qui, quae, quod, *who, which, what.*

campester, -tris, -tre, *of level ground, flat, level.*
despero, -are, -avi, -atus, *give up hope of, despair of, have no hope of.*
huc, *here.*
is, ea, id, *he, she, it; that, this.*
magnitudo, -inis, f., *greatness, extent, size.*
paro, -are, -avi, -atus, *prepare, make ready.*
propter, *on account of.*
tempto, -are, -avi, -atus, *make an attack on, attack, assail, try, attempt.*

Interiores: Plural, masculine, nominative adjective used substantively (A.G. 288). The noun **Galli** is understood (A.G. 288.b). Nominative subject (A.G. 339). Defective comparative adjective (A.G. 130.a).

desperatis campestribus locis propter magnitudinem munitionum: Ablative absolute (A.G. 419-20). **desperatis**: The perfect tense of the participle represents the action as completed at the time indicated by the tense of the main verb (A.G. 489). **propter magnitudinem munitionum**: Prepositional phrase, **propter** with the accusative here means "on account of" (*OLD* **propter** 4). **munitionum**: Possessive genitive with **magnitudinem** (A.G. 343).

loca praerupta: Accusative direct object of **temptant** (A.G. 387). "As the defenses of the plain had been found to be impregnable, the Gauls from the town attacked the less extensive works along the steep slopes of the surrounding hills, probably on the north side." (Kelsey, 432)

ex ascensu: Ablative of *position* with the preposition **ex** (A.G. 429.b).

temptant: The main verb of the coordinate clause **Interiores ... temptant** (A.G. 278.a).

huc: Adverb (A.G. 217.a and 320-21).

ea: Plural, neuter, accusative demonstrative pronoun used substantively meaning "the things" (A.G. 296.2). The pronoun is correlative to the relative clause **quae paraverant** (A.G. 296.d). Accusative direct object of **conferunt** (A.G. 387).

quae paraverant: Relative clause (A.G. 303). **quae**: Plural, neuter, accusative relative pronoun (A.G. 305). The antecedent is **ea**

(A.G. 307). Accusative direct object of **paraverant** (A.G. 387). **paraverant**: The main verb of the subordinate clause (A.G. 278.b). The pronoun **ei**, with **Interiores** as the antecedent, is understood as the subject (A.G. 271.a). The pluperfect denotes an action completed in past time (A.G. 477).

conferunt: The main verb of the coordinate clause **huc ... conferunt** (A.G. 278.a). The pronoun **ei**, with **Interiores** as the antecedent, is understood as the subject (A.G. 271.a).

(86.5-6) Multitudine telorum ex turribus (6) propugnantis deturbant, aggere et cratibus fossas explent, falcibus vallum ac loricam rescindunt.

ac, *and.*

crates, -is, f., *wicker-work, hurdle, fascine, bundle of brushwood. away.*
et, *and.*
expleo, -plere, -plevi, -pletus, *fill up, fill.*
fossa, -ae, f., *ditch, trench, entrenchment, fosse.*
multitudo, -inis, f., *great number, multitude.*
rescindo, -scindere, -scidi, -scissus, *cut down, break up, destroy.*
turris, -is, f., *tower.*

agger, -eris, m., *material for a mound* (earth, timber), *earth.*
deturbo, -are, -avi, -atus, *thrust down, dislodge, drive*
ex, *from.*
falx, falcis, f., *sickle-shaped hook.*
lorica, -ae, f., *breastwork.*
propugno, -are, -avi, -atus, *fight on the defensive.*
telum, -i, n., *dart, spear.*
vallum, -i, n., *rampart, wall, entrenchment.*

Multitudine: Ablative of means (A.G. 409).
telorum: Partitive genitive with **Multitudine** (A.G. 346.a.1).
ex turribus: Ablative of *place from which* with the preposition **ex** (A.G. 426.1).
propugnantis: Plural, masculine, accusative present participle used substantively (A.G. 494.a). The noun **Romanos** is understood (A.G. 288.b). Accusative plural; **-is** for **-es** is the regular form of the present participle (A.G. 117-18). Accusative direct object of **deturbant** (A.G. 387).
deturbant ... explent ... rescindunt: Note the asyndeton between the clauses (A.G. 323.b).
deturbant: The main verb of the coordinate clause **Multitudine ... deturbant** (A.G. 278.a). The pronoun **ei**, with **Interiores** as the antecedent, is understood as the subject (A.G. 271.a).
aggere et cratibus: Two ablatives of means with **explent** (A.G. 409.a). **aggere**: The noun here does not mean the usual "rampart", but "material for a mound (dirt), rubble" (*OLD* **agger** 1). **et**: The conjunction connects the two ablative nouns (A.G. 324.a).
fossas: Accusative direct object of **explent** (A.G. 387).
explent: The main verb of the coordinate clause **aggere ... explent** (A.G. 278.a). The pronoun **ei**, with **Interiores** as the antecedent, is understood as the subject (A.G. 271.a).
falcibus: Ablative of instrument (A.G. 409).
vallum ac loricam: Two accusative direct objects of **rescindunt** (A.G. 387). **ac**: The conjunction connects the two accusative nouns and means "and" (*OLD* **atque** 12).
rescindunt: The main verb of the coordinate clause **falcibus ... rescindunt** (A.G. 278.a). The pronoun **ei**, with **Interiores** as the antecedent, is understood as the subject (A.G. 271.a).

(87.1-2) Mittit primo Brutum adulescentem cum cohortibus Caesar, post cum aliis C. Fabium legatum; postremo ipse, cum (2) vehementius pugnaretur, integros subsidio adducit.

adduco, -ducere, -duxi, -ductus, *bring up, lead.*
alius, -a, -um, *another, other.*
C. Fabius, -i, m., *Gaius Fabius.*
cohors, -hortis, f., *cohort, company,* (the tenth part of a legion).
integri, -orum, m., pl., *those who were unexhausted, fresh men.*

legatus, -i, m., *lieutenant, lieutenant-general.*
post, *after, afterwards, later.*
primo, *at first, in the first place.*
subsidium, -i, n., *support, relief, reinforcement, help, aid.*

adulescens, -entis, m., *the junior.*
Brutus, -i, m., *Brutus.*
Caesar, -aris, m., *Caesar.*
cum, *with; when, while.*
ipse, -a, -um, *he, they,* with or without *himself, themselves.*

mitto, mittere, misi, missus, *send.*
postremo, *at last, finally.*
pugno, -are, -avi, -atus, *fight, combat, engage.*
vehementer, comp. **vehementius**, *vigorously, exceedingly.*

Mittit ... Caesar: The reversal of the normal word order (subject first, verb last) is called hyperbaton (A.G. 596) (Gotoff, 6-10).
Mittit: The main verb of the coordinate clause **Mittit ... Caesar** (A.G. 278.a). Verb first in the emphatic position (A.G. 589.d). The historical present, giving vividness to the narrative, is present in Chapter 87 (A.G. 469). This usage, common in all languages, comes from imagining past events as going on before our eyes (*repraesentatio*) (A.G. 469 Note).
primo ... post ... postremo: A series of three adverbs of time meaning "first ... next ... finally" (A.G. 217.b and 320-21).
Brutum: First accusative direct object of **Mittit** (A.G. 387). See Appendix A.
adulescentem: An accusative noun in apposition to the proper noun **Brutum** (A.G. 282).
cum cohortibus: Ablative of accompaniment with the preposition **cum** (A.G. 413).
Caesar: Nominative subject (A.G. 339). The subject is in the last position in the clause (A.G. 597.b). See Appendix A.

post ... legatum: Coordinate clause, carry down **Mittit** as the main verb (A.G. 278.a).

cum aliis: Ablative of accompaniment with the preposition **cum** (A.G. 413). **aliis**: Plural, feminine, ablative pronoun used substantively meaning "others" (*OLD* **alius2** 1). The noun **cohortibus** is understood.

C. Fabium: Second accusative direct object of **Mittit** (A.G. 387). See Appendix A. **C.**: Abbreviated form of the praenomen **Gaius** (A.G. 108.c).

legatum: An accusative noun in apposition to the proper noun **Fabium** (A.G. 282).

ipse: Singular, masculine, nominative demonstrative pronoun used substantively (A.G. 296.2). The antecedent is **Caesar** (A.G. 297.e). Nominative subject of **adducit** (A.G. 339). The pronoun distinguishes the principal personage (**Caesar**) from subordinate persons (**Brutum ... Fabium**) (A.G. 398.d.3).

cum ... (id) pugnaretur: Temporal clause; the relative adverb **cum** ("when, while") with the imperfect subjunctive describes the circumstances that accompanied the action of the main verb (A.G. 546). **pugnaretur**: The main verb of the subordinate clause (A.G. 278.b). Impersonal use of the intransitive passive verb (A.G. 208.d). Supply **id** as the subject (A.G. 318.c).

vehementius: Comparative adverb (A.G. 218 and 320-21).

integros: Plural, masculine, accusative adjective used substantively (A.G. 288). The noun **milites** is understood (A.G. 387). Accusative direct object of **adducit** (A.G. 387).

subsidio: Dative of the purpose or end. The dative of an abstract noun (**subsidio**) is used to show that for which a thing serves or which it accomplishes (A.G. 382.1).

adducit: The main verb of the main clause (A.G. 278.b).

(87.2-3) Restituto proelio ac repulsis hostibus eo quo Labienum miserat contendit; cohortis IIII ex proximo castello deducit, equitum partem se sequi, partem circumire exteriores munitiones et (3) ab tergo hostis adoriri iubet.

ab, *at.*

adorior, -oriri, -ortus, *fall upon, attack, assail.*

circumeo, -ire, -ivi, or **-ii, -tus**, *surround, encircle.*

contendo, -tendere, -tendi, -tentus, *hasten, make haste, push forward.*

eo, *thither, there.*

et, *and.*

exterior, -ior, -ius, *outer, exterior.*

I, in expression of number, *1.*

Labienus, -i, m., *Labienus.*

munitio, -onis, f., *works of fortifications, entrenchment, defenses.*

proelium, -i, n., *battle, combat, engagement.*

quo, *to which place, where.*

restituo, -uere, -ui, -utus, *restore.*

sui, sibi, se, or **sese**, nom. wanting, *him,* with or without *-self.*

ac, *and.*

castellum, -i, n., *redoubt, fortress, stronghold.*

cohors, -hortis, f., *cohort, company,* (the tenth part of a legion).

deduco, -ducere, -duxi, -ductus, *withdraw, lead, bring.*

eques, -itis, m., *rider, horseman, cavalryman, trooper.*

ex, *from, out of.*

hostis, -is, m., *enemy, foe*; pl., *the enemy.*

iubeo, iubere, iussi, iussus, *order, give orders, bid, command.*

mitto, mittere, misi, missus, *send.*

pars, partis, f., *part, portion.*

proximus, -a, -um, *nearest.*

repello, -pellere, reppuli, repulsus, *drive back, force back, repulse.*

sequor, -qui, -cutus, *follow.*

tergum, -i, n., *back.*

Restituto proelio: Ablative absolute (A.G. 419-20). **Restituto**: The perfect tense of the participle represents the action as completed at the time indicated by the tense of the main verb (A.G. 489).

ac: The conjunction connects the two ablative absolutes and means "and" (*OLD* **atque** 12).

repulsis hostibus: Ablative absolute (A.G. 419-20). **repulsis**: The perfect tense of the participle represents the action as completed at the time indicated by the tense of the main verb (A.G. 489).

eo: Adverb with **contendit** (A.G. 217.a and 320-21).

quo ... miserat: Subordinate clause (A.G. 278.b). For the reference see 86.1-3. **quo**: Adverb, correlative to **eo** meaning "to which place" (*OLD* **quo1** 3.b) (A.G. 215.4 and 320-21). **miserat**: The main verb of the subordinate clause (A.G. 278.b). The pronoun **is**, with **ipse** (**Caesar**) as the antecedent, is understood as the subject (A.G. 271.a). The pluperfect denotes an action completed in past time (A.G. 477).

Labienum: Accusative direct object of **miserat** (A.G. 387). See Appendix A.

contendit: The main verb of the main clause (A.G. 278.b). The pronoun **is**, with **ipse** (**Caesar**) as the antecedent, is understood as the subject (A.G. 271.a).

cohortis IIII: Accusative direct object of **deducit** (A.G. 387). **cohortis**: Accusative plural noun; **-is** for **-es** is the regular form in mixed i-stem nouns (A.G. 71.3). **IIII**: Roman numeral used as an adjective (A.G. 133).

ex proximo castello: Ablative of *place from which* with the preposition **ex** (A.G. 426.1). **proximo**: Defective superlative adjective (A.G. 130.a).

deducit: The main verb of the coordinate clause **cohortis ... deducit** (A.G. 278.a). The pronoun **is**, with **ipse** (**Caesar**) as the antecedent, is understood as the subject (A.G. 271.a).

equitum: Partitive genitive with **partem** (A.G. 346.a.1).

partem ... sequi: Subject accusative with the infinitive after **iubet**. The construction is equivalent to a substantive clause of purpose (A.G. 563.a).

se: Singular, masculine, accusative indirect reflexive pronoun (A.G. 300.2). The antecedent is **is** (**Caesar**), the supplied subject of **iubet** (A.G. 299). Accusative direct object of the infinitive **sequi** (A.G. 387 and 451.3).

partem circumire ... et ... adoriri: A subject accusative with two infinitives after **iubet**. The construction is equivalent to a substantive clause of purpose (A.G. 563.a). **circumire**: "I.e. to make a flank movement and turn the enemy's rear." (Kelsey, 432) **et**: The conjunction connects the two infinitives (A.G. 324.a).

exteriores munitiones: Accusative direct object of the infinitive **circumire** (A.G. 387 and 451.3). **exteriores**: Defective comparative adjective (A.G. 130.b).

ab tergo: Ablative of *position* with the preposition **ab** (A.G. 429.b).

hostis: Accusative direct object of the infinitive **adoriri** (A.G. 387 and 451.3). Accusative plural noun; **-is** for **-es** is the regular form in i-stem nouns (A.G. 65-67 and 74.c).

iubet: The main verb of the coordinate clause **equitum ... iubet** (A.G. 278.a). The pronoun **is**, with **ipse** (Caesar) as the antecedent, is understood as the subject (A.G. 271.a). Notice the asyndeton construction between the verbs **deducit ... iubet** (A.G. 323.b).

(87.3) **Labienus, postquam neque aggeres neque fossae vim hostium sustinere poterant, coactis +una XL+ cohortibus, quas ex proximis praesidiis deductas fors obtulit, Caesarem per nuntios facit certiorem quid faciendum existimet.**

agger, -eris, m., *rampart, mole, mound, dike.*
certus, -a, -um, comp. **-ior**, *certain, positive.*

cohors, -hortis, f., *cohort, company,* (the tenth part of a legion).
ex, *from, out of.*
facio, facere, feci, factus, *do make*; (with **certior**), *inform.*
fossa, -ae, f., *ditch, trench, entrenchment, fosse.*
L, in expression of number, *50.*
neque ... neque, *neither ... nor.*
offero, -ferre, obtuli, oblatus, *offer, present.*
possum, posse, potui, -----, *be able.*
praesidium, -i, n., *fortress, redoubt.*
qui, quae, quod, *who, which, what.*
sustineo, -tinere, -tinui, -tentus, *bear, endure, withstand.*
vis, acc. **vim**, abl. **vi**, f., *strength, force.*

Caesar, -aris, m., *Caesar.*
cogo, cogere, coegi, coactus, *bring together, collect, gather, assemble.*
deduco, -ducere, -duxi, -ductus, *withdraw, lead, bring.*
existimo, -are, -avi, -atus, *think, consider, judge.*
fors, fortis, f., *chance, luck, accident.*
hostis, -is, m., *enemy, foe*; pl., *the enemy.*
Labienus, -i, m., *Labienus.*
nuntius, -i, m., *messenger, courier.*
per, *by* (means of), *through.*
postquam, *when, after.*
proximus, -a, -um, *nearest.*
quis, -----, quid, *who?, what?*
una, *together, in the same place.*
X, in expression of number, *= 10.*

Labienus: Nominative subject of **facit** (A.G. 339). See Appendix A.

postquam ... poterant: Temporal clause; the conjunction **postquam** ("when") with the imperfect indicative denotes a past state of things (A.G. 543.a). **poterant**: The main verb of the subordinate clause (A.G. 278.b).

neque ... neque: The repeated conjunction means "neither ... nor", connecting the two nominative nouns (*OLD* **neque** 7).

aggeres ... fossae: Two nominative subjects of **poterant** (A.G. 339).

vim: Accusative direct object of the infinitive **sustinere** (A.G. 387 and 451.3).

hostium: Possessive genitive with **vim** (A.G. 343).

sustinere: Complementary infinitive after **poterant** (A.G. 456).

coactis ... obtulit: Ablative absolute with a dependent clause.

coactis +una XL+ cohortibus: Ablative absolute (A.G. 419-20). **coactis**: The perfect tense of the participle represents the action as completed at the time indicated by the tense of the main verb (A.G. 489). **una**: Adverb (A.G. 320-21). **XL**: Roman numeral used as an adjective modifying **cohortibus** (A.G. 133).

quas ... obtulit: Relative clause (A.G. 303). **quas**: See below. **obtulit**: The main verb of the subordinate clause (A.G. 278.b).

quas ... deductas: Accusative direct object of **obtulit** (A.G. 387). **quas**: Plural, feminine, accusative relative pronoun used substantively (A.G. 305). The antecedent is **cohortibus** (A.G. 307). **deductas**: Accusative, perfect, passive participle used as a predicate, where in English a phrase or a subordinate clause would be more natural (A.G. 496).

ex proximis praesidiis: Ablative of *place from which* with the preposition **ex** (A.G. 426.1). **proximis**: Defective superlative adjective (A.G. 130.a).

fors: Nominative subject (A.G. 339).

Caesarem ... certiorem: Accusative direct object of **facit** (A.G. 387). **Caesarem**: See Appendix A. **certiorem**: Comparative adjective (A.G. 124).

per nuntios: Prepositional phrase, the personal agent, when considered as instrument or means, is often expressed by **per** with the accusative meaning "by" (means of) (A.G. 405.b).

facit certiorem: The phrase **certiorem facere** is an idiom that means "to inform" (*OLD* **certus** 12.b).

facit: The main verb of the main clause (A.G. 278.b).

quid ... existimet: Indirect question with the subjunctive; the phrase is the object of **facit certiorem** (A.G. 573-75). **quid**: See below. **existimet**: The main verb of the subordinate clause (A.G. 278.b). Present subjunctive; the tense of the subjunctive is normally in secondary sequence after the historical present **facit** (A.G. 575). Here it is in primary sequence through *repraesentatio* (A.G. 485.e and 585.b Note). The pronoun **is**, with **Labienus** as the antecedent, is understood as the subject (A.G. 271.a).

quid faciendum (esse): Accusative/infinitive construction in indirect discourse after **existimet** (A.G. 577 ff.). **quid**: Singular, neuter, accusative interrogative pronoun used substantively (A.G. 148). **faciendum (esse)**: Supply **esse** with the gerundive to form the second periphrastic (passive) present infinitive implying necessity (A.G. 194.b and 196). The tense of the infinitive in indirect discourse is relative to that of the verb of saying (A.G. 584).

(87.3) Accelerat Caesar, ut proelio intersit.

accelero, -are, -avi, -atus, *make haste, hasten.*
intersum, -esse, -fui, -----, *be present at, take part in.*
ut, *so that.*

Caesar, -aris, m., *Caesar.*
proelium, -i, n., *battle, combat, engagement.*

Accelerat Caesar: The reversal of the normal word order (subject first, verb last) is called hyperbaton (A.G. 596) (Gotoff, 6-10). **Accelerat:** The main verb of the main clause (A.G. 278.b). The verb comes in the first position when the idea in it is emphatic (A.G. 598.d).
Caesar: Nominative subject (A.G. 339). The subject is in the last position in the clause (A.G. 597.b). See Appendix A.
ut ... proelio: This is not the only instance of Caesar's personal engagement in warfare in the *BG.* See also the battle of the Sambre river against the Nervii where his personal intervention restored the battle (*BG* 2.25.2-3): **scuto ab novissimis uni militi detracto, quod ipse eo sine scuto venerat, in primam aciem processit centurionibusque nominatim appellatis, reliquos cohortatus milites, signa inferre et manipulos laxare iussit, quo facilius gladiis uti possent.**
ut ... intersit: The conjunction **ut** ("so that") with the subjunctive forms a final (purpose) clause (A.G. 531.1). **intersit:** The main verb of the subordinate clause (A.G. 278.b). Present subjunctive; the tense of the subjunctive is normally in secondary sequence after the historical present **Accelerat** (A.G. 482-85). Here it is in primary sequence through *repraesentatio* (A.G. 485.e and 585.b Note). The pronoun **is**, with **Caesar** as the antecedent, is understood as the subject (A.G. 271.a).
proelio: Dative indirect object of the compound verb **intersit** (A.G. 370).

Chapter 88 forms the climax of the battle of Alesia.

(88.1-2) Eius adventu ex colore vestitus cognito, quo insigni in proeliis uti consuerat, turmisque equitum et cohortibus visis quas se sequi iusserat, ut de locis superioribus haec declivia (2) et devexa cernebantur, hostes proelium committunt.

adventus, -us, m., *coming, approach, arrival.*
cognosco, -gnoscere, -gnovi, cognitus, *learn of, ascertain, know.*

color, -oris, m., *color.*
consuesco, -suescere, -suevi, -suetus, *be accustomed, be wont.*
declivia, -orum, n., pl., *slopes, declivities.*
eques, -itis, m., *rider, horseman, cavalryman, trooper.*
ex, *from, because of.*
hostis, -is, m., *enemy, foe;* pl., *the enemy.*
insigne, -is, n., *sign, mark, signal.*
iubeo, iubere, iussi, iussus, *order, give orders, bid, command.*
proelium, -i, n., *battle, combat, engagement.*
qui, quae, quod, *who, which, what.*
sui, sibi, se, *or* sese, nom. wanting, *him,* with or without *-self.*
turma, -ae, f., *troop, squadron.*
utor, uti, usus, *use, employ.*
video, videre, visi, visus, *see, perceive, observe.*

cerno, cernere, -----, -----, *discern, see, perceive.*
cohors, -hortis, f., *cohort, company,* (the tenth part of a legion).
committo, -mittere, -misi, -missus, *join, begin.*
de, *from.*
devexa, -orum, n., pl., *sloping places.*
et, *and.*
hic, haec, hoc, *this; he, she, it.*
in, *in.*
is, ea, id, *he, she, it; that, this.*
loca, -orum, n., pl., *places.*
-que, *and.*
sequor, -qui, -cutus, *follow.*
superior, -or, -us, *higher, upper.*
ut, *inasmuch as.*
vestitus, -us, m., *clothing, garb.*

Eius ... consuerat: Ablative absolute with a dependent clause.
Eius adventu ex colore vestitus cognito: Ablative absolute (A.G. 419-20). **Eius:** Singular, masculine, genitive demonstrative pronoun used substantively (A.G. 296.2). The antecedent is **Caesar** at 87.3 (A.G. 297.e). Possessive genitive with **adventu** (A.G. 343). **ex colore vestitus:** Ablative of cause with the preposition **ex** (A.G. 404). **colore:** "Ancient purple, corresponding nearly to our scarlet." (Kelsey, 432) **vestitus:** Possessive genitive with **colore** (A.G. 343). "The cloak of the commander (*paludamentum*) differed from that of the soldier only in being more ample, of finer quality, and ornamented; it was ordinarily scarlet in color, and often fringed." (Kelsey, 28) "a reference to the scarlet *paludamentum* worn by the *imperator* (see Pliny, Nat. Hist. 22.3)." (Hammond, 242)
cognito: The perfect tense of the participle represents the action as completed at the time indicated by the tense of the main verb (A.G. 489).
quo ... consuerat: Relative clause (A.G. 303). **quo:** See below. **consuerat:** The main verb of the subordinate clause (A.G. 278.b). Contracted form of **consueverat** (A.G. 181.a). The pronoun **is**, with **Eius** (**Caesar**) as the antecedent, is understood as the subject (A.G. 271.a). The pluperfect denotes an action in indefinite time, but prior to some past time referred to (A.G. 477).
quo insigni: Ablative direct object of the deponent infinitive **uti** (A.G. 410). **quo:** Singular, neuter, ablative relative pronoun (A.G. 305). The antecedent is the neuter noun **insigni** in its own clause (adjectival use) (A.G. 307.b).
in proeliis: Prepositional phrase, **in** with the ablative here means "in" (expressing an abstract location) (*OLD* **in** 26).
uti: Complementary infinitive after **consuerat** (A.G. 456).
turmisque ... cernebantur: Ablative absolute with dependent clauses.
turmisque equitum et cohortibus visis: Ablative absolute (A.G. 419-20). **-que:** The enclitic conjunction connects the two ablative absolutes (A.G. 324.a). **equitum:** Partitive genitive with **turmis** (A.G. 346.a.1). **et:** The conjunction connects the two ablative nouns in the ablative absolute (A.G. 324.a). **visis:** The perfect tense of the participle represents the action as completed at the time indicated by the tense of the main verb (A.G. 489).

quas ... iusserat: Relative clause (A.G. 303). For the reference see 87.2. **quas**: See below. **iusserat**: The main verb of the subordinate clause (A.G. 278.b). The pronoun **is**, with **Eius** (**Caesar**) as the antecedent, is understood as the subject (A.G. 271.a). The pluperfect denotes an action completed in past time (A.G. 477).

quas ... sequi: Subject accusative with an infinitive after **iusserat**. The construction is equivalent to a substantive clause of purpose (A.G. 563.a). **quas**: Plural, feminine, accusative relative pronoun used substantively (A.G. 305). The antecedent is both **turmis** and **cohortibus** (A.G. 307).

se: Singular, masculine, accusative indirect reflexive pronoun (A.G. 300.2). The antecedent is **is** (**Caesar**), the supplied subject of **iusserat** (A.G. 299). Accusative direct object of the infinitive **sequi** (A.G. 387 and 451.3).

ut ... cernebantur: The relative adverb **ut** ("inasmuch as") with the indicative here is causal explaining the preceding ablative absolute (**turmisque equitum et cohortibus visis**) (*OLD* **ut** 21). **cernebantur**: The main verb of the subordinate clause (A.G. 278.b).

de locis superioribus: Ablative of *place from which* with the preposition **de** (A.G. 426.1). **superioribus**: Defective comparative adjective (A.G. 130.b).

haec declivia et devexa: Two nominative subjects (A.G. 339). **haec**: Plural, neuter, nominative demonstrative pronoun used as an adjective modifying both neuter nouns, **declivia** and **devexa** (A.G. 296.1 and a). **declivia**: The neuter noun means "slopes" (*OLD* **declive**). **et**: The conjunction connects the two nominative nouns (A.G. 324.a). **devexa**: Plural, neuter, nominative adjective used substantively meaning "sloping parts" (*OLD* **devexus** 1.b).

hostes: Nominative subject (A.G. 339).

proelium: Accusative direct object of **committunt** (A.G. 387).

committunt: The main verb of the main clause (A.G. 278.b). The historical present, giving vividness to the narrative, is present in Chapter 88 (A.G. 469). This usage, common in all languages, comes from imagining past events as going on before our eyes (*repraesentatio*) (A.G. 469 Note). "Apparently the Romans have sallied out and the Gauls have withdrawn a little in surprise; now the Gauls attack with greater vigor, hoping to win the victory before Caesar can arrive." (Walker, 409)

(88.2) Utrimque clamore sublato excipit rursus ex vallo atque omnibus munitionibus clamor.

atque, *and.*
ex, *from.*

munitio, -onis, f., *works of fortifications, entrenchment, defenses.*
rursus, *in turn.*
utrimque, *from both sides, on both sides.*

clamor, -oris, m., *outcry, loud call, shout, din.*
excipio, -cipere, -cepi, -ceptus, *take up, follow, succeed.*
omnis, -e, *all, the whole of, the entire.*
tollo, tollere, sustuli, sublatus, *raise, send up.*
vallum, -i, n., *rampart, wall, entrenchment.*

Utrimque clamore sublato: Ablative absolute (A.G. 419-20). **Utrimque**: Adverb (320-21). **sublato**: The perfect tense of the participle represents the action as completed at the time indicated by the tense of the main verb (A.G. 489).

clamore ... clamor: The noise of battle is emphasized by the repetition of the noun **clamor**. Iconically, the noise of the battle (**clamore ... clamor**) encloses the battle scene (**ex vallo atque omnibus munitionibus**).

rursus: Adverb (A.G. 216 and 320-21).

excipit: The main verb of the main clause (A.G. 278.b).

ex vallo atque omnibus munitionibus: Ablative of source with the preposition **ex** (A.G. 403.1). **atque**: The conjunction connects the two ablative nouns in the prepositional phrase and means "and" (*OLD* **atque** 12).

clamor: Nominative subject (A.G. 339). The subject is in the last position in the clause (A.G. 597.b).

Nostri ... fuga (88.2-6): This is the climax of this chapter. Notice how the succession of short sentences iconically mirrors the ebb and flow battle. Adcock notes that "The battle reaches its climax, until in a sharp *staccato* come the brief sentences, like blows that hammer defeat into victory. ... There is hardly a word that is not pure prose, but the effect is epic." (Adcock, 68) "Notice throughout this chapter the vividness of style, which is heightened by the omission of conjunctions." (Kelsey, 432)

(88.2-3) Nostri omissis pilis gladiis rem gerunt. (3) Repente post tergum equitatus cernitur; cohortes aliae appropinquant.

alius, -a, -um, *other, different.*

cerno, cernere, -----, -----, *discern, see, perceive.*

equitatus, -us, m., *cavalry.*

gladius, -i, m., *sword.*
omitto, -mittere, -misi, -missus, *lay aside.*
post, *behind.*
res, rei, f., *battle, campaign, military operation.*

appropinquo, -are, -avi, -atus, *approach, come near, draw near.*
cohors, -hortis, f., *cohort, company,* (the tenth part of a legion).
gero, gerere, gessi, gestus, *carry on, carry out, perform, wage.*
nostri, -orum, m., pl., *our men, our side.*
pilum, -i, n., *javelin, pike.*
repente, *suddenly.*
tergum, -i, n., *back,* (with **post**), *in the rear.*

Nostri: Plural, masculine, nominative possessive pronoun used substantively used to denote a special class (A.G. 302.d). Nominative subject (A.G. 339).

omissis pilis: Ablative absolute (A.G. 419-20.1). **omissis**: The perfect tense of the participle represents the action as completed at the time indicated by the tense of the main verb (A.G. 489). **pilis**: "A heavy wooden javelin (**pilum**), with a long iron point which was strong enough to pierce any armor but was likely to bend as it did so. Therefore it could not easily be withdrawn when it had pierced a shield, and could not be thrown back by the enemy. After the battle the javelins were gathered and straightened by the Romans. Each soldier carried but one javelin." (Walker, 24)

gladiis: Ablative of instrument (A.G. 409).

rem: Accusative direct object of **gerunt** (A.G. 387).

gerunt: The main verb of the main clause (A.G. 278.b).

Repente: Adverb (A.G. 320-21).

post tergum: Prepositional phrase, **post** with the accusative here means "behind" (*OLD* **post2** 1). "Of the Romans who have sallied out. The *equitatus* and *cohortes* are those who have followed Caesar." (Walker, 409).

equitatus: Nominative subject (A.G. 339). These are the horsemen which Caesar had sent to attack the enemy's rear at 87.3.

cernitur: The main verb of the simple sentence (A.G. 278.1).

cohortes aliae: Nominative subject (A.G. 339).

appropinquant: The main verb of the simple sentence (A.G. 278.1).

(88.3-5) Hostes terga verterunt: fugientibus equites (4) occurrunt: fit magna caedes. Sedulius, dux et princeps Lemovicum, occiditur; Vercassivellaunus Arvernus vivus in fuga comprehenditur; signa militaria LXXIIII ad Caesarem referuntur: pauci ex tanto numero se incolumes in castra (5) recipiunt.

ad, *to.*

caedes, -is, f., *killing, slaughter, murder, massacre.*

castra, -orum, n., pl., *camp, encampment.*

dux, ducis, m., *leader, general, commander.*

et, *and.*

fio, fieri, factus, *take place, happen, come about, come to pass.*

fugio, fugere, fugi, -----, *flee, run away, make off.*

I, in expression of number, *1.*

incolumis, -e, *safe, unharmed, uninjured, unhurt.*

Lemovices, -um, m., pl., *the Lemovices.*

militaris, -e, *military.*

occido, -cidere, -cidi, -cisus, *kill, slay.*

pauci, -orum m., pl., *few, only a few.*

recipio, -cipere, -cepi, -ceptus, (with se), *return, retreat.*

Sedulius, -i, m., *Sedulius.*

sui, sibi, se, or **sese,** nom. wanting *themselves.*

tergum, -i, n., *back,* (with post), *in the rear.*

verto, vertere, verti, versus, *turn,* (with **terga**), *turn and flee, flee, turn tail.*

X, in expression of number, = *10.*

Arvernus, -i, m., *an Arvernian.*

Caesar, -aris, m., *Caesar.*

comprehendo, -hendere, -hendi, -hensus, *seize, lay hold of, arrest, capture.*

eques, -itis, m., *rider, horseman, cavalryman, trooper.*

ex, *from the number of, from among, of.*

fuga, -ae, f., *flight.*

hostis, -is, m., *enemy, foe;* pl., *the enemy.*

in, *in; into.*

L, in expression of number, *50.*

magnus, -a, -um, *great, large, considerable.*

numerus, -i, m., *body, host, number, amount.*

occurro, -currere, -curri or **-cucurri, -cursurus,** *meet, find, encounter.*

princeps, -ipis, m., *head man, leader, chief, prince.*

refero, -ferre, rettuli, -latus, *bring, carry, convey.*

signum, -i, n., *standard.*

tantus, -a, -um, *so great, so large, such, so extensive.*

Vercassivellaunus, -i, m., *Vercassivellaunus.*

vivus, -a, -um, *living, alive.*

Hostes: Nominative subject (A.G. 339).

terga: Accusative direct object of **verterunt** (A.G. 387). The phrase **terga vertere** is an idiom that means "to turn tail, flee" (*OLD* **verto** 9).

verterunt: The main verb of the simple sentence (A.G. 278.1). Notice the one perfect tense in the midst of the succession of historical presents. The Loeb text reads **vertunt** and the Budé text reads **verterunt**.

fugientibus: Plural, masculine, dative present participle used substantively (A.G. 494.a). The noun **Gallis** is understood (A.G. 288.b). Dative indirect object of the intransitive verb **occurrunt** (A.G. 366).

equites: Nominative subject (A.G. 339).

occurrunt: The main verb of the simple sentence (A.G. 278.1).

fit ... caedes: The reversal of the normal word order (subject first, verb last) is called hyperbaton (A.G. 596) (Gotoff, 6-10).

fit magna caedes: This phrase has occurred at 70.4-5. This terse formulation of the ensuing slaughter is more powerful than a gruesome description of it as it allows the reader to fill in the details with their imagination.

fit: The main verb of the simple sentence (A.G. 278.1). The verb comes in the first position when the idea in it is emphatic (A.G. 598.d).

magna caedes: Nominative subject (A.G. 339). The subject is in the last position in the clause (A.G. 597.b).

Sedulius: Nominative subject (A.G. 339). See Appendix A.

dux et princeps: Two nominative nouns in apposition to the proper noun **Sedulius** (A.G. 282). **et:** The conjunction connects the two nominative nouns (A.G. 324.a).

Lemovicum: Partitive genitive with both **dux ... princeps** of the tribe name **Lemovices** (A.G. 346.a.1). See Appendix A.

occiditur: The main verb of the simple sentence (A.G. 278.1).

Vercassivellaunus ... vivus: Nominative subject (A.G. 339). **Vercassivellaunus:** See Appendix A.

Arvernus: A nominative noun in apposition to the proper noun **Vercassivellaunus** (A.G. 282).

in fuga: Prepositional phrase, **in** with the ablative here means "in" (expressing an abstract location) (*OLD* **in** 26).

comprehenditur: The main verb of the simple sentence (A.G. 278.1).

signa militaria LXXIIII: Nominative subject (A.G. 339). **LXXIIII**: Roman numeral used as an adjective modifying **signa** (A.G. 133).

ad Caesarem: Prepositional phrase, **ad** with the accusative here means "to" (*OLD* **ad** 1). **Caesarem**: See Appendix A.

referuntur: The main verb of the simple sentence (A.G. 278.1).

pauci ... incolumes: Nominative subject (A.G. 339). **pauci**: Plural, masculine, nominative adjective used substantively (A.G. 288). The noun **Galli** is understood (A.G. 288.b). **incolumes**: Plural, masculine, nominative adjective modifying **pauci** but used to qualify the action of the verb, and so has the force of an adverb (A.G. 290).

ex tanto numero: Prepositional phrase, **ex** with the ablative instead of the partitive genitive means "from the number of, from among, of" (A.G. 346.c) (*OLD* **ex** 17).

se: Plural, masculine, accusative direct reflexive pronoun (A.G. 300.1). The antecedent is **pauci**, the subject of **recipiunt** (A.G. 299). Accusative direct object of **recipiunt** (A.G. 387).

in castra: Accusative of *place to which* with the preposition **in** (A.G. 426.2).

recipiunt: The main verb of the simple sentence (A.G. 278.1). The verb **recipere** used reflexively means "to return" (*OLD* **recipio** 12).

(88.5-6) Conspicati ex oppido caedem et fugam suorum (6) desperata salute copias a munitionibus reducunt. Fit protinus hac re audita ex castris Gallorum fuga.

a(b), *from*.
caedes, -is, f., *killing, slaughter, murder, massacre*.
conspicor, -ari, -atus, *catch sight of, see, observe*.
despero, -are, -avi, -atus, *give up on, despair of*.
ex, *from; from, out of*.

fuga, -ae, f., *flight*.
hic, haec, hoc, *this; he, she, it*.

oppidum, -i, n., *fortified town, city*.
reduco, -ducere, -duxi, -ductus, *lead back, conduct back*.
salus, -utis, f., *safety, deliverance*.

audio, -ire, -ivi or **-ii, -itus**, *learn (by hearing), hear of*.
castra, -orum, n., pl., *camp, encampment*.
copiae, -arum, f., pl., *forces, troops*.
et, *and*.
fio, fieri, factus, *take place, happen, come about, come to pass*.
Galli, -orum, m., *the Gauls*.
munitio, -onis, f., *works of fortifications, entrenchment, defenses*.
protinus, *forthwith, at once, immediately*.
res, rei, f., *matter, affair*.
sui, -orum, m., pl., *their men, with or without own*.

Conspicati: Plural, masculine, nominative perfect, deponent participle used substantively (A.G. 494.a). The noun **duces** is understood. Nominative subject (A.G. 339).

ex oppido: Prepositional phrase, **ex** with the ablative here means "from" (indicating the point at or from which an action is performed) (*OLD* **ex** 7).

caedem et fugam: Two accusative direct objects of the participle **Conspicati** (A.G. 387 and 488). **et**: The conjunction connects the two accusative nouns (A.G. 324.a).

suorum: Plural, masculine, genitive possessive pronoun used substantively to denote a special class (A.G. 302.d). Possessive genitive with both **caedem ... fugam** (A.G. 343). This is the relief army.

desperata salute: Ablative absolute (A.G. 419-20). **desperata**: The perfect tense of the participle represents the action as completed at the time indicated by the tense of the main verb (A.G. 489).

copias: Accusative direct object of **reducunt** (A.G. 387).

a munitionibus: Ablative of *place from which* with the preposition **a(b)** (A.G. 426.1).

reducunt: The main verb of the main clause (A.G. 278.b).

Fit ... fuga: The reversal of the normal word order (subject first, verb last) is called hyperbaton (A.G. 596) (Gotoff, 6-10).

Fit: The main verb of the main clause (A.G. 278.b). The verb comes in the first position when the idea in it is emphatic (A.G. 598.d).

protinus: Adverb (A.G. 320-21).

hac re audita: Ablative absolute (A.G. 419-20). **hac**: Singular, feminine, ablative demonstrative pronoun used as an adjective modifying **re** (A.G. 296.1 and a). **audita**: The perfect tense of the participle represents the action as completed at the time indicated by the tense of the main verb (A.G. 489).

ex castris Gallorum: Ablative of *place from which* with the preposition **ex** (A.G. 426.1). "The camp of the relieving army. The Gauls feared an immediate attack." (Walker, 409) **Gallorum**: Possessive genitive with **castris** (A.G. 343). See Appendix A.

fuga: Nominative subject (A.G. 339). The subject is in the last position in the clause (A.G. 597.b).

(88.6-7) Quod nisi crebris subsidiis ac totius diei labore milites essent defessi, (7) omnes hostium copiae deleri potuissent.

ac, *and*.
creber, -bra, -brum, *numerous, frequent*.

deleo, -ere, -evi, -etus, *destroy, annihilate*.
hostis, -is, m., *enemy, foe*; pl., *the enemy*.
miles, -itis, m., *soldier, foot-solider*.
possum, posse, potui, -----, *be able*.

copiae, -arum, f., pl., *forces, troops*.
defetiscor, -i, defessus, *become weary, become exhausted*.
dies, -ei, m. and f., *day*.
labor, -oris, m., *toil, exertion, labor*.
omnis, -e, *all, the entire*.
quod nisi, *if not, unless*.

subsidium, -i, n., *support, relief, reinforcement, help, aid.*   **totus, -a, -um**, *the whole, all, all the, entire.*

Quod nisi: The combination means "if not, unless (A.G. 324.d). **Quod**: The relative adverb (Abut, and, now) is used as a connective particle, referring to what precedes (*OLD* **quod** 1) (A.G. 397.a). **nisi**: See below.

nisi ... essent defessi ... potuissent: Contrary to fact, past time conditional statement (pluperfect subjunctive in both protasis and apodosis) (A.G. 514.C.2).

nisi ... essent defessi: The conjunction **nisi** ("unless") with the subjunctive forms the protasis of the conditional statement (A.G. 512).

nisi: With **nisi** the apodosis is stated as universally true except in the single case supposed, in which case it is (impliedly) not true (A.G. 525.a.1). **essent defessi**: The main verb of the subordinate clause (A.G. 278.b). Pluperfect subjunctive from the deponent verb **defetiscor** (A.G. 190).

crebris subsidiis ac ... labore: Two ablatives of cause (A.G. 404). **ac**: The conjunction connects the two ablative nouns and means "and" (*OLD* **atque** 12).

totius diei: Genitive of quality (measure) with **labore** (A.G. 345.b). **totius**: -ius is the regular genitive singular ending for the adjective **totus** (A.G. 113).

milites: Nominative subject (A.G. 339).

omnes ... copiae: Nominative subject (A.G. 339).

hostium: Partitive genitive with **copiae** (A.G. 346.a.1).

deleri: Complementary infinitive after **potuissent** (A.G. 456).

potuissent: The main verb of the apodosis of the conditional statement (A.G. 512). The main verb of the main clause (A.G. 278.b).

(88.7) De media nocte missus equitatus novissimum agmen consequitur: magnus numerus capitur atque interficitur, reliqui ex fuga in civitates discedunt.

agmen, -minis, n., *column,* (with **novissimum**), *the rear of the column, the rear.*

capio, capere, cepi, captus, *take, get, seize, capture.*

consequor, -sequi, -secutus, *pursue, overtake.*

discedo, -cedere, -cessi, -cessurus, *go away, depart, leave.*

ex, *immediately after, following on.*

in, *to, into.*

magnus, -a, -um, *great, large.*

mitto, mittere, misi, missus, *send.*

nox, noctis, f., *night.*

reliqui, -orum, m., pl., *the rest.*

atque, *and then.*

civitas, -tatis, f., *state, nation.*

de, *immediately after, following.*

equitatus, -us, m., *cavalry.*

fuga, -ae, f., *flight.*

interficio, -ficere, -feci, -fectus, *slay, kill.*

medius, -a, -um, *middle, mid-.*

novus, -a, -um, sup. **-issimus**, *last, at the rear, hindmost.*

numerus, -i, m., *number, amount.*

De media nocte: Prepositional phrase, **de** with the ablative here means "immediately after, following" (*OLD* **de** 4.b). **media**: The adjective designates not what object, but what part of it is meant (A.G. 293).

missus equitatus: Nominative subject (A.G. 339). **missus**: Nominative, perfect, passive, participle used as a predicate, where in English a phrase or a subordinate clause would be more normal (A.G. 496).

novissimum agmen: Accusative direct object of **consequitur** (A.G. 387). **novissimum**: Superlative adjective (A.G. 124). The adjective designates the furthest back portion of the army on the march, "rearguard" (*OLD* **agmen** 5.b).

consequitur: The main verb of the simple sentence (A.G. 278.1).

magnus numerus: Nominative subject of **capitur ... interficitur** (A.G. 339).

capitur: The main verbs of the coordinate clause **magnus ... capitur** (A.G. 278.a).

atque: The conjunction connects the two main verbs and means "and then" (*OLD* **atque** 7).

interficitur: The main verbs of the coordinate clause **interficitur** (A.G. 278.a). Apparently no prisoners were taken during the rout.

reliqui: Plural, masculine, nominative adjective used substantively (A.G. 288). The noun **Galli** is understood (A.G. 288.b). Nominative subject (A.G. 339).

ex fuga: Prepositional phrase, **ex** with the ablative here means "immediately after, following on" (*OLD* **ex** 10).

in civitates: Accusative of *place to which* with the preposition **in** (A.G. 426.2).

discedunt: The main verb of the coordinate clause **reliqui ... discedunt** (A.G. 278.a).

4.R CHAPTER 89: THE SURRENDER OF VERCINGETORIX AND THE BESIEGED ARMY

(89.1-3) Postero die Vercingetorix concilio convocato id bellum se suscepisse non suarum necessitatum sed communis libertatis (2) causa demonstrat et, quoniam sit fortunae cedendum, ad utramque rem se illis offerre, seu morte sua Romanis satis(3)facere seu vivum tradere velint.

ad, *for the purpose of, to be used for.*

causa, -ae, f., abl. with the gen., *for the sake of, for the purpose of.*

communis, -e, *common, in common, public, general.*

convoco, -are, -avi, -atus, *call together, summon, assemble.*

dies, -ei, m. and f., *day.*

bellum, -i, n., *war.*

cedo, cedere, cessi, cessurus, *yield, give up to.*

concilium, -i, n., *meeting, assembly, council.*

demonstro, -are, -avi, -atus, *point out, show, say, explain.*

et, *and.*

fortuna, -ae, f., *fate, chance, fortune, misfortune, adversity.*
is, ea, id, *he, she, it; that, this.*
mors, mortis, f., *death.*
non, *not.*

posterus, -a, -um, *following, the next.*
res, rei, f., *outcome, circumstance, case, event.*
satisfacio, -facere, -feci, -factus, *appease, placate.*
seu ... seu, *whether ... or.*

suscipio, -cipere, -cepi, -ceptus, *undertake, take up.*
trado, -dere, -didi, -ditus, *hand over, give up, deliver, surrender.*
Vercingetorix, -igis, m., *Vercingetorix.*
volo, velle, volui, *wish, desire, mean, intend.*

ille, illae, illud, *that; he, she, it.*
libertas, -atis, f., *freedom, liberty, independence.*
necessitas, -tatis, f., *requirements, demands, need.*
offero, -ferre, obtuli, oblatus, *offer, present,* (with se), *give oneself up.*
quoniam, *since, seeing that, because.*
Romani, -orum, m., pl., *the Romans.*
sed, *but.*
sui, sibi, se, or sese, nom. wanting, *he,* with or without *himself.; himself.*
suus, -a, -um, *his,* with or without *own.*
uterque, -traque, -trumque, *either.*
vivus, -a, -um, *living, alive.*

Postero die: Ablative of *time when* (A.G. 423.1). **die**: The noun **dies** is normally masculine gender (A.G. 97.a).

Vercingetorix: Nominative subject of **demonstrat** (A.G. 339). See Appendix A.

concilio convocato: Ablative absolute (A.G. 419-20). **convocato**: The perfect tense of the participle represents the action as completed at the time indicated by the tense of the main verb (A.G. 489). Kahn claims that the council scene functions as a substitute for choral odes between major episodes. (Kahn, 251) See also 1.4, 14.1, 29.1, 63.5-6, and 75.1.

id ... causa: According to Paul Murphy, the use here of **libertas** is the only instance that is not counterbalanced by the theme of **barbaria**. "Here, at the close, there is no mention of *barbaria*, and *libertas* keeps the dignity that it deserves (P. Murphy, 242). Notice also that "the noun *libertas* rings the book, being invoked as the cause for war at 7.1 and being recalled in defeat at 7.89." (Mannetter, 35).

id bellum: Accusative direct object of the infinitive **suscepisse** (A.G. 387 and 451.3). **id**: Singular, neuter, accusative demonstrative pronoun used as an adjective modifying **bellum** (A.G. 296.1 and a).

se suscepisse: Accusative/infinitive construction in indirect discourse after **demonstrat** (A.G. 577 ff.). **se**: Singular, masculine, accusative direct reflexive pronoun (A.G. 300.1). The antecedent is **Vercingetorix**, the subject of **demonstrat** (A.G. 299). **suscepisse**: Perfect infinitive; the tense of the infinitive in indirect discourse is relative to that of the verb of saying (A.G. 584).

non: Adverb modifying **suarum ... causa**, the negative precedes the word it especially effects (A.G. 217.e, 320-21, and 599.a).

suarum necessitatum sed communis libertatis causa: Two preceding genitives with **causa** in the ablative means "for the sake of" (A.G. 359.b). **suarum**: Plural, feminine, genitive possessive pronoun used as an adjective modifying **necessitatum** (A.G. 302). **sed**: Coordinate conjunction (A.G. 324.d). **libertatis**: For the theme of liberty in Book 7, see **liberius** at 1.3.

demonstrat: The main verb of the main clause (A.G. 278.b). The historical present, giving vividness to the narrative, is present in Chapter 89 (A.G. 469). This usage, common in all languages, comes from imagining past events as going on before our eyes (*repraesentatio*) (A.G. 469 Note).

et: The conjunction connects the two infinitives **suscepisse ... offerre** (A.G. 324.a).

quoniam (id) sit ... cedendum: Causal clause; the conjunction **quoniam** ("since") would normally take the indicative when the reason is given on the authority of the writer or speaker (A.G. 540.a). Here, **quoniam** takes the subjunctive as a subordinate clause in indirect discourse after **demonstrat** (A.G. 580). **sit ... cedendum**: The main verb of the subordinate clause (A.G. 278.b). Present subjunctive of the second periphrastic (passive) conjugation implying necessity (A.G. 194.b). Present subjunctive; the tense of the subjunctive is normally in secondary sequence after the historical present **demonstrat** (A.G. 482-85). Here it is in primary sequence through *repraesentatio* (A.G. 485.e and 585.b Note). The passive of the intransitive verb is used impersonally (A.G. 208.d). Supply **id** as the subject (A.G. 318.c). The verb is here split (tmesis) (A.G. 640).

fortunae: Dative indirect object of the intransitive verb **sit cedendum** (A.G. 366).

ad utramque rem: Prepositional phrase, **ad** with the accusative here implies purpose "for the purpose of, to be used for" (*OLD* **ad** 44). "The conduct of Vercingetorix in defeat shows that he was of the true heroic mould." (Walker, 410)

se: Singular, masculine, accusative direct reflexive pronoun (A.G. 300.1). The antecedent is **Vercingetorix**, the subject of **demonstrat** (A.G. 299). Accusative direct object of the infinitive **offerre** (A.G. 387 and 451.3). The reflexive use of **offerre** means "to give oneself up" (to an authority or higher power) (*OLD* **offero** 7.b).

illis: Plural, masculine, dative demonstrative pronoun used substantively (A.G. 296.2). The antecedent is the implied participants of **concilio convocato** (A.G. 297.e). Dative indirect object of the transitive infinitive **offerre** (A.G. 362 and 451.3).

(se) offerre ... seu ... seu ... velint: Conditional statement in indirect discourse after **demonstrat** (A.G. 589). The protasis, as a dependent clause, is in the subjunctive and the apodosis, as the principal clause, is in the infinitive (A.G. 589).

(se) ... offerre: The apodosis of the conditional statement (A.G. 589.2). Accusative/infinitive construction in indirect discourse after **demonstrat** (A.G. 577 ff.). Carry down the pronoun **se** (**Vercingetorix**) from 89.1 as the accusative subject. **offerre**: Present infinitive; the tense of the infinitive in indirect discourse is relative to that of the verb of saying (A.G. 584). Notice the switch in the tense of the infinitives after **demonstrat** from the perfect (**suscepisse**) to the present (**offerre**).

seu ... seu ... velint: The repeated conjunction **seu ... seu** ("whether ... or") with the subjunctive forms the protasis of the conditional statement in indirect discourse (A.G. 589.1). **seu ... seu**: The repeated conjunction introduces two conditions with a common apodosis and means "whether ... or" (A.G. 324.f). (*OLD* **sive** 4). **velint**: The main verb of the subordinate clause (A.G. 278.b). Present subjunctive; the tense of the subjunctive is normally in secondary sequence after the historical present **demonstrat** (A.G. 482-85). Here it is in primary sequence through *repraesentatio* (A.G. 485.e and 585.b Note). The pronoun **ipsi**, with **illis** (those present at the council) as the antecedent, is understood as the subject (A.G. 271.a).

morte sua: Ablative of means (A.G. 409). **sua**: Singular, feminine, ablative possessive pronoun used as an adjective modifying **morte** (A.G. 302).
Romanis: Dative indirect object of the intransitive compound infinitive **satisfacere** (A.G. 368.2 and 451.3).
satisfacere: Complementary infinitive after **velint** (A.G. 456).
vivum: Singular, masculine, accusative, adjective used substantively (A.G. 288). Carry down **se** from 89.1as the indirect reflexive pronoun (A.G. 288.b). Accusative direct object of the infinitive **tradere** (A.G. 387 and 451.3).
tradere: Complementary infinitive after **velint** (A.G. 456).

Mittuntur ... distribuit (89.3-5): Notice how the voice of the verbs changes between those referring to the beaten Gauls in the passive voice: **mittuntur, tradi, produci, producuntur, deditur,** and **proiciuntur,** and those referring to the victorious Caesar in the active voice: **Iubet, consedit, posset,** and **distribuit.** Compare the use of the active and passive voice at 11.2, 12.4, 12.5, and 62.3-5.

(89.3-5) Mittuntur de his rebus ad (4) Caesarem legati. Iubet arma tradi, principes produci. Ipse in munitione pro castris consedit: eo duces producuntur. (5) Vercingetorix deditur, arma proiciuntur.

ad, *to.*
Caesar, -aris, m., *Caesar.*
consido, -sidere, -sedi, -sessus, *sit down, seat one's self.*
dedo, -ere, -didi, -ditus, *give up, surrender, deliver.*
eo, *thither, there.*
in, *in.*

iubeo, iubere, iussi, iussus, *order, give orders, bid, command.*
mitto, mittere, misi, missus, *send.*

princeps, -ipis, m., *head man, leader, chief, prince.*
produco, -ducere, -duxi, -ductus, *bring out, lead forth.*
res, rei, f., *matter, affair.*

arma, -orum, n., pl., *arms, armor, weapons.*
castra, -orum, n., pl., *camp, encampment.*
de, *about, concerning.*
dux, ducis, m., *leader, general, commander.*
hic, haec, hoc, *this; he, she, it.*
ipse, -a, -um, *he, they,* with or without *himself, themselves.*
legatus, -i, m., *envoy, ambassador.*
munitio, -onis, f., *works of fortifications, entrenchment, defenses.*
pro, *in front of, before.*
proicio, -icere, -ieci, -iectus, *fling, cast, throw down.*
trado, -dere, -didi, -ditus, *hand over, give up, deliver, surrender.*

Vercingetorix, -igis, m., *Vercingetorix.*

Mittuntur ... legati: The reversal of the normal word order (subject first, verb last) is called hyperbaton (A.G. 596) (Gotoff, 6-10).
Mittuntur: The main verb of the simple sentence (A.G. 278.1). The verb comes in the first position when the idea in it is emphatic (A.G. 598.d).
de his rebus: Prepositional phrase, **de** with the ablative meaning "concerning, about" (*OLD* **de** 12). **his**: Plural, feminine, ablative demonstrative pronoun used as an adjective modifying **rebus** (A.G. 296.1 and a).
ad Caesarem: Prepositional phrase, **ad** with the accusative here means "to" (*OLD* **ad** 1). **Caesarem**: See Appendix A.
legati: Nominative subject (A.G. 339). The subject is in the last position (A.G. 597.b).
Iubet: The main verb of the main clause (A.G. 278.b). The verb comes in the first position when the idea in it is emphatic (A.G. 598.d). The pronoun **is**, with **Caesarem** as the antecedent, is understood as the subject (A.G. 271.a).
arma tradi, principes produci: Two subject accusatives with their respective infinitives after **iubet**. The construction is equivalent to a substantive clause of purpose (A.G. 563.a). Notice the asyndeton between the clauses (A.G. 323.b).
Ipse: Singular, masculine, nominative demonstrative pronoun used substantively (A.G. 296.2 and 298.d). The antecedent is **Caesarem** (A.G. 298). Nominative subject (A.G. 339). The pronoun is here emphatic (A.G. 298.d.1).
in munitione: Ablative of *place where* with the preposition **in** (locative ablative) (A.G. 426.3).
pro castris: Prepositional phrase, **pro** with the ablative here means "in front of, before" (*OLD* **pro** 1).
consedit: The main verb of the simple sentence (A.G. 278.1). Notice the one perfect tense in the midst of the succession of historical presents. The Loeb and Budé texts also have **consedit**.
eo: Adverb (A.G. 217.a and 320-21).
duces: Nominative subject (A.G. 339).
producuntur: The main verb of the simple sentence (A.G. 278.1).
producuntur ... deditur .... proiciuntur: Notice the asyndeton construction between the clauses (A.G. 323.b).
Vercingetorix: Nominative subject (A.G. 339). See Appendix A. "Vercingetorix, as we learn from Plutarch (Caes. 27), having arrayed himself in splendid armor, mounted a horse adorned with trappings, passed slowly out of Alesia, and rode around Caesar sitting to receive the prisoners; then, halting before Caesar, he sprang from his horse, laid off his armor, and without a word seated himself at the feet of his conqueror – 'every inch a King!' For six years after this he languished in a Roman dungeon. At length in B.C. 46 he was led along the streets of Rome to grace Caesar's great triumph; then, in accordance with Roman custom, 'while his conqueror was offering solemn thanks to the gods on the summit of the Capitol, Vercingetorix was beheaded at its foot as guilty of high treason against the Roman nation.' Thus ended the career of the greatest of the Gauls, the first national hero of France. A somewhat different and less credible account is given by Dio Cass. XL., 41 and XLIII., 19; cf. also Flor. Ep. I., XLV., 26 (III., X.)." (Kelsey, 432-33)
deditur: The main verb of the simple sentence (A.G. 278.1)
arma: Nominative subject (A.G. 339).
proiciuntur: The main verb of the simple sentence (A.G. 278.1).

(89.5) Reservatis Aeduis atque Arvernis, si per eos civitates reciperare posset, ex reliquis captivis toto exercitui capita singula praedae nomine distribuit.

Aedui, -orum, m., pl., *the Aedui.*
atque, *and.*
caput, -itis, n., *head*; by synecdoche *person, man.*
distribuo, -tribuere, -tribui, -tributus, *distribute, divide, assign, apportion.*
exercitus, -us, m., *army.*
nomen, -inis, n., *name*, (abl.), *under the heading of, by way of, as.*
possum, posse, potui, -----, *be able.*
recipero, -are, -avi, -atus, *recover, regain, get back.*
reservo, -are, -avi, -atus, *keep back, reserve.*
singuli, -ae, -a, *one to each, one apiece.*

Arverni, -orum, m., pl., *the Arverni.*
captivus, -i, m., *captive, prisoner.*
civitas, -tatis, f., *state, nation.*
ex, *from the number of.*
is, ea, id, *he, she, it*; *that, this.*
per, *by* (means of), *through.*
praeda, -ae, f., *booty, spoil, plunder.*
reliquus, -a, -um, *remaining, the rest.*
si, *to see if, in case, on the off chance that.*
totus, -a, -um, *the whole, all, all the, entire.*

Reservatis ... posset: Ablative absolute with a dependent clause. See below at Chapter 90.1-3 for the result of this strategy. "Since these were the leading states of Gaul, their submission would effectually break up all concerted rebellion." (Walker, 410) Sherwin-White notes the importance of winning back the loyalty of the Aedui and Arverni for Caesar's overall strategy of indirect rule (Sherwin-White, 44).
Reservatis Aeduis atque Arvernis: Ablative absolute (A.G. 419-20). **Reservatis**: The perfect tense of the participle represents the action as completed at the time indicated by the tense of the main verb (A.G. 489). **Aeduis**: See Appendix A. **atque**: The conjunction connects the two ablative nouns in the ablative absolute and means "and" (*OLD* **atque** 12). **Arvernis**: See Appendix A.
si ... posset: The conjunction **si** ("to see if, in case, on the off chance that") with the imperfect subjunctive, without an expressed apodosis, indicates an intention or purpose (*OLD* **si** 11). **posset**: The main verb of the subordinate clause (A.G. 278.b). Imperfect subjunctive; the tense of the subjunctive is in secondary sequence and follows the rules for the sequence of tense after the historical present tense of **distribuit** (A.G. 482-85, esp. 485.e). The pronoun **is**, with **Ipse (Caesar)** as the antecedent, is understood as the subject (A.G. 271.a).
per eos: Prepositional phrase, the personal agent, when considered as instrument or means, is often expressed by **per** with the accusative meaning "by" (means of) (A.G. 405.b). **eos**: Plural, masculine, accusative demonstrative pronoun used substantively (A.G. 296.2). The antecedent is **Aeduis atque Arvernis** (A.G. 297.e).
civitates: Accusative direct object of the infinitive **reciperare** (A.G. 387 and 451.3).
reciperare: Complementary infinitive after **posset** (A.G. 456).
ex reliquis captivis: Prepositional phrase, **ex** with the ablative in the partitive sense means "from the number of" (*OLD* **ex** 17).
toto exercitui: Dative indirect object of the transitive verb **distribuit** (A.G. 362).
capita singula: Accusative direct object of the transitive verb **distribuit** (A.G. 387). **capita**: From the noun **caput**, here meaning "a person, individual" by synecdoche ("the use of a part for the whole") (A.G. 641) (*OLD* **caput** 7). **singula**: Distributive numeral used as an adjective (A.G. 136).
praedae nomine: Ablative of quality (descriptive ablative) with a genitive modifier (A.G. 415). **nomine**: The noun **nomine** with the genitive means "under the heading of, by way of, as" (*OLD* **nomen** 24). **praedae**: Appositional genitive, a limiting genitive is sometimes used instead of a noun in apposition (A.G. 343.d).
distribuit: The main verb of the main clause (A.G. 278.b). The pronoun **is**, with **Ipse (Caesar)** as the antecedent, is understood as the subject (A.G. 271.a).

4.S CHAPTER 90: CAESAR RETURNS THE AEDUI AND ARVERNI CAPTIVES; THE CATALOG OF ROMAN DEPLOYMENT AT THE END OF THE CAMPAIGN SEASON

This chapter functions as the anti-climax of the battle of Alesia.

(90.1-2) His rebus confectis, in Aeduos proficiscitur; civitatem (2) recipit.

Aedui, -orum, m., pl., *the Aedui.*
conficio, -ficere, -feci, -fectus, *complete, finish, accomplish, do.*
in, *into the country of.*
recipio, -cipere, -cepi, -ceptus, *recover.*

civitas, -tatis, f., *state, nation.*
hic, haec, hoc, *this*; *he, she, it.*
proficiscor, -ficisci, -fectus, *set out, depart, proceed.*
res, rei, f., *matter, affair.*

His rebus confectis: Ablative absolute (A.G. 419-20). **His**: Plural, feminine, ablative demonstrative pronoun used as an adjective modifying **rebus** (A.G. 426.1 and a). **confectis**: The perfect tense of the participle represents the action as completed at the time indicated by the tense of the main verb (A.G. 489).
in Aeduos: Accusative of *place to which* with the preposition **in** ("into the country of") (A.G. 426.2). **Aeduos**: See Appendix A.
proficiscitur: The main verb of the main clause (A.G. 278.b). The historical present, giving vividness to the narrative, is present in Chapter 90 (A.G. 469). This usage, common in all languages, comes from imagining past events as going on before our eyes (*repraesentatio*) (A.G. 469 Note). The pronoun **is**, with **Ipse (Caesar)** as the antecedent, is understood as the subject (A.G. 271.a).
civitatem: Accusative direct object of **recipit** (A.G. 387).
recipit: The main verb of the simple sentence (A.G. 278.1). The pronoun **is**, with **Ipse (Caesar)** as the antecedent, is understood as the subject (A.G. 271.a).

(90.2) Eo legati ab Arvernis missi quae imperaret, se facturos pollicentur. Imperat magnum numerum obsidum.

ab, *by*.
eo, *thither, there*.
impero, -are, -avi, -atus, *levy, draft, demand*.
magnus, -a, -um, *great, large*.
numerus, -i, m., *number, amount*.
polliceor, -liceri, -lictus, *promise, offer*.
sui, sibi, se, or **sese**, nom. wanting, *they*, with or without *themselves*.

Arverni, -orum, m., pl., *the Arverni*.
facio, facere, feci, factus, *do*.
legatus, -i, m., *envoy, ambassador*.
mitto, mittere, misi, missus, *send*.
obses, -idis, m. and f., *hostage*.
qui, quae, quod, *who, which, what*.

Eo: Adverb (A.G. 217.a and 320-21).
legati ... missi: Nominative subject of **pollicentur** (A.G. 339). **missi**: Nominative, perfect, passive participle used as a predicate, where in English a phrase or a subordinate clause would be more natural (A.G. 496).
ab Arvernis: Ablative of agent with the preposition **ab** after the passive participle **missi** (A.G. 405). **Arvernis**: See Appendix A.
quae imperaret: Relative clause; a subordinate clause in indirect discourse takes the subjunctive (A.G. 303 and 580). **quae**: Plural, neuter, accusative relative pronoun used substantively (A.G. 305). The antecedent is omitted, supply **ea** (A.G. 307.c). Accusative direct object of the normally intransitive verb **imperaret** (A.G. 369 and 387). **imperaret**: The main verb of the subordinate clause (A.G. 278.b). Imperfect subjunctive; the tense of the subjunctive is in secondary sequence and follows the rules for the sequence of tense after the historical present **pollicentur** (A.G. 485.e and 575). The pronoun **is**, with **Ipse (Caesar)** as the antecedent, is understood as the subject (A.G. 271.a).
se facturos (esse): Accusative/infinitive construction in indirect discourse after **pollicentur** (A.G. 577 ff., esp. 580.c). **se**: Plural, masculine, accusative direct reflexive pronoun (A.G. 300.1). The antecedent is **legati**, the subject of **pollicentur** (A.G. 299). **facturos (esse)**: Supply **esse** to form the future, active, infinitive (A.G. 188). The tense of the infinitive in indirect discourse is relative to that of the verb of saying (A.G. 584).
pollicentur: The main verb of the main clause (A.G. 278.b).
Imperat: The main verb of the simple sentence (A.G. 278.1). The verb comes in the first position when the idea in it is emphatic (A.G. 598.d). Notice the impression that the juxtaposition between the verbs **pollicentur** (the Gauls are "promising") and **Iubet** (Caesar is "ordering") makes. The pronoun **is**, with **Ipse (Caesar)** as the antecedent, is understood as the subject (A.G. 271.a).
magnum numerum: Accusative direct object of the normally intransitive verb **Imperat** (A.G. 369 and 387).
obsidum: Partitive genitive with **numerum** (A.G. 346.a.1).

(90.3-4) (3) Legiones in hiberna mittit. Captivorum circiter XX milia (4) Aeduis Arvernisque reddit.

Aedui, -orum, m., pl., *the Aedui*.
captivus, -i, m., *captive, prisoner*.
hiberna, -orum, n., pl., (supply **castra**), *winter-quarters*.
legio, -onis, f., *legion*.
mitto, mittere, misi, missus, *send*.
reddo, -dere, -didi, -ditus, *give back, restore, return*.

Arverni, -orum, m., pl., *the Arverni*.
circiter, *around*.
in, *into*.
milia, -um, n., pl., *thousand, thousands*.
-que, *and*.
X, in expression of number, = *10*.

Legiones: Accusative direct object of **mittit** (A.G. 387).
in hiberna: Accusative of *place to which* with the preposition **in** (A.G. 426.2). **hiberna**: Plural, neuter, accusative adjective used substantively (A.G. 288). The noun **castra** is understood from constant association (A.G. 288.c). "The legions were distributed so as to be a support to one another in case of need, and at the same time so as to command the whole country. The strength of Gaul had been so far broken that little danger was to be apprehended from rebellion." (Kelsey, 433)
mittit: The main verb of the simple sentence (A.G. 278.1). The pronoun **is**, with **Ipse (Caesar)** as the antecedent, is understood as the subject (A.G. 271.a).
Captivorum: Partitive genitive with **milia** (A.G. 346.a.2 and 135.c).
circiter XX milia: Accusative direct object of the transitive verb **reddit** (A.G. 387). **circiter**: Adverb (A.G. 320-21). **XX**: Roman numeral used as an adjective modifying **milia** (A.G. 133). **milia**: Accusative plural; in the plural **mille** declines as a neuter noun (A.G. 134.d).
Aeduis Arvernisque: Dative indirect object of the transitive verb **reddit** (A.G. 362). **Aeduis**: See Appendix A. **-que**: The enclitic conjunction connects the two dative nouns (A.G. 324.a). **Arvernis**: See Appendix A.
reddit: The main verb of the simple sentence (A.G. 278.1). The pronoun **is**, with **Ipse (Caesar)** as the antecedent, is understood as the subject (A.G. 271.a).

T. ... constituit (90.4-8): This catalog is characterized by its "balance and symmetry, especially evident when compared to the catalog of Gallic troops at 7.75. Caesar utilizes short but syntactically full sentences in which he himself is the subject of all the main verbs, which are also all active, and the Roman generals are uniformly the accusative objects. Finally, all seven of the barbarian tribes are the objects of prepositional phrases. There is only one case of asyndeton, the piling up of the three accusatives *C. Antistium Reginum*, *T. Sextium*, and *C. Caninium Rebilum* without a connective, yet even there perfect balance is maintained with a Gallic tribe separating each accusative.

By means of this catalog Caesar is able to present a tripartite hierarchy of power between himself, the Roman generals, and the Gauls through grammatical construction and arrangement. In this locution Caesar is the primary actor, he is the subject of the action verbs: *iubet, attribuit, conlocat, mittit, conlocat* and finally *constituit*, all being very authoritative verbs. Word choice in Caesar should not be ignored and, as John Nordling notes, "The finite form of the verb *iubeo* occurs 178 times, for example, and Caesar is the subject 128 times and that this creates an image of "a virtually omniscient and omnipotent *imperator*." (Nordling, 171-72) Finally, he brings himself to the foreground with the intensive pronoun: *ipse* and the placement at the very end of the catalog is prominent.

The secondary actors, Caesar's generals, are all in the accusative case and dependent on the actions of Caesar, beginning with the most important, Labienus. Each of the Roman generals is assigned a specific and definite sphere of operations and awarded a corresponding Gallic tribe. The planning and organization of Caesar is readily apparent, not only is the deployment of the legions thought out, but the corn supply is provided for as well.

The final members of the catalog, the Gauls, have by this point been grammatically reduced to the objects of prepositions as they have been physically reduced to Roman dependency. Every tribe in this catalog is assigned to a Roman general and, with the exception of the Bellovaci who are the ablative objects of *a* (and who have no Roman contingents within their borders), are the accusative objects of *in*. Earlier in the narrative *in* plus the accusative referring to Gauls usually meant 'against', but here the meaning is "among", further evidence of the final subjugation of the Gauls." (Mannetter, 155-57) Compare this order and hierarchy to the Gallic catalog at Chapter 75.

(90.4-6) T. Labienum cum duabus legionibus et equitatu in Sequanos proficisci iubet: huic (5) M. Sempronium Rutilum attribuit. C. Fabium legatum et L. Minucium Basilum cum legionibus duabus in Remis collocat, ne quam a finitimis Bellovacis calamitatem (6) accipiant.

a(b), *from.*
attribuo, -uere, -ui, -utus, *assign, allot.*
C. Fabius, -i, m., *Gaius Fabius.*
colloco, -are, -avi, -atus, *place, set, post, station.*
duo, -ae, -o, *two.*
et, *and.*

hic, haec, hoc, *this; he, she, it.*
iubeo, iubere, iussi, iussus, *order, give orders, bid, command.*

legatus, -i, m., *lieutenant, lieutenant-general.*
M. Sempronius Rutilus, -i, m., *Marcus Sempronius Rutilus.*
proficiscor, -ficisci, -fectus, *set out, depart, proceed.*

Remi, -orum, m., pl., *the Remi.*
T. Labienus, -i, m., *Titus Labienus.*

accipio, -cipere, -cepi, -ceptus, *receive, accept.*
Bellovaci, -orum, m., pl., *the Bellovaci*
calamitas, -tatis, f., *loss, damage, misfortune.*
cum, *with.*
equitatus, -us, m., *cavalry.*
finitimus, -a, -um, *bordering on, neighboring, adjoining.*
in, *into the country of; among.*
L. Minucium Basilus, -i, m., *Lucius Minucius Basilus.*
legio, -onis, f., *legion.*
ne, *so that ... not.*
quis, -----, quid, *any;* (as adj., **qui, quae,** or **qua, quod**).
Sequani, -orum, m., pl., *the Sequani.*

T. Labienum ... proficisci: Subject accusative with the infinitive after **iubet**. The construction is equivalent to a substantive clause of purpose (A.G. 563.a). **T. Labienum:** See Appendix A. **T.:** Abbreviated form of the praenomen **Titus** (A.G. 108.c). **duabus cum legionibus et equitatu:** Ablative of accompaniment with the preposition **cum** (A.G. 413). **duabus:** Declinable cardinal number used as an adjective modifying **legionibus** (A.G. 132-35). **cum:** A monosyllabic preposition is often placed between a noun and its adjective (A.G. 599.d.2). **et:** The conjunction connects the two ablative nouns in the prepositional phrase (A.G. 324.a).
in Sequanos: Accusative of *place to which* with the preposition **in** ("into the country of") (A.G. 426.2). **Sequanos:** See Appendix A.
iubet: The main verb of the main clause (A.G. 278.b). The pronoun **is**, with **Ipse (Caesar)** as the antecedent, is understood as the subject (A.G. 271.a).
huic: Singular, masculine, dative demonstrative pronoun used substantively (A.G. 296.2). The antecedent is **Labienum** (A.G. 297.e). Dative indirect object of the transitive verb **attribuit** (A.G. 362).
M. Sempronium Rutilum: Accusative direct object of the transitive verb **attribuit** (A.G. 387). See Appendix A. **M.:** Abbreviated form of the praenomen **Marcus** (A.G. 108.c).
attribuit: The main verb of the simple sentence (A.G. 278.1). The pronoun **is**, with **Ipse (Caesar)** as the antecedent, is understood as the subject (A.G. 271.a).
C. Fabium ... et L. Minucium Basilum: Two accusative direct objects of **collocat** (A.G. 387). **C. Fabium:** See Appendix A. **C.:** Abbreviated form of the praenomen **Gaius** (A.G. 108.c). **et:** The conjunction connects the two accusative nouns (A.G. 324.a). **L. :** Abbreviated form of the praenomen **Lucius** (A.G. 108.c). **L. Minucium Basilum:** See Appendix A.
legatum: An accusative noun in apposition to the proper noun **Fabium** (A.G. 282).
cum legionibus duabus: Ablative of accompaniment with the preposition **cum** (A.G. 413). **duabus:** Declinable cardinal number used as an adjective modifying **legionibus** (A.G. 132-35).
in Remis: Ablative of *place where* with the preposition **in** (locative ablative) (A.G. 426.3). **Remis:** See Appendix A.
collocat: The main verb of the main clause (A.G. 278.b). The pronoun **is**, with **Ipse (Caesar)** as the antecedent, is understood as the subject (A.G. 271.a).
ne ... accipiant: The conjunction **ne** ("so that ... not") with the subjunctive forms a negative purpose clause (A.G. 529-31). "The Remi had remained faithful to Caesar, while the Bellovaci had announced their intentions of fighting him." (Walker, 410)

accipiant: The main verb of the subordinate clause (A.G. 278.b). Present subjunctive; the tense of the subjunctive is normally in secondary sequence after the historical present **collocat** (A.G. 482-85). Here it is in primary sequence through *repraesentatio* (A.G. 485.e and 585.b Note). The pronoun **ei**, with **Remis** as the antecedent, is understood as the subject (A.G. 271.a).

quam... calamitatem: Accusative direct object of **accipiant** (A.G. 387). **quam**: Singular, feminine, accusative indefinite pronoun used as an adjective modifying **calamitatem** (A.G. 149). The indefinite **quis, -----, quid** (**qui, quae,** or **qua, quod** when used adjectively) is used after **ne** (A.G. 310.a).

a finitimis Bellovacis: Ablative of source with the preposition **a(b)** (A.G. 403.1). **Bellovacis**: "They were subdued the following year; see Book VIII., Chaps. 6-23." (Kelsey, 433) See Appendix A.

(90.6-7) C. Antistium Reginum in Ambibaretos, T. Sextium in Bituriges, C. Caninium Rebilum in Rutenos cum (7) singulis legionibus mittit.

Ambibareti, -orum, m., pl., *the Ambibareti.*
C. Antistius Reginus, -i, m., *Gaius Antistius Reginus.*

cum, *with.*
legio, -onis, f., *legion.*
Ruteni, -orum, m., pl., *the Ruteni.*
T. Sextius, -i, m., *Titus Sextius.*

Bituriges, -um, m., pl., *the Bituriges.*
C. Caninius Rebilus, -i, m., *Gaius Caninius Rebilus.*
in, *into the country of.*
mitto, mittere, misi, missus, *send.*
singuli, -ae, -a, *one to each, one apiece.*

C. Antistium Reginum: First accusative direct object of **mittit** (A.G. 387). See Appendix A. **C.**: Abbreviated form of the praenomen **Gaius** (A.G. 108.c).

in Ambibaretos: Accusative of *place to which* with the preposition **in** ("into the country of") (A.G. 426.2). **Ambibaretos**: See Appendix A at **Ambluareti**.

T. Sextium: Second accusative direct object of **mittit** (A.G. 387). See Appendix A. **T.**: Abbreviated form of the praenomen **Titus** (A.G. 108.c).

in Bituriges: Accusative of *place to which* with the preposition **in** ("into the country of") (A.G. 426.2). **Bituriges**: See Appendix A.

C. Caninium Rebilum: Third accusative direct object of **mittit** (A.G. 387). See Appendix A. **C.**: Abbreviated form of the praenomen **Gaius** (A.G. 108.c).

in Rutenos: Accusative of *place to which* with the preposition **in** ("into the country of") (A.G. 426.2). **Rutenos**: See Appendix A.

cum singulis legionibus: Ablative of accompaniment with the preposition **cum** (A.G. 413). **singulis**: Distributive numeral used as an adjective modifying **legionibus** (A.G. 136).

mittit: The main verb of the simple sentence (A.G. 278.1). The pronoun **is**, with **Ipse (Caesar)** as the antecedent, is understood as the subject (A.G. 271.a).

(90.7-8) Q. Tullium Ciceronem et P. Sulpicium Cabilloni et Matiscone in Aeduis ad Ararim rei (8) frumentariae causa collocat.

ad, *at, near.*
Arar, -aris, acc. **-im**, m., *the Arar river.*
causa, -ae, f., abl. with the gen., *for the sake of, for the purpose of.*
et, *and.*

in, *among.*
P. Suplicius, -i, m., *Publius Suplicius.*

res, rei, f., (with **frumentaria**) *supply of grain, supplies.*

Aedui, -orum, m., pl., *the Aedui.*
Cabillonum, -i, n., *Cabillonum.*
colloco, -are, -avi, -atus, *place, set, post, station.*
frumentarius, -a, -um, *having to do with grain* or *supplies.*
Matisco, -onis, f., *Matisco.*
Q. Tullius Cicero, -i, -onis, m., *Quintus Tullius Cicero.*

Q. Tullium Ciceronem et P. Sulpicium: Two accusative direct objects of **collocat** (A.G. 387). **Q. Tullium Ciceronem**: This is the brother of the famous orator, Cicero. See Appendix A. **Q.**: Abbreviated form of the praenomen **Quintus** (A.G. 108.c). **et**: The conjunction connects the two accusative nouns (A.G. 324.a). **P. Sulpicium**: See Appendix A. **P.**: Abbreviated form of the praenomen **Publius** (A.G. 108.c).

Cabilloni: Locative case of the city name **Cabillonum, -i**, n. (A.G. 49.a). See Appendix A.

et: The conjunction connects the two locative nouns (A.G. 324.a).

Matiscone: Locative case of the city name **Matisco, -onis**, f. (A.G. 80). See Appendix A.

in Aeduis: Ablative of *place where* with the preposition **in** (locative ablative) (A.G. 426.3). **Aeduis**: See Appendix A.

ad Ararim: Prepositional phrase, with all names of places *at*, meaning *near* (not *in*), is expressed by **ad** with the accusative (A.G. 428.d). **Ararim**: The accusative singular of the third declension masculine i-stem noun **Arar** ends in **-im**, not **-em** (A.G. 73-75, esp. 74.d and 75.a.1). This is the river Saone. See Appendix A.

rei frumentariae causa: A preceding genitive with the ablative of **causa** means "for the sake of" (A.G. 359.b and 404.c).

collocat: The main verb of the simple sentence (A.G. 278.1). The pronoun **is**, with **Ipse (Caesar)** as the antecedent, is understood as the subject (A.G. 271.a).

(90.8) Ipse Bibracte hiemare constituit. His litteris cognitis Romae dierum XX supplicatio redditur.

Bibracte, -is, n. *Bibracte.*
constituo, -stituere, -stitui, -stitutus, *resolve upon, determine, decide.*
hiemo, -are, -avi, -atus, *pass the winter, winter.*
ipse, -a, -um, *he, they,* with or without *himself, themselves.*
reddo, -dere, -didi, -ditus, *award, grant.*
supplicatio, -onis, f., *thanksgiving.*

cognosco, -gnoscere, -gnovi, cognitus, *publish.*
dies, -ei, m. and f., *day.*
hic, haec, hoc, *this; he, she, it.*
litterae, -arum, f., *letter, missive, dispatch.*
Roma, -ae, f., *Rome.*
X, in expression of number, = *10.*

Ipse: Singular, masculine, nominative demonstrative pronoun used substantively (A.G. 296.2 and 298.d). The antecedent is **Caesarem** at 89.4 (A.G. 298). Nominative subject (A.G. 339). The pronoun distinguishes the principal personage (**Caesar**) from the subordinate persons (his lieutenants) (A.G. 298.3). Nominative subject (A.G. 339).
Bibracte: Locative case of the city name **Bibracte, is**, n. (A.G. 80). See Appendix A.
hiemare: Complementary infinitive after **constituit** (A.G. 456 and 563.d). The infinitive is equivalent to a substantive clause of purpose (A.G. 563.d).
constituit: The main verb of the simple sentence (A.G. 278.1).
His litteris cognitis: Ablative absolute (A.G. 419-20). **His**: Plural, feminine, ablative demonstrative pronoun used as an adjective modifying **litteris** (A.G. 426.1 and a). **litteris**: In the plural the noun means "letter (personal or official), missive, dispatch" (*OLD littera* 7) (A.G. 107). **cognitis**: The perfect tense of the participle represents the action as completed at the time indicated by the tense of the main verb (A.G. 489).
Romae: Locative case of the city name **Roma, ae**, f. (A.G. 43.c). See Appendix A.
dierum XX: Genitive of quality (measure) with **supplicatio** (A.G. 346.a.1). **XX**: Roman numeral used as an adjective (A.G. 133).
supplicatio: Nominative subject (A.G. 339). A previous *supplicatio* of 15 days had been declared at *BG* 2.35.4 and one of twenty days at *BG* 4.38.5. "Usually a 'solemn thanksgiving' lasted only three or four days. The longest *supplicatio* previously decreed was in honor of Pompey, at the close of the war with Mithridates (Cic. Prov. Cons. 11, 27)." (Kelsey, 319)
redditur: The main verb of the main clause (A.G. 278.b).

"Thus fell Alesia, after one of the most remarkable sieges on record. Caesar's devices for rendering impassable his lines of defense, in ingenuity and adaptation to the purpose for which they were intended, have never been excelled in the annals of engineering. They are a further evidence of that readiness to meet emergencies and that practical mastery of mechanical details previously shown in the construction of the bridges over the Rhine. Further than this, Caesar's success well illustrates the inevitable superiority of generalship, discipline, persistence, and hard work over vastly greater numbers, even in the face of every disadvantage of position and surroundings. For the Gauls the fall of Alesia was the crowning disaster of a hopeless struggle. They staked all on the relief of the city, and lost. But if Caesar instead of Vercingetorix had suffered complete defeat, little doubt that Gaul would long have remained unconquered, and that the course of European history would have been changed. The siege of Alesia may well rank among the decisive military operations of the world's history." (Kelsey, 433)

APPENDIX A: A LIST OF PEOPLE, PLACES, AND TRIBES WITH A BRIEF DESCRIPTION
Most of these names are not contained in the *OLD*. All references are to the *BG* unless otherwise noted.

Acco, -onis, m., *Acco*, a leader among the Senones. Put to death by Caesar. His death inspires the rebellion in Book 7. 6.4, 44; mentioned in Book 7 only at 7.1.

Aedui, -orum, m., pl., *the Aedui*, a powerful Gallic people, between the upper waters of the Sequana (Seine) and the Liger (Loire), in alliance with the Romans before Caesar's arrival in Gaul. Their influence was increased by him and they were loyal allies until their final defection at 7.55 unites all Gaul against Caesar. They are prominent in Books 1, 2, 5, 6, 7.

Agedincum, -i, n., *Agedincum*, chief city of the Senones, on the Yonne (Icauna), a tributary of the Seine; now *Sens*. 6.44; 7.10, 57, 59, 62.

Alesia, -ae, f., *Alesia*, the chief city of the Mandubii, northeast of Bibracte; now *Alise-Sainte-Reine*. The final battle in Book 7 and Vercingetorix's surrender takes place in Alesia. 7.68-90.

Allobroges, -um (acc. Allobrogas 1.14, 7.64), m., pl., *the Allobroges*, a Gallic people in the northeastern part of 'the province', between the Rhone and the Alps. 1.6, 10, 11, 14, 28, 44; 3.1, 6; 7.64, 65.

Ambiani, -orum, m., pl., *the Ambiani*, a small state in Belgic Gaul, south of the Morini. 2.4, 15; mentioned in Book 7 only at 7.75.

Ambibarii, -orum, m., pl., *the Ambibarii*, a small state on the northwest coast of Gaul. Mentioned only at 7.75.

Ambluareti (Ambivariti, Ambibareti), -orum, m., pl., *the Ambluareti*, a small tribe on the left bank of the upper Liger (Loire), clients of the Aedui. 7.75, 90.

Andes, -ium or **Andi, -orum**, m., pl., *the Andes*, a Gallic people north of the Liger (Loire). The name survives in *Anjou*. 2.35; 3.7; mentioned in Book 7 only at 7.75.

Antistius, -i, m., *Gaius Antistius Reginus*, a lieutenant of Caesar. 6.1; 7.83, 90.

Antonius, -i, m., *Marcus Antonius, Marc Antony* (born 83, died 30 B.C.), who served as a lieutenant of Caesar in Gaul in 52 and 51 B.C., and afterwards in the Civil War; member of the Second Triumvirate, and rival of Octavianus. Mentioned only at 7.81.

Aquitania, -ae, f., *Aquitania*, one of the three main divisions of Gaul. 1.1; 3.11, 20, 21, 23, 26, 27; mentioned in Book 7 only at 7.31.

Arar, -aris, acc. **-im**, m., *the Arar*, now the Saône. It rises in the Vosges Mts., and flows southward into the Rhone. 1.12, 13, 16; mentioned in Book 7 only at 7.90.

Arecomici, -orum, m., pl., *the Arecomici*, a division of the Volcae, in "The province" south of the Cebenna (Cévennes) Mountains. 7.7, 64.

Aremoricus, -a, -um, *Aremoricus*, a name applied to a group of small states along the northwest coast of Gaul (**Aremoricae civitates**) between the Liger (Loire) and the Sequana (Seine). 5.53; mentioned in Book 7 only at 7.75.

Aristius, -i, m., *Marcus Aristius*, a military tribune. 7.42, 43.

Arverni, -orum, m., pl., *the Arverni*, a powerful people about the upper part of the Elaver (Allier), whose chief city, Gergovia, was unsuccessfully besieged by Caesar. 1.31, 35; 7.3-5, 7-9, 34, 37, 38, 64, 66, 75, 77, 89, 90.

Atrebates, -um, m., *the Atrebas*, a Belgic people west of the upper part of the Scaldis (Scheldt). 2.4, 16, 23; 4.21; 5.46; mentioned in Book 7 only at 7.75.

Aulerci, -orum, m., *the Aulerci*, a people in central Gaul in four branches:

Aulerci Brannovices: the *Aulerci Brannovices*, south of the Aedui, near the Arar. Mentioned only at 7.75.

Aulerci Cenomani: the *Aulerci Cenomani*, west of the Carnutes. Mentioned only at 7.75.

Aulerci Diablintes: the *Aulerci Diablintes*, northwest of the Aulerci Cenomani. 3.9.

Aulerci Eburovices: the *Aulerci Eburovices*, near the Sequana (Seine), north of the Carnutes. 3.17, mentioned in Book 7 only at 7.75.

Avaricum, -i, n., *Avaricum*, the largest and most strongly fortified city of the Bituriges, on the river Avara (Yèvre), now *Bourges*; besieged and taken by Caesar, the inhabitants put to the sword. 7.13-32, 47, 52.

Basilus, -i, m., *Lucius Minucius Basilus*, an officer of Caesar, afterwards one of the conspirators against him; murdered in 43 B.C. on account of his cruelty to his slaves. 6.29, 30; mentioned in Book 7 only at 7.90.

Bellovaci, -orum, m., pl., *the Bellovaci*, a powerful Belgic people, between the Sequana (*Seine*), Samar (*Somme*), and the Isara (Oise) Rivers. 2.4, 5, 10, 13, 14; 5.24, 46; 7.59, 75, 90.

Bibracte, -is, n., *Bibracte*, the capital of the Aedui, situated on a mountain now called Mont Beuvray (2,690 ft.). 1.23; 7.55, 63, 90.

Bituriges, -um, m., pl., *the Bituriges*, a people of Central Gaul, across the Liger (Loire) from the Aedui. 1.18; 7.5, 8, 9, 11-15, 21, 29, 75, 90.

Blannovii, -orum, m., pl., *the Blannovii*. Mentioned in Book 7 only at 7.75.

Boii, -orum, m., pl., *the Boii*, a Keltic people widely diffused over Central Europe, whose name survives in *Bohemia*; 32,000 joined the Helvetii in their migration in Book 1, the remnant surviving being settled with the Aedui. 1.5, 25-28, 29; 7.9-10, 17, 75.

Britannia, -ae, f., *Britain*. 2.4, 14; 3.8, 9; 4.20-36; 5.2, 6, 8-23; 6.13; mentioned in Book 7 only at 7.76.

Brutus, -i, m., *Decimus Junius Brutus*, an officer of Caesar, both in the Gallic and Civil War; afterwards guilty of the basest ingratitude and treachery in joining the conspiracy against him. 3.11; 7.9, 87.

Cabillonum, -i, n., *Cabillonum*, an important city of the Aedui on the Arar, now *Châlon-sur-Saône*. 7.42, 90.

Caburus, -i, m., *Gaius Valerius Caburus*, a Gaul who received the Roman citizenship; father of Procillus and Donnotaurus. 1.47; mentioned in Book 7 only at 7.65.

Cadurci, -orum, m., pl., *the Cadurci*, a small state in Aquitania; chief city, Divona, now *Cahors*. 7.4, 64, 75.

Caesar, -aris, m., *Julius Caesar*, was made proconsul in Cisalpine Gaul and Illyricum in 58 B.C. for a five year period, rather than the normal two year span. Upon the death of Metellus Celer, Transapline Gaul was further allotted to Caesar. Caesar was empowered to nominate his own staff, found colonies, and raise an army. 1.7 ff.

Caletes, -um and **Caleti, -orum**, m., pl., *the Caletes*, a people living on the sea-coast at the mouth of the Sequana (Seine). 2.41; Mentioned in Book 7 only at 7.75.

Camulogenus, -i, m., *Camulogenus*, an Aulercan, commander of the Parisii against Labienus. 7.57, 59, 62.

Caninius, -i, m., *Gaius Caninius Rebilus*, a lieutenant of Caesar's in the latter part of the Gallic War, and in the Civil War; made consul by Caesar for a few hours to fill a vacancy on the last day of December, B.C. 45. 7.83, 90.

Carnutes, -um, m., pl., *the Carnutes*, a state in central Gaul, north of the Liger (Loire); chief city, Cenabum. 2.35; 5.25, 29, 56; 6.2, 3, 4, 13, 44; 7.2, 3, 11, 75.

Cavarillus, -i, m., *Cavarillus*, an Aeduan of high rank. Mentioned only at 7.67.

Celtillus, -i, m., *Celtillus*, at one time ruler of the Arverni; father of Vercingetorix. Mentioned only at 7.4.

Cenabenses, -ium, m., *the inhabitants of Cenabum*. Mentioned only at 7.11.

Cenabum, -i, m., *Cenabum*, chief city of the Carnutes, later called *Aurelianensis Urbs*, whence comes the modern name of *Orléans*. 7.3, 11, 14, 17.

Cevenna, -ae, f., *the Cévennes*, a mountain range in southern Gaul about 250 miles long. 7.8, 56.

Cicero, -onis, m., *Quintus Tullius Cicero*, the brother of Marcus Tullius Cicero, the orator, born about 102 B.C.; aedile in 66, praetor in 62 B.C.; became a lieutenant of Caesar in Gaul in 55, made a heroic defense of his camp in 54; held aloof from Caesar in the Civil War, but was reconciled with him in 47; put to death by order of the triumvirs in 43 B.C. 5.24, 27, 38-53; 6.32, 35-42; mentioned in Book 7 only at 7.90.

Cimbri, -orum, m., pl., *the Cimbri*, a Germanic people, originally in the Cimbric peninsula (the present Denmark area), that joined with the Teutones in the invasion of Gaul. 1.33, 40; 2.4, 29; mentioned in Book 7 only at 7.77.

Clodius, -i, m., *Publius Clodius Pulcher*, the enemy of Cicero, who as tribune in B.C. 58 drove the orator into exile; his riotous conduct later disturbed the public peace. Clodius was killed by supporters of Milo, a political rival, on January 18, 52 B.C. Due to the resulting turmoil, the Senate passed the ultimate decree, elected an interrex, armed him, the Tribunes, and Pompey with extraordinary powers to save the city, and authorized Pompey to raise troops throughout Italy (Fuller, pg. 172-73). Mentioned only at 7.1.

Commius, -i, m., *Commius*, an Atrebatian, loyal and useful to Caesar (especially in the British campaigns) till the uprising in 52, when he became a commander in the army raised for the relief of Alesia. 4.21, 27, 35; 5.22; 6.6; 7.75, 76, 79.

Conconnetodumnus, -i, m., *Conconnetodumnus*, a chief of the Carnutes. Mentioned only at 7.3.

Convictolitavis, -is, m., *Convictolitavis*, a prominent Aeduan whose claims to the office of Vergobret were sustained by Caesar. He later rouses the Aeduan state against him. 7.32, 33, 37, 39, 42, 55, 67.

Cotuatus, -i, m., *Cotuatus*, a leader of the Carnutes. Mentioned only at 7.3.

Cotus, -i, m., *Cotus*, an Aeduan, rival of Convictolitavis for the office of Vergobret. 7.32, 33, 39, 67.

Critognatus, -i, m., *Critognatus*, a prominent Arvernian. When trapped in Alesia, he gave a speech urging cannibalism rather than surrender. 7.77, 78.

Curiosolites, -um, m., pl., *the Curiosolites*, a people along the northwest coast of Gaul, north of the Veneti; the name survives in *Corseult*, near St. Malo. 2.34; 3.7, 11; mentioned in Book 7 only at 7.75.

Decetia, -ae, f., *Decetia*, a town of the Aedui, on the Liger (Loire); now Decize. Mentioned only at 7.33.

Diviciacus, -i, m., *Diviciacus*, an Aeduan of great influence, loyal to Caesar, who at his intercession pardoned Dumnorix, his brother, leader of the Aeduan national party which was hostile to Rome. 1.3, 16, 18, 19, 20, 31, 32, 41; 2.5, 10, 14, 15; 6.12; mentioned in Book 7 only at 7.39.

Donnotaurus, -i, m., *Gaius Valerius Donnotaurus*, a Gaul, son of Gaius Valerius Caburus, and leader among the Helvetii. Mentioned only at 7.65.

Elaver, Elaveris, n., *the Elaver*, a tributary of the Liger (Loire), into which it flows from the south after a course of about 200 miles; now *Allier*. 7.34, 35, 53.

Eleuteti, -orum, m., pl., the *Eleuteti*, a people of Central Gaul, clients of the Arverni. Mentioned only at 7.75.

Eporedorigix, -igis, m., *Eporedorigix*,

1) Leader of the Aeduans in the war with the Sequanians; captured by Caesar. Mentioned only at 7.67.

2) An Aeduan of high rank, for a time friendly to Caesar, afterwards one of the commanders of the army raised for the relief of Alesia. 7.38, 39, 40, 54, 55, 63, 64, 76.

Fabius, -i, m., *Fabius*, gentile name of three Romans mentioned in the Gallic Wars:

1) **Quintus Fabius Maximus**, *Quintus Fabius Maximus*. Mentioned only at 1.45.

2) **Gaius Fabius**, *Gaius Fabius*, a lieutenant of Caesar in the Gallic War, and in the first year of the Civil War; no mention is made of him after 49 B.C. 5.24, 46, 47, 53; 6.6; 7.40, 41, 87, 90.

3) **Lucius Fabius**, *Lucius Fabius*, a brave centurion killed at Gergovia. 7.47, 50.

Fufius, -i. m., *Gaius Fufius Cita*, a Roman knight. Mentioned only at 7.3.

Gabali, -orum, m., pl., *the Gabali*, a people east of the Rutini, extending as far as the border of the province; subject to the Arverni. 7.7, 64, 75.

Galli, -orum, m., *the Gauls*, technically only the inhabitants of *Gallia Celtica*, the middle of the three main divisions of Gaul. In Book 7, the term is used generically for all Gauls taking part in the rebellion. 7.1 ff.

Gallia, -ae, f., *Gaul*, the word Gallia was used by the Romans in three different ways. a. In its broadest sense it included *Gallia Cisalpina*, north Italy, and *Gallia Transalpina*, a vast region which comprised all of France, the greater part of Switzerland, and the western portion of Germany, with Holland and Belgium. b. In a narrower sense *Gallia* embraced only *Gallia Transalpina*. c.

In its most restricted use *Gallia* was applied to the *land of the Galli*, the middle part of Gaul. "Camille Jullian believes that its population was only a little less than in the days of Louis XIV - that is, between 20 and 30 millions - and Jérôme Carcopino suggests at least 12 millions. Because these are conjectural figures, all that can be said is that, in the first century B.C., Gaul would appear to have been a well-populated country, a proof of its prosperity and wealth." (Fuller, pg. 97). 7.1 ff.

Gallia Transalpina, -ae, f., *Transalpine Gaul,* according to Caesar, falls into three parts: a. The land of the Belgae, in the northeast, between the Seine, the Marne, and the Rhine. b. The land of the Celtae, or Galli, in the central part between the Seine, the Marne and the Garonne. c. The land of the Aquitani, in the south, between the Garonne and the Pyrenees. 7.1, 6.

Gergovia, -ae, f., *Gergovia,* chief city of the Arverni, situated on a narrow plateau (elevation 2,440 ft.) about six miles south of Clermont-Ferrand. Unsuccessfully besieged by Caesar. Site of a near catastrophic Roman defeat. 7.4, 34, 36-53, 59.

Germani, -orum, m., pl., *the Germans,* natives of Germany. When his Gallic cavalry proved insufficient, Caesar sent for German cavalry. Three times they proved their worth and defeated the Gallic cavalry at critical moments for Caesar. 7. 63, 65, 67, 70, 80.

Germania, -ae, f., *Germany,* bounded, according to the Roman conception, by the Rhine, the Danube, the Vistula, and the Ocean. Caesar sends for cavalry from Germany in order to counteract Vercingetorix's superiority in cavalry. 4.4; 5.13; 6.11, 24, 25, 31; mentioned in Book 7 only at 7.65.

Gobannitio, -onis, m., *Gobannitio,* uncle of Vercingetorix, hostile to his plans but expelled by Vercingetorix. Mentioned only at 7.4.

Gorgobina, -ae, f., *Gorgobina,* a city in the country of the Aedui, inhabited by the Boii who had joined in the Helvetian migration; situated between the Elaver and the Liger, but the exact location is unknown; Napoleon III. places it at St. Parize-le-Châtel. Mentioned only at 7.9.

Helvetii, -orum, m., pl., *the Helvetii,* a Gallic state divided into four cantons, the names of two of which, pagus Tigurinus, pagus Verbigenus, are known. 1.1-29, 30, 31, 40; 4.10; 6.25; mentioned in Book 7 only at 7.75.

Helvi, -orum, m., *the Helvi,* Gallic people in the province, in the southern part of the Cebenna (Cévennes) Mountains. 7.7, 8, 64, 65.

Hispania, -ae, f., *Spain.* 1.1; 5.1, 1, 3, 23; 5.1, 13, 27; mentioned in Book 7 only at 7.55.

Italia, -ae, f., *Italy,* at this period Italia proper extended North only so far as the Rubicon; but Caesar here, as elsewhere in the Gallic War, includes Cisalpine Gaul, which later lost its provincial organization and became a part of Italy (43 BC). 7.1, 6, 7, 55, 65, 57.

Labienus, -i, m., *Titus (Attius?) Labienus,* the most prominent of Caesar's lieutenants in the Gallic War. Plutarch (Caes. xviii.) and Appian (Cel. I. iii.) give to him the credit of the victory over the Tigurini (I. xii.); but their statement does not merit credence in the face of Caesar's own narrative. Labienus gained important successes over the Treveri (B.C. 54-53) and the Parisii (B.C. 52). In the Civil War he went over to the side of Pompey, but displayed small abilities as a commander, and fell at the battle of Munda, B.C. 45. 7.34, 56, 57-62, 86, 87, 90.

Lemovices, -um, m., pl., *the Lemovices,* a Gallic state between the Arverni and the Santones. The name survives in *Lemoges.* 7.4, 75, 88.

Lexovii, -orum, m., pl., *the Lexovii,* a Gallic state on the coast west of the Sequana (Seine), conquered by Sabinus in 56 B.C. 3.9, 11, 17, 29; mentioned in Book 7 only at 7.75.

Liger, -eris, m., *the Liger,* which rises in the Cévennes (Cebenna) mountains, flows northwest, receives as a tributary the Allier (Elaver), flows west, and finally empties into the Atlantic, after a course of more than 500 miles. 3.9; 7.5, 11, 55, 59.

Lingones, -um, m., pl., *the Lingones,* a Gallic state separated from the Sequani by the Arar. One of three tribes that did not join in the rebellion against Caesar. 1.26, 40; 4.10; 6.44; 7.9, 63, 66.

Litiviccus, -i, m., *Litiviccus,* a prominent Aeduan who entered into a conspiracy against Cesar, and took refuge in Gergovia. 7.37-40, 42, 43, 54, 55, 67.

Lucterius, -i, m., *Lucterius,* a Cadurcan, an efficient helper of Vercingetorix in the great uprising of the Gauls, B.C. 52. 7.5, 7, 8.

Lutetia, -ae, f., *Lutetia,* a city of the Parisii on an island on the Seine, *Paris.* 6.3; 7.57, 58.

Mandubii, -orum, m. pl. *the Mandubii,* a Gallic people north of the Aedui; chief city Alesia, now *Alise-Ste.-Reine.* 7.68, 71, 78.

Matisco, -onis, f., *Matisco,* a city of the Aedui, on the Arar (Saône), now *Mâcon.* Mentioned only at 7.90.

Mediomatrici, -orum, m., pl., *the Mediomatrici,* a Gallic people between the headwaters of the Mosa (Meuse) and the Vosegus (Vosges) mountains; chief city, Divodurum, later called Mettis, now *Metz.* Mentioned only at 7.75.

Metiosedum, -i, n., *Metiosedum,* a town of the Senones, on an island in the Sequana (Seine), 28 miles above Paris; later called Melodunum, now *Melun.* 7.58, 60, 61.

Morini, -orum, m., pl., *the Morini,* a powerful Belgic people, on the sea-coast north of the Lys river and opposite Kent. 2.4; 3.9, 28, 4.21, 22, 37, 38; 5.24; 7.75, 76.

Narbo, -onis, m., *Narbo,* capital of 'the province', which was later named from it, *Gallia Narbonensis;* originally a city of the Volcae Arecomici, but made a Roman colony in B.C. 118; now *Narbonne.* 3.20; mentioned in Book 7 only at 7.7.

Nervii, -orum, m., pl., *the Nervii,* a warlike people of Belgic Gaul, south of the Scaldis (Schelde), defeated by Caesar in 57 B.C. at the Sambre with great slaughter; chief city Bagacum, now *Bavay.* 2.4, 15-28, 29, 32. 5.24, 38-52, 56, 58.6.2, 3, 29; mentioned in Book 7 only at 7.75.

Nitiobriges, -um, m., pl., *the Nitiobriges,* a people in Northern Aquitania; chief town Aginum, now *Agen.* 7.7, 31, 46, 75.

Noviodunum, -i, n., *Noviodunum,* name of three cities mentioned in the Gallic War:
1) Of the Aedui, on the right bank of the Liger (Loire); now *Nevers.* Mentioned only at 7.55.
2) Of the Bituriges, on the west side of the Liger, south of the Cenabum; perhaps on the same site as Sancerre. 7.12, 14.
3) Of the Suessionum. Mentioned only at 2.12.

Oceanus, -i, m., *the Ocean,* looked upon by Caesar as one body of water, including the Atlantic ocean, English Channel, and the

North Sea. 7.4, 75.

Ollovico, -onis, m., *Ollovico,* a king of the Nitiobriges. Mentioned only at 7.33.

Osismi, -orum, m., pl., *the Osismi,* a small state in the extreme northwest corner of Gaul. 2.34; 3.9; mentioned in Book 7 only at 7.75.

Parisii, -orum, m., pl., *the Parisii,* a Gallic people on the Sequana (Seine); chief city *Lutetia,* now Paris. 6.3; 7.4, 34, 57, 75.

Petrocorii, -orum, m., pl., *the Petrocorii,* a Gallic people north of the Garumna (Garonne), between the Nitiobriges and the Lemovices; their chief city was Vesunna, now *Périgueux.* Mentioned only at 7.75.

Petronius, -i, m., *Marcus Petronius,* a centurion of the eighth legion, who in the battle before Gergovia gave his life to save his men. Mentioned only at 7.50.

Pictones, -um, m., pl., *the Pictones,* a Gallic people bordering on the Atlantic south of the Liger (Loire), neighbors of the Santoni; the name survives in *Poitou.* 3.11; 7.4, 75.

Pompeius, -i, m., *Gnaeus Pompeius Magnus, Pompey,* Caesar's in-law-in-law and rival, born B.C. 106; conquered by Caesar in the civil war at the battle of Pharsalus, and afterwards murdered in Egypt. 4.1; 6.1; mentioned in Book 7 only at 7.6.

provincia, -ae, f., *the Province,* the part of Transalpine Gaul subdued by the Romans before B.C. 58, lying between the Mediterranean Sea and the upper part of the Rhone, the Cévennes Mountains and the upper part of the Garonne river. 7.1, 6, 7, 56, 59, 64, 65, 66.

Raurici, -orum, m., pl., *the Raurici,* a people along the Rhine, north of the Helvetii. 1.5, 29; 6.25; mentioned in Book 7 only at 7.75.

Redones, -um, m., pl., *the Redones,* a Gallic people in Brittany (Bretagne); the name survuves in *Rennes.* 2.34; mentioned in Book 7 only at 7.75.

Remi, -orum, m., pl., *the Remi,* a Gallic people, about the headwaters of the Axona (Aisne); the chief city, Durocortorum, now *Rheims.* One of three tribes that did not join in the rebellion against Caesar. 2.3-7, 9, 12; 3.11; 5.3, 24, 53, 54, 56; 6.4, 12, 44; 7.63, 90.

Rhenus, -i, m., *the Rhine,* the principal river of Northern Europe, having a course of about 850 miles; twice bridged by Caesar. 1.1, 2, 5, 27, 28, 31, 33, 35, 37, 43, 44, 53, 54; 2.3, 4, 29, 35; 3.11; 4.1, 3, 4, 6, 10, 14, 15, 16, 17, 19; 5.3, 24, 27, 29, 41, 55; 6.9, 24, 29, 32, 35, 41, 42; mentioned in Book 7 only at 7.65.

Rhodanus, -i, m., *the Rhone,* which rises in the Alps near the sources of the Rhine, and passing through Lake Geneva, follows at first a southwesterly direction, then flows south, reaching the Mediterranean after a course of about 500 miles. 1.1, 2, 6, 8, 10, 11, 12, 33; 3.1; mentioned in Book 7 only at 7.65.

Roma, -ae, f., *Rome.* The capital of the Roman Republic. 1.31; 6.12; mentioned in Book 7 only at 7.90.

Ruteni, -orum, m., pl., *the Ruteni,* a Gallic people, west of the Cévennes; part of them were within the limits of the province, and hence were called **Ruteni provinciales.** 1.45; 7.5, 7, 64, 75, 90.

Rutilus, -i, m., *Marcus Sempronius Rutilus,* a cavalry commander. Mentioned only at 7.90.

Santones, -um, or Santoni, -orum, m., pl., *the Santones,* a Gallic people on the sea-coast north of the Garonne; the name survives in *Saintes* and *Saintonge.* 1.10, 11; 3.11; mentioned in Book 7 only at 7.75.

Sedulius, -i, m., *Sedulius,* a leader of the Lemovices, killed before Alesia. Mentioned only at 7.88.

Segusiavi, -orum, m., pl., *the Segusiavi,* a Gallic state, tributary to the Aedui, in the region west of the junction of the Rhone and Saône (Arar). 1.10; 7.64, 75.

Senones, -um, m., pl., *the Senones,* a strong Gallic state south of the Matrone (Marne); chief city Agedincum, now *Sens.* 2.2; 5.54, 56; 6.2-5, 44; 7.4, 11, 34, 56, 58, 75.

Sequana, -ae, f., *the Sequana,* present day *Seine,* the principal river of Northern France. 1.1; 7.57, 58.

Sequani, -orum, m., pl., *the Sequani,* a Gallic state west of the Jura; chief city Vesonito, now *Besançon.* In their strife with the Aedui they secured the aid of Ariovistus, who made them subject to himself. 1.1-3, 6, 8-12, 19, 31-33, 35, 38, 40, 44, 48, 54; 4.10; 6.12; 7.66, 67, 75, 90.

Sextius, -i, m., *Titus Sextius,* a lieutenant. At the time of Caesar's death he was governor of Numidia, a position which he held until the battle of Philippi, B.C. 42. 6.1; 7.49, 51, 90.

Sulpicius, -i, m., *Publius Sulpicius Rufus,* a lieutenant of Caesar in Gaul (first mentioned in 55 B.C.), and afterwards in the Civil War. 4.22; mentioned in Book 7 only at 7.90. *BC.* 1.74; 3.101.

Teutomatus, -i, m., *Teutomatus,* a king of the Nitiobriges who narrowly escaped capture before Gergovia. 7.31, 46.

Teutoni, gen. -um, m., pl., *the Teutons,* see **Cimbri.** 1.33, 40; 2.4, 29; mentioned in Book 7 only at 7.77.

Tolosates, -ium, m., pl., *the Tolosates,* the inhabitants of Tolosa, chief city of the Volcae Tectosages. 1.10; mentioned in Book 7 only at 7.7.

Transalpina Gallia, See **Gallia Transalpina.**

Trebonius, -i, m., *Gaius Trebonius,* quaestor B.C. 60, tribune of the people B.C. 55; in the latter year he proposed the law assigning the provinces, according to the wish of the triumvirs, for five years and was rewarded by Caesar with a lieutenant's commission. He served Caesar in both the Gallic and Civil Wars; though raised by Caesar to positions of trust, he manifested the basest ingratitude in joining the conspiracy that ended the Dictator's life. He was killed by Dolabella at Smyrna in 43 B.C. 5.17, 24; 6.33; 7.11, 81.

Treveri, -orum, m., pl., *the Treveri,* a powerful Belgic people near the Rhine, north of the Mediomatrici; chief town Augusta Treverorum, now *Trier.* One of three tribes that did not join in the rebellion against Caesar. 1.37; 2.34; 3.11; 4.6, 10; 5.2-4, 24, 26, 47, 53, 55-58; 6.2-5, 6-9, 29, 32, 44; Mentioned in Book 7 only two times in 7.63.

Turoni, -orum, m., pl., *the Turoni,* a people on the Liger (Loire), west of the Bituriges. the name survives in *Tours* and *Touraine.* 2.35; 7.4, 75.

Valerius, -i, m., *Valerius,* name of six persons mentioned in the *BG:*

1) **Lucius Valerius Praeconinus**, *Lucius Valerius Praeconinus.* Mentioned only at 3.20.

2) **Gaius Valerius Flaccus**, *Gaius Valerius Flaccus.* Mentioned only at 1.47.

3) **Gaius Valerius Caburus**, *Gaius Valerius Caburus*, a Gaul who received the Roman franchise, B.C. 83. 1.47; mentioned in Book 7 only at 7.65.

4) **Gaius Valerius Procillus**, *Gaius Valerius Procillus.* 1.47, 53.

5) **Gaius Valerius Donnotaurus**, *Gaius Valerius Donnotaurus*, a Gaul, son of Gaius Valerius Caburus. Mentioned only at 7.65.

6) **Gaius Valerius Troucillus**, *Gaius Valerius Troucillus.* Mentioned only at 1.19.

Valetiacus, -i, m., *Valetiacus*, Vergobret of the Aedui, in B.C. 53; brother of Cottus. Mentioned only at 7.32.

Veliocasses, -um, dat. **Veliocassis**, m., pl., *the Veliocasses*, a small state on the north side of the Sequana (Seine); chief town, Rotomagus, today *Rouen.* 2.4; mentioned in Book 7 only at 7.75.

Vellaunodunum, -i, n., *Vellaunodunum*, a city of the Senones, between Agedincum and Cenabum; perhaps *Triguères.* 7.11, 14.

Vellavii, -orum, m., pl., *the Vellavii*, a small state in the Cebenna (Cévennes) Mountains, tributary to the Arverni. Mentioned only at 7.75.

Venelli, -orum, m., pl., *the Venelli*, a Gallic state on the north coast, west of the Lexovii. 2.34; 3.7, 17; mentioned in Book 7 only at 7.75.

Veneti, -orum, m., pl., *the Veneti*, a sea-faring Gallic people, on the west coast; almost exterminated by Caesar. 2.34; 3.7-16, 17, 18; mentioned in Book 7 only at 7.75.

Vercassivellaunus, -i, m., *Vercassivellaunus*, one of the four generals in command of the Gallic army raised for the relief of Alesia; a cousin of Vercingetorix. 7.76, 83, 85, 88.

Vercingetorix, -igis, m., *Vercingetorix*, an Avernian, commander-in-chief of the Gallic forces B.C. 52; greatest general of the Gauls. 7.4, 8, 9, 12, 14-16, 18, 20, 21, 26, 28-30, 31, 33-36, 44, 51, 53, 55, 63, 66-68, 70, 71, 75, 76, 81-90.

Vienna, -ae, f., *Vienna*, chief city of the Allobroges, on the east side of the Rhone; now *Vienne.* Mentioned only at 7.9.

Viridomarus, -i, m., *Viridomarus*, a prominent Aeduan, at first loyal, finally hostile, to Caesar. 7.38-40, 54, 55, 63, 76.

---

[1] Kelsey, Francis W. *Caesar's Gallic War.* Allyn and Bacon, 1898.

[2] Cary, M. and H. H. Scullard. *A History of Rome Down to the Reign of Constantine.* Third edition. St. Martin's Press, New York, 1984.

[3] Fuller, J. F. C. *Caesar: Man, Soldier and Tyrant.* Da Capo Press, N. Y., 1965.

[4] Adcock, F. E. *The Roman Art of War Under the Republic.* Martin Classical Lectures, Volume VIII, Harvard University Press, 1970.

[5] Watson, G. R. *The Roman Soldier.* Cornell University Press, 1969.

[6] Fuller, J. F. C. *Caesar: Man, Soldier and Tyrant.* Da Capo Press, N. Y., 1965.

[7] Taylor, L. R. "The Rise of Julius Caesar". *G&R* 4 (1957): 10-18.

[8] Toynbee, J. M. C. "Portraits of Julius Caesar". *G&R* 4 (1957): 2-9.

[9] *Caesar: The Gallic War.* A New Translation by Carolyn Hammond. Oxford University Press, 1996.

[10] Fuller, J. F. C. *Caesar: Man, Soldier and Tyrant.* Da Capo Press, N. Y., 1965.

[11] Ibid.

[12] Cuff, J. P. "Caesar the Soldier". *G&R* 4 (1957): 29-35.

[13] Sherwin-White, A. N. "Caesar as an Imperialist". *G&R* 4 (1957): 36-45.

[14] *Caesar: The Gallic War.* A New Translation by Carolyn Hammond. Oxford University Press, 1996.

[15] Fuller, J. F. C. *Caesar: Man, Soldier and Tyrant.* Da Capo Press, N. Y., 1965.

[16] *Caesar: The Gallic War.* A New Translation by Carolyn Hammond. Oxford University Press, 1996.

[17] Fuller, J. F. C. *Caesar: Man, Soldier and Tyrant.* Da Capo Press, N. Y., 1965.

[18] Caesar, Julius. *The Civil War.* Translated by A. G. Peskett. The Loeb Classical Library. Harvard University Press, 1979.

[19] Fuller, J. F. C. *Caesar: Man, Soldier and Tyrant.* Da Capo Press, N. Y., 1965.

[20] Caesar, Julius. *Alexandrian, African, and Spanish Wars.* Translated by A. G. Way. The Loeb Classical Library. Harvard University Press, Reprinted 1988.

[21] Fuller, J. F. C. *Caesar: Man, Soldier and Tyrant.* Da Capo Press, N. Y., 1965.

[22] Ibid.

[23]Carson, R. A. G. "Caesar and the Monarchy". *G&R* 4 (1957): 46-53.

[24]Smith, R. E. "The Conspiracy and the Conspirators". *G&R* 4 (1957): 58-70.

[25]Chilver, G. E. F. "The Aftermath of Caesar". *G&R* 4 (1957): 71-77.

[26]Coulter, C.C. "Caesar's Clemency". *CJ* 26 No. 7 (1931): 513-24.

[27]Caesar, Julius. *The Gallic Wars*. Translated by H. J. Edwards. The Loeb Classical Library. Harvard University Press, 1986 or *Caesar: The Gallic War*. A New Translation by Carolyn Hammond. Oxford University Press, 1996.

[28]Caesar, Julius. *The Civil War*. Translated by A. G. Peskett. The Loeb Classical Library. Harvard University Press, 1979.

[29]Caesar, Julius. *Alexandrian, African, and Spanish Wars*. Translated by A. G. Way. The Loeb Classical Library. Harvard University Press, Reprinted 1988.

[30]Suetonius. *The Lives of the Caesars*. Vol. 1: "The Deified Julius". Translated by J. C. Rolfe. The Loeb Classical Library. Harvard University Press, 1979.

[31]Plutarch. *Plutarch's Lives*. Vol. 7: "Caesar". Translated by Bernadotte Perrin. The Loeb Classical Library. Harvard University Press, 1971.

[32]Appian. *Appian's Roman History*. Volume III, Book II, "The Civil Wars". Translated by Horace White. The Loeb Classical Library. Harvard University Press, Reprinted, 1964.

[33]Dio. *Roman History*, Volumes 3-4. Translated by Earnest Cary. The Loeb Classical Library. Harvard University Press, Reprinted, 1961.

[34]Fuller, J. F. C. *Caesar: Man, Soldier and Tyrant*. Da Capo Press, N. Y., 1965.

[35]Gelzer, M. *Caesar: Politician and Statesman*. Translated by Peter Needham. Harvard University Press, 1968.

[36]Yavetz, Z. *Julius Caesar and His Public Image*. London: Thames and Hudson, 1983.

[37]Cicero. *Brutus*. Translated by G.L. Hendrickson. The Loeb Classical Library. Harvard University Press, Reprinted, 1962.

[38]Gotoff, H. C. "Towards a Practical Criticism of Caesar's Prose Style". *ICS* 9. 1 (1984): 1-18.

[39]Williams, M. F. "Caesar's Bibracte Narrative and the Aims of Caesarian Style". *ICS* 10. 2 (1985): 215-226.

[40]Adcock, F. E. *Caesar as a Man of Letters*. Cambridge University Press, 1956.

[41]Conte, G. B. *Latin Literature: A History*. Translated by Joseph B. Solodow. Revised by Don Fowler and Glenn W. Most. The John Hopkins University Press, Baltimore and London, 1994.

[42]Adcock, F. E. *Caesar as a Man of Letters*. Cambridge University Press, 1956.

[43]Kahn, A. D. "'Vercingetorix' - A new Play By C. Julius Caesar". *CW* 64 No. 8 (1971): 249-54.

[44]Rowe, Galen. "Dramatic Structures in Caesar's *Bellum Civile*". *TAPA* 98 (1967): 399-414).

[45]Murphy, C. T. "The Use of Speeches in Caesar's *Gallic War*". *CJ* 45 No. 8 (1949/50): 120-27.

[46]Nordling, J. G. *Indirect Discourse and Rhetorical Strategies in Caesar's BG and BC*, Dissertation at the University of Wisconsin - Madison, 1991.

[47]Deichgräber, K. "Elegantia Caesaris. Zu Caesars Reden und Commentarii". *Gymnasium*, 57 (1950), 112-23.

[48]Rasmussen, D. *Caesars Commantarii: Stil und Stilwandel am Beispiel der Direkten Rede*. Göttingen, 1963.

[49]Siedler, C. W. "Rhetorical Devices in Caesar's Commentaries." *CW* 50 No. 2 (1956): 28-31, and addenda 50 No. 3 (1956): 46-47.

[50]Murphy, P. R. "Themes of Caesar's *Gallic War*". *CJ* 72 No. 1 (1976): 234-43.

[51]Craig, J. D. "The General Reflection in Caesar's *Commentaries*". *CR* 45 (1931): 107-110.

[52]Gotoff, H. C. "Towards a Practical Criticism of Caesar's Prose Style". *ICS* 9. 1 (1984): 1-18.

[53]Schlicher, J. J. "The Development of Caesar's Narrative Style". *CPh* 31 (1936): 212-224.

[54]Eden, P. T. "Caesar's Style: Inheritance Versus Intelligence". *Glotta* 40 (1962): 74-117.

[55]Radista, L. "Julius Caesar and His Writings". *ANRW* 1. 3 (1973): 417-56.

[56]Williams, M. F. "Caesar's Bibracte Narrative and the Aims of Caesarian Style". *ICS* 10. 2 (1985): 215-226.

[57]Keegan, J. T*he Face of Battle*. New York: Viking Press, 1976.

[58]Mannetter, D. A. *Narratology in Caesar*. Dissertation at the University of Wisconsin - Madison, 1995.

[59]Pelling, C.B.R. "Caesar's Battle Descriptions and the Defeat of Ariovistus". *Latomus*, 40 (1981), 741-766.

[60]Suetonius. *The Lives of the Caesars*. Vol. 1: "The Deified Julius". Translated by J. C. Rolfe. The Loeb Classical Library. Harvard University Press, 1979.

[61]Conte, G. B. *Latin Literature: A History*. Translated by Joseph B. Solodow. Revised by Don Fowler and Glenn W. Most. The John Hopkins University Press, Baltimore and London, 1994.

[62]Stevens, S. E. "The *Bellum Gallicum* as a Work of Propaganda". *Latomus* 11 (1952): 3-18, 165-79.

[63]Rambaud, M. *L'art de la Deformation Historique dans les Commentaires de Cesar*. Second edition, Paris, les Belles lettres, 1966.

[64]Balsdon, J. P. V. D. "The Veracity of Caesar". *G&R* 4 (1957): 19-28.

[65]Ibid.

[66]Gardner, J. F. "The Gallic Menace in Caesarian Propaganda". *G&R* 30 No. 2 (1983): 181-89.

[67]Dauge, Y. A. *Le Barbare: Researches Sur la Conception romaine de la Barbarie et de la Civilisation*. Bruxelles: *Latomus* Vol. 176, 1981.

[68]Harmond, J. "Le Portrait de la Gaule dans le 'De Bello Gallico'". *ANRW* 1. 3 (1973): 523-595.

[69]Collins, J. H. "Caesar as Political Propagandist." *ANRW* 1.1 (1972): 922-66.

[70]Conley, D. F. "Causes of Roman Victory Presented in the *Bellum Gallicum*: Caesar the Commander vs. Other Factors". *Helios* 10 (1983): 173-186.

[71]Caesar, J. *C. Iuli Caesaris Commentariorum*. Vol. 1. Ed. Renatus Du Pontet. Oxford Classical Text. Oxford University Press, 1978. Also used in the notes are the Loeb text: Caesar, Julius. *The Gallic Wars*. Translated by H. J. Edwards. The Loeb Classical Library. Harvard University Press, 1986 and the Budé text: Constans, L.-A. *César Guerre Des Gaules*. Tome II. Les Belles Lettres, 2000.

[72]Lewis, Charlton T. *An Elementary Latin Dictionary*. Oxford University Press, 1989.

[73]Kelsey, Francis W. *Caesar's Gallic War*. Allyn and Bacon, 1898.

[74]*Oxford Latin Dictionary*. Oxford at the Clarendon Press, 1968.

[75]Allen and Greenaugh. *Allen and Greenaugh's New Latin Grammar For Schools and Colleges*. College Classical Series. Aristide D. Caratzas, Publisher. Reprinted 1988.

[76]Kelsey, Francis W. *Caesar's Gallic War*. Allyn and Bacon, 1898.

[77]Walker, Arthur Tappan. *Caesar's Gallic War*. Scott, Foresman and Company. 1907.

[78]Birch, C. M. *Concordantia et Index Caesaris*. 2 Vols. Olms-Weidmann, N. Y., 1989.

[79]Kroymann, von Jürgen. "Caesar und das Corpus Caesarianum in der Neueren Forschung: Gesamtbibliographie 1945-1970". *ANRW* 1. 3 (1973): 418-487.